The Handbook of
Historical
Sociolinguistics

CU00797327

Blackwell Handbooks in Linguistics

This outstanding multi-volume series covers all the major subdisciplines within linguistics today and, when complete, will offer a comprehensive survey of linguistics as a whole.

Already published:

The Handbook of Historical Sociolinguistics

Edited by

Juan Manuel Hernández-Campoy
and Juan Camilo Conde-Silvestre

WILEY Blackwell

This paperback edition first published 2014
© 2014 John Wiley & Sons, Ltd

Edition History: Blackwell Publishing Ltd (hardcover, 2012)

Registered Office
John Wiley & Sons Ltd, The Atrium, Southern Gate, Chichester, West Sussex, PO19 8SQ, UK

Editorial Offices
350 Main Street, Malden, MA 02148-5020, USA
9600 Garsington Road, Oxford, OX4 2DQ, UK
The Atrium, Southern Gate, Chichester, West Sussex, PO19 8SQ, UK

For details of our global editorial offices, for customer services, and for information about how to apply for permission to reuse the copyright material in this book please see our website at www.wiley.com/wiley-blackwell.

The right of Juan Manuel Hernández-Campoy and Juan Camilo Conde-Silvestre to be identified as the authors of the editorial material in this work has been asserted in accordance with the UK Copyright, Designs and Patents Act 1988.

All rights reserved. No part of this publication may be reproduced, stored in a retrieval system, or transmitted, in any form or by any means, electronic, mechanical, photocopying, recording or otherwise, except as permitted by the UK Copyright, Designs and Patents Act 1988, without the prior permission of the publisher.

Wiley also publishes its books in a variety of electronic formats. Some content that appears in print may not be available in electronic books.

Designations used by companies to distinguish their products are often claimed as trademarks. All brand names and product names used in this book are trade names, service marks, trademarks or registered trademarks of their respective owners. The publisher is not associated with any product or vendor mentioned in this book.

Limit of Liability/Disclaimer of Warranty: While the publisher and authors have used their best efforts in preparing this book, they make no representations or warranties with respect to the accuracy or completeness of the contents of this book and specifically disclaim any implied warranties of merchantability or fitness for a particular purpose. It is sold on the understanding that the publisher is not engaged in rendering professional services and neither the publisher nor the author shall be liable for damages arising herefrom. If professional advice or other expert assistance is required, the services of a competent professional should be sought.

Library of Congress Cataloging-in-Publication Data
The handbook of historical sociolinguistics / edited by Juan Manuel Hernández-Campoy and Juan Camilo Conde-Silvestre.
        p. cm.
     Includes index.
     ISBN 978-1-4051-9068-8 (cloth) – ISBN 978-1-118-79802-7 (pbk.)
     1. Sociolinguistics–History. 2. Sociolinguistics–Handbooks, manuals, etc. I. Hernández-Campoy, Juan Manuel. II. Conde Silvestre, Juan Camilo.
     P40.H3423 2012
     306.4409–dc23

                                                                    2011037207

A catalogue record for this book is available from the British Library.

Cover image: *Tierradentro*, 2006 (Oil on canvas). Photo © Ignacio Auzike / Getty Images
Cover design by Workhaus

Set in 10/12 pt Palatino by Typesetter
Printed in Malaysia by Ho Printing (M) Sdn Bhd

1   2014

To our Teachers and Students

Contents

List of Plates

List of Figures

List of Maps

List of Tables

Notes on Contributors

Most of the contributors belong to the Historical Sociolinguistics Network (http://www.philhist.uni-augsburg.de/hison/), where we share our research interests.

Jean Aitchison was Professor of Language and Communication at the University of Oxford 1993–2003, and is now an Emeritus Professorial Fellow at Worcester College. Her research and writing are concerned with the mental lexicon, language change, and the language of the media, and she has published a number of books on these topics, such as *Words in the Mind: An Introduction to the Mental Lexicon*, *Aitchison's Linguistics*, *The Articulate Mammal: An Introduction to Psycholinguistics*, *The Word Weavers: Newshounds and Wordsmiths*, *Language Change: Progress or Decay?*, *The Seeds of Speech: Language Origin and Evolution*, *The Language Web: The Power and Problem of Words* (1996 BBC Reith lectures), *A Glossary of Language and Mind*, and *New Media Language* (edited with Diana Lewis).

K. Anipa is Lecturer in Linguistics and Spanish at the University of St Andrews, in the United Kingdom, where he teaches general phonetics and phonology, sociolinguistics, language contact, language and nation, and the history of the Castilian language, as well as medieval and Renaissance Spanish literature. His research interests are in the fields of historical sociolinguistics (variation and continuity in sixteenth- and seventeenth-century Castilian and English, Renaissance writers on language and linguistics, and sociolinguistic behavior in the past), sociolinguistics theorizing and methodology, and the history of linguistic thought and grammatical tradition in Renaissance Spain, England, and France. In addition to articles in leading journals, he is the author of *A Critical Examination of Linguistic Variation in Golden-Age Spanish* and *The Grammatical Thought and Linguistic Behaviour of Juan de Valdés*.

Anita Auer (Ph.D. Manchester) is Assistant Professor in English Language and Linguistics at Utrecht University, the Netherlands. She has taught and lectured in Austria, England, and the Netherlands. Her main focus as a teacher is on the language, literature, and culture of medieval England, the history of English, and change in English, as well as other languages. Auer has published widely on grammar writing and language use during the Modern English period, including the monograph *The Subjunctive in the Age of Prescriptivism*. Her research interests include language variation and change, (socio)historical linguistics, dialectology, language standardization, stylistics, corpus linguistics, and the interface between manuscript and print.

Alexander Bergs is Professor and Chair in English Language and Linguistics at the University of Osnabrück (Germany). His current research interests include language variation and change, constructional approaches to language, the role of context in language, and the syntax/pragmatics interface. His works include books such as *Social Networks and Historical Sociolinguistics*, *Modern Scots*, *Context and Constructions* and *Constructions and Language Change* (both edited with Gabriele Diewald), the two-volume *Handbook of English Historical Linguistics* edited with Laurel Brinton, as well as numerous articles in leading journals such as *English Language and Linguistics*, *Historical Pragmatics*, and *Folia Lingustica Historica*.

David Britain is Professor of Modern English Linguistics at the University of Bern, Switzerland. His research interests embrace language variation and change, varieties of English, dialect contact and attrition, and the linguistics–human geography interface, with particular interest in applying insights from social geography's new Mobilities paradigm to social dialectology. He has published extensively on these areas, including in the journals *Language Variation and Change*, *Journal of Sociolinguistics*, and *Language in Society*. He is editor of *Language in the British Isles*, co-editor (with Jenny Cheshire) of *Social Dialectology*, and co-author of *Linguistics: an Introduction* (with Andrew Radford, Martin Atkinson, Harald Clahsen, and Andrew Spencer). Dave is also currently an Associate Editor of the *Journal of Sociolinguistics*.

Pascual Cantos-Gómez is Professor in Corpus Linguistics at the University of Murcia (Spain), where he teaches corpus linguistics and quantitative approaches to language and linguistics. His research interests include corpus linguistics, statistics, computational lexicography, and computer-assisted language learning, fields in which he has published extensiveiy: books such as *CUMBRE: Corpus lingüísticos del español contemporáneo. Fundamentos, metodología y aplicaciones*, *Lexical Ambiguity, Dictionaries and Corpora*, *Frecuencias del español: Diccionario y estudios léxicos y morfológicos*, and *Statistical Methods in Language and Linguistic Research*, and articles in leading journals, such as *International Journal of Corpus Linguistics*, *Computers and the Humanities*, *Electronic and Telecommunications Research Institute*, *Revue Scientifique et Technique*, and *Bulletin of Hispanic Studies*.

Juan Camilo Conde-Silvestre is Professor in the English Department at the University of Murcia (Spain), where he teaches historical linguistics and the history of English. He has published on a variety of topics in historical sociolinguistics, especially on the social and geographical diffusion of late Middle English changes in progress, on medieval English dialects, and standardization. He is also interested in Old English stylistics and in Middle English lexicology. His publications include the Spanish textbooks *Sociolingüística histórica* and *Crítica literaria y poesía elegíaca anglosajona: Las ruinas, El exiliado errante y El navegante*, and book collections such as *Sociolinguistics and the History of English: Perspectives and Problems* (with J.M. Hernández-Campoy), *Medieval English Literary and Cultural Studies: SELIM XV* (with Nila Vázquez), *Variation and Linguistic Change in English* (with J.M. Hernández-Campoy), as well as articles in leading journals such as *Atlantis, Neuphilologische Mitteilungen, Studia Anglica Posnaniensa, Language in Society* and *Neophilologus*.

Stephan Elspaß (Ph.D. Bonn) is Chair of German Linguistics at the University of Augsburg (Germany). His research interests in the field of German linguistics include grammar, historical and present-day sociolinguistics, language variation and change, phraseology, and language and politics. In recent years, he has received funding for (joint) research projects on dialectometry and on regional grammatical variation in Standard German. Among several books and special journal issues, he is author of *Sprachgeschichte von unten*, co-editor of the volume *Germanic language histories 'from below' (1700–2000)* (with Nils Langer, Joachim Scharloth, and Wim Vandenbussche), and of a special issue of *Multilingua: Journal of Cross-Cultural and Interlanguage Communication* (with Wim Vandenbussche) on "Lower Class Language Use in the Nineteenth Century." He has written over articles (in German and English) in national and international journals and edited volumes.

Laura Esteban-Segura, Lecturer at the Department of English Philology of the University of Murcia (Spain), received her B.A. and M.A. in English Philology (2002, 2004), B.A. in Translation and Interpreting (2004), and M.A. in Specialized Translation and Interpreting (2006) from the University of Málaga, her M.Litt. in English Language and English Linguistics (2007) from the University of Glasgow, and her Ph.D. in English Philology (2008) from the University of Málaga. Her main research interests are in the history of the English language, textual editing, paleography/codicology, manuscript studies, and translation. The more specialist aspects of her research focus on the study of unedited medical manuscripts in Middle English. She has published in international journals such as *English Studies, Neuphilologische Mitteilungen*, and *Studia Anglica Posnaniensia*.

Teresa Fanego is Full Professor of English Language and Linguistics at the University of Santiago de Compostela and since 2005 has been editor of the scholarly journal *Folia Linguistica*. She has published widely on the English of Shakespeare and his contemporaries, English historical syntax, and sentential complement constructions. She is also interested in grammaticalization processes and in functional and cognitive models of grammar. Her articles have appeared in leading journals such as *Diachronica, English Language and Linguistics, Lingua, Studies in Language*, and many others.

Joachim Grzega is Professor of English and General Linguistics at the University of Eichstätt-Ingolstadt (Germany). He founded the *Journal for EuroLinguistiX* and the journal *Onomasiology Online*. His research interests include synchronic and diachronic onomasiology, synchronic and diachronic pragmatics, Eurolinguistics, language teaching, intercultural communication, expert–layperson communication, language and society, and communicative teaching methods. He has published many books and articles in leading journals, such as *Linguistics*, *Anglia*, *Word*, *Zeitschrift für Dialektologie und Linguistik*, and *Zeitschrift für Romanische Philologie*.

Anna Hebda is Assistant Professor in the School of English, Adam Mickiewicz University, Poznań (Poland), and a member of the EmBeR (Emotion – Belief – Reason) project, investigating the conceptualization of abstract categories in Polish and English. Her main research interests include Middle English phonology and dialectology, conceptual metaphor theory, diachronic cognitive semantics and grammaticalization. She has mainly published in the fields of English historical emotionology and the consonantal phonology of medieval English.

Juan Manuel Hernández-Campoy (B.A. and Ph.D. Murcia) is Professor in Sociolinguistics at the University of Murcia (Spain), where he teaches undergraduate courses on English sociolinguistics, varieties of English, and the history of English, as well as on research methods in sociolinguistics for postgraduate students. His research interests include sociolinguistics, geolinguistics, dialectology, and the history of English, fields in which he has published extensively, including books such as *Style-Shifting in Public: New Perspectives on Stylistic Variation* (with J.A. Cutillas-Espinosa), *Diccionario de Sociolingüística* (with P. Trudgill), *Metodología de la Investigación Sociolingüística* (with M. Almeida), *Sociolinguistics and the History of English: Perspectives and Problems* (with J.C. Conde-Silvestre), *Variation and Linguistic Change in English* (with J.C. Conde-Silvestre), *Geolingüística*, and *Sociolingüística Británica*, and articles in leading journals such as *Language in Society*, *Journal of Sociolinguistics*, *International Journal of the Sociology of Language*, *Language Variation and Change*, *Language and Communication*, *Folia Linguistica Historica*, *Sociolinguistic Studies*, *Folia Linguistica*, *Neophilologie Mitteilungen*, and *Spanish in Context*.

Raymond Hickey is Chair of Linguistics at the Department of Anglophone Studies, University of Duisburg and Essen, Germany. His main research interests are varieties of English (especially Irish English) and general questions of language contact, shift, and change. Among his recent book publications are *A Source Book for Irish English*, *Motives for Language Change* (as editor), *A Sound Atlas of Irish English*, *Legacies of Colonial English* (as editor), *Dublin English: Evolution and Change*, *Irish English: History and Present-day Forms*, *Eighteenth-Century English: Ideology and Change* (as editor), and *Varieties of English in Writing: The Written Word as Linguistic Evidence* (as editor).

Brian D. Joseph received his Ph.D. in Linguistics from Harvard University in 1978, working on historical linguistics and Indo-European linguistics, and writing his dissertation on syntactic change in medieval and modern Greek. After a post-doctoral fellowship year at the University of Alberta, he took a position at The Ohio State University, where he has been ever since, becoming the Kenneth E. Naylor Professor of South Slavic Linguistics in 1997 and Distinguished University Professor in 2003. He continues to teach and to do research in historical linguistics, especially on the Greek language, in both its Indo-European context and its Balkan language-contact context, and has published extensively in these areas in journals such as *Language*, *Diachronica*, *Indogermanische Forschungen*, and *Glotta*, among many others. He is co-editor of the *Handbook of Historical Linguistics* and served as editor of *Language* from 2002 to 2009. He is currently co-editor of the *Journal of Greek Linguistics* and managing editor of the Brill series Empirical Approaches to Linguistic Theory and Brill's Handbooks in Linguistics.

Andreas H. Jucker is Professor of English Linguistics at the University of Zurich, where he is also Vice-Dean for Resources of the Faculty of Arts. Previously he taught at the Justus Liebig University, Giessen. His current research interests include historical pragmatics, speech act theory, politeness theory, the language of the new media and the grammar and history of English. His recent publications include *Speech Acts in the History of English* (co-edited with Irma Taavitsainen), *Early Modern English News Discourse*, *Corpora: Pragmatics and Discourse* (co-edited with Daniel Schreier and Marianne Hundt), *Handbook of Historical Pragmatics* (co-edited with Irma Taavitsainen), and *Communicating Early English Manuscripts* (co-edited with Päivi Pahta). He is editor of the *Journal of Historical Pragmatics* (with Irma Taavitsainen), editor of the Mouton series *Handbooks of Pragmatics* (with Wolfram Bublitz and Klaus P. Schneider), and associate editor of the *Pragmatics & Beyond New Series*.

Roland Kehrein is Lecturer in German Linguistics at the Research Centre *Deutscher Sprachatlas* (University of Marburg, Germany), where he teaches in all fields of linguistics and where he is currently employed as managing director of the long-term project Regionalsprache.de (funded by the Academy for Science and Literature, Mainz from 2008 to 2027). His research interests include the phonetics and phonology of prosody as well as variational linguistics and linguistic cartography, in which he has published extensively: articles in leading journals such as *Zeitschrift für Dialektologie und Linguistik* and books such as *Prosodie und Emotionen*, *Language Mapping: An International Handbook of Linguistic Variation* (co-edited with A. Lameli and St. Rabanus), and *Regionalsprachliche Spektren im Raum – Zur linguistischen Struktur der Vertikale*.

Agnieszka Kiełkiewicz-Janowiak is a Lecturer in Sociolinguistics and Associate Professor at the School of English, Adam Mickiewicz University, Poznań (Poland). She is the author of *'Women's Language'? – a Socio-historical View: Private Writings in Early New England* and *A Socio-historical Study in Address: Polish and English*. Her current research interests focus on lifespan sociolinguistics as well as language and gender issues. She is now working on a book on the discourse of ageing.

Nils Langer is a Reader in German Linguistics at the University of Bristol, England. His primary research interests lie within the areas of linguistic purism and the sociolinguistic stigmatization of morphosyntactic constructions in German. Currently he is researching language conflict and language policies in Northern Germany, particularly with regard to the tensions in the use and perception of German vs. Danish and High German vs. Low German in the nineteenth century. He has published books such as *Language and History, Linguistics and Historiography* (co-edited with Steffan Davies and Wim Vandenbussche), *Landmarks in the History of German* (co-edited with Geraldine Horan and Sheila Watts), *Germanic Language Histories from Below* (co-edited with Stephan Elspaß, Joachim Scharloth, and Wim Vandenbussche), *The Making of Bad Language: Lay Linguistic Stigmatisations in German: Past and Present* (with Wini Davies), *Linguistic Purism in the Germanic Languages* (co-edited with Winifred Davies), and *Linguistic Purism in Action – How Auxiliary Tun was Stigmatized in Early New High German*.

Teresa Marqués-Aguado (B.A. and Ph.D. Málaga) is a Lecturer at the University of Murcia (Spain), where she teaches English language as well as some under-graduate courses on historical linguistics. Her research interests lie within the latter, mainly in palaeography, codicology, and manuscript studies. She has published in journals such as *English Studies*, and has collaborated on several volumes centered on her field of research, such as *Textual Healing: Studies in Medieval English Medical, Scientific and Technical Texts* and *Benvenutus Grassus' Treatise on the Use of the Eyes: A Critical Edition*.

Robert McColl Millar is Reader in Linguistics at the University of Aberdeen. His most recent books include *Authority and Identity: a Sociolinguistic History of Europe before the Modern Age, Northern and Insular Scots, Language, Nation and Power,* and *English Historical Sociolinguistics*.

Rajend Mesthrie is Professor of Linguistics at the University of Cape Town, where he teaches courses in sociolinguistics, with special reference to language contact and variation. He was head of the Linguistics Section from 1998 to 2009. He holds a research chair in migration, language, and social change. Amongst his book publications are *Introducing Sociolinguistics* (with J. Swann, A. Deumert, and W. Leap), *World Englishes* (Rakesh Bhatt), *A Dictionary of South African Indian English* and *A Dictionary of Sociolinguistics* (with J. Swann, A. Deumert, and T. Lillis), and the edited collections *Language in South Africa* and *A Concise Encyclopedia of Sociolinguistics*. His current research focuses on the social dialectology of South African English with reference to accelerated post-apartheid social changes. He is a Past President of the Linguistics Society of Southern Africa (2002–9) and a co-editor of the journal *English Today*. He has contributed to *Journal of Sociolinguistics*,

Journal of Pidgin and Creole Languages, *Language Variation and Change*, and *International Journal of the Sociology of Language*.

Anneli Meurman-Solin is a senior researcher in the Research Unit for Variation, Contacts and Change in English (VARIENG) at the University of Helsinki, Finland. She has been a lecturer in English philology in the English Department, University of Helsinki, and a Fellow at the Helsinki Collegium for Advanced Studies. She has compiled two diachronic corpora representing Scottish English and edited the volumes *Connectives in the History of English* (with Ursula Lenker) and *Information Structure and Syntactic Change in the History of English* (with María José López-Couso and Bettelou Los).

James Milroy is Emeritus Professor of Linguistics at the University of Sheffield. After retiring from Sheffield he taught at the University of Michigan. His main research interests have been in Old Norse, Middle English, historical linguistics, the history of English, and sociolinguistics. His publications include *Linguistic Variation and Change: On the Historical Sociolinguistics of English*, *Authority in Language* (with Lesley Milroy), *The Language of Gerard Manley Hopkins*, and many articles: in collections (such as *Standard English: the Widening Debate*) and in various journals, including *Saga-Book of the Viking Society*, *Neophilologus*, *Journal of Linguistics* and *Journal of Sociolinguistics*.

Agnete Nesse is Post doctor at the University of Bergen (Norway), studying the destandardization of Norwegian radio language after 1968. Her research interests include historical linguistics, dialectology, and sociolinguistics, fields in which she has published several books, such as *Bydialekt, Riksmål og Identitet – sett fra Bodø*, and articles in book collections and journals.

Terttu Nevalainen is Professor of English Philology and Academy Professor at the University of Helsinki (Finland). She is the Director of VARIENG, the Research Unit for Variation, Contacts and Change in English, funded by the Academy of Finland National Centres of Excellence Programme (2000–11). Her research interests include English language, the history of English, historical sociolinguistics, variation studies, and corpus compilation and methodology. Besides her work in compiling the *Helsinki Corpus of English Texts* (HC) and the *Corpus of Early English Correspondence* (CEEC), her publications include monographs such as *Historical Sociolinguistics: Language Change in Tudor and Stuart England* (with Helena Raumolin-Brunberg) and *An Introduction to Early Modern English*; co-edited volumes, such as *Types of Variation*, *Letter Writing*, *The Dynamics of Linguistic Variation*, and *The Oxford Handbook of the History of English* (with Elizabeth Traugott); and research articles published in leading journals, such as *English Language and Linguistics*, *Journal of English Linguistics*, and *Language Variation and Change*. She is the English editor of *Neuphilologische Mitteilungen*, published quarterly since 1899, and the editor-in-chief of the e-series *Studies in Variation, Contacts and Change in English*. She also edits the new series Oxford Studies in the History of English.

Nevalainen is the Vice President for Research of the International Society for the Linguistics of English (ISLE).

Mieko Ogura is Professor in Linguistics at Tsurumi University, Yokohama (Japan), where she teaches English historical linguistics, historical linguistics, and phonetics and phonology. She has been working with William S.-Y. Wang for several decades at the Project on Linguistic Analysis, University of California at Berkeley, and the Language Engineering Laboratory, Chinese University of Hong Kong. Her research has centered on language change, primarily that of English, from the perspective of lexical diffusion, in which she has published extensively: books such as *Historical English Phonology: A Lexical Perspective* and *Dynamic Dialectology: A Study of Language in Time and Space* and articles in leading journals such as *Diachronica, Folia Linguistica Historica*, and *Proceedings of the International Conference on English Historical Linguistics, Evolution of Language, Methods and Data in English Historical Dialectology*, and *Language, Evolution, and the Brain*. She is currently interested in interdisciplinary perspectives on language evolution, particularly computational modeling and brain mechanisms. She is currently writing a book on *Language Evolution and Complex Adaptive Systems*.

Minna Palander-Collin is currently professor of English Philology and head of the English Unit at the Department of Modern Languages, and senior researcher at the Research Unit for Variation, Contacts and Change in English (VARIENG), University of Helsinki. Her main research interests include historical sociolinguistics, historical pragmatics, and corpus linguistics, and her latest project focuses on *Language and Identity: Variation and Change in Patterns of Interaction in the History of English*. She has published several articles on these topics and co-edited *The Language of Daily Life in England (1400–1800)* and *Social Roles and Language Practices in Late Modern English*. She is also one of the compilers of the *Corpus of Early English Correspondence*.

Catharina Peersman (Ph.D. K.U.Leuven) is postdoctoral fellow of the Research Foundation – Flanders (FWO) at the K.U. Leuven (Belgium), where she is currently teaching in the interdisciplinary practically-oriented research seminar for Medieval and Renaissance Studies, French Historical Texts and Linguistique appliquée du français. Before that, she was affiliated to the University of Minnesota (Twin Cities Campus) as H. Van Wayenbergh of the Hoover Foundation Fellow for the Belgian American Educational Foundation (2009–10). Her research projects focus on the use and perception of languages in medieval Flanders. While paying particular attention to medieval French, her research also takes into account similar texts written in Latin and Dutch. Dr. Peersman's publications illustrate her interdisciplinary approach, as they include several articles on the rise of written vernaculars in medieval documents (for example, in *Sociolinguistique historique du domaine gallo-roman: Enjeux et methodologies*), as well as a co-authored contribution on *Testing methods on an artificially created textual tradition* (in *The Evolution of Texts: Confronting Stemmatological and Genetical Methods*) and an archival inventory.

Carol Percy is Associate Professor of English at the University of Toronto (Canada), where she teaches courses on eighteenth-century literature and on the history and diaspora of the English language. Her research interests focus on the cultural history of later modern English, including the roles of textbooks, periodicals, and newspapers in the standardization and codification of English. "Consumers of correctness: men, women, and language in eighteenth-century classified advertisements" appeared in *New Perspectives on English Historical Linguistics*. Recent essays in edited collections include "Women's grammars" in *Eighteenth-century English: Ideology and Change*, "How book reviewers became language guardians" in *Social Roles and Language Practices in Late Modern English*, "Learning and virtue: English grammar and the eighteenth-century girls' school" in *Educating the Child in Enlightenment Britain*, and "Mid-century grammars and their reception in the *Monthly Review* and the *Critical Review*" in *Grammars, Grammarians and Grammar-Writing in Eighteenth-century England*.

Helena Raumolin-Brunberg has recently retired from her research post in the Research Unit for Variation, Change, and Contacts in English (VARIENG) at the University of Helsinki. Apart from a three-year period as acting Associate Professor at the Department of Translation Studies (1989–92), she worked as a researcher at the Department of English in Helsinki. Raumolin-Brunberg's research interests include historical sociolinguistics, language change, corpus linguistics, nominal syntax, and Early Modern English, on which she has published over 50 articles. Her doctoral dissertation was entitled *The Noun Phrase in Early Sixteenth-Century English: A Study Based on Sir Thomas More's Writings* (1991). Her other books, co-edited and co-authored with Terttu Nevalainen, include *Sociolinguistics and Language History: Studies Based on the Corpus of Early English Correspondence* and *Historical Sociolinguistics: Language Change in Tudor and Stuart England*. She was one of the compilers of both the Early Modern English section of the *Helsinki Corpus of English Texts* and the *Corpus of Early English Correspondence*. Her recent research has focused on the behavior of individuals under ongoing linguistic change. In this area, she has made longitudinal analyses of individual usage and traced leaders of linguistic change.

Paul T. Roberge is Professor of Germanic Languages and Joint Professor of Linguistics at the University of North Carolina at Chapel Hill. He is also Professor Extraordinary of General Linguistics at the University of Stellenbosch. His teaching and research interests include historical and comparative Germanic linguistics, pidgin and creole languages, sociohistorical linguistics, and Afrikaans. He has also taught and written on the origin and evolution of human language.

Paul Rössler is Professor in German Linguistics at the University of Regensburg (Germany). His research interests include spelling, morphology, standardization, and variation of the German language in sociolinguistic and structural linguistic perspectives, where he has published extensively, including books such as

Schreibvariation Sprachregion Konfession, and articles in book collections and journals.

Hanna Rutkowska has been assistant professor (Polish *adiunkt*) at the School of English, Adam Mickiewicz University (Poznań, Poland) since 2001. In 2003 she published *Graphemics and Morphosyntax in the Cely Letters (1472–78)*, a monograph based on her doctoral dissertation. She is currently working on her post-doctoral project on orthographic standardization in English on the basis of several six-teenth- and seventeenth-century editions of *The kalender of shepherdes*, benefiting from a post-doctoral project grant (N N104 055438) from the Polish Ministry of Science and Higher Education, 2010–12. She has published articles on Middle English and Early Modern English orthography and morphosyntax in journals such as *Folia Linguistica Historica*, *Studia Anglica Posnaniensia* and *SELIM: Journal of the Spanish Society for Medieval English Language and Literature*.

Anni Sairio is a postdoctoral researcher in historical sociolinguistics at the University of Helsinki (Finland). Her research interests include eighteenth-century English, social and cultural factors in language variation and change, social networks, and editing. She is the author of the *Language and Letters of the Bluestocking Network: Sociolinguistic Issues in Eighteenth-century Epistolary English*.

Herbert Schendl is retired Professor in English linguistics at the University of Vienna, where he continues to teach on English historical linguistics. His main research interests include early language variation and change, multilingualism, and historical code-switching, in which he has published extensively: numerous articles on Old English syntax and semantics, historical phonology and mor-phology, historical sociolinguistics, and, especially more recently, historical code-switching, and books including *Code-switching in Early English* (with L. Wright), *Rethinking Middle English* (with N. Ritt), *Historical Linguistics*, and *A Complete Concordance to the Novels of John Lyly*.

Natalie Schilling is an Associate Professor of Linguistics at Georgetown University, Washington, DC, where she teaches a range of courses in sociolinguistics and linguistics, including courses in variation analysis, sociolinguistic field methods, and forensic linguistics. Her research interests include language variation and change, especially stylistic variation, ethnic variation, and regional variation in the Southeastern United States. Her publications include *American English: Dialects and Variation* (with Walt Wolfram), *The Handbook of Language Variation and Change* (with J.K. Chambers and Peter Trudgill), and *Sociolinguistic Fieldwork*, as well as articles in leading journals such as *American Speech*, *Journal of Sociolinguistics*, *Language*, *Language in Society*, and *Language Variation and Change*.

Daniel Schreier has researched and taught at North Carolina State University, the University of Canterbury at Christchurch (New Zealand), the University of Regensburg and the University of Bern. Since 2006, he has been Professor of

English Linguistics at the University of Zurich. His areas of specialization are sociolinguistics and contact linguistics; he has carried out research on such topics as the history and origins of English in the South Atlantic Ocean (Tristan da Cunha and St Helena), earlier New Zealand English, contact-induced phonotactic changes in English around the world and lesser-known varieties of English. He has written several books, such as *The Lesser-known Varieties of English* (with Peter Trudgill, Edgar Schneider and Jeffrey P. Williams), *St Helenian English: Origins, Evolution and Variation*, *Consonant Change in English Worldwide: Synchrony meets Diachrony*, *Isolation and Language Change: Contemporary and Sociohistorical Evidence from Tristan da Cunha English*, and *Tristan da Cunha: History People Language* (with Karen Lavarello-Schreier), and is on the editorial board of the journals *English Worldwide* and *Multilingua*.

Irma Taavitsainen is Professor of English Philology and Deputy Director of the Research Unit for Variation, Contacts and Change in English at the University of Helsinki. Her main research interests focus on historical pragmatics and the development of the special language of medicine. She is the co-editor of the *Journal of Historical Pragmatics* (with Andreas H. Jucker). She is the leader of the Scientific Thought-styles project, and co-compiler of the electronic corpora *Middle English Medical Texts*, *Early Modern Medical Texts 1500–1700*, and *Late Modern English Medical Texts 1700–1800*. She has co-edited several books, including *Medical Writing in Late Medieval English* and *Medical Writing in Early Modern English* (with Päivi Pahta), *Diachronic Perspectives on Domain-specific English* (with Marina Dossena), *Methods in Historical Pragmatics* (with Susan Fitzmaurice), *Diachronic Developments in Address Term Systems* and *Speech Acts in the History of English* (with Andreas H. Jucker), and *Historical Pragmatics* (with Andreas H. Jucker). In addition, she has published articles in various scholarly books and journals.

Matthew Toulmin is Postdoctoral Research Fellow at Serampore College in India, and a linguistics and translation consultant for SIL International. His research interests include Indo-Aryan languages, communication and translation theory, and the design of courses for grassroots language development in the Indian context. He has authored theoretical works including *From Linguistic to Sociolinguistic Reconstruction: the Kamta Historical Subgroup of Indo-Aryan*, as well as several pedagogical works for Serampore College.

Nila Vázquez (B.A. and Ph.D. Santiago de Compostela) is Senior Lecturer in History of the English Language at the University of Murcia (Spain), where she teaches on the history of English and varieties of English. Her research interests include historical linguistics and sociolinguistics, textual scholarship, and electronic editing, in which she has published extensively: books such as *Creation and Use of Historical English Corpora in Spain*, *The* Tale of Gamelyn *of the* Canterbury Tales: *An Annotated Edition* and *Editing Middle English Texts in the 21st Century: New Techniques and Approaches*, and articles in leading journals such as *Studia Anglica Posnaniensia*, *Variants*, *Journal of the Early Book Society* and *Babel*.

Anja Voeste is Professor of Historical Linguistics/German Language History at the Justus Liebig University Giessen, Germany. She graduated in 1998 with a Ph.D. on variation of adjective declension in eighteenth-century German, published as *Varianz und Vertikalisierung: Zur Normierung der Adjektivdeklination in der ersten Hälfte des 18. Jahrhunderts*. For her higher doctorate degree she explored sixteenth-century spelling, published as *Orthographie und Innovation: Die Segmentierung des Wortes im 16. Jahrhundert*, outlining the trendsetting role of the typesetters. Her research focuses on the synthesis of empirical data and theoretical approaches such as historical sociolinguistics and functionalism, sound change and evolutionary theory, spelling history and systems theory, language contact, and discourse analysis.

Richard J. Watts is emeritus professor of Modern English Linguistics, having retired from the chair in that discipline at the University of Bern in 2008. He is the editor of the international journal *Multilingua* and co-editor of the book series, *Language and Social Processes*. He is the author of books such as *Politeness* and *Language Myths and the History of English*, and the co-editor of eight further books such as *Politeness in Language* (with Sachiko Ide and Konrad Ehlich), *Standard English: The Widening Debate* (with Tony Bex), and *Alternative Histories of English* (with Peter Trudgill). He has written around eighty articles on various subjects in linguistics including politeness, pragmatics, sociolinguistics and, more recently, historical linguistics and sociocognitive linguistics.

Roger Wright is Professor (Emeritus) of Spanish at the University of Liverpool (England), where from 1972 to 2008 he taught the language, history and literature of Medieval Spain. His research interests concern the linguistic, philological, sociolinguistic, and historical relations between Latin and the Romance Languages from the end of the Roman Empire until the thirteenth century, on which he has published extensively; his main idea (or discovery) is that Latin and Romance were not conceptually distinguished until the advent of the Carolingian Reforms after 800 A.D. His best-known publications are *Late Latin and Early Romance (In Spain and Carolingian France)* (also published in Spanish translation), *Early Ibero-Romance* and *A Sociophilological Study of Late Latin*. He has written over a hundred articles, and also edited conference proceedings dedicated to these topics.

Preface

TERESA FANEGO

Over the years, the Blackwell Handbooks in Linguistics Series has produced a number of volumes that represent important milestones in the development of linguistic theory and practice in such diverse fields as language variation and change (Chambers, Trudgill and Schilling-Estes 2002), historical linguistics (Joseph and Janda 2003), bilingualism (Bhatia and Ritchie 2005), pragmatics (Horn and Ward 2005), pidgin and creole studies (Kouwenberg and Singler 2008) and language contact (Hickey 2010), among others. The publication of a new volume in the series, devoted to historical sociolinguistics, testifies to the dynamism of this discipline, thirty years after the publication of Suzanne Romaine's groundbreaking work (1982) on the application of sociolinguistic models to historical data.

In the Preface to the proceedings from the first international workshop on historical sociolinguistics (or 'socio-historical linguistics', as it was styled at the time), held in Poznań in 1983 during the Sixth International Conference on Historical Linguistics, Romaine and Traugott (1985: 5) pointed out that the workshop aimed at "bringing together sociolinguists, historical linguists and historians [...], and combin[ing] the rich philological tradition with recent work on quantitative methods, discourse analysis, literacy, as well as with historical phonology, syntax, and pragmatics." This diversity and interdisciplinarity of historical sociolinguistics has no doubt contributed to its ever growing popularity, and has been further nourished and extended in recent times by a number of developments in related fields – corpus linguistics, grammaticalization studies, even Cognitive Linguistics – which have tended to blur the sharp distinction, prevalent during a great part of the twentieth century, between synchrony and diachrony, and between theoretical and applied linguistics.

As the editors of this volume point out in the Introduction, historical sociolinguistics – and historical linguistics in general – has been revolutionized by the emergence of computer-assisted data processing techniques. The compilation of huge historical corpora representing a broad range of genres, dialects, authors, and dates of composition has served to partly overcome the limitations posed by the fragmentary, or otherwise incomplete, data available to historical sociolinguists, as famously noted by Labov (1994: 11). At the same time, from the time of Labov's pioneering research on sound change in Martha's Vineyard (1963) and New York City (1966), and the theoretical treatment of linguistic variation proposed by Weinreich *et al.* (1968), linguistic variation and linguistic change – synchrony and diachrony – have increasingly come to be seen as two different aspects of the same phenomenon. Their interaction is also a fundamental premise of studies involving grammaticalization, as noted by Aitchison (see Chapter 1 in this volume). Grammaticalization, like sociolinguistics itself, has both a synchronic and a diachronic dimension, though "its foundation is diachronic in nature" (Heine 2003: 575); it "focuses on the intersection of 'internal' grammar (structure) and 'external' grammar (use), and insists on gradience and process rather than product" (Traugott 2001: 127), and, being speaker-oriented and concerned with speaker–hearer interaction, touches directly on sociolinguistics, as reflected, for instance, in the wealth of studies exploring the extent to which tenets of grammaticalization can help to explain language change in situations of extreme language contact (see Plag 2002; Heine and Kuteva 2005; Bruyn 2008; also Chapter 24, 28 and 29 in this *Handbook*).

Likewise, interest in the social nature of language is growing among practitioners of Cognitive Linguistics, as might be expected from a linguistic paradigm that proclaims a usage-based approach to language and takes as the basis of its enquiry "language as it is actually used by real speakers in real situations in a specific historical moment" (Kristiansen and Dirven 2008: 3). The social aspects of language variation have thus begun to attract the attention of cognitive researchers, most notably with reference to lexical and lexical-semantic variation (e.g. Speelman, Grondelaers and Geeraerts 2008), but also in realms such as inflectional (Tummers, Speelman and Geeraerts 2005), constructional (Szmrecsanyi 2010), and phonetic variation (Kristiansen 2008). While such studies tend to have a primarily synchronic orientation, some of them (such as Colleman 2010; Robinson 2010) have also started to encompass general social factors involved in change and the interaction of these with cognitive factors, thus contributing to a better understanding of certain variationist phenomena.[1]

To conclude, these and many other aspects of historical sociolinguistics, both theoretical and applied, are covered in this comprehensive and informative reference work. With a list of internationally renowned contributors from around the world, the *Blackwell Handbook of Historical Sociolinguistics* will prove required reading for researchers and advanced students in the fields of historical and non-historical sociolinguistics, language and dialect contact, and language change.

NOTE

1   Note that, interestingly enough, volume 3 (2010) of Labov's *Principles of linguistic change* carries the subtitle *Cognitive and cultural factors.*

REFERENCES

Bhatia, T.K. and Ritchie, W.C. (eds.) (2005) *The Handbook of Bilingualism*, Wiley-Blackwell, Oxford.

Bruyn, A. (2008) Grammaticalization in pidgins and creoles. In S. Kouwenberg and J.V. Singler (eds.), *The Handbook of Pidgin and Creole Studies*, Wiley-Blackwell, Oxford, pp. 383–410.

Chambers, J.K., Trudgill, P., and Schilling-Estes, N. (eds.) (2002) *The Handbook of Language Variation and Change*, Blackwell, Oxford.

Colleman, T. (2010) Lectal variation in constructional semantics: 'Benefactive' ditransitives in Dutch. In D. Geeraerts, G. Kristiansen, and Y. Peirsman (eds.), pp. 191–222.

Geeraerts, D., Kristiansen, G., and Peirsman, Y. (eds.) (2010) *Advances in Cognitive Sociolinguistics*, Mouton de Gruyter, Berlin.

Heine, B. (2003) Grammaticalization. In B.D. Joseph and R.D. Janda (eds.), pp. 575–601.

Heine, B. and Kuteva, T. (2005) *Language Contact and Grammatical Change*, Cambridge University Press, Cambridge.

Hickey, R. (ed.) (2010) *The Handbook of Language Contact*, Wiley-Blackwell, Oxford.

Horn, L., and Ward, G. (eds.) (2005) *The Handbook of Pragmatics*, Blackwell, Oxford.

Joseph, B.D. and Janda, R.D. (eds.) (2003) *The Handbook of Historical Linguistics*, Blackwell, Oxford.

Kouwenberg, S. and Singler, J.V. (eds.) (2008) *The Handbook of Pidgin and Creole Studies*, Wiley-Blackwell, Oxford.

Kristiansen, G. 2008. Style-shifting and shifting styles: A socio-cognitive approach to lectal variation. In G. Kristiansen and R. Dirven (eds.), pp. 45–88.

Kristiansen, G. and Dirven, R. (eds.) (2008) *Cognitive Sociolinguistics. Language Variation, Cultural Models, Social Systems*, Mouton de Gruyter, Berlin.

Kristiansen, G. and Dirven, R. (2008) Cognitive sociolinguistics: Rationale, methods and scope. In G. Kristiansen and R. Dirven (eds.), pp. 1–17.

Labov, W. (1963) The social motivation of a sound change. *Word* 19(3): 273–309.

Labov, W. (1966) *The Social Stratification of English in New York City*, Center for Applied Linguistics, Washington, DC.

Labov, W. (1994) *Principles of Linguistic Change: Internal Factors*, Blackwell, Oxford.

Labov, W. (2010) *Principles of Linguistic Change: Cognitive and Cultural Factors*, Wiley-Blackwell, Oxford.

Plag, I. (2002) On the role of grammaticalization in creolization. A reassessment. In G. Gilbert (ed.), *Pidgin and Creole Linguistics in the 21st century. Essays at Millennium's End*, Lang, New York, pp. 229–46.

Robinson, J. (2010) *Awesome* insights into semantic variation. In D. Geeraerts, G. Kristiansen, and Y. Peirsman (eds.), pp. 85–110.

Romaine, S. (1982) *Socio-historical Linguistics: Its Status and Methodology*, Cambridge University Press, Cambridge.

Romaine, S. and Traugott, E.C. (eds.) (1985) *Papers from the Workshop on Socio-historical Linguistics*. Special issue of *Folia Linguistica Historica* 6(1): 5–180.

Speelman, D., Grondelaers, S., and Geeraerts, D. (2008) Variation in the choice of adjectives in the two main national varieties of Dutch. In G. Kristiansen and R. Dirven (eds.), pp. 205–33.

Szmrecsanyi, B. (2010) The English genitive alternation in a cognitive sociolinguistics perspective. In D. Geeraerts, G. Kristiansen, and Y. Peirsman (eds.), pp. 139–66.

Traugott, E.C. (2001) Zeroing in on multifunctionality and style. In P. Eckert and J.R. Rickford (eds.), *Style and Sociolinguistic Variation*, Cambridge University Press, Cambridge, pp. 127–37.

Tummers, J., Speelman, D., and Geeraerts, D. (2005) Inflectional variation in Belgian and Netherlandic Dutch: A usage-based account of the adjectival inflection. In N. Delbecque, J. van der Auwera, and D. Geeraerts (eds.), *Perspectives on Variation. Sociolinguistic, Historical, Comparative*, Mouton de Gruyter, Berlin, pp. 93–110.

Weinreich, U., Labov, W., and Herzog, M.I. (1968) Empirical foundations for a theory of language change. In W.P. Lehmann and Y. Malkiel (eds.), *Directions for Historical Linguistics: A Symposium*, University of Texas Press, Austin, pp. 95–195.

Introduction

J. CAMILO CONDE-SILVESTRE & JUAN M. HERNÁNDEZ-CAMPOY

Over the last three decades research in the history of languages has been significantly refreshed, not only because new methodologies have developed within linguistics at large, but also because the systematic application of their tenets and tools has often uncovered new aspects to be analysed and interpreted. This is the case of historical sociolinguistics: a hybrid subfield subsisting on the interdisciplinary character of sociolinguistic methodology, whose original goal was, in the words of Suzanne Romaine, "to provide an account of the forms and uses in which variation may manifest itself in a given community over time" (1982: x). Now, thirty years after the publication of Romaine's foundational work *Socio-Historical Linguistics: Its Status and Methodology* (1982), maturity has been obtained thanks to the efforts of other historical sociolinguists[1] – some of them participants in this collaborative volume – who have devoted themselves to the task of elucidating the theoretical limits of the discipline, as well as to applying the tenets and findings of contemporary sociolinguistic research to the interpretation of linguistic material from the past. As a result, the scope of the discipline has widened beyond the study of variation and change to cater for other macrosociolinguistic facets, such as multilingualism, language contact, attitudes to language, and standardization, so that a broader definition of historical sociolinguistics as "the reconstruction of the history of a given language in its socio-cultural context" is, in its simplicity, far more inclusive. The development of historical sociolinguistics has also confirmed the observation – patently obvious, but not always attended to by some late-twentieth-century methods of linguistic research – that the evolution of linguistic systems occurs in systematic connection to the socio-historical situation of their speakers.

One of the most relevant accomplishments of the discipline has been its contribution to enriching the dialogue between the present and the past in linguistic

The Handbook of Historical Sociolinguistics, First Edition. Edited by Juan Manuel Hernández-Campoy and Juan Camilo Conde-Silvestre.
© 2014 John Wiley & Sons, Ltd. Published 2014 by John Wiley & Sons, Ltd.

research. Historical sociolinguistics has revealed that advances at the synchronic level – tracing variation and change in progress, for instance – may lead to a better understanding of diachrony – the *actuation* of historically attested changes – and vice versa: "the use of the present to explain the past," in Labov's words, can be supplemented by the *uniformitarian* principle, to the extent that "[i]f they are relatively constant, day-to-day effects of social interaction upon grammar and phonology [...] continue to operate today the same way they have in the past" (Labov 1972: 274; see also 1994: 21–23). This relaxation of the strict limits of the Saussurean dichotomy has had interesting heuristic consequences. On the one hand, it is fundamental to the strengthening of the limits of the discipline: the present and the past have become interchangeable sources of data for sociolinguistic research and this dialogue has invigorated the versatility of the tools needed to enlighten the processes of variation and change, whether they are well-attested phenomena already catalogued by historical linguists or current processes in progress, interpreted by sociolinguists and dialectologists. On the other hand, in encouraging the application of sociolinguistic methods to materials from the past, historical sociolinguistics has become a locus for monitoring the maturity of sociolinguistics at large, as regards its scientific validity, its paradigmatic quality, and its interdisciplinary nature. This suggests the prospect of refining the interpretation of languages in and through time, social and geographical space, and of improving linguistic theory, as well as of advancing our capacity to understand the nature and structure of language as a human faculty.

In the course of this trajectory historical sociolinguistics has sometimes been blamed for lack of representativeness and its empirical validity has occasionally been questioned. One direction of the problem clearly resides in the strain – shared by all attempts at historical linguistic inquiry – of "making the best use of bad data" (Labov 1994: 11): written materials from the past which have very often survived by mere chance and are isolated from their immediate communicative background, so that their original social and stylistic contexts of production and reception can not really be reconstructed. In addition to these qualms, the historical paradox and the so-called *uniformitarian* principle mentioned earlier have also been part of the controversial issue: How different was the past from the present? To what extent can independent variables be reconstructed for the history of languages without running the risk of anachronism? Are sociolinguistic generalizations meaningful in terms of sociolinguistic universals?

Methodological disputes have not hampered the fruitful development of the field. On the contrary, they have often become a source of additional motivation for researchers to cross discipline boundaries. Indeed, in surmounting these difficulties, historical sociolinguistics has been fortunate in the assistance it has received from the extensive parallel development of other ancillary disciplines: corpus linguistics, on the one hand, and social history, on the other. The links established with these two fields have conferred upon the discipline both 'empirical ease' and 'historical confidence.' It is well known that the developments in computing technology over the last twenty years have radically transformed linguistic research and that the compilation of large electronic corpora has been instrumental in overcoming some of the problems inherent in working with 'bad data' from the past. By allowing researchers to deal simultaneously with almost all the texts that have survived from a given period, corpus linguistics partly solves the fragmentary nature of historical material, ensures that variability in past stages can reliably be reconstructed, and facilitates the selection of the variables that are worthy of analysis. Similarly, the interest of social historians in the structure of groups and communities from the past, together with the reconstruction of demographic and socio-economic structures, has greatly eased the task of the historical sociolinguist, by allowing him/her to reconstruct – on the reliable evidence afforded by contemporary documents (thus non-anachronistically) – the socio-historical circumstances which could have affected linguistic processes in the past.

In parallel to the imperative achievement of 'empirical' and 'historical' validity, most historical sociolinguistic research has been applied to the systematic reconstruction of the social correlates of well-attested changes in different periods of the history of languages. In this respect, data from the past have been correlated with a range of sociolinguistic variables – including not only socio-demographic factors such as age, social status, professional and educational background, gender, domicile, migration history, and networks of personal relationships, but also touching on the diffusion of historical changes, both in time (real or apparent) and space (supralocalization and/or geolinguistic diffusion). There is no doubt that historical sociolinguistic research has enriched the understanding of some of the changes that make up the history of languages, and that, as a result, these processes can no longer be seen as simple shifts from one state to another, but as complex courses whose inception and spread often interact with some of the factors mentioned above. Despite the centrality of variationism to the development of historical sociolinguistics, the field is currently extended to cater for other aspects of language development, often involving macrosociolinguistic issues derived from language contact and multilingualism, standardization and language attitudes, among others, which this handbook also intends to cover. A glance at the publications posted on the e-journal *Historical Sociolinguistics and Sociohistorical Linguistics* (http://www.let.leidenuniv.nl/hsl_shl), launched in 2000 by Ingrid Tieken-Boon van Ostade at the University of Leiden, will familiarize the lay reader with the variety of topics commonly encompassed within the field.

This work is constructed on the foundations established by a number of precedents which it humbly aspires to complement, including the pioneering *Socio-historical Linguistics* (1982) by Suzanne Romaine; Ingrid Tieken-Boon van Ostade's *The Auxiliary Do in Eighteenth-century English: a Sociohistorical-Linguistic Approach* (1987); James Milroy's *Linguistic Variation and Change: on the Historical Sociolinguistics of English* (1992); Tim William Machan and Charles T. Scott's *English in its Social Context: Essays in Historical Sociolinguistics* (1992); Terttu Nevalainen and Helena Raumolin-Brunberg's *Sociolinguistics and Language History: Studies Based on the Corpus of Early English Correspondence* (1996), and their more recent *Historical Sociolinguistics. Language Change in Tudor and Stuart England* (2003); Ernst Håkon Jahr's *Language Change: Advances in Historical Sociolinguistics* (1998); Ulrich

Ammon, Klaus J. Mattheier and Peter H. Nelde's *Historische Soziolinguistik* (1999); Dieter Kastovsky and Arthur Mettinger's *The History of English in a Social Context. Essays in Historical Sociolinguistics* (2000); Ralph Penny's *Variation and Change in Spanish* (2000); Anthony Lodge's *Sociolinguistic History of Parisian French* (2004); Francisco Moreno-Fernández's *Historia Social de las Lenguas de España* (2005); Alexander Bergs' *Social Networks and Historical Sociolinguistics* (2005); J. Camilo Conde-Silvestre and Juan M. Hernández-Campoy's *Sociolinguistics and the History of English: Perspectives and Problems* (2005); and *Sociolingüística Histórica* (2007) by J. Camilo Conde-Silvestre.

The aim of the handbook is to present an up-to-date and in-depth exploration of the extent to which sociolinguistic theoretical models, methods, findings, and expertise can be applied to the process of reconstruction of the past of languages in order to account for diachronic linguistic changes and developments. We therefore expect it to provide the community of scholars and students with a product covering this specific area of research, filling a lacuna in the Wiley-Blackwell language and linguistics collection and to aspire, through the interdisciplinary appeal of the subject-matter, to attract scholars from related fields such as sociolinguistics at large and social history. With contributions from authors belonging to the generation of founders and their intellectual offspring – now themselves internationally acclaimed scholars – and bringing together their own research experience, this handbook exhibits the vitality and growth of the core of the historical sociolinguistic enterprise, illustrating in five parts its different multifaceted pursuits.

In Part I – Origins and Theoretical Assumptions – the discipline of historical sociolinguistics is located at the confluence of two areas, sociolinguistics and historical linguistics, its origins and motivations are outlined, and special emphasis is given to the theoretical assumptions underpinning the reconstruction of the sociolinguistic behavior of historical speech communities. In Chapter 1, Jean Aitchison explores the evolution of two apparently irreconcilable dimensions in the study of language variation and change, diachrony and synchrony, which the scope of historical sociolinguistics attempts to integrate in a kind of complementary distribution. Terttu Nevalainen and Helena Raumolin-Brunberg, in Chapter 2, present the origins, motivations, and main paradigms in this hybrid discipline, providing an outline of the main directions of research. A similar task is accomplished by Robert McColl Millar in Chapter 3, where some concepts and historical applications of macrosociolinguistics are presented and discussed, touching on the connections of the new discipline to social history and the sociology of language.

Part II – Methods for the Sociolinguistic Study of the History of Languages – examines the methods employed by historical sociolinguists when carrying out research, paying special attention to the sources for both linguistic and sociohistorical data and the problems typically encountered when practicing this kind of socially-oriented linguistic archaeology. Juan M. Hernández-Campoy and Natalie Schilling evaluate, in Chapter 4, some problems with the *generalizability* principle – the prospects of extending the results of research conducted with limited material to account for more global trends and processes in the history of language by relying on quantitative methods. Alexander Bergs devotes Chapter

5 to *uniformitarianism* – the claim that "the processes which we observe in the present can help us to gain knowledge about processes in the past" – as a necessary requisite for historical sociolinguistic research, but, paradoxically, also as a possible source of limitations when it verges on anachronism. Pascual Cantos, in Chapter 6, examines linguistic corpora as the most useful tool for overcoming the difficulties inherent in the "bad-data problem" mentioned above. The question of sources is a fundamental issue in historical sociolinguistic research: not all surviving written documents are equally useful, and layers of variation have to be extracted from them, each type of source requiring different approaches and treatments. In this connection, Chapter 7, by Nila Vázquez and Teresa Marqués-Aguado, deals with medieval manuscripts and shows how editorial processes help make the most of them in historical sociolinguistic terms, while Chapters 8 to 11 offer a typology of sources and discuss their treatment for historical sociolinguistics, considered also in chronological sequence: medical, official, and monastic documents as useful materials for research in the Middle Ages (Laura Esteban-Segura), private letters and diaries from the fifteenth century and the early Renaissance onwards (Stephan Elspaß), literary sources throughout the modern period (Kormi Anipa) and, finally, advertisements and newspapers from the eighteenth to the twentieth century (Carol Percy).

Part III – Linguistic and Socio-demographic Variables – demonstrates that by correlating extralinguistic factors, such as socio-demographic and/or context variables, with linguistic variables, historical sociolinguistics is able to detect, locate, describe, and explain the symmetry existing between social variation and linguistic variation in the past in terms of *sociolinguistic variation*; significance being understood as the causality relationship of linguistic and extralinguistic data. In Chapters 12 through 16, results from studies touching on different subsystems are explored in turn by Hanna Rutkowska and Paul Rössler (orthographic variables), Anna Hebda (phonological variables), Anita Auer and Anja Voeste (grammatical variables), Joachim Grzega (lexico-semantic variables), Andreas H. Jucker and Irma Taavitsainen (pragmatic variables). In turn, the independent variables analyzed in sociolinguistic research and their applicability to the history of languages are explored in Chapters 17 through 19 by Agnieszka Kielkiewicz-Janowiak (class, age and gender), J. Camilo Conde-Silvestre (social networks and mobility), and Rajend Mesthrie (race, religion and castes).

Part IV – Historical Dialectology, Language Contact, Change, and Diffusion – is a collection of chapters whose authors are trying to disentangle different facets which touch on languages and dialects in geographical and social motion through time. As is widely known, language change and diffusion have become some of the great unsolved mysteries of linguistic science, and consequently have challenged generations of linguists and philologists. Part IV makes the proper use of the present for the understanding of the past: its chapters examine different ways of using the new concepts and methods developed by sociolinguists and dialectologists to elucidate historical variation and change. In Chapter 20 Paul Roberge studies the teleology of language change, exploring functional and non-functional explanations, while in Chapter 21 Raymond Hickey clarifies the complexities of intralinguistic and extralinguistic factors motivating changes in a speech community and offers a typology. Chapter 22 is devoted by Brian Joseph to a critical analysis of the regularity controversy and the two main models of diffusion that have been of central concern to many linguists: lexical diffusion *vs.* regular (or neogrammarian) change. In Chapter 23, Mieko Ogura deals with the time dimension of these two types of change and its consequences for other socio-linguistic constructs that attend the question of diffusion, such as social networks. In Chapter 24, David Britain examines different models of the geographical diffusion of innovations and changes with a view to tracking their relevance in the past. Chapter 25, by Anneli Meurman-Solin, focuses on the historical reconstruction of regional dialects in contact situations by relying on the perspective afforded by contemporary dialectology and particularly on the use of linguistic atlases. In Chapter 26 Roland Kehrein supplements Meurman-Solin's approach and demonstrates different ways of extracting from linguistic atlases empirical evidence for early dialect change. In Chapter 27, Matthew Toulmin explores aspects of the socio-historical reconstruction of non-European languages. In Chapter 28, Herbert Schendl presents some issues connected to multilingualism, code-switching, and language contact from the perspective of historical sociolinguistics. Chapter 29, by Daniel Schreier, highlights those cases where historical contact between speech communities in the course of migratory movements may give rise to the formation of new linguistic entities, at all levels (new dialect formation). Finally, Chapter 30 in this section is an interesting attempt by Roger Wright to outline the historical evidence of convergence and divergence in world languages with an eye on prospects for the future in this respect.

The last part of the handbook, Attitudes to Language, shows how attitudinal factors in connection to language variation and varieties, mainly on the part of the historical 'language managers' – those professionally involved with languages – have often led to the development of purism and prescriptivism, in obvious connection to standardization, (especially after the eighteenth century), and even to the creation and enforcement of language myths, particularly after the nineteenth century, once the 'scientific' study of languages was established. These constructs, frequently ideologically loaded, are often extended to the evaluation of language systems and may have an effect on sociolinguistic aspects such as the stigmatization of variants and varieties, their maintenance or loss, and even the status of their users. Additionally, language myths may condition our approaches to the study of the history of languages, establishing a canonical selection of the aspects that are worth studying and those that are not. Some of these issues are dealt with in Chapters 31 through 34 by James Milroy (sociolinguistics and ideologies in language history), Richard Watts (language myths), Nils Langer and Agnete Nesse (linguistic purism) and Anni Sairio and Minna Palander-Collin (prestige patterns in language history). Finally, Catharina Peersman, in Chapter 35, traces the origins of these processes through an examination of written vernaculars in Medieval and Renaissance times.

We believe that the *Handbook of Historical Sociolinguistics* constitutes an important step forward in the recognition of the findings and methods of historical sociolinguistics as central to linguistics as a whole. Conceived as a handbook, it aims to be sufficiently comprehensive as to present a reliable guide not only to the work done so far in the field, but also to potential future studies. The scope of the handbook is broad and based on theory, rather than merely on case-studies; by focusing on the most important theoretical, methodological, and definitional topics, aiming at comprehensiveness of reference and avoiding personal research biases, we, as editors, together with the authors with whom we have collaborated, believe it will become a useful textbook for both lay readers and experts alike. With these aims in mind, the contributors have also attempted to combine the recapitulation of already known works with an extension of the scope of the subject into other linguistic and societal areas. Furthermore, despite the obvious preponderance of English as object language of research in the field – as in many other areas of linguistic inquiry – the participation of authors from thirty different universities all over the world (sixteen nations in Europe, America, and Australasia being represented), most of them associated with the Historical Sociolinguistics Network (http://www.philhist.uni-augsburg.de/hison/), ensures that other languages, both Indo-European and non-Indo-European, have become our object of analysis, thus testing the limits of the new discipline in a variety of systems.

As editors, we would like to thank all the contributors to the handbook: their effort has been absolutely invaluable, considering the many different academic commitments we all have. We are also very grateful to Julia Kirk, editor at Wiley-Blackwell, for her assistance throughout the process of editing the handbook, and, of course, Danielle Descoteaux, Wiley-Blackwell's Linguistics Acquisitions Editor, for being so patient and for trusting us, as well as the project. We do appreciate their enthusiasm and encouragement. On behalf of all the contributors to the volume, we wish to dedicate it to our respective teachers and students: from the former we acquired all that we know and became what we are scientifically, while the latter are our main stimulus academically. A plethora of authors from a variety of countries and backgrounds who share their academic professionalism would certainly recognize them both as invaluable sources of motivation for our common intellectual enterprise.

Finally, we hope that this volume not only fulfills its implicit main objective but also helps to introduce new scholars into the field, encouraging research in this promising and vital area.

J. Camilo Conde-Silvestre
Juan M. Hernández-Campoy
Albacete-Murcia-Molina de Segura (Spain)
September 2011

NOTE

1   We here acknowledge the leading role of Jacek Fisiak, Manfred Görlach, Richard Hogg, Merja Kytö, James Milroy, Terttu Nevalainen, Matti Rissanen, Helena Raumolin-Brunberg, Suzanne

Romaine, Michael Samuels, Jeremy Smith, Irma Taavitsainen, Ingrid Tieken-Boon van Ostade or Peter Trudgill, among many others.

REFERENCES

Ammon, U., Mattheier, K.J. and Nelde, P.H. (eds.) (1999) *Historische Soziolinguistik*, Niemeyer, Tübingen.

Bergs, A.T. (2005) *Social Networks and Historical Sociolinguistics. Studies in Morphosyntactic Variation in the Paston Letters (1421–1503)*, Mouton de Gruyter, Berlin/New York.

Conde-Silvestre, J.C. and Hernández-Campoy, J.M. (eds.) (2005) *Sociolinguistics and the History of English: Perspectives and Problems. International Journal of English Studies (IJES). Vol. 5.1*, Editum, Murcia.

Conde-Silvestre, J.C. (2007) *Sociolingüística histórica*, Gredos, Madrid.

Jahr, E.H. (ed.) (1999) *Language Change. Advances in Historical Sociolinguistics*, Mouton de Gruyter, Berlin/New York.

Kastovsky, D. and Mettinger, A. (eds.) (2000) *The History of English in a Social Context. Essays in Historical Sociolinguistics*, Mouton de Gruyter, Berlin/New York.

Labov, W. (1972) *Sociolinguistic Patterns*, University of Pennsylvania Press, Philadelphia.

Labov, W. (1994) *Principles of Linguistic Change. Vol. 1: Internal Factors*, Blackwell, Oxford.

Lodge, A. (2004) *Sociolinguistic History of Parisian French*, Cambridge University Press, Cambridge.

Machan, T.W. and Scott, C.T. (eds.) (1992) *English in its Social Context. Essays in Historical Sociolinguistics*, Oxford University Press, Oxford.

Milroy, J. (1992) *Linguistic Variation and Change. On the Historical Sociolinguistics of English*, Blackwell, Oxford.

Moreno-Fernández, F. (2005) *Historia Social de las Lenguas de España*, Ariel, Barcelona.

Nevalainen, T. and Raumolin-Brunberg, H. (eds.) (1996) *Sociolinguistics and Language History. Studies Based on the Corpus of Early English Correspondence*, Rodopi, Amsterdam.

Nevalainen, T. and Raumolin-Brunberg, H. (2003) *Historical Sociolinguistics. Language Change in Tudor and Stuart England*, Longman Pearson Education, London.

Penny, R. (2000) *Variation and Change in Spanish*, Cambridge University Press, Cambridge.

Romaine, S. (1982) *Socio-historical Linguistics: Its Status and Methodology*, Cambridge University Press, Cambridge.

Tieken-Boon van Ostade, I. (1987) *The Auxiliary Do in Eighteenth Century English. A Sociohistorical Linguistic Approach*, Foris, Dordrecht.

Tieken-Boon van Ostade, I. (ed.) 2000–2010. *Internet Journal. Historical Sociolinguistics and Sociohistorical Linguistics*, www.let.leidenuniv.nl/hsl_shl/index.html [accessed September 12, 2011].

Part I   Origins and Theoretical Assumptions

1 Diachrony vs Synchrony: the Complementary Evolution of Two (Ir)reconcilable Dimensions

JEAN AITCHISON

"Since languages [...] are transmitted from one age to another [...] the relation of the *past* to the *present* enters into the utmost depth of their formation" (Humboldt 1836/1988:40). This statement by the linguistic pioneer Wilhelm von Humboldt in the early nineteenth century shows that the relationship between diachrony and synchrony has long been of concern to linguists – even though Humboldt himself did little more than state the need to deal with both sides of the question. This chapter will explore changing attitudes to this relationship, showing that in the early days of linguistics, diachrony and synchrony were indeed regarded as irreconcilable, though in recent years they have become increasingly integrated.

"The opposition between the two viewpoints – synchronic and diachronic – is absolute and allows no compromise" (Saussure 1915/1959: 125). This dogmatic statement about the need to separate diachrony from synchrony was made by the venerated Swiss linguist Ferdinand de Saussure (1837–1913), in his posthumously published text, *Cours de Linguistique Générale* (1915), which was assembled by his students from their lecture notes. The book is now better known to British and American readers in its translated version *Course in General Linguistics* (1959).

Saussure illustrated his uncompromising statement about the opposition between diachrony and synchrony by his well-known comparison to cuts made through the trunk of a tree. The linguist could make either a horizontal cut, and examine a language at a single point in time, or he could make a vertical cut, and chart the development of selected items over a number of years.

For a long time, this rigid division was largely unquestioned, and still remains a methodological distinction put forward in some textbooks: "[l]anguage can be

The Handbook of Historical Sociolinguistics, First Edition. Edited by Juan Manuel Hernández-Campoy and Juan Camilo Conde-Silvestre.
© 2014 John Wiley & Sons, Ltd. Published 2014 by John Wiley & Sons, Ltd.

viewed either as historically developing, or as a more or less static, synchronic object of investigation" (Hock 1991:30).

Yet the relationship between diachrony and synchrony has varied as linguistic concerns have shifted. In the nineteenth century, attention was focused primarily on diachronic linguistics, largely due to the excitement of finding that changes were not random, but 'regular' in nature. The so-called 'neogrammarians,' a group of scholars centered on Leipzig around 1870, promoted the view that "[a]ll sound changes, as mechanical processes, take place according to laws with no exceptions" (Osthoff and Brugmann 1878, my translation; full text and slightly different translation in Lehmann 1967).

In contrast to the historical fervor of the nineteenth century, for over half of the twentieth century the majority of linguists concentrated on synchronic studies. This was partly in reaction to the earlier historical fixation, and partly because of the urgent need to capture for posterity descriptions of languages that might be likely to die out. Diachronic linguistics continued, but was considered by many to be an optional extra, an inessential subsidiary study.

But in spite of the widespread early twentieth century attention to synchrony, most of the synchronic descriptions were inadequate. They were lacking in coverage in ways that impoverished both synchronic and diachronic studies. The omissions were of two main kinds. First, many synchronic linguists tried to ignore stylistic variation, even though it must have been obvious that any normal speaker could vary the speed and formality of their pronunciation, syntax, and vocabulary, depending on whether s/he was addressing an employer or stranger on the one hand, or friends and family members on the other. Second, the majority of linguists preferred to concentrate on clear-cut cases, ignoring any variation or fuzziness they encountered. In so doing, many of them unwittingly omitted the evidence needed to study changes in progress.

Of course, not all linguists could be accused of these shortcomings. The insightful linguist Edward Sapir famously said: "[a]ll grammars leak" (1921: 38). And the renowned Russian (later American) linguist Roman Jakobson both spoke and wrote realistically about the impossibility of separating diachrony from synchrony. In his memorable lectures at Harvard (1960–61), he impressed his students by standing on one leg and waving the other in the air: "[m]y friends" (this in his inimitable middle-European accent), "[z]is is what a change is like. It is like a step being taken. We do not jump suddenly from one leg to ze other. In a change, you need to look at ze half-way stage, when you are standing on one foot, and ze other is in ze air, like zis" (more leg-waving). In spite of his unforgettable lectures on the topic, his most important published statement on the need to integrate synchrony and diachrony was for a long time accessible only in French, and was not made available in an English translation until 1972 (Jakobson 1949/1972). The paper ended with some key comments on the topic (Jakobson 1949/1972: 138):

> The joining together of the static and the dynamic is one of the most fundamental dialectic paradoxes that determine the spirit of the language. One cannot conceive of the dialectic of linguistic development without referring to this antinomy. Attempts

to identify *synchrony, static* [...] on the one hand, and, on the other *diachrony, dynamic* [...] make of historical linguistics a conglomerate of disparate facts, and create the superficial and harmful illusion of an abyss between the problems of synchrony and diachrony.

Or as another scholar succinctly expressed it more recently: "[t]he linguistic processes that yield change are diachronic extensions of variable processes that are extant in synchronic usage and synchronic grammar" (Guy 2003: 370). As Guy points out, it is now widely accepted that all change involves variation, even though variation does not inevitably lead to change: "[w]e must allow the possibility that some variables persist in active alternation in the speech community, and indeed in the speech of each individual, for generations, without resulting in one variant supplanting all others" (2003: 372).

But perhaps the general lack of knowledge about ongoing changes in the early days was due to the fact that sociolinguistics was a fledgling branch of linguistics, which did not come of age until over halfway through the twentieth century. The person who brought about a revolution in thinking among linguists on this topic was the sociolinguist William Labov. In the 1960s, he addressed the diachrony/ synchrony problem in a (then) novel way and moved historical linguistics in a new direction. He pointed out the need to look not only at completed changes, but also at ongoing alterations:

One approach to linguistic evolution is to study changes completed in the past [...] On the other hand, the questions of the mechanism of change, the inciting causes of change, and the adaptive functions of change, are best analyzed by studying in detail linguistic changes in progress [...] An essential presupposition of this line of research is uniformitarian doctrine: that is, the claim that the same mechanisms which operated to produce the large scale changes of the past may be observed operating in the current changes taking place around us.
(Labov 1965/1972: 268–69) (see Chapter 5 in this *Handbook*)

In a landmark paper (1965/1972), he outlined twelve sound changes, three on rural Martha's Vineyard (an island lying three miles off the east coast of mainland America, and technically part of the state of Massachusetts), and nine in urban New York City. The sound changes were documented across two successive generations: earlier reports in the literature were supplemented by later data obtained by Labov himself. Sound change, he observed, is characterized by the rapid development of some units of a phonetic sub-system, while other units remain relatively constant. Word classes as a whole are affected, rather than individual words. The change is regular, though more in the eventual outcome than in its inception or development.

The changes originated with a restricted subgroup of the speech community, at a time when the separate identity of this group had been weakened. The linguistic form which began to shift was often a marker of regional status with an irregular distribution within the community (Labov 1965/1972: 285). The change then moved throughout the subgroup. He referred to this stage as change from below, that is, change below the level of social awareness[1]. The linguistic variable involved in the change is labeled an 'indicator' which he regarded as a function of group membership.

Succeeding generations of speakers within the same subgroup carried the change further. The variable is now defined as a function of group membership and age level. In cases where the values of the original subgroup were adopted by other groups, the sound change with its associated value of group membership spread to the adopting groups. As the sound change reached the limits of its expansion, the linguistic variable became one of the norms which defined that speech community. The variable was now a 'marker', and began to show stylistic variation.

The movement of the linguistic variable led to readjustments in the distribution of other elements within the system. Later changes, not inevitable, involved 'change from above,' correction towards the prestige model, the linguistic usage of the highest status group.

Labov did not just document changes in progress, he also suggested how to carry out this research. He showed the need to obtain speech samples from a range of different people, in different speech styles. In New York City, he began by selecting a balanced population sample, looking at geographical area, age, ethnic group, and social position, and he obtained different speech styles from each group. Samples of formal speech were relatively easy to document. He and his students found that as interviewers, they were treated as well-educated strangers, and those being interviewed spoke fairly carefully. Even more careful speech was obtained by asking people to read a prose passage, and also word lists. But casual speech was more difficult to capture, and he used several methods. One was a 'danger of death' situation. He asked an informant if s/he had ever seriously thought s/he might be likely to die. As the informants relived a terrifying episode in their lives, they often, without realizing it, moved into a casual style of speech. For example, a woman described a car accident rapidly, using an informal style: "[a]ll I remember is – I thought I fell asleep and I was in a dream […] I actually saw stars, you know, stars in the sky – y'know, when you look up there […] and I was seein' stars" (Labov 1972: 94). Labov was also able to hear casual speech when the informant answered the phone, or talked to her children: "[g]et out of the refrigerator, Darlene! . . . Close the refrigerator, Darlene!" (Labov 1972: 89). He found a street-rhyme useful for the pronunciation of the words *more* and *door*:

> *I won't go to Macy's any more, more, more,*
> *There's a big fat policeman at the door, door, door.*
>
> (Labov 1972: 92)

He also allowed speakers to digress. He found that some speakers, particularly older ones, had favorite topics they wanted to talk about, and these digressions often elicited casual speech.

The early, careful work by Labov on Martha's Vineyard and in New York stimulated a generation of younger linguists to study change, and he is rightly applauded for his inspiration: "[t]he 'synchronic approach' to the study of language change, the study of change in progress, forms one of the cornerstones of research in language variation and change. This approach has had an enormous impact both on our knowledge of the mechanisms of change and on our understanding of its motivations" (Bailey 2002: 312). Another sociolinguist has argued that the study of language change in progress might be "the most striking single accomplishment of contemporary linguistics" (Chambers 1995: 147). Labov's influence is acknowledged in *A Handbook of Language Variation and Change,* a thick volume of over 800 pages, which is dedicated to him: "[f]or William Labov whose work is referred to in every chapter and whose ideas imbue every page" (Chambers, Trudgill and Schilling-Estes 2002: *v*).

Labov's work had an immediate appeal to students and researchers. A key innovation was his emphasis on the need to quantify linguistic variation with reliable statistics, and he established methods for doing this (see Chapter 4 in this *Handbook*). This inspired a whole post-Labovian generation to explore changes which were independent of his original Martha's Vineyard and New York ones. For example, in Britain, Peter Trudgill (1974, 1986) explored English in Norwich, Jenny Cheshire (1982) looked at English verb-endings in Reading, and James and Lesley Milroy examined English in Belfast (e.g. J. Milroy 1992, L. Milroy 1980/1987). Each of these moved the field along in different ways. For example, Trudgill explored over- and under-reporting of changes by people in Norwich, which provided useful insights into attitudes towards change; Cheshire specifically looked at teenagers' use of morphology; James and Lesley Milroy gained the confidence of their informants by saying that the researcher was a 'friend of a friend,' which enabled him/her to be treated as an insider, a trusted participant-observer, who was sometimes prepared to sit quietly for more than an hour, waiting for conversation to begin.

However, it would be a mistake to conclude that all diachronic/synchronic problems had been solved. Labov had looked mainly at how changes moved from person to person, within a community. But now, the progress of change through a language needed further attention. The difficulty was that the spread was never fully complete. In the words of Matthew Chen and William Wang, in any change, there was "the nettlesome problem created by a few recalcitrant forms" (1975: 256). The neogrammarians mostly blamed exceptions on dialect mixture and analogy, though, as Chen and Wang (1975: 256) point out, "more often than not, linguists have used dialect mixture as an excuse for not producing evidence of a substantial nature." And the inadequacy of analogy as an explanation became clear when there was a plethora of exceptions in Chinese, which has virtually no paradigms. The difficulty, as Chen and Wang (1975: 256) explain, is that:

> A phonological innovation may turn out to be ultimately regular, i.e. to affect all relevant lexical items, given the time to complete its course. But more often than linguists have thought, a phonological rule peters out toward the end of its life span, or is thwarted by another change competing for the same lexemes.

They explain this difficulty by hypothesizing a process of lexical diffusion, in which "a phonological innovation extends its scope of operation to a larger and larger portion of the lexicon" (1975: 256) (see Chapter 22 in this *Handbook*). They pointed out that this may have been understood by Sapir, when he had spoken of how a 'drift' gradually "worms its way through a gamut of phonetically analogous forms" (1921: 180). They supported their claim by highlighting changes in Chinese, Welsh, and the altering stress accent in English two-syllable words, where a stress shift has been gradually occurring in words such as *rebel, record*. At first, both nouns and verbs were stressed on the second syllable, though from the sixteenth century onwards, the stress on nouns has increasingly moved to the first syllable, though that on verbs has remained on the second. In short, Chen and Wang emphasized the need to examine the word-by-word behavior of any change, in a process they labeled lexical diffusion (Chen and Wang 1975, summarized in Aitchison 2013) – though Labov has argued that not all changes behave in this fashion (Labov 1994).

Grammaticalization is a further topic that has important implications for the diachrony/synchrony relationship. The older term grammaticization was originally coined by the French linguist Antoine Meillet, and was defined by him as "the attribution of a grammatical character to a previously autonomous word" (Meillet 1912/1948: 131). Yet Meillet's description was too narrow: more than single words tend to be involved, as one of his original examples showed: the change of the Greek words *thelo ina* 'I want/wish that' to the sequence *tha* which is now the future tense marker. Similarly, the English negative *not* was compacted from an earlier *ná wiht* 'not a thing.'

Yet from the diachrony/synchrony angle, the most important point is not the size of the units involved, but the observation that the various stages of the grammaticalization process typically overlap: "[a]lthough it is true that, given enough time, one structure may completely replace another, it is also true that one commonly finds the old and the new structure coexisting, often for a considerable period of time" (Lichtenberk, 1991: 38). There are numerous similar examples, and similar statements in Heine, Claudi, and Hünnemeyer (1991), Heine and Kuteva (2002), Hopper and Traugott (1993/2003), Ramat and Hopper (1998), Traugott and Heine (1991).

As the examples above show, grammaticalization envelops both the form and meaning of words, though there is no need for these two aspects to work simultaneously: they tend to be interleaved and loosely in touch, rather than strict partners (Fischer, 1997). The syntactic sequences found in grammaticalization inevitably vary from language to language. But the semantic concepts involved show surprisingly similar developments across different languages, so much so that a book has been published, with the title *World Lexicon of Grammaticalization* (Heine and Kuteva 2002). For example, ability frequently becomes permission, as in English 'John can come,' spatial concepts become temporal: in English the spatial 'from tree to tree' is paralleled by the temporal 'from year to year,' locative notions may denote existence as in 'there is beer, if you want some,' and similar examples can be found in numerous languages.

A crucial aspect of this type of development is that quite often it is impossible to know whether we are dealing with a synchronic state, or a diachronic happening: one merges into the other. In the example in the paragraph above, it is impossible to tell whether 'John *can* come' is a case of ability or permission. In some cases, the ambiguity may be intentional, as in some samples from Tok Pisin (a pidgin-creole spoken in Papua New Guinea). A toothpaste advertisement possibly exploits the fact that the word *save*, originally 'know' can also mean 'know how to,' 'be skilled at,' 'be accustomed to.' *Colgate i save strongim tit bilong yu* might mean "Colgate [toothpaste] knows how to/ is skilled at/ is accustomed to strengthen your teeth" (Aitchison 2000: 141–42).

Recently, more attention has possibly been paid to the semantic aspects of grammaticalization, and the terms *layering* and *polysemy* have been used for the semantic overlaps which occur, since multiple meanings tend to remain in use synchronically. It has been well explained in papers by Paul Hopper and Elizabeth Traugott: "[w]ithin a broad functional domain, new layers are continually emerging. As this happens, the older layers are not necessarily discarded, but may remain to coexist with and interact with the newer layers" (Hopper 1991). "Meanings expand their range through the development of various polysemies […] these polysemies may be […] quite fine-grained. It is only collectively that they may seem like weakening of meaning" (Hopper and Traugott 1993/2003: 103). This polysemy viewpoint has now replaced the older, outmoded view, that words 'weakened' or 'bleached' as they grew old (Gabelentz 1891).

Polysemy has been defined as "a term used in semantic analysis to refer to a lexical item which has a range of different meanings" (Crystal 2003: 359), though it raises a number of questions, such as how a linguist might distinguish polysemy (one form with several meanings) from homonymy (two lexical items which happen to have the same phonological form). Several proposals have been put forward, but so far, no agreement has been reached. As Nehrlich and Clarke (2003:4) point out: "[t]he precise relationship between polysemy, homonymity, ambiguity and vagueness is still an unresolved issue in lexical semantics." In spite of difficulties of definition, however, examples of polysemy provide excellent evidence for the impossibility of ever separating synchrony from diachrony.

James Pustejovsky may be the linguist who has become best known for his work on polysemy in recent years (Pustejovsky 1995; Pustejovsky and Boguraev 1996). A large amount of attention has been paid to verbs, he claims, but relatively little to other word classes: "[w]e have little insight into the semantic nature of adjectival predication, and even less into the semantics of nominals. Not until all major categories have been studied can we hope to arrive at a balanced understanding of the lexicon" (Pustejovsky 1995: 7).

Pustejovsky is largely right, even though some useful work on nominals has been published (e.g. Wierzbicka 1997). Following on from the observation that nominals have been under-studied, this paper now turns to a case study, exploring how speakers/hearers distinguish nominal polysemy, in a situation where different meanings overlap. This will (hopefully) elucidate how a superficially puzzling situation, the existence of a word with multiple meanings, which seems at first sight to be a synchronic/diachronic mire can be handled by a language's speakers (Aitchison 2003; Aitchison and Lewis 2003).

Aitchison and Lewis (2003) investigated the various usages of the word *disaster* in British English. They used the British National Corpus (BNC) as their main data base: this was supplemented by evidence culled mainly from newspapers (on corpora, see Chapter 6 in this *Handbook*). The initial question was how speakers (and learners) manage to understand which meaning of a polysemous word is intended, and how to use it acceptably. For example, a sequence describing a serious event might be found not far from one which related to social trivia, as in:

> ... the Hillsborough football disaster which killed 95 people. (serious)
> To get a panama hat wet is to court disaster. The hat becomes limp and shapeless. (trivial)

Two main types of clue elucidated the seriousness or triviality of a disaster: topic and collocation. A serious disaster with multiple deaths was above all indicated by a geographical location, as in the Hillsborough football disaster, the Clapham disaster (a rail crash), the Lockerbie disaster (a plane crash), the Zeebrugge ferry disaster (a capsized ferry). The location was sometimes accompanied by an indication of the type of disaster, but not necessarily.

For trivial disasters, the 'disaster' was sometimes fully explained, as in the panama hat problem mentioned above. Others were typically flagged in two ways: first, by the topic of the 'disaster;' second, by the collocating words. Two trivial topics recurred: sporting disappointments, and cookery mishaps:

> The last wicket fell, so it was another *disaster* for England. (cricket, sport)
> The gravy's a *disaster*. It's got too much fat in it. (cookery)

Nobody was ever poisoned in a cookery 'disaster,' the cooks merely produced food that sounded less than delicious.

Collocating words *absolute* or *total* usually indicated that the disaster was a trivial one:

> England must pull itself together if a bitterly disappointing tour is not to become a *total disaster*.

Similarly, the phrases *disaster strikes* or *disaster struck* usually indicated a trivial event:

> *Disaster struck* again for the home side after 57 minutes.

So the attempt to dramatize sporting events, and routine household incidents, partly accounted for the escalation in use and polysemy of the word *disaster*.

But a further factor may have helped to increase its usage. This is the observation that many of the disasters discussed were potential, rather than actual, as shown by the words used with *disaster*, such as *avert, avoid, near, potential, could be*. Again, this seemed to be an attempt to dramatize a non-event:

> A second jet disaster was narrowly averted in Bogota on Thursday.
> When you rescue the old Christmas tree lights from the loft for the umpteenth time, remember that they could be the cause of an electrical disaster.

The findings outlined above relate only to the word *disaster:* other disaster words behave differently. A brief overview of the word *tragedy* suggested that there were no cooking tragedies at dinner parties. Maybe a tragedy would have indicated a 'tragic' outcome, perhaps food-poisoning. Second, our informal discussions (at which we asked speakers of English as a second language to describe some of our 'disasters'), suggest that different types of English use different words for unfortunate events: an Indian informant indicated that the word *calamity* might be appropriate for an over-cooked dinner which disappointed the guests. But at the very least, these 'disasters' show that polysemy can provide a fertile field for future researchers attempting to explore the diachrony/synchrony dimensions.

Conclusion

A once-respected methodological distinction between diachrony and synchrony has become progressively more blurred. Early work which tried to link the two, such as that of Roman Jakobson, was largely unread by the majority of linguists, yet William Labov initiated a key movement in linguistics with his pioneering work on changes in progress, which made sociolinguistics into possibly the most popular branch of modern linguistics. Other linguists, such as Matthew Chen and William Wang, hastened to sweep up some of the few topics unexplored by Labov. They pioneered the approach to the lexicon known as lexical diffusion, which showed how a change spreads over the lexicon, though again with synchronic/ diachronic overlap. The interaction of synchrony and diachrony has been further explored by those working on grammaticalization and meaning change, which show how the various historical stages typically overlap. This has led on to further work, in which the overlapping usages of polysemous words are being explored, with increasing understanding of how speakers and hearers use and understand words with similar form, but different meanings.

This paper has tried to show that diachrony and synchrony are not irreconcilable. They are essentially overlapping processes, and one cannot be understood without the other. This paper started with a quote from the pioneering linguist Wilhelm von Humboldt, so it is relevant to end with another of his memorable comments, which reveals again his farsightedness in setting linguists along the path to understanding the strong links between synchrony and diachrony: "[t]here can no more be a moment of true *stasis* in language, than in the ceaseless effulgence of human thinking itself" (Humboldt 1836/1988: 143).

NOTE

1   The phrase 'change from below' is an unfortunate one, as it has led to a certain amount of misunderstanding about change, an assumption among some that change is led by lower class usage, which is by no means always the case.

REFERENCES

Aitchison, J. (2000) *The Seeds of Speech: Language Origin and Evolution*, Cambridge University Press, Cambridge.

Aitchison, J. (2003) *Words in the Mind: An Introduction to the Mental Lexicon* (3rd edn), Blackwell, Oxford.

Aitchison, J. (2013) *Language Change: Progress or Decay?*(4th edn), Cambridge University Press, Cambridge.

Aitchison, J. and Lewis, D.M. (2003) Polysemy and bleaching. In B. Nerlich, Z. Todd, V. Herman, D.D. Clarke (eds.), *Polysemy: Flexible Patterns of Meaning in Mind and Language*, Mouton de Gruyter, Berlin, pp. 253–66.

Bailey, G. (2002) Real and apparent time. In J.K. Chambers, P. Trudgill, and N. Schilling-Estes (eds.), pp. 312–32.

Chambers, J.K. (1995) *Sociolinguistic Theory: Linguistic Variation and its Social Significance*, Blackwell, Oxford.

Chambers, J.K., Trudgill, P., and Schilling-Estes, N. (eds.) (2002) *The Handbook of Language Variation and Change*, Blackwell, Oxford.

Chen, M. and Wang, W. (1975) Sound change: actuation and implementation. *Language* 51: 255–81.

Cheshire, J. 1982. *Variation in an English Dialect: A Sociolinguistic Study*, Blackwell, Oxford.

Crystal, D. (2003) *A Dictionary of Linguistics and Phonetics* (5th edn), Blackwell, Oxford.

Fischer, O.C.M. (1997) On the status of grammaticalisation and the diachronic dimension in explanation. *Transactions of the Philological Society* 95(2): 149–87.

Gabelentz, G. von der (1891) *Die Sprachwissenschaft. Ihre Aufgaben, Methoden und bisherigen Ergebnisse*, Weigel, Leipzig.

Guy, G.R. (2003) Variationist approaches to phonological change. In B.D. Joseph and R.D. Janda (eds.), *The Handbook of Historical Linguistics*, Blackwell, Oxford, pp. 369–400.

Heine, B., Claudi, U., and Hünnemeyer, F. (1991) *Grammaticalization: A Conceptual Framework*, University of Chicago Press, Chicago.

Heine, B. and Kuteva, T. (2002) *World Lexicon of Grammaticalization*, Cambridge University Press, Cambridge.

Hock, H.H. (1991) *Principles of Historical Linguistics* (2nd edn), Mouton de Gruyter, Berlin.

Hopper, P.J. (1991) *On some principles of grammaticalization*. In E.C. Traugott and B. Heine (eds.), pp. 17–36.

Hopper, P.J. and Traugott, E.C. (1993/2003) *Grammaticalization* (2nd edn), Cambridge University Press, Cambridge.

Humboldt, W. von (1836/1988) *On Language* (translated by P. Heath), Cambridge University Press, Cambridge.

Jakobson, R. (1949/1972) *Principles of Historical Phonology* (translated by A.R. Keiler). In A.R. Keiler (ed.), pp. 121–38.

Keiler, A.R. (ed.) (1972) *A Reader in Historical and Comparative Linguistics*, Holt, Reinhart & Winston, London.

Labov, W. (1965/1972) On the mechanism of linguistic change. In W. Labov (1972), pp. 160–82. Also in A.R. Keiler (ed.) (1972), pp. 267–88.

Labov, W. (1972) *Sociolinguistic Patterns*, University of Pennsylvania Press, Philadelphia.

Labov, W. (1994). *Principles of Linguistic Change. Vol.1: Internal Factors*, Blackwell, Oxford.

Lehmann, W.P. (ed.) (1967) *A Reader in Nineteenth-Century Historical Indo-European Linguistics*, Indiana University Press, Bloomington.

Lichtenberk, F. (1991) *On the gradualness of grammaticalization*. In E.C. Traugott and B. Heine (eds.), pp. 37–80.

Meillet, A. (1912/1948) *Linguistique Historique et Linguistique Générale*, Champion, Paris.

Milroy, J. (1992) *Linguistic Variation and Change: On the Historical Sociolinguistics of English*, Blackwell, Oxford.

Milroy, L. (1980/1987) *Language and Social Networks* (2nd edn), Blackwell, Oxford.

Nehrlich, B. and Clarke, D. (2003) Polysemy and flexibility: introduction and overview. In B. Nerlich, Z. Todd, V. Herman, and D.D. Clarke (eds.), *Polysemy: Flexible Patterns of Meaning in Mind and Language*, Mouton de Gruyter, Berlin, pp. 3–30.

Ostfhoff, H. and Brugmann, K. (1878/1967) *Preface to Morphologische Untersuchungen auf der Gebiete der indogermanischen Sprachen 1*, pp. ii–xx. Translated in W.P. Lehmann (ed.), pp. 197–209.

Pustejovsky, J. (1995) *The Generative Lexicon*, MIT Press, Cambridge, MA.

Pustejovsky, J. and Boguraev, B. (1996) *Lexical Semantics: The Problem of Polysemy*, Clarendon, Oxford.

Ramat, A.G. and Hopper, P. (eds.) (1991) *The Limits of Grammaticalization*, John Benjamins, Amsterdam.

Sapir, E. (1921) *Language*. Harcourt, Brace & World.

Saussure, F. de (1915/1959) *Cours de Linguistique Générale*, Payot, Paris. English translation by W. Baskin (1959), *Course in General Linguistics*, The Philosophical Library, New York.

Traugott, E.C. and Heine, B. (eds.) (1991) *Approaches to Grammaticalization, Vol.1, Focus on Theoretical and Methodological Issues*, John Benjamins, Amsterdam.

Trudgill, P. (1974) *The Social Differentiation of English in Norwich*, Cambridge University Press, Cambridge.

Trudgill, P. (1986) *Dialects in Contact*, Blackwell, Oxford.

Wierzbicka, A. (1997) *Understanding Cultures Through their Key Words*, Oxford University Press, Oxford.

2 Historical Sociolinguistics: Origins, Motivations, and Paradigms

TERTTU NEVALAINEN AND HELENA RAUMOLIN-BRUNBERG[1]

1. Introduction

1.1 Establishing the field

The social nature of human language was recognized by dialectologists and historical and anthropological linguists in the late nineteenth and early twentieth centuries but it took much longer for sociolinguistics to be established as a field of linguistics. The first record of 'sociolinguistics' appeared in the title of a paper published in an anthropological journal discussing India in 1939. Informed by traditions with similar research interests, the field came to be recognized by the 1960s, but the *Oxford English Dictionary* entry for it suggests that its practitioners still felt marginalized at the International Congress of Linguists in 1964: "[t]hose of us who work in the interdisciplinary area of 'socio-linguistics' may feel that we are here at this Congress on sufferance" (OED, Draft version, June 2009, s.v. *socio-linguistics* n.).

The field of historical sociolinguistics, which has emerged over the last thirty years, is yet to have an entry of its own in the OED. However, the historical dictionary records the hyphenated use of *socio-historical* in *The Atlantic Monthly* as early as 1900: "[t]he human life to which we seek to adapt the child is preeminently socio-historical – lived in society, determined by the historical order." (OED, s.v. *socio-historical* adj.). The first books to refer to the field in their titles call it 'socio-historical linguistics' (Romaine 1982, Tieken-Boon van Ostade 1987).

The Handbook of Historical Sociolinguistics, First Edition. Edited by Juan Manuel Hernández-Campoy and Juan Camilo Conde-Silvestre.
© 2014 John Wiley & Sons, Ltd. Published 2014 by John Wiley & Sons, Ltd.

'Historical sociolinguistics' has been consolidated in later works, including Milroy (1992), Machan and Scott (1992), Ammon, Mattheier and Nelde (1999), Jahr (1999), Kastovsky and Mettinger (2000), Nevalainen and Raumolin-Brunberg (2003), Bergs (2005), Willemyns and Vandenbussche (2006), and Conde-Silvestre (2007), as well as the Historical Sociolinguistics Network (HiSoN[2]). Both terms appear in *Historical Sociolinguistics and Sociohistorical Linguistics*[3], the e-journal started by Tieken-Boon van Ostade in 2000.

Unlike the academic specialization of historical sociolinguistics, what might be called 'applied historical sociolinguistics' has a long history: discussions of the social contexts of language use are typically included in language history text-books. These textbooks treat external history and regional variation as essential components of the history of a language. Their production intensified in the course of the twentieth century and reflects the growing market for international languages such as English, where they range from the multiple editions of Baugh's classic *A History of the English Language* (1935; Baugh and Cable 1951/2002) to *The Story of English*, compiled by McCrum, Cran, and MacNeil (1986) with an accompanying, hugely popular television series, and to Crystal's *The Stories of English* (2004). This extensive and clearly influential body of literature falls outside the scope of this chapter, which discusses historical sociolinguistics with an emphasis on the basic research done in the field over the last thirty years with its various cross- and multidisciplinary underpinnings.

1.2 The first three decades

As a sociolinguistic specialization, historical sociolinguistics has followed the overall trends of sociolinguistics at both the macro and the micro level. Romaine's seminal study (1982) focused on the extent to which models of quantitative, variationist sociolinguistics could be applied to historical data. Her approach was theory-oriented and less concerned with reconstructing the social world in which the sixteenth-century Scots texts she analyzed had been produced. Empirically, it was an analysis of the relative pronoun system in seven Middle Scots texts representative of different genres and styles, ranging from official, literary and epistolary prose to serious, religious, and comic verse (1530–50).

Drawing on the increasing availability of multigenre electronic corpora, and hence the possibility of comparing and contrasting registers over time, genre variation became one of the most researched topics in English historical sociolinguistics. Throughout the 1980s, genre continued as the key external variable in sociolinguistically informed studies of language change. One of the methodological issues, no less acute among historical linguists of earlier periods such as Wyld (1920/1936), was how to gain access to maximally speech-like data, a surrogate vernacular, which could shed light on processes of change emanating from the spoken language (e.g. Kytö and Rissanen 1983; Nevalainen and Raumolin-Brunberg 1989).

The 1990s saw a boost in the study of regional variation, and social and demographic history found their place in diachronic variation studies in many languages (e.g. Machan and Scott 1992, Ammon, Mattheier and Nelde 1999, Jahr 1999, Nevalainen and Raumolin-Brunberg 1996). With the increasing use of ego-documents such as personal letters and diaries, studies of language variation and change began to draw systematically on speaker variables such as gender, socio-economic status, education, and mobility.[4] New interests and theoretical orientations such as code-switching and social network analysis were introduced (Milroy 1992, Jahr 1999, Tieken-Boon van Ostade 2000).

In the 2000s, many lines of enquiry in historical sociolinguistics were consolidated. Variationist sociolinguistic work, both quantitative and qualitative, continued across languages (e.g. Nevalainen and Raumolin-Brunberg 2003, Ayres-Bennett 2004, Lodge 2004, Nobels and Van der Wal 2009); extensive social network studies were carried out (Bergs 2005, Sairio 2009); and code-switching research gained ground (Nurmi and Pahta 2004, Schendl and Wright 2011). Drawing on social and demographic history and the sociology of language, macro-level work on a variety of languages flourished, ranging from Penny's (2000) discussion of Castilian and Latin American Spanish from the Middle Ages onwards to McColl Millar's (2010) overview of the linguistic map of Europe before 1500.[5] In recent years, sociopragmatic and interactional phenomena, such as social roles and identity projection, have come to inform research on the micro-level (Nurmi, Nevala and Palander-Collin 2009, Culpeper and Kytö 2010). Many sociolinguistic approaches have been brought together under the umbrella of 'language history from below' (Elspaß *et al.* 2007), contributing to 'alternative histories' of languages, that is, their non-standard, regional and social varieties (Watts and Trudgill 2002).

Being able to connect macro- and micro-level information is necessary not only for theory formation but also, for example, for applications of historical sociolinguistics to studies of disputed authorship (Hope 1994). This dual perspective informs historical sociolinguistic work which addresses issues like the role of the individual in language change and the acquisition of sociolinguistic competence (Raumolin-Brunberg 2005; Nevalainen 2009). In general terms, access to data from a larger reference group, population, or corpus is necessary in studies that endeavor to place individuals, groups of people, or texts within their communities, social networks, genres, or other relevant categories.

2. Principles and Paradoxes

Like any other historical field of enquiry, historical sociolinguistics derives its *raison d'être* from the *principle of uniformitarianism*, which purports that, in a fundamental sense, human beings as biological, psychological, and social creatures have remained largely unchanged over time. Originally introduced in geology in the nineteenth century, the principle is advocated by sociolinguists and historical linguists alike (Labov 1972: 275; Romaine 1988: 1454; Lass 1997: 25; see Chapter 5 in this *Handbook*). In Romaine's formulation:

The linguistic forces which operate today and are observable around us are not unlike those which have operated in the past. This principle is of course basic to purely linguistic reconstruction as well, but sociolinguistically speaking, it means that there is no reason for believing that language did not vary in the same patterned ways in the past as it has been observed to do today. (Romaine 1988: 1454)

It follows from the Uniformitarian Principle that the present can be used to explain the past – and vice versa, as Labov (1972: 161) notes with reference to language change: "the same mechanisms which operated to produce the large-scale changes of the past may be observed operating in the current changes taking place around us." In a later work Labov (1994: 12–13) clarifies the fundamental distinction between *principles* and *generalizations*: principles such as uniformitarianism represent "maximal projections of generalizations," which, in turn, are arrived at inductively from facts of varying levels of abstraction established in the field of enquiry. While the applications of principles are unrestricted in time or space, the inductive processes that create generalizations advance slowly as the data base grows, and a generalization can be disproved by new data that are systematically inconsistent with it. The work of a sociolinguist, both historical and modern, is hence a constant balancing act between what Labov (1994) calls "inductive prudence" and "deductive presumption."

The implications of the Uniformitarian Principle for historical sociolinguistics as a field of study are discussed in the following section. Labov (1994: 21) also draws attention to problems underlying the work of historical linguists, and introduces what he calls the *historical paradox*. He defines it by noting that "[t]he task of historical linguists is to explain the differences between the past and the present; but to the extent that the past was different from the present, there is no way of knowing how different it was." This paradox derives in part from differences in social circumstances between the past and the present, and in part from the historical linguists' typically incomplete and defective data sources. However, at the same time it is worth bearing in mind that although contemporary sociolinguists may have the advantage of knowing the speech communities they study first hand, they, too, have to work out their various analytic distinctions, categories, and classifications and gain access to primary data. In their discussion of the concept of uniformitarianism in diachronic studies Janda and Joseph (2003: 37) make the constructive proposal that we should strive for *informational maximalism*. By this notion they understand:

the utilization of all reasonable means to extend our knowledge of what might have been going on in the past, even though it is not directly observable. Normally, this will involve a heavy concentration on the immediate present, but it is in fact more realistic just to say we wish to gain a maximum of information from a maximum of potential sources: different times and different places – and, in the case of language, also different regional and social dialects, different contexts, different styles, different topics, and so on.

3. Disciplinary Crossings and Hybridity

Taking up the challenge of Labov's historical paradox, we could argue that the task of the historical sociolinguist is precisely to try to discover *how* different the past was. The means of overcoming the paradox are manifold and often complementary, and derive from historical sociolinguistics being a cross-disciplinary area of study, where various paradigms and research orientations come together. These paradigms partly reflect the multiplicity of research approaches in contemporary sociolinguistics and the kindred disciplines they draw on and are associated with.

3.1   *E pluribus unum?*

Bergs (2005: 8–9) considers the hybrid nature of historical sociolinguistics by placing the field at the intersection of linguistics, social sciences, and history; he finds that the areas where these disciplines overlap represent subdisciplines in their respective fields: social sciences and linguistics, linguistics and history, and history and social sciences. Against this background, he views historical sociolinguistics as a potential subdiscipline of its own, which ought to develop its sown aims, methodologies, and theories, divorced from present-day sociolinguistics, on the one hand, and from historical linguistics, on the other (Bergs 2005: 21). The position advanced here is more integrationist. In order to be able to strive for informational maximalism, a variety of perspectives are needed to enrich our understanding of the past, and relevant innovative models and methods are also being developed in other, non-history disciplines. No less importantly, following the principle of uniformitarianism, accounts of the present need to draw on the past and vice versa. Although the historical paradox is obviously valid in that the past was different, real-time research on language change, both trend and panel studies, obliterates a strict division between the present and the past. Moreover, as research findings on an area, locality, or practice accumulate over time, what was the present sixty years ago is now irrevocably a thing of the past.

Figure 2.1 connects historical sociolinguistics with its neighboring fields in more specific terms. These associated fields range from humanities and social science disciplines to methodological specializations such as corpus linguistics. Corpora have a key role to play not only in the quantitative approaches used in variationist sociolinguistics but also, increasingly, in other research paradigms. We do not place historical sociolinguistics directly under *historical linguistics*, as is done, for example, by Jahr (1999), although both specialize in the study of the past and have many interests in common. Focusing on historical *sociolinguistics*, we prefer to approach it as the real-time dimension of sociolinguistics, which enters into varying relations and degrees of integration with other fields, depending on the line of enquiry in question (see further section 4).[6]

Figure 2.1 makes no claims to being exhaustive, which would be neither feasible nor justified in view of the growing versatility of historical sociolinguistic research

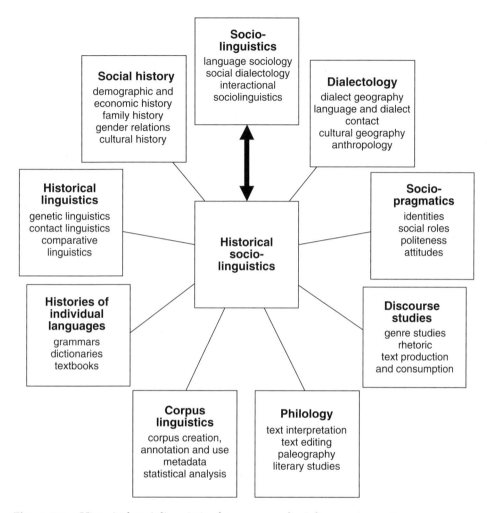

Figure 2.1. Historical sociolinguistics from a cross-disciplinary perspective

and the problems involved in pigeonholing branches of human knowledge. The domains listed under disciplinary labels come in no particular order of preference, and many of them would merit an entry of their own. Other subdisciplines could also have been included, such as cognitive linguistics, while some exert their influence through several fields listed. Sociology, for example, informs not only sociolinguistics and sociopragmatics but also, to the extent that they are always distinguishable, social history and historical sociology. Finally, the modifier 'historical' could have been added to some of the fields to draw attention to the relevance of further specializations such as historical dialectology and historical sociopragmatics.

The influence of the fields of study shown in Figure 2.1 is not a one-way street from the present to the past. When tracing the intellectual history of variationist sociolinguistics, Koerner (1991) finds that the work of William Labov synthesizes various lines of earlier linguistic research, some of them going back to the late nineteenth and early twentieth centuries. The three principal lines that Koerner distinguishes comprise (1) dialect geography and the work of dialectologists such as Wenker, Gauchat, Jaberg, Hermann, and McDavid; (2) sociologically and anthropologically oriented approaches to language change (e.g. Whitney, de Saussure, Meillet, Martinet, and U. Weinreich); and (3) research on bi- and mul-tilingualism (e.g. W. Weinreich, U. Weinreich, Haugen, and Ferguson). Louis Gauchat in fact has the honor of being hailed as the patriarch of variationist lin-guistics (Chambers, Cummins and Tennant 2008). Dialectology and sociolinguis-tics are often found to be so closely intertwined that they merge into social dialectology (Trudgill 1992; Kerswill 2004) or sociodialectology (Ammon and Mattheier 2008). This integration is perhaps even more evident in historical research, where it does not always make sense to separate regional from social variation. In analyzing language variation and change, both matter (Fisiak 1988; Nevalainen and Raumolin-Brunberg 2003; see Chapter 25 in this *Handbook*).

3.2   Material conditions

Philological expertise in text interpreting, editing, and paleography is vital for historical sociolinguistics. Since the data available from the more distant past are all hand-written – as have been, until quite recent times, ego-documents such as letters and diaries – reliable editions are needed to make them accessible to the scholarly community. The electronic era has given the old art of text editing new impetus and new resources. Corpora based on manuscript editions now make increasing use of multimedia techniques to provide the researcher with contextu-alized material such as digital images, which enable the study of different hands and the minutiae of spelling variation. Extensive metadata on the writers are added to maximize the usefulness of text corpora based on documents such as letters (see Beal, Corrigan and Moisl 2007, Nobels and Van der Wal 2009, and Chapters 6–11 in this *Handbook*).

Discourse and genre studies are also relevant to historical sociolinguistics, especially to paradigms with interactional foci. Like many other historical fields of enquiry, historical genre studies operate at the intersection of other fields, including social and literary history, text linguistics, discourse analysis, stylistics, rhetoric, and historical pragmatics and sociolinguistics. In methodological terms, they not only provide frameworks for assessing the linguistic composition (text type) of genres and the changing genre conventions and inventories over time, but also continuity and change in the practices of text production and consump-tion. The following illustrations show that approaches to genre classification and description vary according to research interests and can be used to shed light on related research questions in complementary ways.

As a sociolinguist, Schneider (2002: 73) is interested in the spoken language and its distance from writing. Using five criteria, he proposes a taxonomy of written genres according to their proximity to speech. Trial records come closest to the original speech event on his continuum as they represent real recorded speech with no temporal distance between the speech event and its recording but with different speaker–writer identities. Letters are placed in the middle of the continuum and classified as hypothetic, imagined speech with no temporal distance between the event and its recording by the speaker. Invented, literary dialect comes at the far end of the continuum with the reality of the speech event and its temporal distance from any real speech event left unspecified.

Language and social historians can provide more ample information on the intricate relations between speech and writing in the past, including the complex transmission of trial records; the *Old Bailey Corpus*, for example, benefits from the extensive ground work and metadata produced by social historians (Huber 2007). Interested in compiling a corpus of dialogues, Culpeper and Kytö (2010: 17) cross genre boundaries in their search for features of spoken interaction in writing. They propose a tripartite division of the relevant genres into speech-like (e.g. private correspondence), speech-based (e.g. trial proceedings) and speech-purposed (e.g. plays), which all provide useful data but have their various plusses and minuses.

One of the problems with diachronic work is that genre conventions change over time. Analyzing these changing conventions, Jajdelska (2007), a literary scholar, considers the modes of reading that are reflected in documents such as personal letters and diaries. She distinguishes between writers who punctuated their letters according to the topic, as they spoke it, as opposed to later, typically more educated, writers, who punctuated to disambiguate syntax. In the first case, orality influenced literacy, and in the second, literacy impacted on orality.

What social history and literacy studies can add here is research on the slow rise of full literacy. In 1500, only a very small proportion of the population of Europe could read and write, while the turn of the nineteenth century was already characterized by mass literacy (Houston 1988). At the beginning of this period, authentic records were produced by members of the upper and middle, professional social ranks, who could read and write. However, it was not uncommon even for members of the upper ranks, women in particular, to use a secretary at the time; this has remained the sole option for the illiterate at all times if they needed to communicate in writing.

Wilson (1993a), a social historian, places this lack of direct evidence within the larger context of document genesis. Documents are not simply sources of authority on the past, or witnesses offering direct evidence for the historian to interrogate; what also matter are their effects as reflecting sets of past processes and practices. The research method that adopts this broader approach, he suggests, is investigation of the genesis of these documents, that is, the original context in which the documents were generated. It reveals the boundaries of documents, the relation between what they include and exclude. Wilson (1993a:319) writes:

The difficulties of coverage and representativeness faced by 'history from below' arise from the limitations of content and provenance in the total ensemble of documents. Reconstructing the processes of genesis of the documents provides the most inclusive means available for understanding and explaining those limitations, and hence of allowing for them.

This is one answer to the historical sociolinguist's dilemma of how to cope with deficient data sources, especially those from the more distant past. It is directly reflected in the choice of research paradigms available to historical sociolinguists, our topic in the next section.

4. Paradigms

The division into macro- and micro-sociolinguistics, which goes back to the 1960s, also applies to the study of the past. In a nutshell, macro-sociolinguistics is concerned with the sociolinguistics of society, issues such as societal multilingualism, language policy and standardization, whereas micro-sociolinguistics typically focuses on the sociolinguistics of language, the influence of social interaction in language use (Fasold 1984, 1990). Four sociolinguistic paradigms are commonly distinguished, based on their objects of study, and form a continuum between the macro- and micro-perspectives: the sociology of language, social dialectology, interactional sociolinguistics, and the ethnography of communication. Table 2.1 presents their associated disciplines, principal objects of study, modes of enquiry, and explanatory goals (adapted from Dittmar 1997: 99–100).

The sociology of language is a line of enquiry where a sociolinguistic paradigm cuts across the synchrony/diachrony divide, and research can reach quite far back in time. McColl Millar (2010) discusses the macro-sociolinguistic history of Europe from the first written evidence until 1500. He shows how comparable linguistic circumstances can give rise to quite different linguistic authorities and identities, depending on varying sociolinguistic conditions and the fluctuation between diversity and hegemony.

Burke (2004) concentrates on the period between the invention of printing (c. 1450) and the French Revolution (1789) with a focus on the linguistic construction of communities of different kinds, from nations, regions, churches, and occupations to the international learned community, the 'Republic of Letters'. He notes that individuals were typically members of several communities, some of them in competition or even in conflict. One of the linguistic melting pots was the polyglot armies of the period. For example, the international military language of the Thirty Years' War, current from Poland to Portugal, was based on Romance vocabulary and was transmitted to Sweden and Eastern Europe. Much of this evidence can be retrieved from historical lexicological studies (Burke 2004: 129–30).

The multilingual history of European communities is further sampled in the case studies included in Braunmüller and Ferraresi (2003), which offer a variety of perspectives on multilingualism ranging from medieval Britain and trading centers in the Nordic and Baltic countries to German and Romance language contacts in

Table 2.1. Four sociolinguistic paradigms

Paradigm/ Dimension	Sociology of language	Social dialectology/ Variationist sociolinguistics	Interactional sociolinguistics	Ethnography of communication
Informed by	Sociology	Dialectology, Historical linguistics	Discourse studies	Anthropology
Object of study	status and function of languages and language varieties in language communities	variation in grammar and phonology; linguistic variation in discourse; speaker attitudes	interactive construction and organization of discourse	patterned ways of speaking, sociolinguistic styles/ registers
Describing	norms and patterns of language use in domain-specific conditions	the linguistic system in relation to external factors	organization of discourse as social interaction	situated uses of verbal, para- and nonverbal means of communication
Explaining	differences of and changes in status and function of languages and language varieties	social dynamics of language varieties in speech communities; language change	communicative competence; verbal and nonverbal input in goal-oriented interaction	functional appropriateness of communicative behavior in various social contexts

the Mediterranean. The studies in ten Thije and Zeevaert (2007) focus on receptive multilingualism in language contact situations today and in the past, providing evidence that, for example, the ability to understand one or more foreign languages was commonplace in medieval face-to-face trading contexts in Europe.

While research into multilingualism, language policy and standardization can readily include a diachronic dimension, studies within the other research paradigms shown in Table 2.1 are more constrained by the available data sources. Lack of linguistic materials from the more distant past and the mode of preservation of extant sources severely limit the historical sociolinguist's research agenda: the spoken language and para- and nonverbal information central to much of interactional and ethnographic research is simply not available. However, to a certain extent, the application of a sociolinguistic paradigm to language history is also a matter of the level of delicacy of the analysis. If the contextual analysis of genres, for example, were to be foregrounded and the level of abstraction raised, the ethnographic approach could be used to inform research beyond the late modern period, which is in focus in studies into 'language history from below' (Elspaß *et al.* 2007). It is a sign of the dynamicity of the historical research agenda that it has come to encompass the interactional paradigm in studies of individuals' situated social roles and identities (Palander-Collin, Nevala, and Nurmi 2009: 6–10). The four sociolinguistic paradigms shown in Table 2.1 are hence all in principle applicable to historical research within the limitations imposed on the enterprise by our historical knowledge and the varying quantity and quality of data available.

In the following section we give an extended case study showing how the variationist paradigm can be operationalized in historical sociolinguistics. The prerequisite for doing research of this kind is access to sufficient data sources produced by individual language users. In our experience of compiling and using the *Corpus of Early English Correspondence* (CEEC), personal correspondence provides the 'next best thing' to authentic spoken language and, even with its obvious limitations, makes it possible to extend the variationist paradigm into the more distant past. It enables the researcher to combine macro- and micro level approaches and place individuals within their language communities (Nevalainen 1999; Nevalainen and Raumolin-Brunberg 2003).

5. Language Change and the Individual

It is well known that there is considerable variation in the linguistic usage of contemporaries. The standard list of the determinants of variation includes at least gender, socioeconomic class, status, region, age, migration history, register, style, and genre. However, despite similarities in these external constraints, there can be considerable differences in the participation of individuals in ongoing linguistic changes. For instance, Raumolin-Brunberg and Nevalainen (1997) found great divergence between two early sixteenth-century merchant brothers, John and Otwell Johnson, in their adoption of incoming morphosyntactic forms such as the object pronoun *you*, which came to replace the old subject form *ye* by the end of the century.

One factor that might explain individual differences is their membership in social networks. According to Milroy (1980/1987), the innovators – those who introduce a new form into a network – tend to be marginal members of networks. Labov (2001: 323–411) argues that the linguistic leaders in Philadelphia were central members in their respective networks. These diverging viewpoints may be caused by a difference in focus. While Milroy has looked at the early incipient stage, Labov has examined people who lead the changes at a later phase. On the whole, it seems that the phase of a change at the time of acquisition has an effect on an individual's participation in a change in progress. During a period of very rapid progress, the spectrum of variation between individuals appears to be the broadest (Kurki 2005: 239–40).

In general, individuals can be divided according to the degree of participation in ongoing changes into three groups, progressive, in-between and conservative (Nevalainen, Raumolin-Brunberg, and Mannila 2011). Most people belong to the in-between group and only rarely are the same people progressive or conservative in several simultaneous changes. Recent research has been able to identify a few very progressive people who have led several ongoing changes, such as Queen Elizabeth I in late sixteenth-century England, but such people only form a small minority (Nevalainen, Raumolin-Brunberg, and Mannila 2011).

One of the basic findings concerning language change is its diffusion through variation, both on the societal and individual level. On the individual level this means that the incoming forms appear in the language of individual users as new alternatives to be used alongside the old forms. In other words, during the process of change people tend to have variable grammars. However, the degree of variation, that is, the proportion of alternatives, differs greatly between individuals, and the progressiveness or conservatism of certain people can usually be identified by their more extensive or limited use of the new forms and not as an absolute choice of one or the other variant.

A further interesting question is the stability or instability of individual usage. The behavior of individuals under ongoing linguistic change is often discussed in terms of generational and communal change. 'Generational change' refers to a situation in which there is idiolectal stability despite ongoing change in the community. In 'communal change,' in turn, people change their language in adulthood, altering their language in the same direction. Labov (1994: 83–84) suggests that sound change and morphological change typically follow the pattern of generational change, while lexical and syntactic changes represent the converse pattern, communal change. Although this often seems to be the case, lifespan changes, that is, changes in adulthood, have also been detected, particularly among sound changes in progress (Sankoff and Blondeau 2007).

The well-known concept of 'apparent time' goes back to the generational model, in other words, to the idea that adult speakers' phonology and grammar are fixed. The apparent-time model is a convenient tool with which present-day sociolinguists can examine the diffusion of ongoing linguistic changes by comparing usage across generations of speakers in order to identify the direction and rate of change. Historical research has the advantage of following changes in real time, in other words, how changes actually spread among populations and individuals.

Labov (2007) argues that children and adults participate in linguistic changes in different ways because of their diverging language-learning abilities. Adults have problems in adopting abstract features of language structure, while children learn them at the time of language acquisition or at least before the age of seventeen (Labov 2007: 349).

In a study of quotative *be like* in Toronto English, Tagliamonte and D'Arcy (2007) provide an exciting observation on generational differences. According to them, speakers enhance their use of *be like* when they grow older without changing their grammatical patterns, analyzed with varying constraint rankings. These findings "suggest that adult frequencies of linguistic forms are labile [...], but the grammar underlying them is not" (2007: 213). This would mean that individuals adopt their grammars when young but make quantitative changes between the alternatives during their lifetimes. Diachronic research on historical letters has indeed shown that at least in some morphological changes, both generational and communal types of change are operative at the same time as far as frequencies are concerned (Nevalainen and Raumolin-Brunberg 2003: 86–92; Raumolin-Brunberg 2005).

A further factor worth considering is the variability of grammar at the acquisition phase. According to Nahkola and Saanilahti (2004), categorical linguistic features are inclined to remain categorical in idiolects, whereas features that are acquired as variable tend to change in individual life spans. They also claim that "[t]he more equal the proportions of the rivalling variants are, the more likely it is that one of the variants will increase its proportion and gain dominancy during the speaker's life" (2004: 90).

Figure 2.2 is an illustration of the variability of the linguistic behavior of ten speakers of Early Modern English between 1570 and 1670. The change under examination is the replacement of the indicative third-person singular ending *-th* by *-s* (*he goeth > he goes*; for details, see Nevalainen and Raumolin-Brunberg 2003: 67–68). The graph testifies to great inter-individual variation, most people having variable grammars. There are both progressive and conservative language users among the ten individuals. The graph also shows that, while the proportion of the new form *-s* remains stable in some people's letters during the period from which these letters derive, most people increase the use of the sibilant when they grow older. In the figure, there are two people who did not change their usage at all: Sir Francis Hastings, who systematically resorted to the old variant *-th*, and John Chamberlain, who quite as systematically chose the new *-s* variant. Moreover, Elizabeth, Queen of Bohemia also exhibits high idiolectal stability during her long letter-writing career (for details on the writers, see Table 2.2).

Hastings's conservatism perhaps goes back to his age: he was over fifty years old around 1600, when the higher ranks outside London began to employ *-s*. Chamberlain's advanced use can be understood against his background as a Londoner, a group that, as already mentioned, led this change in this data set (see

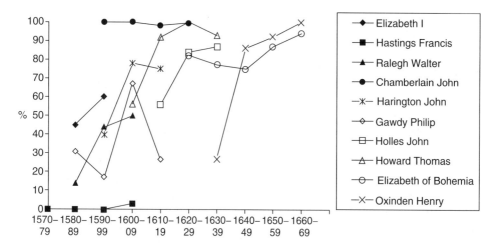

Figure 2.2. The percentage of third-person singular -*s* in ten idiolects, 1570–1669: a longitudinal study at 10-year intervals. CEEC 1998 and Supplement

Table 2.2. Third-person -*s* vs. -*th*: the informants for the longitudinal study[7]

Name	Year of birth	Letters from	Social status	Domicile
Queen Elizabeth I	1533	1585–1596	Royalty	Court
Sir Francis Hastings	1546	1573–1609	Upper Gentry	Leicestershire, Somerset, London
Sir Walter Ralegh	1554	1581–1611	Upper Gentry	Devonshire, Court, (Tower)
John Chamberlain	1554	1597–1625	Lower Gentry	London
Sir John Harington	1561?	1571–1612	Upper Gentry	Somerset, Court
Philip Gawdy	1562	1579–1616	Lower Gentry	East Anglia, London
John Holles, Earl of Clare	1565	1587–1637	Upper Gentry to Nobility	Nottinghamshire, London
Thomas Howard, Earl of Arundel and Surrey	1585	1608–1644	Nobility	Essex, Continent, Court
Elizabeth, Queen of Bohemia	1596	1620–1661	Royalty	Court, Continent
Henry Oxinden	1608	1631–1666	Lower Gentry	Kent

also Nevalainen and Raumolin-Brunberg 2003: 178). During the time when Elizabeth of Bohemia, daughter of James I and wife of a continental prince, began to write letters to her family in England, the use of -s had already become fashionable at Court, and apparently Elizabeth followed this practice.

The remaining seven writers shifted their preferences during the years they wrote the letters that are included in the CEEC (see also Table 2.2). The curve of one of the writers, Philip Gawdy, has a zigzag pattern, while the other six curves go upwards with time. As above, much of the behavior of these people is in line with what we know about the general trajectory of this change. Philip Gawdy's confusion may depend on the fact that he migrated to London from East Anglia, an area where the adoption of -s occurred late (Nevalainen and Raumolin-Brunberg 2003: 178). Ralegh and Harington moved to London from the South West and Holles from Nottinghamshire, and in their cases the migration to London, with its sibilant-preferring practices, may have been a major factor influencing their change of usage. The bulk of the letters of the nobleman Thomas Howard, an art collector, were written during the early decades of the seventeenth century, when a large majority of people had -s as their major variant; whereas Henry Oxinden's Kentish domicile may explain the low share of -s in his early letters, a practice that rapidly caught up with the national average (see also Table 2.2).

6. Concluding Remarks

Now, thirty years since the publication of Romaine's seminal work in 1982, what can we expect from the future of historical sociolinguistics? It may be illuminating to look at how social historians saw *their* future twenty years ago, thirty years into the existence of the new field. Wrightson (1993: 60) discusses the enthusiasm of early social historians in the 1960s, deeply influenced by sociology, social anthropology, and demography:

> For the new social history was not envisaged as a discrete area of study, another specialization in a subject already replete with 'hyphenated histories.' On the contrary it would resist such isolation and compartmentalization. It would be a meeting point; an intersection linking diverse routes to the past. It would thrive upon interconnectedness of the historical process and it would transform understanding of the whole.

However, what the decades that followed in fact saw was professional specialization and compartmentalization both by period and by subject, "each with its own degree of introversion" (Wrightson 1993: 63). One of the future lines of development Wrightson contemplates would be to produce new and more complex forms of integration, of "organic solidarity" but, reading the signs of the time, he is not overly optimistic. What he envisages as the threats posed by this containment are the loss of the interpretative power of the field and its selective appropriation, which might lead to a new kind of marginalization. He nevertheless concludes on the moderately optimistic note that the tools for doing social history are in place:

"[i]f we retain the will to use them well, the job remains as exciting as ever" (Wrightson 1993: 74). The same goes for historical sociolinguistics with the addition that our tools keep evolving with those created in kindred fields – including social history.

NOTES

1   Terttu Nevalainen's work on this chapter was funded by the Academy of Finland's Academy Professorship scheme (2010–2014), and that of Helena Raumolin-Brunberg received funding from the VARIENG Centre of Excellence, funded from the Academy of Finland Centre of Excellence program for 2006–2011. Terttu Nevalainen wrote the first four sections and the conclusion, and Helena Raumolin-Brunberg the penultimate section.
2   http://www.philhist.uni-augsburg.de/hison/ [accessed October 13, 2011].
3   http://www.let.leidenuniv.nl/hsl_shl/ [accessed October 13, 2011].
4   One of the objectives of the Sociolinguistics and Language History project, which we launched at the University of Helsinki in 1993, was to test the relevance of these sociolinguistic variables to real-time change in English between the early fifteenth and late seventeenth century (Nevalainen and Raumolin-Brunberg 1996).
5   The long list includes, for example, the work in Braunmüller and Ferraresi (2003) on various multilingual communities in Europe, Deumert and Vandenbussche (2003) on standardization of Germanic languages, Deumert (2004) on Afrikaans, Lodge (2004) on French, Tuten (2004) on Spanish, and Willemyns and Vandenbussche (2006) on Dutch.
6   It is of course a different matter whether the ultimate goal of some paradigms was to integrate sociolinguistics as part of historical linguistics. This could be the case with the work Labov has carried out within the variationist paradigm, which he connects with the neo-grammarian notion of the regularity of sound change (Labov 1972: 23–24, 1994: 455–460).
7   The system of social status follows that introduced in Nevalainen & Raumolin-Brunberg (2003: 136). The characterization of the Royal Court as one of the domiciles also derives from previous research (Nevalainen & Raumolin-Brunberg 2003: 159).

REFERENCES

Ammon, U. and Mattheier, K.J. (eds.) (2008) *Dialektsoziologie = Sociodialectology = Sociologie du dialecte* [Sociolinguistica 22], Niemeyer, Tübingen.

Ammon, U., Mattheier, K.J., and Nelde, P.H. (eds.) (1999) *Historische Soziolinguistik = Historical Sociolinguistics = La sociolinguistique historique* [Sociolinguistica 13], Niemeyer, Tübingen.

Ayres-Bennett, W. (2004) *Sociolinguistic Variation in Seventeenth-century France*, Cambridge University Press, Cambridge.

Baugh, A.C. (1935) *A History of the English Language*, D. Appleton-Century Company, New York.

Baugh, A.C. and Cable, T. (1951/2002) *A History of the English Language* (5th edn), Routledge, London.

Beal, J.C., Corrigan, K.P., and Moisl, H.L. (eds.) (2007) *Creating and Digitizing Language Corpora, Vol. 2, Diachronic Databases*, Basingstoke, Palgrave-Macmillan.

Bergs, A. (2005) *Social Networks and Historical Sociolinguistics: Studies in Morphosyntactic*

Variation in the Paston Letters (1421–1503), Mouton de Gruyter, Berlin.

Braunmüller, K. and Ferraresi, G. (eds.) (2003) *Aspects of Multilingualism in European Language History*, John Benjamins, Amsterdam.

Burke, P. (2004) *Language and Communities in Early Modern Europe*, Cambridge University Press, Cambridge.

CEEC = *Corpus of Early English Correspondence* (1998) Compiled by T. Nevalainen, H. Raumolin-Brunberg, J. Keränen, M. Nevala, A. Nurmi, and M. Palander-Collin, Department of English, University of Helsinki. http://www.helsinki.fi/varieng/CoRD/corpora/CEEC/index.html [accessed October 13, 2011]

Chambers, J.K., Cummins, S., and Tennant, J. (2008) Louis Gauchat (1866–1942), Patriarch of Variationist Linguistics. *Historiographica Linguistica* 35(1/2): 213–75.

Conde-Silvestre, J.C. (2007) *Sociolingüística histórica*, Gredos, Madrid.

Crystal, D. (2004) *The Stories of English*, Penguin, London.

Culpeper, J. and Kytö, M. (2010) *Early Modern English Dialogues: Spoken Interaction as Writing*, Cambridge University Press, Cambridge.

Deumert, A. (2004) *Language Standardization and Language Change: The Dynamics of Cape Dutch*, John Benjamins, Amsterdam.

Deumert, A. and Vandenbussche, W. (eds.) (2003) *Germanic Standardizations: Past to Present*, John Benjamins, Amsterdam.

Dittmar, N. (1997) *Grundlagen der Soziolinguistik*, Max Niemeyer, Tübingen.

Elspaß, S., Langer, N., Scharloth, J., and Vandenbussche, W. (eds.) (2007) *Germanic Language Histories 'from Below', 1700–2000*, Walter de Gruyter, Berlin.

Fasold, R. (1984) *The Sociolinguistics of Society*. Blackwell, Oxford.

Fasold, R. (1990) *The Sociolinguistics of Language*, Blackwell, Oxford.

Fisiak, J. (ed.) (1988) *Historical Dialectology: Regional and Social*, Mouton de Gruyter, Berlin.

Hope, J. (1994) *The Authorship of Shakespeare's Plays: A Socio-linguistic Study*, Cambridge University Press, Cambridge.

Houston, R.A. (1988) *Literacy in Early Modern Europe: Culture and Education 1500–1800*, Longman, Harlow.

Huber, M. (2007) The *Old Bailey Proceedings*, 1674–1834: Evaluating and annotating a Corpus of 18th- and 19th-century spoken English. In A. Meurman-Solin and A. Nurmi (eds.), *Annotating Variation and Change*, [Studies in Variation, Contacts and Change in English 1] University of Helsinki, Helsinki. http://www.helsinki.fi/varieng/journal/volumes/01/huber [accessed October 13, 2011].

Jahr, E.H. (ed.) (1999) *Language Change: Advances in Historical Sociolinguistics*, Mouton de Gruyter, Berlin.

Jajdelska, E. (2007) *Silent Reading and the Birth of the Narrator*, University of Toronto Press, Toronto.

Janda, R.D. and Joseph, B.D. (2003) On language, change, and language change – or, of history, linguistics, and historical linguistics. In B.D. Joseph and R.D. Janda (eds.), *The Handbook of Historical Linguistics*, Blackwell, Oxford, pp. 3–180.

Kastovsky, D. and Mettinger, A. (eds.) (2000) *The History of English in a Social Context: Essays in Historical Sociolinguistics*, Mouton de Gruyter, Berlin.

Kerswill, P. (2004) Social dialectology/Sozialdialektologie. In U. Ammon, K. Mattheier, and P. Trudgill (eds.), *Sociolinguistics/Soziolinguistik: An International Handbook of the Science of Language and Society, vol. 1* (2nd edn), Walter de Gruyter, Berlin, pp. 22–33.

Koerner, K. (1991) Toward a history of modern sociolinguistics. *American Speech* 66(1): 57–70.

Kurki, T. (2005) *Yksilön ja ryhmän kielen reaaliaikainen muuttuminen. Kielenmuutosten seuraamisesta ja niiden tarkastelussa käytettävistä menetelmistä* [Linguistic real-time change on group and individual level: On following language changes in apparent time and real time, and on the methods used in the study of language change], Suomalaisen Kirjallisuuden Seura, Helsinki.

Kytö, M. and Rissanen, M. (1983) The syntactic study of early American English:

The variationist at the mercy of his corpus? *Neuphilologische Mitteilungen* 84: 470–90.

Labov, W. (1972) *Sociolinguistic Patterns*, University of Pennsylvania Press, Philadelphia.

Labov, W. (1994) *Principles of Linguistic Change, Vol. 1, Internal Factors*, Blackwell, Oxford.

Labov, W. (2001) *Principles of Linguistic Change, Vol. 2, Social Factors*, Blackwell, Oxford.

Labov, W. (2007) Transmission and diffusion. *Language* 83: 344–87.

Lass, R. (1997) *Historical Linguistics and Language Change*, Cambridge University Press, Cambridge.

Lodge, R.A. (2004) *A Sociolinguistic History of Parisian French*, Cambridge University Press, Cambridge.

Machan, T.W. and Scott, C.T. (eds.) (1992) *English in Its Social Contexts: Essays in Historical Sociolinguistics*, Oxford University Press, Oxford.

McColl Millar, R. (2010) *Authority and Identity: A Sociolinguistic History of Europe Before the Modern Age*, Palgrave Macmillan, Basingstoke.

McCrum, R., Cran, W., and MacNeil, R. (1986) *The Story of English*, Viking Penguin, New York.

Milroy, J. (1992) *Linguistic Variation and Change: On the Historical Sociolinguistics of English*, Blackwell, Oxford.

Milroy, L. (1980/1987) *Language and Social Networks* (2nd edn), Blackwell, Oxford.

Nahkola, K. and Saanilahti, M. (2004) Mapping language changes in real time: A panel study on Finnish. *Language Variation and Change* 16(2): 75–91.

Nevalainen, T. (1999) Making the best use of 'bad' data: Evidence for sociolinguistic variation in Early Modern English. *Neuphilologische Mitteilungen* 100(4): 499–533.

Nevalainen, T. (2009) Grasshoppers and blind beetles: Caregiver language in Early Modern English correspondence. In A. Nurmi, M. Nevala, and M. Palander-Collin (eds.), pp. 137–64.

Nevalainen, T. and Raumolin-Brunberg, H. (1989) A corpus of Early Modern Standard English in a socio-historical perspective. *Neuphilologische Mittelungen* 90(1): 61–104.

Nevalainen, T. and Raumolin-Brunberg, H. (eds.) (1996) *Sociolinguistics and Language History: Studies Based on the Corpus of Early English Correspondence*, Rodopi, Amsterdam.

Nevalainen, T. and Raumolin-Brunberg, H. (2003) *Historical Sociolinguistics: Language Change in Tudor and Stuart England*, Pearson Education, London.

Nevalainen, T., Raumolin-Brunberg, H., and Mannila, H. (2011) The diffusion of language change in real time: progressive and conservative individuals and the time-depth of change. *Language Variation and Change* 23: 1–43.

Nobels, J. and van der Wal, M. (2009) Tackling the writer-sender problem: The newly developed Leiden Identification Procedure (LIP). *Historical Sociolinguistics and Sociohistorical Linguistics*. http://www.let.leidenuniv.nl/hsl_shl/Nobels-Wal.html [accessed October 13, 2011]

Nurmi, A. and Pahta, P. (2004) Social stratification and patterns of code-switching in early English letters. *Multilingua* 23: 417–56.

Nurmi, A., Nevala, M., and Palander-Collin, M. (eds.) (2009) *The Language of Daily Life in England (1400–1800)*, John Benjamins, Amsterdam.

OED = *Oxford English Dictionary Online* (2008), Oxford University Press, Oxford, www. oed.com

Palander-Collin, M., Nevala, M., and Nurmi, A. (2009) The language of daily life in the history of English: Studying how macro meets micro. In A. Nurmi, M. Nevala and M. Palander-Collin (eds.), pp. 1–23.

Penny, R. (2000) *Variation and Change in Spanish*, Cambridge University Press, Cambridge.

Raumolin-Brunberg, H. (2005) Language change in adulthood: Historical letters as evidence. *European Journal of English Studies* 9(1): 37–51.

Raumolin-Brunberg, H. and Nevalainen, T. (1997) Social embedding of linguistic changes in Tudor English. In R. Hickey and S. Puppel (eds.), *Language History and*

Linguistic Modelling: A Festschrift for Jacek Fisiak on his 60th Birthday, Mouton de Gruyter, Berlin, pp. 701–717.

Romaine, S. (1982) *Socio-historical Linguistics: Its Status and Methodology*. Cambridge University Press, Cambridge.

Romaine, S. (1988) Historical sociolinguistics: Problems and methodology. In U. Ammon, N. Dittmar, and K.J. Mattheier (eds.), *Sociolinguistics: An International Handbook of the Science of Language and Society*, Walter de Gruyter, Berlin, pp. 1452–69.

Sairio, A. (2009) *Language and Letters of the Bluestocking Network: Sociolinguistic Issues in Eighteenth-century Epistolary English* [Mémoires de la Société Néophilologique 75], Société Néophilologique, Helsinki.

Sankoff, G. and Blondeau, H. (2007) Language change across the lifespan: /r/ in Montreal French. *Language* 83(3): 560–88.

Schendl, H. and Wright, L. (eds.) (2011) *Code-switching in the History of Earlier English*. Mouton de Gruyter, Berlin.

Schneider, E.W. (2002) Investigating variation and change in written documents. In J.K. Chambers, P. Trudgill, and N. Schilling-Estes (eds.), *The Handbook of Language Variation and Change*, Blackwell, Oxford, 67–96.

Tagliamonte, S.A. and D'Arcy, A. (2007) Frequency and variation in the community grammar: Tracking a new change through generations. *Language Variation and Change* 19: 199–217.

Thije, J.D. ten and Zeevaert, L. (eds.) (2007) *Receptive Multilingualism: Linguistic Analyses, Language Policies and Didactic Concepts*, John Benjamins, Amsterdam.

Tieken-Boon van Ostade, I. (1987) *The Auxiliary* do *in Eighteenth-century English: A Sociohistorical-linguistic Approach*, Foris Publications, Dordrecht.

Tieken-Boon van Ostade, I. (2000) Social network analysis and the history of English. *European Journal of English Studies* 4(3): 211–16.

Tieken-Boon van Ostade, I. (ed.) (2000). *Historical Sociolinguistics and Sociohistorical Linguistics*. http://www.let.leidenuniv.nl/hsl_shl [accessed October 13, 2011]

Trudgill, P. (1992/1999) Dialect contact, dialectology and sociolinguistics. In K. Bolton and H. Kwok (eds.), *Sociolinguistics Today: International Perspectives* (1992), Routledge, London, pp. 71–79. Reprinted in J.C. Conde-Silvestre and J.M. Hernández-Campoy (eds.), *Variation and Linguistic Change in English: Diachronic and Synchronic Studies* (CFI8) (1999), Editum, Murcia, pp. 1–8.

Tuten, D.N. (2003) *Koineization in Medieval Spanish*, Mouton de Gruyter, Berlin.

Watts, R. and Trudgill, P. (eds.) (2002) *Alternative Histories of English*, Routledge, London.

Willemyns, R. and Vandenbussche, W. (2006) Historical sociolinguistics: Coming of age? *Sociolinguistica* 20: 146–65.

Wilson, A. (1993a) Foundations of an integrated historiography. In A. Wilson (ed.), pp. 293–335.

Wilson, A. (ed.) (1993b) *Rethinking Social History: English Society 1570–1920 and its Interpretation*, Manchester University Press, Manchester.

Wrightson, K. (1993) The enclosure of English social history. In A. Wilson (ed.), pp. 59–77.

Wyld, H.C. (1920/1936) *A History of Modern Colloquial English* (3rd edn), Blackwell, Oxford.

3 Social History and the Sociology of Language

ROBERT McCOLL MILLAR

1. Social History and Language: Historical Macrosociolinguistics

Since at least the 1940s, a sociological appreciation and analysis of language has become a central sub-field of linguistics. It is a varied field, to the extent that variationist sociolinguistics, in some ways the mainstream – in particular in the English-speaking world – may appear essentially separate from the study of the sociology of language, where individual speakers and their language use are of interest to the extent that they form part of a larger community, whose linguistic behavior may be analyzed in a predominantly sociological manner. Yet without the knowledge of one sub-field, it is difficult to talk intelligently about the other. It is not for nothing that the study of linguistic variation is termed microsociolinguistics by some, just as the impact of society upon language (and language upon society) is termed macrosociolinguistics.

This interaction is arguably even more present when consideration is given to language and language use across time. Although there are some historical linguists who do not consider their topic connected to the times and places in which particular texts were written, this can be a very dangerous oversight. With the knowledge not only about how a particular individual used language, but also a society-wide sense of how written (and spoken) language was viewed, along with the preference that might have been given to a particular variety over others and the social distinctions which may have affected language use, we can truly begin to understand what caused individuals and groups to use language(s) in a particular way.

The Handbook of Historical Sociolinguistics, First Edition. Edited by Juan Manuel Hernández-Campoy and Juan Camilo Conde-Silvestre.
© 2014 John Wiley & Sons, Ltd. Published 2014 by John Wiley & Sons, Ltd.

In this chapter I will in the first instance look at how specific social historical processes might affect language use and language change, then discuss how awareness of these issues affects an informed analysis of diachronic variation and change, before concentrating on some of the macrosociolinguistic forces at work over a considerable historical period. Naturally, in a relatively small space I will not be able to discuss all of even the major themes of historical macrosociolinguistics. I do hope, however, that by combining theoretical discussion with illustrative case studies, I may be able to give a sense of the field's range and potential.

2. Social History and Language Change

Empirical findings – over the last fifty years, in particular – demand that we assume that social historical (or, if you prefer, sociolinguistic) forces underlie (or interact with) all language change. Sometimes, however, we have limited evidence for what these interactions might have been. A good example of this is the First Germanic Consonant Shift, otherwise known as Grimm's Law (see, for instance, McColl Millar 2007: 118–22). It would be very surprising if sociolinguistic forces had not had an input into such a thoroughgoing set of changes. But beyond an awareness that the logjam created by the Roman limes, putting in place a frontier along the Rhine and Danube which has rarely been replicated, meant that people speaking different Germanic dialects (and, indeed, other languages) found themselves living cheek-by-jowl with each other in a way that had not previously happened, which might have meant that, as old political and social structures broke down, the loose network ties associated with sociolinguistic change probably multiplied, there is little more to say: the lack of written evidence for the ongoing change makes any discussion ultimately fruitless (McColl Millar 2010: 99–105).

Rather more helpful information can be gained in searching for sociohistorical explanations for the *Rhenish Fan*, an unusual 'dialect mixing' phenomenon in the Dutch and German varieties spoken along the Rhine, from Upper Alsace down to Holland.[1] In most of the continental West Germanic world a single isogloss runs between traditional dialects with Low German and Dutch consonants and their High German equivalents (modern standardization and educational policy has meant that many people do not follow the traditional use patterns of their home areas, but this change is recent). Thus, north of this *Benrath-line* the original Germanic stops /p/, /t/, /k/ are maintained, in words such as *pund* 'pound', *dorp* 'village', *tijd* 'time', *geslotten* 'shut' and *kind* 'child', *maken* 'make'. South of this line, these stops become affricates or fricatives, depending on the dialect and position in the mouth: *Pfund, Dorf, Zeit, geschlossen, Chind*[2] and *machen*.

In the westernmost parts of the Germanic speaking world, in particular on the west bank of the Rhine, rather more complicated patterns can be found. In Luxembourgish, for instance, while the equivalents to Germanic /k/ are the same as other mainstream High German dialects, Germanic /p/ is retained initially – *pond* 'pound' – but is a fricative finally – *duaref* 'village'; conversely, Germanic /t/

is an affricate initially – *Zeit* 'time' – but a stop finally – *wat* 'what'. In relatively small sections along the Rhine – perhaps 35 to 50 kilometers south to north – this gradual change, unlike the eastern absolute distinction, is played out. The further north a variety is spoken, the more Low German-Dutch features it will have. But right to the historical mouths of the Rhine and Meuse, elements of the High German innovation can be found. Why should this have happened?

In the first instance, a purely language-internal explanation can be invoked. From a viewpoint informed by wave theory, it is normal for a change to be most complete near its point of origin, with 'irregularities' becoming more common the further away from the origin we travel – both in distance and time. Therefore, we can say that the small amount of High German features found at the northern end of the Rhenish Fan represents the final evidence for an 'exhausted' change now played out. But while changes of this type are common, and the Rhenish Fan appears to illustrate one, it does not explain why the changes to the east of the Rhine were so different. In other words, we would expect essentially the same 'gradual change' phenomena on either side of the Rhine. This does not happen, however. An explanation for this discrepancy has again to be sought; on this occasion the only place to turn is social history.

Essentially, the size of the Rhenish fan 'pockets' is interesting, since they are quite uniformly about the size that an average healthy person could walk in a day and then get up the next morning and repeat the process. On many dialect continua this type of formation can be seen as representing a dialect division. But that is not the whole story. At the heart of almost all of the pockets is a city – Strasbourg, Trier, Koblenz, Cologne, and so on. All of these cities were already major centers under the Romans and were major governmental or ecclesiastical centers (or both) which also served as markets of some importance in the Middle Ages.

In the wake of the collapse of Roman central power on the left bank of the Rhine in the fifth century, these centers retained remnants of this authority, even as the speakers of Germanic dialects gradually outnumbered speakers of Latin (and possibly some Celtic speakers). This was probably not a smooth transition, but the western bank of the Rhine retained an urban nature which was not replicated east of the river until somewhat later in the Middle Ages. While this was taking place, the Second Germanic Consonant Shift was beginning to spread from the south. In the Rhenish Fan, local urban authority meant that features of this change were retained in a particular pocket because a strong sense of local identity existed, rather than the more amorphous type of relationship which existed in Germany proper. Moreover, in these pockets, governmental authority was sufficiently strong that local people could be compelled to use the central market. In the east, the change could reach its furthest extent because no (or at least few) sociohistorical forces were present to halt it. In the west the spread of the changes are preserved, as it were, in aspic, in a way which is priceless for historical dialectologists interested in seeing how the change spread – not as a single universal change, but rather as a set of at some level independent changes.

As a final example of how social historical forces can be used to explain linguistic change, the fate of the English <ea> words in the early modern period.

Changes in the pronunciation of the <ea> words are normally analyzed as being part of a major chain-shift termed the 'Great Vowel Shift'[3]. If we look at the distribution of <ea> in the English-speaking world, we can see that most words have the pronunciation /i(:)/, as with *stream*. A small number of words have a lower vowel pronunciation, whether monophthongal, as in Scottish Standard English /e/, or diphthongal, as with Received Pronunciation /eɪ/, in *great* or *steak*. There are also a small number of <ea> words which have /ɛ/ pronunciations, such as *death* or *head*.

In some dialects, in particular most forms of Scots, a similar but different pronunciation pattern is found, where most <ea> words with /ɛ/ in the Standard are pronounced with /i(:)/, so that *head* is /hid/; a few, however, have an /e/ pronunciation, as with /deθ/, *death*. Nevertheless, the overwhelming tendency in all of these dialects is for <ea> to be /i(:)/. There is, however, a rare but important counter-tendency. In traditional dialects from many parts of Ireland and northern Scotland and Orkney, <ea> is normally /e(:)/ or a diphthongal equivalent. How can we explain these strikingly different patterns? How do we explain the mainstream minority usage with /e(:)/ or its diphthongal equivalent?

Space precludes an in-depth discussion of the workings of the Great Vowel Shift, but the considerable amount of evidence from a range of sources for early modern pronunciation, as assembled by Dobson (1957/1968), suggests that two different forms of change were taking place at the same time. The first of these represented a three way merger of <ai/y> words, originally /ai/, as with *hairy* and *may*, <aCe> words, originally /a:/, as in *tale* and *make*, and <ea>, originally /ɛ:/. These merged forms then rose to /e:/. We can therefore say that this pattern is the ancestor of the present Irish and northern Scottish pronunciation patterns. There is considerable evidence that this pattern was prestigious in the London area in the late sixteenth and early seventeenth century.

But a less prestigious pronunciation pattern appears also to have been present in this period. In this similar but divergent pattern <ai/y> words merged with <aCe> words and rose to /e:/; it did not merge with <ea>, however. Instead <ea> rose to /i:/, where it merged with the <ee> words. This is, of course, very close to the majority pattern today. The question then is: how do we explain why a previously less prestigious pattern overcame the more prestigious?

In the late medieval and early modern periods, social mobility became increasingly common in England, largely due to urbanization, the breakdown of feudalism through large-scale demographic changes due to the presence of plague from the 1340s on, the periodic civil wars of the fifteenth century which led to the deaths of many of the old aristocracy and, in the later stages, the economic changes brought about by the discovery of the Americas and new contacts in Asia and beyond. A feature of the sixteenth and seventeenth centuries was the 'new man,' someone from relatively humble origins who attained considerable economic or political power. Examples of this type include Thomas Wolsey, Thomas More, and Thomas Cromwell, each essentially prime minister under Henry VIII (1491–1547), whose own father, Henry VII (1457–1509), was in many ways himself a new man. Later examples include Oliver Cromwell (1599–1658), dictator of the republican

English Commonwealth and John Churchill, first Duke of Marlborough, 'sword' of the 'Glorious Revolution' of 1689–90. The sheer numbers of the new men, coupled with the radicalism in religion and politics which many of their number espoused (as well as the absolutist tendencies of the monarchy in the seventeenth century) led to the English Revolution of 1649 and the 'Glorious Revolution' mentioned above. In both, members of the lower middle classes moved into leadership roles. It can therefore be postulated that the <ea> merging with <ee> patterns was theirs and that its desirability rose with their fortunes, while <ea> with <ai/y> and <aCe> was associated with the 'old order' – the *Tories* as they were called by their enemies – and was therefore eventually outmoded, if not actually abandoned.

This does not explain how this process took place, of course, but we do have some evidence about how the change proceeded. Alexander Gil, an *orthoepist* (someone who corrected people's language) and gifted, although untrained, phonetician, writing in the early years of the seventeenth century, comments on the language of a group of women from the region to the east of London (probably Essex), whom he terms the *Mopsae*. He criticizes the way they pronounce <ea> words higher in the mouth than do more prestigious speakers (Gil 1619/1972: 16). Who the Mopsae were has been a topic of debate for decades among historical linguists. In Shakespeare and other writers of his time *mopsy* is associated with prostitution (or at least sexual availability) among women. While Gil is critical, however, of the Mopsae's pronunciation, there is no real suggestion of 'immorality' inherent in it (indeed, it is very likely that Gil would not have bothered criticizing the English of sex workers, primarily because they would not normally have been his target audience). It would seem likely, although not easily proven, of course, that his comments on the Mopsae's speech represent the establishment's disdain for the lower middle-class pronunciations beginning to filter through society.

But although much of the above is obviously in some sense true, we have to accept that a theoretically conditioned and coherent sociolinguistic analysis of language history is not present. In the rest of this chapter I will be concentrating on macrosociolinguistic analyses of social and historical forces. It is nonetheless necessary to acknowledge the ways in which historical (micro)sociolinguistics has followed the same explanatory paths, moving from an analysis which was history neutral (as seen, to an extent, in Romaine 1982) to one in which an understanding of the social relationships in a particular place and time are one of the central sources for an understanding of sociolinguistic change in that society (see, for instance, Nevalainen and Raumolin-Brunberg 2003). Other chapters in this volume will discuss these issues in greater depth, however.

3. Competition and Conflict between Language Varieties

In the following sections I will discuss some of the central concerns of historical macrosociolinguistics, referring in particular (since it is so central) to the competition and conflict found between language varieties in all societies, the end results of which being as different as the achievement of classical status or the loss of prestige so final that no native speakers remain.

3.1 'Language' and 'dialect'

There are many languages today which could be considered dialects; there are also many varieties termed dialects which could be considered languages (McColl Millar 2005). By general agreement, Norway, Sweden, and Denmark have discrete national languages. Yet Norwegians and Swedes understand each other without great difficulty, and both can, with more effort, understand Danes. Conversely, Cantonese is considered a Chinese dialect, even though it is not mutually intelligible with the prestigious Putonghua (Mandarin) dialect and only marginally intelligible to speakers of other south-eastern dialects.

These apparent anomalies can only be explained with reference to sociohistorical forces. While the separation of Scandinavia into three countries would rarely be challenged now, Norway and Sweden were united under one crown from 1814 to 1906, while Denmark and Norway were fully united from the late Middle Ages until 1814 (with Sweden being part of this union in its earlier history). It is quite possible to imagine 'Scandinavian' a single, standardized language written (and eventually spoken) in a unitary state; because the three-way split has become the norm, although three similar, but different, languages have developed.

On the other hand, because Chinese is almost always written in a logographic script, speakers of different varieties may use a different word for 'tree,' but the same symbol. Moreover, although different varieties of Chinese are not mutually intelligible, their syntactic structures are similar. Thus written mutual intelligibility is possible across far greater distances than spoken. This central point explains why Chinese speakers have retained a writing system so unwieldy, involving considerable time and effort in learning a sufficient number of symbols to read and write relatively complex ideas. The script and the use of the term 'dialects' for cognate languages lie at the heart of being Chinese.

Yet these explanations cannot explain how these relatively extreme situations can be related to rather more muted, but nonetheless not fully straightforward, contexts. The nature of the relationships between different language varieties is dynamic. For instance, the German dialects of Switzerland are not mutually intelligible with standard High German (although all Swiss German speakers can write and, to a degree, speak the standard). Yet few Swiss German speakers would consider their varieties to be separate from German as a whole.

3.2   Diglossia

There is little friction between the two varieties because they are used in different *domains*. It would be considered inappropriate, for instance, to give an academic lecture on inorganic chemistry in your native dialect; equally, however, it is inappropriate (indeed rude or even hostile) to use standard German when speaking in an intimate context with people from your region. Most written domains will be represented by the standard, although some contexts – jokes, political cartoons, and slogans, among others – may be considered best suited to the local variety (Ferguson 1959).

This type of relationship – *diglossia* – exists not only between varieties of the same language. It is not at all uncommon for two (or, indeed, more) different languages to share a diglossic relationship (Fishman 1967). In East Africa, for instance, local languages may be in a diglossic relationship with a lingua franca, such as KiSwahili. In Tanzania KiSwahili is regularly the language of primary education, so that literacy is, to a considerable extent, associated with that language. Yet in a particular place, lack of local language knowledge on the part of, for instance, a politician might make it impossible for him or her to express solidarity. Thus knowledge of both languages and when and where they are used is essential to membership of local networks. At another level, however, KiSwahili is the Low (L) member of a diglossic relationship with English, the official or generally observed High (H) variety nationally and internationally. Individuals may therefore participate in at least three social relationships between languages, but even when they do not have full command of all of the languages, they are still likely to share views on appropriateness with those who can (Mkilifi 1972).

Diglossia is considered to be highly stable. Generally those who live in these situations do not think that there is anything particularly unusual about them, largely due to long-term linguistic hegemony. Yet diglossia can break down. When it does, previously L varieties can become H; how this happens will be discussed in the following. In essence, however, dialects become languages.

3.3   The 'creation' of languages and the process of standardization

Joseph (1987) suggests that, except for the earliest literate languages, all varieties which are considered standard languages, with a codified grammar and orthography, and often with a prescriptive sense of lexical appropriateness, typically expressed in the form of a dictionary, originated as diglossic L. Most L speakers were content with what seems the 'natural' state of affairs, but a 'linguistic avant-garde' shifts towards using L in domains previously associated only with H. Reasons for this can be attributed to a variety of causes, political, economic, and cultural.

When a 'circumstantial' language standardization takes place, where speakers make few conscious decisions to develop a standard (as happens in an 'engineered' standardization), one dialect of the L variety becomes, as Joseph terms it, 'synecdochic,' one standing for all. In general, this dialect is associated with power and prestige. Standard French, for instance, is the descendant of the dialect of Paris, the site for royal power in the later middle ages and early modern periods (McColl Millar 2005: 79–83; Lodge 1993: 85–117). In its various synecdochic forms prior to European intervention, KiSwahili was associated with centralized government (such as that of Zanzibar) or Moslem scholarship (as with Mombasa) (McColl Millar 2005: 154–62).

But even when a common dialect is found, a primarily spoken variety does not have the same level of cultural appropriateness (perceived or actual) in the written form that a long-term H variety has. When a number of the vernaculars of western Europe began to replace Latin as the normal language of scientific discourse in the course of the Early Modern period, many people (including those most in favor of the change) cringed at their own and others' 'uncultured' written language. Under these circumstances, processes such as 'elaboration' and 'acculturation' come into play.

When Rome first became a major player in the eastern Mediterranean world in the second century BCE, its leaders had long admired Hellenistic culture. Many Greek words were borrowed into Latin at that time because of the need for words for new flora and fauna. The perceived need to elaborate also played its part, however, since the need to sound more cultured must have been central to the literacy project of the time (Joseph 1987: 104–5). Kloss (1978) demonstrates that *Ausbau*, 'linguistic development,' takes place through the ongoing 'conquest' of domains within the use of non-literary prose, moving from the 'folksy' and the local to the research-driven and abstract. Although specifically designed to discuss change in the modern era, it can, with some hesitancy, be employed in the analysis of earlier times.

Elaboration and acculturation can sometimes become over-elaboration and over-acculturation. In the eighteenth century, for instance, arbiters of taste for English propelled it towards Latin in relation to structure. Since the two languages are structurally very different, many Latinate features did not survive long. One that did, however, is among the least useful: the 'split infinitive,' quite natural to English, is now avoided in writing because there is no Latin equivalent.

Finally, Joseph (1987) suggests, a mature standard may become an absolute standard. While a mature standard continues to change, remaining fairly close to the spoken form, an absolute standard rarely if ever changes, since it is perceived as being 'perfect' or, at least, is associated with a seminal period in the language's history or with revealed religion. It is often at this point that a linguistic avant-garde supporting a new standard – L – comes into being. An absolute standard is not far from becoming a 'classical language,' undoubtedly greatly admired, but with no native speakers, at least in any meaningful sense.

3.4   *Standard varieties in contact and conflict*

Where there is an educational process designed in favor of a particular language variety, a language must have a standardized form. Otherwise, teaching orthography or a prescriptive grammar would be almost impossible. Nevertheless some languages are more successful in terms of the ways in which the standard form is used – in domains and across regions. A useful example is first millennium BCE Italy (McColl Millar 2010: 55–67).

This period demonstrated a move from considerable diversity in written languages, with Italic languages, other Indo-European languages and non-Indo-European languages being used, to one in which only Latin was written and, eventually, spoken. Generally this change is attributed to the growth of Roman power. This is correct, but does not give full recognition to another feature: Latin, unlike the other Italian written languages, was used in a wide range of domains, both literary and non-literary. In the surviving records of the other Italic languages, written language is used to commemorate acts and treaties and to express ownership. Although Oscan speakers in particular were famous for their *carmina*, presumably spoken 'songs,' there is little evidence of their having recorded them in writing. Etruscan literacy is also not used for much beyond monumental inscriptions or magical-medical 'documents.'

Latin, however, while carrying out all the 'Italian' roles, was also, from early on, used to record speeches and history. Somewhat later, poetry began to be written, often with an epic subject matter. While some impetus for these developments must have come from the nearby Greek traditions, the concentration on legal documents is doubtless based on Rome's being the main city of Latium and, later, of Italy and beyond. But although creative literature eventually came to have considerable ideological importance, particularly in the late Republic and early Principate, the interest in perpetuating the acts of the Roman state remained central to literacy in Latin well into the imperial period. McColl Millar (2010: 206–9) terms this 'civic literacy.'

These developments can be usefully compared with Greek in its classical period. A civic element *was* prominent in Greek literacy. On this occasion, however, it was creative processes which most encouraged the development of a literate culture. Art has always been associated with the elite of a society. The time and expenditure involved is considerable and, until recently, patronage was vital. Even the drama produced in democratic Athens, while obviously attractive to many, merely represents the extension of an elite art-form into the central marketplace. In McColl Millar (2010: 206–9) this state is named 'elite literacy.'

Both civic and elite literacy imply relatively circumscribed literacy levels. But when, as in central Italy, only small amounts of civic material were recorded, true standardization cannot be said to have been accomplished. This is also true for elite literacies. If they combine, however, 'intimate standardizations' result. A written variety has become a true standard, represented in a wide range of domains, but not necessarily to a large number of people.

Economic and political power feeds into the status of a language at this juncture. Linguistic 'maturity' was present in the written use of Rome and Athens when they were city states among city states. But what brought about mass standardization, as described in Figure 3.1 – the use of a written language among large numbers of people, many of whose ancestors had not spoken that language – was the political and economic expansion of states associated with the variety. The power wielded by speakers of these languages led to the appropriation of hegemonic force for the languages.

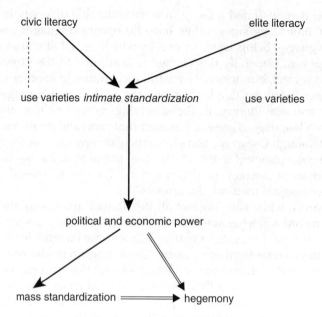

Figure 3.1. A model for the standardization process

3.5 *Standardization and ideology*

Inherent in *engineered* standardization in particular are ideological concerns over how a standardized language should be constituted. Should a language reflect the dialects of the social (and literary) elite, as with French in the eighteenth century, or should it reflect the dialects least affected by urbanization, as with *Landsmaal*, from which *Nynorsk*, one of the two standard varieties of Norwegian, springs? Should a standard represent the desire for a return to an idealized, pristine, time, before capitalism became hegemonic, as again with *Landsmaal*, but also visible in a number of other Nordic languages, or should the planned language represent a self-conscious rejection of the past, focusing instead on the most modern – and often urban – language forms available, as was the case to a degree with Czech? Should a new standard variety embrace H-inputs into its corpus, as planners of Slovak have largely done, or should it reject them, as happened with Czech? Finally, is it possible for a language to exhibit all, or at least most, of these features (Thomas 1991)? In order to test this, we must consider the development of Turkish since the nineteenth century.

As Lewis (1999) points out, in 1919 the Ottoman Empire lay prostrate, its core Turkish lands under threat of dismemberment. The empire's written language, *Osmanlı*, 'Ottoman,' while based on spoken Turkish, was saturated with Arabic and Persian features. Unlettered Turks (probably the majority) had great difficulty in following it.

Many Turks were aware that revolutionary steps had to be taken to protect Turkey's heartland and to realign the country as a literate western nation. Building on Young Turk policies from 1907 on, social, political, and linguistic reform marched shoulder to shoulder toward the objective of national survival and consolidation. As part of this process, Mustafa Kemal, known later as *Atatürk*, seized control of the reforms and remade them in his own image. Having achieved victory against the Greeks in 1921–22, Kemal knew how important the Europeanization of Turkish society was to his plan eventually to overtake the major European powers.

Under the influence of the contemporary Romanization projects in Soviet Central Asia, Kemal's government attempted something breathtaking: the national changeover from one script, written right to left, to another, written left to right, in around a year. Anyone unable to write in the 'Turkish alphabet' would then be considered illiterate; members of the bureaucracy and parliamentarians would lose their jobs if they had not changed scripts. Remarkably, the plan succeeded. What followed this reform was more controversial, however.

Kemal became convinced that the use of Arabic and Persian words and phrases within Turkish acted against his Westernization programme. Like many modern nationalists, he was at heart a linguistic purist who held Romantic ideas about folk speech and its proximity to tradition. Language activists were therefore set the task of finding 'good Turkish' replacements for the 'foreign elements' in the language. This was done in a variety of ways: the use of colloquial and dialectal forms came first; then material from the Turkic languages of central Asia was employed. Almost all of these languages were themselves going through language planning and revitalization processes at the same time, so interaction was considerable. Elements were also derived from other 'Altaic' languages. Thus historical, modernizing, ethnographic *and* elitist features were present in the language reform.

3.6 The inevitable result of planning and standardization: language shift

In the preceding sections we have been primarily concerned with linguistic *winners*, varieties which have succeeded in maintaining or gaining status. Inevitably, however, other varieties must be *losers* in these circumstances. It is to these that we will now turn.

Over the last forty years or so some sociolinguists have become interested in both the sociolinguistic and linguistic nature of language shift. The actual process itself is fairly well understood, although there have not as yet been many attempts at joining up all the sociolinguistic and linguistic findings into one unit. A number of the central findings of the research will nonetheless be summarized in the following.

3.6.1 The process of language shift In the south-eastern Austrian province of Burgenland, a minority of inhabitants are Hungarian speakers. In the settlement of Oberwart (Hungarian Felsőőr) near the present Hungarian frontier, as Gal's seminal study (1979) demonstrates, the majority of inhabitants until the 1950s were Hungarian speakers, but industrial development in the area led to the immigration of German speakers in considerable numbers.

The Oberwart Hungarians are not closely tied culturally or linguistically to the Hungarians over the border in Hungary. Most western Hungarians are Catholics; the people of Oberwart are Calvinists whose ancestors came from the eastern Hungarian territories, in particular Transylvania (now part of Romania). In the seventeenth century, as the Habsburg power on the middle Danube gradually pushed back Ottoman occupation, warrior peasants from Transylvania were transplanted to Burgenland as part of a military frontier. The Oberwart Hungarians were therefore highly distinctive in their new home.

Although Burgenland had long had a German majority, the province was part of the Kingdom of Hungary until it was transferred to Austria in 1919. Prior to this, a Magyarization policy designed to make the other ethnic groups who had settled in the 'crown lands of St. Stephen' Hungarian in language and culture was the ideological norm. Although the fact that the King of Hungary (and Austrian Emperor) was a German speaker may have alleviated the pressure by the Hungarian centre to conform to Hungarian norms in Burgenland, local Hungarian speakers would not have felt the need to learn much German, particularly since peasant life did not require much interaction with outsiders.

After 1919, the new German-language orientation had considerable effects upon the Oberwart Hungarians, in particular in relation to education (although both the First and Second Austrian Republics in theory guaranteed education and other language rights to significant minorities). German would have become useful even to the most inward-looking Hungarian peasant. As economic and political crises plagued Austria, leading up to the 'reunification' of the country with Germany in 1938, German nationalism became increasingly shrill. The minorities may often have felt their interests were served by keeping their heads down and using German outside immediate family circles. This must have only been encouraged by life under the Third Reich, even if Hungary's position as Germany's ally probably gave the Austrian Hungarian minority some protection.

In the aftermath of the Second World War, the Burgenland Hungarians found themselves separated from Hungary by a far less porous frontier than had existed between the wars. At the same time, the Austrian government developed schemes to spread industrial production into agricultural areas. In Oberwart, these schemes encouraged the immigration of many monolingual speakers of German, so that, for the first time, the Hungarian speakers were in the minority. German became increasingly a language regularly used by the younger generations. Strikingly, moreover, Hungarian-speaking women seemed to prefer marrying German-speaking wage-earners than men from their own background. Prior to the large-scale support of agriculture instituted by the EU and its predecessors, the returns from farming were difficult to quantify and there was no immediate correlation between the amount of effort exerted and profitable output, unlike receiving a guaranteed sum of money every week or month. This change led Hungarian-speaking men to marry German-speaking women. While a number of German

Interlocutor

Age	1	2	3	4	5	6	7	8	9	10
14	H	GH		G	G	G	G			G
15	H	GH		G	G	G	G			G
25	H	GH	GH	GH	G	G	G	G	G	G
27	H	H		GH	G	G	G			G
17	H	H		H	GH	G	G			G
13	H	H		GH	GH	GH	GH			G
43	H	H		GH	GH		G	GH	GH	G
39	H	H		H	GH	GH	G	G	G	G
23	H	H		H	GH	H	G		GH	G
40	H	H		H	GH		GH	G	G	G
50	H	H		H	H	GH	GH	GH	G	G
52	H	H	H	GH	H		H	GH	G	G
60	H	H		H	H	GH	GH	GH	G	G
40	H	H	H	H	H	H	H	GH	GH	G
60	H	H		H	H	H	H	H	GH	GH
71	H	H		H	H	H	H	H	H	H

Interlocutors: 1 = God; 2 = grandparents and their generation; 3 = black market clients; 4 = parents and their generation; 5 = age-mate friends, neighbors; 6 = brothers and sisters; 7 = salespeople; 8 = spouse; 9 = children and that generation; 10 = government
Languages: G = German; H = Hungarian

Figure 3.2. Implicational scale for language choice by women speakers in Oberwart (from Gal 1979: 121; Reproduced by permission of Academic Press)

speakers *did* learn Hungarian, the fact that their partners and often their partners' whole families (except, perhaps, the very oldest members) could speak native- or near-native-speaker standard German did not encourage this.

By the 1970s, when Gal was carrying out her research, German was winning out even in wholly Hungarian homes (see Figure 3.2):

What is striking about this table is that language use seems to correlate with a number of features. Most obviously this is the case with age. Older members of the Hungarian community are more likely to speak Hungarian in a wider range of domains. This leads us on to the fact that language-use correlates with domain. All Hungarian speakers use that language when addressing God. Except for some of the youngest speakers, almost all speak Hungarian with their grandparents; many use it with their parents; fewer with their age-mates and brothers and sisters; even fewer with their children. Strikingly, only the oldest people – born when Burgenland was part of Hungary – use Hungarian with government officials (local, provincial, and federal), despite the fact that all Hungarian speakers have the right to expect to be served in that language, if that is their wish. The 'black market' issue will be dealt with shortly.

This is a classic age gradient associated with language shift. Grandchildren know sufficient Hungarian to speak it to their grandparents, but speak it less regularly with their parents, who may have chosen to use German mainly with their children, perceiving the national language as the way forward. As evidenced by their use of German with the authorities, an attempt to fit in and demonstrate their literacy (a trait sometimes not associated with the peasant class by urban dwellers) is also present. The lowest age level in this survey is unlikely to use much Hungarian with their own children. This analysis does not examine a further contributory factor in this language shift, mentioned above: exogamy.

Two domains buck this trend, however. In Austria in the 1970s it was illegal for you to pay anyone other than a registered tradesperson to carry out work associated with that trade. Thus if you paid your neighbor to paint your house and he was not a registered painter, you were considered to have broken the law. Naturally peasants, who tend to develop some ability in a variety of different skills and do not always have ready cash, were inclined to attempt subverting these rules. The authorities naturally expected this subversion, and kept an eye out for it. The Oberwart Hungarians had a great advantage over the monoglot German speakers around them: they could use a language which few other Austrians could understand.

The fact that Hungarian was used almost exclusively by the community in addressing God is not surprising. Austria is a majority Catholic country where the Protestant minority tends to be Lutheran. The Hungarian Calvinists of Burgenland were therefore doubly different from their neighbors: in their religious confession and the language they used in worship. Moreover, until the Second Vatican Council's vernacularization decrees in the mid 1960s, the religious distinction was not between German and Hungarian, but rather between Latin and Hungarian, meaning that Oberwart Hungarians may have considered the use of their language as being not so much a national statement as a religious one.

The use of language in religion has indeed encouraged the continued knowledge of the language among people who regularly use the majority language outside religious domains, as can be seen in communities as far apart as ultra-Orthodox Jews (with Yiddish) in the USA, evangelical Presbyterians in central Scotland (with Gaelic) and, for an extended period, Coptic Christians (with Coptic) in Egypt. The problem is, of course, that, in the secularization so symptomatic of the present era, this association with a way of life from which some members of a community may feel divorced does not augur well for that language.

3.6.2   Towards a theory of language shift   Central to our understanding of the theoretical dimension that lies behind the shift just discussed lies within Dorian's (1981) work on shift away from Gaelic in the East Sutherland region of Scotland, where she introduces the idea of the 'semi-speaker.' Shift *can* be a sudden event, particularly where speaker numbers are low and a traumatic event – disease, famine, natural disasters, genocide – 'dislocates' a considerable proportion of the language's speakers. But it is much more common for there to be a 'grey area' between complete knowledge of a language and complete lack of knowledge.

Dorian found that a number of people within her target group had considerable facility in understanding the local Gaelic, but could not exactly produce the structure of that dialect in the way a native speaker would. When semi-speakers attempted to speak Gaelic, those places where English was particularly different from Gaelic were central to their breakdown in the use of the latter language.

Mostly this was due to lack of recent use. What must originally have been the language of home and family was spoken increasingly infrequently until years might go by between instances of the use of Gaelic. Although the language might literally be the speaker's mother tongue, lack of practice and acculturation to another language led to a partial shift.

The semi-speaker state in fact acts as a continuum between full speakers and non-speakers. Some of Dorian's informants were essentially native speakers who made occasional mistakes in their Gaelic, representing interference from English; others could understand Gaelic well and had a considerable knowledge – both active and passive – of Gaelic lexis, but were incapable of producing a coherent sentence in that language.

But not all semi-speakers are produced by a move away from their childhood language. As Sasse (1992) develops in his model of language shift, in the final stages of a language's life as a language with native speakers, some parents – particularly, perhaps, those who are socially aspirant about their children's futures – may choose *not* to teach the ethnic language to their children. An on-going process exists whereby status differences between language varieties leads on some occasions to the abandonment of the original native language of a group (A) in favor of a more prestigious language (T). In the first instance, the economic, political, and social associations of T (which in some ways is H to A's L, returning to Joseph's views above), focused by an educational system, leads A to be used only in 'homely' contexts, written and spoken, while T tends to be associated with more abstract contexts, achieved through *Ausbau*.

In these circumstances it is almost inevitable that some parents (often aspirational and relatively well educated) choose not to teach their children A, considered doubtless to be of little use or benefit in 'getting on' in T society. Children in these circumstances are still likely to pick up A, but not at quite the level achieved through natural transmission. It is likely, for instance, that they would learn A when somewhat older than when they acquired their native language. Acquisition of A would derive from the language of A-speaking peers and older children, grandparents and their generation, A-using adults, and even, in unguarded moments, their own parents. There might even be considerable peer-pressure to use the 'rough' language. What is almost certain is that those who learn A this way will be unlikely to learn the whole system of the language. Minor rules and exceptions are rarely learnt. Older speakers undoubtedly would consider these speakers language to be 'corrupt.' This process is therefore a major source of semi-speakers.

This might discourage people from using their 'half-learned' variety. But in a situation where the prestige of A is covert and literacy in A, if it is found at all, is uncommon, young people may actually choose to adopt elements of the non-native speaker A as an identity marker. This adoption of forms of the language considered to be in error by elders makes the 'generation gap' even greater. It will also encourage further adoption of non-native forms which encourage rapid change. In the native Australian language Dyirbal, for instance, the historically complex grammatical gender system has been fundamentally simplified in the most recent generations. This is undoubtedly under the influence of English (although it has to be noted that even radical Dyirbal maintains the category of gender, which English has jettisoned entirely); this influence is as likely, however, to be due to the use of Dyirbal by members of the native group who are essentially native speakers of English (see, for instance, Schmidt 1985).

Inevitably, the dislike expressed by elders for the language of the young (not, of course, uncommon with practically every language in the world) discourages more people from teaching A to their children. It has been reported in a number of places in North America, for instance, that 'good,' older, speakers of a local language find the use of that language by the young so obnoxious that they prefer to use the hegemonic language (primarily English, but potentially also French or Spanish) with them (Thomason 2001: 77–85). If enough people feel like this, then A will cease to have native speakers.

But in Sasse's analysis this is not entirely the end. He mentions the 'use of residue knowledge for specialized purposes = ritual, group identification, joke secret language [sic]' after language shift. A good example of this is the language variety Anglo-Romani used by people of Roma background in England and Wales (see, for instance, Kenrick 1979). Serving as a means of excluding outsiders, practically all of Anglo-Romani's vocabulary comes from the ancestral language of its speakers, Romani. But the syntax is essentially English. There was a time when England and Wales had a considerable number of Romani speakers, probably arriving from the fifteenth to sixteenth centuries onward. Unlike Romani speakers on the Continent, however, regular contact was not maintained with other speakers, contact with English speakers becoming increasingly the norm in their everyday existence. Eventually, some time in the late nineteenth to early twentieth centuries, no native speakers of Romani remained. Roma identity continued, however, along with the prejudice and mistrust felt both by 'mainstream' society and people of Romani identity. A use variety, opaque to outsiders, was therefore of considerable advantage to insiders. Lexical elements of Romani – the easiest parts of a language to learn and remember – were perpetuated for precisely this purpose (indeed some believe that the variety had a separate existence before the Roma community shifted from Romani). These theoretical points will now be considered in relation to a language death less well known outside the specialist literature.

3.6.3   Theory in action – Shetland Norn   Until the early to mid eighteenth century, Shetland, an archipelago some 150 kilometers north of the Scottish mainland, had considerable numbers of speakers of Norn, a North Germanic dialect. As discussed by Barnes (1998 and 2010), among others, from at least the fifteenth century on, however, dialects of Scots were spoken there, often associated with the new connection with Scotland forged during the handover of Orkney and Shetland to the Scottish crown (from that of Denmark-Norway) during 1469–71, and these islands' incorporation into the Scottish state in the centuries following. Trading gradually became dominated by Scots speakers during the same period. The Protestant Reformation also came from Scotland and was Calvinist in ideology, unlike the Lutheranism of most Scandinavian state churches (although the Scottish church did at least try to ensure that parish ministers in the more distant parts of Shetland had some knowledge of 'Danish,' and basic liturgical materials at least seem to have been provided for Norn-speaking adherents). Nevertheless, by the mid seventeenth century, Scots (and, initially in writing, Standard English) had a considerable and growing presence in the islands.

This presence was magnified by a series of economic and political events. Until around 1700, Shetland was not fully connected into the economic systems of the British Isles. It maintained close ties with Norway and other Norse-speaking territories and with the Low-German speaking cities of the Hanseatic League. But it was with the Dutch in particular that Shetland had intimate connections. There is a local saying that *Amsterdam wes biggit oot o da back o Bressay* 'Amsterdam was built out of the back of Bressay [the site of Lerwick]'. The great abundance of fish close in to the islands encouraged the first industrial fishery, with Dutch fishermen bringing their catches of herring in particular to Lerwick, the main settlement of the islands, for processing. Moreover, the Scottish state was for long incapable of enforcing its salt tax on the islands. This meant that the Dutch were working essentially duty-free. In the early eighteenth century, however, the state's policing of its prerogatives became much more successful. Although some foreign fishing vessels continued to use the islands, the boom was permanently over. Any remaining contacts with Norway quickly became largely symbolic. It became increasingly rare to hear other Scandinavian dialects being spoken in the islands. Shetland fell into an economic decline which continued for at least a century. In these circumstances, it was practically inevitable that the importance of the spoken and written languages of Scotland – later Britain – would increase in importance even for native speakers of Norn. Thus it could be argued that the death of Norn is a classic example of language shift caused by the high prestige and associated power of T. But there is at least one issue with such a conclusion.

In the late nineteenth century the great Faeroese dialectologist Jakob Jakobsen carried out extensive field work on the Norn lexical elements in the Scots dialects of Shetland. During this fieldwork, he found a number of people in the islands who could recite clauses and even rhymes in Norn. Since these discoveries were made a century and more after the assumed language shift, they are surprising and need some explanation. Some scholars, such as Rendboe (1984), would claim that this demands a later date for the shift. It is striking, however, that no-one mentions this survival anywhere (although that does not necessarily imply that pockets of survival, unnoticed by outsiders, could not have existed). More striking is the fact that the last large-scale Norn recorded, the *Hildina ballad* recorded in the mid-eighteenth century by the Reverend George Low from William Henry, an elderly resident of Foula, was not fully understood by the reciter. Henry could explain what the story was, but could not translate it. In other words, he was at the very most a semi-speaker. Even in outlying districts in 1750, therefore, Norn was moribund.

So what explains the survivals? Let us look again at the curious survival of the Hildina ballad. This is a poem of considerable length and the feat of memory would be considerable even if you understood each word. The fact that Henry learned the poem without understanding it fully implies a considerable feeling of connection, of identity, with its language, which transcended comprehension. By the same token, later survivals of pieces of Norn demonstrate the same sense of connection between person, place, and language. As these recordings became increasingly distant from the time when there were native speakers, they become increasingly incomprehensible. This is something like a feedback loop, becoming increasingly 'corrupted' with each copy from generation to generation. It nonetheless served as a marker that, although Norn speakers were forced by hegemonic forces to switch to Scots entirely, many continued a sense of linguistic difference.

Interestingly, the Scots dialects of Shetland also contain elements – such as /t/ for mainstream Scots /θ/ and /d/ for /ð/ which might be seen as representing the problems which Norn speakers had with the Scots sound pattern during the final shift. The fact that they are retained centuries later may well be constructed (below the level of consciousness) as identity markers.

4. Some Final Thoughts

Language use must be analyzed in its social context. This is never more the case than when dealing with language from the past. Without the connection between the two, it is very difficult not to commit errors in analysis, either historically or linguistically. Historical sociolinguistics of a variationist bent would be at the very least hindered without an understanding of the ecology in which language use is found. Yet historical macrosociolinguistics deserves to be considered as a field by itself, allied but not subjugated to its synchronic equivalent. It is to be hoped that in the future all branches of sociolinguistics will collaborate in ventures which will help us better understand speakers as individuals and groups, along with the language varieties they use, in past and present.

NOTES

1   See, for instance, Chambers and Trudgill (1980/1998: 91–93) and Iverson and Salmons (2006).
2   It should be noted that this pronunciation, with initial /x/, is only found in the more southerly dialects, with a affricate /kx/ being found in a belt to its north and east. However, most High German speakers do not have either pronunciation. The source for this Second Germanic Consonant shift was probably in the south, which explains why it is at its most complete there.
3   It should be noted, however, that some scholars deny the unitary nature of this shift, instead interpreting it as a series of independent changes, but this view does not really affect what is to follow (see McColl Millar (2007: 107–110).

REFERENCES

Barnes, M (1998) *The Norn Language of Orkney and Shetland*, Shetland Times, Lerwick.

Barnes, M. (2010) The Study of Norn. In R. McColl Millar (ed.), *Northern Lights, Northern Words. Selected Papers from the FRLSU Conference, Kirkwall 2009*, Forum for Research on the Languages of Scotland and Ulster, Aberdeen, pp. 26–47.

Chambers, J.K. and Trudgill, P. (1980/1998) *Dialectology* (2nd edn), Cambridge University Press, Cambridge.

Dobson, E.J. (1957/1968) *English Pronunciation, 1500–1700* (2nd edn), Clarendon Press, Oxford.

Dorian, N.C. (1981) *Language Death*, University of Pennsylvania Press, Philadelphia.

Ferguson, C.A. (1959) Diglossia. *Word* 15: 325–40.

Fishman, J.A. (1967) Bilingualism with and without Diglossia. *Journal of Social Issues* 32: 29–38.

Gal, S. (1979) *Language Shift: Social Determinants of Linguistic Change in Bilingual Austria*, Academic Press, New York.

Gil, A. (1619/1972) *Logonomia Anglica*, J. Beale, London. Reprinted in Bror, D. and Gabrielson, A. (eds.) (1972), *Alexander Gill's Logonomia Anglica (1619)*. 2 vols, Almqvist and Wiksell, Stockholm.

Iverson, G.K. and Salmons, J.C. (2006) Fundamental regularities in the Second Consonant Shift. *Journal of Germanic Linguistics* 18: 45–70.

Joseph, J.E. (1987) *Eloquence and Power: The Rise of Language Standards and Standard Languages*, Frances Pinter, London.

Kenrick, D. (1979) Romani English. *International Journal of the Sociology of Language* 19: 111–20.

Kloss, H. (1978) *Die Entwicklung neuer germanischer Kultursprachen seit 1800* (2nd edn), Schwann, Düsseldorf.

Lewis, G. (1999) *The Turkish Language Reform. A Catastrophic Success*, Oxford University Press, Oxford.

Lodge, R.A. (1993) *French, from Dialect to Standard*, Routledge, London.

McColl Millar, R. (2005) *Language, Nation and Power*, Palgrave Macmillan, Basingstoke.

McColl Millar, R. (2007) *Trask's Historical Linguistics*, Hodder Arnold, London.

McColl Millar, R. (2010) *Authority and Identity. A Sociolinguistic History of Europe before the Modern Age*, Palgrave Macmillan, Basingstoke.

Mkilifi, M.H.A. (1972) Triglossia and Swahili–English bilingualism. *Language in Society* 1: 197–213.

Nevalainen, T. and Raumolin-Brunberg, H. (2003) *Historical Sociolinguistics: Language Change in Tudor and Stuart England*, Longman Pearson Education, London.

Rendboe, L. (1984) How 'worn out' or 'corrupted' was Shetland Norn in its final stage? *NOWELE* 3: 53–88.

Romaine, S. (1982) *Socio-historical linguistics: its status and methodology*, Cambridge University Press, Cambridge.

Sasse, H.-J. (1992) Theory of language death. In M. Brenzinger (ed.), *Language Death: Factual and Theoretical Explorations*, Mouton de Gruyter, Berlin, pp. 7–30.

Schmidt, A. (1985) The fate of ergativity in dying Dyirbal. *Language* 61: 378–96.

Thomas, G. (1991) *Linguistic Purism*, Longman, London.

Thomason, S.G. (2001) *Language Contact: an Introduction*, Edinburgh University Press, Edinburgh.

Part II Methods for the Sociolinguistic Study of the History of Languages

4 The Application of the Quantitative Paradigm to Historical Sociolinguistics: Problems with the Generalizability Principle

JUAN M. HERNÁNDEZ-CAMPOY AND NATALIE SCHILLING

Historical sociolinguistics has often been considered to suffer, perhaps inevitably, from lack of representativeness and validity of its findings. This is because the sociolinguistic study of historical language forms must rely on linguistic records from previous periods – most of which will be incomplete or non-representative in some way – as well as on knowledge and understanding of past sociocultural situations that can only be reconstructed rather than directly observed or experienced by the researcher. In this paper, we mention the seven main problems we have to contend with when trying to practice historical sociolinguistic research: i) representativeness, ii) empirical validity, iii) invariation, iv) authenticity, v) authorship, vi) social and historical validity, and vii) standard ideology. But theoretical and procedural problems are also present even in the apparently rigorous methodology of variationist sociolinguistics, as evidenced, for example, in the unevenness with which studies conform or fail to conform to the generalizability principle, as well as the extent to which 'generalizability' in sociolinguistic studies is even possible. Indeed, as Bailey and Tillery (2004: 13) note, "without a body of research that examines the effects of methods on results," we cannot even know how generalizable (i.e. representative and reliable) our studies have been or may be. Hence, we cannot hold historical sociolinguistics to standards with which

The Handbook of Historical Sociolinguistics, First Edition. Edited by Juan Manuel Hernández-Campoy and Juan Camilo Conde-Silvestre.
© 2014 John Wiley & Sons, Ltd. Published 2014 by John Wiley & Sons, Ltd.

sociolinguistics itself cannot comply. As Schneider (2002) states, despite its limitations, historical sociolinguistics is not a second-best solution by inevitable necessity, but just the best solution in those areas of study for which oral records are
not available, especially when studying long-term developments of language variation and change. In fact, in both approaches (diachronic and synchronic sociolinguistics) the goal of illuminating the processes of language change is exactly
the same and the pathways to it are very similar. In Nevalainen and Raumolin-
Brunberg's (2003: 26) words: "[t]rue, historical data can be characterized as 'bad'
in many ways, but we would rather place the emphasis on making the best use
of the data available."

1. Sociolinguistics and the Quantitative Revolution

Schools of thought and historical periods cannot be treated as discrete entities,
with a monolithic nature and abrupt boundaries, since they build upon, and often
begin as reactions against, preceding stages. Even the same phenomena are differently emphasized by different schools, and different aspects of a single theory
may be highlighted by one school and downplayed or neglected by another. This
means, as Lass (1984: 8) suggests, that

> the history of any discipline involves a lot of old wine in new bottles (as well as new
> wine in old bottles, new wine in new bottles, and some old wine left in the old
> bottles). Even ideas that seem at the moment self-evidently true do not arise out of
> nowhere, but are the products of a long series of trial-and-error interim solutions to
> perennial problems, illuminated by occasional flashes of creative insight and inspired
> invention. Improvements or even radical restructuring of a theory does not (or
> should not) imply the rejection of everything that went before.

Kuhn (1962) was in fact very concerned about this nature of science in his thesis
on scientific revolutions and the emergence of new paradigms. Linguistic theory,
as Williams (1992: 40) points out, "has not emerged separately from the social
philosophy of its time. Rather, it must be seen as a manifestation of the ongoing
debate on the nature of society and the social world." In this way, while the nineteenth century philologist, historicist, and comparatist urge in the study of the
nature of language was in overt opposition to the humanism and classicism of the
Renaissance and to seventeenth century rationalism, the structuralist turn at the
beginning of the twentieth century was an alternative to nineteenth-century his-
toricism and comparativism. Even within the same period, different theoretical
trends have followed one another in linguistics, such as the structuralism, functionalism, and generativism of the twentieth century.

In many ways, sociolinguistics also emerged as a kind of reaction against previous paradigms. Different motivations favored the development of this field of
study: i) the dissatisfaction among many linguists in the 1960s with previous
paradigms (e.g. those of Chomsky and Saussure); ii) the redefinition and reformu-

lation of traditional dialectology; iii) the growing interest among linguists in sociology and its scope; and iv) the quantitative revolution. Focusing on this last factor, sociolinguists in the Labovian tradition have sought to adopt scientific methods, to develop a quantitative linguistic perspective in which social, cultural, and contextual factors can be used to describe, explain, and predict patterns of linguistic variation and change (though of course variationists in recent years have stressed that mere correlations of social factors with linguistic phenomena are not in themselves explanations for these phenomena; see, among others, Eckert 2000; Bayley 2002: 134–36).

The principles of *representativeness* and *generalizability* were initially held as fundamental in the methodological rigor of variationist sociolinguistic procedure. Indeed, they are still often regarded as ideals, though sociolinguists have long recognized that achieving genuine statistical representativeness is extremely difficult and indeed is not always necessary to obtain solid results and revealing insights (see Labov 1966; Sankoff 1980: 51–52; Milroy and Gordon 2003: 28–29). As far as representativeness is concerned, all members of the community must have an equal chance of being selected as representative informants; further, informants should be selected preserving the sociological and demographic characteristics of the entire population. With regards to 'generalizability', any sociolinguistic research, according to Wolfram (2004), has to fulfill two particular criteria in order to produce results that can accurately be generalized to the behavior of the entire population, or speech community: in Bailey and Tillery's (2004: 1) words, "reliability (i.e., that the same results would be obtained in repeated observations of the same phenomenon) and subjectivity (i.e., that two different researchers observing the same phenomenon would have obtained the same results)."

For all this, Labov's (1982a: 30) *Principle of Accountability* is crucially important: "all occurrences of a given variant are noted, and where it has been possible to define the variable as a closed set of variants, all occurrences of the variant in the relevant circumstances." That is: "reports of the occurrence of a variant of a linguistic variable must be accompanied by reports of its non-occurrence" (Trudgill 2003: 3).

2. Historical Sociolinguistics and the Difficulties of Reconstructing the Past

Chapters 1 and 2 in this *Handbook* have underlined the hybrid nature of historical sociolinguistics as the convergence of historical linguistics and sociolinguistics (see also Conde-Silvestre 2007: 19–27). Assuming that the evolution of linguistic and social systems always occurs in relation to the sociohistorical situations of their speakers and taking into account the tenet that the past should be studied in order to understand and explain the present (and vice versa), Romaine (1982, 1988) proposed this multidisciplinary discipline. Theoretically, its main objective is: "to investigate and provide an account of the forms and uses in which variation may manifest itself in a given speech community over time, and of how particular functions, uses and kinds of variation develop within particular languages, speech communities, social groups, networks and individuals" (1988: 1453). Methodologically, "the main task of socio-historical linguistics is to develop a set of procedures for the reconstruction of language in its social context, and to use the findings of sociolinguistics as controls on the process of reconstruction and as a means of informing theories of change" (Romaine 1988: 1453). Obviously, as the database for historical sociolinguistic analysis is based on written texts of all kinds from earlier periods, the production of computer-readable corpora has undoubtedly facilitated the development of research (see Chapter 6 in this *Handbook*). In this way, the amount of digitalized corpora available now for historical sociolinguists is a sign of the fruitful relation between linguistics, history, and information technology and their burgeoning growth in recent decades.

Schneider (2002) and Bauer (2002) highlight the potential and problems (pros and cons) of relying on written sources and public corpora (large collections of naturally occurring language data, including those that are computer-readable/searchable) as linguistic data for variationist analysis. The most important disadvantage of datasets of historical documents is that they very often lack representativeness and possibly also validity, since, as noted above, the historical record is incomplete, and written materials may or may not be reflective of the spoken language of the time period under study. As Labov (1972: 98) aptly notes, "[t]exts are produced by a series of historical accidents; amateurs may complain about this predicament, but the sophisticated historian is grateful that anything has survived at all. The great art of the historical linguist is to make the best of this bad data, 'bad' in the sense that it may be fragmentary, corrupted, or many times removed from the actual productions of native speakers."

Nevalainen and Raumolin-Brunberg (Raumolin-Brunberg 1996; Nevalainen and Raumolin-Brunberg 1998; Nevalainen 1999) and Ayres-Bennett (2001) have underlined differences and similarities between historical sociolinguistics and variationist sociolinguistics, with special attention paid to the methodological problems associated with practicing the diachronic approach of the former. Complementing their review, we mention the seven main problems confronting those who practice historical sociolinguistic research, namely: i) representativeness, ii) empirical validity, iii) invariation, iv) authenticity, v) authorship, vi) social and historical validity, and vii) standard ideology.

2.1   *Representativeness*

As noted above, the data used in historical sociolinguistic study often suffer from lack of representativeness. Echoing Labov (1972), Milroy and Gordon (2003: 177) note that "data are often patchy as a consequence of the random preservation of some texts and the equally random loss of others" (see also Schneider 2002: 81–90). Hence, researchers must be careful to assess what types of speaker, population segments, and forms of language their samples encompass, since of course they cannot re-engineer pre-existing datasets.

2.2 *Empirical validity*

The fact that historical sociolinguists must work with text collections whose size is inevitably limited, even those compiled into large computerized corpora, means that we are often limited in terms of quantitative analysis and associated statistical measures (Schneider 2002: 89).The experience of researchers in sociolinguistics suggests that the number of tokens per cell of dependent variables has to be, at least 15 and, ideally, 30 or more, to ensure statistical representativeness. Further, following general social-scientific standards, Labov (1966) suggested the need to use 0.025% of the population to ensure representativeness in terms of independent social factors.

In addition to limitations in linguistic data, there are also limitations in the social data we can obtain in studying past communities. Raumolin-Brunberg (1996) summarizes some of the differences in data, foci, and nature of the conclusions that can be drawn in studying present-day vs. past communities. These are presented here in Table 4.1.

As we can see from the table, not only are we faced with limited linguistic data, in terms of type, amount, and coverage, but also with more limited sociocultural data than can be obtained in the study of current communities (see section 2.3 below for more on the latter issue).

Table 4.1. Sociolinguistic research on current and historical data (from Raumolin-Brunberg 1996: 18; Reproduced by permission of Editions Rodopi B.V.)

	Present-day	*Past*
Object of investigation	Phonological variation and/or change	Grammatical variation and/or change
Research material	Spoken language	Written language
	All people	Only literate people (upper ranks, men)
	Authentic speech: observation, elicitation, evaluation	Randomly preserved texts
Social context	Society familiar, much data available	Social structure to be reconstructed on the basis of historical research
Standardization	Significant element	Significance varies
Associated discipline	Sociology	Social history
Length and result of the change	Unknown	Known

2.3   *Invariation*

The kind of research materials available in the sociolinguistic study of historical vs. present-day communities (written vs. spoken) inevitably affects the object of investigation: phonological vs. grammatical variation and/or change. And given that written language tends to be more conservative, normative, and formal than oral language, the fact of having to rely on written sources constrains the probability of variation (Dees 1971; Arnaud 1980; Roberts and Street 1997; Conde-Silvestre and Hernández-Campoy 1998: 109–10). Hence, we must be careful that we do not overstate the extent of apparent uniformity or the firmness of our conclusions regarding the patterning of the variability we do observe, since in all likelihood, there was probably more variability, perhaps with different patterns, in older spoken language than in the written records that remain. Further, the variation we do find across manuscripts, if any, may be due either to dialectal or other demographic/sociological differences or to stylistic differences across speakers or across time periods (Toon 1976, 1983; Conde-Silvestre and Hernández-Campoy 1998: 109–10).

2.4   *Authenticity (purity in texts)*

Another important fact is that "the linguistic forms in such documents are often distinct from the vernacular of the writers, and instead reflect efforts to capture a normative dialect that never was any speaker's native language. As a result, many documents are riddled with the effects of hypercorrection, dialect mixture, and scribal error" (Labov 1994: 11). The transmission of manuscripts also involves problems, since many of them were copied from earlier ones which are now lost, and in many of them the original dialect may be mixed up with that of the scribe. Manuscripts also show intra-textual variation – that is, different portions of manuscripts appear to be written in different dialects (see Stockwell and Barritt 1951, 1961; Conde-Silvestre and Hernández-Campoy 1998: 110; also Chapter 7 in this *Handbook*). As a result, "the relationship between data derived from various kinds of written source and the data of spoken interaction which forms the basis of much contemporary sociolinguistic work is unclear" (Milroy and Gordon 2003: 177). Of course, sociolinguists have increasingly been questioning traditional notions of 'authentic' language data, since all speech communities are subject to dialect (and language) contact and mixing, and everyday speech is fraught with self-conscious usages of various sorts, including hypercorrections, as well as stylistic variation that can render it impossible to locate a given speaker's 'genuine' vernacular style (see Schilling-Estes 2004).

2.5   *Authorship*

Especially in the case of private correspondence, letters might not have been autographs (hand-written personally by the author) but may instead have been written by an amanuensis (a helper writing from dictation, normally a family clerk or chaplain) due to the widespread illiteracy characteristic of early historical time periods (Hernández-Campoy and Conde-Silvestre 1999; Schneider 2002: 76). For example, in their study of the Middle English *Paston Letters* (Davis 1971), Hernández-Campoy and Conde-Silvestre (1999), found that they had to exercise great care in interpreting patterns of variation found in the writings of one female informant, Margaret Paston (?1400–79). Her writings were, unexpectedly, the most non-standard of the entire collection (which included fifteen members of the Paston family) and hence seemingly divergent from contemporary patterns for the sociolinguistic behavior of women in the current Western industrialized world, at least as noted in very general terms. However, there is external evidence (Davis 1971: xxv; Bergs 2005: 79) strongly suggesting that Margaret did not write the letters herself, but the family clerk and chaplain – James Gloys – or other scribes connected to the family did so for her. In fact, Bergs' (2005: 79–80) analysis suggests that dictation would just affect phonological or graphological variables, but not morpho-syntactic ones. Hence, it would be erroneous to conclude from the analysis that women of Margaret Paston's time were actually less standard in their writing (and possibly speech) than men. Figure 4.1 shows the extent of Margaret Paston's use of vernacular (87%) vs. incipient standard (13%) spelling features – (sh), (wh) and (u) – as compared with three male family members (William Paston I, Clement Paston and John Paston II).

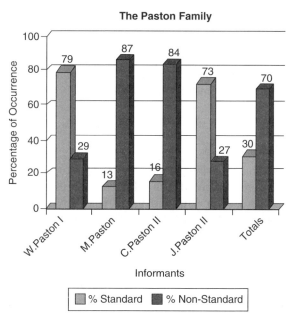

Figure 4.1. Percentage usage of the incipient standard in the Paston Family (from Hernández-Campoy and Conde-Silvestre 1999: 261; Reproduced by permission of Editum)

Table 4.2.   Present-day social class groups in the Western world

Status	Profession
Upper class	Executives, directors, owners, people with inherited wealth
Middle-Middle Class	Professional people: executive managers, employers, bank clerks, insurance workers, school teachers
Lower-Middle Class	Semi-professional people or non-manual workers: lower managers, typists, commercial travelers, office workers
Upper-Working Class	Foremen, skilled manual workers, clerks
Middle-Working Class	(Semi-skilled) manual workers
Lower-Working Class	Laborers, unskilled laborers, seasonal workers

2.6   Social and historical validity: historical and socio-cultural background

Given that "we usually know very little about the social position of the writers, and not much more about the social structure of the community" (Labov 1994: 11), the task of "reconstructing the social information needed to interpret patterns of variation in written texts is not always straightforward" (Milroy and Gordon 2003: 177). If we compare Labov (1966) or Trudgill's (1974) social class groups (see Table 4.2) with those of the past (see Tables 4.3–4.4), such as those characterizing Tudor (1485–1603) and Stuart (1603–1714) England (see Raumolin-Brunberg 1996), the social orders are quite different, which inevitably affects the configuration of independent socio-demographic variables (see also Conde-Silvestre and Hernández-Campoy 2004).

2.7   Standard ideology

Both non-linguists' and linguists' views regarding language systems and their evolution may be influenced by 'the standard ideology' – that is, the notion that certain languages exist in standardized form (J. Milroy 1999, 2001). This notion and surrounding beliefs about the superiority, correctness, clarity, etc. of 'standard' languages have, as Britain (2005) points out, become so entrenched in the way we think that they have become conventionalized and taken for granted. In other words, they have become language ideologies. Linguistic studies of the development of nonstandard dialects are not immune from these ideologies and indeed have been made difficult because histories of languages, until recently, were focused on the history of the standard variety. Non-standard dialects may (unconsciously) be seen as implicitly 'derived from' and even 'perversions of' standard dialects (Britain 2005), despite linguists' overt protestations that all dialects are equally valid.

Table 4.3. Rank and status in Tudor (1485–1603) and Stuart (1603–1714) England (from Raumolin-Brunberg 1996: 26; reproduced by permission of Editions Rodopi B.V.)

Estate		Grade	Title
GENTRY	Nobility	Royalty	
		Duke	Lord, Lady
		Archbishop	
		Marquess	
		Earl	
		Viscount	
		Baron	
		Bishop	
	Gentry proper	Baronet (1611–)	Sir, Dame
		Knight	
		Esquire	Mr, Mrs
		Gentleman	
	Professions	Army Officer (Captain, etc.), Government Official (Secretary of State, etc.), Lawyer, Medical Doctor (Doctor), Merchant, Clergyman, Teacher, etc.	
NON-GENTRY		Yeoman	Goodman, Goodwife
		Merchant	
		Husbandman	
		Craftsman	(Name of Craft: Carpenter, etc.)
		Tradesman	
		Artificer	
			none
		Labourer	(Labourer)
		Cottager	
		Pauper	(none)

Table 4.4.   Social rank and the diffusion of incipient standard spellings in fifteenth-century England (Conde-Silvestre and Hernández-Campoy 2005: 116; reproduced by permission of Editum)

Social Position	Informant
Upper Gentry	Sir William Stonor
	Sir John Paston II
	Sir John Paston III
Lower Gentry	Walter Elmes
	Richard Germyn
Professionals (legal)	Thomas Mull
	Richard Page
Urban Non-Gentry (merchants)	Thomas Betson
	George Cely
	Richard Cely II

In the case of the history of English, as claimed by Lass (1990: 245), "'historical anglistics' has only been interested in the line to the southern British standard. This reflects an old ethnocentrism: straight-line evolution to the southern received standard (which is 'English') and side-paths of antiquarian or specialist interest (leading to the 'dialects')." In reality, as J. Milroy (1999) points out, since approximately the 16th century, the history of English has almost entirely been a history of Standard English. Amongst the number of the 'taken-for-granted characteristics' of histories of English, he includes (J. Milroy 2001: 549; see also Chapter 31 in this *Handbook*):

> English began in the fifth century AD when Germanic tribes settled in Britain
> English has had an unbroken and continuous history since that time and is the same language then as it is now
> English is not a mixed language

One of the consequences of these distorted assumptions has been, on occasion, considerable analytical inaccuracy, since, for example, historical linguists have made claims about dialect developments which rely on these standard histories, rather than examining the histories of the dialects themselves. For example, we have the old-fashioned suggestion by many linguists (especially North American and Irish linguists) that non-rhotic English accents have an /r/-deletion rule rather than an /r/-insertion rule in certain prevocalic contexts. However, given that intrusive /r/ is often inserted in intervocalic contexts in non-rhotic dialects (e.g. *the idear of it* 'the idea of it') and that non-rhoticity is often transferred to second languages, the /r/-deletion analysis is obviously incorrect from a syn-chronic point of view, even though historically non-rhoticity clearly derived from /r/ production. The assumption seems to be that since older forms of English and current Standard American English have non-prevocalic /r/, other dialects derive from this by 'deletion,' an assumption at least partially grounded in 'the standard ideology'.

In Spanish, writers on Andalusian phonology have traditionally focused on 'deletion' of word-final consonants (except /m, n/) and postulated a five-vowel system plus allophony in their dialectological descriptions. Their assumption seems to be that since Standard Spanish has five vowels, southern varieties must also have a five-vowel system. Nevertheless, Hernández-Campoy and Trudgill (2002) show that though consonant deletion is of course the correct diachronic analysis, synchronically speaking, some southern varieties such as Murcian Spanish and Andalusian Spanish do not delete syllable-final consonants but instead do not have them in underlying representation. The diachronic loss of syllable-final consonants had dramatic consequences for the Murcian vowel system, leading to a current system consisting of eight vowels – not five vowels and related allophones. Historical word-final /eC, oC, aC/ became /ɛ, ɔ, æ/, respectively, and the same vowels then began to occur in certain cases word-internally. Hence, an eight-vowel system has developed in conjunction with the loss of syllable-final consonants. The current eight-vowel system of Murcian Spanish is shown in Figure 4.2.

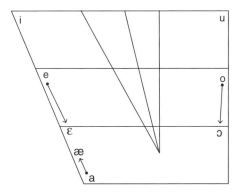

Figure 4.2.   Vowel System of Murcian Spanish

3. Conclusion

Historical sociolinguistics has very often been regarded as limited in its lack of representativeness and empirical validity. In this chapter, we have reviewed some of the main methodological problems encountered when trying to practice historical sociolinguistic research: i) representativeness, ii) empirical validity, iii) invariation, iv) authenticity, v) authorship, vi) social and historical validity, and vii) standard ideology. But, although nowadays the study of language change is practically inconceivable without concurrent consideration of sociolinguistic variation, theoretical and procedural limitations, controversies, and contradictions also exist even within the apparently rigorous scientific field of variationist sociolinguistics, as evidenced, for example, by the following factors:

(a) the unevenness with which the generalizability principle is applied or adhered to (see Bailey and Tillery 2004);
(b) questions surrounding age, time, and language change, including the limitations of apparent time studies of change and the difficulties of conducting studies in real time (see Trudgill 1988; Eckert 1997; Bailey 2002);
(c) ethical issues in sociolinguistic fieldwork (see Labov 1982b; Labov 1984; L. Milroy 1987; Larmouth, Murray, and Murray 1992; Cameron, Frazer, Harvey, *et al.* 1992, 1997; Shuy 1993; Murray and Murray 1996; Josselson 1996; Paulston and Tucker 1997; Wolfram and Fasold 1997; Johnstone 2000; Feagin 2002; Milroy and Gordon 2003);
(d) stylistic variation (see Labov 1972, 2001; Bell 1984, 2001; Coupland 2001a, 2001b, 2007; Johnstone 1996; Eckert 2000; Eckert and Rickford 2001; Rickford and McNair-Knox 1994; Schilling-Estes 2002, 2004; Cutillas-Espinosa and Hernández-Campoy 2006, 2007; Cutillas-Espinosa, Hernández-Campoy, and Schilling-Estes 2010; Hernández-Campoy and Cutillas-Espinosa 2010);
(e) differences in data-gathering procedures and subsequent results, including differences in sampling procedures, interviewer characteristics, and elicitation strategies (such as formal elicitation frames and loosely structured interviews) (see Bailey, Wikle, and Tillery 1997; Montgomery 1998; Bailey and Tillery 1999; Cukor-Avila and Bailey 2001; Bailey 2002; Chambers 2002; Bailey and Tillery 2004); and
(f) issues involved in data processing and analysis, including how spoken data are transformed when transcribed into written form (see Labov 1982a; Hildyard and Olson 1982; or Schneider 2002).

Again, as far as historical sociolinguistics is concerned, we cannot ask of this newer field what we cannot even ask of the more established field of variationist sociolinguistics. Just because there are methodological problems, we should not consider it an empirically invalid and inaccurate field of research. It is crucial in those areas of study for which oral records are not available, especially when studying long-term developments in language variation and change. Further, historical sociolinguistics continues to advance, for example through developments in information technology and sociohistorical study. Despite the limitations mentioned earlier, written records such as *The Helsinski Corpus of English Texts* (HC) provide us with cross-stylistic quantitative correlations (Nevalainen 1995; Nevalainen and Raumolin-Brunberg 1989), while other text collections such as the *Corpus of Early English Correspondence* (CEEC) provide us with correlations of sociohistorical class stratification with linguistic variation (Nevalainen and

Raumolin-Brunberg 1996, 1998, 2003). The diversity of types of interaction and styles reflected in collections of private correspondence, for example the Paston, Cely, and Stonor Letters in late medieval England, is wider than those afforded by official and literary documents and provide us with data for which demographic information about authors can often be traced, hence supplying the data necessary for the proper extension of sociolinguistic methods to historical language states. Additionally, as some scholars show (see Eliason 1956; J. Milroy 1992; Montgomery 1999; Miethaner 2000), written texts can in some ways reflect, though partially, pronunciation characteristics. Even in fairly inconsistent orthographic systems, such as that of English, there are well-established sets of grapheme-phoneme correspondences in writing.

In conclusion, and extending Robert Henry Robins' (1964/1980: 319) quote regarding linguistic studies of five decades ago to today's historical sociolinguistics:

> During these men's lifetimes and through their work we have witnessed striking and encouraging growth, both in the subject itself and in the scholarly interest taken in it. Much remains to be accomplished; new lines of thought open up, and new methods must be devised to follow them; and general linguistic theory must be always keeping pace with methodological progress. The languages of mankind in all their fascinating detail and with all their immense power among the human faculties still present a potentially limitless field for disciplined investigation and systematic study. It is altogether right that they should be the object of scholarly enthusiasm, controlled imagination, and great reverence.

Historical sociolinguistics began in the early 1980s as a hybrid subfield subsisting on historical linguistics and sociolinguistics. Its work is being increasingly done within the field of linguistics and has a growing importance in that field. Now, maturity has been reached thanks to the efforts of a number of historical sociolinguists who, over the past three decades, have devoted themselves to elucidating the theoretical limits of the discipline, as well as to applying the tenets and findings of contemporary sociolinguistic research to the interpretation of linguistic material from the past.

REFERENCES

Arnaud, R. (1980) Quelques observations quantitatives 'en temps réel' sur un changement: L'accroissement d'emploi de la forme progressive dans la première moitié du XIX siècle. Paper presented at the *Xxe Congrès de la Société des Anglicistes de l'Enseignement Supérieur*, Poitiers.

Ayres-Bennett, W. (2001) Socio-historical linguistics and the history of French.

Journal of French Language Studies 11: 159–77.

Bailey, G. (2002) Real and Apparent Time. In J.K. Chambers, P. Trudgill, and N. Schilling-Estes (eds.), pp. 312–32.

Bailey, G. and Tillery, J. (1999) The Rutledge Effect: the impact of interviewers on survey results in linguistics. *American Speech* 74: 389–402.

Bailey, G. and Tillery, J. (2004) Some sources of divergent data. In C. Fought (ed.), pp. 11–30.

Bailey, G., Wikle, T., and Tillery, J. (1997) The effects of methods on results in dialectology. *English World-Wide* 18: 35–63.

Bauer, L. (2002) Inferring variation and change from public corpora. In J.K. Chambers, P. Trudgill, and N. Schilling-Estes (eds.), pp. 97–114.

Bayley, R. (2002) The quantitative paradigm. In J.K. Chambers, P. Trudgill, and N. Schilling-Estes (eds.), pp. 117–41.

Bell, A. (1984) Language style as audience design. *Language in Society* 13: 145–204.

Bell, A. (2001) Back in style: Reworking audience design. In P. Eckert and J.R. Rickford (eds.), pp. 139–69.

Bergs, A. (2005) *Social Networks and Historical Sociolinguistics: Studies in Morphosyntactic Variation in the Paston Letters (1421–1503)*, Mouton de Gruyter, Berlin.

Britain, D. (2005) Standard ideologies in the history of English. Paper given at the *7th Curso de La Variación Sociolingüística: Enfoque Contrastivo*, University of Murcia, November 2005.

Cameron, D., Frazer, E., Harvey, P. *et al.* (1992) *Researching Language: Issues of Power and Method*, Routledge, London.

Cameron, D., Frazer, E., Harvey, P. *et al.* (1997) Ethics, advocacy and empowerment in research language. In N. Coupland and A. Jaworski (eds.), pp. 145–62.

CEEC = *Corpus of Early English Correspondence* (1998) Compiled by T. Nevalainen, H. Raumolin-Brunberg, J. Keränen, M. Nevala, A. Nurmi, and M. Palander-Collin Department of English, University of Helsinki. http://www.helsinki.fi/varieng/CoRD/corpora/CEEC/index.html [accessed October 13, 2011]

Chambers, J.K. (2002) Patterns of variation including change. In J.K. Chambers, P. Trudgill, and N. Schilling-Estes (eds.), pp. 349–72.

Chambers, J.K., Trudgill, P., and Schilling-Estes, N. (eds.) (2002) *The Handbook of Language Variation and Change*, Blackwell, Oxford.

Conde-Silvestre, J.C. (2007) *Sociolingüística histórica*, Gredos, Madrid.

Conde-Silvestre, J.C. and Hernández-Campoy, J.M. (1998) *An Introduction to the History of the English Language II: Middle and Modern English*, Universidad de Murcia and Diego Marín, Murcia.

Conde-Silvestre, J.C. and Hernández-Campoy, J.M. (2004) A sociolinguistic approach to the diffusion of Chancery written practices in late fifteenth-century private correspondence. *Neuphilologische Mitteilungen* 105: 133–52.

Conde-Silvestre, J.C. and Hernández-Campoy, J.M. (2005) Sociolinguistic and geolinguistic approaches to the historical diffusion of linguistic innovations: incipient standardisation in Late Middle English. *International Journal of English Studies* 5.1: 101–34.

Coulmas, F. (ed.) (1997) *The Handbook of Sociolinguistics*, Blackwell, Oxford.

Coupland, N. (2001a) Dialect stylization in radio talk. *Language in Society* 30 (3): 345–75.

Coupland, N. (2001b) Language, situation, and the relational self: theorizing dialect-style in sociolinguistics. In P. Eckert and J.R. Rickford (eds.), pp. 185–210.

Coupland, N. (2007) *Style: Language Variation, and Identity*, Cambridge University Press, Cambridge.

Coupland, N. and Jaworski, A. (eds.) (1997) *Sociolinguistics: A Reader and Coursebook*, Macmillan Press, London.

Cukor-Avila, P. and Bailey, G. (2001) The effects of the race of the interviewer on sociolinguistic fieldwork. *Journal of Sociolinguistics* 5: 254–70.

Cutillas-Espinosa, J.A. and Hernández-Campoy, J.M. (2006) Non-responsive performance in radio broadcasting: a case study. *Language Variation and Change* 18 (3): 317–30.

Cutillas-Espinosa, J.A. and Hernández-Campoy, J.M. (2007) Script design in the media: radio talk norms behind a professional voice. *Language and Communication* 27 (2): 127–52.

Cutillas-Espinosa, J.A., Hernández-Campoy, J.M., and Schilling-Estes, N. (2010) Hyper-vernacularisation in a speaker design context: A case study. *Folia Linguistica* 44: 1–22.

Davis, N.O. (ed.) (1971) *Paston Letters and Papers of the Fifteenth Century* (2 vols.), Clarendon, Oxford.

Dees, A. (1971) *Etude sur l'Evolution des Démonstratifs en Ancien et en Moyen Français*, Wolters-Noordhoff, Groningen.

Eckert, P. (1997) Age as a sociolinguistic variable. In F. Coulmas (ed.), pp. 151–67.

Eckert, P. (2000) *Linguistic Variation as Social Practice*, Blackwell, Oxford.

Eckert, P. and Rickford, J.R. (eds.) (2001) *Style and Sociolinguistic Variation*, Cambridge University Press, Cambridge.

Eliason, N.E (1956) *Tarheel talk: An historical study of the English language in North Carolina to 1860*, University of North Carolina Press, Chapel Hill.

Feagin, C. (2002) Entering the community: fieldwork. In J.K. Chambers, P. Trudgill, and N. Schilling-Estes (eds.), pp. 20–39.

Fought, C. (ed.) (2004) *Sociolinguistic Variation: Critical Reflections*, Oxford University Press, Oxford.

HC = *The Helsinki Corpus of English Texts* (1991) Compiled by M. Rissanen (Project leader), M. Kytö (Project secretary); L. Kahlas-Tarkka, M. Kilpiö (Old English); S. Nevanlinna, I. Taavitsainen (Middle English); T. Nevalainen, H. Raumolin-Brunberg (Early Modern English). Department of English, University of Helsinki. http://www.helsinki.fi/varieng/CoRD/corpora/HelsinkiCorpus [accessed October 13, 2011].

Hernández-Campoy, J.M. and Conde-Silvestre, J.C. (1999) The social diffusion of linguistic innovations in 15th century England: Chancery spellings in private correspondence. *Cuadernos de Filología Inglesa* 8: 251–74.

Hernández-Campoy, J.M. and Cutillas-Espinosa, J.A. (2010) Speaker design practices in political discourse: a case study. *Language and Communication* 30: 297–309.

Hernández-Campoy, J.M. and Trudgill, P. (2002) Functional compensation and Southern Peninsular Spanish /s/ loss. *Folia Linguistica Historica* XXIII: 31–57.

Hildyard, A. and Olson, D.R. (1982) On the comprehension of oral vs. written discourse. In D. Tannen (ed.), *Spoken and Written Language: Exploring Orality and Literacy*, Ablex, Norwood, NJ, pp. 19–33.

Johnstone, B. (1996) *The Linguistic Individual: Self-Expression in Language and Linguistics*, Oxford University Press, Oxford.

Johnstone, B. (2000) *Qualitative Methods in Sociolinguistics*, Oxford University Press, Oxford.

Josselson, R. (ed.) (1996) *Ethics and Process in the Narrative Study of Lives*, Sage, Thousand Oaks, CA.

Kuhn, T.S. (1962) *The Structure of Scientific Revolutions*, University of Chicago Press, Chicago.

Labov, W. (1966) *The Social Stratification of English in New York City*, Center for Applied Linguistics, Washington, DC.

Labov, W. (1972) Some principles of linguistic methodology. *Language in Society* 1: 97–120.

Labov, W. (1982a) Building on empirical foundations. In W.P. Lehmann and Y. Malkiel (eds.), *Directions for Historical Linguistics*, University of Texas Press, Austin, pp. 79–92.

Labov, W. (1982b) Objectivity and commitment in linguistic science: The case of the Black English trial in Ann Arbor. *Language in Society* 11 (2): 165–201.

Labov, W. (1984) Field methods of the project on linguistic change and variation. In J. Baugh and J. Sherzer (eds.), *Language in Use: Readings in Sociolinguistics*, Prentice Hall, Englewoods Cliffs, NJ, pp. 28–66.

Labov, W. (1994) *Principles of Linguistic Change, Volume I: Internal Factors*, Blackwell, Oxford.

Labov, W. (2001) The anatomy of style-shifting. In P. Eckert and J.R. Rickford (eds.), pp. 85–108.

Larmouth, D.W., Murray, T., and Ross Murray, C. (eds.) (1992) *Legal and Ethical Issues in Surreptitious Recording*, University of Alabama Press, Tuscaloosa.

Lass, R. (1984) *Phonology. An Introduction to Basic Concepts*, Cambridge University Press, Cambridge.

Lass, R. (1990) Where do extra-territorial Englishes come from? Dialect input and recodification in transported Englishes. In S. Adamson, V. Law, N. Vincent, and S. Wright (eds.), *Papers from the 5th International Conference on English Historical Linguistics*, John Benjamins, Amsterdam, pp. 245–80.

Miethaner, U. (2000) Orthographic transcriptions of nonstandard varieties: the case of earlier African American English. *Journal of Sociolinguistics* 4: 534–60.

Milroy, J. (1992) *Linguistic Variation and Change: On the Historical Sociolinguistics of English*, Blackwell, Oxford.

Milroy, J. (1999) The consequences of standardisation in descriptive linguistics. In T. Bex and R.J. Watts (eds.), *Standard English: The Widening Debate*, Routledge, London, pp. 16–39.

Milroy, J. (2001) Language ideologies and the consequences of standardisation. *Journal of Sociolinguistics* 5: 530–55.

Milroy, L. (1987) *Observing and Analysing Natural Language*, Blackwell, Oxford.

Milroy, L. and Gordon, M. (2003) *Sociolinguistics: Method and Interpretation*, Blackwell, Oxford.

Montgomery, M. (1998) Multiple modals in LAGS and LAMSAS. In M. Montgomery and T. Nunnally (eds.), *From the Gulf States and Beyond: The Legacy of Lee Pederson and LAGS*, University of Alabama Press, Tuscaloosa, pp. 90–122.

Montgomery, M. (1999) Eighteenth-century Sierra Leone English: another exported variety of African American English. *English World-Wide* 20: 1–34.

Murray, T.E. and Ross Murray, C. (1996) *Under Cover of Law: More on the Legality of Surreptitious Recording*, University of Alabama Press, Tuscaloosa.

Nevalainen, T. (1995) Ongoing work on *The Helsinki Corpus of Early English Correspondence*. Paper presented at the 16th ICAME Conference, Toronto, May 23–28.

Nevalainen, T. (1999) Making the best use of 'bad' data: evidence for sociolinguistic variation in Early Modern English. *Neuphilologische Mitteilungen* 104: 499–533.

Nevalainen, T. and Raumolin-Brunberg, H. (1989) A corpus of Early Modern Standard English in a socio-historical perspective. *Neuphilologische Mitteilungen* 90(1): 67–110.

Nevalainen, T. and Raumolin-Brunberg, H. (eds.) 1996. *Sociolinguistics and Language History: Studies Based on the Corpus of Early English Correspondence*, Rodopi, Amsterdam.

Nevalainen, T. and Raumolin-Brunberg, H. (1998) Reconstructing the social dimension of diachronic language change. In R.M. Hogg and L. van Berger (eds.), *Historical Linguistics 1995. Vol II: Germanic Linguistics*, John Benjamins, Amsterdam, pp. 189–209.

Nevalainen, T. and Raumolin-Brunberg, H. (2003) *Historical Sociolinguistics: Language Change in Tudor and Stuart England*, Longman Pearson Education, London.

Paulston, C.B. and Tucker, G.R. (eds.) (1997) *The Early Days of Sociolinguistics: Memories and Reflections*, Summer Institute of Linguistics, Dallas, TX.

Raumolin-Brunberg, H. (1996) Historical sociolinguistics. In T. Nevalainen and H. Raumolin-Brunberg (eds.), pp. 11–37.

Rickford, J.R. and McNair-Knox, F. (1994) Addressee- and topic-influenced style shift: A quantitative sociolinguistic study. In D. Biber and E. Finegan (eds.), *Sociolinguistic Perspectives on Register*, Oxford University Press, Oxford, pp. 235–76.

Roberts, C. and Street, B. (1997) Spoken and written language. In F. Coulmas (ed.), pp. 168–186.

Robins, R.H. (1964/1980) *General Linguistics. An Introductory Survey* (3rd edn), Longman, London.

Romaine, S. (1982) *Socio-Historical Linguistics: Its Status and Methodology*, Cambridge University Press, Cambridge.

Romaine, S. (1988) Historical sociolinguistics: problems and methodology. In U. Ammon, N. Dittmar, and K.J. Mattheier (eds.), *Sociolinguistics: An International Handbook of the Science of Language and Society* (Vol. 2), Walter de Gruyter, Berlin, pp. 1452–1469.

Sankoff, G. (1980) A quantitative paradigm for the study of communicative competence. In G. Sankoff (ed.), *The Social Life of Language*, University of Pennsylvania Press, Philadelphia, pp. 47–79.

Schilling-Estes, N. (1998) Investigating 'self-conscious' speech: the performance register in Ocracoke English. *Language in Society* 27: 53–83.

Schilling-Estes, N. (2002) Investigating stylistic variation. In J.K. Chambers, P. Trudgill, and N. Schilling-Estes (eds.), pp. 375–401.

Schilling-Estes, N. (2004) Constructing ethnicity in interaction. *Journal of Sociolinguistics* 8 (2): 163–195.

Schneider, E. (2002) Investigating variation and change in written documents. In J.K. Chambers, P. Trudgill, and N. Schilling-Estes (eds.), pp. 67–96.

Shuy, R. (1993) Risk, deception, confidentiality, and informed consent. *American Speech* 68: 103–106.

Stockwell, R.P. and Barritt, C.W. (1951) *Some Old English graphemic-phonemic correspondences*, Battenburg, Norman.

Stockwell, R.P. and Barritt, C.W. (1961) Scribal practice: some assumptions. *Language* 37: 75–82.

Toon, T.E. (1976) The variationist analysis of Early Old English manuscript data. In

W.M. Christie Jr. (ed.), *Proceedings of the Second International Conference on Historical Linguistics*, North Holland, Amsterdam, pp. 71–81.

Toon, T.E. (1983) *The Politics of Early Old English Sound Change*, Academic Press, New York.

Trudgill, P. (1974) *The Social Differentiation of English in Norwich*, Cambridge University Press, Cambridge.

Trudgill, P. (1988) Norwich revisited: recent changes in an English urban dialect. *English World-Wide* 9: 33–49.

Trudgill, P. (2003) *Glossary of Sociolinguistics*, Edinburgh University Press, Edinburgh.

Williams, G. (1992) *Sociolinguistics: A Sociological Critique*, Routledge, London.

Wolfram, W. (2004) The sociolinguistic construction of remnant dialects. In C. Fought (ed.), pp. 84–106.

Wolfram, W. and R.W. Fasold (1997) Field methods in the study of social dialects. In N. Coupland and A. Jaworski (eds.), pp. 89–115.

5 The Uniformitarian Principle and the Risk of Anachronisms in Language and Social History

ALEXANDER BERGS

1. Introduction

The Uniformitarian Principle (UP), sometimes also referred to as the Principle of Uniformity, very simply claims that the processes which we observe in the present can help us to gain knowledge about processes in the past. The reasoning behind this is that we must assume that whatever happens today must also have been possible in the past; whatever is impossible today must have been impossible in the past. If we observe today that water (on earth…) boils at around 100 degrees Celsius, we can assume that it also did so at any given point in the past. This means that when we analyze a historical phenomenon we should first look at known causes in order to explain it, before we turn to unknown causes. This principle, which originated in the natural sciences, has also been applied in the humanities (and in linguistics) when looking at historical developments. In the humanities, however, the Uniformitarian Principle must be taken with a pinch of salt since there is no clear and simple correlate to the laws of nature. The aim of this chapter is to evaluate critically the usefulness of the Uniformitarian Principle in historical linguistics in general, and in historical sociolinguistics in particular. To this end, I will first discuss the history of this principle in linguistics and its traditional uses in historical linguistics. I will then proceed with a discussion of its usefulness in sociohistorical linguistics and the risks associated with it, in

The Handbook of Historical Sociolinguistics, First Edition. Edited by Juan Manuel Hernández-Campoy and Juan Camilo Conde-Silvestre.
© 2014 John Wiley & Sons, Ltd. Published 2014 by John Wiley & Sons, Ltd.

particular, the danger of anachronism. Three case studies on the central and almost ubiquitous concepts of social class, gender, and social networks conclude this chapter.

2. The Uniformitarian Principle in Historical Linguistics

As has been mentioned in the introduction, the UP did not originate in linguistics, but in the natural sciences: in geology, to be precise. One of the earliest studies comes from James Hutton, a Scottish geologist (1726–97), but the principle itself was mainly made famous by Sir Charles Lyell (1797–1875) with his influential and very popular *Principles of Geology* (1830–33). Christy (1983: 1–11) offers a full account of the early developments. One should not forget, however, that some traces of the idea can also be found outside geology, as in David Hume's *A Treatise of Human Nature* (1739). In his *Treatise* he is rather critical of the idea that the laws of nature do not change and claims that

> [i]f reason determin'd us, it wou'd proceed upon that principle, *that instances, of which we have had no experience, must resemble those, of which we have had experience, and that the course of nature continues always uniformly the same.* [But o]ur foregoing method of reasoning will easily convince us, that there can be no *demonstrative* arguments to prove, *that those instances, of which we have had no experience, resemble those, of which we have had experience.* We can at least conceive a change in the course of nature; which sufficiently proves, that such a change is not absolutely impossible.
>
> (Hume 1739/2007: 76, *Treatise*, I, iii, 6)

Apparently, for Hume it was at least *possible* that nature's laws could change – however unlikely that may be. This appears to be somewhat plausible. At the same time, such an 'anything goes' approach is not really useful either in historical studies or in making predictions about future events and states. Thus, at least for practical purposes, we should assume that there are no miracles in nature – and there never have been.

Nineteenth century linguists were probably more impressed by geologists than by David Hume, and picked up the UP quite willingly (see Naumann *et al.* 1992; Nerlich 1990; Christy 1983). Whitney was one of the most outspoken proponents of the principle, and suggested in 1867:

> The nature and uses of speech [...] cannot but have been essentially the same during all periods of history [...] there is no way in which its unknown past can be investigated, except by the careful study of its living present and recorded past, and the extension and application to remote conditions of laws and principles deduced by that study. (Whitney 1867: 24)

Labov also discussed this principle in 1972 and came more or less to the same conclusion: that "the forces operating to produce linguistic change today are of the same kind and order of magnitude as those which operated five or ten thousand years ago" (Labov 1972: 275). Roger Lass offers some of the most recent and extensive theoretical discussions of the UP in his work (1980, 1997). On the basis of a thorough discussion of the natural sciences background, he summarizes two uniformity principles for linguistics: the *General Uniformity Principle* and the *Uniform Probabilities Principle*. These state that (Lass 1997: 28):

> *General Uniformity Principle*
> No linguistic state of affairs (structure, inventory, process, etc.) can have been the case only in the past.
> *Uniform Probabilities Principle*
> The (global, cross-linguistic) likelihood of any linguistic state of affairs (structure, inventory, process, etc.) has always been roughly the same as it is now.

The first principle obviously covers cases that were summarized before as 'whatever is impossible today must have been impossible in the past,' or, alternatively, 'whatever was there in the past must at least be theoretically possible today.' If all languages today have consonants and vowels, all historical languages must also have consonants and vowels. If there is no attested language that lacks negation, we must assume that all languages at all times had ways of negation. However, since our present-day knowledge may be imperfect – we haven't really seen all languages past and present – we might soften this claim a little and say that whoever claims that there was such a language must face the question of why this very special situation should have been possible then and only then. And this is why the second uniformity principle, the *principle of uniform probabilities*, is so valuable. It does not *per se* and absolutely rule out any findings, but it puts a number on them. It is just as unlikely that there would have been a language with no vowels or no negation in 1066 as it is now – almost zero. But just as we discover new and exciting facts about present-day languages we can also discover them about past language stages, so we end up with what we said in our introduction: we should first check all known factors and causes, and only after that, once we have failed, turn for our explanations to unknown factors as causes.

3. Anachronism

What is anachronism? Anachronism in the literal sense translates as 'against time' and usually means an error in chronology, typically placing some state or event earlier in history than it can actually have occurred. If you are shooting a movie about the Roman Empire you certainly do not want any of the actors to wear wrist watches on the set – simply because these did not exist. And the Romans should not go to war with handguns – gunpowder did not reach mainland Europe or even the Islamic world before about 1200. Similarly, potatoes probably did not figure in the diet of people in medieval Europe, because they come from south America and can only have been imported from there after 1492. If you want to claim that some John Doe in Worcestershire in 1275 had jacket potatoes for lunch, you may of course do that, but you need to show convincingly how those potatoes came to England before 1492.

But the danger of anachronism applies not only to historical 'facts' such as potatoes and watches. Ideas and concepts also can be very tricky. When we look at how pre-modern parents actually treated their children and looked upon their development, we must not forget that pre-modern society did not view children in the same way as we do. In the Middle Ages, children before the age of seven were frequently seen as miniature adults who turned into adult humans upon reaching the age of seven (Aries 1962); our 'modern' concept of childhood as such simply did not exist. Therefore, children did not possess the same rights as other human beings. The alternative view was to treat children as adults, and a society might take one or the other of these perspectives. The way people treated their children in pre-modern societies must be seen and evaluated in the context of that society's own moral value system and ideologies (which is, of course, not to say that this system or ideology was or is in any way acceptable). But looking at people's actions from a modern point of view does not do justice to those people and also blurs our view and makes analysis more difficult (since it might, for example, lead us to interpret many actions as wrong, irrational, or immoral). This can also be illustrated by looking at the history of animal rights. Historically, animals could be brought before a court and sentenced for the same offences as humans. Similarly, at certain times in history inanimate or dead things could be legally prosecuted – something we today find unusual or even upsetting. Despite Jardin's convincing arguments (2000) that anachronisms need not always be a bad thing, this still goes to show that different times and cultures may have different perspectives on one and the same thing, and that universally describing – and judging – from one perspective or another may run the danger of anachronism (historically) or perhaps chauvinism (synchronically).

In (historical) linguistics, the concept of anachronism has not been extensively discussed – which is surprising, given that it is a key issue in history as a scientific discipline. Still, one particularly obvious anachronism may be committed in historical linguistics and is occasionally an issue in discussions: that is, positing or assuming language structures which are neither attested nor plausible at the relevant point in time (like the watch in the movie on the Roman empire). So, for example, Old English simply did not have *do*-periphrasis or a fully-fledged system of modal verbs, nor did it have voiced and/or voiceless labio-dental fricative phonemes. Any analysis that assumes the existence of these would first have to justify this assumption in some detail. Conversely, someone who wanted to claim that something that is present in all languages today (such as negation) did not exist in Old English would have to give a detailed account for that. In a word, very unlikely assumptions do not come for free.

In historical *socio*linguistics, however, the whole issue is much more complicated since we are dealing not only with linguistic issues, but also with questions of history and sociology (see Bergs 2005: 8–21). We need to distinguish here between 'factual' anachronisms on the one hand (the 'no watches in ancient Rome' type) and 'constructional' or, perhaps better, 'ideational' anachronisms (the 'no modern childhood in pre-modern times' type). Many of the concepts and models that we use in history and sociology are only constructed during research and may not have any real-life correlates. So, for example, there is no measurable, testable thing called 'social class' apart from the one that we construct and define. The presence or absence of something like 'social class' thus depends both on the definition and the empirical data that we use to evaluate a given state of affairs in relation to our definition. One of the biggest problems that social historians face here is reliable data. With the advent of (modern) anthropology, ethnography, and sociology – among others, in Millar (1771/1990) and, of course, Durkheim (1893, 1895) – we have a metalevel of analysis, and thus also more reliable and comparable descriptions of social constructs such as class. Before that we need other sources to turn to. These include primary historical data, such as historical documents (charters and laws, for example) and archeological findings (tools, clothing, other artifacts, etc.), and secondary data, such as literary products that describe social life (such as Chaucer's *Canterbury Tales*, or Langland's *Piers Plowman*) and other contemporary descriptions of society and societal matters – for instance, William Harrison's *Description of Elizabethan England* (1577), Samuel Pepys's *Diary* (1660–69), or the thirteenth-century *Speculum Doctrinale* by Vincent of Beauvais (c. 1190–1264?). The problem with these sources is, of course, that they need to be interpreted very carefully. So, for example, we need to take care not to confuse historical terms (and their corresponding concepts) with contemporary ones. In the Old English period, before 1100, the term *queen* could refer to women in general. Today, this use is rather rare. But the term can be used today derogatorily for male homosexuals – an option that probably did not exist in Old English. According to the *Oxford English Dictionary* (OED), we find that the word *knight* started its life in Old English meaning 'boy, lad.' It was then used as a term for military servants, and, after the feudal system was fully developed, as an honorable military rank to which only people of noble birth who had undergone an apprenticeship as a squire or page could be raised by the king or other "qualified persons" (OED). Today, the rank "is conferred by the sovereign in recognition of personal merit, or as a reward for services rendered to the crown or country" (OED, s.v. *knight*). This means that when we come across terms such as *queen* or *knight* in historical texts we must be aware of their historical meaning and we must not confuse this with what they mean today. Similarly, when we use these terms today to describe historical entities, we need to make sure how we want these terms to be understood.

In the following sections, I will present three case studies which may illustrate some of the limits and pitfalls of the Uniformitarian Principle in Historical Sociolinguistics.

3.1 Case study 1: social class

Social class has been one of the most discussed factors in modern sociolinguistics (see Ash 2002; Guy 1988; but also Chambers 1995: 34–101; Milroy and Gordon 2003: 88–115). It is used in very influential studies such as Labov (1972, 2001), Trudgill (1974), and Cheshire (1982), who found that a number of salient linguistic variables of English, such as postvocalic (r), (ing), and multiple negation correlate with social class in many varieties. However, social class, despite its conceptual productivity, has never been an easy construct. There is a vast body of studies in sociology, anthropology, political economy, and social history, among others, that discuss social class as a theoretical construct (for an overview, see Georg 2004; Ash 2002; Chambers 1995: 34–101; Marshall, Rose, Newby, and Vogler 1989). Even in contemporary studies, an endless list of complex factors have been suggested as determining an individual's class membership: income, education, parent's education, place of living, even seasonality in the incidence of birth and vacation patterns. While this is not the right place to develop this discussion in greater detail, I think one can still summarize the current situation by pointing out that despite all efforts there is no single, simple determining factor that helps us to utilize social class as a determinant in sociolinguistics. It is not very hard to imagine that the transfer of this complex synchronic concept to diachronic questions and problems is anything but straightforward. Just as there are probably some present-day societies which are not organized in social classes as we know them, there are also historical societies which were not organized along these lines (see Chapter 17 in this *Handbook*).

In the case of England, for example, historians suggest that the term 'social class' only becomes applicable from about the late fifteenth century onwards, perhaps even much later (see Wrightson 1991; Corfield 1991; Britnell 1993). Before that we need to turn away from social class as a 'modern' concept and instead look at how society was actually organized or at least viewed by contemporaries. Nevalainen (1996) and Nevalainen and Raumolin-Brunberg (2003) discuss several different options for Tudor and Stuart England (ca. 1491–1707) which are summarized in Table 5.1:

In her discussion of these three (four) models (Table 5.1), Nevalainen points out that they all have their advantages and disadvantages. Model 1 is obviously quite rough and general, but provides us with the opportunity to study the very important, but also very complex and diverse, group of merchants in greater detail without missing interesting generalizations. Model 2, on the other hand, is a little bit more detailed and distinguishes between 'upper' and 'lower' gentry and clergy – which is certainly justified when we look at the available socio-historical data. Nevalainen (1996: 59) argues that, on the basis of contemporary views, there could be even a third, middling group in the gentry section for esquires. Also, Model 2 introduces the new and interesting category of 'social climbers.' The third model is certainly the most detailed. Like Model 2, it differentiates

Table 5.1.   Models of social stratification in Tudor and Stuart England
(Nevalainen 1996: 58; reproduced by permission of Editions Rodopi B.V.)

Model 1	Model 2	Model 3	Model 4?
(Royalty)	(Royalty)	(Royalty)	
Nobility	Nobility	Nobility	'Better sort'
Gentry	Gentry	Gentry	
	-Upper	-Upper	
	-Lower	-Lower	
	Professions	Professions	
		→Gentry	
		→ Non-Gentry	
Clergy	Clergy	Clergy	'Middling sort'
	-Upper	→Nobility	
	-Lower	→Gentry	
		→Non-Gentry	
Merchants	Merchants	Merchants	
		→Gentry	
		→Non-Gentry	
	Social Climbers	Social Climbers	
Non-Gentry*	Non-Gentry*	Non-Gentry	'Poorest sort'

(*excluding the intermediate ranks of professionals, clergy, and merchants)

within the individual groups and it includes the new category of 'social climbers.' Dividing the professions, clergy and merchants into gentry and non-gentry reflects many of the social changes that we see during Tudor and Stuart England, particularly towards the end of the period when the gentry as a single distinguishable group is backgrounded. However, the complexity of the model also makes it somewhat more difficult to handle, and we need further and more fine-tuned diagnostics in order to determine the group to which somebody belongs. The fourth model arguably reflects a common contemporary, that is, Tudor and Stuart, perspective. Nevalainen (1996: 61) cites Wrightson (1991: 51) as the discoverer of the seventeenth-century writer George King, who had distinguished between no fewer than 26 different ranks in society, but also developed the three broad categories 'better sort,' 'middle sort,' and 'poorest sort.'

It should be pointed out that the issue of social class or social stratification in historical communities is not only a matter of developing categories and labels for the different groups. Different groupings often go together with different attitudes towards societies, or even concrete rules for their organization. Broadly speaking we can say that medieval society in Europe recognized three estates: nobility, clergy, and commoners. Within these groups, people were born into a certain sub-group and usually stayed there for the rest of their lives. For example, the son of a carpenter was usually bound to be a carpenter. The daughter of a spinner was usually bound to be a spinner. The modern concept of social (i.e. upward) mobility did not exist to the same extent as today which means that society as such was also much more stable than today. There were of course some 'social climbers' or 'social aspirers,' but these were much rarer than today and did not constitute a clearly defined sociologically identifiable group. The latter only began to form in Tudor and Stuart England with the rise of the middle class. For most of the Middle Ages, membership of a certain group was clearly marked, even through clothing. This becomes particularly apparent when these distinctions are lost from the fifteenth century onwards. Britnell explains:

> It was observed that, in spite of consumption laws, labourers and servants were dressing in more expensive cloth. One preacher of the early fifteenth century was dismayed that a ploughman who would once have been satisfied with a white kirtle and russet gown was now to be seen as proudly dressed as a squire. Peter Idley, writing about 1445–1450, grumbled that 'a man shall not now ken a knave from a knight.' (Britnell 1993: 169)

All these different models are warranted in the given period, and historical socio-linguists can now choose which of the four models is the most suitable for their particular research question, that is, which of the four is best borne out by the linguistic data that we have. Note that this is also a very fruitful and productive point of collaboration between historians, sociologists, and linguists. Social historians usually develop their models on the basis of the sources mentioned above. These models can then be used by linguists in order to search for possible correlations between linguistic data and social categories. The existence or non-existence of these correlations may in turn serve as helpful clues and additional data for social historians who can fine-tune or revise their models accordingly.

Nevalainen and Raumolin-Brunberg (2003: 140) present the following analysis of the development of the verbal suffixes -(e)s and -(e)th in Early Modern English. Note that -(e)th is the older form and is being replaced by innovative -(e)s. They use Model 2 presented above.

Stratification Model 2 with its fine distinction obviously proves to be very helpful. We can see that in the first period (1520–59), the innovative form -(e)s was used mostly by 'other non-gentry' (58%), but also, and this is interesting, by the nobility (18%) and to a lesser extent also by gentry (8%) and merchants (10%). In general, however, we can say that the middle groups appear to be more conservative than the fringes of the spectrum. In the second period (1640–81) these differences have almost disappeared. However, royalty has not only caught up, but is now the only group with 100% innovative -(e)s. Nobility, gentry, merchants, and other non-gentry have also passed the 90% mark. Again, the middling groups are the most conservative, even though they, too, are clearly above the 80% line. This means, in turn, that the royal group must have seen the steepest increase, while the group of other non-gentry had the slowest. We can only follow Nevalainen and Raumolin-Brunberg in their speculations on why this pattern emerges. It may have been the case that social aspirers (which included three elderly bishops) and clergy were affected by religious language and/or old age, while professionals and lawyers "may have been affected by the conservative language of legal documents" (2003: 140). Possibly *-(e)s* can even be analyzed as a social marker and more common in informal writing (though this hypothesis is very difficult, if not impossible, to test).

This example shows two important things. On the one hand, it provides clear evidence that social stratification *of some sort* was indeed an issue in medieval and Renaissance England. We might even be led to suggest that this was very likely to be true in the uniformitarian sense: probably all human societies exhibit social stratification of some sort. If we wanted to claim that a historical society did not exhibit any kind of social stratification we would have to justify this claim. However, human societies, then and now, are not necessarily all structured in the same way, and even analyses for a single point in time may differ considerably. The study by Nevalainen and Raumolin-Brunberg shows that Models 3 and 4 from Table 5.1 may not have led us to the same picture and the same conclusions, since they would have been too coarse-grained to help us to identify the leading groups in this case. So, in conclusion, we can say that we need to identify the relevant social categories which were important for each individual period and speech community. In a second step, we should also try and utilize these categories (by adjusting the scale on which we use them) so as to arrive at the best (most informative) correlations possible.

3.2   Case study 2: gender

The second case study deals with an equally important and productive category in current sociolinguistics: gender. Despite the fact that the concept of 'gender' is anything but simple and straightforward in modern sociology, cultural studies, and sociolinguistics (see Eckert 1989; Eckert and McConnell-Ginet 2003; and the papers in Holmes and Meyerhoff 2005), it is also the basis for a large number of very valuable and stimulating studies in correlational and qualitative sociolinguistics.

Labov (2001: 263–65) studies the gender differentiation of stable sociolinguistic variables in Philadelphia. He analyzes the following variables: the realization of the voiced interdental fricative as either fricative, affricate/absence, or stop (dh); the realization of the final nasal as either apical or velar (ing); and negative concord (neg). Labov conclusively shows that for (dh), men in general (except for the lower working class group) use more non-standard forms, and that this becomes particularly apparent among middle-working class speakers, both in careful and in casual speech. On the other hand, (ing) comes out as "a strong gender marker for the middle class," where, again, males produce much more non-standard forms than women. Finally, we see that the use of negative concord is also gender-specific, with strongest differences in middle class speakers.

These and numerous other studies led Labov to the development of three principles regarding the linguistic behavior of men and women:

1. For stable sociolinguistic variables, women show a lower rate of stigmatized variants and a higher rate of prestige variants than men (Labov 2001: 266)
2. In linguistic change from above, women adopt prestige forms at a higher rate than men (Labov 2001: 274)
3. In linguistic change from below, women use higher frequencies of innovative forms than men do (Labov 2001: 292).

Ultimately, Labov formulates the corresponding Gender Paradox:

> Women conform more closely than men to sociolinguistic norms that are overtly prescribed, but conform less than men when they are not.
>
> (Labov 2001: 293)

All these principles and the Gender Paradox itself appear to be fairly robust findings with almost universal applicability in contemporary sociolinguistics. In a word, they might qualify as 'laws' across space, culture, and also time. We will now turn to the question of how far this is actually true.

The investigation of gender in modern sociolinguistics is methodologically quite easy. All it takes is a group of speakers which differ – sociolinguistically – only in gender. Roughly speaking, they would have to be from the same social class, from the same area, and they would have to use the same speech style. If we then notice any statistically significant differences in the use of certain variables this should be due to differences in gender. The investigation of gender in language history, in contrast, can be a methodological nightmare (see Chapter 17 in this *Handbook*).

First, we have to acknowledge that data from female speakers becomes rarer the further we go back in time. Cressy (1980: 177) estimates that before 1500 only about 1% of the female English population had something like "signature literacy," that is, they were able to sign their own name. At around 1660, this figure rose to about 10%. By about 1800, the 50% mark may have been reached (cf. Schofield 1973). This has serious consequences for the availability of statistically significant data. However, this need not be a major problem. Even though we do not always have female scribes, we do have female authors, who dictated their texts to scribes. Bergs (2005; forthcoming) argues that the linguistic influence of scribes on the language of authors is not always as large as one might expect. In fact, in the Middle English Paston letters we can see that the morphosyntax of different authors is significantly different, even though the letters were dictated to and written by one and the same scribe. If the scribe had been more influential, we would expect to find more similarities. However, so far this has only been investigated for the Paston Letters and for some morphosyntactic variables (relative clauses and personal pronouns). Future studies could investigate this further.

Second, the data that we have from female speakers does not usually have any male counterparts, so we lack sociolinguistically 'minimal pairs'. Normally we see differences not only in gender, but also in style, text type, and/or region. These factors have to be considered when investigating gender as an external variable.

Third, and most importantly, the gender-related principles presented by Labov crucially rest on the notion of linguistic standards, prestige, stigma, and change from above or below. Generally, modern language communities (especially in the northern hemisphere) are massively influenced by the idea of linguistic standards, norms, and correctness (see Milroy and Milroy 1985/1999). In many studies, linguistic forms are described and analyzed in their relationship to such norms and standards. These, however, did not exist or did not operate in the past as they do now, simply because language standardization, despite its roots in very early language stages (Gneuss 1972; Samuels 1972), is mainly a post-medieval phenomenon. Many pre-modern societies did therefore not have linguistic standards and norms in the sense that modern societies do. This, however, does not mean that people in pre-modern societies did not have any norms they could either observe or deviate from, but the word 'norm' in this case does not have a prescriptivist meaning, but rather should be understood in Coseriu's sense (1962): norms reflect what is common, what is being used and widespread; in brief, the sum of all conventions. In practice, this means that in pre-standardized times we can postulate any number of linguistic communities which have their own specific norms: linguistic usages which speakers of that community expect because of their sheer frequency (but which are not explicitly prescribed!). The fact that speakers were indeed aware of linguistic differences and even attached some value to this or that use or variety becomes very clear when we look at some (in-)famous quotes from literary works (cf. Machan 2003: 111–38):

> "Symond," quod John, "by God, nede has na peer.
> Hym bihoues serve hymself that has na swayn,
> Or elles he is a fool, as clerkes sayn.
> Oure manciple, I hope he wil be deed,
> Swa werkes ay the wanges in his heed;
> And forthy as I come, and eek Alayn,
> To grynde oure corn and carie it ham agayn;
> I pray yow spede us heythen that ye may."

"Simon," said John, "by God, need has no peer" / He has to serve himself that has no slave. / or else he is a fool, as clerks say. / Our manciple, I guess he will be dead, / So ache all the teeth in his head / And therefore have I come, and also Alain, / To grind our corn and carry it home again; / I pray you speed us hence "if you please."
(Geoffrey Chaucer, *Canterbury Tales*, *The Reeve's Tale* I.4026–33, Benson ed. (1986)).

The two clerks, John and Aleyn, come from the north of England and are linguistically characterized as speakers of northern English. We find *na, swa, ham* instead of *no, so, home*, third person singular present tense is expressed by {s} as in *werke-s* instead of {-th} as in *werke-th*, and of course we find lexical items of northern origin: *heythen* instead of *hennes* 'hence,' *werkes* instead of *aches*.

Now it is very tempting to think that Chaucer could have used the dialect features as normal sociolinguistic variables, either as indicators, depending solely on class, or as markers, depending both on class and style. However, this idea presupposes a class system and, more importantly, a linguistic standard that speakers aspire to. While it seems intuitively plausible to assume that at any given point in time speakers had a range of stylistic options at their disposal, it also seems highly implausible that we find social classes in the modern sense before about 1500 (see above). However, people clearly showed some language awareness – particularly an awareness of the differences in language between speakers, at least from different regions. The fact that writers of literature were able to play with dialect features and could actually characterize some of the *dramatis personae* by giving them specific dialect features clearly shows that people were aware of these differences and did expect certain features to be present or absent from the speech of certain speakers – even though there was no such thing as a linguistic standard in the modern sense. In modern sociolinguistics, Dennis Preston developed the concept of 'perceptual dialectology,' the study of what people perceive as different dialects and what they associate with these dialects (Preston 1989, 1999; Niedzielski and Preston 2003). This association or evaluation is not necessarily linked to any standard variety and deviation from this standard, but it seems very likely that speakers who grow up in an environment where language standards and prestige are very highly regarded cannot easily free themselves of these influences when they evaluate language variation and varieties. Nevertheless, it is not unlikely that historical speech communities (whatever these were) also saw themselves in that way, to the point that certain features and varieties were found to be more or less pleasant, rude, honest, boorish, elegant, stand-offish, and so on. It would be worth studying these factors in greater detail – but, again, the problem is that historical periods do not offer much data for that purpose.

In 2003, Tim Machan introduced Einar Haugen's (1972) concept of the ecology of language to historical linguistics (Machan 2003: 9). For Haugen, the ecology of language refers to a very broad sociolinguistic context which includes psycholinguistic, ethnolinguistic, and anthropological aspects of language. According to Haugen, the ecology of language looks at the interplay of language and its environment. The value of this approach is that it undertakes an analysis not only of the sociolinguistic and psycholinguistic aspects of a language, and also of the effects of those aspects on the language itself. The result is a comprehensive picture of language and language users in their 'natural habitat.' Moving away from individual factors and their study in isolation and towards a broader picture thus gives us a chance of capturing even remote and unusual language states, or historical stages which do not offer us the same kind of data that we find in contemporary studies.

Eventually, therefore, we arrive at a point where we have to acknowledge that in all likelihood there was gender-specific language use in the Middle Ages and before, but due to the lack of data on the one hand, and the conceptual problem of standards and 'prestige' on the other, it is hard, if not impossible, to say exactly what those gender differences looked like. The first reliable pieces of evidence again come from Tudor and Stuart England. Nevalainen (1996: 84) demonstrates that at least in the Tudor period we see a clear gender differentiation with many morphosyntactic variables:

In Figure 5.1 we see the two variables *hath* versus *has* and *doth* versus *does* in male and female speakers from six different social groups (note that, due to the lack of data, merchants and professionals have no female representatives). It is very clear that female and male speakers differ significantly in their speech, and this underlines our initial claim that it is unlikely that we would not find any gender related differences at all. Moreover, in Nevalainen's study, women on average use more innovative (-s) forms than men, except for the lower gentry.

Table 5.2.   Approx. percentages of the verbal suffixes
–*(e)s* vs. –*(e)th* from male letter writers in the *Corpus of Early English Correspondence* (CEEC), excluding *have* and *do* (on the basis of Nevalainen & Raumolin-Brunberg 2003: 140)

	1520–1559	*1640–1681*
Royalty		100
Nobility	18	94
Gentry	8	92
Clergy	4	86
Social aspirers	3	88
Professionals	2	86
Merchants	10	92
Other non-gentry	58	92

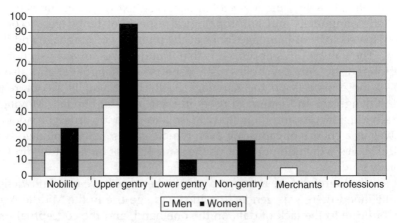

Figure 5.1.   *has* and *does* (%) as opposed to *hath* and *doth* in 1640–80 (adapted from Nevalainen 1996: 84)

How far this has to do with prestige is very difficult to determine. What can be said, however, is that women are, on average, the leaders in this change process.

3.3 Case study 3: social networks

Our final case study deals with social networks. Social networks have been around in modern sociolinguistics for more than thirty years now (for an overview, see Bergs 2005: 22–82; Bergs and Schenk 2004; Freeman 2004). One of the most influential studies is Milroy's work on Belfast (1980/1987). The key idea of social network analysis is that language use is not only determined by fairly stable speaker-related factors such as gender, age, class, education or speech-related factors such as register, genre, or style. Speakers also maintain relations with other people, and these relations form their personal social network. Networks are not fixed and stable entities, but relatively flexible, variable aggregates of relations. The two main factors which have been found to be important in social networking are quantity of contacts and quality of contacts. In other words, it makes a difference how many people somebody knows and how well this person knows his or her contacts. It is usually assumed that quantity and quality are inversely proportional, that is, the more contacts somebody has, the lower is the quality of those links, and vice versa. This is borne out well by our daily experience: you can not have 89 best friends (see Chapter 18 in this *Handbook*).

Determining network structures can be very difficult, even in modern sociolinguistics. There are numerous studies available in sociology which offer an endless array of tools and diagnostics (Wasserman and Faust 1994; Wasserman and Galaskiewicz 1994; Freeman 2004, the journal *Social Networks,* the *International Network for Social Network Analysis INSNA,* www.insna.org). In sociolinguistics, these factors have to be reduced and simplified somewhat in order to make them operable. Milroy, for example, suggests that for Belfast a large number of sociological factors can be determined, but that these need to be turned into a simpler social network strength scale which also reflects the density and multiplexity of an individual's network (Milroy 1980/1987: 140–42). The network strength scale conditions in her study are:

1. Membership of high-density, territorially based cluster.
2. Having substantial ties of kinship in the neighborhood.
3. Working at the same place as at least two others from the same area.
4. Having the same place of work as at least two others of the same sex from the area.
5. Voluntary association with workmates in leisure hours.

Milroy quite rightly points out that "since personal network structure is influenced universally by a great many factors […] one cannot hope to identify and measure all relevant factors. The range of choice actually depends on the local cultural categories which reflect more abstract properties of network structure" (Milroy 1980/1987: 212). This means, in turn, that historical network studies, just like contemporary ones, need to be very careful when they develop their criteria for measuring networks (see Bergs 2005: 31–37).

There is an ongoing debate in sociology and sociolinguistics about what effects different network structures can have on the behavior and attitudes of individuals. The very basic idea is that the number and the quality of the ties a person has should have some influence on the behavior and attitudes of that person. One of the main findings regarding contemporary networks is that dense, multiplex networks (as in traditional village communities where people know each other in a number of different capacities, such as friends, neighbors, workmates, and through joint activities) tend to enforce normative, conservative behavior while loose-knit, monoplex networks (in big cities, with mobile people who may know many people but know most of them in only one capacity or role) tend to foster innovation and change (Granovetter 1973, 1983). Moreover, social network analysis, with its focus on the individual, can go into greater detail about the functional roles of individual network members. We can usually distinguish between central participants, who are very prominent in the network and "extensively involved" (Wasserman and Faust 1994: 173), and average, marginal, and finally, peripheral participants. These can be defined through different degrees of centrality, prestige, involvement, and visibility. Individuals who have ties to two or more different networks can be defined as yet another group of network participants and are usually referred to as 'bridges.' Bridges and peripheral members play an important role in linguistic change. They are the living sources of innovation in their networks as they feel less normative pressure from within their networks and can thus transport linguistic material from one network to another. Central members, on the other hand, are usually more conservative than other network members as they are clearly visible to the other network members and subject to normative pressure from within the network. But once an innovation begins to gain ground, they often change their behavior drastically and act as early adopters of the innovation, as avant garde leaders in the change.

It seems very plausible to assume that speakers have always had individual social networks, based on ties to other members of their speech community. And it seems equally plausible to assume that these networks and ties – despite different features on network strength scales – were basically characterized by very similar factors: the number of ties a given speaker has, and the quality of those ties (good friends, loose friends, socioeconomic dependency, etc.). This is certainly a way in which the uniformity principle makes a lot of sense, even though data problems can make the analysis of historical networks very difficult (see Bergs 2005: 45–52).

Now, it is very tempting to think that networks have also always operated in the same fashion: loose-knit networks facilitate change, tight-knit networks are norm-enforcing, central members are more conservative than bridges, and so on. This idea, however, is problematic. Once again, the whole concept of conservative versus innovative language use in relation to linguistic norms (such as a language standard) crucially depends on the existence of those overtly prescribed linguistic norms and the idea of a language standard as such. These, as we have discussed before, did not exist as they do now before about 1500. This, however, does not necessarily mean that social networks did not play a role in language use and language change before that date, but their role certainly needs to be critically re-evaluated. Before the advent of overtly prestigious language norms, close-knit networks must have had norm-enforcing power in their very small, local communities such as villages and parishes, or perhaps even guilds or religious groups such as the Lollards. One can assume that deviance from these very local (unspoken) norms was not very well regarded. The result would be a number of individual linguistic systems across the country. Loose-knit networks, on the other hand, such as those with members who traveled a lot and did not belong to any particular community, would enable people to develop their own, personal linguistic systems. They could change and adopt their verbal behavior in deliberate acts of identity. Thus, members of close-knit networks felt normative pressures within their groups, and we see the development of group-specific 'standards,' while members of loose-knit networks did not feel this pressure. Close-knit groups could exhibit language variation 'to the point of deviance' without having to fear social sanctions. This can be illustrated on the basis of data from the Paston Letters. The collection of Paston letters contains, among others, the documents of two brothers: John II and John III. They were born in 1442 and 1444, respectively, and of course shared most traditional sociolinguistic factors such as age, gender, education, and place of residence. However, these two brothers had very different lifestyles: the older brother, John II, was a true bon viveur, who left the family home very early, traveled extensively, never actually settled, did not marry or have any children, and gambled and meddled in high-level politics. He often had to send letters home to ask for money. His younger brother was exactly the opposite. He stayed at home, apart from a two-year stay with the Duke of Norfolk, until about his mid-twenties, and acted as secretary to his mother. Later on he mostly stayed in Norwich, married and led a more stable, local life than his traveling brother. This, of course, had some consequences for their networks. John II had more contacts, which could have resulted in more loose-knit networks, and his contacts were of a more uniplex nature, in that they were not very intensive, strong links (see Conde-Silvestre and Hérnandez-Campoy 2004, 2005). John III, in contrast, had a more dense network, and his links as Justice of the Peace and Member of Parliament for his communities, for example, were multiplex and strong. The different lifestyles and networks of the brothers are reflected in their language use. John II uses, on average, more innovative forms such as the new pronouns *them* and *their* instead of *hem* and *here*. His letters exhibit more linguistic freedom and variability. The lack of dense network structures enabled John II to develop this great deal of variability, while the opposite, the dense, multiplex structures that John III found himself in, seem to lead to greater (local) uniformity.

However, all this changed with the development of supra-regional overtly prestigious language norms. Speakers in close-knit social networks like small villages were shielded, as it were, from these supra-regional standards and could maintain their own local norms. This is one reason why traditional dialects can still be found today in more rural areas, but less in urban centers. Today, however, loose-knit networks facilitate innovation in the direction of the standard, at least with upwardly mobile middle class speakers. This means that before about 1500 or 1600, loose-knit networks must have led to greater language diversity; since that time they have led to widespread, supra-local language standards and less diversity. Today, close-knit networks help to maintain vernacular norms, and thus also language diversity, albeit perhaps not on the personal level.

4. Summary and Conclusion

This chapter first presented an outline of the Uniformitarian Principle and its roots in eighteenth-century geology. It was pointed out that the principle is indeed helpful when studying language structures in isolation, but that its applicability in historical sociolinguistics must be viewed with much more caution. Indiscriminating application of the Uniformitarian Principle in this domain may easily result in anachronisms, which were introduced in the following section. It was shown that anachronism may arise both on the factual and on the ideational level.

The chapter concluded with three case studies which exemplify the opportunities and risks of applying the Uniformitarian Principle in historical sociolinguistics. We discussed the role and analysis of the major sociolinguistic factors social class, gender, and social networks in the history of English, mainly between 1300 and 1750. In particular, it became clear that some of the fundamental claims of modern (socio-)linguistics do seem to follow the UP. These include the fact that language must always have been variable, that different social groups and genders had different ways of speaking, and that people have always been aware of these differences, though they may not have evaluated them as we do today. Beyond these very basic facts, however, it seems that every language period and every linguistic community must be investigated independently and in its own right (*pace* Jardin 2000). The actual concepts and functions of class, gender, networks, and, most importantly, norms, standards, and prestige, differ radically in different communities. To assume that we find the rules and mechanisms of modern English in other communities or language periods leads easily to anachronism.

This, however, should not be taken to mean that, because of this implied danger, historical sociolinguistics is a doomed enterprise: on the contrary. With the development of new analytical tools and concepts, such as the ecology of language, we not only gain insights into the past stages of languages, we are also led to reflect on how we see, describe, and analyze contemporary languages.

REFERENCES

Aries, P. (1962) *Centuries of Childhood*, Vintage Books, New York.

Ash, S. (2002) Social class. In J.K. Chambers, P. Trudgill, and N. Schilling-Estes (eds.),

The Handbook of Language Variation and Change, Blackwell, Oxford, pp. 402–22.

Benson, L.D (ed.) (1986) *The Riverside Chaucer*, Clarendon Press, Oxford.

Bergs, A. (2005) *Social Network Analysis and Historical Sociolinguistics*, Mouton de Gruyter, Berlin.

Bergs, A. (forthcoming) The linguistic fingerprints of authors and scribes: a medieval whodunnit. In A. Auer, D. Schreier, and R. Watts (eds.), *Letters, Language and Change in English: Witnessing Sociolinguistic Histories*, Cambridge University Press, Cambridge.

Bergs, A. and Schenk, M. (2004) Network. In U. Ammon *et al.* (eds.), *Soziolinguistik. Ein internationales Handbuch zur Wissenschaft von Sprache und Gesellschaft*, Mouton de Gruyter, Berlin, pp. 438–43.

Britnell, R.H. (1993) *The Commercialisation of English Society, 1000–1500*. Cambridge University Press, Cambridge.

CEEC = *Corpus of Early English Correspondence* (1998) Compiled by T. Nevalainen, H. Raumolin-Brunberg, J. Keränen, M. Nevala, A. Nurmi, and M. Palander-Collin, Department of English, University of Helsinki. http://www.helsinki.fi/varieng/CoRD/corpora/CEEC/index.html [accessed October 13, 2011]

Chambers, J.K. (1995) *Sociolinguistic Theory*, Blackwell, Oxford.

Cheshire, J. (1982) *Variation in an English Dialect: A Sociolinguistic Study*, Cambridge University Press, Cambridge.

Christy, C. (1983) *Uniformitarianism in Linguistics*, John Benjamins, Amsterdam.

Conde-Silvestre, J.C. and Hernández-Campoy, J.M. (2004) A sociolinguistic approach to the diffusion of Chancery written practices in late fifteenth-century private correspondence. *Neuphilologische Mitteilungen* 105(2): 135–52.

Conde-Silvestre, J.C. and Hernández-Campoy, J.M. (2005) Sociolinguistic and geolinguistic approaches to the historical diffusion of linguistic innovations: incipient standardisation in Late Middle English. *International Journal of English Studies* 5(1): 101–34.

Corfield, P.J. (1991) *Language, History and Class*, Blackwell, Oxford.

Coseriu, E. (1962) *Teoría del Lenguaje y Lingüística General*, Gredos, Madrid.

Cressy, D. (1980) *Literacy and the Social Order: Reading and Writing in Tudor and Stuart England*, Cambridge University Press, Cambridge.

Durkheim, E. (1893) *De la division du travail social: Étude sur l'organisation des sociétés supérieures*, Félix Alcan, Paris.

Durkheim, E. (1895) *Les règles de la méthode sociologique*, Félix Alcan, Paris.

Eckert, P. (1989) *Jocks and Burnouts: Social Categories and Identity in the High School*, Teachers College Press, New York.

Eckert, P. and McConnell-Ginet, S. (2003) *Language and Gender*, Cambridge University Press, Cambridge.

Freeman, L. (2004) *The Development of Social Network Analysis: A Study in the Sociology of Science*, Empirical Press, Vancouver.

Georg, W. (2004) Soziale Schicht/Class. In U. Ammon, N. Dittmar, K.J. Mattheier, and P. Trudgill (eds.), *Sociolinguistics. An International Handbook of the Science of Language and Society*, Mouton de Gruyter, Berlin, pp. 377–84.

Gneuss, H. (1972) The origin of Standard Old English and Aethelwold's School at Winchester. *Anglo-Saxon England* 1: 63–83.

Granovetter, M. (1973) The strength of weak ties. *American Journal of Sociology* 78: 1360–80.

Granovetter, M. (1983) The strength of weak ties: a network theory revisited. *Sociological Theory* 1: 201–33.

Guy, G. (1988) Language and social class. In F. Newmeyer (ed.), *Linguistics: The Cambridge Survey IV (Language – The Socio-Cultural Context)*, Cambridge University Press, Cambridge, pp. 37–63.

Haugen, E. (1972) *Ecology of Language: Essays*, Stanford University Press, Stanford.

Holmes, J. and Meyerhoff, M. (eds.) (2005) *The Handbook of Gender*, Blackwell, Oxford.

Hume, D. (1739/2007) *A Treatise of Human Nature: Of the Understanding (Book 1)* (ed. D.G.C. McNabb) (1962), Fontana/Collins, Glasgow.

Jardin, N. (2000) Uses and abuses of anachronism in the history of the sciences. *History of Science* 38: 251–70.

Labov, W. (1972) *Sociolinguistic Patterns*, University of Pennsylvania Press, Philadelphia.

Labov, W. (2001) *Principles of Linguistic Change, Vol. II: Social Factors*, Blackwell, Oxford.

Lass, R. (1980) *On Explaining Language Change*, Cambridge University Press, Cambridge.

Lass, R. (1997) *Historical Linguistics and Language Change*, Cambridge University Press, Cambridge.

Machan, T.W. (2003) *English in the Middle Ages*, Oxford University Press, Oxford.

Marshall, G., Rose, D., Newby, H., and Vogler, C. (1989) *Social Class in Modern Britain*, Routledge, London.

Millar, J. (1771/1990) *The Origin of the Distinction of Ranks*, Thoemmes, Bristol.

Milroy, J. and Milroy, L. (1985/1999) *Authority in Language: Investigating Standard English* (2nd edn), Routledge, London.

Milroy, L. (1980/1987) *Language and Social Networks* (2nd edn), Blackwell, Oxford.

Milroy, L. and Gordon, M. (2003) *Sociolinguistics: Method and Interpretation*, Blackwell, Oxford.

Naumann, B. *et al.* (eds.) (1992) *Language and Earth: Elective Affinities Between the Emerging Sciences of Linguistics and Geology*, John Benjamins, Amsterdam.

Nerlich, B. (1990) *Change in Language. Whitney, Bréal, Wegener*, Routledge, London.

Nevalainen, T. (1996) Social stratification. In T. Nevalainen and H. Raumolin-Brunberg (ed.), *Sociolinguistics and Language History: Studies Based on the Corpus of Early English Correspondence*, Rodopi, Amsterdam, pp. 57–76.

Nevalainen, T. and Raumolin-Brunberg, H. (2003) *Historical Sociolinguistics: Language Change in Tudor and Stuart England*, Longman Pearson Education, London.

Niedzielski, N. and Preston, D. (2003) *Folk linguistics*, Mouton de Gruyter, Berlin.

OED = *Oxford English Dictionary Online* (2008) Oxford: Oxford University Press. www.oed.com

Preston, D. (1989) *Perceptual Dialectology: Nonlinguists' Views of Areal Linguistics*, Foris Publications, Dordrecht.

Preston, D. (ed.) (1999) *Handbook of Perceptual Dialectology, Vol.1*, John Benjamins, Amsterdam.

Samuels, M.L. (1972) *Linguistic Evolution with Special Reference to English*, Cambridge University Press, Cambridge.

Schofield, R.S. (1973) Dimensions of literacy, 1750–1850. *Explorations in Economic History* 10: 437–54.

Trudgill, P. (1974) *The Social Differentiation of English in Norwich*, Cambridge University Press, Cambridge.

Wasserman, S. and Faust, K. (1994) *Social Network Analysis*, Cambridge University Press, Cambridge.

Wasserman, S. and Galaskiewicz, J. (eds.) (1994) *Advances in Social Network Analysis: Research in the Social and Behavioral Sciences*, Sage, Thousand Oaks, CA.

Whitney, W.D. (1867) *Language and the Study of Language: Twelve Lectures on the Principles of Linguistic Science*, Trübner, London.

Wrightson, K. (1991) Estates, degrees and sorts: changing perceptions of society in Tudor and Stuart England. In P.J. Corfield (ed.), *Language, History and Class*, Oxford University Press, Oxford, pp. 30–52.

6 The Use of Linguistic Corpora for the Study of Linguistic Variation and Change: Types and Computational Applications

PASCUAL CANTOS

1. Introduction

Corpus linguistics "differs from other linguistic disciplines, such as sociolinguistics and psycholinguistics, in that it is not defined by the object of study," as it does not study corpora but it rather studies language through corpora (Cantos and Sánchez 2000: 1). Corpus linguistics is the study of linguistic phenomena through large collections of machine-readable texts: linguistic corpora. These are used within a number of research areas, from the descriptive study of the morphology of a language to prosody or language learning, to mention but a few.

A linguistic corpus is a collection of texts which have been selected and brought together, representing a sample of a particular variety or use of language(s) and presented in machine readable form so that this language variety and/or use of language(s) can be studied on the computer. The use of real examples of texts in the study of language is not a new issue in the history of linguistics. However, corpus linguistics has developed considerably in the last decades due to i) the great possibilities offered by the processing of natural language with computers, and ii) the availability of balanced corpora representing varieties of a number of

The Handbook of Historical Sociolinguistics, First Edition. Edited by Juan Manuel Hernández-Campoy and Juan Camilo Conde-Silvestre.
© 2014 John Wiley & Sons, Ltd. Published 2014 by John Wiley & Sons, Ltd.

languages, making it possible to obtain data quickly and easily and also to have this data presented in a format suitable for analysis.

Today, corpus linguistics offers some of the most powerful new procedures for the analysis of language, and the impact of this dynamic and expanding subdiscipline is making itself felt in many areas of language study. Increasing numbers of researchers are seeing the potential benefits of the use of an electronic corpus as a source of empirical language data for their research.

Linguistic corpora allow the extraction and exploration of linguistically felicitous characteristics based on quantitative data. This is a necessary and crucial step in the development of corpus and computational linguistics. Large-scale digital corpora and computational methodologies offer new possibilities for empirical and scientific studies of language. However, the contribution of corpus-based empirical approaches cannot be theoretically significant unless we can show that the quantitative data can be generalized and interpreted as a qualitative account of the linguistic facts. Thus, corpus-based studies can offer both i) qualitative generalizations supported with empirical evidence, and ii) quantitative generalizations which are both replicable and verifiable. On the one hand, a qualitative generalization without a quantifiable prediction is hard to falsify or replicate, but on the other, a quantitative generalization without a qualitative motivation or implication is hard to interpret. Corpora are thus most useful when they enable the linguist to assign a qualitative account to the extracted quantitative generalizations. Nevertheless, the qualitative interpretation of quantitative generalizations is not trivial.

Studies in linguistic variation and change are not an exception, as they also require a familiarity with both the basic tools of qualitative linguistic analysis and quantitative methods for pursuing that analysis to deeper levels (Labov 2008:1; see also Bauer 2002). This chapter will assume a basic familiarity with both sets of tools, and focus upon how they are used to address the major questions of linguistic structure and linguistic change. Given the output of quantitative analyses, we ask, what good are they? What inferences and implications can be found in these numbers that justify the time and energy needed to produce them? What are the principles of quantitative reasoning that allow us to pass from the measurement of surface fluctuations to the underlying forms and principles that produce them?

Language is not a homogeneous phenomenon but a rather complex one displaying great variability. Over the years, however, linguistic variation and change have remained a problem area in linguistics, and linguists in their descriptions of language have tended to abstract away from these variability studies, restricting their goals to the setting up of small-scale hypothetical models which have contributed only a limited number of insights in the phenomenon of language variation, both in the present and in the past. In part, the apparent failure to cope with the complexity of a phenomenon such as language variation can be attributed to the fact that linguists have not been very well equipped to carry out large-scale formal empirical analyses which would enable them to systematically cope with extra-linguistic factors and examine the accompanying linguistic variation.

Corpus-based research has produced some expected results and others that have been unexpected but revealing in the areas of variation regarding the use of grammatical and lexical devices; methodologically these studies offer a prospect for discovering general principles of linguistic change. For instance, Collins (1991) focuses on modals of obligation and necessity such as *must, should, ought, need* and *have (got) to*, and explores their behavior in Australian English as compared to American and British English. Each of these modals has two primary meanings: epistemic, signaling the speaker's certainty and suppositions, and root, indicating obligation, compulsion, or requirement. In their epistemic meanings, *must* and *have (got) to* express a greater degree of conviction than *should* and *ought*. The item *have (got) to* is the main exponent of root obligation in informal speech in Australian English (Collins, 1991: 153). Whereas Quirk *et al.* (1985: 225) claim that *must* does not have a negative form (the form *can't* takes the place of *mustn't*), the Australian corpus contains examples of epistemic *mustn't* in spoken language identical to the number of occurrences of epistemic *can't*. However, *mustn't* does not occur in written data in the Australian corpus. It is not surprising that a change in the context of language use leads to a change in language; this is a well-known historical linguistic process, which can be captured by analyzing spoken language corpora.

Current research findings suggest that the corpus-based approach will be effective in coming to grips with dialect, change, and variety differentiation and will deepen our understanding of register and genre variation (see, among others: Aijmer and Stenström, 2004; Biber, 2006; Biber and Reppen 1998; Biber and Burges, 2000; Conrad and Biber, 2000; McEnery and Wilson, 1996). Corpora have long been recognized as a valuable source for comparison between language varieties as well as for the description of those varieties themselves and their diachronic development. One of the earliest research projects using the LOB (Lancaster-Oslo/Bergen) and Brown corpora was a word-frequency comparison of British and American written English (Hofland and Johansson 1982). Other more complex studies have included the use of the subjunctive in British versus American English (Johansson and Norheim 1988). The construction of corpora of other national varieties of English (the Kolhapur Indian English, the Australian and New Zealand English corpora, and the International Corpus of English) have led to further comparative studies.

Nevertheless, corpus-based approaches may not meet with the same degree of success when dealing with diatypic variation (Meyer 2002: 17–20). Most difficult to deal with may be tenor or the interpersonal dynamics of discourse, mainly because moves in interaction are negotiated as conversations proceed. Furthermore, it is hard to imagine how a corpus-based approach would deal with discourse-based phenomena as opposed to text-based approaches. For example, it is not clear how the phenomena of speaker attitudes, beliefs, and intentions can be dealt with in any corpus-based approach.

We need good corpora and teams of researchers working on analyses before diatypic variation can be better understood. This concern has led some researchers to focus their attention in semantic-pragmatic tagging. In this line of work, Archer and Culpeper (2003) focus their attention on historical corpus linguistics, an area where there are particular difficulties relating to the retrieval of contextual factors (for instance, we cannot ask the speakers!) and where little work has been done on annotation of any kind. They annotated a sub-section of the *Corpus of English Dialogues* (CED), known as the *Sociopragmatic Corpus* (1640–1760), with information related to speaker/hearer relationships, social roles, and sociological characteristics such as gender. Similarly Löfberg *et al.* (2003) and more specifically Archer *et al.* (2003) propose a design for a semantic tagger for Early Modern English texts, containing an 'intelligent' spelling regularizer, that is, a system that has been designed so as to regularize spellings in their 'correct' context. Culpeper and Kytö (2000) examine four speech-related text types (1600–1720) for how linguistically close they are to spoken face-to-face interaction, in terms of lexical repetitions, question marks, interruptions, and several single-word interactive features.

There is a vast range of corpus-based approaches/techniques available to researchers that can be used at the synchronic level (tracing variation and change in progress) in order to better understand diachrony (the actuation of historical change), and vice versa. This link between the present and the past: "the use of the present to explain the past," in Labov's terminology, can be supplemented by the uniformitarian principle, to the extent that "[i]f they are relatively constant, day-to-day effects of social interaction upon grammar and phonology [...] continue to operate today the same way that they have in the past" (Labov 1972: 274; 1994: 21–23; see also Chapter 5 in this *Handbook*). The links between the present and the past are essential in historical sociolinguistics (Nevalainen and Raumolin-Brunberg 2003) for the reconstruction of the English language in some of its social and historical contexts. However, putting this challenging task into practice is not easy, mostly because of the 'bad data problem' (Labov 1994; Fries 1998; Nevalainen 1999; Kytö and Walker 2003). The 'bad data problem' is the key challenge for historical linguists: that of "making the best use of bad data." The researcher engaged in a study of contemporary English can design a balanced, representative sample and has access to information about the social factors and external influences that may impinge on linguistic variation, but whenever we deal with the history of languages we have a much more difficult task. We have to rely on evidence that "survive[s] by chance not design" (Labov 1994: 11), which is often in what Labov terms a "normative dialect," and for which, as Nevalainen (1999) points out, the metadata is lacking. For scholars researching the Late Modern period, these problems are less acute than for medievalists, since more data survives, including documents from less educated, lower-class writers, and the social and historical background is easier to reconstruct. On the other hand, the 'colonial' varieties which emerge during this period (Dollinger 2008) present their own challenge to the researcher: the impossibility of finding sufficient data from the large number of input varieties which influence the formation of Canadian English, for instance. This requires us to "make the best use of bad data" (Labov 1994: 11): written materials from the past, which very often have survived by sheer chance and are isolated from their immediate communicative background, with the result that they can rarely be correlated with the original social and stylistic contexts of production and reception.

Nonetheless, corpus linguistics can fruitfully contribute to overcome the obstacles of the bad data problem; by allowing researchers to process simultaneously almost all the texts that have survived from a given period, corpus linguistics partly solves the fragmentary nature of historical material, and ensures that early varieties can be reliably reconstructed, facilitating the selection of those variables whose analysis is worth undertaking. Particularly useful in this connection is the *Corpus of Early English Correspondence* (CEEC), a collection of personal letters. Personal letters are usually self-contained, authored texts; these characteristics enable the reconstruction of social information (drawn either from the background of authors or from textual cues reflecting different types of interaction) and permit the scholar to piece together a range of styles that, at one end of the continuum, can reflect the oral, informal registers (see Nevalainen and Raumolin-Brunberg 2003: 43–49; Conde-Silvestre 2007: 46–52).

The CEEC has been compiled to facilitate sociolinguistic research into the history of English. The project was originally set up to test how methods developed by sociolinguists of present-day languages could be applied to historical data. The CEEC family of corpora currently covers 400 years from 1400 to 1800, and consists of five daughter corpora. The original corpus, which spans the decades from 1410 to 1680, was completed in 1998, and its sampler version (CEECS) was made publicly available the same year. Based on the original, the *Parsed Corpus of Early English Correspondence* (PCEEC) was released in 2006. The eighteenth-century extension (CEECE) and the supplement to the original (CEECSU), together with their attendant sender and letter databases are nearing completion. The ultimate aim of the compilers is to combine these subcorpora into one structured whole, which will amount to over five million running words. The validity of this corpus for sociolinguistic research has been tested in numerous studies. For instance, Nevalainen and Raumolin-Brunberg in their study "Social stratification in Tudor English" (1996) have attested to the existence of covariation between some morphosyntactic changes of the Early Modern English period and the usual sociolinguistic variables, including age, social status, professional and educational background, gender, domicile, migration history, and networks of personal relationships between informants.

2. Corpora, Variation Studies and Quantitative Techniques

Quantitative methods can "shed new light on the utilization of words in different varieties of English" and can be a starting point of other linguistic studies "as well as for cultural observations" (Hofland and Johansson 1982: 39). Corpus-based variation studies focus on the comparison of the use of objectively countable linguistic features. That is, variationist studies tend to concentrate on the quantitative analysis of extracted tokens. Typical variationist research questions take the form: is variable *x* used differently in corpus *A* compared to corpus *B* (such as corpora from different historical periods, corpora of different regional/national varieties, or written versus oral corpora, different genres)? To be answered, the question has to be translated into a hypothesis –a statement which can be subjected to testing. Depending on the decisions and results of the further tests, the hypothesis may be accepted or rejected.

Hypothesis testing is a type of statistical inference, that is, the drawing of a conclusion based on data. It is one of the most important tools in the application of statistics to problems. Decisions about populations usually have to be made on the basis of sample information, and it is statistical tests that are used in arriving at such decisions. Hypothesis testing is the use of statistics to determine the probability that a given hypothesis is true. The usual process of hypothesis testing consists of four steps.

1. Formulate the null hypothesis H_0 (commonly, that the observations are the result of pure chance; that is, variable x is indistinguishable in corpus A and corpus B, and we assume no variation or lack of change) and the alternative hypothesis H_1 (commonly, that the observations show a real effect combined with a component of chance variation; that is, variable x is measurably and significantly different in corpus A and corpus B; thus we postulate variation or change).
2. Identify the test statistics that can be used to assess the truth of the null hypothesis H_0.
3. Compute the *p-value*, which is the probability that a statistical result at least as significant as the one observed would be obtained assuming that the null hypothesis H_0 were true. The smaller the *p-value*, the stronger the evidence against the null hypothesis.
4. Compare the *p-value* to an acceptable significance value α (sometimes called an alpha value, critical value or level of significance). If $p \leq \alpha$, then the observed effect is statistically significant, H_0 is ruled out, and H_1 is valid; else, if $p > \alpha$, H_1 is rejected, and we accept H_0.

Before considering an example, it is important to note that in order to carry out comparisons we should use similar corpora whenever possible, that is, corpora that are alike or comparable in size, content, and design, in order to avoid too much 'noise' and prevent or reduce the interaction of too many variables. These variables are, in principle, not observable; they are abstract, theoretical labels applied to the relationship or process that links the independent and dependent variables. For instance, if a researcher wants to investigate the differences and similarities in press editorials published in Britain and New Zealand, then (s)he should try to compile two corpora (British press editorials and New Zealand press editorials) that are similar in size, number of documents, topics, and time periods, which are written by native speakers (British people and New Zealanders respectively), and which have similar sized documents and similar distribution regarding authors' sex (male and female). Obviously, the more variables that are controlled and considered *a priori* (that is, in the design and compilation of the corpora), the easier it becomes for the researcher to conclude that differences or

Table 6.1. The Brown Corpus: Text categories, genres and number of texts

Text Category	Genre	Number of Texts
Press	Reportage	44
	Editorial	27
	Reviews	17
Religion		17
Skill and Hobbies		36
Popular Lore		48
Belles-Lettres, Biographies, Memoirs, etc.		75
Miscellaneous: US Government and House Organs		30
Learned Writing		80
Fiction	General	29
	Mystery and Detective Fiction	24
	Science	6
	Adventure and Western	29
	Romance and Love Story	29
Humor		9

similarities between the two corpora are the result of the factor (s)he aims to examine (regional variation, in this case).

In this sense, the national corpora compiled after the *Brown Corpus* design are very positive for variation studies. The *Brown Corpus*, published in 1961, was a carefully compiled selection of current written American English, totaling about a million words drawn from a wide variety of sources. The corpus originally contained 1 014 312 words sampled from fifteen text categories (see Table 6.1) and totaling 500 texts. All works sampled were published in 1961; as far as could be determined, they were first published then, and were written by native speakers of American English. Each sample began at a random sentence boundary in the article or other units chosen, and continued up to the first sentence boundary after 2000 words.

Following the same sampling criteria used in the *Brown Corpus*, we find comparable corpora for other regions (Table 6.2).

A similar working scheme is followed by the *International Corpus of English* (ICE), which started in 1990 with the aim of collecting material for comparative studies of English worldwide. Eighteen research teams around the world are preparing electronic corpora of their own national or regional variety of English. Each ICE corpus[1] consists of one million words of spoken and written English produced after 1989. To ensure compatibility among the component corpora, each team is following a common corpus design, as well as a common scheme for grammatical annotation.

Table 6.2.   Other corpora that are balanced or similar with respect to the Brown Corpus

Region/Variation	Data	Corpus	Size	Compilation Date
British English	written	LOB	1 million words	1970
American English	written	Frown	1 million words	1992
British English	written	FLOB	1 million words	1991
Australian English	written	ACE	1 million words	1989
New Zealand English	written	WCWNZE	1 million words	1991
Indian English	written	Kolhapur Corpus	1 million words	1986

Table 6.3.   Written component of the BNC: publication place, text samples and size

Publication Place	Number of Texts	Size (words)
Unknown	690	14 718 827
UK (unspecific)	263	7 163 111
Ireland	37	570 652
UK: North (north of Mersey-Humber line)	191	3 781 055
UK: Midlands (north of Bristol Channel-Wash line)	93	2 590 345
UK: South (south of Bristol Channel-Wash line)	1853	58 587 808
United States	14	542 134

The corpora balanced with the *Brown Corpus* and those that are part of the ICE project are ideal for canonical comparisons given that all the samples are identical or very similar (in size and composition) except for the variable we want to examine: regional variation. However, it is also possible to use a single corpus[2] for variation studies, if and only if that corpus records information on the variable we want to examine. Consider, for instance, the *British National Corpus* (BNC; 100 million words), where written texts are also characterized according to their place of publication and the type of sampling used (Table 6.3).

The use of the BNC for variation studies is less canonical as the comparisons are not drawn from same-sized samples or (sub)corpora, and the problem of interpreting results is less straightforward. Clearly, the greater the number of variables that differ from one sample or (sub)corpus to another, the more difficult it becomes to say that any differences are the result of the factor we want to examine.

Typical examples of canonical corpus-based variation studies would analyze a specific factor or variable based on equal-sized corpora, such as the LOB versus the Brown corpus. One such example is Hundt's (1998) research on lexical and phonological aspects of New Zealand English (NZE), presenting a careful comparative analysis of four parallel corpora – New Zealand (WCWNZE), British (FLOB), American (Frown), and Australian English (ACE) – in order to single out morphological, syntactic, and lexico-grammatical features typical of an emerging New Zealand standard. NZE is different from other national varieties of English in that it shows preferences for certain variants rather than categorically different grammatical rules. In one of the many studies presented, Hundt focuses on the use of regular and irregular past tense forms of a number of verbs in New Zealand and British English in two equal-sized corpora, one for each variety: WCWNZE and FLOB. The counts show (Table 6.4) that British English (BE) resorts more often than NZE to regular spelling.

With regard to the statistical significance of these differences, we first need to formulate the null hypothesis H_0 (that is, the observations are the result of pure chance) and the alternative hypothesis H_1 (the observations show a real effect combined with a component of chance variation). The differences between NZE and BE, using a chi-squared test[3], show with a certainty of 99% ($\chi^2 = 7.033$; $\alpha = 0.008$), that the use of regular and irregular past tense forms is a clear case of variation between NZE and BE, and we consequently reject H_0.

As an example of a non-canonical comparison, consider the data obtained from the BNC regarding the diachronic usage of the verbal forms *learned/learnt* in British English and tabulated with respect to three different time spans (Table 6.5).

Table 6.4. Regular and irregular past tense form in NZE and BE

	New Zealand English		British English	
	Counts	%	Counts	%
-ed	127	56.4	149	68.7
-t	98	43.6	68	31.3
Total	225	100.0	217	100.0

Table 6.5. Use of regular and irregular past tense forms of *learn* in different time spans

	1960–1974	1975–1984	1985–1993
learned	87	261	4697
learnt	48	108	1961
Total	135	369	6658

Table 6.6.   Sampling size according to time span in the BNC

Time span	Size (in words)
1960–1974	2 056 079
1975–1984	5 401 750
1985–1993	101 731 225
Total	109 189 054

The main problem with non-canonical comparisons is that direct comparisons are not always possible and interpretation of the data is not always that straightforward. A preliminary step could be to normalize the data: as it is very likely that the frequency counts obtained have been extracted from differently-sized samples or (sub)corpora, we need to convert all counts to a common scale. A quick look at the BNC documentation reveals that, indeed, the three time spans also account for different sampling sizes (Table 6.6).

There are various methods for normalizing data, but the easiest in corpus-based approaches is to normalize the data to percentages and/or to a million words: that is, to calculate what the average count would be in a hundred words and/or in a one million word chunk. For example, in order to calculate the percentage rate of usage of *learned* compared to *learnt* for time span 1960–74, we need to multiply the total count of *learned* (87) by 100 and divide it by the total (*learned + learnt* = 135 in 1960–74):

$$learned(1960-1974) = \frac{87*100}{135} = 64.44\%$$

Alternatively, to normalize figures to a million words, we would multiply the total count (87) by one million and divide it by the number of words of the text sample (2,056,079). So the number of occurrences of *learned* in 1960–74 per million would be:

$$learned(1960-1974) = \frac{87*1,000,000}{2,056,079} = 42.31$$

The normalized data and resulting percentages are given in Table 6.7.

The normalized data allows a straightforward comparison and reveals that the use of *learned/learnt* is nearly identical in 1975–84 and 1985–93. The main difference is only apparent between the time spans 1960–74 and 1975–84/1985–93. The data might suggest a trend towards the increased use of the regular form *learned* and, conversely, an under-use of the irregular form *learnt* over time. However, this trend is only evident from 1960–74 to 1975–84, not between 1975–84 and 1985–93.

Table 6.7. Normalized data to one million words and percentages

	1960–1974		*1975–1984*		*1985–1993*	
	Counts	*%*	*Counts*	*%*	*Counts*	*%*
learned	42.31	64.44	48.32	70.73	46.17	70.54
learnt	23.35	35.55	19.99	29.27	19.28	29.45
Total	65.66	100.00	68.31	100.00	65.45	100.00

An important issue is that there is no need to normalize the data[4] when performing a statistical significance test by means of a chi-squared test on frequency counts obtained from corpora of different sizes. The chi-squared test can be used for corpora of any relative size, using the raw frequency counts (the actual number of times each word was observed). So, the chi-squared test on the raw data (Table 6.5) regarding the usage distribution of *learned/learnt* across the three time spans reveals no statistical significance ($\chi^2 = 2.382$; $\alpha = 0.666$). Consequently, we accept H_0 and conclude that the use of regular and irregular past tense forms *learned/ learnt* is not an instance of change across the time spans 1960–74, 1975–84, and 1985–93 in British English.

There is no doubt that the choice of the corpus/corpora (written, spoken, reference, monitor, monolingual, comparable, or parallel) to be used in a study depend(s) upon the research questions being asked. This is an important issue that goes hand in hand with the type of information or data that can be extracted and/or expected from a corpus. Linguistic corpora limit the types of phenomena that can be studied. In principle, we can only extract the linguistic items that are present in the corpus, namely words or types, to use corpus linguistics jargon. Just using raw texts, that is, texts without any additional information such as part-of-speech, syntactic phrase markers, semantic tags, or anaphoric annotation, it would be impossible to retrieve data or samples on common linguistic phenomena such as zero relative as in *the girl Ø I know*, or to distinguish between the word *light* as a noun, verb, or adjective. In contrast, more sophisticated data analysis can be performed using annotated corpora that have been enhanced with various types of linguistic information. This enhancement is carried out using analysts (human and/or computational) imposing a linguistic interpretation upon a corpus. In essence, corpus annotation is the enrichment of a corpus in order to aid the process of corpus exploitation.

Regarding annotating corpora for variation and historical/diachronic studies, note the monograph volume *Annotating Variation and Change* (Meurman-Solin and Nurmi 2007)[5] at the Research Unit for Variation, Contacts and Change in English (VARIENG) from Helsinki University devoted to corpus tagging for variation research and diachronic studies. This volume has shown new ways of benefiting from annotated corpora as well as pinpointing some of the problems of existing annotation schemes. Ideas for developing new types of annotation are also discussed. Meurman-Solin (2007) explores the various problems related to the creation and annotation of the *Corpus of Scottish Correspondence* (CSC). The scheme employed for this corpus involves annotation at many different levels of language, from phrasal to textual. Stenroos (2007) discusses the special questions raised by the Middle English Grammar project, ranging from how to interpret letter shapes in manuscripts to how to define spelling units and headwords for the corpus. Beal *et al.* (2007) present the problems of dealing with language varieties and change, reflecting a high degree of variation when compiling and annotating a corpus of non-standard eighteenth and nineteenth century spoken English: the *Newcastle Electronic Corpus of Tyneside English*. Huber (2007) presents his compilation work of a sociolinguistic corpus of Late Modern spoken English from the *Old Bailey Proceedings* (1674–1834) and explores the need to include information on such issues as methods of shorthand and the publication process in order to assess the closeness of the corpus material to spoken language. Huber also tests the degree of 'spokenness' of his material and the consistency of scribal practices by comparing numbers of contracted forms with scribes and printers. Palander-Collin (2007) approaches the question of annotation from an end-user's point of view, discussing which variables it is desirable to code in a corpus in order to make it easier to systematically study issues such as the interactional features of language and their social embedding in the context of speaker/writer and hearer/reader. Nurmi (2007) looks at the ways in which complex linguistic features could be retrieved and elaborated on through annotation. Her example case is the semantic category of modality, and she discusses both the helpfulness of the available annotation schemes for retrieving examples from corpora and the requirements of an elaborated semantic scheme for the annotation of modal expressions. Feldman and Arshavskaya (2007) explore the ways that temporal categorization can be applied to Russian, and, in the pursuit of cross-linguistic relevance, begin with a model description designed for English, as well as comparing the results to English. Their long-term aim is to develop an algorithm which will allow clauses to be recognized according to time determination.

In what follows, we shall provide a brief recapitulation of corpus-based studies of variation and change in the use of English.

2.1   *Comparing spoken and written language*

Corpus-based studies of variation and change became possible with the availability of the *Brown Corpus*, though, initially, all the research was intra-corpus and within the single variety of written American English. Subsequent availability of the LOB corpus made possible studies of regional variation. When the *Helsinki Corpus of English Texts* and the *London-Lund Corpus* (LLC) became available, it became possible to carry out studies in diachronic variation and comparisons between spoken and written varieties of English, respectively.

Altenberg (1994) analyzed the differences in how the high frequency function word *such* is used in the LOB corpus (written language) and in the LLC (spoken language). Altenberg's findings reveal that in the more formal written texts of the

LOB corpus (informative prose) the use of *such* is more than three times as common as in spontaneous, more informal spoken texts in the LLC. However, the predominance of *such* in written language is restricted to its use as an 'identifier' (*Never has such a thing been done in Israel*), which is seven times more frequent in the LOB corpus than in the LLC; on the other hand, the use of *such* as an 'intensifier' is more common in the LLC (*It's such a beautiful day*). A more in-depth analysis on the use of *such* in different genres in the LLC shows that while 'intensifying' *such* has a similar occurrence in private and public discourse in the LLC, 'identifying' *such* is less common in private conversation.

Similar differences between oral (LLC) and written language (LOB corpus) were found by Kennedy (1998: 183) regarding the distributions of the three main uses of the word *pretty*: as an adjective (*pretty dress*), intensifier before an adjective (*pretty big way*) and intensifier before an adverb (*pretty nicely done*). The data shows that whereas *pretty* as an adjective is eleven times more common in written English than in oral discourse, *pretty* as an adjective intensifier is twice as common in oral language as in written language; *pretty* as an adverb intensifier is used equally in oral and written language.

The availability of larger oral corpora such as the oral component of the BNC has made it possible to carry out more reliable and representative research on oral *versus* written language. For example, Summers (1992) noted that the words *really*, *right* and *just* have a dramatically different usage in speech compared to writing.[6]

Similarities and differences between speech and writing have been the subject of innumerable studies. However, it was not until Biber (1988) that a unified linguistic analysis of the whole range of spoken and written registers in English was provided. Biber's goal was to chart the various ways in which oral and written English vary. To do this, he first identified 67 linguistic features of English in the LOB and LCC. These features were counted in each of the 481 text samples and by means of factor analysis, their patterns of co-occurrence were then identified to establish a number of major dimensions or factors on which texts could vary[7]. Biber identified seven dimensions, numbered in decreasing order of significance: dimension 1 accounts for the largest part of the non-randomness of the data, dimension 2, the next largest, and so on. He calls the first dimension 'involved' versus 'informational' production. Texts with high positive scores are typically spoken, and typically conversations, while texts with high negative scores are academic prose and official documents. The linguistic features with the highest positive weightings are private verbs (such as *assume* and *believe*), *that*-deletion, contractions, present tense verbs, and second person pronouns. The linguistic features with the highest negative weightings are nouns, word length, prepositions, and type-token ratio. Dimension 2 is 'narrative' versus 'non-narrative' discourse, for which past-tense verbs and third-person pronouns are the high-positive features: fiction texts got the high positive scores. Dimension 3 accounts for 'situation-dependent' versus 'elaborated' reference, where the positive linguistic features are time and place adverbials, and the negatives, relative clauses, phrasal co-ordination and nominalizations; broadcasts are the highest-scoring texts and official documents the lowest.

Biber's approach combines corpus-based research with sophisticated statistical analysis and has produced a methodology which can be used to show to what extent any texts are similar or different. Any text can be given a score for any dimension, by counting the numbers of occurrences of the linguistic features in the text and weighting them. Biber has also taken this methodology forward into cross-linguistic and diachronic territories (Biber 1992, 2006; Biber and Finegan 1991). His methodological overview of factor analysis can be summarized in four steps:

1. Gather a set of text samples to cover a wide range of language varieties.
2. Identify and count a set of linguistic features which are likely to serve as discriminators for different varieties in each text sample.
3. Perform a factor analysis to identify which linguistic features tend to co-occur in texts. The output is a set of dimensions or factors, each of which carries a weighting for each of the linguistic features.
4. Interpret each dimension and identify what linguistic features and what corresponding communicative functions on the dimension correspond to.

Finegan and Biber (1995) examine *that* and zero complementizers in object and subject complement positions in Late Modern English. The computerized corpus, ARCHER, which contains approximately 1.7 million words, consists of English texts from ten registers taken from seven periods between 1650 and 1990. Table 6.8 displays the amount of texts analyzed in each register and period.

In their diachronic analysis of part of ARCHER, limiting the description to three registers of British English (letters, sermons, and medical articles) and to a set of verbs (*say, tell* and *know*), they found that throughout the period, clauses with conjunction *that* were preferred to those with zero (Finegan and Biber 1995: 247), especially in the sermons and medicine registers; they contrast their results with studies of present-day English. They also found that discourse factors (such as the subject of the matrix verb, that of the complement clause, intervening elements between the matrix clause, and the subject of the complement clause) were historically relevant to the choice of link.

Table 6.8.   Texts, registers and periods analyzed (adapted from Finegan and Biber 1995: 245)

	1650–1699	1700–1749	1750–1799	1800–1849	1850–1899	1900–1949	1950–1990	*Total*
Sermons	5245	5246	5245	5245	5245	5245	5245	36716
Medicine	8014	17234	7110	26639	32558	20807	18890	131252
Letters	13332	18693	13378	15307	12032	13463	12709	98914
Total	26591	41173	25733	47191	49835	39515	36844	266882

2.2   *Comparing varieties of English: past and present*

The Brown and the LOB corpora made possible the first corpus-based comparative study of equivalent varieties of American and British English, even though they represent only a selection of written genre types. Comparative studies based on these corpora have tended to find fewer grammatical differences between these varieties than many people would have expected. Apart from phonological differences, which cannot be compared in these two corpora of written texts, the main differences are in lexis and spelling.

Hofland and Johansson (1982) studied word frequencies in British and American English, using the Brown and the LOB corpora to identify words that are more typical of one variety of English than the other. Table 6.9 shows that the 25 most

Table 6.9.   Twenty-five most frequent words in the Brown and LOB corpora

Brown Corpus			LOB Corpus		
Rank	Word	Frequency	Rank	Word	Frequency
1	the	69970	1	the	68368
2	of	36410	2	of	35806
3	and	28854	3	and	27908
4	to	26154	4	to	26906
5	a	23363	5	a	23274
6	in	21345	6	in	21373
7	that	10594	7	that	11385
8	is	10102	8	is	10993
9	was	9815	9	it	10505
10	he	9542	10	was	10500
11	for	9489	11	for	9315
12	it	8760	12	he	9078
13	with	7290	13	as	7339
14	as	7251	14	be	7205
15	his	6996	15	with	7199
16	on	6742	16	on	7052
17	be	6376	17	I	6854
18	at	5377	18	his	6271
19	by	5307	19	at	6052
20	I	5180	20	by	5838
21	this	5146	21	had	5391
22	had	5131	22	this	5290
23	not	4610	23	not	5157
24	are	4394	24	from	4995
25	but	4381	25	but	4665

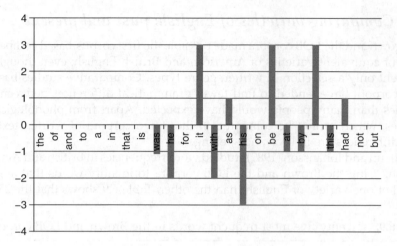

Figure 6.1.   Usage-rank differences between the 25 most frequent words: Brown *versus* LOB

frequent words in both varieties are identical, except for *are*, which does not appear in the LOB corpus, and *from*, which is absent in the Brown.

Further differences are found in the rank ordering of these 25 words. A positive value in the graph (Figure 6.1) indicates that the word is ranked higher in usage in the British variety (LOB) – *it*, *as*, *be*, *I*, and *had* – whereas negative figures signify the opposite: higher usage-ranked in American English (Brown), as in the case of *was*, *he*, *with*, *his*, *at*, *by*, and *this*. We can also perform an analysis to measure the similarity between the 25 most used words in the two corpora: a Spearman rank correlation coefficient measure[8]. Since the rankings for the Brown and the LOB corpus are very similar, the Spearman correlation between them is *0.9787*, nearly 1. It could be concluded that both written English varieties are virtually identical with respect to the rank-usage of the 25 most used words.

If we contrast the frequencies of these top 25 words (Figure 6.2), we find that written British English (LOB) resorts more often to *to*, *in*, *that*, *is*, *it*, *as*, *on*, *be*, *at*, *by*, *I*, *this*, *had*, *not*, and *but*; while written American English uses *the*, *of*, *and*, *a*, *was*, *he*, *for*, *with*, and *his* more frequently. Particularly striking are the overuses in British English of *it* and *I*, though American English uses the definite article *the* far more. Another interesting finding is that the total sums of the 25 most frequent words in both varieties are respectively 338 579 (Brown) and 344 719 (LOB). This means that the top 25 words make up 33.85% of the texts/corpus in American English, compared to 34.47% in British English. That is to say, the written British English of the LOB resorts more often to word repetition of these high frequency words: on average each of them is repeated 13 788 times in British English, compared to 13 543 times in American English.

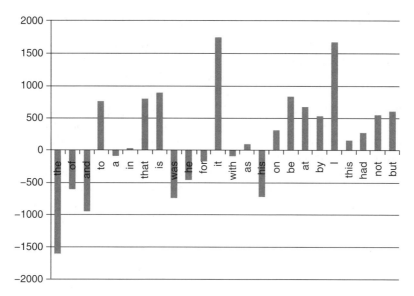

Figure 6.2. Frequency differences between the 25 most used words: Brown *versus* LOB

Hofland and Johansson (1982) have used the chi-squared test as well as Yule's difference coefficient[9] to find vocabulary differences between American English and British English. Some words with high difference coefficients in the LOB (British English) are *accommodation, acquaintances, advertisement, afterwards, alderman, amongst, barrister(s), beforehand, booklet, borough(s), borstal, castle, chap(s), cheque, cinema(s), commonwealth, constable, constituency, councillor(s), cricket,* and *cupboard* among many others. The Brown corpus (American English) exhibited high coefficients for words like *accommodations, afterward, ain't, apartment(s), assignment(s), attorney, auto, automobile(s), barbecue, baseball, basement, billion(s), boost, bulletin, businessman, cafeteria, calendar, campus, carryover, cents, chores, closet, commerce, confederate, congress(ional), congressman, cop(s), cowboy,* and *current.*

Leech and Fallon (1992) also compared the Brown and LOB corpus, analyzing the words used in American and British English, in an attempt to find possible social, political, and cultural differences between the two varieties. They showed that the frequencies of words from everyday domains in the Brown and the LOB corpora mirror the importance of certain concepts in American and British culture. Words concerned with firearms such as *bullet(s), gun(s), rifle(s)* or *shot*, for example, were found to occur much more frequently in Brown than in LOB, and this can certainly be said to reflect the greater interest in this domain in the USA. Leech and Fallon (1992: 30) also pointed out that "the American corpus appears to be more extreme in its 'masculinity' than the British corpus: *he, boy,* and *man* are more fully represented in Brown, whereas *she, girl,* and *woman* are more fully represented in LOB".

2.3   *Analyzing variation in genres, text types and topics*

Genre categories are determined on the basis of external criteria relating to the speaker's purpose and topic; they are assigned on the basis of use rather than on the basis of form (Biber 1988: 170), whereas text types refer to classes of texts that are grouped on the basis of similarities in linguistic form, irrespective of their genre classifications (Biber 1988: 206). Texts from biographies, press reportages, and academic prose might therefore be similar in having a narrative linguistic form and might be grouped together as a single text type, even though they represent three different genres.

Linguistic corpora allow researchers not only to identify ways in which regional or national varieties of English differ from each other, as seen above, but also to study the stylistic distinctiveness of texts from the point of view of different genres and text typology. It is possible to consider groupings of texts that are derived on the basis of linguistic features.

The *Helsinki Corpus of English Texts* was the first historical corpus of English and is one of the most widely used historical corpora of English. It is a structured multi-genre diachronic corpus, which includes text samples, classified by period, from Old, Middle, and Early Modern English. Each sample is preceded by a list of parameter codes giving information on the text and its author. The Corpus is especially useful in the study of the change of linguistic features over long periods. It can be used as a diagnostic corpus giving general information of the occurrence of forms, structures, and lexemes in different periods of English. This information can be supplemented by evidence yielded by more specialized and focused historical corpora, such as ARCHER (*A Representative Corpus of Historical English Registers*). ARCHER is a multi-genre corpus of British and American English covering the period 1650–1999, first constructed by Douglas Biber and Edward Finegan in the 1990s. A number of slightly different versions have been widely used for research on the history of English, up to ARCHER 2 of 2004–5. The current version is known as ARCHER 3.1 and was completed in the summer of 2006. Over the period 2008–11 there will be a new phase of correction, expansion, and tagging, known as ARCHER 3.2.[10]

Among the many quantitative techniques that can be used for analyzing variation in genres and text types are the chi-squared test, Yule's distinctive coefficient, correlation analysis, and factor analysis. We already considered factor analysis in connection with Biber's (1988) research on spoken and written registers in English.

Biber and Finegan (1991) showed that English genres can also be defined or characterized linguistically, not just notionally and subjectively. They used factor analysis to reveal significant linguistic differences between genres and text types. Biber (1993) found, for example, that relative clauses are frequent in official documents and formal speeches, but rare in conversations, while adverbial clauses are frequently used in conversations but hardly at all in press reporting or official documents. Using multidimensional analysis, it is possible to detect systematic differences in the co-occurrence of linguistic patterns in language. The development of genre-based corpora (Brown, LOB, BNC, etc.) has enabled significant research to be carried out involving analyses of discoursal, pragmatic, rhetorical, and genre features (Adel 2006; Breivega *et al.* 2002; Hewings 2001; Hyland 1998; Perez-Llantada and Ferguson 2006; Poos and Simpson 2002; Reppen *et al.* 2002; Simpson and Swales 2001). These studies have implicitly or explicitly shown that the structure and functions of grammar patterns in specialized discourses repre-sent a "fundamentally important part of writers' and speakers' communicative repertoire" (Biber *et al.* 2004: 400).

Oakes (2009: 170–76) used cluster analysis, a type of automatic categorization, in order to group the various genres in the LOB corpus according to the rankings of the most common 89 words in LOB in each genre. The object of cluster analysis is to sort cases (people, things, events, etc.) into groups, or clusters, so that the degree of association is strong between members of the same cluster and weak between members of different clusters. Oakes found that the most similar pair of genres is fiction and romance. The next most similar pair is mystery-and-detective-fiction and adventure-and-western-fiction. In turn, these four genres group together to form a closely related cluster quite distinct from all other genres (press reportage, press editorial, press reviews, humor, etc.).

3. Some Final Remarks

The increasing accessibility of linguistic corpora and the belief that theory must be based on language *as it is* have placed empirical research once again at the forefront of linguistics. The immediate implication of this is that linguists will increasingly demand the use of corpora and statistics in their research.

In this chapter we have tried to examine and exemplify how studies in linguis-tic variation and change can benefit from linguistic corpora and corpus-based investigation. In addition, we have tried to illustrate how quantitative methods go hand in hand with corpus-based approaches, contributing most fruitfully to linguistic analysis and research in variation and change. We have not tried to offer an exhaustive presentation of all the statistical techniques available to linguistics, but to demonstrate the contribution that statistics can and should make to corpus-based studies in the areas of linguistic variation and change.

We have explored some methods and techniques for distinguishing between written and spoken language, regional/national varieties, genres, and text types and topics. We hope we have demonstrated the potential of corpora in the study of linguistic variation and change.

Some readers might be interested in planning their linguistic research using corpora, and several of the techniques introduced here might help their work in similar areas and topics. Furthermore, a quick glance at other corpus-based studies might reveal new potential corpus-based applications within the domain of lin-guistic variation and change.

We end this chapter by reminding the reader that corpus-based linguistic research is only as good as the corpora on which it is based, and grammatical or lexical analysis in linguistic variation and change are only as good as the analytical tools, such as taggers, parsers, and concordancers, which are developed to analyze them (Knowles *et al.* 1996).

NOTES

1   Australia, Canada, East Africa, Fiji, Ghana, Great Britain, Hong Kong, India, Ireland, Jamaica, Malaysia, Malta, New Zealand, Nigeria, Pakistan, Philippines, Singapore, South Africa, Sri Lanka, Trinidad and Tobago, and USA.
2   Bauer (2002: 111–112) provides a short description of electronic corpora. For a more exhaustive list of corpora available see http://www2.lib.udel.edu/subj/ling/internet.htm#corpora [accessed October 13, 2011].
3   The *Chi-squared test* is a widely used statistical test for the comparison of count data, such as word frequencies. It can be extended for comparisons of more than two texts, samples, or corpora (see, for example: Hofland and Johansson 1982; Oakes and Farrow 2007; Cantos *forthcoming*).
4   The chi-squared test can be used as long as the expected values are all five or more (for more details, see Rayson *et al.* 2004).
5   The volume is available at http://www.helsinki.fi/varieng/journal/volumes/01/ [accessed October 13, 2011].
6   For more research on spoken *versus* written English, see also Biber and Finegan (1986), Chafe (1986), Greenbaum and Nelson (1995), Butler (1997), Conrad and Biber (2000), and Biber (2006).
7   For a general overview of all features and dimensions, see *Summary of Factorial Structure* (Biber 1988: 102–103).
8   A correlation coefficient is given as a number between −1 and +1. Coefficients close to ±1 mean that two sets of scores have perfect positive/negative correlation. Scores closer to zero indicate a weaker correlation, while a score of zero means that there is no correlation at all between the two sets of scores.
9   Also known as Yule's distinctiveness coefficient, this is a simple difference coefficient to indicate whether a word might be considered to be over- or under-represented in a corpus (for more details, see Johansson 1980: 26).
10 For a list of recent publications that have made use of ARCHE,R see http://www.llc.manchester.ac.uk/research/projects/archer/publications/ [accessed October 13, 2011].

REFERENCES

Ädel, A. (2006) *Metadiscourse in L1 and L2 English*, John Benjamins, Amsterdam.

Aijmer, K. and Stenström, A.-B. (2004) *Discourse Patterns in Spoken and Written Corpora*, John Benjamins, Amsterdam.

Altenberg, B. (1994) On the functions of *such* in spoken and written English. In N. Oostdijk and P. de Haan (eds.), *Corpus-based Research into Language*, Rodopi, Amsterdam, pp. 223–40.

Archer, D., McEnery, T., Rayson, P., and Hardie, A. (2003) Developing an automated semantic analysis system for Early Modern English. In D. Archer, P. Rayson, A. Wilson and T. McEnery (eds.), *Proceedings of the Corpus Linguistics 2003 conference*, Lancaster, UCREL, Lancaster University, pp. 22–31.

Archer, D. and Culpeper, J. (2003) Sociopragmatic annotation: new directions and possibilities in historical corpus linguistics. In A. Wilson, P. Rayson, and A. McEnery (eds.), *Corpus Linguistics by the Lune: Studies in Honour of Geoffrey Leech*, Peter Lang, Frankfurt, pp. 37–58.

Bauer, L. (2002) Inferring variation and change from public corpora. In J.K. Chambers, P. Trudgill, and N. Schilling-Estes (eds.), *The Handbook of Language Variation and Change*, Blackwell, Oxford, pp. 97–114.

Beal, J., Corrigan, K., Smith, N., and Rayson, P. (2007) Writing the vernacular: transcribing and tagging the Newcastle Electronic Corpus of Tyneside English. In A. Meurman-Solin and A. Nurmi (eds.).

Biber, D. (1988) *Variation across Speech and Writing*. Cambridge University Press, Cambridge.

Biber, D. (1992) On the complexity of discourse complexity: a multidimensional analysis. *Discourse Processes* 15: 133–63.

Biber, D. (1993) The multi-dimensional approach to linguistic analyses of genre variation: an overview of methodology and findings. *Computers and the Humanities* 26: 331–45.

Biber, D. (2006) *University Language. A Corpus-based Study of Spoken and Written Language*, John Benjamins, Amsterdam.

Biber, D. and Burges, J. (2000) Historical change in the language use of women and men: gender differences in dramatic dialogue. *Journal of English Linguistics* 28: 21–37.

Biber, D. and Finegan, E. (1986) An initial typology of English text types. In J. Aarts and W. Meijs (eds.), *Corpus Linguistics II: New Studies in the Analysis and Exploitation of Computer Corpora*, Rodopi, Amsterdam, pp. 19–46.

Biber, D. and Finegan, E. (1991) On the exploitation of computerized corpora in variation studies. In K. Aijmer and B. Altenberg (eds.), *English Corpus Linguistics: Studies in Honour of Jan Svartvik*, Longman, London, pp. 204–20.

Biber, D. and Reppen, R. (1998) Comparing native and learner perspectives on English grammar: a study of complement clauses. In S. Granger (ed.), *Learner English on Computer*, Addison Wesley Longman, London, pp. 145–58.

Biber, D., Conrad, S., and Cortes, V. (2004) *If you look at . . . : lexical bundles in university teaching and textbooks. Applied Linguistics* 25: 371–405.

Breivega, K., Dahl, T., and Flottum, K. (2002) Traces of self and others in research articles. A comparative pilot study of English, French and Norwegian research articles in medicine, economics and linguistics. *International Journal of Applied Linguistics* 12 (2): 218–39.

Butler, C. (1997) Repeated word combinations in spoken and written text: some implications for functional grammar. In C.S. Butler, J.H. Connolly, R.A. Gatward, and R.M. Vismans (eds.), *A Fund of Ideas: Recent Developments in Functional Grammar*, IFOTT, Amsterdam University, Amsterdam, pp. 60–77.

Cantos, P. (forthcoming) *Statistical Methods in Language and Linguistic Research*, Equinox, London.

Cantos, P. and Sánchez, A. (2000) Introduction. *Cuadernos de Filología Inglesa* 9 (1): 1–4.

Chafe, W. (1986) Evidentiality in English conversation and academic writing. In W. Chafe and J. Nichols (eds.), *Evidentiality: The Linguistic Coding of Epistemology*, Ablex, Norwood, NJ, pp. 261–72.

Collins, P. (1991) The modals of obligation and necessity in Australian English. In K. Aijmer and B. Altenberg (eds.), *English Corpus Linguistics: Studies in Honour of Jan Svartvik*, Longman, London, pp. 145–65.

Conde-Silvestre, J.C. (2007) *Sociolingüística histórica*, Gredos, Madrid.

Conrad, S. and Biber, D. (2000) Adverbial marking of stance in speech and writing. In S. Hunston and G. Thompson (eds.), *Evaluation in Text*, Oxford University Press, Oxford, pp. 56–73.

Culpeper, J. and Kytö, M. (2000) Data in historical pragmatics: spoken interaction (re)cast as writing. *Journal of Historical Pragmatics* 1 (2): 175–99.

Dollinger, S. (2008) Taking permissible shortcuts? Limited evidence, heuristic reasoning and the modal auxiliaries in Early Canadian English. In S.M. Fitzmaurice and D. Minkova (eds.), *Studies in the History of the English Language IV. Empirical and Analytical Advances in the Study of English Language Change*, Mouton de Gruyter, Berlin, pp. 357–85.

Feldman, A. and Arshavskaya, K. (2007) English and Russian event annotation: a pilot study. In A. Meurman-Solin and A. Nurmi (eds.).

Finegan, E. and Biber, D. (1995) *That* and zero complementisers in Late Modern English: exploring ARCHER from 1650–1990. In B. Aarts and C.F. Meyer (eds.), *The Verb in Contemporary English. Theory and Description*, Cambridge University Press, Cambridge, pp. 241–57.

Fries, U. (1998) Dialogue in instructional texts. In R. Borgmeier, H. Grabes, and A.H. Jucker (eds.), *Historical Pragmatics*, reprinted from *Anglistentag 1997 Giessen. Proceedings*, Wissenschaftlicher Verlag, Trier, pp. 85–96.

Greenbaum, S. and Nelson, G. (1995) Clause relationships in spoken and written English. *Functions of Language* 2: 1–21.

Hewings, M. (ed.) (2001) *Academic Writing in Context: Implications and Applications*, University of Birmingham Press, Birmingham.

Hofland, K. and Johansson, S. (1982) *Word Frequencies in British and American English*, Longman, London.

Huber, M. (2007) The *Old Bailey Proceedings*, 1674–1834. Evaluating and annotating a sorpus of eighteenth and nineteenth-century spoken English. In A. Meurman-Solin and A. Nurmi (eds.).

Hundt, M. (1998) *New Zealand English Grammar: Fact or Fiction?* John Benjamins, Amsterdam.

Hyland, K. (1998) *Hedging in Scientific Research Articles*, John Benjamins, Amsterdam.

Johansson, S. (1980) The LOB Corpus of British English Texts: presentation and comments. *ALLC Journal* 1: 25–36.

Johansson, S. and Norheim, E.H. (1988) The subjunctive in British and American English. *ICAME Journal* 12: 27–36.

Kennedy, G. (1998) *An Introduction to Corpus Linguistics*. Longman, London.

Knowles, G., Wichmann, A., and Alderson, P. (eds.) 1996) *Working with Speech*. Longman, London.

Kyto, M. and Walker, T. (2003) The linguistic study of Early Modern English speech-related texts. How 'bad' can 'bad' data be? *Journal of English Linguistics* 31(3): 221–48.

Labov, W. (1972) *Sociolinguistic Patterns*, Blackwell, Oxford.

Labov, W. (1994) *Principles of Linguistic Change. Vol 1: Internal Factors*, Blackwell, Oxford.

Labov, W. (2008) Quantitative reasoning in linguistics. http://www.ling.upenn.edu/~wlabov/Papers/QRL.pdf [accessed October 13, 2011].

Leech, G. and Fallon, R. (1992) Computer corpora: what do they tell us about culture? *ICAME Journal*, 16: 1–22.

Löfberg, L., Archer, D., Piao, S. *et al.* (2003) Porting an English semantic tagger to the Finnish language. In D. Archer, P. Rayson, A. Wilson, and T. McEnery (eds.), *Proceedings of the Corpus Linguistics 2003 Conference*, UCREL, Lancaster University, pp. 457–64.

McEnery, T. and Wilson. A. (1996) *Corpus Linguistics*, Edinburgh University Press, Edinburgh.

Meurman-Solin, A. (2007) Annotating variational space over time. In A. Meurman-Solin and A. Nurmi (eds).

Meurman-Solin, A. and Nurmi, A. (eds.) (2007) *Annotating variation and change*. Research Unit for Variation, Contacts and Change in English (VARIENG), University of Helsinki. http://www.helsinki.fi/varieng/journal/volumes/01/index.html [accessed October 13, 2011].

Meyer, C.F. (2002) *English Corpus Linguistics*. Cambridge University Press, Cambridge.

Nevalainen, T. (1999) Making the best use of 'bad' data: evidence for socio-linguistic variation in Early Modern English.

Neuphilologische Mitteilungen 100(4): 499–533.

Nevalainen, T. and Raumolin-Brunberg, H. (1996) Social stratification in Tudor English? In D. Britton (ed.), *English Historical Linguistics. Papers from the 8th International Conference on English Historical Linguistics*, John Benjamins, Amsterdam, pp. 303–26.

Nevalainen, T. and Raumolin-Brunberg, H. (2003) *Historical Sociolinguistics. Language Change in Tudor and Stuart England*, Longman Pearson Education, London.

Nurmi, A. (2007) Employing and elaborating annotation for the study of modality. In A. Meurman-Solin and A. Nurmi (eds.).

Oakes, M. (2009) Corpus linguistics and language variation. In P. Baker (ed.), *Contemporary Corpus Linguistics*, Continuum, London, pp. 159–83.

Oakes, M. and Farrow, M. (2007) Use of the chi-squared test to examine vocabulary differences in English-language corpora representing seven different countries. *Literary and Linguistic Computing* 22: 85–99.

Palander-Collin, M. (2007) What kind of corpus annotation is needed in sociopragmatic research? In A. Meurman-Solin and A. Nurmi (eds.).

Perez-Llantada, C. and Ferguson, G. (eds.) (2006) *English as a Glocalization Phenomenon. Observations from a Linguistic Microcosm,* Prensas Universitarias de Valencia, Valencia.

Poos, D. and Simpson, R. (2002) Cross-linguistic comparison of hedging: some findings from the Michigan Corpus of Academic Spoken English. In R. Reppen, S.M. Fitzmaurice, and D. Biber (eds.), pp. 3–23.

Quirk, R., Greenbaum, S., Leech, G., and Svartvik, J. (1985) *A Comprehensive Grammar of the English Language*, Longman, London.

Rayson P., Berridge, D., and Francis, B. (2004) Extending the Cochran Rule for the comparison of word frequencies between corpora. In *Internationales d'Analyse Statistique des Données Textuelles (JADT 2004)*, Louvain-la-Neuve, Belgium, pp. 926–36.

Reppen, R., Fitzmaurice, S.M., and Biber, D. (eds.) (2002) *Using Corpora to Explore Linguistic Variation*, John Benjamins, Amsterdam.

Simpson, R. and Swales, J. (eds.) (2001) *Corpus Linguistics in North America: Selections from the 1999 Symposium.* University of Michigan Press, Ann Arbor.

Stenroos, M. (2007) Sampling and annotation in the Middle English Grammar Project. In A. Meurman-Solin and A. Nurmi (eds.).

Summers, D. (1992) English in the raw. *Modern English* 1 (4): 14–16.

LINGUISTIC CORPORA CITED

ARCHER = *A Representative Corpus of Historical English Registers* (1990–. First complied by D. Biber and E. Finegan. Now managed as an ongoing project by a consortium of participants at fourteen universities in seven countries. http://www.llc.manchester.ac.uk/research/projects/archer [accessed October 13, 2011].

BNC = *British National Corpus* (1991–94) Compiled by Oxford University Computing Services, Oxford University. www.natcorp.ox.ac.uk [accessed October 13, 2011].

Brown Corpus = *Brown University Standard Corpus of Present-Day American English* (1961–63) Compiled by H. Kučera and W.N. Francis. Department of Linguistics, Brown University, Providence, Rhode Island. http://khnt.aksis.uib.no/icame/manuals/brown [accessed October 13, 2011].

CEEC = *Corpus of Early English Correspondence* (1998) Compiled by T. Nevalainen, H. Raumolin-Brunberg, J. Keränen, M. Nevala, A. Nurmi, and M. Palander-Collin Department of English, University of

Helsinki. http://www.helsinki.fi/varieng/ CoRD/corpora/CEEC/index.html [accessed October 13, 2011].

CED = *Corpus of English Dialogues, 1560–1760* (1996–2006) Compiled by M. Kytö and J. Culpeper. Swedish Research Council/ Vetenskapsrådet, the English Department at Uppsala University, the Arts and Humanities Research Board, UK, and the British Academy. http://www.helsinki.fi/ varieng/CoRD/corpora/CED/index.html [accessed October 13, 2011].

CSC = *Corpus of Scottish Correspondence, 1500–1715* (2000–7) Compiled by A. Meurman-Solin. Department of English, University of Helsinki. http:// www.eng.helsinki.fi/varieng/csc/manual [accessed October 13, 2011].

Helsinki Corpus of English Texts (1984–96) Compiled by M. Rissanen, M. Kytö, L. Kahlas-Tarkka, M. Kilpiö, S. Nevanlinna, I. Taavitsainen, T. Nevalainen, and H. Raumolin-Brunberg. Department of English, University of Helsinki. http:// www.helsinki.fi/varieng/CoRD/corpora/ HelsinkiCorpus/generalintro.html [accessed October 13, 2011].

ICE = *International Corpus of English* (1990–) Project Director G. Nelson. Department of English, The Chinese University of Hong Kong, Shatin, Hong Kong. http:// ice-corpora.net/ice/index.htm [accessed October 13, 2011].

LOB = *Lancaster-Oslo/Bergen Corpus* (1970–78) Compiled at the Universities of Lancaster, Oslo, and the Norwegian Computing Centre for the Humanities at Bergen. http://khnt.hit.uib.no/icame/manuals/ lobman [accessed October 13, 2011].

PCEEC = *Parsed Corpus of Early English Correspondence* (2006) The part-of-speech tagging of the PCEEC was carried out by A. Nurmi (University of Helsinki); the syntactic annotation by A. Taylor (University of York); and the sociolinguistic information for each correspondent was provided by the Helsinki team, and by A. Taylor, assisted by J. Close at York. http://www. helsinki.fi/varieng/CoRD/corpora/CEEC/ pceec.html [accessed October 13, 2011].

Sociopragmatic Corpus, 1640–1760. Compiled by J. Culpeper. Department of Linguistics and English Language, Lancaster University.

7   Editing the Medieval Manuscript in its Social Context

NILA VÁZQUEZ AND TERESA MARQUÉS-AGUADO[1]

1. Introduction

Tim Machan and Charles Scott, in the introduction to their edited volume *English in its social context. Essays in historical sociolinguistics* (1992), point to the methodological differences between general linguistics and sociolinguistics; one of these differences, in their view, is that the former focuses on "formal elements of language and their combinations", that is, 'the code' itself, whereas the latter explores "variation in the forms of the code" (1992: 8). Hence, as Finegan explains (1992: v):

> Its special focus, to be sure, is on the relationships between language and society, and its principal concerns address linguistic variation across social groups and across the range of communicative situations in which men and women deploy their verbal repertoires.

The various types of social variation may be due to differences in the age, sex, cultural level, occupation, ethnic background, and geographical provenance of the speaker. All of us belong to different subgroups of our society at the same time and these groups constantly modify the patterns of the language used in the community. As Chomsky stated, linguistic theory deals with "an 'ideal speaker-listener' in a 'completely homogeneous community'" (1965: 3) but, unfortunately for linguists, this type of ideal speaker does not exist and, more often than not,

The Handbook of Historical Sociolinguistics, First Edition. Edited by Juan Manuel Hernández-Campoy and Juan Camilo Conde-Silvestre.
© 2014 John Wiley & Sons, Ltd. Published 2014 by John Wiley & Sons, Ltd.

these 'completely homogeneous' communities are not easy to find either. In fact, speakers "misspeak," as explained by Machan and Scott, in the sense that mistakes may appear either inadvertently or furnishing an utterance with a "special effect or solidarity" (1992: 9). The first possibility is even clearer when dealing with manuscripts, because, as instances of written rather than of oral production, any mistakes are preserved on the folio, in most cases unconsciously. Several factors such as those mentioned above must therefore be taken into account in the socio-linguistic analysis of a particular sample of language in order to understand the way in which it was produced.

When dealing with historical sociolinguistics, further problems arise, as, on many occasions, it is impossible to ascertain who was responsible for the samples we have to analyze and, consequently, sociolinguistic information about the type of text produced cannot be retrieved, but can be sensed, as discussed later (section 3.3). In this line, Labov mentions the "bad data" problem (1994: 11) since, in his own words, "[h]istorical linguistics can then be thought of as the art of making the best use of bad data" (1994: 11). This difficulty is further compounded with the fact that, as Nevalainen and Raumolin-Brunberg have stressed, "the earlier the period, the thinner the coverage" (2003: 6); that is, the earlier we go back in time, the scantier the written records available, and this reduces our chances of provid-ing a full and detailed account in sociolinguistic terms. Indeed, we have to make do exclusively with written records because of the obvious lack of living speakers of past states of the language. Linguistic innovations are more often than not associated with speakers' oral production, since any changes in the language are commonly first perceived in the oral variety and then come to be reflected in written records (Nevalainen and Raumolin-Brunberg 2003: 2). It is also true that "written language tends to be message-oriented and is deprived of the social and situational contexts in which speech events occur" (Milroy 1992: 45; also in Conde Silvestre 2007: 36), and this has led scholars to consider that 'speechlike genres' should be preferred over traditionally written genres for historical sociolinguistics (we return to this point in section 3.2. with regard to sociolinguistic studies). Finally, and to complicate things even more, the records that have come down to us (be they fragmentary or complete texts) are the outcome of mere accidents of history that are clearly beyond the researcher's control (Milroy 1992: 45; Toon 1992: 30). This may mean that not all genres or varieties are equally represented, nor all social strata evenly represented due to the stratified patterns of literacy in the Middle Ages: whereas members of the upper ranks had access to education and could read and write, those from the lower orders could rarely do so, and gender also played a major role (Nevalainen and Raumolin-Brunberg 1996: 28–29).

Instead of focusing on the 'bad data' problem, more attention should be paid to making the best possible use of the extant material by means of "systematicity in data collection, extensive background reading and good philological work" (Nevalainen and Raumolin-Brunberg 2003: 26). In fact, historical sociolinguistic studies are not deprived of positive aspects. The most relevant is that historical data cannot be manipulated by the researcher, nor can the speaker be influenced by the process of data collection, a problem that has been traditionally referred to as 'the observer's paradox' (Kastovsky and Mettinger 2000: vii).[2] The surviving texts represent genuine communication at a certain stage of the language we are examining. They are as precious for historical linguists as small fossils preserved in amber for biologists, since they allow us to examine the language exactly as it was at a particular stage of its development.

Sometimes, trying to determine the socio-cultural features of a certain manuscript is a losing battle. In contrast, on other occasions, even though we do not have that information to begin with, its authorship, provenance, and other details can be determined after a thorough analysis of its language, style, handwriting, and other features, as explained in section 3. On other occasions, we cannot identify a specific individual as the author of a text, but we are able to locate the author within a particular community at a particular time, as explained in section 3.3. Very frequently, this information is sufficient for a systematic classification of the contents of the work under analysis from different points of view, including the sociolinguistic one.

Following Schneider's classification, the written records used in sociolinguistic studies can be classified into (2002: 72–73): 1) recorded (e.g. trial records), 2) recalled (e.g. travelers' records), 3) imagined (e.g. letters), 4) observed (e.g. utterances cited as characteristic of a certain speech) and 5) invented (e.g. literary works). If we think of the manuscripts dating from the Middle Ages that can be found all over Europe, most of them would belong to categories one, three and five. The focus of this chapter will be mainly on manuscripts that contain these three types of texts, although reflections on other types of texts (such as scientific or legal texts) in sociolinguistic terms will also be made, despite falling outside the scope of Schneider's classification (see also Chapters 8–11 in this *Handbook*).

Schneider (2002: 69) has criticized the works of Milroy (1992) and Romaine (1982) for emphasizing the "socio-political context of language evolution," instead of carrying out a detailed analysis of the particular forms of language at that time. It is true that earlier studies did not pay much attention to the individuals behind the texts and their particular use of the language, tending to comment on the general socio-cultural aspects of the work under analysis. However, this tendency has changed in recent decades, the work of Nevalainen and Raumolin-Brunberg (1996) providing a good example. In their work, the relationship between class stratification and linguistic variation can be clearly observed. With corpora such as the *Helsinki Corpus of English Texts* and the *Corpus of Early English Correspondence*, where a large number of authors are identified,[3] the historical sociolinguist can work more effectively, as the language in the samples can be analyzed by taking into account different social factors (see section 4 on the potential of corpora for sociolinguistic research, and also Chapter 6 in this *Handbook*). Moreover, there is more opportunity for comparative research.

The task of the editors, as we will see below (section 2), turns out to be crucial in any type of historical sociolinguistic study, even though their work is too often neglected. We tend to think of a text as it appears in a certain modern volume but we need to take into account that the 'readable' version we use was initially produced in the Middle Ages and was preserved in a manuscript which an editor had to 'rework' for us to be able to use it now. For instance, as Nevalainen and Raumolin-Brunberg state, "[t]hanks to the editors of letter collections [...] it is possible to identify individual letter writers, trace their social backgrounds [...] in other words, the information without which sociolinguistic analyses and interpretations could not be made" (2003: 29).

As we have already outlined, this chapter is structured into two main sections with minor subsections: a theoretical account of the history of editing procedures and the types of editions available, and a practical approach to various questions where editorial practices, manuscript studies, and sociolinguistic concerns come simultaneously into play.

2. A Brief History of Scholarly Editing and Types of Editions, and their Implications for Historical Sociolinguistic Studies

This section presents an abridged history of editing, as well as an account of various editorial practices. This is relevant insofar as these aspects may help to explain the main features and conventions of the editions available today, and why these are suitable (or not) for particular types of studies, including sociolinguistic ones.

Two basic concepts in the early history of manuscript editing are *emendatio* and *recensio*. The former implies the correction of the copy text, while the latter has to do with the correction of that text by taking into account all the variants in other witnesses and their textual affiliation. Until the eighteenth century, the humanists relied only on *emendatio* without *recensio*. Sometimes, this correction was made following the readings in another copy – *emendatio ope codicum* – but, in most cases, it followed the editor's own conjectures – *emendatio ope ingenii* or *divinatio*. The latter type of approach has been found to be particularly troublesome, especially when trying to use this edited material for subsequent studies, as explained later in this and the next section.

Although Karl Lachmann, who lived in the nineteenth century, is frequently regarded as the father of modern textual criticism, Friedrich August Wolf (1794) was the first philologist to demand editions based on solid diplomatic foundations (see below for a definition), as early as in the eighteenth century.[4] In fact, Lachmann admits that he follows the work of Immanuel Bekker,[5] who was one of Wolf's most talented pupils. These three scholars opted for a *recensio sine interpretatione*, that is, relying exclusively on the manuscript itself and leaving aside the editor's interpretations.

In the twentieth century, with philologists such as Bédier (1928) and Pasquali (1952) and, later on, Bowers (1966) and his followers, a balanced situation emerges. The editor's judgment is taken into consideration again, as long as this 'judgment' is used to evaluate all the different readings in the texts. Thus, in addition to the aforementioned *emendatio* and *recensio*, the scholar has to conform to the *examinatio* of the variants and the *selectio* of the variant which might be closer to the author's original archetype.

In the twenty-first century, we can find examples of good diplomatic and critical editions together with simple electronic editions – mere transcriptions of previous editions – or comprehensive digital editions. In the age of computers and other innovations such as digital photography and x-ray machines, the modern editor can offer the reader a large amount of information, so we find scholarly digital editions[6] which include digital images of the manuscripts, links to translations, notes, and glossaries, links to audiovisual material and many other features.[7] All this material can be stored on a CD-Rom, a DVD or the internet.

When dealing with medieval manuscripts, it must be borne in mind that the production sequence of a text is as important as the authorial one. The figures of the scribe and the medieval editor who would supervise the work of the copyist are as important as the author, for the final output may contain many features that belong to the former and not to the latter. Indeed, the concept of *authorship* during the Middle Ages was not as well established as it is today (Burrow 1982: 36), and authors borrowed freely from others' works.[8] The problem of authorship was further exacerbated by the anonymity of most of the copies that have come down to us. These medieval practices accounted, for instance, for conflated texts.

One of the duties of the modern editor is to try to separate this material and offer it to the reader for further analysis. Following the *Guidelines for Editors of Scholarly Editions* offered by the Modern Language Association's Committee on Scholarly Editions, the reliability of an edition is based on five basic principles: 'accuracy,' 'adequacy,' 'appropriateness,' 'consistency' and 'explicitness,' and all of them must be observed by an editor who wants to produce a 'good' edition (http://www.mla.org/resources/documents/rep_scholarly/cse_guidelines).

Scholarly editing follows two main procedures, the first of which (chiefly facsimile editions or diplomatic editions)[9] is typically associated with single documents and texts where one extant copy remains, while the second (mainly best-text editions and critical editions) is concerned with the comparison of sets of documents. Between these two, there is a wide range of intermediate or 'compromise' editions, to the extent that "most modern editions are rightly a compromise between them" (Hudson 1977: 39). In Petti's words (1977: 34), these represent:

> [...] a useful compromise [...] which provides nearly all that a diplomatic transcription would, but in a more continuous process. It gives scope for editorial interpretation while clearly indicating where this has been carried out.

As far as the former is concerned, the work of the editor focuses on the transliteration of the text in the manuscript. In Moorman's words, a diplomatic edition entails "the faithfully transcribed reproduction as in a facsimile of a single [manuscript] including every spelling variant, every mark of punctuation, every scribal error" (1975: 48). This implies that any relevant feature observed in the manuscript should be reflected in the final output.[10] It is important to notice that, in this type of edition, the output contains very little editorial interpretation. As a general rule, the editor does not take any particular editorial decision on the readings of the text apart from those dealing with the recognition of the letters and other features of the volume.[11] There is a choice between transcribing only the text itself or adding some comments and notes with relevant information on particular details of the manuscript. The more complete the description given, the more useful the edition will be for the reader, especially if aspects which may shed light on socio-linguistic concerns are included – be they linguistic, palaeographical, or codico-logical, etc. This type of edition is particularly recommended in cases where there is just one extant copy.[12]

In contrast, we find editions in which a series of manuscripts is involved. Some medieval works appear in many different witnesses, especially those that enjoyed great popularity in their time. A particularly good example of this is *The Canterbury Tales*, by Geoffrey Chaucer, which survives in 84 manuscripts,[13] belonging to different periods and produced by different hands. It is easy to picture the huge number of variants that these different texts offer. When a scholar is faced with a case like this, a plausible course of action is therefore to prepare either a best-text edition or a critical edition, including a great number of its witnesses, at least the most representative.

The main difference between a best-text edition and a critical edition is that the former lacks the *apparatus criticus* with the different readings and the editor tends to stick too closely to the readings offered in his/her copy text. Blecua describes critical editing as "el arte que tiene como fin presentar un texto depurado en lo posible de todos aquellos elementos extraños al autor" (1983: 19–20).[14] Housman also refers to this discipline as an art: "Textual criticism is a science, and, since it comprises recension and emendation, it is also an art" (1921: 68). This art mainly consists of choosing a base text for the edition and then comparing its readings against those in other surviving material to obtain a better text. As Hanna has pointed out (1992: 122):

> [...] one can thus visualize, not An Edition, but a range of use- or interest-driven possible editions. Such plurality becomes justified because it will approximate, through diversity of approach and method, that plurality which is a property of its subject, texts in manuscript.

In this line, Lass's recent article on corpora compilation based on published editions has been a matter of contention, given his opposition to the random use of editions as if they were historical witnesses. His argument revolves around the tenet that edited texts are "dangerous because of the degree to which they are trusted and characteristically regarded as 'data,' worthy of inclusion in historical corpora," in particular those showing emendation, modernization, alteration of word-division or lineation, reconstruction towards an 'archetype' or any other form of 'normalization' (2004: 22). Yet, he concedes that "[m]y objection throughout is to the reconstruction of *texts*, and their subsequent use as witnesses – not to reconstruction as a source of knowledge of earlier language states at 'system' level" (2004: 24). His final proposal comes to be connected to Petti's model of compromise editions, when he asserts that "a responsible source of historical information" would be "nothing less than a presentation which, whatever its analytical apparatus, is unambiguously resolvable into a diplomatic transcription of a source" (2004: 39).

These statements obviously lead us to consider in section 3 the sort of implications derived from using standard, published editions following a wide array of editorial principles, and what aspects of these should be taken into consideration, especially when dealing with historical sociolinguistic research. In addition, the most frequent types of sociolinguistic research already carried out are highlighted, along with possible future lines of research.

3. Medieval Manuscripts and Historical Sociolinguistic Studies

3.1 Introduction

Connected to the idea of 'speechlike genres' and historical sociolinguistics discussed in section 1, it can be argued that past states of the language may pose certain problems to researchers because of their written nature. Yet, Middle English represents (Machan and Scott 1992: 20):

> [...] the embodiment of the qualities of both orality and textuality [...] Middle English, then, is situated between these extremes: an increasing (although still small) number of individuals was literate in English, and written language, in the form of charters, wills, and letters, was beginning to permeate daily life. Nonetheless, primary orality had been a dominant feature of English culture in the very recent past, and so a sometimes uneasy compromise between orality and textuality is one of the distinctive features of language use in the years 1100 to 1500.

It is also true that the assumptions commonly made on the basis of present-day English developments may not apply to past states of the language, or else scholars may not be able to look into them with the material that has finally come down to the present moment (Nevalainen and Raumolin-Brunberg 2003: 11).

3.2 Types of texts

Not many decades ago, scholars tended to concentrate on literary works which, although often valuable for literary critics and useful to a limited extent for traditional linguists, were rarely of any use for sociolinguists. Now, with the increasing number of editions and collections of trial records and letters, as well as corpora compiled with these text-types (whether in isolation or in conjunction with others), historical sociolinguistics is undergoing a revival. These texts offer unlimited possibilities for learning more about social networks, models of social stratification, geographical movements, and dialectal varieties in the Middle Ages.

The rationale for using these text-types is their closeness to speech, given that there is usually a gap between the activation of a particular language change and its reflection on the written language. Likewise, it is also easier to establish a possible correlation between linguistic variables and the personal circumstances of interlocutors (Conde Silvestre 2007: 45). In this line, Kohnen, for example, has also remarked that "[l]etters have proved to be among the few historical genres which are open to sociolinguistic investigations" (2007). Guild certificates, charters, and other legal texts also fall within the standard scope of sociolinguistics, inasmuch as, although their language probably does not reflect many oral features, much background information can be gathered about the informants. For example, Toon has focused on the information, both historical and sociolinguistic, that can be extracted from the charters passed by Mercian kings in terms of the progressive development of the king's authority and of "the resources enabling the official documentation of that authority" (1992: 37). Another example is that of the guild certificates analyzed by Wright. She examines the spellings associated with particular linguistic features employed by various scribes in an attempt to show that differences in the spelling practices of different scribes working in London may reveal how differently people spoke at the time in the City (1999: 181).[15]

These examples show that these text-types are perfect for comparative studies, whether within the same social group or not, taking as variables sex, provenance, social stratum, profession and so on. It is the editor's task to discover as many details as possible about both the text and its author and to offer them to the reader.

Even though letters and legal documents are those that may pontentially lend themselves particularly well to sociolinguistic research, other text-types (such as scientific texts; see Chapter 8 in this *Handbook*) are also worth mentioning when dealing with editing and sociolinguistic studies. All genres or text-types are the product of a community that imposes, perpetuates, or alters features such as the conventions and standard formulae to be used. If the object of study is language itself (be it in the form of dialectal, phonological, or even pragmatic concerns), other text-types are also likely to be used for research. Let us take, for instance, the process of the vernacularization of science witnessed during the late fourteenth and fifteenth centuries in the British Isles. Although for the most part models from classical writing were imported from the Continent, particular conventions also developed in and left their imprint on the texts written in Britain for the British public. This example can be placed in the wider context of the emergence of written norms, particularly in the new genres of the vernacular language.

3.3 Conditions of production and later use of manuscripts

The importance of social factors in the textual production of any medieval work must also be acknowledged. Some texts are the output of a certain *scriptorium* around the country, and they share the same characteristics. If the scribes are the same or at least similar, the texts will show parallel features, not only as regards their physical appearance but also as regards scribal intrusion or editorial amendments.[16] It is true that researchers might not be able to track the name or social background of the particular scribe (or scribes) in charge of producing a particular copy of a text, but work on similar texts (or different witnesses of the same text) might reveal information about possible *scriptoria* devoted to specific text-types. A case in point is the set of scientific and technical texts linked to a particular *scriptorium*, the so-called 'Chauliac/*Rosarium* type,' commented on by Taavitsainen (2005: 98–104), regarding the production of copies of surgical texts by Chauliac (1300–68), a reputable medieval French surgeon whose surgical treatise was used as core material in university education in the Middle Ages and translated into a number of languages (including Middle English). In fact, his work remained one of the standard textbooks for centuries.

Religious and military mobilizations are also important, because they can account for the fact that monks from different places can be found working together in a monastery, which can make it very difficult to locate a manuscript in a specific *scriptorium*. Likewise city-dwelling copyists may have a different dialectal accent because of their interaction with soldiers coming from different regions or because they come from poorer rural areas. At times, the analysis of documents such as trial records allows for a thorough survey on social movement in the Middle Ages. This type of text is especially suitable for sociolinguistic studies, because we are provided with all the socio-cultural characteristics of the 'speaker,' just as in personal letters with an identified author.

It is also possible for a medieval manuscript to present the editor/researcher with examples of code-switching, also called 'mixed-language,' which reflects the linguistic and social situation of the British Isles during the medieval period, when English, French, and Latin were used (although for different purposes) in the same area (see Chapters 28 and 30 in this *Handbook*). However, Schendl has remarked that this seems to be "rather a specific mode of certain text types than a general phenomenon" when dealing with written texts (2000: 71). It will be again the editor's task to understand and reflect the different languages in a text, which may be of interest from the sociolinguist's point of view when assessing the linguistic situation of the country during the Middle Ages.

Central to the social information that may be gathered from a manuscript is the set of factors and circumstances related to the production of a medieval work, or the context in which it was commissioned, which must be taken into consideration when editing. At the time, manuscripts were not produced on a large scale and with exactly the same contents; instead, they were commissioned by individuals interested in having a copy of a given literary masterpiece, scientific treatise, or religious work. The contents of a codex or manuscript were also determined when ordering the copy, as was the quality with which the contents were to be displayed on the folio. This range of personal interests can help us determine the tastes of particular individuals or certain social groups in terms of text-types. Likewise, the quality of a manuscript may reveal interesting social background information about the owner: copies for display were commonly acquired by middle- or upper-class individuals with (relatively) high economic resources; in contrast, commoner copies would usually be commissioned by people with more limited economic resources. In fact, the prospective use of a manuscript would have conditioned many of its features, from the size of the folios to the decoration employed (colors, miniatures, gilding, etc.). Depending on the text-type, aspects such as "the quality of the vocabulary and the general level of expression" could also be affected by the prospective user, that is, whether this was a professional or a non-professional one; see the General Introduction to the Helsinki Corpus, (1993–98).

When dealing with medical texts, for instance, a clear distinction may be drawn in terms of format and layout between treatises copied for display and those copied to be carried by some medical practitioner as a *vade mecum*. Whereas the former would be rendered in a larger folio with a neat handwriting and colored or gilded letterforms, the latter would probably be of a size easy to carry and written using a cursive script. These differences could also play a major role in the contents of a volume: if a manuscript was intended to be carried by a medical practitioner, its contents would be adapted to his needs (symptoms, courses of action, remedies, alternatives, etc.), whereas copies aimed at display would probably contain lengthy treatises with longer descriptions of patterns of symptoms and so on. Two examples of medical manuscripts will suffice to illustrate this point: Glasgow University Library, MSS 513 and 95, both of which hold the same medical treatise, an *Antidotary* (among others). The size of MS 513 and its other palaeographical and codicological features, such as the script employed or the use of color (not to decorate, but rather to highlight the relevant sections from the point of view of curation and treatment), show that it is a copy to be carried by a medical practitioner. In contrast, the appearance of MS 95 is totally different in terms of size, neatness of handwriting, use of color and gilding, and so on, which show that this is a copy intended for display.

The circumstances in which a manuscript was produced can be of interest for sociolinguistic research, and so can be its later experiences, even centuries later, and this is once again a major concern for editors. The presence of several autographs or signatures (not only on the folios of interest to the editor, but in the entire volume) is a clear indication of the subsequent circulation of a manuscript, especially if it was bound. These signatures reveal who owned a particular codex. If the person is well-known enough, it is possible to ascertain the specific moment and place where the manuscript was when it was signed; otherwise, an approximate date may be established on the basis of the script used. Marginal notes are also of great importance, in that, depending on their nature, they may reveal the way in which manuscripts were read by later readers. Later contributions to a text in the form of glosses are also a key element for an editor, especially in the case of Old English texts. In codicological terms, for instance, interlineation was even increased in size in some cases to allow for the introduction of the glossed text. This coming together of two languages – the glosses normally being in English, while the main text was commonly in Latin – reveals the first attempts to codify meaning from a 'foreign' language into the language commonly spoken by people;

in other words, it encompasses translation practices as well as the first attempts towards building literacy (Toon 1992: 31–32).

If we go back to the *Antidotary* in Glasgow University Library, MS Hunter 513, several autographs can be found in different pages of the manuscript (some in the folios containing the text, some in other folios), and some of them have been identified (Marqués-Aguado 2008: 3–7). In addition, the text was heavily annotated by a series of hands, and this implies that it was carefully read by several later users, especially one of them, who added most of the notes. The facts that this handwriting is clearly later than that of the main text (late fifteenth or early sixteenth century and early fifteenth century, respectively) and that the dialect employed is quite different from that used in the text (East Anglian as opposed to East Midland) suggest that the manuscript circulated widely and that it was frequently used. Moreover, the nature of the notes (some of which correct conceptual or organizational errors in the main text, while others simply focus on the medical information provided) also reveals that a conscious effort was made by a later reader to emend the errors by the scribe of the text so as to make the final product more useful and handy. Accordingly, the use of marginal notes may also be taken as a hint as to which texts were preferred, which gained currency at a particular point in time, and which progressively lost ground over the centuries. Therefore, whenever a medieval work is edited, careful attention must be paid to autographs and marginalia (especially if deployed by later hands), since they may provide information not only about how the text was read and understood by later users, but also about the backgrounds of those users.

3.4   *Dialectology, standardization and sound change*

Middle English was a period characterized by a high degree of variation in terms of writing conventions, a feature that may be linked to uncertainty in writing, associated in turn with the existence of several spoken varieties (Toon 1992: 42). It was only with the advent of printing that dialect-leveling and standardization were finally achieved, because "print shaped the nature of written texts, individual authors, and, it has been argued, thought itself" (Ong 1982 in Machan and Scott 1992: 21). In fact, standardization has been a recurrent topic in historical sociolinguistic studies (Nevalainen and Raumolin-Brunberg 2005: 40), given its key role in the subsequent spread of a standard variety of English which came to triumph in later stages of the language.

This written variation has allowed for the development of extensive research on Middle English dialectology. In fact, Middle English has been referred to as "*par excellence*, the dialectal phase of English in the sense that while dialects have been spoken at all periods, it was in [Middle English] that divergent local usage was normally indicated in writing" (Strang 1970: 224). Dialectal studies have chiefly focused on lexis and have left aside other important aspects, such as personal variables of the informants (sex, age, etc.), but, even so, they still cast light on purely linguistic phenomena.

Variation has been commonly considered an 'obstacle' (Milroy 1992: 132), and non-standard forms as not 'genuine' (Milroy 1992: 143), hence the excessive homogeneization or modernization that may be found in some editions. Yet, in a time of unsettled orthography such as that of Middle English, variation might indeed be used as evidence for ongoing pronunciation changes (one of the main sociolinguistic concerns), as pointed out by Schneider (2002: 77).

3.5   Problems derived from the use of published editions for sociolinguistic studies

Whenever editing, instances of written variation must never be regarded at first sight as potential errors to be corrected. In this line, Lass (2004) warned scholars against the use of any edition as a 'historical witness,' as explained above, and, indeed, it is important to reiterate that not all available editions will be valid for sociolinguistic studies (Nevalainen and Raumolin-Brunberg 1996: 45–46).

Depending on the editorial practice advocated, an edited work will present more or less editorial amendments. On some occasions, the scribe has been assumed to use Anglo-Norman spelling practices, hence his mistakes and the subsequent editorial correction on the grounds of his spellings' not being valid to study English (Milroy 1992: 133). This has been called the *Anglo-Norman Delusion* (Lass 2004: 25). Other editors have considered that language uniformity should be attained, hence the need to introduce corrections which may in many cases delete the variation that characterized Middle English. In this line, Milroy has qualified Scragg's assumption that variants were used by scribes 'at will' by specifying that they were used "according to variable (and historically mixed) conventions" (1992: 134). It is also important to note that an editor must be aware of the fact that two or more scribes may have contributed to a copy of a text so as not to correct spellings that would be characteristic or likely in each scribe's own dialect.

Along with the issue of dialectology and written variation, texts can be found where alternative forms for a verb tense are encountered, such as the third person singular present indicative: <-th>, <-s> or syncopated <-t>. This alternation may be due to several factors, such as the cooperative work of two scribes (each of whom would display a particular form), the perpetuation of some forms from the exemplar along with others introduced by the new copyist(s), or simply the written reflection of the existence of different forms, whether receding or spreading (Milroy 1992: 132). An editorial attempt at homogeneization or selection of the 'best-text' variant might then remove all traces of this possible conflicting situation, which might have been revealing for sociolinguistic studies. Another example furnished by Milroy (though criticized by Schneider (2002: 64) for relying too much on modern evidence from Belfast) is the case of <h>-dropping, or rather, the alternative presence or absence of <h> in syllable initial positions before vowels. He concludes that this alternation may be linked to particular areas and that it might be traced back not to the Anglo-Norman origin of the scribe, but rather to the use of forms of French or Latin origin or to hypercorrection (1992: 141–42).

   Another recurrent problem when editing is the issue of the otiose flourish at the end of some words, which might be taken to be an abbreviation for final <-e>.[17] Editors are usually confronted with the choice of deleting it altogether (judging it to be a mere stroke) transcribing it as <-e> or even transcribing it as a nasal (though only in particular words). Some scholars, such as Parkes (1969: xxix), have argued in favor of transcribing it as a mere stroke or an apostrophe, hence avoiding a decision that might have consequences, not only for the transcription itself, but also for the analysis of the linguistic system employed in a particular text, or even for certain types of sociolinguistic investigation (for instance, the gradually receding use of final <-e> in different types of texts or social contexts). Indeed, such uncertainty may be the reflection of ongoing changes in the language, such as the progressive deletion of inflections, or the alternating choice between <ioun> or <ione>. This alternation may be found in words such as *decisioun/decisione*, or *complectioun/complectione*, to mention just two.

4. Concluding Remarks

In view of the problems with using existing editions for historical sociolinguistic purposes, there is a need to bring to light either unedited texts or else new editions of already published materials that show modernization or excessive homogeneization and correction, since they may provide grounded evidence for certain linguistic developments which have not yet been demonstrated or for which we still lack evidence (Toon 1992: 44) and, by the same token, can also offer reinterpretations and benefit historical sociolinguistics. With this in mind, single- or multi-genre corpora are currently being compiled, and every possible effort should be made towards a careful editing process and a suitable tagging/lemmatization (if deemed necessary). For instance, corpora such as the *Corpus of Early English Correspondence* or the *Helsinki Corpus of Older Scots*, which are sociolinguistically tagged, have already proved to be particularly helpful for sociolinguistic studies by yielding fruitful results. New corpora showing this type of tagging would undoubtedly contribute to sociolinguistic studies.

   Therefore, the user of every edition, whether digital or not, should bear in mind that its text represents a certain socio-cultural and political context, and editors should aim to guide the readers to that particular time during the presentation of the work, for only then will they be fully aware of the real meaning of the text within it.

NOTES

1   Dr. Nila Vázquez is part of the Research Projects 'Variation, Linguistic Change and Grammaticalization', grant HUM2007-60706 (Spanish Ministry of Science and Innovation) and 'Perspectivas sociolingüísticas y aspectos de la investigación en historia de la lengua

inglesa,' grant number 08629/PHCS/08 (Fundación Séneca, Agencia Regional de Ciencia y Tecnología, Región de Murcia, Spain). Dr. Teresa Marqués-Aguado is part of the Research Projects 'Desarrollo del corpus electrónico de manuscritos medievales ingleses de índole científica basado en la colección Hunteriana de la Universidad de Glasgow', grant number FFI2008-02336/FILO (Spanish Ministry of Science and Innovation) and 'Corpus de referencia de inglés científico-técnico en el período medieval inglés', grant number P07-HUM-02609 (regional government of the Junta de Andalucía). These grants are hereby gratefully acknowledged.

2 The data collected by a researcher using modern speakers may be altered by the process itself. In addition, the speaker may be influenced by the interviewer and may adopt more refined speech, thus providing the researcher with non-representative data. Note also Kastovsky and Mettinger's remarks on Tieken Boon-van Ostade's warning against the possible monitoring of the sociolinguistic evidence by modern researchers on account of, for example, "conscious or unconscious editing" (2000: vii).

3 Sometimes the name of the person who is responsible for the text is given, and sometimes some information as regards the sex of the author, his/her provenance, approximate dating of the manuscript and so on is provided.

4 For a detailed study of critical editing before Lachmann, see Morocho-Gayo (1983).

5 In the introduction to his edition of *Tibullus*, Lachmann says: "In any case, if I seem to have made progress in this art beyond Immanuel Bekker, I myself will be pleased and I hope that he will not protest". (1829: iv).

6 Faulhaber (1991) uses the term 'hyperedition' and Marcos-Marín (1986) offers an account of the material available for the edition of texts.

7 An example of such editions (transcription with digitized image, plus a concise manuscript description and the possibility of obtaining various types of lexical information) may be found at http://hunter.uma.es, where the results of the research on the *Corpus of Late Middle English Scientific Prose* are published and regularly updated.

8 A useful definition of the concept of *authorship* and a categorization of the different types may be found in Love (2002: 32–50).

9 "The synoptic edition of a given work is composed of the different diplomatic editions of the manuscripts in which the text appears. In turn, a diplomatic edition consists in the transcription of the lines of a text as close to the original as possible." (Vázquez 2009: 37). An example of the former is the edition of the four witnesses of the Middle English treatise on ophthalmology by Benvenutus Grassus (Miranda-García and González y Fernández-Corugedo, 2011).

10 In the past, it was frequent for editors to regularize and modernize their texts, thus obstructing much linguistic and sociolinguistic research work.

11 This does not mean that this type of editing is not complex. As Buzetti and McGann assert, "[t]he document bears within itself the evidence of its own life and provenance, but that evidence […] will always be more or less obscure, ambiguous in meaning, or even unrecoverable." Available at http://www.tei-c.org/About/Archive_new/ETE/Preview/mcgann.xml [accessed October 13, 2011].

12 As Meahan (2005) suggests in one of his courses, "[a]dhering to the orthographical forms of the witness […] may force the editor into preserving atypical irregularities" as well as some scribal mistakes.

13 For a detailed and updated list of the manuscripts of *The Canterbury Tales*, see Vázquez (2009: 6–9).

14 In other words, 'The art which aims to obtain a clean text, as free as possible from non-authorial elements.'

15 See also section 3.4 on dialectology.

16   See the works by Andrieu (1950), Canfora (2002), and Hammel (1992), among others. This assumption is behind Mooney's work on the compilation of data and subsequent potential identification of late Middle English scribes (2000).
17   See Grieve (1954/1995: ii), Wright (1960: xvii), and Preston and Yeandle (1999: ix), among others. See also Minkova's reflection that "final -*e*'s no longer make sense to the scribe, so he either ignores them or starts piling them up against both earlier and contemporary grammatical norms, unetymologically, and, more interestingly, unmetrically" (1991: 43).

REFERENCES

Andrieu, J. (1950) Pour l'explication psychologique des fautes de copiste. *Revue des Etudes Latines* 28, 279–92.

Bédier, J. (1928) La tradition manuscrite du Lai de l'ombre: Réflexions sur l'art d'éditer les anciens textes. *Romania* 54, 161–96, 321–56.

Blecua, A. (1983) *Manual de crítica textual*, Castalia, Madrid.

Bowers, F. (1966) *Bibliography and Textual Criticism*, Clarendon Press, Oxford.

Burrow, J.A. (1982) *Medieval Writers and Their Work. Middle English Literature and its Background 1100–1500*, Oxford University Press, Oxford.

Buzetti, D. and McGann, J.J. *Electronic textual editing: Critical editing in a digital horizon*, TEI (Text Encoding Initiative) webpage. http://www.tei-c.org/About/Archive_new/ETE/Preview/mcgann.xml12 [accessed March 12, 2009].

Canfora, L. (2002) *Il copista come autore*, Sellerio Editore, Palermo.

Chomsky, N. (1965) *Aspects of the Theory of Syntax*, MIT Press, Cambridge, MA.

Conde Silvestre, J.C. (2007) *Sociolingüística histórica*, Gredos, Madrid.

Corpus of Early English Correspondence (1998) Compiled by T. Nevalainen, H. Raumolin-Brunberg, J. Keränen, M. Nevala, A. Nurmi, and M. Palander-Collin. Department of English, University of Helsinki. http://www.helsinki.fi/varieng/CoRD/corpora/CEEC/index.html [accessed October 13, 2011].

Corpus of Scottish Correspondence, 1500–1715 (2000–7) Compiled by A. Meurman-Solin. Department of English, University of Helsinki. http://www.eng.helsinki.fi/varieng/csc/manual [accessed October 13, 2011].

Faulhaber, C.B. (1991) Textual criticism in the 21st century. *Romance Philology* 45: 123–48.

Finegan, E. (1992) Series foreword. In T.W. Machan and C.T. Scott (eds.), *English in Its Social Contexts*, v–vi.

Grieve, H.E.P. (1954/1995) *Examples of English Handwriting, 1150–1750: With Transcripts and Translations*, Essex Education Committee, Chelmsford.

Hammel, C. de (1992) *Scribes and Illuminators*, British Museum Press, London.

Hanna, R. (1992) Producing manuscripts and editions. In A.J. Minnis and C. Brewer (eds.), *Crux and controversy in Middle English textual criticism*, Brewer, Cambridge, pp. 109–30.

Housman, A.E. (1921) The application of thought to textual criticism. *Proceedings of the Classical Association* 18: 67–84.

Hudson, A. (1977) Middle English. In A.G. Rigg (ed.), *Editing Medieval Texts: English, French and Latin Written in England. Papers Given at the Twelfth Annual Conference on Editorial Problems*, Garland, New York and London, pp. 34–57.

Kastovsky, D. and Mettinger, A. (eds.) (2000) *The History of English in a Social Context. A Contribution to Historical Sociolinguistics*, Mouton de Gruyter, Berlin.

Kohnen, T. (2007) From Helsinki through the centuries: The design and development of English diachronic corpora. In P. Pahta, I. Taavitsainen, T. Nevalainen, and J. Tyrkko (eds.), *Studies in variation*,

contacts and change in English, vol. 2,
http://www.helsinki.fi/varieng/journal/
volumes/02/ kohnen/ [accessed April 10,
2011].

Labov, W. (1994) *Principles of Linguistic
Change. Vol.1: Internal Factors*, Blackwell,
Oxford.

Lachmann, K. (ed.) (1829) *Albii Tibulli libri
quattuor ex recensione Caroli Lachmanni*,
Reimer, Berlin.

Lass, R. (2004) *Ut custodiant literas*: Editions,
corpora and witnesshood. In M. Dossena
and R. Lass (eds.), *Methods and data in
English historical dialectology*, Peter Lang,
Bern, pp. 21–48.

Love, H. (2002) *Attributing Authorship: An
Introduction*, Cambridge University Press,
Cambridge.

Machan, T.W. and Scott, C.T. (1992)
Introduction. In T.W. Machan and C.T.
Scott (eds.), *English in Its Social Contexts*,
pp. 3–27.

Machan, T.W. and Scott, C.T. (eds.) (1992)
*English in its Social Context. Essays in
Historical Sociolinguistics*, Oxford University
Press, Oxford.

Marcos-Marín, F. (1986) Metodología e
informática para la edición de textos.
Incipit 6: 185–203.

Marqués-Aguado, T. (2008) *Edition and
Philological study of G.U.L. MS Hunter 513
(ff. 37v–96v)*, University of Málaga
unpublished Ph.D. thesis.

Meahan, W.P. (2005) *Editing Middle English*,
University of Toronto courses. http://
www.chass.utoronto.ca/~cpercy/
courses/6361meahan.htm [accessed March
12, 2009].

Meurman-Solin, A. (comp.) (1995) *Helsinki
Corpus of Older Scots*, Department of
English, University of Helsinki.

Milroy, J. (1992) *Linguistic Variation and
Change: On the Historical Sociolinguistics of
English*, Blackwell, Oxford.

Minkova, D. (1991) *The History of Final Vowels
in English: The Sound of Muting*, Mouton de
Gruyter, Berlin.

Miranda-García, A. and González y
Fernández-Corugedo, S. (eds.) (2011).
*Benvenutus Grassus' On the well-proven art of
the eye*, Peter Lang, Frankfurt.

Mooney, L.R. (2000) Professional scribes?
Identifying English scribes who had a
hand in more than one manuscript. In D.
Pearsall (ed.), *New directions in later
medieval manuscript studies*, York Medieval
Press, Woodbridge, pp. 131–41.

Moorman, C. (1975) *Editing the Middle English
Manuscript*, University Press of Mississippi,
Jackson.

Morocho-Gayo, G. (1983) La crítica textual
desde el Renacimiento hasta Lachmann.
Anales de la Universidad de Murcia 40:
3–26.

Nevalainen, T. and Raumolin-Brunberg, H.
(eds.) (1996) *Sociolinguistics and Language
History: Studies Based on the Corpus of Early
English Correspondence*, Rodopi,
Amsterdam.

Nevalainen, T. and Raumolin-Brunberg, H.
(2003) *Historical Sociolinguistics: Language
Change in Tudor and Stuart England*,
Longman Pearson Education,
London.

Nevalainen, T. and Raumolin-Brunberg, H.
(2005) Sociolinguistics and the history of
English: A survey. *International Journal of
English Studies* 5(1): 33–58.

Parkes, M.B. (1969) *English Cursive Book
Hands 1250–1500*, Clarendon Press,
Oxford.

Pasquali, G. (1952) *Storia della tradizione e
critica del testo*, Le Monier, Florence.

Petti, A.G. (1977) *English Literary Hands from
Chaucer to Dryden*, Edward Arnold,
London.

Preston, J.F. and Yeandle, L. (1999) *English
Handwriting 1400–1650*, Pegasus Press,
Asheville, NC.

Romaine, S. (1982) *Socio-historical Linguistics.
Its Status and Methodology*, Cambridge
University Press, Cambridge.

Schendl, H. (2000) Syntactic constraints on
code-switching in medieval texts. In I.
Taavitsainen, T. Nevalainen, P. Pahta, and
M. Rissanen (eds.), *Placing Middle English
in Context*, Mouton de Gruyter, Berlin,
pp. 67–86.

Schneider, E. (2002) Investigating variation
and change in written documents. In J.K.
Chambers, P. Trudgill, and N. Schilling-
Estes (eds.), *The Handbook of Language*

Variation and Change, Blackwell, Oxford, pp. 67–96.

Strang, B.M.H. (1970) *A History of English*, Routledge, London.

Taavitsainen, I. (2005) Standardisation, house styles, and the scope of variation in ME scientific writing. In N. Ritt and H. Schendl (eds.), *Rethinking Middle English: Linguistic and literary approaches*, Peter Lang, Frankfurt am Main, pp. 89–109.

The Helsinki Corpus of English Texts (1991) Compiled by M. Rissanen, M. Kytö, L. Kahlas-Tarkka, M. Kilpiö, S. Nevanlinna, I. Taavitsainen, T. Nevalainen and H. Raumolin-Brunberg. Department of English, University of Helsinki. http://www.helsinki.fi/varieng/CoRD/corpora/HelsinkiCorpus [accessed October 13, 2011].

Toon, T.E. (1992) The social and political contexts of language change in Anglo-Saxon England. In T.W. Machan and C.T. Scott (eds.), *English in Its Social Contexts*, pp. 28–46.

Vázquez, N. (2009) *The* Tale of Gamelyn *of the* Canterbury Tales, Edwin Mellen Press, Lampeter.

Wolf, F.A. (1794) *Prolegomena ad Homerum*, Halle.

Wright, C.E. (1960) *English Vernacular Hands from the Twelfth to the Fifteenth Centuries*, Clarendon Press, Oxford.

Wright, L. (1999) Mixed-language business writing: five hundred years of code-switching. In E.H. Jahr (ed.), *Language change. Advances in historical sociolinguistics*, Mouton de Gruyter, Berlin, pp. 99–117.

8 Medical, Official, and Monastic Documents in Sociolinguistic Research

LAURA ESTEBAN-SEGURA

1. Introduction

In sociolinguistics, the gathering of data relies mainly on everyday language: with methodological tools such as interviews, participant observation, and telephone surveys, spoken records are easily obtained. For the historical sociolinguist study-ing early stages of the language this is impossible, since the oral performance of speakers is not available and written documents are the only source of informa-tion. This problem is shared by scholars working in other subdisciplines and approaches within linguistics, especially by historical linguists, for whom the retrieval of language depends on written records preserved over time. These groups have a common interest in assembling solid data, assessing sources, sur-veying style levels, ascertaining the role of editing, and trying to approach speech as thoroughly as possible. They share the difficulty of dealing with considerable chronological gaps in extant material of different periods (Schneider 2002: 68), although there are differences between them in, for example, methods, interests, and goals.

This chapter sets out to survey different types of written documents and to examine their validity for historical sociolinguistic research. Language variation and change, and the circumstances in which they occur, can help us understand historical events and these linguistic phenomena, in turn, can also be interpreted by means of historically attested developments. Taking the tools employed by sociolinguistics for contemporary languages and applying them to the past enables the historical reconstruction of language in its social context (Conde-Silvestre

The Handbook of Historical Sociolinguistics, First Edition. Edited by Juan Manuel Hernández-Campoy and Juan Camilo Conde-Silvestre.
© 2014 John Wiley & Sons, Ltd. Published 2014 by John Wiley & Sons, Ltd.

2007: 10–34).[1] For this purpose, dialectal diversity and divergent developments must be included in historical language description, as this projection of linguistic variability onto the past is what differentiates sociolinguistic approaches from traditional ones (Milroy 1992: 52). The historical texts that can be useful for socio-linguistic analysis are varied; here, medical, official, and monastic documents will be examined. One of the main tenets of the discipline is that linguistic evidence rendered by written sources can be related to extralinguistic parameters, thus delivering insights into the sociohistorical state of the participants involved in the act of communication which a specific text presupposes. Sometimes, especially in early historical periods, material elements are accessible as well as linguistic data and, if possible, should also be considered. Accordingly, the relationship between the manuscript or book and the text should not be forgotten, given that the former can be viewed from a range of perspectives and can provide invaluable informa-tion about the manner of transmission, copies, translations, or commentaries of the text, as well as background on its purpose or function. Examining all the aspects that relate to the making (date, place, scribe) and decoration of manu-scripts and early books,[2] together with the libraries and owners that have ensured their survival, is important, too (Beaud and Fossier 1988: 220). Some of these views are also shared by Verweij (2006: 377):

> [L]es aspects purement matériels d'un manuscrit peuvent nous fournir des données importantes pour en connaître l'histoire. C'est en suivant cette analyse matérielle et historique des manuscrits qu'on peut se figurer la diffusion d'un texte, sa fonction, son usage, les différentes voies que le texte a suivies dans l'histoire. C'est ainsi qu'on peut s'approcher de la réalité historique que le texte a vécue.

This serves to emphasise that history, society, and language are interconnected and, as Guzmán-González (2005: 25) notes, writing (understood as a product of language and society) plays a fundamental role in the study of linguistic change.

2. Medical Documents

In the second half of the fourteenth century, English took over from Latin and French as the language for scientific and practical writings. There was a demand, which had its main impulse in clerical and aristocratic circles, for material in the vernacular, and this situation led to the production of a wide-ranging corpus of works. Writers within religious houses were translating Latin and French works into English (Keiser 1998: 3595).[3] The increase in the amount of material seems to have been greatest in the field of medicine. Written in a vernacular style, medical texts display the usage of native speakers and the analysis of this type of writing can help elucidate the evolution of the vernacular in a multilingual society. The expansion of literacy in the population in England during the fourteenth and fifteenth centuries, reflected in the increasing use of the English language and in the increasing number of surviving manuscripts, is linked to the process of vernacularization. This upsurge in the use of English and in the number of extant vernacular manuscripts may indicate that literacy was becoming more wide-spread and was no longer confined to the top echelons, since "the middle-class was extending its interests and becoming more cultivated" (Parkes 1991: 287–88). Three kinds of literacy can be distinguished: "that of the professional reader, which is the literacy of the scholar or the professional man of letters; that of the cultivated reader, which is the literacy of recreation; and that of the pragmatic reader, which is the literacy of one who has to read or write in the course of trans-acting any kind of business" (Parkes 1991: 275).

The employment of English in the fields of medicine and science constitutes a new set of literacy practices, both by those educated in the universities and by those literate only in English (Jones 2000: 101). It is generally assumed that English medical texts were compiled for healers of a lower level of education than that of university trained doctors, who had Latin textbooks in the fifteenth century and who also wrote their own treatises in the classical language (Norri 1989: 147). However, Jones (2000: 375) argues that, although the shift towards the vernacular during this period has traditionally been regarded as a reflection of the progress of literacy in the general population (i.e. those who did not belong to the medieval category of *litteratus* or 'literate' in Latin), the situation was more complex than that. An illustration of this is the fact that the expansion of literacy and increased accessibility to texts do not account for the use of the vernacular by the *litteratus* and in institutions where Latin literacy was compulsory, such as the universities.[4] In order to understand this changing process, Jones (2004) points out that there is a need to view the whole context of a text, including the manuscript and its socio-historical contexts. She talks of discourse communities[5] rather than audiences (the latter implies a homogeneous group without interaction), as the former would allow connecting "texts and their users in a framework which takes account of people's varying relationships with texts and languages, and which removes the need to force readers into set categories which may be both anachronistic and inaccurate" (2004: 35). Associated with this type of communities are social net-works (involving social ties between specific speakers and how they impinge upon speakers' linguistic usage) and communities of practice (which imply shared practices between members in a variety of contexts) (Mullany 2007: 87–89; see also Chapter 18 in this *Handbook*).

The research that can be carried out may favor a societal view, focusing, for example, on the above-mentioned aspect of multilingualism, or lie at the linguistic end of the continuum including register variation, language and social networks, and different kinds of discourse analysis (Raumolin-Brunberg 1996: 11). These aspects can be discussed in relation to a specific sort of text, the medieval recipe book,[6] which in medieval Western medicine derives from the Greek medical writ-ings of antiquity through Arabic translations. As a consequence, medieval medical recipes form a close-knit textual type with few original texts, in which intertextual-ity can be predicted (Mäkinen 2004: 144). The structure of the recipe books varied. Some followed the principle of *de capite ad pedem*, where the discussion of illnesses was presented starting at the head and moving down to the feet. Other books were built on the practitioner's experience: recipes, notes, commentaries, and so on were sometimes copied erratically, looking chaotic as a result. Recipes could also appear in scientific treatises. Analyzing both the macrostructure and the microstructure of these texts can yield information not only about linguistic usage, but also about external factors, such as the function or purpose for which particular manuscripts were copied. Discourse analysis studies have been carried out by a number of scholars who have have considered, for instance, the structure or organization of recipes (Jones 1997; Esteban-Segura 2008b). Most Middle English recipes follow a standard pattern, consisting of a title, in Latin or English, and a text (Hargreaves 1981: 92). Multilingualism therefore appears in some of these texts, which can display examples of code-switching between English, French, and Latin, reflecting in the way they do this a sociolinguistic correspondence in society (see Hunt 2000; Pahta 2004; see also Chapter 28 in this *Handbook*).

Social constructs, such as status, gender, or age, are present and relevant in medical writings. As far as status is concerned, the target audience of Middle English adaptations and translations included both trained university people conversant with Latin (who used the vernacular version from choice) and lay folk literate only in English. The relationship between communities and texts can also be employed for historical research, as social networks can throw light on the processes of diachronic language change. The dialectal variation characteristic of the Middle English period enables, as Jones (2004: 28–29) suggests, grouping texts and manuscripts within a particular region, and the researcher can rely on the *Linguistic Atlas of Late Mediaeval English* (McIntosh, Samuels, and Benskin: 1986) to help with the task. This would make it possible to establish close-knit groups (such as monastic communities and universities) and more loosely knit ones, and to compare linguistic changes attested in the manuscripts issued by each of the 'communities.' A network of medical texts has been localized, for instance, in late-medieval East Anglia and their analysis can help to determine the diffusion of these changes (see Jones 2000).

On a microstructural level, social considerations of status also occur within texts relating to, for example, the rank or stratum from which the patient comes. An example of this appears in the preparation of recipes, where the choice of ingredients depends on whether the patient is wealthy and can afford them, in which case more expensive or exotic elements can be incorporated into the cures:

(1) And ȝif he bie a riche ma*n*, late hym vse þese electuaries a-morwetide fastinge: [di]anthos, diaciminu*m*, diacalamentu*m*, | þe hoote diacitonicon. And ȝif he bie a simpil ma*n*, ȝif hym diatrionpiperion *and* mel rooset. Also, ȝif he be a riche ma*n*, ȝif hy*m* diamargaritoun, diacameron, diarodon of galienes makyng oþer of julians makyng. (Glasgow, University Library, (G.U.L.) MS Hunter 509, ff. 133r– 133v, in Esteban-Segura 2008a: 241)

(2) And ȝif þou wolt make delicat purgaciou*n*s for hem þat ben norisschyd in delices, make hem in forme of water *and* ȝif it hem to drynke. (G.U.L. MS Hunter 509, f. 17rb, in Esteban-Segura 2008a: 100)

Female roles in medieval society can also be analyzed by looking at the presence of women (or matters relating to women) in texts. Although it has been acknowledged that medical writers paid careful attention to the diseases of women (Getz 1991: lii), the transmission of information dealing with the subject was irregular. One such case appears in the Middle English Gilbertus Anglicus, an adaptation of Gilbertus Anglicus' *Compendium medicinae*, originally written in Latin ca. 1240 and translated into English by an unknown author around 1400. There are more than fifteen extant manuscripts containing the Middle English Gilbertus or parts of it; some of them share other material, as this work was usually combined into compendia (compilations of various texts from different sources into a single manuscript). Information relating to illnesses or conditions specific to women (such as problems in the womb, menstruation, or childbirth) was removed from some of the versions, which circulated without it. The manuscript G.U.L. Hunter 307, for instance, holds a monographic treatise on diseases of women at the end, as well as further reference to them throughout the text, but G.U.L. MS Hunter 509 contains only the scattered information appearing in the text, without the final treatise, and in London, Wellcome Historical Medical Library, MS 537 this information has been deleted and there is almost no reference to women's diseases, or even to women. Thus, a supposedly general treatise that covered all conditions that could affect a person[7] from head to foot, left out discussion of the ailments affecting female patients in several versions. The intended purpose of each individual book could explain such an omission.

As with status, gender differences are also well established and emerge in the texts:

> (3) Oþer take greene aischen bowes *and* leie he*m* on þe fier, *and* take of þe wat*er* þat comeþ out at þe endis of he*m* þe quantite of an ey-henne-schelful, *and* cast þer-to ij sponeful of oile oþer of buttir, and oone sponeful of þe iuys of synegreene, *and* two sponeful of hony, and oon sponeful of wo*m*mannys mylk þat norischiþ a knaue child; if it be for a wo*m*man, a mayde child. *And* do of þis a drope oþere two in his eere *and* stoppe þe eere. (G.U.L. MS Hunter 307, f. 46r)[8]

The same applies if the age of the patient is taken into consideration; thus, some medical procedures are especially appropriate for the very young or very old (example 4). The issue of ethnicity is also tackled in early medical texts (example 5).[9]

> (4) But euacuacioun wiþ ventusis and watir-lechis is able to hem þat ben feble, children & olde men. (London, Wellcome Historical Medical Library, MS 564, f. 152ra, in Taavitsainen, Pahta and Mäkinen 2005)
> (5) Whan þe vrine is þi*n*ne *and* whiȝt, þat ma*n* is male*n*colicus *and* haþ to myche blood. And ȝif he is a blak ma*n*, he is liȝtly wrooþ. (G.U.L. MS Hunter 509, f. 11v, in Esteban-Segura 2008a: 91)

Accessible surveys and editions of historical medical material have enabled the researcher to investigate this specific field of scientific language in recent decades.

The appearance of electronic corpora has added many advantages,[10] such as quick retrieval of data and the possibility of speedier analysis of larger chunks of text. Corpora are being compiled and expanded, which is good news for anyone interested in taking a sociolinguistic approach, since an extensive and systematic electronic corpus offers well-founded coverage for a particular period, and parallel changes can be examined over time (Nevalainen and Raumolin-Brunberg 2003: 11–12).

3. Official Documents

In the preceding section, the development and supremacy of the vernacular over established languages were exemplified with the case of medical writings in medieval England. The opposite (the vernacular not being successful or prevalent) can also occur; to illustrate this, we will look at the linguistic situation in Orihuela, a Spanish town in the Valencian Community, in which Castilian Spanish and Valencian (a variety of Catalan spoken in the Valencian Community) were in contact. Orihuela, located at the southern end of the Community and bordering on the neighboring (and monolingual) Region of Murcia, represents an unusual case if compared to the rest of the towns in the Community where Valencian, the vernacular language, is today more common among the bilingual population. However, in Orihuela, the use of Valencian, which was there the language of administration, was dropped in the seventeenth century in favor of Castilian (Abad-Merino 1994: 16). Providing a sociolinguistic description of a community in which bilingual subjects coexisted with two different linguistic varieties by looking at historical written sources can enable us to account for the situation; linguistic factors are not considered alone, but together with economical, geographical, or historical factors. Abad-Merino (1994) has in fact carried out this analysis by selecting official documents of several types to show the linguistic behavior of professional or social strata.[11] The texts that have been used for the purpose include Books of Correspondence, which hold the letters sent and received by the town hall of Orihuela and different individuals from the Kingdom of Valencia. The range of graphical representations or variants found in these texts gives evidence of the confusion of sounds and, therefore, of phonic interferences between the languages. Thus, the influence of Castilian can be seen in texts written in Valencian and vice versa; an example of interference from Valencian into Castilian is the spelling <t> (representing the voiceless alveolar plosive consonant /t/) for the final voiced alveolar plosive consonant /d/, which should be indicated in writing by means of <d>: *magestat* 'majesty,' *cristiandat* 'Christendom,' *salut* 'health,' *ciudat* 'town,' *universidat* 'university,' *ohit* 'hear,' *voluntat* 'will,' *verdat* 'truth,' *dificultat* 'difficulty,' *solisitut* 'solicitude' (Abad-Merino 1994: 107–8).

Grammatical and lexical interferences are also found, as well as instances of code-switching. The latter is typified by the following fragment taken from a letter written in Valencian, in which switching to Castilian occurs (shown in bold):

(6) **De todo lo que se resolviere y determinare havisarnos an vuestras señorías con toda brevedad advirtiendo a vuestra merced que el síndico de Guardamar a ydo a essa ciudad ha hazer quexas de que el dicho Baltazar Garcia, tiniente, fue a vissitar dicho lugar y hazer autos jurisdictionales en él.**
Ittem. La lletra subsidiaria que la ciutat escriu al jurats de Valencia llegira VM y veura lo que conte y procurara . . . la certificatoria que demanan a ab aquellas **para** lo escriva de Valencia.

(Abad-Merino 1994: 124)

[Your Honours should notify us at your earliest convenience of all that was decided and settled, warning your Worship that the solicitor of Guardamar has gone to that town in order to complain about the fact that the said Baltazar Garcia, lieutenant, went to visit the above place and to make jurisdictional orders in it. Item. The subsidiary letter that the town wrote to the jury of Valencia will reach YW and You will see what it says and procure . . . the certification that is required of those for the scribe of Valencia.]

Although apparently standard, official texts can provide information about different levels and registers of language. This type of document also provides a means of analyzing social and governmental schemata, furnishing details of the linguistic behavior of upper and upper-middle social strata. Depending on the register, features of orality may also become apparent in the letters, which could be classified into different fields, such as social uses (recommendation, greetings and congratulation, condolences), finances, government, or law.

Other useful sources for historical research are the books in which the administration of public funds (local expenditure, civil servants' salaries, bureaucratic and judicial expenses, etc.) was recorded; in addition, administrative and sacramental books, the latter including christening and marriage certificates, kept in parishes and churches can give clues about the language used by the clergy. Extralinguistic parameters, such as profession, cultural level, age, and gender, are readily available in the case of the sort of official documents mentioned so far.

The compilation and study of this type of written sources can be a productive way of reconstructing a social situation from the past and is, as Abad-Merino (1994: 321) notes, an essential – and the only – source for addressing diachronic linguistic questions. Her research, based on official writings, evaluates language use and alternation in a bilingual community over a period of time and identifies Castilian (considered to be more prestigious) as the common language employed by the inhabitants of Orihuela in contrast to the vernacular. The results of this historical sociolinguistic approach corroborate the validity of official sources for assessing linguistic change.

4. Monastic Documents

Medical texts, which have been dealt with above, may represent a type of monastic document, since some of the works were copied in monastery scriptoria and were used there as well. Many texts contain marginalia, which vouch for their continuing or renewed use. Rodríguez-Álvarez and Domínguez-Rodríguez (2005: 45–46) have highlighted the significance of the metatext – the annotations, glosses, deletions, etc. made to a text, especially those added by readers from a later period – as well as the text itself, as an excellent basis for the study of the changing state of a language. As these scholars suggest, annotations can "shed light on the changing vocabulary, morphology, grammatical constructions and even on stylistic preferences." But they can also supply social data about the producers and the readership or audience, as well as adding "a reader perspective and an interactiveness to the texts which is otherwise missing" (Claridge 251: 2008).[12]

A different use of monastic records is the account of sign language collected in *Monasteriales Indicia*, which provides helpful information on monastic life in the early Middle Ages, especially in Anglo-Saxon England. The text, written in Old English and preserved in a manuscript from the mid-eleventh century, contains an explanation of the signs employed by monks who followed the Benedictine Rule. This provides the cultural context behind the compilation: the Rule regarded silence as an essential feature for divine contemplation and a requisite for the regulation of religious life, and was imposed in church, during meals, and in the dormitory. Signs were permitted as replacements for words only in cases of severe necessity and as their use became widespread, so it became necessary to codify this system of communication in writing (Conde-Silvestre 2001: 146–47). The text therefore reveals details of reformed monastic life and religious communities, which can be of service when studying the relationship between language (taking signs to be a form of language and communication) and society.

The Anglo-Saxon Gospels, which go back to the tenth century and exist in several copies (see Skeat 1871: v–xiii), represent another type of monastic writing. Little is known about the purpose and audience of the work since, as Liuzza (1998: 5) points out, "there is unfortunately no explicit testimony regarding either the intention of the author or the reception of the Old English Gospels."[13] Nevertheless, a need to understand the sacred text could explain the use of the vernacular, hence stressing its importance as a means of communication. The adaptation of the Gospels from Latin into Old English is found in three of the four main dialects of the period, namely West Saxon, Northumbrian, and Mercian (but not in Kentish). The West-Saxon text is a translation, whereas the Northumbrian dialect is attested in the interlinear glosses of the Lindisfarne and Rushworth versions; Mercian features only occur in the Rushworth version and are restricted to the glosses to Matthew, Mark 1–2:15 and John 18:1–3 (Kuhn 1945: 631). The *Lindisfarne Gospels* provide evidence of a change in progress: the gradual replacement of -*th* forms of the present-indicative paradigm by -*s* forms.[14] Two instances of this are the verbs *utgaas* and *worðias* in examples (7) to (10) and (11) to (14) respectively.

(7) Of þære heortan **cumaþ** yfle geþancas. mann-slyhtas. únriht-hæmedu. forligru. stale. lease gewitnyssa. tállice word (West Saxon)[15]

(8) of hearte forðon **utgaas** smeaunga yfle morður uif-giornis derne legra ðiofunta leasa witnesa ebolsung (Lindisfarne)[16]

(9) of heorta ut **gaeþ** geþohtas yfele morþur unriht-hæmed forlaegennisse stale lyge gewitnisse hefalsunge (Rushworth)

(10) de corde enim exeunt cogitationes malæ homicidia adulteria fornicationes furta
      falsa testimonia blasphemiae (Latin)
      [Out of the heart come evil thoughts, murder, adultery, wantonness, theft, false
      testimony, slander]
(11) Ða andswarode he hi*m* ; Wel witegod isaias be eow licceteru*m* swa hit awriten
      is ; Þis folc me mid weleru*m* **wurðað**. soðlice hyra heorte is feor fra*m* me. (West
      Saxon)[17]
(12) soð he onduearde cuoeað to him wel gewitgade of iuih legerum suæ awritten
      is folc ðis mið muðum mec **worðias** hearta uutet*lice* hiora long is fro*m* me
      (Lindisfarne)[18]
(13) soð he & worde cwæð him forðon wel gewitgade esaias of iow legerum swa
      awriten is folche ðis mið muðe mec **weorðas** heorte wutud*lice* hiora long from
      me (Rushworth)
(14) at ille respondens dixit eis bene prophetauit esaias de uobis hypocritis sicut
      scriptum est populus hic labiis me honorat cór autem eorum longe est á me.
      (Latin)
      [Then he answered him, Isaiah was right when he predicted about you hypo-
      crites, as it is written: these people worship me with their lips, but their hearts
      are far from me.]

According to Cole (2010), subject type has not been regarded as a conditioning
factor to account for -*s*/-*th* variation, but it could be worthwhile adopting such
an approach, as research on variation in the *be* paradigm in varieties of Modern
English shows that subject type is a decisive determinant in the selection of verbal
morphology. A graded subject hierarchy, for instance, determines processes of
default singulars or subject–verb nonconcord in present-day English,[19] such as
was-leveling (Chambers 2004). As Cole (2010) suggests, internal constraints affecting variation in modern varieties could also influence historical processes of regularization, thus reflecting universal tendencies.

The *Rushworth Gospels*, on the other hand, have been approached from the
perspective of social network analysis (Smith 1996: 26–29) by taking into account
the language employed by one of the scribes, Farman, whose portion of glossing
differed linguistically from the Northumbrian variety used by Owun, the other
scribe of the interlinear gloss. Kuhn (1945: 641–42) has pointed out that Farman,
a Mercian, inserted many Saxonisms into his glosses as a result of his attempt "to
imitate the language of his temporal and ecclesiastical superiors." According to
Smith (1996: 29), Farman hyperadapted because he aspired to West Saxonism and
his hypercorrection, typical of "socially mobile, upwardly aspiring people" (1996:
26), could be explained by weak cultural ties.

Continuing with Old English, the analysis of written documents has allowed
delimiting the language of smaller circles, such as the 'Mercian literary dialect,' the
'Alfred Circle' and, the 'Winchester Circle,' which, as proposed by Lenker (2000:
225), would be similar to social networks. Lenker has applied the network model
to the tenth-century language variety found at Winchester, also referred to as the
'Winchester School,' which "emerges as a tight-knit, localised network cluster
which functions as a mechanism of norm enforcement and maintenance" (2000:
226) and has reflected on the diffusion of the group norms across monasteries.

5. Concluding Remarks

Several of the conclusions reached by Schneider (2002: 90) in the analysis of written records and the problems arising when these sources are used in the study of language variation and change are also relevant for historical sociolinguistics:

> It is necessary to assess the characteristics of text types and individual texts in the light of their historical and culture-specific settings; it is necessary to judge the representativeness of one's sample as well as the validity of a group of texts or a single source, and it is necessary to consider the possible effects of these factors upon the representation of a given linguistic level or feature with care, judgment, and reluctance: it is to be expected that these vary greatly from one source to another, from one goal of analysis to another. Mostly the nature of the sources available will determine, sometimes limit, what can be achieved with them.

The potential for historical sociolinguistic analysis offered by different text types (some of which have been illustrated in this chapter) is becoming clearer, especially given the growing number of historical corpora and the editing of unpublished material in a variety of contexts (medicine, law, etc.), which are major sources of evidence and provide new resources and challenges for researchers.

However, many issues, not just those strictly linguistic, remain to be addressed in the historical reconstruction of language structure. Texts exist within a particular textual culture and this should be taken into consideration. Marginalia, for instance, can account for reading practices in different periods; the same could be said of libraries and archives. Such resources may shed light on social and economic conditions, thus linking language and social history. The evolution of language has been continuous, from its starting-point as speech, then manuscript, print, and, ultimately, screen, and these stages bear witness to diverse social situations. The feasibility of relating all of them is an advantage for the modern scholar.

Milroy (1992: 222) set a major task for historical sociolinguists, namely, to connect linguistic change with social change in order to elucidate "the conditions under which linguistic change takes on particular patterns, including patterns of rapid and slow change". The possibility of analyzing new (types of) texts currently being compiled and/or edited (together with those already available) may allow scholars to detect internal variation within texts and thus permit the application of sociolinguistic approaches or principles to the historical study of language. This novelty makes the task empirically feasible and promises a stimulating and encouraging future for historical sociolinguistics.

Acknowledgements

I am grateful to the Spanish Ministry of Science and Innovation (grant number FFI2008-02336/FILO) and to the Autonomous Government of Andalusia (grant number P07-HUM-02609) for research funding. I would like to thank Professors

Juan Manuel Hernández-Campoy and Juan Camilo Conde-Silvestre (University of Murcia) for reading drafts of the article and providing helpful comments. Grateful acknowledgement is also made to the Keeper of the Special Collections Department at Glasgow University Library for kindly permitting the reproduction of the digitized images from manuscripts Hunter 307 and Hunter 509 (their copyright resides with the University of Glasgow).

NOTES

1   According to Romaine (2005: 1696), "language is both a historical and social product, and must therefore be explained with reference to the historical and social forces which have shaped its use." This is the central premise of historical sociolinguistics.

2   An example of a decorated folio from a medical manuscript is shown in Plate 8.1.

3   Roberge (2006: 2307) puts forward three main reasons that can account for language change; they can be summarized as (i) speakers' conscious intervention; (ii) speakers' unconscious intervention; (iii) contact with other languages. The promotion of vernacular literacy, which would result in a variety serving as a medium of communication, would belong to the first group.

4   Jones pays special attention to the vernacularization of medicine in late-medieval East Anglia, which appears to have been both the cause and effect of shifting literacy practices. Some of these shifts can be recognized from the growth of literate medicine, professional literacy, expansion of current practices, translation, and changes in institutional practices (see Jones 2000: 375–81).

5   An example of the notion of discourse community – a group of people sharing certain practices of language use, which are conventionalized by means of stylistic codes and canonical knowledge (Bizzell 1992: 222) – is provided by Fitzmaurice (2010), who studies the characteristics of the discourse community of essay writers and journalists in eighteenth-century literary London. By taking into account "the linguistic behaviours and rhetorical concerns of a group of speakers in early eighteenth-century London," she connects social networks and coalitions to the broader discourse community (2010: 107).

6   Jones (1997: 5) comments that the language of medieval medical recipe books has been neglected and that, although such books may not possess much literary merit, they were works in use during the late-medieval period which can provide insights into how the language was employed by a part of the professional classes. Hargreaves (1981: 92) remarks that the inquiry into medical recipes may shed light upon different facets of social history, such as the organization of the cheap book trade and the history of medicine. From these views, the link between language and society is indisputable.

7   The word *man* and masculine pronouns to refer to the patient are generally employed in these texts; a generic sense might be intended, but it seems more likely that the main targets were male patients, especially when women's illnesses were left out.

8   Transcription and edition of the text by the author.

9   Ethnicity is one of the social factors interacting with linguistic factors in language change, as proposed by Roberge (2006: 2308), in addition to socioeconomic status, occupation, education, age, gender, social mobility, communication network structure, contextual style, topic, and medium of expression.

10   Nevalainen (1996: 4–5) referred to the lack of sufficient quantity of appropriate materials as one of the reasons for the underrepresentation of social information in early texts. With the

emergence of computerized resources, such as *Middle English Medical Texts* (MEMT) (Taavitsainen, Pahta, and Mäkinen 2005) and *Early Modern English Medical Texts* (EMEMT) (Taavitsainen *et al.* 2010), and the availability of a wide array of historical corpora on different genres and registers, also providing sociolinguistic information, this problem can be partly solved (see http://www.helsinki.fi/varieng/CoRD/corpora/index.html, where descriptions of corpora and subcorpora are supplied).

11 Montoya-Abad (1986) has also analyzed the linguistic alternation between Castilian and Valencian in the seventeenth century from a sociolinguistic perspective by scrutinizing official documents held in the town archives of Elda, Petrel, Monforte, and Orihuela (in Alicante, Spain).

12 An example of the marginalia found in a medical manuscript is supplied in Plate 8.2.

13 However, he also remarks that the work was copied, read, and used, as indicated by textual evidence. Its uses may have included "devotional reading," "pastoral instruction," and/or "liturgical recitation" (Liuzza 1998: 6–7), probably among monks and parish priests through whom the Gospels might have reached a general lay audience (1998: 15).

14 This change may be present in the Rushworth version as well, since it is derived from the Lindisfarne gloss.

15 Matthew 15:19 (In Skeat 1887: 128).

16 The fragments corresponding to the Lindisfarne, Rushworth, and Latin versions are from Skeat (1887: 129).

17 Mark 7:6 (In Skeat 1871: 52).

18 The fragments corresponding to the Lindisfarne, Rushworth, and Latin versions are from Skeat (1871: 53).

19 Chambers (2004: 129) includes default singulars in his enumeration of vernacular universals, the latter originating "in the context of sociolinguistic dialectology as generalizations about intralinguistic variation" (2004: 127).

REFERENCES

Abad-Merino, M. (1994) *El cambio de lengua en Orihuela. Estudio sociolingüístico-histórico del siglo XVII*, Universidad, Secretariado de Publicaciones, Murcia.

Beaud, J. and Fossier, L. (1988) Livre médiéval et informatique. In J. Glénisson (ed.), *Le livre au Moyen Âge*, CNRS, Paris, pp. 220–21.

Bizzell, P. (1992) *Academic Discourse and Critical Consciousness*, University of Pittsburgh Press, Pittsburgh.

Chambers, J.K. (2004) Dynamic typology and vernacular universals. In B. Kortmann (ed.), *Dialectology Meets Typology: Dialect Grammar from a Cross-linguistic Perspective*, Mouton de Gruyter, Berlin, pp. 127–45.

Claridge, C. (2008) Historical corpora. In A. Lüdeling and M. Kytö (eds.), *Corpus Linguistics: An International Handbook, Vol. 1*, Walter de Gruyter, Berlin, pp. 242–59.

Cole, M. (2010) An investigation into *-s/-th* variation in the glosses to the *Lindisfarne Gospels*. Paper presented at the 22nd International Conference of the Spanish Society for Mediaeval English Language and Literature (SELIM), Universidad de La Rioja, September 30–October 2, 2010.

Conde-Silvestre, J.C. (2001) The code and context of *Monasteriales Indicia*: A semiotic analysis of late Anglo-Saxon monastic sign language. *Studia Anglica Posnaniensia* 36: 145–69.

Conde-Silvestre, J.C. (2007) *Sociolingüística histórica*, Gredos, Madrid.

Esteban-Segura, L. (2008a) *G.U.L. MS Hunter 509 (ff. 1r–167v): An Edition and Philological Study*, Universidad de Málaga Ph.D. thesis.

Esteban-Segura, L. (2008b) Textual analysis of recipes in G.U.L. MS Hunter 509: A sample study. Paper presented at the 32nd International AEDEAN [*Asociación Española de Estudios Anglo-Norteamericanos*] Conference, Universitat de les Illes Balears, November 13–15, 2008.

Fitzmaurice, S. (2010) Coalitions, networks, and discourse communities in Augustan England: The *Spectator* and the early eighteenth-century essay. In R. Hickey (ed.), *Eighteenth-century English: Ideology and Change*, Cambridge University Press, Cambridge, pp. 106–32.

Getz, F.M. (ed.) (1991) *Healing and Society in Medieval England: A Middle English Translation of the Pharmaceutical Writings of Gilbertus Anglicus*, University of Wisconsin Press, Madison, WI.

Guzmán-González, T. (2005) Out of the past: A walk with labels and concepts, raiders of the lost evidence, and a vindication of the role of writing. *International Journal of English Studies* 5(1): 13–31.

Hargreaves, H. (1981) Some problems in indexing Middle English recipes. In A.S.G. Edwards and D. Pearsall (eds.), *Middle English Prose: Essays on Bibliographical Problems*, Garland, New York and London, pp. 91–113.

Hunt, T. (2000) Code-switching in medical texts. In D.A. Trotter (ed.), *Multilingualism in Later Medieval Britain*, Brewer, Cambridge, pp. 131–47.

Jones, C. (1997) *An Analysis of the Language and Style of a Late-medieval Medical Recipe Book: Glasgow University Library MS Hunter 117*, University of Glasgow M.Phil. dissertation.

Jones, C. (2000) *Vernacular Literacy in Late-medieval England: The Example of East Anglian Medical Manuscripts*, University of Glasgow Ph.D. thesis.

Jones, C. (2004) Discourse communities and medical texts. In I. Taavitsainen and P. Pahta (eds.), pp. 23–36.

Keiser, G.R. (1998) Works of science and information. In A.E. Hartung (ed.), *A Manual of the Writings in Middle English, 1050–1500*, vol. 10, Connecticut Academy of Arts and Sciences, New Haven, pp. 3593–967.

Kuhn, S.M. (1945) *e* and *æ* in Farman's Mercian glosses. *PMLA* 60(3): 631–69.

Lenker, U. (2000) The monasteries of the Benedictine reform and the 'Winchester School.' Model cases of social networks in Anglo-Saxon England? *European Journal of English Studies* 4(3): 225–38.

Liuzza, R.M. (1998) Who read the Gospels in Old English? In P.S. Baker and N. Howe (eds.), *Words and Works: Studies in Medieval English Language and Literature in Honour of Fred C. Robinson*, University of Toronto Press, Toronto, pp. 3–24.

McIntosh, A., Samuels, M.L., and Benskin, M. (1986) *A Linguistic Atlas of Late Mediaeval English*, 4 vols., Aberdeen University Press, Aberdeen.

Mäkinen, M. (2004) Herbal recipes and recipes in herbals – intertextuality in early English medical writing. In I. Taavitsainen and P. Pahta (eds.), pp. 144–73.

Milroy, J. (1992) *Linguistic Variation and Change: On the Historical Sociolinguistics of English*, Blackwell, Oxford.

Montoya-Abad, B. (1986) *Variació i desplaçament de llengües a Elda i a Oriola durant l'Edat Moderna*, Institut d'Estudis Juan Gil-Albert, Alicante.

Mullany, L. (2007) Speech communities. In C. Llamas, L. Mullany, and P. Stockwell (eds.), *The Routledge Companion to Sociolinguistics*, Routledge, London, pp. 84–91.

Nevalainen, T. (1996) Introduction. In T. Nevalainen and H. Raumolin-Brunberg (eds.), pp. 3–9.

Nevalainen, T. and Raumolin-Brunberg, H. (eds.) (1996) *Sociolinguistics and Language History: Studies Based on the Corpus of Early English Correspondence*, Rodopi, Amsterdam.

Nevalainen, T. and Raumolin-Brunberg, H. (2003) *Historical Sociolinguistics: Language Change in Tudor and Stuart England*, Longman/Pearson Education, London.

Norri, J. (1989) Premodification and postmodification as a means of term-formation in Middle English medical prose. *Neuphilologische Mitteilungen* 90(2): 147–61.

Pahta, P. (2004) Code-switching in medieval medical writing. In I. Taavitsainen and P. Pahta (eds.), pp. 73–99.

Parkes, M.B. (1991) *Scribes, Scripts and Readers: Studies in the Communication, Presentation and Dissemination of Medieval Texts*, Hambledon Press, London.

Raumolin-Brunberg, H. (1996) Historical sociolinguistics. In T. Nevalainen and H. Raumolin-Brunberg (eds.), pp. 11–37.

Roberge, P.T. (2006) Language history and historical sociolinguistics. In U. Ammon, N. Dittmar, K.J. Mattheier, and P. Trudgill (eds.), *Sociolinguistics: An International Handbook of the Science of Language and Society*, vol. 3, Walter de Gruyter, Berlin, pp. 2307–15.

Rodríguez-Álvarez, A. and Domínguez-Rodríguez M.V., (2005) A Middle English text revised by a Renaissance reader: John Wotton's annotations to British Library MS Sloane 249 (ff. 180v–205v). *International Journal of English Studies* 5(2): 45–70.

Romaine, S. (2005) Historical sociolinguistics. In U. Ammon, N. Dittmar, K.J. Mattheier, and P. Trudgill (eds.), *Sociolinguistics: An International Handbook of the Science of Language and Society*, vol. 2, Walter de Gruyter, Berlin, pp. 1696–703.

Schneider, E.W. (2002) Investigating variation and change in written documents. In J.K. Chambers, P. Trudgill, and N. Schilling-Estes (eds.), *The Handbook of Language Variation and Change*, Blackwell, Oxford, pp. 67–96.

Skeat, W.W. (ed.) (1871) *The Gospel According to Saint Mark in Anglo-Saxon and Northumbrian Versions Synoptically Arranged, with Collations Exhibiting All the Readings of All the MSS*, Cambridge University Press, Cambridge.

Skeat, W.W. (ed.) (1887) *The Gospel According to Saint Matthew in Anglo-Saxon, Northumbrian, and Old Mercian Versions, Synoptically Arranged, with Collations Exhibiting All the Readings of All the MSS*, Cambridge University Press, Cambridge.

Smith, J. (1996) *An Historical Study of English. Function, Form and Change*, Routledge, London.

Taavitsainen, I. and Pahta, P. (eds.) (2004) *Medical and Scientific Writing in Late Medieval English*, Cambridge University Press, Cambridge.

Taavitsainen, I., Pahta, P., Hiltunen, T., Mäkinen, M., Marttila, V., Ratia, M., Suhr, C., and Tyrkkö, J. (eds.) (2010) *Early Modern English Medical Texts* (CD-ROM), John Benjamins, Amsterdam.

Taavitsainen, I., Pahta, P., and Mäkinen, M. (eds.) (2005) *Middle English Medical Texts* (CD-ROM), John Benjamins, Amsterdam.

Verweij, M. (2006) La matérialité des manuscrits. Conséquences pour l'histoire et pour les éditions critiques. In T. van Hemelryck and C. van Hoorebeeck (eds.), *L'écrit et le manuscrit à la fin du Moyen Âge*, Brepols, Turnhout, pp. 367–77.

Appendix

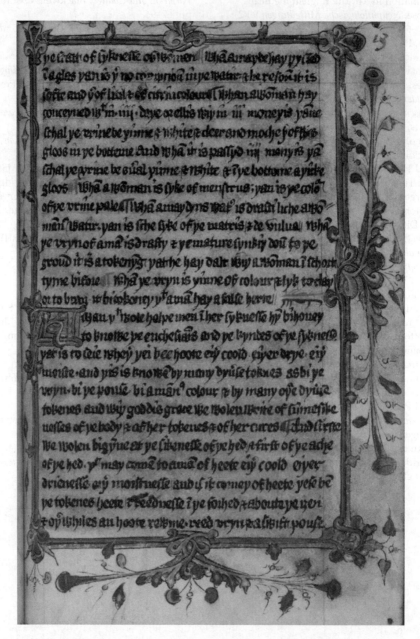

Plate 8.1.   Decorated folio (f. 13r, G.U.L. MS Hunter 307; reproduced by permission of the University of Glasgow)

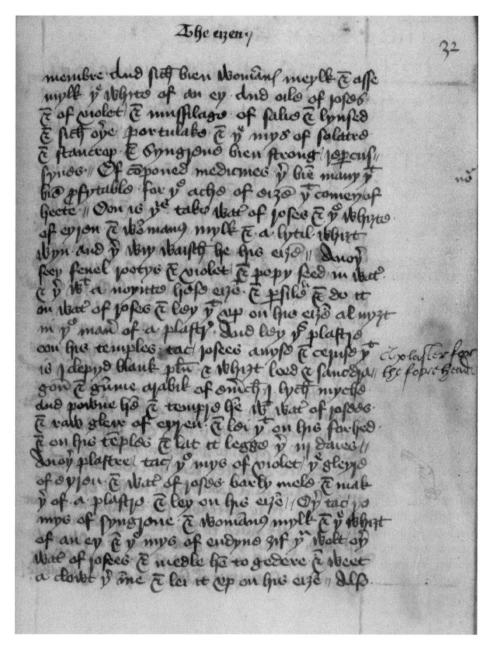

Plate 8.2. Folio with marginalia (f. 32r, G.U.L. MS Hunter 509; reproduced by permission of the University of Glasgow)

9 The Use of Private Letters and Diaries in Sociolinguistic Investigation

STEPHAN ELSPASS

1. Introduction

In portraying the modern period, most language histories of the Western hemisphere tell the story of *printed* languages. A complete account of language history, viewed from the perspective of its agents, can only be achieved if we attempt to consider as many text sources from as many different times, varieties, regions, domains, and text types as possible. This chapter discusses the special role of *handwritten* text sources such as private letters, diaries, and similar ego-documents in historical sociolinguistics. They are special, firstly, because they are as close to speech as non-fictional historical texts can possibly be and therefore cast light on the history of natural language. Secondly, they can fill "blank spaces" (Van der Wal 2006) left by traditional historical linguistics' teleological perspective on language histories and its focus on literary texts and formal texts from higher registers. Moreover, they can constitute the basis of a 'language history from below' in its own right. The first part of the chapter (sections 2 to 4) is devoted to the question of how the analysis of such private text sources contributes to broader perspectives in historical sociolinguistics. Section 5 will give a brief survey of example corpora and studies of historical private letters and diaries from different languages. Section 6 will be concerned with basic criteria for editing and designing corpora of such texts.

The Handbook of Historical Sociolinguistics, First Edition. Edited by Juan Manuel Hernández-Campoy and Juan Camilo Conde-Silvestre.
© 2014 John Wiley & Sons, Ltd. Published 2014 by John Wiley & Sons, Ltd.

2. The (Hi)story of Speech Retold Through Private Letters and Diaries

Historical linguists will agree that speech is primary, writing secondary, and that "in a default setting, the study of language variation and change starts out from performance data" (Schneider 2002: 67). In principle, historical linguistics, concerned with language history of the time before speech recorders were developed (i.e. pre-twentieth century), has always had to rely on written sources. The analysis of present-day spoken records has proved of additional benefit in that it contributes to a better understanding of the general processes of language variation and language change.

Having to depend on written documents, however, does not mean that it is impossible to study the history of speech from such sources. The traditional distinction between 'spoken language' and 'written language' is simplistic and even misleading. To arrive at an adequate understanding of the nature of 'speech,' 'spoken language,' and/or 'orality,' it is essential to place these notions into an integral model. Such a model is provided by Koch and Oesterreicher (1985, 1994) and their notion of 'language of immediacy' (*Sprache der Nähe*) vs. 'language of distance' (*Sprache der Distanz*). For an appreciation of the relation between historical 'language of immediacy' and the history of speech, it will be necessary to give a brief outline of Koch's and Oesterreicher's model.

Firstly, the model differentiates between language medium and language conception. Verbal language is transmitted either by voice or by the written word, so the phonic and the graphic medium constitute a strict dichotomy. The linguistic conception of a text, however, can be established only relative to prototypical texts of 'immediacy' (orality, informality, unplannedness) and prototypical texts of 'distance' (literateness, formality, plannedness). These prototypical texts – for example, an intimate conversation as a prototype of a text of 'immediacy' and a legal contract as a prototype of a text of 'distance' – constitute the two poles of the conceptional continuum. On a scale between these two poles, all kinds of text types can be located according to their degree of linguistic 'immediacy' or linguistic 'distance,' respectively. Whether a given text is more immediate (oral, informal, unplanned) or more distant (literate, formal, planned) is subject to a combination of scalar values of such parameters as formality, spatial or temporal distance, private or public setting of the communication, familiarity of the communication partner, spontaneity, and free or fixed topics.[1] The distinction between the conceptual poles of the continuum is primary to an understanding of the 'orality' or 'writtenness' of language. The medium is secondary, as a written text can be read out and a recording of a spoken text can be transcribed at any time (thus the notion of 'medium transferability'). Although there "is a great affinity between conceptional immediacy and speech, on the one hand, and conceptional distance and script, on the other hand," this does not "invalidate the fundamental rule: that medium and conception are independent of each other" (Oesterreicher 1997: 195). Conceptional differences between utterances and their underlying communicational parameters are regarded as anthropological constants in all speech communities, that is, as linguistic universals. Consequently, even "societies that have no recourse to writing" can be said to "employ different conceptional strategies in different types of situations and utterances" (Oesterreicher 1997: 193).

From Koch's and Oesterreicher's (1985, 1994) model and its underlying parameters it becomes evident that familiarity and maximum cooperation of communication partners in symmetrical communicative settings are typical characteristics of 'language of immediacy.' Thus, letters, diaries, and other ego-documents from the private sphere are the types of texts that investigators will specifically have to look out for when searching for "material as close to actual speech as possible, only in written form," which could help to fill missing links in diachronic corpora (Sević 1999: 340).[2] Other types of letters and diaries are less 'oral' because of the specific communicative circumstances in which and for whom they were written. Thus, in composing formal letters (such as letters of reference, letters of thanks or congratulations), letters in asymmetrical communicative settings (letters of appeal), or diaries undertaken for institutional purposes (such as business ledgers or military records), writers usually draw on discourse traditions with highly formalized discourse patterns and routines.

In tracing orality in written records, it appears to be worthwhile to focus on writing by semi-literate rather than highly literate or even professional writers. Although such writers may have only mastered a small portion within the whole range of written text types of their time, they were not totally uninfluenced by contemporary text traditions, particularly with respect to formulaic usage (cf. e.g. Dossena 2007). In general, however, their writing can be assumed to be the least influenced, and, still less, dominated by traditions of a 'writing of distance,' so that their private texts can be regarded as the most 'oral' written sources in language history (for a discussion of such sources, see Schneider 2002: 76–77).

A fundamental problem in working with private documents or any other historical documents that have come down to us is the question of authorship. For instance, even if letters were signed with an identifiable name, "we can't always be sure whether the people whose names appear at the end of these letters were the actual writers" (Fairman 2000: 64). This observation holds for letters in asymmetrical communicative settings such as letters of appeal, in particular, as people would tend to hire professional writers when, for instance, an allowance would depend critically on the 'correct' form of the written request. In principle, such a caveat also applies to private letters. In symmetrical written communication, however, grammatical correctness, spelling, or particular sets of formulae were not crucial to a successful communicational act, so that even barely literate people would take up pen or pencil to write down texts of private interest.

As a final point, fictional 'ego-documents' (like epistolary novels) may be excluded altogether from text corpora of 'historical speech' on the grounds that the original authorship of a historical text and the authenticity of the historical communicational situation are prerequisites for constituting such corpora. Furthermore, Oesterreicher and other scholars have repeatedly stated that the "authentic immediacy" of private texts can never be matched by the "mimesis of immediacy or simulated orality" of fictional texts (Oesterreicher 1997: 205).

To summarize, private letters and diaries written by semi-literate writers seem to have the highest potential to render authentic sources of historical orality. Historical orality is primary: the (hi)story of writing has to be matched against it (see section 4). Language historians will not come across such 'oral' texts frequently, but these texts do exist and many are still waiting to be unearthed from archives or private collections.

3. The Sociohistorical Dimension of Private Texts

In terms of socio-demography, traditional language historiography has clearly concentrated not only on printed texts, but also on texts of writers from the upper classes in society (see Chapter 17 in this *Handbook*). From a practical point of view, this appears to be legitimate, as for a long time only members of the elites were literate (not that all of them were), and even from the time when members of the lower ranks learned to read and write, upper class writers have always written more texts than writers from the lower classes. In addition, documents written by elite writers have come down to us in greater numbers for different reasons, but mainly because they were traditionally attributed a higher value than texts from 'ordinary' writers. Even today – and every day – large quantities of private documents written by 'common people' are destroyed, while the correspondence of people such as professional writers, artists, and politicians have a greater chance of being preserved in private or public archives.

From early modern times, however, reading and writing were no longer a privilege of the upper and upper middle classes, who probably never constituted more than five per cent of the population anywhere, including western and central Europe. At the end of the Middle Ages, some parts of central Europe could already claim literacy rates of 20 per cent of the population (for Germany, see Maas 2003: 2408). As a result of mass literacy drives in the late eighteenth and the nineteenth century (see Arnove and Graff 1987), not only members of the social elite, but a large proportion of the 'ordinary' population (farmers, artisans, soldiers, housemaids etc.) were able to read and to put pen to paper – although they had rarely reason or opportunity to do so in the 'average' life of a village, town, or city. For the production of texts for personal needs, a knowledge of different registers of writing was not necessary. Thus, from early modern times diary writing is well-documented even among the lower ranks of society, and when face-to-face interaction was interrupted in times of warfare or migration, ordinary people took extensively to letter writing (see section 5). In the context of mass migration in the nineteenth century and the two world wars in the twentieth century, in particular, the sheer mass of people from the lower and lower middle classes produced a volume of letters which is unprecedented in the history of writing. Corpora of nineteenth-century private letters certainly represent the first text sources in western language history which give us an authentic and representative picture of written language as it was used by the vast majority of the population.

Texts such as those referred to in this chapter usually do not constitute part of the cultural memory of western societies. The long-standing disregard or even ignorance of documents written by members of the lower ranks of society can be explained by practical factors (such as those mentioned above), but also by a narrow view of what was 'of value' in an account of a nation's language history. This has meant that not only historians, but also historical linguists, have long had an image of 'the illiterate masses,' who were able to speak only vernaculars, but barely contributed to the history of our modern languages.

4. Private Documents as a Basis for a Language History 'from Below'

Rather than just supplementing existing language histories with some aspects of orality or listening to voices other than those of the elites, private documents, especially those written by non-professional writers, can serve as text sources fundamental to a radically different approach to language history in its own right, which has been termed 'language history from below' (Elspaß 2005a; Elspaß, Langer, Scharloth, and Vandenbussche 2007). This approach implies a change of perspective from a 'bird's eye' to a 'worm's eye' view and combines the two aspects already outlined above.

Firstly, the view 'from below' argues for a different starting point for the description of language history and the explanation of language change. The shift of perspectives involves an acknowledgment of language registers of 'historical orality' which are basic to human interaction and which are prototypically represented by speech in face-to-face-interaction. Language of immediacy is ontogenetically and phylogenetically primary in all speech communities; it is the place where language variation and change occur, typically, inherently, and daily. It therefore appears natural to take 'historical orality,' as represented in private documents, as a starting-point not only for writing historical grammars (Ágel and Hennig 2006), but for the pursuit of historical linguistics itself. Language of immediacy is the unmarked case, language of distance is the marked case. Traditional language histories are "very biased and partial historical descriptions of the elaborate and distance-orientated variety that develops or has developed into the standard form of the respective languages" (Oesterreicher 1997: 198). Private letters, diaries and similar sources have thus come into focus as historical text sources which can tell the (hi)story of orality and, based on this, its relationship with the (hi)story of literate writing as well as the changes in orality under the influence of writing. This would include phenomena like "second orality" (Ong 1982), oral varieties and registers which – having emerged in the age of electronic media such as telephone, radio, and television – are essentially based on conceptionally written language, but used in the spoken medium and thus eventually encompassing elements from both 'orality' and 'writtenness.'

Secondly, in concentrating on texts by writers from the middle and lower ranks of society, the 'language history from below' approach is also a long overdue emancipation of the vast majority of the population in language historiography. As traditional language histories are overwhelmingly histories of distance-orientated varieties, they are also accounts of the 'winners' of national language histories, resembling the one-sidedness of war reports from the perspective of the victorious generals only. The teleological view of traditional language historio-graphy and its concentration on texts – for modern times mostly printed texts – of elite writers and on literary or administrative texts was thus motivated and at the same time affirmed by linguistic myths, linguistic purism, and the standard language ideology (see Milroy and Milroy 1985: 22–23; Milroy 1992: 124–25) in the wake of modern nation state-building (see Durrell 2000 and Milroy 2005 for the German and the British case; see Chapters 31–33 in this *Handbook*). Therefore, the 'language history from below' approach is an attempt to write "alternative histories" (Watts and Trudgill 2002), which is a necessary counterweight to the tendency of traditional language historiography to ignore or trivialize the histories of minority languages, varieties, and registers that did not win the race, and to ignore or shrug off linguistic variation and digressions from the dominating varie-ties as corrupted language, and therefore non-valuable data for linguistic research.

The study of historical language variation and change on the 'non-standard' level, as represented in letters and diaries, has gained particular significance when viewed against present-day variation and change of modern standard languages. Given that new variants constantly emerge in printed standard varieties (often via prior diffusion through 'oral' texts on the internet), and that not all new variants can be attributed to L1:L2 contact, researchers have developed an increasing inter-est in the origin of such variants in varieties prior to the modern standard ones. It is a widespread conviction that a deeper insight into linguistic developments of the past – and late modern periods, in particular – is necessary "to explain the present" (Nevalainen and Kahlas-Tarkka 1999; Beal 2007). Ágel (2001: 319) has termed the underlying methodological principle "the principle of viability:"

> Jede linguistische Beschreibung (bzw. Erklärung) muss mit der Beschreibung (bzw. Erklärung) der Geschichte des zu beschreibenden (bzw. zu erklärenden) Phänomens konform sein.
>
> Every linguistic description (or explanation) has to fit into the description (or explanation) of the history of the phenomenon under description (or explanation). (my translation)

It is of particular interest in this context, that in documents such as private letters and diaries, linguistic variants emerge which, in an act of "sanitary purism" (Milroy 2005: 324–26), had been cleaned off the linguistic surface of standard textbooks, dictionaries, and grammars, and thus have gone practically unnoticed by traditional historiography and grammarians (see Elspaß 2005a: 196–460 and Elspaß 2005b: 35–40 for examples from German).

To sum up, within the framework of Historical Sociolinguistics and a 'language history from below' approach in particular, the study of 'language of immediacy' in private letters, diaries and similar ego-documents can bring to light not only previously unknown historical variation, but – even more importantly – appears to be the only way to disclose the linguistic foundations of modern languages in their full varietal spectra.

5. Existing Corpora, Collections and (Case) Studies

This section gives a brief outline of text types in the realm of ego-documents, with examples of text editions and case studies from different languages. It concentrates on corpora and studies of sources from the western hemisphere.

Where letters are concerned, 'language of immediacy' is best represented by private letters (see section 2). Only a few examples of such letters have come down to us from antiquity, such as the private letters of Roman soldiers (see Pighi 1964; Adams 1977). Private letters from the early modern period mostly stem from members of the higher ranks of society. In the biggest corpus of English letters from this period, the Helsinki *Corpus of Early English Correspondence* (CEEC 1998), which comprises over 6,000 letters from the early fifteenth century to the end of the seventeenth, more than two thirds of the 778 writers were members of the gentry, nobility or clergy. From the end of the seventeenth century onwards, letters from those of lower rank come into view. For instance, the collection of more than 38 000 Dutch 'sailing letters,' which were confiscated during the wars fought between the Netherlands and England from the second half of the seventeenth to the early nineteenth century, contains about 15 000 private letters "written by men, women and even children of all social ranks, including the lower and middle classes."[3] Studies of eighteenth-, nineteenth- and early twentieth-century private letters from the lower ranks of society, thus those comprising the largest proposition of society, are available for languages such as English (e.g. Montgomery 1995; García-Bermejo Giner & Montgomery 1997; Allen 2006; Dossena 2007), German (Schikorsky 1990; Elspaß 2005a, 2007; McLelland 2007), Dutch (Van der Wal 2006, 2007, Nobels 2013), Cape Dutch (Deumert 2004), Finnish (Nordlund 2007), Russian (Yokoyama 2008), Danish (Sandersen 2007), Canadian French (Martineau 2007), Canadian English (Dollinger 2008), Spanish (Cano Aguilar 1996; López Álvarez 2000; Moyna 2009, 2010) and Italian (e.g. Spitzer's 1921 study on prisoner-of-war letters).[4] We draw special attention to letter collections which were not compiled for the purpose of linguistic analysis in the first place, such as volumes of emigrants' letters edited by social historians (see Fitzpatrick 1994; Helbich, Kamphoefner and Sommer 1988). In general, a closer collaboration between social historians and linguists in tracking down, editing and analyzing such sources can prove fruitful (see, for instance, Graser and Tlusty 2012).

Whereas private letters are characterized by dialogue and 'a social practice' between the correspondents (Barton and Hall 2000), private diaries are strictly monologic by nature. Such texts may be as informal in style and unplanned in their conception as private letters, but they are usually less 'oral.' A look at some numbers for English ego-documents from the British Isles may suffice to illustrate the amount of such source material available to language historians. The "total number of British diarists and autobiographers included in a new census or database covering the period 1500–1900 will be well over 5000" (Houlbrooke n.d. [2008]). Again, the vast majority of these writers were male and "belonged to the gentry or the wealthier of the middle ranking social groups" (Houlbrooke n.d. [2008]). For the period between 1790 and 1900, 850 autobiographies and diaries by working class writers are documented in a bibliography by Burnett, Vincent and Mayall (1984). Only 67 of these texts qualify as 'working-class diaries' that were presumably not written to be printed. In general, the term 'diary' covers different types of monological texts, such as personal diaries (with mostly private content), family books (recording events of family life), account books and private chronicles with irregular entries (thus hardly 'journals' in the strict sense) that comprise events of family and village life, interspersed with weather reports and news about wars and accidents. It is the latter type of diary which seems to have gone unnoticed for a long time. So-called 'peasant diaries,' for instance, are in evidence as far back as the sixteenth century (see Lorenzen-Schmidt and Poulsen 2002) but have been paid little attention. A prominent example of such a text is the seventeenth-century "Denkelbok" ('memorabilia book') by Hartich Sierk, a member of the rural 'upper class' of his home region in the northernmost part of Germany. His diary-cum-chronicle, written mostly in Low German, is a concoction of legal matters, minor and major events, and other things, such as notes about purchases and sales (see Maas 1995). Therefore, when Schneider (2002: 78) writes that historical diaries by unprofessional writers are rare, because "the very habit of writing a diary is untypical of semi-literate writers," he certainly has personal diaries in mind, not family books, account books, or private chronicles. Ágel and Hennig (2006: 40–49) have in fact used such an ego-document by a seventeenth-century artisan to illustrate their method of establishing the degree of 'immediacy' in historical texts.

A major difference between personal diaries and the latter types of diaries is that these were not only read by the original writers, but also used by other family members of the same and subsequent generations. The tradition of handing down private and other *handwritten* documents from one generation to the next within families and other small personal networks is closely linked to the century-long practice of learning to read and write largely by copying old family scripts. This practice can account for the fact that such texts display traces not only of historical speech (see section 2), but also of conservative grammar and spelling (Messerli 2000: 245; Elspaß 2005a: 345–48, 427–39) and outdated formulae (Elspaß 2005a: 158–74; Dossena 2007). Even written varieties on the verge of extinction did apparently survive for some time in such private texts, such as Low German in the north of Germany in the late seventeenth century, illustrated by Hartich Sierck's "Denkelbok," or even in the eighteenth century (see Denkler and Elspaß 2004).

A comprehensive account of existing collections of private letters, diaries, and similar ego-documents is, as indicated, not yet possible, as year by year new text sources come to light, often in the context of new research projects.[5]

6. Criteria for Corpus Design and Editing

For a historical-sociolinguistic analysis of private letters, diaries and other ego-documents, investigators would want to draw on as many texts as possible. The size of the corpus is, of course, limited by the number of texts that have come down to us. If a reasonable amount of sources is available to the investigator, he or she has the choice of designing the corpus according to his or her needs. Unlike a book editor working with manuscripts, a linguist is not subject to restrictions of place, order of texts, and so on. In electronic corpora, for instance, collections of letters can be edited unabridged and arranged chronologically, thematically, or by correspondents, according to the requirements of the investigator's research aims. To study letters as dialogic text forms, for instance, one would seek a comprehensive collection of letters between two correspondents (see Schikorsky 1999). For a network analysis, it would be necessary to consider as many letters from one or more personal networks (as in the *Corpus of Cape Dutch Correspondence*; see Deumert 2004).

Editors and corpora-builders have to observe some general standards for editing and adapting historical texts such as private letters and diaries (see Woesler 1998: 946):

1. The text source and its archival records must be identified.
2. A standardized form of presenting relevant information about the text must be employed, for example in a standardized header or file name.
3. The editorial principles – and deviations from general principles, in particular – must be stated.
4. Any deviation from the wording or spelling of the original text (if any is necessary, see below) and variants in other manuscripts of the same text, such as fair copies, must be listed in a critical apparatus.

As for quality criteria, it goes without saying that for linguistic analysis, (historical) manuscripts must be presented in an authentic form, that is, unabridged and without any changes to spelling, grammar, or style:

a) For limitations of space, many printed editions of letters and diaries tend to omit lengthy formulae, quotes, and other prefabricated language. Such language material may also appear tedious for a reader who is interested in a content analysis. Linguistically, however, it is highly telling. Firstly, fixed expressions and formulaic language can constitute text types as well as single texts. Therefore, a study of formulaic language may disclose not only the verbal rituals of a period and changing patterns of textual constitution, but also the extent to which a writer was familiar with the conventions and fashions of formal letter-writing of that period (see Elspaß 2005a: 152–96; Dossena 2007). Secondly, a study of grammatical, lexical, and spelling variation in historical texts must take into account the difference between variants within and outside formulaic language of the text. For instance, in nineteenth-century German emigrants' letters, it has been demonstrated that certain grammatical markers, such as dative and genitive markers, were used far less in 'creative language' than in fixed and formulaic expressions; in fact, some forms of genitives and datives were clearly limited to a set of routine formulae (Elspaß 2005a: 317–20, 336–39, 348–54).

b) There is some dispute as to whether manuscripts should be presented as 'quasi-facsimiles' or not. Hunter (2009: 72–85) argues that it is not necessary to reproduce, for example, ligatures or tildes to denote a duplication of *n* or *m* and makes a case for even expanding abbreviations, such as M^{tie} to *Majestie*. Many linguists, however, consider such interventions as too far-reaching. Fairman (2007) distinguishes between interpretive and literal transliterations and uses a "basically interpretive one" – because "a strictly literal transliteration would be too confusing" (2007: 173) – which still reproduces features such as authors' abbreviations, upper and lower case writings, and deletions. We might ask ourselves whether a fully literal transcription is in fact really possible or whether all transcriptions are not interpretive in some way or another. Thus, Fairman's (2007) guideline for transliterators may be modified as follows: transliterators should always be aware of the extent to which they transliterate interpretively, and make the readers aware of that too.

Further quality criteria depend on the type of linguistic analysis. For a variationist analysis, for instance, Schneider (2002: 71; see also Chapter 6 in this *Handbook*) identified four basic criteria:

1. Texts should be as close to speech, and especially vernacular style, as possible [...]
2. To facilitate correlations with extralinguistic parameters, the texts should be of different origins [...]
3. Texts must display variability of the phenomenon under investigation [...]
4. With quantification being the staple methodology of variationism, texts must fulfill certain size requirements.

With respect to these criteria, private letters and diaries certainly rank as two of the best text types available for variationist analysis. The quantities of nineteenth- and twentieth-century emigrant and war letters, for instance, which have survived in many languages allow for correlative studies of context parameters such as age, sex, social class, and regional origin of the writers.

In general, investigators and corpus builders should strive for as much information about the writers as possible and make it available to the reader and the user of the corpus (as far as the printed page allows). The Helsinki *Corpus of Early English Correspondence* (CEEC), for instance, records each writer's provenance, social and family status, education, social mobility, age, gender, and relation to the recipient. Of course, in publishing such personal data, editors and corpora-builders have to consider legal and ethical issues. The writers of historical letters and diaries certainly never imagined and presumably never wished that their texts would one day be published. Apart from possible legal restrictions, each private historical document must therefore be treated with due respect.

NOTES

1   For details see Koch and Oesterreicher (1985: 19–23, 1994: 588), and similar ideas in Biber (1995: 283–288); for a method to operationalize the degree of 'immediacy' and case studies, see Ágel and Hennig (2006).
2   In an attempt to reconstruct historical speech, the analysis of various other text types has been suggested, for example vernacular inscriptions (historical cartoons, in particular) or court records. In mere quantitative terms, however, such sources will certainly not match the amount of text in historical letters and diaries.
3   http://www.brievenalsbuit.nl/ [accessed July 7, 2013].
4   The study of historical variation and change may, however, not be restricted to private letters, see Fairman's work on mainly nineteenth-century English pauper letters (2000, 2007).
5   In 2008, the major international project "First person writings in European context," funded by the European Science Foundation, started with research groups in the Czech Republic, Denmark, France, Germany, Great Britain, Italy, Lithuania, the Netherlands, Poland, the Russian Federation, Spain, and Switzerland; see http://www.firstpersonwritings.eu/ [accessed July 7, 2013].

REFERENCES

Adams, J.N. (1977) *The Vulgar Latin of the Letters of Claudius Terentianus*, Manchester University Press, Manchester.

Ágel, V. (2001) Gegenwartsgrammatik und Sprachgeschichte. Methodologische Überlegungen am Beispiel der Seriali-sierung im Verbalkomplex. *Zeitschrift für Germanistische Linguistik* 29: 293–318.

Ágel, V. and Hennig, M. (eds.) (2006) *Grammatik aus Nähe und Distanz. Theorie und Praxis am Beispiel von Nähetexten 1650–2000*, Niemeyer, Tübingen.

Allen, B. (2006) *The Acquisition and Practice of Working-class Literacy in the Nineteenth-century Sussex Weald*, University of Sussex Ph.D. thesis.

Arnove, R.F. and Graff, H.J. (eds.) (1987) *National Literacy Campaigns. Historical and Comparative Perspectives*, Plenum Press, New York and London.

Barton, D. and Hall, N. (eds.) (2000) *Letter Writing as a Social Practice*, John Benjamins, Amsterdam.

Beal, J. (2007) To explain the present: 18th and 19th-century antecedents of 21st-century levelling and diffusion. In J.L. Bueno Alonso, D. González Álvarez, J. Pérez-Guerra, and E. Rama Martínez (eds.), *'Of varying language and opposing creed': New Insights into Late Modern English*, Peter Lang, Bern, pp. 25–46.

Biber, D. (1995) *Dimensions of Register Variation. A Cross-linguistic Comparison*, Cambridge University Press, Cambridge.

Burnett, J., Vincent, D., and Mayall, D. (1984) *The Autobiography of the Working Class. An Annotated, Critical Bibliography. Vol. 1: 1790–1900*, Harvester Press, Brighton.

Cano Aguilar, R. (1996) Lenguaje 'espontáneo' y retórica epistolar en cartas de emigrantes españoles a Indias. In T. Kotschi, W. Oesterreicher, and K. Zimmermann (eds.), *El Español hablado y la cultura oral en España e Hispanoamérica*, Vervuert/Iberoamericana, Frankfurt/Madrid, pp. 375–404.

CEEC = *Corpus of Early English Correspondence* (1998) Compiled by T. Nevalainen, H. Raumolin-Brunberg, J. Keränen, M. Nevala, A. Nurmi, and M. Palander-Collin Department of English, University of Helsinki. http://www.helsinki.fi/varieng/CoRD/corpora/CEEC/index.html [accessed July 7, 2013].

Denkler, M. and Elspaß, S. (2004) Perspektiven ländlicher Schriftlichkeit. Ein münsterländisches Anschreibebuch aus der zweiten Hälfte des 17. Jahrhunderts. In R. Damme and N. Nagel (eds.), *'westfeles vnde sassesch'. Festgabe für Robert Peters zum 60. Geburtstag*, Verlag für Regionalgeschichte, Bielefeld, pp. 181–206.

Deumert, A. (2004) *Language Standardization and Language Change. The Dynamics of Cape Dutch*, John Benjamins, Amsterdam.

Dollinger, S. (2008) *New-dialect Formation in Canada: Evidence from the English Modal Auxiliaries*, John Benjamins, Amsterdam.

Dossena, M. (2007) 'As this leaves me at present' – Formulaic usage, politeness, and social proximity in nineteenth-century Scottish emigrants' letters. In S. Elspaß, N. Langer, J. Scharloth, and W. Vandenbussche (eds.) (2007), pp. 13–29.

Durrell, M. (2000) Standard language and the creation of national myths in nineteenth-century Germany. In J. Barkhoff, G. Carr, and R. Paulin (eds.), *Das schwierige neunzehnte Jahrhundert. Germanistische Tagung zum 65. Geburtstag von Eda Sagarra im August 1998. Mit einem Vorwort von Wolfgang Frühwald*, Niemeyer, Tübingen, pp. 15–26.

Elspaß, S. (2005a) *Sprachgeschichte von unten. Untersuchungen zum geschriebenen Alltagsdeutsch im 19. Jahrhundert*, Niemeyer, Tübingen.

Elspaß, S. (2005b) Language norm and language reality. Effectiveness and limits of prescriptivism in New High German. In N. Langer and W.V. Davies (eds.), pp. 20–45.

Elspaß, S. (2007) Everyday language in emigrant letters and its implications on language historiography – the German case. *Multilingua* 26-2/3: 151–65.

Elspaß, S., Langer, N., Scharloth, J., and Vandenbussche, W. (eds.) (2007) *Germanic language histories 'from below' (1700–2000)*, Mouton de Gruyter, Berlin.

Fairman, T. (2000) English pauper letters 1800–34 and the English language. In D. Barton and N. Hall (eds.), *Letter writing as a social practice*, John Benjamins, Amsterdam, pp. 63–82.

Fairman, T. (2007) Writing and 'the Standard': England, 1795–1834. In W. Vandenbussche and S. Elspaß (eds.), *Lower Class Language Use in the 19th century*, Special issue of *Multilingua. Journal of Cross-Cultural and Interlanguage Communication* 26-2/3: 167–201.

Fitzpatrick, D. (1994) *Oceans of Consolation. Personal Accounts of Irish Migration to Australia*, Cornell University Press, Ithaca.

García-Bermejo Giner, M.F. and Montgomery, M. (1997) British regional English in the nineteenth century: the evidence from emigrant letters. In A.R. Thomas (ed.), *Issues and Methods in Dialectology*, University of Wales Bangor, Department of Linguistics, pp. 167–83.

Graser, H. and Tlusty, B.A. (2012) Slanderous street songs of the 16th century. Social history and the history of language 'from below.' In N. Langer, S. Davies, and W. Vandenbussche (eds.), *Language and History, Linguistics and Historiography*, Peter Lang, Oxford, pp. 363–388.

Helbich, W., Kamphoefner, W.D., and Sommer, U. (eds.) (1988) *Briefe aus Amerika. Deutsche Auswanderer schreiben aus der Neuen Welt 1830–1930*, Beck, München (English edition (1991): *News from the Land of Freedom. German Immigrants Write Home*, Cornell University Press, Ithaca).

Houlbrooke, R. (n.d. [2008]) First person writings in European context – Britain: 'ego-documents' and life writing 1500–1900. http://www.firstpersonwritings.eu/greatbritain/greatbritain_project.htm [accessed February 28, 2010].

Hunter, M. (2009) *Editing Early Modern Texts. An Introduction to Principles and Practice*, Palgrave Macmillan, Basingstoke.

Koch, P. and Oesterreicher, W. (1985) Sprache der Nähe – Sprache der Distanz. Mündlichkeit und Schriftlichkeit im Spannungsfeld von Sprachtheorie und Sprachgeschichte. *Romanistisches Jahrbuch* 36: 15–43.

Koch, P. and Oesterreicher, W. (1994) Schriftlichkeit und Sprache. In H. Günther and O. Ludwig (eds.), *Writing and Its Use. An Interdisciplinary Handbook of International Research*, vol. 1., Mouton de Gruyter, Berlin, pp. 587–604.

Langer, N. and Davies, W.D. (eds.) (2005) *Linguistic Purism in the Germanic Languages*, Mouton de Gruyter, Berlin.

López Álvarez, J. (2000) Cartas desde América: La emigración de asturianos a través de la correspondencia: 1899–1925. *Revista de dialectología y tradiciones populares* 55: 81–120.

Lorenzen-Schmidt, K.J. and Poulsen, B. (eds.) (2002) *Writing Peasants. Studies on Peasant Literacy in Early Modern Northern Europe*, Landbohistorisk selskab, Gylling.

Maas, U. (1995) Bäuerliches Schreiben in der Frühen Neuzeit. Die Chronik des Hartich Sierk aus den Dithmarschen in der ersten Hälfte des 17. Jahrhunderts. In W. Raible (ed.), *Kulturelle Perspektiven auf Schrift und Schreibprozesse: Elf Aufsätze zum Thema Mündlichkeit und Schriftlichkeit*, Narr, Tübingen, pp. 65–96.

Maas, U. (2003) Alphabetisierung. Zur Entwicklung der schriftkulturellen Verhältnisse in bildungs- und sozial-geschichtlicher Perspektive. In W. Besch, A. Betten, O. Reichmann, and S. Sonderegger (eds.), *Sprachgeschichte. Ein Handbuch zur Geschichte der deutschen Sprache und ihrer Erforschung*, vol. 3 (2nd edn), Mouton de Gruyter, Berlin, pp. 2403–18.

Martineau, F. (2007) Variation in Canadian French usage from the 18th to the 19th century. *Multilingua* 26-2/3: 203–27.

McLelland, N. (2007) "Doch mein Mann möchte doch mal wissen . . . " A discourse analysis of 19th-century emigrant men and women's private correspondence. In S. Elspaß, N. Langer, J. Scharloth, and W. Vandenbussche (eds.) (2007), pp. 45–68.

Messerli, A. (2000) Das Lesen von Gedrucktem und das Lesen von Handschriften – zwei verschiedene Kulturtechniken? In A. Messerli and R. Chartier (eds.), *Lesen und Schreiben in Europa 1500–1900. Vergleichende Perspektiven*, Schwabe, Basel, pp. 235–46.

Milroy, J. (1992) *Linguistic Variation and Change. On the Historical Sociolingustics of English*, Blackwell, Oxford.

Milroy, J. (2005) Some effects of purist ideologies on historical descriptions of English. In N. Langer and W.V. Davies (eds.), *Linguistic Purism in the Germanic Languages*, Mouton de Gruyter, Berlin, pp. 324–42.

Milroy, J. and Milroy, L. (1985) *Authority in Language. Investigating Language Prescription and Standardisation*, Routledge, London.

Montgomery, M. (1995) The linguistic value of Ulster emigrant letters. *Ulster Folklife* 41: 1–16.

Moyna, M.I. (2009) Back at the Rancho: Language maintenance and shift among spanish speakers in post-annexation California (1848–1900). *Revista Internacional de Lingüística Iberoamericana* 14: 165–84.

Moyna, M.I. (2010) Varieties of Spanish in Post-Annexation California (1848–1900). In D. Villa and S. Rivera-Mills (eds.), *Spanish of the Southwest: A Language in Transition*, Iberoamericana/Vervuert, Madrid and Frankfurt, 27–44.

Nevalainen, T. and Kahlas-Tarkka, L. (eds.) (1999) *To Explain the Present: Studies in the Changing English Language in Honour of Matti Rissanen. Mémoires de la Société Néophilologique de Helsinki*, Société Néophilologique, Helsinki.

Nobels, J. (2013) *(Extra)Ordinary Letters. A view from below on seventeenth-century Dutch*, LOT, Utrecht.

Nordlund, T. (2007) Double diglossia – lower class writing in 19th-century Finland. *Multilingua* 26-2/3: 229–46.

Oesterreicher, W. (1997) Types of orality in text. In E. Bakker and A. Kahane (eds.),

Written Voices, Spoken Signs, Harvard University Press, Cambridge, MA, pp. 190–214.

Ong, W.J. (1982) *Orality and Literacy. The Technologizing of the Word*, Methuen, London.

Pighi, G.B. (1964) *Lettere Latine d'un soldato di Traiano*, Zanichelli, Bologna.

Sandersen, V. (2007) Writing ability and written language of Danish private soldiers in the Three Years' War (1848–50). *Multilingua* 26-2/3: 247–78.

Schikorsky, I. (1990) *Private Schriftlichkeit im 19. Jahrhundert: Untersuchungen zur Geschichte des alltäglichen Sprachverhaltens 'kleiner Leute,'* Niemeyer, Tübingen.

Schikorsky, I. (ed.) (1999) *'Wenn doch dies Elend ein Ende hätte' Ein Briefwechsel aus dem Deutsch-Französischen Krieg 1870/71*, Böhlau, Cologne.

Schneider, E.W. (2002) Investigating variation and change in written documents. In J.K. Chambers, P. Trudgill, and N. Schilling-Estes (eds.), *The Handbook of Language Variation and Change*, Blackwell, Oxford, pp. 67–96.

Sević, R.B. (1999) Early collections of private documents: The missing link in the diachronic corpora. In C. Beedham (ed.), *Langue and parole in synchronic and diachronic perspective. Selected Proceedings of the XXXIst Annual Meeting of the Societas Linguistica Europaea, St Andrews 1998*, Pergamon, Amsterdam, pp. 337–47.

Spitzer, L. (1921) *Italienische Kriegsgefangenenbriefe. Materialien zu einer Charakteristik der volkstümlichen italienischen Korrespondenz*, Hanstein, Bonn (Italian edition: Spitzer, L. (1976) *Lettere di Prigionieri di Guerra Italiani 1915–18*, Boringhieri, Turin).

Van der Wal, M. (2006) *Onvoltooid verleden tijd. Witte vlekken in de taalgeschiedenis*, Koninklijke Nederlandse Akademie van Wetenschappen, Amsterdam.

Van der Wal, M. (2007) Eighteenth-century linguistic variation from the perspective of a Dutch diary and a collection of private letters. In S. Elspaß, N. Langer, J. Scharloth, and W. Vandenbussche (eds.) (2007), pp. 83–96.

Watts, R. and Trudgill, P. (2002) *Alternative Histories of English*, Routledge, London.

Woesler, W. (1998) Editionsprinzipien für deutsche Texte der Neuzeit II: nichtliterarische Texte. In W. Besch, A. Betten, O. Reichmann, and S. Sonderegger (eds.), *Sprachgeschichte. Ein Handbuch zur Geschichte der deutschen Sprache und ihrer Erforschung*, vol. 1. (2nd edn), Mouton de Gruyter, Berlin, pp. 941–48.

Yokoyama, O.T. (2008) *Russian Peasant Letters. Texts and Contexts*. 2 vols, Harrassowitz, Wiesbaden.

10 The Use of Literary Sources in Historical Sociolinguistic Research

K. ANIPA

'In linguistic matters consistency (so-called) means inaccuracy'
– Daniel Jones (*An English Pronouncing Dictionary*, 1917)

1. Introduction

It is common knowledge amongst professional linguists that linguistic theory and observation of data go hand in hand and that neither can exist independently (see Lass 1980: ix). For Milroy and Gordon (2003: 22), "the methods of investigating language are at every stage bound up with theoretical concerns," to the extent that separating them "is not practiced or even desired in sociolinguistics;" so fundamental is the issue that some scholars have made much more explicit declarations about it: "The actual data collection or analysis is often less important than the thought and discussion about methodology that should precede it" (Johnstone 2000: 17). This explains why discussions of theory and methodology are not confined to specific parts of the present volume.

Although historical sociolinguistics has achieved a degree of maturity, it remains a relatively young subfield; hence, theoretical-methodological reflections continue to be vital in underpinning its *objective knowledge* basis (Popper 1972/1979: 25). Present-day sociolinguistics – the obvious template for historical sociolinguistics – is still haunted by numerous problems, a handful of which will be outlined after this introduction, followed by the presentation of a promising theoretical-methodological model. The chapter will then consider briefly a few issues specific to literary data, before proceeding to illustrate the model with a modest micro-study of variation in the language of a Renaissance literary figure.

The Handbook of Historical Sociolinguistics, First Edition. Edited by Juan Manuel Hernández-Campoy and Juan Camilo Conde-Silvestre.
© 2014 John Wiley & Sons, Ltd. Published 2014 by John Wiley & Sons, Ltd.

It is presumed that readers will be fully conversant with the essential conceptual distinction to be made between *historical sociolinguistics* and traditional *historical linguistics*.

2. Theoretical and Methodological Parameters

A quick survey of the early works in the subfield reveals that, in order to carve a space alongside the canons of present-day sociolinguistics and traditional historical linguistics, the pioneers naturally set their eyes firmly on theory and methodology. The opening paragraph of Romaine (1982: ix) began with a statement of her early interest in "claims about the epistemological status of sociolinguistic methodology and, in particular, the so-called empirical foundations of a sociolinguistic theory;" it closed with one about "the scope of sociolinguistic theory and the relevance of sociolinguistic methods to problems in historical syntax." Correspondingly, her first and concluding chapters were largely devoted to theory and methodology. She wrote:

> There are a great many methodological and theoretical problems arising from the nexus of sociolinguistics and historical linguistics [...] Not all the issues I have raised are resolved, but judging from the literature, some at least have not previously been recognized as issues and given the serious attention they merit.
>
> (Romaine 1982: x)

Bearing this in mind will shelter our subfield from premature stagnation. The many *unresolved* issues raised by Romaine (which are not exhaustive) do not end with simply being read about.

J. Milroy's (1992) contribution built on important earlier works (Milroy and Milroy 1985a, 1985b/1999). He highlighted the concept of speaker innovation,[1] which drew attention to over-concentration on change and an imbalance in the very essence of sociolinguistics, that is, variation (see also J. Milroy 1999: 23).

For their part, Nevalainen and Raumolin-Brunberg (1996: 5) have contributed by, amongst other things, proposing "a historical sociolinguistics that studies the actual processes of diachronic language change in their social contexts." Arguing that Romaine's approach is more linguistic than sociohistorical, that J. Milroy's is more sociolinguistic than historical, and that neither work contained any references to the social history of the periods in question, they noted:

> One of the aims [...] is to bridge the gap between different research traditions and actually *do* historical sociolinguistics that is both empirical in the variationist sense, and social in the sense modern sociolinguists understand the concept. What we consider the most important contribution of our own is the systematic use that we intend to make of the information that social historians can offer us. (Nevalainen and Raumolin-Brunberg 1996: 5)

As regards sources of data, they believed that making use of personal letters from the past should reflect present-day sociolinguistic contexts more closely than Romaine's selection of textual genres for that purpose.

2.1 Inherent and inherited problems

"Who controls the past controls the future: who controls the present controls the past" (after George Orwell 1949: 38). The implications of this observation for historical sociolinguistics are palpable: we must first navigate problems in present-day sociolinguistics, achieve satisfactory application to the past, which, in turn, will help us project towards the future of the languages we investigate. Apart from well-known problems inherent in historical sociolinguistics itself, one essential dimension of the works of Romaine and others is the explicit acknowledgement of a range of problems in contemporary sociolinguistics itself (see Lass 1980; Romaine 1982, 1984; Milroy and Milroy 1985a; Cameron 1990; J. Milroy 1992, 2002; Hudson 1980/1996; and Oksaar 1999). The risk of historical sociolinguistics inheriting those problems, or of us unwittingly transposing them onto it, is real and disconcerting.

Within the limited space of this chapter, only the following four crucial problems will be considered briefly:

(i)   The ontological status of the object of linguistic investigation – language.
(ii) Confusion between *synchronic* and *diachronic* analyses.
(iii) Distortion of the concepts of linguistic *variation* and linguistic *change*.
(iv) The epistemological status of sociolinguistics itself.

Problem (i) might appear surprising, but it is indeed a fact that linguists have not been able to agree on what constitutes language or a language – "what we heedlessly and somewhat rashly call 'a language'," as Martinet put it (in Weinreich 1953: vii; see also Lass 1980: 129 and Asher 1994: s.v. *Language*). That might well explain why Saussure created one himself – a mythical one at that (Crowley 1990).[2] His idealization of language was the culmination of a fairly long intellectual tradition, which, having expert intellectual roots, has profoundly affected our conceptualization of the object of study (see J. Milroy 1992: 22–23; 1999: 24). Hudson (1980/1996: 34) links the problem to the ideology of standard languages and draws attention to its effects as follows:

> The irony, of course, is that academic linguistics is likely to arise only in a society with a standard language, such as Britain, the United States or France, and the first language to which linguists pay attention is their own – a standard one.[3]

Watts (2007: 511) also reflects on the same problem and expresses the need for soul-searching from sociolinguists "if we are to make further progress" (see also Cameron 1995).

Problem (ii) represents confusion of the most important set of Saussurean concepts, whereby *synchronic* has come to equate to *present-day* and *diachronic* to *historical*, to the extent that the notion of conducting a synchronic study of historical materials may sound strange to many.[4] Saussure repeatedly emphasizes the primacy of synchronic analysis and how it constitutes a speaker-centered perspective – the very core of sociolinguistic philosophy:

> Il est évident que l'aspect synchronique prime l'autre [c.-à-d., l'aspect diachronique], puisque pour la masse parlante il est la vraie et la seule réalité [...] La première chose qui frappe quand on étudie les faits de langue, c'est que pour le sujet parlant leur succession dans le temps est inexistante: il est devant un état. Aussi le linguiste qui veut comprendre cet état doit-il faire table rase de tout ce qui l'a produit et ignorer la diachronie [...] La synchronie ne connaît qu'une perspective, celle des sujets parlants, et toute sa méthode consiste à recueillir leur témoignage.
>
> [It is self-evident that the synchronic aspect [of languages] overrides the other [i.e., the diachronic aspect], because, for the masses of speakers, it is the true and only reality [...] The first striking factor in the study of linguistic realities is that for the speaker diachrony does not exist: what he has before him is a state [of language]. Also, a linguist who wishes to understand that state has to ignore diachrony by brushing aside whatever brought about that state [...] Synchrony only views facts from one perspective, which is that of the speaker, and the linguist's methodology invariably focuses on collecting the speaker's testimony.]
>
> (Saussure 1915/1972: 117–28)

Crystal's (2003: s.v. *Synchronic*) statement that "one could carry out a synchronic description of the language of Chaucer, or of the sixteenth century, or of modern-day English," therefore mirrors Saussure's own insistence on the status of these fundamental concepts. Thus, whilst *diachronic* invariably implies *historical*, the latter does not necessarily imply the former (see also Chapter 1 in this *Handbook*).

Problem (iii) is closely connected with (ii). Linguistic variation, crisply defined by Labov (1972: 271) as "the option of saying 'the same thing' in several different ways," can sometimes lead to change, but this does not imply that work on variation must *automatically* include change; the development of present-day sociolinguistics along largely diachronic lines of investigation has, perhaps inadvertently, been detrimental to the notion of "alternative ways of expressing (near-)synonymy" (Nevalainen and Raumolin-Brunberg 1996: 4; see also Raumolin-Brunberg 1991: 23, and, in particular, J. Milroy 1992: 162), which legitimately comprises the twin concepts of *linguistic continuity/linguistic innovation* (with possible change in progress). At any given time, a language overwhelmingly represents continuity.[5] Romaine (1982: 200) rightly considered the distortion to be a dangerous development in sociolinguistics:

> A very dangerous line of argumentation seems to have developed within sociolinguistics [...] with respect to the nature of variation and change. For some, the implicational relationship between the two holds equally well in both directions so that not only does change imply variation, but also variation implies change. Most sociolinguistic studies in recent years are looking for, and usually report, instances of change in progress on the basis of different rates of variation for age groups, social

classes, etc., while relatively few studies have devoted themselves to the analysis of situations in which change does not occur.

This dangerous development is reflected in the fact that we have the well-established phrase 'variation and change,' whilst 'variation and continuity' is virtually non-existent (see J. Milroy 1992: 10–11). Part of its uncomfortable effect is that, whilst present-day sociolinguistics plays an ambitious role of linguistic forecasting (largely in defiance of the linguistic equivalence of quantum decoherence),[6] such a role appears contrived for its historical counterpart, whose operations are always *post hoc* (see Lass 1980: 89–90). In effect, sociolinguistics suffers from the lack of an established theoretical framework for investigating and describing *stable variation*, which is an indisputable reality of languages. This is no small matter.

Problem (iv) is equally crucial, because at the mention of sociolinguistics, the first thing that comes to mind is the Labovian paradigm. Cameron (1990: 82–83) defines it in the following passage:

> To make sociolinguistics synonymous with the Labovian quantitative paradigm is to beg the question [...] For most people in the field (and especially most linguists in the field) 'sociolinguistics' does indeed mean primarily if not exclusively 'Labovian quantitative sociolinguistics.'

One often has to remind oneself that the Labovian paradigm is not the only way of doing sociolinguistics and that it has even been found wanting in important respects, its major shortcomings being collectively labeled the *correlational fallacy*. Scholars point out that, since statistical correlations apply only to collectives and are not reducible to individuals, a fundamental problem arises when they are applied to individuals and when they are treated as covering laws expressing regularities that govern particular instances. Romaine (1984: 36) observes in that respect:

> Correlations between linguistic variables and social categories do not explain anything of the social meaning speakers convey in linguistic structure [...] Social scientists have been all too often misled into thinking that only the knowledge obtained from an empiricist epistemology can provide the basis for real explanation. I do not believe, as Labov (1980) appears to, that progress in linguistics is dependent on developing new quantitative methodology for analyzing variation.

Thus, the unqualified adoption of the Labovian paradigm may constitute another burden of an inherited problem for historical sociolinguistics. Although his characterization of historical materials as 'bad data' has been replicated across the literature, it must be understood that historical data may only be bad if they are studied within the correlational paradigm (a fundamental methodological problem that epitomizes the proverbial pouring of new wine into old bottles). Consequently, methodological refinements still remain extremely important for historical sociolinguistics.

2.2 Self-segregation

One drawback for our subfield is the tendency to label more inclusive historical accounts with the tag *alternative*, or a similar qualifier (Watts and Trudgill 2002 and Elspaß *et al.* 2007 readily come to mind as examples). It is true that to be able "to challenge accepted beliefs [established by] the hegemony of the traditional discourse" about the history of languages we need deconstruction, then reconstruction (Watts 2007: 495); but since deconstruction, reconstruction, and counter-discourses are all *means to an end*, rather than ends in themselves, any special labels based on them might cause more harm than good. It is strategically helpful to avoid such labels, as the consequent connotative implications go well beyond what is immediately apparent.

2.3 Inappropriate nomenclature

There is also the need to shun such terms as 'archaism,' 'dialectalism,' 'low-class speech,' 'provincialism,' 'rusticism,' and 'vulgarism' (see J. Milroy 2002), for, ingrained as these qualifiers are, they remain purely ideological constructs from pre-sociolinguistics discourse, largely unbecoming to linguistic professionals and which sociolinguists must not perpetuate. These terms are connotation-laden and lead to what James Milroy calls biased selectivity; they represent linguistic value judgments (the *bête noire* of sociolinguistic philosophy) which derive from millennia-old, ugly social attitudes of members of the privileged minority classes' derision of and disdain towards the majority of society. The objective reality is that when it comes to language usage, each and every native speaker is effectively an authority (see Priestley 1762, cited by Baugh and Cable 1994: 278); even Saussure (1915/1972: 20–21) admits to this fact:

> Dans la vie des individus et des sociétés, le langage est un facteur plus important qu'aucun autre. *Il serait inadmissible que son étude restât l'affaire de quelques spécialistes; en fait, tout le monde s'en occupe peu ou prou.*
> [In the life of individuals and societies, language is the most important factor of all. It would be unacceptable that its study should remain in the hands of just some specialists; as a matter of fact, everyone more or less engages in it]. (My italics)

Historical sociolinguistics is the best equipped to address the treatment of languages as if, in the words of James Milroy (2002: 12–13), they do not belong "to all its speakers – only to a select few;" likewise, Crystal's (2002: 241) wish for "a more inclusive and representative historical linguistics" can only be effectively answered by historical sociolinguistics.

2.4 Hudson's micro-model

To the problems outlined above the finest tip of micro-sociolinguistics provides the much-needed solutions. The micro-model reduces the subject matter of sociolinguistics to particular linguistic items as used by individuals, a model expounded in a cogent and incisive exposition by Hudson (1980/1996) in his well-known work *Sociolinguistics*. Pointing out that both sociologists and sociolinguists would agree on the need to keep individuals firmly in the centre of interest whilst talking about large-scale abstractions and movements, he compares the importance of the individual in sociolinguistics to the individual cell in biology: if we do not understand how the individual behaves, we shall not be able to understand how collections of individuals behave either. He specifies that, unlike the individual cell, the individual speaker is molded much more by experience than by genetic make-up. From the uniqueness of people's sociolinguistic past, each individual constructs a more or less subconscious mental map arranged in a multi-dimensional social space. The particular map that each individual draws will reflect his or her own personal experience.

The individual is, however, not simply a social automaton controlled by this map, nor is the map itself an unselective record of past experience. Rather, individuals *filter* their experience of new situations through their existing map, and two people could both hear the same person talking, but be affected in different ways (see Oksaar 1999: 5–6). This leads to the operation of the forces of individualism and conformity within individuals, so that the amount of variation found within any given community will depend on the relative strengths of these two forces.

Hudson notes that human linguistic behavior is much more complex than many of us linguists think, though it may well be that those with less professional commitment to linguistics will find that their current common-sense view of language fits the facts quite well. He painstakingly demonstrates the extensive over-lapping of linguistic items in usage, so that it is impossible to pin down in reality a number of well-established concepts in modern sociolinguistics (see Martinet's very important declaration in Weinreich 1953: vii). A selection of Hudson's (1980/1996: 68–69) key conclusions follow:

> The search for a 'true' definition of the speech community, or for the 'true' boundaries around some assumed speech community, is just a wild goose chase [...] Language must be 'in the individual' for various reasons – because each individual is unique, because individuals use language so as to locate themselves in a multi-dimensional social space. (29)
>
> There is no way of delimiting varieties, and we must therefore conclude that varieties of language do not exist. All that exists are people and items, and people may be more or less similar to one another in the items they have in their language. *Though unexciting, this conclusion is at least true.* (My italics) (39)
>
> One person's dialect is another person's register. For example, the items which one person uses under all circumstances, however informal, may be used by someone else only on the most formal occasions. (47)
>
> Are languages always kept separate in speech? Here too we find that the variety-based view is far too rigid to do justice to human linguistic behaviour. (51)
>
> It is still possible to use terms like 'variety' and 'language' in an informal way [...], without intending them to be taken seriously as theoretical constructs. (68–69)

The above are key observations and show that there are still many common notions in our discipline – speech community, the delimitation of languages, their locus, their varieties, and the formal–informal stylistic dichotomy – that cannot stand objective scrutiny.

One difficulty that Hudson notes (if we wish to refine the micro-model so as to obtain psychologically real variables) is that it entails an ambitious task of gathering data on all the variants of all variables of every speaker that we set out to investigate:

> Armed with the individual's vocabulary list, we can then ignore any words in which they never use [a given variant], thereby guaranteeing that our figures really do show the proportion of real choices that they make in favour of each variant. The result would be wonderfully clean data, but of course there is a fundamental flaw in this programme: it is simply impossible because the individual inventories would take too long.
>
> (Hudson 1980/1996: 173)

However, we need not look hard to see the applicability of Hudson's theoretical-methodological model to historical sociolinguistics, which, by the nature of the source of its data, automatically irons out the only flaw in an otherwise perfect approach in sociolinguistics and allows us to produce wonderfully clean data. We have a fairly clear idea of the limits of the usage of the individual(s) we set out to investigate, because our main source of data is written language (literary or other-wise). And although the writings of a given individual constitute just a tiny frac-tion of their entire language use, that is the only material available to us, for obvious reasons. Thus, unlike speech, written records are not open-ended. Even for prolific writers like Cervantes or Shakespeare, the record of their language is closed-ended, and investigating it is made even easier with modern electronic software. Thus, wonderfully clean data, impossible in present-day sociolinguis-tics, is perfectly obtainable in historical sociolinguistics, even for several individu-als in the course of a single project. The micro-model, therefore, sticks out as ideal for historical sociolinguistics, as it does away with most of the inherent and inher-ited problems that the subfield has been grappling with, such as the effort to reconstruct past dialectal patterns and social structures via textual genres or glean-ings from social histories.

The potential of the micro-model can be viewed as parallel to that of quantum mechanics (the "theory of the very small," to poach Stephen Hawking's words, 2008), whose overall contribution has been described as the most successful theory in the history of science, based on the behavior of atomic objects. The success, however, carries a psychological challenge:

> It is also a theory that challenges our imagination. It seems to violate some funda-mental principles of classical physics, principles that eventually have become a part of western common sense since the rise of the modern worldview in the Renaissance.
> (Faye 2008: 1)

The Uncertainty Principle, whereby quantum mechanics "introduces an unavoidable element of unpredictability or randomness into science" (Hawking 1988: 60), is now common knowledge. Most interestingly, physicists now compare the behavior of atoms, in terms of being hard to predict with certainty, to that of humans. They openly declare that in the quantum world common sense is frequently violated. Hawking (2008) tellingly states: "At the very tiny level, our universe is like a crazy dance of waves [...] Particles appear and disappear at random; and at this level, nothing is certain, not even existence."

Sociolinguistics can, similarly, compare linguistic behavior to the erratic behavior of particles and build into its methodological framework 'the theory of the very small' and the concepts of randomness. Hudson's micro-model appears to be the best candidate for an objective description of perhaps the fuzziest and most sophisticated of all human phenomena – language and linguistic behavior – and eliminates the burden of expecting neat, regular patterns all the time. As humans have the propensity to see patterns and regularity in nature, it is easier to view things from afar, from where large-scale patterns are more easily seen. As we get closer, however, such patterns more often than not dissipate. An analogy may be made with star constellations, which for millennia have been viewed as forming given shapes of objects; but the now familiar fact that real interstellar distances in those apparent patterns are vast, even running into light years, to the extent that whole galaxies can collide (usually called 'galactic cannibalism' in astronomy) without their constituent stars coming close to each other, let alone colliding, renders the patterns mirage-like phenomena (although this view may raise a further ontological question: is a mirage reality or not?). From his philosophical vantage point, Popper (1972/1979: 23–24) states in this respect:

> It was first in animals and children, but later also in adults, that I observed the immensely powerful need for regularity – the need which makes them seek for regularities; which makes them sometimes experience regularities even where there are none; which makes them unhappy and may drive them to despair and to the verge of madness if certain assumed regularities break down.

In a similar vein, Labov's (1989) discussion of variations in one feature of the English spoken in Philadelphia has attracted some critical comments from Hudson (1980/1996: 30). Arguing against the over-generalization of his findings, Hudson observes that, although Labov's data are beyond dispute, they only seem to show that individuals in Philadelphia are very similar as far as this one feature is concerned. A similar criticism is implied in his reference to Labov's use of the whole of New York City as a single speech community with a 'community grammar.'

The micro-framework does not ignore the big picture. It provides for it in the sense that the big picture can only be built up gradually, by the accumulation of micro-studies – a concept best expressed by Martinet as "the aggregate of millions of such microcosms many of which evince [...] aberrant linguistic comportment" (see Weinreich 1953: vii). The process must be slow, but it is realistic, nevertheless. The model eliminates the bulk of the problems that prompted Romaine to view sociolinguistics as an aesthetic rather than a scientific pursuit, given that the alleged empirical foundations advocated by Labov are based on "a mistaken idea of what constitutes the method of natural science and the nature of the issues which can properly be empirical in a linguistic theory" (1982: 274). The model by Hudson provides for Romaine's (1982: 282) suggestions that we need to avoid *scientism* and the development of a *non-deductivist epistemology*. It also responds to her warning that "[s]ociology has no solutions to offer to our problems" and that "there are no ready-made sociological theories for linguists to plug their data into" (1982: 36).[7] All in all, the micro-framework has the potential to do away with many of the thorny, and still unresolved, issues that have led some scholars to advocate the demythologization of sociolinguistics (see Cameron 1990).

3. Literary Sources

In an article entitled "Early collections of private documents: the missing link in the diachronic corpora?," Sevic (1999: 337) declares that "[t]he author finds the use of literary texts as material for diachronic study inadequate," a statement that is fairly representative of a widespread view amongst (socio)linguists. Of course historical sociolinguistics would be missing the plot if it aimed to replicate the type of data and results achievable in present-day sociolinguistics (see Feyerabend 1978, cited by Romaine 1982: 105). It is clear that, for example, by the very nature of their science, paleontologists cannot expect to find live zebras (as present-day macrobiologists do) dating back to pre-Ice Age epochs; but that restriction does not render them despondent and make them lament over the fossilized remains of a mammoth or footprints of a baby tyrannosaurus, as doing so would imply a serious identity crisis.

It must be noted that the complementary relationship between speech and writing has been part of philosophical debate since antiquity. From the time of Augustine to the Renaissance and beyond, philosophers drew on ancient debates in developing their semiotic philosophies in logic, with the relative status between spoken words and writing being a roller coaster over centuries. Literature, fiction-based or not, is an integral part of language and of the language in which it is written. It is also a manifestation of language use and linguistic behavior and, therefore, a legitimate source of data for (socio)linguistic research. The argument against the validity of literary sources comes across as just as worthless as Saussure's conviction that spoken language was not valid for linguistic research (see note 2): an argument that apparently appeared important and learned at the time, but which one would presume that no serious professional sociolinguist would be keen to be associated with in this day and age. In a word, there is no worthwhile debate to engage in on the issue, beyond the broad ontological question of what constitutes a language (see section 2.1 above).

Part of the reason for the unnecessary debate is that we tend to lose sight of the fact that literature played a prominent role in the configuration of what we now know as standard languages (see Baugh and Cable 1951/1994; Milroy and Milroy 1985b/1999; Watts 2007) and the creation of their pillars – authoritative lexicographical works (beginning with those of Edward Phillips and, later, Samuel Johnson, in the case of English) and grammars. Moreover, we lose sight of the fact that, paradoxically, the very ideology that feeds the anti-literature argumentation in linguistics had its origins in literature itself (see Close 2000 and Moreno García del Pulgar 2009).

In effect, Romaine (1982: 14–21) did justice to this issue, arguing convincingly that speech and writing are the same language embodied in different channels, and that, if written language is an instance of language, then the same techniques apply to all instances of language. She sees a reminiscence of the language–literature overlap in the controversy over the boundary between sociology and sociolinguistics, and acknowledges the inevitability of such overlaps in virtually any discipline that deals with human phenomena. She asserts that, in the case of literature, the linguist will be interested in the language as such in the first instance, whilst the literary critic is interested in the language as literature.

That being the case, attention should be drawn to the fact that even aspects such as figures of speech and rhetorical devices, universally recognizable as typical literary phenomena, should also be readily identifiable as functional sociolinguistic devices. This is because each literary device, be it an *anadiplosis*, a *hyperbole*, a *polysyndeton*, a *tautology*, or indeed *silence* (in any of its nuances), reflects an expressive linguistic function that is ascertainable in real-life human interactions. In other words, the various shades of effects that they create are an integral part of how people tailor language to different functional and interactional ends, including the art of negotiating ubiquitous tactical and strategic power relations. Thus, far from being restricted to the discipline of literary criticism, these devices represent characteristics of language usage in speech and at all levels of writing. There remains a great deal more in literary sources to be explored and exploited by the (historical) sociolinguist, without necessarily having to pay homage to the established literary terminology, for obvious reasons.

3.1   Sample size

According to Romaine (1982: 11),

> The difference in competing linguistic theories lies not so much in the denial or admission of the existence of variation per se (as one might believe from reading the work of Labov, for example), but rather in disagreement about which types of variation can and are to be included within the scope of linguistic theory as fundamental […] The remaining variation, i.e. the non-fundamental, is then excluded as irrelevant, or, at worst, non-existent.

We must resist importing this practice into historical sociolinguistics, since to do so would amount to setting out to reconstruct at least parts of a challenging jigsaw puzzle, but then discarding pieces of it, because they look ugly or are too small. How to avoid unhelpful practices is a real methodological challenge. In present-day sociolinguistics, samples of data that are often excluded from analyses include those that are considered either too small or too large. In practice, there is no consensus amongst sociolinguists as regards sample size (see Milroy and Gordon 2003). Romaine (1982: 111) cites Albo as concluding that in some cases more than 100 tokens may not be enough, whilst in others, fewer than ten, and even two, tokens might show contrastive patterns of usage for a given variable for an individual speaker.

This problem brings into focus the common remark found in research based on historical written data, concerning the high frequency of certain variants. The usual treatment is that since those variants might be stereotypical, they are not representative of normal usage and therefore cannot be taken seriously. This view requires reconsideration, because the conventional evaluation of such stereotypes has been almost entirely carried out within the parameters of the quantitative-correlational paradigm. In the micro-model, however, this supposedly serious problem becomes largely irrelevant, because the stereotypical variants will be viewed as part of the author's sociolinguistic behavior.

3.2   Fictional characters

One interesting question about using literary data in sociolinguistics is that of the status of fictional characters. One wonders whether it is legitimate to refer to, say, the language of Sancho Panza or Cleopatra (see Crystal 2008). Such linguistic attributions are not uncommon, but it can be argued that such language may only be used for informal reference, without regarding it as serious sociolinguistic reality. The simplest way to conceptualize the issue is that by attributing language to characters we effectively put ourselves in the untenable situation of having to refer to the language of non-human entities, since these do appear in literature (Anipa 2005: 282–83).

3.3   A study of variation in Shakespeare's language

In examining variation in Shakespeare's language, I find it irresistible to use his name as a point of departure. The idea of Shakespeare's and his contemporaries' inability to write his name 'correctly,' as the debate over this issue tends to indicate (see Kathman, 1996) is not even worth contemplating by the historical sociolinguist. Setting aside severely abbreviated forms of his name, the following are the different variants that are readily recognizable.

1. Shakespeare	2. Shakespere	3. Shakespear
4. Shakspeare	5. Shackspeare	6. Shakspere
7. Shackespeare	8. Shackspere	9. Shackespere
10. Shaxspere	11. Shexpere	12. Shakspe~
13. Shaxpere	14. Shagspere	15. Shaksper
16. Shaxpeare	17. Shaxper	18. Shake-speare
19. Shakespe	20. Shakp	21. Shaxberd
22. Shak-speare	23. Shakspear	24. Schaksp.
25. Shakespheare	26. Shakespe	27. Shakspe

From a sociolinguistic viewpoint, the question as to which of these was *the* spelling of Shakespeare's name is irrelevant, but, assuming it was posed, the answer would emphatically be: *all of them*.

Table 10.1 displays variation in 20 variables from 13 of Shakespeare's plays. The data are extracted from the *Oxford Shakespeare Concordances*; the plays are presented in the "conjectured order of composition" (see Wells *et al.* 1986/2005: xliii),[8] for ease of cross-referencing and "pattern-hunting;" the variables are defined by their modern English forms; fictional characters in the plays have been ignored and the entire language exclusively attributed to the author. The issue of grapheme-phoneme correspondence, "an area where precise conclusions are unattainable" (Crystal 2005: xlvii; see also Salmon 1986), is not considered here. What we are interested in is a snapshot of linguistic variation across a number of Shakespeare's plays over a twenty-year period, as well as the implications thereof.

3.4   Discussion

In the light of Jones's declaration used as epigraph for this chapter, the display and celebration of inconsistency in a language should contribute towards knowledge of a more accurate picture of it. This, in turn, contributes towards redressing the long-standing imbalance in the traditional representation of language usage in the past. At a glance, the variation displayed in Table 10.1 appears to be substantial; but on closer examination, the picture turns out to be deceptive. The data can be analyzed and interpreted in diverse ways, but due to severe restriction imposed by space this section will be brief and confined to just three domains, all designed to test the real continuity–change dichotomy of variation:

i.   Examination of the degree of variation in individual texts.
ii. Comparison of usage in texts (b) and (m), in search of any shift in choice over an eighteen-year period.
iii. Consideration of the zero occurrences of some variants.

For domain (i), we have these percentages of variation: (a) 100%, (b) 44.4%, (c) 33.3%, (d) 44.4%, (e) 50.0%, (f) 52.6%, (g) 38.9%, (h) 52.9%, (i) 61.1%, (j) 68.7%, (k) 43.8%, (l) 52.6% and (m) 31.2%. Text (a) has a special status, however, as it was used as the basis for determining the variables to be examined, hence the 100% variation. Moreover, the percentages are calculated on the actual number of variables featured in each text (i.e. minus non-occurrences). Another point of interest is that variables (12) and (17) have identical variants across the texts, including (a).

The analysis for domain (ii) reveals that, apart from the fairly close percentages (44.4% : 31.2%) in the degree of variation over eighteen years, these texts have identical variants in eight of the 20 variables (40%). In variables (3) and (13), of which text (b) has only one variant each, text (m) has more than one. Conversely, text (m) has one variant each in variables (4), (9) and (20), whilst text (b) has more than one. In one variable, (20), where they both have multiple variants, the difference lies in text (b) having one more than (m); and in another variable, (7), they both have just one variant, which, however, do not coincide.

Domain (iii) is also of great interest and can be accorded a two-way examination. Horizontally, the zero occurrence of variables in all the texts ranges from one to eight, with the absence of variables (1) and (8) being the most prominent. Vertically, the zero occurrence ranges from two to four, with texts (j), (k), and (m) most prominent.

3.4.1   Reflection   The three aspects of the data examined have revealed a great deal about variation in Shakespeare's English, precisely by *not* revealing much variation across the texts he composed approximately between 1591 and 1611. In other words, we have evidence of *stable variation* in Shakespeare's English (as far as the variables studied are concerned) over a period of twenty years. First, by scoring the lowest degree of variation (31.2%), text (m) presents an interesting front, for being the latest text studied with the least amount of variation. This is deceptive, since it is one of the texts with four non-occurring variables, whilst text (c), close to the lower end of the chronology, and with the second lowest degree of variation (33.3%), has only two non-occurring variables. This presents a higher denominator for the calculation. Second, at first sight, text (m) appears to display a set of relatively more modern variants, but a closer examination – as in domain (ii) of the analysis – shows that there is hardly any difference. Third, the analysis reveals that neither the horizontal nor the vertical aspects of non-occurrence of some variables bear any relationship to chronology. Rather, the most likely factor must be that of topic, since it cannot be argued, for instance, that *afford* and *deceased* were fading out of Shakespeare's English. Thus, even the broad notion of change *in progress* cannot be ascertained in the data used.

If we add to all these indicators the fact that the texts examined include several 'reported texts', we have strong evidence of *linguistic continuity* and virtually none for linguistic change over the twenty-year period. It is indeed inattention to continuity that has led to erroneous labeling as innovations of various features of modern languages, which are, in reality, *'retentions* [from the past]' (Poplack, Van Herk, and Harvie 2002: 89). In that connection, Crystal (2008) discusses a number of modern myths about Shakespeare's English and reveals that the proportion of real change in his English over the past four centuries amounts to less than 10%. He asserts: "[a]ll fluent modern English speakers, native or non-native, have an immensely powerful start, in that they already know over 90% of the language that Shakespeare uses" (2008: 15).

This is a sample of synchronic study of Shakespeare's English, which reveals that he went back and forth in his choice of the variants available to him. Such linguistic behavior transcends certain common sociolinguistic concepts such as 'innovators,' 'early-adopters,' 'laggards' and 'resisters' – an over-simplification of human ingenuity and creativity, for, in effect, "each individual is a battle-field for conflicting linguistic types and habits" (Martinet, in Weinreich 1953: vii). It mirrors the 'uncertainty principle,' whereby the same speaker can simultaneously act as an innovator, a laggard and even a resister, a phenomenon designated as 'the

Table 10.1. Variation in Shakespeare's Language

List of variables	Variants in SHAKESPEARE					
	a. TSH* 1590-1	b. RIC3* 1592-3	c. LLL 1594-5	d. KRS 1595	e. MND 1595	f. 1 KHF 1596-7
1. afford	-o-/-oo-	-oo-	-o-/-oo-	-o-	X	-o-
2. amazed	-z'd/-zed	X	-zde	-zd/-zed/ -zde	-z'd/-zed	-z'd
3. among	'mong/-g/ -gst	-g	-g	-gst	-g	'mongst/ -g/-gst
4. ask	-k/-ke	-ke	-ke	-ke	-ke	-ke
5. beauty	-ie/-y	-ie/-y	-ie	X	-y	-ie/-y
6. brief	-eef/-ief/ iefe	-eef/-ief/ -iefe	X	-ief/-iefe	-ief/-iefe	-ief/-iefe
7. courtesy	courtesie/ courtsie/ curtesie/ curtsie	curtesie	courtecie/ courtesie/ courtisie/ curtesie/ curtsie	courtesie/ curtesie	courtesie/ curtesie/ curtsie	courtesie/ curtesie
8. deceased	-sed/-st	X	X	X	-st	-s'd
9. endure	en-/in-	en-/in-	en-/in-	en-	en-	en-
10. extreme	-e-/-ea-	-e-/-ea-	-ea-	-ea-	-e-/-ea-	-ea-
11. favour	-or/-our	-our	-our	-our	-our	-or/-our
12. go	-o/-oe	-o/-oe	-o/-oe	-o/-oe	-o/-oe	-o/-oe
13. I think	methinkes/ me-thinkes	methinkes	methinkes	methinkes	methinks	methinkes
14. know	-o/-ow	-ow	-ow	-ow/-owe	-ow/-owe	-ow
15. obey	-ay/-ey	-ey	-ay	-ey	X	X
16. only	onelie/ onely/only	onely	onelie/ onely/ only	onely	onely/ only	onely/ only
17. shall	-l/-ll	-l/-ll	-l/-ll	-l/-ll	-l/-ll	-l/-ll
18. through	-o-/-ou-	-ou-	-ou-	-ou-	-ou-	-ou-
19. while	-le/-l'st	-le/-les/ -l'st	-le	-le/-lst	-les/-lst	-le/-les/ -l'st
20. year	-eare/-eere	-eare/-eer/ -eere	-eere	-eare/ -eere	-ear	-eare/ -eere

Notes: (1) a = *The Taming of the Shrew*; b = *Richard III*; c = *Love's Labour's Lost*; d = *Richard II*; e = *A Midsummer Night's Dream*; f = 1 *Henry IV*; g = *The Merchant of Venice*; h = 2 *Henry IV*; i = *Hamlet*; j = *Measure for Measure*; k = *Pericles*; l = *All's Well that Ends Well*; m = *The Tempest*. (2) Asterisks indicate 'reported texts'. (3) Zero occurrences are represented by 'X'.

g. MVE 1596-7	h. 2 KHF 1597-8	i. HAM* 1600-01	j. MME 1603-4	k. PER* 1607	l. AWE 1606-7	m. TEM* 1610-11
X	X	X	X	X	-oo-	X
-z'd	X	-z'd	-z'd	X	-z'd	-zed
'mong/-g	-g/-gst	-g	X	-gst	-g/-gst	'mong/-g
-ke	-ke	-ke	-k/-ke	-ke	-ke	-ke
-y	X	-ie/-y	-ie/-y	-ie	-ie/-y	-y
X	-ief	-eef/-ief/-iefe	-ief/-iefe	-ief/-iefe	-eef/-ief/-iefe	X
courtesie/curtesie	courtesie/curtesie/curtsie	courtesie/curtesie	courtesie/curtesie/curtsie	courtesie/curtesie	courtesie/curtesie	courtesie
-sed	-st	X	X	X	X	X
X	en-/in-	en-	X	en-	en-	en-
-ea-	-ea-	-e-	-e-	-e-	-e-	X
-our	-or/-our	-or/-our	-or/-our	-our	-our	-our
-o/-oe	-o/-oe	-o/-oe	-o/-oe	-o/-oe	-o/-oe	-o/-oe
methinkes	methinkes	methinks	methinkes/methinks	X	methinkes/methinks	methinkes/methinks
-ow/-owe	-ow	-ow/-owe	-ow	-ow/-owe	-ow	-ow
-ey	-ey	-ay/-ey	-ey	-ey	-ey	-ey
onely	onely/only	onely/only	onelie/onely	onely	onelie/onely/onlie	onely
-l/-ll	-l/-ll	-l/-ll	-l/-ll	-l/-ll	-l/-ll	-l/-ll
-ou-	-ou-	-ou-	-ou-	-ou-	-ou	-ou-
-les/-lst	-le/-les	-le/-les/-l'st	-le/-les/-lst	-le/-les	-le/-l'st	-le/-les
-eere	-eare/-eere	-ear/eere/-ere	-eare/-eere	-eare/-eere/-eer	-eare/-eere	-eere

tug-of-war theory of variability,' illustrated diagrammatically by Anipa (2001: 22–37).

The case of Shakespeare is, therefore, a manifestation of that intra-personal linguistic tug-of-war. The eventual acceptance of the fact that, at the micro-, individual level, it is sometimes *impossible* to determine why an individual switches from one variant to another, will be a quantum leap for sociolinguistics.[9] Normal humans are susceptible to an open-ended range of temperaments and attitudes, all with indeterminate shades of idiosyncratic variation.

Expanding on the concept of 'states of a language' – on which synchronic analysis focuses – Saussure acknowledged its approximate nature, saying that 'Cela peut être dix ans, une génération, un siècle, davantage même […] Bref, la notion d'état de langue ne peut être qu'approximative' ('That could be ten years, a generation, a century, even more […] In a word, the notion of state of language can only be a matter of approximation') (1915/1972: 142–43). That being the case, it may be possible to discover some change in progress, when variation is studied in Shakespeare's complete works; any such indication would be confined to the variable(s) studied, rather than being characterized with a blanket statement such as 'language change.'[10] A relatively promising enterprise would be to conduct micro-studies on the usage of many of Shakespeare's contemporaries and those of a generation before and after, and compare them, in order to determine possible changes in progress in any items.

4. Conclusions

Firmly grounded in the probing ideas of Suzanne Romaine and others over the past few decades, as well as in Hudson's micro-theoretical-methodological model, this chapter has unashamedly rekindled and brought to the fore some important pending issues in present-day sociolinguistics that should not be taken for granted in the configuration of historical sociolinguistics. It has illustrated the micro-framework with a modest study of variation in Shakespeare's language. With so many unresolved issues surrounding sociolinguistics, it becomes clear that we are not quite yet in control of the present, the prerequisite for controlling the past. The inherited burden is substantial and the problems so fundamental that keeping them in focus can only benefit historical sociolinguistics in its long-term theoretical-methodological refinement.

Unlike traditional historical linguistics, which archetypically does so, historical sociolinguistics need not concentrate on *change* within a diachronic paradigm, since a focus on change naturally neglects continuity, which, paradoxically, accounts for the bulk of any language at any given time. It is not only possible, but also realistic, to study historical data synchronically as snapshots of inclusive linguistic repertoires available to past users of a language. This operation parallels the technique of composite images to display extensive phenomena that cannot be captured otherwise – like Martinet's 'millions of microcosms.' And, whether or not Shakespeare and his contemporaries were sufficiently educated to write the words *beauty, courtesy, go* or his surname 'correctly' can never be a worthwhile issue to the historical sociolinguist.

In the light of supposed 'adulteration' of Shakespeare's scripts by compositors, copyists, editors, printers, etc., from his own time (see, for example, Salmon 1986), one might ask to what extent the data presented in this study reflect Shakespeare's own language.[11] To address this concern, it must be borne in mind that the uncertainty itself has always been based on the questionable assumption that Shakespeare's written language must be necessarily (and radically) different from those of his contemporaries. Having said that, if we assume that Shakespeare's plays are a collective testimony to late sixteenth- and early seventeenth-century English (because they equally reflect the language of a few others who might have tampered with his manuscripts), that is not too bad a testimony to go by.

Romaine's pioneering work was very bold, as is Hudson's on the micro-model, and, indeed, Jones's assertion about inaccuracy in consistency. It is a much-needed attitude for real progress, for, as the philosopher Hume (1740/1938: 4) observed,

> [b]old attempts are always advantageous in the republic of letters, because they shake off the yoke of authority, accustom men to think for themselves, give new hints, which men of genius may carry further, and by the very opposition, illustrate points, wherein no one before suspected any difficulty.

NOTES

1 Compare Saussure's (1915/1972: 139) 'dans l'histoire de toute innovation on rencontre toujours deux moments distincts: 1° celui où elle surgit chez les individus; 2° celui où elle est devenue un fait de langue' ('there are always two distinct facets in the history of any innovation: one is when an innovation emerges in the usage of individuals, whilst the other is when it has become an integral part of the language'). (My translation from French here and throughout the chapter.)

2 Chambers (1995: 32–33) views Saussure's idealization of language as typifying the axiom of categoricity in linguistics and characterizes it as "a convenient fiction, erected in order to simplify reality in hopes of making data manageable and analyzable." He asserts that sociolinguistics is indeed the linguistics of the real thing – Saussure's *parole*. And in an extraordinary feat of frankness, Saussure openly admits to the fact that linguistics (i.e. of his mythical *langue*) is only possible if usage variation is strictly shunned: "Non seulement la science de la langue peut se passer des autres éléments du langage, mais *elle n'est possible que si ces autres éléments n'y sont pas mêlés*" ('Not only can the science of language do without other elements [i.e. the elements of speech], but it is only possible if such elements are not allowed to interfere with it') (p. 31) (my italics). See also Chambers' discussion of the identity problem of non-social linguistics (1995: 27–28).

3 In the same vein, Milroy and Milroy (1999: 19) observe: "it seems appropriate to speak more abstractly of standardisation as an *ideology*, and a standard language as an idea in the mind rather than a reality – a set of abstract norms to which actual usage may conform to a greater or lesser extent."

4   Occasionally in the linguistics literature one comes across the phrase "synchronic present-day studies" (see Jahr 1999: v), which, unless employed to contrast with "synchronic historical studies," exemplifies the confusion.

5   Saussure declares in that respect (echoing Baudouin de Courtenay's concept of 'dynamic stability'): "Ce qui domine dans toute altération, c'est la persistance de la matière ancienne; l'infidélité au passé n'est que relative. Voilà pourquoi le principe d'altération se fonde sur le principe de continuité" ('The dominant force in any phenomenon of change is the persistence of the old material; disloyalty to the past is only marginal. That is why the theory of change is based on the theory of continuity') (1915/1972: 109).

6   Interference phenomena in quantum mechanics (and in philosophy, etc.) are related to spontaneous interactions between a system and its environment that lead to the suppression of interference, since there are situations in which interference effects are suppressed. In the context of sociolinguistics, it translates into the fact that there is no guarantee that a given speaker innovation (see J. Milroy 1992) will successfully make it to language change; the process is a constant tug-of-war both between and within speakers (see Anipa 2001: 22–37), the outcome of which is shrouded in indeterminacy (see Raumolin-Brunberg 1991: 23); this creates an effective degree of equilibrium that keeps each language together and prevents it from disintegrating overnight, as it were.

7   A familiar issue about the sociologist's concept of society – borrowed by sociolinguistics – is its being conceptualized as a unified and harmonious mass of individuals, a misconception of reality, since society is the site and object of conflict, in the manner in which Bakhtin understands it (see Crowley 1990: 45). Martinet viewed such macro-concepts as having made "investigators blind to a large number of actual complexities" (see Weinreich 1953: vii).

8   Given the lack of consensus in the scholarship on Shakespeare about the nature of the early texts and their order of composition, it seems satisfactory to go by the dates that these specialists have arrived at.

9   One concept that has yet to be considered in sociolinguistic behavior is that of the law of diminishing returns, operating below the level of conscious awareness. In that respect, quantification would assume a special relevance.

10 Even though we are yet to agree on the definition of a language, it is self-evident that calling just a few linguistic features 'a language' is highly questionable from a scientific point of view and, thus, should better be avoided.

11 But that also brings up the challenge of whether we can effectively talk about the language of, say, The Queen or the UN Secretary-General, who do not usually write the scripts of their speeches themselves.

REFERENCES

Anipa, K. (2001) *A Critical Examination of Linguistic Variation in Golden-Age Spanish*, Lang, New York.

Anipa, K. (2005) A study of intra-personal variation in Cervantes (grapho-phonology). In R. Wright and P. Ricketts (eds.), *Studies in Ibero-Romance linguistics dedicated to Ralph Penny*, Juan de la Cuesta, Newark, DE, pp. 277–98.

Asher, R. (1994) *Encyclopedia of Language and Linguistics*, Pergamon Press, Oxford.

Baugh, A. and T. Cable (1951/1994) *A History of the English Language* (4th edn), Routledge, London.

Cameron, D. (1990) Demythologizing sociolinguistics: why language does not reflect society. In J. Joseph and J.T. Taylor (eds.), pp. 79–93.

Cameron, D. (1995) *Verbal Hygiene*, Routledge, London.

Chambers, J.K. (1995) *Sociolinguistic Theory*, Blackwell, Oxford.

Close, A. (2000) *Cervantes and the Comic Mind of his Age*, Oxford University Press, Oxford.

Crowley, T. (1990) That obscure object of desire: a science of language. In J. Joseph and J.T. Taylor (eds.), pp. 27–50.

Crystal, D. (2002) Broadcasting the nonstandard message. In R. Watts and P. Trudgill (eds.), pp. 233–44.

Crystal, D. (2003) *A Dictionary of Linguistics and Phonetics*, Blackwell, Oxford.

Crystal, D. (2005) The language of Shakespeare. In S. Wells, G. Taylor, J. Howett, and W. Montgomery (eds.), pp. xlv–lxiv.

Crystal, D. (2008) '*Think On My Words': Exploring Shakespeare's Language*, Cambridge University Press, Cambridge.

Elspaß, S., Langer, N., Scharloth, J., and Vandenbussche, W. (2007) *Germanic Language Histories 'from Below' (1700–2000)*, Walter de Gruyter, Berlin.

Faye, J. (2008) Copenhagen interpretation of quantum mechanics. In E.N. Zalta (ed.), *Stanford Encyclopedia of Philosophy*, Fall 2008 edition. http://plato.Stanford.edu/archives/fall2008/entries/qm-copenhagen/ [accessed August 31, 2008].

Feyerabend, P. (1978) *Against Method*, Verso, London.

Hawking, S. (1988) *A Brief History of Time: From the Big Bang to Black Holes*, Bantam, London.

Hawking, S. (2008) *Stephen Hawking and the theory of everything. Master of the Universe*, Channel Four Television Corporation Television Documentary.

Hudson, R.A. (1980/1996) *Sociolinguistics* (2nd edn), Cambridge University Press, Cambridge.

Hume, D. (1740/1938) *An Abstract of a Treatise of Human Nature* (reprinted with an introduction by J.M. Keynes and P. Sraffa), Cambridge University Press, Cambridge.

Jahr, E.H. (ed.) (1999) *Language Change: Advances in Historical Sociolinguistics*, Mouton de Gruyter, Berlin.

Johnstone, B. (2000) *Qualitative Methods in Sociolinguistics*, Oxford University Press, Oxford.

Jones, D. (1917) *An English Pronouncing Dictionary*, Dent, London.

Joseph, J.E. and Taylor, T.J. (eds.) (1990) *Ideologies of Language*, Routledge, London.

Kathman, D. (1996) The spelling and pronunciation of Shakespeare's name. http://shakespeareauthorship.com/name1.html#top [accessed October 2, 2008].

Labov, W. (1972) *Sociolinguistic Patterns*, University of Philadelphia Press, Philadelphia.

Labov, W. (ed.) (1980) *Locating Language in Time and Space*, Academic Press, New York.

Labov, W. (1989) Exact description of the speech community: Short a in Philadelphia. In R. Fasold and D. Schiffrin (eds.), *Language change and variation*, John Benjamins, Amsterdam, pp. 1–57.

Lass, R. (1980) *On Explaining Language Change*, Cambridge University Press, Cambridge.

Martinet, A. (1953) Preface. In U. Weinreich (eds.), *Languages in contact*, Linguistic Circle of New York, New York.

Milroy, J. (1992) *Linguistic Variation and Change. On the Historical Sociolinguistics of English*, Blackwell, Oxford.

Milroy, J. (1999) Towards a speaker-based account of language change. In E.H. Jahr (ed.), pp. 21–36.

Milroy, J. (2002) The legitimate language: giving a history to English. In R. Watts and P. Trudgill (eds.), pp. 7–25.

Milroy, J. and Milroy, L. (1985a) Linguistic change, social network and speaker innovation. *Journal of Linguistics* 21: 339–84.

Milroy, J. and Milroy, L. (1985b/1999) *Authority in Language* (3rd edn), Routledge, London.

Milroy, L. and Gordon, M. (2003) *Sociolinguistics: Method and Interpretation*, Blackwell, Oxford.

Moreno García del Pulgar, M. (2009) La Princesa de Salerno y algunas damas de la corte del Adelantado de Murcia. La obra poética de Acevedo en LB1. In J. Snow and R. Wright (eds.), *Late Medieval Spanish Studies in Honour of Dorothy Sherman Severin*, University Press, Liverpool, pp. 74–85.

Nevalainen, T. and Raumolin-Brunberg, H. (eds.) (1996) *Sociolinguistics and Language History. Studies Based on the Corpus of Early English Correspondence*, Rodopi, Amsterdam.

Oksaar, E. (1999) Social networks, communicative acts and the multilingual individual. Methodological issues in the field of language change. In E.H. Jahr (ed.), pp. 3–20.

Orwell, G. (1949) *Nineteen Eighty-Four: A Novel*, Secker and Warburg, London.

Poplack, S., Van Herk, G., and Harvie, D. (2002) Deformed in the dialects: an alternative history of non-standard English. In R. Watts and P. Trudgill (eds.), pp. 87–110.

Popper, K.R (1972/1979) *Objective Knowledge: An Evolutionary Approach* (2nd edn), Clarendon Press, Oxford.

Priestley, J. (1762) *Theological and Miscellaneous Works*. 25 vols. XXIII. n.p.

Raumolin-Brunberg, H. (1991) *The Noun Phrase in Early Sixteenth-Century English. A Study Based on Sir Thomas More's Writings*, Société Néophilologique, Helsinki.

Romaine, S. (1982) *Socio-Historical Linguistics: Its Status and Methodology*. Cambridge University Press, Cambridge.

Romaine, S. (1984) The status of sociological models and categories in explaining linguistic variation. *Linguistische Berichte* 90: 25–38.

Salmon, V. (1986) The spelling and pronunciation of Shakespeare's time. In S. Wells, G. Taylor, J. Howett, and W. Montgomery (eds.), pp. xlii–lvi.

Saussure, F. de (1915/1972) *Cours de Linguistique Générale*, Payot, Paris.

Sevic, R.B. (1999) Early collections of private documents: The missing link in the diachronic corpora? In C. Beedham (ed.), *Langue and Parole in Synchronic and Diachronic Perspective*, Pergamon, Amsterdam, pp. 337–47.

Watts, R. and Trudgill, P. (eds.) (2002) *Alternative Histories of English*, Routledge, London.

Watts, R. (2007) Deconstructing episodes in the 'history of English.' In S. Elspaß, N. Langer, J. Scharloth, and W. Vandenbussche (eds.), pp. 495–513.

Weinreich, U. (1953) *Languages in Contact*, Linguistic Circle of New York, New York.

Wells, S., Taylor, G., Howett, J., and Montgomery, J. (1986/2005) *William Shakespeare. The Complete Works* (2nd edn), Clarendon Press, Oxford.

11 Early Advertising and Newspapers as Sources of Sociolinguistic Investigation

CAROL PERCY

1. Introduction: Sociolinguistic Studies of Modern Newspapers

Why study the language of newspapers? With their 'large target audiences' and many text types (such as advertisements and death notices), newspapers effectively reflect the breadth of contemporary language and culture (Rademann 1998: 49). Moreover, newspapers not only reflect but influence their readers: language has pragmatic as well as semantic functions, conveying attitude as well as content (Cotter 2003: 47). Finally, in competition with other newspapers and other media, newspapers must attract and keep the attention of their readers (Ungerer 2000: vii). In sum, newspapers might attract, inform, influence, and/or entertain readers.

In turn, linguists can study newspapers in various ways. Indeed, in order to demonstrate the sociolinguistic potential of newspapers, I begin this chapter with an overview of modern sociolinguistic studies. Monographs about modern media language include those by Bell (1991: 5–7), Fowler (1991), Fairclough (1995: 20–34), Reah (2002), Herring (2003), and Richardson (2007). Some perspectives specifically illuminate the linguistics of persuasion: among sociolinguistic approaches to modern media language, Critical Discourse Analysis focuses on "how media discourse conveys ideological and political meanings" (Herring 2003: 7). Linguists have also considered the evaluative functions of features like modals and stance adverbials (Belmonte 2007: 2). Other approaches to media language are less

The Handbook of Historical Sociolinguistics, First Edition. Edited by Juan Manuel Hernández-Campoy and Juan Camilo Conde-Silvestre.
© 2014 John Wiley & Sons, Ltd. Published 2014 by John Wiley & Sons, Ltd.

explicitly ideological: structural studies, for instance, commonly establish characteristics and prototypes of different newspaper text types (Belmonte 2007: 3). Linguistically-oriented studies of newspaper language can inform our understanding of newspapers and their social roles.

Linguistic studies of newspapers can also illuminate the dynamics of language variation and change. Reportage and editorial material from newspapers are among the registers represented in such major modern corpora as the *British National Corpus* (BNC), *the International Corpus of English* (ICE), and the *Brown* and *Lancaster-Oslo/Bergen* (LOB) 'family' of corpora. In these multidimensional corpora, news reports and editorials represent language that was printed, public, and, respectively, more or less informative or influential. Newspapers have also been used by individual linguists: an important example of the use of newspapers in diachronic studies is Bauer's *Watching English Change: An Introduction to the Study of Linguistic Change in Standard Englishes in the Twentieth Century* (1994). More recently, online newspapers have been used as corpora by linguists. In a relatively early study of these resources, Rademann (1998) assessed their "benefits and pitfalls" for linguists. Some linguists use these corpora of periodicals to track the appearance of new words and phrases (Baayen and Renouf 1996, Bauer 2002), the role of the media in this innovation (Renouf 2007b), and even diachronic changes in recent news reportage (Kehoe 2006). A number of scholars have explained their methods for finding and analyzing specific linguistic patterns in online newspapers with such tools as "GlossaNet"[1] (Fairon and Singler 2006) and on the web generally with "WebCorp"[2] (Renouf and Kehoe 2006; Kehoe 2006; Morley 2006; Renouf 2007a; Renouf, Kehoe and Banerjee 2007). Commercial publishers of English language reference tools have also drawn on such contemporary media: along with John Sinclair, Renouf indeed co-directed the Collins COBUILD project's groundbreaking use of corpora for use in commercial lexicography. However, the methodological and financial difficulties that confront individual humanities scholars in a digitizing world are spelled out by team members of the Perseus Project, one of the leading initiatives in humanities computing (Crane, Babeu, and Bamman 2007). Online newspapers are powerful tools for linguistic research, but using them requires much methodological innovation and reflection. The possibilities and difficulties of coordinating different kinds of contemporary corpora to track ongoing grammatical change are discussed by Mair (2006). Findings from commercial collections of newspapers cannot be compared easily with the findings from the corpus linguistic tradition.

2. Overview: Linguistic Studies of Early Newspapers

Historical newspapers have also attracted the attention of linguists. They will probably continue to do so because of the increasing availability to individual scholars of such expansive and expensive digital collections as the *17th and 18th Century Burney Collection Newspapers*, the *Eighteenth Century Journals collections*, the *Times Digital Archive, 1785–1985*, and (for the United States) the *Historical*

Newspapers Collection. For lucky instructors at subscribing institutions, these online newspapers are accessible and appealing undergraduate teaching resources (see Curzan 2000). Collections of digitized historical newspapers are proliferating on the internet, sometimes requiring a subscription: many (including Google's) are listed on a useful series of metapages produced by XooxleAnswers: *Newspaper Archives.* One open historical corpus that draws on historical newspapers is Mark Davies' *Corpus of Historical American English,* which has the architecture and inter-face of the *British National Corpus* (BNC) and corresponds to a Corpus of Contemporary American English. For scholars in many disciplines, these resources are "powerful new research tools" (Popik 2004).

Because proliferating digital resources present new methodological challenges, some scholars have published advice for potential users of online historical news-papers. MacQueen (2004) argues that such very large collections as the *Times Digital Archive* are invaluable for tracing the diachronic development of such infrequent lexical items as the word *million*; he also acknowledges such disadvan-tages as relatively poor proofreading and the conflation of search terms in the "plural look-up feature." Even when online newspapers are carefully processed, the spelling variation characteristic of earlier English provides data for linguists but poses problems for users, as Fries and Schneider (2000: 19–23; Schneider 2002) remind us. Computational linguists rise to the challenge of using word tokens (often variably spelled) to identify not merely word types but also semantic fields. Crane and Jones (2006) provide strategies for processing proper nouns in an electronic corpus of eighteenth-century newspapers; Newman and Block (2006) demonstrate how automated word searches might identify discrete topics for historians. Finally, some corpus linguists have drawn attention to the lack of com-parability of different commercial newspaper corpora, and to the difficulty of using them in combination with existing linguistic corpora (Lindquist and Levin 2000; see also Mair 2006, among others).

To date, the most prominent studies of the early English newspaper have drawn on structured corpora compiled in Europe. The oldest and best-known corpus is the *Zurich English Newspaper* (ZEN) Corpus (1661–1791) (Fries and Schneider 2000; Lehmann, auf dem Keller and Ruef 2006). Covering an earlier period than ZEN, the *Florence Early English Newspapers* (FEEN) corpus (1641–61) was originally an extension of it (Brownlees 2001). Such corpora have been compiled with specific research aims in mind. ZEN's starting date suggests that one such aim involved language change generally: 1661 connects ZEN to the Brown and LOB corpora of English from 1961 (Fries and Schneider 2000: 7). Like most newspaper corpora, however, to date ZEN has been more often used to illuminate the development of journalism and its specific linguistic conventions. Its end date of 1791 was chosen to overlap with the starting date of the *Times Digital Archive,* 1785–1985. Similarly, the material in FEEN has allowed Brownlees to identify and analyze emergent conventions of the earliest English journalism.[3] In contrast, the three-century span of the *Rostock Corpus of English Newspapers* (1700–2000) facilitates large-scale diachronic investigations: it was constructed specifically "to explore the roots of popular English journalism" by finding linguistic correlates for popular and prestige readership such as personal pronouns, lexical diversity, and sentence length and complexity (Schneider 1998; Schneider 2000b: 335). As we will see below, users of these corpora have often tracked the development of now-established conventions within the genre: these include the development of the headline, the 'inverted pyramid' of the news story, and such subgenres as the advertisement and the death notice.

As well as attesting to the development of English language journalism, historical corpora containing early newspapers have also contributed to linguists' understanding of language change. Scholars such as Fitzmaurice (2007) have explored the roles of social networks in language change: her *Network of Eighteenth Century English Texts* (NEET) contains essays from *The Spectator* among other writings connected with its editor Joseph Addison. Other corpora have been constructed to facilitate diachronic linguistic studies. The LOB corpus is being extended back in time from 1961 to 1931 (Leech and Smith 2005), for instance. Because some twentieth-century text types do not clearly correspond to earlier ones, Leech and Smith (2005: 90) question whether the corpora in the LOB/Brown 'family' could be extended into the eighteenth century. However, news reportage has a long time-depth and is thus a key category in the well-known *Representative Corpus of Historical English Registers* (ARCHER). Such register studies, as Nevalainen explains (2000: 39), are predicated on the assumption that "the key to understanding the social embedding of language change is to get as close as possible to authentic, everyday communication between people" (see also Biber and Conrad 2001). The register of news reportage has an interesting if indirect relationship with everyday language. Newspapers were relatively widely read; Tieken-Boon van Ostade (2009: 142–43) connects them with the spread of literacy. In the ARCHER corpus, in contrast to the three categories of 'speech-based' writing, news reportage represents the category of 'popular exposition' as one of seven categories of written language. Using ARCHER, Biber and Finegan (2001: 75) have argued that over time, such popular written registers as news reportage have become increasingly a more 'popular' register, adopting "more 'oral' characteristics." As Curzan summarizes, register studies "have enhanced our understanding of the history of English and the changing relation of spoken and written language" (2008: 600–2).

Early newspapers are not represented in all stratified historical corpora. News reportage is absent, for instance, from *the Corpus of Early American English* (Kytö 1993) and the *Corpus of Nineteenth Century English* (CONCE) (Kytö, Rydén, and Smitterberg 2006: 6). These structured corpora are associated with the pioneering Helsinki Corpus of English, which features text types that span the period from Old English (OE) to 1710 and which does not include news (Kytö 1996). The absence of news reportage from these particular corpora highlights the importance of comparability across diachronic corpora. However, because newspapers reflect local norms or trends of language, they are integral to some other diachronic corpora constructed to chart the development of regional norms, for instance, in early Australia (Fritz 2006) and Ontario, Canada (Dollinger 2006). Dollinger (2008: 101–2) has constructed his *Corpus of Early Ontario English* (CONTE) to be comparable with ARCHER. Making corpora comparable facilitates the study of both diachronic and diasporic developments.

The remainder of my survey will elaborate on the approaches to historical newspapers that I have surveyed above. I focus on historical-linguistic approaches, but necessarily draw attention to work that has been done in other fields, especially by historical pragmatists. As Herring (2003: 5) observes, "[l]anguage change can operate simultaneously on multiple levels – lexical, structural, semantic, discourse-pragmatic, ideological, generic." Indeed, it has not been very easy to identify and acquire all the articles that I would like to have seen because applied-linguistic studies of historical newspaper language appear in quite dispersed venues.[4] Some articles appear in collections of essays on corpus linguistics (e.g. Renouf and Kehoe 2006) or in the *ICAME Journal*, others in the *Journal of Historical Pragmatics* or in collections reflecting pragmatic approaches, such as Ungerer (ed.) (2000), Brownlees (ed.) (2006), and Jucker (ed.) (2009). Moreover, because the study of media language can illuminate 'media' as well as 'language,' linguistic analyses of historical newspaper language can and have appeared in such disciplinary journals as *Media History* (see Raymond 2005: 15). However, despite this evidence of cross-disciplinary collaboration, scholars in different disciplines sometimes do not take advantage of each other's conclusions about similar topics. For instance, without citing corpus linguists, Matheson (2000) can describe the development of journalistic style, and the 'inverted pyramid' gets separate treatment by the pragmatists Ungerer (2002) and Jucker (2005) and the journalist Pöttker (2003). Finally, much fine work is so current that it is not yet accessible.[5] One of my aims in this survey is to synthesize some of the key trends in work to date. Another is to make a bibliography of work available in one place.

3. Linguistic Perspectives on Early Journalism

Newspapers first appeared in England in the seventeenth century, although the earliest "serial news pamphlets [...] between 1620 and 1642" were called not newspapers but 'corantos' (Brownlees 2005: 71; Fries and Schneider 2000: 4–6). A number of linguists have considered how this earliest English news writing differed from such similar genres as the private newsletter and the published polemical pamphlet. In connection with her work on early English correspondence, Nevalainen (2002: 73) has considered how the language of these public news serials differed from the private newsletter: unsurprisingly, early published newsletters had spelling that was more standardized than that of contemporary manuscript newsletters. Contrasting a sample of newspapers with contemporary polemical pamphlets, Claridge (2000: 26, 42) characterizes newspapers as relatively more 'informational' than 'interpersonal' or 'involved:' such linguistic markers of involvement as the first-person singular pronoun appear much less frequently in newspapers than in pamphlets. Early journalists were writing for an unknown audience, and their language reflected that.

Many linguistic studies of early newspapers draw on the *Florence Early English Newspapers* (FEEN) corpus and are listed on the web page of its compiler and main user, Nicholas Brownlees. In several, he accounts for the occasional stylistic foregrounding of more 'oral' or 'interpersonal' language in the otherwise 'informational' register of early corantos and later newsbooks (Brownlees 2005). As Jucker (2006: 120) has established, in comparison to modern genres, direct and reported speech occurred less often in early newspapers and was attributed to a socially narrower range of speakers. When it was used, direct speech (or representations of it) could add drama to a report, but Brownlees (2005: 72) notes a few instances where the speech is stylistically elevated and perhaps works to distance readers from the "regal" or "semi-divine" speaker. Direct speech could also function as a persuasive "truth-authenticating" device: in the case of King Charles I's trial, Brownlees observes that direct speech was attributed mostly to speakers the journalist wishes to sketch as sympathetic (2005: 78–79). Brownlees also observes that a very few news writers in the Civil War period occasionally used such interpersonal features as direct address, the second person pronoun, and parenthetic comments; these features, he argues, served to establish both connection and consensus with readers, "to reinforce the communicative impact of an ideologically charged message" (2005: 82–83; see also Brownlees 2006). These early journalists stood out from their peers: Brownlees' studies highlight the innovations of Thomas Gainsford (1566–1624) and some later anonymous writers, while Fries and Schneider (2000: 5) contrast the lively style of the professional editor of the *Post Man* with that of the civil servants who logged the *London Gazette* (first published in 1665). However, scholars emphasize that, in general contrast with modern genres, early news writing remained more 'informational' and less 'interpersonal.' Drawing on the Rostock Corpus (1700–2000) for her diachronic study of the imperative, Bös (2009: 131) finds its personalizing, persuasive, and structural functions more common in later newspapers. 'Oral' features were not the only techniques used to reach the readers of newspapers. The representation of in-groups and out-groups in early newsbooks is the subject of a semantic category analysis by Prentice and Hardie (2009). Comparisons with *like* and *as* similarly establish common ground with the reader; like other 'interpersonal' features of news reportage, they are more common in later texts (Claridge 2009: 112). Journalists' increasing exploitation of these more 'interpersonal' features to strengthen relationships with readers has also been observed in comparable genres of English newspaper writing through the twentieth century (Fowler 1991, quoted by Brownlees 2005: 75).

Görlach defines the newspaper as a "conglomerate supertype as well as a cluster of more or less clearly distinct individual text types" (2002: 83). Many scholars have used corpora of early newspapers to track the diachronic development of some of these text types. The headline is perhaps the most prominent feature of the modern English newspaper, and its development has been relatively well studied. According to Ungerer (2000: ix), over time the English headline has "become easier to comprehend and more attractive as an attention-getting device," perhaps as a response to increased competition (reported by Studer 2003: 20). Of the contemporary headline's separate elements, perhaps most notable are the distinctive syntax of its attributive noun phrases and its present-tense verb. Bailey (1996: 54) claims that the introduction of this "historic" or "dramatic" present into the headline reflects another way in which newspaper writing was becoming more oral. In his accessible explanation of the headline's modern form, Bailey (1996: 53–54) draws on the early work of Straumann (1935) when reporting that the characteristic present-tense verbs appeared first in the nineteenth-century United States. The headline's development in Britain, specifically in the nineteenth- and twentieth-century *Times*, is summarized by Simon-Vandenbergen (1981). Thanks to the development of the ZEN and Rostock corpora, the form and function of earlier headlines have been examined more recently. In her study of post-1800 headlines, Schneider (2000a: 56–61) focuses on how features other than finite verbs could convey "action" in headlines; she uses a semantic rather than grammatical scheme of classification. Studer's empirical study of earlier eighteenth-century headlines seeks to qualify statements like Schneider's (2000a: 52) that headlines proper were "extremely" rare in the eighteenth century. According to Studer, many early headlines structured rather than summarized their corresponding text (2003: 22; Studer 2005); by the mid-eighteenth century, headlines had more "varied" "pragmatic" functions which included such "performative" functions as giving notice. Studer and Schneider have used corpora of early newspapers to classify historical headlines on their own terms.

As well as the headline, scholars have attended to the development of such other newspaper text classes (Fries 2001) as death notices (Fries 1990, 2006), crime reports (Fries 2009), and advertisements (see below). Corpus-based studies of particular linguistic features often help to characterize newspaper text types: in Fries and Lehmann's study of lexical diversity in early newspapers, the class of advertisements was distinguished with the most diverse vocabulary (2006: 99), while Studer (2008: 226) found that modality correlated with "specific news contexts." Some studies of linguistic variables note how they can organize text types (Gieszinger 2000: 95–96, auf dem Keller 2004, Mäkinen 2008: 58, Bös 2009: 129, Fries 2009: 15–19). However, although corpus-based linguistic studies have allowed scholars to establish prototypes for specific text types in earlier periods (Mäkinen 2008, Wright 2009), they have also confirmed that early and modern genres do not always correspond. For instance, although *whereas* or past participles like *stolen* frequently begin eighteenth-century announcements of crimes (Fries 2009: 15–19), those announcements blur the boundary between what we now would consider news and advertisements.

4. Linguistic Perspectives on Early Advertisements

Advertising is an important economic engine of print journalism. Advertisements are prominent in many early newspapers: for instance, the *Daily Advertiser*, founded in 1730, effectively made news out of advertisements (Fries and Schneider 2000: 6). Advertisements' content highlights what is perceived to be of value in contemporary society, and research about advertisements is thus prominent in many academic disciplines. Advertisements' value as cultural-historical sources is evident in the work of economic historians (Church 2000), historians (Andrew 1997, 1998; Plumb 1975) and educational historians (Skedd 1997), book historians (Ferdinand 1997; Tierney 1995, 2001), and literary scholars (Doherty 1992). Suggestive connections between journalistic and literary methods of persuasion, and between advertisements and literature, are drawn by the literary scholar Mathison (1998) and the historian Donna Andrew (1998), who has examined how anonymous advertisers looking for public charity characterized themselves with literary tropes of sensibility. The linguistic features of advertisements can also index key aspects of contemporary culture. A diachronic study of personal advertisements tracks changing social values and gender relations in the last century of Australian society (Vlčková 2002). Class relations in early Britain and North America are illuminated by Wright's (2009) study of employment advertisements in eighteenth-century London and Mäkinen's (2008) study of nineteenth-century American advertisements for runaway slaves. By abstracting prototypes from their corpora, Mäkinen and Wright illuminate the development of their text types as well as emphasizing their function: advertisers needed their advertisements to be effective, and advertisements were generally very conservative (Mäkinen 2008: 87–88). There is general consensus that advertisements needed to attract readers' attention, to inform them about something, and to influence them to take action (Gieszinger 2000: 85–86). Leech's (1966) linguistic perspective on advertising has informed the work of many historical linguists. But to what extent are advertisements 'universal' across time and space? According to Momma and Matto (2008: 6), advertisements change their form and format as fast as material culture and media technology. Auf dem Keller (2006) describes some changes in the textual structure of book advertisements in the ZEN corpus. And can linguistic features in advertisements index more substantial changes in culture itself?

Whether and when a distinctively 'consumer society' took shape in English-speaking culture is a matter of interest and debate in a number of disciplines (see Church 2000). According to McKendrick, Brewer, and Plumb (1982) the eighteenth century saw a "consumer revolution," the "birth of a consumer society." Prominent literary scholars take such a transformation for granted: Campbell (2002), Lamb (2004), and Benedict (2007), for instance, link issues of identity and community to aspects of eighteenth-century advertising, and it seems to be the case that among the narrower range of commodities that were advertised in newspapers, books and patent medicines were prominent (Church 2000: 627–28).

Applied linguists, coming from a tradition of comprehensive and methodical analysis of data and keen to chart prototypical categories, are quite well placed to identify such a transformation. A study of eighteenth-century medical advertisements (Fries 1997: 60) documents the rise of the brand names that were to become much more common in subsequent centuries (Church 2000: 633). Moreover, in the eighteenth century advertisements are relatively "inconspicuous" (Görlach 2002: 96), not yet distinct from news as a text type (Gieszinger 2000: 86, 105; Fries 2009: 15–19). Some linguistic features attest at least to changing demographics in commercial culture. It is a truism that over time advertisements were "directed increasingly towards a broadening social status" (Church 2000: 634). In an unpublished conference paper, Palander-Collin (2008) has identified and analyzed the terms in which eighteenth-century advertisers represented and thereby flattered and influenced their audience, using such key words as 'nobility' and 'ladies.' The relatively elite status of eighteenth-century newspaper readers is also suggested by the prominence of Latin and French in advertisements for books and medicines (Fries 2007: 129–30). Latinate words are prominent among the adjectives so typical of advertisements of all periods (Fries 1997: 63–67, Gieszinger 2001: 141–44, Gotti 2005: 31–32). While reminding us that this apparent 'formality' in eighteenth-century advertisements needs to be measured in terms of the prose of the period, Görlach (2002: 99) draws attention to the culture-specific persuasive power of this "semi-learned diction" (2002: 96) and syntax that is almost "legal" in its involvement (2002: 95). According to a number of applied linguists, the language of eighteenth-century advertisements was less 'involved' and more 'informational' than that of contemporary advertisements. For instance, Gieszinger reports fewer questions (2000: 95–96), and Gotti (2005: 34) and Bös (2009: 117–19) report fewer imperatives. Moreover, even when imperative forms were used, they *usually* ordered potential customers not to buy a product but to seek information about it (Gotti 2005: 34). Such an increase in linguistic 'involvement' is often correlated with the demographic expansion of newspapers documented elsewhere for the nineteenth century (see Görlach 2002: 98), with the perhaps related rise in frequency of more 'involved' features in news discourse generally, mentioned above, and with increasing competition within and among media.

Advertisements can also attest to what we might term the 'language ecology' of their culture. The content of eighteenth-century advertisements for books, medicines, and employment suggest that classical and modern languages were perceived to be valued by readers (Fries 2007: 129–30; Percy 2004); from this, we might infer the relatively elite status of many newspaper readers. Evidence from historical American advertisements conveys a sense of the linguistic assimilation of British immigrants (Read 1938), the linguistic ecology of early Louisiana (Bailey 2003) and the presence there of anglophone slaves (Picone 2003), as well as the naming practices of runaway slaves farther north (see Laversuch 2006). These sources are just a few among many that use historical advertisements as evidence to reconstruct which languages and dialects were spoken at the time.

5. Newspapers as Repositories of Attitudes Towards Language

The social capital of correct English, along with the importance of the classics and modern languages, can be seen in classified advertisements of the later eighteenth century. In a qualitative study (Percy 2004), advertisements, especially those for teachers and for schools, indicate that by the 1760s correct language had become a commodity for some contemporary Londoners. In advertisements for their schools, some educational entrepreneurs featured grammar as one sign of an effective education (Percy 2009a). Advertisements confirm the diffusion of normative attitudes.

The social stigma of incorrect language is perhaps an even more prominent topic in newspapers, old and new. Because journalists report – and sometimes create – newsworthy or entertaining information, news stories can be useful sources of information about attitudes to language. Such early eighteenth-century serials as *The Tatler* and *The Spectator* were key media for the transmission of normative attitudes (see Fitzmaurice 1998). Jonathan Swift complained anonymously in *The Tatler* about the incorrect language of some of his contemporaries; as the eponymous Spectator, Joseph Addison expressed normative attitudes about grammatical usage in a number of essays. The ambiguous status of these papers – were they newspapers? magazines? – has been demonstrated by Fitzmaurice (2007). In a cluster analysis, Fitzmaurice (2010: 51) reveals that keywords in *Spectator* essays tended to be more literary, in contrast to more 'current' political keywords in contemporary serial publications. For reasons of space, this chapter cannot consider the role of magazines in historical sociolinguistics. Elsewhere I have summarized the roles of eighteenth-century book reviews in disseminating prescriptive ideals. Some reviewers constructed their linguistic authority in part by contrasting reviews with the newspaper, whose language was represented as ephemeral and incorrect (Percy 2009b).

Like Addison in the previous century, nineteenth-century journalists turned language variation into news: in overviews of usage, Gilman (1989: 9a) and Finegan (1980, 1998, 2001) highlight the fights stirred up by nineteenth-century writers such as Henry Alford in Britain and Edward S. Gould and Richard Grant White in the United States. Like book reviews, early journalism is a useful medium for conveying linguistic attitudes, for instance to Pittsburgh English in the early twentieth century (Johnstone and Danielson 2001). As institutions, newspapers and their editors have a long history as upholders and disseminators of linguistic standards: Bell (1991: 67–83) mentions standardizing as one of the aspects of editing news. According to Gilman (1989: 9a), newspapers' roles as codifiers of style began formally with William Cullen Bryant's 1877 list of words to avoid, *Index Expurgatorius*. However, as Bryant himself complained, merely by adopting and thus authorizing certain spellings a newspaper could (or could be perceived to) disseminate them. The spellings recommended by Noah Webster may have become entrenched less by his textbooks than by newspapers' use of them (quoted in Mencken 1936: 387; see also Anson 1990). Webster's spellings were still debatable – and thus newsworthy – in the 1850s (Mencken 1936: 387).

However, as popular and ephemeral texts, newspapers have also been criticized for their language, which might on occasion be more current than correct. Like the eighteenth-century book reviewers, Fowler "found much to dislike in the prose of contemporary newspapers" (Gilman 1989: 10a). The remainder of this chapter will summarize how early newspapers have furnished evidence for contemporary linguistic practices.

6. Early Newspapers and Early Modern English: Synchronic Perspectives

Because newspapers report on current events, they reflect contemporary linguistic practices and innovations. Along with other media, newspaper quotations authorize the current usage codified in some modern dictionaries and grammars for both native speakers and learners of English (Mukherjee 2006: 342). As we have seen, newspapers feature in the records of written and spoken English that make up the "Collins Word Web" drawn on by the COBUILD dictionaries and grammars. The *Longman Spoken and Written English Corpus* is likewise marketed as the authoritative source for such works of reference as the *Longman Grammar of Spoken and Written English* (Biber *et al.* 1999); on the publisher's website, the Longman Dictionaries generally are marketed as drawing on the Longman Corpus Network, which features newspapers among its 'real-life sources.'[6] Historical newspapers are likewise important sources for such historically oriented dictionaries as the *Oxford English Dictionary* (OED): of its 'top 1000 sources,' the most frequently quoted is *The Times*, which provides the first evidence for 1634 words and for 7405 senses of words.[7] Historical newspapers are also drawn on by historical dictionaries reflecting the English of other regions: these include the *Scottish National Dictionary* (Grant and Murison 1931–76)[8] and the *Dictionary of American Regional English* (Cassidy 1985–). Histories of various Englishes also draw on newspapers among other evidence: New York newspapers fill about a column of the index to Mencken's *American Language* (1936: index, xviii–xix). In contrast to modern corpus-based dictionaries, editors and authors of books and reference works on the history of the English language use historical newspapers relatively casually.

Some linguistic studies of older English newspapers index trends that are cultural as well as linguistic. Corpus-based studies of early newsbooks illuminate the politics of Cromwell's Commonwealth. *Mercurius Fumigosus*, a seventeenth-century newsbook, proved a useful source of ephemeral contemporary slang for Tony McEnery;[9] he (2006: 67–68) uses this information to expose the selective enforcement of the Blasphemy Act in Cromwell's Commonwealth. Analyzing representation of 'outgroups' in early journals of the Commonwealth period, Prentice and Hardie (2009) contribute to our understanding of their ideology. Cultural information can be gleaned from notices and advertisements as well as from news. Studying death notices in the ZEN corpus, Fries (2006) identifies some euphemisms that not only characterize that text class but also convey cultural attitudes to death. Fries (2007) has also written about foreign words in English newspapers, a topic that reveals the importance of classical and European culture in England, particularly as reflected in book advertisements. As part of her ongoing work on London English, Wright (2006, 2009) has studied eighteenth-century newspaper advertisements. Her work identifies words and phrases characteristic of these text classes, and incidentally illuminates the changing nature of urban life. Wright (2006) defines prepositions like *backside* and *over against* while using advertisements as evidence for the transition from hanging signs to street addresses. Other kinds of advertisements anatomize social relations in the eighteenth century: servitude in London and slavery in America, for instance. Wright's analysis of employment advertisements not only defines such employment jargon as *can bear confinement* (2009: 47–50), but also and especially illuminates the subtleties of such socially-loaded terms as *genteel* (33–36) and *character* (36–39) and *person* (32). Mäkinen's (2008: 40–45) anatomy of runaway slave advertisements includes a section on how they were named, classified, and described. Methodical analyses of newspaper language can enhance our understanding of earlier cultures.

7. Early Newspapers and Diachronic Studies of Early Modern English

7.1   Lexis and orthography

Newspapers can also track diachronic linguistic change: their long time-depth makes them an important resource for scholars from many disciplines. Non-linguists have used words in newspapers to index cultural trends. The historian Andrew (1997) uses early English newspapers among other resources to track changing attitudes to adultery or what was also called *gallantry*. The literary scholar Mathison (1998) connects the increasing frequency and sophistication of Scottish advertisements for patent medicine with the consumer revolution discussed above. Mathison's focus is not only commercial but political: he links the political and medical authority of words like 'royal' and 'British' with Scotland's relatively recent Union with Britain. References to London in Newcastle newspaper advertisements had a similar function (Berry 2002: 6). Lexical analysis helps literary scholars explore the significance of 'London' and 'Britain' to advertisers in Newcastle and Scotland.

Corpora containing newspapers have encouraged historical linguists to track and explain the emergence of orthographical norms beyond London or Britain – both what we might think of as the final stages of national standardization as well as the early stages of international divergence. Spelling had been standardized relatively early across genres of written English. Scholars have been keen to trace and to explain the stabilization of the relatively few orthographical variants that remained in eighteenth-century Britain (Fries and Schneider 2000: 19–23) and thus in early America (Anson 1990), Australia (Fritz 2006: 33–35), and Canada (Dollinger 2008: 124–27).

Several scholars have compared spelling practices as witnessed in newspapers with the precepts of such authors of popular reference books and textbooks as Samuel Johnson and Noah Webster. Fischer and Schneider (2002) have used the ZEN corpus to track the disappearance of the <-ick> spelling in words like *musick*, thereby raising the possibility that it was the practices of the press rather than the prescriptions of codifiers like Johnson that influenced and crystallized spelling in Britain. Moving beyond Britain, Anson (1990) uses sources including northeastern American newspapers to dispel the myth that Webster had an immediate and dramatic impact on American spelling of words like *honor*. Fritz (2006: 33–35) similarly downplays the idea that American usage influenced Australian spellings in <-or>, like Anson using nineteenth-century newspapers to demonstrate that there was still a great deal of variability in orthographical practice well after Webster. Dollinger (2008: 126) makes a case for orthographic nationalism in early Ontario, using corpus evidence of spelling shifts to attribute the shift from <-or> to <-our> spellings to anti-American sentiment after the War of 1812. These studies have qualified or dispelled some myths about why language changes, in particular questioning the influence of certain individuals and their codifying texts. These exercises have also reminded us of the symbolic value of certain spelling variants after most orthographical practice in public writing was standardized.

7.2   *Grammar*

Linguists have also used the long-lived genre of the newspaper to track grammatical change. In her recent overview of later modern English, Tieken-Boon van Ostade (2009: 143) briefly identifies the quickly-produced genre of the newspaper as a potentially excellent source for tracking such grammatical change from below as the emergence of the passive progressive. The development and dissemination of prepositional aspect constructions in Irish and Hiberno-English are traced by Pietsch (2008), who draws on a corpus of late-eighteenth-century New York newspaper advertisements alongside other texts likely to reflect change from below. Hoffmann (2002) has used corpora of fiction and non-fiction, including the ZEN corpus, to trace the grammaticalization of complex prepositions: according to Hoffmann, these become more common in non-fiction than in fiction. In its focus on text types, Hoffman's contrast of genres corresponds to other grammatical studies involving newspapers.

   Indeed, in contrast to spelling, there is more grammatical variation across text types. A number of scholars have been able to draw on the ARCHER corpus to track grammatical variation and change. While some, like Krug (2000: 32–33), use only the registers that correspond most closely to spoken English, others (Moore 2007: 125–26) draw on the seven more 'written' categories that include news reportage. It is beyond the scope of this survey to summarize the studies that have drawn on ARCHER, but a long and current bibliography of studies that have drawn on it is available online. Although ARCHER is not publicly available for copyright reasons, its association with a consortium of institutions has facilitated its use by a range of scholars and thus the comparability of disparate linguistic studies. The evident centrality of ARCHER to the historical-linguistic community suggests that we can expect further illumination of the roles of early newspapers in language change.

Acknowledgements

In preparing this chapter, the author is grateful for Joshua Wasserman's assistance with the references and for Roberta Facchinetti's and Andreas Jucker's comments on an earlier draft. Any and all remaining errors are her own responsibility.

NOTES

1   http://glossa.fltr.ucl.ac.be/ [accessed 14.10.11].
2   www.webcorp.org.uk/ [accessed 14.10.11].
3   Brownlees, N. Web page. http://www.dipfilmod.unifi.it/CMpro-v-p-116.html [accessed July 24, 2009].
4   Nevertheless, a number of individual scholars have been helpfully productive in this field. I have been grateful for assistance from my research assistant Anna Guy.
5   I must thank Andreas H. Jucker for generously giving me access to the second proofs of his edited collection on *Early Modern News Discourse* (see Jucker 2009).
6   http://www.pearsonlongman.com/dictionaries/corpus/index.html [accessed 14.10.11].
7   www.oed.com
8   Available online as part of the *Dictionary of the Scots Language* project, www.dsl.ac.uk/
9   McEnery, T. Web page. *Mercurius Fumigosus:* Slang decoded. http://www.lancs.ac.uk/fass/projects/newsbooks/dict.htm [accessed July 24, 2009].

REFERENCES

Andrew, D.T. (1997) 'Adultery à-la-mode:' Privilege, the Law and Attitudes to Adultery 1770–1809. *History* 82(265): 5–23.

Andrew, D.T. (1998) 'To the Charitable and Humane' Appeals for Assistance in the Eighteenth-Century London Press. In H. Cunningham and J. Innes (eds.), *Charity, philanthropy and reform. From the 1690s to 1850*, Macmillan and St. Martin's, New York, pp. 87–107.

Anson, C.M. (1990) *Errours* and *endeavors*: a case study in American orthography. *International Journal of Lexicography* 3(1): 35–63.

Baayen, R.H. and Renouf, A. (1996) Chronicling *The Times*: Productive lexical innovations in an English newspaper. *Language* 72(1): 69–96.

Bailey, R.W. (1996) *Nineteenth-century English*, University of Michigan Press, Ann Arbor.

Bailey, R.W. (2003) The Foundation of English in the Louisiana Purchase: New Orleans, 1800–1850. *American Speech* 78(4): 363–84.

Bauer, L. (1994) *Watching English Change: An Introduction to the Study of Linguistic Change in Standard Englishes in the Twentieth Century*, Longman, London.

Bauer, L. (2002) Inferring variation and change from public corpora. In J.K. Chambers, P. Trudgill, and N. Schilling-Estes (eds.), *The Handbook of Language Variation and Change*, Blackwell, Oxford, pp. 97–114.

Bell, A. (1991) *The Language of News Media*, Blackwell, Oxford.

Belmonte, I.A. (2007) Newspaper Editorials and Comment Articles: a 'Cinderella' Genre? *RÆL – Revista Electrónica de Lingüística Aplicada. Volumen Monográfico 1: Different Approaches to Newspaper Opinion Discourse* 6: 1–9. http://www.aesla.uji.es/rael [accessed 14.10.11]

Benedict, B.M. (2007) Encounters with the Object: Advertisements, Time, and Literary Discourse in the early Eighteenth-Century Thing-Poem. *Eighteenth-Century Studies* 40(2): 193–207.

Berry, H. (2002) Promoting taste in the provincial press: National and local culture in eighteenth-century Newcastle upon Tyne. *British Journal for Eighteenth-Century Studies* 25(1): 1–17.

Biber, D. *et al.* (eds.) (1999) *Longman Grammar of Spoken and Written English*, Longman, New York.

Biber, D. and Conrad, S. (2001) Register variation: a corpus approach. In D. Schiffrin, D. Tannen, and H. Ehernberger Hamilton (eds.), *The Handbook Of Discourse Analysis*, Blackwell, Oxford, pp. 175–96.

Biber, D. and Finegan, E. (2001) Diachronic relations among speech-based and written registers in English. In S. Conrad and D. Biber (eds.), *Variation in English: Multidimensional Studies*, Longman, London, pp. 66–83.

Bös, B. (2009) 'Place yer bets' and 'Let us hope' imperatives and their pragmatic functions in news reports. In A.H. Jucker (ed.), pp. 115–33.

Brownlees, N. (2001) Extending the ZEN Corpus (1641–1650): A Progress Report. http://cecl.fltr.ucl.ac.be/Events/icamepr.htm#zen [accessed July 24, 2009].

Brownlees, N. (2005) Spoken discourse in early English newspapers. *Media History* 11(1/2): 69–85.

Brownlees, N. (2006) Polemic and propaganda in Civil War news discourse. In N. Brownlees (ed.), pp. 19–42.

Brownlees, N. (ed.) (2006) *News Discourse in Early Modern Britain: Selected Papers of Conference on Historical News Discourse 2004 (CHINED)*, Peter Lang, Bern.

Campbell, J. (2002) Domestic intelligence: newspaper advertising and the eighteenth-century novel. *Yale Journal of Criticism* 15(2): 251–92.

Cassidy, F.G. (ed.) (1985) *Dictionary of American Regional English*, Belknap Press of Harvard University Press, Cambridge, MA.

Church, R. (2000) Advertising consumer goods in nineteenth-century Britain: reinterpretations. *Economic History Review* 53(4): 621–45.

Claridge, C. (2000) Pamphlets and early newspapers: political interaction vs news reporting. In F. Ungerer (ed.), pp. 25–43.

Claridge, C. (2009) 'As silly as an Irish Teague' comparisons in early English news discourse. In A.H. Jucker (ed.), pp. 91–114.

Cotter, C. (2003) Prescription and practice: motivations behind change in news discourse. *Journal of Historical Pragmatics* 4(1): 45–74.

Crane, G., Babeu, A., and Bamman, D. (2007) eScience and the humanities. *International Journal on Digital Libraries* 7(1): 117–22.

Crane, G. and Jones, A. (2006) The challenge of Virginia Banks: An evaluation of named entity analysis in a 19th-century newspaper collection. In G. Marchionini, M.L. Nelson, and C.C. Marshall (eds.), *Proceedings of the 6th ACM/IEEE-CS Joint Conference on Digital Libraries*, New York, NY: ACM Press, pp. 31–40. http://dx.doi.org/10.1145/1141753.1141759 [accessed December 28, 2010)].

Curzan, A. (2000) English historical corpora in the classroom. *Journal of English Linguistics* 28(1): 77–89.

Curzan, A. (2008) Corpus-based linguistic approaches to the history of English. In H. Momma and M. Matto (eds.), pp. 596–607.

Doherty, F. (1992) *A Study in Eighteenth-century Advertising Methods. The Anodyne Necklace*, Edwin Mellen, Lewiston, NY.

Dollinger, S. (2006) Oh Canada! Towards the corpus of early Ontario English. In A. Renouf and A. Kehoe (eds.), pp. 7–25.

Dollinger, S. (2008) *New-dialect Formation in Canada: Evidence from the English Modal Auxiliaries*. John Benjamins, Amsterdam.

Facchinetti, R. and Rissanen, M. (eds.) (2006) *Corpus-based Studies of Diachronic English*, Peter Lang, Bern.

Fairclough, N. (1995) *Media Discourse*, Edward Arnold, London.

Fairon, C. and Singler, J.V. (2006) "I'm like, 'Hey, it works!':" Using GlossaNet to find attestations of the quotative (*be*) *like* in English-language newspapers. In A. Renouf and A. Kehoe (eds.), pp. 325–36.

Ferdinand, C.Y. (1997) *Benjamin Collins and the Provincial Newspaper Trade in the Eighteenth Century*, Clarendon Press, Oxford.

Finegan, E. (1980) *Attitudes Toward English Usage: The History of a War of Words*, Teachers College Press, New York.

Finegan, E. (1998) English grammar and usage. In S. Romaine (ed.), *Cambridge History of the English Language (vol. 4:*

1776–1997), Cambridge University Press, Cambridge, pp. 536–88.

Finegan, E. (2001) Usage. In J. Algeo (ed.), *Cambridge History of the English Language (vol. 6: English in North America)*, Cambridge University Press, Cambridge, pp. 358–421.

Fischer, A. and Schneider, P. (2002) The dramatick disappearance of the <-ick> spelling, researched with authentic material from the Zurich English Newspaper Corpus. In A. Fischer, G. Tottie, and H.M. Lehmann (eds.), pp. 139–50.

Fischer, A., Tottie, G., and Lehmann, H.M. (2002) *Text Types and Corpora. Studies in Honour of Udo Fries*, Tübingen, Narr.

Fitzmaurice, S.M. (1998) The commerce of language in the pursuit of politeness in the eighteenth century. *English Studies* 79(4): 309–28.

Fitzmaurice, S.M. (2007) Questions of standardization and representativeness in the development of social networks based corpora: The story of the Network of Eighteenth-Century English Texts. In C. Beal, K.P. Corrigan, and H.L. Moisl (eds.), *Creating and Digitizing Language Corpora, vol. 2*, Palgrave Macmillan, Basingstoke, pp. 49–81.

Fitzmaurice, S.M. (2010) Mr. Spectator: identity and social roles in an early eighteenth-century community of practice and the periodical discourse community. In P. Pahta, M. Nevala, A. Nurmi, and M. Palander-Collin (eds.), *Social Roles and Language Practices in Late Modern English*, John Benjamins, Amsterdam, pp. 29–53.

Fowler, R. (1991) *Language in the News: Discourse and Ideology in the British Press*, Routledge, London.

Fries, U. (1990) Two hundred years of English death notices. In M. Bridges (ed.), *On Strangeness*, Narr, Tübingen, pp. 57–71.

Fries, U. (1997) 'Electarum mirabile' praise in 18th-century medical advertisements. In J. Aarts, I. de Mönnink, and H. Wekker (eds.), *Studies in English Language and Teaching. In Honour of Flor Aarts*, Rodopi, Amsterdam, pp. 57–73.

Fries, U. (2001) Text classes in early English newspapers. *European Journal of English Studies* 5(2): 167–80.

Fries, U. (2006) Death notices: the birth of a genre. In R. Facchinetti and M. Rissanen (eds.), pp. 157–70.

Fries, U. (2007) Foreign words in early English newspapers. In S. Dollinger, J. Hüttner, and U. Smit (eds.), *Tracing English Through Time: Explorations in Language Variation. In Honour of Herbert Schendl on the Occasion of his 65th Birthday*, Braumüller, Vienna, pp. 115–32.

Fries, U. (2009) Crime and punishment. In A. Jucker (ed.), pp. 13–30.

Fries, U. and Lehmann, H.M. (2006) The style of 18th-century English newspapers: lexical diversity. In N. Brownlees (ed.), pp. 91–104.

Fries, U. and Schneider, P. (2000) ZEN: preparing the Zurich English Newspaper Corpus. In F. Ungerer (ed.), pp. 3–24.

Fritz, C. (2006) Favoring Americanism? <ou> vs. <o> before <l> and <r> in Early English in Australia: a corpus-based approach. In A. Renouf and A. Kehoe (eds.), pp. 27–44.

Gieszinger, S. (2000) Two hundred years of advertising in *The Times*: the development of text type markers. In F. Ungerer (ed.), pp. 85–109.

Gieszinger, S. (2001) *The History of Advertising Language: The Advertisements in* The Times *from 1788 to 1996*, Peter Lang, Frankfurt am Main.

Gilman, E.W. (1989) A brief history of English usage, in *Webster's Dictionary Of English Usage*, Merriam-Webster, Springfield, MA, pp. 7–11.

Görlach, M. (2002) A linguistic history of advertising, 1700–1890. In T. Fanego, B. Méndez-Naya, and E. Seoane (eds.), *Sounds, Words, Texts and Change: Selected Papers from 11 ICEHL, Santiago de Compostela, 7–11 September 2000*, John Benjamins, Amsterdam, pp. 83–104.

Gotti, M. (2005) Advertising discourse in eighteenth-century English newspapers. In J. Skaffari *et al.* (eds.), pp. 23–38.

Grant, W. and Murison, D.D. (eds.) (1931–76) *The Scottish National Dictionary : Designed Partly on Regional Lines and Partly on Historical Principles, and Containing All the Scottish Words Known to Be in Use or to Have Been in Use Since c.1700. 10 vols,*

Scottish National Dictionary Association, Edinburgh.

Herring, S.C. (2003) Media and language change. *Journal of Historical Pragmatics* 4(1): 1–17.

Hoffmann, S. (2002) In (hot) pursuit of data: complex prepositions in Late Modern English. In P. Peters, P. Collins, and A. Smith (eds.), *New Frontiers of Corpus Research*, Rodopi, Amsterdam, pp. 127–46.

Johnstone, B. and Danielson, A. (2001) *'Pittsburghese' in the Daily Papers, 1910–2001: Historical Sources of Ideology About Variation.* ERIC (Educational Resources Information Center, US Department of Education) Document database. Accession no. ED464484.

Jucker, A.H. (2005) News discourse: Mass media communication from the seventeenth to the twenty-first century. In J. Skaffari *et al.* (eds.), pp. 7–21.

Jucker, A.H. (2006) 'But 'tis believed that…' speech and thought presentation in Early English newspapers. In N. Brownlees (ed.), pp. 105–25.

Jucker, A.H. (2009) Newspapers, pamphlets and scientific news discourse in Early Modern Britain. In A.H. Jucker (ed.), pp. 1–9.

Jucker, A.H. (ed.) (2009) *Early Modern English News Discourse. Newspapers, Pamphlets and Scientific News Discourse*, John Benjamins, Amsterdam.

Kehoe, A. (2006) Diachronic linguistic analysis on the web using WebCorp. In A. Renouf and A. Kehoe (eds.), pp. 297–307.

Keller, C. auf dem (2004) *Textual Structures in Eighteenth-century Newspaper Advertising: A Corpus-based Study of Medical Advertisements and Book Advertisements*, Shaker, Aachen.

Keller, C. auf dem (2006) Changes in textual structures of book advertisements in the ZEN corpus. In A. Renouf and A. Kehoe (eds.), pp. 143–62.

Krug, M.G. (2000) *Emerging English Modals: A Corpus-based Study of Grammaticalization*, Mouton de Gruyter, New York.

Kytö, M. (1993) Early American English. In M. Rissanen, M. Kytö, and M. Palander-Collin (eds.), *Early English in the Computer Age: Explorations Through the Helsinki Corpus*, Walter de Gruyter, Berlin, pp. 83–91.

Kytö, M. (1996) *Manual to the Diachronic Part of the Helsinki Corpus of English Texts: Coding Conventions and Lists of Source Texts (3rd edn)*, University of Helsinki Department of English. http://khnt.hit.uib.no/icame/manuals/HC/#con11 [accessed September 1, 2009].

Kytö, M., Rydén, M., and Smitterberg, E. (eds.) 2006) *Nineteenth-century English: Stability and Change*, Cambridge University Press, New York.

Lamb, J. (2004) The crying of lost things. *English Literary History* 71(4): 949–67.

Laversuch, I.M. (2006) Runaway slave names recaptured: an investigation of the personal first names of fugitive slaves advertised in the Virginia Gazette between 1736 and 1776. *Names* 54(4): 331–62.

Leech, G. (1966) *English in Advertising: A Linguistic Study of Advertising in Great Britain*, Longman, London.

Leech, G. and Smith, N. (2005) Extending the possibilities of corpus-based research on English in the twentieth-century: a prequel to LOB and FLOB. *ICAME Journal* 29: 83–90.

Lehmann, H.M., auf dem Keller, C., and Ruef, B. (2006) ZEN Corpus 1.0. In R. Facchinetti and M. Rissanen (eds.), pp. 135–55.

Lindquist, H. and Levin, M. (2000) Apples and oranges: on comparing data from different corpora. In C. Mair and M. Hundt (eds.), pp. 201–12.

MacQueen, D.S. (2004) Developing methods for very-large-scale searches in Proquest Historical Newspapers Collection and Infotrac *The Times* Digital Archive: The case of *two million* versus *two millions*. *Journal of English Linguistics* 32(2): 124–243.

Mair, C. (2006) Tracking ongoing grammatical change and recent diversification in present-day standard English: the complementary role of small and large corpora. In A. Renouf and A. Kehoe (eds.), pp. 355–76.

Mair, C. and Hundt, M. (eds.) 2000) *Corpus Linguistics and Linguistic Theory*, Rodopi, Amsterdam.

Mäkinen, S. (2008) *Generic Features of Eighteenth Century American Runaway Slave Advertisements* (Pro Gradu thesis), University of Turku Department of English.

Matheson, D. (2000) The birth of news discourse: changes in news language in British newspapers, 1880–1930. *Media, Culture and Society* 22(5): 557–73.

Mathison, H. (1998) Tropes of promotion and wellbeing: advertisement and the eighteenth-century Scottish periodical press. *Prose Studies* 21(3): 206–25.

McEnery, T. (2006) The moral panic about bad language in England, 1691–1745. *Journal of Historical Pragmatics* 7: 89–113.

McKendrick, N., Brewer, J., and Plumb, J.H. (1982) *The Birth of a Consumer Society: The Commercialization of Eighteenth-century England*, Europa, London.

Mencken, H.L. (1936) *The American Language: An Inquiry into the Development of English in the United States*, A.A. Knopf, New York.

Momma, H. and Matto, M. (2008) History, English, language: studying HEL today. In H. Momma and M. Matto (eds.), pp. 3–10.

Momma, H. and Matto, M. (eds.) (2008) *A Companion to the History of the English Language*, Wiley-Blackwell, Chichester.

Moore, C. (2007) The spread of grammaticalized forms: The case of *be + supposed to*. *Journal of English Linguistics* 35(2): 117–31.

Morley, B. (2006) WebCorp: a tool for online linguistic information retrieval and analysis. In A. Renouf and A. Kehoe (eds.), pp. 283–96.

Mukherjee, J. (2006) Corpus linguistics and English reference grammars. In A. Renouf and A. Kehoe (eds.), pp. 337–54.

Nevalainen, T. (2000) Gender differences in the evolution of standard English: evidence from the corpus of early English correspondence. *Journal of English Linguistics* 28(1): 38–59.

Nevalainen, T. (2002) English newsletters in the seventeenth century. In A. Fischer, G. Tottie, and H.M. Lehmann (eds.), pp. 67–90.

Newman, D.J. and Block, S. (2006) Probabilistic topic decomposition of an eighteenth-century American newspaper. *Journal of the American Society for Information Science and Technology* 57(6): 753–67.

Palander-Collin, M. (2008) Persuasive language in early advertisements. Paper presented at 15th ICEHL (International Conference on English Historical Linguistics), University of Munich, August 24–30, 2008.

Percy, C. (2004) Consumers of correctness: men, women, and language in eighteenth-century classified advertisements. In C. Kay, S. Horobin, and J. Smith (eds.), *New Perspectives on English Historical Linguistics: Selected Papers from 12th ICEHL, Glasgow, 21–26 August 2002 (vol. 1)*, John Benjamins, Amsterdam, pp. 153–76.

Percy, C. (2009a) Learning and virtue: English grammar and the eighteenth-century girls' school. In M. Hilton and J. Shefrin (eds.), *Educating the Child in the British Enlightenment: Beliefs, Cultures, Practices*, Ashgate, Aldershot, UK and Burlington, VT, pp. 77–98.

Percy, C. (2009b) Periodical reviews and the rise of prescriptivism: the *Monthly* (1749–1844) and *Critical Review* (1756–1817) in the eighteenth century. In I. Tieken-Boon van Ostade and W. van der Wurff (eds.), *Current Issues in Late Modern English*, Peter Lang, Bern, pp. 117–50.

Picone, M.D. (2003) Anglophone slaves in francophone Louisiana. *American Speech* 78(4): 404–33.

Pietsch, L. (2008) Prepositional aspect constructions in Hiberno-English. In P. Siemund and N. Kintana (eds.), *Language Contact and Contact Languages*, John Benjamins, Amsterdam, pp. 213–36.

Plumb, J.H. (1975) The new world of children in eighteenth-century England. *Past and Present* 67(1): 64–95.

Popik, B. (2004) Digital historical newspapers: A review of the powerful new research tools. *Journal of English Linguistics* 32(2): 114–23.

Pöttker, H. (2003) News and its communicative quality: the inverted pyramid – when and why did it appear? *Journalism Studies* 4(4): 501–11.

Prentice, S. and Hardie, A. (2009) Empowerment and disempowerment in the Glencairn Uprising: a corpus-based critical analysis of Early Modern English news discourse. *Journal of Historical Pragmatics* 10(1): 23–55.

Rademann, T. (1998) Using online electronic newspapers in modern English-language press corpora: benefits and pitfalls. *ICAME Journal* 22: 49–72.

Raymond, J. (2005) Introduction: networks, communication, practice. Special issue on news networks in Early Modern Britain and Europe. *Media History* 11(1/2): 3–19.

Read, A.W. (1938) The assimilation of the speech of British immigrants in colonial America. *Journal of English and Germanic Philology* 37: 70–79.

Reah, D. (2002) *The Language of Newspapers* (2nd edn), Routledge, London.

Renouf, A. (2007a) Corpus development 25 years on: From super-corpus to cyber-corpus. In R. Facchinetti (ed.), *Corpus Linguistics 25 Years On*, Rodopi, Amsterdam, pp. 27–50.

Renouf, A. (2007b) Tracing lexical productivity and creativity in the British media: the chavs and the chav-nots. In J. Munat (ed.), *Lexical Creativity, Texts and Contexts*, John Benjamins, Amsterdam, pp. 61–89.

Renouf, A. and Kehoe, A. (eds.) (2006) *The Changing Face of Corpus Linguistics*, Rodopi, Amsterdam.

Renouf, A., Kehoe, A., and Banerjee, J. (2007) WebCorp: an integrated system for web text search. In M. Hundt, N. Nesselhauf, and C. Biewer (eds.), *Corpus Linguistics and the Web*, Rodopi, Amsterdam, pp. 47–67.

Richardson, J.E. (2007) *Analysing Newspapers: An Approach from Critical Discourse Analysis*, Palgrave Macmillan, New York.

Schneider, K. (1998) Introducing the Rostock Historical Newspaper Corpus: From 1700 to today. http://www.tu-chemnitz.de/phil/english/chairs/linguist/real/independent/llc/Conference1998/Papers/Schneider.htm [accessed July 24, 2009].

Schneider, K. (2000a) The emergence and development of headlines in British newspapers. In F. Ungerer (ed.), pp. 45–65.

Schneider, K. (2000b) Popular and quality papers in the Rostock Historical Newspaper Corpus. In C. Mair and M. Hundt (eds.), pp. 321–37.

Schneider, P. (2002) Computer-assisted spelling normalization of 18th-century English. In P. Peters, P. Collins, and A. Smith (eds.), *New Frontiers of Corpus Research*, Rodopi, Amsterdam, pp. 199–213.

Simon-Vandenbergen, A.M. (1981) *The Grammar of Headlines in* The Times, *1870–1970*, Koninklijke Academie voor Wetenschappen, Letteren en Schone Kunsten van Belgie, Brussels.

Skaffari, J. *et al.* (eds.) (2005) *Opening Windows on Texts and Discourses of the Past*, John Benjamins, Amsterdam.

Skedd, S. (1997) Women teachers and the expansion of girls' schooling in England, c1760–1820. In H.J. Barker and E. Chalus (eds.), *Gender in Eighteenth-century England: Roles, Representations and Responsibilities*, Longman, London, pp. 101–25.

Straumann, H. (1935) *Newspaper Headlines: A Study in Linguistic Method*, George Allen and Unwin, London.

Studer, P. (2003) Textual structures in eighteenth-century newspapers: a corpus-based study of headlines. *Journal of Historical Pragmatics* 4(1): 19–44.

Studer, P. (2005) Text-initiating strategies in eighteenth-century newspaper headlines. In J. Skaffari *et al.* (eds.), 65–79.

Studer, P. (2008) *Historical Corpus Stylistics: Media, Technology and Change*, Continuum, London and New York.

Tieken-Boon van Ostade, I. (2009) *An Introduction to Late Modern English*, Edinburgh University Press, Edinburgh.

Tierney, J. (1995) Book advertisements in mid-18th-century newspapers: the example of Robert Dodsley. In R. Myers and M. Harris (eds.), *A Genius for Letters. Booksellers and Bookselling from the 16th to the 20th Century*, Oak Knoll Press, DE, pp. 103–22.

Tierney, J. (2001) Advertisements for books in London newspapers, 1760–1785. *Studies in Eighteenth-century Culture* 30: 153–64.

Ungerer, F. (2000) Introduction. In F. Ungerer (ed.), pp. vii–xiv.

Ungerer, F. (ed.) (2000) *English Media Texts – Past and Present: Language and Textual Structure*, John Benjamins, Amsterdam.

Ungerer, F. (2002) When news stories are no longer stories: the emergence of the top-down structure in news reports in English newspapers. In A. Fischer, G. Tottie, and H.M. Lehmann (eds.), pp. 91–104.

Vlčková, J. (2002) Social values, their linguistic coding and changes through time: Australian personal ads over the span of one hundred years. *Brno Studies in English* 28: 91–102.

Wright, L. (2006) Street addresses and directions in mid-eighteenth century London newspaper advertisements. In N. Brownlees (ed.), pp. 199–215.

Wright, L. (2009) Reading late eighteenth-century want ads. In A.H. Jucker (ed.), pp. 31–55.

LINGUISTIC CORPORA CITED

ARCHER = *A Representative Corpus of Historical English Registers* (1990–) First compiled by D. Biber and E. Finegan. Now managed as an ongoing project by a consortium of participants at fourteen universities in seven countries. http://www.llc.manchester.ac.uk/research/projects/archer [accessed June 2, 2011].

BNC = *British National Corpus* (1991–94) Compiled by Oxford University Computing Services, Oxford University. www.natcorp.ox.ac.uk [accessed June 2, 2011].

Brown Corpus = *Brown University Standard Corpus of Present-Day American English* (1961–63. Compiled by Henry Kucera and W. Nelson Francis. Providence, Rhode Island: Department of Linguistics, Brown University. http://khnt.aksis.uib.no/icame/manuals/brown [accessed June 2, 2011].

COHA = *The Corpus of Historical American English* (2008–) M.D. Mark. 400+ million words, 1810–present. http://corpus.byu.edu/coha [accessed July 30, 2010].

CONTE = *Corpus of Early Ontario English* http://faculty.arts.ubc.ca/sdollinger/CONTE.htm [accessed June 2, 2011].

Historical Newspapers. ProQuest. Web site. ProQuest http://www.proquest.com/en-US/catalogs/databases/detail/pq-hist-news.shtml [accessed June 2, 2011].

Eighteenth Century Journals Portal. Adam Matthew Digital. Web site. http://www.amdigital.co.uk/Collections/Eighteenth-Century-Journals-Portal.aspx [accessed July 24, 2009].

ICE = *International Corpus of English* (1990–) Project Director G. Nelson. Department of English, The Chinese University of Hong Kong. http://ice-corpora.net/ice/index.htm [accessed June 2, 2011].

LOB = *Lancaster-Oslo/Bergen Corpus* (1970–78) Compiled at the Universities of Lancaster, Oslo and the Norwegian Computing Centre for the Humanities at Bergen. http://khnt.hit.uib.no/icame/manuals/lobman [accessed June 2, 2011].

Longman Spoken and Written English Corpus http://www.pearsonlongman.com/dictionaries/corpus/index.html [accessed June 2, 2011].

Newspaper Archives. XooxleAnswers. Web page. http://xooxleanswers.com/newspaperarchives.aspx [accessed July 30, 2010].

OED = *Oxford English Dictionary* Online www.oed.com [accessed June 2, 2011]

Times Digital Archive, 1785–1985. Gale Cengage. Web page. http://www.gale.cengage.com/DigitalCollections/products/Times/ [accessed June 2, 2011)].

17th and 18th Century Burney Collection Newspapers. Gale Cengage. Web page. http://www.gale.cengage.com/servlet/ItemDetailServlet?region=9&imprint=000&titleCode=M355E&cf=e&type=4&id=242587 [accessed July 24, 2009].

Part III Linguistic and Socio-demographic Variables

12 Orthographic Variables

HANNA RUTKOWSKA AND PAUL RÖSSLER

1. Introduction

The view that "structured variability is the essential property of language that fulfills important social functions and permits orderly linguistic change" (Milroy and Gordon 2003: 4) constitutes the foundation of modern sociolinguistics. Such variability exists not only at the generally recognized levels of phonology, morphology, and syntax, but also at the level of orthography. The orthographic system of a natural language (if it has one) has more or less complex interrelations with the phonology, morphology, syntax, and lexicon, as well as the semantics and pragmatics, of that language, despite the attempts of the early structuralists to treat writing, and consequently also orthography, as an extra-linguistic component (Saussure 1915/1993: 41, Sapir 1921/1949: 20, Bloomfield 1933: 21). Thus it seems reasonable to consider orthographic variation to be worth a detailed examination. But at the same time orthography, more than any other aspect of language, is likely to be influenced by external factors such as language planning which impose change from above the level of consciousness. Therefore it should be emphasized, with Jeremy Smith, that "the evolution of orthography can be understood only when the dynamic interaction between extra- and intra-linguistic processes and pressures is brought into consideration" (1996: 78).

Traditionally, the value of historical orthographic evidence for linguistic purposes has been judged most frequently according to the (assumed) accuracy with which it reflects pronunciation differences between dialects. This was the approach taken, for example, by authors such as Zachrisson (1913), Wyld (1936), and Dobson (1957–68), who focused mainly on the structural description of grapho-phonemic correspondences. The description of at least some elements of the social context

The Handbook of Historical Sociolinguistics, First Edition. Edited by Juan Manuel Hernández-Campoy and Juan Camilo Conde-Silvestre.
© 2014 John Wiley & Sons, Ltd. Published 2014 by John Wiley & Sons, Ltd.

of orthographic variation is present in all these works; but social factors such as age, gender, education, and rank have only recently become part of the methodological framework used in investigating orthographic variants.

The present chapter deals with several different aspects of orthographic variation and its usefulness for historical linguists and sociolinguists. First we will explain the technical terms connected with orthography, orthographic systematicity, and orthographic variation, including a tentative definition of an orthographic variable. Then we will present theoretical approaches to the orthographic variable as a unit of sociolinguistic study, and offer an overview of sociolinguistic studies on orthographic variation, ordered chronologically with respect to the periods examined. Because most historical sociolinguistic studies on orthographic variants deal with aspects of standardization, particular attention is paid to this.[1] Finally, we will suggest some possibilities for future research.

2. Orthography: Theoretical Preliminaries

2.1   *What is orthography?*

An *orthography* is a spelling norm which consists of all the standardized and codified graphic representations of a language. These graphic representations are related not only to the basic spelling units with distinctive function and phonemic reference, the graphemes, but also to larger units such as morphemes. They can also include capitalization,[2] whether to spell compound words as single items or separate morphemes, word division at the end of lines, and punctuation. Among experts, the latter is sometimes seen as part of the orthography and sometimes as separate (Eisenberg and Günther 1989, Gallmann 1996, Kohrt 1987, Maas 1992, Nerius 2007).

Spelling involves the graphic realizations of all spoken items, whereas *orthography* is limited to a more or less binding norm that can lead to criticism in case of non-compliance. Orthography depends on the practices of a community of writers within a certain period and has to be established and accepted by this community. Thus each orthography is part of the spelling of a language, but not every spelling system features an established orthography (Eisenberg and Günther 1989).

The word *orthography* can be used to refer both to a spelling norm and to a branch of linguistic study which deals with all aspects of a spelling norm, looking into the relation between writing practices beyond the norms, codification, and official standardization, as well as the criteria which form the basis of the standardization processes. As a spelling norm, orthography is made up of explicit rules, which have different degrees of generalization. The degree of generalization can be low, as in the spelling of individual words in orthographic dictionaries. High degrees of generalization are found in the general rules which are intended to establish a norm for the spelling of large classes of linguistic items. In dictionaries, these rules are mostly presented explicitly, before the lists of entries. These different degrees of generalization can lead to further regulations for domains which lack general rules, in, for example, the spelling of foreign loans. Ideally, such individual regulations should only be established in the absence of general rules, but in reality most involve the application of already existing general orthographic rules. Some aspects, such as the rules for word division at the end of lines, are general orthographic rules which apply to any word, but even so are often also repeated within the dictionaries, which can lead to the orthography being codified there twice (Kohrt 1987, Stetter 1996: 694).

2.2   *Orthographic principles and variability*

Different principles form the basis of the general orthographic rules (Augst 1985), and they are not always completely consistent. The interplay of these partly antithetic principles can lead to problems that cannot always be completely avoided, even by giving different weighting to the principles. An example is the German orthography in use until 1996 and afterwards, as well as the reform of the reform undertaken in 2006 (Güthert 2006, Dudenredaktion 2006). The greater the demand to harmonize as many aspects of a written language as possible, the more difficult it is to formulate the general orthographic rules without contradictions, because they are based on partly conflicting and overlapping principles.

2.1.1   The principles behind the general orthographic rules   Most current orthographic systems of European languages consist of the interaction of the following principles (Glück 2005, Bußmann 2008[3]), illustrated here with German and English examples:

(a) The phonetic principle. Only alphabets designed to represent sounds, such as the IPA (International Phonetic Alphabet), follow this principle strictly and systematically. There are many cases in German and English orthography which do not follow this principle: for example, the character <s> represents both the voiced fricative [z] and the unvoiced [s] (in English *lose* and *loose*); in particular combinations, such as <st> and <sp>, it corresponds to the apical fricative [ʃ] in German; and in the trigraph <sch> in German, and the digraph <sh> in English, it also represents [ʃ]. That is, despite the overall tendency towards a one-to-one relationship between speech sound and character, there is no complete congruence. The degree of such congruence in the orthographic systems of European languages varies greatly.

(b) The phonological principle. Here, one phoneme corresponds to one character. In German orthography, this principle is realized in, for example, the correspondence of the allophones [ç] and [x] to one digraph <ch>, as well as the use of one graph, <r>, for all the allophonic variants of this /r/ phoneme, such as [r] and [R]. This principle can also be found in English, where, for instance, <l> represents both [l] and [ɫ].

(c) The etymological principle, which respects morpheme constancy; that is, in etymologically related words the root is spelled the same; for example, German sg. *Rad* and pl. *Räder*, despite the word-final devoicing of the /d/ in the singular; English sg. *child* and pl. *children*, despite the difference in the vowel quality ([aɪ] in the singular, [ɪ] in the plural).

(d) The historical principle. Writers in a later period sometimes take over orthographic features from earlier periods, often with a different function. In New High German, for instance, the digraph <ie> represents the fact that the vowel [iː] is long, whereas in Middle High German it represented the falling diphthong [ɪɐ]. During the monophthongization of this diphthong in Early New High German the graph <e> after <i> was left with no function to fulfill, and could thus be used with a new function, indicating vowel length. Likewise, in Southern British English, the <r> in the sequence <ir> in such words as *bird* and *first*, can be considered to represent the length of the vowel [ɜː], which has developed from the Middle English [ir].

(e) The principle of heterography. Homophones are visually distinguished by having different spellings. Thus, for example, German *Leib* 'body' vs. *Laib* 'loaf', English *brake* vs. *break*. This principle often overlaps with principles (c) and (d).

(f) The principle of economy, whereby certain spellings are shortened. Thus, for example, *du reißt* instead of *du *reißst* 'you rip' in German, and *eighteen* instead of **eightteen* in English. In this respect, the American English spelling system allows a higher degree of such spelling simplification than the British counterpart. Crystal (1995: 205) mentions that the forms *signalled, diagrammed, kidnapper* co-exist alongside *signaled, diagramed, kidnaper* in American English, whereas in British English only the former are considered correct.

(g) The graphostylistic (or graphotactic) principle, which implies that specific character strings are considered incompatible. Thus, for instance, no double characters of <i, u, w, ch, sch, ß> are allowed in German, and English words do not end in <j, q, u, v>, or a single <z> (Carney 1994: 67).

(h) The pragmatic principle. Different spelling in recipient-specific contexts. Thus, for example, the capitalization of pronouns of distant address in German (*Sie* 'you') versus the use of small letters in pronouns of close address (*du* 'you'). From 1996 to 2006 this *du* was the only valid spelling in German orthography, whereas since 2006 both spellings in pronouns of close address have been allowed (*du, Du* 'you'). In contrast with this, the capitalization of all nouns in German is based on **(i)** the grammatical principle, because in this case the part of speech (the syntactic function) is what requires the capitalization. Capitalization of proper nouns in turn is part of **(j)**, the semantic principle.

2.2.2 *Categories and functions of orthographic variants* Historically, orthography arises later than spelling. Orthography, in the sense of a codified norm consisting of only few or no variants, emerges from earlier, non-codified, and profoundly varying writing customs within a speech community (Elmentaler 2000, Mihm 2000, Nerius 1996). This more or less complex selection process can be influenced by both linguistic and extra-linguistic factors, such as politics, the economy, the media, and science. Nowadays inconsistent writing in such contexts as schools or administration is regarded as defective, so much so that consistent writing has become a national symbol in many countries (Eisenberg 2006, Friedrich 1996): "[s]tandardized orthography as normed and verifiable writing goes along with a rigid norm-consciousness that accepts one and only one spelling as the correct one: variatio *non* delectat." (Voeste 2007: 296). On the other hand, most phases in the history of writing have been characterized by graphic variation and heterogeneity. Even in modern times, despite the fact that the written standards of particular languages are usually well established, orthographic variation is not extinct. The nature of the variation depends on several factors. Orthographic variants can be divided into categories according to their functions, and with reference to several sociolinguistic subsystems. We can distinguish (a) diachronic, (b) diatopic, (c) diaphasic, (d) diastratic, (e) diasituative, and (f) aesthetic variants:

(a) In cases where there coexist old, established forms with new, emerging ones, we refer to them as diachronic variants. The simultaneity of both the old and the new forms helps guarantee acceptance for the writer and comprehensibility for the reader, particularly if the modern form is not yet entirely established. For instance, contemporary German orthography allows numerous alternative spellings of foreign words, such as *Ketchup/Ketschup*, *Spaghetti/Spagetti, Hämorrhoiden/Hämorriden*, to ensure that both the older orthography in use before 1996 and the new one, which has been in use since then, are recognized. Similarly, British English allows variants such as *hiccup/hiccough, jail/gaol, focused/focussed*, though the first variant in each set (which is not always the more recent) is considerably more common (Tieken-Boon van Ostade 2009: 37). However, whereas both *-ise* and *-ize* are considered correct and are equally popular in British English[4], in American English only *-ize* can be used in words such as *generalize* and *characterize*.

(b) Different regional pronunciation can give rise to diatopic variants in the written forms, such as the distinct written features in the northern and the southern parts of Germany during the late Early New High German period. For example, the Early New High German monophthongization [uɐ̯] > [uː] became a kind of confessional shibboleth, distinguishing between the northern 'protestant' monophthong written as <u> and the southern 'catholic' diphthong written as <ue>/<uo> (Macha 1998, 2004; Rössler 2005). These regional features do not necessarily have to be interpreted as characteristic of the sender's, (that is, the author's, printer's or typesetter's) language; the regional variants can also be chosen as a courtesy to the addressee – the reader in general – or to satisfy the censor or the patron, particularly in the early modern period (Möller 1998). In English, there is the codified and politically approved diatopic division into two spelling systems, British and American[5], including the respective use of such characteristic spelling variants as those in *colour/color, theatre/theater, catalogue/catalog, aeroplane/airplane* and *tyre/tire* (Crystal 1995: 307, McArthur 2006: 375). However, it is also noteworthy that the existence of only these two major spelling systems in English is not unanimously acknowledged by linguists. Fritz (2006), for example, challenged the assumption that forms such as *honor, center,* and *apologize* in Australian spelling are due to American influence, and claimed that a standard developed in Australia independently.

(c) The different phases in a writer's life indicate diaphasic variability. Everyone experiences an intensive diaphasic shift during the phase of writing acquisition, whereas other phases of life affect us less in this respect (Friedrich 1996, Mayr 2007). In addition to this individual diaphasic variability, writing differences between generations can be classified as diaphasic variants as well. Due to the German orthographic reforms undertaken within the last two decades, different generations follow different spelling practices; this is because those who learned the old orthography – especially if they did so many years before the reform of 1996, and are not forced to deal with the new one (for instance, in educational situations) – tend to continue using the former spelling, even if it is no longer meant to be valid.

(d) Diastratic variants concern social differences. As a result of the writer's social background, the level of education differs. This can have an impact on the writing style, and also the ability to follow orthographic instructions (Hernández-Campoy and Conde-Silvestre 1999).

(e) Diasituative variants can be distinguished on the basis of the different registers and genres of written texts. That is, the spelling can vary according to the writer's intention and the communicative function of the text. For instance, in British English, the form *program* (which was borrowed from American usage) is reserved for computing-related contexts, and *programme* is used in the remaining senses of the word, whereas American English uses *program* in every meaning (OED Online: www.oed.com). To take another example, Crystal (1995: 340) described the spelling system of Canadian English as a combination of British and American features, with different variants dominant in particular provinces; the British spelling model is followed in scientific journals, and the American in popular publications. Similarly, advertising texts tend to differ from the orthographic norm because of their intention to catch the addressee's (the consumer's) eye.[6] In contrast, legal texts follow the orthographic standard strictly, in order to underline their normative value.

(f) Particularly in the Early New High German of the sixteenth and seventeenth centuries, spelling variability corresponded to an aesthetic principle (similar to modern advice to use lexical alternatives): "[v]ariatio delectat meant more than just giving pleasure to the eye. It meant demonstrating one's writing skills through the calculated use of alternation" (Voeste 2007: 303). Voeste relates the importance of aesthetic principles to the emergence of regulated, visually shaped spelling variants: "[s]ome of those aesthetic patterns became an integral part of today's orthography: you still must not extend the right margin of a word if the left one already shows a cluster of three or four consonants, cf. *Schwahn, *Strohm, *Schahl" (Voeste 2007: 305). In today's languages, with their well-established orthographic standards, the use of non-standard variants can be deliberate (Beaugrande 2006: 43), or even constitute "a powerful expressive resource" capturing some of "the 'immediacy,' the 'authenticity' and 'flavor' of the spoken word in all its diversity" (Jaffe 2000: 498). The power of non-standard orthography can be experienced in everyday contexts, for example in trade-names (see Carney 1994: 446–48), TV commercials, and internet chat rooms. It can also be found in printed material, such as in poetry (Tom Leonard, Ernst Jandl), or popular fiction (Irvine Welsh), and is used, for instance, as a tool for drawing the reader's attention to his protagonists' ethnicity, as well as their otherness and alienation with regard to mainstream society values.

2.3   The orthographic variable as a linguistic variable: definition, classification, and sociolinguistic approaches

Having discussed the most significant principles and rules governing orthographic systems, as well as the types and functions of orthographic variants, it seems appropriate to relate orthographic variation more closely to sociolinguistic terminology and methodology. In order to make this possible, it is first of all necessary to refer to the notion of *linguistic variable* as central to sociolinguistic study. A linguistic variable is "a structural unit, parallel to such units as the phoneme and noun phrase in linguistic theory" (Milroy and Gordon 2003: 4–50; see also Chambers and Trudgill 1980/1994: 145–49, Chambers 1995/2009: 11–25). The term was defined by Labov (1966). However, the use of the term *orthographic variable* is a recent development in sociolinguistics.[7]

As Stenroos rightly points out, "[t]he description of orthography is a field undergoing development, and so far there seems to be no one established system of terminology in use." (2004: 263). Likewise, no consensus has yet been achieved as regards the definition of an orthographic variable, nor has the classification of orthographic variables yet been standardized. However, on the basis of the first sociolinguistic studies of orthographic variants (to be discussed in the following sections), one can propose a tentative definition as follows: an orthographic variable is a feature of an orthographic system of a given language, related to the phonological, morphological, or lexical levels of that language system, and realized by different variants under specific extra-linguistic circumstances. Like the more general term *linguistic variable*, it can be considered to denote an abstract entity realized by two or more variants, which "are not always predictable by phonological, morphological, or any other kind of linguistic conditioning" (Chambers 1995/2009: 17). The extra-linguistic variables which can be correlated with orthographic variables in a sociolinguistic analysis of a text include time of production, geographical location, demographics (sex, age, rank), social networks, text type (and genre), style, register, and medium (e.g. handwritten vs. printed). The types of orthographic variables present in a text, and thus amenable to investigation, as well as their distribution, seem to depend on the extra-linguistic factors involved, as the following sections will show. The typology and distribution of orthographic variables can also differ across languages.

In fact, there has only recently been a growing recognition of the usefulness of orthographic variation for linguistic, especially sociolinguistic, investigations. But authors examining the distribution of orthographic variants according to extra-linguistic factors rarely use the term *orthographic variable*, and even those who do use it do not offer a clear-cut definition of it. For example, Stenroos (2004 and 2006) investigated the realizations of the variables (th) and (gh) in Middle English texts, and Hernández-Campoy and Conde-Silvestre (1999) examined the variables (sh), (wh), and (u) in Early Modern English documents, referring to the word-initial, word-final, and occasionally word-medial orthographic variants found in a number of lexemes. These correspond to orthographic realizations of particular phonemes, or, in terms of placement, the onsets, codas, and nuclei of the syllables which they represent. For instance, the variable (wh) may refer to the Middle English spellings <wh>, <qw>, <qu> in the word WHICH, presumably pronounced as the labio-velar semivowel /w/. Thus the term *orthographic variable* is not equivalent to *grapheme*, as different graphemes (including their allographs) or combinations of graphemes can be variants of the same variable. Neither is it necessarily directly related to the phoneme, though in the example given above it is compatible with that unit of the phonological system. Nevertheless, an ortho-graphic variable may also comprise orthographic realizations of morphological categories, such as: the preterite and past participle ending {-ed} (Oldireva-Gustafsson 2002, Sairio 2009: 226–61); whole lexical items, for instance (much), (such), and (which) in former stages of English (Taavitsainen 2004, Conde-Silvestre and Hernández-Campoy 2004, Hernández-Campoy and Conde-Silvestre 2005). It may even operate at the level above the word boundary, for example contracted vs. non-contracted forms of auxiliary verbs such as *don't* and *do not* (Sairio 2009: 262–91).

3. Overview of Historical Sociolinguistic Studies on Orthographic Variation

This section gives an overview of approaches to orthographic variation in histori-cal documents in English. In view of the fact that there exist few studies on orthographic change conducted within a strict sociolinguistic methodological framework, we discuss also those studies whose authors explicitly recognize and consider social, textual, and stylistic factors as conditioning the distribution of orthographic variants. Because the time of production of the texts under consid-eration determines, to a large extent, the focus and methodology of particular studies, we have decided to divide this part of the chapter into several sub-sections referring roughly to successive historical periods. Particular emphasis is put on the stages of orthographic standardization, as this is the main area of inter-est of the existing studies on orthographic variation.

3.1 *Orthographic variation in medieval texts*

"[M]edieval writing does not produce variants; it is variance" (Cerquiglini 1989: 111, quoted by Nichols 1990: 1). The orthographic variation abounding in the extant Old and Middle English manuscripts has been investigated from two main points of view: 1) as a tool for determining the pronunciation of these language users, who left only written evidence behind them, and 2) as evidence in its own right. In both cases much emphasis has been laid on the abundance of regional variation in the documents. The former approach was clearly adopted by Toon (1992: 429), according to whom Old English scribes' "spelling in the absence of the pressures of a standard would be roughly phonetic 'transcriptions' of speech patterns," and by Luick (1914–40: §27), who claimed that in Middle English "one wrote as one spoke". Apart from those linguists who considered "orthographic variation as (roughly) mirroring phonological" (Lass 1997: 65), and examined it in order to reconstruct speech, others claimed that "not all spelling variation has any potential equivalent in speech" (Stenroos 2002: 456), and investigated the orthographic variation as evidence in its own right. The most monumental work published with that aim so far is definitely *A Linguistic Atlas of Late Mediaeval English* (McIntosh, Samuels, and Benskin 1986, henceforth LALME), which maps the dialects of English documents written in the period c. 1350–c. 1450, showing the regional distribution of dialectal variants and indicating the place of origin of both manuscripts and their scribes. It has been followed by several other large projects, such as *A Linguistic Atlas of Early Middle English* (LAEME[8]), prepared by Margaret Laing, Roger Lass, and Keith Williamson, a project running at the Institute for Historical Dialectology at the University of Edinburgh, and the *Middle English Grammar Corpus* (MEG-C[9]) by Merja Stenroos and her team at the University of Stavanger (in cooperation with the University of Glasgow).

Unfortunately, although the early texts do contain a huge number of orthographic variants, it is hard to correlate them with the social variables usually taken into consideration by sociolinguists analyzing modern languages, because of both the lack of surviving information and the relative social homogeneity of medieval scribes in terms of sex, class, education, and occupation (Hogg 2006: 395, Laing and Lass 2006: 419). However, historical linguists have proposed a variationist approach with a modified set of extra-linguistic variables, adjusted to the existing limitations as well as to the specific circumstances under which the medieval documents were produced. A noteworthy attempt to consider Old English from a sociolinguistic perspective was made by Hogg (2006: 395–416), who admitted the limitations of Old English dialectology, but did suggest that incorporating variables such as style, register, and text type into the analysis of variation in very early texts could provide important sociolinguistic insights into Old English. Laing and Lass, discussing the achievements and perspectives of early Middle English dialectology, emphasize that the variables relevant for examining medieval documents are "tied directly to the sources" and comprise "the intricate relations between the scribes' native varieties and their transcribing of languages other than English, the text genres, the provenance of exemplars and the different modes of copying" (2006: 419–20). They also point to the ability of textual scholars, paleographers, and codicologists to contribute more specific variables useful in the sociolinguistic analysis of the variation found in medieval documents, such as the order to which a given scribe belonged (such as Franciscan or Benedictine), the kind of script he used, and the particular scriptorium where he wrote. This is proved by research reported, for example, in Dumville (1993), Blake and Thaisen (2004), Traxel (2004), and Thaisen (2005).

In fact, the orthographic variation in certain early Middle English documents proves to be so pervasive and the relations between the variants and their phonological interpretations so complex that traditional, structural terminology does not seem sufficient for descriptive and explanatory purposes. Therefore, in order to analyze the orthographic variants in medieval texts, the authors of LAEME abandoned the division into *graphemes* and *phonemes*, and introduced the concepts of *litteral substitution sets* (LSS) and *potestatic substitution sets* (PSS), denoting sets of orthographic variants used to realize sounds, and sets of phonological (or phonetic) interpretations of spellings, respectively, with reference to particular lexical items recorded in medieval texts (Laing 1999, Laing and Lass 2003, 2006: 431–32, Lass and Laing 2007). The notion of LSS was borrowed by Stenroos (2006) in her study of fricative spellings, where she correlated the sets of spellings for the orthographic variables (th), (y), and (gh) with extra-linguistic variables, including region, chronology, and text type. That study (see also Stenroos 2002 and 2004) is a result of work on the first part of the Middle English Grammar project mentioned above, which aims at a detailed description of orthographic variants found in English medieval documents from a sociolinguistic perspective. More precisely, the compilers of MEG-C attempt to include "various categories of extra-linguistic information in the database." Stenroos (2004: 259) calls the assumed procedure "a standard one for variationist enquiry, even though the parameters employed are necessarily different from those used in the study of present-day languages." Instead of "the usual sociolinguistic variables, age, sex, and class," reflecting "the kinds of information retrievable for written medieval texts," date, genre/ text type, script, and manuscript ownership are used.

We can expect ongoing projects such as LAEME and MEG-C, as well as transcription and digitization projects such as the Canterbury Tales Project and the Málaga-Glasgow-Oviedo project (see Caie 2008: xi–xvi), to contribute more studies focused on particular texts and comparative studies considering numerous representative samples of documents. This will bring a refinement of the methodology and further explanation of the complexity of medieval orthographic systems in correlation with extra-linguistic variables (see also Chapters 6–8 in this *Handbook*).

3.2   Aspects of standardization of orthography

The political and socio-historical changes brought about by the Renaissance affected virtually all aspects of human activity in Europe, and are also reflected in the language of written texts dating from that period. In the medieval period, English had no orthographic standard in any sense approaching its modern definition. Instead, dialectal variation was rife. The situation began to change in the fifteenth century when the process of standardization commenced. It took over two centuries to complete, including the stages of selection, acceptance, functional elaboration, and codification (Haugen 1966/1972: 110, Leith 1983/1997: 31–34).

3.2.1   *Selection and acceptance* The English Renaissance is usually dated to the sixteenth and seventeenth centuries (Baugh and Cable 1951/2002: 200–52), but important changes in social attitudes to the English language are already notice-able several decades before 1500. After the adoption of English as the official language in most of the important institutions in the fourteenth century (Baugh and Cable 1951/2002: 143–51), there appeared a need for a national standard. As a result of "communicative pressures" developed due to that need, "the fifteenth century saw a gradual shift from the richly diverse spellings of the Middle English period to a more muted set of variations where more exotic forms of rare currency were purged in favour of those more commonly used," leading to the rise of spell-ing which "lacks precise dialectal 'colouring'" in the late fifteenth century (Smith 2006: 134).

The growing uniformity of spelling conventions, involving "the suppression of optional variability" (Milroy and Milroy 1985: 8), affected different types of texts at different times. The earliest efforts at standardization are recorded in govern-ment documents. According to a traditional view (Fisher 1977), a set of forms typical of those documents, often referred to as Chancery English (or Chancery Standard), was "familiarized throughout the country," and came "to be emulated, apparently because of the authority with which the Chancery was regarded" (Corrie 2006: 111). The impact of Chancery English has recently been reassessed by Benskin (2004: 36), who claims that "[t]he development of a written standard, even in the offices of government, was more complex and less determined than it has sometimes been made to appear." It is now generally recognized that the process of standardization involved the selection of linguistic features from a range of local varieties, for example the dialect originating in the Central Midlands, functioning as incipient standard norms (Samuels 1963/1969, 1972: 165–70, 1981: 43; Benskin 1992, 2004; Hope 2000; Conde-Silvestre and Hernández-Campoy 2004: 4).[10]

The gradual development of more uniform spelling practices in the late Middle and Early Modern English periods is embedded in a general socio-historical setting characterized by an increase in social mobility, growing literacy (enhanced by the introduction of printing and the greater availability of books), and a con-sequent multiplication of text types and genres. That period proves more rewarding than the Middle Ages for sociolinguistic research, thanks to the growing diversity with regard to the social variables, for example rank, education, and sex, available for correlation with orthographic (and other linguistic) variation. That opportunity has been taken up by several linguists, who have attempted to relate those variables to the orthographic variants recorded in extant documents. The adoption of prestigious spellings in the writings of particular individuals was studied, for example, by Gómez-Soliño (1981, 1985, 1986, 1997), Rodríguez (1999), and Nevalainen (2002). However, the first studies evaluating the fifteenth-century orthographic variation within a strictly sociolinguistic framework appeared only a few years ago. Hernández-Campoy and Conde-Silvestre (1999, 2005) and Conde-Silvestre and Hernández-Campoy (2004) examined the diffusion of incipient standard orthographic practices in late fifteenth-century private correspondence, by correlating selected graphemic innovations with the variables of age, gender, style, social status, and social networks, and adopting the model of social stratification developed and put into practice by Nevalainen (1996), Raumolin-Brunberg (1996), and Nevalainen and Raumolin-Brunberg (1996). Hernández-Campoy and Conde-Silvestre (2005: 110) selected personal correspondence as the basis for their study, because that genre offers relatively detailed personal information on their authors. The orthographic variants chosen for the analysis were first (see Hernández-Campoy and Conde-Silvestre 1999) referred to as the realizations of the variables (sh), (wh), and (u) in particular lexical items, namely SHOULD, SHALL, WORSHIP, SHE, WHICH, SUCH, and MUCH; whereas in the later studies (Conde-Silvestre and Hernández-Campoy 2004 and Hernández-Campoy and Conde-Silvestre 2005) they analyze the progress in the standardization of orthographic variants in fifteen lexical items –(should), (which), (such), (much), (though), (these), (self), (yet), (them), (it), (will), (not), (her), (any), and (through) – treated as orthographic variables. The authors conclude that the variable of social rank (including class and occupation), as well as the establishment of weak ties within the loose-knit networks promoting social mobility, played an important role in the diffusion in time of incipient standard spellings, with the most mobile members of the upper gentry and also urban non-gentry (merchants) appearing as "prominent in the use of the spellings that would become standard practices" (Hernández-Campoy and Conde-Silvestre 2005: 126). Another variable identified as important for the diffusion of standard spellings is style, since the "increase in the use of early standard variants in the course of time is parallel to their extension from formal to informal documents" (Hernández-Campoy and Conde-Silvestre 2005: 126).

3.2.2 *Functional elaboration and codification* The stages of selection and acceptance of a widely recognized language variety, including its characteristic orthographic variants, are naturally followed by its functional elaboration and codification. In English the standardization process was complex, because the functional elaboration started before the process of selection and acceptance had allowed for the identification of one and only one nationally recognized standard. In particular, even if the 'Chancery standard' remained the main inspiration for the orthographic choices in legal documents (Fisher 1977), the Central Midland Standard "was the only one that had achieved the status of a literary standard" (Samuels 1963/1969: 411). On the basis of her study on spellings in scientific documents, Taavitsainen (2000: 131) indicated that it is the latter incipient standard that seems to have been elaborated, "widening the functions of the vernacular to the prestige area of learning."

Taavitsainen (2004) continued her study on the process of vernacularization, including the elaboration of a new, scientific register in English, and attempted to relate the orthographic realizations of particular lexemes – SUCH, MUCH, ANY, SELF etc. – to the variables of register and genre (and text type). She examined several fifteenth-century scientific treatises, and concluded that dialect mixing was one of the characteristic features of the scientific discourse developing at that period. She related the evidence of conflicting spellings to social factors, and showed that the complex dialectal picture of manuscripts correlated with contemporary immigration patterns to and from London, the main metropolis (Taavitsainen 2004: 211–12). On the basis of numerous East Midland spellings shared by several surgical manuscripts, she also postulated that they may have been produced in a single scriptorium, by the scribes representing "a discourse community of a high professional level" (Taavitsainen 2004: 237). That study also confirmed the influence of the Central Midland Standard on the orthographic forms used in Early Modern English scientific writings. Although Taavitsainen's studies on orthographic variants – correlated with the variable of register and text type – show that considerable potential is offered by such research, few similar studies[11] are available as yet.

The arrival of printing in the latter half of the fifteenth century allows for the introduction of medium (handwritten vs. printed) as another extra-linguistic variable in studies on Renaissance and later documents. Osselton (1984) compared the spellings in the public (printed) writings and private correspondence of several authors (such as Johnson, Gray, Addison, Defoe, and Dryden). He concluded that in the seventeenth and eighteenth centuries there existed two standards of spelling, one used in public writings (based to a large extent on printers' practices) and the other in private letters, with the latter allowing a much wider range of spelling variants than the former. Like most other linguists interested in orthographic variation in historical texts, Osselton did not use the term *orthographic variable* in his study, but with hindsight the variants he analyzed were grouped into several variables, including capitalized vs. non-capitalized nouns, the orthographic realizations of the past tense/past participle inflectional ending {-ed} in weak verbs, and of the derivational suffix {-al}, as well as abbreviated vs. full forms of particular lexical items such as AND, WHICH, THOUGH, and THROUGH. He correlated those with extra-linguistic factors, including first of all the medium and the time of production, but referred also to the age of the authors, and to style. He did not distinguish particular text types in the printed medium, and the only text type that he analyzed, as regards handwritten documents, seems to have been a private letter. Osselton arrived at the conclusion that "epistolary spelling is a graphic system which leads its own linguistic life" (1984: 125), which can point to inherent features of that genre (cross-correlating with style). He also discovered "a time-lag of between 50 and 100 years between epistolary and printers' spelling" (1984: 132)[12]. Apparently, although "initially printing proved only a hindrance in the move towards orthographic uniformity" (Scragg 1974: 64), over the following two hundred years the situation must have changed considerably.

The existence of the double spelling standard in English in the eighteenth century, one in printed texts and the other in private letters, was confirmed by further studies. Tieken-Boon van Ostade (1996, 1998) examined the letters of Sarah Fielding, Robert Lowth, Laurence Sterne, and James Boswell, and compared their spelling practices with those of contemporary printers. She concluded that "[t]he epistolary spelling system is characterized by a greater amount of variation than the printers' system" (1998: 464), and that the most frequent areas of variation include, for example, the spellings of the preterite and past participle, different spelling rules in processes of word-formation, the distribution of double and single consonants, the presence or absence of an apostrophe in the genitive singular and in contracted verb forms, and different rules of capitalization (Tieken-Boon van Ostade 1998: 463–64, 2006a: 255–57).[13]

Further studies also revealed the importance of variables such as style, genre, text type, and register specificity for the distribution of orthographic variants. Tieken-Boon van Ostade stated that the frequency of abbreviations and contractions used in a letter was likely to be determined by its level of formality, with informal letters (especially drafts) and short formal notes containing more contracted forms than letters (especially formal ones) that were actually sent to their addressees (2003, 2006b: 233, 241, see also 1998: 460–61)[14]. She also noticed that some abbreviations appeared in most letters (such as those referring to names of months), whereas others were used only in those which dealt with scholarly matters (Tieken-Boon van Ostade 2006b: 239). Other recent studies correlating orthographic variables (particularly the use of contractions and abbreviations) with the variables of text type, gender, and style, include Oldireva-Gustafsson (2002) and Sairio (2009: 217–93).

Markus (2006) also analyzed the distribution of various kinds of abbreviated forms (compared to the full forms of the same lexemes, e.g., *wt* vs. *with*, *&* vs. *and*) in a corpus of correspondence, in correlation with the variables of chronology and the author's sex. He found that women use fewer abbreviations than men, and that abbreviations were less frequent in the sixteenth century than in the fifteenth and the seventeenth. The reason for such uneven distribution may have been the subject matter of the letters, with male-written business letters being particularly common in the fifteenth-century part of the corpus, referring to units of currency such as pounds, shillings, and pence, and showing a higher number of abbreviation tokens (2006: 123). In his conclusion, Markus (2006: 125–26) draws the reader's attention to the importance of the register variable, claiming that abbreviations are a characteristic feature of letters, especially business letters, where they function as gesture-saving instruments and make part of a simplified linguistic code typical of English for Specific Purposes (ESP).

As regards the variable of sex and its correlation with spelling habits, it has often been assumed that women used to spell more phonetically and be generally worse spellers than men, tending to use non-standard or dialectal forms (Zachrisson 1913: 43, Görlach 2001: 78)[15]. Sönmez (2000: 405) warned that such statements are usually based on impressionistic perceptions, and that the gender differences may be exaggerated. She points to the fact that previous studies on spelling variables in correlation with gender compared different text types (for instance, public writings by men with private writings by women, as few public writings by women are available), which must have considerably affected the results of such studies, where "what has been labelled a difference between men and women's spelling habits is more a difference between text types" (2000: 408)[16]. Accordingly, she emphasized the importance of using adequate methodologies and observing them strictly in order to obtain reliable results.

The process of codifying the orthographic variants that were considered correct was both triggered and strongly supported by the grammarians, spelling reformers, and lexicographers, whose proposals concerning the regularization of spelling are considered crucial for the orthographic standardization of English (Brengelman 1980, Carney 1994: 467)[17], given the lack of a single academic authority which could impose particular spelling patterns and usages.[18] As a result of the influence of grammars, spelling books, and dictionaries – printed, reprinted, and disseminated by a growing number of publishing houses[19] – the level of orthographic variation dropped considerably in the second half of the seventeenth century. The increase in consistency was so significant that it is usually considered that the orthographic standardization in English had been completed by the end of the seventeenth century (Scragg 1974: 80, Görlach 2001: 78). Indeed, most spellings in printed documents had become stable by that time. Nevertheless, it has recently been emphasized that the completion of standardization can be applied mainly to printed texts, whereas "[d]eviant spelling continued in letters and diaries, even among the educated" (Görlach 2001: 78, see also Salmon 1999: 44, and Tieken-Boon van Ostade 2009: 46–50). Moreover, writing about nineteenth-century English, Mugglestone (2006: 278) claimed that "while public printed texts manifest greater stability, even these are not devoid of change." Thus, the variables of medium and text type continued to determine the level of orthographic variation in Late Modern English.

Together with the growing recognition of the codified orthographic variants, 'correct' spelling started to be associated with intellectual and cultural sophistication, and dialectal as well as idiosyncratic spellings began to be stigmatized and considered unacceptable among well-educated speakers (Francis 1958: 561, Blake 1981: 124, Görlach 1999: 487, Fritz 2006: 238, Tieken-Boon van Ostade 2009: 47).[20] In this way the notion of 'spelling error' appeared.

Although mostly unpopular, the orthographic norms of modern languages are now profoundly prescriptive (Leiss and Leiss 1997). To disregard officially codified orthographic rules in specific contexts, for example in a school or in an office, is socially penalized, because "[i]f you cannot spell you are thought to be uneducated and, by a further savage twist, unintelligent" (Carney 1994: 79). Every literate individual internalizes the basically external, codified spelling norm during his or her socialization in school. Thus a strong individual awareness of the orthographic norm develops, which stabilizes it in the speech community at large. On the one hand, this enforces the congruence of spelling norm and writing customs, but on the other, the increasing discrepancy between the old tradition of handwritten idiosyncrasy and the relatively recent development of a variety of new text types, especially in digital media, may allow one to expect some confusion on the part of writers about which spelling is appropriate to the text type. However, most writers can easily distinguish between different contexts and text types and thus can keep texts which require an explicitly codified orthographic norm apart from texts that lack a codified orthography, but still have implicit spelling conventions, such as internet chats and SMS messages. Compared to the relatively little variation within modern, contemporary codified orthography, we can see that orthographic variation is increasing and has a positive image in these new text types in digital media. In this text type the heterographic function – unlike the capitalization of nouns or nuclei of noun phrases – does not operate for grammatical reasons alone, since it also transfers nonverbal or conceptually spoken forms into writing, such as ☺ and other emoticons (Rössler 2000, Crystal 2001). Moreover, in contrast to earlier periods in the history of the English language, the use of non-standard spellings, capitalization, and punctuation, is usually fully conscious, and serves particular stylistic purposes.

4. Conclusions

The features of orthography outlined in the first part of this chapter do not exist outside their time. They are the result of a historical development (Coulmas 1982). The high demand for prescriptiveness, accurate codification, and little variability, as normal features of modern, contemporary orthographic systems, results from the interplay which existed for centuries between writing customs and increasing codification, right up to the establishment of an orthographic norm. Whereas presenting distinct forms in writing can help to differentiate between dialects and languages in general, in the early stages the writing of a dialect or a language mainly uses spellings which already exist in foreign languages. Thus the writing systems of most contemporary European languages have their foundations in the Latin writing system. The inconsistencies of the orthographies of these languages partly follow from the lack of a clear-cut match between their graphemic and phonemic systems. Particularly since the beginning of the modern age several factors have affected the development of writing and thus the history of orthographic variation:

(a) As soon as the national languages gained their conceptual identity separate both from Latin, as the lingua franca of the élite, and from local dialects, the focus on writing and on standardization in orthography increased.
(b) The invention and spread of printing, which enabled an enormous increase in written documents, as well as an increase in the number and regional origins of readers, caused a reduction in variant spellings for typographic and economic reasons.
(c) As a result of printing, and later of the introduction of compulsory education, literacy increased. These developments also contributed to the increasing standardization of orthography.
(d) The shift from reading aloud to silent reading added to the autonomy of writing compared to speech. An example of increasing autonomy is the use of heterography as a feature of visual reception to distinguish cases of homophony, as in German *Lid* 'eyelid' vs. *Lied* 'song', or English *see* vs. *sea*.

(e) The original function of punctuation, as an indicator of when to breathe when reading aloud, decreased, and began to be used increasingly to mark grammatical structures (Gallmann 1996).

(f) As morphemes became more visually consistent, so the semantic elements became more comprehensible and readable. That is, readers could recognize the words as wholes rather than needing to decode the sounds one by one; it became possible to read and understand words without being able to pronounce them.

(g) With the process of nation-building, the orthography of a national language became a political concern. As a consequence of this, many states have established orthographic laws valid for particular contexts, such as school and public authorities.

The studies on orthographic variation and change reviewed in the later part of this chapter deal only with the selected historical developments listed above, with particular emphasis on some aspects of standardization; other developments still need more detailed examination from a sociolinguistic perspective. However, the increasing number of studies that have appeared in recent years show that, after a period of neglect due to the established tradition of treating orthographic change as "something secondary, merely a reflection of the spoken mode" (Stenroos 2006: 9), the phenomenon has started to raise more interest among linguists, including historical sociolinguists. Studies on orthographic variables and their correlation to extra-linguistic factors have already led to important insights into sociolinguistic phenomena, such as the process of standardization of the English language. In view of the recent flowering of corpus linguistics, it can be hoped that new, more reliable and easily searchable electronic editions of numerous historical documents will facilitate future research in the area, including the investigation into the correlation between particular orthographic variants and other variables such as style, register, text type, age, and gender. It can also be expected that the proliferation of scientific investigations will contribute to the refinement and increased consistency of the terminology and the theoretical frameworks used for describing and explaining orthographic change.

NOTES

1   Most of the examples provided in this chapter deal with the history of English.

2   In German, capitalization provides morphological information, since all the words which belong to the word class of nouns are capitalized.

3   See Ruszkiewicz (1976) and Sgall (1987) for discussions of alternative sets of principles governing orthographic systems.

4   Tieken-Boon van Ostade's (2009: 38) research on the basis of the *British National Corpus* (BNC) shows that both variants yield nearly equal numbers of hits.

5   For political and ideological reasons, these can be considered two separate standards.

6 Yet another context and text type which requires different orthographic conventions can be found in computer-mediated communication (Crystal 2001, Herring 2001).
7 This term was used earlier in experimental psychology, applied theoretical linguistics, psycholinguistics, and language acquisition (see Templeton and Scarborough-Franks 1985, and Luelsdorff 1990).
8 http://www.lel.ed.ac.uk/ihd/laeme1/laeme1.html [accessed November 18, 2009].
9 http://www.uis.no/research/culture/the_middle_english_grammar_project/meg-c/ [accessed October 14, 2011].
10 See also studies on dialectal orthographic features in particular texts and their connection with the developing standard in English, Raumolin-Brunberg and Nevalainen (1990), Lucas (1994), Heikkonen (1996), Nevalainen (1996), and Rutkowska (2003).
11 See Rissanen's (1999) remarks on spellings in early statutes.
12 The latter correlation did not apply to all the variables examined.
13 Orthographic variation has also been examined in studies comparing handwritten and printed texts. Detailed comparisons of orthographic systems and degree of standardization in several editions of early English printed books can be found in, for example, Blake (1965), Aronoff (1989), Horobin (2001), and Rutkowska (2005).
14 See also Haugland (1995) for an elaborate discussion of the treatment of contractions and abbreviations in grammars of the sixteenth to eighteenth centuries, including the prescriptive and proscriptive recommendations of contemporary grammarians and spelling reformers.
15 See Sönmez (2000: 406–407) for examples of such comments from modern as well as sixteenth- and seventeenth-century authors.
16 Tieken-Boon van Ostade's research (2006a: 257) also shows that "[g]enteel women did not on the whole spell worse than men."
17 But compare Scragg (1974: 81), who claimed that "English spelling seems to have been particularly resistant to the interference of linguistic philosophers." See also Osselton (1985: 50) on conflicting advice in the seventeenth- and eighteenth-century spelling books on the rules concerning capitalization.
18 In contrast to England, in other European countries official bodies were established for the codification of national languages, such as the Accademia della Crusca (founded in 1582), the Académie Française (1635), and the Real Academia Española (1713).
19 For evidence concerning the role of printers in the standardization of English spelling see, for example, Osselton (1985), Salmon (1989), and Tieken-Boon van Ostade (1998).
20 The stigmatization of non-standard spellings was also a characteristic of developing standards in other European languages. See Posner (1997: 55) who states that "[a]ccurate spelling was a moral question" and "one of the most important criteria for success" in nineteenth-century France.

REFERENCES

Aronoff, M. (1989) The orthographic system of an early English printer: Wynkyn de Worde. *Folia Linguistica Historica* 8(1–2): 65–98.

Augst, G. (1985) Graphematik und Orthographie. Interdisziplinäre Aspekte gegenwärtiger Schrift- und Orthographieforschung, Niemeyer, Tübingen.

Baugh, A.C. and Cable, T. (1951/2002) *A History of the English Language* (5th edn), Routledge, London.

Beaugrande, R. de. (2006) Speech versus writing in the discourse of linguistics.

Miscelánea: *A Journal of English and American Studies* 33: 31–45.

Benskin, M. (1992) Some new perspectives on the origins of standard written English. In J.A. van Leuvensteijn and J.B. Berns (eds.), *Dialect and Standard Language in the English, Dutch, German and Norwegian Language Areas*, North Holland, Amsterdam, pp. 71–105.

Benskin, M. (2004) Chancery Standard. In C. Kay, C. Hough, and I. Wotherspoon (eds.), *New Perspectives on English Historical Linguistics: Selected Papers from 12 ICEHL, Glasgow, August 21–26, 2002. Volume 2: Lexis and Transmission*, John Benjamins, Amsterdam, pp. 1–40.

Blake, N. (1965) English versions of Reynard the Fox in the fifteenth and sixteenth centuries. *Studies in Philology* 62: 63–77.

Blake, N. (1981) *Non-standard Language in English Literature*, Deutsch, London.

Blake, N. and Thaisen, J. (2004) Spelling's significance for textual studies. *Nordic Journal of English Studies*. 3(1): 93–107.

Bloomfield, L. (1933) *Language*, Holt, Rinehart and Winston, New York.

Brengelman, F.H. (1980) Orthoepists, printers, and the rationalization of English spelling. *Journal of English and Germanic Philology* 79: 332–54.

BNC = British National Corpus (1991–94) Compiled by Oxford University Computing Services, Oxford University. www.natcorp.ox.ac.uk [accessed February 20, 2010].

Britton, D. (ed.) (1996) *English Historical Linguistics 1994: Papers from the 8th International Conference on English Historical Linguistics*, John Benjamins, Amsterdam.

Bußmann, H. (2008) *Lexikon der Sprachwissenschaft* (4th edn), Kröner, Stuttgart.

Caie, G.D. (2008) Prologue. In T. Marqués-Aguado, A. Miranda-García, and S. González (eds.), *Benvenutus Grassus: The Middle English Ophthalmic Treatise on the Use of the Eye in G. U. L. MS Hunter 513 (ff. 1r-37r)*, Universidad de Malaga, pp. xi–xvi.

Carney, E. (1994) *A Survey of English Spelling*, Routledge, London.

Cerquiglini, B. (1989) *Eloge de la variante: histoire critique de la philologie*, Seuil, Paris.

Chambers, J.K. (1995/2009) *Sociolinguistic Theory* (2nd edn), Wiley-Blackwell, Oxford.

Chambers, J.K. and Trudgill, P. (1980/1994) *Dialectology*. Cambridge University Press, Cambridge.

Conde-Silvestre, J.C. and Hernández-Campoy, J.M. (2004) A sociolinguistic approach to the diffusion of Chancery written practices in late fifteenth century private correspondence. *Neuphilologische Mitteilungen* 105: 133–52.

Corrie, M. (2006) Middle English: dialects and diversity. In L. Mugglestone (ed.), pp. 86–119.

Coulmas, F. (1982) *Über Schrift*, Suhrkamp, Frankfurt am Main.

Crystal, D. (1995) *The Cambridge Encyclopedia of the English Language*, Cambridge University Press, Cambridge.

Crystal, D. (2001) *Language and the Internet*, Cambridge University Press, Cambridge.

Dobson, E. (1957–68) *English Pronunciation 1500–1700. Volumes 1–2*, Oxford University Press, Oxford.

Dudenredaktion (2006) *Die deutsche Rechtschreibung* (24th edn), Dudenverlag, Mannheim, Leipzig, Wien, Zürich.

Dumville, D. (1993) *English Caroline Script and Monastic History: Studies in Benedictinism A. D. 950–1030*, The Boydell Press, Woodbridge.

Eisenberg, P. (ed.) (2006) *Niemand hat das letzte Wort. Sprache – Schrift – Orthographie*, Wallstein, Göttingen.

Eisenberg, P. and Günther, H. (eds.) (1989) *Schriftsystem und Orthographie*, Niemeyer, Tübingen.

Elmentaler, M. (2000) Zur Koexistenz graphematischer Systeme in der spätmittelalterlichen Stadt. In M. Elmentaler (ed.), *Regionalsprachen, Stadtsprachen und Institutionssprachen im historischen Prozess*, Edition Praesens, Vienna, pp. 53–72.

Francis, W.N. (1958) *The Structure of American English*, The Ronald Press Company, New York.

Fisher, J.H. (1977) Chancery English and the emergence of standard written English. *Speculum* 50: 870–99.

Friedrich, B. (1996) Aspekte und Probleme des Schreibunterrichts: Rechtschreiben. In H. Günther and O. Ludwig (eds.), pp. 1249–60.

Fritz, C. (2006) The convention's spelling conventions: regional variation in 19th-century Australian spelling. In R. Facchinetti and M. Rissanen (eds.), *Corpus-based Studies of Diachronic English*, Peter Lang, Bern, pp. 231–52.

Gallmann, P. (1996) Interpunktion (Syngrapheme). In H. Günther and O. Ludwig (eds.), pp. 1456–67.

Glück, H. (ed.) (2005) *Metzler Lexikon Sprache. Stuttgart* (3rd edn), Metzler, Weimar, pp. 461–62.

Gómez-Soliño, J. (1981) Thomas Wolsey, Thomas More y la lengua inglesa estándar de su época. *Revista Canaria de Estudios Ingleses* 3: 74–84.

Gómez-Soliño, J. (1985) William Caxton y la estandarización de la lengua inglesa en el siglo XV. *Revista Canaria de Estudios Ingleses* 10: 95–118.

Gómez-Soliño, J. (1986) La normalización lingüística en la época de Enrique VIII. In S. Onega (ed.), *Estudios literarios ingleses. Renacimiento y barroco*, Cátedra, Madrid, pp. 19–44.

Gómez-Soliño, J. (1997) Pastons, Celys and the standard language in the late fifteenth century. In M. Giménez Bon and V. Olsen (eds.), *Proceedings of the IXth International Conference of the Spanish Society for Medieval English Language and Literature*, Universidad del País Vasco, Vitoria-Gasteiz, pp. 117–39.

Görlach, M. (1999) Regional and social variation. In R. Lass (ed.), pp. 459–538.

Görlach, M. (2001) *Eighteenth-century English*, C. Winter, Heidelberg.

Günther, H. and Ludwig, O. (eds.) (1996) *Schrift und Schriftlichkeit. Writing and Its Use. Ein interdisziplinäres Handbuch internationaler Forschung*, Walter de Gruyter, Berlin.

Güthert, K. (2006) Zur Neuregelung der deutschen Rechtschreibung ab 1. August 2006. extra edn. *(Sprachreport. Informationen und Meinungen zur deutschen Sprache 22)*.

Haugen, E. (1966/1972) Dialect, language and nation. In J. Pride and J. Holmes (eds.), *Sociolinguistics*, Penguin, Harmondsworth, pp. 97–111.

Haugland, K. (1995) Is't allow'd or ain't? On contraction in early grammars and spelling books. *Studia Neophilologica* 67(2): 165–84.

Heikkonen, K. (1996) Regional variation in standardization. A case study of Henry V's Signet Office. In T. Nevalainen and H. Raumolin-Brunberg (eds.), pp. 111–27.

Hernández-Campoy, J.M. and Conde-Silvestre, J.C. (1999) The social diffusion of linguistic innovations in 15th century England: Chancery spellings in private correspondence. *Cuadernos de Filología Inglesa* 8: 251–74.

Hernández-Campoy, J.M. and Conde-Silvestre, J.C. (2005) Sociolinguistic and geolinguistic approaches to the historical diffusion of linguistic innovations: incipient standardisation in Late Middle English. *International Journal of English Studies* 5(1): 101–34.

Herring, S. (2001) Computer-mediated discourse. In D. Schiffrin, D. Tannen and H.E. Hamilton (eds.), *The Handbook of Discourse Analysis*, Blackwell, Oxford, pp. 612–34.

Hogg, R. (2006) Old English dialectology. In A. van Kemenade and B. Los (eds.), pp. 395–416.

Hope, J. (2000) Rats, bats, sparrows and dogs: biology, linguistics and the nature of Standard English. In L. Wright (ed.), pp. 49–56.

Horobin, S. (2001) The language of the fifteenth-century printed editions of *The Canterbury Tales*. *Anglia* 119 (2): 249–58.

Jaffe, A. (2000) Introduction: non-standard orthography and non-standard speech. *Journal of Sociolinguistics* 4 (4): 497–513.

Kohrt, M. (1987) *Theoretische Aspekte der deutschen Orthographie* (RGL 70), Niemeyer, Tübingen.

Labov, W. (1966) The linguistic variable as a structural unit. *Washington Linguistics Review* 3: 4–22. http://www.eric.ed.gov/PDFS/ED010871.pdf [accessed September 23, 2011].

Laing, M. (1999) Confusion *wrs* confounded: litteral substitution sets in early Middle English writing systems. *Neuphilologische Mitteilungen* 100: 251–70.

Laing, M. and Lass, R. (2003) Tales of the 1001 nists. The phonological implications of litteral substitution sets in 13th-century South-West-Midland texts. *English Language and Linguistics* 7(2): 1–22.

Laing, M. and Lass, R. (2006) Early Middle English dialectology: problems and prospects. In A. van Kemenade and B. Los (eds.), pp. 417–51.

Lass, R. (1997) *Historical Linguistics and Language Change*, Cambridge University Press, Cambridge.

Lass, R. (ed.) (1999) *The Cambridge History of the English Language. Volume 3: 1476–1776*, Cambridge University Press, Cambridge.

Lass, R. and Laing, M. (2007) Introduction. Part I: Background. Chapter 2: Interpreting Middle English, in *A Linguistic Atlas of Early Middle English, 1150–1325* (compiled by M. Laing and R. Lass), University of Edinburgh. http://www.lel.ed.ac.uk/ihd/laeme1/laeme1.html [accessed November 18, 2009].

Leiss, E. and Leiss, J. (1997) *Die regulierte Schrift. Plädoyer für die Freigabe der Rechtschreibung*, Palm and Enke, Erlangen and Jena.

Leith, D. (1983/1997) *A Social History of English* (2nd edn), Routledge, London.

Lucas, P. (1994) Towards a standard written English? Continuity and change in the orthographic usage of John Capgrave, O.S.A. (1393–1464). In F.M. Fernández, M. Fuster, and J.J. Calvo (eds.), *English Historical Linguistics 1992: Papers from the 7th International Conference on English Historical Linguistics, Valencia, 22–26 September 1992*, John Benjamins, Amsterdam, pp. 91–103.

Luelsdorff, P. (1990) Principles of orthography. *Theoretical Linguistics* 16(2–3): 165–214.

Luick, K. (1914–40) *Historische Grammatik der englischen Sprache*, Bernhard Tauchnitz, Stuttgart.

Macha, J. (1998) Schreibvariation und ihr regional-kultureller Hintergrund: Rheinland und Westfalen im 17. Jahrhundert, in *Zeitschrift für deutsche Philologie* 117. Sonderheft Regionale Sprachgeschichte, 50–66.

Macha, J. (2004) Konfession und Sprache: Zur schreibsprachlichen Divergenz um 1600. In K.J. Mattheier and H. Nitta (eds.), *Sprachwandel und Gesellschaftswandel – Wurzeln des heutigen Deutsch*, Iudicium, München, pp. 161–76.

Maas, U. (1992) *Grundzüge der deutschen Orthographie*, Niemeyer, Tübingen.

Markus, M. (2006) Abbreviations in Early Modern English correspondence. In M. Dossena and S.M. Fitzmaurice (eds.), *Business and Official Correspondence: Historical Investigations*, Peter Lang, Bern, pp. 107–29.

Mayr, S. (2007) *Grammatikkenntnisse für Rechtschreibregeln? Drei deutsche Rechtschreibwörterbücher kritisch analysiert*, Niemeyer, Tübingen.

McArthur, T. (2006) English world-wide in the twentieth century. In L. Mugglestone (ed.), pp. 360–93.

McIntosh, A., Samuels, M., and Benskin, M. (1986) *A Linguistic Atlas of Late Medieval English* (LALME), Aberdeen University Press.

MEG-C = *The Middle English Grammar Corpus* (2009) (compiled by M. Stenroos, M. Mäkinen, S. Horobin, and J. Smith), University of Stavanger, http://www.uis.no/research/culture/the_middle_english_grammar_project/ [accessed November 11, 2010].

Mihm, A. (2000) Zur Deutung der graphematischen Variation in historischen Texten. In A. Häcki Buhofer (ed.), *Vom Umgang mit sprachlicher Variation: Soziolinguistik, Dialektologie, Methoden und Wissenschaftsgeschichte. Festschrift für Heinrich Löffler zum 60. Geburtstag*, Francke, Tübingen and Basel, pp. 367–90.

Milroy, J. and Milroy, L. (1985) *Authority in Language: Investigating Language Prescription and Standardisation*, Routledge, London.

Milroy, L. and Gordon, M. (2003) *Sociolinguistics: Method and Interpretation*, Blackwell, Oxford.

Möller, R. (1998) *Regionale Schreibsprachen im überregionalen Schriftverkehr. Empfängerorientierung in den Briefen des*

Kölner Rates im 15. Jahrhundert, Böhlau, Cologne.

Mugglestone, L. (2006) English in the nineteenth century. In L. Mugglestone (ed.), pp. 274–304.

Mugglestone, L. (ed.) (2006) *The Oxford History of English*, Oxford University Press, Oxford.

Nerius, D. (1996) Orthographieentwicklung und Orthographiereform. In H. Günther and O. Ludwig (eds.), pp. 720–39.

Nerius, D. (ed.) (2007) *Deutsche Orthographie* (4th edn), Olms, Hildesheim.

Nevalainen, T. (1996) Social stratification. In T. Nevalainen and H. Raumolin-Brunberg (eds.), pp. 57–76.

Nevalainen, T. (2002) What's in a royal letter? Linguistic variation in the correspondence of King Henry VIII. In K. Lenz and R. Möhlig (eds.), *Of dyuersitie & chaunge of langage*, Universitätsverlag C. Winter, Heidelberg, pp. 169–79.

Nevalainen, T. and Raumolin-Brunberg, H. (1996) Social stratification in Tudor English? In D. Britton (ed.), pp. 303–26.

Nevalainen, T. and Raumolin-Brunberg, H. (eds.) (1996) *Sociolinguistics and Language History: Studies Based on the Corpus of Early English Correspondence*, Rodopi, Amsterdam.

Nichols, S.G. (1990) Introduction: philology in a manuscript culture. *Speculum* 65: 1–10.

Oldireva-Gustafsson, L. (2002) *Preterite and Past Participle Forms in English: 1680–1790*, Uppsala Universitet, Stockholm.

Osselton, N. (1984) Informal spelling systems in Early Modern English: 1500–1800. N. Blake and C. Jones (eds.), *English Historical Linguistics: Studies in Development*, CECTAL, University of Sheffield, pp. 123–37.

Osselton, N. (1985) Spelling-book rules and the capitalization of nouns in the seventeenth and eighteenth centuries. In M.-J. Arn, H. Wirtjes, and H. Jansen (eds.), *Historical & Editorial Studies in Medieval & Early Modern English*, Wolters-Noordhoff, Groningen, pp. 49–61.

OED Online = Oxford English Dictionary Online. www.oed.com [accessed February 12, 2010].

Posner, R. (1997) *Linguistic Change in French*, Clarendon Press, Oxford.

Raumolin-Brunberg, H. (1996) Historical sociolinguistics. In T. Nevalainen and H. Raumolin-Brunberg (eds.), pp. 11–37.

Raumolin-Brunberg, H. and Nevalainen, T. (1990) Dialectal features in a corpus of Early Standard English? In G. Caie *et al.* (eds.), *Proceedings from the Fourth Nordic Conference for English Studies*, University of Copenhagen Department of English, pp. 119–31.

Rissanen, M. (1999) Language of law and the development of Standard English. In I. Taavitsainen, G. Melchers, and P. Pahta (eds.), *Writing in Non-Standard English*, John Benjamins, Amsterdam, pp. 189–204.

Rodríguez, G. (1999) Spelling variables and conformity to the standard in the late fifteenth century. In A. Bringas López *et al.* (eds.), *'Woonderous Ænglisce' SELIM Studies in Medieval English Language*, Universidade de Vigo, pp. 145–99.

Rössler, P. (2000) Von der Virgel zum Slash. Zur Zeichensetzung zwischen Gutenberg und Internet, in *Zeitschrift für Germanistik. 3*, Peter Lang, Bern, pp. 508–20.

Rössler, P. (2005) Schreibvariation – Sprachregion – Konfession. Graphematik und Morphologie in österreichischen und bayerischen Drucken vom 16. bis ins 18. Jahrhundert, Peter Lang, Bern.

Ruszkiewicz, P. (1976) *Modern Approaches to Graphophonemic Investigations in English*, Uniwersytet Śląski, Katowice.

Rutkowska, H. (2003) *Graphemics and Morphosyntax in the* Cely Letters *(1472–88)*. Peter Lang, Frankfurt am Main.

Rutkowska, H. (2005) Selected orthographic features in English editions of the *Book of good maners (1487–1507)*, *SELIM* 12 (2003–4), pp. 127–42.

Sairio, A. (2009) *Language and Letters of the Bluestocking Network: Sociolinguistic Issues in Eighteenth-century Epistolary English*, Société Néophilologique, Helsinki.

Salmon, V. (1989) John Rastell and the normalization of early sixteenth-century orthography. In L.E. Breivik, A. Hille, and S. Johansson (eds.), *Essays on English language in honour of Bertil Sundby*, Novus Forlag, Oslo, pp. 289–301.

Salmon, V. (1999) Orthography and punctuation. In R. Lass (ed.), pp. 13–55.

Samuels, M. (1963/1969) Some applications of Middle English dialectology. *English Studies* 44: 81–94. Reprinted in *Approaches to English historical linguistics*, R. Lass (ed.) (1969), Holt, Rinehart and Winston, New York, pp. 404–18.

Samuels, M. (1972) *Linguistic Evolution with Special Reference to English*, Cambridge University Press, Cambridge.

Samuels, M. (1981) Spelling and dialect in the late and post-middle English periods. In M. Benskin and M. Samuels (eds.), *So Meny People, Longages and Tonges. Philological Essays in Scots and Medieval English Presented to A. McIntosh*, Middle English Dialect Project, Edinburgh, pp. 43–54.

Sapir, E. (1921/1949) *Language: An Introduction to the Study of Speech*, Harcourt, Brace and World, New York.

Saussure, F. de (1915/1993) *Troisième Cours de Linguistique Generale (1910–11) d'après les cahiers d'Emile Constantin/ Third Course of Lectures on General Linguistics (1910–11): From the Notebooks of Emile Constantin* (eds. E. Komatsu and R. Harris), Pergamon Press, Oxford.

Scragg, D. (1974) *A History of English Spelling*, Manchester University Press, Manchester.

Sgall, P. (1987) Towards a theory of phonemic orthography. In P.A. Luelsdorff (ed.), *Orthography and Phonology*, John Benjamins, Amsterdam, pp. 1–30.

Smith, J. (1996) *An Historical Study of English: Function, Form and Change*, Routledge, London.

Smith, J. (2006) From Middle to Early Modern English. In L. Mugglestone (ed.), pp. 120–46.

Sönmez, M.J.-M. (2000) Perceived and real differences between men's and women's spellings of the early to mid-seventeenth century. In D. Kastovsky and A. Mettinger (eds.), *The History of Englishin a Social Context: A Contribution to Historical Sociolinguistics*, Mouton de Gruyter, Berlin, pp. 405–39.

Stenroos, M. (2002) Free variation and other myths: interpreting historical English spelling. *Studia Anglica Posnaniensia* 38: 445–68.

Stenroos, M. (2004) Regional dialects and spelling conventions in Late Middle English: searches for (th) in the LALME data. In M. Dossena and R. Lass (eds.), *Methods and Data in English Historical Dialectology*, Peter Lang, Bern, pp. 257–85.

Stenroos, M. (2006) A Middle English mess of fricative spellings: reflections on thorn, yogh and their rivals. In M. Krygier and L. Sikorska (eds.), *To Make his Englissh Sweete upon his Tonge*, Peter Lang, Frankfurt am Main, pp. 9–35.

Stetter, C. (1996) Orthographie als Normierung des Schriftsystems. In H. Günther and O. Ludwig (eds.), pp. 687–97.

Taavitsainen, I. (2000) Scientific language and spelling standardisation. In L. Wright (ed.), pp. 131–54.

Taavitsainen, I. (2004) Scriptorial 'house-styles' and discourse communities. In I. Taavitsainen and P. Pahta (eds.), *Medical and Scientific Writing in Late Medieval English*, Cambridge University Press, Cambridge, pp. 209–40.

Templeton, S. and Scarborough-Franks, L. (1985) The spelling's the thing: knowledge of derivational morphology in orthography and phonology among older students. *Applied Psycholinguistics* 6: 371–90.

Thaisen, J. (2005) Orthography, codicology, and textual studies: The Cambridge University Library, Gg.4.27 *Canterbury Tales. Boletín Millares Carlo* 24–25, Las Palmas, pp. 379–94.

Tieken-Boon van Ostade, I. (1996) Social network theory and eighteenth-century English: the case of Boswell. In D. Britton (ed.), pp. 327–37.

Tieken-Boon van Ostade, I. (1998) Standardization of English spelling: the eighteenth-century printers' contribution. In J. Fisiak and M. Krygier (eds.), *Advances in English historical linguistics 1996*, Mouton de Gruyter, Berlin, pp. 457–70.

Tieken-Boon van Ostade, I. (2003) Lowth's language. In M. Dossena and C. Jones (eds.), *Insights into Late Modern English*, Peter Lang, Bern, pp. 241–64.

Tieken-Boon van Ostade, I. (2006a) English at the onset of the normative tradition. In L. Mugglestone (ed.), pp. 240–73.

Tieken-Boon van Ostade, I. (2006b) 'Disrespectful and too familiar?' Abbreviations as an index of politeness in 18th-century letters. In C. Dalton-Puffer, D. Kastovsky, N. Ritt, and H. Schendl (eds.), *Syntax, Style and Grammatical Norms: English from 1500–2000*, Peter Lang, Bern, pp. 229–47.

Tieken-Boon van Ostade, I. (2009) *An Introduction to Late Modern English*. Edinburgh University Press, Edinburgh.

Toon, T. (1992) Old English dialects. In N. Blake (ed.), *The Cambridge History of the English Language. Volume 2: 1066–1476*, Cambridge University Press, Cambridge, pp. 409–51.

Traxel, O. (2004) *Language Change, Writing and Textual Interference in Post-Conquest Old English Manuscripts: The Evidence of Cambridge University Library, Ii. l. 33*, Peter Lang, Frankfurt am Main.

van Kemenade, A. and Los, B. (eds.) (2006) *The Handbook of the History of English*, Blackwell, Oxford.

Voeste, A. (2007) Variability and professionalism as prerequisites of standardization. In S. Elspaß, N. Langer, J. Scharloth, and W. Vandenbussche (eds.), *Germanic Language Histories 'from Below' 1700–2000*, Walter de Gruyter, Berlin, pp. 295–308.

Wright, L. (ed.) (2000) *The Development of Standard English, 1300–1800: Theories, Descriptions, Conflicts*, Cambridge University Press, Cambridge.

Wyld, H. (1936) *A History of Modern Colloquial English* (3rd edn), Blackwell, Oxford.

Zachrisson, R. (1913) *Pronunciation of English Vowels 1400–1700*, W. Zachrissons boktryckeri, Göteborg.

13 Phonological Variables

ANNA HEBDA

1. The Notion of a Phonological Variable

No matter when one looks at a language or what language one looks at, "it is variable and in a state of change" (Milroy 1992: 2). This inherent heterogeneity, which is far from haphazard or unstructured, manifests itself through linguistic variables, which can be perhaps best defined as "a set of related dialect forms all of which mean the same thing and which correlate with some social grouping in the speech community" (Britain 2002). These 'related dialect forms' need not necessarily be words, however, even though the phrase 'mean the same thing' might suggest otherwise. What is meant by the synonymy indicated here, in the context of linguistic variables, is the fact that the use of one variant (or another) of a given variable does not entail a difference in meaning. Consequently, any linguistic unit whose realization varies depending on the context, be it a phoneme, a morpheme, a lexeme, or a phrase, comprises a linguistic variable.

A *phonological variable* is an umbrella-term for a set of complementarily distributed variant forms of a phoneme, in other words, its allophones (see also Kerswill 2006). Phonological variability, attributable to differences in vocal tract anatomy, the linguistic context, and the geographical and social background of the speaker (see Foulkes 2006 for details), typically manifests itself through a number of discrete alternants or a continuum of variants ranging along a given phonetic dimension. While the former – alternation between discrete forms (including 'zero') – seems to be a feature of variability within the consonant inventory (take, for example, *h*-dropping or the realization of (ng) as [ŋ] or [n] in English), continuous variables are found among vowel phonemes whose allophones vary in their height and advancement (Milroy and Gordon 2003: 138), as in the case

The Handbook of Historical Sociolinguistics, First Edition. Edited by Juan Manuel Hernández-Campoy and Juan Camilo Conde-Silvestre.
© 2014 John Wiley & Sons, Ltd. Published 2014 by John Wiley & Sons, Ltd.

of the pre-lateral (e) in Norwich English pronounced as either [ɛ], [ɜ] or [ʌ] (Trudgill 1974), or Seoul Korean (o) realizable as [o] or [u] in bound-morphemes (Labov 1966/2006).

The awareness of phonological variation goes back to the Middle Ages, one of the earliest comments thereon coming from Trevisa's (c. 1385) translation of Higden's *Polychronicon*:

> Hyt semeþ a gret wondur houȝ Englysch, þat ys þe burþtonge of Englysch men and here oune longage and tonge, ys so dyuers of soun in þis ylond, and þe longage of Normandy ys comlyng of anoþer lond and haþ on maner soun among al men þat spekeþ hyt aryȝt in Engelond. Noþeles *þer ys as meny dyuers maner Frensch yn þe rem of Fraunce as ys dyuers manere Englysch in þe rem of Engelond* . . . [my italics, AH] (Kaiser 1961: 517),

Nevertheless, it was not until the 1960s that a more systematic sociolinguistic analysis of phonological variability began. Labov's (1963) seminal study on the pronunciation of (au) and (ai) on Martha's Vineyard showed the predominance of the centralized [əu, əi] variants in middle-aged Yankee fishermen living around Chilmark. Three years later, a study on the distribution of word-final and post-vocalic (r) in the English of New York City revealed a correlation between rhoticity and the level of formality and social status. Another sixteen years passed, however, before sociolinguists embraced the idea of incorporating diachronic data into their research, with Romaine's (1982) *Socio-historical Linguistics* paving the way for diachronically-oriented variationist sociolinguistic analyses.

The remainder of this chapter is essentially devoted to outlining the tasks undertaken by historical sociolinguistics, the difficulties it faces in reconstructing phonological variation, and ways of overcoming problems inherent in the use of 'bad data' (Labov 1994). Given that, as Foulkes (2006) observes, a great deal of what is known about variation today comes from research on English, discussions of variation are of necessity biased towards diachronic material related to this language, though reference is also made to Parisian French and Arabic. For the sake of clarity, the case studies overviewed here have been grouped together on the basis of the time frame within which the analyzed data fall, and presented in the resulting chronological order.

2. On the (Im?)possibility of Historical Sociolinguistics

Given that the relationship of linguistic to extralinguistic variables falls within the scope of sociolinguistics, historical sociolinguistics must, by definition, investigate this same relationship from a diachronic perspective. In other words, while sociolinguistics inquires into the social uses of language (Chambers 1995/2003) in the sense of the linguistic choices people make, historical sociolinguistics is interested in what determined those choices in the past, the extralinguistic constraints involved being geographical background and mobility, gender, age, ethnic group membership, and the social network and socio-economic class of the speaker (Raumolin-Brunberg 1996).

Yet, influential as they may be, not all the external factors that are critical from the point of view of sociolinguistics will be applicable in historical sociolinguistic studies or equally relevant for all historical periods[1]. As early as 1988, for example, Hogg questioned the plausibility of considering sociolinguistic variation with reference to Old English dialects, and in 2006 he reiterated this concern:

> [N]o present-day analysis of dialect variation could be conducted without reference to social variation. This will include the kinds of variation which are induced by, for example, class features or gender, or age. For Old English little of this makes much sense, even though we would like it to. (Hogg 2006: 395)

In the same vein, in their discussion of the problems and prospects of Early Middle English dialectology, Laing and Lass (2006: 418) stressed the underprivileged position of historical studies in view of the constraints on the available range of extralinguistic variables:

> In modern dialect studies, the social dimension may involve variables such as age, sex, class, religion, occupation, economic status, education, and ethnicity. In the context of historical dialectology 'social milieu' must be taken more generally to refer to the whole historical background. It is rarely possible to achieve the fineness of resolution typical of studies of contemporary language states. Variables will differ according to which historical vernacular is under scrutiny and at what period.

Nevalainen and Raumolin-Brunberg (2005: 34), in turn, point out that even though there must have always been a relationship between linguistic and social variation, it is unlikely that languages in the past varied "according to the social divisions of present-day western societies." Nevalainen (2006: 559) further adds that knowing that the past differed from the present is by no means tantamount to knowing the extent to which it was different: consider, for example, Labov's notion of the *Historical Paradox*[2] (1994: 20–21).

Two points seem to be at issue here, namely the specificity of historical data and the general level of literacy in the past. Although, as Wyld (1927: 21) observed, "the drama of linguistic change is enacted not in manuscripts nor inscriptions, but in the mouths and minds of men," any branch of linguistics whose name includes the constituent 'historical' will of necessity deal with written evidence alone. Using this kind of data in sociolinguistic research carries a number of implications (see Schneider 2002: 69). First of all, writing is much less of a social activity than speaking, with spoken exchanges by default taking place between participants in social contexts and, therefore, being more context-dependent (Milroy 1992: 5). Moreover, written language is said to show less variability because the speaker (or the writer/author/scribe, for that matter) has considerably more time to carefully pre-plan both the contents and the form of the message to be conveyed. Finally, written and oral language are believed to fulfill different functions; unlike speech events, written language is seen as goal- rather than listener-oriented (Milroy 1992: 45; Brown 1982: 77). What follows is that the written medium is more explicit and independent of situational context because the "function of writing is to communicate messages outside the immediate interpersonal context" (Milroy 1992: 40).

There is also the problem of the representativeness of historical data and the researcher's (lack of) control over the database. While sociolinguists working on and with speakers of present-day English can control their samples for a number of independent variables, such as age, gender, socioeconomic status, geographical background or ethnic group membership, a linguist who inquires into the past states of a language has no choice but to work with whatever testimonies that have survived. Given that the earliest extant English texts are inscriptions and glossaries going back to the seventh and eighth centuries, and that there is a paucity of evidence from the North before the fifteenth century, the database will inevitably be imbalanced, with certain regions, periods of time, text-types, and genres represented better than others (Milroy 1992: 45).

The need for "making the best use of bad data" (Labov 1994: 11) has been widely recognized by historical linguists. Hogg (2006: 395), Laing and Lass (2006: 418), and Nevalainen (2006: 559), to name but a few, underline the lack of access to the actual speech of informants and the increasing obscurity of the social context the further back one moves in time. They also point to the relative social homogeneity of the surviving (early) material, attributable to a low level of literacy in the Middle Ages. Witnesses from before the sixteenth century are mostly "the output of literate, adult, English Catholics largely inhabiting closed institutions (monasteries, professions) where class stratification would be of little importance" (Laing and Lass 2006: 419). This, obviously, affects the type of language transmitted to the point of the near-nonrecoverability of ordinary people's linguistic habits (Hogg 1992: 20; see also Chapter 4 in this *Handbook*).

The significance of the general level of literacy mentioned above (see Parkes 1973) consists in the direct influence it exerts on the contents of the database in terms of authorship. According to Cressy (1980), for example, in sixteenth-century England ten times as many men as women could sign their names, and the literacy rate among females amounted to a mere 1%. Although the level of literacy increased over the next 150 years by 9% and 20% for women and men respectively, it was only the affluent who knew how to read and write, with the poor still remaining illiterate for the most part. Interestingly, as Raumolin-Brunberg (1996: 25) observes, "the overall literacy of women was at the same level as that of men of the lowest social ranking." This, as well as the fact that in the Middle Ages, by and large, authors preferred to remain anonymous, has serious consequences for diachronic linguistic studies, especially those with a sociolinguistic bent. If the authorship of a given text is unknown, and one can only speculate (using common sense and the knowledge of the socio-political context of the time) that it was composed or written down by a trained male copyist, most likely a monk or clerk, it is rather difficult to consider the dependence of linguistic variation on age, gender, or socio-economic status (see also Hogg 2006: 295).

That said, and on a less somber note, even if modern sociolinguistics operates on extralinguistic variables largely unavailable to scholars working with diachronic data, this is not to say that historical sociolinguistics is impracticable. If Whitney's proposal (1867: 1–2, as quoted in Labov 1994: 22) that "[t]he factors that produced changes in human speech five thousand or ten thousand years ago cannot have been essentially different from those which are now operating to transform living languages" is valid, and the uniformitarian principle has long been accepted by linguistics, the orderly heterogeneity that is so characteristic of modern speech communities must have always been there, even if constrained by different external factors. It is then precisely those extralinguistic factors that need to be "reconstructed on the basis of what we know about the past societies themselves" (Nevalainen and Raumolin-Brunberg 2005: 34) for every vernacular at every period[3] (see also Chapter 5 in this *Handbook*).

Recovering the variables that constrained linguistic variation in the past is attainable insofar as the existing knowledge of the socio-political context allows it. One cannot fail to mention here the contribution made by social, cultural, and economic history, on the findings of which historical sociolinguistics heavily draws (Nevalainen 2006: 559). Sometimes, however, the information on relevant (even if less common) extralinguistic factors, such as the order or scriptorium to which a scribe belonged, is encoded in the sources themselves (Laing and Lass 2006). No wonder, then, that, questioning the applicability of the Labovian framework to witnesses from before the sixteenth century, Laing and Lass (2006: 419–20) argue for the establishment of tenable parameters on the basis of the available material, seeing such variables as "the intricate relations between the scribes' native varieties and their transcribing of languages other than English, the text genres, the provenance of exemplars, and the different modes of copying" as capable of replacing some of the traditional ones.

The exclusively written character of data is insurmountable, although in Romaine's (1988) view textual material should be studied, not as a poor reflection of spoken language, but as valuable research fabric in its own right. Surely, as Nevalainen (2006) notes, sociolinguistic variation does not manifest itself in speech alone, and phenomena such as stylistic or register variation lend themselves to sociolinguistic analyses, provided the evidence is relatively heterogeneous in terms of text-types and genres.

This last condition becomes much less of a problem once large, diachronically oriented and generically diversified electronic corpora come into play. A systematic sizeable database comprising (samples of) texts that differ in terms of date, type, provenance, and genre considerably facilitates the collection of vast amounts of data, and can be searched for socially-motivated explanations for the attested linguistic variation (Milroy 1983). Today, diachronic corpora, such as *The Helsinki Corpus of English Texts*, *The Helsinki Corpus of Older Scots*, *The Corpus do Português* (www.corpusdoportugues.org) or *The Base de Français Médiéval database* (http://bfm.ens-lyon.fr/), are compiled in such a way that they are conducive to a variationist analysis, which means that texts are not only as close to speech as possible[4], but also display linguistic variability and meet the requirement of representativeness, understood as a composite of appropriate size and diverse authorship. As a result, such corpora satisfy the requirements for empirical, social, and historical validity, making historical sociolinguistics possible (Nevalainen 2006; Nevalainen and Raumolin-Brunberg 2005: 35).

3. Sociolinguistics as an Explanatory Tool in Diachronic Phonological Studies

The last part of the present chapter is designed to show what can be done and what has already been done in the field of sociohistorical phonological studies. It offers an overview of selected contributions exploring the social context of phonological variation in the Middle Ages, the Renaissance, and the twentieth century.

3.1   *The Middle Ages: phonological variation before the twelfth century – the case of Old English*

One of the earliest studies seeking a sociolinguistic explanation for diachronic phonological variation (dialect contact seen as belonging to the domain of socio-linguistics) is Bennett's (1955) paper on the development of the Germanic initial *f, þ*, and *s* in southern England. Bennett sees the voicing of initial fricatives found in Kent and the south-western dialects of Old and Middle English as potentially attributable to the contact between the Juto-Frisians and Low Franconians (Bennett 1955: 351). Given the presence in Old and Middle Low Franconian of forms such as OLF *vuss* 'fox,' MLF *zo* 'so' or MLF *vor* 'for,' Bennett finds it possible that the Juto-Frisians may have acquired more than just the lower Rhenish cultural traits when passing through the Lower Rhine (or the Low Franconian) area on their way to Britain.

Toon (1983), in turn, examines linguistic variation in the first English texts, applying the Labovian quantitative paradigm to his analysis. He specifically focuses on the diffusion of features typically considered Mercian[5] and approaches the issue from the perspective of Mercian hegemony. Clearly, in Toon's (1983: 21) view, too little significance has been attached to the period of Mercia's political dominance, which has resulted in its role in the development of English being grossly underestimated.

In a detailed description of Mercia's path to supremacy, Toon (1983: 25–40) stresses the comprehensive development of the kingdom under Æðelbald (855–60) and Offa (757–96). During eighty years of relative peace, he says, Mercia flour-ished in terms of hard and soft infrastructure. The building of towns and the growth of fortifications were paralleled by cultural and literary achievements. The requirement that priests "know the mass, the rite of baptism, the Creed, and the Lord's Prayer in English," formulated at the Synod of Clovesho in 747, stimulated the compilation of Latin–Old English glossaries and the production of Psalters and Bibles intended "for use at state occasions" (Toon 1983: 38). Moreover, a considerable amount of secular poetry was composed, to survive later in West Saxon versions. At the same time, successive rulers asserted their kingship through genealogies, king-lists, and legislation, thereby institutionalizing their power:

> Every aspect of Mercian cultural development was used by the Mercian kings to celebrate the glory of the social institution of kingship. Powerful kings enabled the Anglo-Saxon peoples to build a society and culture based on peace rather than constant intertribal hostility. Because culture and its benefits derived from the overlords, eighth-century culture, throughout England, was Mercian culture; eighth-century literacy especially was Mercian literacy. (Toon 1983: 38)

As follows from his claim that "[a] text produced anywhere in southern England during the period of Mercian supremacy must be considered in some respects a Mercian text," Toon (1983: 42) regards the development of English literacy under the Mercian kings as instrumental in the spread of Mercian dialect features. Consequently, this is exactly how he explains the <o>-spellings for the pre-nasal West Germanic *a and the raising of æ to e found in Kentish charters. Since in the charters from before the Mercian hegemony the WGmc *a is regularly spelled <a>, for example in *Cantuarorium* 'the people of Kent,' and in the manuscripts produced during the period of Mercian political control over southern England the same segment is rendered as <o>, Toon (1983: 94) sees the shift as caused by the influence of the dominant culture.[6] By the same token, the raising of OE æ < WGmc *a to e attested in the Kentish charters written under Mercian domination is interpreted by Toon (1983: 152) as reflecting the Mercian 'second fronting'[7]:

> These data would indicate that the Kentish were at first slow to learn the second fronting from the politically dominant Mercians, but then quickly imitated the speech of their masters and fully extended the raising to any æs from all sources.

Toon's hypothesis has been refuted by both Hogg (1988) and Trousdale (2005). Trousdale (2005) criticizes, first and foremost, the choice of variationist sociolinguistics as a framework within which to analyze 'Kentish raising.' Far from claiming that Old English sociolinguistics is impossible, he warns against treating extant OE manuscripts as if they resembled in any way the informants used in modern sociolinguistic interviews, and points to the necessity of reconstructing the linguistic system of the variety under study, as well as the social context in which that variety was embedded. Having discussed the drawbacks of using the variationist paradigm in research on OE data, Trousdale looks to the Continent for the reason behind the raising of æ in Old Kentish (2005: 70–74). With some genetic evidence implying the possibility of Frisian migrations spreading northwards through Kent, he postulates dialect contact as a potential factor in its merger with a mid vowel.

Hogg (1988) likewise doubts the connection between the change of short æ to e in late Kentish and 'second fronting.' He does acknowledge the significance of Mercian literacy, noting, for example, that "it was only in Mercia that the scholarly tradition of the North had been able to survive, and [that] there is precious little evidence to support any such tradition in the South" (Hogg 1992: 6), but he insists that 'Kentish raising' is a process independent from 'second fronting' (Hogg 1988: 197–98). Having analyzed four ninth-century Kentish charters which show variability between <æ> and <e> for *æ*, Hogg (1988: 197) proposes that the <æ>-spellings are an attempt on the part of a Mercian(-trained) scribe, speaking (or at least familiar with) Kentish, to show the difference between the post-'second fronting' *e* < *æ* and a slightly raised (but still audibly lower) Kentish *æ*. Although he recognizes the capacity of Mercian to influence other varieties, Hogg (1988: 198) thinks 'second fronting' to be unrelated to 'Kentish raising,' considering the latter "a locally-restricted sound change affecting equally /æ/ and /æ:/."

Despite the criticism that Toon's (1983) approach received, his work certainly contributed to an increase in interest in the application of modern sociolinguistic tools to analyses of diachronic data. Schendl (2002), for instance, seems to share Toon's sentiments about the marriage of the variationist framework and studies on Old English phonology. Using the insights of modern sociolinguistics, Schendl tries to determine why the Old English reflexes of Germanic diphthongs developed differently from the complex vowels that resulted from 'breaking' or 'palatal diphthongization.' Having proposed two alternative solutions, namely a reversal of a partial merger of the lexical sets with original Germanic diphthongs and 'broken' monophthongs[8] or a reversal of a so-called 'near-merger,' he focuses on the second option and goes on to characterize the concept briefly. The nature of near-mergers leads Schendl (2002: 275) to conclude that if one were assumed for the OE reflexes of PGmc diphthongs, and fractured long monophthongs, as well as for the umlauted and broken descendants of short PGmc vowels, its reversal would explain the later divergent development of the two classes.

3.2 Phonological variables between the twelfth and sixteenth centuries on the basis of Middle English and Parisian French

At more or less the same time as Toon's (1983) work, Milroy published his paper (1983) on the sociolinguistic history of *h*-dropping in English, providing another voice very much in favor of approaching historical data from the point of view of social dialectology. A subscriber to the belief that "one can use the present state of a language to reflect back upon the past of that language," Milroy (1983: 37) remarks that to the extent that analyzing vast amounts of present day evidence in detail can facilitate detecting changes in progress and "perhaps [...] offer explanations of a social kind for such changes," the ever-growing body of generically diversified historical corpora should make the same goal tenable in the case of diachronic material.

In the latter part of his paper, Milroy (1983) discusses *h*-dropping as a contact phenomenon, attributable to the simplification of the segmental phonology induced by the Norman Conquest and the resulting linguistic situation in England. Considering the spread of the process in terms of the Labovian model of social diffusion, Milroy (1983: 47–48) observes that once *h*-loss began, it probably diffused from the middle- to the lower middle and lower orders of society, first gaining ground in politically and commercially significant urban centers. Despite its relative commonness, however, in the sixteenth century *h*-dropping came to be regarded as a sign of maleducation, whereby (h) acquired the status of a stylistic variable to be retained in formal styles (Milroy 1983: 50).

The diffusion of phonological innovation, or more precisely, the principles that governed it in medieval Lincolnshire, is the leitmotif of Conde-Silvestre and Pérez-Raja's (2008) paper on the transitional areas in and social history of Middle English dialectology. The paper is an attempt to establish how such socio-historical factors as social mobility, urbanization, migration, or the organization of the land may have contributed to the peculiarity of the linguistic profile of the county. The authors point out that the specificity of Lincolnshire lies not only in its being home to the Northern and East Midland varieties of Middle English, but also in its receptivity to dialect variants that spread from neighboring areas. Focusing on the development of two Old English variables, namely (ɑ:) and (o:), and their distribution in Lincolnshire during the Middle English period, Conde-Silvestre and Pérez-Raja (2008) notice the slightly puzzling presence of /ɔ:/ forms (ME *lǭng* < OE *lang*) as far north as Lindsey, and the apparent fronting of /o:/ > /y:/ as far south as northern Kesteven (to reach southern Kesteven and Holland in the sixteenth century) (Conde-Silvestre and Pérez-Raja 2008: 716–17). Using the social network approach (Milroy 1980/1987) and Granovetter's (1973) theory of strong and weak ties, the authors explain the cumbersome diffusion of /o:/- and /y:/-pronunciations as caused by the density of the population in Lincolnshire, the urbanization of the county between the tenth and late twelfth centuries, the migration of people to the rapidly expanding towns, and a related loosening of interpersonal ties within networks (Conde-Silvestre and Pérez-Raja 2008: 717–25).

An enterprise similar in nature, although of a noticeably larger format, is Lodge's sociolinguistic history of Paris (2004). Lodge seeks to identify the major macro-level tendencies in Parisian French from the Middle Ages to the twentieth century (2004: 4). The analysis of a considerable body of mid-thirteenth mid-fourteenth century evidence (administrative documents from the *Prévôté de Paris*) reveals that the Parisian vernacular of that time has its roots in the hinterland dialect of Paris (HDP) with which it shared the palatalization of Latin [ka] > [ʃa], the diphthongization of Latin [o] > [ow] > [œ], the epenthetic *d* in [ndr] as in *vendredi* 'Friday,' and the raising of stressed Latin [a] > [e]. Other traits of the speech of mediaeval Paris, such as [wa] ~ [wɛ] in *soir* 'evening,' or [jo] ~ [o] in *eau* 'water,' turn out to have been dialectal forms brought to the city following its twelfth-century "economic and demographic take off" (Lodge 2004: 39, 58–70).

Having established that the dialect of fourteenth-century Paris was a product of koinéization, Lodge sets out to determine how this composite came about. To that end, he discusses the features of the vernacular (and the social attitudes towards them) against the background of the development of the city in terms of size, urbanization, industrialization, and social structure, correlating "as far as possible linguistic variation and change in the city with historical changes in social and demographic structure" (2004: 10).

3.3   The Renaissance: a linguistic 'beauty contest'

Sixteenth-century Europe witnessed the emergence of national standard varieties and the establishment of language academies (such as the Academia della Crusca, Florence, 1582). A desire arose to regularize spelling and maintain the purity of the language. Orthoëpists in England called for the rationalization of orthography, and in France a number of publications appeared stressing the shortcomings of French in comparison with Italian, which was perceived as more orderly and refined (Lodge 2004: 126). How important it was, at least for some people or in some circles, to use the standard language, for instance, follows from Puttenham's (1589) *The Arte of English Poesie* (quoted here after Barber 1976/1997: 13), where he advises a poet on the kind of language he should use:

> [N]either shall he take the termes of Northern-men, such as they vse in dayly talke, whether they be noble men or gentlemen, or of their best clarkes all is a matter: nor in effect any speach vsed beyond the riuer of Trent, though no man can deny but that theirs is the purer English Saxon at this day, yet it is not so Courtly nor so currant as our Southerne English is, no more is the far Westerne mans speach: ye shall therfore take the vsuall speach of the Court, and that of London and the shires lying about London within lx. myles, and not much aboue. I say not this but that in euery shyre of England there be gentlemen and others that speake but specially write as good Southerne as we of Middlesex or Surrey do, but not the common people of euery shire, to whom the gentlemen, and also their learned clarkes do for the most part condescend.

This quotation testifies to the ongoing regional variation in spoken English, even among upper-class speakers, which was, however, obliterated (to the point of non-existence) in the written mode, as a result of a general movement towards linguistic standardization. The same was the case with social variation, whose (unsurprising) existence finds indirect confirmation in Puttenham's urging a poet to model his tongue on the language of "the better brought vp sort, such as the Greekes call *charientes* men ciuill and graciously behauoured and bred" as opposed to "a craftes man or carter, or other of the inferiour sort, [who], though he be inhabitant or bred in the best town and Citie in this Realme [...] do[es] abuse good speaches by strange accents or illshapen soundes, and false ortographie" (Barber 1976/1997: 21).

With the regularization of the writing system, the evidence for regional and social linguistic variation largely disappeared, save for private correspondence[9], which, being less formal, was more tolerant of non-standard forms. Occasionally, traces of heterogeneity surfaced in poetry and drama, when poets and playwrights found it necessary to reproduce the regional or social dialect of a character. That these reproductions were accurate is, however, doubtful, and they should therefore not be taken at face value, as Barber (1976/1997: 22) remarks. More accurate and revealing (if utterly critical) comments concerning language variation came from orthoëpists and language reformers, such as Alexander Gil (1565–1635), John Hart (d. 1574), Théodore de Bèze (1519–1605), Geoffroy Tory (c.1480–c.1533), and Étienne Tabourot (1547–90).

In English, for example, the zero realization of the glottal fricative (h) word finally or in combination with /t/, after a front vowel, as in *nyght* 'night' and word finally or in combination with /t/, after a back vowel, as in *plough*, was looked down upon and considered "the barbarous speech of your country people" (Coote 1596/1968: 21, after Lass 1999: 117). This (h) was also variably realized as Ø when syllable-initial in stressed positions, as in *aard* 'hard,' *and* 'hand,' a phenomenon attested already in Early Middle English, but *h*-dropping did not come to be regarded as vulgar or provincial until the eighteenth century (Lass 1999: 118; see also Milroy 1983; Johannesson 2000; Crisma 2007).

Another stigmatized zero-pronunciation was the removal of post-vocalic /r/. According to Lass (1999: 114), word-final/pre-consonantal (r) began to be realized as zero in the fifteenth century, with occasional deletion featuring mostly in private letters written by women. The process was not recognized as a feature of the standard until the middle of the eighteenth century, and some like Walker (1791) were fairly critical towards it as late as 1790. By the end of the century post-vocalic /r/ was commonly elided (except when between vowels), but the zero pronunciation remained variable for the next seventy years (Lass 1999: 115).

In sixteenth-century Parisian French, in turn, two of the features of the vernacular mentioned above, namely the variables [jo] ~ [o], as in *beau* 'nice, pretty,' and [wa] ~ [wɛ], in *voirre* 'see,' became highly salient and, consequently, overtly stigmatized (Lodge 2004: 119–20). While the pronunciation [jo] was described by Bèze (1584/1972: 52, 53) as defective and, as such, best avoided, [wa] was considered downright vulgar, and its spelling incorrect: "Pour *voirre* ou, comme d'autres l'escrivent, *verre*, on prononce vulgairement a Paris et on escrit tres mal *voarre*" (after Lodge 2004: 120).

The fact that the emergence of a standard language ousted evidence of regional or social variation from most written records of the sixteenth and seventeenth centuries certainly makes phonological sociolinguistic analyses difficult, but not entirely impossible. In a paper on *t/d* deletion and insertion in Late Medieval and Renaissance Scottish English, for example, Meurman-Solin (1997) uses corpus evidence to trace the pattern of diffusion in two tendencies in formal and informal prose witnesses. Since the texts she investigates represent fifteen different genres, from parliamentary acts and burgh records to diaries, official letters, and the Bible, the study makes it possible to correlate *t/d* loss and epenthesis with the external variable 'setting'[10] (1997: 111). Careful examination of 346 *t*-stem verb types elicited from the *Helsinki Corpus of Older Scots* (1450–1700) points to the spread of deletion from formal to informal styles (a change from above), with the frequencies rising in the sixteenth century parallel to the increasing divergence of Scottish English from the Northern English dialect (Meurman-Solin 1997: 122).

3.4   *When 'modern' and 'present day' are centuries apart: phonological variation in nineteenth-century English and the twentieth-century Arabic of Jordanian women*

The problem of the southern voicing of initial fricatives in English, explained by Bennett (1955) through dialect contact, returns in Voitl's (1988) paper on the history of the process seen as a conflicting tendency between regional pronunciation and social attitude. The voicing, which in its Late Middle English heyday covered Essex, Worcestershire, Hertfordshire, the largest south-western part of Buckinghamshire, the south-western corner of Northamptonshire, the southern half of Warwickshire and Shropshire, and possibly Suffolk (Fisiak 1985), began to recede southward and westward in the nineteenth century, the original area considerably decreasing in size.

Interested in determining why the feature receded, Voitl (1988) examines sociohistorical and demographic developments in the region. He observes that, being a highly marked phenomenon not infrequently used to portray the 'country bumpkin' type in EModE drama (Voitl 1988: 576), the voicing must have been prone to stigmatization and the influence of the prestigious standard pronunciation. Judging by the chronology and the direction in which the feature receded, Voitl (1988: 576–80) comes to the conclusion that it was closely related to the nineteenth-century explosion and increasing mobility of population due to the onset of industrialization, and the influence of linguistic standardization through education.

Today the role of elegance and prestige is still a factor in the linguistic choices people make, as follows from Al-Wer's (1999) study of the distribution of four phonological variables in the speech of Jordanian women. The socio-political and demographic situation in Jordan has been shaped, as Al-Wer (1999: 39–40) observes, by the Arab–Israeli conflicts of 1948 and 1967, with a total of 1 150 000 Palestinian refugees seeking shelter in Jordan upon the incorporation of the West Bank into the Kingdom of Jordan, and its loss almost twenty years later. The Palestinian community was eventually granted full Jordanian citizenship (including the right to vote) and came to play an increasingly important role in the political and economic development of the country, especially in larger cities, where most Palestinians settled. Consequently, urban Palestinian, whose features diffused rapidly, began to gain ground as the more prestigious variety, associated with such qualities as finesse, modernity, elegance, and liberation (Al-Wer 1999: 41).

In research conducted in 1987 on 116 indigenous Jordanian women from the towns of Sult, Ajloun, and Karak, Al-Wer (1999) analyzed the realization of (q) pronounced as [g] or [ʔ], (θ) articulated as [θ] or [t], (ð) realized as [ð] or [d], and (ʤ) surfacing as [ʤ] or [ʒ]. In each case, the first allophone is the conservative Jordanian variant, the second representing the innovative urban Palestinian pronunciation (1999: 39). The study showed a correlation between the gender and identity of a speaker and his/her receptivity to linguistic innovations, though not to the same extent for every variable considered.

4. Conclusion

Diachronic sociolinguistics is a relatively new discipline, one that has been developing for the past 25 years or so. Yet not every aspect of language seems equally conducive to historical sociolinguistic analyses (Hernández-Campoy and Conde-Silvestre 2005). Phonological variability, which is easily tractable, recordable, and analyzable in the case of present-day linguistic data, must be reconstructed from spelling evidence and rhymes when the only sources available are written. The specificity of historical data (written mode, unknown authorship) makes sociolinguistic analyses particularly difficult, especially with regard to witnesses predating the year 1500. With regard to studies on English, for example, Nevalainen (2006: 561) admits that "both for reasons of the available data sources and the changes that have taken place in the language, orthographic and morphosyntactic variation have to date proved to be the major areas of interest."

Be that as it may, work by Toon (1983), Voitl (1988), Romaine (1984, 1996), Meurman-Solin (1997), J. Milroy (1983), Conde-Silvestre and Hernández-Campoy (2002), Schendl (2002), Lodge (2004), Trousdale (2005), and Conde-Silvestre and Pérez-Raja (2008), to name but a few, clearly indicates that such studies are not only needed but, first and foremost, feasible. With the increasing number of diachronic corpora and growing knowledge of the socio-political and demographic reality of the past, it should be possible to address the issue of phonological variation in a more comprehensive manner than hitherto.

NOTES

1 See Trousdale (2005) for a criticism of the application of the Labovian paradigm to Old English sociolinguistics.
2 According to Labov (1994: 11), "[t]he task of historical linguistics is to explain the differences between the past and the present; but to the extent that the past was different from the present, there is no way of knowing how different it was."
3 The product of a small, socially homogenous, close-knit network, diachronic data require an approach resting not so much on the standard extralinguistic variables as factors relevant in the context of the social organization of a given stage of human history (Laing and Lass 2006).
4 See Schneider (2002: 57–58) for a typology of text types on the basis of their proximity to spoken language.
5 Although Toon (1983: 25) uses the traditional dialect labels such as Mercian or West Saxon throughout his work, he questions the validity of the division into Northumbrian, Mercian,

West Saxon, and Kentish, given the tribal nature of Anglo-Saxon society in the eighth century.

6 The number of <o>-spellings drops considerably with the decay of Mercian supremacy (Toon 1983: 94).

7 Second fronting, mostly found in the *Vespasian Psalter*, *St. Chad*, *Royal Glosses*, and the *Epinal* and *Corpus Glossaries*, consisted in the fronting of Early Old English *a* to *æ* and the raising of EOE *æ* to *e* (Campbell 1959/1983: 64–66).

8 Schendl (2002: 273) observes that competing forms of the kind *ald ~ eald* or *heofon ~ hefen* imply the existence of an alternating class. Members of an alternating class are believed to have the potential for a reversal of a merger.

9 See García-Bermejo Giner and Montgomery (2001) on English; or Ernst (1996) on French.

10 The external variable 'setting' refers to the social milieu in which the events described in a text take place and has two parameter values, namely 'formal' and 'informal' (Meurman-Solin 1997: 111).

REFERENCES

Al-Wer, E. (1999) Why do different variables behave differently? Data from Arabic. In Y. Suleiman (ed.), *Language and society in the Middle East and North Africa*, Curzon Press, London, pp. 38–57.

Barber, C. (1976/1997) *Early Modern English*, Edinburgh University Press, Edinburgh.

Bennett, W.H. (1955) The Southern English development of Germanic initial [f s þ]. *Language* 31: 367–71.

Bèze, T. de (1584/1972) *De Francicae Linguae recta pronuntiatione tractatus*, Slatkine Reprints, Geneva.

Britain, D. (2002) *Sociolinguistic variation*. http://www.llas.ac.uk/resources/gpg/1054 [accessed August 2010].

Brown, G. (1982) The spoken language. In R. Carter (ed.), *Linguistics and the Teacher*, Routledge and Kegan Paul, London, pp. 75–87.

Campbell, A. (1959/1983) *Old English Grammar* (3rd edn), Clarendon Press, Oxford.

Chambers, J.K. (1995/2003) *Sociolinguistic Theory* (2nd edn), Blackwell, Oxford.

Conde-Silvestre, J.C. and Hernández-Campoy, J.M. (2002) Modern geolinguistic tenets and the diffusion of linguistic innovations in Late Middle English. *Studia Anglica Posnaniensia* 38: 147–77.

Conde-Silvestre, J.C. and Pérez-Raja, M.D. (2008) Transitional areas and social history in Middle English dialectology: the case of Lincolnshire. *Neophilologus* 92: 713–27.

Coote, E. (1596/1968) *The English Schoole-Maister*, Scolar Press, Menston.

Cressy, D. (1980) *Literacy and the Social Order: Reading and Writing in Tudor and Stuart England*, Cambridge University Press, Cambridge.

Crisma, P. (2007) Were they 'dropping their aitches'? A quantitative study of h-loss in Middle English. *English Language and Linguistics* 11(1): 51–80.

Ernst, G. (1996) Problèmes d'édition de textes à caractère privé des XVIIe et XVIIIe siècles. Unpublished paper read to the Groupe d'études en Histoire de la Langue française, Paris.

Fisiak, J. (1985) The voicing of initial fricatives in Middle English. In W. Viereck (ed.), *Focus on England and Wales*, John Benjamins, Amsterdam, pp. 5–28.

Foulkes, P. (2006) Phonological variation: a global perspective. In B. Aarts and A. McMahon (eds.), *The Handbook of English Linguistics*, Blackwell, Oxford, pp. 625–69.

García-Bermejo Giner, M.F. and Montgomery, M. (2001) Yorkshire English two hundred years ago. *Journal of English Linguistics* 29: 346–62.

Granovetter, M. (1973) The strength of weak ties. *American Journal of Sociology* 78(6): 1360–80.

Hernández-Campoy, J.M. and Conde-Silvestre, J.C. (2005) Sociolinguistic and geolinguistic approaches to the historical diffusion of linguistic innovations: Incipient standardisation in Late Middle English. *International Journal of English Studies* 5 (1): 101–34.

Hogg, R. (1988) On the impossibility of Old English dialectology. In G. Bauer, D. Kastovsky, and J. Fisiak (eds.), *Luick Revisited: Papers Read at Schloß Liechtenstein 15–18.9.1985*, Narr, Tübingen, pp. 183–203.

Hogg, R. (1992) Phonology and morphology. In R. Hogg (ed.), *The Cambridge History of the English Language. Vol. 1. The Beginnings to 1066*, Cambridge University Press, Cambridge, pp. 67–167.

Hogg, R. (2006) Old English dialectology. In A. van Kemenade and B. Los (eds.), pp. 395–416.

Johannesson, N.L. (2000) On the time-depth of variability: Orm and Farmon as h-droppers. In M. Ljung (ed.), *Language structure and variation*, Almqvist and Wiksell International, Stockholm, pp. 107–19.

Kaiser, R. (ed.) (1961) *Medieval English: An Old English and Middle English Anthology* (Revised edn), Rolf Kaiser, Berlin.

Kerswill, P. (2006) Standard and non-standard English. In D. Britain (ed.), *Language in the British Isles* (2nd edn), Cambridge University Press, Cambridge, pp. 34–51.

Labov, W. (1963) The social motivation of a sound change. *Word* 19: 273–309.

Labov, W. (1994) *Principles of Linguistic Change, Vol. I: Internal Factors*, Blackwell, Oxford.

Labov, W. (1966/2006) *The Social Stratification of English in New York City* (2nd edn), Cambridge University Press, Cambridge.

Laing, M. and Lass, R. (2006) Early Middle English dialectology: problems and prospects. In A. van Kemenade and B. Los (eds.), pp. 417–51.

Lass, R. (1999) Phonology and morphology. In R. Lass (ed.), *The Cambridge History of the English Language. Vol. 3. 1476–1776*, Cambridge University Press, Cambridge, pp. 56–186.

Lodge, R.A. (2004) *A Sociolinguistic History of Parisian French*, Cambridge University Press, Cambridge.

Meurman-Solin, A. (1997) A corpus-based study on t/d deletion and insertion in Late Medieval and Renaissance Scottish English. In T. Nevalainen and L. Kahlas-Tarkka (eds.), *To Explain the Present*, Société Néophilologique, Helsinki, pp. 111–25.

Milroy, J. (1983) On the sociolinguistic history of /h/-dropping in English. In M. Davenport, E. Hansen, and H.F. Nielsen (eds.), *Current Topics in English Historical Linguistics*, Odense University Press, Odense, pp. 37–51.

Milroy, J. (1992) *Linguistic Variation and Change: On the Historical Sociolinguistics of English*, Blackwell, Oxford.

Milroy, L. (1980/1987) *Language and Social Networks* (2nd edn), Blackwell, Oxford.

Milroy, L. and Gordon, M. (2003) *Sociolinguistics: Method and Interpretation*, Blackwell, Oxford.

Nevalainen, T. (2006) Historical sociolinguistics and language change. In A. van Kemenade and B. Los (eds.), pp. 558–88.

Nevalainen, T. and Raumolin-Brunberg, H. (2005) Sociolinguistics and the history of English: a survey. *International Journal of English Studies* 5(1): 33–58.

Parkes, M.B. (1973) The literacy of the laity. In D. Daiches and A. Thorlby (eds.), *The Medieval World: Literature and Western Civilization*, Aldus Books, London, pp. 555–77.

Raumolin-Brunberg, H. (1996) Historical sociolinguistics. In T. Nevalainen and H. Raumolin-Brunberg (eds.), *Sociolinguistics and Language History*, Rodopi, Amsterdam, pp. 11–37.

Romaine, S. (1982) *Socio-historical Linguistics: Its Status and Methodology*, Cambridge University Press, Cambridge.

Romaine, S. (1984) The sociolinguistic history of t/d deletion. *Folia Linguistica Historica* 5: 221–55.

Romaine, S. (1988) Historical sociolinguistics: problems and methodology. In U. Ammon, N. Dittmar, and K.J. Mattheier (eds.), *Sociolinguistics: An International Handbook of the Science of Language and Society*, vol. 2, Walter de Gruyter, Berlin, pp. 1452–69.

Romaine, S. (1996) Internal vs. external factors in socio-historical explanations of change: a fruitless dichotomy? In J. Ahlers *et al.* (eds.), *Proceedings of the Twenty-First Annual Meeting of the Berkeley Linguistics Society*. General Session and Parasession on Historical Issues in Sociolinguistics/ Social Issues in Historical Linguistics, Department of Linguistics, University of California, Berkeley, pp. 478–91.

Schendl, H. (2002) Some sociolinguistic considerations on Old English phonology. In J. Hladký (ed.), *Language and function*, John Benjamins, Amsterdam, pp. 269–78.

Schneider, E. (2002) Investigating variation and change in written documents. In J.K. Chambers, P. Trudgill, and N. Schilling-Estes (eds.), *The Handbook of Language Variation and Change*, Blackwell, Oxford, pp. 67–90.

Toon, T.E. (1983) *The Politics of Early Old English Sound Change*, Academic Press, New York and London.

Trousdale, G. (2005) The social context of Kentish raising: issues in Old English sociolinguistics. *International Journal of English Studies* 5(1): 59–76.

Trudgill, P. (1974) *The Social Differentiation of English in Norwich*, Cambridge University Press, Cambridge.

van Kemenade, A. and Los, B. (eds.) (2006) *The Handbook of the History of English*, Blackwell, Oxford.

Voitl, H. (1988) The history of voicing of initial fricatives in Southern England: a case of conflict between regional and social dialect. In J. Fisiak (ed.), *Historical Dialectology: Regional and Social*, Mouton de Gruyter, New York, pp. 555–600.

Walker, J. (1791) *A Critical Pronouncing Dictionary and Expositor of the English Language*, London.

Whitney, W.D. (1867) *Language and the Study of Language*, Charles Scribner and Co., New York.

Wyld, H.C. (1927) *Short History of English*, John Murray, London.

14   Grammatical Variables

ANITA AUER AND ANJA VOESTE

1. On What They Are

Speakers have linguistic rules at their disposal which allow them to adjust their language behavior to specific situations. It is one of the tasks of sociolinguistics to describe and explain these alternative ways of saying the same thing in different contexts. In this respect, the concept of variables fulfils an important function.

A variable, in general, is a parameter which conceptualizes a certain pattern of variation in language use. It is defined as a set of at least two variants which may be used alternatively. A *grammatical* variable, in particular, is a set of at least two *grammatical*, that is, *morphological* or *syntactic* variants, which may be used alternatively. Variation is caused by external (non-linguistic, such as diatopic, diastratic, diasituative, or diaphasic) determinants as well as by internal (linguistic) factors, such as the position of the variant in a given context or the frequency of occurrence. The external and internal factors which determine the choice of a variant are called *constraints* on variability. External and internal constraints may interact, as the following example shows: in seventeenth-century French it was considered 'elegant' to put the negative particles *ne* and *pas* both in front of a following infinitive: 'pour **ne pas** tomber dans les inconveniens,' instead of 'pour **ne** tomber **pas** dans les inconveniens' (Vaugelas 1647: 409). This change was caused by an *external* constraint, which, in this particular case, is the prestige factor. At the same time, the change was restricted by an *internal* factor, namely the nature of the verb. Even the most elegant and fashionable *gentilhomme* limited the construction to lexical verbs and hesitated to use it with modal verbs and auxiliaries (*'pour **ne pas** être tombé dans les inconveniens') (for details see Hirschbühler and Labelle 1994 and Ayres-Bennett 2004b: 219).

The Handbook of Historical Sociolinguistics, First Edition. Edited by Juan Manuel Hernández-Campoy and Juan Camilo Conde-Silvestre.
© 2014 John Wiley & Sons, Ltd. Published 2014 by John Wiley & Sons, Ltd.

Grammatical variables may be classified, firstly, according to the levels of grammar at which they occur: phonology (see Chapter 13 in this *Handbook*), morphology, or syntax. Such a classification may also follow more subtle models of grammar which contain additional, intermediate levels, such as morphophonemics and morphosyntax (see Winford 1984; Cheshire 1987). Secondly, grammatical variables may be classified according to the types of variants they contain (for such an attempt see Wolfram 1991: 23–24; 2006: 334). With respect to this classification, a distinction between *paradigmatic* and *syntagmatic* variables can be made. In the *paradigmatic* case, the variants are independent from each other; one variant out of a given set of possible variants is chosen (V_1 or V_2 or . . .) – with the extreme case of only one variant being possible (V_1 or V_0) (see Figure 14.1 below).

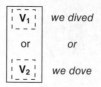

Figure 14.1.   'Simple' paradigmatic variants

Variants of a paradigmatic variable may be simple and holistic, but they may also be complex, when they consist of at least two sequenced elements. In this special case, variability arises from the permutations of the elements, which means that all variants are different linear sequences of these elements. This is exemplified in Figure 14.2 below.

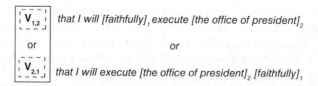

Figure 14.2.   'Complex' paradigmatic variants

Variants of different paradigmatic variables may be combined to *syntagmatic* variants. As Figure 14.3 shows, the co-occurrence of these variants makes up new variants that are multipart and interdependent.

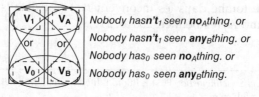

Figure 14.3.   Syntagmatic variants

Classifications of variables – whether according to the level of grammar or to the type of variants – are conceptual tools for the linguist: they structure the world of *linguistic* entities. A first set of empirical research hypotheses could be formulated as to the relationships between these different linguistic entities and external, social factors. A second set of hypotheses could be formulated as to the possible correlations between the different levels or types of variants – phonological/morphological/syntactic or paradigmatic/syntagmatic respectively – and their potential role as Labov's (1972) *indicators* (carrying little or no social significance), *markers* (that are of social and/or stylistic import), or *stereotypes* (well known popular characterizations of the speech of particular groups). These hypotheses still await testing.

2. The Evolution of the Concept

When sociolinguists focused on variability in the 1960s, the initial challenge was to understand and define the connection between variables and social factors. In these early stages, researchers tended to neglect the *internal* linguistic relationship between the variants in favor of 'sociolinguistic profiling,' that is, the task of specifying the language profiles of selected and well-defined groups of language users. This *external* perspective implies that the conceptual accuracy of the genuinely *linguistic* part of the theory was not of primary importance. It was thus acceptable that variables contained alloforms stemming from different abstract classes, like allophones of different phonemes (Labov 1966: 53).

Shortly afterwards, however, inspired by transformational-generative theories of grammar, the interest shifted from 'external' to 'internal.' It became of great importance that the variants which were tied together in a variable should be *linguistically* well-defined; more precisely, they were to be based on a common underlying form. According to the 'variable rule' (Labov 1969; Cedergren and Sankoff 1974; Sankoff 1978), all variants of a variable had to be derived *via* one and the same linguistic (phonological, grammatical) rule. These new theoretical concerns as regards the orderly and well-defined linguistic basis of variables had the consequence that social constraints were treated as 'external' in the double sense of the word, that is, as social determinants and as mere paraphernalia: sociolinguistic profiling had thus lost its initial significance (for a critical view see Wolfram 1991, 1993).

The linguistic discussion about how to bundle variants in a variable soon arrived at the central question of the semantic premises of this procedure. There was an early consensus that the referential meaning of the variants had to be identical (Weiner and Labov 1983; Sankoff and Thibault 1977; Laberge 1980; Bolinger 1977) in order to prevent the selection of one variant over another because of subtle semantic differences. As regards the semantic aspect, phonological and non-phonological (morphological, syntactic, and lexical) variants differ in a fundamental way. The story of phonological variables is a relatively happy one (see Chapter 13 in this *Handbook*): phonological variants can be handled with greater ease because they are realizations of a *phoneme*. Phonemes, as the smallest contrastive unit, distinguish meanings of words, but they have no semantic content themselves: their allophones and variants never convey a different referential meaning *per definitionem*.

Phonological variables are therefore ideal candidates for variation analyses, but the postulate of semantic equivalence poses much more difficult problems regarding non-phonological variants. This raises the question of whether syntactic variants like 'The liquor closet was broken into,' 'The liquor closet got broken into,' 'They broke into the liquor closet' (Weiner and Labov 1983) are to be considered as semantically equivalent. These problems, however, are not only of a theoretical nature. Against the background of the behaviorist assumption, which argues that there is a close connection between language skills and mental abilities (imagined as 'internalized speech'), the mere fact of a differential distribution of language variants in different social groups was in danger of being misinterpreted as evidence of "more or less intelligence, more or less expressive power, more or less verbal ability" (Lavandera 1978: 181). As Lavandera argued, the claim of referential equivalence was a precaution against the reproach that linguistic analysis functions as a carrier of social prejudice (Lavandera 1978: 179). She contested the *semantic* equivalence of non-phonological variants and recommended a looser formulation of the criterion of *referential* equivalence which allows research into variables "above and beyond phonology" – a view that has been generally adopted ever since.[1]

Not all segments of the linguistic community were engaged in these discussions. As dialectologists and descriptive linguists had always, especially in the historical perspective, accepted variables as an unproblematic, quasi-natural fact and circumstance of practical language use, they did not participate in, let alone drive, the theoretical debates on the nature of variables. Theoretical linguists, on the other hand, tended to neglect the empirical fact of variability because its integration into their conceptual framework proved to be difficult, and because there was not much to gain in this field for their central interest: the modeling of linguistic competence as an idealized capacity (*I-language*), not the performance of actual utterances (*E-language*) (see Chomsky 1986). In spite of the debates on their nature and the uneven participation in the discussions, variables are regarded as a most useful heuristic construct, widely accepted as an integral element in the investigation of variability.

3. Research Problems in the Historical Dimension

Historical sociolinguists cannot always apply the theoretical concept of grammatical variables and the quantitative methods of synchronic sociolinguistics in a cut and dried way to their historical data (see Chapters 1 and 2 in this *Handbook*). There are more significant theoretical as well as methodological problems to be solved with respect to the historical investigation of variability. We will address some of the most important issues here, proceeding from rather general, to more methodological, theoretical questions.

3.1   Basic theoretical questions

The modern sociolinguistic concept needs to be applied *mutatis mutandis* to the study of the diachronic dimension. The following cautions have to be kept in mind.

All research into the variability of a *language* in the diachronic dimension pre-supposes the continuity of one and the same, more or less homogeneous 'language entity' over a more or less significant period of time. Only based on these premises and within this framework is it possible to formulate hypotheses with respect to the change and/or stability of 'a certain language' in general, and its variability in particular. This may sound like conventional wisdom, which is valid with respect to all historical research, but the historical sociolinguist has to take into account that variability 'happens' in historically developed speech communities whose homogeneity and continuity is not to be taken for granted and must be thoroughly scrutinized.

Research into the variability of language practice in a given, concrete historical speech community in the diachronic dimension has to consider that the range of variability may comprise more than the variants of *one* language. Historical socio-linguists need more complex frames of reference when the variability is situated in a multiethnic and multilingual context and the vernacular in question was in competition with other, perhaps more dominant literary languages. One mainly thinks of Latin as *the* complementary literary language of religion, politics, and culture in early modern Europe, but cases like the historical language situation in Ottoman Bulgaria show that the picture may even be more complicated: Bulgarian served as the vernacular, Greek was the language of the Orthodox Church[2] as well as the *lingua franca* of commerce, while Turkish was the language of administra-tion. Historical sociolinguists therefore have to take into account that the historical data of a vernacular may be only one part in a much more complex picture of bi- or multilingualism. The amount of variability may not be particularly notice-able with regard to the individual languages, but is certainly noticeable with regard to the skills of the historical scribes and speakers: their competence reaches beyond the borders of one language.

Another difficulty of applying sociolinguistic concepts to historical data is the linguistic profiling of individual practices in the historical dimension. Historical sociolinguistic research has to consider that variability has not always or every-where been an expression of individuality to the same extent as it is today. Medieval scribes, for instance, were not modern individuals in the sense that they were free to choose stylistic variants according to their personal preference or as a way of developing and showing a personal profile. Not only did they not wish to make such choices: the mere possibility was beyond their horizon (see Chapters 4 and 7 in this *Handbook*). Scribes in pre-modern societies used variants, varieties, and even different languages according to rules which were more or less 'given' by the *usus* or by the instructions to be found in administration, law, and religion. It is arguable whether linguistic variants have always been linked to external, social factors at all. At times when status was denoted by privileges, vested rights, and dress codes, language may not have played as pivotal a role as a status symbol as it does today (see Chapter 5 in this *Handbook*). Wealth, accoutrements, physical strength, spirituality, or other attributes may have played the role we now attribute to linguistic variables.

The turning point in the perception of language as a bearer of social significance in Europe seems to have occurred in early modern times. Taking European language histories as an example, a development of great importance can be illustrated: a significant and perhaps necessary precondition for the change to a 'modern' use of variants as an expression of individuality is the reflective use of language. Let us assume that all variants had been equal and all speakers had used their vernacular 'only' as a means of daily communication. This changed by the time the first publications on vernaculars were released. Grammars and dictionaries proved to speakers that language was more than just a means of communication, and the vernacular gained, as it were, a totally new life. This happened in a quite tangible and material way in the sense that rules and forms were printed on paper and could now be picked up and consulted in a reference book. This was a fundamental condition for language to become a status symbol. It meant, as Knoop (1987) put it, that deviant oral and written forms became for the first time 'discriminable' in both meanings of the word: one could distinguish (recognize) them, and one could separate (reject) them. This can be seen as the starting point of standardization. The authors of grammars became increasingly sensitive towards the social, regional, and stylistic differences between variants. They thus provided us with rich information for historical sociolinguistic studies.

One might presume that variants had been pigeonholed right from the start into two different categories: good and bad. Thus, the early prescriptive grammarians might have determinedly sorted out the variants and promoted the good ones, while simultaneously denouncing the bad ones that ought not to be used. If one asks scholars who have taken a closer look into how meta-linguistic attitudes were expressed in early modern grammars, dictionaries, usage and style guides (see Ayres-Bennett 2004a for French and Davies and Langer 2006 for German), it becomes clear that the prescriptive grammarians only had a very rudimentary idea of what was a *good* grammatical construction. This means that during the course of standardization, prestigious variants were never explicitly recommended as exemplary. Instead, meta-linguistic comments in prescriptive grammars largely consisted of negative labels that were ascribed to the *unacceptable* variants; these stigmatized variants were primarily of a diatopic or diastratic nature. Judgments such as 'plebeian,' 'vulgar,' 'absurd,' 'contrary to the rule,' 'unpleasant,' 'patched up,' 'offending the ear' or 'lower Saxon,' 'from the March,' 'Silesian' for German (Voeste 1999a, 1999b) are the tools to distinguish *mauvais usage* or *schlechtes Deutsch*. Contemporaries were thus mainly informed *ex negativo* and were therefore required to draw the correct conclusions from these stigmatizations – as today's linguist is also obliged to do.

Moreover, it might be premature to surmise that early modern times naturally brought forth 'modern' criteria of evaluation. Prescriptive grammarians did not usually rely on functional linguistic explanations, and, in most cases, their judgments were not even new but based on traditional evaluation criteria, the origins of which lie in Latin rhetoric (Haas 1980). It is no coincidence that typical arguments referred to euphony, analogy, *consuetudo* (to common use) or to the *auctoritas* or *vetustas* (to the language as used by established writers). For seventeenth-century French, Ayres-Bennett (2004b: 223) was able to show that their orientation towards tradition led the grammarians and *remarqueurs* to express a preference for older constructions they did not even favor in their own literary works. As most prescriptive grammarians neither drove nor kept pace with actual changes, hunting through their reference books for functional explanations as to why a particular variant should be preferred over others may be a wild goose chase.

However, although prescriptive grammarians did not trigger linguistic norms, they played an important role in the propagation of common linguistic standards as status symbols in their own right. They were regarded as linguistic authorities – a respectable position which allowed them to support and solidify the so-called process of *verticalization* (Reichmann 1988, 1990). Reichmann uses this term to describe the fundamental change from the 'peaceful coexistence' of variants to a hierarchy in which only a single variant is deemed correct, carrying all the prestige and advancing the limitation or even elimination of variation.

3.2   *Methodological questions*

In many cases – and at least with respect to some periods of history – methodological problems are caused by the relatively small quantity of written sources. In other words, the theme may be there but the variations are lacking. Very often the empirical evidence is simply not sufficient to allow a comparative sociolinguistic and stylistic interpretation. Because of these sometimes considerable empirical difficulties, the historical linguist has to choose the appropriate technique of data collection and data description suitable to his purpose of analyzing variables.

3.2.1   *Data capture*

3.2.1.1   Intra-, inter-, and cross-textual data collection   When data in significant quantities are available, the first step is to record possible variants of a variable. In the historical perspective, there are three common procedures for the analysis variables:

(1) An *intra-textual* investigation examines the frequency and range of variants in one text or a corpus of texts that has been compiled for this purpose and is treated as a single text. Such a procedure might be used for the study of a specific variable in a text such as the Nuremberg chronicle (1493) or in a corpus of texts such as the *lettres provinciales*, a collection of 18 letters from Blaise Pascal to Antoine Arnauld (1656–57). As illustrated in Figure 14.4 below, the

Die seltzame History

ff / vnnd was der sinn derselben Geschrifften zů
teutsch also. Nach der zeit des Königs von Franck
reich/genant Otto/da was zů Potiers in Franck
reich ein edler Graue wol erkandt/genant Eme-
rich/ein wolgelerter Herr / vnnd besonder in der
kunst Astronomia/das er sich des Himmels lauff
vnd der künfftigen ding vil wisst zůberichten. Der
selb was auch an gůt gar reich/vnd het mit jagen
grosse kurtzweil. Er het auch nur ein Son vnd eine einige Tochter/die er gar lieb het/Der Sohn
hiess Bertram/vnd die Tochter hiess Blantsette/
die was ein schöne vnd zůchtige Jungfraw. Nun
was in dem Land / zů Potiers vil grosser Wäld
vnd auch Hölzer/vnd besonder so heisst ein wald
Der Kürbsforst / in dem selben Wald was gesess-
sen ein gar edler G
Graue von dem V   *mit vil Kindern*
gůt arm/vnd was
Er was aber ein vernünfftiger weiser redlicher
Herr/vnd der gar bescheidenlich nach gůter ord-
nung lebt / vnd sich vnd seine kinder ehrlich hin-
zoge mit wenig gůts/darumb er wol erkant ward/
vnd auch von aller menigklich geehret / vnd gar
wol gehalten. Der selb Graue was auch des selben Stammens vnd Geschlechts des vorgenan-
ten Grauen von Potiers/vnd seines Schilts vnd
Helms genoss / wenn er was sein rechter öhem.
Nun betrachtet der
von Potiers /das s   *mit vil Kinden*
Vorst arm wer / vn
den / vnd gedacht wie er jhn seiner Kinder eins
theils wölt entladen / vnd jhm etwas zů statten
vnd

Figure 14.4.   Intra-textual variable analysis[3]

variants are compared with regard to their specific contexts in order to explain their particular use. This procedure is particularly useful for the detection of possible internal factors that trigger the choice of a variant.

(2) In the case of an *inter-textual* variable analysis, the results of two or more intra-textual investigations are compared. This method is chosen if a linguist wants to compare the choice of variants found in the Nuremberg chronicle to other incunabula, thereby changing the external determinants such as time or place. In this way, it is possible to detect differences among these individual texts in the range of variants and their distribution. Above all, this allows the scholar to identify external factors and thus to ascertain diatopic, diastratic, or other important sociolinguistic characteristics of the texts under investigation.

(3) A *cross-textual* variable analysis compares the variants in different versions of the same text. The main purpose of this method is to focus on the *alterations* from one version to another in order to detect a pattern of deliberate changes.

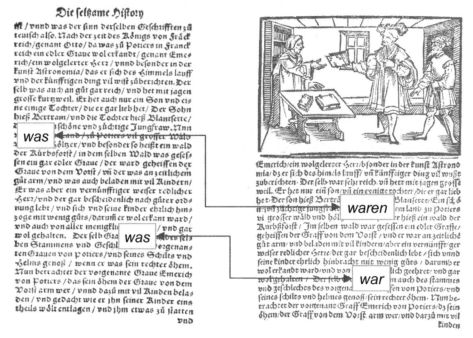

Figure 14.5. Cross-textual variable analysis[4]

As a precondition, it requires successive textual records, such as concept, draft, first manuscript, and fair copy, or different copies or editions of the same text. This method is favored by scholars such as those working on the tradition of the Bible or on European legends like *Melusine* or *Tristan and Iseult* which were retold in numerous sources. In contrast to an intra- and inter-textual analysis, this method seeks to compare the variants as single items in different versions line by line and paragraph by paragraph (see Figure 14.5 for an illustration). This approach, comparing different versions, is particularly suited to uncovering differences and similarities between texts when such differences are not evident in an inter-textual examination. Consider the following example: the inter-textual findings may show no differences in frequency and range of variants and both versions may contain three variants used with more or less the same frequency. Nevertheless, a cross-textual analysis might reveal that single variants were replaced by one of the two others, although the overall distribution by number remained the same. If corresponding alterations were made repeatedly, one can reasonably assume that the internal or external constraints for this variable must have changed. If one succeeds in linking such patterns to their determining factors, be they internal or external, an important step towards an explanation of variation can be taken.

3.2.1.2   Variation and change: applying the apparent-time model   The interplay
between language variation and language change is of great significance, since
language change originates in variation. One of the major difficulties of taking a
historical perspective is deciding whether a variable is part of an ongoing process
of language change. Regardless of what variables we are dealing with, the process
of language change implies a period of transition during which both old and new
variants coexist. It should be noted here that, although language change is not
possible without variation, variation does not necessarily result in language
change. Accordingly, a distinction should ideally be made between stable variation[5] and dynamic variation (Labov 2001: 85), but this is in most cases possible
only after observing the particular variation over a longer period of time. For the
study of dynamic variation, there are two types of change that should be differentiated. Labov (1994: 83) makes the following distinction:

(a) Changes from generation to generation; in an age cohort or generation, indi-
    viduals maintain a certain frequency of a variant throughout their lifetime.
    Nevertheless, a comparison of successive generations reveals an ongoing
    change in the choice of variants. This type of dynamic variation is linked to
    language acquisition and is called 'generational change.'
(b) Changes in which the whole community modifies its choice of variants simul-
    taneously – for instance, by acquiring and increasingly using a new variant.
    This means that individuals do not maintain the same patterns during their
    lifetime and that each generation implements the change at the same time.
    This second type is called 'communal change.' With regard to grammatical
    variables, Labov (1994: 84) points out that the first type is more likely to be
    found in morphological changes, whereas the second would be expected in
    syntactical changes.

In a historical study, the quantity of data might be too limited to verify diachronic changes in a real-time analysis and to decide whether language change
has taken place, and if so, what type of change. One way to circumvent this
problem is to apply an apparent-time analysis to historical data.[6] Present-day
sociolinguists use the apparent-time construct as an elegant and effective method
for investigating a supposed real-time change. Instead of investigating language
use over a longer period of time, the apparent-time method can be used to simulate diachronic change by comparing the use of variants by different generations
at a given point in time. The apparent-time model has been applied to historical
data, as is shown by the following studies of English and French.

Based on the correspondence of the Celys (1472–88), a wealthy family of London
wool merchants, Bailey (1989) investigated the evolution of *are* in Early Modern
English. He was able to show that the older generation of the Cely family consistently used the *be* variant as a plural form while, at the same time, several other
variants (*ben, beth, is, are*) were used by the younger Celys. By applying the
apparent-time model, Bailey's study revealed differences in the use of variants

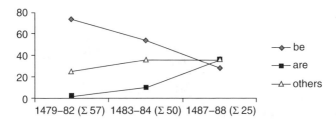

Figure 14.6. Plural forms used by William Cely during three different time periods (source: Bailey 1989:161, based on Hanham 1975; Reproduced by permission of The University of Tennessee Press)

between the older and the younger generation: the *are* variant, a northern form which eventually became the standard present tense plural form, had not been used by the older Cely generation, whereas it had already emerged in the correspondence of the younger Cely family members. Backed up by knowledge of the further development of *are*, Bailey could draw the conclusion that a real-time change had taken place and that it could be a generational one.

In order to determine if a change is generational or communal, it may be possible – if there is enough data – to compare the variables of individuals in two or more time tranches. There is no standard as to how far apart these time tranches should be and how many years such a time span should cover; scholars have not handled this problem in a consistent way. Let us return to the evolution of *are* in Early Modern English. Bailey (1989), for instance, compared three different time tranches that cover a period of nine years in total (see Figure 14.6) in order to demonstrate an increasing use of the *are* variant by one of the younger Celys. Such a change in the habit of individuals during their lifetime could theoretically speak for a communal change – but since, as we have seen, the older generation of Celys retained the *be* variant to the exclusion of all others, this cannot be the case. Instead, other internal or external factors must have interfered.

The apparent-time model may, of course, also be applied when data in significant quantity are available for a longer period of time. In this case, the linguist is in an advantageous position that makes it possible to look into the (historical) future: to couple both time models and compare apparent-time and real-time data. If the results of an apparent-time and a real-time analysis are congruent, one can reasonably assume that there are no other internal or external constraints that need to be taken into consideration. But if the results are incongruent, other internal or external factors may be interfering, and these must be explored. Using the example of a syntactic variable in seventeenth-century French ('je **le** veux faire' vs. 'je veux **le** faire'),[7] Ayres-Bennett (2004b: 208–23) coupled both methods. In an apparent-time approach, she analyzed the distribution of both word-order variants in different age groups over a time span of twenty years (1600–19). She then repeated this method in two successive chronological tranches (1640–59 and 1680–99).

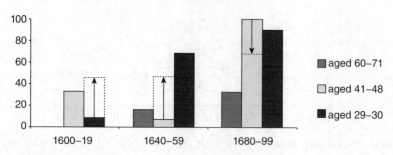

Figure 14.7.   The increase of the variant Finite Verb+Pronoun+Infinitive in real but not in apparent time (source: Ayres-Bennett 2004b: 208–219; Reproduced by permission of Nodus)

By comparing the chronological tranches, she could prove a diachronic increase in the use of the new variant from around 10% to 80% in total in the course of the century. But although she found this significant increase of the variant in question in real time, there was no evidence for an apparent-time change. Comparing the different age groups in each tranche, very different behavior in the choice between the old and new variant could be observed. In Figure 14.7, we emphasize the discrepancies in the apparent-time analysis by arrows. In each cohort, there should have been an age-related increase of the new variant, with the younger authors (aged 29–30) leading. Using the apparent-time model, Ayres-Bennett could prove that the choice of the new word order had not been triggered by age alone. The discrepancies between the apparent-time and the real-time study are an important and valuable clue indicating that other internal or external factors were relevant in this process of change.

3.2.2 Looking for explanations   Imagine that, in an investigation, we had taken all the steps mentioned above – first identifying the potential variants of a variable; then determining whether (a) we are dealing with variation that remains stable over time, or whether (b) a process of language change has taken place. The next step is to investigate which external and internal factors play a role, or, to put it differently, with which exogenous and endogenous factors the linguistic variants can be correlated. While this plan seems straightforward, its implementation may be quite a challenge. After all, the range of potential correlating decisive factors is daunting. This great diversity attests to the interplay between language and numerous social factors such as class, ethnicity, religion, age, gender, and social grouping. Moreover, the linguist has to consider the pragma-linguistic context, which may lead language users to abandon their first choice of variant. While one particular communication situation requires the use of a specific variant, another situation may require a different one. The language user is thus not necessarily tied to a variant, but selects the appropriate one for the particular situation from a more or less restricted set of possibilities.

However, even if we take all of these socio- and pragma-linguistic conditions into account, and even if we succeed some day in describing all of these conditions, historical sociolinguists will still struggle with a crucial task – namely, the integration of the dynamics of time and space into their theory. External factors such as class, ethnicity, religion, age, and gender are indeed of great importance, but they cease to be useful categories if we view them as 'abstractions' outside time and space. They function in historical contexts, in concrete historical constellations, and each does so at its own level of intensity. We will illustrate the problem by focusing on the external factor *age*. Whether a person is young, middle-aged, or elderly may at first glance seem part of a relevant category which is not bound by time and space. However, like any other external factor it can only take effect in historical contexts, in tangible historical constellations. In the chronological perspective, for instance, an identity-endowing language used by young people presupposes the existence of a youth culture. As long as adolescents were treated as immature adults, such a language variety was nonexistent; in fact, the very existence of a youth language was inconceivable. Only when adolescence was recognized as an age in its own right were the historical conditions provided for adolescence to become an external factor that can shape a variety. Similarly, if we take the spatial and thereby cultural perspective into account, we will also be presented with important spatial differences. For instance, in a comparison of young adult members of different cultures, Ota *et al.* (2000) and McCann *et al.* (2004) found markedly different age identities, which led to the conclusion that adolescence may be considered as a more meaningful social category in some cultures than in others and thus might have quite different effects on language. Accordingly, in the case of a rural Xhosa society in South Africa, van Eeden (1991) showed that the sequence of initiation rituals was considered more important than mere biological age.[8]

Generally speaking, before we can explain the dynamics of linguistic variables in time and space, we have to consider carefully these historical and spatial constellations; in other words, we have to correlate our socio- and pragma-linguistic 'micro-variables' with historical and spatial 'macro-variables.'

The adolescence example shows that the linguistic behavior of language users does not accord with the categories laid down in sociolinguistic studies in every case. On the contrary, language may respond much more flexibly to social demands than our 'yardsticks' show us. But this statement of flexibility requires modification: language is flexible only within the scope of its typological possibilities. Just as we have to consider that exogenous processes have a crucial effect on language development, we must not overlook endogenous prerequisites. Systemic long-term tendencies of language change can be reinforced, accelerated as well as decelerated and halted by historical processes. To visualize this process, imagine tennis balls rolling down a hill: their motion and trajectory is determined by gravitation, which may be compared to endogenous, systemic tendencies.

On their way, though, the tennis balls hit obstacles which redirect them; they accelerate on steep slopes and decelerate in flat areas. These obstacles and the terrain may be seen as exogenous tendencies. The tennis balls thus follow different paths that have different effects on their movement. Similarly, the acceleration or deceleration may proceed in an asynchronous manner in different communication spheres, which is still traceable in different text types or genres. This may explain why linguistic development may appear contradictory: some linguistic features decrease quickly in selected text types – as is, for instance, the case with the inflectional subjunctive in English (Auer 2009) – while persisting in other text types in which they fulfill a differentiating function.

Let us assume that, despite all these challenges, we succeeded in correlating the variant of a variable to a well-defined social category. We are not faced with any problems as long as the selection of variants remains stable. However, if the language starts changing, we need to explain why one variant is chosen over another. Let us return to the example of the Cely letters and the evolution of *are* in Early Modern English. Bailey (1989: 167) explains the replacement of the older plural form *be* with *are* as a movement towards transparency. Early Modern English "achieved greater transparency by borrowing the *are* which northern immigrants brought with them, using it for the indicative plural and restricting *be* to the subjunctive and infinitival uses" (1989:168). It is indeed tempting to provide a functional explanation *a posteriori* by stating that the older variants which underwent the change had been irregular, opaque, or redundant. Dahl (2004) even suggests the term "verbosity," as opposed to "linearity," for the use of redundant variants. From a cross-linguistic perspective, a variant exhibits verbosity if it requires more linguistic effort (such as greater phonetic weight) than is usually the case. Accordingly, a change towards more regularity, transparency, and explicitness may be considered functional.

However, 'functional' may refer to more than just 'efficient in transmitting information' (as regards speed, completeness, or adequacy). Particularly from a sociolinguistic point of view, 'functional' may comprise a wide range of other aspects that influence the speaker's choice, such as aesthetic criteria, striving for prestige, the labeling of group affiliations – and the possible political and social power interests behind these motives. 'Functional' may even come into conflict with the principle of linguistic economy. It is precisely because variants are 'costly' to produce that they are apt to indicate the prominent social status and prestige of the speaker/writer who is obviously able to afford this blatant waste of resources. In terms of evolutionary psychology, these variants are seen as costly or *Góngorist* signals.[9] Millar (2002: 184) cites a vivid example of costly signals from the American *Young Man's Own Book* (Anonymous 1832), a guide to polite behavior from the 1830s. This manual illustrates and advises how to express condolences if you want to be a man of fashion. Saying "I am sorry for your loss"

> may be civil, but it is nevertheless vulgar. A man of fashion will express the same
> thing more elegantly [...]. He will advance, [...] and with a peculiar composure of
> voice and countenance, begin his compliments of condolence with "I hope, sir, you

will do me the justice to be persuaded, that I am not insensible of your unhappiness, that I take part in your distress, and shall ever be affected when *you* are so." (202; also in Millar 2002: 184)

It may well be that the basic mechanism of language change is functionality. But, as historical sociolinguists, we understand 'functionality' not only as technical efficiency in information transmission. We include a number of alternative functions such as marking of prestige and social inclusion or exclusion. Thus, language change is the permanent process of adapting and readapting language to its external means and ends. Language change is a trial and error process: successful inventions are incorporated and become common parlance, but they do so for a limited period of time only in response to a specific historical setting. As the external contexts of language do not remain constant, language also continues changing.

4. Conclusions

Historical sociolinguistics has made considerable progress in the last decades in the investigation of correlations between grammatical variants and non-linguistic social and cultural factors. Increasing numbers of these external factors have been tested as regards their potential influence on the choice of linguistic variants: class, ethnicity, religion, age, gender, social grouping, network, community of practice, power relations, solidarity, prestige, level of formality, medium, style, register, and topic. Despite all these achievements, we see two principal problems inherent in the historical sociolinguistic paradigm, especially in the quantitative approach: historical sociolinguistics increasingly concentrates on the investigation of micro-variables and tends to neglect the concrete, that is, the specific historical macro-configurations that form the background of the linguistic variables and their non-linguistic determinants. It thus places the micro-variables, as it were, *beyond historical time*. Without attention to the specific historical context, one might assume that Elizabeth I was typical of English women in the Renaissance, and, observing that she used a lot of new language variants, conclude that women in general were in the vanguard of language change (see Nevalainen 2006: 575).

Studies in historical sociolinguistics often result in the detection of correlations between grammatical variants and external factors. Correlations, however, are not explanations in the sense of answers to why-questions, specifying cause and effect. When we find a colleague leaving every time we enter the cafeteria, we should not conclude that she is avoiding our company for lunch. The description of correlations is a necessary step, but in the long run it is in no way sufficient. Historical sociolinguistics *as a science* should go beyond this point and provide explanations, or at least look for them. Historical sociolinguists should also ask why people behaved "linguistically as they have been found to do in study after study" (Cameron 1990: 81). Why, and how, do grammatical variables 'reflect' society?

NOTES

1 A grammatically less restricted interpretation is also given by Romaine (1981, 1984), who argues on the basis of the functional equivalence of communicative intentions. For a detailed discussion, see Winford (1984, 1996), Cheshire (1987), and Serrano (1997/98).

2 The Ottomans did not normally require Christians to become Muslims. For a general overview, see Crampton (1997) and Lord Kinross (2008).

3 Variants of the German dative plural 'children', cf. *Die schöne und liebliche Histori oder wunderbarliche Geschicht, von der Edlen und schönen Melusina*. 1577. Straßburg: Müller, Aiij^v. (Munich, Bayerische Staatsbibliothek, Rar. 1192)

4 Variants of the German preterite form in 3rd person plural and singular, cf. *Die schöne und liebliche Histori oder wunderbarliche Geschicht, von der Edlen und schönen Melusina*. 1577. Straßburg: Müller, Aiij^v (Munich, Bayerische Staatsbibliothek, Rar. 1192) (on the left) and *Melusina. Von Lieb und Leyd/ Ein schöne und lustige Histori. Ausz Frantzösischer Spraach in Teutsch verwandelt.* [ca. 1580. Frankfurt am Main: Egenolff Erben], Aij^v. (Göttingen, Niedersächsische Staats- und Universitätsbibliothek, 8 FAB III 2023) (on the right)

5 Age grading is a classic example of stable variation; see Hockett (1950). Adolescents in each generation, for instance, use a higher proportion of stigmatized variants than speakers of other ages. This does not usually lead to language change. See also Cheshire (2005).

6 See Raumolin-Brunberg (1996). For a critical view of the application of the apparent-time model in historical sociolinguistics see Valli (1983), Blanche-Benveniste and Jeanjean (1987), and Ayres-Bennett (2004b). For a discussion, see also Ashby (1991).

7 The Old French word order Pronoun + Finite Verb + Infinitive ('je **le** veux faire') was replaced by the ordering Finite Verb + Pronoun + Infinitive ('je veux **le** faire') during the seventeenth century, which can be described as an instance of the demise of clitic climbing (Kayne 1975).

8 See also the literature cited in Cheshire (2005).

9 *Góngorism* (named for the Spanish writer Luis de *Góngora*, 1561–1627) or *culteranismo* was a stylistic movement during the Spanish baroque. It became notorious for its use of ostentatious vocabulary and alien syntactic order (*hyperbaton*) used for emphasis. A well-known example of hyperbaton in English is attributed to Winston Churchill: *This is the sort of English up with which I will not put.* And few among us will be unfamiliar with the many French polite phrases such as *dans l'attente de votre réponse, je vous prie de croire, Madame, à l'expression de mes sentiments les plus distingués.*

REFERENCES

Anonymous (1832) *Young Man's Own Book. A Manual of Politeness, Intellectual Improvement, and Moral Deportment*, Key and Biddle, Philadelphia.

Ashby, W.J. (1991) When does variation indicate linguistic change in progress? *Journal of French Language Studies* 1: 1–19.

Auer, A. (2009) *The Subjunctive in the Age of Prescriptivism. English and German Developments in the Eighteenth Century*, Palgrave Macmillan, Basingstoke.

Ayres-Bennett, W. (2004a) Sociolinguistic variation in the work of the French seventeenth-century *remarqueurs*. In G. Haßler and G. Volkmann (eds.), *History of Linguistics in Texts and Concepts – Geschichte der Sprachwissenschaft in Texten und Konzepten*. Vol. I. Nodus, Münster, pp. 131–40.

Ayres-Bennett, W. (2004b) *Sociolinguistic Variation in Seventeenth-Century France*, Cambridge University Press, Cambridge.

Bailey, G. (1989) Sociolinguistic constraints on language change and the evolution of *are* in Early Modern English. In J.B. Trahern, Jr. (ed.), *Standardizing English. Essays in the History of Language Change. In Honour of John Hurt Fisher*, University of Tennessee Press, Knoxville, pp. 158–71.

Blanche-Benveniste, C. and Jeanjean, C. (1987) *Le Français Parlé: Transcription et Édition*, Didier, Paris.

Bolinger, D. (1977) *Meaning and Form*, Longman, London.

Cameron, D. (1990) Demythologizing sociolinguistics: why language does not reflect society. In J. Joseph and T. Taylor (eds.), *Ideologies of language*, Routledge, London, pp. 79–93.

Cedergren, H.J. and Sankoff, D. (1974) Variable rules: performance as a statistical reflection of competence. *Language* 50: 333–55.

Cheshire, J. (1987) Syntactic variation, the linguistic variable, and sociolinguistic theory. *Linguistics* 25: 257–82.

Cheshire, J. (2005) Age and generation-specific use of language. In U. Ammon, N. Dittmar, K. Mattheier and P. Trudgill (eds.), *Sociolinguistics: An Introductory Handbook of the Science of Language and Society*, Mouton de Gruyter, Berlin, pp. 1552–63.

Chomsky, N. (1986) *Knowledge of Language*, Praeger, New York.

Crampton, R.J. (1997) *A Concise History of Bulgaria*, Cambridge University Press, Cambridge.

Dahl, Ö. (2004) *The Growth and Maintenance of Linguistic Diversity*, John Benjamins, Amsterdam.

Davies, W.V. and Langer, N. (2006) *The Making of Bad Language. Lay Linguistic Stigmatisations in German: Past and Present*, Peter Lang, Frankfurt.

Haas, E. (1980) *Rhetorik und Hochsprache. Über die Wirksamkeit der Rhetorik bei der Entstehung der deutschen Hochsprache im 17. und 18. Jahrhundert*, Peter Lang, Frankfurt.

Hanham, A. (ed.) (1975) *The Cely Letters 1472–1488*, Oxford University Press, Oxford.

Hirschbühler, P. and Labelle, M. (1994) Change in verb position in French negative infinitival clauses. *Language Variation and Change* 6: 149–78.

Hockett, C. (1950) Age-grading and linguistic continuity. *Language* 26: 449–59.

Kayne, R.S. (1975) *French Syntax: The Transformational Cycle*, MIT Press, Cambridge, MA.

Kinross, Lord (2008) *The Ottoman Centuries. The Rise and Fall of the Turkish Empire*, Folio Society, London.

Knoop, U. (1987) Beschreibungsprinzipien der neueren Sprachgeschichte. Eine kritische Sichtung der sprachwissenschaftlichen, soziologischen, sozialhistorischen und geschichtswissenschaftlichen Begrifflichkeit. *Germanistische Linguistik* 91/92: 11–41.

Laberge, S. (1980) The changing distribution of indefinite pronouns in discourse. In R.W. Shuy and A. Schnukal (eds.), *Language Use and the Uses of Language*, Georgetown University Press, Washington, DC, pp. 248–59.

Labov, W. (1966) *The Social Stratification of English in New York City*, Center for Applied Linguistics Washington, DC.

Labov, W. (1969) Contraction, deletion, and inherent variability of the English copula. *Language* 45: 715–62.

Labov, W. (1972) *Sociolinguistic Patterns*, University of Pennsylvania Press, Philadelphia.

Labov, W. (1994) *Principles of Linguistic Change, Vol. 1. Internal Factors*, Blackwell, Oxford.

Labov, W. (2001) *Principles of Linguistic Change, Vol. 2. Social Factors*, Blackwell, Oxford.

Lavandera, B. (1978) Where does the linguistic variable stop? *Language in Society* 7: 171–82.

McCann, R. *et al.* (2004) Cultural and gender influences on age identification. *Communication Studies* 55 (1): 88–105.

Millar, S. (2002) Eloquence and elegance: ideals of communicative competence in spoken English. In R. Watts and P. Trudgill (eds.), *Alternative Histories of English*, Routledge, London, pp. 173–90.

Nevalainen, T. (2006) Historical sociolinguistics and language change. In A. van Kemenade and B. Los (eds.), *The Handbook of the History of English*, Blackwell, Oxford, pp. 558–88.

Ota, H., Harwood, J., Williams, A., and Takai, J. (2000) A cross-cultural analysis of age identity in Japan and the United States. *Journal of Multilingual and Multicultural Development* 21, 33–43.

Raumolin-Brunberg, H. (1996) Apparent time. In T. Nevalainen and H. Raumolin-Brunberg (eds.), *Sociolinguistics and Language History. Studies based on the Corpus of Early English Correspondence*, Rodopi, Amsterdam, pp. 93–109.

Reichmann, O. (1988) Zur Vertikalisierung des Variantenspektrums in der jüngeren Sprachgeschichte des Deutschen. In H.H. Munske, *et al.* (eds.), *Deutscher Wortschatz. Lexikologische Studien*, de Gruyter, Berlin, pp. 151–80.

Reichmann, O. (1990) Sprache ohne Leitvarietät vs Sprache mit Leitvarietät: ein Schlüssel für die nachmittelalterliche Geschichte des Deutschen? In W. Besch (ed.), *Deutsche Sprachgeschichte. Grundlagen, Methoden, Perspektiven*, Peter Lang, Frankfurt am Main, pp. 141–58.

Romaine, S. (1981) On the problem of syntactic variation: a reply to Beatriz Lavandera and William Labov. *Working Papers in Sociolinguistics* 82: 1–38.

Romaine, S. (1984) On the problem of syntactic variation and pragmatic meaning in sociolinguistic theory. *Folia Linguistica* 18: 409–37.

Sankoff, D. (1978) Probability and linguistic variation. *Synthèse* 37: 217–38.

Sankoff, G. and Thibault, P. (1977) L'alternance entre les auxiliaries *avoir* et *être* en français parlé à Montréal. *Langue Française* 34: 81–108.

Serrano, M.J. (1997/98) On the variability of syntax: some theoretical remarks. *CAUCE. Revista de Filologia y su Didáctica* 20/21: 1053–73.

Valli, A. (1983) Un exemple d'approche du problème des variantes syntaxiques en linguistique diachronique. *Recherches sur le Français Parlé* 5: 125–46.

van Eeden, J.A. (1991) *Ageing and Seniority in a Rural Xhosa Community*, HSRC Centre for Gerontology, University of Cape Town Medical School.

Vaugelas, C. F. de (1647) *Remarques sur la langue françoise utiles à ceux qui veulent bien parler and bien escrire*, Camusat and le Petit, Paris (facsimile Slatkine, Paris, 1934).

Voeste, A. (1999a) How to explain historical processes of consolidation in 18th century morphology: the German adjective declension. *Linguistik Online* 4(3). http://www.linguistik-online.de/3_99/voeste.html [accessed September 25, 2011].

Voeste, A. (1999b) *Varianz und Vertikalisierung. Zur Normierung der Adjektivdeklination in der ersten Hälfte des 18. Jahrhunderts*, Rodopi, Amsterdam.

Weiner, E.J., and Labov, W. (1983) Constraints on the agentless passive. *Journal of Linguistics* 19: 29–58.

Winford, D. (1984) The linguistic variable and syntactic variation in creole continua. *Lingua* 62: 267–88.

Winford, D. (1996) The problem of syntactic variation. In J. Arnold *et al.* (eds.), *Sociolinguistic Variation: Data, Theory, and Analysis: Selected papers from NWAV 23 at Stanford*, CSLI Publications, Stanford, pp. 177–92.

Wolfram, W. (1991) The linguistic variable: fact and fantasy. *American Speech*, Vol. 66, 1: 22–32.

Wolfram, W. (1993) Identifying and interpreting variables. In D.R. Preston (ed.), *American Dialect Research*, John Benjamins, Amsterdam, pp. 193–221.

Wolfram, W. (2006) Variation and language: overview. In K. Brown (ed.), *Encyclopedia of Language and Linguistics. Vol. 13* (2nd edition), Elsevier, Amsterdam: pp. 333–41.

15 Lexical-Semantic Variables

JOACHIM GRZEGA

1. Introduction

Several articles in Cruse *et al.*'s (2002–5) handbook describe the specific word-stocks for various languages at various periods as well as for some specific social groups. This chapter strives for a more theoretical approach to the correlation of lexical-semantic variables and social groups. For example, the combination of sociolinguistics and historical linguistics has helped explain the spread of lexical innovations in terms of prestige (see Labov 1994, 2001, 2010) and social networks (see Milroy and Milroy 1985). What has not been so thoroughly explored, though, is the formulation of a model that tries to integrate all sorts of lexical, or lexemic, change (semantic changes, borrowings, word-formations) – especially as regards the very first phase of lexemic change, in other words: the actual lexemic innovation. The following paragraphs shed light on recent suggestions for such an overall model, predicated on results from cognitive, pragmatic, and sociolinguistic studies. It will therefore be called the *Cognitive and Social Model for Onomasiological Studies (CoSMOS)*.

The study of lexical-semantic variables in the frame of historical sociolinguistics leads to the field of onomasiology in its classical sense: the study of designations, where the linguist starts with an extralinguistic concept and looks for its formal verbalizations. In a wider sense, onomasiology also covers the function-to-form direction, or concept-to-form direction, in diachronic pragmatics and in diachronic morphology and syntax. The second approach toward words is known as semasiology: starting with the form and asking for the contents it covers, or the concepts it denotes. The onomasiological approach is the view of an encoding speaker, while the semasiological is the view of a decoding listener. Since lexical

The Handbook of Historical Sociolinguistics, First Edition. Edited by Juan Manuel Hernández-Campoy and Juan Camilo Conde-Silvestre.
© 2014 John Wiley & Sons, Ltd. Published 2014 by John Wiley & Sons, Ltd.

innovation has to do with encoding ideas into words, this chapter will look mainly at onomasiological frameworks.

As already indicated, CoSMOS, as an overall model, covers the formal, cognitive, and social aspects of the forces and the processes involved in lexical changes. Therefore, the chapter will first present the CoSMOS model in full. For readability, the first part will include the illustration of just one example. The succeeding sections will focus on the sociolinguistic elements in the forces of lexical change and on the sociolinguistic aspects of the processes of lexical change. These two parts will provide examples from various languages and cultures. The subsequent section will shed light on the interaction between social aspects and the spread of innovations.

2. A General Model of Processes and Forces in Lexical Change: CoSMOS

A comprehensive theory of lexical, or lexemic, change was presented in Grzega (2004), which describes the forces (causes, reasons, goals) as well as the formal and cognitive-associative processes of lexemic change (see also the English summaries in Grzega 2004: 281–87 and Grzega 2007). It discusses and revises works from all periods of linguistics. Its aim is to bring together the benefits from structural, variational, and cognitive linguistics and draw up a new integrated onomasiological theory of lexemic change. The basic ideas are seen as universal, and critically incorporate ideas by Brent (1992) and Brown (2001). The study is therefore based on the analysis of several hundred examples from English, German, the Romance languages and others.

The fundamental onomasiological process is illustrated in CoSMOS (Grzega 2007: 19), which starts with a concrete referent in context (see Figure 15.1):

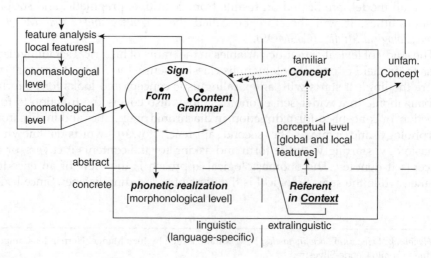

Figure 15.1.   The CoSMOS model

The following sections describe how CoSMOS is to be read, illustrating each phase with terms for the concept THE SEASON AFTER SUMMER AND BEFORE WINTER.

Phase 1

The starting-point is either a thought, or concept, or a specific referent in context. The term 'context' covers the speaker-hearer situation, the type of discourse, the communicative goal, and the syntactical context[1].

> Example: I need to refer to the season outside. My context is: We are in the sixteenth century. It is a day in September. I am addressing a general English-speaking audience (some of them speak French, too; some even know some Latin).

Phase 2

The speaker classifies the referent through processing its more basic, 'global' and its more specific, 'local' traits. The speaker then categorizes the referent using some kind of mental checklist for the absence or presence of specific features and by comparing the overall image of the referent with other images already in the mind. This is the **perceptual level**.

> Example: It's no longer summer, but it's not winter yet. The temperature has generally fallen, days are shorter and nights are longer, precipitation gradually increases. Leaves have turned reddish, brownish, yellowish, and greenish and are falling from the trees. Many crops are being harvested. It is THE TRANSITION PERIOD BETWEEN SUMMER AND WINTER.

Phase 3

If the (concrete) referent can be identified as the member of a familiar (abstract) concept, the speaker may use an already existing designation or opt for creating a new designation, sometimes more, sometimes less consciously: this is reminiscent of Labov's difference between 'pressure from above'/'overt prestige' (change either above the level of conscious awareness and/or motivated by the speech of a socially higher class) and 'pressure from below'/'covert prestige' (change either below the level of conscious awareness or motivated by the speech of the peer group) (Labov 1966; 2001: 517–18). The decision will be based on a cost–benefit analysis, in which the speaker reflects on the goals of the designation in this specific speaker–hearer constellation and the utterance it is embedded in: do I want to sound like the hearer? do I want to sound different from others? should the designation be precise or vague? do I want to sound primitive, elaborate, polite, impolite? do I want to simply take the first word that comes to my mind? The cost–benefit analysis can be described as 'linguistic economy.' If the speaker does not want to coin an innovation consciously, but does not have the best word at hand, a word whose semantics is close might be used on the spur of the moment, in the hope that the hearer may infer the suitable meaning from the context of the interaction. This results in what Traugott and Dasher (2002) call 'pragmatic polysemies,' which may sometimes lead to new, fossilized semantic polysemies. In fact, Traugott and Dasher see 'invited inferencing' as the principal mechanism of semantic change. However, in the case of intentional conscious innovation the speaker then goes through several levels of a word-finding, or name-giving, process.

> Example: The term *autumn* already exists, but it is a foreign term, a learned term which is not very explicit and not necessarily generally intelligible. However, my communicative goals are that I want to use a term that my audience might under-stand more easily and I want to give this transitional period a new short name because I will refer to it frequently. What can I call this period to achieve my com-municative goal?

The motor of language change in general (not lexemic changes alone) can be said to be of an economic nature: speakers connect a speech act with a certain goal and a certain effect in a certain speaker–hearer constellation. Speakers like to achieve this effect as efficiently as possible, respecting – according to their needs – maxims such as 'make your contribution convincing/credible/emphatic,' 'make clear what you mean,' 'show yourself in the best possible light,' 'be polite/dominant/ obsequious,' 'express yourself in a sophisticated/humorous manner' (on these maxims see Grice 1975 and Keller 1995). In fact, there seems to be a supra-principle that could be termed 'pressure of acceptance' or rather the supra-goal of 'get accepted,' either because the group you want to be accepted by recognizes your style as similar to theirs and different from others or because the group you want to be accepted by admires the fact that you are different from them. In the former case, the speaker pursues a maxim of statics ('Speak like the audience. Don't innovate'), in the latter, the speaker observes a maxim of dynamics ('Do not speak like the audience. Innovate'). The less informal and the less private a communica-tive situation, the more important this supra-goal becomes. The maxim for dynam-ics may trigger linguistic changes, which may secondarily be generally conserved in the language through a maxim for statics. Enduring linguistic change can either be planned (see the contributions in Coulmas 1989), or may simply occur as a by-product.

The coinage of a new designation can be instigated by various, potentially concurrent, forces. Early attempts at listing such forces were unsystematic and did not always neatly separate processes from forces (see the overview in Grzega 2004: 163–65). Geeraerts' (1997: 102–12) list of causes of lexical change is unfortunately not very fine-grained and basically differentiates simply between conscious and subconscious explanatory factors. Blank (1997: 345 and 1999: 70) is the first to establish a comprehensive empirical-based, cognitive-linguistic catalog of forces triggering semantic change. Grzega's works (2002a and 2004) are the first to strive for an empirically based, comprehensive, and systematic catalog of forces for all types of lexemic change. The CoSMOS catalog of forces, sometimes more conscious, sometimes less, contains the following items (the socio-historically relevant items will be further explained in section 3:

- Onomasiological fuzziness: this refers to the observation that sometimes speakers have difficulties in classifying the referent or attributing the right word to the referent and thus mix up designations.
- Dominance of the prototype: this refers to the fuzzy difference between superordinate and subordinate term due to the high prominence of the prototype of a category in the real world.
- Social reasons: this refers to contact situations with social 'undemarcation' effects.
- Institutional and non-institutional linguistic pre- and proscriptivism: this covers legal and peer-group linguistic pre- and proscriptivism, aiming at social 'demarcation.'
- Flattery.
- Insult.
- Disguising language: this is a paraphrase for 'misnomers,' words which hide uncomfortable aspects of a concept by avoiding morphemes that trigger uncomfortable associations.
- Taboo: this includes both avoiding sanctioned expressions and expressions for concepts you should not talk about.
- Aesthetic-formal reasons: this covers the avoidance of words that are phonetically similar or identical to words with negative connotations.
- Communicative-formal reasons: this refers to the abolition of the ambiguity of forms in context, 'homonymic conflict and polysemic conflict.'
- Word play/punning.
- Excessive length of words.
- Morphological misinterpretation: this is traditionally referred to as 'folk-etymology' and means the (subconscious) creation of transparency by alterations within a word).
- Logical-formal reasons: this expresses the strive for lexical regularization or morphological consociation between words.
- Desire for plasticity: this refers to the creation of a salient or memorable motivation of a name.
- Anthropological salience of a concept: this could also be termed 'natural salience' and expresses the anthropologically explainable emotional character of a concept.
- Culture-induced salience of a concept: this could also be termed 'cultural importance' or simply 'cultural salience' and refers to the fact that a thing may be very important not to all humans, but only to a specific sociocultural group.
- Changes in the referents (or changes in the world).
- World-view change (or changes in the categorization of the world).

- Prestige/fashion: this covers the prestige of another language or variety, of certain word-formation patterns, or of certain figurative patterns, such as centers of expansion.

The forces from the catalog can be linked with maxims of social-communicative behavior, such as Grice's conversational maxims (see Table 15.1; the question mark before a force indicates that the force can only be linked with the maxim in the corresponding row).

Using the 'word death' metaphor, we could position these factors on a conscious–subconscious continuum, where the gradual subconscious loss of a word can be compared to 'natural (designation) death' and where the conscious avoidance of a word can be compared to '(designation) murder;' these two extremes embrace several intermediate degrees (see Figure 15.2; a question mark before a force indicates that the respective force, also occurring at another level, could potentially be located on this level of consciousness, too).

Phase 4

The next phase in the name-giving process is again an analysis of the specific traits of the concept (= **feature analysis**) – with a focus on the local traits. This step is skipped if the speaker simply borrows a word from a foreign language or variety that is used for the concept in question; it can also be skipped if the speaker simply picks an already existing designation and reduces its form.

> Example: There is no clear-cut end of summer and no clear-cut beginning of winter, but the period in between typically shows falling temperatures, days are shorter and nights are longer, precipitation gradually increases, leaves change their colors from green into brown, red and yellow and finally fall, most crops are harvested. In France they call it *automne*; in Latin *autumnus*.

Phase 5

The speaker will then highlight one or two features as a basis for the designation. Štekauer (1998, 2001) and Štekauer *et al.* (2005) refer to this as 'naming in a more abstract sense.' The designation motives could be termed 'iconemes.' These are commonly based on similarity, contrast, partiality, and contiguity/contact relations, which can affect the linguistic side as well as the extralinguistic and the abstract side as well as the concrete. In Štekauer's model this is called the 'onomasiological level.' Here again, the speaker keeps in mind the extralinguistic context. The concrete associations may or may not be initiated by a model, which may be of the speaker's own language or a foreign one.

> Example: I want to inform. I want to be understood by a general audience. I cannot simply use the unmotivated French or Latin term for a general audience. I need to look for a transparent formation. Trees loose their leaves, leaves fall from the trees. This iconeme serves well for a general audience, as no specialist knowledge is needed for this.

Table 15.1. Forces of lexical change and the Gricean Maxims

Maxim	Rather subconscious violation	Rather conscious violation	Conscious violation	Rather subconscious observance	Rather conscious observance	Conscious observance
Quality (truth of content) (persuasion)	onomasiological fuzziness, dominance of the prototype	?flattery	word-play, disguising language			
Quantity (appropriate quantity in content) (persuasion)		?anthropological salience of a concept	word-play, ?disguising language, ?flattery		desire for plasticity, culture-induced salience, recategorization, communicative-formal forces	
Manner/modality (order of utterance, appropriate quantity in form) (representation)	social reasons, dominance of the prototype	?anthropological salience of a concept	word-play, taboo, disguising language, ?flattery	logical-formal reasons, morphological misinterpretation, recategorization, length	desire for plasticity	communicative-formal forces, aesthetic-formal forces
Image (of speaker)						disguising language, taboo, fashion, aesthetic-formal motives, word-play, pre- and proscriptivism
Relation (between speaker and hearer)			word-play, ?insult	social reasons	insult	flattery, taboo, aesthetic-formal motives, pre- and proscriptivism
Aesthetics (of form)					anthropological salience of a concept	word-play, taboo, aesthetic-formal forces, fashion

subconscious

['*natural word-death*' = lack of motivation]

subconscious 'creation of lexical life' with '*involuntary word-slaughter, negligent lexicide*' = onomasiological fuzziness, dominance of the prototype, social reasons, morphological misinterpretation; subconscious '*creation of lexical life*' = logical-formal reasons; onomasiological analogy

relatively conscious 'creation of lexical life' = ?logical-formal reasons, anthropological salience/emotionality of a concept, desire for plasticity, culture-induced salience of a concept, flattery, insult, word play, excessive length; onomasiological analogy

'*creation of lexical life*' with '*(voluntary) word-slaughter*' = communicative-formal reasons, prestige/fashion

'*first-degree word murder, first-degree lexicide*' and '*creation of lexical life*' = non-institutional linguistic pre- and proscriptivism, institutional linguistic pre- and proscriptivism, taboo, aesthetic-formal reasons, world view change, disguising language; [conscious '*creation of lexical life*' = change in things, new concept, ?world view change]

conscious

Figure 15.2.   Forces of lexical change on a conscious-subconscious continuum

Phase 6

The next step leads to what Štekauer (1998, 2001) and Štekauer *et al.* (2005) call the "onomatological level" ('naming in a more concrete sense'). Here, the speaker selects concrete morphemes, keeping in mind the speaker-hearer situation, the type of discourse, the communicative goal, and the syntactical context.

> Example: I want to be understood by a general audience. I cannot use unmotivated French or Latin morphemes for a general English audience. I do not want to use a term with high-register connotation. I want to use a brief word. I take the verbal morpheme {fall} and use it as a noun.

Theoretically, the speaker can reduce the form of an already existing designation for the concept, combine forms to a new lexeme, or simply use an already existing word and enlarge its usage. The last two options can be achieved through several types of process, which are founded on the speaker's own language, on a model from a foreign language, or on no model at all:

6.1 Adoption of an already existing word
 a from the speaker's own language (semantic change)[2];
 b from a foreign language, including dialects and jargons (loanword):
 i 'true loan;'
 ii 'incomplete loan' (traditionally called 'morphological pseudo-loan');
 iii 'mis-loan' (folk-etymological formal change of a loan, folk-etymological semantic extension due to a loan that is only phonetically similar);
 iv 'creative loan' (traditionally called a 'lexical pseudo-loan').
6.2 Syntactical recategorization (traditionally also known as 'zero derivation' or 'conversion').
6.3 Composition (*lato sensu*, the combination of existing morphemes)[3].
6.4 Blendings (overlapping of already existing lexemes)[4].
6.5 Back-derivation.
6.6 Reduplication (covering rhyming and alliterating combinations).
6.7 Morphological alteration (e.g. number change, gender change).
6.8 Wordplaying[5].
6.9 Phonetic-prosodic alteration (e.g. stress shift in English *ímport* vs. *impórt*).
6.10 Graphic alteration (e.g. English *discrete* vs. *discreet*).
6.11 Phraseologism.
6.12 Root creation (including onomatopoetic and expressive words).
6.13 Clarifying compounds (tautological compounds).
6.14 Formal shortening of already existing designations[6].

These processes may be combined. In Grzega's (2004) classification, amelioration of meaning (elevation), deterioration of meaning (degeneration), strengthening of meaning (hyperbole), and weakening of meaning (litotes) are dismissed as types of processes, as they are seen as in part subjectively classified and subsumable under other types of semantic change.

Phase 7

In this phase, the word is provided with a fixed form-content relation and certain grammatical traits – the **sign** is completed.

Example: *fall*: /fɔːl/, 'season after summer and before winter; action of falling,' noun, regular.

Phase 8

Eventually, the sign is *phonetically realized* in a concrete context. This may be influenced by a foreign sound model.

Example: [fɔːɫ]

3. Sociocultural Forces of Lexemic Change

To summarize, the causes of and motives for lexemic change (Grzega 2004: 163–274) are formal, cognitive, and sociocultural in nature. By and large, sociocultural forces are at work either when there are changes within a social group or when there is interplay between two social groups. From the catalog of forces given in the CoSMOS model, the following are sociocultural:

- Dominance of the prototype. For example, as the apple is the most salient fruit in Europe this led to formations such as Dutch *sinaasappel* ~ German *Apfelsine* 'China-apple' for 'orange' (the expression *pomme de Sine* 'apple from China' in the neighboring and prestigious French language could have served as a model for these eighteenth-century usages) and German *Erdapfel* ~ Dutch *aardappel* ~ French *pomme de terre* 'earth-apple' for 'potato' (originally, the terms referred to other fruits growing in the ground).
- Social reasons. In ethnic contact zones (geographically or socially adjacent), we find, for example, the use of Hungarian *palacsinta* 'crêpe' in Austria (in the form of *Palatschinken*) and the use of Austrian *Creme-(Schnitte)* 'cream slice' in Hungary (in the form of *krémes*) (which goes back to the blend of the two cuisines in the Austro-Hungarian empire 1867–1918) or the vast number of French words that entered the English language in England's phase of French–English bilingualism from the twelfth to the fifteenth centuries (in such contact situations both social groups, not just the demographically or hierarchically dominant one, can be the donor language group).
- Pre- and proscriptivism, either non-institutional (in the form of debates on 'good' language in countries all around the world) or institutional (in the form of language laws, such as France's Toubon Law from 1994, which strongly restricts the use of Anglicisms in official documents, or in the form of publications by language academies such as Italy's *Accademia della Crusca*, founded in 1582, Germany's *Fruchtbringende Gesellschaft*, founded in 1617, France's *Académie française*, founded in 1635, and Spain's *Real Academia de la Lengua*, founded in 1713).
- Flattery, such as Italian *Ciao* and German dialectal *Servus*, originally meaning '(your) servant' for 'hello/goodbye' (*ciao* is a regular North Italian continuant of Latin *s(c)lavus* 'servant,' the southern German and originally Latin *servus* seems to go back to the administrative Latin letter-style in the nineteenth century – Latin had not yet lost its status as language of administration in all parts of Europe).
- Insult, like derogatory words for 'a weak and ineffectual man' such as English *pantywaist* and *softy*, Italian *rammollito* 'soft' and German *Weichei* 'soft egg,' or derogatory words for 'nose' such as Italian *nappa* 'tassel,' German *Zinken* 'beaked burin,' US English *beak* 'a bird's mouth' and British English *hooter* 'horn,' which, in turn, is a word for a woman's breast in the US; or derogatory words for 'Interlocutor!/You!' such as *fellow!*, which, in the fourteenth century,

was a term that showed solidarity and a certain casualness, but by Shakespeare's time had become impolite if said to someone who was not a member of the lower classes of society.

- Disguising language (called *mots-menteurs* 'lying words' by Dauzat 1949: 214), such as the twentieth-century German coinage *Minuswachstum* 'minus growth' for 'recession' in a time where economic growth is seen as the norm.
- Taboo, such as using a form meaning 'sleep with someone' to denote 'have sex with someone,' in several languages around the world at various periods in history, in order to avoid a more unequivocal term.
- Cultural salience (vs. natural salience), such as the twentieth-century replacement of English *professor*, French *professeur*, German *Professor* by the shorter English *prof*, French *prof*, German *Prof* among (the now large group of) people in the secondary and/or tertiary education system.
- Prestige/fashion, such as the longstanding prestige of French culture and language in the realm of fashion and the eventual prestige shift to Anglo-American culture is reflected in the change of German designations for 'hairdresser:' from indigenous *Bartscherer* and *Bader* (both no longer used in German) to the fourteenth-century Gallicism *Barbier* and the seventeenth-century coinages *Frisierer* (a loan blend with a French word as the stem and an indigenous agent-noun suffix) and *Perückenmacher* (a loan blend with a French word as first element: the word was borrowed into Russian as *parikmakher* in the seventeenth century, but is no longer present in German) to finally eighteenth-century *Friseur* (another Gallicism), nineteenth-century *Coiffeur* (still another Gallicism), and twentieth-century *Hairstylist* (an Anglicism)[7].
- Aesthetic-formal reasons, such as eighteenth-century English *ass* > *donkey* (to avoid homonymy with *arse*), twelfth-century French *pesteur* 'baker' > *boulanger* 'white-bread-maker' for 'baker' (to avoid a homonymy with *péter* 'fart,' when /s/ before a fortis consonant started to become unstable in pronunciation).
- Changes in the referents, such as the mid-day meal: nineteenth-century English *dinner* > *lunch* and nineteenth-century French *dîner* > *déjeuner* (because the main meal of the day was no longer eaten around noon, but in the evening, while the meal at noon was smaller, often being the first meal of the day; in several dialects the original use of the words is retained). More generally, changes in the referents mean changes in a society and may be preceded by a change in the connotation of an existing word.
- World-view change, such as the reclassification of the whale and the dolphin as mammals instead of fishes with the development of scientific biology and with the spread of scientific knowledge over society in general during the twentieth century. Such a world-view change may also have been triggered by a prior change somewhere else in the lexical system, or by a prior change in the connotation of an existing word.

As already noted, some of these forces are subconscious, others are conscious. Of the latter, some illustrate people's creative nature (finding a more effective synonym aside from the usual designation), some are proof of their destructive side (deleting, or avoiding, the usual designation).

4. Sociocultural Aspects of the Processes of Lexical Change

Society consists of different social groups and can change demographically and culturally. This brings about different preferences for name-giving processes at different times and in different societies or social groups. Frequently, contact between different cultures or social groups play a role. While in Anglo-Saxon times new concepts from another culture (especially Christian culture) were mostly expressed using indigenous words or morphemes, the English from the thirteenth century onwards favored borrowings from French, Latin, and Greek. And in the current age of globalization, English is the source of many new designations in languages around the world (again, of course, with exceptions such as Chinese). It is only recently that lexicologists have begun to study preferences for name-giving patterns from a strictly onomasiological perspective (Štekauer *et al.* 2005 and Körtvélyessy 2009).

Different speech communities not only favor but also offer different models. In his etymological-onomasiological grid, Koch (2001, 2002) distinguishes between the cognitive-associative dimension (contiguity and similarity), the formal dimension (suffixation, prefixation, and composition), and the stratification dimension (indigenous material vs. borrowed elements). In other words, each new coinage is classified on three dimensions: the formal aspect, the cognitive-associative aspect, and the stratification aspect. Koch (2001: 25) claims that borrowings are very often neutral in their cognitive as well as in their formal dimension, in other words, they are simply adopted without any major formal or semantic change (e.g. nineteenth-century English *café* < French *café*, twentieth-century Italian *mouse* 'computer device' < English *mouse* 'animal; computer device,' both were imported from the donor culture together with their names). In this approach the distinctions between 'foreign word' and 'loan word' and between 'loan translation' and 'loan rendering' become irrelevant. Positive relations between the stratification dimension and both the formal and the cognitive-associative dimension are reminiscent of the classical opposition between importation and substitution, yet they introduce new problems when importation and substitution are seen in all sorts of formal and cognitive combinations: the problem is the difficulty of identifying, or spotting, the role of cognitive-associate models. While formal influence from another language or variety is easy to see (such as English *café*, Italian *mouse*, German *Sombrero*), foreign influence in the cognitive-associative dimension is hard to determine: did the meaning twentieth-century German *Maus* 'rodent' extend to 'computer device' due to the influence of English *mouse* or was it an independent development? Is it really the case that the relation of taxonomic subordination played a role in the importation of Spanish *sombrero* 'hat' into twentieth-century German? If Germans really took *Sombrero* directly from Spanish and not via English, it appears that German speakers, when importing the prototypical Mexican hat and searching for a name for it, just copied the word that Mexicans used to denote their prototypical member of the category 'hat,' namely the basic level term *sombrero*.[8] Perhaps the German-speakers did not know that the word referred not to a specific kind of hat, but to any type of hat, or that they did know, but that they also knew that the typical Mexican hat is broad-brimmed. From a semasiological perspective the development from Spanish *sombrero* 'hat' to German *sombrero* 'specific kind of hat (viz. with a broad brim, as worn in Mexico)' is an instance of specialization; from an onomasiological viewpoint this sense relation is very unlikely to be present in the minds of Germans. This suggests, again, that people do not adopt meanings, but references; in other words, not lexemes, but designations for a specific concept or referent (see Schelper 1995: 241). Therefore it is debatable whether, alongside the cognitive and formal relations, the stratification aspect should be seen as a third, equipollent dimension – except perhaps for fully bilingual societies. While semantic change and word-formation are phenomena connected with CoSMOS's onomasiological and onomatological levels, respectively, influence from a foreign tongue can occur at any of the stages of the word-finding, or name-giving, process.

Hermann Paul (1920: 392) sketched a distinction between the borrowing of actual foreign (external) forms and the borrowing of the internal structure of a foreign word – a distinction that would later be known as importation vs. substitution (see also Stanforth 2002: 806). However, it was not until Betz (1949, 1959), Haugen (1950, 1956), and Weinreich (1953) that the landmark theories on loan influence were formulated (see the two survey articles by Oksaar 1996: 4 and Stanforth 2002).

On the basis of his importation–substitution distinction[9], Haugen (1950: 214) distinguished three basic groups of borrowings: (1) loanwords, showing morphemic importation without substitution; (2) loanblends, showing morphemic substitution and importation; and (3) loanshifts, showing morphemic substitution without importation. In addition, Weinreich (1953: 47) differentiated between two mechanisms of lexical interference, namely those initiated by words that seem to be simple and those initiated by words that seem to be compound (including phrases). Haugen later refined his model (1956). His suggestions are included in Figure 15.3 and the comments that follow it. Hock and Joseph (1996: 275) investigated the forces that drive speakers in their choice of adoption or adaptation: they conclude that adoption is favored when there is a high similarity between the structure of the donor and the target language as well as political dominion and prestige, while adaptation is preferred when there is a low similarity of the structures of donor and recipient language as well as linguistic nationalism, or purism (see also Hock 1986: 409). Finally, Duckworth (1977) adds "partial substitution" to Betz's model so that we get the following nomenclature (see Figure 15.3; Haugen's terms are added in square brackets):

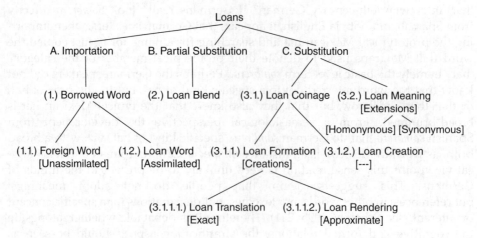

Figure 15.3. Types of borrowing

Betz and Duckworth define these categories as follows:

1.1. Non-integrated or weakly integrated words from a foreign language, such as English *ballet* in the form [bæˈleɪ], *envelope* in the form [ˈɑːnvəloʊp], *fiancé* in the form [fiˈɑ̃nseɪ] (all from prestigious French, in the seventeenth, eighteenth and nineteenth centuries respectively); twentieth-century Spanish *hippie* [ˈxipi] and *whisk(e)y* (both from British culture, the origin of both hippies and whisky); nineteenth-century English *weltanschauung* (< German *Weltanschauung*, at that time Germanophone philosophers were the most renowned), sixteenth-century English *sympathy* (< Greek *sympatheia*; Greek, together with Latin, has developed as the main source for creating technical terms in all academic fields since Humanism) and fifteenth-century English *compassion* (< Latin *compassio* < Greek *sympatheia*, possibly via French *compassion*); twentieth-century Italian, (American) Spanish and (especially American) Portuguese *mouse* 'computer device' (< American English *mouse* 'rodent; computer device,' the US being a dominant power in the computer industry).

1.2. Fully or strongly integrated words from a foreign language, such as English *ballet* in the form [ˈbæleɪ], *envelope* in the form [ˈenvələʊp], *fiancé* in the form [fiˈɔntseɪ] (all from French); Spanish *jipi* [ˈxipi] and *güisqui* (both from prestigious English).

2. Composite words, in which one part is borrowed and another substituted, such as Old English *Saturnes dæg* 'Saturday' (< Latin *Saturnis dies*, probably already in use when the Romans and Germanic tribes were direct neighbors on the European continent), twentieth-century German *Showgeschäft*, literally 'show-business', and *Live-Sendung*, literally 'live-broadcast' (< English *show business*

and *live broadcast*, due to the high prestige and model character of the US entertainment industry in the second half of the twentieth century).

3.1.1.1. Translation of the components of the foreign word, such as Old English *Mōnan dæg* 'Monday' (< Latin *Lunae dies*), twentieth-century French *gratte-ciel* and Spanish *rasca·cielos* both literally 'scrape-sky' (< English *sky-scraper*), nineteenth-century English *world view* (< German *Welt·anschauung*), fourteenth-century German *Mit·leid* 'sympathy' (< Latin *com·passio* < Greek *sym·patheia*), American Spanish *manzana de Adán* (< English *Adam's apple* vs. European Spanish *nuez [de la garganta]* literally: 'nut [of the throat]').

3.1.1.2. Translation of part of the components of the foreign word, such as fourteenth-century English *brother·hood* (< Latin *frater·nitas* [= Latin *frater* 'brother' + suffix]), twentieth-century German *Wolken·kratzer* literally: 'clouds-scraper' (< English *sky·scraper*).

3.1.2. Coinage independent of the foreign word, but created to replace a foreign word (so, strictly speaking, this does not fall into the group of 'foreign model' coinages), such as seventeenth-century English *brandy(-wine)* (to avoid *cognac* as a loan from French).

3.2. Indigenous word to which the meaning of the foreign word is passed on, such as Old English *cniht* 'servant + disciple of Jesus' and *heofon* 'sky, abode of the gods + Christian heaven' (< Latin *discipulus* 'student, disciple of Jesus' and *caelum* 'sky, abode of the gods, Christian heaven,' when the Latin Christian texts were disseminated in England); seventeenth-century German *Fall* 'action of falling + grammatical case' (< Latin *casus* 'action of falling, grammatical case;' Latin as a continued core source for technical terms since the Middle Ages to the present day); twentieth-century German *Maus*, (especially European) Spanish *ratón*, (European) Portuguese *rato*, Polish *mysz*, Dutch *muis*, Hungarian *éger*, Russian *mysh'* and French *souris* 'rodent + computer device' (< English *mouse* 'rodent, computer device').

Borrowings may come not only from another language, but also from a variety of the same language, that is, the variety of another social group. This is taken into account by Schöne (1951), Deroy (1956: 113, 116) and Hock (1986: 380, 388), but is often ignored in the literature. Some linguists deliberately exclude the possibility of borrowing from another variety from their definition of borrowing; Gusmani (1973: 7), for example, argues this on the grounds that otherwise virtually every word would be a borrowing, from one idiolect to another.

Some of the categories are hard to keep apart, especially when it comes to separating foreign words from loanwords. The crucial difference is the degree of integration. However, 'integrated' in what sense? In linguistic respects (system) (Weinreich 1953: 54) or in sociolinguistic respects (acceptance by speech community) (Polenz 1967: 72; Cannon 1999: 330) or in both (Gusmani 1973: 23)? Discussions do at least show that with these categories we are confronted with 'fuzzy edges,' to adopt a label from cognitive linguistics. In other words, there are prototypical, clearly foreign words such as English *coup d'état* (< French) and prototypical loanwords like Old English *wīn* 'wine' (< Latin *vīnum*; probably already borrowed when the Romans and Germanic tribes were direct neighbors on the European continent, in the fifth century or earlier) and many intermediate stages along a continuum (see also Deroy 1956: 224). This adaptation seems to be achieved through the interplay of generation-independent increase in usage frequencies (ousting competing lexemes) and phonological-morphological integration (see also Poplack and Sankoff 1984: 128–31).

When it comes to hybrid composites, mention can also be made of "tautological compounds" (Gusmani 1973: 51; Glahn 2000: 46): compounds where a native morpheme is added to a foreign morpheme, the sense of the former being already encompassed in the latter. Examples are Middle English *peacock* (first element from Latin *pavo* 'peacock'), Old English *porlēac* 'porridge' (first element from Latin *porrus* 'porridge' + Old English *lēac* 'porridge'). It has been said that 'tautological compounds' are coined because speakers do not (or no longer) know the exact meaning of the foreign word (Carstensen 1965: 265; Fleischer and Barz 1995: 126; Tesch 1978: 127). This is plausible, but it cannot be the only reason. Does the choice between *crimson* and *crimson red* depend on the speaker's knowledge of the exact meaning of *crimson*? Moreover, the formal extension of *pea* to *peacock* does not necessarily make the identification of the corresponding concept easier.

It is difficult to integrate 'pseudo-loans' into such models (Grzega 2003). Pseudo-loans have been grouped into three types (Carstensen 1980a, 1980b, 1981): (i) semantic pseudo-loans: a foreign word gains a sense it did not possess in the original language: for example, the twentieth-century German words *Start* in the sense of 'take-off,' *Oldtimer* in the sense of 'veteran car,' *checken* in the sense of 'understand,' and *to strafe* in the sense of 'to attack by shooting from airplanes flying low in the sky' (after German *Gott strafe England* 'God may punish England;' (ii) lexical pseudo-loans: the word looks foreign or is coined with foreign components, but does not exist as such in the foreign language. Examples include twentieth-century German *Handy* 'cell phone' and *Showmaster* 'host,' fifteenth-century English *difficult* (back-formation from *difficulty*; in French the adjective is *difficile*); (iii) morphological pseudo-loans: combinations of lexical morphemes that are not exactly the same as the formations in the foreign language, such as twentieth-century German *Happy-End* for English *happy ending*, twentieth-century English *blitz* (ellipsis of German *Blitzkrieg*). Pseudo-loans can be considered as a process of 'borrowing' encouraged by a foreign language's prestige and rules (Schottmann 1977: 27). Since the twentieth century, this status is accorded to (American) English in everyday language and by Latin/Greek for technical terms, which, to a large degree, could also be termed pseudo-loans, as the things did not even exist in Latin and Ancient Greek times (e.g. English *telephone*, French *télé-phone*, Italian *telefono*, Spanish *teléfono*, Dutch *telefoon*, German *Telefon*, Polish *telefon*).

It needs to be stressed that the above three-fold classification is understandable in terms of an analytical, synchronic approach. A synthetical, onomasiological perspective, however, explains 'pseudo'-loans differently. Here it is vital to check the source language at the time of the first attestation of the word in the target language. This also includes the exact analysis of semantic pseudo-loans: was the deviant sense already present at the point of borrowing (that is, was the foreign word misunderstood or misused?) or is the deviant sense a later, secondary, independent, and conscious development in the target language? (see also Carstensen 1965: 256; Bellmann 1971; Höfler 1990: 99).

Consequently, lexical pseudo-loans such as German *Handy* and *Showmaster* are not (necessarily) to be considered as reflexes of existing foreign words. What is clear is that they have been coined with foreign material (perhaps due to the prestige of the foreign language). In fact, we can observe that these are always morphologically motivated words: a word can be understood as a pseudo-loan only if it shows (at least in part) motivation. 'Morphological pseudo-loans,' as they have been called, are either secondary developments or genuine minor changes in the morphological structure. Thus, in *happy ending*, the derivational suffix *-ing* may not have been felt necessary for comprehension and was thus omitted in German *Happy End*. As to semantic pseudo-loans, a more in-depth treatment of the examples above suggests that German *Oldtimer* and German *Start* both were borrowed with their original English senses, but show secondary semantic extensions based on similarity between the original concept denoted and the secondary one.

In summary, we can distinguish between morpho-lexical pseudo-loans, where the word in the replica language does not exist in the model language, such as German *Handy* 'cellular phone,' German *Showmaster* 'host', and sem(antic)o-lexical pseudo-loans, where the (composite) word in the replica language does exist in the model language, but is 'mis-used' in the replica language. In any case, one should only speak of semo-lexical pseudo-loans when the aberrant sense is already there at the time of the 'borrowing' process. When the aberrant sense is secondary, we have an example of semantic change.

The example of German *auspowern* '1. to impoverish, 2. to elbow out' illustrates the force of folk-etymology that is said to be especially prominent with loans. This word was originally used in sense 1 only and pronounced ['aospovɐn]. It is a nineteenth-century derivation of the German reflex of French *pauvre* [povr] 'poor.' With the growing prestige of (American) English, however, the word was, in the late twentieth century, folk-etymologically more and more frequently realized as ['aospaʊɐn] (cf. English *power*). Sixteenth-century English *gooseberry* seems to represent an apt example from English, regardless of whether the ultimate source is German (dialectal) *Krausbeere*, Dutch *kruisbezie* or French *groseille*. Taking into account the weak motivation for naming this specific berry after the goose and the strong similarity of the sounds in the English and foreign words, it seems hard to deny any relation. Another case is seventeenth-century French *contredanse* (French *contre* 'counter, opposite') from English *country dance*. For the most part, though, folk-etymologies are not triggered by the name-giver and borrower, but by the speech community, which subsequently tries to adopt the word.

5. Social Aspects and the Spread of Innovations

The spread of an innovation (and its speed) seems to depend on the prestige of the innovator and the structure of the social networks in which the innovation starts (see Milroy and Milroy 1985; Labov 2001; Ogura and Wang 2008; and Chapter 24 in this *Handbook*). Special mention should be made of the spread of loanwords as these include integration processes of various kinds, phonetic, morphosyntactic, semantic, stylistic, and social. Often – perhaps almost always – a speech community fails to reproduce the foreign sound chain, a fact that was observed by Paul (1920: 394). As a consequence, the clear integration of a foreign phoneme – in Haugen's (1950: 226) terminology 'phonemic importation' – is comparatively rare (see also Deroy 1956: 239). This includes the combination of sounds, or phonotactic rules. Japanese, for example, allows only the syllabic form consonant-vowel-(vowel)-(/n/) and has therefore integrated English *strike* in the twentieth century as *suturaiku*. On the other hand, the combination of initial [s] plus consonant is mostly kept in loanwords in present-day Austrian Standard German (e.g. *Start*). The selection of grammatical patterns is an issue in inflectional languages, and the solutions are not always straightforward: German *E-Mail*, for instance, is used either as a feminine noun like its semantic cognate German *die* Post 'mail, post' or as a neuter noun like its semantic cognate German *das* Schreiben 'letter.' Bellmann (1971: 36) and Tesch (1978: 128) noted that a word also needs to be integrated semantically: what position does it take in a word-field? How does it or should it differ from already existent lexemes on the denotational, connotational, and collocational levels (for example, German technical *Appendicitis* vs. everyday *Blinddarmentzündung* 'appendicitis'). In brief, the effects and roles of the aspects of integration described here vary not only from language to language, but also from region to region, social class to social class, and generation to generation. By and large, however, as already stated, integration seems to be achieved in a simultaneous progress on the usage frequency level (banning competing lexemes) and the phonological-morphological level (see also Poplack and Sankoff 1984: 128–31).

6. Conclusion

In conclusion, the choice of variants and the coinage of new variants for a certain lexical-semantic variable are deeply connected to sociocultural, or sociohistorical, aspects. This starts with the categorization of a referent: a referent is classified into one or more culture-bound, or society-bound, concepts. If the classification is followed by a lexemic innovation, this may be linked to sociocultural factors, too. Lexemic innovations may be caused by what the society's world looks like (objectively), by what it looks like for a speaker or a society (subjectively), by what a speaker or a society wants the world to look like, by what a speaker or a society wants the language to look like, or by how the speaker wants to be perceived by an audience. Lexemic innovations may also be triggered by other societies, due either to direct contact with people from neighboring cultures or to the prestige of a culture that may be near or distant. For a lexemic innovation, a speaker or a society may resort to another society's variants for a lexical-semantic variable as a cognitive-associative or a formal model for a lexemic innovation. Finally, the spread of an innovation is an entirely social process: it depends on how the society cherishes the innovation and the innovator.

NOTES

1 This comes close to what Nerlich and Clarke 1992 call a 'meta-semantic expert system.'

2 The adoption of an already existing lexeme of the speaker's own language (semantic change) occurs in various subtypes: (i) metaphor ('similar-to' relation); (ii) metonymy ('neighbor-of' relation); (iii) synecdoche ('part-of' relation); (iv) generalization and specialization ('kind-of' relation); (v) cohyponymic transfer ('sibling-of' relation); (vi) antiphrasis and auto-antonymy ('contrast-to' relation); (vii) conceptual recategorization. Semantic change also includes the phenomenon traditionally known as 'semantic loan,' the copy of an instance of polysemy found in a donor language. The ideas for the sub-organization of semantic change in Grzega (2000, 2004) owe a lot to the work of Blank (1997, 1999, 2001) and Koch (2002).

3 This covers the two phenomena traditionally referred to as 'compounds' and 'derivations,' 'loan translations' and 'loan renditions.' Several types of compositions can then be distinguished: (i) 'complete complex structure,' or complex composites: complete determinative composites with a base and a so-called mark, consisting of a determining component and a determined component; (ii) 'incomplete complex structure 1': composites with absence of determining component of the mark; (iii) 'incomplete complex structure 2': composites with absence of determined component of the mark; (iv) 'incomplete complex structure B': composites with absence of the base; (v) 'simplex structure,' or simplex composites: no determinative relationship between the elements; and (vi) 'copulative structure': copulatives composites. The ideas for the sub-organization of word-formation (Grzega 2002b, 2004) owe a lot to the works by Štekauer (1998, 2001).

4 In a broad sense, this includes the phenomena traditionally known as *folk-etymologies*, although these arise unintentionally.

5 This process must not be confused with the force triggering the change; wordplaying refers strictly to a play with forms that cannot be subsumed under any of the other processes mentioned here, such as the English backslang word *earth* 'three.'

6 Among these, the following sub-types can be distinguished: (a) morpheme deletion (ellipsis); (b) morpheme shortening (clipping); (c) morpheme symbolization (acronyms, including alphabetisms, and short forms).

7 The major prestige languages in the history of Europe are Latin, French, and English, and to a limited degree, Italian, German, and Arabic (see Grzega 2006: 73–120).

8 That prototypical members are normally referred to by the corresponding basic level term and not by the subordinate level term is deducible from a number of studies; see, among others, Mangold-Allwinn *et al.* (1995: 126, 153).

9 Hock and Joseph (1996: 275) use the terms *adoption* and *adaptation*.

REFERENCES

Bellmann, G. (1971) *Slavoteutonica*, de Gruyter, Berlin.

Betz, W. (1949) *Deutsch und Lateinisch: Die Lehnbildungen der althochdeutschen Benediktinerregel*, Bouvier, Bonn.

Betz, W. (1959) Lehnwörter und Lehnprägungen im Vor- und Frühdeutschen. In F. Maurer and F. Stroh (eds.), *Deutsche Wortgeschichte, vol. 1* (2nd edn), Schmidt, Berlin, pp. 127–47.

Blank, A. (1997) *Prinzipien des lexikalischen Bedeutungswandels am Beispiel der romanischen Sprachen*, Niemeyer, Tübingen.

Blank, A. (1999) Why do new meanings occur? A cognitive typology of the motivations for lexical semantic change. In A. Blank and P. Koch (eds.), *Historical semantics and cognition*, Mouton de Gruyter, Berlin, pp. 61–90.

Blank, A. (2001) Pathways of lexicalization. In M. Haspelmath *et al.* (eds.), pp. 1596–1608.

Brent, B. (1992) *Ethnobiological Classification: Principles of Categorization of Plants and Animals in Traditional Societies*, Princeton University Press, Princeton.

Brown, C.H. (2001) Lexical typology from an anthropological point of view. In M. Haspelmath *et al.* (eds.), pp. 1178–90.

Cannon, G. (1999) Problems in studying loans. *Proceedings of the Annual Meeting of the Berkeley Linguistics Society* 25. 326–36.

Carstensen, B. (1965) *Englische Einflüsse auf die deutsche Sprache nach 1945*, Winter, Heidelberg.

Carstensen, B. (1980a) German morphological adaptation of English lexical material. In W. Hüllen (ed.), *Understanding Bilingualism*, Peter Lang, Frankfurt am Main, pp. 13–24.

Carstensen, B. (1980b) Semantische Scheinentlehnungen des Deutschen aus dem Englischen. In W. Viereck (ed.), *Studien zum Einfluß der englischen Sprache auf das Deutsche*, Narr, Tübingen, pp. 77–100.

Carstensen, B. (1981) Lexikalische Scheinentlehnungen des Deutschen aus dem Englischen. In W. Kühlwein, G.

Thome, and W. Wilss (eds.), *Kontrastive Linguistik und Übersetzungswissenschaft*, Fink, München, pp. 175–82.

Coulmas, F. (ed.) (1989) *Language Adaptation*, Cambridge University Press, Cambridge.

Cruse, D.A., Hundsnurcher, F., Job, M., and Lutzeier, P.R. (eds.) (2002–5) *Lexicology: An International Handbook on the Nature and Structure of Words and Vocabularies/ Lexikologie: Ein internationales Handbuch zur Natur und Struktur von Wörtern und Wortschätzen*, Walter de Gruyter, Berlin.

Dauzat, A. (1949) *Précis d'histoire de la langue française et du vocabulaires français*, Larousse, Paris.

Deroy, L. (1956) *L'emprunt Linguistique*, Les Belles Lettres, Paris.

Duckworth, D. (1977) Zur terminologischen und systematischen Grundlage der Forschung auf dem Gebiet der englisch-deutschen Interferenz: Kritische Übersicht und neuer Vorschlag. In H. Kolb and H. Lauffer (eds.), *Sprachliche Interferenz: Festschrift für Werner Betz zum 65. Geburtstag*, Niemeyer, Tübingen, pp. 36–56.

Fleischer, W. and Barz, I. (1995) *Wortbildung der deutschen Gegenwartssprache* (2nd, revised edn), Niemeyer, Tübingen.

Geeraerts, D. (1997) *Diachronic Prototype Semantics: A Contribution to Historical Lexicology*, Clarendon Press, Oxford.

Glahn, R. (2000) *Der Einfluß des Englischen auf gesprochene deutsche Gegenwartssprache*, Peter Lang, Frankfurt am Main.

Grice, H.P. (1975) Logic and conversation. In P. Cole and J.L. Morgan (eds.), *Syntax and Semantics, vol. 3*, Academic Press, New York, pp. 41–58.

Grzega, J. (2000) Historical semantics in the light of cognitive linguistics: Aspects of a new reference book reviewed. *Arbeiten aus Anglistik und Amerikanistik* 25: 233–44.

Grzega, J. (2002a) Some aspects of modern diachronic onomasiology. *Linguistics* 44: 1021–45.

Grzega, J. (2002b) Some thoughts on a cognitive onomasiological approach to word-formation with special reference to English. *Onomasiology Online* 3: 1–29. www.onomasiology.de [accessed June 30, 2009].

Grzega, J. (2003) Borrowing as a word-finding process in cognitive historical onomasiology. *Onomasiology Online* 4: 22–42. www.onomasiology.de [accessed June 30, 2009].

Grzega, J. (2004) *Bezeichnungswandel: Wie, Warum, Wozu? – Ein Beitrag zur englischen und allgemeinen Onomasiologie*, Winter, Heidelberg.

Grzega, J. (2006) *Eurolinguistischer Parcours: Kernwissen zur europäischen Sprachkultur.* Frankfurt, IKO.

Grzega, J. (2007) Summary, supplement and index for J. Grzega (2004). *Onomasiology Online* 8: 18–196. www.onomasiology.de [accessed June 30, 2009].

Gusmani, R. (1973) *Aspetti del prestito linguistico*, Libreria Scientifica, Naples.

Haspelmath, M., König, E., Oesterreicher, W., and Raible, W. (eds.) (2001) *Language Typology and Language Universals: An International Handbook/Sprachtypologie und sprachliche Universalien: Ein internationales Handbuch*, Walter de Gruyter, Berlin.

Haugen, E. (1950) The analysis of linguistic borrowing. *Language* 26: 210–31.

Haugen, E. (1956) Review: Helmut Gneuss, *Lehnbildungen und Lehnbedeutungen im Altenglischen*, Berlin 1955. *Language* 26: 210–31.

Hock, H. (1986) *Principles of Historical Linguistics*, Mouton de Gruyter, Berlin.

Hock, H.H. and Joseph, B.D. (1996) *Language History, Language Change, and Language Relationship: An Introduction to Historical and Comparative Linguistics*, Mouton de Gruyter, Berlin.

Höfler, M. (1990) Zum Problem der Scheinentlehnung. *Archiv für das Studium der neueren Sprachen und Literaturen* 227: 96–107.

Keller, R. (1995) *Zeichentheorie: Zu einer Theorie semiotischen Wissens*, Francke, Tübingen/Basel.

Koch, P. (2001) Bedeutungswandel und Bezeichnungswandel: Von der kognitiven Semasiologie zur kognitiven

Onomasiologie. *Zeitschrift für Literaturwissenschaft und Linguistik* 121: 7–36.

Koch, P. (2002) Lexical typology from a cognitive and linguistic point of view. In D.A. Cruse *et al.* (eds.) (2002–5), vol. 1, pp. 1142–78.

Körtvélyessy, L. (2009) Productivity and creativity in word-formation: A sociolinguistic perspective. *Onomasiology Online* 10: 1–22 www.onomasiology.de [accessed June 30, 2009].

Labov, W. (1966) *The Social Stratification of English in New York City*, Center for Applied Linguistics, Washington DC.

Labov, W. (1994) *Principles of Linguistic Change, Vol. 1. Internal Factors*, Blackwell, Oxford.

Labov, W. (2001) *Principles of Linguistic Change, Vol. 2. Social factors*, Blackwell, Oxford.

Labov, W. (2010) *Principles of Linguistic Change, Vol. 3. Cognitive and cultural factors*, Blackwell, Oxford.

Mangold-Allwinn, R., Baratteli, S., Kiefer, M., and Koelvin, H.G. (1995) *Wörter für Dinge: Von flexiblen Konzepten zu Benennungen*, Westdeutscher Verlag, Opladen.

Milroy, J. and Milroy, L. (1985) Linguistic change, social network and speaker innovation. *Journal of Linguistics* 21: 339–84.

Nerlich, B. and Clarke, D.D. (1992) Outline of a model for semantic change. In G. Kellermann and M.D. Morrissey (eds.), *Diachrony with Synchrony: Language History and Cognition*, Peter Lang, Frankfurt am Main, pp. 125–41.

Ogura, M. and Wang, W.S.-Y. (2008) Dynamic dialectology and social networks. In M. Dossena, R. Dury, and M. Gotti (eds.), *English Historical Linguistics 2006. Volume III: Geo-historical variation in English*, John Benjamins, Amsterdam, pp. 131–51.

Oksaar, E. (1996) The history of Contact Linguistics as a discipline. In H. Goebl, P.H. Nelde, Z. Stary, and W. Walck (eds.), *Kontaktlinguistik/Contact Linguistics/ Linguistique de contact*, Mouton de Gruyter, Berlin, pp. 1–12.

Paul, H. (1920) *Prinzipien der Sprachgeschichte* (5th edn), Niemeyer, Tübingen.

Polenz, P. von (1967) Fremdwort und Lehnwort sprachwissenschaftlich betrachtet. *Muttersprache* 77: 65–80.

Poplack, S. and Sankoff, D. (1984) Borrowing: the synchrony of integration. *Linguistics* 22: 99–135.

Schelper, D. (1995) *Anglizismen in der Pressesprache der BRD, der DDR, Österreichs und der Schweiz: Eine vergleichende, typologische und chronologische Studie*, Ph.D. dissertation Université Laval, Québec.

Schöne, M. (1951) *Vie et Mort des Mots*, Presses Universitaires de France, Paris.

Schottmann, H. (1977) Die Beschreibung der Interferenz. In H. Kolb and H. Lauffer (eds.), *Sprachliche Interferenz: Festschrift für Werner Betz zum 65. Geburtstag*, Niemeyer, Tübingen, pp. 13–35.

Stanforth, A.W. (2002) Effects of language contact on the vocabulary: An overview. In D.A. Cruse *et al.* (eds.), vol. 1, pp. 805–13.

Štekauer, P. (1998) *An Onomasiological Theory of Word-formation in English*, John Benjamins, Amsterdam.

Štekauer, P. (2001) Fundamental principles of an onomasiological theory of English word-formation. *Onomasiology Online* 2 www.onomasiology.de [accessed June 30, 2009].

Štekauer, P., Chapman, D., Tomaščíková, S., and Franco, Š. (2005) Word-formation as creativity within productivity constraints: sociolinguistic evidence. *Onomasiology Online* 6: 1–55 www.onomasiology.de [accessed June 30, 2009].

Tesch, G. (1978) *Linguale Interferenz: Theoretische, terminologische und methodische Grundlagen zu ihrer Erforschung*, Narr, Tübingen.

Traugott, E.C. and Dasher, R.B. (2002) *Regularity in Semantic Change*, Cambridge University Press, Cambridge.

Weinreich, U. (1953) *Languages in Contact: Findings and Problems*, Mouton, The Hague.

16 Pragmatic Variables

ANDREAS H. JUCKER AND IRMA TAAVITSAINEN

1. Introduction

In this chapter we discuss pragmatic variables and their role in socio-historical linguistics and neighboring fields such as historical pragmatics, comparing them with socio-demographic variables. In recent years, the analysis of pragmatic units in the history of English and other languages has gained ground, and such analyses implicitly or explicitly make reference to contextual features to account for their occurrence and use.

For the purpose of this chapter we are using a broad, Continental European view of pragmatics. The Anglo-American view of pragmatics is largely restricted to topics such as implicature, presupposition, speech acts, and deixis. This conception of pragmatics is also called the "component view" (see Huang 2007: 4, 2010: 341): pragmatics is seen as a component of linguistic analysis parallel to semantics, syntax, and morphology.

The wider continental European conception of pragmatics can be defined as "a general cognitive, social, and cultural perspective on linguistic phenomena in relation to their usage in forms of behaviour" (Verschueren 1999: 7). Here, the social and cultural context of language use plays a significant role. Pragmatics is seen as a functional perspective on all levels of language; this approach is therefore called the "perspective view" (Huang 2007: 4, 2010: 341). It encompasses a much larger range of potential pragmatic variables than the more restricted view of Anglo-American pragmatics. Mey – like Verschueren also a proponent of the Continental European conception of pragmatics – defines it as the study of "the use of language in human communication as determined by the conditions of

The Handbook of Historical Sociolinguistics, First Edition. Edited by Juan Manuel Hernández-Campoy and Juan Camilo Conde-Silvestre.
© 2014 John Wiley & Sons, Ltd. Published 2014 by John Wiley & Sons, Ltd.

society" (2001: 6). We will argue below that these conditions of society are a crucial part of what we want to call pragmatic variables.

We shall begin by discussing language variation and language variability as theoretical points of departure (section 2) and by defining the difference between socio-demographic variables and linguistic variables (section 3). In section 4, we discuss variability studies and their applicability to pragmatics, and in section 5, we will give an overview of relevant work on a range of linguistic units (expressions, utterances, discourses or conversations, and discourse domains).

2. Variation and Variability in Language

The variationist view serves as the basis of all sociolinguistic studies. Language and language use are patterned both socially and linguistically and the principles behind these patterns can be discovered by relating linguistic variation to underlying socio-demographic parameters. The range of possibilities from which choices can be made varies over time, as new variants emerge and old ones fade away. This is true at all levels of linguistic description. At the level of phonology, some people start to pronounce a word in a slightly different way and thus produce a choice between different pronunciations. Over time, the new pronunciation may oust the old pronunciation after a relatively short or long period of coexistence. The same is true at the level of morphology, where innovations in inflectional or derivational morphemes lead to new word forms, or at the level of the lexicon, where new words or new meanings for old words may offer choices within a language. This variability in language has been termed "orderly heterogeneity" by Weinreich, Labov, and Herzog (1968). The patterns of this heterogeneity can be discovered through a systematic empirical investigation of attested variants in relation to various parameters.

Pragmatics brings an additional perspective to the variationist paradigm. Variability as a property of language has been defined as the range of possibilities from which choices can be made and is a dynamic notion, as "at any given moment in the course of interaction, a choice may rule out alternatives or create new ones" (Verschueren 1999: 59). Thus it is closely connected to one of the core issues of pragmatics: negotiability. The underlying socio-linguistic parameters cannot explain the shifts, instead, appeals must be made to contextual cues and pragmatic principles. Variability can be observed in all pragmatic aspects of language use, in speech act realizations as well as conversational implicatures.

3. Linguistic and Socio-demographic Variables

The linguistic tool for the investigation of this variability in language is the linguistic variable. A linguistic variable is an item in the structure of language that can be realized in different ways, either by different speakers or by the same speaker on different occasions. Prototypical examples are words or morphemes that have different pronunciations, such as the final sound in the pronunciation of words like *working* or *running*, which can be realized as an alveolar nasal [n] or as a velar nasal [ŋ]. Similarly, the pronunciation of words such as *bar* or *barn* can include an [r] or not, [Ø]. But linguistic variables are not restricted to pronunciation. Well-known cases are different realizations of the relative pronoun – *who*, *that*, *whom*, Ø – the realization of copula *be* – *is*, *be*, Ø – in sentences such as *She is happy*. What all these variables have in common is that the basic meaning of the sentence that contains them does not change according to which variant is used. In Labov's (1972: 271) words, "social and stylistic variation presuppose the option of saying 'the same thing' in several ways: that is, the variants are identical in reference or truth value, but opposed in their social and/or stylistic significance." This requirement of 'sameness' is easier to apply to phonological variation than to variation at higher levels of linguistic analysis (see Lavandera 1978), as phonological units do not carry independent meanings. Units at higher levels have meanings, and, therefore, the choice of one unit rather than another may be guided by considerations of meaning.

After the identification of the linguistic variable, the next step in the analysis is to find out who uses the different realizational variants, in order to correlate the linguistic variable with socio-demographic variables of region, social class, ethnicity, age, or gender (see the other chapters in Part III of this *Handbook*). In this step, researchers ascertain, for instance, how often members of one particular social class on average use each of the variants of a given variable and how this compares to the members of other social classes.

Typically, linguistic variables are treated as dependent variables. They comprise the linguistic items under investigation, and the investigation focuses on how their realization depends on the socio-demographic variables of the speakers, the latter therefore being the independent variables, which are properties of the different groups of speakers whose use of the linguistic variable is under investigation. But linguistic variables can also be treated as independent variables if their influence on the realization of some other linguistic variables is under investigation. The choice between the genitive and the *of*-construction (*the reports' publication* versus *the publication of the report*), for instance, has been shown to depend both on socio-demographic variables (occurrence in up-market or down-market newspapers), on linguistic variables (type of internal modification of both parts of the construction) and on specific pragmatic variables (the end-focus and the end-weight principles) (Jucker 1993).

4. Pragmatic Variation and Variational Pragmatics

Pragmatic variables are of a different type altogether and much less is known about them. In fact, Schneider and Barron (2008b: 2–3) have pointed out that so far variationists have rarely investigated pragmatic variables, while pragmaticists have rarely investigated the social or regional distribution of their units of investigation.

> In short, dialectology has focused overwhelmingly on the central levels of the language system, i.e. on pronunciation, vocabulary and grammar, whereas language use in terms of communicative functions, linguistic action and interactive behaviour has been almost completely ignored. This applies to traditional dialect geography as well as to contemporary social dialectology, and also to the study of national varieties of pluricentric languages.
>
> (Schneider and Barron 2008b: 3)

One reason for this almost complete lack of work by variationists on pragmatic variables may be their preoccupation with the analysis of "saying 'the same thing' in several ways" (Labov 1972: 271, see above). Pragmatic variables rarely – if ever – provide clear cases of saying the same thing in several ways, and they are, therefore, less obvious candidates for variationist studies (but see section 5 below).

Schneider and Barron (2008b: 4–7) identify the same lack of work on the variation of communicative functions on the side of the pragmaticists. In the first decades of the relatively brief history of research in pragmatics, the focus was on universal principles of communication and on establishing frameworks of analysis with universal applicability[1]. In reaction, later work started to look more carefully at cross-cultural variation, as in the work by Wierzbicka (1985) on Australian English in comparison to Polish, or Blum-Kulka *et al.*'s (1989) and Trosborg's (1994) work on a whole range of languages.

> Problematically, however, underlying much cross-cultural pragmatic research is a basic assumption that language communities of native speakers are homogeneous wholes. Language variation is, thus, abstracted away.
>
> (Schneider and Barron 2008b: 5)

Schneider and Barron (2008b: 2) rightly identify this lack of work both on the side of the variationists and on the side of the pragmaticists as a serious research gap and propose to fill it by setting up a field of variational pragmatics. In such a research paradigm, communicative functions, speech actions, and communicative principles would be investigated in the context of their intra-language variability involving all levels of socio-demographic differentiation: regional, social, and ethnic, as well as gender- and age-related differentiation. Schneider and Barron's (2008a) seminal volume on variational pragmatics covers only regional differentiation, but the other levels clearly also provide very promising research opportunities.

In view of the dearth of relevant work, it is not surprising that pragmatic variables have not yet established themselves as commonly recognized research tools. In fact, such variables would comprise both dependent (i.e. realizational) and independent (i.e. contextual) variables. Realizational pragmatic variables are a special type of the linguistic variables described above, but with a focus on a pragmatic unit of a language instead of a phonological, morphological, or syntactic unit. Relevant examples are address terms (*tu* versus *vous* in French, for instance), discourse markers, different types of speech acts or different types of politeness strategies. For these variables it is perhaps even more difficult than for other non-phonological variables to claim that they comprise options of saying 'the same thing'. Thus the question is whether we can postulate any conditioned variation for realizational pragmatic variables at all.

For address terms such as *tu* and *vous*, a truth-conditional equivalence can be assumed whichever pronoun is being used in addressing someone because both pronouns are used to refer to the addressee. The choice between the two is clearly conditioned by a variety of factors, such as familiarity of the speaker with the addressee, and the power differential between them.

It is usually claimed that discourse markers, at least the prototypical ones, lack propositional meaning. The choice of one discourse marker rather than another, therefore, could also serve as a realizational pragmatic variable to the extent that it is possible to spell out the conditions under which one marker is chosen rather than another.

Pragmatic variables can also take the form of independent (contextual) variables that influence the realization of specific linguistic items. This type of pragmatic variable comprises contextual elements. Using the same examples again, the conditions that govern the choice between *tu* and *vous* can be seen as a pragmatic context variable in the intended sense. Another would be the principle of placing communicatively more important information towards the end, which influences the choice between the genitive and the *of*-construction.

In the narrow, mainly Anglo-American view, contextual pragmatic variables would be restricted to the linguistic context. There is, however, clearly an overlap with the stylistic variables mentioned above. The formality of a situation conditions the realization of linguistic units at all levels. In the broader, mainly Continental European, view of pragmatics, a much larger range of contextual variables can be taken into consideration, including the social roles of the conversational participants, their relationships, the developing power differential in a conversation, and even cultural considerations.

In the context of historical studies, the problems of identifying pragmatic variables are considerably exacerbated. In many cases, we do not have sufficient information about the socio-demographics of the speakers and addressees of recorded interactions, or we have only limited access to the common ground that they must have shared in order to interpret each other's utterances.

In the following section, we will survey a range of relevant work that could be re-conceptualized in terms of pragmatic variables even though – as a rule – this term is not used in this research, and in fact in this section we extend the discussion somewhat.

5. Units of Analysis

Jucker (2008) proposed a categorization of the pragmatic units under investigation, which parallels the classical structuralist levels of linguistic analysis from phonetics and phonology to morphology, syntax, and semantics. In pragmatic-conversational analysis, the following levels are distinguished: expression, utterance, discourse, and discourse domain. The following exposition uses this categorization and focuses on the linguistic features that have been discussed in the literature and can be re-conceptualized as pragmatic variables.

5.1   Expressions

Our smallest unit of analysis contains address terms and inserts (Biber *et al.* 1999: 1082). Pronouns of address are perhaps the most obvious candidates as pragmatic variables. In many languages their choice is dependent on purely socio-demographic factors. In German, for instance, up to a certain age a young person is addressed with the T-form, and in Swedish the king is always addressed with the polite and distant third person ('His Majesty'), although otherwise the demo-cratic T-form is used throughout society. In some languages, however, there is room for negotiating interpersonal relations and their moment-by-moment changes with the choice of pronouns, as, for instance, in Middle and Early Modern English. There is a great deal of research that investigates the precise conditions of their use: who uses *ye* and who uses *thou* in which situations, and what the motivations for shifts expressing transient states of mind could be. For example, there are several studies on address in Shakespeare and Chaucer (e.g. Brown and Gilman 1989; Busse 2002; Jucker 2006; Mazzon 2000, 2003; Stein 2003).

On a theoretical level, Burnley (2003) traces pathways of choice paying atten-tion to socio-demographic parameters and discourse-based choices of T-forms, but his flow chart also includes momentary shifts for affective, rhetorical, or generic reasons (2003: 29). French is likely to have given models to English texts, but the area has not been studied in depth. Medieval verse texts did not give support for the arbitrariness of the choice or random mixing of *tu* and *vus*, but pronouns "occur mostly in blocks of matching speeches and sudden changes seem to be properly motivated" (Hunt 2003: 57).

Inserts can be grouped into several major functional types with overlapping shades of meaning, and individual members of this category can be versatile and take on different conversational roles. For example, the most common of the present-day interjections, *oh*, has an exclamatory function expressive of the speaker's emotion, but also functions as a discourse marker to introduce utter-ances, or as a response to a previous utterance. Often it combines with other inserts. The core function today appears to convey surprise, unexpectedness, or emotional arousal in response to something the speaker has just found out or noticed. According to Biber *et al.* (1999: 1083–84), *ah* and *wow* are less routine expressions with a greater intensity of emotional involvement than *oh*.

Both interjections and discourse markers have received a great deal of attention in historical studies. They have been examined from different perspectives, taking their modern functions as a point of departure, but elaborating various aspects. However, their dependence on socio-demographic variables has not been inves-tigated to any great extent. Holmes' early paper (1986) on the function of the discourse marker *you know* in women's and men's speech in present-day New Zealand English is a notable exception in this respect.

So far, studies on both modern languages and historical stages of particular languages have mainly focused on the pragmatic negotiation of meanings, speakers' attitudes and on how they reflect a change in the situation at hand. Person (2009) takes modern conversation analysis as his guideline and discusses the uses of *oh* in Shakespeare's plays. He distinguishes the same functions as Heritage (1984; see also 1998, 2002), and lays special emphasis on the discourse marker function of signaling a change of state to show that the speaker has experienced a change of mental status and is responding to a remark that has brought something new to the situation. It works locally and signals a momentary shift in the interactants' negotiation of meaning.

Lutzky (2008) is one of the rare historical studies that directly correlates the use of a discourse marker with socio-demographic variables. On the basis of her data from Shakespeare, she claims that the discourse marker *marry* was predominantly used by the lower ranks of society and mostly in conversations with social superiors. And even though she could not detect any differences in the frequency of *marry* between male and female speakers, she observed that it was used more often in mixed-gender than in same-gender interactions.

Aspects of written language and conventionalized genre-specific uses of interjections have been the focus of Taavitsainen's studies (1995, 1998). Gender aspects have also been touched upon, as the functions of 'aahs' and 'oohs' change in romantic prose over a long diachronic perspective from a text-sequencing function to gender-specific uses. Romantic heroines in Gothic novels express emotions by frequent exclamations. The feature of excessive outbursts of emotion is developed in a caricature by Jane Austen (1775–1817) in *Northanger Abbey*, gaining a new function in character description at the same time (Taavitsainen 1998).

5.2   *Utterances*

The utterance level is represented by historical speech act studies. The first diachronic studies were published at the turn of the millennium, and a great deal has been published since then (see, for example, Arnovick 1999, and the papers in Jucker and Taavitsainen 2008). Studies have mostly focused on methodology and data problems, and have been conducted on individual speech acts, such as requests, apologies, insults, and compliments. However, studies that correlate the use of specific speech acts with socio-demographic variables are still quite rare. For present-day English, it has been shown, for instance, that women pay and receive more compliments than men (Holmes 1988, 1995), and that their compliments are of a different kind.

Taavitsainen and Jucker (2008) pointed out the same tendency in a historical study on English fictional materials. In a corpus of literary texts from Early Modern and Late Modern English, compliments also turned out to be gendered speech acts. Both male and female authors include compliments in their fiction. Female characters receive praise for their looks and often turn it down as flattery, while in the few cases that men receive compliments, they accept it by bowing.

The descriptions are firmly embedded in social practices and norms of appropriate behavior.

Some work has already been carried out that suggests that in the eighteenth century, in particular, general patterns of linguistic behavior and communicative behavior depended very much on the social class of the speaker. Watts (1999), for instance, argues that the use of 'polite' language was closely connected to the social class of the speakers.

> Politeness was an attribute of the legitimate language variety within the early eighteenth century linguistic marketplace in Britain, access to which was equivalent to access to high social status from which power could be exercised.
>
> (Watts 1999: 6)

Taavitsainen and Jucker (2010) argue in a similar vein that the political and socio-demographic changes of the eighteenth century were closely connected with the rise of the politeness culture. The growing wealth and influence of the middle classes was linked to the right type of linguistic behavior: the rising social classes set themselves off from the rest by enforcing among themselves polished manners and polite conversations.

> [P] politeness was associated with and often identified with gentlemanliness since it applied to the social world of gentlemen and ladies [...] Not all gentlemen were polite since 'politeness' was a criterion of proper behavior. The kernel of 'politeness' could be conveyed in the simple expression, 'the art of pleasing in company,' or, in a contemporary definition, 'a dextrous management of our Words and Actions, whereby we make other People have better Opinions of us and themselves.'
>
> (Klein 1994: 3–4)

A major challenge for researchers is presented by the fact that speech acts are always interpreted within the larger context of the talk exchange. The interactants have a considerable amount of common ground and each knows that the other shares this. For the outside analyst it becomes imperative to reconstruct as much as possible of this common ground, but the further removed the speech community under investigation from the researcher's own speech community, the more difficult this reconstruction process becomes. A particularly clear instance of this is provided by ironic utterances and sarcasm. The interpretation of such utterances always relies on a large amount of common ground, which for the outside observer can often only be grasped on the basis of contextual clues. The researcher has to assess utterances in their discourse context in order to catch their transient meanings. Sometimes the analyst can learn more about the intended or perceived force of an utterance if the perlocutionary effects on the audience are recorded in the texts under scrutiny.

At the level of entire utterances, it becomes increasingly problematic to talk of "saying 'the same thing' in several ways" (Labov 1972: 271). Kohnen's (2008a, 2008b) research on requests, for instance, looks at alternative forms of forming requests in Old English: directive performatives, such as 'I ask you to . . . ,' constructions involving a second-person pronoun plus *scealt/sculon*; constructions with *uton* 'let's' plus infinitive; and impersonal constructions with *(neod)þearf* 'it is necessary for x.' These forms are set in relation to the type of society of the Anglo-Saxon world, a society characterized by mutual obligation and kinship loyalty as well as the Christian values of *caritas* and *humilitas*. This stands in contrast to negatively polite requests, such as "Could you say that again" (BNC KPG 912[2]), typical of present-day British English. All these ways of trying to get the addressee to do something that he or she might not have done without the request share a core of functional equivalence even if they cannot be said to be different ways of saying the same thing.

5.3 *Conversation*

Historical conversation analysis emerged as a field of study at about the same time as historical pragmatics. It is sometimes referred to as historical dialogue analysis (Jucker, Fritz and Lebsanft 1999a; Kilian 2005) or historical discourse analysis (Brinton 2001). Conversation analysis has been extended to historical materials both in the form of dialogues and conversations recorded in historical sources and in the form of written language, which has in itself come to be regarded as a legitimate object of study for dialogue and conversation analysts. It is the dialogic nature of language use that the analysis is concerned with (see Jucker, Fritz and Lebsanft 1999a: 1; Kilian 2005).

Conversation analysis can yield a great deal for the analysis of historical materials, as its methodology offers a conceptual framework for the analysis of the whole context of the occurrence of a particular linguistic feature and makes it possible to locate instances of language use in the conversational structure, at the level of turns and larger sequences. Such sequences and multiple ways of performing an action have been studied by Lebsanft (1999), who sets out to analyze one particular form of dialogue, bargain dialogues. His case study is based on the late medieval farce of *Maistre Pierres Pathelin* (ca 1456–60), a famous French comic drama. He defines a bargain dialogue as an exchange in which a vendor and a customer discuss and agree on the conditions under which an object is handed over from the vendor to the customer in return for another object that may count as a payment (1999: 284). He argues that the kernel structure of such bargaining has a very long history and exists in many different social and historical contexts, although the precise details of who may interact in such an exchange and the nature of the objects that are exchanged differs from one social and historical context to another[3]. In this case, therefore, the socio-demographic variables of the participants of the interaction influence the way in which the entire bargaining dialogue is performed.

Other studies have concentrated on how pragmatic context variables, which could be conceptualized as independent variables, have a bearing on how conversations develop. Seppänen (2003), for instance, works in the framework of conversation analysis and applies its principles to the analysis of demonstrative pronouns of addressing and referring in older Finnish dialect material. The field notes recording dialectal speech in the nineteenth century did not include the contextual facts of the speech situation, but conversational data from the 1950s and 1980s proved helpful as they provided parallel cases of language use in situations where, in addition to the speaker and the addressee, other people were present. It is likely that the earlier instances of demonstrative pronouns were uttered in similar multi-person contexts and were not directed to an addressee in the normal sense at all, but distanced and extended so that the target is not only the person involved but also the others present. The speaker is actually asking for the audience's permission for the action mentioned (*Lähtiskös tää Tuomas nuotalle?* 'Now would this Tuomas like to come with me and have a look at the fishing net?'). In another case the person referred to with the demonstrative pronoun was put in the limelight by way of teasing, changing his position from an addressee to an object of attention. The shifts are subtle, but show that the insights gained with modern video techniques have relevance to historical interpretations. The examples come from the early days of dialect research, but similar patterns of vernacular address survive as multipurpose references in multi-person conversational situations.

5.4 Discourse domains

By 'discourse domains' we understand the entire repertoire of texts and genres at the disposal of a discourse community, the discourse patterns that the members of these communities used, and how both the repertoire and the patterns change over time (Jucker 2008: 901–2). In several discourse domains, practices have undergone fundamental change. In particular, the discourse domains of scientific news discourse have received scholarly attention. In seventeenth-century England, semi-private correspondence was an important means of delivering news and exchanging opinions through networks in discourse communities that were small and in which the members knew one another personally. The practice was carried over into the published form as scientists reported on their findings and discussed current issues in the *Philosophical Transactions*. These patterns are regularly discussed in the context of the structures of society that were undergoing changes at the time. The increasing prosperity of the upper middle classes provided more opportunities for scientific pursuits, and the socio-demographic characteristics of these authors were certainly relevant to the developments of scientific news discourse in the Early Modern period (see, for instance, Moessner 2009; Valle 1999, 2006; Gotti 2006).

The reception of scientific doctrines forms the other side of the coin, and has been approached by studies on appropriation, or how common cultural sets such as scientific doctrines were understood and acted upon (Taavitsainen 2005). Texts have plural uses and are perceived in different ways by different audiences. Medical historians are interested in how medical knowledge spread into private households during social visits, and how recipes were circulated in letters and recorded into notebooks for private use. Manuscript recipe collections provide intriguing evidence of early modern women's literacy practices at various levels of proficiency (Leong and Pennell 2007). Another example of societal differentiation can be found in the appropriations of the humoral theory. Knowledge spread from learned sources to the highly educated classes in society (including the Queen, Elizabeth I), but in their letters medical terms acquired more abstract senses in metaphors about the affairs of state, whereas almanacs give evidence of a different type of appropriation of the same doctrines in the form of simple rules of thumb for the right timing of actions (Taavitsainen, 2011).

6. Conclusion

We have argued that sociolinguistically informed variability studies have so far not significantly extended to include pragmatic units, presumably as the result of the difficulty of arguing that two different pragmatic units constitute different ways of saying basically the same thing. At the same time, pragmaticists have not paid any systematic attention to socio-demographic variables that might correlate with the pragmatic units that they analyze. This lack of interaction between studies on linguistic variation and pragmatics is even more pronounced in historical linguistics.

Against this background, we have tried to identify pragmatic variables at the different levels of descriptions from expressions to utterances, conversations, and discourse domains, and we have pointed out some studies that – in one way or another – appeal to socio-demographic variables or pragmatic context variables as explanations. At the level of expressions and utterances, address terms, inserts such as discourse markers and interjections, and individual speech acts have been treated as pragmatic variables, in that their occurrence has been correlated with the socio-demographic features of the speakers and other contextual variables. Similarly, pragmatic context variables, such as the presence of certain people in an interaction, have been identified as influencing speech production. The identification of a set of variants for individual variables is not always easy. In the case of the address terms *you* and *thou* it is relatively straightforward, but in the case of different forms of performing a request or different politeness strategies the identification of variants may be highly problematic.

At the level of conversation, we identified different forms of dialogues, such as bargain dialogues, as pragmatic variables, whose precise form of enactment is correlated with the socio-demographic variables of the interactants. And on the level of discourse domains, entire repertoires of texts and genres, and patterns of the dissemination of knowledge and information, form the core of what might be called 'pragmatic variables' that can be correlated with the social background of their users.

The work that we have summarized above does not usually invoke the notion of pragmatic variables at all, but we hope to have shown that it might usefully be reconceptualized in these terms. We believe that historical pragmatic studies would gain a lot by considering the sociolinguistic concept of the variable. In many cases it might allow for more rigorous definitions of the elements under investigation and their variants, and an even clearer understanding of how they correlate with the socio-demographic features of the users of the language. And for sociolinguistic studies, an extension to pragmatic variables might provide a rich new area of investigation.

NOTES

1   Such as Grice's (1975) work on cooperation in communication or Brown and Levinson's (1987) framework for the description of politeness.
2   The reference is to the *British National Corpus* (http://www.es.uzh.ch/services/corpling.html [accessed October 14, 2011]).
3   See also Bös (2007) for an analysis of bargaining dialogues in Early Modern English service encounters.

REFERENCES

Arnovick, L.K. (1999) *Diachronic Pragmatics. Seven Case Studies in English Illocutionary Development*, John Benjamins, Amsterdam.

Biber, D., Johansson, S., Leech, G., Conrad, S., and Finegan, E. (1999) *Longman Grammar of Spoken and Written English*, Longman, London.

Blum-Kulka, S., House, J., and Kasper, G. (eds.) (1989) *Cross-Cultural Pragmatics: Requests and Apologies*, Ablex, Norwood, NJ.

Bös, B. (2007) *What do you lacke? what is it you buy?:* Early Modern English service encounters. In S.M. Fitzmaurice and I. Taavitsainen (eds.), *Methodological Issues in Historical Pragmatics*, Mouton de Gruyter, Berlin, pp. 219–40.

Brinton, L.J. (2001) Historical discourse analysis. In D. Schiffrin, D. Tannen, and H.E. Hamilton (eds.), *The Handbook of Discourse Analysis*, Blackwell, Oxford, pp. 138–60.

Brown, R. and Gilman, A. (1989) Politeness theory and Shakespeare's four major tragedies. *Language in Society* 18.2: 159–212.

Brown, P. and Levinson, S.C. (1987) *Politeness. Some Universals in Language Usage*, Cambridge University Press, Cambridge.

Brownlees, N. (ed.) (2006) *News Discourse in Early Modern Britain. Selected Papers of*

Conference on Historical News Discourse 2004 (CHINED), Peter Lang, Bern.

Burnley, D. (2003) The T/V pronouns in later Middle English literature. In I. Taavitsainen and A.H. Jucker (eds.), pp. 27–45.

Busse, U. (2002) *Linguistic Variation in the Shakespeare Corpus. Morpho-Syntactic Variability of Second Person Pronouns*, John Benjamins, Amsterdam.

Gotti, M. (2006) Disseminating early modern science: specialized news discourse in the *Philosophical Transactions*. In N. Brownlees (ed.), pp. 41–70.

Grice, H.P. (1975) Logic and conversation. In P. Cole and J.L. Morgan (eds.), *Syntax and Semantics 3: Speech Acts*, Academic Press. New York, pp. 41–58.

Heritage, J. (1984) A change-of-state token and aspects of its sequential placement. In J.M. Atkinson and J. Heritage (eds.), *Structure of Social Action. Studies in Conversation Analysis*, Cambridge University Press, Cambridge, pp. 299–345.

Heritage, J. (1998) *Oh*-prefaced responses to inquiry. *Language in Society* 27: 291–334.

Heritage, J. (2002) *Oh*-prefaced responses to assessments: a method of modifying agreement/disagreement. In C.E. Ford, B.A. Fox, and S.A. Thompson (eds.), *The*

Language of Turn and Sequence, Oxford University Press, Oxford, pp. 196–224.

Holmes, J. (1986) Functions of *you know* in women's and men's speech. *Language in Society* 15: 1–22.

Holmes, J. (1988) Paying compliments: a sex preferential politeness strategy. *Journal of Pragmatics* 12.4: 445–65.

Holmes, J. (1995) *Women, Men and Politeness*, Longman, London.

Huang, Y. (2007) *Pragmatics*, Oxford University Press, Oxford.

Huang, Y. (2010) Pragmatics. In L. Cummings (ed.), *The Pragmatics Encyclopedia*, Routledge, London, pp. 341–45.

Hunt, T. (2003) The use of *tu/vus* in the Anglo-Norman *Seinte Resureccion*. In I. Taavitsainen and A.H. Jucker (eds.), pp. 47–59.

Jucker, A.H. (1993) The genitive versus the *of*-construction in British newspapers. In A.H. Jucker (ed.), *The Noun Phrase in English. Its Structure and Variability*, Special issue of *anglistik + englischunterricht* 49: 121–36.

Jucker, A.H. (ed.) (1995) *Historical Pragmatics. Pragmatic Developments in the History of English*, John Benjamins, Amsterdam.

Jucker, A.H. (2006) 'Thou art so loothly and so oold also': The use of *ye* and *thou* in Chaucer's *Canterbury Tales*. *Anglistik* 17.2: 57–72.

Jucker, A.H. (2008) Historical pragmatics. *Language and Linguistics Compass* 2.5: 894–906.

Jucker, A.H., Fritz, G., and Lebsanft, F. (1999a) Historical dialogue analysis: roots and traditions in the study of the Romance languages, German and English. In A.H. Jucker, G. Fritz, and F. Lebsanft (eds.), pp. 1–33.

Jucker, A.H., Fritz, G., and Lebsanft, F. (eds.) (1999b) *Historical Dialogue Analysis*, John Benjamins, Amsterdam.

Jucker, A.H. and Taavitsainen, I. (eds.) (2008) *Speech Acts in the History of English*, John Benjamins, Amsterdam.

Kilian, J. (2005) *Historische Dialoganalyse*, Niemeyer, Tübingen.

Klein, L. (1994) *Shaftesbury and the Culture of Politeness. Moral Discourse and Cultural Politics in Early Eighteenth-Century England*, Cambridge University Press, Cambridge.

Kohnen, T. (2008a) Directives in Old English: Beyond politeness? In A.H. Jucker and I. Taavitsainen (eds.), pp. 27–44.

Kohnen, T. (2008b) Tracing directives through text and time: towards a methodology of a corpus-based diachronic speech-act analysis. In A.H. Jucker and I. Taavitsainen (eds.), pp. 295–310.

Labov, W. (1972) *Sociolinguistic Patterns*, Blackwell, Oxford.

Lavandera, B. (1978) Where does the sociolinguistic variable stop? *Language in Society* 7: 171–83.

Lebsanft, F. (1999) A Late Medieval French bargain dialogue (*Pathelin* II), Or: Further remarks on the history of dialogue forms. In A.H. Jucker, G. Fritz, and F. Lebsanft (eds.), pp. 269–92.

Leong, E., and Pennell, S. (2007) Recipe collections and the currency of medical knowledge in the Early Modern 'medical marketplace.' In M.S.R. Jenner and P. Wallis (eds.), *Medicine and the Market in England and its Colonies, c. 1450 –c. 1850*, Palgrave Macmillan, Basingstoke, pp. 133–52.

Lutzky, U. (2008) The discourse marker *marry*: a sociopragmatic analysis. *VIEWS* 17.2: 3–20.

Mazzon, G. (2000) Social relations and form of address in the *Canterbury Tales*. In D. Kastovsky and A. Mettinger (eds.), *The History of English in a Social Context. A Contribution to Historical Sociolinguistics*, Mouton de Gruyter, Berlin, pp.135–68.

Mazzon, G. (2003) Pronouns and nominal address in Shakespearean English: a socio-affective marking system in transition. In I. Taavitsainen and A.H. Jucker (eds.), pp. 223–49.

Mey, J. (2001) *Pragmatics. An Introduction* (2nd edn), Blackwell, Oxford.

Moessner, L. (2009) The influence of the Royal Society on 17th-century scientific writing. *ICAME Journal* 33: 65–87.

Person, R.R., Jr. (2009) 'Oh' in Shakespeare: a conversation analytic approach. *Journal of Historical Pragmatics* 10.1: 84–107.

Schneider, K.P. and Barron, A. (eds.) (2008a) *Variational Pragmatics. A Focus on Regional Varieties in Pluricentric Languages*, John Benjamins, Amsterdam.

Schneider, K.P. and Barron, A. (2008b) Where pragmatics and dialectology meet. Introducing variational pragmatics. In K.P. Schneider and A. Barron (eds.), pp. 1–32.

Seppänen, E.L. (2003) Demonstrative pronouns in addressing and referring in Finnish. In I. Taavitsainen and A.H. Jucker (eds.), pp. 375–99.

Stein, D. (2003) Pronominal usage in Shakespeare: between sociolinguistics and conversational analysis. In I. Taavitsainen and A.H. Jucker (eds.), pp. 251–307.

Taavitsainen, I. (1995) Interjections in Early Modern English: from imitation of spoken to conventions of written language. In A.H. Jucker (ed.), pp. 439–65.

Taavitsainen, I. (1998) Emphatic language and romantic prose: changing functions of interjections in a sociocultural perspective. *European Journal of English Studies* 2.2: 195–214.

Taavitsainen, I. (2005) Genres and the appropriation of science: *loci communes* in English in the late medieval and early modern period. In J. Skaffari, M. Peikola, R. Carroll, R. Hiltunen, and B. Wårvik (eds.), *Opening Windows on Texts and Discourses of the Past*, John Benjamins, Amsterdam, pp. 179–96.

Taavitsainen, I. (2011) Dissemination and appropriation of medical knowledge: Humoral theory in early modern medical writing and lay texts. In I. Taavitsainen and P. Pahta (eds.), *Medical Writing in Early Modern English*, Cambridge University Press, Cambridge, pp. 94–114.

Taavitsainen, I. and Jucker, A.H. (eds.) (2003) *Diachronic Perspectives on Address Term Systems*, John Benjamins, Amsterdam.

Taavitsainen, I. and Jucker, A.H. (2008) "Methinks you seem more beautiful than ever:" compliments and gender in the history of English. In A.H. Jucker and I. Taavitsainen (eds.), pp. 195–228.

Taavitsainen, I. and Jucker, A.H. (2010) Expressive speech acts and politeness in eighteenth-century English. In R. Hickey (ed.), *Eighteenth-Century English: Ideology and Change*, Cambridge University Press, Cambridge, pp. 159–81.

Trosborg, A. (1994) *Interlanguage Pragmatics. Requests, Complaints and Apologies*, Mouton de Gruyter, Berlin.

Valle, E. (1999) *A Collective Intelligence. The Life Sciences in the Royal Society as a Scientific Discourse Community, 1665–1965*. University of Turku.

Valle, E. (2006) Reporting the doings of the curious: authors and editors in the Philosophical Transactions of the Royal Society of London. In N. Brownlees (ed.), pp. 71–90.

Verschueren, J. (1999) *Understanding Pragmatics*, Arnold, London.

Watts, R.J. (1999) Language and politeness in early eighteenth century Britain. In M. Kienpointer (ed.), *Ideologies of Politeness*, special issue of *Pragmatics* 9.1: 5–20.

Weinreich, U., Labov, W., and Herzog, M. (1968) Empirical foundations for a theory of language change. In W.P. Lehmann and Y. Malkiel (eds.), *Directions for Historical Linguistics: A Symposium*, University of Texas Press, Austin, pp. 95–188.

Wierzbicka, A. (1985) Different cultures, different languages, different speech acts. *Journal of Pragmatics* 9: 145–78.

17 Class, Age, and Gender-based Patterns

AGNIESZKA KIEŁKIEWICZ-JANOWIAK

1. Introduction

In reconstructing the past, sociolinguists have to rely on concepts that will adequately describe historical realities and, most importantly, capture the complex relationships between language and society, without falsely assuming that for any historical period those relationships are comparable to those of the present day. In other words, present-day descriptions and understandings of social variables and relations should not be too readily taken as valid for historical periods. Instead, the meaning of a variable has to be recovered from the historical text that is the subject of linguistic analysis, as well as from the background writings of the historical period under study. Social variables such as social class, gender, and age, commonly referred to in sociolinguistic accounts of language variation as components of speaker characteristics and important aspects of social context, should not be flattened and distorted by looking at them through a modern lens (see also Chapter 5 in this *Handbook*).

To further the study of historical sociolinguistic variation it is important to add socio-historical depth to flat demographic dimensions, increase awareness of the social aspects of these dimensions, and make students of language understand that it is indeed these aspects that have consequences for language use patterns. One way to tackle this task is to read the historical text to understand it (and others like it) from its own perspective and through its own discourse.[1]

The study of written sources, given the absense of spoken data, has yielded much insight into the sociolinguistic patterns of earlier periods (see Chapters 8–11 in this *Handbook*). In particular, historical corpora that represent private rather than

The Handbook of Historical Sociolinguistics, First Edition. Edited by Juan Manuel Hernández-Campoy and Juan Camilo Conde-Silvestre.
© 2014 John Wiley & Sons, Ltd. Published 2014 by John Wiley & Sons, Ltd.

public genres have helped us to overcome both the problem of access to less formal styles and a larger array of authors' social backgrounds. Their results give overall pictures of variation and outline trends in sociolinguistic change (see Nevalainen and Raumolin-Brunberg 2003). Alternatively, in ethnographic studies of historical text and society, special attention is given to retrieving information about the authors and their speech communities from the texts they have themselves written (Tieken-Boon van Ostade 2006a, 2009; Sairio 2009).

The texts which will be used for reference in this chapter have the common feature of having been privately written (mostly) by (female) authors of varied social backgrounds in late eighteenth- and early nineteenth-century New England. This collection of private writings reflects the randomness of the availability of historical texts and attempts to show the implications of an unsystematic choice of data. Specifically, the corpus of texts drawn on here shifts the focus of the discussion to women's history, rather than (as in most historical studies so far) men's.

2. Data

The historical sociolinguist has to deal with the unsystematic character of the linguistic as well as the social information in their data: the problem of 'bad data' was pointed out by Labov (1994: 11) and discussed by Nevalainen (1999: 499) and Nevalainen and Raumolin-Brunberg (2003: 26–27) (see also Chapter 4 in this *Handbook*).

Historical sociolinguistics has to tackle the problem of data scarcity and randomness. Efforts made by historical researchers to retrieve texts from manuscripts, create archives and, ultimately, annotated corpora are invaluable (see Chapters 6–7 in this *Handbook*). Large quantitative studies of sociolinguistic variation have been completed on the basis of impressively large corpora, such as the Corpus of Early English Correspondence (CEEC) or the Corpus of Nineteenth-Century English (CONCE).[2] Examples of monographs or collections of articles reporting on research based on these corpora include Nurmi, Nevala and Palander-Collin (2009), Okulska (2006a, 2006b), Kytö *et al.* (2006), and Fitzmaurice (2002).

The socially unrepresentative character of historical texts is often due to the elite educational and social backgrounds of their authors. Members of lower social ranks and women are, as a rule, under-represented. The researcher who wants to rely on a balanced text sample needs to be aware of how male and female authors are unequally represented in the existing texts. For example, only about 20% of the material in the Corpus of Early English Correspondence was written by women (Palander-Collin 1999). In the first place, the total amount of text that has ever been written by women is less than that written by men, due to women's incomplete education: for example, in late eighteenth- and early nineteenth-century United States the ability to read, but not to write, was an educational priority for women. Secondly, women's writings were often private (diaries or letters) and never published, so present-day researchers do not find them in printed form and need to make the effort to access material preserved in manuscripts, often as parts of the less accessible, private collections (see Chapter 9 in this *Handbook*).

The imbalance in historical knowledge about women and men may be illustrated by the case of a married couple representing an early nineteenth-century Boston merchant family. The husband, Henry Lee, is much better known to posterity because of his career in trade and public service. We learn about Mary Jackson Lee chiefly as Henry's wife, though she was also a member of an aristocratic family and received an education no worse than her husband's. However, reading through her letter-journal[3] reveals a wealth of social and private history that no history book has recorded.[4]

The language material preserved is for the most part stylistically unbalanced, with informal styles under-represented. Corpus compilers have therefore striven to include informal and conversational data or even create corpora dedicated to representing oral interaction (see Culpeper and Kytö 1997, 2010; Jucker *et al.* 1999).

2.1   The study of private writings

It is important to note that writings which were not intended for publication are also more likely to represent authors who would otherwise be underrepresented: members of the lower social ranks or women. Because they often refer to 'ordinary life,' these texts give researchers a great opportunity to obtain first-hand information and details of their informants' lifestyles. In fact, many of the available texts written for private circulation, such as the journal of Esther Edwards Burr, written in 1754–57 (Karlsen and Crumpacker 1984: 19) have only recently been rediscovered as historical sources.

Raumolin-Brunberg (2005: 40) recommends letters, rather than other genres, for longitudinal studies because "as it is often the case with literary genres, the genre conventions may change over time." Furthermore, she considers the fact that (early modern) letters deal with everyday matters to be an additional advantage of this genre. Indeed, the historical detail given by the authors whose linguistic patterns are studied gives much credibility to findings about the "social embedding" of language (see also Dossena and Tieken-Boon van Ostade 2008). The study of private writings has also been shown to be useful in uncovering how language changes over the lifespans of individuals (Raumolin-Brunberg 2005, 2009).

Letters and other private writings can provide a detailed social picture of the people involved. For instance, by looking closely at linguistic references to relationships (such as forms of address or identity markers) the researcher can uncover the relationships of power and solidarity, and thus reconstruct the social rank system (see Nevalainen and Raumolin-Brunberg 1995; Nevala 2004, 2009; Tieken-Boon van Ostade 2006a: 253, 2006b; Palander-Collin 2009; for power relations as retrieved from the discourse of historical correspondence see also Tiisala 2004; Hakanen and Koskinen 2009; Okulska 2010).

In general, private writings, having limited audiences and not being intended for publication, have been considered relatively more informal (than published texts) and very useful in the reconstruction of the spoken vernacular of their time

(Tieken-Boon van Ostade 2000a: 450; Palander-Collin and Nevala 2005; Okulska 2006c). The study of private writings uncovers detailed ethnographic evidence of historical life. An ethnographically oriented text analysis shows how each private document tells a unique story about the people involved (Kiełkiewicz-Janowiak 2002, 2003).

An example of a text recovered for socio-historical analysis is the diary of Martha Ballard, a midwife from Maine, which spans 27 years from 1785 to 1812, and tells a fascinating story of Martha's professional and private life. This is a case of an individual collection which is longitudinal and very systematic in nature.[5] However, private writings and letters have often been preserved only randomly. For example, Mary Jackson Lee scrupulously recorded (by copying into her journal) the letters she sent to her husband. Yet only some of Henry Lee's letters to her, written over the long period of his absence from home, have been pre-served.[6] A unique example of texts from the under-represented social ranks may be collections of letters by the so-called 'factory girls,' the New England textile mill workers who wrote letters to their families and friends back home in their native villages (Dublin 1982/1993, 1994).

2.2   Qualitative and quantitative methodologies

Systematic, quantitative analyses of historical texts have been conducted either with particular socio-demographic variables in focus (Nevalainen and Raumolin-Brunberg 1996; Biber and Burges 2000), or as portraits of the language of a histori-cal period, considering specific linguistic variables (Kytö *et al.* 2006). These studies present corpus-based empirical research.

With the random and quantitatively unbalanced composition of a text corpus, it is sometimes impossible to report any statistically significant results for the occurrence of variables. Often, rather than comparing a range of texts, it is better to treat them separately, depending on the language data contained within them. Close attention may then be given to the socio-historical information embedded in the texts. This makes each source text truly unique and its author(s) a worth-while object of special historical interest. Such qualitative, micro-scale approaches are highly valued (Eckert 2000; Holmes and Meyerhoff 2003), if only to comple-ment quantitative, larger scale analyses.

2.3   The study of individual cases

Tieken-Boon van Ostade recommends the study of texts written by individual authors. In her systematic studies of the (formal and informal) letters of individual authors, she juxtaposes the language of people "from all layers of society, ranging from those who were highly educated to those who were barely able to spell. All these people wrote letters" (2006a: 243).

There exist other corpora centered on the writing of individuals, which also include texts written by members of the central figure's more or less immediate environment. For example, Bax (2005), Tieken-Boon van Ostade (2000b, 2003), and

Fitzmaurice (2000) have analyzed collections devoted to Samuel Johnson (1709–84), Sarah Fielding (1710–68), Robert Lowth (1710–87), and Joseph Addison (1672–1719). Bergs (2005) investigated the Paston letters in the context of the Paston family network in the Middle English period and Sairio (2009) edited and studied the correspondence of Elizabeth Montagu (1718–1800) and the members of her Bluestocking circle. Such collections provide the basis for reconstructing the social networks of the text's authors and identifying their roles in the sociolinguistic processes evidenced in their writings (see Chapter 18 in this *Handbook*).

A qualitative micro-scale study of individuals and their writings emphasizes social diversity and the uniqueness of individual experience. However, analyses of the backgrounds and the language of individual speakers can only provide an illustration of the workings of a community in the process of communication. The individual speaker "can only be understood as the product of a unique social history, and the intersection of the linguistic patterns of all the social groups and categories that define that individual" (Labov 2001: 34).

3. Social Class

In modern sociolinguistic studies, social stratification has often been represented in terms of social class. The difficulty of assigning individuals to any social groupings lies in selecting the criteria, which are likely to be differently relevant in different societies. Many sociolinguists have discussed that particular problem where social class is concerned (Milroy 1980: 14; Trudgill 1983).

Guided by social historians (Burke 1992) and their recommendations to avoid the use of the economically-based concept of class in the context of pre-industrial societies, historical sociolinguists have more often referred to social rank or social order (see Conde-Silvestre and Hernandez-Campoy 2004), a hierarchical category based on a number of historically relevant criteria.

Assuming that social stratification conditioned language variation in the past, historically adequate models are required. Nevalainen (1996) has proposed models of social stratification for early modern England (see also Nevalainen and Raumolin-Brunberg 2003: 136). Nevala (2004) demonstrates how elements of these models "originate from history" (2004: 19) by referring to the distinction between the "better sort," the "middling sort" and the "poorest sort:" indeed, by the early eighteenth century the term 'sort' was well-established in the English vocabulary for describing social groups (Wrightson 1991). The criteria for constructing models of social stratification may be drawn from source texts which show how the people of a certain era considered their societies to be hierarchical or in any way divided.

The texts might also indicate whether one's social rank was seen as acquired by birth, and only later confirmed by one's educational and occupational status, or whether it could be changed at any time by marriage or by other acts of social mobility. The popular thinking about historical societies involves relatively greater fixedness of the social rank divisions expressed by the belief that one was primarily 'born into' a rank and allowed little chance of upgrading one's status. However, research into individual life stories reveals flexibility. Socio-historical models of social stratification include the dynamic category of "social climbers" or "social aspirers" (Nevalainen 1996: 61). For a detailed discussion of social mobility, both upward and downward, between 1400 and 1800, see Nevala (2004: 23–26).

A close examination of the situation of women illustrates the potential for change and social opportunity. In the New England corpus referred to earlier (see Kiełkiewicz-Janowiak 2002), 'factory girls' are a striking case of people seeking (and often achieving) social advancement. At the beginning of the nineteenth century these (unmarried) young women, living in rural areas, chose to leave their crowded farmhouses and work at the textile mills to save money for their marriage dowries and sometimes to support their families back home (Dublin 1994). Ultimately, they used the opportunity – unique at the time – offered to women by the rapidly growing textile industry to work outside the home and thus secure for themselves social and financial independence. This provided new opportunities for women to raise their status in ways other than a socially advantageous marriage.[7]

The daughters of more socially aspiring families were sent off to schools (female academies, later also seminaries), while the housework was relegated to the lower-class members. In the early nineteenth century, these educational options were open mostly to the daughters of the emerging middle class. However, the more women who could graduate from seminaries and enter the teaching profession, the more girls from the lower stations got the chance to learn to read and write in common schools. Thus, the new occupational and educational opportunities becoming available to women in early New England brought about changes in the social order.

Many factory women sought to continue education during their stay in a mill town. This was one way of both raising their reputation and improving their prospects for their future status. In addition, the workers themselves organized 'improvement circles,' institutions for self-education and for sharing literary interests. In the early years of the nineteenth century, due to the expansion of literacy, reading was becoming available to ever wider social spheres. Young women with just elementary education were eager to learn more through reading. Literature for women held out the promise of social advancement by promoting middle class values and lifestyles.

For adults of either sex, letter-writing manuals (called 'letter-writers') proved of enormous use in helping them to conduct business communication as well as private correspondence. One such manual popular in America was W.H. Dilworth's *The complete letter-writer* (1794), widely reprinted and imitated by other authors. Dierks (2000) claims that the popularization of letter manuals "threw open the social boundaries around letter writing in terms of class, gender, and life cycle." Furthermore, "the expansion of letter writing reflected an unprecedented unleashing of aspiration for upward mobility" (2000: 32–33).

The above example suggests that the social order should in fact be approached as resulting from the changing opportunities available to members of past societies (education and work). Moreover, as in present-day accounts of social hierarchies, social distinctions do not only derive from one's level of economic prosperity but also from declarations of respect or disregard for others. Today's social attitudes are probed by direct questionnaires, while those of the past may only be gleaned indirectly – from the source texts, which offer detailed information about changing social realities and people's attitudes to them.

4. Gender

The patterns of male and female language use have long been contrasted in sociolinguistic research. Early correlational studies regarded sex as a demographic category and compared male and female language patterns (Fischer 1958; Wolfram 1969; Trudgill 1974). It was becoming clear, however, that linguistic patterns distributed according to the sex of the speaker are to be accounted for by reference to the social characteristics of the speakers (their social roles, their attitudes, their preferences) in the larger societal context.[8]

In more recent sociolinguistic work gender, rather than sex, has been taken as the variable of significance to language variation: sex is a (biological) feature of an *individual*, but gender – as a social concept – is more about *group* characteristics.

Women and men are often socially perceived and defined as separate social groups. Not only in everyday life but also in research, priority has been given to the (social) differences between women and men.[9] Consequently, drawing a sharp gender contrast homogenizes women (or men) as a social group. However, documents testify to an immense variety of backgrounds, roles, and expectations. The analysis of texts helps us realize and appreciate the complexity of the social conditioning of language variation.

For historical sociolinguists too it became obvious that, rather than simply indicating the sex of the speaker, researchers should define gender in terms of a set of social roles and characteristics usually ascribed to, and accepted by, women and men within a given society. Explorations of how historical societies were gendered have been conducted. One problem is how to get access to the information about people's gender identities rather than referring to the demographic data on their sex. Another task has been to show how, in the past, gender identity arose in interaction with other social variables. Finally, the reconstruction of the unique relationships between gender and language use in the specific historical context is a challenge. In fact, the analysis and comparison of individual cases suggests that more attention should be given to intra-group variation. Women in two opposed social groups will often differ in language use more from each other than from men,[10] because people choose to assert their membership in different groups in context-dependent and variable ways.

In the context of investigations of past societies it is easy to overlook some aspects of internal variation. One example of a historically major social divide within a gender group is marital status. A comparison of the life of married and unmarried women in early New England shows a dramatic difference, pointing to the relative attractiveness of the life of those women who were unmarried. Largely irrespective of their social status, single women had more time to maintain social contacts. For the elite women this was an important obligation,[11] while rural women and those of lower status were free to socialize after they had finished helping with the housework and farm work. Single women were also allowed to take up waged employment, which was not an option open to married women. This gave unmarried women more economic independence, greater mobility and generally greater variety in social experience. In contrast, marriage meant complete subordination of the wife to the husband (Cott 1977). The woman's possessions became her husband's on marriage; only single women over eighteen and widows could own property.[12] Nevertheless, most women wished to marry.[13] Besides imposing total economic dependence (on the husband's wealth or indigence), the married state promised a new sphere of self-sovereignty: the home. When considering women's social networks as affecting their language practices this 'marital status divide' should be understood in its context. Alexis de Tocqueville, who visited the United States in 1831 to prepare a report about the American penitentiary system, took the opportunity to make many political and social observations, such as these remarks about the married state in a letter to his sister from New York (June 9, 1831):

> When a woman marries, it's as if she entered a convent, except however that it is not taken ill that she have children, and even many of them. Otherwise, it's the life of a nun; no more balls; hardly any more society; a husband as estimable as cold for all company; and that to the life eternal. I ventured the other day to ask one of these charming recluses just how, exactly, a wife could pass her time in America. She answered me, with great *sang-froid*: in admiring her husband.
>
> (excerpt from de Tocqueville in Pierson 1938: 144)

The social circumstances of women's and men's lives were recognizably different not only with respect to legal rights (inheritance, for example), but also in their access to and quality of education. The popular notion of literacy today involves the ability to read and write. In the context of the eighteenth-century United States, however, they must be viewed as separate skills, with reading considered as basic. Both men and women were taught to read, though for different purposes: it was supposed to help men to conduct business and participate in public life, whilst women were to be able to read the Bible. At the turn of the century most of the population of New England could read (Lockridge 1974); writing, however, remained the preserve of men.[14] Many women never learned any writing beyond scribbling their own signature. In fact, reading aloud was one of the skills considered important in the education of young women and it was encouraged as a way to provide pleasure to members of the family.[15]

An important part of women's education was acquired at home. What was instilled in the fair sex, besides the ability to read, was the particular concern for propriety. That at least some women were aware of the gender difference in communicative skills is illustrated by Mary Jackson Lee's explicit comments on her ability to communicate with others. Reporting to her husband on a conversation she had about religion with her brother-in-law, Mary Jackson Lee suggested that men communicated better than women as they did not care so much for "forms:"

> I am so ignorant of the proper use of language that I can never support any conversa-
> tion as I shd. like to – [...] – I think that he in common with most of your sex has too
> great a contempt for forms they are perhaps in them selves considered unimportant
> but as a <u>means</u> of exciting devotional feelings they are of infinite use [...] – you men
> can better get along without all this than we can.
>
> (Mary Jackson Lee Journal 74)

In current studies of language use in context, a lot of attention has been given to the communicative styles used by males and females, and their perception as gendered (Holmes and Stubbe 2003; Talbot 2003; Mullany 2007). Feminine and masculine communicative styles have often been related to gendered socialization processes (Maltz and Borker 1982). Historical texts, though they do not directly document the relation between socialization and language use, do record people's expectations of social appropriateness. In the case of women, a major source of social pressure on women was encoded in the ideology of femininity. For centuries it had been deemed desirable for a woman to be unimposing and considerate to others. This precept, at the level of linguistic behavior, involved listening rather than speaking, understanding rather than arguing.

However, when invited to speak, women were expected to display the virtue of 'sympathy.' Donawerth (2002) studied the works of Lydia Sigourney of Connecticut, a writer on morals and a poet. Sigourney, a teacher at a girls' school, in her *Letters to my pupils* (1837/1851), explains what she means by "fitly spoken words," which she recommends to her pupils: she meant "words that give pleasure" (p. 49), "words that convey instruction" (p. 50) and "words that soothe sorrow" (p. 52).

In their speech women were believed to excel in an 'ornamental' way. The admiration for women's linguistic excellence emerged as early as the eighteenth century and fully developed in the nineteenth (Bailey 1991). Women were *expected* to be more 'refined' than men in the area of 'forms' – conventions defining the rituals of social life, which included dress, gesture, and conversation. In England, one desirable attribute of a gentlewoman was the ability to speak with *grace* and *elegance*. Such characteristics were present in 'polite' (i.e. non-localized) rather than 'provincial' accents (Mugglestone 1995). Mugglestone describes how the notion of 'refinement' was reflected in the nineteenth century grammarians' prescriptions about pronunciation: it was supposed to be like the speech of the 'refined circles,' "clear, distinct, well-modulated" (Nichols 1874, as quoted by Mugglestone 1995: 169), but also "soft, gentle and low" (as prescribed by another manual; Mugglestone 1995: 173). American women's pronunciation likewise generated approving or, more frequently, disapproving comment. In general, American English, increasingly distinct from the English spoken in Britain, received considerable attention from language observers and commentators. However, the elocution of women was particularly censured.

Harvey Newcomb, a clergyman who wrote several conduct books for young women and men, had a lot to say about proper language use in his book entitled *How to be a lady: a book for girls, containing useful hints on the formation of character* (1850). Most importantly, Newcomb forcefully warned girls against talkativeness and affectation:

> There is another very uncomfortable habit, which, for the want of a better name, I shall call NOISINESS. It is made up of talkativeness, loud laughing, humming patches of song-tunes, and in general, a noisy, bustling activity. Talkativeness itself is a very bad habit for a little girl or a young lady. It is a good thing to be sociable; and to converse freely and affably at the proper time, and in the proper place.
>
> (Newcomb 1850: 93)

Affectation is frequently manifested by "the hesitancy of speech," which makes the worst of impressions on the interlocutor: "[t]he more simple and unaffected your style is, provided it be pure and chaste, the better you will appear. Affectation will only make you ridiculous." (Newcomb 1850: 199). Other common sins in polite conversation are "coarse jesting, rudeness, vulgarity" and "[t]he use of low expressions, ungrammatical language, and a sort of chimney-corner dialect" (Newcomb 1850: 97–98).

In the process of female socialization, which in the nineteenth century continued throughout a woman's life, much attention was given to sensitivity to the needs of others, to being responsive and agreeable. Explanations of how to achieve this aim involved prescriptions of linguistic behavior: listen carefully rather than speak, but when speaking, use language appropriately, and avoid hurting the feelings of interlocutors. In terms of modern theory, these expectations could be linked to linguistic politeness: "[b]eing linguistically polite involves being a considerate participant in interaction" (Holmes 1995: 25).

Another requirement was for a woman to improve herself constantly for the sake of those for whom she was a moral authority. The reading of books and consulting of grammars was designed to ensure the linguistic aspect of this self-improvement. In fulfilling these assigned roles, women had to pay more attention to language skills than men. This is indicated by the amount of (moral and linguistic) instruction directed specifically at women. In the times of the doctrine of domesticity, they may have perceived this as not only their obligation but also as a chance to elevate their social position. All this social pressure exerted on women would be expected to result in the formation of a unique 'women's language.' Common to most women would be those elements of the genderlect which express the important values of the feminine ideal.

In modern language and gender studies, questions have been posed concerning social explanations of gender variation such as: Does women's relatively frequent use of high prestige variants depend on their access to the prestige norm? Do all women aspire to the same social identity, performed through similar patterns of language use? In my investigation of 'women's language' in late eighteenth- and early nineteenth-century New England (Kiełkiewicz-Janowiak 2002), I considered these issues against the historical background: did the 'separate spheres' rule in early New England determine men's and women's access to public life and to the public use of language? Is it true that the nineteenth-century ideology of femininity influenced most women's perceptions of their social identity? Finally, were these perceptions actually reflected in women's preferred patterns of language use? Freedom to define and redefine one's identity irrespective of institutionally assigned roles (in the family, at work, and so on) may be different at different periods in history. For example, Nevalainen (1999: 510) suggested that "the notions of sex and gender may have been closer in the early modern era than they are today." It seems probable that in the New England of the late eighteenth and early nineteenth century, gender roles were more strictly imposed on women than they are today.

The following is another example of how source texts facilitate the understanding of the local historical context. Klein (1996: 100) questions whether eighteenth-century women were indeed restricted to the private sphere and the home, juxtaposing "theory versus practice, articulated norms versus actual behaviors, knowledge versus action," and suggesting that "high theory and prescriptive literature represent only one layer of a society's knowledge" (1996: 100). He goes on to consider what 'public' and 'private' meant in the eighteenth century. Where 'public' meant "related to the State and its agencies," women were explicitly excluded. However, he also enumerates three other modes of public sphere: 'civic' – "pertaining to the shared or the common or pertaining to society as a whole," 'economic' – related to the market and the division of labor, and 'associative' – involving the company of others. He argues that "the distinction between the private and the public did not correspond to the distinction between home and not-home" (Klein 1996: 103–4), adding that women may have spent more time at home but that did not mean spending more time in private.

5. Stereotyping Class, Gender, and Age

Most sociolinguistic enquiries that have compared the language of women and that of men have concluded that the differences are relatively small and the similarities numerous. However, as well as actual behavioral patterns, there exist powerful gender stereotypes, whose impact should not be overlooked. These stereotypes perpetuate and magnify the gender effect in our perception, so that a relatively small gender difference is believed to bring about a true contrast. Such perceptions also lead to the formation of strong expectations, which have the power of self-fulfilling prophecies. The resulting social pressures for gendered behavior are hard to ignore. Similar relationships between social stereotypes and the perception of actual behavior are relevant to the social awareness of class and age-specific language patterns.

In the case of social rank, it may be important to learn from the historical source texts whether people conceived of social order mainly in terms of difference rather than similarity. This is reflected in their attitudes to members of other social ranks and also in their social aspirations, which will motivate social mobility. Linguistic attitudes are an indicator of the societal and individual perceptions of social dynamics and the potential for change. However, the role of social stereotypes in affecting perceptions and, further, behavioral patterns, is a complex one.

Stereotyped beliefs about class, gender, and age, and the implications for their effect on language, are partially retrievable from the historical source texts. A socio-cultural phenomenon which is of interest here is the popularity of normative publications and prescriptions on language use. Tieken-Boon van Ostade (2006a) recommends looking at complete records of texts by individuals, particularly those who were socially (and geographically) mobile. She describes cases of both upward and downward social mobility, where people faced different speech norms and where some, like William Croft, "may have consciously sought new linguistic models, working hard to adopt the desired norm" (2006a: 247), or Robert Lowth, whose "awareness of what was appropriate language is evident from his most formal letters" (2006a: 247). Significantly, Tieken-Boon van Ostade observes, on the basis of eighteenth-century private letters by literary figures, that "writers were not yet constrained by normative writings" and concludes that "[g]rammars such as those by Lowth and his contemporaries primarily served the function of making accessible new linguistic norms to those who sought social advancement, rather than controlling the language *per se*" (2006a: 270).

6. Intertwined Variables

There are numerous studies focusing on social status and gender as the guiding variables related to linguistic variation (Labov 1984; Eckert 1989). What is often left in the background is their interconnectedness, which, if recognized, helps to highlight the heterogeneity of established social groupings. Gender, in particular, is a notable example of a variable which leads researchers all too readily to assume that all women and all men share the same social and psychological characteristics (see James 1996 for a critique of this approach; see also Cheshire and Gardner-Chloros 1997).

The complexities of the impact of both social class and gender on linguistic variation were noted in the debate over the notion of prestige and apparent gender differences in preferences for more prestigious variants. Lesley Milroy (1992: 171) argued against explanations based on gendered orientations to prestige: there is no one-to-one correspondence between variables and their social functions and "it does not seem rational to account for the interacting effect of sex and class by invoking some stereotyped notion of the status consciousness of women."

Considering gender in relation to social status demonstrates the heterogeneity of femininity and masculinity as social characteristics, in present-day and past societies alike. However, the social perceptions of gender groups are often very different and the contrasts (rather than the similarities) are constantly perpetuated in the process of socialization. Also, in sociolinguistic research, gender-based divisions have sometimes been claimed to override differences in social rank (Milroy and Milroy 1993), while in fact it seems best to treat them in conjunction.

In historical sociolinguistic research, researchers have suggested that both social rank and gender have major significance for social and linguistic behavior (Nevalainen and Raumolin-Brunberg 2003; Raumolin-Brunberg 2006; Palander-Collin 1999; Nurmi, Nevala, and Palander-Collin 2009; for a general overview see Okulska 2006d). Nevalainen (2006a), in a review of the social embedding of some ongoing language changes in Tudor England (-*(e)th* and -*(e)s* variation, *thou* and *you*, periphrastic *do*), singles out gender as a prominent factor in the change in the third person verbal ending, where women were the first to promote the incoming form -*(e)s*. However, women's advantage in spreading language change was conditioned by their access to education and thus to the "learned and literary domains of language use" (Nevalainen 2006a: 208–9).

It follows that, for historical periods, the interconnection between gender and social rank must be evaluated in the given historical context. The legal rights, educational opportunities, occupational patterns, social mobility, and networking – all typical correlates of social rank – were in the past markedly different for women and men (Cott 1977; Rogers 1982; see also Laurence 1994: 227–35). Education, for one, has been claimed to be socially stratified. In Tudor and Stuart England, children's training depended on their social background and gender (Nevalainen and Raumolin-Brunberg 2003: 41). Similarly, in eighteenth- and nineteenth-century America, people's educational backgrounds related strictly to both their gender and social status. For instance, the statistics of literacy in early New England uniformly reveal a difference between male and female literacy.[16] This points to an asymmetry in the access to schooling of boys and girls, which in turn reflects social attitudes to their education.[17] Sairio (2009: 46) observes an inequality in the legal and educational status of women and men in eighteenth-century England. She claims that the gender distinction had major significance in that period and goes on to assert that "relationships between people of the same sex were likely to be more familiar than those between people of different sex, particularly when the individuals were roughly on the same level of the social scale" (Sairio 2009: 47).

In past societies, the social status of women derived from the rank of their fathers (if unmarried) or their husbands (if married) (Nevalainen and Raumolin-Brunberg 2003: 37). This perception is documented by historical texts but is also perpetuated by social scientists who have often, in view of the lack of records, felt obliged to assume women's status to be the same as that of their men. In fact, the women's social circumstances were determined by their family's social rank as well as their gender. In particular, men's and women's roles in society were perhaps more distinct two hundred years ago than they are today, due to the ideology of 'separate spheres.'

The changes in the American economy which occurred at the turn of the eighteenth century drove men away from their homes and strengthened women's attachment to the domestic sphere. The requirements of motherhood as well as the social pressures on women to secure the moral well-being of the next generations of Americans kept the majority of mothers (but also sisters) in the home, to a large extent irrespective of their social status. Their fathers, brothers, and husbands, on the other hand, were obliged to make money outside the home. In the nineteenth century, women appropriated the whole domestic sphere (or rather, had it left to them) – the negotiation of domestic space between men and women took place much later, nearer the middle of the nineteenth century.

As private writings document, next to family care and household chores, women in New England performed important social duties. The participation in the life of the immediate community as well as various religious groups kept women's social activity close to the home but by no means restricted it to the private sphere. The distinction between the private and the public spheres was not, at least for women, to be equated with that between the home and the wider community (see Klein's argument, above). In other words, their private sphere was filled with community life. Explanations of linguistic patterns in terms of the structure of the social networks therefore need to take this into account.

7. Language Change: Class, Gender, and Age

The social variables of class, gender, and age have all been discussed as relevant to the processes of language change. Studying these processes of change calls for a dynamic model of social class which accounts for mobility as a major context of that change. In fact, being mobile may be more important than class membership for initiating and spreading language change. Insights from micro- and macro-scale analyses of historical texts allows for the reconstruction of social networks on the basis of individual life stories, on which historical sociolinguistics, of necessity, has to focus. Close observation of individual network patterns reveal mobility in relation to social rank (see Chapter 18 in this *Handbook*).

The relative participation of speakers of particular ranks in the processes of initiating and spreading linguistic change may have been different in the past from today. Nevalainen (2006b: 570) observes that the upper ranks of society have rarely been studied in investigations of modern languages. However, analyses of historical corpora suggest that the upper ranks do participate in the diffusion of linguistic changes, particularly supralocal ones (Nevalainen 2006b: 571).

Nevalainen and Raumolin-Brunberg (2003: 150–54) have questioned the usefulness of social rank in accounting for some language changes (such as the loss of multiple negation) and highlighted the role of speaker characteristics that may be viewed as components of rank: the level of education and the professional status of the leaders of change.

In early New England, at the turn of the eighteenth century, the educational policies, and their institutional and social implementation, had an impact on the relative rank of women. After the Revolution, the need for the education of girls and women was established as a national cause in the US.[18] With the increase in female literacy and the expansion of schools for girls, many grammar books were devoted specifically to the education of girls and young women.[19] For example, an 'accidence' by Caleb Bingham was first published in Boston in 1785. Bingham's *Young Lady's Accidence* was designed to be taught at a girls' school, as the title indicates: "Designed principally, for the use of Young Learners, more especially those of the FAIR SEX, though proper for either" (Bingham 1785/1981: title page). One of the major concerns of teachers and learners of writing was spelling: "among persons moving in good society, and who may be supposed to have received a tolerable education, although to spell correctly be no merit, to spell incorrectly is a great disgrace" (*Complete Art of Polite Correspondence* 1857 edition of Cooke 1796, quoted from Bailey 1996: 64).

Clearly, the social capital afforded by teaching prestige language habits has for long been recognized and appreciated. The acknowledgement of the special role of women as in-home educators put them in a position of responsibility to 'care for forms.' This may be related to modern explanations of gender differentiation in language, such as those based on the idea of women's greater reliance on the symbolic capital of language because of their lesser access to power and greater social and psychological insecurity (for a review of explanations, see Labov 2001: 275–78) or "their greater assumption of responsibility for the upward mobility of their children" (Labov 2001: 178).

A major research aim of socio-historical studies on language and gender is to test – on the basis of historical data – the hypotheses about gender differentiation in modern languages. As interest was increasingly devoted to the dynamics of the relations between the social and the linguistic, gender differences came to be described as small but sociolinguistically significant. Researchers' attention was turned to the supposedly specific role of women in the processes of language change.

Research into present-day gender variation in language has amply demonstrated that gender is intertwined with social rank in its significance for the processes of language change (Labov 2001). Milroy and Milroy (1993) have suggested that it may be that women, by adopting innovations, actually create prestige rather than adopting forms that are prestigious. Their data testify to women's association with forms that gain supralocal usage.

Labov's formulation of the 'gender paradox' (2001: 293) refers to the notion of women's tendency to conform (or not) to sociolinguistic norms. Their conformist (or non-conformist) behavior depends on whether these norms are overtly prescribed and if so, when. While Labov observed in the earliest stages of a sound change a relative independence of speaker's sex and social class, he concluded that interaction between the two is highest at a later stage, in changes "where the stigmatized or prestige form is recognized and discussed in the speech community" (Labov 2001: 320). In other words, social status becomes more relevant when a change rises above the level of public awareness. It is then that women's role in leading the change is noticeable, as they turn out to be responding to the social status of linguistic variables more actively and more rapidly than men (Labov 2001: 321).

If the gendered tendencies in language change are ultimately due to women's and men's different socialization patterns, as suggested by some authors

(L. Milroy 1999), descriptions of gender-appropriate behavior in different communities, especially societal expectations and pressures about language use, are highly relevant to explaining the mechanism of change.[20] However, women's special role in change involving prestige linguistic forms is based on the presumption that they have access to the high prestige norm (Labov 1990). In the case of women in the past, this access is often questionable (see Nevalainen 2006a). In historical studies of language and gender, much attention has been given to men's and women's different contact with the standard language via education and schooling. In her investigation of language change, Nevalainen (2000: 53) draws the following conclusion: "[w]omen were not in the forefront of the professionally led change away from multiple negation in Early Modern English. This gender difference may be best explained in terms of the two sexes' differential access to education in general and to professional specializations in particular."

An understanding of historical gender roles may provoke a reconsideration of the hypothesis about the process of language change being gendered. It seems that, historically, women had been assigned a predominant role in the education of children. More and more grammar books were written with the purpose of assisting mothers (or, more generally, caregivers) to fulfill their role as educators of (their own) children (Tieken-Boon van Ostade 2010). An example is a book (published in 1800 in London) whose purpose is spelled out in the title: *The Child's Grammar, Designed to Enable Ladies Who May Not Have Attended to the Subject Themselves to Instruct Their Children*. The home was the place where young people were to learn cultivated language and the home upbringing was blamed for any neglect in this respect. We can presume that all members of the family were supposed to watch their language for the sake of the children, but it was the mother's responsibility to teach and, when necessary, to correct errors.

> Home is the place where we form many, if not the most of our habits, both of action and speech. These habits we carry into the world. They cling to us like leeches. [...] Be assured, my young friends, that your language at home will give character and tone to your language abroad, and that your language in the most refined circles in which you may mingle will tell a sure tale of your home language.
>
> (Weaver 1854: 154)

If nineteenth-century women did have greater responsibility (than men) for the acquisition of linguistic skills by children, then the hypothesis of women's preference for prestigious language forms as driven by their care for the well-being of the children needs to be seriously considered within this historical context.

Systematic studies of historical language corpora that include private writings, such as the Corpus of Early English Correspondence, prove fruitful for testing hypotheses about the gender effect in the processes of language change. Nevalainen and Raumolin-Brunberg (2003) review previous studies as well as their own investigation of the gender pattern as relevant to language change in English in Tudor and Stuart times. They examine a number of changes: those that turn out to be gender-affiliated are so from the "new and vigorous stage" of the change through to "its (near-)completion" (2003: 130). The authors also claim a "female advantage in language change regardless of the social embedding of the process" (2003: 131) and follow Milroy and Milroy's (1993) hypothesis about the priority of gender over social class, declaring that gender overrides rank in Tudor and Stuart England. Overall, in the period investigated, the pattern of female advantage in the process of language change "was already clearly in evidence" (Nevalainen and Raumolin-Brunberg 2003: 131).

Sometimes, when the social circumstances of change are closely examined, the 'gender effect' proves less relevant than other factors. Nevalainen's work (1999) has shown that the change in the third person verb marking from –(e)th to –(e)s was stratified by social rank as well as by gender (see also Kytö 1993). The patterning of this change has, however, been much more adequately described as being related to the speakers' geographical origins and social mobility in England from the early fifteenth century and through the sixteenth, as well as the migration of the northern population south and to London (see Nevalainen and Raumolin-Brunberg 2003: 38–40; Nevalainen 2006a: 184–93).

In general, hypotheses about the processes of socially conditioned historical language change (for instance, the hypothesis about the special role of women as leaders of change) have sometimes been questioned due to insufficient and/or unrepresentative data. However, studies of individuals in historical periods have a particular, and quite exceptional, advantage over studies of present-day speakers: historical corpora make available data that may cover the whole lifetime of informants, as in the case of the Corpus of Early English Correspondence, in which some letter collections span fifty years (Raumolin-Brunberg 2005: 40). This presents the researchers with true 'real-time' data which are not easily accessible for descriptions of ongoing current change.

Sociolinguistics has appealed to speaker age to describe how change is taken up by speakers of certain age cohorts and is then transmitted to successive generations. Tracing language change has benefited much from apparent time studies which, however, rest on the assumption that people's language patterns remain relatively stable from adolescence through adulthood (see Chapter 23 in this *Handbook*). While this may be an acceptable idealization for sound patterns, lexical and syntactic features do change in adulthood and speakers, at any stage of their lives, are often very aware of new words entering their vocabulary.

Historical corpora prove particularly useful in refining our descriptions of language change and the apparent time methodology (see Raumolin-Brunberg 1998) by giving researchers the opportunity to observe change in real time. Additionally, they offer data for longitudinal studies of individuals. Raumolin-Brunberg (2005) pointed out this great advantage of historical sources and refined the description of a change which happened over the lives of adults who lived between 1570 and 1670. By looking at the age of the speakers Raumolin-Brunberg demonstrates the gradual shift in their use of the present indicative third person singular verbal suffix, from -(e)th to -(e)s, which is relatively well documented in the historical corpus. Raumolin-Brunberg argues that a quantitative analysis of six generations of speakers, as well as that of each generation of speakers, suggests that the change in question is both generational and communal (Raumolin-Brunberg 2005: 44).

Moreover, an investigation of individual usage reveals variation that can be explained in terms of the authors' social and geographical contexts and that is, in general, consonant with the tendency for an overall increase of the use of the -(e)s suffix. Raumolin-Brunberg shows how empirical evidence from historical corpora gives the lie to the idea that speakers do not change language patterns in adulthood. She finds some corroboration for her findings from recent research done on change in idiolects in a modern language: Nahkola and Saanilahti (2004) claim that "categorical linguistic features are inclined to remain categorical in the idiolect [...] If a speaker acquires a feature with little or no variation in it, no major changes are likely to take place during the speaker's lifetime" (2004: 90). However, if speakers acquire a truly variable feature, that is, one with no one prevailing variant, they are likely to shift during their lifetime.

Raumolin-Brunberg concludes that her quantitative results confirm the idea that features acquired as categorical do not change in an individual's lifetime. However, she points out that change is instigated by innovators, and "there is no evidence that these innovators are children" (Raumolin-Brunberg 2005: 47). Admittedly, investigations of children's language patterns on the basis of historical corpora are difficult.

8. Conclusions

While assuming that we can use the present to understand the past, we cannot make hasty generalizations about the quality of correlations between a present-day society and language as being the same as those between a past society and its language. In other words, in accounts of both modern and historical language variation an in-depth social understanding of a given demographic dimension must be the basis of linguistic explorations.

Earlier sociolinguistic studies viewed the non-linguistic variables which correlate with linguistic variation in a deterministic way. More recently, especially with the rising popularity of discourse-analytic approaches, demographic categories have come to be treated as complex social dimensions which are mediated through language and discourse, and are, in fact, discursively constructed and negotiated. The study of historical discourses provides data for the rethinking of social variables and their relation to linguistic patterns. Ultimately, both in studies of present-day languages and historical varieties, sociolinguists are challenged by the versatility of social dimensions and the interrelations between different non-linguistic variables, as well as the complexity of their relationships with language patterns.

Historical sociolinguistics has provided many insights into the history of the social embedding of language. Its sensitivity to geographical and historical local context and the careful consideration of the mechanisms through which social context affects speakers' linguistic choices may lead to the recognition of universal or panchronic sociolinguistic patterns.

From the point of view of the social conditioning of language variation it is a major drawback of historical sources that they under-represent the less literate members of society, such as lower rank speakers and women. One way to circumvent this would be to look closely into the (often unpublished) texts authored by the socially backgrounded and read their stories. More generally, reading the complete textual records of individual lifetimes is rewarding, and adds to our understanding of the (linguistic) developments of an individual over a lifespan, which so far have been under-appreciated.

Analyses of historical texts show much intra-individual and in-group variation, reveal details of contextual factors, and draw vivid pictures of individual behavior. This complements quantitative work on linguistic features and contributes to the reconstruction of collective patterns of sociolinguistic stability and change. Moreover, historical sociolinguistics offers methodological benefits to the study of language change, in that it makes it possible to study change in both real and apparent time, and thus enables us to test and refine the latter method.

The traditional studies of sociolinguistic variation in terms of the variables of gender, age, and social class, have given way to more dynamic approaches based on social networking and social mobility (see Chapter 18 in this *Handbook*). Historical sociolinguists have drawn (socio)linguists' attention to some elements of the social context as, in different historical times, relevant in different ways for linguistic phenomena. Recovering these dynamic processes of sociolinguistic conditioning from historical text is a challenge. To relate to earlier studies, the researcher must at least recognize the interrelationships between the traditional variables and show how they interacted to produce complex language variation patterns.

NOTES

1   See Watts' application of Foucault's (2002) idea of an 'archive' in historical sociolinguistics, at http://homepages.vub.ac.be/~rvosters/conf_brugge.pdf
2   CEEC is a corpus of letters covering the period between 1410 and 1681; it contains 2.7 million words and was created at the University of Helsinki (Nevalainen and Raumolin-Brunberg 1996). CONCE is a multi-genre, one-million-word corpus, compiled at Uppsala University and the University of Tampere (Kytö *et al*. 2000).
3   The manuscript of Mary Jackson Lee's letter-journal is owned by the Massachusetts Historical Society and has been published in microform as a part of the *Microfilm edition of the Lee family papers (1535–1957)*.
4   It was a common practice in the eighteenth and the nineteenth centuries to keep copies of letters in order to record what had been written and when, as a letter usually took long to reach the addressee. These copies of letters sent out were put together to create the so-called letter-journals. Letter-journals might alternatively be collections of unsent letters, kept for the addressee to read later.

5   Martha Ballard's diary has been turned into an internet resource: it is available online from a magnificent history web site (*Martha Ballard's Diary Online* at www.dohistory.org), developed and maintained by the Film Study Center at Harvard University, which offers the manuscript of the diary itself as well as its transcription and numerous links to primary documents and other archival sources associated with the period in question. One extremely useful feature of the website is its search engine, which locates words or strings of words in the whole diary or in selected portions of the text. Martha's diary daily entries include about 430 000 words. For more information see Petrik's (2000) review of the site at http://www.albany.edu/jmmh/vol3/dohistory/dohistory.html [accessed October 14, 2011].

6   A part of the New England corpus referred to here is the journal by Mary Jackson Lee, an aristocratic Boston housewife, dated 1813–1816 (c. 84 000 words), consisting of copies of letters she wrote to her husband, Henry Lee, and 40 letters (c. 17 200 words) written by Henry Lee to his wife between 1812 and 1813 (edited by Morse 1926). See also : *Microfilm edition of the Lee Family Papers, 1535–1957*. Massachusetts Historical Society.

7   Mary Paul, for example, from rural Vermont, decided to look for a better fortune in the Lowell textile factory. In a letter to her father, seeking his consent, she argued:
    I think it would be much better for me than to stay about here. I could earn more to begin with than I can anywhere about here. I am in need of clothes which I cannot get if I stay about here and for that reason I want to go to Lowell or some other place. We think if I could go with some steady girl that I might do well. (Mary Paul's letter of September 13, 1845; quoted from Dublin 1993: 124).

8   Eckert (1990: 246–247) very aptly explains how researchers, in descriptions of language variation, have sometimes referred to survey categories, such as class, age, or sex, rather than more directly to their social significance. Instead, it is the social practices of speakers that should be relevant to linguistic variation: "[l]ike age, sex is a biological category that serves as a fundamental basis for the differentiation of roles, norms, and expectations in all societies. It is these roles, norms and expectations that constitute gender, the social construction of sex" (1990: 246).

9   For a discussion of how and why gender difference, rather than similarity, is preferred in popular publications and foregrounded in research results, see Cameron (2008: 41–58).

10   Eckert (1989) pointed to the difference between women in disparate social groups (female Jocks and female Burnouts), stressing the interconnection of gender with other social variables.

11   Some young women of merchant families did not particularly like this duty. Cott (1977: 52–53) quotes an ambitious daughter of the Lee family complaining of the idleness of a woman's life: "a young man can occupy himself with his business, and look forward to his life and prospects, but all we have to do is to pass our time agreeably to ourselves."

12   Although Massachusetts law provided protection to widows, in practice widowhood was a source of property-related problems and women frequently preferred to remarry. For a study of the status of widows in early eighteenth-century Massachusetts, see Keyssar (1974).

13   According to Cott (1977), at the turn of the eighteenth century around 90% of American women were married.

14   Statistics concerning literacy need to be taken with caution. In many studies, the estimates of literacy are based on counting signatures (more recently labeled as 'signature literacy'), which is an indicator of the ability to read (Nevalainen and Raumolin Brunberg 2003: 42, referring to Reay 1998).

15   Donawerth (2002: 8) shows that, according to Lydia Sigourney (1851), training in elocution for women was related to the need of their being "clearly understood" when they read aloud to family members.

16   By 1750 the literacy rate for males was about 75% and for females 65%. By 1815 male literacy reached 90%–95% and female literacy 80%–90% (Gilmore-Lehne 1999).

17   In the times of the American Revolution, only about half of New England women could sign their names (Lockridge 1974; Cott 1977). However, after the American Revolution, primary education for women expanded widely and became seen as important because women were recognized as the first teachers of their own, and others', children.

18   Webster himself was very committed to the education of young women. He wanted to eradicate illiteracy (among both men and women) and endorsed plans for providing equal educational opportunities for women (Unger 1998).

19   See also Percy (1994, 2003) and Tieken-Boon van Ostade (2000c) for information about "women's grammars" – grammar books written in eighteenth-century England by women and/or for women.

20   For example, Kiełkiewicz-Janowiak and Pawelczyk (2009) showed how in the local Polish context it is women rather than men who have been made responsible for the cultivation and enforcement of the linguistic norm. The study shows Polish society to be particularly linguistic-norm oriented, with women being assigned (and having taken on) the special role of caring educators, responsible for both their own children and the generations to come. The pronounced Polish concern with standardness and linguistic appropriateness ("the cult of the norm") combined with the 'Polish mother' ideology has defined the special role of women in spreading the prestigious variants (Kiełkiewicz-Janowiak and Pawelczyk 2009: 9).

REFERENCES

Bailey, R.W. (1991) *Images of English: A Cultural History of the Language*, Cambridge University Press, Cambridge.

Bailey, R.W. (1996) *Nineteenth-Century English*, University of Michigan Press, Ann Arbor.

Bax, R. (2005) Traces of Johnson in the language of Fanny Burney. *International Journal of English Studies* 5(1): 159–81.

Bergs, A. (2005) *Social Networks and Historical Sociolinguistics. Studies in Morphosyntactic Variation in the Paston Letters (1421–1503)*, Mouton de Gruyter, Berlin.

Biber, C. and Burges, J. (2000) Historical change in the language use of women and men: gender differences in dramatic dialogue. *Journal of English Linguistics* 28: 21–37.

Bingham, C. (1785/1981) *The Young Lady's Accidence. A Short and Easy Introduction to English Grammar*, Greenleaf and Freeman, Boston. [Reprinted in 1981 by Scholars' Facsimiles and Reprints, Delmar, NY.]

Burke, P. (1992) *History and Social Theory*, Polity Press, Cambridge.

Cameron, D. (2008) *The myth of Mars and Venus: Do Men and Women Really Speak Different Languages?* Oxford University Press, Oxford.

Cheshire, J. and Gardner-Chloros, P. (1997) Communicating gender in two languages. In H. Kotthoff and R. Wodak (eds.), *Communicating Gender in Context*, John Benjamins, Amsterdam, pp. 249–81.

Conde-Silvestre, J.C. and Hernandez-Campoy, J.M. (2004) A sociolinguistic approach to the diffusion of Chancery written practices in late fifteenth century private correspondence. *Neuphilologische Mitteilungen* 105(2): 133–52.

Cooke, Rev. T. (1796) *The Universal Letter-Writer: or, New Art of Polite Correspondence . . .* , Printed for A. Millar, W. Law and R. Cater, London; Printed for Wilson, Spence, and Mawman, York.

Cott, N. (1977) *The Bonds of Womanhood: "Woman's Sphere" in New England, 1780–1835*, Yale University Press, New Haven, CT.

Culpeper, J. and Kytö, M. (1997) Towards a corpus of dialogues, 1550–1750. In H. Ramisch and K. Wynne (eds.), *Language in Time and Space: Studies in Honour of*

Wolfgang Viereck on the Occasion of his 60th Birthday, Franz Steiner Verlag, Stuttgart, pp. 60–73.

Culpeper, J. and Kytö, M. (2010) *Early Modern English Dialogues. Spoken Interaction as Writing*, Cambridge University Press, Cambridge.

Dierks, K. (2000) The familiar letter and social refinement in America, 1750–1800. In D. Barton and N. Hall (eds.), *Letter Writing as a Social Practice*, John Benjamins, Amsterdam, pp. 31–41.

Donawerth, J. (2002) Nineteenth-Century United States conduct book rhetoric by women. *Rhetoric Review* 21(1): 5–21.

Dossena, M. and Tieken-Boon van Ostade, I. (eds.) (2008) *Studies in Late Modern English Correspondence: Methodology and Data*, Peter Lang, Bern.

Dublin, T. (ed.) (1982/1993) *Women's Letters, 1830–1860* (2nd edn), Columbia University Press, Washington, DC.

Dublin, T. (1994) *Transforming Women's Work: New England Lives in the Industrial Revolution*, Cornell University Press, Ithaca, NY.

Eckert, P. (1989) *Jocks and Burnouts: Social Categories and Identity in the High School*, Teachers College Press, New York.

Eckert, P. (1990) The whole woman: sex and gender differences in variation. *Language Variation and Change* 1(3): 245–67.

Eckert, P. (2000) *Linguistic Variation as Social Practice*, Blackwell, Oxford.

Fischer, J.L. (1958) Social influences on the choice of a linguistic variant. *Word* 14: 47–56.

Fitzmaurice, S. (2000) *The Spectator*, the politics of social networks, and language standardization in eighteenth-century England. In L. Wright (ed.), *The Development of Standard English, 1300–1800: Theories, Descriptions, Conflicts*, Cambridge University Press, Cambridge, pp. 195–218.

Fitzmaurice, S. (2002) *The Familiar Letter in Early Modern English*, John Benjamins, Amsterdam.

Foucault, M. (2002) *Archaeology of Knowledge*, Routledge, London.

Gilmore-Lehne, W. (1989) *Reading Becomes a Necessity of Life: Material and Cultural Life in Rural New England, 1780–1835*, University of Tennessee Press, Knoxville.

Hakanen, M. and Koskinen, U. (2009) From 'friends' to 'patrons' transformations in the social power structure as reflected in the rhetoric of personal letters in 16th- and 17th-century Sweden. *Journal of Historical Pragmatics* 10(1): 1–22.

Holmes, J. (1995) *Women, Men and Politeness*, Longman, London.

Holmes J. and Meyerhoff, M. (eds.) (2003) *The Handbook of Language and Gender*, Blackwell, Oxford.

Holmes, J. and Stubbe, M. (2003) *Power and Politeness in the Workplace: A Sociolinguistic Analysis of Talk at Work*, Pearson, London.

James, D. (1996) Women, men and prestige speech forms: a critical review. In V. Bergvall, J. Bing, and A. Freed (eds.), *Rethinking Language and Gender Research: Theory and Practice*, Longman, London, pp. 98–125.

Jucker, A.H., Fritz, G., and Lebsanft, F. (eds.) (1999) *Historical Dialogue Analysis*, John Benjamins, Amsterdam.

Karlsen, C.F. and Crumpacker, L. (eds.) (1984) *The Journal of Esther Edwards Burr*, Yale University Press, New Haven, CT.

Keyssar, A. (1974) Widowhood in eighteenth-century Massachusetts: a problem in the history of the family. *Perspectives in American History* 8: 83–119.

Kiełkiewicz-Janowiak, A. (2002) "Women's Language"? A Socio-historical View: Private Writings in Early New England*, Motivex, Poznań.

Kiełkiewicz-Janowiak, A. (2003) Language and society in the diaries of two women in early New England. In M. Dossena and C. Jones (eds.), *Insights into Late Modern English*, Peter Lang, Bern, pp. 331–49.

Kiełkiewicz-Janowiak A. and Pawelczyk, J. (2009) Socio-cultural conditioning of the sex/prestige pattern: the local Polish context. In J. de Bres *et al.* (eds.), *Proceedings of the 5th Biennial International Gender and Language Association Conference IGALA 5, Wellington 2008*, (CD edn), Victoria University, Wellington, NZ.

Klein, L.E. (1996) Gender and the public/private distinction in the eighteenth century: some questions about evidence and analytic procedure. *Eighteenth-Century Studies* 29(1): 97–109.

Kytö, M. (1993) Third-person singular verb inflection in early British and American English. 5(2): 113–39.

Kytö, M., Rudanko, J., and Smitterberg, E. (eds.) (2000) Building a bridge between the present and the past: a corpus of 19th-century English. *ICAME Journal* 24: 85–97.

Kytö, M., Rydén, M., and Smitterberg, E. (eds.) (2006) *Nineteenth-Century English: Stability and Change*, Cambridge University Press, Cambridge.

Labov, W. (1984) Research methods of the project on linguistic change and variation. In J. Baugh and J. Sherzer (eds.), *Language in Use: Readings in Sociolinguistics*, Prentice Hall, Englewood Cliffs, NJ, pp. 28–53.

Labov, W. (1990) The intersection of sex and social class in the course of linguistic change. *Language Variation and Change* 2(2): 205–54.

Labov, W. (1994) *Principles of Linguistic Change, Vol. 1: Internal Factors*, Blackwell, Oxford.

Labov, W. (2001) *Principles of Linguistic Change Vol. 2: Social Factors*, Blackwell, Oxford.

Laurence, A. (1994) *Women in England 1500–1760. A Social History*, Phoenix, London.

Lockridge, K.A. (1974) *Literacy in Colonial New England*, Norton, New York.

Maltz, D. and Borker, R. (1982) A cultural approach to male–female miscommunication. In J. Gumperz (ed.), *Language and Social Identity*, Cambridge University Press, Cambridge, pp. 196–216.

Milroy, L. (1980) *Language and Social Networks*, Blackwell, Oxford.

Milroy, L. (1992) New perspectives in the analysis of sex differentiation in language. In K. Bolton and H. Kwok (eds.), *Sociolinguistics Today: International Perspectives*, Routledge, London, pp. 163–79.

Milroy, L. (1999) Women as innovators and norm-creators: the sociolinguistics of dialect leveling in a northern English city. In S. Wertheim, A.C. Bailey, and M. Corston-Olivier (eds.), *Engendering Communication: Proceedings from the*

Fifth Berkeley Women and Language Conference, Berkeley Women and Language Group, Berkeley, CA, pp. 361–76.

Milroy, J. and Milroy, L. (1993) Mechanisms of change in urban dialects: the role of class, social network and gender. *International Journal of Applied Linguistics* 3: 57–77.

Morse, F.R. (1926) *Henry and Mary Lee. Letters and Journals with Other Family Letters 1802–1860*, privately printed, Boston.

Mugglestone, L. (1995) 'Talking proper': *The Rise of Accent as Social Symbol*, Clarendon Press, Oxford.

Mugglestone, L. (ed.) (2006) *The Oxford History of English*, Oxford University Press, Oxford.

Mullany, L. (2007) *Gendered Discourse in the Professional Workplace*, Palgrave Macmillan, Basingstoke.

Nahkola, K. and Saanilahti, M. (2004) Mapping language changes in real time: a panel study on Finnish. *Language Variation and Change* 16(2): 75–91.

Nevala, M. (2004) *Address in Early English Correspondence: Its Forms and Socio-pragmatic Functions*, Société Néophilologique, Helsinki.

Nevala, M. (2009) Altering distance and defining authority: person reference in Late Modern English. *Journal of Historical Pragmatics* 10(2): 238–59.

Nevalainen, T. (1996) Social stratification. In T. Nevalainen and H. Raumolin-Brunberg (eds.), pp. 57–76.

Nevalainen, T. (1999) Making the best use of 'bad' data: evidence for sociolinguistic variation in Early Modern English. *Neuphilologische Mitteilungen* 100(4): 499–533.

Nevalainen, T. (2000) Gender differences in the evolution of standard English: evidence from the Corpus of Early English Correspondence. *Journal of English Linguistics* 28(1): 38–59.

Nevalainen, T. (2006a) Mapping change in Tudor English. In L. Mugglestone (ed.), pp. 178–211.

Nevalainen, T. (2006b) Historical sociolinguistics and language change. In A. van Kemenade and B. Los (eds.), *The*

Handbook of the History of English, Blackwell, Oxford, pp. 558–88.

Nevalainen, T. and Raumolin-Brunberg, H. (1995) Constraints on politeness. The pragmatics of address formulae in Early Modern English correspondence. In A.H. Jucker (ed.), *Historical Pragmatics*, John Benjamins, Amsterdam, pp. 541–601.

Nevalainen, T. and Raumolin-Brunberg, H. (1996) The Corpus of Early English Correspondence. In T. Nevalainen and H. Raumolin-Brunberg (eds.), pp. 39–54.

Nevalainen, T. and Raumolin-Brunberg, H. (eds.) (1996) *Sociolinguistics and Language History. Studies Based on the Corpus of Early English Correspondence*, Rodopi, Amsterdam.

Nevalainen, T. and Raumolin-Brunberg, H. (2003) *Historical Sociolinguistics: Language Change in Tudor and Stuart England*, Pearson Education, London.

Newcomb, H. (1850) *How to Be a Lady: A Book for Girls, Containing Useful Hints on the Formation of Character* (8th edn), Gould, Kendall, and Lincoln, Boston.

Nichols, T.L. (1874) *Behaviour: A Manual of Manners and Morals*. London.

Nurmi, A., Nevala, M., and Palander-Collin, M. (eds.) (2009) *The Language of Daily Life in England (1400–1800)*, John Benjamins, Amsterdam.

Okulska, U. (2006a) *Gender and the Formation of Modern Standard English. A Sociolinguistic Corpus Study with Early Modern English in Focus*, Peter Lang, Frankfurt am Main.

Okulska, U. (2006b) Textual strategies in the diplomatic correspondence of the Middle and Early Modern English periods: the narrative report letter as a genre. In M. Dossena and S.M. Fitzmaurice (eds.), *Business and Official Correspondence: Historical Investigations*, Peter Lang, Bern, pp. 47–76.

Okulska, U. (2006c) Diachronic corpus research: towards a holistic reconstruction of the spoken modality of English. In A. Duszak and U. Okulska (eds.), *Bridges and Barriers in Metalinguistic Discourse*, Peter Lang, Frankfurt am Main, pp. 181–200.

Okulska, U. (2006d) Historical corpora and their applicability to sociolinguistic,

discourse-pragmatic, and ethno-linguistic research. *Poznan Studies in Contemporary Linguistics* 41: 87–109.

Okulska, U. (2010) Performing the world of politics through the discourse of institutional correspondence in Late Middle and Early Modern England. In U. Okulska and P. Cap (eds.), *Perspectives in Politics and Discourse*, John Benjamins, Amsterdam, pp. 173–97.

Pallander-Collin, M. (1999) Male and female styles in 17th-century correspondence: I THINK. *Language Variation and Change* 11(2): 123–41.

Palander-Collin, M. (2009) Variation and change in patterns of self-reference in early English correspondence. *Journal of Historical Pragmatics* 10(2): 260–85.

Pallander-Collin, M. and Nevala, M. (eds.) (2005) *Letters and Letter Writing*. Special issue of *European Journal of English Studies* 9/1.

Percy, C. (1994) Paradigms for their sex? Women's grammars in late eighteenth-century England. *Histoire Epistémologie Langage* 16: 121–41.

Percy, C. (2003) The art of grammar in the age of sensibility: *The Accidence . . . for Young Ladies* (1775). In M. Dossena and C. Jones (eds.), *Insights into Late Modern English*, Peter Lang, Bern, pp. 45–82.

Petrik, P. (2000) Web site review of DoHistory, *Journal for MultiMedia History*, http://www.albany.edu/jmmh/vol3/dohistory/dohistory.html [accessed October 14, 2011].

Pierson, G.W. (1938) *Tocqueville and Beaumont in America*, Oxford University Press, New York.

Raumolin-Brunberg, H. (1998) Social factors and pronominal change in the seventeenth century: the Civil War effect? In J. Fisiak and M. Krygier (eds.), *Advances in English Historical Linguistics*, Mouton de Gruyter, Berlin, pp. 361–88.

Raumolin-Brunberg, H. (2005) Language change in adulthood: historical letters as evidence. *European Journal of English Studies* 9(1): 37–51.

Raumolin-Brunberg, H. (2006) Leaders of linguistic change in Early Modern England.

In R. Facchinetti and M. Rissanen (eds.), *Corpus-based Studies of Diachronic English*, Peter Lang, Frankfurt am Main, pp. 115–34.

Raumolin-Brunberg, H. (2009) Lifespan changes in the language of three early modern gentlemen. In A. Nurmi, M. Nevala, and M. Palander-Collin (eds.), *The Language of Daily Life in England (1450–1800)*, John Benjamins, Amsterdam, pp. 165–96.

Reay, B. (1998) *Popular Cultures in England 1550–1750*, Longman, London.

Rogers, K.M. (1982) *Feminism in Eighteenth-Century England*, University of Illinois Press, Urbana.

Sairio, A. (2009) *Language and Letters of the Bluestocking Network. Sociolinguistic Issues in Eighteenth-Century Epistolary English*, Société Néophilologique, Helsinki.

Sigourney, L. (1837/1851) *Letters to My Pupils: with Narrative and Biographical Sketches*, New York.

Talbot, M. (2003) Gender stereotypes: reproduction and challenge. In J. Holmes and M. Meyerhoff (eds.), pp. 468–86.

Tieken-Boon van Ostade, I. (2000a) Sociohistorical linguistics and the observer's paradox. In D. Kastovsky and A. Mettinger (eds.), *The History of English in a Social Context: A Contribution to Historical Sociolinguistics*, Mouton de Gruyter, Berlin, pp. 441–61.

Tieken-Boon van Ostade, I. (2000b) Social network analysis and the language of Sarah Fielding. *European Journal of English Studies* 3(4): 291–301.

Tieken-Boon van Ostade, I. (2000c) Female grammarians of the eighteenth century. *Historical Sociolinguistics and Sociohistorical Linguistics* 1(1), http://www.let.leidenuniv.nl/hsl_shl/femgram.htm [accessed October 14, 2011].

Tieken-Boon van Ostade, I. (2003) Lowth's language. In M. Dossena, M. Gotti, and C. Jones (eds.), *Insights into Late Modern English*, Peter Lang, Frankfurt am Main, pp. 241–64.

Tieken-Boon van Ostade, I. (2006a) English at the onset of the normative tradition. In L. Mugglestone (ed.), pp. 240–73.

Tieken-Boon van Ostade, I. (2006b) Disrespectful and too familiar? Abbreviations as an index of politeness in eighteenth-century letters. In C. Dalton-Puffer, N. Ritt, H. Schendl, and D. Kastovsky (eds.), *Syntax, Style and Grammatical Norms: English from 1500–2000*, Peter Lang, Frankfurt am Main, pp. 229–47.

Tieken-Boon van Ostade, I. (2009) *An Introduction to Late Modern English*, Edinburgh University Press, Edinburgh.

Tieken-Boon van Ostade, I. (2010) Age and the codification of the English language. In A. Duszak and U. Okulska (eds.), *Language, Culture and the Dynamics of Age*, Mouton de Gruyter, Berlin, pp. 349–74.

Tiisala, S. (2004) Power and politeness: language and salutation formulas in correspondence between Sweden and the German Hanse. *Journal of Historical Pragmatics* 5(2): 193–206.

Trudgill, P. (1974) *The Social Differentiation of English in Norwich*, Cambridge University Press, Cambridge.

Trudgill, P. (1983) *On Dialect: Social and Geographical Perspectives*, Blackwell, Oxford.

Unger, H.G. (1998) *Noah Webster: The Life and Times of an American Patriot*, John Wiley & Sons, New York.

Weaver, G.S. (1854) *Hopes and Helps for the Young of Both Sexes*, Fowlers and Wells, New York.

Wolfram, W. (1969) *A Sociolinguistic Description of Negro Speech in Detroit*, Center for Applied Linguistics, Arlington, VA.

Wrightson, K. (1991) Estates, degrees, and sorts: changing perceptions of society in Tudor and Stuart England. In P.J. Corfield (ed.), *Language, History and Class*, Blackwell, Oxford, pp. 30–52.

18 The Role of Social Networks and Mobility in Diachronic Sociolinguistics[1]

JUAN CAMILO CONDE-SILVESTRE

1. The Social Network Hypothesis in Sociolinguistic Research

In the late 1970s, when synchronic sociolinguistic research was yielding mature fruit, James and Lesley Milroy carried out a joint research project in Belfast which, in addition to providing a complete description of vernacular varieties from that city, afforded scholars new methodological tenets integrated into a micro-sociolinguistic approach to the study of language variation and change (J. Milroy and L. Milroy 1985; J. Milroy 1992; 1998). Among these principles are:

(a) The maintenance of a distinction between stability and change in the study of languages: while accepting that change is inherent in languages, a well-grounded approach should also consider the maintenance of linguistic states, so that studying the circumstances contributing to the perpetuation of languages would also contribute to our understanding of the conditions under which changes are *actuated*.

(b) The importance of analyzing separately (i) the linguistic behavior of speakers, as the proper actors of changes in language, and (ii) the systemic aspects affected, and, as a result, the establishment of a fundamental distinction between 'innovation' and 'change:' the former is any spontaneous verbal act by an individual which may reach others in interaction with him or her, while

The Handbook of Historical Sociolinguistics, First Edition. Edited by Juan Manuel Hernández-Campoy and Juan Camilo Conde-Silvestre.
© 2014 John Wiley & Sons, Ltd. Published 2014 by John Wiley & Sons, Ltd.

the latter follows from the diffusion of the innovative variant once it has reached social significance (see also Chapter 22 in this *Handbook*).

(c) The importance of seeking the origins of innovations by observing 'natural language' (L. Milroy 1991), that is, the linguistic behavior of speakers in inter-action. In this respect, the study of spontaneous, context-bound speech acts pragmatically or phatically oriented towards listeners and contributing to reinforce social relationships gains prominence.

As an heuristic consequence – a means to secure the micro-sociolinguistic analysis of individual speakers in everyday interaction – the sociological construct 'social network' was added to the list of independent variables that were already being applied in sociolinguistic research: age, gender, ethnicity, socio-economic status, style, and so on. This follows from the application of the notion in other fields, such as anthropology, social psychology, and economic and business studies, where social networks refer to the type, strength, and length of the inter-personal contacts (ties) that individuals establish both inside and outside their usual circle: the fabric of personal links and relationships between individuals (Hernández-Campoy and Almeida 2005: 64–65; Conde-Silvestre 2007: 164–76).[2] A social networks is close-knit and dense if most of its members keep some relation-ship with the others, so that if several individuals from the same network talk about a third or fourth party, it is likely that all of them have some acquaintance with him or her. Networks can also be loose-knit and less dense, when the mutual conversance of their members is less widespread: some of them have relationships with others, while others have only sporadic, brief bonds. Finally, networks can be multiplex or uniplex depending on the social domains in which interpersonal contact is established: in the workplace, the neighborhood, within groups of friends, kin, or family, in one or more than one capacity at the same time. Finally, the ties that bind individuals from the same network can be strong or weak, depending on a variety of factors, such as duration, periodicity, emotional inten-sity, intimacy, reciprocity, or the function of the relationships (Boissevain 1974; 1987).

James and Lesley Milroy (1985) applied social networks to the interpretation of language variation and change in Belfast. They took as a premise the sociological observation that the structural properties of networks – their density, multiplexity, reciprocity, and so on – may influence the behavior of their individual members and, following Granovetter's (1973, 1982) theory of strong and weak ties, studied the links between networks and the *actuation* and diffusion of linguistic changes in the city between 1975 and 1982. They showed that individuals receive pressure from members of their own social network to maintain the linguistic variety that they normally use. This norm-enforcing pressure is stronger when the ties between speakers are dense and multiplex and, accordingly, the network is close-knit, with many strong ties: virtually everybody knows everyone else in the group and their mutual relationship affects more than one sphere (profession, family, friends, etc.). Such situations tend to be "hostile to influence from outside" (Tieken-Boon van Ostade 2006: 251) and usually result in resistance to innovation, including language change. There are, however, individuals who, by virtue of their social and spatial mobility, may establish weak, uniplex ties within loose-knit networks, and they are more exposed to linguistic innovations originating outside the group: "their mobility brings them into contact with other social networks and hence with different speech norms which may influence their own language and that of those around them" (Tieken-Boon van Ostade 2006: 251). The conclusion reached by James and Lesley Milroy has become a basic principle of contemporary sociolinguistic research: loose-knit networks favor the diffusion of innovations and, since interpersonal contacts within them require less effort and affect more speakers of different linguistic varieties and social status, their characteristic weak ties provide the bridges across which linguistic innovations can spread (J. Milroy and L. Milroy 1985: 363–66; L. Milroy 1980/1987; L. Milroy and J. Milroy 1992: 5–10; L. Milroy 2002).

In the terminology adopted by James and Lesley Milroy there is a crucial distinction between 'innovators' and 'early adopters.' Innovators are those who first introduce a new form into a group. They tend to be peripheral members of networks who are not highly affected by pressures to maintain vernacular local norms coming from inside. In contemporary western societies – and perhaps in the past as well – innovators tend to be socially and geographically mobile speakers, who remain on the edges of several networks and thus enjoy an enhanced capacity to establish a high number of uniplex, weak ties: as a result they are highly exposed to and conscious of innovations. Members of the highest and lowest social layers, however, tend to belong to close-knit, dense networks and to establish strong(er) multiplex ties within them, which favor resistance to innovations. Early adopters are usually the central, influential network members who start to use the innovation while establishing strong ties with others within their own close-knit network, while being at the same time weakly tied to innovators from outside (J. Milroy and L. Milroy 1985: 364–70; L. Milroy 2002: 562–63). This means that, once an innovation has been accepted by the early adopters, it diffuses rapidly outwards, from the center to the periphery, in a kind of "expanded centrality" which takes the innovation back to the margins, from where it spreads to other networks by way of the weak ties with their peripheral members (Labov 2001: 364).[3]

2. The Social Network Hypothesis in Historical Sociolinguistic Research

Historical sociolinguists are not unaware of the difficulties inherent in drawing connections between social networks and the patterning of linguistic variation and change in the past. Apart from the methodological complexities affecting the discipline – the 'bad data' problem in historical linguistic research – there are numerous obstacles to determining the extent and type of interpersonal relations in past times. Not only is it hard for researchers to reconstruct the socio-economic hierarchies of the past, even if some relevant evidence is available (see Chapter 5 in this *Handbook*), it is also difficult to determine the fabric of personal relationships that an individual could have established with those in his or her environment, and impossible to identify either the social domains where interaction took place or the degree of intimacy, all of which are factors that have become basic transactional components of the social network hypothesis in sociolinguistic research.

However, it is not totally irrational to assume – following the generalizability and uniformitarian principles (see Chapters 4 and 5 in this *Handbook*) – that, just as all human beings have a natural tendency to establish a variety of social relationships, the notion of social network could have a universal application. It is also reasonable to suppose that networks in the past, as in the present, would have consisted of links and bonds between individuals – metaphorically expressed as the 'dots-and-lines model' – and that, just as networks in the present show different patterns, depending on the ties between their members (loose-knit or close-knit), contacts involving speakers from the past would have also yielded different network structures that correlated with the development of some historically attested changes (Tieken-Boon van Ostade 2000a: 211–12). Moreover, the possibility of extending social networks to historical sociolinguistic research increases if they are taken as a general analytic construct, stripped of their quantitative component. With this methodological purpose in mind, Alexander Bergs (2000: 41; 2005: 44–47) has distinguished two dimensions of social networks in historical linguistics. The structural dimension captures the presence or absence of relationships as well as the physical appearance of the network, such as whether it is close-knit or loose-knit, the density of its fabric, and the situation of speakers at the center or periphery. Theoretically, it would not be impossible to reconstruct these elements for the past, provided that information can be gathered on "who is part of a given network and who is in contact with whom" (Bergs 2005: 46). In contrast, the transactional or attitudinal dimension is difficult to reconstruct. The personal aspects of relationships from the past, such as periodicity, intensity, reciprocity, and even function, depend on private or intimate facets and are based on notions – family, kinship, neighborhood, friendship, acquaintance, intimacy – which differ from society to society and from period to period. Just as in any other type of sociolinguistically-oriented research in the history of languages, the anachronistic fallacy should be avoided and, where networks are concerned, it must be borne in mind that "what constitutes an important transaction today need not necessarily have been an important transaction six hundred years ago" (Bergs 2005: 46; see also Bax 2000: 283, and Chapter 5 in this *Handbook*).

Heuristically useful, in this respect, is the distinction between 'ego-centric' and 'socio-centric' networks established by Barnes (1972). The former corresponds to the usual 'dots-and-lines model,' while the latter, at a more general level, does not necessarily rely on the establishment of proper links, but on the effects that the global, inclusive structure of networks has on the behavior (linguistic or otherwise) of groups and populations: "it is the concentration of indirect linkages, through a configuration of relations with properties that exist independently of particular agents which should be at the centre of attention" (Scott 1997: 75; see also Bergs 2005: 52).

These methodological distinctions afford at least three possible applications of social networks in historical (socio-)linguistic research. Firstly, networks can be used to describe communal change: global and *ad hoc* connections can be established between the prototypical organizations of society prevalent in a historical speech community and either the stability of linguistic structures or the rapid development of changes in different languages or periods of their history. As a result, historical and typological linguists have been able to find social motives for either the conservatism inherent in some languages or the highly innovative quality of others. If weak ties and loose networks facilitate innovation and change, and strong ties within close-knit networks facilitate maintenance, then "phases of stability should correspond to phases with stronger network structures, while phases of change should correspond to phases with weaker network structures" (Bergs 2005: 53). Secondly, a socio-centric application of networks is appropriate when the information available can only be ascribed to the group and network structures are included for consideration. For instance, it has been possible to establish the factors which could have favored social and geographical mobility as well as the establishment of weak ties between individuals in some speech communities and to relate them successfully to the implementation of historically attested language changes. Thirdly, it is sometimes possible – if sufficient linguistic and social data are available and they can be individuated – to reconstruct the ego-centric dimension of social networks from the past, to locate their central and peripheral members and, by analyzing their written production, to notice their degree of involvement in the diffusion of changes, either as innovators or as early adopters. In the following sections, some contributions to historical sociolinguistics that have relied on social networks within these directions of research will be discussed.

2.1   *From the typological to the socio-centric approach*

Meta-theoretically, social networks have proved useful for identifying the possible links between the basic patterning of social structures in historical communities and the long-term development of changes in the history of languages. This typological application derives from one of the conclusions reached by James and Lesley Milroy: dense and close-knit social networks with strong multiplex ties between their members tend to promote the stability of linguistic systems, while loose-knit networks with weak uniplex ties favor the diffusion of innovations and the *actuation* of language changes. A supra-individual application of this tenet has allowed historical linguists to explore the connections between types of communities from the past and the rate of change in their respective language histories: small and isolated communities, little affected by colonization or contact with other groups would not exhibit as many changes (or as many abrupt ones) as those which have historically been open to external influence – subject to industrialization, urbanization, epidemics, internal wars, immigration, and so on – with the result that their members had more opportunities to establish weak ties within loose-knit networks, at least in theory (J. Milroy and L. Milroy 1985: 375; Andersen

1988; Trudgill 2002: 709, 723). A well-known example is given by James and Lesley Milroy when they compare Icelandic, a conservative language with few changes attested since the late thirteenth century, and English, which has undergone radical changes in grammar and phonology over the last seven centuries. The authors try to relate these differences to the social patterning historically prevalent in both communities. In medieval Iceland, institutions tended to remain communal and social differences were not sharp. Textual evidence is interesting: in the medieval sagas, a complete genealogy of the main characters is given when they are introduced for the first time, and attention is often paid to ancestors, relatives, and friends: these relationships connect with each other in complex ways, both within a single text and intertextually. This may be taken as a clue that people – even if they belonged to distant geographical communities – could have been strongly tied with links of kinship, friendship (or, very often, enmity), acquaintance, and so on. This is posited by Lesley and James Milroy as a sensible reason behind the conservative nature of Icelandic (1985: 376–77). The sociological history of English is quite different, since the language was affected by the successive settlements by Danes (9th–10th centuries) and Normans (11th–13th centuries). James and Lesley Milroy claim that the coexistence of the native population with new settlers would have favored the development of unfocused group norms that have accompanied a higher rate of innovation and change in the history of English (1985: 378).

The idea that, in typological terms, immigration and contact with foreign communities favor the diffusion of innovations and changes – perhaps by loosening formerly dense network structures – has also been put forward in the field of Hispanic studies. Ralph Penny has proposed (2000: 63–67) that the reconquest by northern Christians of parts of Muslim Spain (12th–13th centuries) must have been accompanied by a major southwards displacement of the Castilian population. This may have meant, according to Penny, that the prototypical close-knit networks that characterized the personal relationships of Castilians while they inhabited the self-contained northern regions of the peninsula could have dissolved into loose-knit ones as soon as they occupied the central areas. An acknowledged result of this probable new sociological reality was the quick adoption in the reconquered territories of socio-political innovations, such as the replacement of Roman codes by Germanic customary law and a certain degree of receptiveness towards Muslim influences. Penny also believes that some linguistic developments in Castilian could be related to the new patterning of social networks: for instance, the change from Latin initial [f-], which still remains in the conservative northern varieties of Spanish, into [h-] or [Ø], typical of early Castilian.[4]

A parallel case in medieval England is provided by Lincolnshire: a characteristic transitional area in dialectological terms, which throughout the Middle English period received innovations from the south, west and north. Conde-Silvestre and Pérez-Raja (2008) have studied the socio-economic and demographic history of late Anglo-Saxon and early Norman Lincolnshire to assess the receptivity of the area to linguistic innovations. They point to some factors, such as the formation of nucleated villages and urban centers, the existence of communication routes crossing the county and an apparently greater mobility of some sections of the population, as the possible reasons behind the formation of unfocused group norms which favored the diffusion of innovations in the area.

The demographic, socio-economic, and urban development of London during the late Middle Ages and the Renaissance is another widely studied case of changing sociological circumstances which can safely be connected to a number of language changes attested in English between 1500 and 1700 (Nevalainen and Raumolin-Brunberg 2000; 2003: 38–40). From the fourteenth century onwards, London became a center for the export of corn, wool, and textiles, within a large international network that spread into the Netherlands and across the North Sea, to the extent that commerce, manufactures, and national wealth began to be concentrated in the area. The resulting prosperity is reflected in demography: the population rose from around 35,000, with a density of 56.2 per square mile in 1377 – when London was still part of the county of Middlesex – to nearly 80,000 in 1545 (86.7 per square mile) when the metropolitan area had extended to include Westminster and Southwark-Lambeth. Historical geographers estimate that these figures may have undergone a fivefold increase in 1700, possibly reaching 500,000 – one tenth of the total population of the country (Keene 2000: 99; Beier and Finlay 1986; Nevalainen 2000a: 258). The increase in population was due to the arrival of immigrants, especially from the north: people on temporary visits for business purposes, such as political, legal, or financial contacts and betterment migrants in search of social advancement, were also attracted to the metropolis. This population mixture within such a densely populated city, must have created a fluid social structure – the establishment of weak ties within loose-knit networks – that favored the diffusion of certain language changes into and out of London earlier than other areas of Britain (Conde-Silvestre and Hernández-Campoy 2002). For example, Terttu Nevalainen and Helena Raumolin-Brunberg have reconstructed the geographical diffusion southwards between the late fifteenth and the seventeenth century of morphological features such as the spread (found in the *Corpus of Early English Correspondence*) of the pronominal object form *you* into the subject function to the detriment of *ye*, and the diffusion of the third person singular present indicative ending -(*e*)*s* vs. -(*e*)*th*. As shown in Figures 18.1 and 18.2, both variants diffused earlier in texts by London writers during the central decades of the sixteenth century. In the case of the pronoun (Figure 18.1) the percentage of the incoming form *you* in texts from London is well above 50% in the period 1520–59, while hardly reaching 10% in texts from East Anglia and the North. In the case of -(*e*)*s*, a northern innovation (Figure 18.2), Londoners seemed to have accepted this earlier than East Anglians, particularly in the period 1579–1660, when it spread vigorously in letters written by correspondents from the city (Nevalainen and Raumolin-Brunberg 2000; Nevalainen 2000a; 2000b).

It seems that London behaved as a catalyst for both innovations, unlike other areas of the country, where diffusion was slower. One plausible explanation for this process of 'supralocalization' could be related to the new demographic and socio-economic circumstances of the metropolis and their effects on the typology of interpersonal relationships (social networks) of some of its inhabitants.[5] In this

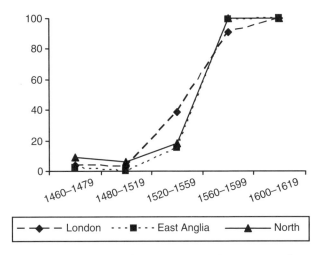

Figure 18.1. Geographical diffusion of *you*, 1460–1619 (source: Nevalainen 2000a: 262; reproduced by permission of Routledge)

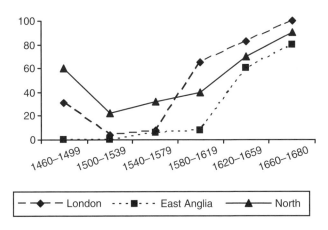

Figure 18.2. Geographical diffusion of *-(e)s*, 1460–1680 (source: Nevalainen and Raumolin-Brunberg 2003: 178; reproduced by permission of Longman Pearson Education)

way, this type of analysis can pass beyond the mere exercise of drawing the typological correspondences of broad sociological patterns at the communal level. Attempts are made at tracing the progress of actual changes in real communities whose social structures have been shattered by diverse reasons. In this respect, there is additional evidence that some individuals changed their verbal behavior soon after they arrived in London. This is the case of one member of the Paston family from Norfolk, John Paston III (1444–1504) (see below), who adopted the incipient standard spelling <-ght> in words like *myght* (vs. *myt*, *mygth*) and *thowght* (vs. *thowt*) and started to use *th*-forms of the plural personal pronoun (*them, their*) after 1467, when he had already been in London for some time, where these forms were prevalent. It is not wholly implausible that his social networks became looser in the city and that he was more disposed to adopt such linguistic innovations (Davis 1954: 68; Conde-Silvestre and Hernández-Campoy 2004: 145).

2.2   *From the socio-centric to the ego-centric application of social networks in historical sociolinguistic research*

Considering the sociological contexts that favor the spread of linguistic innovations, historical sociolinguists have been able to identify – provided that sufficient data is available – certain individuals who, in view of their social and geographical mobility, could have established weak ties in loose-knit networks and, accordingly, could have behaved as proper innovators.

Alexander Bergs (2000; 2005) has recently completed a project to reconstruct the typical network structures of some members of the Paston family of Norfolk. By scrutinizing the large corpus of extant correspondence written by the members of the family between 1421 and 1503, Bergs identifies biographical details which could have favored innovative or conservative linguistic behavior. In addition, he establishes connections with changes in progress during the transition from late Middle to early Modern English. This is clearly a socio-centric analysis, in that the transactional component of networks is not considered, but it clearly evolves into the ego-centric model, since the personal and social circumstances surrounding each speaker single him or her out as a proper innovator in connection with actual linguistic behavior. In this way, Bergs establishes a "tentative network checklist," in the light of the effect that biographical aspects could have had both on each member's prototypical network structures – close-knit or loose-knit – and on the type of links – weak or strong, uniplex or multiplex – that they were likely to have made. Among other components Bergs (2005: 72–75) considers:

(a) Gender: in the late English Middle Ages, male speakers would travel more frequently than women and might establish weaker, uniplex ties in less dense networks.

(b) Education and degree of literacy: the more educated is the individual, the more contacts and roles he or she has. Higher education would have involved more and weaker ties in less dense networks.

(c) Place of residence: "the larger the place of living, the more ties the speaker has, the less dense the network appears to be and the less multiplex" (2005: 73).

(d) Marital status and reference group: for either sex, marriage would probably have meant fewer (stronger) ties, of higher density and multiplexity. However, marriage would not necessarily mean that speakers remained within their family circle; some established reference groups outside it, thus increasing the number of weak and uniplex ties in their networks, whose density would also decrease.

(e) Travel frequency and travel destinations: spatial mobility in the Middle Ages may have been much greater than is generally assumed; in parallel to the local-national-international continuum it could increase the number of (weak) ties established by an individual as well as lowering the density and multiplexity of his or her networks.

(f) Offices and clusters. The former refers to "the number of prestigious or official positions a given person occupied" (2005: 74): ties would increase and the network's density would decrease in proportion to the prestige and the supralocalization of the office. The latter denotes the speaker's membership of one or more social or institutional groups, correlating with a higher number of ties of greater density but lower multiplexity.

(g) Contact with high-prestige actors and with the leaders of linguistic innovations would increase the number of weak uniplex ties, while contact with low-prestige individuals and with conservative speakers would extend the number of multiplex and strong ties and hinder the adoption of innovations.

The story of the Paston family (Table 18.1) offers a fascinating example of social mobility in the late English Middle Ages. Clement Paston, the founder of the family, was a yeoman farmer in Richard II's day (1367–1400). However, he managed to have his son, William Paston I (1387–1444), trained as a lawyer,

Table 18.1. Relative connectors in three generations of the Paston family (Bergs 2000: 243; reproduced by permission of Routledge)

		that	*which*	*the which*	*whose*	*whom*	*who*	*ratio*
I	Agnes (1400?–1479)	59.4	29.7	1.6	3.1	3.1	3.1	1.46
	William I (1378–1444)	60.0	23.3	3.3	6.6	3.3	3.3	1.50
II	William II (1436–1496)	63.3	30.3	–	0.9	4.6	0.9	1.73
	John I (1421–1466)	59.2	30.7	2.3	3.8	2.3	1.9	1.45
	Margaret (1420?–1484)	76.7	12.5	7.6	1.5	1.4	0.3	3.29
III	John II (1442–1479)	51.6	44.9	–	1.4	1.2	0.9	1.07
	John III (1444–1504)	55.9	33.3	0.7	1.4	6.2	2.4	1.26
	Edmond II (1445?–1495)	30.0	50.0	5.0	–	50.0	10.0	0.43
	Walter (1456?–1479)	54.5	36.4	9.1	–	–	–	1.20
	William III (1459?–??)	48.8	27.9	9.3	2.3	2.3	9.3	0.95

and the latter rose to become a sergeant of the Court of Common Pleas. William's own business and his marriage to Agnes Berry (1400?–79), the daughter of a Hertfordshire knight, made him the wealthy owner of several manors in Norfolk. This account of the family origins shows that their social position had risen significantly by the fifteenth century, when two of William's grandsons, John Paston II (1442–79) and John Paston III (1444–1504) became courtiers in the service of King Edward IV.

One of the linguistic innovations analyzed by Bergs is the spread of different forms of the relative connector in the Paston correspondence. Table 18.1 shows the advance of this Middle English change in progress along the different generations of the family. Throughout Middle English, *that* behaved as the universal relative connector, used with all types of clauses and antecedents. However, *that* soon started to coexist with the interrogative pronouns, which, following a common trend in Latin and French, came to be used with this function. Chronologically, not all interrogatives were used as relative connectors at the same time: the earliest attested forms were *which* and the northernism *the which*, then the object and possessive forms *whom* and *whose* – helping to disambiguate the lack of case marking of *that* – and finally, in the late fifteenth century, the subject *who* extended to acquire the function, beginning with its ritualistic use in formulaic religious language, as in this letter from Margaret Paston to her son John II (1470) "God bryng vs oute of it, who haue yow in his keepyng" (Davis 1971, vol. 1: 350). Figures in the right-hand column (ratio) are calculated by dividing the occurrences of the Middle English common form *that* by those of the *wh*-forms, so that the lower the figure for each speaker, the more innovative his or her linguistic behavior would have been.

It is not surprising that, in parallel to the chronology of this change, the lowest ratio corresponds to the third-generation members of the family, born between 1442 and 1459. There are, however, some striking differences. Particularly significant are those between the three brothers John Paston II (1.07), John Paston III (1.26), and Edmond Paston (0.43), in that their innovative or conservative behavior cannot be related to age. However, we can make sense of this by looking at their biographies. John Paston II (1442–79) had a high profile political career: it started at the court of Edward IV (1442–83) between 1461 and 1463, when he was knighted; it later took him to London, where he was MP for Norfolk between 1467–68; in this year he accompanied Princess Margaret to Bruges on the occasion of her marriage and in the following decade he seems to have travelled extensively on diplomatic missions to the continent: Calais, Bruges, and Neuss (1472, 1473); in the early 1470s he was also present in battles of the War of the Roses, particularly at Barnet (1471); later in the decade he was an MP again, this time for Yarmouth (Davis 1971: lviii–lix). This picture of "a careless bon vivant without interests in Norfolk affairs and a serious concern for the family" (Bergs 2005: 66) includes some of the 'tentative characteristics' which, according to Bergs, could have correlated with the establishment of weak and uniplex ties in loose-knit social networks: a courtly education, prestige official positions, unmarried status, and reference groups outside the Paston family and far from its area of influence in Norfolk. Particularly prominent, in this respect, is his social and extensive geographical mobility (travel frequency and destinations) which would include long stays in an already heavily populated London (Conde-Silvestre and Hernández-Campoy 2004: 149). The frequent travels of John Paston III (1444–1504) took him throughout the country (Wales, Newcastle) and abroad in the service of the Duke of Norfolk (1463–64): in fact, he was also in Bruges accompanying Princess Margaret in 1468, and at the battle of Barnet (1471), where he was wounded. An interesting difference from his brother John II is that in the 1470s and 80s he remained in the family's manors in Norfolk, acting as his mother's secretary and later running the family business, although he occasionally visited London and Calais as MP for Norwich (1485–86), Sheriff of Norfolk and Suffolk or councillor to the Lord High Admiral, the Earl of Oxford. In 1487, after his participation in the battle of Stoke, he was knighted, and in the 1490s he performed several duties as deputy of the Earl. His last service to the King was attending the arrival of Catherine of Aragon in 1498. He married twice: to Margery Brews in 1477 and when she died in 1495, to Agnes, daughter of Nicholas Morley of Glynde, (Davis 1971: lix–lx). This biographical profile also points to an individual educated at court, who occupied prestige social positions and enjoyed some degree of social and geographical mobility; this may mean that John Paston III could have also established some weak, uniplex ties in loose-knit networks. Nevertheless, his connections to reference groups within the Paston family and the Norfolk states, where he led a "more stable, controlled and responsible" life than his brother (Bergs 2005: 67), may imply that some of the networks in which he participated might have been territorially restricted to this area (close-knit and more dense), and within them he could have established stronger ties, at least in contrast to his brother (Conde Silvestre and Hernández Campoy 2004: 150).

The biographies of the Paston brothers and the possibility that they established different types of networks during the course of their lives could be the reason for differences in their linguistic behavior, especially in the choice of the most innovative relative connectors in the late fifteenth century: 1.26 for John III vs. 1.07 for John II. However, their linguistic behavior is not radically different when other variables are considered (Bergs 2005: 250–51). Furthermore, John III's linguistic behavior is occasionally less conservative than his brother's, particularly as regards the adoption of the spelling practices that were to become standard (Conde Silvestre and Hernández Campoy 2004: 144–45). I believe that other factors, such as contact with high-prestige actors and with the leaders of linguistic innovations, must be considered. It is well-known that many of the new graphemes originated among members of the legal profession in London, whence they diffused to other areas and domains (Rissanen 1999; Conde-Silvestre 2007: 337–39). In this connection, Davis (1954) highlighted John III's capacity for establishing close contacts with lawyers from London, and this may explain his involvement in the diffusion of the spelling innovations. It could also explain, according to Bergs (2000: 245), Edmond Paston II's highly innovative behavior. Regarding the use of relative connectors, Edmond is the most innovative speaker, showing the lowest ratio

(0.43); he is also advanced in extending the old interrogative *who* to the relative function beyond its ritualistic religious usage. This clearly does not correlate with much experience of travelling or long periods in London; in fact, he spent most of his adult life in Norfolk, where he "led a quiet, orderly, 'normal' life" (Bergs 2005: 68). The basic difference from his brothers is his education: in contrast to John II and John III's upbringing at court, Edmond was educated at Cambridge and at the Staple Inn in London, where he might have first come across those linguistic trends that were to become normative.

Finally, in sharp contrast to the three brothers stands their mother's linguistic repertoire. Margaret Paston (1420?–84) is clearly the most conservative speaker, with a ratio of 3.29. This should not be unexpected, not only on account of her gender and the absence of higher education, but also because of her lack of geographical mobility and the fact that she remained within the family's reference group throughout her life. Margaret was a "self-determined businesswoman," who remained in Norfolk and, according to the internal evidence of the letters, travelled only once, to visit her husband when he was imprisoned in London in 1465. Her social networks must have been very dense, with strong multiplex ties, which clearly correlates with her preference for traditional, even archaic, language forms (Bergs 2005: 64, 248).

These socio-centric applications of networks in historical sociolinguistic research successfully relate some biographical characteristics of individuals to the degree of innovation in their linguistic repertoire. Speakers who are ahead of the rest in the choice of linguistic innovations – such as John Paston II – tend to exhibit high mobility, extensive contacts and, in general, a lifestyle which could have facilitated the establishment of weak ties in loose network structures. In contrast, conservative speakers – such as Margaret Paston – led orderly lives, without apparent mobility, and their personal relationships may have adopted a different patterning: dense networks with stronger ties. It goes without saying that these conclusions must remain at the speculative level, given that the complete, actual networks of the speakers cannot be reconstructed and that the prominence of different external factors may have differed for each of the variables affected.

2.3 Ego-centric applications of social networks in historical sociolinguistic research

Another productive direction of research is based on the classical ego-centric representation of social networks – the dots-and-lines model – and attempts to reconstruct as many dimensions of the social networks of individuals from the past as possible. In the case of English, the eighteenth century has become a favorite period for a number of reasons. Firstly, some sections of the population enjoyed increased social and geographical mobility which brought them "in contact with different norms of speech, with the potential for their own language to change in response" (Tieken-Boon van Ostade 2006: 247). Secondly, in contrast to previous centuries, many written documents with attested authorship, of a personal and even intimate character – letters and diaries, for example – have survived and have provided the historical sociolinguist with the biographical information needed to reconstruct both the relationships between individuals and the properties of their links: the structural and the transactional components of social networks. Moreover, using these resources, scholars have been able to speculate on the possible connection between individuals, as central or peripheral members of their networks, as well as changes in progress.

An interesting example is Susan Fitzmaurice's analysis of the interpersonal relationships of the politicians and writers associated with *The Spectator* in the years 1710–14. Rather than a collection of proper ego-based networks, Fitzmaurice recognizes that she is dealing with a 'coalition,' in the sense coined by Boissevain (1974: 171): a group of people formed "in order to achieve a particular goal or to pursue a particular common agenda [...] during a particular period of time" (Fitzmaurice 2000a: 266, 273). This means that the relationships enacted focus on common interests, so that the members' attitude towards this target plays a crucial role on both the coalition structure and its effects. The people behind *The Spectator* project clearly developed common alliances with particular goals in mind, either in search of personal promotion or of literary and political success in association with the *Whigs* (Fitzmaurice 2007).[6] *The Spectator* became one of the cornerstones of English culture in the first part of the eighteenth century; it enjoyed high prestige and soon became a model in questions of refinement, taste, manners, and opinions for the middle classes. As such, *The Spectator* seems to have also affected language, in that grammarians often drew examples of correctness from its pages (Wright 1994). In connection with this, Fitzmaurice aims to detect how this coalition enforced adherence to a set of norms established mainly by its most powerful, central members, as reflected in their surviving written production, compiled electronically: the *Network of Eighteenth Century English Texts* corpus.

At the center of this coalition (see Figure 18.3) was Joseph Addison (1672–1719): in fact most quotes from *The Spectator* by contemporary authors were attributed to him and, accordingly, his linguistic repertoire was regarded as worthy of imitation (Wright 1997; Fitzmaurice 2000b: 201). Joseph Addison and Richard Steele (1672–1729) became friends when they were students at Charterhouse and Oxford University; their early friendship bore fruit in their collaboration in *The Spectator* and was reinforced by their geographical proximity: this closeness is represented by the thick double-tipped arrow linking them in the illustration. A similar relationship must have existed between Addison and Edward Wortley (1713–76): they met in France and maintained an enduring mutual friendship which, however, was not always accompanied by geographical proximity, thus the arrow is also double-tipped but slightly thinner. Through Wortley, Addison and Steele must have also met Wortley's mother, Lady Mary Wortley Montagu (1689–1762), who occasionally made contributions to the periodical and, for this reason, appears at the periphery of the coalition. The ties that bound Addison to some outstanding members of the Whig party, such as the playwright William Congreve (1670–1729),

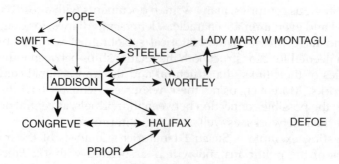

Figure 18.3.   A historical coalition around *The Spectator* and Joseph Addison (1710–14) (source: Fitzmaurice 2000b: 209; reproduced by permission of Cambridge University Press)

Charles Montagu (1661–1715), the Duke of Halifax, and the civil servant and diplomat Matthew Prior (1664–1721), can be traced back to 1700 when he joined the influential *Kit-Cat* club. These ties, which are also attested in surviving private correspondence, afford interesting examples of asymmetrical relationships, showing that writers like Addison and Congreve could have been attracted to this group of influential politicians in search of sponsorship and protection; the arrow is drawn so as to indicate this asymmetry. Asymmetry also defines the relationship between Addison and Alexander Pope (1688–1744): he must have been seeking the protection of an influential writer like Addison, who, in turn, wished to recruit young writers for *The Spectator* group. Finally, the ties linking Addison, Steele, and Jonathan Swift (1667–1745) are peculiar: all three were acquainted, but they are unlikely to have experienced any kind of mutual friendship. On the contrary: their relationship was characterized by the rivalry to be expected between members of opposing parties, Swift being a celebrated Tory. This is why he also occupies a peripheral position.

Fitzmaurice's research concludes with the analysis of a linguistic change in progress in the early eighteenth century. She considers the distribution of relative connectors in the correspondence of members of this coalition and their adherence to the rules of correctness favored by prescriptive grammarians. By the 1700s the interrogatives *who(m)* and *which* were well-established in their relative function; they still coexisted with *that* and with the Ø-relative, although grammarians wholly disapproved of the latter and criticized the former as "hazardous and hardly justifiable" (Lowth 1762: 137, in Fitzmaurice 2000b: 202). The distribution of these forms in the writings of members from the coalition also exhibits significant differences that could be related to their central or peripheral position. For instance, peripheral members such as Edward Wortley Montagu and his mother, Lady Mary, as well as Alexander Pope were especially fond of *that* and the Ø-relative. In contrast, central members, like Steele, Congreve, and Addison himself, tended to be well ahead in their adherence to pronouncements by the grammarians. Differences between them can also be observed. Addison, for instance, makes copious use of *who(m)* and *which*, but does not completely avoid the use of *that*, although he sometimes prefers to omit the relative altogether. Congreve, however, sticks to the prestige new forms: he uses *who(m)* and *which* three times more than *that*, and systematically avoids the Ø-relative. Their position in the network around *The Spectator* allows Fitzmaurice to characterize their linguistic behavior as typical of the innovators or of the early adopters. Congreve occupied a peripheral position and established strong ties only with Addison and Lord Halifax. His biographical profile is that of a person with ample contacts, in touch with politicians from both parties and involved in a variety of circles: literary, theatrical, and courtly. Such mobility would have made him a peripheral member of several loose-knit networks, who established weak ties with their central actors. As such, he could have had access to linguistic innovations which might have been diffused through the weak ties he established with members of other groups. Addison, however, occupied the central position, and, as such, could have played the role of early adopter, taking an innovation from peripheral members such as Congreve and diffusing it to the rest by way of his centrality (2000a: 267–68).

Other scholars have reconstructed specific networks and have also speculated on the roles of their members as innovators or early adopters. Ingrid Tieken-Boon van Ostade (1987; 1991; 1996), for instance, has studied the biography of the eighteenth-century novelist Samuel Richardson (1689–1761) and his connections to different circles, in association with his linguistic behavior. Richardson was an unconfident person, with few, weak ties to other people, most of them established within loose-knit networks (1996: 330). His social mobility is also well-attested: as a printer in his youth he had been in touch with the upper classes who were later to back him in his literary career. Tieken-Boon van Ostade also considers some members of his closer circle, paying particular attention to those who were central in other networks. For instance, Richardson became a friend of Samuel Johnson (1709–84), who was at the center of a network of friends and admirers. Richardson was also closely linked to Henry Fielding's sister, Sarah (1710–68). As a result, Tieken-Boon van Ostade detects Richardson's linguistic influence on their repertoire: Johnson could have followed Richardson's earliest use of *to do* as auxiliary in negative sentences – he even quotes from his novels in the *Dictionary of the English Language* (1755) (Tieken-Boon van Ostade 1987: 167–69; 1996: 330–31). Sarah Fielding also followed Richardson's orthographical practices – in particular, she used <'d> in the preterit and past participle forms of weak verbs as well as similar patterns of capitalization – possibly acknowledging his authority as printer (Tieken-Boon van Ostade 2000b: 300). Some entries in the *Oxford English Dictionary* also confirm this influence: the compound *over-indulged*, for instance, is first recorded in Richardson's *Pamela* (1741) and the quotation following it in the *OED* is from Sarah Fielding's *The Countess of Dellwyn* (1759) (Tieken-Boon van Ostade 2006: 267–69; 2009: 105). The situation is parallel to that traced by Fitzmaurice in *The Spectator* coalition: Richardson (like Congreve) would be an innovator who diffused the changes in progress to the central members of the social networks at whose periphery he was placed. This must have been the role played by Samuel Johnson or Sarah Fielding, who, like Addison, could have behaved as early adopters: their centrality in their respective networks would have contributed to the diffusion of innovations to the rest. For example, the linguistic influence of Johnson over the language of Fanny Burney (1752–1840) as regards the use of *to do* as negative auxiliary has also been confirmed by Tieken-Boon van Ostade (2006: 261, 269) and Randy Bax (2005); just as some linguistic traits of the diarist Mrs Hester Lynch Thrale (1741–1821) were also likely to have been influenced by Johnson, such as the old-fashioned spelling *-ick* instead of *-ic* in words like *musick* or *publick* (Bax 2002; Tieken-Boon van Ostade 2009: 109).

There are several recent research projects applying the social network hypothesis to eighteenth-century English. Tieken-Boon van Ostade and Bax (2002), for instance, have scrutinized the biography and correspondence of bishop Robert Lowth (1710–87) and his circle and have detected patterns of influence within the social networks in which he participated (Tieken-Boon van Ostade and Bax 2002; Tieken-Boon van Ostade 2005). Anni Sairio (2008; 2009a; 2009b) has studied the diffusion of the progressive construction, preposition stranding and pied-piping in a corpus of letters by members of the Bluestocking coterie (1738–78): a group of politicians, poets, scholars, and educated women from the gentry gravitating around Elizabeth Montagu (c.1718–1800). Trinidad Guzmán and Santiago González (2005) have dealt with the treatment of 'assigned gender' – the use of gendered marks such as third person singular and relative pronouns in the personification of objects – within the large scholarly network of eighteenth-century English grammarians. Froukje Henstra (2008) has studied the correspondence of Horace Walpole (1717–97) and his family and has proposed a specific network checklist to trace the diffusion of some linguistic features overtly prescribed or recommended by eighteenth-century grammarians: the alternation *you was* vs. *you were*, the *be/have* variation in perfective constructions and the confusion of preterit and past participle forms in perfective and passive constructions, as in 'I might have *broke* my neck.' Finally, Lynda Pratt and David Denison (2000) rely conceptually on the notion of social network in their study "The language of the Southey-Coleridge circle." They trace the use of the incoming progressive passive in the *Corpus of Late Eighteenth-Century Prose*, a collection of writings by early romantics, including Robert Southey, Samuel Coleridge, William Wordsworth, Charles Lamb, Robert Lowell, John Keats, Percy Bysshe Shelley, Mary Shelley, their kin, friends and correspondents, mainly located around the Clifton area of Bristol between the 1790s and 1810s. They note that the progressive passive construction was for members of this group a symbol of identity and that it may have diffused outwards from them to other members of the speech community at large (2000: 416–17).

All in all, these studies confirm that, despite methodological difficulties, social networks can be applied in historical sociolinguistic research, although – as I have tried to show in this chapter – the scope and reliability of results depends on the time depth and the availability of biographical, social, and linguistic data.

NOTES

1   The financial support of Fundación Séneca, Agencia Regional de Ciencia y Tecnología, Región de Murcia (Spain) is gratefully acknowledged (research project 08629/PHCS/08).

2   The possibility of applying the idea of social networks in sociolinguistic research was created by the theory of linguistic accommodation developed in the 1970s by social psychologists such as Howard Giles. In a nutshell, the theory proposes that the expressive elections made by speakers may be partly conditioned by their desire to create some distance from others (linguistic divergence), due to social or power differences or for the assertion of their own personal identity. Alternatively, it could lead to linguistic convergence, as a manifestation of solidarity, social equality, the need for approval or simply imitation of speakers who enjoy social prestige in the community. See Coupland (1996) for a complete review.

3   In contrast with this approach, Labov proposed that the profile of innovators corresponds to individuals who are able to establish weak ties both inside and outside their network. The elusive nature of weak ties has recently led him to abandon the distinction between innovators and early adopters. instead proposing the more generic label "leaders of linguistic change" (2001: 362).

4   See also Imhoff (2000) for an a typological application of social networks to the situation of Navarro-Aragonese in the same period and circumstances.

5   See also the suggestion by Helena Raumolin-Brunberg (1998) that the English Civil War (1642–49) could have also contributed to a rapid diffusion of innovations in the mid-seventeenth century. The war could have led to the development of language changes acceler-ated in catastrophic historical circumstances which, by favouring the displacement of populations – soldiers and refugees on the move – tend to affect and loosen the social bonds between individuals, promoting contact between speakers of diverse social and geographical origins. In the same way, Bergs believes that the War of the Roses (1455–85) could also have had disruptive effects for the social structures prevalent in late medieval England, which would have fostered the rapid development of innovations and changes in the fifteenth century (2005: 49).

6   'Coalitions' from the past are easier to reconstruct than ego-based networks, if only because problematic issues, such as degrees of friendship or intimacy, are avoided, and because many surviving documents reflect common enterprises of this kind, involving guilds, monastic establishments, communities of merchants, and political clubs. In a sense, the concept of coalition may be a diachronic counterpart of 'communities of practice:' a construct which has also been successfully applied in synchronic sociolinguistic research. Communities of prac-tice like social networks, are defined in terms of the interaction between individuals, but their reconstruction transcends the structural aspects – type of relationship, intensity, reciprocity – to consider attitudinal and performative factors. As a result, communities of practice take into account the subjective experience of their members as regards the limits between their own community and others, and their construction depends on the type of activities commonly involving them (including linguistic activity). This means that a community of practice is not a typical independent variable which may or may not correlate with linguistic variables, but that language use plays a fundamental role in its definition (Eckert 2000; Meyerhoff 2002). This attitudinal component makes the concept difficult to apply in historical

sociolinguistic research, although Susan Fitzmaurice (2002; 2007), among others, has attempted to reconstruct some historical communities in connection with the development of pragmatic markers.

REFERENCES

Andersen, H. (1988) Center and periphery: adoption, diffusion and spread. In J. Fisiak (ed.), *Historical Dialectology*, Mouton de Gruyter, Berlin, pp. 39–83.

Barnes, J. (1972) Social networks. *Module in Anthropology* 26: 1–29.

Bax, R.C. (2000) A network strength scale for the study of eighteenth-century English. *European Journal of English Studies* 4(3): 277–89.

Bax, R.C. (2002) Linguistic accommodation. The correspondence between Samuel Johnson and Hester Lynch Thrale. In T. Fanego, B. Méndez Naya, and E. Seoane (eds.), *Sounds, Words, Texts and Change. Selected Papers from 11 ICEHL*, John Benjamins, Amsterdam, pp. 9–23.

Bax, R.C. (2005) Traces of Johnson in the language of Fanny Burney. *International Journal of English Studies* 5(1): 159–81.

Beier, A.L. and Finlay, R. (eds.) (1986) *London 1500–1700: The Making of the Metropolis*, Longman, London.

Bergs, R.T. (2000) Social networks in pre-1500 Britain: problems, prospects, examples. *European Journal of English Studies* 4(3): 239–51.

Bergs, A.T. (2005) *Social Networks and Historical Sociolinguistics. Studies in Morphosyntactic Variation in the Paston Letters (1421–1503)*, Mouton de Gruyter, Berlin.

Boissevain, J. (1974) *Friends of Friends. Networks, Manipulators and Coalitions*, St. Martin's Press, New York.

Boissevain, J. (1987) Social networks. In U. Ammon and K.J. Mattheier (eds.), *Sociolinguistics. An International Handbook of the Science of Language*, Mouton de Gruyter, Berlin, pp. 164–69.

Chambers, J.K., Trudgill, P., and Schilling-Estes, N. (eds.) (2002) *The Handbook of Language Variation and Change*, Blackwell, Oxford.

Conde Silvestre, J.C. (2007) *Sociolingüística histórica*, Gredos, Madrid.

Conde Silvestre, J.C. and Hernández Campoy, J.M. (2002) Modern geolinguistic tenets and the diffusion of linguistic innovations in late Middle English. *Studia Anglica Posnaniensia* 38: 147–77.

Conde Silvestre, J.C. and Hernández Campoy, J.M. (2004) A sociolinguistic approach to the diffusion of Chancery written practices in late fifteenth-century private correspondence. *Neuphilologische Mitteilungen* 105(2): 135–52.

Conde Silvestre, J.C. and Pérez Raja, M.D. (2008) Transitional areas and social history in Middle English dialectology: the case of Lincolnshire. *Neophilologus* 92: 713–27.

Coupland, N. (1996) Accommodation theory. In J.J.-O. Östman and J. Verschueren (eds.), *Handbook of Pragmatics Online*, John Benjamins, Amsterdam. http://www.benjamins.com/online/hop/ [accessed September 28, 2011].

Davis, N. (1954) The language of the Pastons. In J.A. Burrow (ed.), *Middle English Literature. British Academy Gollancz Lectures*, Oxford University Press, Oxford, pp. 45–70.

Davis, N. (ed.) (1971) *Paston Letters and Papers of the Fifteenth Century*, Clarendon, Oxford.

Eckert, P. (2000) *Linguistic Variation as Social Practice*, Blackwell, Oxford.

Fitzmaurice, S. (2000a) Coalitions and the investigation of social influence in linguistic history. *European Journal of English Studies* 4(3): 265–76.

Fitzmaurice, S. (2000b) *The Spectator*, the politics of social networks and language standardisation in eighteenth-century England. In L. Wright (ed.), pp. 195–218.

Fitzmaurice, S. (2002) Politeness and modal meaning in the construction of humiliative discourse in an early eighteenth-century network of patron–client relationships. *English Language and Linguistics* 6(2): 239–65.

Fitzmaurice, S. (2007) The world of the periodical essay: social networks and discourse communities in eighteenth-century London. *Historical Sociolinguistics and Socio-Historical Linguistics* 7. http://www.let.leidenuniv.nl/hsl_shl/periodical%20essay.htm [accessed September 28, 2011].

Granovetter, M. (1973) The strength of weak ties. *American Journal of Sociology* 78: 1360–80.

Granovetter, M. (1982) The strength of weak ties: a network theory revisited. In P.V. Marsden and N. Lin (eds.), *Social Structure and Network Analysis*, Sage, London, pp. 105–30.

Guzmán González, T. and González, S. (2005) 'Why the Furies were made female.' An approach to gender assignment in 18th-century language treatises from sociolinguistic epistemology. In E. Borkowska and M.J. Álvarez Marín (eds.), *The Margins of Europe. Cultural and Linguistic Identities*, University of Silesia Press, pp. 89–109.

Henstra, F. (2008) Social network analysis and the eighteenth-century family network. A case study of the Walpole family. *Transactions of the Philological Society* 108(1): 29–70.

Hernández-Campoy, J.M. and Almeida, M. (2005) *Metodología de la investigación sociolingüística*, Comares, Málaga.

Imhoff, B. (2000) Socio-historic network ties and medieval Navarro-Aragonese. *Neuphilologische Mitteilungen* 101: 443–50.

Keene, D. (2000) Metropolitan values: migration, mobility and cultural norms, London 1100–1700. In L. Wright (ed.), pp. 93–114.

Labov, W. (2001) *Principles of Linguistic Change. Vol. 2: Social Factors*, Blackwell, Oxford.

Lowth, R. (1762) *A Short Introduction to Grammar*, A. Millar, R. and J. Dodsley, London.

Meyerhoff, M. (2002) Communities of practice. In J.K. Chambers, P. Trudgill, and N. Schilling-Estes (eds.), pp. 526–48.

Milroy, J. (1992) *Linguistic Variation and Change. On the Historical Sociolinguistics of English*, Blackwell, Oxford.

Milroy, J. (1998) Explaining linguistic variation to explain language change. *Sociolinguistica* 12: 39–52.

Milroy, J. and Milroy, L. (1985) Linguistic change, social network and speaker innovation. *Journal of Linguistics* 21: 339–84.

Milroy, L. (1980/1987) *Language and Social Networks* (2nd edn), Blackwell, Oxford.

Milroy, L. (1991) *Observing and Analysing Natural Language*, Blackwell, Oxford.

Milroy, L. (2002) Social networks. In J.K. Chambers, P. Trudgill, and N. Schilling-Estes (eds.), pp. 549–72.

Milroy, L. and Milroy, J. (1992) Social network and social class: toward an integrated sociolinguistic theory. *Language in Society* 21: 1–26.

Nevalainen, T. (2000a) Mobility, social networks and language change in early Modern England. *European Journal of English Studies* 4(3): 253–64.

Nevalainen, T. (2000b) Processes of supralocalisation and the rise of standard English in the early modern period. In R. Bermúdez-Otero *et al.* (eds.), *Generative Theory and Corpus Studies. A Dialogue from the 10th ICEHL*, Mouton de Gruyter, Berlin, pp. 329–71.

Nevalainen, T. and Raumolin-Brunberg, H. (2000) The changing role of London on the linguistic map of Tudor and Stuart English. In D. Kastovsky and A. Mettinger (eds.), *The History of English in a Social Context. Essays in Historical Sociolinguistics*, Mouton de Gruyter, Berlin, pp. 280–337.

Nevalainen, T. and Raumolin-Brunberg, H. (2003) *Historical Sociolinguistics. Language Change in Tudor and Stuart England*, Longman/Pearson Education, London.

Penny, R. (2000) *Variation and Change in Spanish*, Cambridge University Press, Cambridge.

Pratt, L. and Denison, D. (2000) The language of the Southey-Coleridge circle. *Language Sciences* 22: 401–22.

Raumolin-Brunberg, H. (1998) Social factors and pronominal change in the seventeenth century: the Civil War effect? In J. Fisiak and M. Krygier (eds.), *Advances in English Historical Linguistics*, Mouton de Gruyter, Berlin, pp. 361–88.

Rissanen, M. (1999) The language of law and the development of standard English. In I. Taavitsainen, G. Melchers, and P. Pahta (eds.), *Writing in Non-Standard English*, John Benjamins, Amsterdam, pp. 189–204.

Sairio, A. (2008) A social network study of the eighteenth-century Bluestockings: the progressive and preposition stranding in their letters. *Historical Sociolinguistics and Socio-Historical Linguistics* 8. http://www.let.leidenuniv.nl/hsl_shl/Sairio.htm [accessed September 28, 2011].

Sairio, A. (2009a) *Language and Letters of the Bluestocking Network. Sociolinguistic Issues in Eighteenth-century Epistolary English*, Societé Neophilologiqué, Helsinki.

Sairio, A. (2009b) Methodological and practical aspects of historical network analysis. A case study of the Bluestocking Letters. In A. Nurmi, M. Nevala, and M. Palander-Collin (eds.), *The Language of Daily Life in England (1400–1800)*, John Benjamins, Amsterdam, pp. 107–35.

Scott, J. (ed.) (1997) *Social Network Analysis. A Handbook*, Sage, London.

Tieken-Boon van Ostade, I. (1987) *The Auxiliary Do in Eighteenth Century English. A Sociohistorical Linguistic Approach*, Foris, Dordrecht.

Tieken-Boon van Ostade, I. (1991) Samuel Richardson's role as linguistic innovator: a sociolinguistic analysis. In I. Tieken-Boon van Ostade and J. Franklin (eds.), *Language Usage and Variation*, Rodopi, Amsterdam, pp. 45–57.

Tieken-Boon van Ostade, I. (1996) Social network theory and eighteenth century English: the case of Boswell. In D. Britton (ed.), *English Historical Linguistics 1994. Papers from the 8th ICEHL*, John Benjamins, Amsterdam, pp. 327–37.

Tieken-Boon van Ostade, I. (2000a) Social network analysis and the history of

English. *European Journal of English Studies* 4(3): 211–16.

Tieken-Boon van Ostade, I. (2000b) Social network analysis and the language of Sarah Fielding. *European Journal of English Studies* 4(3): 291–301.

Tieken-Boon van Ostade, I. (2005) Of social networks and linguistic influence. The language of Robert Lowth and his correspondents. *International Journal of English Studies* 5(1): 135–57.

Tieken-Boon van Ostade, I. (2006) English at the onset of the normative tradition. In L. Mugglestone (ed.), *The Oxford History of English*, Oxford University Press, Oxford, pp. 240–73.

Tieken-Boon van Ostade, I. (2009) *An Introduction to Late Modern English*, Edinburgh University Press, Edinburgh.

Tieken-Boon van Ostade, I. and Bax, R. (2002) Of Dodley's projects and linguistic influence: the language of Johnson and Lowth. *Historical Sociolinguistics and Socio-Historical Linguistics* 2. http://www.let.leidenuniv.nl/hsl_shl/johnson%20lowth.htm [accessed September 28, 2011].

Trudgill, P.J. (2002) Linguistic and social typology. In J.K. Chambers, P. Trudgill, and N. Schilling-Estes (eds.), pp. 707–28.

Wright. L. (ed.) (2000) *The Development of Standard English, 1300–1800. Theories, Descriptions, Conflicts*, Cambridge University Press, Cambridge.

Wright, S. (1994) The critic and the grammarians: Joseph Addison and the prescriptivists. In D. Stein and I. Tieken-Boon van Ostade (eds.), *Toward a Standard English*, Mouton, The Hague, pp. 243–84.

Wright, S. (1997) Speaker innovation, textual revision and the case of Joseph Addison. In T. Nevalainen and L. Kahlas-Tarkka (eds.), *To Explain the Present. Studies in the Changing English Language in Honour of Matti Rissanen*, Societé Neophilologique, Helsinki, pp. 483–503.

19   Race, Ethnicity, Religion, and Castes

RAJEND MESTHRIE

1. Race: A Conceptual Overview

Race is a notoriously difficult concept, seemingly simple in its everyday sense of
"each of the major divisions of humankind, having distinct physical characteristics" (*Oxford South African Concise Dictionary* 2006: 970), yet a far more precarious
notion in a strictly academic and scientific sense. In fact there is a tradition of
rejecting race as a useful and definable concept in sociology and anthropology,
with analysts referring instead to *ethnicity*, which carries much less scientific (or
pseudo-scientific) baggage. By way of parallel, linguists have long had to live with
the ill-defined concept of 'a language' (both in demarcating 'a language' from 'a
dialect' and one 'language' from another closely related one). Writing about race
and language therefore carries a double terminological difficulty: technically one
should be discussing conceptualizations of race in relation to conceptualizations
of language. Carmen Fought (2006:10) cites Smelser *et al.*'s (2001: 3) definition of
race as follows: "race is a social category based on the identification of (1) a physical marker transmitted through reproduction and (2) individual, group and cultural attributes associated with that marker." Biologists use the term 'species' for
"a group of living organisms consisting of similar individuals capable of exchanging genes or interbreeding [...] e.g. Homo sapiens" (*Oxford South African Concise
Dictionary* 2006: 1139). This sense of species differs from race, except in the more
colloquial phrase 'the human race.' So if we were to reconcile the definitions of
'race' (as a popular term) and 'species' (as a technical term) as given above we
would have to consider race to really mean 'sub-species' in abstract biological
terms. These subspecies or races are not 'givens,' rather they are historical and
geographical aggregations. Individual human subgroups referred to as "major

The Handbook of Historical Sociolinguistics, First Edition. Edited by Juan Manuel Hernández-Campoy
and Juan Camilo Conde-Silvestre.
© 2014 John Wiley & Sons, Ltd. Published 2014 by John Wiley & Sons, Ltd.

divisions of humankind" are that way because over vast stretches of time they lived in proximity to one another, exchanged genetic material (to put it impruriently), thus contributing to a common genetic sub-pool. In the course of time this led to different cultural styles and further differentiation of languages.

Yet things need not have turned out this way, given other historical and geographical circumstances. The only biological givens are that the exchange of like genetic material produces similar offspring. There is no *biological* constraint governing the exchange of like and unlike genetic material within a species. So if our world had been smaller with one small land mass accessible to all people, it is conceivable that there would be no 'races' in the sense of 'sub-species' or divisions of humankind, since there would have been no physical barriers to enhance differentiated genetic pools. Even in a larger world such as ours, less physical isolation and more frequent social and sexual contact would have most likely resulted in a continuum of physical types, rather than easily identifiable 'races.' There are signs that in an age of aviation and mass migration this is starting to happen (but the effects will only be discernible over multi-millennia, all other things being equal). To summarize: race is a mosaic of biological (genetic) considerations, mediated by social relationships resulting from history and geography.

It is quite clear that in the modern world there is no clear-cut relationship between race (accepting for argument's sake the popular notion of the term) and language. This is so because of the phenomenon of language shift. A whole group may over time exchange one language for another – seldom willingly, most often by force of circumstances. Such circumstances include the migration of a group of people who become a minority in a new territory in which some other language is dominant. The process of language shift usually takes a few generations, though it may be effected in as little as one generation. Yet language shift need not involve a genetic shift. Thus, the community of speakers of English as a home language is not genetically homogeneous: even within a single territory like the United Kingdom, English-speakers reflect a spectrum of humanity. However, given the history of the world, the further back in time we go, the stronger appear to be the correlations between language families (aggregates of languages that can be defined by the traditional methods of historical and comparative linguistics) and specific groups of speakers defined by certain physical characteristics. It was traditional in twentieth-century linguistics not to speculate on the origins of language; even Chomsky, who is best known for positing one underlying linguistic competence for all humans, did not feel it profitable to speculate on the reasons for this – the time depth for the possible origins of language(s) and for their subsequent divergence is too great to be meaningfully illuminated by the traditional methods of historical linguistics. However, linguists are now being forced into the speculative realm, given biologists' acceptance of the 'Out of Africa' theory, that all of present-day humankind shares a common ancestry with *one* female, dubbed 'the African Eve.' Archaeological evidence increasingly shows Africa to be the likely cradle of humankind, and it is becoming less reckless linguistically to speculate on a common origin for all of humankind's ancient languages, with subsequent periods of divergence. The extent to which this correlates with notions of race (without the argument becoming circular) will be an interesting development in future historical linguistics. In a more contemporary setting, linguists and sociologists prefer to work with the concept of ethnicity, rather than race, and it is now necessary to turn to this concept.

2. Ethnicity

Edwards (1985: 6) writes insightfully about the concept of ethnicity, characterizing it as "a sense of group identity deriving from real or perceived bonds such as language, race or religion." The term 'race' here refers to perceptions of physical differences relating to differential histories in a distant past. An ethnic group is often thought of as a distinct category of people in a larger society whose culture is usually different from its own. This view equates ethnicity with minorities: dominant groups seldom portray themselves as having ethnicity. Nationhood becomes the relevant concept here, a kind of ethnicity of the majority, or ethnicity writ large[1]. Thus ethnicity can be a problematic concept, no less troublesome than race, but in different ways. Smelser *et al.* (2001: 3) tease out race from ethnicity as follows: "race is a form of ethnicity, but distinguished from other forms of ethnicity by the identification of distinguishing physical characteristics, which, among other things, make it more difficult for members of the group to change their identity."

Ethnicity is different from race in that it is a social category, tied to group identities. As Morris (1968: 167) stresses: "The members of such a group are, or feel themselves, or are thought to be, bound together by common ties of race or nationality or culture." The labeling and the identity may not always come from within: an ethnic group may be 'othered' into existence by dominant groups. Turning to sociolinguistic matters, we can ask to what extent language is a defining feature of ethnicity. Appel and Muysken (1985: 15) put it crisply: "the relation between language and ethnicity is accidental. Language may or may not be in the group's cultural bag." That is to say, two distinct ethnic groups could well share a common language (such as Indian and White South Africans in the province of KwaZulu-Natal, South Africa). However, matters are more complex than this. Within the same territory speaking different languages must confer different sense of ethnicities. The relation is thus necessary but not sufficient: language difference implies some ethnic difference; but ethnic difference need not imply language difference. However, we are using 'language' in a broad sense here, masking the fact that it is always differentiated by the prime sociolinguistic categories of class, gender, region, age, and so on. In fact it is hard to conceive of a serious and sustained sense of ethnic differentiation that does not include some linguistic differentiation. At a relatively simple level this would extend to greetings and religious or cultural terminology (see section 6); at a more interesting level for sociolinguistics it would extend to issues of accent and syntax. This time the logical relation is reversed: ethnic differentiation implies some linguistic differentiation at the level of dialect (actually, of social dialect), but dialect differentiation need not imply a different ethnicity (it could, for example, mark class and regional differentiation). The Indian and White varieties of English in KwaZulu-Natal are, as we shall see, quite distinctive, despite ready mutual intelligibility today.

Sociologists have long warned against conceiving of ethnicity as something fixed and primordial. Edwards quotes Steinberg's (1982: 256) rather strong conclusion that "ethnicity is willingly set aside for socioeconomic advancement" and that ethnic groups "have been all too willing to trample over ethnic boundaries [...] in the pursuit of economic and social advantage." A post-modern approach would instead emphasize the view that ethnicity is not a static phenomenon, it is something that people 'do,' something that is played out differently in different situations, is not necessarily stable, and need not have fixed boundaries.

3. Race, Ethnicity and 'Color'

Color and race are sometimes conflated, and color distinctions have played a major role in categorizations of people in countries such as the United States, Sri Lanka and, above all, South Africa. Yet it is important to note that there is no 'objective correlative' of color outside the perceptions (and misperceptions) of the societies concerned. Even terms like 'black' and 'white' are not semantically transparent, nor other terms like 'brown' or 'colored.' In British India, for example, the indigenous population were referred to as either 'black' or 'brown' (see Chaudhary 2009: 425, 528). There is also a lack of agreement regarding the nomenclature of color, both officially and – more importantly for sociolinguistics – in ordinary discourse. In Britain the main categories at one time (around the 1960s) used to be 'white' versus 'colored,' while in the United States the primary distinction used to be between 'white' and 'black.' This was not just a difference of surface terminology: in the United Kingdom, people of Asian origin would have been considered 'colored' (perhaps less so now), whereas in the United States they would not have been considered 'black' (and would fall into a group marked 'Asian'). A further distinction was often made in colonial societies between a group intermediate between colonizer and colonized – that is, those of multiple ancestries. In India this group was called 'Anglo-Indian' or 'Eurasian,' in Sri Lanka 'burghers,' and in South Africa the term is "colored." The racial terminology of apartheid South Africa thus had 'white,' 'black,' 'colored,' and 'Asian' at its core. The non-congruency of the three systems can be seen in Figure 19.1.

Thus the categorizations do not fit into any neat generalization, except that the 'white' group is more or less treated as uniform, compared to 'non-whites' – to

United Kingdom	white	colored		
United States	white	black		Asian
South Africa	white	black	colored	Asian

Figure 19.1. Race/color terms in three territories in the 1960s

cite another colonial categorization. If we factor in other indigenous people, further complications arise. In the United States the category 'native American' falls outside the classification (or would form a fourth category). In South Africa, however, the indigenous Khoe-San are treated as part of the Colored population, rather than 'black.' The maximum number of terms in the racial-color scheme is not in fact four. Namibia, formerly known as South West Africa, has five: 'white' – 'black' – 'colored' – 'baster' – Asian. The term 'baster' denotes a group whose origins lie in the nineteenth-century migrations of families originally having Dutch (or Afrikaner) fathers and Khoe mothers. It comes from Afrikaans *baster*, related to English *bastard*, though the Namibian ethnonym does not carry this derogatory nuance. In South Africa such families would have been classified 'colored,' but the 'baster' people took their auto-ethnonym (a self-bestowed ethnic label) with them into Namibia. They remain distinct from the Coloreds of Namibia who are latter-day migrants from South Africa.

All this shows that race and color are fuzzy concepts, not at all biologically clear-cut, and dependent upon power and cultural relations within a territory. Sociologists, anthropologists, and linguists therefore feel more comfortable in working with ethnicity as a variable with categorizations that are somewhat subjective but used by communities themselves. There is also a sense in which the categorizations are unstable, as in the phenomenon of 'passing.' This usually refers to the attempt of a person of mixed ancestry to be accepted as part of a dominant white group, but other types of passing are possible too. In apartheid South Africa some people with fair complexions classified 'colored' tried to escape this stigma and the limitations it imposed on their social and economic opportunities by passing for 'white' (Watson 1970). They could do so only if they were fair skinned, and at great personal cost: they would have had to conceal their backgrounds and not visit those family members who remained on the 'colored' side. With economic restrictions also being severe on 'black' people, some succeeded in passing as 'colored:' this would involve taking a new first name and surname and concealing their contacts with family members who spoke an African language such as Xhosa or Zulu. Language does turn up as an issue in the phenomenon of passing: Watson (1970) recounts how 'colored' people had to give up speaking Afrikaans (or bilingual speech drawing on Afrikaans and English) in favor of English only. Likewise 'black' people would have had to gain fluency in Afrikaans in order to 'pass' successfully. Existing sociological studies do not mention accent as a feature in passing, but this barrier would also have had to be surmounted. I will have more to say on the unstable relation between language and ethnicity in South Africa at the end of section 4 below.

4. Ethnic Dialects and Social Networks

The persistence of an ethnic variety has less to do with characteristics of groups than with social networks. Linguistic work utilizing the social networks of speakers was pioneered by Lesley Milroy (1980). Rather than studying individual speakers as part of an abstract social group defined by social class, Milroy examined how their speech behavior correlated with the nature of their everyday social contacts. She outlined two different types of social networks, close-knit and loose-knit. These are determined by two factors. Firstly, 'density' or the number of contacts one has within the network: a maximally dense network relationship is one in which one has regular contacts with all members. One's friends' acquaintances are one's own too. A minimally dense equivalent is when one does not have much contact with one's friends' acquaintances. The second factor is whether the relationships within the network are 'multiplex' or not. In a multiplex relation, one member interacts with another in several roles. A neighbor might also be a friend, a co-worker and an active member of the same religious group. Milroy demonstrates convincingly that close-knit networks require loyalty to local ways of speaking, whereas loose-knit networks have more diffuse norms and are more open to linguistic innovations (see Chapter 18 in this *Handbook*). Initially a common background, including language background, may indeed be responsible for an ethnic accent or dialect (more usually termed 'ethnolect'). However, it is not ethnicity alone which sustains accents and styles of talking, but the nature of the interaction within the network. The proportion of one's everyday communication with in-group members as opposed to out-groups also makes a difference to the ethnolect. Le Page and Tabouret-Keller (1985: 13), describing the acts of identity which promoted a focused versus a more diffuse social dialect, put this more elegantly: language involves a series of acts of identity in which people both reveal their personal identity and their search for meaningful social roles.

A salient example of a historical reconstructed ethnolect alluded to earlier is South African Indian English, which will serve to illustrate the complex and dynamic nature of language in ethnicity and the effects of westernization and globalization on minorities today. The community dates back to the 1860s, when large numbers of Indians were shipped to the colony of Natal as a labor force to establish and work in large plantations, the chief of which produced sugar. Later some Indians were allowed into the colony as ordinary workers or traders, rather than indentured laborers. Coming from five different parts of India, Indians were first divided by ethnicity, on the basis of a common region and common language of the area (present-day Tamil Nadu, Andhra Pradesh, Bihar and Uttar Pradesh, Gujarat, and the Maharashtran Coast; the languages being Tamil, Telugu, Bhojpuri-Hindi, Gujarati, Urdu, and Konkani). Distinct ethnicities saw people retain their languages for over a hundred years and practice different regional customs and religious observances, a large degree of endogamy (marriage within a group) according to region of origin (and therefore home language) and distinctive (but overlapping) patterns of naming, styles of cooking, and so forth. For a hundred years or so the question 'Are you Tamil, Telugu, Gujarati, Hindustani, or Muslim?' was an important one socially. There was a kind of unity in diversity in this period, since, although they felt themselves to be internally diverse, Indians were treated as a more or less uniform group by the state, employers, and others. Common experiences and prejudices against them led to an increasing sense of unity from the 1960s onwards. Around this time came a change in social networks, which were less focused on speakers of the same ancestral language as on fellow Indians living together, under relatively rigid apartheid restrictions. There was a decrease in the hitherto relatively strong patterns of endogamy, with intermarriage between Telugu and Tamil, and Tamil and Hindi speakers becoming more frequent. English gained ground as the most common language in use within the community (which could now be characterized as showing diversity within unity), to the extent that the ancestral languages declined fairly drastically. Most relevant for this chapter is the nature of the English that stabilized, which I have characterized (Mesthrie 1992) as an incarnation of an Indian language (or at least an 'Indian' dialect of English). This extends to all aspects of the variety, which I characterize very briefly below:

a. **Accent**: weakened retroflexion of consonants /t/ and /d/; dental stops rather than dental fricatives; aspiration patterns of /p t k/ that differ from that of white speakers in the province; open vowels in place of final schwa (Mesthrie 2004).
b. **Morphology**: salient items such as *y'all* for second person plural pronoun, with genitive form *yall's*; *should* as past tense habitual auxiliary, meaning 'used to' (Mesthrie 1992).
c. **Syntax**: lack of *do*-support and auxiliary inversion in informal speech. Greater use of topicalization and fronting.
d. **Discourse**: salient use of tags like *an' all* (not unique to the dialect, but felt to be so by other speakers); shortened tag *isn't* for 'isn't it/she/he;' use of *be + -ing* for conversational historic present in narratives.
e. **Pragmatics**: notions of politeness and respect embedded in semantics and syntax of kinship terms (Mesthrie 1992).
f. **Vocabulary**: kinship terms like *māma* 'maternal uncle;' culinary terms like *sugarcane herbs* for a particular type of herb whose leaves are cooked; religious terms like *Kāvady* for a particular South Indian festival.
g. **Semantics**: slightly different meanings attached to words like *boy, girl, aunty, uncle*, to ways of reckoning age relative to a birthday, to definitions of salient culinary concepts like *curry, chutney, herbs* etc.

However, an ethnolect is not a static, closed system. Firstly, it is embedded within a larger language universe: South African Indian English (henceforth SAIE) is recognizable as a form of South African English (SAE) with which it obviously shares a great deal of special vocabulary, vowel realizations, morphosyntax, and discourse and other conventions. A few brief examples follow:

a. **Shared special vocabulary**: *robot* 'traffic light,' *stop-street* 'compulsory four way traffic stop,' *donga* 'ravine, steep walled dry water course,' *plus-minus* 'approximately.'
b. **Vowel realizations**: centralized /ɪ/ except in velar and glottal environments, [e] rather than [ɛ] as the usual realization of the DRESS vowel, lowering of /e/ before /l/.

c. **Morphosyntax**: *busy* as a semi-auxiliary in 'non-busy durative activities' (e.g. *I was busy relaxing*), *them* as associative plural marker (e.g. *Roy and them came over last night*); *by* with the meaning 'at,' rather than 'past' (e.g. *He left it by the house*).

d. **Discourse and other conventions**: *shame* as a marker of sympathy or warmth in relation to something just said by an interlocutor (e.g. *'Oh shame, isn't she sweet with her baby'* – Branford 1991: 284).

Secondly, the ethnolect is itself subject to internal variation by class, gender, and region. The biggest difference between male and female speech is in the use of slang, which is almost universal among young males, but not very common among their female age-mates. Class differences have yet to be studied in detail; but some salient markers include lowering of the NURSE vowel in some middle-class speech, but seldom in working-class speech. Mesthrie (1992) documented a vast array of forms that are basilectal, and therefore characteristic of speakers who are older, less educated, rural, and bilingual in English and an Indian language. These are mostly eschewed by acrolectal speakers (younger, middle-class, and urban), except in the most informal situations with a basilectal interlocutor. As the community becomes increasingly English-dominant these 'contact' or 'lectal' differences are transformed into a class continuum. This is a major, if largely unseen, kind of language change, since it involves shifts in the stylistic repertoires of families over time, without necessarily producing new linguistic forms. What changes is the proportion of speakers belonging to different lects or styles.

Thirdly, in terms of region, the Indian English dialect in KwaZulu-Natal, where the majority of its speakers reside, is distinct from that of other areas where Indians live (Johannesburg, Port Elizabeth, Cape Town). A simple example is the word for 'hot or spicy' (as opposed to food that is merely hot in terms of stove or oven temperature). In KwaZulu-Natal a term like *kaaro* or *thitta* survives (from Tamil and Bhojpuri-Hindi respectively) in informal speech; in formal speech speakers may use terms like *pungent* (a colonial expression that has survived in India and South Africa) or *chilli-hot*. These terms are less common in other city centers. In Cape Town the equivalent term amongst Indians is *strong* (e.g. *Is the curry too strong?*), while in Johannesburg the term is simply *hot*. The numbers and distribution of speakers also affects the ethnolect. In its heartland, KwaZulu-Natal province, SAIE is a focused, independent ethnolect. In other cities, where it is numerically weaker, it tends to share features with other varieties of English, especially 'Colored' English.

Fourthly, like all language varieties, an ethnolect is open to change. For example, retroflexion of consonants remains salient amongst the oldest speakers, less so among younger speakers (and least among young middle-class speakers). Finally, with changes in sociopolitical arrangements, an ethnolect may lose speakers to the mainstream. SAIE was a focused variety during the period of apartheid (1948–94), which prescribed where people would be born, brought up, educated, what kinds of work they would do, where and whom they would marry, and where they would be buried or cremated. Stronger control of social networks cannot be imagined. With the collapse of legal apartheid (and even a little before) social networks that were once multiplex and dense became much more diffuse. Parents from the middle classes in South Africa have opted to send their children to exclusive private schools or relatively high fee-paying, former 'white' government schools (called *Model C* in South Africa). This has brought students who would formerly have been consigned to speaking different ethnolects into contact with each other. As Mesthrie (2010) shows, many 'black' and Indian and some 'colored' speakers have crossed over into the 'white' sociolectal space. Such speakers are often labeled *coconuts* by friends and peers who do not share this predilection. The term, like the American *Oreo*, refers to one who is allegedly 'dark on the outside, white on the inside.' At the middle-middle and upper-middle social class levels (but probably not the lower-middle and working-class levels) White South African English is gaining speakers from the other ethnolects in this way. This is not a purely mechanical process, however, since individuals may resist such identity and linguistic change. In other cases 'white' students have been reported to be adopting some features of their new schoolmates, especially in slangy and rebellious styles. It remains to be seen whether this influences other informal styles. Some Indian, black, and colored speakers also report a high degree of style-shifting, especially if they go back to their 'traditional' neighborhoods after school. One speaker I interviewed is certain that she is bidialectal in SAIE and White SAE. She would be laughed at by her white friends if she spoke in her neighborhood style at school (except perhaps in jest) and would be mocked by her Indian neighborhood friends if she spoke in the manner of (mainly) white girls at school. So while class seems to trump ethnicity at the upper- and middle-middle class level, and while ethnicity resists class incursions at the working-class levels, bidialectalism seems a way out for some speakers whose social networks are evenly balanced (via neighborhood and school). This is one way of resisting the 'coconut' label, and the identity conflict it implies.

5. Caste

Caste is a topic that has been insufficiently studied in sociolinguistics: studies have tended to be more anthropological and based on vocabulary specialization, whereas a focus on interaction, accommodation/divergence and style shifting are matters awaiting detailed study. Writing about eighty years ago, Dutt (1931: 3) provided a useful characterization of the caste system of India of the time:

> Without attempting to make a comprehensive definition it may be stated that the most apparent features of the present day caste system are that members of the different castes cannot have matrimonial connections with any but persons of their own caste; that there are restrictions, though not so rigid as in the matter of marriage, about a member of the caste eating and drinking with that of a different caste; that in many cases there are fixed occupations for different castes; that there is some hierarchical gradation among the castes, the most recognized position being that of the Brahmans at the top; that birth alone decides a man's connection with his caste

for life, unless expelled for violation of his caste rules, and that transition from one caste to another, high or low is not possible. The prestige of the Brahman caste is the corner-stone of the whole organisation.

From a sociohistorical point of view the kind of socialization permitted within a rigidly observed caste system is important. Hereditary membership of a caste, commensality rules (concerning who one dines with, accepts food from, and so on), hierarchical arrangements of castes, occupational specialization (determined to a large extent by birth) and endogamy (marriage within a caste or even sub-caste grouping) leave little room for open social networks. Just as race or ethnicity – as I have argued – can be linked closely to territorial and social patterns, so too can caste. The obvious restrictions on socialization will result in differential linguistic patterns that go beyond specialization in occupational terminology to affect patterns of phonology, morphology, and discourse. In their study of caste dialects of Tamil in South India, Bright and Ramanujam (1964/1972) argued that Brahmin dialects frequently preserve non-native phonology in loanwords, while non-Brahmin dialects innovate in the phonology of native words. They proposed (1964/1972: 163) that 'upper and lower class dialects innovate independently of one another, and in two ways, [...] conscious and unconscious. Of these types of change, the more conscious variety is regularly the mark of the upper-class dialect. The less conscious changes apparently may affect both upper and lower dialects.'

One dimension neglected by the authors that also plays a role in creating and sustaining such differences is what we might call a linguistic ideology (see Blommaert 2005). The caste of Brahmins invest a significant amount of energy into maintaining a sense of linguistic differentiation from the other castes. This is done linguistically by studying Sanskrit, the ancient language of India, to the extent that it impacts upon one's speech repertoire. Sanskrit is used to create a formal and erudite register of the everyday languages that is often unintelligible to those who speak the languages but lack advanced education (see Chaudhary 2009: 568). From the examples provided by Bright and Ramanujam (1964/1972), it is clear that the higher castes actively suppress regular phonological processes of the modern vernaculars, in favor of more archaic rules. So, for example, consonant clusters may be restored where they have been lost in the vernaculars, and older suffixes deployed in favor of newer phonologically reduced ones. Together with differences in syntax, these produce a variety that carries some of the aura of Sanskrit (which means 'the cultured or polished language') as against the popular form of the vernaculars, which are often characterized (or perhaps stereotyped) as, for example, 'mixed,' or 'rough.' Sociolinguists would expect these ideological differences to hold only in formal styles, where consciousness of speech is high, and that at the vernacular level, in the intimacy of hearth and home, things might be different, with significantly less investment in formal speech. However, the whole caste edifice is very much geared towards the production and sustaining of difference even in homes, where servants of different castes may be employed. From anecdotal evidence, children of Brahmin families who use a more 'popular' word, phrase, or pronunciation are severely chastised by elders.

We should, however, be careful in over-exoticizing caste. Modern India has made compromises and reforms, especially with the ideals of Gandhi in the first half of the twentieth century, the outlawing of caste by the first independent government in the mid-twentieth century, and the protests of the lower castes and outcastes in the late twentieth century (the Dalit Movement continues its search for greater freedoms, opportunities, and respect). Although caste differs from class in that it blocks social mobility, there is a sense in which class may well be gaining ground at the expense of caste in a globalizing and economically-changing India. Furthermore, the degree of social mobility across classes in the West should not be exaggerated. The social system of the United States in the first half of the twentieth century is often characterized as a color-caste system (especially in relation to blacks and whites), though there was class mobility, mainly amongst whites. And South Africa's former apartheid system displayed obvious parallels to caste in its policy of racial hierarchy, commensality (no 'mixed' dining), hereditary membership, endogamy, and a large degree of job reservation. Finally, some of the differences described along caste lines by Bright and Ramanujam (1964/1972) also hold true for the differences between middle- and working-class western speakers (see Kroch 1978).

The bigger generalization is that where networks across social groups are constrained by custom or law, there is a proliferation of social dialect differentiation within the same geographical space. For apartheid South Africa, my study of the syntax of different English varieties (of whites, blacks, coloreds, and Indians) shows sharp boundaries in the social dialects separated in their histories (whether L1 or L2 or shifting from L2 to L1) and in social space. This has been reported on with some amazement by David Crystal (1995: 356), but it appears that syntax is no less open to social differentiation than accent.

6. Religion and Language

The study of religious language is fascinating for several reasons. Within a language, it is remarkable how often a special register is developed to talk about faith and belief. The transcendental nature of religious discourse, its heavy reliance on metaphor, and the frequently archaic syntax that goes with it in language after language are of great linguistic interest. Hand in hand with this are the intonation, rhythms, and phonological changes associated with formality and solemnity. There are also societies in which the domain of religion requires not just a transcendental stylistic shift but a complete shift to an archaic language: the cases of Latin in the Catholic Church, Classical Greek in the Orthodox Church, Hebrew in Judaism, Sanskrit in Hinduism, Pali in Buddhism and Classical Arabic in Islam are well known. The motivations are both symbolic (the words of God are appropriately expressed in an archaic language) as well as literal (the ancient language preserves the words of God, or at least the most literal interpretations of his words).

In line with the emphasis in the rest of this chapter it is necessary to ask about the relation between communities defined along religious lines within a particular geographical area and their language or social dialect. This time the emphasis is less on the special register of religion, but on everyday discourse (the vernacular). To what extent does religion act as a badge in non-religious discourse within a community? In the first place, religious sub-communities will find ways of expressing certain things differently: the word for 'God,' for example, or 'church' versus 'temple' or 'mosque,' or in greeting and leave taking. In Cape Town, people of the Islamic faith tend to use words like *kanallah* for 'please, by the Grace of Allah,' *shukran* 'thanks' and *maaf* for 'asking for forgiveness' when speaking English. Speakers might intersperse other Arabic exclamations like *salaam walaykum* (greetings), *inshallah* 'God willing' and *hamdullilah* 'by the Grace of Allah.' These lexical items serve to act as identifiers, though they may be used by people of non-Islamic faith: beggars seem to have learnt the first set to widen their range of potential sympathizers, and the greeting *Salaam walaykum* may (rarely and in marked linguistic fashion) be used by non-Muslims to Muslims. On the whole this is a small and rather self-conscious set of lexical items, mostly pertaining to greetings and exclamations. The real issue for a sociolinguist is whether the language in such a context can be characterized by different phonologies and syntaxes on religious grounds in the vernacular style, all other things being equal. The answer seems to be 'no': where phonologies are differentiated it is more in the formal religious register (e.g. the insertion of a sound in certain lexical sets from the associated classical language). It does not appear to be the case that there are any informal syntactic and phonological differences on purely religious grounds between the informal English of Muslims and Christians in Cape Town. The most famous case of religious bifurcation is, of course, that of Hindi and Urdu in India. These two varieties, which are associated with Hinduism and Islam respectively and written in different scripts, differ in their religious registers, lexicon of culture, and literary lexis. In these matters Hindi draws on Sanskritic vocabulary, whereas Urdu draws on Persian and Arabic. But at the everyday colloquial spoken level, one would be hard pressed to separate the two. In discourse that does not involve religion or writing (such as speech between friends, or a popular song or movie), it would be futile to debate whether it was Hindi or Urdu that is being used. The attaching of a label is a reflection of language and cultural ideologies, when in fact, all other things being equal, social network trumps religion in the vernacular context.

7. Conclusion

Race, ethnicity, caste, and religion all have an impact on language. I have tried to show that race is a particularly problematic term. What appear to be distinct races do not derive their identity from a strict biological definition, rather they evolved historically out of gene pools constrained by long-term geographical and social patterns. In fact, from a conceptual point of view, even the most hardened tracks pertaining to language in relation to ethnicity, caste, and religion are socio-geographic and historical in nature. These act as constraints on social networks and interaction, which remain the guiding force to our understanding of ordinary colloquial speech habits.

NOTE

1   The term 'minority' in sociology and political science is sometimes extended to demographic majorities who are not in power, and whose culture is different from that of the dominant group.

REFERENCES

Appel, R. and Muysken, P. (1985) *Language Contact and Bilingualism*, Edward Arnold, London.

Blommaert, J. (2005) *Discourse: A Critical Introduction*, Cambridge University Press, Cambridge.

Branford, J. (with Branford, W.) (1991) *A Dictionary of South African English* (4th edn), Oxford University Press, Cape Town.

Bright, W. and Ramanujam, A.K. (1964/1972) Sociolinguistic variation and language change. In *Proceedings of the Ninth International Congress of Linguists*, Cambridge, MA. Reproduced in J.B. Pride and J. Holmes (eds.) (1972), *Sociolinguistics*, Penguin, Harmondsworth, pp. 157–66.

Chaudhary, S. (2009) *Foreigners and Foreign Languages in India: A Sociolinguistic History*. Foundation Books, New Delhi.

Crystal, D. (1995) *The Cambridge Encyclopedia of the English Language*, Cambridge University Press, Cambridge.

Dutt, N.K. (1931) *Origin and Growth of Caste in India. Vol 1*, Kegan Paul, Trench and Trubner, London.

Edwards, J. (1985) *Language, Society and Identity*, Blackwell, Oxford.

Fought, C. (2006) *Language and Ethnicity*, Cambridge University Press, Cambridge.

Kroch, A. (1978) Towards a theory of dialect differentiation. *Language in Society*. 7: 17–36.

Le Page, R. and Tabouret-Keller, A. (1985) *Acts of Identity: Creole-based Approaches to Language and Ethnicity*, Cambridge University Press, Cambridge.

Mesthrie, R. (1992) *English in Language Shift: the History, Structure and Sociolinguistics of South African Indian English*, Cambridge University Press, Cambridge.

Mesthrie, R. (2004) South African Indian English: phonology. In E. Schneider, K. Burridge, B. Kortmann, R. Mesthrie, and C. Upton (eds.), *A Handbook of Varieties of English vol 1: Phonology*, Mouton de Gruyter, Berlin, pp. 953–63.

Mesthrie, R. (2010) Sociophonetics and social change: deracialisation of the GOOSE vowel in South African English. *Journal of Sociolinguistics*. 14(1):3–33.

Milroy, L. (1980) *Language and Social Networks*, Blackwell, Oxford.

Morris, H.S. (1968) Ethnic groups. In D.L. Sills (ed.), *International Encyclopedia of Social Sciences*, Free Press, New York, pp. 167–72.

Oxford South African Concise Dictionary (2006) Oxford University Press, Cape Town.

Smelser, N., Wilson, W., and Mitchell, F. (eds.) (2001) *America Becoming: Racial Trends and their Consequences. Vol 1*, National Academy Press, Washington, DC.

Steinberg, S. (1982) *The Ethnic Myth*, Atheneum, New York.

Watson, G. (1970) *Passing for White: a Study of Racial Assimilation in a South African School*, Tavistock, London.

Part IV Historical Dialectology, Language Contact, Change, and Diffusion

20 The Teleology of Change: Functional and Non-Functional Explanations for Language Variation and Change

PAUL T. ROBERGE

1. Two General Properties of Language: Variability and Lability

In 1960 Charles F. Hockett set himself the task of reconstructing the "communicative habits of the remote ancestors of the hominid line" (1960: 89) and working out the sequence by which ancestral forms of communication became language, as our species evolved. To do this, he formulated a set of thirteen design features that all languages share. Among the features that are unique to human language is what he called "traditional transmission." The human genome carries the mental capacities for the acquisition of language "and probably also a strong drive toward such acquisition" (1960: 90). However, the detailed conventions that make up individual languages are transmitted extragenetically across generations. Language emerges from an interaction between mind and external phenomena (Hurford 2003: 50). The proportion of what the innate language faculty brings to acquisition vis-à-vis what is learned from experience has long been a subject of debate. The language faculty is biologically based and invariant, but it is at the same time "open, consistent with a range of phenotypical shapes" (Lightfoot 2006: 4). In the case of learned behaviors, the phenotype interacts in complex ways with an environment that is itself variable (Kirby and Christiansen 2003: 274). It is

The Handbook of Historical Sociolinguistics, First Edition. Edited by Juan Manuel Hernández-Campoy and Juan Camilo Conde-Silvestre.
© 2014 John Wiley & Sons, Ltd. Published 2014 by John Wiley & Sons, Ltd.

therefore natural that human language, involving, as it does, a large learned component, exhibits a great deal of variation across our species. Variability manifests itself not only cross-linguistically but within what we conventionally idealize as "a (given) language."

As a consequence of cultural transmission, environmental heterogeneity, and variability, human languages change rapidly, at least relative to communication systems in other species, which are largely unlearned and probably changing at rates little different from other biologically evolved characteristics (Odling-Smee and Laland 2009: 116).

I follow Jackendoff (2002: 236) in assuming that language arose in our species primarily in the interests of facilitating communication. Accordingly, the most significant aspects of language should be those that make the encoding of propositional information possible, viz. a mental dictionary (lexicon) and a formal combinatorial system (grammar) that generates phrases, sentences, and complex words. Yet, if language evolved to enhance the transfer of information between individuals, one might expect stability of form and meaning to be part of its design, especially in communities where culturally transmitted knowledge is a critical resource for survival. Because evolution could have produced linguistic structures that are more resistant or even impervious to "corruption" over time, lability must have been selected for (Dunbar 2003: 230).

Fitch (2010: 228) points out that highly structured social systems are among the traits shared by most primates, probably dating back to the Eocene Epoch (c. 56 to 34 million years ago). Sociality represents "an early, stable feature of the primate lineage, with implications continuing to modern humans. Coping with complex groups has long been an important selective force for greater intelligence in primates" (Fitch 2010: 228). The most plausible selectional pressure for high rates of language change is the need to differentiate groups. Citing the spatial model of Nettle and Dunbar (1997) and Nettle (1999), Dunbar (2003: 231) asserts that dialects are particularly well designed to act as badges of group membership and authenticity, which "allow everyone to identify members of their [resource] exchange group;" local varieties are difficult to learn well by adult outsiders, generally have to be acquired young, "and change sufficiently rapidly that it is possible to identify an individual not just within a locality but also within a generation within that locality."

2. Explanation

"Linguists, like all scientists, are generally not satisfied with simply describing things; they also want somehow to explain them," wrote Eli Fischer-Jørgensen (1975: 387) in her history of phonological theory. From an evolutionary perspective, this means identifying the adaptive significance of the features of human language design in order to understand why language should be inherently labile and variable. Historical linguistics, by contrast, concerns itself with language traditions of communities of speakers with fully evolved brains and language faculty.

According to Lass (1997: 111–12), the history of a language *qua* semiotic system is an account of its replication over time. Perfect success in this endeavor would result in apparent stasis; language change is therefore a failure of exact replication in the transmission of features across time (see also Kroch 2001: 699). From this perspective, explanation is based on the study of relationships between successive, idealized states of a language. But explanations can be of many kinds.

The usual focus has been on explaining particular changes or change types (Lass 1997: 325), which starts with the collection and analysis of data from corpora of written and/or spoken language in order to document what happened. This is followed by an attempt to understand why it happened. The analytical procedure entails a determination of the linguistic, pragmatic, cultural, and social factors that have conditioned each change event (Andersen 2006: 84). If a pattern of change can be characterized not as an isolated case but as an example of a more general phenomenon or process, it is considered better understood. The possibility of generalization is to some extent an explanation (Fischer-Jørgensen 1975: 387; Andersen 2006). A deeper understanding would be achieved if the observed (type of) change could be shown to have some motivation from the point of view of production, system optimization, or communicative efficacy. A still higher degree of understanding would be reached if these proposals are underpinned by a general theory that elaborates the mechanisms by which 'errors' of replication occur and is sufficiently robust to account for their diffusion across populations; it would be a further advance if that theory could specify the constraints on possible changes in full modern human language.

3. Explanation of a Nonfunctional Kind

One explanation that has a long historical tradition is simply drift, the gradual accumulation of accidental, "almost imperceptible, weakly-profiled" mutations in pronunciation and meaning over long periods of time (Malkiel 1981: 535). In the canonical neogrammarian view, sound change occurs when minute deviations from the norm in the speech signal repeat themselves in large numbers of morphemes (Osthoff and Brugmann 1878: xiii). As purely phonetically determined, mechanical processes, sound changes are regular and independent of grammatical and semantic factors, although they may, of course, have significant effects on the morphosyntax of a language. Apparent exceptions should be attributable to impinging "lawful" forces operating within the same language (Paul 1920: 71) and the effects of analogy and borrowing. Intrinsically sporadic types of sound change (dissimilation, metathesis, haplology) can be systematically exempted from the regularity hypothesis, which Hockett (1965) characterized as one of the major breakthroughs in the history of linguistics. As Lass (1997: 134) has pointed out, the neogrammarians did succeed in isolating "a subtype of change that in the end proved to be critical for uncovering language relations and reconstructing history" – see also Halle (1962), Longobardi (2003: 105), and Ohala (2003: 669).

Bloomfield (1933) endorsed the neogrammarian conception of sound change, which he considered a scientifically justifiable foundation of historical linguistics. Hill (1936), Hoenigswald (1960), and Moulton (1967), among others, applied the structuralist approach to phonology in its diachronic aspect. But the traditional view was largely retained by Hockett as late as 1965, when he saw the normal variability of articulation, leading to allophonic drift, as the principal cause of sound change. In general, post-Bloomfield American structuralists concentrated on a descriptive account of distributional structure, that is, "the occurrence of parts (ultimately sounds) relative to other parts" (Harris 1954: 146). Explanation was treated gingerly, as speculative and inexact; for Joos (1950: 702) it lay beyond the linguist's charge: "[w]e try to describe precisely; we do not try to explain. Anything in our description that sounds like explanation is simple loose talk – deliberately loose, perhaps, for the sake of persuasion by analogy – and is not to be considered part of current linguistic theory."

While American structuralists occupied themselves primarily with the description of finite corpora, Noam Chomsky proceeded from a fundamental characteristic of human language – speakers are capable of producing and comprehending an infinite number of sentences – and sought to gain insight into deeper organizing principles. The project of developing a theory that has explanatory adequacy brought with it several requirements. A child capable of language acquisition must have (*inter alia*) "some initial delimitation of a class of possible hypotheses about language structure" and a method for selecting one of these hypotheses consistent with the primary linguistic data (Chomsky 1965: 30). Correspondingly, a theory of language must specify (*inter alia*) the form of the grammar of a possible human language and a way of evaluating alternative proposed grammars (Chomsky 1965: 31). The criterion for selection was the overall formal simplicity of the description. In phonology the evaluation measure entailed considerations of markedness as well as the number of features required (Chomsky and Halle 1968). Such a proposal is a hypothesis about the nature of language. Children seek maximally general and natural rules in selecting a grammar that is compatible with the primary linguistic data.[1]

From the generative viewpoint, language "has no existence apart from its mental representation" (Chomsky 1968: 81); its history is perforce an account of the internalized grammars of successive generations of speakers. In generative phonology the traditional model of sound change was firmly rejected (see Postal 1968); the structuralist practice of comparing autonomous phoneme inventories at different stages of a given language was dismissed as irrelevant (King 1969: 30). In contradistinction to the neogrammarians and structuralists, generativists have been greatly interested in theorizing the diachrony of syntax; see Lightfoot (1979: 21–42) for a critical survey of important early work. In the 'classical' generative framework, change originates in a series of individual, low-grade innovations on the part of adult speakers. These innovations, which formally reflect the addition of single rules to adult grammar, are passed on to the next generation. Children will either acquire the adult grammar 'as is' or more likely simplify it, thereby introducing a minimal discontinuity between generations. But the new generation is also capable of restructuring a grammar so as to effect more significant changes (Halle 1962; Closs 1965: 402, 414–15).

Several problems turned up in connection with these proposals. Equating linguistic change with rule change – addition, simplification (generalization), reordering, and loss (Closs 1965: 412; Kiparsky 1968; King 1969) – explains nothing (Andersen 1973: 766, 790; Lightfoot 1979: 41). To say that a rule is added to the grammar begs the question of how innovators got the rule in the first place. This should invite some consideration of the cognitive processes (mechanisms) that mediate or facilitate grammar assembly, modes of inference, and properties of the primary linguistic data. Against the backdrop of the highly abstract notion of explanatory adequacy in classical generative theory (given by the notational conventions and evaluation metric), some scholars, such as Wang (1969) and Ohala (1974), emphasized the necessity of physiologically and acoustically grounded explanations in historical phonology[2]. Weinreich, Labov, and Herzog (1968: 144–46) criticized the generative conception of change as unrealistic. Investigation of the grammatical knowledge of an idealized native speaker-hearer necessarily isolates the individual parent-model and child-learner from their speech community and dissociates historical developments from their social context. The fact is that children derive their input from many sources and revise their grammars many times as they mature. In the preadolescent years it is the influence of the peer group that determines vernacular patterns. A further problem is the unexamined assumption that change is completed within a single generation.

What is needed, according to Andersen (1973: 767), is a model of change that recognizes, on the one hand, that the verbal behavior of speakers is determined by the grammars they have assembled and, on other hand, that grammars are determined by the verbal behavior from which they are inferred. The L1-learner's goal is not to acquire an exact or optimized replica, but only a grammar that is consistent with the data of experience. Innovation is explainable on the basis of structural ambiguities in the corpus of utterances that constitute the input for L1-acquisition (see also Timberlake 1977). The potential for multiple structural analysis is a cause of change by virtue of the fact that it allows for abductive innovations (reinterpretations of structure) and deductive innovations (manifestations or applications of the new interpretations). Such innovations can lead to 'evolutive changes,' which are entirely explainable in terms of the linguistic system. Their subsequent diffusion to other groups, however, falls under the rubric of 'adaptive change,' for which we must seek explanations outside of the linguistic system.

In the light of these considerations it would seem important to distinguish between the instantiation of change and its propagation. As regards the former, one explanatory strategy has been to scrutinize the mechanisms that give rise to innovation, which Andersen (2006: 67) defines as "the introduction by a speaker, into grammar or usage, of a new variant, or […] the modification of an existing variant." Innovations are of the following types: neologism (lexical coinage, borrowing, "exploratory expressions" in the sense of Harris and Campbell 1995: 72–75), extension (application of existing linguistic resources in new usages), and reanalysis (made in acquisition, through abduction, when a surface linguistic pattern is structurally indeterminate). Harris and Campbell (1995: 50–54) agree on reanalysis and extension (although they do not define these terms in quite the same way) but elevate borrowing as a mechanism of equal rank. The transfer of structural features across language boundaries has ordinarily been considered separately from the instantiation and diffusion of change within monolingual speech communities. One reason for the separation is that structural borrowing may be constrained by linguistic factors that do not present themselves in the latter scenario. But the differences may turn out to be a matter of degree rather than kind (see Thomason 2003: 687–88). When languages come into intimate contact, innovations can arise through the agentivity of recipient-language speakers and/or speakers of the source language. In the latter case van Coetsem (2000) speaks of the imposition of features on the recipient language. Language contact is often a catalyst for reanalysis and extension as well (Harris and Campbell 1995: 51). By whatever mechanism, any innovation arising out of contact will lead to change only through its adoption by a sufficient number of speakers and its transmission to the cohorts who follow them:

> If one believes in accommodation theory and in the role of 'linguistic missionaries' [i.e., innovators and early adopters in the terminology of Milroy and Milroy 1985: 367; J. Milroy 1992: 184–85] in spreading features from one network of communication to another and thereby causing change, then the basic explanation is that contact among idiolects is the fundamental cause of language change.
>
> (Mufwene 2000: 71)

When contact among languages is involved, the pool of features may become larger, but the process of competition and selection is the same, operating at the level of individuals before affecting the community.

Contemporary generative theory proceeds from its original premise that change occurs between the generations, when children learning a language construct a grammar different from that of their elders (Lightfoot 2003: 496). According to Lightfoot (2006: 10, 45), the data that children encounter during L1-acquisition constitute a triggering experience that causes the 'linguistic genotype' (Universal Grammar) to develop into a 'linguistic phenotype,' a person's mature grammar or internal language (I-language, the mental system). Rather than learn whole systems, children infer parameter settings from the data resident in external language (E-language), which is "a function of the various grammars in the child's environment and of people's *use* of those grammars and does not reflect any single system" (Lightfoot 2006: 12). Children scan utterances for cues, or elements of structure that are necessary for them to fix parameters in certain ways (Lightfoot 2006: 14, 77–78).

In the Principles and Parameters framework, the goal of diachronic syntax is to explain how and why parameter settings change (Pintzuk 2003: 509). Roberts (2007: 121) wishes to show that all the major types of syntactic change involve parameter change, which is "the principal explanatory mechanism in diachronic syntax." Reanalysis is usually a symptom of a change in the value of a parameter: "Given the central idea that parameters unify clusters of surface grammatical properties, this implies that a parameter change may manifest itself as a cluster of reanalyses" (123). The cause of parameter resetting lies in perturbations in the linguistic environment, which may be due to other structural changes, shifting stylistic patterns, or language contact. Lightfoot (2003: 497) claims that changes involving new parameter settings tend to occur more rapidly than other changes (such as grammaticalization or deflection) and evince the S-curve pattern observed by Kroch (1989). Scholars investigating historical texts from a variationist perspective, such as Kroch (1989, 2001) and Pintzuk (1999, 2003), have documented a competition between alternative parameteric values – "two distinct grammatical options in areas of grammar that do not ordinarily permit optionality" (Pintzuk 2003: 516) – until the change is fully diffused. Systematic variation over time (which can in many cases be measured quantitatively) supports the hypothesis that parameter values do not change abruptly.

4. Function, Teleology, and Preference

The term *function* has had several meanings in linguistics. In its logico-mathematical sense it refers to a mapping (Keller 1997: 14), that is, a correspondence between two variables such that one quantity (input) determines another quantity (output); or, to put the matter another way, exchanges of values under one variable are correlated with exchanges of values under another variable (Haas 1975: 28). Unlike the mathematician's definition of function, the linguistic notion is basically a teleological one, entailing, as it does, the tasks or roles of linguistic elements in a system that maps meaning onto form (Jakobson 1932/1962: 232; Haas 1975: 29; Lass 1980: 65; Keller 1997). Teleology is not identified with purpose in the sense of conscious intent. Rather, defining the function of an element within the system of which it is part "amounts to a teleological explanation" (Andersen 1973: 789). It has been customary in linguistics to distinguish 'teleology of function' from 'teleology of purpose' (Andersen 1973; Lass 1980: 80–83).

Prague School linguists were greatly interested in language change and were especially concerned with the development of phonological systems. As early as the 1920s, Roman Jakobson (1928/1962: 1) called for the replacement of the neogrammarian mechanistic view of change with a teleological one:

> Language (and in particular its sound system) cannot be analyzed without taking into account the purpose which that system serves [...] The overlapping between territorially, socially, or functionally distinct linguistic patterns can be fully comprehended only from a teleological point of view, since every transition from one system to another necessarily bears a linguistic function.

In American structuralism it was thought that the description of syntagmatic co-occurrence and paradigmatic substitution ceases to be precise if it becomes mixed up with functional considerations (Haas 1975: 25). In European structuralism no sound change can be understood without reference to the system that undergoes it; and each change is purposeful (Jakobson 1932/1962: 232). When the asymmetry of physiology disturbs systemic equilibrium, there may follow a cycle of changes that aim at its restoration. With regard to the resilience or attenuation of phono-logical oppositions, Martinet (1952, 1953, 1955/1970) attached much importance to functional load (degree of utilization), the efficient use (economy) of distinctive features, which is manifest in a tendency toward symmetrical arrays of phonemes, and the tendency to maintain a safe phonetic distance between phonemes.

In Hock's view (1986/1991: 164–65), changes conditioned by phonological structure unfold through a series of "tactical decisions" in response to situations that prevail at a given time rather than as implementation of some preconceived "grand plan" or "strategy." The results of such decisions may accrue with enough "critical mass" to establish a clear surface-structure target for further changes (see also Aitchison 1987: 29, and Chapter 21 in this *Handbook*). A "two-mora conspir-acy" in Pali, for example, comprised three phonetically quite distinct changes (vowel shortening, cluster simplification, and epenthesis) that eliminated tri-moric syllable rhymes. Certain syntactic changes, too, may be oriented toward a goal (Hock 1986/1991: 361–70). The 1970s saw attempts to explicate Sapir's notion of a general drift to language – "the unconscious selection on the part of its speakers of [individual] variations that are cumulative in some special direction" (1921: 155) – as typological shift (see Roberge 1985 for references and discussion). Drifts, we were told, reflect the accumulation of short-term changes or a single long-term process working toward some well-characterized typological goal. Aitchison (1987: 29), too, examines situations in which different rules conspire to produce a common effect. There comes a point at which certain types of rules proliferate, and language is akin to "a snowball rolling down a hill, accumulating snow, and virtually unable to alter its course."

Lass (1980: 80) points out that teleological arguments often fail to distinguish between goals and *de facto termini* (see also Haider 1998: 98, 2001). Chain shifts can have the effect of maintaining contrast, although it will prove difficult to establish that speakers effect the wholesale realignment of a phonological system (in lieu of merger) in order to retain its preexisting diacritic relations. Labov (1994: 218–21) finds mechanical explanations of the principles of chain shifting to be more consistent with the available data. Invoking typological harmony or consist-ency does not constitute an explanation, unless one imputes to language history an institutional memory, allows for the operation of 'unconscious rationality' (Itkonen 1982, 1983), or personifies language itself as an agent. Typologically mixed languages exist and remain stable over the long haul; there is further dis-cussion of these criticisms in Lightfoot (1979: 385–405) and Lass (1980: 80–83, 1987). Aitchison (1987: 19, 29), who does draw the proper distinction, points out that social factors may direct a language toward one or another set of options that are predetermined by its existing structure. Specification of the developmental options at each stage and identification of incipient conspiracies might shed light on the phenomenon of drift. Linguistic structure and the responses to the options selected are governed by the cognitive infrastructure, and genuine explanation will require us to find out a lot more about the level of mind.

The term 'functional' also refers to theories claiming that the processes of lan-guage operate so as to preserve meaning (Guy 2003: 392). On this view, reductive phonological processes are likely to be constrained, if not blocked outright in environments in which they would produce homophony or efface surface grammatical distinctions (see Kiparsky 1982: 88–92; see also Roberge 1985, Labov 1994: 547–68, and Guy 1996 for reviews of the literature). To cite a stock example, some varieties of American English do not permit deletion of post-consonantal final /-t, -d/ (or do so only sporadically) if the final segment represents the weak preterital suffix: *past/pas', find/fin'* but not *passed/*pass', fined/*fin'*. In other varieties – most notably African American Vernacular English – this suffix, too, is deletable, but not as often as coronal stops in final clusters of monomorphemic words (Labov 1972: 216–26, 1994: 552–55). Guy (1996, 2003: 392–94), however, problematizes a functional interpretation of this pattern, having found that the suffix of the weak past participle shows essentially the same frequency of deletion as the preterital suffix, despite its redundancy in periphrastic tense constructions (*Kendall has pass(ed) the examination*). The grammatical conditioning inheres in formal structure (root + suffix), not the information-carrying capacity of the exponents. The larger point is that functional hypotheses predict a tendency for speakers to select variants in such a way as to maintain meaning. Labov (1994: 568) concludes that the weight of evidence shows the opposite. Overall, conservation of meaning does not exert a significant effect on the selection process. In most cases, when variation turns to change, languages manage to retain their referential power "by one route or another" (Labov 1994: 568). Further to the problematic nature of this *explanans*, see Lass (1980: 66–70), Kroch (1989), and Guy (1996).

It has long been thought that the direction of change is subject to and potentially determined by system-internal and system-external preferences (see also Chapter 21 in this *Handbook*). Markedness involves inclusive relationships between two poles of an opposition (e.g., /p/ : /b/, singular/plural), in which the marked member contains an extra feature or property ([+voice], {PLURAL}), or between syntactic constructions, in which one usage is expected (unmarked) in a given environment and the other (marked) usage is exceptional or innovative. Naturalness is a gradient concept that subsumes phonetic plausibility, constructional iconicity, morphotactic and morpho-semantic transparency, and form–meaning biuniqueness. Although markedness and naturalness are conceptually independent in their strict senses (see Andersen 2008), one finds considerable overlap in the literature. For many writers, markedness has to do with the relative frequency of features, cross-linguistically, based on statistical observation. Moreover, "the usual equation is that unmarked features are more natural and marked features are less natural, but this equation is clearly too simplistic" (Thomason 2001: 65).

In phonology, changes from less natural to more natural encompass the maximization of optimal syllable structure (CV or CVC) and the selection of 'easier' articulations over 'harder' ones. An optimal lexicon would manifest itself in meaning–form biuniqueness ('one meaning, one form') and the avoidance of homophony. Underlying natural morphological change is a semiotic preference for formal transparency. Accordingly, redundant, "opacifying" (Dressler 2003: 464) morphophonological alternations should evince a greater susceptibility to loss than material bearing primary inflectional meaning, as, for example, in the minimization of allomorphy within paradigms (Middle English *wif*, gen. sg. *wives* [wi:vəs], pl. *wives* > Modern English *wife, wife's* [waɪfs], *wives*). By the same token, the favored trajectory of morphological change should be in the direction of constructional iconicity. The inflectional relationship *cow* + {PLURAL} is more transparently realized by the diagrammatic, secondary form *cows* than by historical, now archaic *kine* (cf. Middle English *cū, kū*, pl. *kyn*). Such changes have been characterized as functional (Dressler 2003: 461, 471) insofar as they are targeted at preferred states within their domain.

Lass (1980: 35, 80–83) rejects the explanatory significance of putative (universal) natural tendencies on grounds that they are *post hoc* and nonpredictive. Any change of the type 'abnatural' > '(more) natural' counts as an instantiation of the preference; and no failure to optimize can be a counterexample. As with teleology of function generally, preferences are nonexplanatory if they are not identifiable independently of their empirical manifestations. Vennemann (1983: 13) acknowledges the necessity of deriving preferences "from the theorems of nonlinguistic theories, such as phonetic theories, theories of learning, semiotic theories, theories of communication, etc." Some linguists believe that absolute prediction is neither realistic nor appropriate as a standard of proof in historical linguistics (see Aitchison 1987; Harris and Campbell 1995: 321–25 for discussion). For any given variable, the natural value should be the more likely candidate for selection than the abnatural value. Given two comparable pathways of change, the natural one should be more likely to occur than the reverse. These trends represent not a global change toward more natural systems but rather local improvements. What they predict, Dressler (2003: 463) assures us, is testable empirically and should reach statistical significance at a minimum.

Optimality Theory (OT), which attributes cross-linguistic variability to differential rankings within a universal set of constraints, explicates language change in terms of constraint re-ranking over time. Applications of OT to historical linguistics (originally in phonology but later also in syntax) constitute a burgeoning literature (Holt 2003) and have generated disagreement over the model's explanatory adequacy – see, especially, the critical assessments of McMahon (2000) and Gess (2003). Haspelmath (1999), however, seeks to establish a correspondence between linguistic optimality and 'user optimality.' Languages show variation in all areas of grammar; frequency of use is determined by the usefulness of linguistic structures; high-frequency variants may become obligatory in a process of functional selection, on analogy with the biological notion of natural selection.

The idea that grammatical structures are adapted to the needs of language users has also been promulgated by Croft (2000, 2006). But the transfer of theoretical concepts from evolutionary biology to historical linguistics has encountered resistance (Andersen 2006) and will doubtless remain controversial.

5. Functionalism

Researchers working under the label of 'functionalism,' such as Givón (1995), Dik (1989/1997) and Halliday (1985/2004), do not specifically constitute a school but represent a trend in linguistics that is broadly unified by a common perspective regarding the instrumentality of language. A natural language is an instrument of social interaction (Dik 1989/1997: volume 1, page 5); it exists by virtue of its being deployed for the expression and communication of thoughts. Change is a product of purposeful language use in concrete situations, in fulfillment of language's discourse and communication functions. Keller's (1990/1994) 'invisible hand' explanation obtains from an analysis of speakers' rational choices in communicative behavior, which are "functional in the teleological sense," and of the "unintended macro-structural consequences" of their choices (Keller 1997: 16–17). For other functionalist perspectives on change, see the heterogeneous collection of articles in Gvozdanović (1997). Along a separate front, precepts of functionalism are discernable in studies that examine the semantic-pragmatic bases of grammaticalization, which "can be interpreted as the result of a process which has problem-solving as its main goal" (Heine, Claudi, and Hünnemeyer 1991: 150; see Hopper and Traugott 1993/2003: 71–98 for a good survey). Mithun (2003) stresses the inseparability of cognitive and discourse factors in the development of syntactic constructions and looks to the expressive needs of speakers to account for the extension of existing patterns to new environments.

Much can be said in favor of grounding proposals in speaker intentionality (if this can be rigorously determined) and in the contextual circumstances surrounding actual language use. But there remains the danger of what Haspelmath (1999: 188) calls the "teleological fallacy": "[u]seful or needed things are not sufficiently explained by their usefulness or need for them." Conversion of functional statements into full explanations requires a theory of selection from independently existing and competing linguistic structures.

6. Explanation in Historical Sociolinguistics

By using the present to explain the past under license of the uniformitarian principle (Labov 1975), the social study of variation has adopted a panchronic perspective (see also Chapter 5 in this *Handbook*). Weinreich, Labov, and Herzog (1968) laid out a comprehensive research program for the study of language change. Structured heterogeneity is the basic assumption; it is "an integral part of the linguistic economy of the community, necessary to satisfy the linguistic demands of every-day life" (Labov 1982: 17). The variable use of forms within a single language is structured along demographic, contextual, linguistic, and interactional dimensions. Linguistic variables correlate systematically with region, socioeconomic status, ethnicity, gender, and age, as has been massively documented in the literature. Intersecting variation by users is variation according to use and degree of formality, which in traditional variationist studies has been referred to as register and style. Aspects of the linguistic system – formally known as variable constraints (Labov 1972: 218) or independent linguistic constraints – may influence variation apart from social factors and context. A speaker's control of the variants and the constraints on their occurrence is part of 'competence,' not 'performance.'

Adequate explanation of language change must address five fundamental problems: (i) "the set of possible changes and possible conditions for changes which can take place in a structure of a given type" (Weinreich, Labov, and Herzog 1968: 101) (the problem of universal constraints); (ii) intervening stages between instantiation of a change and its completion – in other words its spread from an innovating subgroup within a speech community to other subgroups: the transition problem; (iii) correlation of variants that are constitutive of linguistic variables with features of the linguistic environment and extralinguistic characteristics of the speaker and the situation – the embedding problem; (iv) the social valuation of the variants themselves and speaker attitudes generally – the evaluation problem; (v) why change should take place in a particular language at a particular time but not in other languages with the same structural conditions, or in the same language at some other point in time – the actuation problem.

The actuation problem presents an explanatory challenge that "can be regarded as the very heart of the matter" (Weinreich, Labov, and Herzog 1968: 102). It can be studied through the analysis of social networks, which are the sum of relationships which individuals have contracted with others (L. Milroy 1980/1987, 2001: 370) (see also Chapter 18 in this *Handbook*). Group identification through language can be very strong. Chambers (1995/2003: 266) asserts that "the underlying cause of sociolinguistic differences, largely beneath consciousness, is the human instinct to establish and maintain social identity." People feel a need

> to show they belong somewhere, and to define themselves, sometimes narrowly and sometimes generally. It is not enough to mark our territory as belonging to us [...] We must also mark ourselves as belonging to the territory, and one of the most convincing markers is by speaking like the people who live there. (Chambers 1995/2003: 266)

Close-knit networks support the maintenance of low-status vernaculars in rural and urban communities despite pressure from superposed prestige varieties. A corollary of a network's capacity for norm enforcement is that the loosening of its structure will open up a conduit for change. Innovators are weakly linked to the group, whereas early adopters have strong ties within it. Once these central figures adopt an innovation from more marginal persons, it is disseminated "from the inside outwards" (Milroy and Milroy 1985: 367).

Other sociolinguists interested in explanation have likewise emphasized the primacy of speakers as active agents. In the model of Le Page and Tabouret-Keller (1985), individuals have priority. Well-defined social groups cannot be presupposed. Speakers direct their verbal behavior so as to resemble or distance themselves from the individuals and groups with which they interact. In so doing, they exhibit the effects of individual and communal acts of identity. More recently, Eckert (2000, 2008) has redirected attention to the social meaning of variation. The enterprise is not one of seeking explanations for structural changes in the construction of meaning, but rather one of examining what speakers do with the elements of such changes as a function of social practice. Labov's pioneering study (1963) of the centralization of /ay/ on the island of Martha's Vineyard and how it indexed local authenticity is an early demonstration of the power of variation in social change. Renewed interest in variation as an indexical system that embeds ideology in language should contribute in an essential way to the widening of perspectives in historical explanation.

7. Explanation in Macrosociolinguistics

New patterns of usage may come about through deliberate intervention on the part of institutions, political and cultural elites, and individual 'language strategists,' in accordance with prescriptive articulations (ideologies) and with desired practical outcomes. In some precolonial societies of the Pacific an important distinction is that between 'exoteric' and 'esoteric' languages. The former are available for intergroup communication; the latter

> [a]re restricted to a well-defined group who often contribute to its exclusiveness by making it difficult for outsiders to learn. To sustain an esoteric language requires considerable social effort, as it involves formal teaching, monitoring and correcting. (Mühlhäusler 1996: 39)

Another, obvious case in point is the cultivation of superposed varieties of language. The process of vernacular elevation is one of enhancing the status of a selected or constructed (*koineized*) variety of language and increasing its referential and expressive power by means of adlexification and stylistic elaboration. The end result is the establishment of a received set of orthographic and linguistic norms that define a unitary medium of wider communication in high-level domains, such as government administration, religion, education, *belles lettres*, and scientific inquiry.

Here, as with speaker agency at the microsociolinguistic level, one may speak of teleology of purpose. Explanation may take us far beyond the linguistic facts and into a study of the political, social, and cultural conditions underlying language choice, maintenance, shift, and standardization.

8. Conclusion

At one level, historical sociolinguistics constitutes a part of general sociolinguistics. Its underlying premise is that linguistic and social factors are closely interrelated and must be studied in their mutual interaction. The bases of linguistic change are typically assumed to lie in low-level variability of speech (as claimed by the neogrammarians), ambiguities in the primary linguistic data that allow multiple analysis, innovation (in the sense of Andersen 2006), and language contact. The role of systemic function (such as phonological symmetry, margin of safety in chain shifts, and preservation) is acknowledged. So far, historical sociolinguistics has been primarily interested in accounting for shifting patterns of usage over time and their social meanings rather than in the mechanisms of change or its particular linguistic trajectory (based on considerations of naturalness, universal preferences, optimality, and so on). This is perhaps as it should be, especially if one adopts the view that change is implemented by speakers and takes place in speech, which is a social activity (J. Milroy 1992; Milroy and Milroy 1985). But at another level, historical sociolinguistics must be situated within a general theory of language change that unifies internal, social, cognitive, and discourse principles.

Lightfoot (1999: 218) writes that historical linguistics seems more concerned with explanations than other sub-disciplines in our field. In the early twenty-first century the problem of how to explain language change and the justification of proposed explanations remain central to the scholarly enterprise. Beyond observational, descriptive, and explanatory adequacy, there is a fourth level of achievement to be attained, to wit, historical adequacy. Of the biologically possible human languages, why do we have precisely the ones we have? And beyond that fundamental question lies the phylogenesis of the language faculty, or evolutionary adequacy (Longobardi 2003: 103).

NOTES

1   A grammar is observationally adequate if it accounts for the data in a given corpus. A descriptively adequate grammar makes distinctions between well-formed and infelicitous linguistic structures, according to the intuitions of native speakers. Explanatory adequacy is achieved if the theory provides a general basis for the selection of a descriptively adequate grammar from among the observationally adequate ones (Chomsky 1965: 25).
2   Ohala (2003) brings the problem of phonetic factors in the initiation of sound change up to date.

REFERENCES

Aitchison, J. (1987) The language lifegame: prediction, explanation and linguistic change. In W. Koopman *et al.* (eds.), pp. 11–32.

Andersen, H. (1973) Abductive and deductive change. *Language* 49: 765–93.

Andersen, H. (2006) Synchrony, diachrony, and evolution. In O.N. Thomsen (ed.), pp. 59–90.

Andersen, H. (2008) Naturalness and markedness. In K. Willems and L. de Cuypere (eds.), *Naturalness and Iconicity in language*, John Benjamins, Amsterdam, pp. 101–19.

Bloomfield, L. (1933) *Language*, Holt, Rinehart & Winston, New York.

Chambers, J.K. (1995/2003) *Sociolinguistic Theory: Linguistic Variation and its Social Significance* (2nd edn), Blackwell, Oxford.

Chomsky, N. (1965) *Aspects of the Theory of Syntax*, MIT Press, Cambridge, MA.

Chomsky, N. (1968) *Language and Mind*, Harcourt, Brace, Jovanovich, New York.

Chomsky, N. and Halle, M. (1968) *The Sound Pattern of English*, Harper & Row, New York.

Christiansen, M.H. and Kirby, S. (eds.) (2003) *Language Evolution*, Oxford University Press, Oxford.

Closs, E. (1965) Diachronic syntax and generative grammar. *Language* 41: 402–15.

Croft, W. (2000) *Explaining Language Change: An Evolutionary Approach*, Longman, Harlow.

Croft, W. (2006) The relevance of an evolutionary model to historical linguistics. In O.N. Thomsen (ed.), pp. 91–132.

Dik, S. (1989/1997) *The Theory of Functional Grammar* (2nd edn), 2 vols, Mouton de Gruyter, Berlin.

Dressler, W.U. (2003) Naturalness and morphological change. In B.D. Joseph and R.D. Janda (eds.), pp. 461–71.

Dunbar, R.I.M. (2003) The origin and subsequent evolution of language. In M.H. Christiansen and S. Kirby (eds.), pp. 219–34.

Eckert, P. (2000) *Linguistic Variation as Social Practice: The Linguistic Construction of Identity in Belten High*, Blackwell, Oxford.

Eckert, P. (2008) Variation and the indexical field. *Journal of Sociolinguistics* 12: 453–76.

Fischer-Jørgensen, E. (1975) *Trends in Phonological Theory*, Akademisk forlag, Copenhagen.

Fitch, W.T. (2010) *The Evolution of Language*, Cambridge University Press, Cambridge.

Gess, R. (2003) On re-ranking and explanatory adequacy in a constraint-based theory of phonological change. In D.E. Holt (ed.), pp. 67–90.

Givón, T. (1995) *Functionalism and Grammar*, John Benjamins, Amsterdam.

Guy, G.R. (1996) Form and function in linguistic variation. In G.R. Guy, C. Feagin, D. Schiffrin, and J. Baugh (eds.), *Towards a Social Science of Language: Papers in Honor of William Labov, vol. 1*, John Benjamins, Amsterdam, pp. 221–52.

Guy, G.R. (2003) Variationist approaches to phonological change. In B.D. Joseph and R.D. Janda (eds.), pp. 369–400.

Gvozdanović, J. (ed.) (1997) *Language Change and Functional Explanations*, Mouton de Gruyter, Berlin.

Haas, W. (1975) Phonology and general linguistics: On the notion of 'linguistic function.' In W.U. Dressler and F.V. Mareš (eds.), *Phonologica 1972*, Fink, Munich/Salzburg, pp. 25–33.

Haider, H. (1998) Form follows function fails – as a direct explanation for properties of grammar. In P. Weingartner, G. Schurz, and G. Dorn (eds.), *The Role of Pragmatics in Contemporary Philosophy*, Hölder-Pichler-Tempsky, Vienna, pp. 92–108.

Haider, H. (2001) Not every why has a wherefore – Notes on the relation between form and function. In W. Bisang (ed.), *Aspects of Typology and Universals*, Akademie Verlag, Berlin, pp. 37–52.

Halle, M. (1962) Phonology in generative grammar. *Word* 18: 54–72.

Halliday, M.A.K. (1985/2004) *An Introduction to Functional Grammar* (3rd edn), Edward Arnold, London.

Harris, A.C. and Campbell, L. (1995) *Historical Syntax in Cross-Linguistic Perspective*, Cambridge University Press, Cambridge.

Harris, Z. (1954) Distributional structure. *Word* 10: 146–62.

Haspelmath, M. (1999) Optimality and diachronic adaptation. *Zeitschrift für Sprachwissenschaft* 18: 180–205.

Heine, B., Claudi, U., and Hünnemeyer, F. (1991) From cognition to grammar: Evidence from African languages. In E.C. Traugott and B. Heine (eds.), *Approaches to Grammaticalization vol. 1*, John Benjamins, Amsterdam, pp. 149–87.

Hill, A.A. (1936) Phonetic and phonemic change. *Language* 12: 15–22.

Hock, H.H. (1986/1991) *Principles of Historical Linguistics* (2nd edn), Mouton de Gruyter, Berlin.

Hockett, C.F. (1960) The origin of speech. *Scientific American* 203: 88–96.

Hockett, C.F. (1965) Sound change. *Language* 41: 185–204.

Hoenigswald, H.M. (1960) *Language Change and Linguistic Reconstruction*, University of Chicago Press, Chicago.

Holt, D.E. (ed.) (2003) *Optimality Theory and Language Change*, Kluwer, Dordrecht.

Hopper, P.J. and Traugott, E.C. (1993/2003) *Grammaticalization* (2nd edn), Cambridge University Press, Cambridge.

Hurford, J.R. (2003) The language mosaic and its evolution. In M.H. Christiansen and S. Kirby (eds.), pp. 38–57.

Itkonen, E. (1982) Short-term and long-term teleology in linguistic change. In J.P. Maher, A.R. Bomhard, and E.F.K. Koerner (eds.), *Papers from the Third International Conference on Historical Linguistics*, John Benjamins, Amsterdam, pp. 85–118.

Itkonen, E. (1983) *Causality in Linguistic Theory: A Critical Investigation into the Philosophical and Methodological Foundations of 'Non-Autonomous' Linguistics*, Indiana University Press, Bloomington.

Jackendoff, R. (2002) *Foundations of Language: Brain, Meaning, Grammar, Evolution*, Oxford University Press, Oxford.

Jakobson, R. (1928/1962) The concept of the sound law and the teleological criterion. In R. Jakobson, pp. 1–2.

Jakobson, R. (1932/1962) Phoneme and phonology. In R. Jakobson, pp. 231–33.

Jakobson, R. (1962) *Selected Writings, vol. 1*, Mouton, The Hague.

Joos, M. (1950) Description of language design. *Journal of the Acoustical Society of America* 22: 701–8.

Joseph, B.D. and Janda, R.D. (eds.) (2003) *The Handbook of Historical Linguistics*, Blackwell, Oxford.

Keller, R. (1990/1994) *Sprachwandel: Von der unsichtbaren Hand in der Sprache* (2nd edn), Francke, Tübingen.

Keller, R. (1997) In what sense can explanations of language change be functional? In J. Gvozdanović (ed.), pp. 9–20.

King, R.D. (1969) *Historical Linguistics and Generative Grammar*, Prentice-Hall, Englewood Cliffs, NJ.

Kiparsky, P. (1968) Linguistic universals and linguistic change. In E. Bach and R.T. Harms (eds.), *Universals in Linguistic Theory*, Holt, Rinehart & Winston, New York, pp. 170–202. Reprinted in P. Kiparsky (1982), pp. 13–43.

Kiparsky, P. (1982) *Explanation in Phonology*, Foris, Dordrecht.

Kirby, S. and Christiansen, M.H. (2003) From language learning to language evolution. In M.H. Christiansen and S. Kirby (eds.), pp. 272–94.

Koopman, W., van der Leek, F., Fischer, O., and Eaton, R. (eds.) (1987) *Explanation and Linguistic Change*, John Benjamins, Amsterdam.

Kroch, A.S. (1989) Reflexes of grammar in patterns of language change. *Language Variation and Change* 1: 199–244.

Kroch, A.S. (2001) Syntactic change. In M. Baltin and C. Collins (eds.), *The Handbook of Contemporary Syntactic Theory*, Blackwell, Oxford, pp. 699–729.

Labov, W. (1963) The social motivation of a sound change. *Word* 19: 273–309. Reprinted in Labov (1972), pp. 1–42.

Labov, W. (1972) *Sociolinguistic Patterns*, University of Pennsylvania Press, Philadelphia.

Labov, W. (1975) On the use of the present to explain the past. In L. Heilmann (ed.), *Proceedings of the Eleventh International Congress of Linguists, vol. 2*, Il Mulino, Bologna, pp. 825–51.

Labov, W. (1982) Building on empirical foundations. In W.P. Lehmann and Y. Malkiel (eds.), *Perspectives on Historical Linguistics*, John Benjamins, Amsterdam, pp. 17–92.

Labov, W. (1994) *Principles of Linguistic Change I: Internal Factors*, Blackwell, Oxford.

Lass, R. (1980) *On Explaining Language Change*, Cambridge University Press, Cambridge.

Lass, R. (1987) Language, speakers, history and drift. In W. Koopman *et al.* (eds.), pp. 151–76.

Lass, R. (1997) *Historical Linguistics and Language Change*, Cambridge University Press, Cambridge.

Le Page, R.B. and Tabouret-Keller, A. (1985) *Acts of Identity: Creole-Based Approaches to Language and Ethnicity*, Cambridge University Press, Cambridge.

Lightfoot, D. (1979) *Principles of Diachronic Syntax*, Cambridge University Press, Cambridge.

Lightfoot, D. (1999) *The Development of Language: Acquisition, Change, and Evolution*, Blackwell, Oxford.

Lightfoot, D. (2003) Grammatical approaches to syntactic change. In B.D. Joseph and R.D. Janda (eds.), pp. 495–508.

Lightfoot, D. (2006) *How New Languages Emerge*, Cambridge University Press, Cambridge.

Longobardi, G. (2003) Methods in parametric linguistics and cognitive history. *Linguistic Variation Yearbook* 3: 101–38.

Malkiel, Y. (1981) Drift, slope, and slant: background of, and variations upon, a Sapirian theme. *Language* 57: 535–70.

Martinet, A. (1952) Function, structure, and sound change. *Word* 8: 1–32.

Martinet, A. (1953) Concerning the preservation of useful sound features. *Word* 9: 1–11.

Martinet, A. (1955/1970) *Économie des changements phonétiques: Traité de phonologie diachronique* (3rd edn), Francke, Bern.

McMahon, A. (2000) *Change, Chance, and Optimality*, Oxford University Press, Oxford.

Milroy, J. (1992) *Linguistic Variation and Change: On the Historical Sociolinguistics of English*, Blackwell, Oxford.

Milroy, J. and Milroy, L. (1985) Linguistic change, social network and speaker innovation. *Journal of Linguistics* 21: 339–84.

Milroy, L. (1980/1987) *Language and Social Networks* (2nd edn), Blackwell, Oxford.

Milroy, L. (2001) Social networks. In R. Mesthrie (ed.), *Concise Encyclopedia of Sociolinguistics*, Elsevier, Amsterdam, pp. 370–76.

Mithun, M. (2003) Functional perspectives on syntactic change. In B.D. Joseph and R.D. Janda (eds.), pp. 552–72.

Moulton, W.G. (1967) Types of phonemic change. *To Honor Roman Jakobson: Essays on the Occasion of his Seventieth Birthday, vol. 2*, Mouton, The Hague, pp. 1393–1407.

Mufwene, S.S. (2000) Creolization is a social, not a structural, process. In I. Neumann-Holzschuh and E.W. Schneider (eds.), *Degrees of Restructuring in Creole Languages*, John Benjamins, Amsterdam, pp. 65–84.

Mühlhäusler, P. (1996) *Linguistic Ecology: Language Change and Linguistic Imperialism in the Pacific Region*, Routledge, London.

Nettle, D. (1999) *Linguistic Diversity*, Oxford University Press, Oxford.

Nettle, D. and Dunbar, R.I.M. (1997) Social markers and the evolution of reciprocal exchange. *Current Anthropology* 38: 93–98.

Odling-Smee, J. and Laland, K.N. (2009) Cultural niche construction: evolution's cradle of language. In R. Botha and C. Knight (eds.), *The Prehistory of Language*, Oxford University Press, Oxford, pp. 99–121.

Ohala, J.J. (1974) Experimental historical phonology. In J.M. Anderson and C. Jones (eds.), *Historical Linguistics: Proceedings of the First International Conference on Historical Linguistics, vol. 2*, North-Holland, Amsterdam, pp. 353–87.

Ohala, J.J. (2003) Phonetics and historical phonology. In B.D. Joseph and R.D. Janda (eds.), pp. 669–86.

Osthoff, H. and Brugmann, K. (1878) Vorwort, in *Morphologische Untersuchungen auf dem Gebiete der indogermanischen Sprachen, Theil 1*, S. Hirzel, Leipzig, pp. iii–xx.

Paul, H. (1920) *Prinzipien der Sprachgeschichte* (5th edn), Max Niemeyer, Halle/Salle.

Pintzuk, S. (1999) *Phrase Structures in Competition: Variation and Change in Old English Word Order*, Garland, New York.

Pintzuk, S. (2003) Variationist approaches to syntactic change. In B.D. Joseph and R.D. Janda (eds.), pp. 509–28.

Postal, P.M. (1968) *Aspects of Phonological Theory*, Harper & Row, New York.

Roberge, P.T. (1985) Grammatical prerequisites to phonological change? *Zeitschrift für Dialektologie und Linguistik* 52: 188–217.

Roberts, I. (2007) *Diachronic Syntax*, Oxford University Press, Oxford.

Sapir, E. (1921) *Language: An Introduction to the Study of Speech*, Harcourt, Brace & World, New York.

Thomason, S.G. (2001) *Language Contact*, Georgetown University Press, Washington, DC.

Thomason, S.G. (2003) Contact as a source of language change. In B.D. Joseph and R.D. Janda (eds.), pp. 687–712.

Thomsen, O.N. (ed.) (2006) *Competing Models of Linguistic Change: Evolution and Beyond*, John Benjamins, Amsterdam.

Timberlake, A. (1977) Reanalysis and actualization in syntactic change. In C.N. Li (ed.), *Mechanisms of Syntactic Change*, University of Texas Press, Austin, pp. 141–77.

van Coetsem, F. (2000) *A General and Unified Theory of the Transmission Process in Language Contact*, Carl Winter, Heidelberg.

Vennemann, T. (1983) Causality in language change: theories of linguistic preferences as a basis for linguistic explanation. *Folia Linguistica Historica* 4: 5–26.

Wang, W.S.-Y. (1969) Competing changes as a cause of residue. *Language* 45: 9–25.

Weinreich, U., Labov, W., and Herzog, M.I. (1968) Empirical foundations for a theory of language change. In W.P. Lehmann and Y. Malkiel (eds.), *Directions for Historical Linguistics*, University of Texas Press, Austin, pp. 95–188.

21 Internally- and Externally-Motivated Language Change

RAYMOND HICKEY

1. Introduction

The field of historical sociolinguistics has been well served in recent years. There are several volumes which deal with this topic, starting with the seminal study by Romaine (1982) and culminating in monographs by Nevalainen and Raumolin-Brunberg (2003) and Conde-Silvestre (2007). There have been edited volumes such as Jahr (1998), special issues of journals like Conde-Silvestre and Hernández-Campoy (2005), and individual studies carrying the label 'historical sociolinguistics' in their titles, such as Bergs (2005). There is a network[1] of scholars engaged in historical sociolinguistics, and continuing work in the field is attested by new publications such as McColl Millar (2012).

Given this range of research it would seem appropriate to consider just what changes in language fall within the orbit of historical sociolinguistics. It appears to be a consensus opinion that all types of external change should be included: by implication, internal changes would be excluded. The relationship between these two sources of change has been pursued in a number of dedicated publications, such as Gerritsen and Stein (1992), Dorian (1993), Yang (2000), Pargman (2002), Jones and Esch (2002), and Torgersen and Kerswill (2004). In overviews of historical linguistics the issue is usually examined, for example in Chapter 11 of Campbell (1998/2004), 'Explaining linguistic change,' there is a section entitled 'Internal and external causes' (Campbell 1998/2004: 316–26); in Croft (2001: 166–74) there is a section 'Communities, societies and the internal/external distinction in language change,' to mention two well-known overviews of historical linguistics and language change of the past decade. Sources of change are also central to the

The Handbook of Historical Sociolinguistics, First Edition. Edited by Juan Manuel Hernández-Campoy and Juan Camilo Conde-Silvestre.
© 2014 John Wiley & Sons, Ltd. Published 2014 by John Wiley & Sons, Ltd.

comprehensive, three-volume work by Labov (1994, 2001, 2010), especially the first two volumes.

1.1　Approaching the internal–external division in language change

This chapter is exploratory in nature. It considers the issue of motivation for language change, specifically asking whether a clear distinction can be drawn between internally- and externally-motivated language change. The question is essentially one which considers the 'behavior of speakers' versus the 'properties of languages' (J. Milroy 1992: 16) and it is obvious that the simple labels 'internally-motivated' and 'externally-motivated' language change do not do justice to the complex and intricate relationship between how speakers act linguistically in their community and the postulated abstract level of structure which is taken to provide the basis for their behavior. It is clear, then, that linguistic reality is too complex to be fully captured by a simple binary division of change types into 'internal' and 'external' (Dorian 1993: 131). Indeed, these two labels should not be understood as forming a mutually exclusive dichotomy,[2] but rather as referring to two possible sources which can be identified in language change, the description of whose differential interaction is an essential part of accounting for this change.

1.2　What is 'internally-motivated change'?

Any change which can be traced to structural considerations in a language and which is independent of sociolinguistic factors can be classified as internally-motivated.[3] A change which would appear to be triggered and guided by social considerations can be labeled 'externally-motivated.' Obvious examples include both accommodation by speakers towards a social group with certain linguistic features, as well as dissociation from other social groups whose speech is regarded as undesirable. Accommodation leads to the adoption of features already present in the group being accommodated towards, or to the development of intermediary features, while dissociation can result in the development of new features not already present in the speech of the group engaged in dissociation.

In this chapter individual examples of language change will be discussed for the purposes of illustration. Specifically, instances where a mixture of motivations can be recognized will be examined in the hope of throwing light on the interrelationship of the two sources of change. There are inherent advantages to understanding different sources for language change and what course this change can take. For instance, considering social motivation as a central factor can improve the understanding of apparently counterintuitive instances of change, or at least of changes that would not be expected on purely language-internal, structural grounds. In addition, social factors can help to account for the reversal of change and for the important issue of non-change. As James Milroy states: "In order to account for differential patterns of change at particular times and places, we need first to take account of those factors that tend to maintain language states and resist change" (J. Milroy 1992: 10). This was stated more explicitly somewhat later by the same author: "[I]f we pose the more basic question of why some forms and varieties are *maintained* while others change, we cannot avoid reference to society" (J. Milroy 1993: 220).

Language change is not just about the rise of new features but about any type of alteration to the configuration of a language. Thus mergers (see section 3.4. below) are types of change, and the more general processes of dialect leveling and new dialect formation (Hickey 2003a) represent equally valid instances of change, although the amount of variation in a community is reduced in both these cases.

1.3   What is 'externally-motivated change'?

Any variation and change in a language which can be connected with the community or society using that language can be labeled 'externally-motivated.' Naturally, such a broad definition covers a whole range of change types. In modern sociolinguistics, such change would be traced to reactions that speakers show to the speech of different social groups – see classical sociolinguistic investigations such as Labov (1966/2006) and Trudgill (1974).

External motivation for language change seems most likely on the level of sounds, because speakers' pronunciation is immediately available for assessment by others, so differences in pronunciation can lead to change across speaker groups, via accommodation (Trudgill 1986: 1–38) or dissociation (Hickey 2000, forthcoming). The situation is not necessarily different in principle on the level of grammar. But given that the number of tokens which could theoretically trigger change across groups is smaller and that these do not appear in speech with the same degree of frequency and predictability as do phonetic features, the significance of grammatical features as triggers of change is less. Scholars dealing with morphosyntactic change therefore stress the role of token occurrence in establishing change: "Frequency determines which linguistic tokens and abstract types (structures) become automated and entrenched within the processing system" (Fischer 2006: 325).

In past periods of history, social differences would not necessarily have been the same as at present, so much of the research in historical sociolinguistics is about vernacular speech and the interaction of speakers, often without the class differences obvious in modern western societies. Historical investigations in this vein tend to use private documents, frequently egodocuments (personal letters, diaries, autobiographies, memoirs, and travelogues), to trace change across a given period. Examples include the personal correspondence which provides the data basis for Nevalainen and Raumolin-Brunberg (2003) (see also Chapter 9 in this *Handbook*). This type of change seems to have been *community-internal*, that is to have occurred within a speech community without any outside influence. However, there is also *community-external* change, which originates from outside the speech community in question. Such change is due to language or dialect contact (on the latter, see studies such as Britain 1997).

1.3.1 The case of language contact The influence of one language on another is not necessarily about primary social differences between speakers. For instance, language contact can lead to change which does not appear to have been determined by social factors, as in the case of Old English and Old Norse in the ninth and tenth centuries in Scotland and the north of England. There can of course be contact which is connected with social differences, such as that of French and English in England and of French and Irish in Ireland (Hickey 1997). Many loans into both English and Irish were imposed from above through the second-language varieties of English and Irish spoken by the French communities in late medieval England and Ireland.

Language contact scenarios (Myers-Scotton 2002; Winford 2005; Matras 2009; Hickey, ed. 2010) are often regarded as leading to convergence between languages, although some authors favor a single source for change rather than more than one (Lass and Wright 1986). Nonetheless, it is fruitful to consider instances of possible convergence to exercise the arguments for and against this scenario. A case in point is the development of non-initial stress in Southern Irish. Here, long vowels developed in Middle Irish through the loss of consonants and compensatory lengthening, as in Old Irish *sochaide* /'sɔxɪðə/ > *sochaí* /'sɔxi:/ 'host, crowd; society.' These long vowels later attracted stress in the south – /'sɔxi:/ > /sɔ'xi: / – but not in the north and west. However, the south is the area where the contact with the Anglo-Normans was greatest, and Norman French had non-initial stress, cf. *avan'tage* > Irish *buntáiste* /bun'tɑːʃtʲə/ 'advantage,' with a long second vowel stressed in the south. Instances of convergence in contact would thus seem to be both internally and externally motivated.[4]

1.4 Where does change begin?

Speakers are the agents of change. It goes without saying that speakers change language and that the term 'language' is an abstraction over the collective behavior of a speech community. It is salutary to remember that when one is dealing with structural and developmental tendencies in language it is in the linguistic behavior of speakers that these are manifested (J. Milroy 2003).

Change begins with variation in the speech of speakers, ultimately that of individual speakers. But continuously occurring variation in speech only leads to established instances of change in some cases. And it is communities (or sub-communities) who carry it forward. So change must reach a certain threshold to become established. While it is not possible to predict change, accounting for change which has already occurred is a legitimate pursuit for linguists.

1.4.1 Awareness of change Among speakers who are not linguistically alert there would seem to be no obvious awareness of different sources for language change. Indeed, if anything, socially triggered change may evince greater awareness as speakers are liable to be conscious of the social forces involved. Additionally, one can point to prescriptivism as one prominent cause for awareness of change.

But prescriptivism tends to have a retarding influence on change rather than promoting it and does not have a dynamic quality; rather it is frequently characterized by attempting to reverse changes which are already well underway.

Various instances of grammaticalization in the late modern period became the target of objections by prescriptive authors, such as the progressive passive, seen in *the house was being built* rather than *the house was building*, which was remarked on negatively in the late eighteenth century when it was coming into use (Traugott 1972: 178). The same is true of other grammatical phenomena which gained the attention of prescriptivists: split infinitives (*to seriously consider the matter*), future continuous with *going* (*we're going to be involved a lot in that process*), quantifier *lots of* (*there's lots of talk about ecology these days*).[5] Prescriptive comments generally stem from an awareness of the presence of these structures in colloquial speech and from the resulting attempt to exclude them from more formal registers of language.

Prescriptivism can also lead to a static situation where a change does not go to completion and where both the incoming and the outgoing forms/structures are possible in a language; this is the case with the censure of sentence final prepositions in English or the insistence of a specific form of oblique *who*, both seen in *The man with whom she was talking* versus *The man who she was talking with*.

Sociolinguistic censure, in the form of prescriptivism, may also stop a development entirely, or at least exclude it from standard forms of a language. A clear instance of this is *tun* 'do' as an auxiliary which was extensive in Early Modern High German (Langer 2001) and which is only found in vernaculars in present-day German, for example *Ich tue dir das Geld morgen bringen* 'I do you-DATIVE the money tomorrow bring-INFINITIVE' which would be: *Ich bringe dir das Geld morgen* 'I bring you-DATIVE the money tomorrow' in standard German, without the use of an auxiliary 'do' *tun* (first person singular: *tue*).

1.4.2 Salience and markedness

Salient features are those that speakers recognize as typical of a variety or language and to which they may react positively or negatively. Such features may be the result of natural phonetic processes (such as those discussed in 3.1 below). For instance, a velarized [ɫ] is often mentioned by speakers of Castilian Spanish as being typical of Catalan and is thus a salient feature of the latter. Marked features, on the other hand, are those which are typologically unusual. For instance, the lowering of /u/ to /ʌ/ (see the discussion in 3.2 below) is cross-linguistically unusual and is not found in the major European languages, although southern British English and varieties of English connected with it show the shift.

Negative and positive salience are frequently associated with stigma and prestige respectively. It should be pointed out, however, that 'prestige' does not have to be associated with publicly recognized power groups in a society, but can be located on a smaller scale and on a local level, as shown by Eckert (2000) in her examination of adolescents and by James and Lesley Milroy in their investigations of working-class social networks in Belfast.[7]

2. Assessing the Principles of Change

If all instances of variation had an equal chance of becoming established as an item of change then the results would be random without recognizable patterning. But this is obviously not the case. So there appear to be preferences for certain types of variation to establish themselves as change in a speech community. It is true that no type of change can in principle be excluded from occurring, as Andersen (1988) has shown in his discussion of several instances of 'unlikely' changes. However, there are cross-linguistically common changes. The question then is why certain kinds occur more frequently than others. Whatever the role of social factors in the actuation, propagation and termination of change it does not seem possible to correlate any of these factors with specific kinds of change. For example, it would be untenable to maintain that lower-middle class hypercorrection always favors the production of non-prevocalic /r/. This may be the case in the United States, but it is not so in Britain, to quote two countries with obviously contrasting social assessments of non-prevocalic /r/.

If external factors are not responsible for the relative occurrence of change types, then the reasons must be sought among internal factors, that is, these types must be causally connected to structural features of language (in phonology and morphosyntax) or to contingencies of language production (in phonetics).

It is obvious that there are regularities in language change. These have different causes on different levels of language. In phonetics, regularities are generally associated with speech production and perception, which also interact with the structural properties of the sound system of a language. Consider the fact that intervocalic consonants have a tendency to become voiced. Cross-linguistically, the rise of voiced intervocalic consonants is much more common than the reverse, so that a development like /afa/ > /ava/ is more likely than /ava/ > /afa/. Examples abound from the Romance languages and in early forms of English, Danish, and Finnish. The 'internal' motivation for this type of change lies in the tendency for voice, present on both sides of a segment, to spread to a consonant, thus rendering it voiced. There is usually more resistance to this spread if the originally voiceless segment is also long, hence the lesser tendency for geminates to voice compared with simplex consonants, as in Latin *peccatum* which became Irish *peaca* 'sin' (with the shift of a geminate to a simplex consonant retaining voicelessness) and Latin *sacerdos* which became Irish *sagart* 'priest' (with the voicing of the simplex /k/ of the Latin original).

Of course, additional factors may play a role here; for instance, if the voiced consonant is followed by a voiceless one, the latter can induce voicelessness in the preceding consonant. If the voiceless element then disappears, the change might look like a straightforward case of devoicing. In Irish this change can be recognized with many words, as in *fágtha* [fɑghə] 'left' which developed into [fɑːkiː] by the [h] devoicing the preceding [g] and then disappearing.

Another case of phonetic motivation is the greater tendency of low vowels rather than high ones to lengthen. In the Irish of Cois Fhairrge, west of Galway city (Hickey 2011), all low vowels are long, irrespective of their systemic status, but the corresponding high vowels show a distinction in phonetic length; for example *fear* /fʲar/ [fʲæːr] 'man' and *tá* /tɑː/ [tɑː][8] 'is,' but *duine* /dɪnə/ [dɪnə] 'person' and *mín* /mʲiːnʲ/ [mʲiːnʲ] 'smooth.'

This tendency can, of course, interact with others to produce different results in different languages or stages of a language. Where vowel length is conditioned by phonetic environment, long vowels may result, as in late Old English, where short high vowels before voiced clusters, typically /nd/, were lengthened, yielding shifts like *blind* /blɪnd/ > /bliːnd/, *mind* /mɪnd/ > /miːnd/, and thus producing hypercharacterized syllables (see Lass 1984: 250–60).

There may also be system considerations in operation. A language with a systemic length distinction for vowels may show lowering with lengthening. For example, in early Middle English, vowels in open syllables were lowered and also lengthened, like *nosu* /no.zu/ > *nose* /nɔː.zə/ 'nose,' *stelan* /ste.lan/ > *stele* /stɛː.lə/ 'steal' (on this open syllable lengthening, see Minkova 1982).

Analogous regularities in change can be found on other levels of language. From semantic/pragmatic investigations it is known that over time, structures are co-opted by speakers to increasingly express their own attitudes and beliefs (Lyons in Traugott 2003: 125). One of the best-known cases of this is the development of *while* from a purely temporal adverb in Old English, *hwilum*, to expressing speaker attitudes as in *While I like linguistics, I think I'll take literature for my orals*. Another similar development is the shift from deontic to epistemic modality (Traugott 1989) with English modals like *must*, for example *I must do this first* (deontic) versus *He must be home by now* (epistemic – 'it must be the case that he is home by now') which is a common direction of change for modals (Fischer 2006: 261).[9]

When the developments alluded to above were in their early stages they represented innovations, but did not constitute change[10] until they spread and became part of the system in the languages concerned. This transition from variation to system was captured neatly by Kiparsky in his comments on developments in phonology: "[N]atural phonological processes, originating in production, perception, and acquisition, result in inherent, functionally controlled variability of speech. 'Sound change' takes place when the results of these processes are internalized by language learners as part of their grammatical competence" (Kiparsky 1988: 389).

2.1 Structural regularity and change

If there are changes which are triggered by strictly language-internal considerations, they must be ultimately traceable to properties of the system. Inasmuch as such changes appear in early childhood when speakers are establishing their internal language systems, they can be associated with structural regularity. In different terms, it is difficult to conceive of internally-motivated language change which in itself produces irregularity. However, what may very well be the case is that change on one level – for example, certain types of phonetic change such as lenition in syllable rhymes or fortition in syllable onsets – can lead to detrimental change on higher levels, notably in morphology. For instance, there was lenition of intervocalic fricatives in Old English, seen in word pairs like *wif* [wiːf] : *wifas* [wiːvas] (present-day *wife* [waif] : *wives* [waivz]). This development resulted in an alternation of voiceless and voiced fricatives between singular and plural in English, which increased the degree of irregularity in English morphology and which in time became opaque in its motivation, as the original rule no longer applied in later forms of English: *roof* [ruːf] : *rooves* [ruːvz] but *cuff* [kʌf] : *cuffs* [kʌfs]. This voicing of intervocalic fricatives is a prime example of internally-motivated language change. Nonetheless, it cannot be ruled out that the change spread by one group showing this change and others picking it up from this group. If this were the case then the change, viewed across the whole society of the time, would have had a mixture of internal and external motivation. In retrospect it is not possible to determine if this was indeed the case.

The type of change which is quintessentially associated with the promotion of structural regularity is undoubtedly analogical change (see Campbell 1998/2004: 103–21). Proportional analogy, as attested in the migration of suffixal verbs into a class of vowel-alternating verbs ('strong' verbs) on the basis of phonetic similarity in some non-standard varieties of English (vernacular English in the Lower South of the United States, for example), can be seen in shifts like *bring : brought > bring : brung* by analogy with *sing : sung*. Other instances would be *dive : dived > dive : dove* by analogy with verbs like *strive : strove*.

Analogy can also promote feature maintenance over time. Consider the case of the dental fricatives of English: these have a low functional load, which means that minimal pairs like *teeth : teethe* are relatively rare. However, the distinction in voice for fricatives is central to the phonology of English, as pairs like *cease : seize, sip : zip; vet : wet, life : live* (adj.) clearly show. A similar argument could be used for the maintenance of /θ, ð/ in Castilian Spanish, where the two fricatives match other sets of fricatives such as /s, z/ and /x, ɣ/ (on the development of fricatives in forms of Spanish, see Penny 1991/2002: 96–110).

2.2   The actuation problem

This problem can best be formulated in the words of Weinreich, Labov, and Herzog in their seminal study of the social motivation for language change: "Why do changes in a structural feature take place in a particular language at a given time, but not in other languages with the same feature, or in the same language at other times" (1968: 102). For externally-motivated change social reasons can be suggested, such as the imitation of a group showing certain features or speakers distancing themselves from a group with other features. Why this social motivation should become active when it does might be explained by further factors in the society in question, such as rapid change in social structure and relative prosperity, as was the case in Dublin during the 1990s.

The actuation of change must be triggered by external factors. If change were purely internal and determined by preferred structural properties of language or developmental tendencies (to establish these properties), it would be difficult to account for why certain internally-motivated changes take place when they do and not at other times and in other languages. For instance, if increasing sonority for consonants in intervocalic position is a developmental tendency in language, why did this occur in Old English (see discussion above) when it is not active in present-day English? This question could be repeated for a whole range of changes in some forms of English but not in others. For instance, why did the Scottish Vowel Length Rule only arise in Scotland, or why did Canadian Raising only become fully established in Canada?

3. Evaluating Instances of Change

The following sections examine further instances of change and assess their possible motivation from the perspective of internal and external factors. In this context, a major question is whether one can exclusively assign the trigger for a change to either an internal or external cause. If a change can be associated with a general principle of language structure and/or development over longer periods of time, then internal motivation is at play, though not exclusively, as the examples show.

3.1 *Phonetically natural processes*

By the late Middle English period, a number of words which had a short mid front vowel, /ɛ/, appear with a corresponding high vowel, /ɪ/, with adjustment of the spelling in most cases: for example *enke> ink, streng > stringe, þenken > think; Engelande > England (e = /ɪ/).* This nasal raising was probably triggered by the fact that the nasal cavity is open for nasals and an anti-resonance occurs, which interacts with that in the oral cavity. This anti-resonance sets in between 800 and 2000 Hz (Fry 1979: 118–19; Lieberman 1977: 177) and has the effect of depressing the first formant of the flanking vowel. Consider in Table 21.1 the following representative values for the first and second formants of five common vowels (Fry 1979: 79).

So there is internal motivation here: nasals depress F1, causing raising of /ɛ/ to /ɪ/ which in turn results in homophony with word pairs like *pen* and *pin.* But of course this raising does not occur in every language, so its appearance in a language or variety implies that this tendency was favored at some time by the

Table 21.1. Typical formant values for vowels (in Hertz)

	F1	F2		F1	F2
/i/	360	2100	/o/	600	900
/e/	570	1970	/u/	380	950
/a/	750	1750			

speech community in question. This happened in late Middle English, and in the southern United States and in south-west Ireland as well. But its appearance, as an established feature, must have been triggered externally, because the internal argument alone cannot explain why nasal raising did not occur elsewhere in the anglophone world.

3.2 Variation and the threshold for change

The lowering of Early Modern English /u/. In the south of England during the first half of the seventeenth century (Dobson 1968/1985: II.585–90), the short high back vowel in the STRUT lexical set (Wells 1982: I.131–32) was lowered, and continued to be so during the following centuries, leading ultimately to [ʌ]. This movement would appear to be motivated by external factors. The initial lowering of the high back vowel /u/ would probably have been triggered by a preference for a slightly lowered realization of the /u/-vowel, which was within the normal range of target realizations for this high back vowel. With time the preference was enlarged and the lowered realizations were adopted by increasingly large sections of the southern English population. At some later point the phonetic distance to the original [ʊ] realization of the /u/-vowel was so great as to constitute a separate systemic unit in those varieties showing the shift, namely /ʌ/. The distinction was strengthened by the contrast of words like *put* [pʊt] and *putt* [pʌt]. This shift cannot be assigned an internal explanation, not even partially, because the lowering of /u/ is not known to be a general developmental tendency in vowel systems of the world's languages.

   The TRAP vowel in the past two centuries. Variation in the target realizations of segments can become sociolinguistically significant if this variation is associated with a particular grouping in society. A case in point involves the vowel of the TRAP lexical set, which at least from the late eighteenth century and throughout the nineteenth showed a raised vowel in the region of /ɛ/ in southern varieties of British English. This was commented on by prescriptivists of the time, notably Thomas Sheridan and John Walker (Hickey 2009a) and was typical of early forms of what was later termed 'Received Pronunciation' (RP). But the raised TRAP vowel did not lead to a merger with the vowel of the DRESS lexical set, so the raising was in principle reversible.

   For more conservative forms of RP in the early twentieth century, a raised vowel in the TRAP lexical set was typical (Bauer 1994: 120–21), but after the Second World War this older form of speech was increasingly out of tune with contemporary usage, which was showing a lowered vowel in the region of /æ/. This tendency towards lowering and centralization of the TRAP vowel has continued with values close to [a] not unusual in southern British English in the early twenty-first century.

3.3 Urban British English

Urban forms of British English show a number of innovations in their local ver-naculars. These are generally regarded as south-eastern features which have radiated out from the London area (the discussion about origin is not of relevance here: see Beal 2007 for further information). Three of the spreading features are the following.

TH-fronting. This is a label for the shift of voiceless /θ/, as in *think* [θɪŋk], to a voiceless labio-dental fricative: [θɪŋk] > [fɪŋk]. This shift can be considered to have an internal motivation, as the shift leads to more audible friction, so the /f/ has a perceptual advantage over /θ/. It is attested in other varieties of English (in African American English as voiced /ð/ > /v/).

T-glottaling. In intervocalic position the shift of /t/ to /ʔ/ is a widespread feature, occurring not only in vernacular London English and other urban varieties influenced by it, but also in Scottish English and in local forms of Dublin English. T-glottaling leads to the loss of an oral gesture for /t/, with glottalic closure the only remaining consonantal feature. Whether this can be regarded as a form of lenition is a matter of debate. In London English the shift of /t/ is straight to /ʔ/. In Dublin English, by contrast, /ʔ/ is part of a lenition cline which starts at /t/ and proceeds through /t̞/ (an apico-alveolar fricative) to /h, r/, then to /ʔ/ and possibly zero (see section 4.1 below). Here the case for considering T-glottaling as an instance of lenition is more plausible. However, in all three varieties of English the shift can be regarded as stemming from an internal development in the sound system, which then spread as the shift became a signal for vernacular metropolitan speech (at least in London and Dublin), and was then emulated by other urban groups outside the capital (in the case of London).

H-dropping. An endemic feature in urban varieties of English, which is of some vintage, is the loss of word-initial /h-/ as in *hand* [ænd, æn?], *hit* [ɪt, ɪʔ] or *hall* [ɔːl, ɔːɫ]. This may well have been the result of less-than-target realizations of the glottal fricative by some speakers in the first group to show H-dropping. Given that the loss of /h-/ is phonetically gradual – there are degrees of fricative reduction – it could be interpreted as a sociophonetic feature rather than a structure-driven development within the sound system. If there was a structural tendency in sound systems to lose /h-/, the phenomenon would be much more widespread. However, in varieties of English it is a specifically British phenomenon. H-dropping is a highly salient feature, perhaps because of the amount of homophony it leads to (but see next section), and was already the subject of negative sociolinguistic comment in the nineteenth century (Mugglestone 1995/2003), something which blocked its establishment as a feature of both Australian and New Zealand English.

3.4 *The special case of mergers*

In the sociolinguistic literature on mergers (Labov 1994: 293–417) it is agreed that these are not the object of sociolinguistic comments. It would seem that speakers are generally not aware of the merging of sounds, even if this leads to some homophony. The motivation for mergers is not easy to determine. Among the many instances from the history of English and its present-day forms, two will be mentioned here, which illustrate somewhat different trends.

3.4.1 *Merger of* which *and* witch   At the beginning of the twenty-first century there are very few varieties of English which maintain a consistent distinction between the initial sounds in words like *which* and *witch*. The difference is between a voiceless labiovelar fricative [ʍ] (written *wh-*) and a voiced one [w] (written *w-*). The distinction is known to have existed in conservative forms of American English, but it is highly recessive, even in traditional forms of English in both the United States and Canada. In Ireland *which* and *witch* are now homophones for all young speakers of supraregional Irish English (Hickey 2003b), leaving Scotland the sole anglophone region in which this distinction is still maintained consistently by large numbers of speakers.

In all cases where homophony of *which* and *witch* has arisen, the resulting single sound is voiced: [w]. This would imply that the change is motivated by the regulation of the relationship between vowels and glides, all of which are voiced in those varieties which have no voiceless [ʍ]. Because of the high sonority of vowels and glides, it is not surprising that the merger is to the voiced member of the pair, [w]. Furthermore, there was already a phonotactic restriction which applied to [ʍ]: it only occurred in absolute word-initial position, whereas [w] was, and is, found in post-consonantal position, as in *twin* [twɪn].

3.4.2 *Merger of* morning *and* mourning   Among present-day varieties of English only a small number still have a distinction between the vowels in *morning* [ɔ:] and *mourning* [o:], again vernacular forms of Irish and Scottish English. In all cases where the distinction is missing it is the higher vowel – [o:] – which is found (see Table 21.2).

Table 21.2.   Four long vowel systems in the history of English

		Front		Back
Late Middle English outset	Level 1	i:		u:
	Level 2	e:		o:
	Level 3	ɛ:		ɔ:
	Level 4		a:	
System after *meat* → *meet*	Level 1	i:		u:
	Level 2	e:		o:
	Level 3			ɔ:
	Level 4		a:	
System after *morning* → *mourning*	Level 1	i:		u:
	Level 2	e:		o:
	Level 3		a:	
System with later diphthongization and /a:/ retraction	Level 1	i:		u:
	Level 2	eɪ		əʊ
	Level 3		ɑ:	

An internal motivation for this merger can be provided. Consider that in the early modern period (at different times for different varieties) the distinction between inherited [ɛ:] and [e:] – as in *meat* and *meet* respectively – was lost, with the two vowels merging to [e:], which was then raised to [i:]. The net effect of the merger was to remove a systemic unit /ɛ:/ from the sound system of English. The merger of *morning* and *mourning* did the same, but among back vowels, so that varieties with the latter merger have a more symmetrical distribution of vowels across phonological space.

The merger of both Middle English /e:, ɛ:/ and /o:, ɔ:/ did produce several cases of homophony, so an argument based on the avoidance of homophony would not account for the developments considered here (J. Milroy 1992: 14–15). Equally, the retention of distinct pronunciations[11] in some vernacular varieties can hardly be motivated by this argument either because, if it were, one would have to offer reasons why in principle one set of varieties maintained the distinctions while others did not.

3.5   Constructing systemic knowledge and reanalysis

For the present section quite different changes are to be considered. These are instances of reanalysis, a phenomenon typically located in first language acquisition when children (Louden 2003) are constructing systemic knowledge for the language of which they are becoming native speakers.

The Celtic mutations. In the pre-written period of the Celtic languages a series of sandhi changes at the beginning of words led to regular phonetic alterations which correlated with grammatical categories such as gender (with nouns) and tense (with verbs) (Hickey 1995, 2003c). For instance, feminine nouns showed a shift to fricative when preceded by the definite article, but masculine nouns did not. Modern Irish examples can be used to illustrate this principle: *an cháin* /xɑːnʲ/ (< *cáin* /kɑːnʲ/, fem.) 'the tax' but *an cabhlach* /kaulˠəx/ (< *cabhlach*, masc.) 'the navy'; a verb example is *glanaim* /glˠanˠəmʲ/ 'I clean' but *ghlan mé* /ɣlˠanˠ mʲeː/ 'I cleaned.' At the time these changes were occurring, the inherited inflections of Indo-European were waning, so that at some stage across all the Celtic regions, language learners began to interpret the initial alterations as indicators of key grammatical categories, and not inherited suffixes, which means that they reanalyzed the grammatical system of Irish. As a result, the initial mutations became part of the system of Irish and, due to parallel developments, of the other Celtic languages as well.

Change in word-class in present-day English. Reanalysis can also occur in adult speech and there are some examples from present-day English. A well-known instance is the word *fun* which has migrated to the class of adjectives in recent years (Aarts *et al.* eds., 2004). The trajectory for this change may have begun with equative sentences where *fun* was used as part of the second noun phrase. But where the latter consisted of the bare noun *fun*, it was open to interpretation as a predicative adjective as in *The party was loud*.

(1) a. *The party was great fun.* (equative sentence)
NP1 = NP2
(Noun) (Adjective + Noun)
  b. *The party was fun.*
Noun1 = Noun2
Or: Noun + Verb + Adjective?

An interpretation of *fun* as an adjective is clear when it began to appear in attributive position as well:

(2) a. *The fun party we went to.*
  b. *Partying is a fun thing to do.*

The clinching evidence for *fun* as adjective is its use in comparative and superlative forms: *A funner type of mobile, The funnest thing I've ever heard.*

  This change seems to be entirely internal: there does not appear to be any external social motivation for *fun* to migrate to a new word-class. However, once it had done this, and especially when it appeared in the comparative and superlative, censorious comments arose, condemning the newly established usage.

4. The Interaction of Internal and External Factors

4.1 Lenition in Dublin English

In positions of high sonority – intervocalically and post-vocalically before a pause – alveolar stops are lenited in all forms of southern Irish English (Hickey 2009b). Lenition can be seen as a scale with the full plosive /t/ at one end and zero at the other, with identifiable stages in between. The entire lenition cline is found in vernacular Dublin English as follows ([t̞] = apico-alveolar fricative).

(3) Vernacular Dublin English

t	–	t̞	–	ʔ	–	h/r	–	Ø
button		*but*		*water*		*water*		*what*

For non-local, more standard varieties of Irish English, lenition is only attested for the first stage, that is to a fricative, with one or two lexicalized cases where [h] is found, such as in the word for *Saturday* which has internal [h] in Irish.

(4) Supraregional southern Irish English

t	–	t̞	(–	h, lexicalized)
button		*but*	(–	*Saturday* ['sæhə̆de], Irish *Sahairn*)

Why was the path of lenition not continued in supraregional southern Irish English? The answer would seem to lie in the maintenance of phonetic distance to local, vernacular Dublin English. Supraregional Irish English arose out of middle-class Dublin English usage during the late nineteenth and early twentieth centuries (Hickey 2005), so early supraregional speakers would have been aware of vernacular Dublin English and would have been motivated to avoid phonetic merging with it in the area of lenition, for instance by not tolerating glottalization as an advanced stage of *t*-lenition, as in (3) above. This development shows that the natural (internal) phonetic process of lenition was halted for external social reasons.

4.2   Vowels before /r/ in Dublin English

During the 1980s a new pronunciation of southern Dublin English developed in which central vowels were retracted and low back vowels raised. This accent came to be known as the 'Dublin 4' accent (later just 'D4') after a prosperous suburb of south Dublin where the accent was supposedly common. Shortly afterwards, the name of the suburban railway known as the *Dart* (an acronym deriving from *Dublin Area Rapid Transport*), a commuter train mainly in the southern parts of the city, came to be used for the supposed accent of the people who lived in the southside suburbs. The label *Dartspeak* was coined and found favor among Dubliners. This label was then given a particular pronunciation with a retracted and rounded vowel, [dɔːɹtspiːk], and came to be written *Dortspeak*, – much commented on by journalists, broadcasters, and writers.

   The retraction and raising of vowels was unconditional in this change and was found in many nouns with a vowel plus /r/, as in *smart* [smɒːɹt] ~ [smɔːɹt]. But if one considers advanced varieties of Dublin English today, one finds a central vowel before /r/, [smaːɹt].

(5) Retraction and fronting of vowels before *r*
     Early 'Dublin 4' accent (1980s)
     initial retraction and raising before /r/: *smart* [smɒːɹt] ~ [smɔːɹt]
     Later new Dublin English accent (late 1990s, 2000s)
     no raising but fronting before /r/: *smart* [smaːɹt]

What is remarkable here is that the remainder of the vowel shift in Dublin continued along its trajectory (general raising along a back path) and became established as the new supraregional form of Irish English for virtually all speakers born after 1980: *born* [bɒːrn] > [bɔrn] > [boːrn], *point* [pɒɪnt] > [pɔɪnt] > [poɪnt].

   The question as to why the retraction and raising of /ar/ was discontinued in new Dublin English of the 1990s can be answered by considering external factors. As the 1990s proceeded and Ireland entered a period of unprecedented economic prosperity, 'Dortspeak' became less and less 'trendy' and began to date. Salient features of this pronunciation, such as the retracted /a/ vowel before /r/, were no longer 'cool' and young speakers began to avoid them (Hickey 2003d). The pronunciation of *Dartspeak* as [dɔːɹtspiːk], – *Dortspeak* – is now regarded as 'stuffy' and 'uncool' and the present pronunciation of *Dartspeak* is [daːɹtspiːk] with a central vowel before the /r/ in the first syllable.

5. Summary

It is a commonplace to state that language use is characterized by continual variation. Virtually all of this is entirely otiose. But occasionally some items of variation become established by spreading from single speakers or small groups to larger sections of a community. When this happens, the variation becomes sociolinguistically significant. Speakers are unconsciously aware of any social value superimposed on variation by its being indicative of a certain subgroup or subgroups in their speech community.

If items of variation, such as phonetic segments, show differing degrees of distance from outset values, then speakers appreciate the relative distance to the originals: some items of variation will be closer to the outset and others somewhat further away. This fact allows speakers to grasp the trajectory of a change, which is generally only visible to analysts viewing it retrospectively.

By and large the variation in a language which can become sociolinguistically significant and lead to change across a community is regular, but this does not necessarily hold for every individual case; indeed closely-knit communities and networks can carry irregular changes forward if these accrue identificational value in the community/network in question.

While the variation in a language is largely regular it cannot be predicted for every individual instance. In the pool of variation in a language at any one time there will be some which is irregular, seen in the context of the language system at the time. For instance, ejective plosives would be highly irregular with respect to the sound system of present-day English and are unlikely to establish themselves, but they did so in historical stages of Caucasian languages, for example.

The non-occurrence of change is as important as its occurrence. There are certainly regular tendencies in language, particularly in syllable structure and in the realization of phonetic segments, but the lack of change in the direction of these tendencies in a community is significant as well. For instance, the maintenance of complex grammatical inflections in German, compared to the remaining Germanic languages, is not the result of random behavior by speakers of the language, but by the role of these inflections in the unconscious identity of the German language.[12]

During a period of change, sociolinguistic factors can be at play and affect the patterning that results from the change. In the case of the Dublin Vowel Shift, discussed above, the stigma attached to the retraction of /a/ before /r/ led to the removal of just this instance from the general retraction of low back vowels (section 4.2 above).

Patterning in multi-item change implies regularity but the latter does not have to be total by any means. Speakers can handle a considerable amount of irregularity and lexicalization, as was seen with the lexicalized realizations of /t/ as [h] in supraregional varieties of Irish English (section 4.1 above).

6. Conclusion

Viewed from the standpoint of speakers, change can in principle take place (i) during early childhood, when language learners construct systemic knowledge of the language they are exposed to, and (ii) after this phase of their lives, when children begin to participate in the groupings of the society they are entering, or later on when they have become integrated into this society as adults.

Change from the first phase is generally *reanalysis*, as shown with the Celtic mutations discussed above, and is independent of social factors, because early language learners do not interact linguistically with social groupings at this stage of their lives. Given that reanalysis is a change in the language system of a generation compared with preceding generations, it is not a type of change that occurs widely in adulthood after speakers have established their linguistic systems, though there are individual examples (see section 3.5 above).

There is no overall name for the types of change which can take place after language learners have passed their childhood. Different factors are at play during different phases of life: language behavior during adolescence (Eckert 2000) is not the same as that during speakers' adult lives. Changes which may enter the speech of middle-aged speakers are generally lexical, possibly grammatical, and rarely phonetic, compared to the changes young adults engage in while they are establishing themselves socially and professionally. But all these kinds of change take place with speakers who act within a community embedded in a society.

Finally, one can consider whether the distinction between internally and externally motivated change is valid as a binary dichotomy. The answer is both 'yes' and 'no.' In early childhood, change is internal and system-driven and definitely free of external motivation. However, in adolescence and later life, change is both internal and external: social factors determine whether variation, inherent in all languages, is carried over a threshold, after which it becomes change in the community in question. The actuation, propagation, and conclusion of change is determined by social factors, but its linguistic course is connected with structural properties and developmental preferences which exist across languages and which ultimately have to do with language production and processing. Again, social considerations may be at work here and promote irregularity and disturb symmetry and patterning, especially if there is strong social motivation for this disturbance arising and being maintained. Lastly, it should be emphasized that change should be seen in the context of non-change, that is, what is altered and what is maintained in a language are of equal significance, and depend ultimately on how speakers react to inherent variation in their speech community.

Acknowledgements

My thanks go to Juan Manuel Hernández-Campoy and Juan Camilo Conde-Silvestre for accepting this contribution to the present volume at a late date, for their encouragement to deal with the current topic and for their comments on the contents. They are not to be associated with the shortcomings of the chapter.

NOTES

1   See the web site at http://www.philhist.uni-augsburg.de/hison/ [accessed October 14, 2011].
2   I thus agree with Thomason and Kaufman who reject the "untenable position that an external cause excludes an internal one" (1988: 61).
3   In historical linguistics, most attention has been given to internally motivated change. This has been challenged recently by prominent sociolinguists, some of whom have offered explanations for the concentration on internal change well into the twentieth century: "It has been quite usual to speak of historical descriptions as consisting of two types: *internal* and *external*, and of these it is the internal accounts that have been the most intellectually challenging and highly valued" (J. Milroy 1993: 219).
4   Dorian (1993: 135) mentions that "…there is a natural tendency to assign convergent change to external motivation and divergent change to internal motivation," though it is doubtful whether this simplistic division of types can be upheld in the face of data where divergent change is triggered by contact.
5   My thanks go to Elizabeth Traugott for pointing out these examples as relevant to the current discussion.
6   Eckert (2000: 226–228) offers a succinct critique of the undifferentiated use of the terms 'stigma' and 'prestige.'
7   For general information on their investigations of social networks, see L. Milroy (1980/1987); and for further information on prescriptivism and the relationship of vernaculars to standards, see Milroy and Milroy (1985/1999).
8   The distinction in relative frontness and backness of the low vowels is not relevant to the point being made here.
9   Fischer (2006: 263) regards this development as a genuine case of grammaticalization, as it involves a category – that of core modals – and not a single word such as *while*.
10   On the distinction between 'innovation' and 'change,' see J. Milroy (1993: 232–234).
11   Consider in this context, the merger of up to five vowels to one, /iː/, a well-known characteristic of Modern Greek (J. Milroy 1992: 37).
12   In this particular instance, processes of standardization, which favor the retention of inflections, played a role.

REFERENCES

Aarts, B., Denison, D., Keizer, E., and Popova, G. (eds.) (2004) *Fuzzy Grammar – A Reader*, Oxford University Press, Oxford.

Andersen, H. (1988) Center and periphery: adoption, diffusion, and spread. In J. Fisiak (ed.), *Historical Dialectology*, Mouton de Gruyter, Berlin, pp. 39–83.

Bauer, L. (1994) *Watching English Change. An Introduction to the Study of Linguistic Change in Standard Englishes in the Twentieth Century*, Longman, London.

Beal, J.C. (2007) 'To explain the present': nineteenth-century evidence for 'recent' changes in English pronunciation. In J. Pérez-Guerra, D. González-Álvarez, J.L.

Bueno-Alonso, and E. Rama-Martínez (eds.), *'Of Varying Language and Opposing Creed.' New Insights into Late Modern English*, Peter Lang, Bern, pp. 25–46.

Bergs, A. (2005) *Social Networks and Historical Sociolinguistics: Studies in Morphosyntactic Variation in the Paston Letters (1421–1503)*, Mouton de Gruyter, Berlin.

Britain, D. (1997) Dialect contact and phonological reallocation: 'Canadian Raising' in the English Fens. *Language in Society* 26: 15–46.

Campbell, L. (1998/2004) *Historical Linguistics. An Introduction* (2nd edn), MIT Press, *Cambridge*, MA.

Conde-Silvestre, J.C. (2007) *Sociolingüística histórica*, Gredos, Madrid.

Conde-Silvestre, J.C. and Hernández-Campoy, J.M. (eds.) (2005) *Sociolinguistics and the History of English: Perspectives and Problems*. Special issue of *International Journal of English Studies*, Vol 5:1.

Croft, W. (2001) *Explaining Language Change: An Evolutionary Approach*, Longman, London.

Dobson, E.J. (1968/1985) *English Pronunciation 1500–1700. Vol.1 – Survey of the Sources. Vol.2 – Phonology* (2nd edn), Oxford University Press, Oxford.

Dorian, N.C. (1993) Internally and externally motivated change in contact situations: doubts about dichotomy. In C. Jones (ed.), *Historical Linguistics: Problems and Perspectives*, Longman, London, pp. 131–55.

Eckert, P. (2000) *Linguistic Variation as Social Practice. The Linguistic Construction of Identity in Belten High*, Blackwell, Oxford.

Fischer, O. (2006) *Morphosyntactic Change: Functional and Formal Perspectives*, Oxford University Press, Oxford.

Fry, D. (1979) *The Physics of Speech*, Cambridge University Press, Cambridge.

Gerritsen, M. and Stein, D. (eds.) (1992) *Internal and External Factors in Syntactic Change*, Mouton de Gruyter, Berlin.

Hickey, R. (1995) Sound change and typological shift: initial mutation in Celtic. In J. Fisiak (ed.), *Linguistic Typology and Reconstruction*, Mouton de Gruyter, Berlin, pp. 133–82.

Hickey, R. (1997) Assessing the relative status of languages in medieval Ireland. In J. Fisiak (ed.), *Studies in Middle English Linguistics*, Mouton de Gruyter, Berlin, pp. 181–205.

Hickey, R. (2000) Dissociation as a form of language change. *European Journal of English Studies* 4.3: 303–15.

Hickey, R. (2003a) How do dialects get the features they have? On the process of new dialect formation. In R. Hickey (ed.), pp. 213–39.

Hickey, R. (2003b) How and why supraregional varieties arise. In M. Dossena and C. Jones (eds.), *Insights into Late Modern English*, Peter Lang, Frankfurt, pp. 351–73.

Hickey, R. (2003c) Reanalysis and typological change. In R. Hickey (ed.), pp. 258–78.

Hickey, R (2003d) What's cool in Irish English? Linguistic change in contemporary Ireland. In H.L.C. Tristram (ed.), *Celtic Englishes III*, Winter, Heidelberg, pp. 357–73.

Hickey, R. (ed.) (2003) *Motives for Language Change*, Cambridge University Press, Cambridge.

Hickey, R. (2005) *Dublin English: Evolution and Change*, John Benjamins, Amsterdam.

Hickey, R. (2009a) Telling people how to speak. Rhetorical grammars and pronouncing dictionaries. In I. Tieken-Boon van Ostade and W. van der Wurff (eds.), *Current Issues in Late Modern English*, Peter Lang, Frankfurt, pp. 89–116.

Hickey, R. (2009b) Weak segments in Irish English. In D. Minkova (ed.), *Phonological Weakness in English. From Old to Present-day English*, Palgrave Macmillan, Basingstoke, pp. 116–29.

Hickey, R. (ed.) (2010) *The Handbook of Language Contact*, Wiley-Blackwell, Chichester.

Hickey, R. (2011) *The Dialects of Irish: Study in a Changing Landscape*, Mouton de Gruyter, Berlin.

Hickey, R. (forthcoming) Dissociation and supraregionalisation. In J.K. Chambers and Natalie Schilling-Estes (eds.), *The Handbook of Language Variation and Change* (2nd edn), Wiley-Blackwell, Chichester.

Jahr, E.H. (ed.) (1998. *Language Change: Advances in Historical Sociolinguistics*, Mouton de Gruyter, Berlin.

Jones, M.C. and Esch, E. (eds.) (2002) *Language Change: The Interplay of Internal, External and Extra-linguistic Factors*, Mouton de Gruyter, Berlin.

Kiparsky, P. (1988) Phonological change. In F.J. Newmeyer (ed.), *Linguistics: The Cambridge Survey, Vol. 1: Linguistic Theory: Foundations*, Cambridge University Press, Cambridge, pp. 363–415.

Labov, W. (1966/2006) *The Social Stratification of English in New York City* (2nd edn). Cambridge University Press, Cambridge.

Labov, W. (1994) *Principles of Linguistic Change. Vol. 1: Internal Factors*, Blackwell, Oxford.

Labov, W. (2001) *Principles of Linguistic Change. Vol. 2: Social Factors*, Blackwell, Oxford.

Labov, William. (2010). *Principles of Linguistic Change. Vol. 3: Cognitive and Cultural Factors*, Wiley-Blackwell, Chichester.

Langer, N. (2001) *Linguistic Purism in Action. How Auxiliary* tun *was Stigmatized in Early New High German*, Walter de Gruyter, Berlin.

Lass, R. (1984) *Phonology*, Cambridge University Press, Cambridge.

Lass, R. and Wright, S. (1986) Endogeny vs. contact: Afrikaans influence on South African English. *English World Wide* 7: 201–23.

Lieberman, P. (1977) *Speech Physiology and Acoustic Phonetics: An Introduction*, Macmillan, New York.

Louden, M.L. (2003) Child language acquisition and language change. *Diachronica* 20.1: 167–83.

Matras, Y. (2009) *Language Contact*, Cambridge University Press, Cambridge.

McColl Millar, R. (2012) *English Historical Sociolinguistics*, Edinburgh University Press, Edinburgh.

Milroy, J. (1992) *Linguistic Variation and Change: On the Historical Sociolinguistics of English*, Blackwell, Oxford.

Milroy, J. (1993) On the social origins of language change. In C. Jones (ed.), *Historical Linguistics*, Longman, London, pp. 215–36.

Milroy, J. (2003) On the role of the speaker in language change. In R. Hickey (ed.), pp. 143–57.

Milroy, J. and Milroy, L. (1985/1999) *Authority in Language* (3rd edn), Routledge, London.

Milroy, L. (1980/1987) *Language and Social Networks* (2nd edn), Blackwell, Oxford.

Minkova, D. (1982) The environment for open syllable lengthening in Middle English. *Folia Linguistica Historica* 3: 29–58.

Mugglestone, L. (1995/2003) *'Talking Proper.' The Rise of Accent as Social Symbol* (2nd edn), Oxford University Press, Oxford.

Myers-Scotton, C. (2002) *Contact Linguistics: Bilingual Encounters and Grammatical Outcomes*, Oxford University Press, Oxford.

Nevalainen, T. and Raumolin-Brunberg, H. (2003) *Historical Sociolinguistics: Language Change in Tudor and Stuart England*, Longman Pearson Education, London.

Pargman, S. (2002) *Internal and External Factors in Language Change*, University of Chicago (Department of Linguistics), Chicago.

Penny, R. (1991/2002) *A History of the Spanish Language* (2nd edn), Cambridge University Press, Cambridge.

Romaine, S. (1982) *Socio-historical Linguistics: Its Status and Methodology*, Cambridge University Press, Cambridge.

Thomason, S.G. and Kaufman, T. (1988) *Language Contact, Creolization, and Genetic Linguistics*, University of California Press, Berkeley.

Torgersen, E. and Kerswill, P. (2004) Internal and external motivation in phonetic change: dialect levelling outcomes for an English vowel shift. *Journal of Sociolinguistics* 8.1: 23–53.

Traugott, E.C. (1972) *A History of English Syntax. A Transformational Approach to the History of English Sentence Structure*, Holt, Rinehart and Winston, New York.

Traugott, E.C. (1989) On the rise of epistemic meanings in English: an example of subjectification in semantic change. *Language* 57: 33–65.

Traugott, E.C. (2003) From subjectification to intersubjectification. In R. Hickey (ed.), pp. 124–39.

Trudgill, P. (1974) *The Social Differentiation of English in Norwich*, Cambridge University Press, Cambridge.

Trudgill, P. (1986) *Dialects in Contact*, Blackwell, Oxford.

Weinreich, U., Labov, W., and Herzog, M. (1968) Empirical foundations for a theory of language change. In W.P. Lehmann and Y. Malkiel (eds.), *Directions for Historical Linguistics*, University of Texas Press, Austin, TX, pp. 95–189.

Wells, J.C. (1982) *Accents of English*. 3 vols, Cambridge University Press, Cambridge.

Winford, D. (2005) Contact-induced changes: Classification and processes. *Diachronica* 22.2: 373–427.

Yang, C.D. (2000) Internal and external forces in language change. *Language Variation and Change* 12: 231–50.

22 Lexical Diffusion and the Regular Transmission of Language Change in its Sociohistorical Context

BRIAN D. JOSEPH

1. Introduction

As far as language is concerned, 'transmission' can be understood, in its most general sense, as the passing of language across populations; 'language' here really means particular linguistic features, but the features can add up, as it were, so that large portions of language or even the entire language itself can be transmitted. With this last point in mind, regarding the transmission of the entire language, a stricter sense of transmission can be identified, referring to the passing of language across generational populations, that is, the acquisition of language by children based on what they hear spoken around them by parents and caretakers who represent older generations. Thus, in this more restricted sense, transmission as a term belongs to the realm of first language acquisition, while in its broader sense, transmission can be taken to include what might be called 'diffusion,' referring to the spread of language and language features within and across various nongenerationally based sectors within society, in effect, then, the spread across social dimensions.

The terminology adopted here thus follows the important lead of Labov (2007). There, Labov defines transmission in terms of the notion of 'linguistic descent,' which, following in the footsteps of Bloomfield (1933) and Hoenigswald (1960), is formulated thus by Ringe, Warnow, and Taylor (2002: 63), as cited by Labov (2007: 346):

The Handbook of Historical Sociolinguistics, First Edition. Edited by Juan Manuel Hernández-Campoy and Juan Camilo Conde-Silvestre.
© 2014 John Wiley & Sons, Ltd. Published 2014 by John Wiley & Sons, Ltd.

> A language (or dialect) Y at a given time is said to be descended from language (or dialect) X of an earlier time if and only if X developed into Y by an unbroken sequence of instances of native-language acquisition by children.

The notion of diffusion, by contrast, represents "the importation of elements from other systems" (Labov 2007: 346) and as such is "a secondary process, of a very different character" (Labov 2007: 347) from transmission. Transmission, by virtue of the definition adopted for linguistic descent, is the primary, internal, means of language change and "is the result of the ability of children to replicate faithfully the form of the older generation's language" with allowances for change via 'incrementation,' a process in which "successive cohorts and generations of children advance [a] change [evident in variable elements in the language] beyond the level of their caretakers and role models" (Labov 2007: 346). In this way, continuity and descent are still maintained but with an allowable basis for observed change. Although Labov's work represents a terminological breakthrough,[1] there is far more to say about both key notions; accordingly, diffusion, in various guises, is discussed in greater detail below in sections 3 and 4, with one apparent manifestation taken up in section 4, while some crucial foundational notions about language in general and about transmission in the stricter sense are first discussed in section 2, to lay the appropriate groundwork.

2. More on Transmission (and Diffusion) and Lineal Descent

In making sense of transmission, it is important to recognize that language has both an individual, that is, a psychological/cognitive, side, and a communal, or social, side. It is, of course, individuals who speak, but in the usual case,[2] they speak to some other person, and often to several other people; moreover, the individual is typically part of a speech community, or actually several intersecting speech communities, as determined by the social 'circles' s/he moves in, involving family, friends, occupational contacts, people with shared interests, and the like, and by the demographically defined groups s/he belongs to, based on gender, socioeconomic class, attitudes, practices, geography, age, and other socially determining factors.

Transmission can therefore be understood as spread of a language within the psychological dimension of the acquisition of the language by, and its development within, an individual, based on input in the ambient environment provided in part by an older generation of speakers. The qualifier 'in part' is needed because in the view of language acquisition advocated here an older generation of caretakers (typically but not necessarily parents) provides at least a baseline of input to a language-learning child, but further input and reinforcement of forms, representations, structures, and such also come from the child's peer group as s/he grows and develops. This approach takes its cue from that advocated by Labov, namely that the social development of the child is crucial to full language development; it is significant that Labov's definition of 'incrementation,' given above, refers to 'cohorts' and not just language-learning 'individuals' or 'generations.' In this regard, of course, we must take note of the oft-cited and admittedly somewhat attractive view, put forward by Halle (1962) and taken up by most generativists since – see the work of David Lightfoot (1997, 1999) – that a certain type of development in the individual acquisition of language – namely 'imperfect learning' – is the locus of change; nonetheless, the observation made by Labov (2007: 346n.4) concerning this view of language change is particularly damning:

> Halle (1962) argued that linguistic change is the result of children's imperfect learning [...]: that late additions to adults' grammars are reorganized by children as a simpler model, which does not exactly match the parents' original grammar. Although Lightfoot (1997, 1999) argues for this model as a means of explaining completed changes, such a process has not yet been directly observed in the study of changes in progress.

Continuing along similar lines of explanation, then, we can say that diffusion generally represents spread within the social side of language; in section 4 below, we focus on a slightly different use of the term to denote a particular type of diffusion, one that has attracted considerable attention and which offers a dimension along which these two senses clash/converge. But in order for that focus to make sense, further details on transmission are necessary.

As the definition given above from Ringe, Warnow, and Taylor (2002) suggests, the notion of 'lineal descent' – what can more emphatically be called 'direct lineal descent'[3] – is a crucially important notion in historical linguistics. As indicated, it refers to those cases in which we can demonstrate, or at least safely assume, an unbroken chain of generational transmission between one stage of a language and some later stage. If such a chain can be established, it allows us to talk confidently about change, in that we know that an earlier speech-form and a later one are directly connected by a series of language-developmental – that is to say, transmissional – events from one generation to another, or, more realistically, from one socially determined language-learning cohort to another.

Just why this notion is crucial to work in historical linguistics can be illustrated by examining the sort of straight-line connection described above that appears to obtain between Ancient Greek (AGk) and Modern Greek (MGk), inasmuch as MGk represents a changed form of its predecessor, AGk. That is, MGk certainly owes much to the vocabulary and grammar of AGk, even if it has innovated and borrowed to get to where it is today. But what does 'predecessor' mean in this context? Such a term seems to suggest that AGk was a monolith and it has changed over time into another monolith, MGk. However, like all languages, Ancient Greek was hardly monolithic, and it encompassed rather considerable variation, including a number of different geographically determined dialects, the main ones being Attic-Ionic, Doric, Aeolic, and Arcado-Cypriot.[4] Moreover, MGk itself encompasses numerous dialects, including Peloponnesian Greek (the basis for much of the present-day standard language), Northern Greek, Southeastern

Greek, Cretan, and so on,[5] as well as subdialects for various locales. Can we thus map in a lineal way from any given AGk dialect, say the Doric dialect found all over ancient Crete, to any given modern dialect, say the present-day dialect of Greek spoken in Crete? Most likely not, since it was the ancient Attic-Ionic dialect that ended up predominating in the Hellenistic period (roughly 300BC – 300AD) and serving as the basis for the variety of Greek known as the Koine that spread over Greek-speaking territory in that era and was the foundation for the modern dialects, including Standard Modern Greek and, significantly, modern Cretan.[6] Thus although related, and part of the same sub(-sub-)branch of the Hellenic family tree, ancient Cretan and modern Cretan are not lineally connected by an unbroken sequence of transmission across stages of the language. Thus, one cannot map directly from an ancient Cretan form onto a form found in modern Crete, since Ancient Doric essentially died out (though see below), being replaced by the Koine in Hellenistic times. That means that ancient Cretan < καί > (*kai*) 'and' did not yield modern Cretan [tʃE], whereas we can be sure that Attic-Ionic < καί > (*kai*) yielded Modern Standard Greek [cE]. Similarly, despite the apparent modern look to the ancient Cretan form αϜτον (*aFton*) 'this,'[7] where the Ϝ ('digamma,' a 'w'-like sound), suggesting a pronunciation [aw], seems to antici-pate the modern [av]/[af] pronunciation for the orthographic <αυ>, the modern forms surely derive from Koine pronunciations. That is, the reason for caution is that for all we know, both ancient Cretan καί and αϜτον could have changed or been replaced within ancient Cretan, only to then be replaced by the Koine pred-ecessors to the modern standard forms as speakers in Hellenistic times shifted to use of the Koine in place of their indigenous dialect.[8] It is the case, though, that in practice, in discussing the origin of some modern form, we might let ancient forms from any dialect stand in for Attic-Ionic forms if the particular form is not directly attested in Attic-Ionic,[9] but in principle one can only tell that a given form at language stage n has changed into a particular form at language stage $n + x$[10] if the line of descent can be established.[11] Importantly, in this regard, it must be recognized that the ancient Doric dialect does have a lineal descendant in modern times, in the form of the Tsakonian variety of Greek, spoken now in parts of the eastern Peloponnesos. Thus, Ancient Doric and modern dialects of the north do not really constitute a path of direct lineal descent, but Ancient Doric and Tsakonian do, as do Ancient Attic-Ionic and the modern Cretan and modern northern dia-lects (among others).

The line of linguistic transmissional descent can be broken by any kind of event that leads to the substitution of a speech-form (dialect or language) that is external to the form of speech that the older generation would otherwise pass on to the next generation. The speech-form used by adults can be altered or affected by an external source, but if there is complete substitution of the external for the native speech-form, the transmission of that native form is broken. For instance, one dialect or language in a region may gain ascendancy over others based on politi-cal, economic, and/or social value associated with it, and such a situation often leads speakers – adult speakers, that is – to give up their native dialect or language in favor of the prevailing one. This is essentially what happened in the case of

Greek, in that the Hellenistic Koine was based largely on Attic-Ionic, due in large part to the adoption of Athenian Greek – the dialect of Athens, the economic and cultural center of ancient Greece – as the court language by Philip of Macedon, whose son, Alexander the Great, carried out conquests that led to the spread of an altered form of Attic-Ionic throughout an extensive empire encompassing most of the eastern Mediterranean area and stretching to India.[12] In the case of Tsakonian, its isolation in the rugged country of the eastern Peloponnesos contributed to keeping at bay the Koine – and into the early part of the twentieth century, Standard Modern Greek.[13] It can be noted that in some works on language contact, such as Thomason and Kaufman (1988), the uprooting of a language (or languages) that occurs in creole formation is seen as a serious break in transmission, such that there is no continuity at all.

A question that needs to be asked is: just what is it that makes the descent lineal and unbroken in the typical case? As suggested already, it is transmission through generations. This transmission takes place in the individual first language learner, of course, but it actually takes place in many individual first language learners throughout the speech community. That baseline of language from generational transmission then gets smoothed out, and added to and elaborated on, in the social interactions that the child first-language learner engages in as s/he becomes part of a peer group, part of a sector of a larger domain of speakers. In that way, s/he becomes involved in interactions with other sectors of society, including older speakers, and thereby begins assimilating to the established norms but also deviating from them in certain respects. In short, s/he is becoming a fully functioning member of a speech community as features enter his/her speech through diffusion from other speakers or become reinforced in his/her usage through contact with them. And, since, in the typical case, significant numbers of individual learning speakers are going through this exact same process of assimilating to a peer group cohort within a larger speech community, the cohort emerges as the carrier of continuity with earlier states of the language, giving the unbroken lineal descent that generational transmission entails. Lineal descent is thus a phenomenon based in part on the individual and in part on the socially defined cohort.[14]

Admittedly this scenario for language-learning may seem to make it hard to maintain a sharp division between transmission and diffusion, in that diffusion – the learning of the norms of a speech community – is involved in language development at a somewhat later stage for the socially defined cohort, after a baseline has been established in each child. Nonetheless, if this is what is involved in the usual path of lineal trans-generational transmission, this simply is what one must recognize and work with. Diffusion as a 'secondary process' (see above, section 1), however, in the typical case, involves adult speakers of one language in contact with adult speakers of another. As Labov (2007: 349) puts it:

> The contrast between the transmission of change within languages and diffusion of change across languages is the result of two different kinds of language learning. On the one hand, transmission is the product of the acquisition of language by young

children. On the other hand, the limitations of diffusion are the result of the fact that most language contact is largely between and among adults.

We can then distinguish between 'primary diffusion,' the diffusion involved in the learning – with some breaking – of societal norms by the (young) first-language learning cohort, and 'secondary diffusion,' the diffusion involved when adult speakers (with fully formed language) come into contact with speakers of different dialects and different languages altogether.

3. More on Diffusion

Diffusion and, more generally, transmission are therefore at the heart of how language goes beyond the individual and becomes part of the social. That movement from the individual to the social deserves further attention and elaboration.

Diffusion as a term applies to the spread of features from individual to individual, from individual to group, or from group to group. Thus, in this sort of spread of linguistic features, certain aspects of language move from being individual idiosyncrasies, in a sense, to being properties of a wider range of individuals, that is, part of the language use of a group, variously defined. As indicated above in section 1, under one interpretation, transmission subsumes diffusion, but also takes in the situation in which there is 'movement' of language between generations.

In this sort of spread, language comes to be rooted not just in one generation but in a wider range of individuals of different ages; since society at large – any sizeable social group, that is – offers a continuum of ages at any given point, ranging from newborns to octogenarians (and older), the transmissional spread of language across generations guarantees a widening of the age of speakers in a given community.

Diffusion moreover interacts with transmission; a restricted type of diffusion – that involved in bringing the emerging usage of an individual in line with a speech community's general linguistic practices, referred to here as 'primary diffusion' – is part and parcel of the transmission process. But there is a key difference between transmission and diffusion in general: while transmission takes place over a relatively short period of time within an individual's development,[15] diffusion, specifically what is called here 'secondary diffusion,' continues across an individual's lifetime. It has been shown empirically, for instance by Sankoff and Blondeau (2007), that language change goes on throughout an individual's lifetime, and not just in trivial ways pertaining to the addition of new lexical items;[16] much of that change in later life is due to the influence of other speakers, and thus represents change by ('secondary') diffusion.[17] Admittedly, some linguists argue here that such changes in adulthood are changes only in language behavior and not in language knowledge (Hale 2007: 40). Still, it is worth asking how one knows that language knowledge is not affected except insofar as it is manifested in language behavior. A similar sort of objection is voiced by Klein

(2010: 721), whose words, even though directed by purely practical concerns, are instructive:

> [T]he model for understanding linguistic change from the perspective of I[nternalized]-language is the interstitial relationship between adjacent generations [...] I like to distinguish this situation – call it microdiachrony – from the traditional enterprise of diachronic linguistics – call it macrodiachrony – which looks at linguistic stages separated by many generations, producing huge saltations between one stage of attestation and another. Under the latter circumstances the attainment of any insight into I-language is, for all intents and purposes, impossible. We are left to do the best we can with E[xternalized]-language: the data we have.

Returning to diffusion, it must be recognized, further, as being possible along any of the dimensions along which individuals interact with or 'bond' with others. That is, diffusion can occur, for example, across social class lines, across geographic lines, and across age boundaries. Diffusion of this last type, across age boundaries, would involve established speakers, as with the spread in American English (and elsewhere) of quotative *like* (as in 'I'm like, what's going on here?!'), with its apparent origins in youth-based usage (Schourup 1983; Romaine and Lange 1991). These paths of diffusion line up with the sets of social contacts and group 'memberships' that an individual has, and with his/her social network, in the sense of Milroy (1980).

Understanding diffusion is also important for getting a handle on just what the notion of 'change' entails, as far as language is concerned. That is, one can recognize that in any 'change event' there is not only the initial appearance of an innovative altered (generally competing) form but also the spread of the use of that form by a wider range of speakers. Yet at what point or points in that 'event' can one talk about a 'change' having occurred? One view might well say that the initial emergence of the innovation is the change, that is, something that the language system alone gives (whether or not the impetus is system-internal or system-external); this is essentially the view taken in Hale (2007). By contrast, a competing view might well say that only with the spread of an innovation is there 'real' change; this is essentially the view that Labov (1994) has repeatedly advocated. In the former view, the innovation alone is all that is of interest to linguistics, and the spread is a matter, perhaps, of sociology. In the latter view, both elements – innovation and spread – are crucial to there being a change; that is, there may be many innovations that go nowhere,[18] in the sense of not spreading to any other speakers, and which thus do not constitute in any substantive sense a 'change' in the language.

It is not necessary to take a stance on the otherwise foundational and important question of how to define 'real change' in order to recognize the distinction insisted on here between diffusion and transmission. Whether a sociological phenomenon or a (socio)-linguistic one, diffusion has an impact on language. Similarly, except in cases of a societal break – as in Thomason and Kaufmann's (1988) view of creolization – or the loss of actual speakers and a speech community (as is happening, and presumably has happened, repeatedly now and in the past as languages 'die'[19]), language transmission will occur, regardless of how 'change' is defined. The issue of what 'change' is in actuality is an important one, but it is orthogonal to the transmission/diffusion dichotomy discussed here.

4. One Particular Non-Social Type of Diffusion and its Status

Work in the nineteenth century in comparative philology, especially but not exclusively with regard to Indo-European languages, yielded several important results that helped to establish a scientific footing for linguistics. Among these achievements were the recognition that genealogical[20] language relationships could be mapped in a family-tree-like diagram, much as manuscript families were classified by classical scholars, and that undergirding much – but not all, as is seen below – of the recognition of these relationships was the discovery of the regularity of sound change. 'Regularity' here refers to the fact that once the parameters for a sound change are appropriately restricted so that it operates in specifiable phonetically determined contexts, all candidate forms for a given sound change can be seen to undergo that change. What this discovery did for genealogical relationships was to offer clear sets of innovations that systematically distinguished clusters of languages (or dialects, for that matter) as separate and distinct from other clusters. Although such clusters could also be identified on the basis of morphological, syntactic, or even semantic or lexical innovations, none of those domains show regularity in the same way that sound change does. Accordingly, the identification of sound changes took on a particular importance for recognizing tree-like branchings-off of distinct speech communities from a unified proto-language starting point.

The notion of direct lineal descent discussed above also plays a role here, since, as indicated, the only way to be able to speak meaningfully about language change along a branch of a family tree is if there is an unbroken line of generational transmission linking one linguistic stage at a higher node in a tree with a later linguistic stage. There is thus a connection between lineal descent and family-tree-like diachronic branching events, and a key element in that connection is sound change, and in particular that kind of change event involving sound that is phonetically driven and adheres to Neogrammarian regularity, what I have elsewhere referred to as 'sound change proper.'[21]

Challenges to the Neogrammarian view of sound change, therefore, indirectly constitute challenges to the tree-like conceptualization of language (and dialect) relationships. One famous challenge was Johannes Schmidt's (1871) 'Wellentheorie' ('wave theory'), the suggestion that language changes do not occur with the regularity and systematicity across a whole language-acquiring cohort that would result in tree-like neat branchings; rather, according to Schmidt's theory, they occur in waves of propagation – that is, in a type of diffusion in our sense – from some innovating center. Despite the fact that these two approaches to representing the results of change – the tree representation associated with Neogrammarian practices and the wave theory representation with its concentric circles of propagation – are often viewed as opposed to one another, in principle both can be right, but can refer to different kinds of change events. In particular, tree representations may be appropriate for innovations that are based in transmission – and therefore primary diffusion – while wave-model representations may be appropriate for innovations that are based in Labovian (secondary) diffusion.

Nonetheless, other challenges are possible to the Neogrammarian view of sound change and the representations of relationships based on it. In particular, what has come to be called 'lexical diffusion' is just such a challenge. This is a type of diffusion that has not so far been mentioned here, but has figured prominently from time to time in the historical linguistic and sociolinguistic literature,[22] and involves diffusion along the purely linguistic dimension of the lexicon. Lexical diffusion is the view that sound change is not implemented uniformly and abruptly across all candidate tokens of a given affected sound in a specified phonetic conditioning environment, that is to say, in all words and morphemes containing that sound and meeting the specified conditions for the sound change. As a result, it does not necessarily lead to regularity for a given sound change, since not all candidate forms need be affected by the change; rather, in the view of those advocating lexical diffusion, a sound change moves within the lexicon from one word meeting the conditioning environment to another and another and another. Crucially, some candidate words could fail to undergo the change: the diffusion of the sound change could weaken and stop before reaching the full extent of the lexicon. Sound change is thus, in the words of Wang (1969: 14), "phonetically abrupt [but] lexically gradual." The challenge to regularity would thus be seen in a putative case of words with nearly identical phonological environments but different behavior with regard to a relevant sound change, as if, for instance, the [æ] of *sad* and *saddle* in English were to develop differently. In such a case, one might claim that the difference in syllable structure – [æ] is in a closed syllable in *sad* but an open syllable in *saddle* – makes a difference. Thus, especially problematic would be a putative case involving true homophones, two distinct words that happen to have the same phonological realization, such as *seed* and *cede* in English, if it could be shown that they developed differently due to sound change and sound change alone.

The reason that such cases are problematic is to be found in a key element of the Neogrammarian view of regular sound change, namely that the only allowable conditioning is of a purely phonetic nature. That means that if sound change were sensitive to meaning or to the part of speech or if it could just ignore phonetics, then it would be necessary to abandon the view that sees sound change as regular *because* it is simply a mechanistic adjustment in articulation that would be replicated, almost automatically, across all places where the adjustment that the sound change entails is called for. There is thus considerable importance to be placed on the hypothesis of lexically diffuse sound change, and there have accordingly been attempts to either reconcile Neogrammarian sound change with lexical diffusion, as in Labov (1981), or to reinterpret lexical diffusion in such a way as to make it irrelevant to the Neogrammarian claims about sound change, as in Kiparsky (1988, 1995/2003), who argues that lexical diffusion is simply a type of analogical change. My own views are closer to Kiparsky's on this, and as an ardent Neogrammarian, I have my own wrinkle on a solution to the challenge that lexical diffusion poses.[23] But first I offer a few somewhat tangential but still not insignificant observations.

First, as a historical note, it is worth remembering that although for many Wang is associated with bringing lexical diffusion before the eyes of the modern linguistic world, the notion of gradual spread through the lexicon has historical antecedents. Wang himself (1969: 14) acknowledges that Sturtevant (1917: 79) envisioned such a type of gradualness, and even if not part of Neogrammarian doctrine about sound change, the positing of lexically diffuse propagation of sound change was on occasion part of Neogrammarian practice. Prokosch (1938: 63, 67) discusses exceptions in Gothic to Verner's Law regarding the voicing of spirants following unaccented syllables in pre-Germanic, prior to a shift of the accent to root syllables. The forms *waurþum* 'we became' and *waurþans* 'having become' are such exceptions, and, citing Hirt (1931) approvingly, Prokosch (1938: 67) states that "we must assume [...] that in these words Gothic had root accent sooner than other Germanic languages," an assumption that would seem to entail that there were words in Gothic, namely those that do show the accent-conditioned Verner's effects, such as *sibun* 'seven,' that acquired root accent later. This assumption, then, is tantamount to saying that the accent shift to the root was accomplished sooner in some words than in others, that is, that the accent shift was a lexically diffuse sound change.

Second, if sound change were an essentially lexical, not phonetic, phenomenon, then in principle we might expect to see far more irregularity in the spread and propagation of change than we usually do, since the lexicon is a repository for the idiosyncratic aspects of language; as a result, under the hypothesis of lexical diffusion, there need not be any predictability to the spread of a sound change.[24]

Moreover, to pick up on Prokosch's suggestion of a variable realization of the shifting of Germanic accent, the sort of variability that lexical diffusion could in principle introduce can be assessed sociolinguistically. At first, though, when one looks at lexical diffusion from the point of view of sociolinguistics and the social dimensions of diffusion, such as those mentioned here throughout, it might seem that there is really no social dimension to lexical diffusion; that is, a first take on lexical diffusion is that it is not really an issue for sociolinguistics: the spread of a sound change through the lexicon would seem to be irrelevant to language in its social setting, being instead just a system-internal matter. However, on a different level, lexical diffusion would matter sociolinguistically since in the posited spread of a sound change word-by-word for individual speakers, it would be surprising if all speakers showed the spread in exactly the same way, to the exact same set of lexical items. Thus with lexical diffusion we might expect there to be considerable variation within the speech community as to which words are pronounced in one way or in a different way, and that variability would be expected to feed into processes of social evaluation by speakers.

Finally, a further important observation is that many types of language change are lexically diffuse. Morphological change, especially involving analogy, is notoriously diffuse and lexically restricted in its realization, and analogical changes that affect just a few lexical items are commonplace. As an extreme case, one can even find instances where just a single form was analogically affected; for instance, the AGk nominative form *Zeus* (chief god of the Greek pantheon) was the basis for the analogical remaking of the nominative of the word for 'month' in the Elean dialect to *meus*, replacing an expected *meis. Similarly, there can be lexically based exceptions, suggesting lexically diffuse spread, for syntactic changes: the general fronted positioning of subject pronouns in English before imperative verbs, as in 'You get me a cold soda right now!' did not affect a few (now-)fixed expressions, such as 'Mind you' or 'Believe you me.'[25] And Joseph (1983) demonstrates that the replacement of the infinitive by finite verb forms in Post-Classical and Medieval Greek diffused through the grammar of Greek in such a way as to affect some constructions, and thus some complement-taking lexical items, before others. The fact of expected diffusion with morphological and syntactic change means that claims of lexical diffusion really only represent a challenge to established views with regard to sound change, since it is only Neogrammarian doctrine on sound change that turns regularity into an issue. Moreover, the hypothesis of lexical diffusion is of real interest only if one takes a Labovian view rather than a Halean view (see above) as to where real change is to be located; if change is defined on the point of origination of an innovation – Hale's view above – then any dimension of spread belongs to a different domain of inquiry.[26]

As for how to reconcile lexical diffusion with Neogrammarianism, as a first step, one can build on this last observation and recognize that there can certainly be a *diffusionary effect* to the way a change, of any sort, is realized in the lexicon at large. As just noted, most changes are indeed lexically gradual; moreover, there are many ways in which the pronunciation of a lexical item can change that do not have to do with phonetically driven Neogrammarian-style sound change. Besides the workings of analogy, there are socially determined processes that can affect the pronunciation, the phonetic realization, of a word. For instance, in hypercorrection, the perceived prestige of a (generally standard) dialect and concomitant concern about stigmatized usage can drive (insecure) speakers to alter forms that are acceptable in standard usage. An example involving an isolated lexical item, and thus highly relevant here, is the widespread Midwestern American English pronunciation [kjúpan] for *coupon*, more standardly with [ku-] in the first syllable, presumably an extension based on urbane-sounding pronunciations with yod after alveolars as in [tjun] *tune*; note that it does not extend to all [ku]-initial words, as forms like *coot, cooed,* or *kook* seem never to occur with [kj]. [27]

Similarly, attitudes about the verbal portrayal of foreign words can change, as in the case of nativizing pronunciations as opposed to pronunciations that are truer to the foreign origin. For example,[28] in the 1950s, the official news agency of the Soviet Union, abbreviated as TASS, standing for *Telegrafnoye agentstvo Sovetskovo*

Soyuza 'Telegraphic Agency of the Soviet Union,' was pronounced, when uttered as a word, for instance by newscasters, as [tæs], whereas in the 1990s, in the post-Soviet era, one could hear instead [tas]. This difference in pronunciation was not a matter of a general change in pronunciation, since, in English, phonetically similar words like *lass* or *pass* retained their [æ] and did not become [las]/[pas], and to say it was a lexically diffuse sound change that just happened to affect this one word would in essence deplete the notion of lexical diffusion of any empirical content. Rather, what seems to have happened is that *TASS* was recognized as the foreign word it was and an attempt was made to give it, as such, a pronunciation more like that in its source language of Russian, hence [tas]. The attitude about how to deal with such obvious foreignisms changed and affected the pronunciation of this one word, and differentiated it from words that were not obvious foreignisms like *lass*, *pass*, and others.

Thus merely finding that a change is realized in just a subset of its potential candidates, when the change is characterized in terms of phonetic environment, is not enough to warrant a claim of lexical diffusion. It is for that reason that the terminological distinction made above is called for, by which 'sound change,' encompassing all possible ways in which a word's phonetic realization could be altered, is differentiated from 'sound change proper,' taking in the far narrower scope of just those changes in pronunciation induced by the phonetic environment and realized across all candidate forms.[29] Similarly, such examples point to the need to distinguish the effects of diffusion (i.e. *diffusionary effects*), as caused by various sorts of processes (other than sound change) altering the pronunciation of words, from *lexical diffusion* per se as a special mechanism of change, as a special type (or subtype) of sound change. And, in cases where that distinction is made, positing lexical diffusion can actually be a less compelling explanation than invoking a naturally diffusionary type of change, such as analogy.

To illustrate, a return to Prokosch and his concerns about Germanic is helpful. Prokosch's comments and his invocation of Hirt, as noted earlier, were made in the context of discussing exceptions to Verner's Law in Gothic. These exceptions constitute a case where a difference between the effects of a sound change on isolated forms, as opposed to what is seen in forms that participate in morphological alternations involving the affected sound, becomes important. In particular, they bear on how explanatory a construct lexical diffusion is. In the case of Verner's Law, as seen above, its effects occur uniformly in all morphologically isolated forms that meet the environmental conditions for the change, such as *sibun* 'seven' (pre-Germanic *sefún, from Proto-Indo-European *septm̥), but only sporadically in verb forms, in which there were accentual alternations that changed the conditions for Verner's Law between different related grammatical categories. Thus, while *þarf*/*þaurbum* 'need' show Verner's Law effects inflectionally between first person singular and plural preterit forms, and *filhan* 'to hide'/*fulgins* 'hidden' do so derivationally, *wairþan* 'to become' does not (rather: *warþ*/*waurþum*/*waurþans*). A lexical diffusion account could be constructed that would say simply that Verner's Law never made it to the lexeme *wairþan*, but that is rather unsatisfying, as it gives no basis for why that lexeme should have been late to be affected by

Verner's Law. Instead, one can posit analogy, a mechanism of change for which lexically diffuse realization is expected, as being operative here, leveling out pre-sumed allomorphy between *warþ* / **waurdum* (allomorphy like that in *þarf* / *þaurbum*). In fact, analogy provides a more satisfying account here, since it explains why isolated forms always show Verner's Law; such forms have no alternating related form on which analogical restoration of the voiceless fricative could be based, so they will necessarily show the voiced fricatives created by Verner's Law, under the assumption of regular (abrupt, in Wang's terms) realization of the sound change at the start. Moreover, analogy provides a natural account of variation seen in one verb, where one finds both expected (per Verner's Law) third person sin-gular *áih* 'he has' and unexpected *áig*, and in the plural both expected first person *áigum* but also unexpected *áihum*. A lexical diffusion account would be hard-pressed to explain this variation, but, using analogy, one need only start with an original alternating paradigm *áih* / *áigum* and assume leveling out of the alterna-tion in different directions. Such bidirectional leveling is seen in English, where some verbs that originally had dental preterits have analogically developed past tense forms marked by vowel change alone; for instance, alongside original *dived*, analogical *dove* has developed. This is counter to the more typical directionality of analogy in English toward new dental preterit forms, as with original *clomb* being replaced by analogical *climbed*. [30]

Even seemingly nonalternating forms can be subject to different environmental influences due to their occurring in different positions in a phrase or sentence in connected speech ('sandhi') or with different intonational contours or other 'suprasegmental' effects. Interestingly Prokosch is willing to recognize such effects in his account of the voicing of the original initial [θ] to [ð] in English in a single lexical class, that of deictics and pronouns (*the, this, then, thou, thee*, etc.). As he puts it (1938: 62), "[OE [θ]] became voiced [...] initially only in words which are relatively unstressed in a sentence [...] Here the whole word is 'lenis,' and there-fore the weak spirant is voiced." This means that a richer basis needs to be con-sidered for the phonetic conditioning environment for sound changes (proper).

Recognizing such richer bases leads to a final point: in the end, fine-grained phonetic detail, including what occurs in connected speech (as opposed to just looking at words in isolated citation forms), matters significantly for sound change (proper), even though we tend to look for very general statements of the condi-tions on sound changes. The 'big bang' theory of sound change, proposed by Janda and Joseph (2003) (see also Janda 2003:419–21), starts with that need to take into account the fine phonetic detail of an environment and turns it into a virtue, saying that sound changes start as phonetically determined 'events' in very 'small' environments – the big bang – and in the aftermath of the big bang of a phonetic event there can be generalization along various lines. [31] One of those lines of generalization can be further continuation of the phonetic trajectory initiated by the 'big bang,' leading to the most commonly observed situation – what was referred to above as 'sound change proper,' that is, Neogrammarian regular sound change – where one sees a fairly broadly realized and phonetically conditioned change in the realization of certain elements. Other lines of generalization are possible, such as phonological, in which the phonetic grounding is lost but sound-based categories are still involved, or morphological, in which analogy and grammar come into play leading often to what is sometimes (erroneously – see Hock 1976) referred to as "grammatically conditioned sound change," or social, in which diffusion and (re)definition of the value of the change according to social categories occur. Moreover, a phonetic big bang event allows for 'lexical diffusion' without violating Neogrammarian tenets. A 'lexically diffuse' change would simply be a sound change proper that in the aftermath of the big bang was generalizing (diffusing) along lexical lines but was never fully generalized. The Neogrammarian sound change proper is to be viewed as distinct from the aftermath, so there would be no violation of the principle of regularity of sound change; regularity would be defined in such a case on the phonetics of that particular 'big bang.' In this view, then, diffusion – really, generalization along various paths – is essential, but it occurs after the defining 'moment' for a sound change, after the 'big bang.'

5. Conclusion

It should be clear from the foregoing that transmission and diffusion are crucial notions in historical linguistic investigations: transmission and diffusion together, in a sense, give the historical dimension to language. Successful transmission in part depends on primary diffusion, establishing lineal descent, and that sets the stage for possible secondary diffusion, which, in the usual case where there is no wholesale shift to another language (or dialect) but only the accretion of material from one into another, preserves lineal descent. Further, in its most usual sense, diffusion necessarily involves spread across different socially defined groups. Transmission and diffusion are thus essential to practices and studies at the intersection of historical linguistic investigation and sociolinguistic investigation, that is, the meeting ground we might call historical sociolinguistics.

An examination of the different dimensions of diffusion leads to a need to consider the one type of nonsocial diffusion, namely lexical diffusion, and the upshot of that discussion is to cast doubt on the need to recognize lexical diffusion as a mechanism of change distinct from analogy and other inherently diffusionary types of change. From a practical standpoint, this result liberates (socially inclined) students of diffusion from having to consider linguistic dimensions to spread, except those associated with generalization in the aftermath of the big bang of a sound change, and it thereby allows them to concentrate on just social dimensions to diffusion. Historical sociolinguistics can thus be practiced with an emphasis on the social side of the history. The spread of sound change in its aftermath, for instance, can still be analyzed in socially diffusionary ways, along socially determined paths relating to speakers' lines of social interaction, but the purely linguistic dimension of spread through the lexicon need not be taken account of; it can be profitably viewed as a type of analogy, a process that can lead to diffusionary effects in the lexicon, independent of social concerns.

This result means further that diffusion, now limited to socially determined diffusion, is not a problem for Neogrammarianism because sound changes have always had to be relativized to particular speech communities. Socially determined diffusion simply means that a richer sense of 'speech community' is needed as far as sound change is concerned, but other linguistic phenomena point in that direction anyway.

This sociolinguistically satisfying result has a further consequence that is satisfying from the perspective of historical linguistics; the Neogrammarian hypothesis of the regularity of sound change is foundational to so much else in historical linguistic methodology,[32] so the ability to remove lexical diffusion from the playing field, while allowing social diffusion to remain in play, means that Neogrammarian doctrine can be preserved, including the associated notion of lineal transmission, and with it the methodological edifice that it supports and all the important results that have flowed from that edifice over decades of research.

Historical sociolinguistics as a paradigm for understanding the passage of a language and its speakers through time depends on a degree of rigor on the historical, the social, and the purely linguistic levels of analysis. Being able to identify and separate out different causes for different kinds of effects thus strengthens the paradigm, as it emboldens practitioners by giving clearer direction to their investigations.

NOTES

1   Given the enormous contributions of Labov's research program over the past nearly fifty years to our understanding of language change in its social setting, Labov (2007) quite characteristically also offers important conceptual and empirical breakthroughs.
2   That is, excluding talking to oneself and talk contained in dreams.
3   I have used this expression for years in my teaching of historical linguistics but I am not sure exactly of its ultimate source. My first historical linguistics teacher, Isidore Dyen, used 'lineal descent' in the course entitled "Historical Linguistics" (course number: Linguistics 51a) that I took during my senior year at Yale University in the autumn of 1972 (and I have it in my notebook from that class). I do not know if the addition of 'direct' is my embellishment or was used by Dyen; I wonder too if there was any influence from Leonard Bloomfield (Dyen's colleague at Yale after World War II) but leave that an open question for now. Hale (2007: 27) has a detailed discussion of what 'descent' means in linguistic terms.
4   I am deliberately leaving aside Northwest Greek, as in some accounts it is subsumed under Doric, as well as, for different reasons – having to do with difficulty in placing them accurately – Mycenaean Greek and Pamphylian Greek.
5   See Newton (1972) and Trudgill (2003) for details and some discussion. The rather meager listing given here (pared down for the sake of convenience) leaves out a large number of regional and other varieties of Greek that might well be called 'Modern Greek dialects.'
6   See Browning (1969/1983) and Horrocks (1997/2010) for information on the formation of the Koine and the historical development of Modern Greek more generally.
7   This form occurs in one of the earliest Cretan inscriptions, from Drerus, dating from the sixth century BC.

8 Hale (2007: 30–31) terms this the problem of 'non-lineal descent;' see also Janda and Joseph (2003: 19) for further general discussion.

9 The reasoning behind such a practice is that in the absence of evidence to the contrary, an Attic-Ionic form corresponding to the attested non-Attic-Ionic form is likely to have occurred but just to be accidentally missing from the documentary record on the dialect. Attestation is, after all, a matter of historical accident; see Janda and Joseph (2003: 15–16) for some relevant discussion.

10 This view sees a language as consisting of a series of synchronic stages where each stage is replaced, actually replicated with possible alteration, by another, and that by another and so on, with diachrony being the movement of the language through these successive synchronic stages. See Joseph (1992) and Hale (2007: 5–6) for discussion (and diagrams).

11 Klein (2010: 721n.1) makes this same point; see also Hale (2007). Although illustrated here with Greek, similar concerns hold for virtually every linguistic tradition; Crystal (1995: 29) has this to say on this problem in the history of English: "Most of the Old English corpus is written in the Wessex [West Saxon] dialect [...] however, it is one of the ironies of English linguistic history that modern Standard English is descended not from West Saxon but from Mercian [...] the dialect spoken [...] in [...] [and] around London."

12 There are archaisms in some modern dialects that escaped the leveling out that occasioned the formation of the Hellenistic Koine – see Andriotis (1974) and Shipp (1979) for various examples.

13 Pernot (1934) is the most authoritative presentation of Tsakonian grammar before there was serious influence – evident in small amounts even in Pernot's time – from the standard language on the form of Tsakonian. Present-day Tsakonian is still distinctive, but shows ever-increasing standard language influence.

14 As noted earlier in this section, one can identify a fairly extreme generativist view of the relation between language acquisition and language change, namely the view that Labov (2007) criticizes (see above). That particular view goes awry, in my opinion, because it focuses too much on the individual and not enough (if at all) on the individual in a social group and a larger speech community. If an innovation in an individual were actually to arise due to the 'imperfect learning' scenario but then were to go nowhere in terms of spread within the cohort, one has to wonder how significant it is; see below for discussion of what constitutes 'real' change.

15 It is a matter of some debate just how long this 'critical period' is, and, for that matter, if there really is such a 'critical period' or if observable differences between first and second language acquisition are to be explained in ways other than in psychological/maturational terms.

16 A somewhat more theoretical and conceptual discussion of change through the lifetime is offered in Janda and Joseph (2003: 174n.133), where reference is also made to an early modern case study (Robson 1975).

17 This is not to say that older speakers are incapable of making system-internal changes, as that is most assuredly not the case. Problems older speakers may have with the retrieval of forms no doubt contribute to some instances of analogical regularization, for instance.

18 There are random fluctuations in production evident even in the same speaker uttering the same form at different times throughout the course of a day; such fluctuations are, in a sense, system-produced innovations, but in the typical case, they do not spread and thus are mere ephemera.

19 The scare quotes around 'die' are in recognition of the fact that almost every way of referring to a situation in which a language fails to be transmitted generationally is ideologically charged in some way or other.

20 The term 'genealogical' seems to be gaining in use among historical linguists; I actually prefer the term 'genetic,' with the etymological sense of Greek *genetikós* 'pertaining to

origins' being operative, but the modern biological sense of 'genetic' interferes with that earlier meaning in ways that can lead to misunderstandings.

21   The need for a terminological distinction here comes from the fact that there can be numerous ways in which the sounds of a word undergo change, such as analogy – an essentially morphologically driven process – but only one guarantees regularity, and that is phonetically driven sound change, sound change of the Neogrammarian type, 'sound change proper.' See further below for more discussion, and footnote 29.

22   See Wang (1969, 1979), the various papers in Wang (1977), and, most recently, Phillips (2006); also Chapter 23 in this *Handbook*.

23   I have benefitted in this presentation of lexical diffusion not only from the cited works of Kiparsky and Labov, but also from Phillips (2006), with its fine summary of the literature on the lexical dimension in sound change and its careful treatment of various factors that might play a role in the paths of diffusion through the lexicon. That I disagree with her ultimate conclusions about, for instance, needing to keep lexical diffusion distinct from analogy, is no indication of anything less than admiration for the carefully reasoned work.

24   Though see Phillips (2006) regarding frequency as a possible predictive factor.

25   Of course, subject pronouns do not usually occur at all with imperatives; *mind you* and *believe you me* therefore also constitute exceptions to the more general imperatival subject deletion, since subjectless *Mind!* (e.g. *Mind your manners!*) has a different meaning from *mind you!* (and note: *Mind you your manners), and subjectless *Believe me!* lacks the emphatic nature and pragmatic 'intimacy' that *believe you me* adds to an utterance.

26   One necessary embellishment on Hale's view is that spread could not be a purely sociological matter if it includes the (presumably) nonsocially driven spread through the lexicon.

27   Hypercorrection may well have an analogical component, as it is generally based on patterns of correspondences involving dialects perceived as having different social values; see Hock and Joseph (1996/2009: 181–2) for some discussion.

28   I thank my friend and colleague Neil Jacobs for this example. See Janda, Joseph, and Jacobs (1994) for some discussion of various ways in which attitudes about forms perceived as foreign can affect their realization.

29   Kiparsky (1988: 369) describes this distinction as follows: "certain historical processes which *look* like sound changes are in reality not sound changes in the technical sense at all, but arise by other mechanisms."

30   Prokosch (1938: 63) suggests that the existence of alternations could block the operation of the sound change as opposed to undoing its effects; such a preventative view of the conditioning of sound change is counter to Neogrammarian tenets, because it posits conditioning that is nonphonetic in nature. While attractive, such an account clearly could not work for the *áih/áig/áigum/áihum* set of forms, so it is simpler to assume only restorative power for analogy rather than both restorative and preventative powers.

31   This comes close to the nineteenth-century view of dialectologists that "every word has its own history," in the sense that each word can define – or, within phrases, participate in – its own almost unique fine-grained phonetic environment. In the typical case, however, the fine phonetic detail is replicated to a certain extent in other words of similar structure, allowing for some generalization of environments across words. Clearly, the finer the detail one focuses on, the harder it is to generalize; the view taken here is that one starts with narrowly defined environments and things generalize from there. See Kiparsky (1988: 368–370) for a discussion of how the Neogrammarian view of sound change and this dialectological claim can be seen as compatible.

32   For instance, recognizing the regularity of sound change allows for the determination of the type of change involved in a given phenomenon, for example analogy as opposed to sound change (proper), it allows for the sorting out of borrowings from inherited lexical items, and it provides a basis for establishing the relative chronology of sound changes, all key elements in the practicing historical linguist's toolkit.

REFERENCES

Andriotis, N. (1974) *Lexikon der Archaismen in neugriechischen Dialekten*, Osterreichische Akademie der Wissenschaften, Vienna.

Bloomfield, L. (1933) *Language*, Holt Rinehart, New York.

Browning, R. (1969/1983) *Medieval and Modern Greek* (2nd edn), Cambridge University Press, Cambridge.

Crystal, D. (1995) *The Cambridge Encyclopedia of the English Language*, Cambridge University Press, Cambridge.

Hale, M. (2007) *Historical Linguistics: Theory and Method*, Blackwell, Oxford.

Halle, M. (1962) Phonology in generative grammar. *Word* 18: 54–72.

Hirt, H. (1931) *Handbuch des Urgermanisch Vol. 1*, Carl Winters Universitätsverlag, Heidelberg.

Hock, H.H. (1976) Review of R. Anttila (1972) *An Introduction to Historical and Comparative Linguistics* (Macmillan, New York). *Language* 52(1): 202–20.

Hock, H.H. and Joseph, B.D. (1996/2009) *Language Change, Language History, and Language Relationship. An Introduction to Historical Linguistics* (2nd edn), Mouton de Gruyter, Berlin.

Hoenigswald, H. (1960) *Language Change and Linguistic Reconstruction*, University of Chicago Press, Chicago.

Horrocks, G. (1997/2010) *Greek. A History of the Language and its Speakers* (2nd edn), Wiley-Blackwell, Chichester.

Janda, R.D. (2003) 'Phonologization' as the start of dephoneticization – or, on sound change and its aftermath: of extension, generalization, lexicalization, and morphologization. In B. Joseph and R. Janda (eds.), pp. 401–22.

Janda, R.D. and Joseph, B.D. (2003) Reconsidering the canons of sound change: towards a Big Bang Theory. In B. Blake and K. Burridge (eds.), *Historical Linguistics 2001. Selected Papers from the 15th International Conference on Historical Linguistics, Melbourne, 13–17 August 2001*, John Benjamins, Amsterdam, pp. 205–19.

Janda, R.D., Joseph, B.D., and Jacobs, N. (1994) Systematic hyperforeignisms as maximally external evidence for linguistic rules. In S. Lima, R. Corrigan, and G. Iverson (eds.), *The Reality of Linguistic Rules*, John Benjamins, Amsterdam, pp. 67–92.

Joseph, B.D. (1983) *The Synchrony and Diachrony of the Balkan Infinitive: A Study in Areal, General, and Historical Linguistics*, Cambridge University Press, Cambridge.

Joseph, B.D. (1992) Diachronic explanation: putting speakers back into the picture. In G. Davis and G. Iverson (eds.), *Explanation in Historical Linguistics*, John Benjamins, Amsterdam, pp. 123–44.

Joseph, B.D. and Janda, R.D. (eds.) (2003) *The Handbook of Historical Linguistics*, Blackwell, Oxford.

Kiparsky, P. (1988) Phonological change, in *Linguistics: The Cambridge survey, I: Linguistic theory: Foundations*, Cambridge University Press, Cambridge, pp. 363–415.

Kiparsky, P. (1995/2003) The phonological basis of sound change. In J.A. Goldsmith (ed.), *The Handbook of Phonological Theory*, Blackwell, Oxford, pp. 640–70. Reprinted in B.D. Joseph and R.D. Janda (eds.), pp. 313–42.

Klein, J.S. (2010) Review of G. Ferraresi and M. Goldbach (eds.) (2008), *Principles of Syntactic Reconstruction* (John Benjamins, Amsterdam). *Language* 86(3): 720–26.

Labov, W. (1981) Resolving the Neogrammarian controversy. *Language* 57: 267–308.

Labov, W. (1994) *Principles of Linguistic Change. Vol. 1: Internal Factors*, Blackwell, Oxford.

Labov, W. (2007) Transmission and diffusion. *Language* 83(2): 344–87.

Lightfoot, D. (1997) Catastrophic change and learning theory. *Lingua* 100: 171–92.

Lightfoot, D. (1999) *The Development of Language: Acquisition, Change, and Evolution*, Blackwell, Oxford.

Milroy, L. (1980) *Language and Social Networks*, Blackwell, Oxford.

Newton, B. (1972) *The Generative Interpretation of Dialect. A Study of Modern Greek Phonology*, Cambridge University Press, Cambridge.

Pernot, H. (1934) *Introduction à l'étude du dialecte tsakonien*. Paris.

Phillips, B.S. (2006) *Word Frequency and Lexical Diffusion*, Palgrave Macmillan, New York.

Prokosch, E. (1938) *A Comparative Germanic Grammar*, Linguistic Society of America, Baltimore.

Ringe, D., Warnow, T., and Taylor, A. (2002) Indo-European and computational cladistics. *Transactions of the Philological Society* 100: 59–129.

Robson, B. (1975) Jenepher revisited: adult language change. In R.W. Fasold and R.W. Shuy (eds.), *Analyzing Variation in Language. Papers from the Second Colloquium of New Ways of Analyzing Variation*, Georgetown University Press, Washington, pp. 283–90.

Romaine, S. and Lange, D. (1991) The use of *like* as a marker of reported speech and thought: A case of grammaticalization in progress. *American Speech* 66: 227–79.

Sankoff, G. and Blondeau, H. (2007) Language change across the lifespan: /r/ in Montreal French. *Language* 83(3): 560–88.

Schmidt, J. (1871) *Die Verwandtschaftsverhältnisse der indogermanischen Sprachen*, H. Böhlau, Weimar.

Schourup, L. (1983) *Common Discourse Particles in English Conversation*. Ph.D. dissertation, Ohio State University (published 1984 as *Ohio State University Working Papers in Linguistics* 28).

Shipp, G.P. (1979) *Modern Greek Evidence for the Ancient Greek Vocabulary*, Sydney University Press, Sydney.

Sturtevant, E. (1917) *Linguistic Change*, University of Chicago Press, Chicago.

Thomason, S.G. and Kaufman, T. (1988) *Language Contact, Creolization, and Genetic Linguistics*, University of California Press, Berkeley and Los Angeles.

Trudgill, P. (2003) Modern Greek dialects: a preliminary classification. *Journal of Greek Linguistics* 4: 45–63.

Wang, W.S-Y. (1969) Competing changes as cause of residue. *Language* 45(1): 9–25.

Wang, W.S-Y. (ed.) (1977) *The Lexicon in Phonological Change*, Mouton, The Hague.

Wang, W.S-Y. (1979) Language change – a lexical perspective. *Annual Review of Anthropology* 8: 353–71.

23 The Timing of Language Change

MIEKO OGURA

1. Introduction

The most explicit hypothesis on how sound change comes about was proposed by the Neogrammarians working in Germany in the mid-1870s. The Neogrammarian hypothesis has essentially two parts: lexical regularity and phonetic gradualness. We will not repeat the various arguments that have been offered recently to show the difficulties of the Neogrammarian hypothesis – see Ogura (1987), and also Chapter 22 in this *Handbook*. In view of the unsatisfactory state of the mechanism that the Neogrammarians advocated, other processes for implementing sound change have been proposed. Empirical investigations over the past four decades on a variety of languages, using large amounts of data, have shown that there must be a process which is implemented in a manner that is lexically gradual, diffusing across the lexicon. This is an inevitable consequence of admitting phonetic abruptness; in his seminal article Wang (1969) called this process 'lexical diffusion.'

The chronological profile of lexical diffusion may be represented by the S-curve slope. When the change first enters the language, the number of words it affects may be small. The change gradually diffuses, going slowly at first. Then, as it spreads, it accelerates, picking up speed in mid-stream. In the most active period, the change moves quickly through a large number of lexical items. It then gradually slows down again, and tapers off at the end (Chen 1972). The diffusion process is comparable to epidemics of infectious diseases, and the standard model of an epidemic produces an S-curve.

Chen and Wang (1975: 256) argue that "one of the most neglected aspects of historical linguistics, which professes to be a study of language evolving across

The Handbook of Historical Sociolinguistics, First Edition. Edited by Juan Manuel Hernández-Campoy and Juan Camilo Conde-Silvestre.
© 2014 John Wiley & Sons, Ltd. Published 2014 by John Wiley & Sons, Ltd.

time, is the time element itself." Nevalainen and Raumolin-Brunberg (2003: 56–57) admit that the accurate timing of linguistic changes has not been a central issue in historical linguistics and that there is still a great deal of truth in Chen and Wang's argument. Further, they state that despite the abundance of diachronic studies dealing with individual linguistic changes over time, it is not easy to find publications that concentrate on the temporal aspects of change, such as timing, rate of change, and the S-curve.

Language change is basically a speaker-to-speaker social propagation in time and space. As early as 1917, Sturtevant (1917: 82) already stated that "[t]he two processes of spread from word to word and spread from speaker to speaker progress side by side until the new sound has extended to all the words of the language which contained the old sound in the same surroundings." Therefore lexical diffusion must have its trace in a population and its real mechanism should be studied both in the diffusion from word to word and in the diffusion from speaker to speaker in progress (Shen 1990).

In lexical diffusion, the change catches on gradually, both within a language and when moving from speaker to speaker in the community. The lexical diffusion model is defined along two dimensions: diffusion from word to word in a single speaker, which we call W(ord)-diffusion, and diffusion from speaker to speaker of a single word, which we call S(peaker)-diffusion. When W-diffusion is slower than S-diffusion, the difference is greater between words. When W-diffusion is faster than S-diffusion, the difference is greater between speakers. Figure 23.1 schematically shows the S-curve progress of two-dimensional diffusion through time (t) when W-diffusion is faster than S-diffusion (W > S), W-diffusion is slower than S-diffusion (W < S), and the rate of W-diffusion and S-diffusion is equal (W = S) (Ogura and Wang 1998).

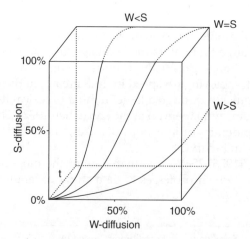

Figure 23.1.   S-curve progress of two-dimensional diffusion through time (Ogura and Wang 1998: 333; reproduced by permission of Mouton de Gruyter)

In this chapter, we first discuss S-curve progress of language change and its snowball effect in relation to word frequency in W-diffusion, based on the development of periphrastic *do* and the development of *-(e)s* in the third person singular present indicative in English. Then we deal with the effects of social networks in S-diffusion, based on simulation and historical data from English. Historical sociolinguistics deals with language use and language users in particular in their social contexts (Nevalainen and Raumolin-Brunberg 2003: 2). It is mainly concerned with S-diffusion in our model. As stated above, however, S-diffusion and W-diffusion are closely related. Thus our discussion in this chapter is concerned with both S-diffusion and W-diffusion. From this perspective, we would like to examine the core concepts in historical sociolinguistics along the time dimension.

People acquire their linguistic habits mainly at their 'critical age' for language acquisition. By the age of puberty, individuals have normally acquired their linguistic system (Hockett 1950). An individual's linguistic pattern is, to a certain degree, the reflex of the linguistic pattern during his language learning period. Therefore, the linguistic differences in different ages, from young to old, should reflect an increase of new linguistic features. If there is ongoing change with a time span about the length of a lifetime, we can use differential behavior of speakers in various age groups as a time indicator to study the correlated lexical gradualness. This is an apparent-time study of linguistic change (Shen 1990; Labov 1994: 43–72, 2001: 75–78). Apparent-time studies work well in ongoing changes in present-day data, but problems arise in historical linguistics because of insufficient background data (Nevalainen and Raumolin-Brunberg 2003: 85).

Linguistic change in real time is the cumulative effect of the transmission of change across generations. It can best be traced by using corpora that cover a long time span. The real-time variable has, however, attracted less systematic attention in recent years than it deserves (Nevalainen 2006). Further, the transmission of change across generations has not been discussed or even recognized in the literature (Labov 2001: 415–45). Our discussion in this chapter focuses on large-scale developments in real time, and language transmission and change are investigated through simulation and historical corpora.

2. S-curve Progress, Snowball Effect, and Word Frequency in W-diffusion

2.1 *The development of periphrastic do*

Kroch (1989), using a mathematical function, the logistic, examines whether changes occur sequentially across the various contexts, or simultaneously in all contexts. He further presents two possibilities in the latter scenario: either changes spread at the same rate or at different rates; he proposes that changes occur simultaneously and spread at the same rate in all contexts.

Ogura (1993) examines the validity of the simultaneous equal activation scenario for the S-curve progress that Kroch (1989) proposes, and claims that changes

Table 23.1.   The development of periphrastic *do* in various types of sentences (Ellegård 1953: 161; reproduced by permission of Almqvist and Wiksell)

Period	Date	Aff.decl.		Neg.decl.		Neg.q.		Aff.q.		Neg.imp.	
		do	*n*	*do*	*s*	*do*	*s*	*do*	*s*	*do*	*s*
0	1390–1400	6	45000	0	–	0	–	0	–	0	–
1	1400–1425	11	4600	0	177	2	15	0	10	0	52
2	1425–1475	121	45500	11	892	2	23	6	136	3	279
3	1475–1500	1059	59600	33	660	3	24	10	132	0	129
4	1500–1525	396	28600	47	558	46	32	41	140	2	164
5	1525–1535	494	18800	89	562	34	22	33	69	0	101
6	1535–1550	1564	19200	205	530	63	21	93	114	0	72
7	1550–1575	1360	14600	119	194	41	7	72	56	4	39
8	1575–1600	1142	18000	150	479	83	45	228	150	8	117
9	1600–1625	240	7900	102	176	89	6	406	181	65	119
10	1625–1650	212	7200	109	235	32	6	116	24	5	10
11	1650–1700	140	7900	126	148	48	4	164	43	17	16
12	1710	5	2800	61	9	16	0	53	3	28	0

Aff.decl. = affirmative declarative sentences
Neg.decl. = negative declarative sentences, main group
Neg.q. = negative direct adverbial and yes/no questions
Aff.q. = affirmative direct adverbial and yes/no questions
Neg.imp. = negative imperatives, main group

in the different contexts initiate at different times and the later a change begins, the greater the rate of change becomes. Our data as well as Kroch's are based on Ellegård's extensive and monumental study *The Auxiliary Do: The Establishment and Regulation of its Use in English* (1953), which collects the periphrastic *do*-forms and non-periphrastic ('simple') forms from prose texts from 1390 through 1710, showing their relative frequencies in several contexts and grouping the texts into thirteen periods. The results are summarized in Table 23.1, and displayed graphically in Figure 23.2. For negative declaratives, negative questions, affirmative questions and negative imperatives, the number of tokens of the *do*-forms (abbreviated as 'do') and simple forms (abbreviated as 's') are given, and for affirmative declaratives, the number of tokens of the *do*-forms and the total number of tokens of *do*-forms plus simple forms (abbreviated as 'n') are given.

The data in Table 23.1 are fitted from period 0 through period 12 for affirmative declaratives, from period 1 through period 12 for negative declaratives, negative questions and affirmative questions, and from period 2 through period 12 for negative imperatives to the logistic function, which transforms the curve into a

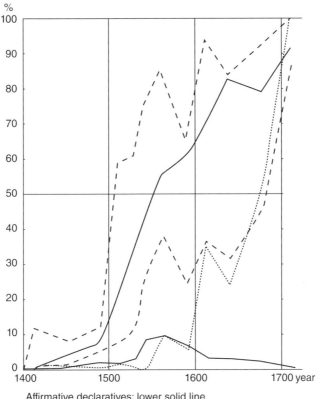

Figure 23.2.   The development of periphrastic *do* (Ellegård 1953: 162; reproduced by permission of Almqvist and Wiksell)

linear function of time by the so-called 'logistic transform of frequency.' Table 23.2 shows the slope and intercept parameters of the fits calculated by logit modeling in Statistical Analysis System (SAS). The slope represents the rate of change, whereas the intercept measures the frequency of the changed form at the fixed point in time, $t = 0$ of the logistic function. When we compute the estimates for the parameters, we interpret the periods in Table 23.1 as the years from the reference point in time ($t = 0$), in our case, the year 1175, when the first written example of all the sentence types appeared (see below).

Table 23.3 shows the estimates of the slope and intercept parameters obtained by Kroch (1989). He fixes the zero point in time at 1350, and uses a univariate version of the maximum likelihood fit in the VARBRUL program. He considers

Table 23.2. Slope and intercept parameters of logistic regressions on the data in Table 23.1

	Affirmative declaratives	Negative declaratives	Negative questions	Affirmative questions	Negative imperatives
slope	3.41	5.90	6.90	7.73	13.44
intercept	−23.61	−36.45	−40.14	−46.15	−82.72

Table 23.3. Slope and intercept parameters of logistic regressions obtained by Kroch (1989)

	Affirmative declaratives	Negative declaratives	Negative questions	Aff. trans. adv.and yes/no q.	Aff. intrans. adv.and yes/no q.	Affirmative wh-object q.
slope	2.82	3.74	3.45	3.62	3.77	4.01
intercept	−8.32	−8.33	−5.57	−6.58	−8.08	−9.26

that there is a grammatical reanalysis in period 7, and cuts off the data after that[1].

We take all the periods for which Ellegård provides data, and fit the data to the logistic curve. As shown in Table 23.2, it turns out that different contexts do have different slopes, that is, different rates of change. When we look at the starting point of the changes, we find a clear correlation between each of them and the rates of change. According to Visser (1963–73: 1411–76), the earliest dates of *do* periphrasis in writing were: affirmative declaratives, c.1175; negative declaratives, c.1280; negative questions, c.1370; affirmative questions, c.1380; negative imperatives, c.1422.

Our results in Table 23.2, together with the earliest dates of *do* periphrasis of the five sentence types, show that the later a change starts, the sharper its slope becomes, that is, the later a change starts, the greater the rate of change. This shows the 'snowball effect' of lexical diffusion: diffusion across more and more contexts at faster rates in later starting contexts.

The examples above are sporadic and they are the earliest dates at which the form is attested in the surviving written sample, which is not the same thing as the earliest dates of the actual change. Moreover, a linguistic phenomenon probably becomes noticeable in written texts long after it has become fairly widespread in spoken language. Even so, we may assume that these citations show the earliest appearances of periphrastic *do* which started undergoing the change at different times, based on the following statistical argumentation.

Suppose we assume with Kroch that the change began simultaneously in all environments, and proceeded with uniform slope. When the rate of occurrence of the change is very low in the earliest periods, it is only likely to show up in the surviving sample in environments with lots of data. At some later period, when the probability of the innovation rises, we would expect a case to occur in the middle frequency environment, and at still later times in the low frequency environments.

If the number of occurrences of tokens in each environment in the sample does not reflect the actual frequency, the premise of the logical conclusion should be the simultaneous start of the changes. However, if the number of occurrences of tokens in each environment reflects the actual frequency, the situation is different. If we cannot get an example in the middle and low frequency environments at the earliest periods, it means that the actual change has not appeared in those environments. At some later period, when the probability of the innovation rises, an example occurs in the middle frequency environment, which means that the actual change has first appeared in the middle frequency environment. We may assume that the premise of the logical conclusion should be the sequential start of the changes.

The total number of occurrences of tokens in each environment in Table 23.1 reflects the actual frequency of tokens. Given the actual frequency of tokens in each environment reflected in Table 23.1 and the uniform rate of change, we can predict that the change in each environment started sequentially. Thus, there is little probability for Kroch's assumption that the change began simultaneously in all environments and proceeded with uniform rate; note that the earliest dates in Visser's data are not the outcome of a common starting date.

We may gather from Table 23.1 that the changes appeared earlier in the contexts where the larger number of tokens occur. Affirmative declaratives, in which change initiated first in all contexts, have the largest number of tokens. The change then started in negative declaratives, which have the second largest number of tokens, then in questions, both negative and affirmative, and finally in negative imperatives, which have the smallest number of tokens. Within each context, there is a significant tendency for the high frequency words to change late and therefore to have a sharper slope. Table 23.4 shows the development of the *do*-form in the *say*-group, which consists of the high-frequency verbs *say*, *mean*, *do*, and *think*, and the main group, which consists of the remaining low-frequency words in affirmative *wh*-object questions. A blank means that the example has not been found yet. As mentioned above, the early example in the main group is found in c.1380, though the data on the main group in Table 23.4 do not show the occurrence of *do* periphrasis in periods 1 and 2. The first occurrence of *do* periphrasis in the *say*-group in Table 23.4 is found in period 3, which means that there is a lag of about one hundred years in the *say*-group.

Table 23.5 shows slopes and intercepts for the *say*-group and the main group. We can say that the high-frequency words resisted the *do*-form, but once they started to change, the rate of change turned out to be greater than that of the low frequency words.

Table 23.4. The development of the *do*-form in the *say*-group and the main group of affirmative *wh*-object questions (Ogura 1993: based on the data given by Ellegård 1953 in the data section in Part III; reproduced by permission of John Benjamins)

Period	Date	say-group		main group	
		do	*s*	*do*	*s*
1	1400–1425		0	0	1
2	1425–1475		19	0	28
3	1475–1500	1	39	1	24
4	1500–1525	2	27	4	36
5	1525–1535	0	33	6	22
6	1535–1550	0	45	8	32
7	1550–1575	3	51	22	14
8	1575–1600	7	56	39	27
9	1600–1625	25	93	28	30
10	1625–1650	15	39	24	32
11	1650–1700	24	20	11	3
12	1710	7	4	4	0

Table 23.5. Slope and intercept parameters of logistic regressions on the data in Table 23.4

	say-group	*main group*
Slope	10.49	6.82
Intercept	−65.19	−41.33

The above results can be confirmed in negative declaratives. Ellegård classifies the negative declaratives into two groups, the *know*-group, which seems to have resisted the *do*-form, including verbs such as *know, do, doubt, care, list, fear, skill, trow,* and *boot,* and the main group, which consists of the rest of the verbs. Ellegård's data in Tables 23.1 and 23.6 show that 22% of the total number of tokens for negative declaratives (5672 tokens for the main group and 1620 tokens for the *know*-group) are tokens of the *know*-group. He gives lexical information on the 1512 tokens of the total number of the 1620 *know*-verbs. The frequency of the nine *know*-verbs is as follows: *know,* 869 tokens; *do,* 212 tokens; *doubt,* 229 tokens; *care,* 127 tokens; *list,* 15 tokens; *fear,* 47 tokens; *skill,* 5 tokens; *trow,* 3 tokens; *boot,* 5 tokens. Although Ellegård does not give lexical information on the main group verbs, we may assume that *know, do, doubt, care, list,* and *fear* are the most frequent

Table 23.6.   The development of the *do*-form in the *know*-group of negative declaratives (Ogura 1993: based on the data given by Ellegård 1953 in the data section in Part III; reproduced by permission of John Benjamins)

Period	Date	know-*group*	
		do	*s*
1	1400–1425		31
2	1425–1475		191
3	1475–1500	3	178
4	1500–1525	0	144
5	1525–1535	0	133
6	1535–1550	11	211
7	1550–1575	5	88
8	1575–1600	14	227
9	1600–1625	22	135
10	1625–1650	5	80
11	1650–1700	27	80
12	1710	17	18

Table 23.7.   Slope and intercept parameters of logistic regressions on the data of the *know*-group and the main group of negative declaratives

	know-*group*	*main group*
Slope	8.06	5.90
Intercept	−51.14	−36.45

words in negative declaratives. Three items in the *know*-group, *skill*, *trow*, and *boot*, are not frequent words. Though they are included in the *know*-group, they have no effect on the parameter estimates.

Table 23.6 shows the development of the *do*-form in the *know*-group. A blank means that the example has not been found yet. As mentioned above, the early form in the main group is found c.1280, though the data on the main group in Table 23.1 do not show the occurrence of *do* periphrasis in periods 0 and 1. The first occurrence of the *know*-group in Table 23.6 is found in period 3, which means that there is a lag in the *know*-group of about two hundred years.

Table 23.7 shows slopes and intercepts for the *know*-group and the main group. The *know*-group, which started later, has a sharper slope and, therefore, a greater rate of change.

Table 23.8.   The overall distributions of the -*(e)th* and -*(e)s* endings in non-sibilant verbs in EModE (Ogura and Wang 1996: based on the data from the Early Modern English section of the Helsinki Corpus; reproduced by permission of John Benjamins)

freq	EModE I-th	EModE I-s	EModE II-th	EModE II-s	EModE III-th	EModE III-s
1084-21 (33 types)	1103 tokens	29 tokens (2.6%)	932 tokens	331 tokens (26.2%)	251 tokens	697 tokens (73.5%)
20-3 (176 types)	384 tokens	6 tokens (1.5%)	282 tokens	166 tokens (37.1%)	28 tokens	339 tokens (92.4%)
2-1 (262 types)	116 tokens	0 tokens (0%)	72 tokens	25 tokens (25.8%)	5 tokens	121 tokens (96.0%)

2.2   The development of -s in the third person singular present indicative

The snowball effect and the interaction between word frequency and environments can also be found in the development of -*(e)s* in the third person singular present indicative. Based on the data from the Early Modern English (EModE) section of the Helsinki Corpus, Ogura and Wang (1996) give the overall distributions of the -*(e)th* and -*(e)s* forms by sub-periods for the non-sibilant verbs, which are divided into three groups according to word frequency as shown in Table 23.8. The percentages of the -*s* forms for the total tokens for each sub-period are given for each of the three groups of the non-sibilant verbs. For example, there are 33 types of non-sibilant verbs whose word frequency is from 1084 to 21. The -*(e)th* and -*(e)s* forms occur in 1103 tokens and 29 tokens respectively in EModE I for the 33 types. Thus -*(e)s* forms occur in 2.6% of the total tokens which are the sum of the occurrences of the -*(e)th* and -*(e)s* forms (1103 + 29) in EModE I.

Within the non-sibilant verbs, most of the -*(e)s* forms in EModE I (1500–70) occur in the most frequent 33 words, whose word frequency is from 1084 to 21. Only three words have -*(e)s* in EModE I among the 438 infrequent verbs. The change started slowly from a handful of high-frequency words. Holmqvist considers that *have, do,* and *say* are the laggers of the change, which has become a well-established view so far. But our data show that *have, do,* and *say* are by far the most frequent words, and that the most frequent verbs started to change first.

However, once the infrequent verbs got started, they changed more quickly than the frequent verbs. Most of the less frequent 176 verbs whose word frequency is from 20 to 3 show the -*(e)th* forms in EModE I. Many of them started to change in EModE II (1570–1640), and completed the change in EModE III (1640–1710). The least frequent 262 verbs whose word frequency is 2 or 1 never show the -*(e)s* forms in EModE I and rarely in EModE II. Many of them quickly changed

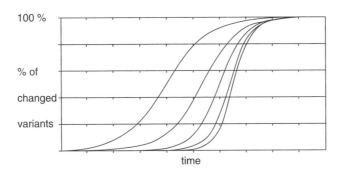

100 %

% of

changed

variants

time

Figure 23.3. An idealized diagram of snowball effect in lexical diffusion (Ogura and Wang 1996: 132; reproduced by permission of John Benjamins)

into the -*(e)s* forms and completed the change in EModE III. The -*(e)th* forms are rare in EModE III in the 438 infrequent verbs. On the other hand, the most frequent 33 verbs often still show the -*(e)th* forms in EModE III. The verbs *do* and *have*, in particular, show the -*(e)th* forms nearly 50% and more than 50% of the total tokens respectively in EModE III.

Figure 23.3 is an idealized diagram of the snowball effect in lexical diffusion. The abscissa shows the time and the ordinate shows the percentage of changed variants. Each S-curve represents the rate of change of each word through the population (S-diffusion), and the time interval between each word represents the rate of change through the lexicon (W-diffusion). The acceleration effects on the rate of change operate both through the population and the lexicon.

2.3 *Word frequency*

Our next task is to show that word frequency plays a role in determining the leaders and the laggers in W-diffusion. Hooper (1976) shows that reductive phonetic change such as schwa-deletion in the sequences -*ary*, -*ery*, -*ory* and -*ury* tends to affect high-frequency words first, whereas analogical change such as the weakening of strong verbs tends to affect low-frequency words first. Furthermore, she suggests that reductive sound change, affecting high-frequency words first, has its source in production, whereas analogical change in the leveling of strong verbs into weak ones is due to imperfect learning. Bybee (2002) discusses the problem further, based on the larger number of exemplars that could be found in experience.

Phillips (1984) distinguishes phonological change in (a) physiologically motivated changes, where the frequent words change first, and (b) non-physiologically motivated changes, where the infrequent words change first. She gives several instances of non-physiologically motivated changes which affect infrequent words first: the glide deletion after alveolar stops as in *tune, duke*, the unrounding of Middle English /ö(:)/, formation of diatones, that is, noun-verb pairs where the stress falls on the first syllable for the noun but the second (or third) syllable for the verb, as in *address, permit,* or *subject.* Phillips (2001; 2006) attempts to refine her hypothesis, namely that sound changes that require analysis – whether syntactic, morphological, or phonological – during their implementation affect the least frequent words first, while the rest affect the most frequent words first. However, the interaction between word frequency and environments operates not only in changes that affect the least frequent words first, but also in those that affect the most frequent words first, as already shown in the development of *-(e)s* in the third person singular present indicative and the changes mentioned below. Thus her remarks are factually incorrect.

Ogura (1987: 141–201) examines the interplay of phonetic factors and word frequency in the snowball effect of the shortening of Early Modern English /u:/, where the most frequent words change first. Ogura and Wang (1995) show that semantic change begins in the frequent words first, among synonymous words. Semantic change is a pragmatic process, that is, it is context-dependent. Thus it is in frequent words that semantic change is most likely to occur first. We may synthesize these investigations and assume that:

a) Productively or physiologically motivated change, pragmatically motivated change, and socially motivated change occur in high-frequency words first. Productively or physiologically motivated change and pragmatically motivated change are the result of linguistic production, and socially motivated change affects linguistic production externally. If all of these changes are concerned with linguistic production, words that are used frequently will have more opportunity to be affected by these processes.
b) Perceptually motivated change and cognitively motivated change affect low-frequency words first. Perceptually or cognitively unfavorable forms can be learned and maintained in their unfavorable forms if they are of high frequency in the input. However, if their frequency of use is low, they may not be sufficiently available in experience to be acquired. Thus they may be more susceptible to change on the basis of perceptually or cognitively favorable forms.

Words that are used frequently are experienced with corresponding frequency by language users, so frequent words spread through interactions among people. When a change starts from high-frequency words, it takes a long time to complete because the unchanged variants of high-frequency words are maintained, so frequent words also tend to become laggers, as shown in the development of *-(e)s* in the third person singular present indicative. When the change starts from low-frequency words, speakers observe unchanged variants of high-frequency words for a long time, and the high-frequency words become laggers of the change.

The directions for lexical diffusion with regard to word frequency may yield some evidence concerning the actuation of change. There is a great divergence of views on the origin of periphrastic *do,* where the change started in infrequent verbs. Most of the views have been summarized by Ellegård (1953) and Visser

(1963–73: 1411–17). We assume that the crucial factor in the development of the modal auxiliary was the collapse of the subjunctive mood in the course of Middle English (ME), which led to the use of modals in place of the subjunctive inflection. When the modals lost their status as main verbs and became syntactic auxiliaries, appearing in the INFL[ection] position, which contains tense and agreement, main verbs were no longer raised to the INFL position, and the tense marking of main verbs was effected via a transfer of the affix from INFL to the verb in its deep structure position. This transfer was blocked by the sentence negator *not*, and periphrastic *do* was inserted to provide lexical support for the affixes in INFL in negative declaratives. Periphrastic *do* arose from cognitively motivated changes affecting the underlying structure. Several views have been presented on the origin of *-(e)s* in the third person singular present indicative, where the change started in the most frequent verbs. We assume that the change must have been motivated socially, perhaps as an adoption from Old Norse (ON) in the face-to-face interactions of ordinary English people with their Danish counterparts (see section 3.4.2).

Finally, we would like to explain the rapid mid-stream change of S-curve progress. Ogura (1995) shows, based on the development of ME /i:/ and ME /u:/ words at 311 sites in England, that there is no significant ordering relation among words through which the change moves quickly in mid-stream, and the order of the change of words varies among individuals. Gell-Mann (1992) was perhaps the first to suggest the relevance of Kolmogorov Complexity to the study of language evolution. Kolmogorov Complexity favors the development of methods for inductive inference, based on the search for the simplest interpretation of observed data, and has been applied to representations of any kind: logical, linguistic, probabilistic, or pictorial. When regularity exists in the observed data, the hypothesis will capture this regularity, when justified, and allow for generalization beyond what was observed. Thus we assume that speakers, after they observe a small number of changed words, generalize the change into more and more words without necessarily having observed all the relevant words, with the result that the order of the generalization varies among individuals. By an appeal to the concept of Kolmogorov Complexity the rapid mid-stream change can be explained as a kind of phase transition.

3. Social Networks in S-diffusion

3.1 *Social networks*

All complex adaptive systems consist of a network of interacting agents, and the structures of networks determine the spread of, for example, information and diseases (see also Chapter 18 in this *Handbook*) The random network theory of Erdos and Rényi (1959), as shown in Figure 23.4c, has dominated scientific thinking about networks since its introduction in 1959. Granovetter (1973), however, proposed that society is structured into highly connected clusters by strong ties,

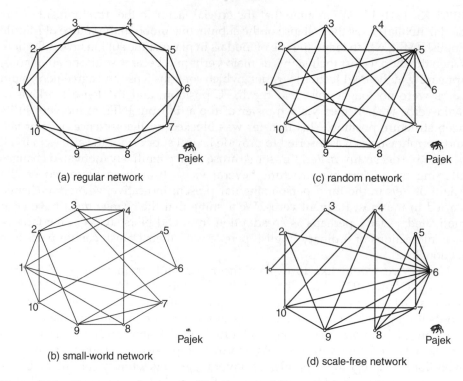

(a) regular network

(c) random network

(b) small-world network

(d) scale-free network

Figure 23.4.   Four types of networks (Ke, Gong, and Wang 2004 version)

and a few external links connect these clusters to other networks by weak ties. This is the model Lesley Milroy (1980/1987) and James and Lesley Milroy (1985) used in their analysis of Belfast vernacular.

Based on the analysis of large-scale complex networks in the real world, researchers have recently found two new types of network: small-world networks and scale-free networks. To explain the ubiquity of clustering in most real networks, Watts and Strogatz (1998) proposed a small-world network that reconciled high clustering with the haphazard character of random network. They started from a circle of nodes, where each node is connected to its immediate and next-nearest neighbors in a regular network, as shown in Figure 23.4a. To make this world a small one, a few regular links were rewired, connected to randomly selected nodes, as shown in Figure 23.4b. These long-range links offer the crucial shortcuts between distant nodes, shortening the average length between all nodes.

Barabási and Albert (1999) proposed the scale-free network shown in Figure 23.4d. This model brings together Erdos and Rényi's (1959) random network with Granovetter's (1973) clustered society. Each network starts from a small nucleus and expands with the addition of new nodes. These new nodes, when deciding where to link, prefer the nodes that have more links. Because of growth and preferential attachment, a few hubs, that is, nodes with a large number of links, emerge. The degree, or number of links of a node, follows a power law, in which most nodes have only a few links held together by a few highly connected hubs.

In this section we investigate how different structures of social networks affect functionally biased and socially biased change. Our analysis combines simulated and historical data from English. To the best of our knowledge, this is the first attempt to connect recently-developed network theory to large-scale historical change. Our historical data constitute the empirical basis for theories (Ogura 1990, Ogura and Wang 2004, 2008), and computer simulations allow us to create scenarios in which a large number of entities interact in an observable way (Wang and Minett 2005).

Labov (2001: 325–65) is critical of social network studies by L. Milroy (1980/1987), J. Milroy and L. Milroy (1985), J. Milroy (1992) and others, because they assume that social networks would replace other measurements based on such social variables as class, age, gender, and ethnicity, and because most of them are devoted to one or two isolated groups of around a dozen speakers. We assume that such social variables as class, age, gender, and ethnicity are the factors that actuate changes. Social networks are really concerned with the implementation of changes, though they are closely associated with other social variables.[2] So far, social network studies have focused on change in progress and a limited number of speakers. We would like to examine the long-term effects of large-scale social networks on historical change by using both simulated and empirical data.

3.2   Computational modeling of social networks and language change

Ke, Gong, and Wang (2004/2008) examine the effects of different types of social networks on diffusion processes by simulation. They construct a learning model, which is a modification of Nettle (1999b). Each agent is included in an age stage from 1 to 5. Agents at stage 1 are infants who only learn from their teachers; agents at stage 2 both learn and teach others. Agents at both stages 1 and 2 are learners, and a critical period for the learning of language is assumed. Agents at stages 3–5 are adults, who only teach learners. The ratio between adults and learners is 3:2. After each time step, all agents advance in age by one stage. After stage 5, agents die, and new infants at stage 1 are born, so that the population size never changes.

We give an illustration of the way how a learner learns from his connected neighbors. When there are both 'u' (unchanged) and 'c' (changed) forms in the input, the learner will learn a form which has a higher fitness. The fitness of a form is measured by a function of incorporating the functional value and the frequency of that form in the learner's connected neighborhood. For example, in a network with 10 agents as shown in Figure 23.5, the learner with a black dot is connected with 4 agents, three of which use 'u''s and one of which uses 'c.' If the functional values for 'c' and 'u' are 4 and 1, then the learner will learn the 'c' form, because fitness value for 1 'c' is 4 (= 4 × 1) and that for 3 'u''s is 3 (= 1 × 3).

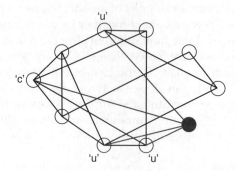

Figure 23.5.   Learning model (Ke, Gong, and Wang 2004 version)

Ke, Gong, and Wang (2004/2008) only consider functional bias as a learning strategy, but we can extend their model to a socially biased change. The difference is that functional bias is an unconscious non-intentional functional selection by learners, while social bias is intentional interaction among learners.

Figure 23.6 shows the diffusion dynamics in four types of networks under three conditions. In all conditions the network size (N) is 500 agents, and the average number of links for each agent (k) is 20. The x axis is the number of generations, and the y axis is the percentage of changed forms used by the population. The results of 20 runs are shown for each condition. Functional or social bias is varied, and the number of innovators is determined for each condition such that the innovation can spread throughout in the whole population:

Condition 1 Functional or social bias (B) is 20 and there is only 1 innovator (I).
Condition 2 Functional or social bias is 10 and there are 10 innovators.
Condition 3 Functional or social bias is 2 and there are 100 innovators.

When we compare the diffusion processes of a small-world network and a scale-free network under each condition, we find that the differences between them become greater as functional or social bias becomes weaker. Under Condition 1, both networks show a sharp S-curve. Under Condition 2, both networks show an S-curve pattern of diffusion, but a small-world network shows a slower rate. Under Condition 3, a small-world network shows a gradual diffusion, while a scale-free network shows an S-curve diffusion, though there are many unsuccessful diffusions. Thus, we may assume that the weaker the functional or social bias, the greater the effects of different network structures on diffusion processes of change.

3.3   Case studies: functionally biased change

Linguistic selection is unconscious functional selection between available variants by learners. Languages become adapted to the productive, perceptual, and cognitive abilities of human beings in their transmission across generations. Languages

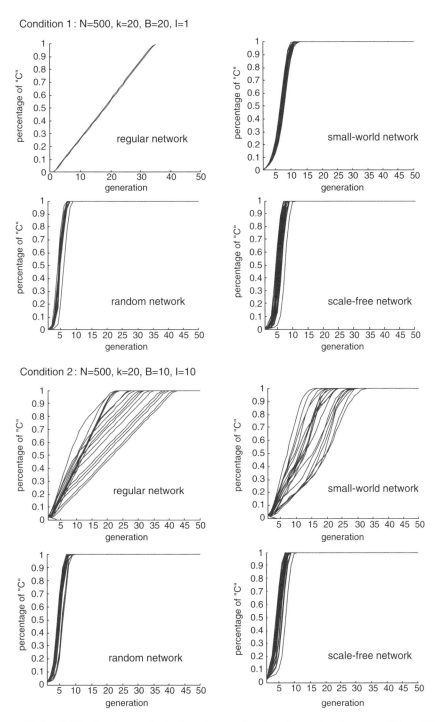

Figure 23.6. Diffusion dynamics in four types of networks under three conditions (Ke, Gong, and Wang 2004/2008: 940–42; reproduced by permission of Global Science Press)

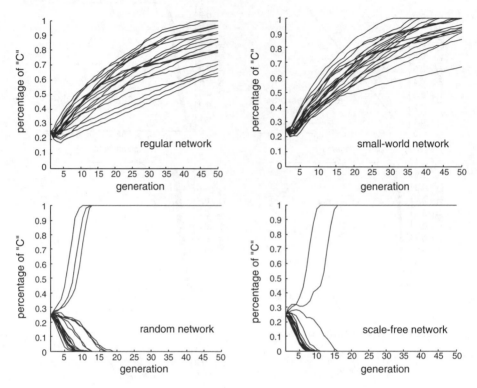

Figure 23.6.   (*Contiued*)

tend towards uniformity, because every language will discover the same optimal functionally-selected compromise (Nettle 1999b: 33).

For instance, the driving force of the Great Vowel Shift, which appeared in the thirteenth century and was complete by the sixteenth, is maximum perceptual contrast among the vowels in the system. The word order change from OV to VO in Old English is an adaptation to a perceptual constraint on center-embedding. Simplification of noun and verb declensions in Middle English is the result of imperfect learning of English by Scandinavian settlers. The extension of the verbal noun *-ing(e)* ending to the present participle form *-and(e)*, *-end(e)* and *-ind(e)* in Middle English was actuated by the interaction between imperfect learning by the child and perceptual saliency (for details, see Ogura 1990; Ogura and Wang 2004; 2008).

We do not recognize any differences in these changes between the diffusion patterns in London and other parts of the country. In contrast, the rapid spread of new forms throughout the country suggests a rather strong functional bias. Before 1500 the vast majority of the population lived in the country, though internal migration was common and urbanization was on the increase (Nevalainen and Raumolin-Brunberg 2003: 34–35). We may assume that this rural and agricultural society formed a small-world network. The above changes correspond to the case of a small-world network under Condition 2 in Figure 23.6.

3.4 Case studies: socially biased change

The changes arising from social factors spread by cooperation through the interactions of individuals. The size of the neighborhood determines the number of individuals that interact, and socially influential people have an increased probability of being imitated by their neighbors. Hence, successful changes spread locally. Without socially influential people, a considerable number of innovators are necessary for the change to spread.

3.4.1 Change by socially influential people Speakers model themselves on those with whom they wish to associate and identify, and with whom their aspirations are bound up (Nettle 1999a: 100). Socially influential people are from time to time the bearers of new variants. Even rare variants get adopted and spread through entire communities in an S-shaped curve, and convergence is rapid.

An example is the development of West Germanic **a* before nasals in the Mercian speech community. Toon (1983) finds evidence of the shift from *a* to *o* in Mercia and suggests that Mercian political domination could effect the same change in Kent. The data from Kentish charters before the period of Mercian control are scant but unanimously use *a* forms. However, there is a change in the charters produced under Mercian domination, which almost exclusively have *o* spellings between 803 and 824. Lowe (2001) criticizes Toon's dating of the charters after 833, when Mercian influence began to decline. Toon's statistics should be revised, but we still find that charters dating from 833–50 and 859–68 show fluctuations between *o* and *a*, in favor of *o* and *a* respectively. It must be noted that under Mercian control in 803–24 the change spread very quickly. The rapid change from *a* to *o* without the coexistence of an older form suggests a strong social bias (see also Chapter 13 in this *Handbook*). The change corresponds to a case under Condition 1 in Figure 23.6. Network structures do not affect the diffusion processes, and we cannot see any difference between a small-world network and a scale-free network.

3.4.2 Change by a massive immigration flow The effects of different structures of a small-world network and a scale-free network can be recognized clearly in the development of *-(e)s* in the third person singular present indicative. The *-(e)s* form first emerged in the tenth century in Northumbrian texts. The change had not yet spread even to the northernmost part of the East Midlands at the beginning of the thirteenth century, but in the course of the thirteenth and fourteenth centuries the *-(e)s* form gradually displaced the old ending over the whole of Lincolnshire (Holmqvist 1922: 49–73). In the century from 1350 to 1450, *-th* was the regular ending in Norfolk, but we can also find *-(e)s* there (Holmqvist 1922: 49–73, 100–17;

McIntosh, Samuels, and Benskin 1986: Vol. I, Maps 645 and 646). Thomason and Kaufman (1988: 37–45) state that if there is strong long-term cultural pressure from source-language speakers on the borrowing-language speaker group, structural features may be borrowed as well, including features of inflectional morphology. We assume that the -(e)s form is an adoption from ON during the course of face-to-face interactions between ordinary English people and their Danish counterparts. They formed a small-world network and the diffusion occurred gradually in the area of Danish settlements. This is a case of small-world network under condition 3 in Figure 23.6, with little social bias and a large number of innovators.

Based on *The Corpus of Early English Correspondence*, Nevalainen and Raumolin-Brunberg (2003: 157–84) show the replacement of -(e)th by -(e)s in verbs other than *have* and *do* in London (the City, the suburbs outside the walls, and Southwark), the Court (among members of the royal family, courtiers, and other high-ranking government officials), East Anglia, and the North. Their findings are reproduced in Figure 23.7.

In the latter half of the fifteenth century, -(e)s is the majority form in the North and is also found in one third of the cases in London. But, surprisingly, in the first half of the sixteenth century, the data show a sudden dip of -(e)s in the North and London. We assume that this increased occurrence of -(e)th in the North was a change brought about by influential people of the upper ranks in London, and that it was a superposed dialect. In London, the diffusion of -(e)s took about 80 years at the start of the diffusion process from the sub-period 1500–39 to 1580–1619, partly because of the -th form from the upper ranks, and partly because of the high probability of unsuccessful diffusions of the -(e)s with little social bias in a scale-free network. But the diffusion of the -(e)s form gained ground, and its sudden take-off, when a great number of verbs were affected, took place during

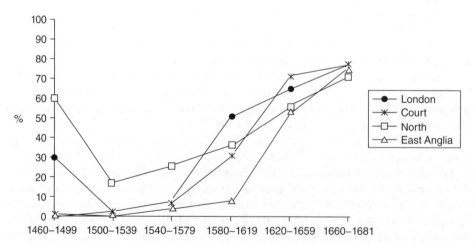

Figure 23.7.　Replacement of -(e)th by -(e)s in verbs other than *have* and *do* (Nevalainen and Raumolin-Brunberg 2003: 178; reproduced by permission of Longman Pearson Education)

40 years or so in the sub-periods 1580–1619 to 1620–59. The change started from the lower ranks (Nevalainen and Raumolin-Brunberg 2003: 144), and was the result of a large number of migrants to the capital from the North. The Court was slow in adopting the *-(e)s* form, but once it started to change, it changed faster, which shows a snowball effect. The gradual increase in the *-(e)s* form in the North should also be noted; this is different from the S-curve diffusion in London, the Court, and East Anglia. This can be explained by the existence of a small-world network in the North.

The growth of London in the late sixteenth and seventeenth centuries was remarkable. The number of inhabitants in the late Middle Ages was about 50 000, growing to c. 200,000 in 1600 and to 500,000 by 1700.[3] London's growth depended on a steady flow of migrants. Sixteenth and seventeenth century court records suggest that only 15% of Londoners were born there (Coleman and Salt 1992: 27). One English adult in eight in 1550–1650 and one in six in 1650–1750 had some experience of life in London (Wrigley 1967: 49). In the late fifteenth and sixteenth centuries a large number of the immigrants came from the North. The number of apprentices sent from the North to London was high until the seventeenth century. Power's study (1986), based on John Stow's *Survey of London* (1603) testifies to occupational clustering. This phenomenal growth of the population gave rise to changes in the social network structures of London, forming a scale-free network. The change started from the lower ranks, occupied by laborers from the North, and diffused rapidly, constituting an instance of a scale-free network under Condition 3 in Figure 23.6, where most people have only a small number of links, held together by a small number of highly connected people.

4. Conclusion

After presenting some theoretical preliminaries in section 1, we dealt with S-curve change in W-diffusion in Section 2, basing our discussion on historical data from English. We also discussed the so-called snowball effect: the later the change, the more words change, and words that change later, change faster. The relation with word frequency was also considered.

Section 3 dealt with the role of social networks in S-diffusion. We examined how different structures of social networks affect both functionally biased and socially biased changes based on the evidence afforded by both simulation and historical data from English. We showed that the weaker the functional or social bias, the greater the effects of different network structures on diffusion processes of change.

Acknowledgements

I wish to thank William S-Y. Wang for helpful suggestions and comments. I am also grateful to the editors for valuable comments. The research in this chapter is supported by grants from the Human Frontier Science Program and the Ministry of Education, Culture, Sports, Science and Technology of Japan.

NOTES

1   For criticisms of Kroch's view, see Ogura (1993).
2   On actuation and implementation of change, see Chen and Wang (1975).
3   The sources for these population estimates are Beier and Finlay (1986: 3), Finlay and Shearer (1986: 39), Rappaport (1989: 61), and Coleman and Salt (1992: 27).

REFERENCES

Barabási, A.-L. and Albert, R. (1999) Emergence of scaling in random networks. *Science* 286: 509–12.

Beier, A.L. and Finlay, R. (1986) The significance of the metropolis. In A.L. Beier and R. Finlay (eds.), pp. 1–33.

Beier, A.L. and Finlay, R. (eds.) (1986) *London 1500–1700: The Making of the Metropolis*, Longman, London and New York.

Bybee, J. (2002) Word frequency and context of use in the lexical diffusion of phonetically conditioned sound change. *Language Variation and Change* 14: 261–90.

Chen, M.Y. (1972) The time dimension: contribution toward a theory of sound change. *Foundations of Language* 8: 457–98.

Chen, M.Y. and Wang, W.S.-Y. (1975) Sound change: actuation and implementation. *Language* 51: 255–81.

Coleman, D. and Salt, J. (1992) *The British Population: Patterns, Trends, Processes*, Oxford University Press, Oxford.

Ellegård, A. (1953) *The Auxiliary Do: The Establishment and Regulation of its Use in English*, Almqvist and Wiksell, Stockholm.

Erdos, P. and Rényi, A. (1959) On random graphs I. *Publicationes Mathematicae (Debrecen)* 6(2): 290–97.

Finlay, R. and Shearer, B. (1986) Population growth and suburban expansion. In A.L. Beier and R. Finlay (eds.), pp. 37–59.

Gell-Mann, M. (1992) Complexity and complex adaptive systems. In J.A. Hawkins

and M. Gell-Mann (eds.), *The Evolution of Human Language*, Addison-Wesley Redwood City, CA, pp. 3–18.

Granovetter, M. (1973) The strength of weak ties. *American Journal of Sociology* 78: 1360–80.

Hockett, C.F. (1950) Age-grading and linguistic continuity. *Language* 26: 449–57.

Holmqvist, E. (1922) *On the History of the English Present Inflections Particularly -th and –s*, Carl Winter, Heidelberg.

Hooper, J. (1976) Word frequency in lexical diffusion and the source of morphophonological change. In W. Christie (ed.), *Current Progress in Historical Linguistics*, North Holland, Amsterdam, pp. 95–105.

Ke, J., Gong, T., and Wang, W.S.-Y. (2004/2008) Language change and social networks. *Communications in Computational Physics* 3(4): 935–49. [An early version was presented at the International Conference on the Evolution of Language in Leipzig, 2004.]

Kroch, A. (1989) Reflexes of grammar in patterns of language change. *Language Variation and Change* 1: 199–244.

Labov, W. (1994) *Principles of Linguistic Change, Vol.1: Internal Factors*, Blackwell, Oxford.

Labov, W. (2001) *Principles of Linguistic Change, Vol. 2: Social Factors*, Blackwell, Oxford.

Lowe, K.A. (2001) On the plausibility of Old English dialectology: the ninth-century Kentish charter material. *Folia Linguistica Historica* 32: 67–102.

McIntosh, A., Samuels, M.L., and Benskin, M. (1986) *A Linguistic Atlas of Late Medieval English (LALME)*. Vols. 1–4, Aberdeen University Press, Aberdeen.

Milroy, J. (1992) *Linguistic Variation and Change: On the Historical Sociolinguistics of English*, Blackwell, Oxford.

Milroy, J. and Milroy, L. (1985) Linguistic change, social network and speaker innovation. *Journal of Linguistics* 21: 339–84.

Milroy, L. (1980/1987) *Language and Social Networks* (2nd edn), Blackwell, Oxford.

Nettle, D. (1999a) Using social impact theory to simulate language change. *Lingua* 108: 95–117.

Nettle, D. (1999b) *Linguistic Diversity*, Oxford University Press, Oxford.

Nevalainen, T. (2006) Historical sociolinguistics and language change. In A. van Kemenade and B. Los (eds.), *Handbook of the History of English*, Blackwell, Oxford, pp. 558–88.

Nevalainen, T. and Raumolin-Brunberg, H. (2003) *Historical Sociolinguistics: Language Change in Tudor and Stuart England*, Longman, London.

Ogura, M. (1987) *Historical English Phonology: A Lexical Perspective*, Kenkyusha, Tokyo.

Ogura, M. (1990) *Dynamic Dialectology: A Study of Language in Time and Space*, Kenkyusha, Tokyo.

Ogura, M. (1993) The development of periphrastic *do* in English: a case of lexical diffusion in syntax. *Diachronica* 10: 51–85.

Ogura, M. (1995) The development of Middle English *i:* and *u:* a reply to Labov (1992, 1994). *Diachronica* 12: 31–53.

Ogura, M. and Wang, W.S.-Y. (1995) Lexical diffusion in semantic change: with special reference to universal changes. *Folia Linguistica Historica* 16: 29–73.

Ogura, M. and Wang, W.S.-Y. (1996) Snowball effect in lexical diffusion: the development of -*s* in the third person singular present indicative in English. In D. Britton (ed.), *English Historical Linguistics 1994: Papers from the 8th International Congress on English Historical Linguistics*, John Benjamins, Amsterdam, pp. 119–41.

Ogura, M. and Wang, W.S.-Y. (1998) Evolution theory and lexical diffusion. In J. Fisiak and M. Krygier (eds.), *Advances in English Historical Linguistics*, Mouton de Gruyter, Berlin, pp. 315–44.

Ogura, M. and Wang, W.S.-Y. (2004) Dynamic dialectology and complex adaptive system. In M. Dossena and R. Lass (eds.), *Methods and Data in English Historical Dialectology*, Peter Lang, Bern, pp. 137–70.

Ogura, M. and Wang, W.S.-Y. (2008) Dynamic dialectology and social networks. In M. Dossena, R. Dury, and M. Gotti (eds.), *English Historical Linguistics 2006, Vol. III: Geo-Historical Variation in English*, John Benjamins, Amsterdam, pp. 131–51.

Phillips, B.S. (1984) Word frequency and the actuation of sound change. *Language* 60: 320–42.

Phillips, B.S. (2001) Lexical diffusion, lexical frequency, and lexical analysis. In J. Bybee and P. Hopper (eds.), *Frequency and the Emergence of Linguistic Structure*, John Benjamins, Amsterdam, pp. 123–36.

Phillips, B.S. (2006) *Word Frequency and Lexical Diffusion*, Palgrave Macmillan, New York.

Power, M.J. (1986) The social topography of Restoration London. In A.L. Beier and R. Finlay (eds.), pp. 199–233.

Rappaport, S. (1989) *Worlds within Worlds: Structures of Life in Sixteenth-century London*, Cambridge University Press, Cambridge.

Shen, Z. (1990) Lexical diffusion: a population perspective and a mathematical model. *Journal of Chinese Linguistics* 18(1): 159–200.

Sturtevant, E.H. (1917) *Linguistic Change*, University of Chicago Press, Chicago.

Thomason, G.S. and Kaufman, T. (1988) *Language Contact, Creolization, and Genetic Linguistics*, University California Press, Berkeley.

Toon, T.E. (1983) *The Politics of Early Old English Sound Change*, Academic Press, New York.

Visser, F.Th. (1963–73) *An Historical Syntax of the English Language* 4 vols., E.J. Brill, Leiden.

Wang, W.S.-Y. (1969) Competing changes as a cause of residue. *Language* 45: 9–25.

Wang, W.S.-Y. and Minett, H. (2005). The invasion of language: emergence, change and death. *Trends in Ecology and Evolution*, 20(5): 263–69.

Watts, D.J. and Strogatz, S.H. (1998) Collective dynamics of 'small-world' networks. *Nature* 393: 440–42.

Wrigley, E.A. (1967) A simple model of London's importance in changing English society and economy 1650–1750. *Past and Present* 37: 44–70.

24 Innovation Diffusion in Sociohistorical Linguistics

DAVID BRITAIN

1. Using the Present to Explain the Past

The study of linguistic diffusion – how, both at the level of a person's social network ties and on a broader spatial scale, new linguistic structures spread from speaker to speaker and from community to community – has, like many other areas of historical sociolinguistics, developed by drawing heavily on present-day approaches and applying them to historical contexts from which we no longer have living speakers – *using the present to explain the past*. Just as Labov (1975, 1994) used contemporary techniques (sociolinguistic methods, spectrographic vowel analysis, etc.) to deconstruct the paradox of the apparent merger then demerger of long /aː/ and Early Modern English <ēa> spelt forms deriving from ME /ɛː/, so historical sociolinguistics, in order to examine feature spread, has applied present-day diffusion models to the spread of linguistic innovations of times past and has examined historical patterns of mobility and migration which (may help us to) account for those diffusions.

Labov (1975:850) argued, back in the early days of variationist sociolinguistics, not only that the 'rational character' of language could only be understood by "turning back to the secular world and to the real speakers in it," armed with the tools and technologies that the modern age had provided (such as recording devices, acoustic analysis, survey methodologies and reliable sample frames), but also that this approach and these tools could help us understand questions of the past too:

The Handbook of Historical Sociolinguistics, First Edition. Edited by Juan Manuel Hernández-Campoy and Juan Camilo Conde-Silvestre.
© 2014 John Wiley & Sons, Ltd. Published 2014 by John Wiley & Sons, Ltd.

We should have no hesitation in projecting this understanding to past events that are no longer accessible to direct observation. Granted that the world of everyday speech is rational, there is no reason to think that it was any less so in the past. If there are contradictions in the historical record, we have no doubt that they can be resolved: the most likely route to such a resolution is through a deeper understanding of the use of language in the ordinary world of the present. Only when we are thoroughly at home in that everyday world, can we expect to be at home in the past. (Labov 1975: 850)

Diffusion has been at the centre of the sociolinguistic enterprise from the very start. Weinreich, Labov, and Herzog (1968: 187) present the understanding of diffusion as one that should be "taken as central to our thinking" about language change, helping us to grasp the complexity of its variability and speed. Students of innovations that diffused centuries past have, as we shall see, listened carefully to Labov's appeal to project modern understandings, modern methodological approaches, and modern theoretical premises to past events.

In this chapter, I examine research on dialect diffusion in its sociohistorical context, focusing on what has often in the literature been referred to as 'expansion diffusion' – features spreading from person to person via everyday contacts and routine or relatively small-scale mobilities. 'Relocation diffusion' (the spread of features from one place to another by the migration of its speakers) is covered by Daniel Schreier in Chapter 29 in this *Handbook*, though it is recognized that the linguistic outcomes and the theoretical concerns of both are (very) similar (see Gerritsen 1988 for a discussion of relocation versus expansion diffusion).

It is highly questionable whether the distinction between relocation and expansion diffusion is a useful or theoretically sustainable one, since: (a) expansion diffusion involves mobilities, albeit rather mundane, everyday, routine ones (see Britain 2010a, 2012, 2013); some of these mobilities are hard to distinguish and tease apart[1]; and some forms of apparent relocation diffusion are small-scale and mundane (moving to the next village). The linguistic consequences of expansion diffusion are very similar in type, albeit perhaps less radical and dramatic, to those triggered by long-distance relocation diffusions that bring together radically distinct varieties of language. This chapter, though, in looking at smaller-scale and more mundane mobilities, contrasts with the rather more dramatic (sometimes forced) migrations of the relocation diffusion dealt with by Schreier, but theoretically they are from the same stable.

I begin by looking briefly at how social dialectologists today examine the diffusion of linguistic innovations (see further Britain 2012). This has traditionally involved two levels of inspection: firstly, examining the process of innovation itself – where is the innovator socially located in networks of speakers in communities? (the level of local interaction); and secondly, examining how scholars have modeled the spread of innovations from location to location – how does a feature spread from city A to town B to village C, for example? (the level of spatial diffusion). Then I investigate, in the context of some of the problems with present-day approaches, the difficulties that historical sociolinguists face in examining diffusion – quite understandably, they lack vital evidence in putting together the diffusion puzzle for contexts of innovation and diffusion that have long since passed. There follows a presentation of some of the rich historical sociolinguistic research which has examined diffusion.

2. Diffusion Modeling in Contemporary Social Dialectology

2.1 The innovator in the community

Milroy (1992:169) argued that there was an important distinction between 'innovation' on the one hand and 'change' on the other: an innovation, he suggests, is "an act of the speaker which is capable of influencing linguistic structure," whereas a change is a structural alteration in the language system. Adherence to this distinction has a number of consequences: firstly, it forces us to recognize that it is speakers that innovate and not languages – *speakers* create new linguistic forms (that may or may not be adopted by others), languages do not, so we must place speakers (and their positions in society, their networks, their mobilities) at center stage in our theorization; secondly, changes result from the spread of successful innovations, but there are also, necessarily, unsuccessful innovations that ultimately have no effect on the linguistic system; and thirdly, change can only be spotted *after* the act of speaker-innovation, and *after* the innovation has been embedded within the linguistic system through diffusion – diffusion then begins before change can be spotted (the act of successful innovation is not observable).

The sociolinguistic literature has been in some disagreement about the exact social locus of innovating individuals. Through different means, those working in the Labovian approach via social class, and the Milroyian approach via social network, came to agree that linguistic changes tended to be led by the 'central' classes in society – the upper working classes and the lower middle classes. Using social class approaches, it was found that whilst changes from above appeared to be embedded most in the grammars of the upper social class groups, it was the lower middle class groups that tended to push these changes forward most vigorously. Conversely, with changes from below, it was often the upper working class groups that were the most instrumental in their promotion[2]. Labov (2001: 32) called this the 'curvilinear hypothesis': "the crucial division in the society from the point of view of language change was not middle class vs. working class, but rather centrally located groups as against peripherally located groups." Meanwhile, examining change from the perspective of weak and strong social network ties, James and Lesley Milroy (Milroy and Milroy 1985) argued that change is most likely to spread in those sections of society where social network ties are weakest, and most likely to be resisted in those sections where network ties were stronger and more multiplex. They argued that weak ties were most probably characteristic of the central classes – the very same ones that Labov, Trudgill, and others had argued were leaders of change via a social class approach.

The disagreement in the contemporary sociolinguistic literature has emerged in locating innovators within social networks themselves (see Milroy 1992; Labov 2001). Milroy has argued that changes diffuse across weak links between strong networks: "weak ties between groups regularly provide bridges through which information and influence are diffused" (1992: 178). Labov, on the other hand, has argued that promoters of change are likely to be people who have strong ties, not just locally but also beyond: "the leaders are people who are not limited to their local networks, but have intimate friends in the wider neighborhood" (2001: 360; see further Britain 2012; and also Chapter 18 in this *Handbook*).

2.2   Spatial diffusion of innovations

While (urban) sociolinguistics expanded dramatically in the 1960s and 1970s, the investigation of spatial aspects of language change did not. Labov, in a reflection on the first twenty years of variationist sociolinguistics, claimed that "the study of heterogeneity in space has not advanced at the same tempo as research in single communities" (Labov 1982: 42), and since the study of spatial diffusion necessitated a multilocality perspective, few sociolinguistic scholars worked in this field, with Peter Trudgill and Jack Chambers being highly notable, but somewhat lonely, exceptions. Indeed, in their own retrospective on geolinguistics in the first edition of *Dialectology* (Chambers and Trudgill 1980: 205–7), they admitted that the field was still very much in its infancy. I examine some of the reasons for this theoretical lag elsewhere (Britain 2009a, 2009b).

Sociolinguistic approaches to the spatial paths by which innovations diffuse have drawn largely from economic geography, adopting models which have been used, for example, to examine the adoption of new agricultural technologies, of motor-cars, or of new medicines. Trudgill's pioneering work (1974b), for example, draws on the Swedish socio-historical geographer Torsten Hägerstrand's work (1952) on the diffusion of the adoption of motor-cars in southern Sweden in the early twentieth century. Along with this economic geographical modeling of spatial diffusion, Trudgill also introduced to sociolinguistics the gravity model, a formula the aim of which was to allow us to predict the likely linguistic influence one place would have on another, bearing in mind their populations and their distances apart. He applied these techniques to examine the spread of phonological changes both in southern Norway and eastern England, and, recognizing that gravity models were not altogether unproblematic, adapted them to allow for the pre-existing linguistic similarity or otherwise of the two places being entered into the gravity model. These approaches have been extremely influential in the study of innovation diffusion, with many works drawing inspiration from his methods and from the gravity model approach (see, for example, Callary 1975; Bailey *et al.* 1993; Hernández-Campoy 1996, 1999, 2003; Kerswill 2003; Labov 2003; Larmouth 1981). As we will see, this approach has been influential in historical sociolinguistics too.

The literature has also proposed a number of different typologies of spatial paths along which innovations spread (see further Britain 2009a, 2010a, 2012):

- The wave model: innovations spread from origin point A in a wave action, reaching nearby places before more distant places, just as ripples spread out from the place where a stone is dropped into a pool of water. It is certainly an appealingly iconic model, but evidence for it is relatively limited: Trudgill (1986: 50–51), for example, proposes this as the mechanism behind the extremely slow advance in British English of the fronting of the STRUT vowel to the north of London in East Anglia (see also Labov 2003; Bailey *et al.* 1993).
- The urban hierarchy or cascade model: innovations spread from city to city and percolate down an urban hierarchy to towns, villages, and isolated settlements, arguably because interactions between cities are greater than between cities and their small town and rural hinterlands. Kerswill (2003) has argued that the urban hierarchy model is behind the spread of the fronting of both voiceless and voiced interdental fricatives in England (and beyond) (see also Trudgill 1986: 53–57; Hernández-Campoy 2003; Labov 2003; Callary 1975).
- The cultural hearth model: this has been proposed by Ron and Barbara Horvath (1997, 2001, 2002) to account for the behavior of changes such as /l/ vocalization in Australia, where the change appears to take hold first in both urban and rural areas in a focal area, before then spreading hierarchically beyond.
- The counterhierarchical model: changes diffuse *up* the urban hierarchy, beginning in rural areas, rather than *down* as the more commonly attested cascade model, above, suggests. The smoothing of triphthongs to diphthongs and long monophthongs in northern East Anglia is mentioned by Trudgill (1986: 47–50) as an example of such a diffusion in England.

The contemporary human geographical literature has not looked kindly on the adoption of innovation diffusion modeling in the Hägerstrandian vein, arguing that such approaches fail to "cut through the connective tissue of the world in such a way that its fundamental integrities are retained" (Gregory 1985: 28; see also Blaikie 1978; Gregory 1981/2000). Space precludes me from examining this critique in detail, but it centers around: i) the downplaying in much innovation diffusion work of the richness and complexity of social life and social interactions; ii) non-adoption of innovations being often regarded as the result of a lack of impulse of the innovation rather than the active rejection of it by communities of speakers; iii) a lack of sensitivity to the historical contingency of the factors which motivate innovations to diffuse in certain ways; and iv) a general avoidance (until recently) of conceptualizing innovation diffusion as a form of contact, whereby a new form and a conservative form clash, rather than as an exercise simply of replacing a conservative form with an innovative one (see further Trudgill 1986: 57–82; Britain 2009a, 2010b, 2012).

Another theme in current diffusion studies that has received recent impetus is the examination of the linguistic consequences of the diffusion of innovations on the linguistic system. Alongside adoption and rejection, processes associated with dialect contact and koineization are now being examined in the diffusion literature. Trudgill's (1986) dialect contact model had always conceptualized diffusion as a form of contact, likely to lead to similar outcomes as other forms of dialect contact (see above, and Chapter 29 in this *Handbook*), and he exemplified outcomes of diffusion that were clearly instances of koineization, such as interdialect, merger, and simplification. Labov (2007) contrasted the typologies of diffused changes with those associated with regular adult to child transmission of linguistic features. Through an examination of the linguistic contexts in which /a/ had been raised, he compared US communities that had adopted the change as a result of diffusion and migration with more stable urban contexts that had expanded and spread the change within the community itself. He found that they were typologically distinct – the former were of a simplifying kind, the latter showed regular, but small-scale incrementations of the contexts in which the new variant of raised /a/ could be found. His work therefore reiterated the view that diffusion had linguistic consequences, not just for the conservative form being eroded as a result of diffusion, but also for the diffusing innovation itself. That diffusion could lead to such simplification was not new, but Labov's demonstration of the contrast between diffusion and transmission gave an important boost to research on the structural consequences of the former.

3. A Jigsaw with Missing Pieces: Diffusion and the Historical Paradox

Studies of spatial innovation diffusion in the contemporary sociolinguistic mold have relied on certain methodological approaches and certain types of evidence. Almost all examine evidence from the spoken language – see Labov (2003) for an exception in the sociolinguistic tradition of diffusion studies – emanating from speakers of different social backgrounds, as much as possible interacting in relatively informal 'styles.' All rely on evidencing diffusion as the "spatial diffusion of ratios" (Trudgill 1974b: 222), examining and comparing proportions of use of the different innovative and conservative variants in play. All involve collecting similarly stratified samples of data from a number of different locations in a similar way at a similar time. The work of Ron and Barbara Horvath is exemplary in this regard – very similar sets of recordings of similar reading passages and word-lists, containing relevant tokens of /l/ vocalization in different linguistic environments, all collected from similarly stratified samples of speakers in a large number of urban centers in Australia and New Zealand, all analyzed in the same way (1997, 2001, 2002, 2003).

But historical sociolinguists ply their trade in non-optimal conditions, of course, Labov (1982: 20; 1994: 11) describing the field as the "highly developed" art of "making the best use of bad data" (see Conde-Silvestre 2007: 35–40; and also Chapter 4 in this *Handbook*). He outlines a number of these non-optimal conditions: i) the fact that historical documents largely survive by luck and not by design: is the sample of data we have from period X in the past therefore representative of that period or not?; ii) the question of the gap between the written forms preserved in the historical documents and the actual speech of those writers, given what we know about speech–writing differences: do writers in period X in the past write in the same way as they speak, and what can these writings tell us about the masses as opposed to the literates? iii) the question of how consistently different writers represent the same sounds; iv) the question of the lack of negative evidence: does the fact that structural feature A is not found in the historical documents from period X mean that it was absent from the speech of that time, or simply that no documents that may have contained it survived to illustrate its presence? and v) the question of social structure and patterns of interaction: how different was the past from the present? how can we access the intimate complexities of social interactions in the way that, for example, present-day ethnographic work on communities of practice attempts to achieve?

The requirements of present-day diffusion studies are also difficult if not impossible for the historical sociolinguist to meet – there is no spoken data evidence, just indirect evidence of how the language may (but may not) have been spoken; the data available are not neatly stratifiable in the way a contemporary sociolinguistic corpus may be; some social classes are (much) better represented than others; we know less about the individuals themselves; and we do not have comparable amounts of data from a sufficient number of discrete locations to securely plot the geographical paths of diffusion.

But in many ways, the exploration of these issues in historical sociolinguistics is yet another demonstration of using the present to explain the past. We can examine what the present-day tells us that we need in order to conduct such work; we thereby realize the extent of the difficulties and gaps involved, and apply present-day findings to earlier times (for example, by learning from work on the differences between the spoken and written language or on the established patterns of social stratification in language variation), fully aware of the problems and proceeding cautiously in the circumstances[3]. Thereby, historical linguists piece together the puzzle of language change in the past, recognizing that very many of the pieces are missing, but learning from the present-day picture what the historical one may have looked like.

4. Putting the Pieces Together: Investigations in Historical Innovation Diffusion

Here, then, I present a few of the many studies that have examined the diffusion of innovations in the historical context, concentrating on the social positions of the innovators, their roles in their respective social networks, and the spatial diffusion of innovations in historical work based firmly on sociolinguistic principles.

4.1 Evidence for the curvilinear hypothesis

Raumolin-Brunberg (2006) examines the claim that changes begin in the central classes of society through an examination of three changes in progress from the early fifteenth to the early seventeenth centuries, namely the use of object pronoun *you* as a subject pronoun, the replacement of the third person present-tense suffix *-eth* with *-s*, and the use of *my* and *thy* in place of *mine* and *thine* in pre-vocalic positions (see also Raumolin-Brunberg and Nevalainen 2007). She finds that in the case of *you* and *-s*, change did indeed, according to the *Corpus of Early English Correspondence* (CEEC 1998) data, begin in what she describes as the "interior social groups [...] middle-ranking people" (2006: 131; see also Nevalainen and Raumolin-Brunberg 2003: 149, Nevalainen 1996: 73). It turns out this grouping comprises merchants and lawyers, who are, in her classification, immediately below the nobility and royalty. She shows that some of the changes spread from these 'middle ranks' to lower-ranking groups – such as the use of *-s* – and others spread from the middle upwards – such as the use of *you* as a subject pronoun (Raumolin-Brunberg 2006: 122). Interestingly, Conde-Silvestre and Hernández-Campoy (2004), in an investigation of the diffusion of incipient standard spellings in the fifteenth century, also argue for the critical role of lawyers and contact with the legal profession in the promotion of diffusion, as does Nevalainen (2000: 355) herself, in work highlighting lawyers as the promoters of single as opposed to multiple negation. One question that arises from this apparently important inno-vating role for lawyers across these studies is whether this group really was socio-linguistically more innovative in general, or whether the finding stems from their important position in the written linguistic marketplace as language 'brokers,' having to routinely command a range of written styles addressed to a range of different audiences.

4.2   Innovation in weak or strong network ties?

Through an examination of the usage rates of different changes at different stages in their progress, Raumolin-Brunberg (2006) is neatly able to tease apart the puzzle over the likely strength of network ties of those who are the most likely to be innovators. She showed that when the changes were at the incipient stage[4], the leaders (individuals using the innovation more than 30% of the time) were usually individuals whose social histories suggest a good deal of mobility and many but rather weak network connections into their local communities. These findings appear to support Milroy's (1992) position with respect to the role of network strength in innovation promotion. However, she then contrasts this finding with an examination of so-called 'new and vigorous leaders' (individuals using the innovation more than 50% of the time at a stage of the change's progress where the average use of the innovation is between 15% and 30%). This group of indi-viduals comprises, she claims, largely influential, central figures, with strong and multiplex connections within their social networks, supporting Labov's (2001) view, discussed earlier, that leaders are people with "a high degree of interaction within the block they live in and a large proportion of wider contacts off the block" (Raumolin-Brunberg 2006: 131). Perhaps, she argues, these positions are not in conflict after all, but are reflective of different stages in the life-cycle of a linguistic change.

4.3   *Evidence for spatial patterning of innovation diffusion*

Here, it must be said, the historical sociolinguistic evidence is less detailed and less able to provide evidence in favor of one or other of the different spatial models outlined above. Whilst there is great evidence of diffusion of forms from one place to another, such research seems characterized by place categories so large-scale that it is difficult to ascertain where exactly the locus of the change may have been, whether that locus was urban or rural, or, importantly here, whether the change diffused hierarchically, or in a wave-like way, or in some other manner. Nevalainen and Raumolin-Brunberg (2003), for instance, examined London's role as a 'magnet' in comparison to 'East Anglia (Norfolk and Suffolk)' and 'the North.' Of course this is largely the result of a lack of sufficient data, but does haze attempts at more fine-tuned diffusion modeling.

Their extensive historical sociolinguistic work shows ample evidence of the direction of linguistic innovations, however. Two changes diffusing southwards from the North to London were third person singular -*s* and the use of *my* and *thy* in place of *mine* and *thine* (see also Raumolin-Brunberg 2006; Raumolin-Brunberg and Nevalainen 2007). East Anglia, however, seemingly 'in between' 'the North' and London, was not affected by these innovations at this stage, and this prompted the Helsinki researchers (2003: 178) to suggest that this was an example of the urban hierarchy effect in action, with the innovation 'hopping' from the North to the South, missing the intervening East Anglia. Whilst this is an appealing hypothesis, I am not sure it is a sustainable one, for the reason, simply, that the parts of East Anglia under investigation, Norfolk and Suffolk, are not 'in between' the North and London at all, but were somewhat sheltered from influence along the North-to-London route by the fenlands. Bergs (2006: 20–21) presents maps showing that road connections between East Anglia and the North were poor, that the road route to East Anglia from the North involved almost coming as far south as London before heading north(east)wards again, and that the fenlands made a more direct East Anglia to the North route rather problematic –see Britain (2001) on role of the fenlands as barrier, linguistic and social. In essence, East Anglia was, by road at least, further away from the North than London, and the fact that it received -*s* forms later is not unexpected but is not in itself evidence of the urban hierarchy in action. In contrast with -*s* and *my/thy*, however, Nevalainen and Raumolin-Brunberg (2003: 170) find that the use of the present plural indicative *are* form of BE did diffuse from the North to East Anglia before reaching London, a diffusion they argue 'percolated' southwards.

They also show (2003) that, like today, the linguistic influence of London on its hinterland was immense (see also Nevalainen and Raumolin-Brunberg 2000). A number of variables that they studied in the *Corpus of Early English Correspondence* (CEEC) provided evidence of London leading the way, but in many cases it appears it was the influence of the Court that was crucial: the use of subject pronoun *you* was vigorously adopted both in London and in the Court (2003: 172), but an innovative gerundive form (2003: 173), single negation (2003: 175), relative pronoun *which* (2003: 176) and preposition + *wh-* (2003: 177) were all most vigorously adopted by the Court, with London often lagging well behind.

So historical sociolinguistic work, lacking the depth of data from a number of distinct individual sites that enables multi-locality diffusion studies, has not (yet at least) been so readily able to refine our understandings of the geographic routes of innovation diffusions.

5. Conclusion

When systematic, corpus-based, sociolinguistically-informed variation analysis is carried out, it is clear that we can draw significant insights from historical patterns of variation, despite the problematic nature of the data we have to work with, and it is clear that many findings that we have accumulated through empirical work in contemporary communities appear to hold true in historical contexts too. Research such as that carried out on the *Corpus of Early English Correspondence* (CEEC) has highlighted, for example, the robustness of the curvilinear hypothesis, the origins of linguistic change in the central social classes of society, and may even have helped to resolve debates around the network structures that 'support' the promoters of linguistic changes, by distinguishing between changes in the incipient stages – which seem to be led by speakers with weak networks as predicted by Milroy (1992) – and those in the (later) new and vigorous stages, led by speakers with strong networks both locally and beyond (supporting Labov's 2001 view). The promotion sites of some linguistic changes have also been isolated to some degree, highlighting the important role of the Court and of the legal profession (perhaps reflecting the inevitably written nature of the data), of London on its hinterland, but also of the North, not only the site of some linguistic features which made their way to the capital, but also the home of many thousands of migrants to London at the time.

This significant influence of the North on London, not a characteristic of twenty-first century English (as far as we know at this point and with our current knowledge), reminds us, however, of a very important principle that contemporary diffusion modeling has largely ignored – innovations are speaker-led, and to track their geographical journeys we need to track the speakers who use them. Our studies of demographic history tell us that human mobility patterns are historically contingent, and we should, therefore, expect to find different diffusion routes depending on the predominant migratory and mobility patterns at that particular point in history. Throughout the period covered by the data in the *Corpus of Early English Correspondence*, 1400–1680, migration to the ever-growing London was significant and dramatic, and this trend continued right through to the early twentieth century, with other urban centers joining in to benefit from the rural exodus from the time of the Industrial Revolution onwards. That the North, a significant donor of migrants to London, has influenced the capital linguistically, should not be seen as surprising in the context of this demography. But these migration patterns no longer hold. Northern Europe in general but Britain in particular have been experiencing more than half a century of counter-urbanization, with millions of urbanites escaping to the countryside, presumably carrying their dialects with them. Bergs (2006: 28) argued that, perhaps more important than establishing evidence for the urban hierarchy model or wave-like diffusion, is a sensitivity in diffusion studies to what he calls the "human thread," the "actual way(s) and path(s) of travelling speakers." The importance of such meaningful mobility is increasingly being recognized by geographers and social scientists (see Cresswell 2006; Urry 2007), though its implications for sociolinguistics are still being explored. Spatial patterns of innovation diffusion, if we are to take the *socio* in sociolinguistics seriously, if we fully take on board the idea that it is *speakers* who innovate and not languages, need to be able to reflect historical trends in human mobility and be flexible to local conditions created by those mobilities (Britain 2013). The patterns of innovation diffusion found in historical sociolinguistic work certainly enable us to see just how much the past can learn from the present. The past, however, can also remind those of us working on contemporary variation and change that our analytical and theoretical assumptions may well treat as universal processes which are in fact historically contingent, such as the geographical routes taken by new linguistic features. We need to conceptualize innovators 'on the move,' recognizing that throughout time they have not always moved in the same direction.

NOTES

1   For example, Champion, Coombes, and Brown (2009) show that commuting (often mentioned as a cause of *expansion* diffusion) and urban-to-rural home moves (as a migration, a type of *relocation* diffusion) are often engaged in by the very same people.
2   See, for example, the analysis of (r) in New York City, a change from above, in Labov (1966), and (e) in Norwich, a change from below, in Trudgill (1974a).
3   See Raumolin-Brunberg (1996) for an excellent discussion of the methodological problems that historical sociolinguistics faces, an account of 'using the present to explain the past' and an excellent summary of social, cultural, and linguistic conditions in the early modern English period.
4   In her data, the incipient stage is where, across the data set as a whole, the innovation was used in less than 15% of possible cases.

REFERENCES

Bailey, G., Wikle, T., Tillery, J., and Sand, L. (1993) Some patterns of linguistic diffusion. *Language Variation and Change* 3: 359–90.

Bergs, A. (2006) Spreading the word: patterns of diffusion in historical dialectology. In M. Filppula, J. Klemola, M. Palander, and E. Penttilä (eds.), *Topics in Dialectal Variation:*

Selection of Papers from the Eleventh International Conference on Methods in Dialectology, University of Joensuu Press, Joensuu, pp. 5–30.

Blaikie, P. (1978) The theory of the spatial diffusion of innovations: a spacious cul-de-sac. *Progress in Human Geography* 2: 268–95.

Britain, D. (2001) Welcome to East Anglia! two major dialect 'boundaries' in the Fens. In P. Trudgill and J. Fisiak (eds.), *East Anglian English*, Boydell and Brewer, Woodbridge, pp. 217–42.

Britain, D. (2009a) Language and space: the variationist approach. In P. Auer and J. Schmidt (eds.), *Language and Space: an International Handbook of Linguistic Variation*, Mouton de Gruyter, Berlin, pp. 142–62.

Britain, D. (2009b) 'Big bright lights' versus 'green and pleasant land'? The unhelpful dichotomy of 'urban' vs 'rural' in dialectology. In E. Al-Wer and R. de Jong (eds.), *Arabic Dialectology*, Brill, Leiden, pp. 223–48.

Britain, D. (2010a) Conceptualisations of geographic space in linguistics. In A. Lameli, R. Kehrein, and S. Rabanus (eds.), *The Handbook of Language Mapping*, Mouton de Gruyter, Berlin, pp. 69–97.

Britain, D. (2010b) Contact and dialectology. In R. Hickey (ed.), *The Handbook of Language Contact*, Blackwell, Oxford, pp. 208–29.

Britain, D. (2012) Diffusion. In A. Bergs and L. Brinton (eds.), *English Historical Linguistics: An International Handbook*, Berlin: Mouton de Gruyter, pp. 2031–2043.

Britain, D. (2013) The role of mundane mobility and contact in dialect death and dialect birth. In D. Schreier and M. Hundt (eds.), *English as a Contact Language*, Cambridge: Cambridge University Press, pp. 165–181.

Britain, D. and Cheshire, J. (eds.) (2003) *Social Dialectology: In Honour of Peter Trudgill*, John Benjamins, Amsterdam.

Callary, R. (1975) Phonological change and the development of an urban dialect in Illinois. *Language in Society* 4: 155–70.

CEEC = *Corpus of Early English Correspondence*. (1998) T. Nevalainen, H. Raumolin-Brunberg, J. Keränen, M. Nevala, A. Nurmi, and M. Palander-Collin, Department of English, University of Helsinki. http://www.helsinki.fi/varieng/CoRD/corpora/CEEC/index.html [accessed October 14, 2011].

Chambers, J.K. and Trudgill, P. (1980) *Dialectology* (1st edn), Cambridge University Press, Cambridge.

Champion, A., Coombes, M., and Brown, D. (2009) Migration and longer-distance commuting in rural England. *Regional Studies* 43: 1245–59.

Conde-Silvestre, J.C. (2007) *Sociolingüística histórica*, Gredos, Madrid.

Conde-Silvestre, J.C. and Hernández-Campoy, J.M. (2004) A sociolinguistic approach to the diffusion of Chancery written practices in late fifteenth-century private correspondence. *Neuphilologische Mitteilungen* 105: 133–52.

Cresswell, T. (2006) *On the Move: Mobility in the Modern Western World*, Routledge, London.

Gerritsen, M. (1988) Sociolinguistic developments as a diffusion process. In U. Ammon, N. Dittmar, and K. Mattheier (eds.), *Sociolinguistics: an International Handbook of the Science of Language and Society*, Berlin, Walter de Gruyter, pp. 1574–91.

Gregory, D. (1985) Suspended animation: the stasis of diffusion theory. In D. Gregory and J. Urry (eds.), *Social Relations and Spatial Structures*, Macmillan, London, pp. 296–336.

Gregory, D. (1981/2000) Diffusion. In R. Johnston, D. Gregory, G. Pratt, and M. Watts (eds.), *The Dictionary of Human Geography* (4th edn), Blackwell, Oxford, pp. 175–78.

Hägerstrand, T. (1952) *The Propagation of Innovation Waves*, Gleerup, Lund.

Hernández-Campoy, J.M. (1996) *Modelos de Difusión Geográfica de las Innovaciones Sociolingüísticas en los Acentos del Reino Unido*, Universidad de Murcia, Murcia.

Hernández-Campoy, J.M. (1999) Geolinguistic models of analysis of the spatial diffusion of sociolinguistic innovations. *Studia Anglica Posnaniensia* 34: 7–42.

Hernández-Campoy, J.M. (2003) Exposure to contact and the geographical adoption of standard features: two complementary approaches. *Language in Society* 32: 227–55.

Horvath, B. and Horvath, R. (1997) The geolinguistics of a sound change in progress: /l/ vocalisation in Australia. In C. Boberg, M. Meyerhoff, and S. Strassel (eds.), *A Selection of Papers from NWAVE 25*. Special issue of *University of Pennsylvania Working Papers in Linguistics*, 4: 109–24.

Horvath, B. and Horvath, R. (2001) A multilocality study of a sound change in progress: the case of /l/ vocalisation in New Zealand and Australian English. *Language Variation and Change* 13: 37–58.

Horvath, B. and Horvath, R. (2002) The geolinguistics of /l/ vocalisation in Australia and New Zealand. *Journal of Sociolinguistics* 6: 319–46.

Horvath, B. and Horvath, R. (2003) A closer look at the constraint hierarchy: order, contrast, and geographical scale. *Language Variation and Change* 15: 143–70.

Kerswill, P. (2003) Dialect levelling and geographical diffusion in British English. In D. Britain and J. Cheshire (eds.), pp. 223–44.

Labov, W. (1966) *The Social Stratification of English in New York City*, Center for Applied Linguistics, Washington, DC.

Labov, W. (1975) On the use of the present to explain the past, in *Proceedings of the 11th International Congress of Linguists* (ed. L. Heilmann), Il Mulino, Bologna, pp. 825–51.

Labov, W. (1982) Building on empirical foundations. In W. Lehmann and Y. Malkiel (eds.), *Perspectives in Historical Linguistics*, John Benjamins, Amsterdam, pp. 79–92.

Labov, W. (1994) *Principles of Linguistic Change. Vol.1: Internal Factors*, Blackwell, Oxford.

Labov, W. (2001) *Principles of Linguistic Change, Vol. 2: Social Factors*, Blackwell, Oxford.

Labov, W. (2003) Pursuing the cascade model. In D. Britain and J. Cheshire (eds.), pp. 9–22.

Labov, W. (2007) Transmission and diffusion. *Language* 83: 344–87.

Larmouth, D. (1981) Gravity models, wave theory and low-structure regions. In H. Warkentyne (ed.), *Methods IV: Papers from the 4th International Conference on Methods in Dialectology*, University of Victoria, Victoria, pp. 199–219.

Milroy, J. (1992) *Linguistic Variation and Change: On the Historical Sociolinguistics of English*, Blackwell, Oxford.

Milroy, J. and Milroy, L. (1985) Linguistic change, social network and speaker innovation. *Journal of Linguistics* 21: 339–84.

Nevalainen, T. (1996) Social stratification. In T. Nevalainen and H. Raumolin-Brunberg (eds.), pp. 57–75.

Nevalainen, T. (2000) Processes of supralocalisation and the rise of Standard English in the early Modern period. In R. Bermudez-Otero, D. Denison, R. Hogg, and C. McCully (eds.), *Generative Theory and Corpus Studies: A Dialogue from 10 ICEHL*, Mouton de Gruyter, Berlin, pp. 329–71.

Nevalainen, T. and Raumolin-Brunberg, H. (eds.) (1996) *Sociolinguistics and Language History: Studies Based on the Corpus of Early English Correspondence*, Rodopi, Amsterdam.

Nevalainen, T. and Raumolin-Brunberg, H. (2000) The changing role of London on the linguistic map of Tudor and Stuart England. In D. Kastovsky and A. Mettinger (eds.), *The History of English in a Social Context: A Contribution to Historical Sociolinguistics*, Mouton de Gruyter, Berlin, pp. 279–337.

Nevalainen, T. and Raumolin-Brunberg, H. (2003) *Historical Sociolinguistics: Language Change in Tudor and Stuart England*, Longman Pearson Education, London.

Raumolin-Brunberg, H. (1996) Historical sociolinguistics. In T. Nevalainen and H. Raumolin-Brunberg (eds.), pp. 11–38.

Raumolin-Brunberg, H. (2006) Leaders of linguistic change in early modern England. In R. Facchinetti and M Rissanen (eds.), *Corpus-based Studies of Diachronic English*, Peter Lang, Bern, pp. 115–34.

Raumolin-Brunberg, H. and Nevalainen, T. (2007) From *mine* to *my* and *thine* to *thy*: loss of the nasal in the first and second person possessives. *Austrian Studies in English* 95: 303–14.

Trudgill, P. (1974a) *The Social Differentiation of English in Norwich*, Cambridge University Press, Cambridge.

Trudgill, P. (1974b) Linguistic change and diffusion: description and explanation in sociolinguistic dialect geography. *Language in Society* 3: 215–46.

Trudgill, P. (1986) *Dialects in Contact*, Blackwell, Oxford.

Urry, J. (2007) *Mobilities*, Polity, London.

Weinreich, U., Labov, W., and Herzog, M. (1968) Empirical foundations for a theory of language change. In W. Lehmann and Y. Malkiel (eds.), *Directions for Historical Linguistics*, University of Texas Press, Austin, pp. 97–195.

25 Historical Dialectology: Space as a Variable in the Reconstruction of Regional Dialects

ANNELI MEURMAN-SOLIN

1. Introduction

In the context of historical sociolinguistics, 'space' is a complex variable, and can rarely be claimed to be an autonomous conditioning factor. Texts represent particular localities or regions to varying degrees, depending on how closely they relate to other texts, their registers and conventions of writing, and other localities and regions. Such contacts may be direct or indirect, close or loose. Similarly, features characterizing informants can be related to social variables in terms of varying degree of representativeness, depending on how much reliable information is available about the informants, their social, economic, and cultural context, and the textual history and social functions of the texts they use for communication in their particular communities and networks. The history of a text, its writer and addressee, relationships between texts, writers, and addressees, and the functions and the social and communicative contexts of writing are all interrelated in various ways. 'Space' is a construct based on these various interrelated dimensions (see Britain's definition, below, and also Chapter 24 in this *Handbook*).

The main consequence of considering 'space' an independent variable is that parameters of 'space' are generally accepted as valid for the identification and naming of language varieties, although the areas in which these are used are chiefly or exclusively demarcated by political criteria. Regional varieties tend to be objectified or reified, and their naming and description tend to reflect the

The Handbook of Historical Sociolinguistics, First Edition. Edited by Juan Manuel Hernández-Campoy and Juan Camilo Conde-Silvestre.
© 2014 John Wiley & Sons, Ltd. Published 2014 by John Wiley & Sons, Ltd.

perspective from which their history is traditionally written and their position in the hierarchy of languages and varieties on the continuum from standardized to non-standard (Meurman-Solin 2004b: 27; forthcoming a; see also Milroy 1999; Benson 2001). Moreover, linguistic descriptions of local and regional varieties tend to highlight distinctive features rather than providing a comprehensive account of all the features of a particular variety. This comparative angle may direct the researcher's attention away from what is common and frequent. Yet, in the history of a regional variety such as Scottish English, the investigation of anglicization, as in Devitt (1989), is just one of the many relevant perspectives required for exploring the development of this variety with regard to time, place, and social milieu.

Another consequence of reification, historicization, and hierarchicization is the general practice of dividing countries and regions into dialect areas and accepting these as established, although the criteria originally used for drawing maps of dialect areas may be considered outdated on the basis of evidence extracted from large digital corpora and the advance of theory and methodology. For example, areal division which is valid with respect to Modern Scots (Dossena 2005; Meurman-Solin forthcoming a) may not be appropriate for the identification of patterns of variation and change in earlier periods. The above critical remarks on periodization thus also apply to the interpretation of recorded data with reference to a fixed set of geographical areas – for information on the use of co-ordinates, see the websites of the *Linguistic Atlas of Early Middle English* (LAEME), the *Linguistic Atlas of Older Scots* (LAOS), and the *Linguistic Atlas of Late Medieval English* (LALME).

That 'space' cannot be conceived of exclusively in terms of the physical world can be illustrated by Britain's (2002: 604) three dimensions of 'spatiality': physical, social, and perceptual space (see Table 25.1).

Table 25.1.   The three dimensions of 'spatiality' (based on Britain 2002: 604)

Euclidean space	the objective, geometric, socially divorced space of mathematics and physics
Social space	the space shaped by social organization and human agency, by the human manipulation of the landscape, by the contextualization of face-to-face interaction, by the creation of a built environment, and by the relationship of these to the way the state spatially organizes and controls at a political level
Perceived space	how civil society perceives its immediate and not so immediate environments – important given the way people's environmental perceptions and attitudes construct, and are constructed by, everyday practice

Definitions of social and perceived space succinctly illustrate how necessary it has become for linguists to work with experts in other fields of study. In historical sociolinguistics, the language-external variables used by scholars are best defined by integrating new knowledge provided by researchers working in disciplines such as geography and social, economic, and cultural history (see Chapter 3 in this *Handbook*). Linguists have indeed become more aware of the complex nature of language-external variables, and of their scalar nature in particular. While some variables can be defined quite precisely, others are still based on hypotheses or knowledge which draws on as yet only partially-reconstructed stages of social, cultural, and economic history. As a consequence, a given data set may have varying degrees of relevance, depending on how much reliable information we have about particular extralinguistic features that have influenced that data set.

A further concept which has general relevance in defining functions of 'space' in historical sociolinguistics is that of 'community type.' As argued in Meurman-Solin (2004b), while letters written by informants defined as representatives of 'speech communities' permit us to identify idiolectal grammars (grammars of individuals whose language is only available in private documents), those written by members of 'discourse communities' also reflect grouplectal preferences. Language use in texts of the latter kind is affected by the conventionalized practices of professional coalitions, writers sharing similar communicative goals and applying similar genre-specific rules of writing, or groups who strictly follow a specific prescriptivist trend. Texts created by members of a particular discourse community can no longer be examined solely with reference to the variables of time and space, since at least some of their linguistic choices have been influenced by "inherited, borrowed, or recontextualized discourses, English or foreign" (Meurman-Solin 2004b: 28).

The term 'text community' refers to literate people in a particular place and time who share a particular range of written texts. For example, in fifteenth- and sixteenth-century Scotland, the identification of a text community may be based on information about the consumption of literary texts and texts representing religious instruction. A better method for reconstructing text communities is to browse through bundles of documents put together in the archive of a particular family, administrative body, or other institution. Such bundles typically contain legal documents and letters to officials or friends and relatives, but also more or less unedited reports, notes, pro memoria-type documents, diaries, and memoirs. Text communities have tended to be defined on the basis of edited texts, whereas many unedited texts, both manuscripts and early printed works, have frequently been marginalized, despite their integral social and communicative function in their historical context, as they do not have the status of texts or genres traditionally included in the canon.

In my view, the conceptual framework provided by the three community types permits us to assess the relevance and validity of databases more reliably. We will become aware of the extent to which the range of texts varies between communities. A representative diachronic database would, in theory, comprise the full range of once-functional texts relevant to the expression of the communicative purposes of the various text, discourse, and speech communities in a given geographical area. In practice, this full range will remain beyond recovery, and it is therefore necessary to provide at least some direct or indirect evidence of the major gaps (see section 2).

By defining communities in terms of which written texts verifiably had a social and communicative function among the literate members of that community, and by using such a representative compilation of texts as data, it is possible to deobjectify and dehistoricize a language variety. To use Scots as an example, a particularly important consequence of de-reification in the description of the Scottish English variety is that the internal heterogeneity of this variety will be given due attention from both the intrasystemic and the intersystemic perspective (cf Jones 1997).

To summarize this section, now that sophisticated tools for data retrieval and analysis have been developed in corpus linguistics, the conceptualization of language varieties in terms of entities and hierarchies is no longer a valid methodological approach. In modern corpus-based diachronic research, language varieties are first described in great detail, carefully avoiding a comparative angle in which a particular variety is described in reference to how it relates to a variety that – in hierarchical and historical terms – has been recognized as a standard, or norm. In this exercise, the supranational, national, regional, local, and idiolectal levels of analysis are mutually complementary, each providing a different body of language-external information for interpreting linguistic evidence. Of these sets of information, those related to community type, contacts and networks are particularly important (see section 3). When there is not enough language-external information to enable us to understand and define a particular variable (for example, to localize a particular informant), instead of giving a hypothetical parameter value to such a variable, it is advisable to resort to the so-called 'fitting technique' (see section 3). The grouping of informants must always be based on reliable information; if such information is lacking, the analysis should be restricted to the idiolectal level.

2. Diatopic and Diastratic Representativeness of Diachronic Corpora

There are always gaps in diachronic databases that represent what Fleischman (2000: 34) calls "text languages," languages which exist exclusively in written texts. It is important to try to reconstruct the loci of such gaps in order to understand how this absence of data may affect the description and analysis of correlations between linguistic choices and sociolinguistically relevant language-external variables. For example, as Laing (2004: 51), the compiler of the LAEME corpus, points out, "[f]or the study of linguistic variation in early Middle English, the range of accessible sociolinguistic variables is small. We are concerned only with the output, in English, of the literate – at this period a small subset of the population. Moreover, they would have been from a relatively homogeneous social milieu: adult, largely male, English-speaking, many also French-speaking, and either clerics or professionals."

In general, large corpora are based on earlier editions, it usually being too expensive and time-consuming for scholars to start the compilation process by transcribing texts from original manuscripts. It is also noteworthy that far fewer editions of non-literary texts than of literary texts are available. Moreover, even among non-literary texts, only those with particular historical significance have been considered sufficiently valuable to be edited. This has led to an imbalance between genres in general-purpose corpora, with only a small proportion of those text-types which typically resist standardizing trends longer than others.

The validity of the variable of 'space' can be usefully assessed by relating it to other variables. Let us examine representativeness by using 'space' and 'gender' as tools. A browse through the correspondence in family archives makes it immediately obvious that only a very small proportion of letters, mostly by well-known male writers, have been included in editions and family memoirs. This bias decreases the relevance of the data for historical dialectology, given that women and members of the lower social ranks are often excluded from editions. This can be illustrated using the work of Sir William Fraser, who has edited a large selection of correspondence in a series of Scottish family memoirs. In the *Memoirs of the Montgomeries of Eglinton*, of a total of 248 sixteenth- and seventeenth-century family letters, 28 per cent (69 letters) are by female writers, and a further 13 per cent are letters by men to female addressees (Meurman-Solin 2001b: 26–27).

Gaps may be there for other reasons too. For example, as Marshall (1983: 57) points out, "[t]he study of female literacy is […] handicapped, for while families throughout the centuries would go to great trouble to preserve the records of property, sooner or later they usually threw away as being of no importance the personal letters of women." In Scotland, the earliest known autograph letters by women to have been preserved, the important letters to Mary of Lorraine, the Queen Dowager, by the Countesses of Huntly and Erroll, Lady Home and Catherine Bellenden, date from as late as the 1540s. The linguistic and stylistic competence of these writers suggests, however, that there must have been at least some predecessors of their own sex who shared their skill (Meurman-Solin 2001b: 21–22).

The representativeness of a database also varies depending on which of the traditional variables in sociolinguistics is used as a criterion. Thus, the relation of 'space' to 'time' and 'gender' can only be examined by taking full account of statistical information about literacy. For example, before the 1650s, female illiteracy in both Scotland and England was generally more than 90 per cent (Houston 1985: 57). According to Houston (1985: 60), in the period from 1640 to 1699, the percentage of illiterate female deponents from the social ranks of professional people and gentry was 24 in northern England and 35 in Lowland Scotland. By 1770, there was a 100 per cent literacy rate in these groups in England, whereas 25 per cent were still illiterate in Scotland.

Both the quantity and the quality of digital corpora have improved in recent years. Nonetheless, only rather rarely do linguists ask whether modern methods developed by disciplines such as sociolinguistics, dialectology, or discourse stylistics can be applied to data that has not been compiled with the theoretical framework of these fields of study in mind. The relevance of this question has been completely understood by the compilers of the *Corpus of Early English Correspondence* (CEEC) (see, for example, Nevalainen and Raumolin-Brunberg 1996; 2003), a corpus that has been structured to rigorously reflect recent theoretical and methodological developments in historical sociolinguistics.

Another important prerequisite is that there should be no basic contradiction between the theoretical and methodological approaches to the research for which the corpus is claimed to be valid and the annotation system applied to the data. For example, the generally large degree of variation recorded in regionally representative correspondence usually requires a tagging and parsing system which is sensitive to categorial fuzziness and polyfunctionality. The use of automatic or semi-automatic taggers and parsers tends to re-establish and redistribute conventionalized ways of analyzing and categorizing linguistic data. As described in Meurman-Solin (2007a, 2007b), in the tagging system applied to the *Corpus of Scottish Correspondence* (CSC), the tags indicate fuzziness and polyfunctionality by referring to co-ordinates on a cline, so that there is no need to insist on membership of a single category. The order of these co-ordinates is carefully controlled, and the hierarchy between different types of information is transparent; core properties precede components providing contextual information. The co-ordinates permit the positioning of a particular feature in variational space and the tracing of developments over time. No tag is merely an interpretation of a particular occurrence in a particular context, but provides information about the different stages in processes of change, the co-ordinates thus faithfully reflecting historical continua.

As regards other diachronic corpora that provide valid data for historical sociolinguistics, I would like to mention *A Corpus of Nineteenth-century English* (CONCE), which comprises seven genres: correspondence, scientific writing, history writing, fiction, trial proceedings, parliamentary debates, and drama comedy. This corpus thus includes representatives of speech-related and non-speech-related genres, and formal and informal written genres (Kytö, Rydén, and Smitterberg 2006). Corpora comprising trial proceedings are especially useful as data for studies written from the sociolinguistic angle: such corpora include the *Old Bailey Proceedings* (Huber 2007), the *Salem Witchcraft Trials* (Rosenthal 2009), and the electronic text edition of *English Witness Depositions, 1560–1760* (Kytö, Walker, and Grund 2007). The last-mentioned has been explicitly designed for exploring regional variation (see Kytö, Grund, and Walker 2007).

The corpora compiled at the Institute for Historical Dialectology at the University of Edinburgh have provided data for two linguistic atlases, *A Linguistic Atlas of Early Middle English* (LAEME) and *A Linguistic Atlas of Older Scots* (LAOS). In her discussion of the various planes in which historical dialectology must operate, Laing (2004: 49) summarizes as follows:

Regional differences occur when changes over time are projected onto a geographical landscape. Linguistic change itself involves interactions within speech communities. This introduces a further dimension – social milieu and the variation that results from the intricacies of language use […]. Dialectology must take into account all three analytical planes: how linguistic forms change through time (diachronic); how they vary across space (diatopic); how the interactions of the speakers and writers of the language produce and define this variation (diastratic).

Most importantly, Laing (2004: 49) stresses the challenging nature of historical dialectology as follows (for further information, see Laing 2008; Laing and Lass 2006, 2009):

> In dialect studies of modern languages, this social dimension may involve variables such as age, sex, class, religion, occupation, economic status, education and ethnicity. For historical dialectologists social milieu must refer to the whole historical background. The fineness of resolution typical of contemporary regional or sociolinguistic variation studies is not available to the historical dialectologist. In addition extra-linguistic variables will differ according to which historical vernacular is under study and at what period.

In the Edinburgh atlas projects, in addition to the focus on 'the whole historical background,' close attention is paid to the history of each text as well as its inter-textual relations.

3. Methodology

Lass (2004: 29) argues that the reconstruction of historical texts is inherently difficult by pointing out that this exercise "is of necessity an attempt at *the reconstruction of utterances*":

> We can perhaps (generally in a very coarse-grained way, and with at least residual uncertainty) reconstruct the systems underlying the utterances we *receive* as part of the historical legacy. But we cannot reconstruct any utterance *per se*. This is simply because utterances (prose works, poems, letters, shopping lists, marginalia, graffiti) are contingent and spatiotemporally located objects.

He concludes that "the background richness of any utterance precludes reconstruction, because we cannot know the variables constituting this background" and that "environments provoking the utterance are layers or intersecting sets of conditions: e.g. social milieu, occasion, individual choice. We cannot retrodict the composition of a text" (Lass 2004: 30). In Lass's view (2004: 31), "any reconstructed text is not an utterance but a system-object;" as a consequence "textual 'originals' remain unreconstructable."

The challenge of reconstructing utterances leads us to the conclusion that methods traditionally considered appropriate in the description of diatopic variation and change will have to be complemented by those originally developed

472 Historical Dialectology, Language Contact, Change, and Diffusion

within quite different disciplines, such as historical pragmatics, historical stylistics, and historical sociolinguistics. In addition to providing new methods and approaches, interdisciplinary collaboration permits us to understand more precisely such concepts as 'distance,' 'contact,' and 'networks.'

But let us first examine ways of defining the basic variables. My earlier studies drawing on corpora of early Scottish English have shown that, in general, no straightforward correlation between linguistic variation and sociolinguistically-defined conditioning factors is evident (Meurman-Solin 2000a, 2000b, 2001b). Therefore, in my present approach, diastratic variation is seen as complementing our understanding of the diffusion of linguistic features over time and space. In other words, the primary language-external variables are 'time' and 'space' (for the concept of 'spacetime,' see Williamson 2004), while the secondary ones are the author's 'age,' 'gender,' and so on. During my discussion of the principles of corpus compilation in the manual of the *Corpus of Scottish Correspondence*, I suggested that some degree of hierarchical ordering should be introduced into how language-external variables are conceptualized. In the corpora related to my collaboration with the Institute for Historical Dialectology at the University of Edinburgh, time and space were considered primary because a frame of reference provided by diachronically and diatopically securely anchored texts, the so-called primary witnesses, is required for positioning texts whose history is unknown or based on hypothetical knowledge.

Anchor texts, or 'primary witnesses,' can be localized on the basis of prima facie extra-linguistic evidence of an association with a place and a given date; ideally, anchor texts are also distributed relatively evenly over time and space and have a relatively fixed social and communicative function. A 'secondary witness' is a text which must be localized on linguistic grounds, as it lacks any or sufficient extra-linguistic indications of its provenance and/or date. In other words, if an informant cannot be localized using language-external criteria, it may be possible to position his or her idiolect in a particular geographical area according to linguistic criteria by applying the 'fitting technique' (see Williamson 2000, 2001; Laing and Williamson 2004).

The notion of texts as witnesses is useful, as it permits the possibility that new evidence will be found that may alter the strength of the case for providing valid parameter values for sociolinguistically relevant variables. In corpora, a text is generally presented as a permanent member of a specific group or category, filling a slot in the compiler's schema. However, despite the fact that the corpus space is carefully demarcated and compartmentalized by the compiler, the user of a particular corpus should first see the texts as floating in extra-linguistic space and then proceed to fix them for a particular study by including only those textual witnesses that meet the criterion of having a valid relationship between the language-external variables defining them and the research question. The user of the corpus may see the set of variables in terms of a hierarchical system, finding some of them particularly relevant and others marginal or not valid for a particular research hypothesis. The user may also see some factors as more closely interrelated than others; he or she may claim that some binary variables are independent, while others form a network in which the conditioning effect of one is dependent on the converging effect of another (for more information, see the manual of the CSC corpus: Meurman-Solin 2007a).

Most variables are inherently scalar by nature. As regards the socio-cultural context, a text represents a particular locality or region to a varying degree, depending on the extent to which it relates to other texts and styles and conventions of writing. In terms of the study of letters, for example, linguistic findings can only be interpreted with reference to space or other sociolinguistically defined variables when conventions of epistolary discourse, which are partly borrowed or recontextualized from other discourses, or the influence on letter-writing of models, both British and European, have also been thoroughly studied. In the genre of letters, the practices of polite society are an important influence on linguistic and stylistic preferences (see Palander-Collin 1999; Nevala 2004; Meurman-Solin and Nurmi 2004; Palander-Collin and Nevala 2005).

In practice, a particular historical text is usually localized using information about the geographical origin of its writer or scribe. However, straightforward decisions are rarely possible. The scarcity of prosopographical information about some authors and scribes, especially female writers, may make the localization of a particular text by language-external factors difficult. For example, as a result of marriage (or marriages), women may have moved from one place to another. Moreover, since we do not usually know where and when a female informant became literate, it may be impossible to tell which area the spelling practices she learned belong to and whether they relate to her pronunciation. In general, in the absence of more detailed information, appurtenance to a particular family along with the geographical spread of the lands which that family owned are often the main criteria for defining the parameter values of variables such as the geographical origin and social class of an individual. However, informants cannot be classified purely by their origin; parameters related to mobility – both geographical and social –also have to be taken into account.

'Space' can also be conceptualized in terms of a particular author's networks (Tieken-Boon van Ostade 2005; Sairio 2009a, 2009b). It is possible to reconstruct an informant's social networks, including the geographical spread of such networking. For example, as amply illustrated by Meurman-Solin (2001b), close contacts with the royal court are clearly reflected even in women's language in early Scottish correspondence. However, in the case of numerous women and younger sons in particular, this connection can only be posited to the extent that such information is provided by their correspondence.

A further aspect reflecting the complexity of the concept of 'space' is the idea of viewing the dimension of distance as a social, economic, and cultural construct, rather than as a concept defined purely geographically (Meurman-Solin 2000a, 2000b). Distance may have a more important conditioning effect than, for example, a particular place, social class, or cultural context. This can be illustrated by the network of family castles scattered around on the map of Scotland. Their position may give the impression of places on the periphery or isolation, but their distance from administrative centers varies depending on a particular family's or family member's role in national politics, the economy, or culture. Thus, the concepts of economic and social distance must be applied in order to explain differences between members of self-contained tightly-knit speech communities and those regularly in contact with people originating from various areas within the rather diffusely-patterned administrative and economic framework. Scalar values may have to be created to avoid the streamlining effect of discrete categories. Network theory provides us with one formulation of the concept of 'distance,' but further research is required to understand all the implications.

As suggested in section 1, the concept of 'space' should be related to community type, in diachronic studies usefully categorized into 'speech community,' 'discourse community,' and 'text community.' Methodologically, particular linguistic features can be studied by drawing on a subcorpus of texts which represents a particular community type. For example, as suggested in Meurman-Solin (2004b: 28), "the best informants for reconstructing practices of a speech community can be found in texts written in private settings by non-professional, preferably less trained and relatively inexperienced writers." Phonetic spellings and other features reflecting the spoken idiom recorded in letters by these informants are usually not attested in texts influenced by shared scribal practices or, in the case of early printed works not available in manuscript, by the preferences of printers (for information on recorded phonetic spellings, see Meurman-Solin 1999, 2001b, and 2005).

In addition to variables traditionally viewed as relevant in sociolinguistics (age, gender, rank, and so on), diastratic variation may be conditioned by the range of social functions of writing in various localities and regions in different time periods. However, to my knowledge, this topic has not been studied in detail. An obvious example is the restricted number of functions for which sixteenth-century Scottish women used their writing skills. These women mostly wrote letters to their relatives, and, somewhat later, kept account books and recorded their daily life in their personal diaries (Meurman-Solin 2001a: 16). In cases of this kind, language use – or rather, what is preserved of language use – can be assumed to be essentially conditioned by the limited social functions of writing. In profiling areas with reference to types of writing, it may also be useful to investigate whether the social and communicative functions of texts can be related to the social features of informants, although no hypothesis about direct correlation between the two can be made. With information about the diffusion of genres over time and space, it is possible to explore whether a particular set of genres, or a particular discourse community type, relates to the social, economic, and cultural structures of the population in a particular place at a given time. It is necessary at the very least to try to assess whether a poor range of genres in a particular locality or region reflects a poor range of communicative functions or instead reflects the fact that a considerable number of historical texts have been lost for one reason or another (on the reconstruction of gaps, see section 2).

Another factor which may make it impossible to interpret linguistic findings purely with reference to sociolinguistic variables is that of variation in the informants' linguistic competence and stylistic literacy. It is often possible to detect variation resulting from the writers' inexperience and lack of training, particularly when data can be explored in diplomatically transcribed and digitized manuscripts. When a preference for particular variants is systematic, such variation can partly be explained by the informants' pronunciation practices (Meurman-Solin 2001b), but sporadically chosen variants may reflect the informants' ignorance of standard spelling. Stylistic literacy has not gained the status of a significant conditioning factor quite as unquestionably as the traditionally selected variables in sociolinguistics. Nonetheless, I would like to claim that, in letters in particular – a genre representing an exceptionally wide range of informant types – linguistic choices may reflect the writer's ability to apply the rules of this particular discourse community rather than those of the local or regional norm, a particular age group, a particular gender, or a particular social class. Of course, there is often close correlation between membership in a particular social class and opportunities for becoming stylistically literate, but methodologically the two variables should be kept distinct.

Finally, to relate dimensions of space and spatiality to social variables, it is useful to take into account contextual factors which have been shown to be relevant in research on the ethnography of communication, including situational aspects and factors that define the participant relationship. In describing the wider framework, linguists require information about opportunities for education, the consumption of culture, and the ideas and practices of polite society.

4. Concluding Remarks

Further interdisciplinary work will provide new knowledge which will help us to formulate valid definitions of sociolinguistically relevant language-external variables. It is hoped that special effort will be taken to investigate these variables at local, regional, national, and supranational levels, avoiding the trend to focus exclusively on prestigious standardized varieties. Community type, distance, and the nature of contacts and ensuing networks will have to be examined in order to conceptualize these less traditional variables in scalar terms. Recent research in the field of geography provides insights on concepts such as 'distance,' and other fields offer us views on other sociolinguistically relevant variables. However, an even more immediate challenge is to understand the implications of the imbalance between the knowledge we have of the social history of localities and regions of minor political importance and, for example, that of Metropolitan London. More information about hierarchies and communication between various types of towns as well as more or less densely populated rural areas is also urgently required.

Quantitative evidence presented as reflecting correlation with a particular language-external variable will have to be complemented by an assessment of intra- and intersystemic pressures at the purely linguistic level (cf. major trends reflected in the typology of adverbial subordinators, as discussed in Meurman-Solin 2004a and 2004b). Features of discourse have also been shown to trigger preferences for a particular linguistic feature, which may be unrelated to the conditioning of sociolinguistically defined variables. For example, the relative *who* in Scots, which was introduced in the mid-sixteenth century, first occurred in stylistically marked discourse types, namely fixed letter-closing formulae, mostly with *God* as antecedent (Meurman-Solin 2000b; for converging evidence in English, see Bergs 2005). As shown by Meurman-Solin (2007c), beside their use in clauses functioning as postnominal modifiers, relative pronouns may also occur as realizations of anaphoric reference at sentence level. This use as a so-called relative connective has been attested in narrative texts in particular, a particular style of writing thus correlating with a particular linguistic choice. Moreover, in defining the linguistic category of such polyfunctional items as the utterance-initial connectives *and*, *but*, and *for*, the appropriate level of analysis may be text and discourse organization; in this case, linguistic variation and change is conditioned by preferred practices of writing in a particular prose register or genre in a particular time-period (Meurman-Solin forthcoming b; see also Lenker 2010).

In general, it may be difficult to distinguish between a dialect-specific feature and a feature borrowed from a set of conventionalized practices employed by a discourse or text community. Moreover, a generally large degree of variation even at the idiolectal level, which may also reflect the flexible use of interchangeable variants, may prevent us from identifying systematic preferences which would justify claims about dialect-specificity. As Meurman-Solin (2004b: 32–39) illustrates, drawing on a corpus of sixteenth- and seventeenth-century Scottish letters, there are three different kinds of evidence. Firstly, a more or less established set of features is shared by informants originating from the various regions, regularly representing a clear majority; only a low proportion of variants of a particular linguistic item may be distinctive features of a particular dialect area. Secondly, a set of prestigious variants favored by influential discourse communities have been recorded spreading across regions; in the case of Scottish English, these usually reflect anglicization. Thirdly, geographical and social mobility have been shown to affect the idiolectal repertoires of linguistic features. The last two trends lead to mixed-speech type patterns of variation. Thus, spelling practices which originate from a relatively widespread set of orthographic conventions in the administrative and cultural centers of the south-east of Scotland spread to other regions. As regards mobility, the findings suggest that, in interpreting internal heterogeneity in specific geographical areas, the varying degrees of socio-economic distance correlate with particular linguistic choices.

REFERENCES

Benson, P. (2001) *Ethnocentrism and the English Dictionary*, Routledge, London and New York.

Bergs, A. (2005) *Social Networks and Historical Sociolinguistics. Studies in Morpho-syntactic Variation in the Paston Letters (1421–1503)*, Mouton de Gruyter, Berlin.

Britain, D. (2002) Space and spatial diffusion. In J.K. Chambers, P. Trudgill, and N. Schilling-Estes (eds.), *The Handbook of*

Language Variation and Change, Blackwell, Oxford, pp. 603–37.

CEEC = *Corpus of Early English Correspondence* (1998) Compiled by T. Nevalainen, H. Raumolin-Brunberg, J. Keränen, M. Nevala, A. Nurmi, and M. Palander-Collin, Department of English, University of Helsinki. http://www.helsinki.fi/varieng/CoRD/corpora/CEEC/index.html [accessed October 3, 2011].

CONCE = *A Corpus of Nineteenth-Century English*. Compiled by M. Kytö, Uppsala University and J. Rudanko, University of Tampere.

CSC = *Corpus of Scottish Correspondence, 1500–1715* (2007) Compiled by A. Meurman-Solin. Department of English, University of Helsinki. http://www.eng.helsinki.fi/varieng/csc/manual [accessed October 3, 2011].

Devitt, A.J. (1989) *Standardizing Written English. Diffusion in the Case of Scotland 1520–1659*, Cambridge University Press, Cambridge.

Dossena, M. (2005) *Scotticisms in Grammar and Vocabulary*, John Donald Publishers, Edinburgh.

Dossena, M. and Lass, R. (eds.) (2004) *Methods and Data in English Historical Dialectology*, Peter Lang, Bern.

Fleischman, S. (2000) Methodologies and ideologies in historical linguistics: on working with older languages. In S.C. Herring, P. van Reenen, and L. Schøsler (eds.), *Textual Parameters in Older Languages*, John Benjamins, Amsterdam, pp. 33–58.

Houston, R.A. (1985) *Scottish Literacy and the Scottish Identity. Illiteracy and Society in Scotland and Northern England, 1600–1800*, Cambridge University Press, Cambridge.

Huber, M. (2007) The Old Bailey Proceedings, 1674–1834: Evaluating and annotating a corpus of 18th- and 19th-century spoken English. In A. Meurman-Solin and A. Nurmi (eds.), *Annotating Variation and Change. Studies in Variation, Contacts and Change in English*, 1. http://www.helsinki.fi/varieng/journal/volumes/01/huber/ [accessed October 3, 2011].

Jones, C. (ed.) (1997) *The Edinburgh History of the Scots Language*, Edinburgh University Press, Edinburgh.

Kytö, M., Rydén, M., and Smitterberg, E. (eds.) (2006) *Nineteenth-Century English: Stability and Change*, Cambridge University Press, Cambridge.

Kytö, M., Grund, P., and Walker, T. (2007) Regional variation and the language of English witness depositions 1560–1760: constructing a 'linguistic' edition in electronic form. In P. Pahta, I. Taavitsainen, T. Nevalainen, and J. Tyrkkö (eds.), *Towards Multimedia in Corpus Studies. Studies in Variation, Contacts and Change in English*, 2. http://www.helsinki.fi/varieng/journal/volumes/02/kyto_et_al/ [accessed October 3, 2011].

Kytö, M., Walker, T., and Grund, P. (2007) English witness depositions 1560–1760: An electronic text edition. *ICAME Journal* 31: 65–85.

LAEME 2.1 = *A Linguistic Atlas of Early Middle English, 1150–1325* (2008) Compiled by M. Laing and R. Lass. Edinburgh: The University of Edinburgh. http://www.lel.ed.ac.uk/ihd/laeme1/laeme1.html [accessed October 3, 2011].

Laing, M. (2004) Multidimensionality: time, space and stratigraphy in historical dialectology. In M. Dossena and R. Lass (eds.), pp. 49–96.

Laing, M. (2008) The Middle English scribe: *sprach er wie er schrieb*? In M. Dossena, R. Dury, and M. Gotti (eds.), *English Historical Liguistics 2006. Volume III: Geo-historical Variation*, John Benjamins, Amsterdam, pp. 1–44.

Laing, M. and Lass, R. (2006) Early Middle English dialectology: problems and prospects. In A. van Kemenade and B. Los (eds.), *The Handbook of the History of English*, Blackwell, Oxford, pp. 417–51.

Laing, M. and Lass, R. (2009) Shape-shifting, sound change and the genesis of prodigal writing systems. *English Language and Linguistics* 13 (1): 1–31.

Laing, M. and Williamson, K. (2004) The archaeology of medieval texts. In C.J. Kay and J.J. Smith (eds.), *Categorization in the History of English*, John Benjamins, Amsterdam, pp. 85–145.

LALME = *A Linguistic Atlas of Late Mediaeval English* (1986) 4 vols. Compiled by A.

McIntosh, M.L. Samuels and M. Benskin, Aberdeen University Press, Aberdeen. http://www.lel.ed.ac.uk/research/ihd/projectsX.shtml [accessed October 11, 2011].

LAOS = *A Linguistic Atlas of Older Scots* (2007) Compiled by K. Williamson, University of Edinburgh http://www.lel.ed.ac.uk/ihd/laos1/laos1.html [accessed October 3, 2011].

Lass, R. (2004) *Ut custodiant litteras*: Editions, corpora and witnesshood. In M. Dossena and R. Lass (eds.), pp. 21–48.

Lenker, U. (2010) *Argument and Rhetoric. Adverbial Connectors in the History of English*, Mouton de Gruyter, Berlin.

Marshall, R.K. (1983) *Virgins and Viragos. A History of Women in Scotland 1080 to 1980*, Collins, London.

Meurman-Solin, A. (1999) Letters as a source of data for reconstructing early spoken Scots. In I. Taavitsainen, G. Melchers, and P. Pahta (eds.), *Writing in Nonstandard English*, John Benjamins, Amsterdam, pp. 305–22.

Meurman-Solin, A. (2000a) On the conditioning of geographical and social distance in language variation and change in Renaissance Scots. In D. Kastovsky and A. Mettinger (eds.), *The History of English in a Social Context. A Contribution to Historical Sociolinguistics*, Mouton de Gruyter, Berlin, pp. 227–55.

Meurman-Solin, A. (2000b) Geographical, socio-spatial and systemic distance in the spread of the relative *who* in Scots. In R. Bermúdez-Otero, D. Denison, R.M. Hogg, and C.B. McCully (eds.), *Generative Theory and Corpus Studies: A Dialogue from 10ICEHL*, Mouton de Gruyter, Berlin, pp. 417–38.

Meurman-Solin A. (2001a) Structured text corpora in the study of language variation and change. *Literary and Linguistic Computing* 16(1): 5–27.

Meurman-Solin, A. (2001b) Women as informants in the reconstruction of geographically and socioculturally conditioned language variation and change in sixteenth- and seventeenth-century Scots. *Scottish Language* 20: 20–46.

Meurman-Solin, A. (2004a) Towards a variationist typology of clausal connectives. Methodological considerations based on the Corpus of Scottish Correspondence. In M. Dossena and R. Lass (eds.), pp. 171–97.

Meurman-Solin, A. (2004b) Data and methods in Scottish historical linguistics. In E. Barisone, M.L. Maggioni, and P. Tornaghi (eds.), *The History of English and the Dynamics of Power*, Edizioni dell'Orso, Alessandria, pp. 25–42.

Meurman-Solin, A. (2005) Women's Scots: gender-based variation in Renaissance letters. In S. Mapstone (ed.), *Older Scots Literature*, John Donald Publishers, Edinburgh, pp. 424–40.

Meurman-Solin, A. (2007a. *Manual to the Corpus of Scottish Correspondence*. http://www.eng.helsinki.fi/varieng/csc/manual [accessed October 3, 2011].

Meurman-Solin, A. (2007b) Annotating variational space over time. In A. Meurman-Solin and A. Nurmi (eds.), *Annotating Variation and Change. Studies in Variation, Contacts and Change in English*, 1. http://www.helsinki.fi/varieng/journal/volumes/01/meurman-solin/ [accessed October 3, 2011].

Meurman-Solin, A. (2007c) Relatives as sentence-level connectives. In U. Lenker and A. Meurman-Solin (eds.), *Connectives in the History of English*, John Benjamins, Amsterdam, pp. 255–87.

Meurman-Solin, A. (forthcoming a) Early Modern English dialects. In L. Brinton (ed.), *Historical Linguistics of English: An International Handbook, Volume 2*, Mouton de Gruyter, Berlin.

Meurman-Solin, A. (2012) The Connectives, *And, For, But*, and *Only* as Clause and Discourse Type Indicators in 16th- and 17th-Century Epistolary Prose. In A. Meurman-Solin, M.J. López-Couso, and B. Los (eds.), *Information Structure and Syntactic Change in the History of English*, Oxford University Press, New York.

Meurman-Solin, A. and Nurmi, A. (2004) Circumstantial adverbials and stylistic literacy in the evolution of epistolary discourse. In B.L. Gunnarsson *et al.* (eds.),

Language Variation in Europe. Papers from ICLaVE 2, Universitetstryckeriet, Uppsala, pp. 302–14.

Milroy, J. (1999) The consequences of standardization in descriptive linguistics. In T. Bex and R.J. Watts (eds.), *Standard English. The Widening Debate*, Routledge, London, pp. 16–39.

Nevala, M. (2004) *Address in Early English Correspondence. Its Forms and Socio-pragmatic Functions*, Société Néophilologique, Helsinki.

Nevalainen, T. and Raumolin-Brunberg, H. (1996) The corpus of Early English correspondence. In T. Nevalainen and H. Raumolin-Brunberg (eds.), *Sociolinguistics and Language History. Studies Based on the Corpus of Early English Correspondence*, Rodopi, Amsterdam, pp. 39–54.

Nevalainen, T. and Raumolin-Brunberg, H. (2003) *Historical Sociolinguistics. Language Change in Tudor and Stuart England*, Longman Pearson Education, London.

Palander-Collin, M. (1999) *Grammaticalization and Social Embedding*: I THINK *and* METHINKS *in Middle and Early Modern English*, Société Néophilologique, Helsinki.

Palander-Collin, M. and Nevala, M. (eds.) (2005) *Letters and Letter Writing*. Special issue *of European Journal for English Studies* (EJES) 9(1).

Rosenthal, B. (ed.) (2009) *Records of the Salem Witch-Hunt*, Cambridge University Press, Cambridge.

Sairio, A. (2009a) *Language and Letters of the Bluestocking Network. Sociolinguistic Issues in Eighteenth-Century Epistolary English*, Société Néophilologique, Helsinki.

Sairio, A. (2009b) Methodological and practical aspects of historical network analysis: A case study of the Bluestocking letters. In A. Nurmi, M. Nevala, and M. Palander-Collin (eds.), *The language of daily life in England (1400–1800)*, John Benjamins, Amsterdam, pp. 107–35.

Tieken-Boon van Ostade, I. (2005) Of social networks and linguistic influence: The language of Robert Lowth and his correspondents. *International Journal of English Studies* 5(1): 135–57.

Williamson, K. (2000) Changing spaces: linguistic relationships and the dialect continuum. In I. Taavitsainen, T. Nevalainen, P. Pahta, and M. Rissanen (eds.), *Placing Middle English in Context*, Mouton de Gruyter, Berlin, pp. 141–79.

Williamson, K. (2001) Spatio-temporal aspects of Older Scots texts. *Scottish Language* 20: 1–19.

Williamson, K. (2004) On chronicity and space(s) in historical dialectology. In M. Dossena and R. Lass (eds.), pp. 97–136.

26 Linguistic Atlases: Empirical Evidence for Dialect Change in the History of Languages

ROLAND KEHREIN

1. Introduction – A Short History of Linguistic Atlases[1]

The development of dialectology was strongly supported by the idea of the death of dialects as communication systems.[2] Thus, the primary goal of early linguistic atlases, in the beginning exclusively dialect atlases – apart from depicting regional differences in language – was the documentation of the oldest available forms of spoken language. The same applies to early dialect lexicon projects (so-called *Idiotika*), created to preserve the prevalent form of speech of the relevant time period (see Richey 1754: xliii–cliv). The emergence of German dialectology is worth noting insofar as its theoretical and methodological developments resulted in the first linguistic atlas in the contemporary sense of the term, namely an "intended combination of maps, based on an objective or narrative" (Ormeling 2010: 37), in this case the areal distribution of languages/dialects or linguistic phenomena: Georg Wenker's *Sprachatlas der Rheinprovinz nördlich der Mosel und des Kreises Siegen* (1878). It is no surprise that this atlas deals with an area where an extreme heterogeneity of dialects was (and to some extent still is) to be found, including the Moselle-Franconian, the Ripuarian, and the Lower Franconian dialect formations. Accordingly, it is not surprising that the first linguistic atlas dealing with Romance dialects of the Rhone valley, "a region in the contact zone between Switzerland, Italy and Savoy where Romance varieties are spoken"

The Handbook of Historical Sociolinguistics, First Edition. Edited by Juan Manuel Hernández-Campoy and Juan Camilo Conde-Silvestre.
© 2014 John Wiley & Sons, Ltd. Published 2014 by John Wiley & Sons, Ltd.

(Lameli 2010: 577), was edited just two years later: Jules Gilliéron's *Petit Atlas phonétique du Valais roman (sud du Rhône)* (1880).[3] Subsequently, both Wenker and Gilliéron implemented the first 'large-area atlases'[4] covering a complete political territory: the late nineteenth-century German empire in the case of Wenker (*Sprachatlas des Deutschen Reichs*, 1888–1923) and France in that of Gilliéron (*Atlas linguistique de la France: ALF*, 1902–10). Despite the tremendous influence of both works on the linguistic cartography of later generations, both atlases had some methodological shortcomings, such as Wenker's indirect method of data collection and the restriction of data to forty sentences, or the investigation of only 639 locations throughout France by Gilliéron. Subsequent atlas projects[5] therefore tried, firstly, to overcome these shortcomings and, secondly, to combine the methodological advantages of both atlases: a dense net of survey locations (as in Wenker's atlas) and directly collected data from voluminous questionnaires (as in Gilliéron's atlas). A consequence of these methodological developments was the restriction to smaller areas in contrast to Wenker's and Gilliéron's atlases.

All in all, after the initial works of Wenker and Gilliéron, the history of linguistic cartography and linguistic atlases represents a continuous process of theoretical and methodological progress visible in many different traces in different parts of the world.[6] Beginning by collecting and documentating[7] the oldest, invariably solitary, variants for certain items per location,[8] Jaberg and Jud were already moving on to investigating some locations twice. Furthermore, they always valued the presence of informants' wives, who often made comments on the answers, and thus allowed the collection of linguistic variants for individual items. These are represented and explained in commentary texts that form part of the maps' legends (Jaberg and Jud 1928: 210). Hans Kurath (1938: 3) – explicitly naming the *ALF* (Gilliéron and Edmont 1902–10) and the *AIS* (Jaberg and Jud 1928) as models for his own work – went a step further when collecting data for his *Linguistic Atlas of New England (LANE)*: he introduced two important innovations, the first of which is the collection of data from two, sometimes three, informants per location, chosen according to social and educational criteria. One of them was "aged and unschooled (illiterate, if possible) and the other middle-aged and possessing a grammar school or even a high school education. Moreover, cultured informants have been included in 38 communities" (Kurath 1938: 3–4, 1939: 44). All informant responses – further classified into response types (spontaneous, suggested and the like) – were depicted on one map (per topic). The second innovation entailed the making of phonographic recordings of more than half of the informants as a supplement to the direct transcriptions. This first truly pluridimensional approach – since all data were included in the maps – was developed further in the survey for the *Linguistic Atlas of the Gulf States* (Pederson, McDaniel, and Adams 1977), which as well as requiring speakers to have been born locally, applied social criteria to the choice of speakers, in original terms: age (two to four generations), sex, ethnic group (four different groups), social class (five levels), education (three levels), and social experience (two levels).[9] With the extensive pluridimensional atlases executed by Harald Thun in South America (e.g., Thun and Elizaincín 2000)[10] on the one hand, and the digitally supported creation of 'dynamic language atlases' culminating in a Geolinguistic Information System (to be described later in some detail) on the other, this process of historical development has currently reached a preliminary conclusion. The more recent types of atlases help linguists study language variation dependent on certain extralinguistic factors and to interpret such variation diachronically as language change, using the apparent-time hypothesis with pluridimensional atlases (comparing speakers from different generations) or real-time language change with dynamic language atlases (comparing linguistic data collected at different times).

2. Applying Linguistic Atlases to the Study of Language or Dialect Change

2.1   *Interpreting map images as the results of language change*

Kurath mentions the historical interpretation of maps as one aim of his *LANE*. Since he observes that many characteristics of the pronunciation and lexicon of the "provincial dialects of colonial times" (the mid to late seventeenth century) were still present at the beginning of the twentieth century, Kurath (1938: 6) claims that:

> [t]he present distribution of dialect features by sections, by social levels and by age groups, as documented in the *Linguistic Atlas of New England*, will enable us to determine the trends of the present and of the recent past in the speech of New England. The determination of these trends will in turn make possible the reconstruction, in its main features, of the linguistic structure of New England before the industrial era [...], so that ultimately the British sources of New England speech can be determined.

Returning to Europe, we find a different kind of historical interpretation of linguistic atlases.

> [I]t was the tradition of the Neogrammarians to project the present-day language on[to] a reconstructed, historical proto-system. The reason for this is that present-day phenomena can be explained as the result of language change.
> (Veith 1994/2006: 522; see also Kirk 2001: 351)

In the case of the German dialects, these putative proto-systems are usually Middle High German for vowels and West Germanic for consonants, because these are the periods immediately prior to substantial sound changes. Consequently, the descriptions of phonetic/phonological inventories of village and regional grammars within the Neogrammarian tradition were structured according to the historical 'sounds' and the relevant paragraphs were often entitled "The historical development of the sounds" or the like. This structure was adopted by many atlas projects: the topics of such maps were, for instance, dialectal equivalents of Middle High German *î* as represented by one or more lexemes. The resulting map images could thus be viewed as the outcome of regional processes of divergence from the relevant proto-systems. The most prominent interpretations of such diachronic relations between the areal distribution of linguistic phenomena and a reconstructed proto-system are the staged isoglosses of the Second Sound Shift (also called High-German Sound Shift). These isoglosses reflect the provisional endpoint of a profound large scale sound shift that took place roughly between the seventh and ninth centuries, in which the varying degree to which the Germanic plosives /p, t, k/ shifted resulted in a series of geographic steps. It constitutes a case of broad linguistic differentiation.

To view every regional divergence among dialectal equivalents as a result of 'real language change' is of course highly questionable, if not inadequate, since we know that in the history of German and its dialects there has never been a single system that could be taken as the starting point for such processes of divergence. It seems more appropriate to treat such proto-systems as a means with which to compare two 'synchronically' observable systems, to establish a *tertium comparationis*, or a diasystem[11] – as Weinreich (1954) calls it – without a diachronic interpretation.

2.2 Interpreting map images as intermediate stages in ongoing language change

In addition to the interpretation of map images as the result of changes, from the very beginnings of the development of linguistic atlases there were attempts to interpret static map images (*Kartenbilder*) dynamically.[12] Map images have thus been viewed as representing a particular state within an ongoing process of language (or dialect) change – either on the basis of the shape of isoglosses on individual maps or (more often) using the combination of isoglosses from different maps to calculate dialectal differentiation (Ivić 1962). The processes hypothesized were either related to language-external phenomena or could be explained in language-internal terms.

Earlier accounts involved the interpretation of certain shapes of (bundles of) isoglosses with reference to extra-linguistic factors. These extra-linguistic factors were then interpreted as significant factors in linguistic change, a 'snapshot' of which could be observed on linguistic maps. The terminology applied suggests that these processes were considered to be movements of language (or a linguistic phenomenon) itself, in that scientists speak of *Sprachbewegung* (language movement), *Ausbreitung sprachlicher Eigentümlichkeiten* (spread of linguistic features), or *sprachliche Strömungsvorgänge* (language flows; Becker 1942). In the context of the *ALF* (Gilliéron and Edmont 1902–10), phrases like "linguistic biology" or "life of language" can be observed (Swiggers 2010: 275). These 'movements', however, were related to extra-linguistic factors, above all transportation infrastructure (*Verkehrswege*) or other cultural connections (such as the presence of a bigger city, borders between areas of different religious denomination, or political units) and sometimes the migration of certain ethnic groups (Haag 1900; Wrede 1903; Frings 1924; Aubin, Frings, and Müller 1926; and as a kind of summary, Bach 1934). Moreover, such cultural landscapes (*Kulturräume*) were viewed as inseparably linked to the people who lived there and constructed them and therefore as socio-cultural, not geographical landscapes (Bach 1934: § 55).[13] This approach could be labeled socio-cultural dialectology, as distinct from sociolinguistics, in which the individual – more or less independent of their relation to location – plays a domi-nant role. This tradition remained vital until the second half of the twentieth century (Gluth, Lompa and Smolka 1982). The most important isogloss contours related to external factors rested upon the two basic shapes of *circle* and *border line:* a stellate shape, progressive stages, wedge, fan, preceding or following islands, cone and tube (Gluth, Lompa and Smolka 1982; see also Goossens 1969 and Weijnen 1977 for typologies of map configurations). Figure 26.1 shows an example of a typical staged tube configuration, in which, along the river Rhine, southern forms for three different phenomena 'invade' northern areas. This means that the assumed direction of the linguistic movement follows the river's flow. However, it is noteworthy that in most cases the suspected direction of movement is the weak point in such analyses. The depicted configuration could also be interpreted as moving in the opposite direction, the tube-building forms being relics of declining areas.

A famous example of language-internal explanations is the development of the lexical expression for *cock* in Gascony: Gilliéron and Roques (1912) describe the establishment of new lexical items referring to *cock* to avoid homonymy with expressions for *cat* which should have arisen from two phonological develop-ments predicted by sound laws.[14] Goossens (1977: 95–97) classifies typical relations between isoglosses of linguistic items involved in language-internal explanations as either *coincidence* between different isoglosses (as in the *cock* example), or as

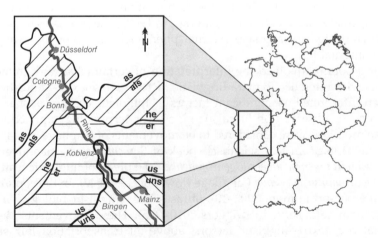

Figure 26.1.   Example of several isoglosses forming a tube configuration

scars indicating that an observable band between two isoglosses developed from a former clash of linguistic forms causing a 'wound' in the respective system.

In their *Atlas of North American English (ANAE)*, Labov, Ash, and Boberg (2006: 43–44), describing and explaining horizontal structures and processes of merger, distinguish three types: 'bundling' (the degree of coincidence among isoglosses that are defined by separate features), 'complementation' (the degree to which they do not overlap, defining mutually exclusive dialect areas) and 'nesting' (when the spatial distribution of one feature is contained entirely within that of another, establishing an implicational relationship).

However, such dynamic interpretations of isogloss shapes and coincidence or discrepancy of a number of isoglosses, or of isoglosses and extra-linguistic features, always remain speculative to some degree and need to be reassessed in the light of additional data.

2.3   Apparent-time analyses using bi- or pluridimensional atlases

One of the explicit goals of pluridimensional geolinguistics and pluridimensional linguistic cartography is "to extend the plane superficies of monodimensional geolinguistics to a three-dimensional linguistic space" (Thun 2010: 522), thus combining the merits of dialectology and sociolinguistics and considering numerous social variables in many, areally distributed localities. The most important aspect here is the interpretation of dialect differences between speakers from two or more generations as dialect change in apparent time (Labov 1994: 43–72). In a very early analysis, Terracher (1914) was able to demonstrate striking differences between the morphological systems of two generations that can be directly ascribed to intermarriage in the older generation (Swiggers 2010). Analyses according to the apparent-time hypothesis would, in principle, also have been possible on the basis of the data collected for the *LAGS* (Pederson, McDaniel, and Adams 1986–92) and the *LANE* (Kurath, Hanley, Bloch, *et al.* 1939–43). But as Labov, Ash, and Boberg (2006: 4) mention in a broad criticism of the missing connection between linguistic atlas projects and 'general linguistics,' the 'substantial findings' of these atlas projects "were not followed by many papers that built on the linguistic implications of their results." As a consequence, the *MRhSA* (Bellmann, Herrgen, and Schmidt 1994–2002) was the first linguistic atlas for which analyses – together with numerous subsequent related studies – ultimately resulted in a fundamentally new theory of language variation and change, the 'Linguistic Dynamics Approach' (see Schmidt 2010a, and below). In this atlas, data from two social groups were collected, one group consisting of traditional informants for dialectological studies (NORM speakers of about 70 years of age), the other comprising members of a younger and professionally more regionally mobile generation (craftsmen about 40 years old). One of the fundamental findings when the apparent-time dialectal variation between the two social groups is interpreted is a dialect convergence that leans not towards the national oralization norm of Standard German, but rather involves the spread of certain (prestigious) local dialectal forms, resulting in horizontal structures of regional (rather than earlier local) dialects (Schmidt 1993; Bellmann 1997).[15] Most interestingly, this kind of horizontal convergence between dialects – as opposed to vertical convergence upon the standard language – is also one of the basic findings of the *ANAE* (Labov, Ash, and Boberg 2006: 10).[16]

2.4   Real-time analyses combining linguistic maps from different points in time and the creation of dynamic language atlases

The first linguistic atlas which offers an opportunity to compare linguistic data from two points in time over a span of several decades is Günter Bellmann's *Schlesischer Sprachatlas* (1965–67). In this atlas, the author combines data he collected directly with data from Wenker's survey. The latter are printed on tracing paper that can be laid over the maps based on new materials. Data from the late-nineteenth-century atlas compiled by Wenker can thus be directly compared to data collected in the early 1960s.

The *ANAE* (Labov, Ash, and Boberg 2006), in addition to apparent-time interpretations, also includes maps depicting merger processes, in which currently collected data are compared to historical data from Kurath and McDavid (1961) and from "a survey of long distance telephone operators carried out by Labov in 1966" (Labov, Ash, and Boberg 2006: 66). This information is inserted into the maps in the form of lines, delimiting regions in which the distribution of the several phenomena either matches or differs from their distribution in recent times.[17]

While the examples mentioned represent more or less manual ways of comparing data and are thus restricted to isolated phenomena or map subjects, the application of digital media enables linguists to overcome such restrictions. As an exemplary case, the following paragraphs will describe the constitution of a modern dynamic language atlas, the *Digitaler Wenker-Atlas* (*DiWA*), with regard to its contents and basic technical features.[18]

In terms of historical background, Wenker's comprehensive survey of German dialects at the end of the nineteenth century (nearly 50,000 survey locations) for his *Sprachatlas des Deutschen Reichs* became the foundation of nearly every subsequent dialectological study on German dialects, despite the fact that the original atlas – consisting of two copies, each containing 1,659 map sheets on which linguistic information had been drawn manually and differentiating up to 22 colors per map sheet – was never published, due to the large size of the maps (each map sheet extended over about 60 × 60 centimeters and a complete map consisted of three map sheets) and color depth.

The primary objective of the *DiWA* project (Schmidt and Herrgen 2001–9) was thus the digital reproduction, publication, and archiving of the historical hand-drawn maps. This objective was achieved in 2003, by which time, all of the map sheets had been digitized and saved as (600 dpi, 24-bit color) TIFF files. As part of the publication process the images were georeferenced. This converted the bitmap files into geographically 'intelligent' map files, in which each pixel – in addition to RGB color information – contains information about the geographic coordinate it depicts. This enabled us to tackle the second main objective of the project: combining the historical maps with numerous additional sources of linguistic and non-linguistic information. Such information can be georeferenced and thereby linked to any place of interest on the map. The following types of additional data are combined with the historical maps in the *DiWA*:

- maps from more recently published German small-area dialect atlases (confined to maps of phenomena directly comparable to Wenker's maps);
- sound recordings of the 40 sentences on which Wenker's survey was based (such recordings had been collected since the 1930s in many locations from all over the German-speaking area);
- bibliographical references, where known publications deal with the relevant locations or regions;
- non-linguistic maps which may turn out to be relevant for explanations of language change.

The online system in which the *DiWA* (www.diwa.info) is published operates on the basis of an Image Web Server, processing files in the ECW (Enhanced Compressed Wavelet) file format, a quasi-standard in GIS technology. Apart from seamless zooming and scrolling on the map, the user can overlay several maps and compare them by changing their opacity. These maps can either be several historical maps or historical and recent maps, enabling the user to gain either a synchronic view of certain phenomena or look at 100 years of dialect development. In applying *DiWA*, real-time analyses can be conducted for those parts of the German-speaking area, depicted in Figure 26.2, where the areas of Wenker's survey and recent regional atlases overlap.

Thanks to the highly productive discipline of language geography and cartography and the constant enhancing of its methodology, linguists from all over the world can now in principle analyze language dynamics in real-time studies of linguistic data from time spans covering up to more than a century. Early atlases from the late nineteenth or the early twentieth century play the most important role in these diachronic comparisons. Such 'historical' atlases exist at least for Japan (*Phonetic Dialect Atlas*, Language Research Commission 1905, and *Grammatical Dialect Atlas*, Language Research Commission 1906; see Onishi 2007), parts of North America (*LAGS* (Pederson, McDaniel, and Adams 1986–92) and *LANE* (Kurath, Hanley, Bloch, *et al.* 1939–43)), Danish dialects (Bennike and Kristensen 1898–1912), Poland (Małecki and Nitsch 1934), Slovenia (Tesnière 1925) and France and neighboring areas covered by Romance dialects (*ALF* (Gilliéron and Edmont 1902–10), *AIS* (Jaberg and Jud 1928–40)).[19] The prospects for linguistic analysis on this time-scale provide completely new opportunities for an overall theory of language change, probably even leading to new theories

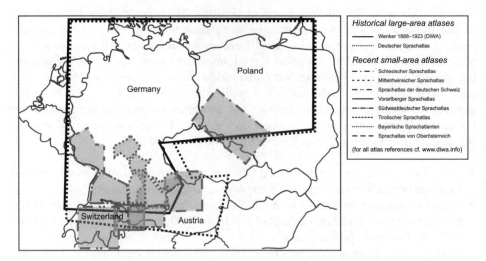

Figure 26.2.   Historical (black) and recent (gray and shaded) German dialect atlases currently available in *DiWA*

about language itself. One such theory, the Linguistic Dynamics Approach, resulting from empirical studies employing these modern research tools, will be introduced in the following section.

3. Preliminary Results of Analyses within the Framework of the *Digitaler Wenker-Atlas (DiWA)* and Theoretical Advances

Schmidt (2010a) describes four types of diachronic developments of dialects which can be observed in a real-time comparison of linguistic atlases, which I can only sketch here. An important pre-condition for valid real-time comparisons is to ensure that only directly comparable phenomena (phenomena that can be linked by a diasystem, thus forming a linguistic variable) at identical places are compared (Schmidt 2010b).

Schmidt does not describe dialect change towards Standard German (that is, the loss of dialect forms), because this is completely in line with the general hypothesis of dialect decline in German. In contrast to this general hypothesis, his first type is the preservation of dialectal features in quite a few cases and in all regions where diachronic comparisons can be drawn. The schematized illustration of such cases in Figure 26.3 indicates the most important precondition for such stability: the isogloss involved has to coincide with the historical boundary between two different dialect formations (*Dialektverbände*), thus forming an important horizontal structural boundary between different linguistic systems. Schmidt takes one of the areally staged isoglosses of the Second Sound Shift as an example,

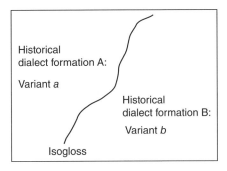

Figure 26.3. Type 1: stability of isoglosses over a period of more than 100 years (adapted from Schmidt 2010a: 208)

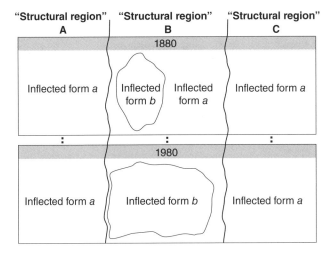

Figure 26.4. Type 2: development away from both the standard language and the old dialect (adapted from Schmidt 2010a: 208)

the lemmas *das*, *was*, and *es* (respectively corresponding to Moselle Franconian *dat*, *wat*, *et* as opposed to Rhenish Franconian *das*, *was*, *es*).

The second type of diachronic development of dialect phenomena also contradicts the dialect loss hypothesis. As illustrated in Figure 26.4, in this case a dialectal phenomenon *b* is distributed within a structural region B together with a dialectal phenomenon *a*. The latter is both the predominant form in the surrounding structural regions (A and C) and in Standard German. Contrary to all expectations, the highly peculiar form *b* spreads all over the area of structural region B, displacing the competing phenomena in just one century, or just two or three generations (given that Wenker's informants were students at the end of

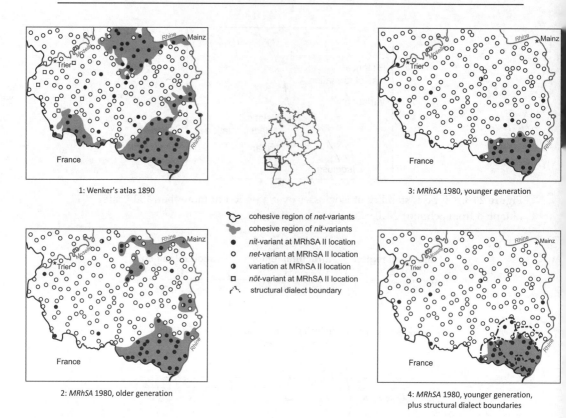

1: Wenker's atlas 1890

3: *MRhSA* 1980, younger generation

2: *MRhSA* 1980, older generation

4: *MRhSA* 1980, younger generation, plus structural dialect boundaries

∾ cohesive region of *net*-variants
∾ cohesive region of *nit*-variants
● *nit*-variant at MRhSA II location
○ *net*-variant at MRhSA II location
◑ variation at MRhSA II location
□ *nöt*-variant at MRhSA II location
⌐∿ structural dialect boundary

Figure 26.5.   Distribution of variants *nit* and *net* for Standard German *nicht* in the Middle-Rhine area at different periods of time (read column by column)

the nineteenth century and the two generations interviewed for the *MRhSA* (Bellmann, Herrgen and Schmidt 1994–2002) were born between 1900 and 1910 or 1940 and 1950, respectively).

A subtype of Schmidt's type 2 development is horizontal accommodation between neighboring dialects, in which local dialects disperse to regional dialects without the direct engagement of the supraregional standard language. As can be seen in Figure 26.5, the lemma *nicht* in the southern Middle-Rhine area is represented by two dominant variants, *nit* and *net*. If we compare the distribution of these variants in Wenker's atlas (1890s) to the distribution attested by the older generation of the *MRhSA* (NORM speakers in 1980) we can observe variation within the latter and in some cases the substitution of former *i*-vowels by *e*-vowels. Taking the younger *MRhSA* informants into consideration, the number of locations where this substitution takes place is even higher.[20] This displacement stops exactly at the structural boundaries of the southern Palatinate area (*Pfälzisches Reliktgebiet*), which forms a linguistically relatively conservative region.

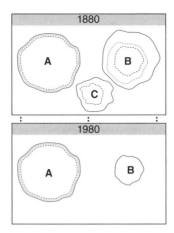

Figure 26.6.   Type 3: broad-scale transformation of the phonological structure of dialect areas (adapted from Schmidt 2010a: 209)

Unlike types 1 and 2, the third type of development involves "phonological change and shifts in the phonological boundaries between former dialect formations" (Schmidt 2010a: 209). Since such development is described by a reference to the idealized Middle High German phonological system serving as a diasystem, this kind of observation forms the sequel to descriptions made by Moulton (1961), among others. This time, however, it is based on (at least) two sets of empirical data related only by the Middle High German diasystem (see Figure 26.6). In the case of dialect area A, in the older data all of the isoglosses for words containing the old dialectal phonemes involved coincide: stability in the phonological system can be observed even 100 years later. In the other two areas the situation is different: the isoglosses reflecting the different occurrences of a phoneme already had different shapes at the earlier time. As a consequence, a century later, change in several lexemes or the loss of the phoneme altogether can be observed. This may result in shifts within the overall phonological systems of the dialects, or even within the dialect formations involved. Schmidt concludes:

> The clarity of this finding is striking. (1) For phonologically relevant phenomena (i.e., phonemic splits and mergers) the old aphorism 'every word has a history of its own' implies that a very long term (in this instance phonological) change is in progress. A long-standing language change process has not yet been completed. (2) The phonological transformation proceeds via a lexeme-for-lexeme phonological redistribution. (Schmidt 2010a: 210).

The final type of development is somewhat exceptional in that the factor of old boundaries between dialect formations is not significant at all. In a comprehensive study of the interplay between the inflectional morphology of verb and pronoun constructions, often resulting in syncretism, in dialects across large parts of middle and southern Germany, Rabanus (2008) was able to demonstrate that, firstly, changes spread across dialect boundaries and secondly, that a language-internal factor alone was responsible for an inhibition of this process, namely the preservation of the functional distinction of 'minimal sentences.'

All the processes mentioned so far can be explained in terms of the Linguistic Dynamics Approach.[21] Instead of trying to describe static systems and possible diachronic relations between single elements of those systems (as in the Saussurean dichotomy synchrony vs. diachrony), this theory takes the variability of language and linguistic variation as a given, thus transcending the Saussurean concept of synchrony. Synchronic systems are viewed as theoretical reductions, inadequate to the task of describing language, which is fundamentally characterized by variability. The central idea of the Linguistic Dynamics Approach is therefore the notion of 'synchronization:' "the calibration of competence differences in the performance act" (Schmidt 2010a: 212). With this concept, communicative interaction is systematically taken into account as a possible starting point for all processes of language change. In detail, synchronization is subdivided into three related concepts: 'micro-,' 'meso-,' and 'macrosynchronization.' On the premise of the cooperative principle in communication, it is assumed that speakers produce utterances that are comprehensible for their communicative partners (drawing upon speakers' assumptions about their interactors' knowledge, expectations, and so forth). If an element of an utterance turns out not to be part of the interlocutor's competence he/she will signal a lack of understanding. This will lead to a reformulation or an explanation by the initial speaker. In this way, the interlocutors' individual competencies are adjusted *moment by moment* – stabilized in case of the first speaker, modified in case of the interlocutor. Such "calibration of the individual competencies within a single interaction" (Schmidt 2010a: 212) is called microsynchronization and forms the basis of the other two types of synchronization. Individuals usually interact in a restricted number of groups (communities of practice or other peer groups) at particular periods of their lives. In these, individual acts of microsynchronization that are directed in identical directions occur repeatedly and may lead to a permanent change in an individual's and his interlocutors' individual competencies: "[s]uch a series of parallel acts of synchronization, performed by individuals in personal contact situations, leading to the establishment of common context-dependent linguistic knowledge, we term *mesosynchronization*" (Schmidt 2010a: 213). Finally, the concept of macrosynchronization comprises the processes by which members of a linguistic community orient themselves to a common written and oral norm.

Speakers' knowledge about varieties and styles is established on the basis of synchronization acts, especially mesosynchronizations. This means that, unlike structuralist attempts to define linguistic varieties which tried to cope with heterogeneity by breaking "down the object of description [i.e., linguistic varieties] even further to the 'idiolect' level" (Weinreich 1954: 389), by applying the notion of synchronization, varieties may be conceptualized as dynamic systems. Schmidt gives the following definition of 'full varieties:'[22]

Full varieties can be specified as sectors of linguistic knowledge defined by independent prosodic/phonological and morphosyntactic structures on the basis of which individuals or groups of speakers interact in particular situations. The full varieties of a language are semi-discrete and interdependent. The minimal and necessary criterion is the presence of at least one 'idiovarietal' element or structural feature in the prosodic/phonological or morphosyntactic subsystems. (Schmidt 2010a: 215).

This definition thus combines the linguistic level with the levels of individual competence and language use. In opposition to varieties, 'styles' or 'speech levels' (*Sprechlagen*) merely "arise from conventional allophonic and allomorphic variation within a full variety in correlation with social, contextual and spatial factors" (Schmidt 2010a: 215).

There is empirical evidence attesting to the existence of horizontal or vertical borders between different varieties: linguistic hyperforms. These show up as mistakes when a speaker attempts to produce a specific form from a specific variety that he or she regards as most appropriate in a concrete interaction. These varieties may be either Standard German or a dialect. Such mistakes may be interpreted as lack of individual knowledge and evidence for the evidence of a different linguistic variety.

4. Prospects: From Linguistic Atlases to Geolinguistic Information Systems

In principle, traditional linguistic atlases contain information about the informants' competence in a particular, usually dialectal, variety. This means that the data represent linguistic forms which are already quite well established within the dialect community, even if they differ from variants documented at an earlier point in time. Such stable arrangements, which represent the results of language change processes in general, take some time to form (in the case of phenomena that have changed between an older and a more recent dialect atlas). It is thus conceivable that, when asked, informants know certain variants but do not use them in their everyday communication. This means that competence and performance can diverge. That is why the Research Center *Deutscher Sprachatlas* has set out to collect a broad range of data on current 'real spoken everyday language' from defined social groups recorded in different interactive contexts and to integrate these data into a Geolinguistic Information System (together with language atlas data). This comprehensive survey forms part of the *Regionalsprache.de* (*REDE*) project, which has been developed for 19 years with two main elements:

(1) The integration of regional language data, far exceeding the amount of material that is already part of the *DiWA* (Schmidt and Herrgen 2001–9) system. Subject to validity checks, any data which colleagues are prepared to make available to us will be considered for inclusion. These data can be in the form of linguistic maps and atlases, sound recordings of regionally marked speech

on different levels of the vertical dimension, or publications dealing with variational linguistic issues (serving as a georeferenced bibliography in the first instance, perhaps also linked to digitized publications). The data – including data previously only published on printed maps – will be gradually integrated into databases (Nickel 2008).

(2) The new survey mentioned above. Data are currently being collected from representative male speakers from three generations:[23] one speaker at least 65 years old representing a generation of NORMs; two middle-aged speakers (45–55-year-old policemen) representing people of a middle educational level working in a communicative job, such as answering emergency calls (Kehrein 2006); and a speaker from a younger generation, around 20 years old, the age at which the most important period of linguistic conditioning is believed to end. These speakers are recorded in five defined situations – six, including the emergency calls for the policemen. In these situations, the dialectal and Standard German competencies of the speakers are explored, using the forty sentences which Georg Wenker invented for his comprehensive survey in the late nineteenth century and the tale "The North Wind and the Sun," which is read aloud. The additional situations are constructed, through choice of interlocutors and the formality of the situation, so as to force the informants to use different speaking styles ranging from the dialect to Standard German.[24] All new recordings will also be integrated into the system described.

All the data available in the Geolinguistic Information System will be made accessible via several types of indexes: phonetic-phonological, morphosyntactic and historical, using the Middle High German vowel system and the Germanic consonant system as diasystems (see section 2.1 above). Thus, all the data are directly comparable and analyzable from diachronic, diatopic, and diastratic perspectives. Together with an online mapping tool, the opportunities provided far exceed the mere comparison of maps. While the aim of pluridimensional cartography was to link sociolinguistics and linguistic cartography, the Geolinguistic Information System currently being developed additionally opens up the historical dimension.

NOTES

1   Since the potential of an atlas to assist studies of language change essentially depends on the collected data, I will deal only with the methodology underlying the data collection for the atlas projects mentioned and disregard the different methods of data presentation on maps. For these issues, the interested reader is referred to the comprehensive contributions by Kirk (2001), and Girnth (2010).

2   In this chapter the term 'dialect' is used to refer only to local or regional dialects.

3   As Lameli (2010) points out, there were linguistic maps before Wenker and Gilliéron, the first of which he identifies as the work of ten Kate (1723), which shows a classification of

European languages. Julius Klaproth's *Asia polyglotta. Sprachatlas* (1823) is one of the earliest works explicitly entitled as an 'atlas.' It contains only one map, however, which depicts the different groups of speakers to be found in the region of interest and which can also be "understood as a 'register' which refers to the contents of the table and helps to interpret the regional picture in more depth" (Lameli 2010: 570). The same 'register' function holds true for Schmeller's single supplementary map of comparative descriptions of Bavarian dialect grammars (1821). These, like numerous other publications, old and new, and sometimes referred to as 'atlases', do not fit the definition given above, these earlier examples rather being a kind of encyclopedic work.

4   The major distinction between 'small-area atlases' and 'large-area atlases' was first suggested by Hotzenköcherle (1962).

5   The first influential atlases for Europe were the *Sprach- und Sachatlas Italiens und der Südschweiz* (*AIS*; Jaberg and Jud 1928–1940) in the Romance tradition and the *Sprachatlas der deutschen Schweiz* (*SDS*; Hotzenköcherle, Schläpfer, Trüb, and Zinsli 1962–1997; the project was begun as early as 1935) in the German tradition. Jaberg and Jud, the editors of the *AIS*, may even be considered the first to display a rudimentary pluridimensional approach (cf. Thun 2000: 81; 2010). This is also true of the *SDS* survey, in which different social groups were queried at a restricted set of locations. However, these were considered on only a few maps and were merely referenced in the maps' legends.

6   For a comprehensive overview see the *International Handbook of Linguistic Variation: Language Mapping*, edited by Lameli, Kehrein, and Rabanus (2010).

7   These types of atlases can be called 'monodimensional linguistic atlases' since they limit the extralinguistic variables to areality (cf. Thun 2010). However, Wenker's immediate successors had already enriched the atlas data by their systematic extralinguistic embedding. This "led to the elaboration of the subdiscipline of social linguistics (Soziallinguistik) under Wrede's direction, whose most important output is the *Deutsche Dialektgeographie* [....] book series" (Lameli 2010: 579). This series was founded in order to systematically document complete dialectal systems in so called dialect grammars (*Ortsgrammatiken*). Moreover, the *SDS* (Hotzenköcherle, Schläpfer, Trüb, and Zinsli 1962–1997) was accompanied by the sound recordings collected and published by the Zurich *Phonogrammarchiv* (Phonogrammarchiv der Universität Zürich 1952). Hotzenköcherle's explicit claim to relate linguistic findings to extralinguistic phenomena in space is reflected by the close connection of the *SDS* to folklore projects.

8   Describing the methodology of traditional linguistic atlases as restricted to the consideration of the oldest speakers (a NORM: 'non-mobile rural old male' speaker; see Chambers and Trudgill 1980/1998: 29) is not quite in line with the facts: Wenker, for example, polled school pupils (via teachers), and Jaberg and Jud deliberately chose speakers between 45 and 60 years of age, because older speakers were often less suitable due to mental and physical aging. They also emphasize that, for a number of reasons, women in general made better informants (Jaberg and Jud 1928: 189–193).

9   For a more detailed treatment of the *LAGS*, see Kirk (2001).

10   Additional examples of bi- or pluridimensional linguistic atlases include the *Linguistic Atlas of the Seto Inland Sea* (Japan; Fujiwara 1974) or the German *Mittelrheinischer Sprachatlas* (*MRhSA*; Bellmann, Herrgen, and Schmidt 1994–2002).

11   Moulton (1961, 1962) applies the diasystem notation to describe regional differences between whole phonological subsystems in Swiss dialects. Peter Wiesinger's (1970, 1983) horizontal dialect classifications are also based on diasystematic comparisons of adjacent dialects.

12   Schirmunski (1962: 120) makes an early reference to the dynamics of the linguistic map ('Dynamik der Sprachkarte') which appears when the regional distribution of linguistic phenomena are compared across several maps.

13   This point of view is quite in line with modern sociolinguistic conceptualizations of linguistic space (see Britain 2010).
14   Additional examples of language change explained on the basis of language (system) internal factors can be found in the studies by Moulton (1961, 1962).
15   On the basis of this atlas and a comparison of the dialect maps, Girnth (2000) develops a theory of grammaticalization.
16   For recent and extensive overviews of potential findings from the study of pluridimensional linguistic atlases, see Thun (2010) and Mang and Wollin (2010).
17   Another analysis applying linguistic atlas data from several decades is described in Ebata (2008).
18   For a detailed description of the *DiWA*, see Kehrein, Lameli, and Nickel (2005), Rabanus (2005), Nickel (2008) and Rabanus, Kehrein, and Lameli (2010).
19   In some regions the diachronic perspective can be extended even further, since linguistic atlases of historical language states exist such as the *Linguistic Atlas of Late Medieval English* (*LALME*; McIntosh, Samuels, and Benskin 1986) and the *Historischer Südwestdeutscher Sprachatlas* (*HSS*; Kleiber, Kunze, and Löffler 1979).
20   The three surveys were conducted at a different number of locations. Following the methodological principle mentioned above, comparison is restricted to those locations polled in all three surveys (that is, for the *MRhSA* younger generation). The shaded areas indicate the distribution of features when all relevant locations are considered.
21   The Linguistic Dynamics Approach is presented in detail in Schmidt and Herrgen (2011).
22   "Full varieties must be distinguished from [...] sectoral varieties such as technical jargons (*Fachsprachen*), which are based on a full variety (whether standard or dialect) and feature restricted, sectoral, usually lexical distinctions and substitutions, and in which an individual's competence is subject to continual, lifelong change" (Schmidt 2010a: 215).
23   Male speakers were selected because 90 percent of police staff answering emergency calls in the relevant age group were men.
24   Since the collection of these data is very time-consuming, the number of informants has to be limited. However, by applying standardized methods of data collection and analysis, supplementary investigations can easily be directly incorporated into the *REDE* project. One such project (*Sprachvariation in Norddeutschland, SiN*) is currently running in the Low German language area (see Elmentaler, Gessinger, Macha *et al.* 2006).

REFERENCES

Aubin, H., Frings, T., and Müller, J. (1926) *Kulturströmungen und Kulturprovinzen in den Rheinlanden: Geschichte, Sprache, Volkskunde*, Röhrscheid, Bonn.

Auer, P. and Schmidt, J.E. (eds.) (2010) *Language and Space: An International Handbook of Linguistic Variation*, vol. 1: *Theories and Methods*, Mouton de Gruyter, Berlin.

Bach, A. (1934) *Deutsche Mundartforschung. Ihre Wege, Ergebnisse, Aufgaben*, Winter, Heidelberg.

Becker, H. (1942) Über Trichterwirkung. Eine besondere Art von Sprachströmung. *Zeitschrift für Mundartforschung* 18: 59–67.

Bellmann, G. (1965–67) *Schlesischer Sprachatlas*. 2 volumes, Elwert, Marburg.

Bellmann, G. (1997) Zur Technik und Aussagefähigkeit zweidimensionaler Dialekterhebung und Dialektkartographie am Beispiel des Mittelrheinischen Sprachatlasses. In G. Stickel (ed.), *Varietäten des Deutschen. Regional- und Umgangssprachen*, de Gruyter, Berlin, pp. 271–90.

Bellmann, G., Herrgen, J., and Schmidt, J.E. (eds.) (1994–2002) *Mittelrheinischer Sprachatlas (MRhSA). Unter Mitarbeit von G. Drenda, H. Girnth und M. Klenk.* 5 volumes, Niemeyer, Tübingen.

Bennike, V. and Kristensen, M. (1898–1912) *Kort over de danske Folkemål med Forklaringer,* Gyldendalske Boghandel and Nordisk Forlag, Copenhagen.

Britain, D. (2010) Conceptualizations of geographic space in linguistics. In A. Lameli, R. Kehrein and S. Rabanus (eds.), pp. 69–97.

Chambers, J.K. and Trudgill, P. (1980/1998) *Dialectology* (2nd edn), Cambridge University Press, Cambridge.

Ebata, Y. (2008) The new method and findings of geolinguistics, using linguistic atlases from every decade with regard to the phrase "It *will be* fine tomorrow". *Dialectologia et Geolinguistica* 16: 34–48.

Elmentaler, M., Gessinger, J., Macha, J. *et al.* (2006) Sprachvariation in Norddeutschland. Ein Projekt zur Analyse des sprachlichen Wandels in Norddeutschland. In A. Voeste and J. Gessinger (eds.), *Dialekt im Wandel. Perspektiven einer neuen Dialektologie,* Redaktion OBST, Duisburg, pp. 159–78.

Frings, T. (1924) *Rheinische Sprachgeschichte,* Baedeker, Essen.

Fujiwara, Y. (1974) *A Linguistic Atlas of the Seto Inland Sea,* 3 volumes, University of Tokyo Press, Tokyo.

Gilliéron, J. (1880) *Petit Atlas phonétique du Valais roman (sud du Rhône),* Champion, Paris.

Gilliéron, J. and Edmont, E. (1902–10) *Atlas linguistique de la France (ALF).* Paris. (Reprinted 1968, Forni, Bologna).

Gilliéron, J. and Roques, M. (1912) *Etudes de géographie linguistique d'après l'Atlas linguistique de la France,* Champion, Paris.

Girnth, H. (2000) *Untersuchungen zur Theorie der Grammatikalisierung am Beispiel des Westmitteldeutschen,* Niemeyer, Tübingen.

Girnth, H. (2010) Mapping language data. In A. Lameli, R. Kehrein, and S. Rabanus (eds.), pp. 98–121.

Gluth, K., Lompa, M., and Smolka, H.-H. (1982) Verfahren dialektologischer

Karteninterpretation und ihre Reichweite. In W. Besch *et al* (ed.), *Dialektologie. Ein Handbuch zur deutschen und allgemeinen Dialektforschung,* vol. 1, Walter de Gruyter, Berlin, pp. 485–500.

Goossens, J. (1969) *Strukturelle Sprachgeographie. Eine Einführung in Methodik und Ergebnisse,* Winter, Heidelberg.

Goossens, J. (1977) *Deutsche Dialektologie,* Walter de Gruyter, Berlin.

Haag, K. (1900) 7 Sätze über Sprachbewegung. *Zeitschrift für hochdeutsche Mundarten* 1: 138–41.

Hotzenköcherle, R. (1962) *Einführung in den Sprachatlas der deutschen Schweiz,* Francke, Bern.

Hotzenköcherle, R., Schläpfer, R., Trüb, R., and Zinsli, P. (1962–97) *Sprachatlas der deutschen Schweiz (SDS).* 8 volumes, Francke, Bern.

Ivić, P. (1962) On the structure of dialectal differentiation. *Word* 18: 33–53.

Jaberg, K. and Jud, J. (1928) *Der Sprachatlas als Forschungsinstrument. Kritische Grundlegung und Einführung in den Sprach- und Sachatlas Italiens und der Südschweiz,* Niemeyer, Halle (Saale).

Jaberg, K. and Jud, J. (1928–40) *Sprach- und Sachatlas Italiens und der Südschweiz (AIS).* 8 volumes, Ringier, Zofingen.

Kehrein, R. (2006) Regional accent in the German language area – how dialectally do German police answer emergency calls? In F. Hinskens (ed.), *Language Variation – European Perspectives. Selected papers from the Third International Conference on Language Variation in Europe (ICLaVE 3),* John Benjamins, Amsterdam, pp. 83–96.

Kehrein, R., Lameli, A., and Nickel, J. (2005) Möglichkeiten der computergestützten Regionalsprachenforschung am Beispiel des Digitalen Wenker-Atlas (DiWA). In G. Braungart *et al.* (eds.), *Jahrbuch für Computerphilologie* 7, Mentis, Paderborn, pp. 149–70.

Kirk, J.M. (2001) Maps: dialect and language. In R. Mesthrie (ed.), *Concise Encyclopedia of Sociolinguistics,* Elsevier, Amsterdam, pp. 350–62.

Klaproth, J. (1823) *Asia polyglotta. Sprachatlas*, A. Schubart, Paris.

Kleiber, W., Kunze, K., and Löffler, H. (1979) *Historischer Südwestdeutscher Sprachatlas (HSS). Aufgrund von Urbaren des 13. bis 15. Jahrhunderts. Band II: Karten*, Francke, Bern and Munich.

Kurath, H. (1938) *Linguistic Atlas of New England. Prospect*, Brown University for the American Council of Learned Societies, Providence.

Kurath, H. (1939) (with the collaboration of M.L. Hansen, J. Bloch, and B. Bloch) *Handbook of the Linguistic Geography of New England*, Brown University for the American Council of Learned Societies Providence.

Kurath, H., Hanley, M.L., Bloch, B., *et al.* (1939–43) *Linguistic Atlas of New England (LANE)*. 3 volumes, Brown University for the American Council of Learned Societies, Providence.

Kurath, H. and McDavid, R.I. (1961) *The Pronunciation of English in the Atlantic States. Based upon the collections of the Linguistic Atlas of the Eastern United States*, University of Michigan Press, Ann Arbor.

Labov, W. (1994) *Principles of Linguistic Change. Volume 1: Internal Factors*, Blackwell, Oxford.

Labov, W., Ash, S., and Boberg, C. (2006) *The Atlas of North American English (ANAE). Phonetics, Phonology and Sound Change. A Multimedia Reference Tool*, Mouton de Gruyter, Berlin.

Lameli, A. (2010) Linguistic atlases – traditional and modern. In P. Auer and J.E. Schmidt (eds.), pp. 567–92.

Lameli, A., Kehrein, R., and Rabanus, S. (eds.) (2010) *Language and Space: An International Handbook of Linguistic Variation*, vol. 2: *Language Mapping*, Mouton de Gruyter, Berlin.

Language Research Commission (ed.) (1905) *Phonetic Dialect Atlas (PDA)*, Publisher unknown, Tokyo.

Language Research Commission (ed.) (1906) *Grammatical Dialect Atlas (GDA)*, Publisher unknown, Tokyo.

Małecki, M. and Nitsch, K. (1934) *Atlas językowy Polskiego Podkarpacia. Cz. 1: Mapy*,

cz. 2: Wstęp, objaśnienia, wykazy wyrazów [Linguistic Atlas of the Polish Subcarpathian Region. Part 1: Maps, Part 2: Introduction, Explanation, Indexes of Words], Polska akademija umiejętności, Kraków.

Mang, A. and Wollin, M. (2010) Sprachraum and sociodemographic variables. In A. Lameli, R. Kehrein, and S. Rabanus (eds.), pp. 607–26.

McIntosh, A., Samuels, M.L., and Benskin, M. (1986) (with the assistance of M. Laing and K. Williamson) *A Linguistic Atlas of Late Mediaeval English (LALME)*. 4 vols., Aberdeen University Press, Aberdeen.

Moulton, W.G. (1961) Lautwandel durch innere Kausalität: die ostschweizerische Vokalspaltung. *Zeitschrift für Mundartforschung* 28(3): 227–51.

Moulton, W.G. (1962) Dialect geography and the concept of phonological space. *Word* 18: 23–32.

Nickel, J. (2008) Das 'Informationssystem Sprachgeographie': (Endlich) ein Kartographiepgrogramm für die Variationslinguistik. In S. Elspaß and W. König (eds.), *Sprachgeographie digital. Die neue Generation der Sprachatlanten*, Olms, Hildesheim, pp. 181–96.

Onishi, T. (2007) Mapping Japanese dialects, in *Geolinguistics Around the World. Proceedings of the 14th NIJL International Symposium, Tokyo (Japan)*, The National Institute for Japanese Language, Tokyo, pp. 1–6.

Ormeling, F. (2010) Visualizing geographic space and the nature of maps. In A. Lameli, R. Kehrein, and S. Rabanus (eds.), pp. 21–40.

Pederson, L., McDaniel, S.L., and C.M. Adams (eds.) (1986–92) *Linguistic Atlas of the Gulf States (LAGS)*, 7 vols., University of Georgia Press, Athens, GA.

Phonogrammarchiv der Universität Zürich (1952) *Der sprechende Atlas. Plattentext in verschiedenen schweizerdeutschen Dialekten*, Phonogrammarchiv, Zürich.

Rabanus, S. (2005) Sprachkartographie des Deutschen: Von Schmeller bis zum Digitalen Wenker-Atlas. In C. Di Meola et al. (eds.), *Perspektiven Eins. Akten der 1.*

Tagung Deutsche Sprachwissenschaft in Italien (Rom, 6.–7. Februar 2004), Istituto Italiano di Studi Germanici, Rome, pp. 345–63.

Rabanus, S. (2008) *Morphologisches Minimum. Distinktionen und Synkretismen im Minimalsatz hochdeutscher Dialekte*, Steiner, Stuttgart.

Rabanus, S., Kehrein, R., and Lameli, A. (2010) Creating digital editions of historical maps. In A. Lameli, R. Kehrein, and S. Rabanus (eds.), pp. 375–85.

Richey, M. (1754) *Idiotikon Hamburgense oder Wörterbuch zur Erklärung der eigenen, in und um Hamburg gebräuchlichen, Nieder-Sächsischen Mund-Art. Jetzo vielfältig vermehret, und mit Anmerckungen und Zusätzen Zweener berühmten Männer, nebst einem Vierfachen Anhange, ausgefertiget*, Conrad König, Hamburg.

Schirmunski, V.M. (1962) *Deutsche Mundartkunde. Vergleichende Laut- und Formenlehre der deutschen Mundarten*, Akademie, Berlin.

Schmeller, J.A. (1821) *Die Mundarten Bayerns grammatisch dargestellt*, Thienemann, Munich.

Schmidt, J.E. (1993) Zweidimensionale Dialektologie und eindimensional-vertikale Analyse. Ein exemplarischer Vergleich. In W. Viereck (ed.), *Verhandlungen des Internationalen Dialektologenkongresses Bamberg, 29.7.–4.8.1990*, volume 1, Steiner, Stuttgart, pp. 454–67.

Schmidt, J.E. (2010a) Language and space: the linguistic dynamics approach. In P. Auer and J.E. Schmidt (eds.), pp. 201–25.

Schmidt, J.E. (2010b) Linguistic dynamic maps and validation. In A. Lameli, R. Kehrein, and S. Rabanus (eds.), pp. 385–401.

Schmidt, J.E. and Herrgen, J. (2011) *Sprachdynamik. Eine Einführung in die moderne Regionalsprachenforschung*, Erich Schmidt, Berlin.

Schmidt, J.E. and Herrgen, J. (eds.) (2001–9) *Digitaler Wenker-Atlas (DiWA)*. Bearbeitet von A. Lameli, T. Giessler, R. Kehrein *et al*. Erste vollständige Ausgabe von G. Wenkers "Sprachatlas des Deutschen Reichs". 1888–1923

handgezeichnet von E. Maurmann, G. Wenker und F. Wrede, Forschungszentrum Deutscher Sprachatlas, Marburg. www.diwa.info [accessed November 1, 2010].

Swiggers, P. (2010) Mapping the Romance languages of Europe. In A. Lameli, R. Kehrein, and S. Rabanus (eds.), pp. 269–300.

ten Kate, L. (1723) *Anleiding tot de Kennisse van het verhevene deel der Nederduitsche sprake*. 2 volumes, Wetstein, Amsterdam.

Terracher, A. (1914) *Les aires morphologiques dans les parlers du Nord-Ouest de l'Angoumois (1800–1900)*, Champion, Paris.

Tesnière, L. (1925) *Atlas linguistique pour servir à l'étude du duel en slovène*, Champion, Paris.

Thun, H. (2000) Altes und Neues in der Sprachgeographie. In W. Dietrich and U. Hoinkes (eds.), *Romanistica se movet . . . Festgabe für Horst Geckeler zu seinem 65. Geburtstag*, Nodus, Münster, pp. 69–89.

Thun, H. (2010) Pluridimensional cartography. In A. Lameli, R. Kehrein, and S. Rabanus (eds.), pp. 506–24.

Thun, H. and Elizaincín, A. (2000) *Atlas Diatópico y Diastrático del Uruguay (ADDU). I, 1–2: Consonantismo y vocalismo del español*, Westensee-Verlag, Kiel.

Veith, W.H. (1994/2006) Dialect atlases. In K. Brown *et al.* (eds.), *Encyclopedia of Language and Linguistics*, volume 3 (2nd edn), Elsevier, Oxford, pp. 517–28.

Weijnen, A. (1977) *The Value of the Map Configuration*, Katholieke Universiteit, Nijmegen.

Weinreich, U. (1954) Is a structural dialectology possible? *Word* 10: 388–400.

Wenker, G. (1878) *Sprachatlas der Rheinprovinz nördlich der Mosel sowie des Kreises Siegen. Nach systematisch aus ca. 1500 Orten gesammeltem Material zusammengestellt, entworfen und gezeichnet*, Manuscript (published online in 2009, www.diwa.info).

Wenker, G. (1888–1923) *Sprachatlas des Deutschen Reichs*, Manuscript (published online 2001–5, www.diwa.info).

Wiesinger, P. (1970) *Phonetisch-phonologische Untersuchungen zur Vokalentwicklung in den deutschen Dialekten*, 2 volumes, Walter de Gruyter, Berlin.

Wiesinger, P. (1983) Die Einteilung der deutschen Dialekte. In W. Besch, U. Knoop, W. Putschke, and H.E. Wiegand (eds.), *Dialektologie. Ein Handbuch zur deutschen und allgemeinen Dialektforschung*, 2 volumes (1982/1983), Walter de Gruyter, Berlin, pp. 807–900.

Wrede, F. (1903) Der Sprachatlas des Deutschen Reichs und die elsässische Dialektforschung. *Archiv für das Studium der neueren Sprachen und Literaturen* 57(111). 29–48.

27 Historical Sociolinguistic Reconstruction Beyond Europe: Case Studies from South Asia and Fiji

MATTHEW TOULMIN

1. Introduction

Throughout the twentieth century, the comparative method (CM) served as the standard method of historical linguistic reconstruction.[1] Given the right historical sociolinguistic conditions, the results of comparative reconstruction are impressive (see, for example, Pawley and Ross 1993). Even in the successful cases, however, historical linguists understand that the results of CM reconstruction constitute a simplification of language history. Moreover, given a certain set of sociolinguistic conditions, not only might the CM simplify language history, it might distort it altogether.

The application of the CM to dialect continua has proved particularly problematic, and exposes historical sociolinguistic flaws in the assumptions that underlie the method. In this chapter, the CM is critically examined and revised in the light of research into dialect continuum history in India,[2] with further illustration from Fiji. The CM is not discarded, but re-constituted within a sociohistorical framework of language (and dialect) reconstruction.

The Handbook of Historical Sociolinguistics, First Edition. Edited by Juan Manuel Hernández-Campoy and Juan Camilo Conde-Silvestre.
© 2014 John Wiley & Sons, Ltd. Published 2014 by John Wiley & Sons, Ltd.

2. Theoretical and Methodological Considerations

2.1   *Understanding the dialect continuum*

A dialect continuum (or 'chain') involves variable, non-discrete boundaries between speech communities. Masica describes the Indic, or Indo-Aryan, situation as follows:

> Lacking clearcut geographical units of the European type where dialectal variants can crystallize in semi-isolation, or longstanding political boundaries, the entire Indo-Aryan realm (except for Sinhalese) constitutes one enormous dialect continuum, where continued contact inhibits such crystallisation, and differentiated dialects continue to influence one another. The speech of each village differs slightly from the next, without loss of mutual intelligibility, all the way from Assam to Afghanistan. (Masica 1991:25; see also Shapiro and Schiffman 1981).

The dialect continuum is a historical sociolinguistic configuration of closely related lects and their speakers.[3] Their histories are characterized by recurrent speaker interaction, and barriers to communication between adjacent lects are weak or non-persistent. Within a dialect continuum, two seemingly paradoxical processes are at work: *localizing* processes which create and maintain linguistic differentiation; and *integrating* processes of dialect leveling, which sustain unification. Saussure (1915/1966: 281) termed these two forces '*l'esprit de clocher*' ('spirit of the [town] church spire') and '*la force d'intercourse*' ('force of communication').

To use a different metaphor, both centrifugal ('center-fleeing') and centripetal ('center-seeking') forces act concurrently in a dialect continuum. The forces involved are social in nature and pull the speaker's linguistic conventions in two directions at one and the same time. The centripetal forces pull the speaker's conventions in the direction of more inclusive and 'global' social norms. These forces support the propagation of innovations across a wider range, and support the maintenance of shared linguistic features within a wider community of speakers. The centrifugal forces move in the opposite direction, towards more localized and exclusive usage. These forces support the maintenance of conservative local features (even in the face of wider pressures to replace them) as well as the propagation of innovative local features.

Given this depiction of the dialect continuum, the possibility of common changes occurring subsequent to, or concurrent with, divergence emerges as a completely natural and regular possibility. Frequently, dialect continua do not adhere to a 'family tree' model of language splits and discrete subgroups (Ross 1997). Instead, lects in the continuum split and reintegrate, undergo differentiation and leveling, depending on the historical sociolinguistic forces at work through speakers (cf. social network theory as developed by Lesley Milroy 1980/1987 and James Milroy 1992, 1997). The non-discrete nature of language history in a dialect continuum is, however, deeply problematic for reconstruction by the traditional CM, as we shall see.

2.2   An empirical problem for the CM

The Comparative Method (CM) is the most successful tool in the historical linguist's kit. Broadly defined, the method works as follows:

1) Collate and interpret correspondences between phonemes in putative cognate sets;
2) Reconstruct proto-phonemes and subsequent changes which account for the correspondences as regular phonological reflexes;
3) Interpret the reconstructed proto-phonemes as a (contemporaneous) protophonology of a protolanguage;
4) Reconstruct the protolexicon by substituting the reconstructed proto-phonemes in the appropriate positions of the constructed cognate sets.[4]

Step 3 introduces the assumption that reconstructed proto-phonemes form a contemporaneous system. Behind this assumption lies the idea that normal language phylogeny consists of the discrete differentiation of languages. Accordingly, common inherited features and reconstructed common 'proto-features' are assumed to predate differentiation. In the case of dialect continua these assumptions are erroneous and threaten the reliability of the CM (broad definition). The rest of this section provides illustrations of the problem of applying the CM in a dialect continuum.

   In his doctoral dissertation, Southworth (1958) applied the CM to a reconstruction of the historical relations between four major Indo-Aryan lects: Panjabi (Punjabi), Hindi, Bengali, and Marathi. The result is a reconstructed 'protophonology' for a 'protolanguage,' which he uses to reconstruct 'proto-words.' However, on comparing these results with ancient written records for Middle and Old Indo-Aryan, it becomes apparent that "the protolanguage cannot be assumed to represent any Indic dialect which could actually have existed; it combines different chronological stages [...] and different dialectal representations" (1958: 160). The method leads Southworth to reconstruct lexical items such as *két 'field' and *gin- 'count,' which correspond to Sanskrit *kṣétra* and *gr̥nti* respectively.[5] The problem is that the reconstructed items combine non-contemporaneous phonological features, so the reconstruction is not historically accurate. (For a fuller description of the problem exposed by Southworth, see Toulmin 2009: section 3.3.1.) In this instance, the CM fails to reach its goal of reconstructing reliable linguistic history.

   The implications of this failure of the CM are considerable. Southworth only knew the reconstructed protolanguage was historically fallacious because written records existed with which he could compare his reconstruction. In the case of lects with little or no historical writings, no such comparison is possible, and fallacious reconstruction may go unnoticed. Is the CM still useable? Can its results be interpreted in a way that avoids the kind of historical distortions illustrated above? It is not the intention of this chapter to throw the baby of the CM out with the bathwater of unrealistic underlying sociolinguistic assumptions. One failure of a method does not invalidate its many successes. Nonetheless, CM reconstruction rests on assumptions about language phylogenesis (historical descent) which need to be revised in the light of modern sociolinguistic theories of language change. In particular, the family tree model of discrete language divergence is an unreliable guide for sequencing change events, because a widely shared feature may have been propagated more recently than a highly localized feature. Alternative methods for sequencing linguistic changes are needed, based on empirically verified sociolinguistic principles of language change.

2.3   *Reconstructing the history of 'a language'*

Croft (2000) draws on concepts from evolutionary biology to outline a sociohistorical theory of language change. A central concept, requiring careful definition for language change theory, is 'the language' itself. Croft compares two types of definition for 'a language,' analogous to two types of definition for 'a species' in evolutionary biology. These definitions in turn give rise to different models of language descent and, we may add, different approaches to reconstruction. An essentialist approach defines 'a language' in terms of structural linguistic properties. A population-based approach defines 'a language' as the utterances used by a population of interacting speakers. Following the second definition, speaker interaction defines the boundaries of a language, rather than linguistic features *per se*. The population-based definition of a language has no problem with the sociolinguistic phenomena of variation and heterogeneity within 'the language,' because it is not those (or any other) linguistic features which define the boundaries of 'a language,' but, rather, the patterns of speaker interaction.

The population-based definition, however, creates a different methodological challenge for historical sociolinguists. 'The language' is defined by the interactions between speakers, but whilst a sociolinguist may study *present* patterns of speaker interaction, the language historian has no direct access to *past* interactions. Principles and methods of reconstruction are required, therefore, which seek *post facto* evidence for historical patterns of speaker interaction. Now, just as linguistic traits do not in themselves define a language, so too, the *post facto* evidence (including the distribution of linguistic traits) does not *in itself* define the phylogeny (historical descent) of 'the language.' Those traits are clues, to be explained through the reconstruction of realistic historical sociolinguistic scenarios, and it is these reconstructed scenarios (of speakers propagating linguistic traits through their interactions) which define the language's phylogeny. Accordingly, language phylogeny (as here defined) cannot be established by the CM alone, for the CM, as traditionally defined, examines only the linguistic traits. A further step is required, studying the range of those traits and explaining their distribution through realistic historical sociolinguistic scenarios.

The definition and use of the CM by historical linguists has yet to come fully to terms with sociolinguistics; but with the maturing of historical sociolinguistics the time is right for this development. There is no inherent conflict between the CM and historical sociolinguistics: the latter, indeed, provides the framework for a more reliable application of the CM. Whilst historical sociolinguistic scenarios have at times figured in historical reconstructions (see Lehmann 1962/1992: 127; and Bloomfield 1933: 344–345), the connection has tended towards the *ad hoc*, and lacked theoretical integration and methodological discipline.

2.4 Understanding the sociolinguistic processes of language change

An integration of the CM and historical sociolinguistics is based on a non-essentialist and sociohistorical theory of language change. The discussion here focuses on the models of change articulated by Croft (2000) and Enfield (2003). Though using different terminologies, they endorse models with basically the same components[6].

In the evolutionary model presented by Croft (2000), language change is composed of two basic mechanisms: 'altered replication' and 'differential selection.' The first of these processes involves "the creation of a novel variant by altered replication of a lingueme in an utterance" (2000: 238). This process, referred to below as 'novel variation,' is a necessary (but not sufficient) condition for language change (see also Weinreich, Labov, and Herzog 1968: 188). The second process is 'differential selection,' which entails the increase in frequency of a novel variant in speakers' utterances. Croft and Enfield refer to this mechanism as 'propagation,' a term which is adopted in the methodology outlined below.[7] Propagation of a variant is a social process, and "begins when the generalization of a particular alternation in a given subgroup of the speech community assumes direction and takes on the character of orderly differentiation" (Weinreich, Labov, and Herzog 1968: 187).

When propagation of a linguistic variant occurs in the speech community, this is a significant event in the historical descent (phylogeny) of the language. Indeed, if a language is defined as the population of utterances, and if linguistic phylogeny is concerned with relations of historical descent in 'the language,' then it must be the (sociolinguistic) propagation of the trait rather than the (linguistic) trait itself which defines linguistic phylogeny. Accordingly, it is the second process of change – propagation (or differential selection) – which is the necessary and sufficient cause of phylogenetically significant language changes. Change without propagation is possible – it is called drift – but it is of no phylogenetic significance if we adopt a population-based definition of 'a language.'

The task for historical sociolinguistic reconstruction, therefore, is to utilize historical sociolinguistic diagnostics, applied to linguistic changes reconstructed by, for example, the CM, towards the reconstruction of historical propagation events within speech communities. The necessary concepts and methods for this task are the subject of the next section.

2.5 Summary of a new theoretical framework for the CM

Linguistic phylogeny was defined above as the differential transmission of linguistic material through speaker interaction over the course of history. In order to reconstruct linguistic phylogeny, certain key terms are defined in this section, on which the method of reconstruction is based.

Speaker interaction enables *propagation* of novel variants, by means of social networks of speaker interaction (Croft 2000: 8; following the work of J. Milroy 1992, 1997, and L. Milroy 1980/1987). When an innovative feature is propagated through a web of interconnected networks of speaker interaction, this is termed a 'Propagation Event' (PEvent, my term). The geographical and social extent of a PEvent is its range.

The theoretical accompaniments of a PEvent are the 'Propagation Network' – the population of interacting speakers who participated in the change – and a 'Propagation Defined Language' – the population of utterances used by the members of the Propagation Network (Croft 2000: 26). The propagation defined language (henceforth PDLanguage, my term) does not necessarily represent a structurally homogenous entity, because it is not defined by its overall linguistic homogeneity but by a PEvent.

A phylogenetic subgroup of lects shares a common ancestral PDLanguage (defined by a PEvent) as part of their linguistic histories. If a propagation network (PNetwork, my term) is more limited in range than antecedent PNetworks, then this constitutes a phylogenetic division; if the new PNetwork is broader than the antecedent PNetworks, then this is a phylogenetic reticulation. Whether by division or reticulation, the new PNetwork defines a new PDLanguage, which must figure in the phylogenies of descendent lects. Note that under this theoretical approach, phylogenetic reticulations define a subgroup of lects in the same way as do phylogenetic divisions. The theoretical maxim 'once a subgroup, always a subgroup' does not hold within a dialect continuum, and a non-essentialist theory of linguistic phylogeny does not insist that it should hold.

A crucial task for the linguistic historian is the sequencing of PEvents. Only by the reconstruction of PEvents *in a sequence* can we reconstruct a coherent and plausible account of language history. PEvents may be sequenced based on linguistic, textual, or sociohistorical grounds. Innovations may be sequenced on linguistic grounds if the linguistic output from one innovation 'bleeds' or 'feeds' the input for another linguistic innovation. For example, we may reconstruct *s > h for PDlanguages A and B, and *h > Ø for PDLanguage A. If the dataset for PDLanguage A entails a 'feeding' relation between the two changes (*s > *h > Ø) then we have linguistic grounds for sequencing *s > h before *h > Ø.

Innovations may also be sequenced on textual grounds, though this is not without its problems: for instance if the written register is artificially distanced from spoken norms. In general the following principle should be followed when sequencing innovations based on textual evidence: assume that the text was at least partially archaic, and that the vernaculars of the time were more progressive in the use of innovative features than is attested by the text. The presence of an innovative feature in an historical text is good evidence that the feature had occurred in some lect at the time of writing. But if an innovative feature is absent from an historical text, this is not necessarily evidence that the innovation had *not* occurred in the vernaculars of the day. It is entirely plausible that the written norms lagged behind the spoken norms of the day.

Thirdly, the sequencing of innovations may be based on sociohistorical criteria. This chapter is pre-eminently concerned with the development of methods for applying sociohistorical criteria to reconstruct the sequence of innovations. The range of PNetworks does not remain stable over history: there is widening and narrowing as a result of changes in the structure of the speech community. A 'change in the structure of the speech community' constitutes a 'Speech Community Event' (SCEvent; see Ross 1997, 1998), and the directionality of SCEvents may entail a sequencing of PNetworks, and hence a sequencing of PEvents. For example, as we shall see later, the change in the course of a river can lead to changes in the structure of a Speech Community, which results in different PNetworks before and after the SCEvent. If we can sequence the PNetworks, then we can sequence the PEvents which define those PNetworks.

With these theoretical concepts now before us, we can turn to the methods for diagnosing and reconstructing historical PEvents and language phylogeny. The CM must be stripped of essentialist assumptions concerning 'a language,' 'a proto-language,' subgrouping, and linguistic phylogeny.

CM (non-essentialist definition):

(1) construct correspondences between phonemes in putative cognate sets;
(2) reconstruct proto-phonemes and subsequent changes which account for the correspondences as regular phonological reflexes.

Under this narrow definition the CM is stripped of as many assumptions about subgrouping as possible,[8] so as to prevent covert chronologies from sneaking into the reconstruction without warrant. When interpreting correspondences in a dialect continuum situation, the linguistic historian must keep in mind that shared features may have been more recently innovated than divergent features. Further criteria must be satisfied before the sequencing of shared and divergent features can be established. The CM (non-essentialist definition) is then integrated within a historical sociolinguistic framework for reconstruction:

I.   Reconstruct **linguistic innovations** (e.g. by the CM [non-essentialist definition]).
II. Scrutinise in as much detail as possible the **dialectological range** of the innovations.
III. Evaluate whether the innovations are diagnostic of **Propagation Events**. Look at: linguistic complexity of the innovation, ecological distinctiveness of the novel variant, and the historical sociolinguistic plausibility of propagation within the range.
IV. Investigate whether there are **linguistic grounds** ('bleeding' and 'feeding'), or **textual grounds** for a particular sequencing of changes.
V.   Investigate **sociohistorical grounds** for sequencing the PEvents in a certain way.

Do sociohistorical considerations make one possible sequence of PEvents more plausible than other possible sequences? Conside

(i) the possible permutations of SCEvents (divisions and integrations) which would account for the disjunction in PNetworks,

(ii) the relative plausibility of each possible permutation, and

(iii) the relative plausibility of a SCEvent as against the concurrent existence of multiple PNetworks within a complex Speech Community.

Accordingly, reconstruct the chronology of PEvents by selecting the most plausible historical sociolinguistic explanation.

VI. Bring together and harmonise the sequencing of PEvents based on linguistic, textual and sociohistorical criteria, within a unified account of language history.

3. Case Studies

3.1   Case study 1: proto Kamta and the New Indo-Aryan dialect continuum

This method is now applied to the reconstruction of phylogenetic relations within a small subgroup of New Indo-Aryan (NIA), which for historical reasons (outlined below) is termed the Kamta subgroup. The lects within this subgroup, spoken across northern Bangladesh, western Assam, northern West Bengal, north-eastern Bihar, and south-eastern Nepal, are known by a variety of names, including Rajbanshi, Rangpuri, Deshi, Surjapuri, Dhekri, Kamrupi, and Kamatapuri. For ease of reference, this group of names will be referred to below as KRDS (Kamta, Rajbanshi, Deshi, Surjapuri).

Synchronically, the KRDS lects within this subgroup are quite similar to each other, though nonetheless differentiated in phonology, morphosyntax, and lexicon.[9] The subgroup is geographically situated between the speech zones of Asamiya (Assamese), Bangla (Bengali), and various Bihari lects including Maithili (Map 27.1). The lects are often claimed by Asamiya speakers and scholars as dialectally subordinate to Asamiya, and by Bangla speakers and scholars as dialectally subordinate to Bangla. In certain sections of the speech community, speakers claim their lect to be a distinct language called 'Rajbanshi;' others agree on its independent status but call the language 'Kamta' or 'Kamtapuri;' still others refer to it generically as *deshi bhasha*, 'local language.'

3.1.1   The proto Kamta stage of language history   Phonological and morphological comparison of cognate forms in eight (geographically defined) KRDS lects, and comparison with the related language history of Bangla and Asamiya, yields five linguistic innovations that are common to all eight KRDS lects, and which are diagnostic of propagation events based on the complexity and ecological distinctiveness of the changes (see further Toulmin 2009: section 7.3). These five changes, taken together, provide robust evidence for a stage in language history ancestral

Map 27.1. The region where lects of the Kamta subgroup are spoken, with international boundaries and district names marked

to the eight lects, and distinct from neighboring languages; this stage is termed proto Kamta for historical reasons given further below.

- Third person pronominal stem (plural, nominative) *-mʰra, for example in Cooch Behar > /umra/ 'they (there)' /imra/ 'they (here).'
- Third person pronominal stem (plural, oblique) *-mʰa-, for example in Cooch Behar > /umar, imar/ 'their.'
- Innovative cognate forms within the (secondary) system of agreement suffixes, inflected for singular and plural number as well as first person:
  e.g. /dekh-il-**uŋ**/ 'I saw' vs. /dekh-il-**oŋ**/ 'we saw' {Cooch Behari lect}.
- Locational pronominals based on *-t̪ʰɛ + kuna > *- t̪ʰɛkuna.
- Second person singular imperative verbal suffix /-ek/ < *-ɛkɔ < *-ɛ '2 singular' + *-kɔ.

The wide distribution of these features across lects that are no longer sociolinguistically integrated is evidence for an ancestral, antecedent propagation network. The fact that these innovations are not shared with the neighboring lects (Bangla and Asamiya), however, is evidence that the ancestral proto Kamta PNetwork was distinct from proto Bangla and proto Asamiya PNetworks.

Examination of the sociohistorical record for the region yields information relevant to the sequencing of the proto Kamta PNetwork. The ancestors of the contemporary speakers of these lects were, at an earlier time, speakers of a Tibeto-Burman language (van Driem 2001). For the changes listed above to be unique to, but common throughout the KRDS region, these unique changes must have occurred after the Aryanization (conversion to Aryan religion and language) of a significant proportion of the ancestral population.

Sociohistorical records are not explicit regarding the timing and pace of the language shift from Tibeto-Burman to Indo-Aryan. Nevertheless we may surmise that a major factor in this regard was the shift of the ancient Kamrupa seat of government from Guwahati (to the east in today's Assam) to Kamatapur (near Cooch Behar in Map 27.1) around AD 1255.[10] Prior to this, the capital had been located near Guwahati, and had been a driving force for Aryanization of speech in the Brahmaputra valley (Clark 1969: 197). The capital was the center, both religiously and politically, from which Aryan influence radiated outwards. The shift of capital westwards to Kamatapur in the thirteenth century established a new center of cultural influence, and must have given a great impetus to the Aryanization of the Tibeto-Burman peoples in this region. Geographically located at the heart of what would become the KRDS-speaking area, Kamatapur as capital would have been a point of social reference for the surrounding villages, and a force for social integration, to a degree that Guwahati as capital had not been, on account of its considerable distance to the east. It is sociohistorically plausible, therefore, that Indo-Aryan influence greatly increased in the KRDS area after the change of capital and that this increased Aryanism gave rise to the proto Kamta speech community and its language (see further Toulmin 2009, section 7.3.1.1). This historical event provides a *terminus post quem* of AD 1255 for the proto Kamta PNetwork and PDLanguage.

The second event which is relevant to dating these changes, and which provides a *terminus ante quem* for the proto Kamta PNetwork is the expansion of the Kamta-Koch kingdom in the mid-sixteenth century. In the present day, the five innovations described above are distributed as far west as Morang of Nepal, and as far east as western Assam. The sociolinguistic conditions for a propagation over that area were absent both before and after the Kamta-Koch sociopolitical expansion of the sixteenth century. It is sociohistorically most plausible, therefore, that the unique proto Kamta changes were innovated before the sixteenth-century expansion, and exported throughout the regions occupied by the Kamta-Koch armies (see further Toulmin 2009, section 7.3.1.2). Accordingly, the proto Kamta PNetwork and PDLanguage is dated by this method as approximately AD 1250–1550. This dating hypothesis receives some confirmation from the letter of Maharaja Nara Narayana to the Ahom king, written in AD 1555, which attests some of the innovative features (see further Toulmin 2009, 7.3.1.3).[11]

3.1.2   Sequencing changes in 'the western corridor of change'   While there are some innovations which define the KRDS lects as a subgroup, there are also many innovations by which the lects are differentiated. The most complex array of isogloss boundaries within the KRDS area is found in a geographical corridor approximately 50 kilometers wide, which separates western KRDS lects from central or midlands KRDS lects. This area of criss-crossing ranges of historical propagation events is termed here KRDS's 'western corridor of change'. The main phonological and morphological innovations, whose ranges of propagation terminate in this corridor, are given in Map 27.2. The isogloss boundaries are labeled, and the key explains whether the innovation is found to the east (marked by 'e')

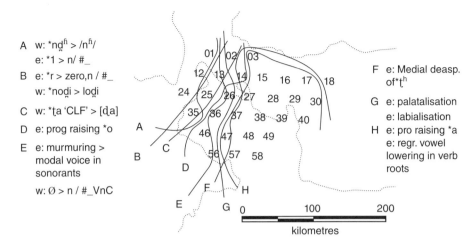

Map 27.2. Isogloss boundaries in KRDS's western corridor of change (Toulmin 2009, figure 7.6)

or to the west (marked by 'w') of the boundary line. A summary of the linguistic character of each innovation is also given in the map; the details are to be found in Toulmin (2009).

Confronted by such a complex dialectological pattern of innovations we might determine this to be the limit beyond which we cannot reconstruct language history. Note that the relative chronology of the changes cannot be established on linguistic grounds, because in general the changes do not bleed or feed into each other. Sociohistorical considerations, however, can provide a basis for sequencing the changes.

Upon inspection, some of the isoglosses can be seen to run in a north-south direction, as exemplified in Maps 27.3–27.4: dark shading indicates near categorical presence of the change in the data collected for that site; light shading indicates that the change is variable in the data for that site.

The western limit of these north-south running lines does not correspond with contemporary socio-political, geographical, or social boundaries; but it does correspond with the *old* course of the river Tista. This old river ran from north to south, and was, until around AD 1787, second only to the Brahmaputra river in terms of size and political importance for the KRDS region. The old Tista river functioned as an ethnic and political boundary during several historical periods: during early medieval times, it formed the boundary between the kingdoms of Kamrupa and Gauda. It also formed the boundary between the Koch and Gaur kingdoms before the expansion made by Biswa Singha's sons (Whyte 2002: 25). After the fragmentation of the greater Koch kingdom, this river for a time separated the Koch kingdom from Mughal Bengal (Nathan 1936: 804; Bhattacharya 1943: 241).

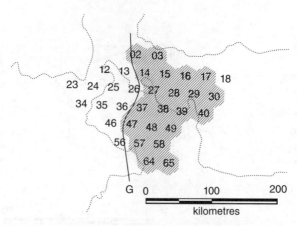

Map 27.3.   Dialect geography of phonological innovation: *C > Cʲ / i _ a (see PI 6, Toulmin 2009; reproduced by permission of Pacific Linguistics)

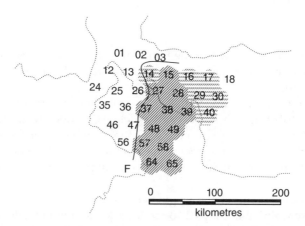

Map 27.4.   Dialect geography of phonological innovation: loss of aspiration for intervocalic consonants (see PI 10, Toulmin 2009; reproduced by permission of Pacific Linguistics)

As reported in the Gazetteers, large earthquakes and floods during AD 1787 had a major impact on the course and unity of the Tista river system, effectively splitting a major river into several smaller rivers. This event had a catastrophic effect on the lives of the inhabitants of the low lying flood-plains. Clark (1969) cites Henry Frowde's statement in the Imperial Gazetteer of India that one sixth of the local population died in the disaster.

On the one hand, then, we have the geographical course of the Tista river system which was a pre-modern political boundary and ran north to south until AD 1787. On the other hand, we have the dialect geography of several innovations which (1) are diagnostic of Propagation Events, and (2) share substantial portions of their western boundary quite exactly with this old course of the river Tista. Based on these correspondences in geography, I propose that the Tista was, before its division, a sufficient boundary to hinder interaction between speakers living on either side such that local changes propagated among speakers on one side were not adopted by speakers on the other. It may be mentioned in support of this argument that

(i)   the rivers of today's north Bengal are in general fast running, and among them the Tista is at times "exceptionally violent" (Clark 1969: 98);

(ii) the previous channel of the Tista was considerably wider than any of the present-day rivers of north Bengal (not including the Brahmaputra in the east); and

(iii) this major river had also functioned as a socio-political boundary at several points in the history of the region before its shift in course.

A causal connection between (a) the zone of interaction bounded by the old course of the Tista and (b) the propagation of innovations shown in Maps 27.3–27.4 (and other changes besides), provides a *terminus ante quem* for the associated innovations. The shift in the Tista's course would have resulted in a major restructuring of patterns of social interaction across North Bengal and the Cooch Behar kingdom. For the old course of the Tista to have so precisely conditioned the extent of propagation of linguistic changes, those changes must have been propagated before the river changed course. The easternmost limit of KRDS's western corridor of change is accordingly dated as prior to AD 1787 (when the river shifted its course).

The western limit of the corridor does not run in a north-south direction but from north-east to south-west, and may be defined by the isoglosses A, B and C of Map 27.3. The range of propagation of these innovations does not correspond with major geographical features, but rather with the major socio-political boundaries established by the British after they secured control of the region in AD 1773.

Notice that the ranges of propagation demonstrated by isoglosses A, B and C divide sites on the north-west from sites to the east and south. The region had only been divided along these lines – between Bihar in the north-west, and Dinajpur and Rangpur in the east and south –since the time of British rule in this area (AD 1773). The district of Dinajpur (Dinagepour) is shown in James Rennell's 1781 Bengal Atlas with these boundaries (see Rennell and Ambashthya 1975). The western limit of Dinajpur at that time followed a small river called Nagar (Nagore), which today forms the international border between West Bengal and Bangladesh (delineated in the maps included here). Prior to British rule, the river Nagar had no significance as a boundary between administrative divisions – on the contrary, it flowed directly through the center of the Sarkar (Mughal equivalent of a district) called Tajpur (see Habib 1982: plate 11). In short, the western limit of KRDS's western corridor of change corresponds very poorly with the Mughal administrative divisions, and much more neatly with the British reorganization of districts.

On the basis of these geographical observations, I propose a causal correspondence between the borders of district organization established by the British and the extent of propagation shown in isoglosses A, B, and C in Map 27.2. The same pattern of propagation was not found in the set of north-south changes (Maps 27.3–27.4), and this is plausible because the two patterns reflect historically distinct networks of speaker organization and interaction. The historical changes which best account for this change in speaker organization and interaction occurred at the end of the eighteenth century when: (1) the river Tista shifted its course, and (2) the British administration restructured the district boundaries. These restructured district boundaries provide a plausible sociohistorical cause for the occidental limit of the western corridor of change.

However, the impact of this administrative reorganization on patterns of social interaction and linguistic performance would hardly have been instantaneous. It probably took a few generations for the new socio-political boundaries to stamp their mark on patterns of interaction and linguistic propagation. We may assume, though, that the impact on speaker interaction of the administrative reorganization would have been exacerbated by the catastrophic events of AD 1787. An earthquake and flooding which killed one sixth of the local population would have caused major destruction of villages and led to considerable rebuilding of lives within the region. The rebuilding would have been both of physical aspects like houses and farms, but also of social events such as family relations. It is plausible that this rebuilding phase sped up the process of reshaping patterns of social interaction (and hence propagation events) along the new district lines.

This reconstruction relies heavily on the principles and methods outlined above for sociohistorical seriation of linguistic changes, which can be summarized as follows:

If   PNetworks are reconstructed with a disjunction in their ranges,
And   an SCEvent is, on balance, more sociohistorically plausible than the
        co-existence of these PNetworks within a complex speech community,
And   a particular directionality of SCEvent (either SC division or integration)
        is more plausible for sociohistorical reasons,
Then   this plausible directionality of the SCEvent also supports a particular
        sequencing of the PEvents.

In the case of KRDS's western corridor of change, there is a disjunction in ranges, with sociohistorical reasons for considering a particular directionality of SCEvent to be more plausible than the alternatives. The SCEvents reconstructed above for the corridor of change are (a) earlier division along the old Tista river course; with (b) subsequent reintegration between communities on either side after the river shifted course, this reintegration also influenced by colonial reorganization of district boundaries.

This particular directionality of SCEs is more plausible than the alternative scenarios, given what we know of the social history of the area. The directionality of SCEvents entails a particular chronological relation between the linguistic

PEvents: PEvents associated with the old river course preceded PEvents associated with the reorganized districts. The changes that preceded the shift in river course in AD 1787 must also have occurred subsequent to the division of the proto Kamta Speech Community in AD 1550 (following the expansion of the Koch kingdom).

Sociohistorical methods make possible the reconstruction of KRDS language history in greater detail and with greater reliability than a traditional application of the CM, which does not consider sociohistorical phenomena. In the case of KRDS, the sociohistorical reconstruction relies on a combination of attested and hypothetical (plausible) sociohistorical scenarios. In areas which lack documented social history, the same method can be applied but must rely to a greater extent on hypothetical scenarios and arguments about plausibility.

3.2 Case study 2: Geraghty's reconstruction of Fijian language history

The use of social history as a means of establishing the chronology of linguistic changes is not entirely new to historical linguistics. Inferences of this kind can be found in several studies but the methodology for developing them has nowhere (that I know of) been made explicit and proceduralized. Geraghty (Geraghty 1983: 351) cites Pawley and Sayaba (1971) as combining an "analysis of the linguistic situation with archaeological and topographical considerations," resulting in the hypothesis that "most of the favourable coastal regions of all the main islands of Fiji had been settled by 1000 BC."

Geraghty (1983) is a historical study of the related but differentiated lects spoken across the Fijian islands. Geraghty reconstructs (by the CM) distinct sets of innovations, with distinct ranges of propagation, which define (in my terms) PNetworks and PDLanguages. He proposes a sequencing of these PNetworks on the basis of plausible historical sociolinguistic scenarios. An illustrative subset of the PNetworks which he reconstructs is shown in Figure 27.1, with distinct ranges of propagation placed in different rows[12].

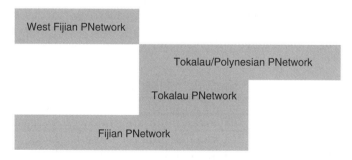

Figure 27.1.   Selected PNetworks reconstructed by Geraghty (1983)

Geraghty rejects the tree-model of language phylogeny as a reliable principle for sequencing these PNetworks:

> Exclusively shared features merely serve to suggest that languages were once in contact, and if features are shared exclusively by languages which are not in contact, those features constitute strong evidence that the languages were once in contact. In a dialect chain such as exists in Fiji, however, all adjoining communalects have generally maintained some degree of contact, so any observed innovation can be attributed to any time between the establishment of the dialect chain and the present. *A feature found all over Fiji, therefore, may be a recent innovation.* (Geraghty 1983: 277, emphasis added).

Instead (in part following Pawley and Sayaba 1971), he gives a sociohistorical argument based on topographical considerations, which can account for the disjunction between ranges of PNetworks. Viti Levu (the largest island of the Fijian archipelago) is divided from north to south by a mountain range; correlating with the topography, the Fijian languages are phylogenetically divided into west Fijian and Tokalau languages. The existence of a common PNetwork joining Tokalau (eastern) Fijian with Polynesian languages must be sequenced both in relation to the division of west and eastern Fijian PNetworks, and in relation to the unification of a single Fijian PNetwork.

Based on the contemporary distance separating Polynesian languages from Fiji – and the unsustainability of propagation among only these speech communities over so great a distance – an ancestral community (Pre-Proto-Polynesian) is inferred as having migrated from (north-)eastern Fiji to Tonga *after* the propagation of the Tokalau-Polynesian common innovations. Thus, this proto-community carried with them the proto-Tokalau-Polynesian innovations, but not any subsequent innovations that were propagated in eastern Fiji. The eastern (Tokalau) PEvents are then inferred, for simplicity of reconstruction, as occurring after the migratory division from pre-proto Polynesian. The unified Fijian PNetwork is reconstructed as a more recent occurrence on the basis of sociohistorical considerations, summarized by Ross as follows:

> After the geographic separation of Pre-Proto-Polynesian [PNetwork] from the Tokalau/Polynesian [PNetwork], the growing [Fijian] population filled up the coastal strip of Viti Levu and spread up the mountain valleys, so that the West Fijian [PNetwork] and the Tokalau Fijian [PNetworks] were gradually rejoined and innovations again began to spread across the mountain barrier between the two [PNetworks]. (1997: 229)[13].

Sociohistorical considerations, therefore, combine with the broader phylogenetic picture to justify the sequencing of a unified Fijian PNetwork as a more recent occurrence than the division of Fijian communication into west and east PNetworks. Despite the lack of written historical records for these language communities, sociohistorical scenarios contribute significantly to the sequencing of language history; and the methods used by Pawley and Sayaba (1971), Geraghty (1983), and

Ross (1997, 1998) are consonant with the more formalized procedure of sociohistorical sequencing of linguistic changes outlined in this chapter.

4. Conclusion

The phenomenon of sociolinguistic propagation events cutting across prior historical divisions of lects is not uncommon. In such cases, historical linguists need additional criteria, ones that go beyond the purely linguistic, for disambiguating the sequence in which changes were more likely to have occurred. Oftentimes sociohistorical criteria can (and do) provide a good basis for sequencing changes in language history, as has been demonstrated in the major case study of KRDS, and the shorter illustration from Fiji.

The integration of sociohistorical and linguistic criteria in reconstruction must not be *ad hoc*, but well grounded in theory, and well disciplined in method. The CM is a powerful tool for historical reconstruction, but its results must be interpreted without capitulating to essentialist models of language phylogeny. Note that in the framework put forward above, the CM (non-essentialist definition) is allowed to run its course in reconstructing the linguistic particulars of innovations before sociohistorical criteria and methods enter into the analysis. This is an important methodological point, which ensures the independence of the disciplines whilst synthesizing their results in a single model.

As disciplines, historical linguistics and historical sociolinguistics both deal with the phenomenon of language change; but they attend to distinct (yet related) types of data, and these data types entail distinct methods of analysis (see Ross 1998: 158). An optimum framework for reconstruction will make use of all the relevant data types – linguistic, sociolinguistic, archaeological, topographical, biological, and so on – whilst systematically managing the interaction and independence of the methods which best address each data type.

NOTES

1 My thanks go to Dr Bethwyn Evans, Dr Harold Koch, and Professor Malcolm Ross for reviewing an earlier draft of this chapter.
2 For an expanded articulation of the argument and methods outlined in this chapter, see Toulmin (in preparation).
3 Following Ross (1997: 212), "the term 'lect' and the corresponding adjective 'lectal' [are used] to cover both 'language' and 'dialect' since there is no objective way to draw a boundary between the two."
4 For similar but more exhaustive algorithms of the CM, see Ross and Durie (1996) and Koch (1996).
5 The symbol $\underset{\circ}{r}$ is used in Indic studies for 'syllabic r.' The open circle below the *r* is not to be confused with the IPA convention for 'voiceless.'

6   These studies in turn build on the works of Weinreich, Labov, and Herzog (1968), Thomason and Kaufman (1988), Milroy (1992), Keller (1994), and others.
7   Trask (2000: 159) terms this process 'implementation of change'.
8   The hedging words are necessary here because even in step (2) we cannot avoid some minimal considerations of subgrouping. See further Toulmin (in preparation, section 3.3.2, footnote 10).
9   For synchronic descriptions, see Wilde (2008) and Toulmin (in preparation).
10 Nowadays, this area is completely Aryanized, though with pockets of Tibeto-Burman speakers still inhabiting the thick jungle areas of Jalpaiguri to the north of Cooch Behar.
11 Maharaja Nara Narayana (son of Viswa Singha) was the second ruler of the Koch dynasty, from which Koch Bihar (Cooch Behar) takes its name.The Koch kingdom reached its zenith under Nara Narayana's reign through the military genius of Sukhladhvaj – the King's brother and commander-in-chief of the Koch armies.In AD 1555 Maharaja Nara Narayana sent a letter to Ahom king Sukampha. It is the oldest extant prose in the language of Kamta-Koch Bihar.
12 This analysis is also indebted to the re-presentation of Geraghty's work in Ross (1997).
13 Note that for the sake of consistency in this chapter, I have substituted my term 'PNetwork', for Ross's term 'linkage'.

REFERENCES

Bhattacharya, S.N. (1943) State of Bengal under Jahangir. In R.C. Majumdar and J.N. Sarkar (eds.), *The History of Bengal*, University of Dacca.

Bloomfield, L. (1933) *Language*, George Allen and Unwin, London.

Clark, R.H. (1969) *A Study of the Religious Customs and Practices of the Rajbangshis of North Bengal*, Hartford Seminary Foundation dissertation, Hartford, CT.

Croft, W. (2000) *Explaining Language Change: An Evolutionary Approach*, Longman, Harlow.

Durie, M. and Ross, M.D. (eds.) (1996) *The Comparative Method Reviewed: Regularity and Irregularity in Language Change*, Oxford University Press, New York.

Enfield, N.J. (2003) *Linguistic Epidemiology: Semantics and Grammar of Language Contact in Mainland Southeast Asia*, Routledge, London and New York.

Geraghty, P.A. (1983) *The History of the Fijian Languages*, University of Hawaii Press, Honolulu.

Habib, I. (1982) *An Atlas of the Mughal Empire: Political and Economic Maps with Detailed Notes, Bibliography and Index*, Oxford University Press, Delhi.

Keller, R. (1994) *On Language Change: The Invisible Hand in Language* (trans. B. Nerlich), Routledge, Abingdon and New York.

Koch, H. (1996) Reconstruction in morphology. In M. Durie and M.D. Ross (eds.), pp.218–263.

Lehmann, W.P. (1962/1992) *Historical Linguistics: An Introduction* (3rd edn), Routledge, Abingdon and New York.

Masica, C.P. (1991) *The Indo-Aryan Languages*, Cambridge University Press, Cambridge.

Milroy, J. (1992) *Linguistic Variation and Change: On the Historical Sociolinguistics of English*, Blackwell, Oxford.

Milroy, J. (1997) Internal vs external motivations for linguistic change. *Multilingua* 16(4): 311–323.

Milroy, L. (1980/1987) *Language and Social Networks* (2nd edn), Blackwell, Oxford.

Nathan, M. II. (1936) *Baharistan-i-Ghaybi: A History of the Mughal Wars in Assam, Cooch Behar, Bengal, Bihar and Orissa During the reigns of Jahargir and Shahjahan* (trans. M.I. Borah), Government of Assam, Department of Historical and Antiquarian Studies, Shillong.

Pawley, A. and Ross, M.D. (1993) Austronesian historical linguistics and culture history. *Annual Review of Anthropology* 22: 425–459.

Pawley, A. and Sayaba, T. (1971) Fijian dialect divisions; eastern and western. *Journal of Polynesian Society* 80(4): 405–436.

Rennell, J. and Ambashthya, B.P. (1975) *Memoir of a Map of Hindustan or the Mughal Empire and his Bengal Atlas*, N.V. Publications, Patna.

Ross, M.D. (1997) Social network and kinds of speech-community event. In R. Blench and M. Spriggs (eds.), *Archaeology and Language I: Theoretical and Methodological Orientations*, Routledge, London and New York, pp. 209–261.

Ross, M.D. (1998) Sequencing and dating linguistic events in Oceania: the linguistics/archaeology interface. In R. Blanch and M. Spriggs (eds.), *Archaeology and Language II: Archaeological Data and Linguistic Hypotheses*, Routledge, London and New York, pp. 141–173.

Ross, M.D. and Durie, M. (1996) Introduction. In M. Durie and M.D. Ross (eds.), pp. 3–38.

Saussure, F. de. (1915/1966) *Cours de linguistique générale* (3rd edn), Payot, Paris.

Shapiro, M.C. and Schiffman, H.F. (1981) *Language and Society in South Asia*, Motilal Banarsidass, Delhi.

Southworth, F.C. (1958) *A Test of the Comparative Method (A Historically Controlled Reconstruction Based on Four Modern Indic Languages, Panjabi, Hindi, Bengali and Marathi)*, Yale University Dissertation.

Thomason, S.G. and Kaufman, T. (1988) *Language Contact, Creolization, and Genetic Linguistics*, University of California Press, Berkeley.

Toulmin, M. (2009) *From Linguistic to Sociolinguistic Reconstruction: The Kamta Historical Subgroup of Indo-Aryan*, Pacific Linguistics, Canberra.

Toulmin, M. (in preparation) Rajbanshi/ Kamta, as spoken in India and Bangladesh. In T. Oranskaia (ed.), *New Indo-Aryan Languages*, Nauka, Moscow.

Trask, R.L. (2000) *The Dictionary of Historical and Comparative Linguistics*, Edinburgh University Press, Edinburgh.

van Driem, G. (2001) *Languages of the Himalayas: An Ethnolinguistic Handbook of the Greater Himalayan Region*, Brill, Leiden and Boston.

Weinreich, U., Labov, W., and Herzog, M.I. (1968) Empirical foundations for a theory of language change. In W.P. Lehmann and Y. Malkiel (eds.), *Directions for Historical Linguistics*, University of Texas Press, Austin, pp. 95–195.

Whyte, B.R. (2002) *Waiting for the Eskimo: An Historical and Documentary Study of the Cooch Behar Enclaves of India and Bangladesh*, The School of Anthropology, Geography and Environmental Studies, University of Melbourne.

Wilde, C.P. (2008) *A Sketch of the Phonology and Grammar of Rājbanshi*, Department of General Linguistics, University of Helsinki.

28 Multilingualism, Code-switching, and Language Contact in Historical Sociolinguistics

HERBERT SCHENDL

1. Introduction

The development of historical sociolinguistics has greatly advanced our understanding of the social dimension of earlier stages of language and of the social foundation of linguistic change. The compilation of large electronic corpora of historical texts, such as the *Helsinki Corpus of English Texts* (1991), but also of more specialized corpora such as the *Corpus of Early English Correspondence* (CEEC 1998), have enabled quantitative sociolinguistic studies of earlier stages of English in the tradition of Labovian sociolinguistics, taking speaker variables such as age, gender, and social status into account (see Nevalainen and Raumolin-Brunberg 2003). However, as the contributions to the present *Handbook* impressively illustrate, a wide range of further topics in historical linguistics have been addressed from a sociolinguistic point of view, including, more recently, questions of multilingualism, language contact, and of early code-switching (see also Chapter 3 in this *Handbook*). The present chapter will focus on historical code-switching as a recently developed subfield of historical sociolinguistics, which is closely linked to historical multilingualism and language contact. The main emphasis will be placed on the situation in medieval and early modern Britain, since this is a particularly well-researched area and period, though selected aspects from other European regions from these periods will also be addressed. This focus seems justified, since

The Handbook of Historical Sociolinguistics, First Edition. Edited by Juan Manuel Hernández-Campoy and Juan Camilo Conde-Silvestre.
© 2014 John Wiley & Sons, Ltd. Published 2014 by John Wiley & Sons, Ltd.

the theoretical and methodological questions discussed on the basis of the British situation are also of more general relevance and illustrate wider issues of the field.

2. Multilingualism and Language Contact

In many modern, especially Western, societies multilingualism is often considered a marginal and unwanted phenomenon, though on a world-wide scale it is rather the norm than the exception: monolingualism has even sometimes been labeled an 'aberration.' There is strong evidence that this was even more true of earlier historical stages, including medieval Europe[1].

Due to well-known political, demographic, and cultural developments in classical antiquity, multilingualism was already a widespread phenomenon in the Roman Empire (and before), though its specific nature depended on local conditions[2]. The collapse of the Roman Empire and the migrations and conquests of the Germanic tribes, as well as the Arabic invasions of Spain and Sicily in the medieval period, brought numerous vernacular languages into close contact, which left its traces in numerous European languages[3]. The spread of Christianity established Latin in most European countries as the language of religion, education, and culture and frequently resulted in a multilingual, often diglossic situation with Latin as a prestigious High language coexisting with one or more vernacular languages of low(er) status.

Thus, for example, the linguistic landscape of Britain between the late fifth century and the end of the eleventh was characterized by the increasing dominance of the various Old English dialects, competing with the lower status Celtic languages, but also with Old Norse in parts of the Midlands. Latin and, from the ninth century onwards, increasingly the West-Saxon form of Old English were used in the written medium. After the Norman Conquest of 1066, French established itself as the prestige vernacular for almost three centuries, though increasingly yielding its privileged position to English; however, for most of the period – and well into the sixteenth century – Latin continued to dominate as the language of literacy, though partly challenged by French and increasingly by English (on early language contacts in Britain, see Filppula 2010; Conde-Silvestre 2007). The linguistic situation in the later Middle English period is generally seen as triglossic, with Latin, French, and English predominantly used in specific domains (see Rothwell 1994; Wright 2000), though the use of any particular language in a particular domain was in general not categorical and, even more importantly, changed over the period.[4]

This brief sketch has of course neglected the regional and social dimensions of the complex multilingual situation in medieval Britain, as well as the fact that the political structure changed greatly from a number of more or less independent kingdoms in the early Anglo-Saxon period to an increasingly centralized political power. If we consider medieval Britain as a whole, there were large predominantly monolingual areas, within which socially determined multilingualism may have existed within certain social groups but also on the part of individuals. Furthermore, multilingualism in speech has to be distinguished from that in writing, the latter being the main topic of this chapter.

Any multilingual situation is inseparably linked to the social context in which it exists, that is, to factors such as the relative status of the languages involved, the power relations between the speakers of the different languages, the number and prestige of multilingual speakers, or the use of particular languages in specific domains. Equally, language contact and contact-induced linguistic change are to a large degree determined by such extralinguistic factors, though the relative influence of social and of language internal factors on contact-induced linguistic change is still controversial (Thomason 2001, 2008). The very different results of medieval language contact between English and Celtic on the one hand and between English and French on the other is clearly due to the different social contexts in which the two language pairs interacted, including factors leading to imperfect learning (Thomason 2001: 66–75).

One of the central questions to ask in the sociolinguistic analysis of multilingual societies is "[w]ho speaks what language to whom and when" (Fishman 1965: 428). All the relevant factors we need to answer this question are, again, social or sociolinguistic, irrespective of whether we are investigating modern multilingual speech communities or earlier ones, though the difficulties are clearly much greater when studying earlier multilingual societies.

An important factor influencing language choice in multilingual contexts is the relative status of the different languages, which for earlier multilingual societies can generally only be measured qualitatively; however, with a large enough written corpus, a quantitative diachronic analysis of language choice in a specific text type over a certain period may provide a welcome complement to qualitative analysis. John H. Fisher, for example, demonstrated that the changing status of French and English – which is directly linked to an ongoing shift from French to English – is reflected in the change of their absolute and relative frequencies in the Rolls of Parliament, a well-attested administrative text type, during the Hundred Years' War (Fisher 1977).[5]

Interesting insights into the relation between social status and language choice, and thus indirectly into the relative status of English and French in early fifteenth-century England, can be derived from a group of about sixty letters on the subject of a Welsh rebellion in the early fifteenth century (see Schendl 2002b). Written by and to men of different social standing, ranging from lower officials to members of the church and the nobility up to King Henry IV and the Prince of Wales, they were addressed "both to social equals and to social superiors and inferiors" (2002b: 249) and thus reflect social variables which have an influence on the choice of language. All letters by lower officials to higher ones in this corpus are in English, as are most of the answers of these higher officials. However, in the letters of the higher officials to socially still higher recipients (including the King), French was generally used, while the King and the Prince of Wales used exclusively French in their letters in this group (for details, see Schendl 2002b: 250–51, for the two letters showing code-switching see sections 3.2 and 3.3 below). It is important to emphasize that such patterns are often text-type related and cannot be generalized to other text types.

3. Multilingualism and Code-switching

3.1   *General remarks*

A frequent contact phenomenon in multilingual societies is code-switching: the use of more than one language in a specific communicative event (for recent surveys, see Gardner-Chloros 2009; Matras 2009: 101–145; and on contact and code-switching, Gardner-Chloros 2010). Though code-switching is generally regarded as being typical of speech, its use in written modern texts has been increasingly the topic of recent research (Callahan 2004; Sebba, Mahootian, and Jonsson, forthcoming). Modern research has approached code-switching from different perspectives, such as the structural and the psycholinguistic, but it has first and foremost been investigated as a social phenomenon (see Bullock and Toribio 2009a: 14–17). This also applies to most research into early code-switching in a number of languages, including English, where the sociocultural embedding of texts and text types as well as the social factors influencing code-choice and code-switching have been central aspects of research.

Direct evidence of early code-switching is obviously restricted to written mixed-language texts, which have survived in great numbers from inscriptions and texts from antiquity (Adams 2003; Adams, Janse, and Swain 2002) and even more extensively in a wide range of text types from different parts of Europe from medieval to modern times. Most of these mixed-language texts result from what Adams (2003: 9) has called "élite bilingualism:" they were produced by the educated and literate multilingual part of the population. The sociohistorical study of such early written evidence of code-switching is a quite recent development, mainly since the 1990s (for brief surveys, see Schendl 2002a, and the Preface to Schendl and Wright 2011), though a number of earlier studies paved the way (such as Stolt 1964; Lüdi 1985, 1989). Particularly extensive research has been conducted for early English (see Schendl and Wright 2011), but there are also a large number of studies on other countries and regions, such as the Roman Empire (Adams 2003), Switzerland (Lüdi 1985, 1989), France (Trotter 2006), Italy (Lazzerini 1971; Kämmerer 2006), Germany (Stolt 1964; Kämmerer 2006); for an illustration of a variety of early code-switched texts from European countries, see Schendl (2004a).

Like historical sociolinguistics in general, sociolinguistic research into early code-switching requires an interdisciplinary approach, combining historical linguistics with sociolinguistics and social history (Nevalainen and Raumolin-Brunberg 2003: 8). As in the sociolinguistic analysis of monolingual discourse in multilingual contexts, a central question of historical code-switching is again the question of "[w]ho speaks what language to whom and when" (see section 2); in other words, we not only have to analyze which social factors, both macro- and microlinguistic, make speakers and writers choose language A instead of language B, but also under which social conditions they additionally opt for a code-switched discourse. In other words, both code choice and code-switching in multilingual societies are dependent on similar sociolinguistic factors, irrespective of whether the involved languages have equal status or differ in prestige and in their domains of use. Multilingual speakers are the carriers of language contact in a multiplicity of situations, but most importantly, in their use of code-switching.

3.2   Code-switching and language shift

In section 2 we pointed out that language shift may be reflected in the changing frequencies in the use of competing languages in a particular text type, such as the Rolls of Parliament, where we find a dramatic decrease in French-language documents and a corresponding increase in English documents between the 1420s and the 1440s, leading finally to the complete disappearance of French from this text type. It is not only such quantitative changes of monolingual documents that can be indicators of an ongoing language shift, but also the appearance or increase of mixed-language documents (for the relation between language shift and code-switching, see Myers-Scotton 1993: 223–24.) For example, among the 61 vernacular letters relating to the Welsh rebellion of the early fifteenth century (see section 2 above), 11 are monolingual in English, 48 in French, while two predominantly French letters addressed to King Henry IV by the archdeacon of Hereford in 1403 show extensive code-switching into English.[6] As discussed in Schendl (2002b: 247–48, 257–59), monolingual English letters are attested only from the 1390s onwards, so that there seems to be a clear temporal correlation between the first use of English in non-official letters and that of the appearance of French/English mixed letters, with French increasingly replaced by English during the reign of Henry V. Interestingly, King Henry himself shifted in his non-official correspondence from French to English, especially from 1417 onwards, probably for political reasons. A similar correlation between the increasing use of the vernacular in text types where Latin had earlier predominated exists with mixed-language sermons (also known as 'macaronic sermons') from late medieval England (Schendl 2002a: 70–71) and also with medical texts, where the overlap between the increase of code-switching and the increasing vernacularization of this text type is also clearly observable (see Voigts 1996: 814; Pahta and Taavitsainen 2004: 12; and Chapters 7 and 8 in this *Handbook*). Such a correlation between a shift from French to German and the increase of code-switching had also been observed by Lüdi (1985: 165–68) in fifteenth-century administrative documents from the Swiss town of Fribourg.

3.3   Attitudes towards early code-switching

Unlike many modern Western societies, where code-switching is often evaluated negatively or even stigmatized, multilingual speech seems to have been viewed more neutrally or even positively in earlier European societies, especially in the period before the standardization of vernacular languages – at least when it resulted from 'elite bilingualism.' Such earlier attitudes towards switching can be recovered at least indirectly by sociolinguistic analysis, for example by looking at the social and educational status of the producers and recipients of code-switched texts and their relative power relations, by analyzing the text types in which code-switching is attested, and by its sociolinguistic functions. This type of analysis is particularly promising in the case of early letters, an interactive text type which is often closer to speech. Non-official letters in particular provide interesting evidence not only for the status of languages in multilingual settings, but also for attitudes towards code-switching. Though the vernacular was used for letter writing rather late – in England only from the end of the fourteenth century (see section 3.2) – quite a number of multilingual letters have survived from medieval and early modern Europe, all of which support the social accept-ance and acceptability of code-switching in this text type, even among the upper social ranks. As briefly mentioned in 3.2, among the earliest bilingual vernacular letters from England are two letters in French addressed by Richard Kingeston, archdeacon of Hereford, to King Henry IV in 1403, which code-switch extensively into English. Since there can be hardly any doubt that letters to the King would have been carefully checked before being sent off, this extensive code-switching must have been a conscious choice by the author and cannot have been considered as inappropriate in addressing the King (for a discussion of the possible function of switching in these letters, see section 3.4.2 below, and Schendl 2002b). Similarly, in an Italian letter by Pope Sixtus IV to Galeazzo Maria Sforza, dated 1474, we find a number of switches from the vernacular into Latin, a frequent pattern also found in the late Middle English Paston letters, particularly those written by Friar John Brackley to Sir John Paston, a member of the Paston family (of gentry status), in the late 1450s. Even more telling in regard to the acceptability of code-switching are the multilingual letters of the Emperor Maximilian II from around the middle of the sixteenth century, addressed to one of his ambassadors; here we find fre-quent switches from the German matrix language both into Latin and Castilian (for illustrating samples, see Schendl 2004a). Though each of these cases must be analyzed in its specific sociolinguistic context, especially in regard to the relative status of sender and receiver, their relative power relations and the status of the languages involved, such examples must be regarded as proof of the wide social acceptability of code-switching in letters, even among the highest ranks of society and in various European countries in the late medieval and early modern periods.

Other formal and non-formal text types where code-switching frequently occurs both in early Britain and on the continent are 'macaronic' sermons and other religious texts, accounts, and medical and scientific texts, as well as a variety of literary texts. In spite of their wide range of functions and their different status, all these texts speak against any social stigmatization of code-switching in the medieval and early modern periods.

3.4 The empirical study of early code-switching

3.4.1 The data problem The linguistic foundation of any sociohistorical analy-sis of early code-switching is a sufficient and reliable amount of mixed-language data which satisfy "the requirement of *empirical validity*" (Nevalainen and

Raumolin-Brunberg 2003: 9, original emphasis). There are, however, a number of restrictions especially on medieval mixed-language data, such as the limited literacy of particular parts of society (especially with regard to gender), and partly in regard to text types. Furthermore, we often have only limited information not only on important social variables concerning the producers and the recipients or audiences of the texts, but also on their purpose or mode of delivery.

As for the accessibility of code-switching data from the history of English, only a small part of mixed-language material has been edited so far; early editions are often unreliable, particularly in their rendering of the abbreviations in medieval manuscripts (see Wright 1995, 1998). While the sociolinguistic analysis of earlier monolingual English texts can rely on an increasing number of electronic corpora (see section 1, and Chapter 6 in this *Handbook*), there are still no purpose-built mixed-language corpora of earlier texts. Nevertheless, even basically 'monolingual' corpora such as the *Helsinki Corpus* and the *Corpus of Early English Correspondence* provide a wide range of code-switched data, though they lack specific mixed-language text types such as 'macaronic' sermons and poems and mixed-texts with Latin or French as the matrix language, such as the two mixed-language letters to King Henry IV discussed above (studies on early code-switching based on these two electronic corpora include Pahta and Nurmi 2006; Pahta and Nurmi, 2011 for a critical assessment of such corpus studies, see Schendl and Wright, 2011).

3.4.2   Some social functions of early historical code-switching   As stated above, a sociolinguistic analysis of early code-switching attempts to uncover the socio-cultural embedding of mixed language texts, the social factors which influence this multilingual strategy and, last but not least, the social functions of switching. These questions can only be answered on the basis of extralinguistic information on social parameters, which is, however, often incomplete or even lacking, particularly since for certain text types in particular periods of language history few mixed-language texts survive. As for other areas of historical sociolinguistics, Labov's 'uniformitarian principle,' the view that insights from the present can be used to explain the past, has been widely accepted for the analysis of historical code-switching (see Lüdi 1985: 172; Machan 1994: note 5; Schendl 2002a: 60–61; and Chapter 5 in this *Handbook*). Though the basic principles governing this strategy can be regarded as valid, this does not mean that there are no differences between early and present-day switching, but as Nevalainen and Raumolin-Brunberg (2003: ix) point out, "in recent years the past has also established its relevance to the present," and this also applies to historical code-switching research.

In view of the uneven distribution of switching in different text types, historical analyses should concentrate on particular text types either at a given point of time or – if the data allow – diachronically over time. In the following we will illustrate some specific functions in a few selected text types in the early history of English. However, the basic problems encountered in such an analysis will be the same for other early European languages.

Administrative texts are among the most frequent text types to show early code-switching, not only in Britain but also in various continental countries. Among the earliest studies are George Lüdi's analyses of switching in numerous 'town protocols' from the multilingual Swiss town Fribourg from the fourteenth and fifteenth centuries (Lüdi 1985, 1989). Medieval Britain offers a particularly rich source of mixed-language administrative texts, from the Old English charters (Schendl 2004b) to a variety of administrative text types in the Middle English period, in particular different types of accounts (see Wright 1995, 1998), wills, inventories, and similar documents.

Tenth-century charters – documents granting land or specific privileges to individuals or institutions – offer an interesting case of language choice and code-switching: While the Old English royal charter was typically written in Latin,[7] and the writ, a specific non-royal document granting land, was always in the vernacular, other non-royal charters were less restricted in their choice of language. Among these non-royal documents, the 75 land leases granted by Oswald of Worcester over a period of about 30 years are of particular linguistic interest, since a majority of them show code-switching, sometimes extensive and varied, primarily from Latin to Old English, less frequently the other way round; see example (1), a lease to Eadric dating from 988 (manuscript BL Cotton Tiberius, A xiii).[8]

(1) [Q]uandam rurusculi partem, tres uidelicet, mansas et dimidiam. in loco. quem illius terrae soliculae Cloptun uocitant, 7 .vi. *æcras mædwan for ongean ða mylne æt Eanulfes tune 7 healfe mylene æt Bluntesige into Cloptune*, libenti concedo animo, cum omnibus ad eum utilitatibus rite pertinentibus, […] Eadrico, meo uidelicet ministro

    [A] certain share of a small estate, namely three and a half hides, in the place which the inhabitants of this land call Clopton, and 6 *acres of meadow opposite the mill at Alveston and half the mill at Bluntesige to Clopton*, I gladly grant with all rights belonging to it, […] to Eadric, my minister

A functional analysis of switching in Oswald's leases has shown that we have to distinguish between the micro-level functions (such as indication of date, definition of property, and possible sanctions for the breach of the lease) and the macro-level function; the latter is linked to the respective status and domains of Latin and Old English, which were to a certain extent in a diglossic distribution in multilingual Anglo-Saxon England (Nevalainen and Raumolin-Brunberg 2005: 37). On this macro-level, the alternating use of Latin as the language of authority and the Church and Old English as the language of lay society is consciously used to build a linguistic bridge between two different social and political spheres, namely the ecclesiastical authority of Oswald and the See of Worcester and the members of the secular society, "whose allegiance Oswald's leasing policy was trying to secure" (Schendl 2011: section 6). It is this macro-level which is of particular relevance for the sociohistorical analysis of switching in Oswald's leases.

The majority of the accounts and inventories from the Middle English period show a particular type of code-switching, in which the language of (closed-class) function words such as prepositions was originally Latin or French while nouns, and later also verbs and noun modifiers, were in English. Though we find a trend towards the increasing use of English, the extensive use of abbreviations and suspension marks often neutralizes the languages, since word stems are often identical in Latin, French, and English, while the language-specific morphology is hidden by the abbreviation system (Wright 1995, 1998). According to Wright, this medieval mixed-language business text type was found Europe-wide and functioned not only as a supra-regional code in multilingual Britain, but even as an international trade language, which only disappeared with the increasing emergence of the new English standard language.

Sermons are another frequent mixed-language text type found in medieval (and partly early modern) Britain as well as on the continent (Wenzel 1994; Kämmerer 2006; Lazzerini 1971; Stolt 1964). Since the production, purpose, and audience of these multilingual sermons as well as the languages involved differ from one country to another, the following brief discussion will be limited to bilingual sermons from England dating from the late fourteenth to the late fifteenth century. Example (2) from Wenzel (1994: 274) gives a sample from the early fifteenth-century sermon *De cello querebant* (manuscript Oxford, MS Bodley 649):

(2) Set bene nouistis quod *be* vitis *neuer so likinge* in [blank], rami *neuer so fair ne so lusti*, ex quo est gracilis et fere nullius fortitudinis, nisi supportentur *railis*, cito possunt *be blow doun and broke*. Þes *railis* nichil aliud sunt nisi comunitas regni, populus qui est sub gubernacione dominorum, quos oportet fundari in humili-tate, pati *wytout grangynge and grennynge* superiorum correcciones si delinquant, *þai most obey to her gouernouris* in omnibus licitis et supportare vites domini corpore *and catel*.

But you know well that, *be* the vine *ever so pleasant*, the branches *ever so fair or so cheerful*, because it is delicate and has practically no strength, unless they be supported *by rails*, they can be *blown down and broken*. *These rails* are nothing else than the community of the realm, the common people who are under the rule of the lords, who must be rooted in humility, suffer *without groaning and gnashing of teeth* against the correction by their superiors if they have done wrong; *they must obey their governors* in everything that is lawful and support the vines of their lord with their body *and goods*.

Though the question of whether these sermons were preached in their mixed-language form to a multilingual audience (Wenzel 1994) or instead used as reading matter (Fletcher 1994; Schendl forthcoming a) is controversial, these mixed sermons constitute a particular mode of bilingual discourse of this clerical multi-lingual audience or readership, whose main macro-level function is "to express dual or multiple group-membership or to establish in-group feeling in certain communicative situations or for certain communicative purposes" (Schendl forth-coming a; for this general function see also Poplack 1980).

In section 3.2 we discussed the relevance of mixed-language letters for discovering attitudes towards early code-switching. However, as an interactive text type, letters also show various sociolinguistic functions of switching. The switches to English in the French letters to Henry IV discussed above occur especially when the writer becomes emotionally involved with his message, while the French passages are predominantly objective accounts of events or facts. The text and translation are from Hingeston (1860: I. 155–59).

(3) [P]lease a vostre tresgraciouse Seignourie entendre que a jourduy, apres noo[ne] [...] q'ils furent venuz deinz nostre countie pluis de CCCC des les rebelz de Owyne, Glyn, Talgard, et pluseours autres rebelz [...]

Qar, mon tresredoute Seigneur, vous trouverez pour certein que si vous ne venez en vostre propre persone pour attendre [apres] voz rebelx en Galys, vous ne trouverez un gentil que veot attendre deinz vostre dit Countee.

War fore, for Goddesake, thinketh on 3our beste Frende, God, and thanke Hym as He hath deserved to 3owe; and leveth nought that 3e ne come for no man that may counsaille 3owe the contrarie; for, [...] the Walshmen supposen and trusten that 3e schulle nought come there,[...]

Tresexcellent [...] Seignour, autrement say a present nieez.

[M]ay it please your most gracious Lordship to consider that to day, after noon [...] there were come into our county more than four hundred of the rebels of Owen, Glynn, Talgard, and many other rebels besides [...] For, my most dread Lord, you will find for certain that, if you do not come in your own person to await your rebels in Wales, you will not find a single gentleman that will stop in your said county.

Wherefore, for God's sake, think on your best friend, God, and thank Him, as He hath deserved of you; and leave nought that you do not come for no man that may counsel you the contrary: for, [...] the Welshmen suppose and trust that you shall not come there, [...]

Most excellent [...] Lord, I know nothing besides at present.

The function of switching in the two mixed-language letters can be interpreted as "marking personalization vs. objectivization" (Romaine 1990/1995: 164), with the function of English being personalization, and that of French that of a "marker of objectivization" (Schendl 2004a: 258).

As mentioned above, the scarcity of data and of extralinguistic social information often makes the sociohistorical analysis of medieval texts difficult, though the above discussions should have shown that, even in this early period, such an approach can yield valuable results. With the great increase of data and extralinguistic information from the early modern period onwards (Nevalainen and Raumolin-Brunberg 2003: 29–30), such an approach becomes even more relevant for the analysis of early code-switching. This is convincingly illustrated in two recent detailed studies of code-switching practices in English texts from the eighteenth century. Pahta and Nurmi (2009) investigate the interpersonal communication of the musician and music historian Charles Burnley (1726–1814) as attested in fifty letters to a variety of people. Drawing "on insights gained in research in interactional sociolinguistics" (2009: 27), the authors show that the code-switching practices in these letters vary according to the relationship between Burnley and the recipients of his letters, switching being "more frequent in letters written between correspondents who have a close relationship;" furthermore, switching is related to "particular types of social memberships and relationships" (2009: 27). Nurmi and Pahta (2010) study a variety of texts from different registers and genres in both the private and public domain by the clergyman and scholar Thomas Twining (1734–1804). Like the previous study, code-switching patterns reflect different social roles and functions "as an index of the communicative situation and the interpersonal relationship between the interlocutors" (2010: 135).

As for early bilingual speech, a unique and particularly interesting corpus has survived in Martin Luther's (1483–1546) so-called "table talks" (*Tischgespräche*), his conversations with friends and students on a variety of topics over dinner. Luther's German/Latin mixed conversations were written down by some of his pupils and thus constitute a unique documentary record of the bilingual discourse of an influential sixteenth-century German cleric. Their detailed analysis by Birgit Stolt in 1964 can be seen as the beginning of historical code-switching research, though it still stands outside the framework of historical sociolinguistics. Written dialogues from earlier periods based on natural speech such as Luther's are extremely rare. However, invented dialogues as found in drama and in a variety of verse and prose narratives can also provide interesting data, as long as we are aware that invented dialogues do not represent real speech, though they may be close to it. Diller's (1997/98) study of code-switching in medieval drama analyses the functions of English, French, and Latin and thus reveals their status and level of prestige. Putter (2011) shows how code-switching in direct speech passages in Geoffrey Chaucer and William Langland was used as a strategy for negotiating the speaker's position towards other participants in the exchange as well as towards the speaker's own utterances.

4. Conclusion

Language contact and contact-induced changes have often been viewed primarily from the point of view of their linguistic results and as being mainly due to language-internal factors. However, both early multilingualism and one of its most typical strategies, code-switching, can only be fully understood if we approach these changes from a sociolinguistic point of view. Though earlier periods of language certainly present problems for such an approach, particularly because of the scarcity not only of data but especially of sociolinguistic and social information on the context of multilingual discourse, we have tried to illustrate that even for these early periods, historical sociolinguistics provides an important research paradigm for multilingual practices, including code-switching. After long neglect as an object of historical linguistic research, recent studies in this field have clearly shown its importance for a deeper understanding of various aspects of historical multilingualism. Furthermore, such research opens up the important diachronic dimension of one of the most prolific fields of modern sociolinguistic research.

NOTES

1   For accounts on earlier multilingualism, see Braunmüller and Ferraresi (2003), Metcalfe (2003), Trotter (2000), and the contributions in Hickey (2010: 359–836); for more recent multilingual colonial settings, see Trudgill (2010).
2   On multilingualism in the Roman empire, see Adams (2003), and the contributions in Adams, Janse, and Swain (2002).
3   For the role of Arabic in multilingual Sicily and its replacement by Latin, see Metcalfe (2003).
4   For accounts of multilingualism and language contact in other regions see, for example, Metcalfe (2003), Braunmüller and Ferraresi (2003).
5   For instance, in 1422, 76% were in French, 13% in English; while by 1440 the figures were approximately reversed, with only 14% in French, 62% in English, and the rest in Latin (Fisher 1977).
6   There are two earlier mixed-language letters, one from the late 1370s and another one from around the early 1380s (Schendl 2002b: 257).
7   Except for the so-called boundary-clause, which by that time was always in the vernacular even in otherwise Latin, English, or mixed charters. These boundary clauses specified the boundaries of the granted land and were thus the communicatively most salient part of a charter; this may have been the main reason for their being written in the vernacular. For more details, see Schendl (2011: sections 3.2 and 4.1.1).
8   For detailed discussion of syntactic and sociolinguistic aspects of code-switching in these leases, see Schendl (2011), where the following example is given and discussed under (35). Here as in other examples, switches from the matrix language are indicated by italics.

REFERENCES

Adams, J.N. (2003) *Bilingualism and the Latin Language*, Cambridge University Press, Cambridge.

Adams, J.N., Janse, M., and Swain, S. (eds.) (2002) *Bilingualism in Ancient Society: Language Contact and the Written Word*, Oxford University Press, Oxford.

Braunmüller, K. and Ferraresi, G. (eds.) (2003) *Aspects of Multilingualism in European Language History*, John Benjamins, Amsterdam.

Bullock, B.E. and Toribio, A.J. (2009a) Themes in the study of code-switching. In B.E. Bullock and A.J. Toribio (eds.), pp. 1–17.

Bullock, B.E. and Toribio, A.J. (eds.) (2009b) *The Cambridge Handbook of Linguistic Code-switching*, Cambridge University Press, Cambridge.

Callahan, L. (2004) *Spanish/English Codeswitching in a Written Corpus*, John Benjamins, Amsterdam.

CEEC = *Corpus of Early English Correspondence* (1998) Compiled by T. Nevalainen, H. Raumolin-Brunberg, J. Keränen, M. Nevala, A. Nurmi, and M. Palander-Collin Department of English, University of Helsinki. http://www.helsinki.fi/varieng/CoRD/corpora/CEEC/index.html

Conde-Silvestre, J.C. (2007) *Sociolingüística histórica*, Gredos, Madrid.

Diller, H.-J. (1997/98) Code-switching in medieval English drama. *Comparative Drama* 31.4: 500–537.

Filppula, M. (2010) Contact and the early history of English. In R. Hickey (ed.), pp. 432–53.

Fisher, J.H. (1977) Chancery and the emergence of standard written English in the fifteenth century. *Speculum* 52: 870–99.

Fishman, J.A. (1965) Who speaks what language to whom and when. *La Linguistique* 1(2): 67–88.

Fletcher, A.J. (1994) 'Benedictus qui venit in nomine Domini:' A thirteenth-century sermon for Advent and the macaronic style in England. *Mediaeval Studies* 56: 217–45.

Gardner-Chloros, P. (2009) *Code-switching*, Cambridge University Press, Cambridge.

Gardner-Chloros, P. (2010) Contact and code-switching. In R. Hickey (ed.), pp. 188–207.

The Helsinki Corpus of English Texts (1991) Compiled by M. Rissanen, M. Kytö, L. Kahlas-Tarkka, M. Kilpiö, S. Nevanlinna, I. Taavitsainen, T. Nevalainen, H. Raumolin-Brunberg. Department of English, University of Helsinki. http://www.helsinki.fi/varieng/CoRD/corpora/HelsinkiCorpus

Hickey, R. (ed.) (2010) *The Handbook of Language Contact*, Wiley-Blackwell, Chichester.

Hingeston, F.C. (ed.) 1860) *Royal and Historical Letters During the Reign of Henry the Fourth, King of England and of France, and Lord of Ireland*. Vol. I: A.D. 1399–1404, Longman, London.

Kämmerer, C.M. (2006) *Codeswitching in Predigten des 15. Jahrhunderts. Mittellatein-Frühneuhochdeutsch, Mittellatein-Altitalienisch/Altspanisch*, Logos Verlag, Berlin.

Kerswill, P. (2002) Koineization and accommodation. In J.K. Chambers, P. Trudgill, and N. Schilling-Estes (eds.), *The Handbook of Language Variation and Change*, Blackwell, Oxford, pp. 669–702.

Lazzerini, L. (1971) 'Per latinos grossos': Studio sui sermoni mescidati. *Studi di Filologia Italiana* 2: 219–339.

Lüdi, G. (1985) Mehrsprachige Rede in Freiburger Ratsmanualen des 15. Jahrhunderts. *Vox Romanica* 44: 163–88.

Lüdi, G. (1989) Ein historisches Beispiel für Polyglossie: Stadtsprachen in Fribourg/Freiburg i. Ue. im XIV./XV. Jahrhundert. In P.H. Nelde (ed.), *Historische Sprachkonflikte*, Dümmler, Bonn, pp. 37–55.

Machan, T. (1994) Language contact in Piers Plowman. *Speculum* 69(2): 359–85.

Matras, Y. (2009) *Language Contact*, Cambridge University Press, Cambridge.

Metcalfe, A. (2003) *Muslims and Christians in Norman Sicily: Arabic Speakers and the End of Islam*, Routledge Curzon, London.

Myers-Scotton, C. (1993) *Duelling Languages: Grammatical Structure in Codeswitching*, Oxford University Press, Oxford.

Nevalainen, T. and Raumolin-Brunberg, H. (2003) *Historical Sociolinguistics: Language Change in Tudor and Stuart England*, Longman Pearson Education, London.

Nevalainen, T. and Raumolin-Brunberg, H. (2005) Sociolinguistics and the history of English. *International Journal of English Studies* 5: 33–58.

Nurmi, A. and Pahta, P. (2010) Preacher, scholar, brother, friend: Social roles and code-switching in the writings of Thomas Twining. In P. Pahta, M. Nevala, A. Nurmi, and M. Palander-Collin (eds.), *Social Roles and Language Practices in Late Modern English*, John Benjamins, Amsterdam, pp. 135–62.

Pahta, P. and Nurmi, A. (2006) Code-switching in the Helsinki Corpus: a thousand years of multilingual practice. In N. Ritt, H. Schendl, C. Dalton-Puffer, and D. Kastovsky (eds.), *Medieval English and its Heritage: Structure, Meaning and Mechanisms of Change*, Peter Lang, Frankfurt am Main, pp. 203–20.

Pahta, P. and Nurmi, A. (2009) Negotiating interpersonal identities in writing: code-switching practices in Charles Burnley's correspondence. In A. Nurmi, M. Nevala, and M. Palander-Collin (eds.), *The Language of Daily Life in England (1400–1800)*, John Benjamins, Amsterdam, pp. 27–52.

Pahta, P. and Nurmi, A. (2011) Multilingual discourse in the domain of religion in medieval and early modern England: a corpus approach to research on historical code-switching. In H. Schendl and L. Wright (eds.).

Pahta, P. and Taavitsainen, I. (2004) Vernacularisation of scientific and medical writing in its sociohistorical context. In I. Taavitsainen and P. Pahta (eds.), *Medical and Scientific Writing in Late Medieval*

English, Cambridge University Press, Cambridge, pp. 1–18.

Poplack, S. (1980) Sometimes I'll start a sentence in Spanish y termino en español: toward a typology of code-switching. *Linguistics* 18: 581–618.

Putter, A. (2011) Code-switching in Langland, Chaucer and the *Gawain* poet: diglossia and footing. In H. Schendl and L. Wright (eds.).

Romaine, S. (1990/1995) *Bilingualism* (2nd edn), Blackwell, Oxford.

Rothwell, W. (1994) The trilingual England of Geoffrey Chaucer. *Studies in the Age of Chaucer* 16: 45–67.

Schendl, H. (2002a) Mixed language texts as data and evidence in English historical linguistics. In D. Minkova and R. Stockwell (eds.), *Studies in the History of the English Language: A Millennial Perspective*, Mouton de Gruyter, Berlin, pp. 51–78.

Schendl, H. (2002b) Code-choice and code-switching in some early fifteenth-century letters. In P.J. Lucas and A.M. Lucas (eds.), *Middle English from Tongue to Text*, Peter Lang, Frankfurt, pp. 247–62.

Schendl, H. (2004a) English historical code-switching in a European perspective. In C.B. Dabelsteen and J.N. Jorgensen (eds.), *Languaging and Language Practices*, University of Copenhagen, Copenhagen, pp. 188–202.

Schendl, H. (2004b) Hec sunt prata *to wassingwellan*: Aspects of code-switching in Old English charters. *VIEWS (Vienna English Working PaperS)* 13 (2): 52–68 (also published in *Historical Sociolinguistics and Sociohistorical Linguistics* 5 (2005), http://www.hum2.leidenuniv.nl/hsl_shl/)

Schendl, H. (forthcoming a) Code-switching in late medieval macaronic sermons. In J. Jefferson and A. Putter (eds.), *Multilingualism in Later Medieval Britain: Sources and Analysis*, Brepols, Turnhout.

Schendl, H. (2011) Beyond boundaries: code-switching in the leases of Oswald of Worcester. In H. Schendl and L. Wright (eds.).

Schendl, H. and Wright, L. (eds.) (2011) *Code-switching in Early English*, Mouton de Gruyter, Berlin.

Sebba, M, Mahootian, S., and Jonsson, C. (eds.) (forthcoming) *Language Mixing and Code-switching in Writing: Approaches to Mixed-language Written Discourse*, Routledge, London.

Stolt, B. (1964) *Die Sprachmischung in Luthers Tischreden. Studien zum Problem der Zweisprachigkeit*, Almquist and Wiksell, Stockholm.

Thomason, S. (2001) *Language Contact*, Edinburgh University Press, Edinburgh.

Thomason, S. (2008) Social and linguistic factors as predictors of contact-induced change. *Journal of Language Contact – Thema* 2: 42–56.

Trotter, D.A. (ed.) (2000) *Multilingualism in Later Medieval Britain*, D.S. Brewer, Woodbridge.

Trotter, D. (2006) *Si le français n'y peut aller*: Villers-Cotterêts and mixed-language documents from the Pyrenees. In D.J. Cowling (ed.), *Conceptions of Europe in Renaissance France: A Festschrift for Keith Cameron*, Rodopi, Amsterdam, pp. 77–97.

Trudgill, P. (2010) *Investigations in Sociohistorical Linguistics. Stories of Colonisation and Contact*, Cambridge University Press, Cambridge.

Voigts, L.E. (1996) What's the word? Bilingualism in late-medieval England. *Speculum* 71: 813–26.

Wenzel, S. (1994) *Macaronic Sermons: Bilingualism and Preaching in Late-medieval England*, University of Michigan Press, Ann Arbor.

Wright, L. (1995) A hypothesis on the structure of macaronic business writing. In J. Fisiak (ed.), *Medieval Dialectology*, Mouton de Gruyter, Berlin, pp. 309–21.

Wright, L. (1998) Mixed-language business writing: five hundred years of codeswitching. In Ernst Håkon Jahr (ed.), *Language Change: Advances in Historical Sociolinguistics*, Mouton de Gruyter, Berlin, pp. 99–118.

Wright, L. (2000) Bills, accounts, inventories: everyday trilingual activities in the business world of later medieval England. In D.A. Trotter (ed.), pp. 149–56.

29 The Impact of Migratory Movements on Linguistic Systems: Transplanted Speech Communities and Varieties from a Historical Sociolinguistic Perspective

DANIEL SCHREIER

Migratory movements and linguistic systems in contact have a quasi-symbiotic relationship. Population movements (emigration, immigration, or cross-migration) lead to modifications in language varieties (varieties spoken by those on the move as well as varieties spoken where they move to), such as via koinéization, pidginization, and/or creolization; as a consequence, groups of speakers (or to be more precise: their languages, dialects, and sociolects) come into unprecedented contact and the resulting patterns of social dispersion and diffusion shape the ultimate sociolinguistic outcome of the new variety. At the same time, the nature of the linguistic systems in contact has a strong impact on the output, that is, on the koiné or the creole; the nature of the systems (their structural similarity, genetic parallelisms, and phonological overlap, for example) strongly determines the nature of the processes triggered, such as the adoption of majority forms and the leveling out of minority forms, or when systems undergo regularization and restructuring. Moreover, migratory movements and interaction of linguistic systems are directly interwoven when it comes to parameters such as the total proportions of speaker groups in contact (and the sociolinguistic balance of input

The Handbook of Historical Sociolinguistics, First Edition. Edited by Juan Manuel Hernández-Campoy and Juan Camilo Conde-Silvestre.
© 2014 John Wiley & Sons, Ltd. Published 2014 by John Wiley & Sons, Ltd.

varieties), the implementation of founder effects, social stratification (and the manifestation of social variation in transplanted communities), or incipient norm-enforcement via the formation of newly emerging social networks.

This chapter looks at general patterns of relocation diffusion and one possible outcome of population movements (koinéization). It discusses some major mechanisms involved in new-dialect formation and the impact of both social and linguistic factors (the structural properties of the systems in contact and the social set-up of the newly emerging community). I will start with a reconstruction of the earliest contact scenario of English (from the fifth century onwards), then outline some relevant general principles, both in terms of sociolinguistic processes and sociohistorical factors, and provide a discussion of the evolution of New Zealand English (NZE) as a case in point. In conclusion, I will present some current controversies in the field and discuss their theoretical implications.

1. The Emergence of Old English: Earliest Migration Patterns and Dialect Contact

It is well known that Old English formed as an amalgam of inputs spoken by the founder Germanic populations (Angles, Saxons, Jutes, Frisians, and others: see Map 29.1). English must have been a contact-derived language from its earliest phase, though it is debated how extensive these contacts were. Baugh and Cable (1951/1993: 50), for instance, state: "the English language has resulted from the fusion of the dialects of the Germanic tribes who came to England [...] It is impossible to say how much the speech of the Angles differed from that of the Saxons or that of the Jutes. The differences were certainly slight". This is supported by the general picture drawn in most textbooks, in which the kingdoms of Anglo-Saxon England (Wessex, Kent, Mercia, and Northumbria) are presented as fairly homogeneous sociopolitical entities with, it is alleged, sociolinguistic unity – the dialects of Old English (West Saxon, Kentish, Mercian, and Northumbrian respectively) – a traditional idea that goes back to Sweet (1885). Campbell (1959: § 256), on the other hand, emphasizes that "dialectal names [...] in this book [are] used practically without territorial significance." In the same vein, Hogg (1988: 189) stresses that "we must get away from the idea of four more or less homogeneous and discrete speech-communities. What we have to do, rather, is see each individual text, or small group of texts, as separate entities – although, of course, no text is an island." Similarly, Jucker (2000: 16) states that there are "clear dialectal differences. Normally four different dialect areas are distinguished [...] In reality, the situation will have been more complex, with differences within these areas and gradual rather than abrupt shifts from one area to the other. There can be little doubt that the dialectal differences in the spoken language of the day were more pronounced than in the written records that have survived from this period."

This can only mean that Old English emerged via dialect contact, that it was a contact-derived variety from its earliest stages. This view is expressed by Crystal

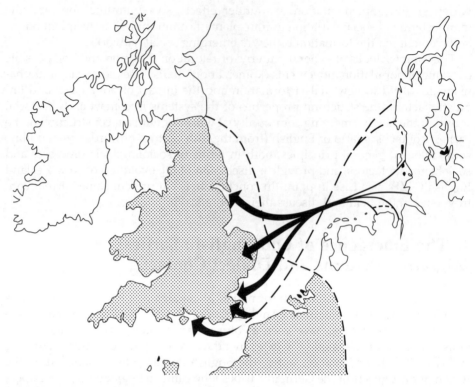

Map 29.1. Early migration patterns and dialect contact in Old English (adapted from Baugh and Cable 1951/1993: 42–48)

(2004: 41), who argues that "we must regard dialect mixing as a normal part of the Old English situation." How can this be substantiated? Toon (1992) reports evidence from spelling variations within a single text written by an individual, such as in the will of a Kentish scribe by the name of Abba (presumably written in the early ninth century). Toon finds that Abba uses both the northern <o> spelling and the southern <a> variant, alternating between the two, for example, *ond him man selle* and *ond mon selle him* 'and to him one gives,' sometimes on the same line. The spelling <mon> is typical in Mercian and Northumbrian texts, as is <man> in West Saxon and Kentish, and the fact that both are found in the same text strongly implies mixing (see also Hogg 2006, and Chapter 13 in this *Handbook*). Nevertheless, the evidence is scant, mostly for methodological reasons (the paucity of surviving documents and aspects related to authorship, authenticity, and so on), and one needs to interpret these findings with great care[1]. As for so much else, a language user's motivation for using both northern and southern forms will never be verified, but there is little doubt that English has undergone mixing and dialect contact from its earliest stages.

2. Exploring Types of Movements and their Consequences

One complicating factor for sociohistorical reconstruction of these processes (let alone their prediction) is that, though demographic stability is a prerequisite (see below), population movements are as diverse as the sociolinguistic processes they give rise to. An important consideration is the type of colonialism in question, a general distinction can be drawn between 'settler colonialism' and 'exploitation colonialism' and their outcomes (Mufwene 2001; Schneider 2007). The first, settler colonialism, involves a policy (often planned at government level) of conquering a land for settlers with the aim of setting up society similar to that in the colonial power's home territory. The motives for settler colonialism are manifold; one is simply to ease the pressure of a growing population and its needs, as suggested by Robert Hakluyt in 1582[2]:

> Yea if wee woulde beholde with the eye of pitie howe al our Prisons are pestered and filled with able men to serue their Countrie, which for small roberies are dayly hanged vp in great numbers euen twentie at a clappe out of one jayle (as was seene at the last assises at Rochester) we woulde hasten and further euery man to his power the deducting of some Colonies of our superfluous people into those temperate and fertile parts of America, which being within six weekes sayling of England are yet unpossessed by any Christian: and seeme to offer themselues vnto vs, stretching neerer vnto her Maiesties Dominions, then to any other part of Europe.
>
> (Hakluyt 1582)

By the same token, the possibility of acquiring overseas possessions and financial gain were important economic pull-factors, while persecutions and religious dissent, political turmoil, or simply finding somewhere to put what Hakluyt referred to as "our superfluous people" were the most important push-factors. In settler colonies, governments or agencies such as the East India Company typically strove to establish a local infrastructure and to follow British models wherever possible (in architecture, legislature, political organization, and so on), thus extending and preserving territorial sovereignty as well as possible. This practice had permanent sociolinguistic and ideological effects – such as identity construction (Schneider 2007) – and was in sharp contrast with exploitation colonialism, a policy of conquering territories with the intention of exploiting natural and human resources by force, for immediate profit, such as by extracting cheap raw materials and enslaving the native population. Imperialist powers have sometimes chosen one type of colonialism, sometimes the other, or have even pursued both at the same time. The British Empire provides a good example: it carried out settlement policies mainly in areas such as North America and Australasia, where it invested heavily, building modern infrastructures and often displacing the native population. For such purposes, it ignored the Indian subcontinent and Africa, which were densely populated. The 'scramble for Africa' in the late nineteenth century is a particularly pertinent example. At that point hardly colonized at all, Africa (and south-east Asia) became the primary target of 'New Imperialism' (in 1875) when Benjamin Disraeli bought the Suez Canal shareholdings of an indebted Egyptian company in order to secure control of this strategic waterway. The two most important European holdings in Africa at the time were French-controlled Algeria and Britain's Cape Colony. In an unprecedented colonial rush, almost the whole continent was colonized within thirty years, leaving Ethiopia and Liberia as the only territories not under formal European control when World War I began.

In 1914, Great Britain emerged with not only the largest overseas empire (India), but also the greatest gains in the 'scramble for Africa:' between 1885 and 1914, it had taken nearly 30% of Africa's population under control (compared to 15% for France, 9% for Germany, 7% for Belgium, and 1% for Italy), Nigeria alone contributing 15 million people, more than the whole of French West Africa or the German colonial empire combined. This happened in many other locations, since colonization was a truly global phenomenon; Map 29.2 shows the colonial powers and their possessions at the end of World War II. Overseas possessions were held by Great Britain, France, Portugal, Spain, the Netherlands, Belgium, and the United States of America and it was not until the 1960s that most colonies actively sought and obtained political independence.

The areas subjected to New Imperialism were typically ruled by a small colonial population, who had sole access to education, administration, and social privileges, and their economies were oriented almost exclusively toward the export of agricultural goods. This meant that the vast majority of the population did not have access either to social privileges or to the English language.

Different types of socio-political engagement in colonies had distinct sociolinguistic consequences, particularly for contact-induced language variation and change (which manifests itself most obviously in processes such as borrowing). Thomason and Kaufman (1988: 75–77) suggest that there is a direct connection

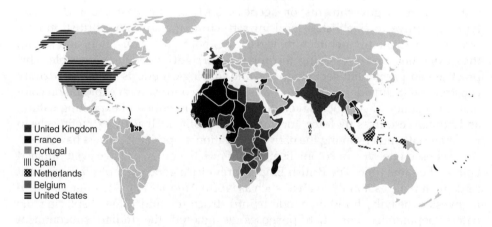

Map 29.2. Colonization as a global phenomenon in 1945

between the type of contact and the borrowing mechanism triggered, differentiating between[3]:

(1) casual contact: non-basic vocabulary, content-words, mostly nouns;
(2) slightly more intense contact: adverbial particles, conjunctions, foreign phonemes in foreign words;
(3) more intense contact: prepositions, pronouns, low numerals, derivational morphemes, foreign inflectional endings in foreign words, restructuring of the phonemic system under foreign influence, stress rules, syllable structure;
(4) strong cultural pressure: massive lexical and structural borrowing;
(5) very strong cultural pressure: borrowing to the point of typological reorientation, in extreme cases resulting in language death.

3. Exploring the Sociolinguistic Processes Induced by Population Movements

Several stages can be identified in the formation of contact-derived dialects. First of all, the total number of variants present in the contact scenario represents a pool out of which the first native speakers select features during the initial formation phase (Mufwene 2001). None of the input varieties 'wins out' at this stage; were it to do so, then all but one variety present in the contact scenario would disappear without a trace and the newly developing variety would be the equivalent of one of its inputs. Riograndenser Hunsrückisch would merely be a transplanted (and systemically unaltered) form of a Rhineland-Palatinate German dialect in Brazil, Australian English exported Cockney, Québec French the equivalent of a regional variety found in France, Brazilian the equivalent of Portuguese, and so on. This is hardly ever the case, since speakers accommodate to each other, as a result of which features are combined in novel ways by the first generations of native-born speakers. The usual outcome is that the inputs undergo a stage of *mixing*, driven by mechanisms such as feature selection and retention. Consequently, contact between linguistic systems triggers selection processes of features from several co-existing varieties (Kerswill 1996, 2002), and this may be influenced by factors such as total number of features present, the salience, stigma, and prestige of individual variables, sociodemographic characteristics and social mobility. Fully-developed koinés, the end-product of *focusing* (Le Page and Tabouret-Keller 1985; see below), have thus adopted features from at least two (very often, more) donors. Put differently, a crystallizing contact-based overseas variety combines a mixture of features (phonetic/phonological, grammatical, morphological, and/or lexical) that derive from some or all the dialects present in the original contact situation.

Another important process in this context is *leveling*: the majority of variants found in a diffuse mixture situation gradually disappear as features are permanently selected (Trudgill 1986; Siegel 1987; Britain 1997). Contact-induced language change has strong tendencies towards regularity and transparency. Though the precise nature of what determines leveling is still unknown, there is consensus that status (stigma or prestige) and frequency are important criteria. Variants that are regionally or socially marked are usually not maintained (Mesthrie 1993) and those with the widest social and geographical distribution have the highest chances of surviving the selection process (Trudgill 1986). The surviving form is usually the one found in the majority of inputs (Mesthrie 1993; Siegel 1987), and this led Trudgill (2004) to adopt an extreme (and controversial) hypothesis, namely that it is the frequency of features *alone* that accounts for adoption. Social factors (prestige, status, social network structures, and so on), as a consequence, would simply be irrelevant (further discussion below).[4]

New Zealand English (NZE; see below) provides a pertinent case of leveling. Schreier, Gordon, Hay, and Maclagan (2003) analyzed the maintenance of voiceless labiovelar /hw-/ fricatives (minimal pairs *Wales ~ whales, witch ~ which*) in three regions of New Zealand (Otago/Southland, Canterbury, and the North Island) and found considerable regional variation in the early twentieth century. Whereas speakers from the North Island and Canterbury were predominantly using /w/ (so that the /hw/ ~ /w/ merger was practically completed by 1950), speakers from the Southland and Otago regions had high levels of /hw-/ well into the second half of the century. The regional distribution of the variable was explained by population demographics and ancestral effects, in particular the total input strength of /hw-/-retaining donor dialects. A high overall presence of /hw-/ variants in the inputs was found to have an enhancing effect on the adoption and maintenance of the phoneme. The strong presence of /hw-/ in the Otago/Southland dialect region was explained by high input frequency and the disproportionally high input of Scottish settlers, who made a distinction between /hw-/ and /w-/. In the other regions, however, /hw-/ was not adopted, simply because the social configuration and the local contact and mixture situations were different. The inputs were mainly from the South of England, where /hw-/ was a minority feature, and this enhanced leveling-out in the local forms of NZE.

Another important process involved is what some label 'simplification' (Trudgill 1986), which may be preferably considered as a manifestation of regularization. Simplification is not an ideal term since the outcome of new-dialect formation is not necessarily 'simpler' than any of the corresponding input forms. Rather, a given property of a variant X, whether phonetic/phonological, lexical, or grammatical, is subject to less variation than it originally was in the input varieties, for instance, when there is reduction of a quantitative range of forms. Siegel (1987: 14) maintains that simplification is not well understood and argues that it should be investigated quantitatively rather than qualitatively (adopting a variationist perspective to trace a putative decrease in variability) and viewed as a diachronic process, with reference to earlier evolutionary phases of a variety (or of the input varieties). This problem is also recognized by Britain (1997: 41), who states that simplification represents "an increase in grammatical regularity and decrease in formal complexity," and Mühlhäusler (1997: 236), who claims that:

Simplification only refers to the form of the rules in which a language is encoded, indicating optimalization of existing rules and the development of regularities for formerly irregular aspects, for example, grammaticalization of the lexicon. Simplification is a dynamic concept. It expresses the fact that *as one moves along a developmental continuum, more and more regularities appear.* (Emphasis added)

A good example of phonological regularization in overseas varieties comes from devoicing of inter-vocalic alveolar plosives in Afrikaans (Booij 2002). In Dutch, voiceless alveolar plosives (/t/) are voiced in intervocalic environments: /t/ > [d]/V_V. Dutch plural formation commonly involves the affixation of an *-en* marker and changes the phonological environment from /-VC#/ to /-VCV#/. If a singular form ends in /d/, then the corresponding plural form maintains it. A voiceless /t/, however, assimilates to [d], as in *hoed* 'hat', *hoeden* 'hats'. Afrikaans, in contrast, has regularized this assimilation rule so that the phonological environment has no effect on the alveolar plosive: *hoed* 'hat', *hoeden* 'hats' or *stad* 'city', *statten* 'cities'. Afrikaans is thus more regular than its ancestral variety Dutch, in that it has reduced the number of phonological rules and does not make phonological contrasts in this particular environment (Booij 2002). Similarly, a striking case of morphosyntactic regularization is found in Tristan da Cunha English, which regularized the past tense paradigm of *be* (with pivot form *was*) to the extent that *were* was categorically absent from the speech of Tristanians born before World War II (Schreier 2002).[5]

Feature selection and retention are not the only processes operating in long-term contact situations. A new dialect affiliates with its inputs by drawing features from them, but it is erroneous to assume that it is linguistically predetermined by the distinctive properties of the varieties in contact. Contact-derived dialects may develop their own dynamics, namely when "contact between two dialects leads to the development of forms that actually originally occurred in neither dialect" (Trudgill 1986: 62). Some variants are "not actually present in any of the dialects that contribute to the mixture but [...] arise out of interaction between them" (Trudgill *et al.* 2000), and this has been amply documented by Britain (1997) in Fens English in Great Britain. According to Trudgill (1986), 'interdialectalisms' represent intermediate variants of original forms (and thus originate in incomplete or faulty accommodation) and can be classified as manifestations of overgeneralization and hyperadaptation[6]. Therefore, mixing and leveling alone cannot be offered as explanations for all the features of a newly developing variety. Any theory that attempts to arrive at a general outline of contact-induced language change needs to leave room for independent innovation patterns.

These processes contribute to new-dialect formation and are thus part of what Le Page and Tabouret-Keller (1985) call 'focusing.' Speakers of a fully focused variety are in agreement about normative structures and have a strong awareness that their dialect differs from others on linguistic grounds. Focused varieties often have a 'proper' name and are accompanied by processes of standardization and codification; these reinforce attitudes towards outsiders and foster a strong sense of local identity on the part of a speech community's members. In so-called diffuse communities, by contrast, speakers display considerable heterogeneity, having little (or no) consensus on linguistic norms and the status of the variety. Le Page and Tabouret-Keller (1985) illustrate this with the case of multilingual Belize, where English, Creole, and Spanish coexist. There is a continuum between acro- and basilectal varieties, no consensus on the usage of high-standard norms, no clear demarcation between the coexisting varieties and little or no agreement as to which of the varieties is used in a given context or interaction. The maintenance of multiple varieties in a contact setting is therefore a crucial factor in determining whether a variety focuses or remains diffuse, which has implications for the development of overseas varieties in general. According to Kerswill and Williams (1992, 2000), the initial stages of any dialect mixture situation are characterized by extreme diffuseness. There is no agreement on shared norms in a newly founded community and language usage is characterized by the coexistence of a number of distinct variants. Variability may then be reduced when accommodation patterns between speakers in face-to-face interaction increase and social networks are implemented.

4. New-dialect Formation: New Zealand as a Case in Point

NZE is the youngest of the 'inner-circle' varieties of English around the world, in the sense that it has undergone structural nativization (Schneider 2007) only quite recently. European expansion into the Pacific began in the late eighteenth century, but by the 1830s, European residents in New Zealand numbered only around 2000. It was only after the Treaty of Waitangi in 1840 that British sovereignty was proclaimed over the country and the European population of New Zealand began to grow. This growth occurred at a remarkable rate, however; by 1872, the European population had reached 256 000 and by 1881 almost half a million (Belich 1996: 278). In the early years of colonization, Auckland became the seat of government and it was to remain the most populous settlement. However, the period between 1840 and 1852 was also characterized by the colonizing efforts of bodies in Britain that organized emigration to central and southern New Zealand. Most of the immigrants who arrived in these years came to planned settlements. Although their numbers were not great when compared with later immigration, they laid out early patterns in the areas where they settled, particularly in Otago and Canterbury, thus potentially establishing founder effects (see below).

The 1871 census indicates that the vast majority of migrants in New Zealand came from the British Isles, the English forming the largest ethnic group (51%). The Scots, who made up 10% of the population of the British Isles, constituted 27.3% of the migrants in New Zealand and were mainly concentrated in Otago and Southland. The Irish, who in 1871 made up 18.8% of the total UK population, constituted about 22% of the New Zealand migrant population. The Welsh were often conflated with the English in official records but, even allowing for this, the percentage of Welsh migrants was insignificant. By 1871, the North Island provinces generally had more New Zealand-born people than the South Island, and Otago and Southland had significantly more immigrants from Scotland than the other provinces. Canterbury, in contrast, was planned to be "English, Anglo-Catholic, and Conservative" (Sinclair 1959/1991: 92) and had a majority of immigrants from England (55%, mostly from the South of England, in particular the south-east), though the difference between this and other provinces in the North Island was not as strong as the predominance of Scots in Otago and Southland. Here, the Scots made up between 60% to 80% of the total population, mostly living off agriculture (Olssen 1984: 71). The other large group consisted of miners, mostly from England and Ireland, who made up about 24% of the male workforce (Olssen 1984: 71).

New Zealand's North Island, on the other hand, has a notably different social history and was characterized by higher sociodemographic fluctuation. Wellington was the earliest New Zealand Company settlement and one of the first sites of European involvement. Places like Dannevirke, in contrast, were planned settlements, set up for government-assisted immigrants from Scandinavia in the 1870s. Political insecurities and struggles with the local Maori population hindered colonization of much of the North Island, but the stationing of British soldiers soon attracted more European settlers. Numbers rose dramatically in the 1860s, after war had broken out between the Maori and the British troops. The colonial government launched an ambitious scheme to recruit soldier settlers and to repatriate them on land confiscated from the Maori. By the mid-1860s, there were some 12 000 Imperial troops, together with 4 000 local soldiers. According to McGibbon (2000: 325), "most of those who enlisted were young single men born in Great Britain and from the lower stratum of Victorian society, laborers and semi-skilled workers attracted by the promise of a free farm." On their discharge soldiers were allotted land (the amount determined by rank), though many did not stay long enough to obtain legal ownership.

Economically, the provinces of the North Island long lagged behind Otago and Canterbury, where the wool and meat industry yielded high profits. The discovery of gold in the South Island in 1861 increased growth in the economy and the population. In the 1870s, a government immigration scheme was set up to boost the population in the wealthier provinces of the south, and there was a massive influx of new immigrants to Otago and Canterbury. The situation was to change from the 1880s on, when the success of refrigerated shipping made the export of dairy produce possible. After 1901, increasingly dense settlement and industrial development gave the Northern provinces an economic advantage, which led to demographic restructuring and a pre-eminent socio-political role of the North Island.

Sociolinguistically, NZE is a showcase for the study of new-dialect formation mechanisms. Though some (see Hammarström 1980) have argued for monogenetic origins, taking the view that Australian English (and, by implication, NZE) basically represent varieties of transplanted Cockney, most linguists would agree that NZE originated in a context of dialect transplantation, contact and mixture, so that it can be classified as a contact dialect (or *koiné*): "While NZE is undoubt-edly southern English in origin, [and] it shows features which are found through-out the south of England [...] *NZE really is a mixed dialect, taking input from throughout Britain*" (Bauer 1999: 304; emphasis added). In the words of Trudgill *et al.* (2000: 302), it "is the result [...] of a complex series of processes involving dialect contact between different British Isles varieties of English, followed by dialect mixture, new-dialect formation, and then by subsequent linguistic changes." The scenario that gave rise to this variety of Southern Hemisphere English thus involved several transplanted inputs; their phonological and mor-phosyntactic properties served as a feature pool from which NZE drew its fea-tures. Pre-eminent among these varieties was the English of south-east England, or London, to be more precise. Bauer (1994: 388) states that "phonologically speak-ing, New Zealand English is a variant of the southeast England system", a claim clearly supported by the qualitative and quantitative analysis reported in the ONZE ('Origins of New Zealand English') project (Gordon, Campbell, Hay *et al.* 2004). Apparent-time data of nineteenth-century NZE (the database used by the ONZE team) is indicative of early rudimentary *leveling* (of socially and regionally marked variants, such as the /v ~ w/ merger) and extreme variability in the speech of the first locally-born generation, which is characterized by unique and often idiosyncratic combinations of features from distinct dialect regions of the British Isles. The impact of language contact was slight, manifesting itself mostly on the lexical level (Bauer 1994). Following the course of focusing and new-norm adoption, NZE (like other post-colonial varieties, such as Australian English) underwent regional uniformity and leveling on a nationwide scale, as a result of which regionality does not (yet) correlate with language variation in present-day NZE: "New Zealand, like Australia, is more remarkable for the absence of regional differences" (Gordon and Deverson 1998: 126). This has also been openly remarked on in the case of earlier American English[7] as well as in that of Australian English: "Australians are for practical reasons almost completely unmarked by region within their speech community" (Bernard 1989: 255). Indeed, this seems to be a highly diagnostic feature of the early evolutionary phase of 'inner-circle' overseas varieties (see Schneider 2007 for an in-depth comparison and theoretical analysis of these varieties) and one that sets them apart from others developing in multi-lingual contexts.

5. Population Movements, Koinéization and Historical Sociolinguistics: Current Debates

All contact settings differ for linguistic, sociolinguistic, and demographic reasons, and this is one of the reasons, perhaps the most important, why a coherent theory of new-dialect formation has not yet been formulated. The reason this is such a complex task is that linguistic developments are ultimately unpredictable, simply because speakers' attitudes and behavior are unpredictable. Nevertheless, several theories have been developed, focusing on and integrating the factors above (or a combination of them) and a lively debate has sprung up as to which is most important in determining the evolutionary path of koinéization and what would be the main driving force behind this process.

Perhaps the most important question of all is why an emerging contact dialect would select features from input A and not input B, develop structure X at the expense of structure Y, and so on. Some thirty years ago, the idea was first put forward that the linguistic properties of the varieties in contact are a decisive factor; Bernard (1981: 20), for instance, claimed that "the ingredients of the mixing bowl [in AusE and NZE] were very much the same, and at different times and in different places the same process was carried out and the same end point achieved." This idea has been developed elsewhere. In their discussion of the formation of NZE, Trudgill, Gordon, Lewis, and Maclagan (2000: 299) follow this line of thinking and argue in favor of a linguistically deterministic model, suggesting that the product of koinéization is primarily determined by the inputs that contribute to the new dialect:

> [D]ialect mixture and new-dialect formation are not haphazard processes. We demonstrate that, given sufficient linguistic information about the dialects which contribute to the mixture, and sufficient demographic information about the proportions of the different dialects, it is possible to make predictions about what the outcome of the mixture will be.

A koiné would thus be 'preconditioned' by its ancestral varieties so that it reflects the proportions of the input mixture. Trudgill *et al.* argue that new-formation mechanisms are linguistically driven and/or motivated. They go as far as to claim that all that is required in order to predict new-dialect formation is that sufficient demographic information is available on the overall proportions of transplanted donor varieties. In other words, the directionality of koinéization would be exclusively governed by factors such as social demography and feature frequency. An extreme version of this claim is made by Trudgill (2001: 44), when he says that "[w]e have not found it at all necessary to call on social features 'prestige' or 'stigma' as explanatory factors, nor have we had to have recourse to notions such as 'identity'." In this line of thinking, social factors play no role whatsoever except among the original adult immigrants, who, however, are not instrumental in new-dialect formation (see below). Following such a view, one would have to exclude the impact of social factors altogether (with the exception of sociodemographics, of course), an extreme position Trudgill has subsequently modified:

> Linguistic change in general, of course, is not deterministic [...] a theory of linguistic change cannot be genuinely deterministic in the sense that it is impossible for a theory to predict "that a change will occur, which change will occur, when a change will occur" (Harris and Campbell 1995: 321). I concur wholeheartedly with this point of view [...] I do not even suggest that the outcomes of language contact and dialect contact are normally deterministic. My claim about determinism is made solely with

respect to the unusual type of situation in which colonial varieties develop, in tabula rasa environments, out of dialect mixtures. (Trudgill 2004: 26–27)

All in all, though, Trudgill claims that the evolution of NZE is predictable given that there is reliable information on the demographic mix of the English, Scottish, and Irish immigrants in the early colonial period from 1840 to the 1870s. Predicting the outcome (that is, contemporary NZE) depends on finding out where the settlers came from, what dialects they spoke, and in what proportions they settled in the newly set up colonies. This view has not gone unchallenged and several scholars have argued that it is erroneous to focus exclusively on feature frequency in the input varieties. Schreier (2008) has pointed out that such an approach cannot account for *reallocation*, when more than one original variant survives the leveling process, as discussed by Trudgill (1986). If leveling were solely driven by the frequency with which a feature occurs in the dialects in contact, then it would be impossible to explain (1) why minority features can survive the selection process, and (2) how independent developments should arise in general.

Others have argued that identity and nation-building are crucial factors. Domingue (1981: 150) states that dialect differences may be leveled out as a result of "the need for unification among speakers of different dialects in a new environment." Along similar lines, Siegel (1985) focuses on social criteria in his study of dialect contact in North Malaitan migrants to Fiji. In their places of origin, they spoke mutually intelligible varieties (regional dialects). Upon emigration to Fiji, however, leveling and koinéization occurred side-by-side with social restructuring, a new sense of identity sprung up and the linguistic outcome of these sociocultural changes saw the development of the koiné Wai. Contact between speech communities with similar dialects may therefore lead to koinéization only if certain *social* conditions are met. In Scandinavia, for instance, typologically related varieties with a high degree of mutual intelligibility have been in contact for centuries, yet koinéization has not taken place, at least not on a general level, and this emphasizes the contribution of factors that are non-linguistic: social, sociopsychological, political, economic, cultural, and demographic.

A social approach can also account for reallocation since the functional redistribution of minority features as socially or stylistically distinctive variants can be socially motivated. This has been documented by Domingue (1981) for Mauritius Bhojpuri, where the total number of coexisting variants was not reduced after regional forms of Hindi became reinterpreted as indicators of formality and style (see also Britain and Trudgill 1999).

Mufwene (2001) emphasizes that the social relationships between individual ethnic groups have consequences for the directionality and future development of contact-derived varieties. From a creolist perspective, he argues that the predominance of lexical input from the superstrate variety is a linguistic reflection of the unequal balance between the different ethnic groups present, which attests to the influence and high prestige of the socially powerful group. This explains why English or French were most important for lexical selection in places where they were spoken by a minority of the general population only (such as Mauritius and

Jamaica). Processes of feature selection thus reflect the asymmetrical power relationships between the contact groups; the less influential groups (the speakers of
substrate varieties) accommodate more extensively than more powerful members
of the community. In such a view, social criteria (prestige, access to target, stratification, and so on) are paramount, a point also made by Thomason and Kaufman
(1988: 35), who emphasize the importance of extra-linguistic factors: "[i]t is the
sociolinguistic history of the speakers, and not the structure of their language,
that is the primary determinant of the linguistic outcome of language contact.
Purely linguistic considerations are relevant but strictly secondary overall."
Hickey (2003) subscribes to this point of view. He accepts that the proportions of
different groups among the colonizers are an important factor in the eventual
crystallization of new norms, while at the same time rejecting the idea that the
social embedding of new-dialect formation should not matter at all. Hickey sees
a shortcoming in Trudgill's claims that the status and prestige of individual colonizers as well as the social standing of colonizing populations are irrelevant.
Documenting the chronology of Irish settlements in New Zealand, he suggests
that the earliest forms of settlement may well have been socially stratified. He
argues in favor of a social approach to koinéization and suggests that the distinct
prestige patterns attributed to donor dialects had a decisive impact on the future
development of new-dialect formation. This would explain why, for example,
Irish English, though arriving early and socio-demographically prominent in
large settlements such as Auckland, disappeared without making an impact, the
social stigma of its speakers being too great.

Hickey explains norm-emergence and stabilization by what he refers to as
"supraregionalization:" "[D]ialect speakers progressively adopt more and more
features of a non-regional variety which they are in contact with. There does not
have to be direct speaker contact" (2003: 236). With regard to the second generation – the children of the first locally-born children, who are instrumental in
forming a focused, stable new dialect – Hickey says that the new variety can "be
seen as a product of unconscious choices made across a broad front in a new
society to create a distinct linguistic identity" (Hickey 2003: 215), thus strongly
rejecting Trudgill's argument against identity factors (see also Schneider 2007). A
supraregional form of NZE, according to Hickey, would have emerged in the
melting pot settlements, which had mixed populations of high density and size,
and then spread to rural settlements that subsequently became dialectally
distinctive.

A final unresolved issue deals with causation, given that dialect and language
contact do not automatically lead to the formation of a stable contact-based variety.
The stabilization and expansion of koinés, for instance, depends on factors such
as sociodemographic stability and limited access to non-local norms. Increasing
mobility rates, as a result of renewed or ongoing colonialism, trade, emigration,
or political expansion, continuously affect the outcome, altering its evolutionary
path or causing it to disappear. Crucially, sociodemographic dynamics are practically always ongoing; new settlers or colonists arrive and earlier ones leave, so
the community's linguistic and social configuration is continuously transformed

and stays in a state of flux. This, needless to say, poses problems for research and challenges all sociolinguistic theory-building. The new-dialect formation process ends abruptly when the community in which a koiné has developed disperses or relocates.

More complicated still, there is not even a way to predict whether focusing will occur or not. Norm-emergence and stabilization may not operate even when the setting seems ideal, as in communities that have sufficient time depth, that are self-contained and not swamped by waves of immigrants. The Norwegian Arctic territory of Spitsbergen (Svalbard), for instance, has not developed a koiné, though it has existed for over a century now (Mæhlum 1992). The reason is that families stay only for ten years on average, which means that the locally-born children move away before focusing can occur. Children have an "unclear dialect identity" (Mæhlum 1992: 123), identifying both with 'home' in Norway and with Spitsbergen. Though the initial stage – stage I in the model suggested by Trudgill (2004) – may be triggered (young children's speech is reported to be greatly influenced by that of their parents, and to be more heterogeneous and internally inconsistent), they are not given sufficient time to drive forward stages II and III (stabilization and nativization). Mæhlum (1992: 123) argues that they use code-switching, dialect mixing, and a version of standard East (Oslo) Norwegian as "strategies of neutrality" instead. The Dutch polders, to give another example, have not seen the development of a locally distinctive stable variety, though the conditions meet all these criteria; Scholtmeijer (1992, 1997) explains this as a consequence of high mobility and extensive contacts outside the community. Moreover, Sudbury (2000: 368) found in her pioneering research on Falklands Islands English (FIE) that "the Falklands accent has not yet focused [...] FIE has not become a fully focused variety like the rest of the southern hemisphere Englishes." This contradicts Trudgill's (2004) argument, even for the revised version about new-dialect formation under *tabula rasa* conditions. The Falkland Islands come as close as possible to such a scenario, since there was no permanent population when they were colonized by the British in the 1840s. FIE is a case where new-dialect formation simply did not happen even though the conditions were ideal: dialect contact, insularity, sociodemographic stability, and a time depth of more than a century and a half. The fact that FIE did not focus (Sudbury 2000, 2001) shows how unpredictable koinéization really is.

Following Kerswill (2001), successful koinéization depends on three criteria. First of all, the trajectory and tempo of koinéization is influenced by "the kind and level of social integration of the new community" (Kerswill 2001: 695). Social homogeneity favors stabilization, while heterogeneity and social stratification have an impeding effect. Second, "children's access to peer groups is crucial" (Kerswill 2001: 695). Koinéization depends on loose and open social networks, so that children interact freely with others and older children or adolescents can serve as role models in the absence of stable norms in the speech of adults. Compulsory schooling may also have an effect (Britain 1997: 165, though this has been contested in Gordon, Campbell, Hay *et al.* 2004). The third point concerns "the degree of difference between the input varieties [that] will affect the amount of accommodation that individuals have to engage in" (Kerswill 2001: 695). Their distinctiveness both systemically and structurally, and their degree of mutual intelligibility, are thus crucial. Taking all this into account, Kerswill (2001) emphasizes that the social embedding of a community (its networks and emerging communities of practice, social stratification, in-group prestige, and so on) is an important factor to set off koinéization, either speeding it up or slowing it down.

To conclude, contact-induced change depends on a number of external factors, the duration and intensity of the contact scenario being most important, and is shaped in a complex interplay of sociodemographic and socio-psychological as well as language-internal and structural-systemic parameters. Most researchers in this field would agree that contact varieties are ultimately shaped by their social histories; the selection and evolution of structural characteristics reflects not only the properties and proportions of the input varieties (though they are certainly essential) but also, and perhaps more importantly, the intricate social set-up of a newly emerging community.

NOTES

1   Crystal (2004), for instance, considers the possibility that Abba dictated his will to a Mercian scribe working in Kent, who then mixed his native variant with that of Abba.
2   A very similar type of discourse was later found in debates as to whether and how to settle Australia (the well-known convict colonies).
3   Similar ideas have been developed by Schneider (2007), who formulated a five-step model of the emergence of New Englishes, with identity construction as a driving force.
4   For instance, such an explanation cannot account for independent developments (see below) or cases of *reallocation* (Trudgill 1986), when more than one original variant survives the leveling process. Reasons for reallocation are reanalysis and functional redistribution, either as social or stylistic variants, or as phonological variants in complementary environments (Britain 1997). This has been documented by Domingue (1981) for Mauritius Bhojpuri, where the total number of coexisting variants was not reduced, because former regional variants of Hindi were reinterpreted as indicators of (in)formality and style.
5   One notes the interplay of simplification and regularization. A past *be* paradigm that has undergone regularization (we *was*, the fishermen *was*, etc.) is also in a way simpler. Put differently, there is no process of simplification that does not also entail regularization, which raises the question of whether it is necessary to keep the two terms distinct.
6   Perhaps the most well-known case here is hypercorrection, which occurs when speakers misinterpret and incorrectly generalize rules by applying them to inappropriate contexts (Trudgill 1986: 66).
7   "The characters chiefly noted in American speech by all who have discussed it, are, first, its general uniformity throughout the country, so that dialects, properly speaking, are confined to recent immigrants, to the native whites of a few isolated areas and to the negroes of the South" (Mencken 1921: 28).

REFERENCES

Bauer, L. (1994) English in New Zealand. In R.W. Burchfield (ed.), *The Cambridge History of the English Language, Vol V: English in Britain and Overseas, Origins and Developments*, Cambridge University Press, Cambridge, pp. 382–429.

Bauer, L. (1999) On the origins of the New Zealand English accent. *English World-Wide* 20: 287–307.

Baugh, A.C. and Cable, T. (1951/1993) *A History of the English Language* (4th edn), Routledge, London.

Belich, J. (1996) *Making Peoples: A History of the New Zealanders from Polynesian Settlement to the End of the Nineteenth Century*, Penguin, Auckland.

Bernard, J.R. (1981) Australian pronunciation. In A. Delbridge, J. Bernard, D. Blair, *et al.* (eds.), *Macquarie Dictionary*, Macquarie Library, Sydney, pp. 18–27.

Bernard, J.R. (1989) Quantitative aspects of the sounds of Australian English. In P. Collins and D. Blair (eds.), *Australian English: The Language of a New Society*, University of Queensland Press, St Lucia, pp. 187–204.

Booij, G. (2002) The balance between storage and computation in the language faculty. Science Prestige Lecture given at the University of Canterbury, Christchurch, July 30 2002.

Britain, D. (1997) Dialect contact and phonological reallocation: 'Canadian raising' in the English Fens. *Language in Society* 26: 15–46.

Britain, D. and Trudgill, P. (1999) Migration, new dialect formation and sociolinguistic refunctionalization: *Reallocation* as an outcome of dialect contact. *Transactions of the Philological Society* 97: 245–56.

Campbell, A. (1959) *Old English Grammar*, Clarendon Press, Oxford.

Crystal, D. (2004) *The Stories of English*, Allen Lane, London.

Domingue, N. (1981) Internal change in a transplanted language. *Studies in the Linguistic Sciences* 4 (2): 151–59.

Gordon, E., Campbell, L., Hay, J., *et al.* (2004) *New Zealand English: Its Origins and Evolution*, Cambridge: Cambridge University Press.

Gordon, E. and Deverson, T. (1998) *New Zealand English and English in New Zealand*, New House, Auckland.

Hakluyt, R. (1582) *Divers Voyages Touching the Discoverie of America and the Ilands Adjacent unto the Same, Made First of All by Our Englishmen and Afterwards by the Frenchmen and Britons: With Two Mappes Annexed Hereunto*, T. Woodcocke, London.

Hammarström, G. (1980) *Australian English: Its Origin and Status*, Helmut Buske, Hamburg.

Harris, A.C. and Campbell, L. (1995) *Historical Syntax in Cross-linguistic Perspective*, Cambridge University Press, Cambridge.

Hickey, R. (2003) How do dialects get the features they have? On the process of new dialect formation. In R. Hickey (ed.), *Motives for Language Change*, Cambridge University Press, Cambridge, pp. 213–39.

Hogg, R. (1988) On the impossibility of Old English dialectology. In D. Kastovsky and G. Bauer (eds.), *Luick Revisited: Papers Read at Schloß Liechtenstein 15–18.9.1985*, Narr, Tübingen, pp. 183–203.

Hogg, R. (2006) Old English dialectology. In A. van Kammenade and B. Los (eds.), *The Handbook of the History of English*, Blackwell, Oxford, pp. 395–416.

Jucker, A.H. (2000) *History of English and English Historical Linguistics*, Klett, Stuttgart.

Kerswill, P. (1996) Children, adolescents and language change. *Language Variation and Change* 8: 177–202.

Kerswill, P. (2002) Koineization and accommodation. In J.K. Chambers, P. Trudgill, and N. Schilling-Estes (eds.), *The Handbook of Language Variation and Change*, Blackwell, Oxford, pp. 669–702.

Kerswill, P. and Williams, A. (1992) Some principles of dialect contact: evidence from the new town of Milton Keynes. In I.

Philippaki-Warburton and R. Ingham (eds.), *Reading Working Papers 1992*, University of Reading: Department of Linguistic Science, pp. 68–90.

Kerswill, P. and Williams, A. (2000) Creating a new town koiné: children and language change in Milton Keynes. *Language in Society* 29: 65–115.

Le Page, R. and Tabouret-Keller, A. (1985) *Acts of Identity. Creole-based Approaches to Language and Identity*, Cambridge University Press, Cambridge.

Mæhlum, B. (1992) Dialect socialization in Longyearbyen, Svalbard (Spitsbergen): a fruitful chaos. In E.H. Jahr (ed.), *Language Contact and Language Change*, Mouton de Gruyter, Berlin, pp. 117–30.

McGibbon, I. (ed.) (2000) *The Oxford Companion to New Zealand Military History*, Oxford University Press, Auckland.

Mencken, H.L. (1921) *The American Language: An Inquiry into the Development of English in the United States* (revised edn), Random House, New York.

Mesthrie, R. (1993) Koineization in the Bhojpuri-Hindi diaspora – with special reference to South Africa. *International Journal of the Sociology of Language* 99: 25–44.

Mufwene, S.S. (2001) *The Ecology of Language Evolution*, Cambridge University Press, Cambridge.

Mühlhäusler, P. (1997) *Pidgin and Creole Linguistics*, Battlebridge, London.

Olssen, E. (1984) *A History of Otago*, McIndoe, Dunedin.

Schneider, E.W. (2007) *Postcolonial English: Varieties Around the World*, Cambridge University Press, Cambridge.

Scholtmeijer, H. (1992) *Het Nederlands van de Ijsselmeer Polders*, Mondiss, Kampen.

Scholtmeijer, H. (1997) Language in the Dutch Polders: why dialects did not mix. Paper presented at the workshop *Migration as a factor in connection with convergence and divergence processes of dialects in Europe*, Heidelberg, Germany, October 17–21, 1997.

Schreier, D. (2002) Past *be* in Tristan da Cunha: the rise and fall of categoricality in language change. *American Speech* 77: 70–99.

Schreier, D., Gordon, E., Hay, J., and Maclagan, M. (2003) The regional and sociolinguistic dimension of /hw-/ maintenance and loss in early 20th century New Zealand English. *English World-Wide* 24: 245–69.

Schreier, D. (2008) *St Helenian English: Origins, Evolution and Variation*, Benjamins, Amsterdam and Philadelphia.

Siegel, J. (1985) Koines and koineization. *Language in Society* 14: 357–78.

Siegel, J. (1987) *Language Contact in a Plantation Environment*, Cambridge University Press, Cambridge.

Sinclair, K. (1959/1991) *A History of New Zealand* (4th edn), Penguin, Auckland.

Sudbury, A. (2000) Dialect contact and koinéization in the Falkland Islands: development of a southern hemisphere English. Ph.D. dissertation, University of Essex.

Sudbury, A. (2001) Falkland Islands English: a southern hemisphere variety? *English World-Wide* 22 (1): 55–80.

Sweet, H. (1885) *The Oldest English Texts*, Kessinger Publishing, London.

Thomason, S.G. and Kaufman, T. (1988) *Language Contact, Creolization, and Genetic Linguistics*, University of California Press, Los Angeles.

Toon, T.E. (1992) Old English dialects. In R.M. Hogg (ed.), *The Cambridge History of the English Language (Vol. 1): The Beginnings to 1066*, Cambridge University Press, Cambridge, pp. 409–51.

Trudgill, P. (1986) *Dialects in Contact*, Blackwell, Oxford.

Trudgill, P. (2001) On the irrelevance of prestige, stigma and identity in the development of New Zealand English phonology. *New Zealand English Journal* 15: 42–46.

Trudgill, P. (2004) *New Dialect Formation: The Inevitability of Colonial Englishes*, Edinburgh University Press, Edinburgh.

Trudgill, P, Gordon, E., Lewis, G., and Maclagan, M. (2000) Determinism in new-dialect formation and the genesis of New Zealand English. *Journal of Linguistics* 36: 299–318.

30 Convergence and Divergence in World Languages

ROGER WRIGHT

There is no generally agreed precise definition of what counts as a 'World' Language. For the purposes of this chapter, they can be defined as languages spoken over a wide geographical area, often as a result of previous colonization, and in many cases by native speakers of some other language. The category now includes Spanish, Portuguese, French, and English, but with reference to historically earlier periods the label has been applied to Latin, and more loosely also to Proto-Indo-European, the distant ancestor of the Indo-European languages. 'Divergence' is a natural and probably inevitable process whereby languages change in different ways in different places, leading to geographical variation; it needs to be distinguished from 'fragmentation' (also called 'break-up,' as in Trask 2000), a term which is used to refer to the process whereby a language ends up splitting into one or more subsequent languages, which is not at all inevitable. 'Convergence' is the opposite process, whereby different dialects or languages become more similar over time.

1. Divergence in Proto-Indo-European

The scientific study of historical linguistics began with the intellectual realization that the relationship between what we now call the Indo-European languages implied a common ancestor. The reconstruction of that ancestor, 'Proto'-Indo-European (PIE), on the basis of attested written descendants, developed from an erudite sport into a complex branch of philology. The reconstructions came to be treated as discoveries rather than hypotheses, and so, given this prehistoric starting point, attention turned to how and why the common PIE basis diverged and

The Handbook of Historical Sociolinguistics, First Edition. Edited by Juan Manuel Hernández-Campoy and Juan Camilo Conde-Silvestre.
© 2014 John Wiley & Sons, Ltd. Published 2014 by John Wiley & Sons, Ltd.

fragmented into the many separately identifiable languages categorizable as Indo-European. The experience gained from these investigations in turn led to the rise of historical linguistics.

Proto-Indo-European has been the prime field of endeavor for many historical linguists, which explains several assumptions that have appeared natural to subsequent workers studying other language families. These include the beliefs that the development of PIE into a large number of daughter languages represents a universal tendency, that such fragmentation is the default case, and that it is therefore normal for all languages over time to split into daughter languages. The resulting languages form collectively a 'family' in each case, and the continued discovery of such inter-related families in many parts of the world has reinforced the assumption.

The development from a single language containing wide geographical variation to several separate languages is something that has happened naturally in several historical contexts, and it is worth studying the phenomenon and establishing when, how, and why it is likely to happen. There has been a tendency to assume that all attested languages must be part of some wider family, which has led to many of them being incorporated in modern accounts into wider family units out of a feeling of vicarious parental responsibility. This has been allied to another commonly held view, for which necessarily there is no direct linguistic evidence, that all languages must have derived from a common ancestor which existed about 200 000 BC in the brains and mouths of the original ancestors of the whole human race. And it is easy to share the feeling, reinforced by a natural respect for Occam's razor, that human history is neater if all humans and all human languages have the same common ancestor, rather than arising independently in unrelated groups in different places. The evidence is compatible with the former view, but only because at that time depth the evidence is inconclusive either way. Over 200 000 years all visible traces of cognate relationships are likely to have faded away. Perhaps there was once a single human language ('Proto-World'). Perhaps all languages developed divergently from this, and are thus related. The evidence is not there to support these claims now, but by the nature of the argument none of these theories can be conclusively refuted. Their appeal partly relies on an instinctive feeling that divergence to the point of break-up over time is inevitable and ubiquitous and must be a universal.

Yet isolate languages, those that have no known relative from which they would have diverged and fragmented in the past, are not uncommon, if we identify as isolates all those that have eluded convincing attempts to incorporate them into a wider grouping. Basque is one such: Trask (1997) debunked the theories that tried to ally Basque with some other attested language family. The fact that Basque cannot be allotted to any otherwise attested family does not in itself disprove the theory that all languages have arisen by diverging from a single common source; it merely shows that there is no evidence which could be used to prove it. Trask (2000), Nichols (1992), Janson (2002), and others have developed the theme with enthusiasm, pointing out that until the last few thousand years there were relatively many isolate languages in the world, each spoken by a relatively small number of people. It is possible in all these cases that the language had a distant ancestor which fragmented, and that all the sister languages thus created died out without trace, except for the attested survivor. By its very nature, that hypothesis cannot be disproved either; we cannot demonstrate that such languages did not exist on the grounds that there is no evidence for their existence, since the lack of such evidence defines the category.

So there are two questions left pending at this stage: (1) why should languages diverge and fragment at all, when it would be more convenient if they didn't? and (2) why have some languages failed to diverge and fragment? At this point sociohistorical considerations need to come into play: prehistoric sociolinguistics, in effect, although nobody has ever called it that. From this point of view, the reason why PIE fragmented into many different languages is straightforward; the speakers themselves diverged geographically and fragmented into different communities which lost touch with each other. Conversely, those speech communities that preserved a single language, however internally variable and divergent, did so because they stayed physically together.

This explanation seems obvious, and is probably essentially right, although in the PIE case it risks being circular. There may or may not be archaeological evidence to support a theory that a particular prehistoric linguistic community has, or has not, split at a particular time; and it is not clear how far we can use the argument in the reverse direction, to argue on the basis of roughly datable linguistic evidence that communities are likely to have diverged geographically by that point (see Justus and McWhirter 2000). But it makes good sense, as such an explanation for the development of divergence into fragmentation relies on the most basic universal tenet of historical linguistics: that spoken languages change.

There has been considerable argument about what it is that actually changes during a linguistic change. There is no generally accepted answer; but one possible perspective is that a linguistic change is both an individual change, in the separate brains of everyone involved, and a social change, as the speakers tacitly agree with each other to use the new feature. Under this perspective, lexical and semantic changes occur in the individual lexical entries in the brain of every speaker, which explains why not all speakers adopt new words (lexical change) or new meanings for existing words (semantic change) at exactly the same time; we may all speak the same language, but we don't all share the same brain. Sound changes operate in the phonological section of each lexical entry for the words affected, which helps explain why lexical diffusion of sound changes is possible at all. It is true that morphosyntactic changes (other than in irregular verbs) are not located in the speaker's lexicon in the same way, which helps explain why they take longer to actuate than the phonetic, lexical, and semantic changes, although they are still most plausibly located in each individual's mental competence. If an innovation is successful, that is because individual speakers gradually adopt it; often, although not necessarily, they also subsequently lose the corresponding feature which had fulfilled the same function hitherto. That community can then use the novel feature intelligibly in their speech. But other groups who have physically lost touch with them will never hear it, and are therefore not likely to adopt it. This is how eventual fragmentation between different languages deriving from a common ancestor was possible at all in prehistoric times.

This scenario implies that similar linguistic novelties in physically separate communities are not likely to occur spontaneously. They can do so, but it is plausible to hypothesize that the initial, dialectal, stages of such a change predate the physical split of the communities concerned, whereas differential developments are usually initiated later than that separation; for example, the general loss of the distinction in Romance languages between long [a:] and short [a] began to occur before the Western and Eastern Latin-speaking communities separated physically from each other, because it happened in Rumanian as well as the Western Romance languages; but other phenomena which occurred in the Western languages but not in Rumanian are correspondingly likely to have begun later than that.

Proto-Indo-European qualifies to be called a 'World Language,' in that it came to be spoken over a wide area; other reconstructed prehistoric ancestors of geographically widespread families include Pama-Nyungan in Australia and Niger-Congo in Africa, which probably fragmented in a roughly similar way. PIE first comes onto the radar in a relatively small region (probably in or near the Caucasus), and then spreads to cover a huge area from Scotland to Persia and beyond, which is why the family was eventually allotted that collective name. During the expansion, some of those speakers met speakers of non-PIE languages such as Etruscan and Basque, and if such contacts led to linguistic interference within PIE, the consequences would have been different in different places. PIE thus became a World Language while simultaneously losing internal cohesion; a speaker from Scotland would never have known one from Persia, and may only rarely, if ever, have met one from continental Europe. By the first millennium BC it is likely that they would not have been mutually comprehensible if they had. There is no evidence, for example, that any Romans realized that the languages spoken by their Germanic and Celtic neighbors were related to Latin; those who did not speak Latin or Greek were designated as Barbarians, whether their language was of Indo-European origin, as Germanic and Celtic were, or not, as with the Aquitanian Basques or the Berbers in the Maghrib. Intellectually curious Romans could realize that the other languages in their Italic subfamily, spoken in the Italian peninsula, had some kind of relationship with Latin, but even so it is thought by modern specialists (such as Clackson and Horrocks 2007) that Latin and Oscan, for example, were not mutually comprehensible in imperial times. We can conclude, then, that the divergence and fragmentation of a World Language, going beyond normal language-internal variation, is possible, because in the Indo-European case it undoubtedly happened.

2. Convergence in Latin

Latin also became a very widely spoken language. The Roman Empire, however, and the Late Latin (Early Romance) speaking regions during the succeeding centuries, were different in most sociolinguistic respects from the Indo-European area of two millennia before. The Latin-speaking area also ranged at one point from Scotland to Persia, but Latin-speakers, unlike the fragmented Indo-European groups, were often in contact with others from elsewhere. The most obvious context in which people travelled far from home and met speakers from elsewhere involved soldiers in the army, who were usually sent away from their own home region; thus the Vindolanda tablets found in Northern England do not attest first-century British Latin, because the identifiable protagonists had come there from elsewhere. Clackson and Horrocks (2007) mention the calculation that at any one time over 40% of the adult population of the Empire were located somewhere different from their birth region. There was not, in short, the physical separation of communities from each other which was intrinsically connected to the fragmentation of PIE.

A further factor which prevented the effective fragmentation of Latin for several centuries lay in the written mode; there have been varying estimates of the proportion of literate Roman citizens, but the latest analyses tend to be relatively bullish (see Ward-Perkins 2005: 151–68). Writing allows communities who are not in physical contact to remain in communication, although in itself it is unlikely in the long run to prevent differentiation in speech (see Milroy 2001, and also Chapter 31 in this *Handbook*). There had not been any such effect within Indo-European; by the time that any Indo-European language was committed to writing, irreversible divergence had already occurred. But the study of Latin has always been primarily a branch of philology, since the primary data are necessarily in written form. Some historical linguists trained in the comparative method, such as Hall (1974), Agard (1984) and De Dardel (1996), reacted by ignoring those data and reconstructing 'Proto'-Romance in the same way as their predecessors had reconstructed PIE, on the basis of written Romance data from a much later time; they succeeded in establishing Latin phonetics, and resurrecting some lexical items, but their attempts to reconstruct the morphosyntactic development of spoken Latin have been unconvincing. Arguing on phonetic grounds, they also postulate a remarkably early divergence of Latin into separate Romance languages, claiming, for example, that Sardinian had diverged to become a separate language by the third century BC. Syntactic evidence does not lead to the same conclusion, and other historians and historical sociolinguists point out that Sardinia was not cut off during the Roman Empire, concluding that definitive divergence, as opposed to normal geographical variation, cannot be seriously postulated for that time (see Herman 1990).

Yet the reconstructionists discovered genuine features, and their approximate datings for their first arrival may often be right. But at times they probably mistook the normal variation found within a natural ensemble of sociolinguistic continua for the starker phenomenon of divergence between whole linguistic 'systems' (dialects or languages). They came to such conclusions because they thought that reconstructing a particular feature for a certain time and place implied that the pre-existing feature which fulfilled that function must have fallen out of use at the same time as the arrival of the corresponding new feature: for example, an epenthetic front vowel before the start of a word beginning in [sC-], as in

Spanish *estar* < Latin *stare*; or the use of the preposition *de* rather than a genitive inflection to mean 'of;' or the use of *quod* plus a finite verb rather than an accusative plus infinitive construction. They only rarely took into account the possibility of monolingual internal variation between the old and the new phenomena. Thus the recent advent of historical sociolinguistics has led to a decline in the prestige of Proto-Romance reconstruction, as Michel Banniard trenchantly exemplifies (1992, 1997, although Banniard calls his field 'retrospective' rather than 'historical' sociolinguistics). It is probably now generally accepted, for example, that the [esC-] realization of /sC-/, *de* meaning 'of,' and *quod* + finite verbs, indeed came into Latin during the early empire as available variants, within the sociolinguistic continua of styles and registers, but without the existing [sC-] pronunciations, genitive inflections and ACC + INF constructions quickly disappearing as a consequence. The arrival of the new, as sociolinguistics has insisted and historical linguistics has often attested, does not necessarily or even commonly coincide with the loss of the old (see Penny 2000). Indeed, the old feature need never disappear. In these cases, [sC-] has indeed been lost in Spain, but survives in France and Italy (where the consonants found after initial /s-/ include several unavailable in Latin, so we can see that in Italy the development has subsequently turned round and traveled in the other direction); genitives have been lost in nouns, but not in pronouns (e.g. French *leur* and Italian *loro* < Latin *illorum*); accusative and infinitive constructions survive after verbs of perceiving (such as Spanish *las vi sonreír*, 'I saw them smile'). Thus we can conclude that the existence of variation within normal sociolinguistic continua explains the discoveries which reconstructors such as Hall (1983) and De Dardel (1996) attributed to an early divergence between Latin and Romance. They saw genitives as by definition Latin, and *de* meaning 'of' as by definition Romance, unable to conceive that both features could fit inside the same language or that the resulting stylistic and sociolinguistic variation was normal. There are texts that combine genitives and *de* within the same document, until the twelfth century in the Iberian Peninsula, but not because the writers were cavalierly mixing two different languages; their single language was inherently variable and contained both features.

3. Divergence in Romance

The definitive Latin-Romance divergence had to wait till long after the end of the Empire. Romanists and Latinists do not envisage much geographical divergence within the period of the Empire itself (see Wright 2003). Adams (2007) studied the regional diversification of imperial Latin in detail, and concluded that the relatively minor attested features of geographical divergence cannot have greatly disrupted communication between speakers from different areas. Normal diatopic variation had always existed anyway:

> The regional diversity of the language can be traced back at least to 200 BC and was not a new development of the Empire [...] the essential point is that the language

always showed regional as well as social, educational and stylistic variations. The Romance languages in the modern sense came into being [...] when some regional varieties were codified in writing, and particularly when certain of them acquired the status of standard languages.

(Adams 2007: 684)

That is, the continuum was only broken many centuries later.

Adams's conclusions are not all new, but this perspective seems unattractive to those linguists who assume that divergence to the point of fragmentation is an almost inevitable consequence of change. And the picture has also been nuanced recently by the growing realization of an accompanying truth: that, given continuing contact between speakers, convergence is also likely (see Fusco *et al.* 2000). There is not a contradiction or paradox here; whether there is convergence or divergence depends on sociohistorical circumstances, such as whether communities are in contact or not, and sociophilological ones, such as whether different areas share a writing system.

'Convergence' here is not being used to refer (as it sometimes is) to the areal similarity of unrelated languages in the same region, but to the progressive assimilation of cognate variants within a larger language (cp. Thomason and Kaufman 1988); it can even sometimes lead to the formation of a new dialect. Such convergence is essentially the familiar phenomenon that mutually intelligible speakers of different geographical dialects tend naturally to accommodate their speech to each other's habits. If a Liverpudlian meets an Australian on a train, their ability to understand each other's English will improve over the journey, and they can sometimes end up speaking slightly more like each other; for instance, the Liverpudlian might adopt the Australian's upwardly rising intonation pattern at the end of a remark which introduces a referent new to the discourse. Such convergence is normal in armies. The Roman armies included soldiers from all areas, as the modern Greek army has soldiers from Epirus, Corfu, the Peloponnese, Salonica, Crete, and so on; initially they smile at each other's accents, but soon learn to get along. In the past, such accommodation only had significant consequences if many speakers met physically in this way; but in the modern world television may occasionally have such an effect, as watching *Neighbours* helped some Liverpudlians understand Australian English, although on the whole television has almost no effect on production (as opposed to reception), and, even then, mainly on vocabulary.

The later Roman Empire may have been particularly propitious to such convergence. Adams himself (2007) is relatively skeptical about this, but Herman (1990) was led by his encyclopedic knowledge of epigraphy to support the hypothesis. Herman felt able to identify different geographical areas as the original home of certain linguistic developments; for example, African Latin led the way in the dephonologization of vowel length, Pannonia in losing the dative/ablative distinctions, the Venice area in the reorganization of the vowel aperture system, and Rome in consonantal sandhi phenomena; but the evidence also led Herman to the view that such changes usually spread to become empire-wide by the late fourth century AD. Thus many features of Early Romance were found all over the Latin-speaking area, including all the examples adduced above, epenthetic [esC-], *de* for 'of' and the use of the complementizer *quod* plus a finite verb. The presence over the western Christian world of the same written norm helped slow down tendencies to divergence, as a largely standardized liturgy, Bible, and other texts, accentuated existing tendencies to geographical uniformity; in Banniard's words (2001: 15), "from the triple convergence of Biblical Latin, uncultivated Latin and cultivated Latin, a language of general communication was born." Then the Early Romance-speaking geographical area became progressively smaller from the fourth to the eighth centuries, as Germanic, Greek, and, later, Arabic advanced into Latin's original territory from the North, East, and South respectively; thus theirs was a diametrically opposite kind of space to that of the geographically ever-expanding Proto-Indo-European speakers of the remote past. The evidence, internal and external, suggests that convergence had led to a more internally coherent speech community, although necessarily variable, in 400 AD than in 1 AD, and that Latin (Early Romance) remained a single multivariable language until about 800 AD.

This maintenance of unity was not achieved because the language had refrained from evolving. Latin evolved spectacularly, in phonetics and morphology in particular, over the intervening centuries, and was highly variable along several complex continua. But although it had begun to diverge internally, it had not yet fragmented into separate languages, and many of the evolutions, however significant and far-reaching in themselves, were similar in different places. Romania is the exception; those speakers were physically out of touch with Western Romance.

Tree-branches rarely converge, so convergence does not fit the tree-diagram model. This may be one reason why this convergent scenario has been resisted by those Romanists who want to date definitive divergence and fragmentation to an earlier period. Another is an assumption held by some specialists as well as laymen, that language change is usually caused by contact with other languages. In the Romance case this feeling has inspired 'substratum' theories, which propose that the divergence of Romance languages could be traced to the influence of the different languages spoken in different areas before the Romans arrived. Unfortunately, we know little about many of these languages, and apart from some features of intonation, and some lexical items (particularly toponyms), no feature of Romance was ever shown to have been caused by a pre-existing language that stopped being spoken during the Empire. Influence from surviving 'adstratum' languages is more plausible, but may be limited to the choice between already existing variants, as when bilingual Basque Latin speakers preferred to use the existing allophone [h-] rather than [f-] as the realization of Latin /f-/ because of features of their Basque. There was bound to be some substratum influence, of course, at an initial stage; the pre-existing language would influence the Latin used by first- and second-generation Latin learners, as Adams (2007) showed for Punic-Latin bilinguals in third-century AD North Africa, but it is probable that their descendants in subsequent generations, who by then knew Latin as a first language, lost those traits, and then participated in the general convergence.

The effect of later 'superstratum' languages on the divergence of Early Romance has proved less easy to dismiss. Germanic played some role in the separate identity of Old French, for example. But although the distinct conceptual identity of Ibero-Romance coincided chronologically with the presence there of many Arabic-Romance bilinguals, it has proved difficult to show that the distinctiveness of any Ibero-Romance feature was directly caused by Arabic. Adams is undoubtedly right: the arrival of separately identified Romance languages, fragmented out of Latin, came rather later, perhaps in the late twelfth century, and was connected with what we know to have been the deliberate invention of separate new ways of writing, differently in different places. In Janson's view (2002; see also Wright 2003), the deployment of these different writing methods led to the subsequent idea that there were several different Romance languages; in Banniard's converse view (1997), the conceptual distinctions came first and inspired the distinctiveness of the writing systems which we now refer to as Old French, Old Provençal, Old Sicilian, and so on.

Thus the definitive fragmentation of Latin into the Romance languages did not happen in the same way or for the same reason as the break-up of PIE (although both were, of course, based on changes that had already happened in different ways in different places), but with the deliberate development of separate writing systems. Without these, the language could perhaps have continued to be regarded as a multivariable 'Latin' (or 'Romance') with a single written standard, taught and learnt largely logographically; in the same way as most speakers of modern Chinese will tell you that Chinese is one language, despite the enormous internal spoken variability over wide geographical distances, while most linguists on the other side of the world prefer to decide (on linguistic rather than sociolinguistic grounds) that Chinese is six or seven different languages. In such circumstances, it is not obvious who has the casting vote, the native speakers or the theoretical linguists; is Chinese one language, or has it fragmented? Chinese certainly counts as a World Language, both in numbers of speakers and in geographical extension – unless it isn't one language at all. So the Chinese government has an interest in promoting the idea of convergence rather than divergence.

PIE and Latin are untypical cases of fragmentation, despite their central interest for historical sociolinguistics, in that the eventual results of the process are generally known. The future development of current World Languages is not clear at all. The increasing importance of the written mode, and the growing interest shown by language-planning politicians, make it difficult to tell if the future will be like the past. The uniformitarian hypothesis, that, other things being equal, the nature of linguistic communities in the past was probably similar to the nature of linguistic communities in the present, is helpful until the other things are not equal at all, including, most notably, the interventions of politicians and the increasing relevance of literacy.

Historical linguists and sociolinguists are in any event reluctant to predict the future. This is sensible, because we may well be embarrassingly proved wrong. Yet the practitioners of the discipline sometimes like to claim that it is 'predictive.' This does not mean that we claim to know the future, but that we could have predicted features of the present had we been speaking the language several hundred years ago. Inevitably, this is often a circular argument, in that what we think we know about a language state of the past has itself usually been established by arguing backwards on the basis of present evidence.

4. The Future

4.1 *Spanish*

The prospects for the future are at best ambiguous. In the world of mass media and the Internet, many speakers of even the most widely-spread World Languages can hear the dialects, accents, vocabulary, and other peculiarities of a wide range of geographical variants all the time; in that sense, reception is convergent. Vocabulary converges to some extent for the same reason; English English-speakers and Spanish Spanish-speakers now understand better than before much American vocabulary which we are unlikely to use actively. Geographical syntactic variation, although it exists, is relatively unimportant and unnoticed, and syntactic variants are almost always easy to understand even when noticed; even in the long development of Romance languages from Latin, syntactic changes were few and progressed slowly (as contrasted with morphological developments, which were spectacular).

Intellectuals in Spain and in Spanish America have at times been worried that Spanish, as a World Language, might diverge and then subsequently fragment in America as Latin eventually did in Europe; they were particularly worried between 1848 and 1927, when the Chileans were operating different spelling rules. But since the chilenos abandoned these, the possibility has seemed less imminent. Even though some of them tend to call their language *chileno*, the general view in Chile, and in the rest of the Spanish-speaking world, is that Spanish is and will remain a single variable international language, with one written standard and political support for its global identity. This view has been explicitly expressed at government level (although governments probably have less influence on spoken language than they believe, and their vision of the future may, of course, be wrong). Each Spanish-speaking country in the Americas has an *Academia de la Lengua*, but under the leadership of the *Real Academia Española* in Madrid they have collectively agreed to co-operate and maintain a single written standard. The intention is not necessarily to refrain from reforming the written language at all, as conservative purists would prefer, but to reform it, if they do, the same way in every country. For example, if the *Academias* ever decide to drop the initial letter *h-* from spellings, which never represents any speech sound, they will all drop it together. Evolution without divergence. That's the deliberate intention, and unless some future global catastrophe reduces all intra-Hispanic contacts, divergence in the written mode, at least, will be prevented. But even without this official activity, spoken Spanish dialects seem to have been generally converging anyway; some of the more individual developments reported a century ago appear to be stable, or in retreat, in the present millennium. (For the historical sociolinguistic development of Spanish, see Penny 2000; Del Valle and Gabriel-Stheeman 2002; for contemporary Spanish sociolinguistics, see Stewart 1999; Pountain 2003; for Latin-American Spanish, see Lipski 1994).

The above refers to Spanish as a World Language. Within Spanish in Spain there is more linguistic diversity than there is in Spanish America, and there are political counter-movements in the other direction. In the North, Catalan and Galician have had their status as separate languages within the pan-Romance continuum affirmed by post-Franco politicians and standardized with written norms; they, and their Aragonese and Asturian neighbours, whose political support and linguistic status are less secure, developed divergently from Latin, as did Castilian (Spanish), and the *patois* in France. But the local modes of speech in the Southern Iberian Peninsula are sociohistorically in a different category, because these developed not from Latin but from the Northern Spanish varieties brought south during the Medieval Reconquest of Muslim Spain, particularly in the thirteenth century. Linguists outside the area think it obvious that the ways in which people speak in informal contexts and registers in Extremadura, Seville, Granada, Murcia, and the Canary Islands are kinds of Spanish, varying within normal sociolinguistic continua. But some southern local patriots, understandably annoyed at being told by Northerners that they speak Spanish badly, now claim that they are not speaking Spanish at all; that their communities are in fact speaking *extremeño, andaluz, canario,* and so on, rather than Spanish. It is politically incorrect to disagree with them in some circles, but many of their neighbors are annoyed to be told that they are not speaking Spanish at all. These arguments are political, not linguistic. Dialects are to some extent political constructs anyway, of course, and, within a dialect continuum, dialect borders where isoglosses bundle along political frontiers are not the norm (unless caused by large population movements); but even so, it is possible that these local patriots will get their political way, establish separate written systems, and create the fragmentation within Spanish that the Spanish Americans, through adopting opposite policies aimed ultimately at convergence, are intending to avoid.

4.2 Portuguese

Spanish became a World Language after Columbus; Portuguese is also a World Language with a similar pedigree, and now the fifth most widely spoken language in the world. But the forces for convergence and divergence in the Portuguese-speaking world present a different picture from those operating within Spanish. The recent well-intentioned attempts to preserve linguistic, or at least orthographic, unity throughout Portugal, Brazil, and the Portuguese African territories (and Goa, Macao, and East Timor) have created chaos, particularly in Portugal itself. The far more numerous Brazilians do not wish to be told what to do by the relatively tiny number of European Portuguese-speakers; the relatively well-educated European Portuguese do not wish to be told to follow any of the habits of largely illiterate (up to 80%) speakers in third-world Brazil. The arguments have become political and heated. Whereas hardly any English-speakers care much whether a playhouse is a *theater* or a *theatre*, such questions can seem hugely significant in many Romance-speaking communities, and Portuguese-speakers can come close to blows over whether there should be a written accent on *idéia*. Since official spelling rules in Portugal have to be approved in Parliament, they are literally laws. A misprint is technically an offence. In 2008 a delegation of worried linguists went to see the President of Portugal to seek his support against the legal imposition of the new *acordo ortográfico da Língua Portuguesa* (1990; approved by Parliament in 1991). The cause of the anti-*acordo* linguists is probably lost, but the feeling remains widespread in Portugal; what is the point of unifying the spelling systems when the ways people speak are so different in Portugal and in Brazil? Brazilian Portuguese is less complex than European Portuguese in several ways, particularly in phonology, and internally varies widely; although Portuguese-speakers from Europe tend to understand most Brazilians, Brazilians often find European Portuguese hard to follow, more so than American Spanish- and English-speakers find their European counterparts. In practice, linguistic analysts usually now refer to either Brazilian Portuguese or European Portuguese, and do not claim that their analyses for one hold for the other. There are a few convergent features, particularly in the vocabulary used in journalism, but some of the socio-political factors are so strongly anti-convergent that Portuguese may turn out in the future to be not just pluricentric but the only World Language that actually fragments, rather than simply diverging, and thus stops being a World Language at all (Clyne 1992: *Revue Belge* 2001).

4.3   French

The Chinese would see the point in forestalling that; so would the French. French was chronologically the next language to become a World Language. Its future is ostensibly under conscious direction (see Lodge 1993; Walter 1994). Since the *Académie Française* was founded in 1634–35, prestigious French linguists have not only told French-speakers what to write, but also what to say. And they may even have had an effect. No other similar state institution has so much practical influence, at least: when the Spanish *Academia* ran a weekly five-minute broadcast entitled *Se dice así* ('This is how to say it') in the early 1970s, intended to correct infelicitous divergent spoken usage, it was very popular, but nobody seems to have actually changed their spoken habits as a result. Yet the geographical homogeneity of spoken as well as written language in France has increased over the years, as a result of the general intellectual atmosphere that led to the existence of the *Académie* as much as of the *Académie* itself, partly because regional Romance *patois* were sociolinguistically downgraded so much in the early twentieth century that these have much less covert prestige now than their English or Spanish equivalents. The *Académie* has recently, however, accepted the possibility of a few differing but equally correct usages within standard French, whose variability can thus now be seen as inherent rather than attesting dialect mixture. The differences between the spoken and written French of standard French-speakers are large; not only in the wide divergence between the standard orthography and the phonetic transcriptions of the same words, but in the morphology and syntax used when speaking and writing. In many other contexts, such differences between sets of linguistic data would appear so great that sociolinguists would be tempted to classify the two as separate diastratically-distinguished languages, in the same way as Romanists view Latin and Old French as co-existing separate entities in the competence of ninth-century Carolingian intellectuals. Yet no linguist in France seems to have been tempted seriously to suggest that they are separate languages. That is, French is still one language, but only because everybody thinks it is. French is a World Language spoken in many continents and several far-flung islands whose speech is often hard for visitors to understand, but the sociopolitical idea of *La Francophonie* (a word coined in 1880), in the singular, with its one written standard, seems to be more powerful than any facts on the ground. The linguistic status of creoles can, however, lead to differences of specialist opinion. The overall result is that French is increasingly like Chinese, in that there is officially one worldwide language despite the spoken variability, and the universally-advocated written forms are consequently in essence logographic, with decreasing isomorphism between the alphabetic constituents and the phonetic representations of most lexical items. In Portugal some linguists talk of *lusofonías* in the plural, and definitive divergence may well now be under way; but it will take political and cultural earthquakes to introduce such an acceptance of divergence within French, particularly if we are in an age of gradual convergence in practice.

4.4   English

English is now often described as a (or even 'the') World Language. It is indeed spoken in many parts of the world (McArthur 2002; Trudgill 1998, 2006). But it is a decidedly unusual one; more people speak it as a second language than as a first. Substratum effects among first-generation attempted bilinguals are common now, particularly in Asia, as they were in the Latin of third-century Libya; McArthur's *Oxford Guide to World English* (2002) provides many neat examples. The point of the world-wide attempts to learn English is that it is the international language of the moment. Although English is pluricentric, a perceived lack of divergence may well be essential in order to preserve its world-wide status, whether or not we think that it is diverging in practice. It has become common for sociolinguists to finesse this possibility by referring to the multiply varying kinds of English in the plural, as *Englishes*. The presence of a single international standardized written form is as valuable to the unity of English as it was to the Late Latin world (Wright 2004); in the early seventh century Isidore of Seville could write his encyclopedia (the *Etymologiae*) in standard Latin, and have it read avidly by the literate minority in both Romance and non-Romance speaking places precisely because that was the single established written mode; in the same way David Crystal (1997) can write his encyclopedias in standard English spelling and grammar and be understood with profit anywhere in the world. The fact that the text of both encyclopedias contains words whose standard orthographic form is rather different from a phonetic transcription of their author's natural speech is not a drawback; such semi-logographic systems are entirely practical, even if their component parts were originally alphabetical in inspiration. They show how essential standardized and mainly unreformed orthographic systems are for languages spoken over a wide area, since these can for some practical purposes overcome the geographical variability and potential divergence of the spoken counterparts. If English spelling were ever in the future to be generally reformed on a phonographic model in which spelling approximated pronunciation, those reformed modes would have to be markedly different in different places, as the first attempts at written Romance had to be, and that would lead, as it did in Romance, to the idea that these were not just several new ways of writing the same language but several new languages. Divergence would then have occurred to the point of fragmentation.

But other than in orthography, it would be a mistake to create a separate internationally-valid World English standard deliberately different from the usage of native speakers. There is a possibility of this happening. If the developing 'Euro-English,' or the management-speak register spoken by bureaucrats, comes to have more prestige than the natural speech of native speakers, this could have the same unfortunate consequences as the development of artificial Medieval Latin *grammatica* had in Europe, when the natural speech of native Romance-speakers lost sociolinguistic prestige in comparison with the imposed archaizing standard. The establishment of Medieval Latin, conceptually distinct from Early Romance, was probably what finally catalyzed the divergence of Latin and Romance as diastratically separate languages, to the continuing disadvantage of non-Latinate Romance-speakers everywhere. David Crystal (1998) has implied that this will inevitably occur to English, but he may not be right about that; looking to the future here is essentially guesswork.

Even so, it is not unreasonable to suggest that in the native English-speaking world convergence may after all end up winning. The mass media might allow it to be an international phenomenon. American, Australian, and Indian English habits are better understood in Britain now than they used to be fifty years ago. Some of the more individual features of rural dialect English speech are less noticeable now (in Britain) than they were two hundred years ago. There is a countervailing tendency in the divergent speech of big cities in the United States, however, and everywhere local varieties of speech have more prestige than they used to. Despite this, if we avoid spelling reforms and linguistically-conscious political separatism, even though English is a very widely-spoken and widely varying World Language it may manage to avoid divergence to the point of fragmentation, and remain internally variable; complex but monolingual.

5. Conclusion

The history of the main World Languages over the last few thousand years suggests that both divergence and convergence are natural processes. The difference in practice between natural divergence (which is inevitable) and eventual subsequent fragmentation (which is not) depends on whether or not the speakers are cut off from communicating with each other, whether or not there is a unified written mode, and whether or not the language can escape the more unfortunate effects of political interference.

REFERENCES

Adams, J. (2007) *The Regional Diversification of Latin, 200 BC – AD 600*, Cambridge University Press, Cambridge.

Agard, F.B. (1984) *A Course in Romance Linguistics*, Georgetown University, Washington.

Banniard, M. (1992) *Viva Voce: communication écrite et communication orale du IVe au IXe siècle en Occident latin*, Études Augustiniennes, Paris.

Banniard, M. (1997) *Du latin aux langues romanes*, Nathan, Paris.

Banniard, M. (2001) Action et réaction de la parole latinophone: démocratisation et unification (IIIe–Ve siècles). *An Tard* 9: 115–29.

Clackson, J. and Horrocks, G. (2007) *The Blackwell History of the Latin Language*, Blackwell, Oxford.

Clyne, M. (ed.) (1992) *Pluricentric Languages: Differing Norms in Different Nations*, de Gruyter, Berlin.

Crystal, D, (1997) *The Cambridge Encyclopaedia of Language*, Cambridge University Press, Cambridge.

Crystal, D. (1998) *English as a Global Language*, Cambridge University Press, Cambridge.

De Dardel, R. (1996) *A la recherche du protoroman*, Niemeyer, Tübingen.

Del Valle, J. and Gabriel-Stheeman, L. (eds.) (2002) *The Battle over Spanish between 1800 and 2000*, Routledge, London.

Fusco, F., Orioles, V., and Parmeggiani, A. (eds.) (2000) *Processi di convergenza e differenziazione nelle lingue dell'Europa medievale e moderna*, Forum, Udine.

Hall, R.A., Jr. (1974) *External History of the Romance Languages*, Elsevier, New York.

Hall, R.A., Jr. (1983) *Proto-Romance Morphology*, John Benjamins, Amsterdam.

Herman, J. (1990) *Du latin aux langues romanes*, Niemeyer, Tübingen.

Herman, J. (2000) *Vulgar Latin*, Penn State University Press, Pennsylvania.

Janson, T. (2002) *Speak: A Short History of Languages*, Oxford University Press, Oxford.

Justus, C.F. and McWhirter, D.A. (2000) Indo-European religious dialect divisions. *General Linguistics* 40: 19–51.

Lipski, J. (1994) *Latin-American Spanish*, Longman, London.

Lodge, R.A. (1993) *French, from Dialect to Standard*, Routledge, London.

McArthur, T. (2002) *The Oxford Guide to World English*, Oxford University Press, Oxford.

Milroy, J. (2001) Language ideologies and the consequences of standardization. *Journal of Sociolinguistics* 5: 530–55.

Nichols, J. (1992) *Linguistic Diversity in Space and Time*, Chicago University Press, Chicago.

Penny, R. (2000) *Variation and Change in Spanish*, Cambridge University Press, Cambridge.

Pountain, C. (2003) *Exploring the Spanish Language*, Arnold, London.

Revue Belge de Philologie et d'Histoire 79(3) 2001, *Les langues pluricentriques*.

Stewart, M. (1999) *The Spanish Language Today*, Routledge, London.

Thomason, S. and Kaufman, T. (1988) *Language Contact, Creolization and Genetic Linguistics*, University of California Press, Berkeley.

Trask, R.L. (1997) *The History of Basque*, Routledge, London.

Trask, R.L. (2000) *The Dictionary of Historical and Comparative Linguistics*, Edinburgh University Press, Edinburgh.

Trudgill, P. (1998) World English: convergence or divergence? In H. Lindqvist *et al.* (eds.), *The Major Varieties of English*, Växjö University Press, Växjö, pp. 29–36.

Trudgill, P. (2006) *The Inevitability of Colonial Englishes*, Edinburgh University Press, Edinburgh.

Walter, H. (1994) *French Inside Out*, Routledge, London.

Ward-Perkins, B. (2005) *The Fall of Rome and the End of Civilization*, Oxford University Press, Oxford.

Wright, R. (2003) *A Sociophilological Study of Late Latin*, Brepols, Turnhout.

Wright, R. (2004) Latin and English as World languages. *English Today* 20(4): 3–19.

Part V   Attitudes to Language

31 Sociolinguistics and Ideologies in Language History

JAMES MILROY

According to most linguistic scholars, ideological attitudes and beliefs have no place in linguistics: their influences must be rigorously excluded. When Saussure laid down the principles of the subject, he was emphatic about this: "[m]y definition of language" he insisted, "presupposes the exclusion of everything that is outside its organisation or system – in a word everything known as 'external linguistics'" (1916/1983: 20). Most formal linguists have tried to obey these requirements, and for this reason much of the so-called 'autonomous' linguistics of the last century or so has consisted of formal statements of rules and relationships, with no overt reference to the world outside language.

Much, but not all, of historical linguistic theorizing has also been inward-looking. Since the nineteenth century, linguistic changes have preferentially been explained as caused by factors internal to language structure rather than by speaker activity in social settings. Internal or 'endogenous' explanations have been preferred to external explanations (Lass 1997). So, for example, a phonological change may be said to be due to assimilation, dissimilation, stress-shift, or some other language-internal phenomenon, with no attention, or only occasional slight and speculative attention, to the social conditions that might have helped to trigger it. Furthermore, in what has been called 'genetic' linguistics, the requirement that each language must have a single parent language has led to neglect of the effects of language and dialect contact on language change (see Mufwene 2001, 108–9).

Despite the axioms of autonomous linguistics, however, descriptive and historical linguists have frequently allowed ideological positions to influence their

The Handbook of Historical Sociolinguistics, First Edition. Edited by Juan Manuel Hernández-Campoy and Juan Camilo Conde-Silvestre.
© 2014 John Wiley & Sons, Ltd. Published 2014 by John Wiley & Sons, Ltd.

methods and conclusions. This is particularly noticeable in accounts of histories of languages, often in books designed for undergraduates and written by distinguished scholars. Typically, popular accounts glorify the past, tying the history of a language to the 'glorious' history of the nation and to literary achievements, and, although language is not literally a living organism, we may be told that it has a life, that it has had 'growth' and has made 'progress' (Jespersen 1938). A recent book on English (Bragg 2003) is subtitled 'the biography of a language.'

However, there are more subtle ideological influences on the thinking of linguists, some of them arising from neogrammarian and structuralist positions, and it is possible to argue that the general assumptions that underlie the whole subject are ideologically influenced. For example, the idea that a language is a self-contained system of interdependent parts, and that it is wholly distinct from every other language, may be ideologically driven – arising from researchers' personal experience of the national languages of major nation-states. There are many situations in which the distinctions between languages are unclear, and there is a tendency to think of these situations, including pidgin and creole language situations, as abnormal. Thomason and Kaufman (1988: 147–66), for example, consider creole languages as resulting from transmission that is not 'normal' transmission. This is a blatantly social judgment, made on the basis of sociopolitical conditions that are considered to be abnormal: there is no reason to suppose that there is anything *linguistically* abnormal about mixed or multilingual language situations (for a discussion, see especially Mufwene 2001). Joseph and Taylor insist (1990: 2) – correctly, I believe – that the whole subject, while claiming to be non-ideological, is in fact ideologically influenced.

In what follows, we shall first consider a frequently invoked concept that has proved to be problematic in the work of language historians and sociolinguists – the concept of 'prestige' as used in explaining linguistic changes. We then proceed to consider certain ideological processes, and in the light of these processes, we go on to discuss specific ideological influences on the work of linguists.

1. The Concept of Prestige in Socio-Historical Argumentation

One of the background influences on allegedly neutral descriptions of language change is the idea that some language forms and varieties may have greater prestige than others. It is clear that speaker/listeners attribute greater or lesser prestige to different varieties of language and, indeed, to different languages, and descriptive linguists have, almost routinely, used the idea of prestige in their attempted explanations for linguistic changes. Prestige, however, is a social, not a linguistic, concept. Whether a linguistic form is believed to have high or low prestige depends, not on its linguistic shape, but on the perceived social status or importance of the speakers who use it. In using the concept, linguists are making assumptions about social structure and other matters that are external to language structure – social class differences, for example – even when they do not explicitly discuss and explain these things.

In traditional historical linguistics, the conceptualization of prestige has been unidirectional, with linguistic influences regarded as moving in one direction only. Thus, it has been assumed that the higher social classes determine the direction of change, as, notably, in the following: "a new king may ascend the throne and his subjects begin to follow his speech rather than that of his predecessor" (Sturtevant 1917: 30). Sturtevant was a great language scholar, but his account of the speech community is narrow and elitist: he was clearly in the grip of an ideology based on consciousness of social class distinctions:

> Just as fashions in dress are binding upon all members of a given class and are imitated by all who look up to that class, so fashions in language are binding upon all people of culture and are followed by other members of the community to the best of their ability. (Sturtevant 1917: 26).

The view that upper-class forms are dominant has been highly influential in traditional historical reasoning and is still sometimes prominent, for example, in the idea found among historians of English that modern 'Received Pronunciation' (RP) is the direct descendant of the speech of the Elizabethan royal court.

> The speech of the Court, however, phonetically largely that of the London area, increasingly acquired a prestige value and in time, lost some of the local characteristics of London speech. It may be said to have been finally fixed, as the speech of the ruling class, through the conformist influence of the public schools of the nineteenth century.
>
> (Gimson 1962/1970, 84–85)

This appears to suggest that changes in this variety have been triggered internally with no influence from outside. It is implied that the elite variety has existed for centuries immune to influences from other varieties, which have been too low-status to be able to have an effect on it (on RP, see further below). Indeed, in English historical linguistics, this emphasis on elite language led to a situation in which only the polite language of relatively educated speakers and writers could be included in historical descriptions of a language. The language of the uneducated was not part of history: it could be ignored or rejected. This ideologically-driven tendency to reject or ignore relevant evidence has been called the process of "erasure," to which we shall also return below.

It seems that the traditional conceptualization of sociolinguistic space has been unidimensional and unidirectional – a space in which elite groups set the tone in language, as well as in dress and other cultural matters, and in which lower groups strive to follow their lead, and much of what is accepted as the histories of major languages has been influenced by this narrow conceptualization. The most important difficulty with it is that it has been widely shown that linguistic changes do not necessarily, or even normally, originate in the elite variety, but often appear to spread into it 'from below.' Modern English RP (the high-prestige British accent mentioned above), for example, now often has the glottal stop (for word-final [t]) and 'intrusive [r]' (as in 'law[r] and order'), which both originated in lower-class usage and would horrify Victorian RP speakers if they heard them. Henry Alford (1864/1889: 35–36) considered intrusive [r] to be "a worse fault even" than h-dropping and viewed it as a London vernacular ('Cockney') feature. This usage, along with the glottal stop and other features, has now penetrated the high prestige variety from the speech of lower social classes. As Strang (1970: 164) commented:

> . . . since the function of a prestige variety […] is to be the mark of a metropolitan elite, it may seem strange that the source of most innovations proves to be vulgar or dialectal speech.

'Strange' indeed, but true. William Labov (1994: 78) comments that "no cases have been recorded in which the highest-status social group acts as the innovating group."

The fact that language change does not usually come from elite varieties has been a stumbling block in historical linguistics. Strang (1970: 164), for example, has noted that if change comes about in the elite variety, it can only come from 'socially inferior' varieties. She then goes on to attach the term 'prestige' to forms current in the socially inferior varieties from which the elite variety borrows. Here we are very close to a logical contradiction, which, we might feel, renders the term 'prestige' almost meaningless: the high prestige variety, it is proposed, borrows from lower-prestige varieties because some of the forms in the lower-prestige varieties have higher, not lower, prestige. Therefore, in some respects, the higher-prestige variety must have lower prestige!

William Labov's attempted solution to this apparent contradiction is to postulate two distinct kinds of linguistic change – 'change from above' and 'change from below' – but we should notice that his characterization of the linguistic innovator (1980: 261) still depends heavily on the idea of prestige in a speech community characterized in terms of socio-economic class.

Those who lead sound changes are the speakers who have the highest status in their communities, as measured by a social class index, according to Labov: the most advanced speakers among these "are the persons with the largest number of local contacts within the neighborhood, yet who have at the same time the highest proportion of their acquaintances outside the neighborhood" (Labov 1980: 261). He goes on to comment: "[t]hus we have a portrait of individuals with the highest local prestige who are responsive to a somewhat broader form of prestige at the next larger level of social communication" (Labov 1980: 261–62).

Although this is a great advance on the assumptions of traditional historical linguistics, there are objections to many aspects of Labov's model, which have been widely discussed (by Milroy and Milroy 1985 and J. Milroy 1992a, for example), including its relative blindness to the effects on language of ideological positions and its continuing dependence on the notions of class and prestige. It can be suggested that our explanatory frameworks should avoid relying on the notion of prestige and focus more on the indexicality of linguistic variables as used by social groups independently of the social status of such groups. Emphasis on socio-economic class is a considerable limitation on any sociolinguistic model, since class is not a universal in all societies.

2. Ideological Processes

Recently, linguistic anthropologists have devoted much attention to ideologies of language, considering, for example, nationalistic beliefs about the histories of, and origins of, particular languages (see, for example, Schieffelin, Woolard and Kroskrity 1998). The most important work in the context of this chapter is research into ideological influences on the scholars who first described the languages of colonial peoples. Irvine and Gal (2000: 35–36) note that linguistic ideological positions are held not only by the speakers of languages, but also by the "linguists and ethnographers who have mapped the boundaries of languages and provided descriptive accounts of them." They have suggested that these scholars have been influenced by certain ideological *processes*, of which two are specially relevant here. These are 'iconization' and 'erasure.'

We have already noticed some features of language histories that are broadly affected by iconization: for example, the idea that the history of a language is intimately linked with the history of a people, and if that national history is glorious, then the history of the language is also necessarily glorious. As for erasure, Irvine and Gal (2000: 38) describe it as follows:

> [T]he process in which ideology, in simplifying the sociolinguistic field, renders some persons or activities (or sociolinguistic phenomena) invisible. Facts that are inconsistent with the ideological scheme either go unnoticed or get explained away. So, for example, a social group or a language may be imagined as homogeneous, its internal variation disregarded.

This is a very common process in historical language description, and in what follows we shall notice several instances of it.

2.1   The ideology of the standard language

The notion of 'standard language' has had a considerable influence on historical language description, and I have discussed it elsewhere, including Milroy (2001), on which much of the following account is based. There has been some vagueness and confusion as to what the properties of a 'standard language' might be, and, commonly, the standard form of a language is characterized as the variety with the highest prestige. Although the standard may indeed be perceived as carrying high prestige, it should be noticed that high prestige is not the key defining linguistic property of a standard variety. If in a given case the standard variety is found to be identical with the highest prestige variety, it does not follow that high prestige is the most important factor in the process of standardization or in what constitutes a 'standard.' This is clear if we look at standardization in fields other than language: we would not apply the notion of prestige to sets of electric plugs, for example, although they are certainly standardized, and many things that are not standardized (such as hand-made objects) may actually be the ones that acquire the highest prestige. Standardization consists of the imposition of *uniformity* upon a class of objects – in this case language – which are, in the nature of things, variable. To the extent that a language variety is standardized, it will show a higher degree of structural invariance than other varieties. Thus, usually, a standard variety recognizes only one form of any word, pronunciation, or grammatical structure as the accepted form, and other variants, which may actually exist abundantly in the language, are rejected. Uniformity of structure is the key property of an ideal standard language, and, unlike prestige, this is a property of the language system itself, not of the social groups of speakers who use it.

Notably, some of the interpretations of variation recently proposed by quantitative sociolinguists are not clear on the relation of 'standard' to prestige. Variation in the speech community has been interpreted on a scale of prestige, which derives from the socio-economic class of speakers, but this scale is frequently interpreted as though it were identical to a scale of 'standard' to 'non-standard.' Labov's model of linguistic change, for instance, is predicated on a speech community organized in terms of social class. For example, changes from above "are introduced by the dominant social class, often with full public awareness" (Labov 1994: 78). Labov's account of language differences according to sex of speaker invokes 'standard' and 'prestige' as effectively the same thing, or at least closely associated: "men use more nonstandard forms than women, less influenced by the social stigma against them; or, conversely, women use more standard forms, responding to the overt prestige associated with them" (Labov 1990: 210). The assumption here seems to be that the scale from 'standard' to 'non-standard' is strongly associated with the scale of prestige. I have elsewhere (2001: 533) suggested that, as that quantitative paradigm uses the concept of prestige in this way, its interpretations appear to be to this extent dependent on the standard ideology.

As a result of its relative uniformity of structure, a standard variety is highly functional. It can be used in a wide variety of functions, whereas non-standard varieties generally cannot. It is the variety that is normally used in writing, and it can therefore be used to communicate over long distances and periods of time. We can say that it acquires 'prestige' from these things, but if so, this kind of prestige is not, strictly speaking, the same phenomenon as the prestige derived from the high social status of speakers. It is more precise to say that the functional flexibility of the standard gives it a high utilitarian *value*: an economic metaphor is more appropriate here than one based on social prestige. If, for example, one group uses more standard structures than another, this may be because these forms are perceived to be more generally functional and therefore to have a higher practical value in communication.

The development over time of a standard variety of a language leads to a situation in which this variety can be seen as identical with the language as a whole, and this fact is of great importance in historical linguistics. It is the variety that is routinely taught to non-native speakers, and native speakers use it as a point of reference, even if they speak a variety that is quite deviant from the standard. A community in which there is a general consciousness of a standard may be described as a 'standard language culture.' It is necessary to recognize this as a distinct phenomenon, because there are many language situations in the world in which standard languages do not exist or are not relevant. The cultures in which professional linguists live are, however, standard language cultures, so there has been considerable influence of the standard ideology on their underlying assumptions. This ideology, and other ideologies that may contribute to it, had a particularly strong influence on the work of the linguists who in the nineteenth century determined the principles of historical linguistics and produced historical descriptions of major languages and their relationships to one another.

There are several underlying assumptions in structural linguistics that seem to coincide with aspects of the standard ideology. The chief assumption is that a language is a coherent self-contained entity – a system of interdependent parts – in which everything holds together. Each individual language is considered to be clearly distinct from every other language. It looks as though these assumptions are particularly appropriate to standard varieties of languages, and other varieties may not fit the requirements so well; in our own research in Belfast (Milroy 1992a: 97–109), I was at pains to emphasize the fact that non-standard varieties incorporate greater variability than standard English. Thus, it is possible that some of the axioms of structural linguistics are themselves affected by ideology – arising from the standard language culture. Research in unstandardized language situations has shown that there can be a great deal of indefiniteness as to what constitutes a given language and which language is which. The languages that are not standardized do not necessarily exhibit definable boundaries and are not wholly describable in the ways that are conventional in language description.

2.2   *Unstandardized language situations*

Among those who have studied such situations, George Grace's work on Pacific languages is important. He has shown that there are difficulties in dealing with certain Austronesian languages in neogrammarian and structuralist terms. This is discussed in Milroy (2001: 540) and summarized here (see also Chapter 27 in this *Handbook*). The difficulties include the impossibility of fitting some of them into a historical 'genetic' family-tree model, even when they seem to be quite closely related to one another. The boundaries of specific languages also often seem to be unclear, and Grace mentions (1990: 169) a particular case in which "the language as a whole had no truly separate existence in the minds of its speakers." He also found it puzzling (1991: 15) "that in some areas the people seemed to have no conception of what their language is and no sense of belonging to a linguistic community." Peter Mühlhäusler discusses similar questions, citing (1996: 334) a comment by Heryanto (1990: 41): "[l]anguage is not a universal category or cultural activity, though it may sound odd, not all people have a language in a sense of which this term is currently used." Where there is no 'standard language culture,' it seems that 'languages' may be much less well defined than the European languages conventionally described by linguists. Using European language descriptions as the model, we may have been forcing these Pacific languages into much more rigidly defined patterns than they actually possess in the nature of things. Standard or near-standard varieties, of course, being codified, exhibit definite boundaries and orderliness, and these can conveniently provide the model for the structuralist view of languages as self-contained systems of interdependent parts.

Mühlhäusler (1996: 328) also mentions certain beliefs that in his view have not been "helpful in the study of the traditional languages of the Pacific area." These are: the belief in distinct word-classes; the belief in the possibility of using the same descriptive labels for all languages; the belief in the separability of languages and other non-linguistic phenomena; and the belief in the existence of separate languages. We need to consider the possibility that what Mühlhäusler calls 'beliefs' arise very largely from linguists' dominant experience of standard or near-standard varieties in largely European settings.

One of the most illuminating discussions of the imposition of European ideological assumptions on non-standard language cultures is that of Irvine and Gal (2000). They discuss in some detail early European scholars' assumptions of their own cultural superiority and their belief that what they called 'tribes' must be monolingual, with, preferably, one language for each 'tribe' (this is an aspect of iconicization). Furthermore, in the mapping project they describe, linguistic information that could not be made to fit into a map could be ignored (erasure). In reality, in these situations, scholars should be prepared to encounter and describe multilingualism and language mixing, but the principles of traditional scholarship did not generally allow for these phenomena. They tended to be *erased* from the record.

Indeed – as I have suggested elsewhere (Milroy 2005: 331) – the structuralist emphasis on single languages has been so strong that even scholars who were explicitly concerned with language-contact phenomena – Haugen and Weinreich, for example – were capable of thinking of language-mixing as something abnormal – almost pathological. This is clear in the wording of passages such as the following (Weinreich 1953: 60, my emphasis):

> [A] bilingual's speech may *suffer* from the *interference* of another vocabulary through mere *oversight*; that is, the limitations on the distribution of certain words to utterances belonging to one language are *violated*. In affective speech, when the speaker's attention is almost completely diverted from the form of the message to its topic, the transfer of words is particularly common.

The bilingual speaker, it seems, is not respecting the separate integrity of the languages he is using, so his speech is *suffering*. He is allowing one language to *interfere* with another, and this is an *oversight*. In this, one of the languages is being *violated*. The languages involved are seen as separate entities independent of the speakers who use them, and the speaker's probable success in communicating in this way in the circumstances of the conversation is, apparently, not the main interest. The linguist's primary interest here seems to be in language systems as coherent internally-structured entities, rather than on how speakers succeed in communicating in bilingual/multilingual situations – drawing on the totality of the linguistic resources available in their communities in order to do so.

3. Ideological Influences on Historical Linguistics

The influence of the standard ideology on traditional historical descriptions of major modern languages cannot be overstated. Indeed, it can be reasonably suggested that the practice of writing broad descriptive language histories has in itself been a contribution to the standard language culture. This is certainly true of 'popular' histories of English, such as Bragg (2003) and many others, and it is also true of more rigorous accounts, such as those in elementary undergraduate textbooks. Potter (1950) is a good example. In such accounts, the history of the language becomes an inspiring story of the growth and development from obscure and humble beginnings to the language of a great empire and the most important language in the world. Other European languages are treated similarly by their historians. Typically, there is considerable emphasis on literary history, and great authors, such as Chaucer and Shakespeare in the case of English (rather than millions of speakers throughout history), are credited with having greatly influenced the language. Although dialectal forms of the language are sometimes admired, the standard ideology is an essential part of the background to these histories, and much attention is usually devoted to the origin and development of the standard variety. There is a great deal of careful and important scholarly work that contributes to these histories, but, however impressive it may be, we find here also that evidence that does not relate directly to the standard is often undervalued, dismissed, or ignored. We now consider some examples, some of which are discussed in more detail in J. Milroy (2002).

H. C. Wyld (an influential historian of English) made it quite clear that Standard English was in his view the most important variety and devoted his attention to describing its history. The "dialects," he felt, were "of very little importance," and "the main objects of our solicitude" should be "the language of Literature and Received Standard Spoken English" (1914/1927: 16). It is of course true that the standard variety, being the basis of the written language, is in certain respects (most of them non-linguistic) the most important variety, but it is not true that the dialects are of very little importance. By ignoring them we produce an incomplete history of English. The history that scholars, such as Wyld and his successors, actually did give to the language was mainly a history of one variety – a relatively well-defined variety – the standard. Conventional histories of this kind contribute to what may be called the process of "legitimization" of the language (as represented by the standard variety).

The extent to which traditional scholars were prepared to argue away evidence that did not fit in with their conceptualization of the standard is actually quite remarkable. Some decades ago, I noticed that initial <h> spellings were very variable in many Middle English (ME) texts: <h> was often omitted where it was historically expected (as in *om* for 'home') or added where it was not expected (as in *halle* for 'all'). This strongly suggests that in some dialects initial [h] before vowels was omitted in speech. Wyld (1920/1936: 294–96) cites many examples of this spelling phenomenon, but considers Middle English evidence unreliable because of Norman scribes, and concludes that "the present day vulgarism" could not have been widespread before the late eighteenth century. The rejection of evidence because of the alleged activities of Anglo-Norman scribes is in fact very widespread in textual editing, dialectology, and onomastics, and it seems to originate in a paper by W. W. Skeat (1897) in which a number of early ME spelling characteristics, including variation in <h> use, are overtly ascribed to the inability of Norman scribes to pronounce English correctly; as late as the early fourteenth century, about two and a half centuries after the Conquest. Cecily Clark (1992) has referred to this as "the myth of the Anglo-Norman scribe," and I have discussed it in several places (Milroy 1983, 1992b). If we take the sociolinguistic view that a language is variable at all times, it is clearly quite acceptable to suggest that initial [h] loss could have happened early in some varieties, but not others, and remained variable in English thereafter. Furthermore there is no need to assume that it was always a 'vulgarism' – as traditional scholars probably believed. Similar arguments about variability also apply to [w] for [hw], as in *what, when*. Although Roger Lass (1999: 123–24) claims that the first good evidence for this is from 1701, there is one ME text (*The Bestiary* c. 1300) in which there are no <wh> spellings at all, but many <w> spellings, in over 800 lines, and there are many other texts in which <w> spellings are common. Recently, Donka Minkova (2004) has shown, from alliterative evidence in Old English (OE) poetry, that a variant in [w] was probably already present in OE.

Erasure, however, can be practiced without the help of Anglo-Norman scribes. E.J. Dobson's account of early Modern English (EModE) pronunciation explicitly sets out to describe a variety he calls Early Modern Standard English. This variety appears to be characterized in prestige terms, that is, it is seen as the dialect of the higher social classes. Amongst other things, Dobson notices a number of spellings in which <a> and <e> appear to be confused, and this might suggest that in some words they sounded the same in, say, 1550–1600. He is anxious not to accept this possibility: "Undoubted instances are few," he comments, "when they occur they must depend on the *dialectal and vulgar* developments described in Note 2 above" (1957/1968, II, 552: my emphasis). In other remarks, Dobson makes it clear that the possible instances of raising of [a] to [e] or lowering of [e] to [a] must be characterized as 'vulgar' and rejected (1957/1968, II: 551), because the writer concerned was 'Cockney.' But the "most important objection" to the possible merger or overlap of [a] and [e], "and it alone is a decisive one," he claims:

> [M]ust be that no Englishman could conceivably use *e* as a means of representing [æ]
> [...] No English-speaking child learning to spell [...] would write *ket* for [kæt]; the

distinction between [æ] and [e] is an absolute one for him (since otherwise he could not distinguish [...] *man* from *men*.

(Dobson 1957/1968, II: 549)

This is very odd, as Dobson is referring to occasional spellings by native English-speaking persons who actually *did* write <a> for <e> or <e> for <a>, and he gives no evidence for his negative claim. The sociolinguistic solution to this problem is, of course, to recognize EModE /a/ as a variable, with the possibility of merger with /e/ in some varieties or in certain lexical sets (see Milroy 1992a: 145–56).

It is sad that by using these rather desperate arguments to reject inconvenient evidence, Dobson is in fact rejecting ('erasing') information that can greatly enrich our knowledge of the phonemic and allophonic structure of Early Modern English. One of the effects of this kind of scholarship is to project the structure of present-day standard English on to past states of language, suggesting that these past states were largely invariant in structure, the researcher being free to use any argument that occurs to him/her to reject any evidence that does not fit in. The social bias also is extremely clear in the explicit rejection of 'vulgar' and dialectal evidence. Dobson's careful and valuable academic work is dominated by the standard ideology.

The erasure of non-standard variants and varieties by this means had subtle and far-reaching effects on language historians, and many examples of its influence could be cited from the histories of English used as undergraduate textbooks in the last half-century or so. The following seemingly harmless comments are perhaps sufficient to demonstrate the point:

> Many consonants have disappeared in Modern English. Perhaps the most important change of this kind is the loss of *r* medially before consonants and finally unless the next word begins with a vowel [...] Initial *h* is generally pronounced as an aspirate in present-day English. (Brook 1958: 98, 99).

This is not actually true, as many regional varieties in England and South Wales, almost all Irish and Scottish English, and most North American varieties are 'rhotic' (they pronounce [r] medially before consonants and finally), and many regional varieties in England and Wales do not pronounce initial [h]. Brook, as a dialectologist, knew both of these facts, so how could he ignore them? It seems that the expression 'Modern English' (above) stands effectively for 'modern standard or near-standard British English.' It is assumed here without comment that a history of 'English' is effectively a history of *standard* English, and that comments of this kind, although inaccurate, will be accepted by readers as a kind of 'common sense.' In this kind of account, therefore, people who do not pronounce their [h]s do not count as speakers of English.

4. Legitimization

Once the standard language has been established and codified, it becomes important to prescribe its 'correct' forms, and members of standard language cultures develop a strong sense of what is 'right' or 'wrong' in usage. The selection of one variety as the standard variety and the diffusion of this variety through codification and prescription lead to a sense of legitimacy of this variety, and – by the same token – the relegation of other varieties to possible illegitimacy or dubious legitimacy. Manuals of usage are effectively law-codes, and using non-standard forms is analogous to disobeying the statutes enshrined in law-codes. The process involved in this can be called 'legitimization.' The standard language comes to be looked upon as identical with the language as a whole and is the legitimate form: other varieties are not at this stage seen as lawful manifestations of the language. For English, this is particularly true of urban varieties, which, according to Wyld (1914/1927: 16), are merely 'modified standards' – vulgar and ignorant attempts to speak the standard variety: in his view they do not have independent histories of their own. Thus, they are not legitimate varieties of language. Because there is a dominant lawful variety of a language, the term 'correctness,' which is often used in reference to linguistic forms, has legalistic – and sometimes moral – overtones.

Apart from the synchronic imposition of prescriptive grammars and social sanctions against those who do not conform, there is, however, another influence on legitimization (hinted at above), which has the effect of giving even greater power and status to the language, usually in its standard variety. This can be called 'historicization.' Histories of a language and language family trees become from this point of view part of the process of legitimization. If a language can be shown to possess a known history, this strengthens the sense of the lawfulness of a language (and recall that many of the world's languages do not have written histories). The language has not just appeared from nowhere: it is related to other languages and has an attested lineage. Claims about the long and continuous history of English, in particular, are common in the nineteenth century and still occur. The same is true of many other European languages. As I have pointed out elsewhere (Milroy 2005), it is also desirable that the language should be as 'pure' as possible (on purism see, further, Chapter 33 in this *Handbook*), relatively unaffected by language contact, and there are currently strong national movements dedicated to cleanse many languages of foreign borrowings – now especially borrowings from English.

5. Conclusions

In the present context, the most important insight of sociolinguistics is the principle that *language is variable at all times*. In historical description, however, there has been a strong tendency to search for an 'original' invariant form. As we have seen, historians have tended to show a preference for a unilinear or single-stranded accounts as far as possible, with efforts to argue away any evidence that might tend to complicate the picture, and they have also displayed a highly class-conscious conviction that the true history of a language consists of only high-prestige or educated language. In matters of greater detail, however, the conventional account has displayed other characteristics. First, there has been a tendency to define a sound change as something that takes place in a whole language rather than in a given variety or a 'speech community.' It has also been usual to fix a rather precise date for each change and to describe a relative chronology of changes, with fairly exact dates specified for each change.

Thus, it has been thought reasonable to ask such questions as: 'What was the pronunciation of Middle English /a/?' . . . and then to conclude, for example, that it was either definitely a back vowel or definitely a front vowel. Sociolinguistic experience, however, would suggest that ME /a/, together with many other phonemes, was variable; therefore it could have been front in some dialects and back in others; it may also have varied in tongue-height and in the degree to which it overlapped with other phonemes, and changes that had already happened in one variety could have been reversed through the influence of another variety.

Sociolinguistic insights have extremely important implications for the way in which historical language description is practiced. Using these insights, we may find that it is no longer necessary to show that a sound change in English – such as [h]-loss before vowels or before [w] – took place once and for all in the language at one particular time, and insist that it could not have happened before that time. These particular changes, it seems, have been in progress for many centuries, sometimes completed in some varieties and sometimes – possibly – reversed, and there are many other small phonetic changes that may have gone back and forward in the same way.

The true history of a language is necessarily a social history, and therefore sociolinguistic insights can contribute enormously to it. In recent years, sociolinguistic researchers (there are many examples in the present *Handbook*) have been making many extremely detailed and valuable contributions to our knowledge of what happened in the past, and, using sociolinguistic insights and methods, there is much more for us to do.

REFERENCES

Alford, H. (1864/1889) *The Queen's English* (3rd edn), George Bell, London.

Bragg, M. (2003) *The Adventure of English*, Hodder and Stoughton, London.

Brook, G.L. (1958) *History of the English Language*, André Deutsch, London.

Clark, C. (1992) The myth of the Anglo-Norman scribe. In M. Rissanen, O. Ihalainen, T. Nevalainen, and I. Taavitsainen (eds.), *History of Englishes: New Methods and Interpretations in Historical Linguistics*, Mouton de Gruyter, Berlin, pp. 117–29.

Dobson, E.J. (1957/1968) *English Pronunciation 1500–1700* (2 volumes) (2nd edn), Clarendon Press, Oxford.

Gimson, A.C. (1962/1970) *An Introduction to the Pronunciation of English* (2nd edn), Arnold, London.

Grace, G. (1990) The 'aberrant' (vs. 'exemplary') Melanesian languages. In P. Baldi (ed.), *Linguistic Change and Reconstruction Methodology*, Mouton de Gruyter, Berlin, pp. 155–73.

Grace, G. (1991) How do languages change? (More on 'aberrant languages'). Paper presented at the Sixth International Conference on Austronesian Linguistics, Honolulu.

Heryanto, A. (1990) The making of language: developmentalism in Indonesia. *Prism* 50: 40–53.

Irvine, J. and Gal, S. (2000) Language ideology and linguistic differentiation. In P.V. Kroskrity (ed.), *Regimes of Language*, School of American Research Press, Santa Fe, NM, pp. 35–84.

Jespersen, O. (1938) *Growth and Structure of the English Language*, Teubner Verlag, Stuttgart.

Joseph, J.E. and Taylor, T. (eds.) (1990) *Ideologies of Language*, Routledge, London.

Labov, W. (1980) The social origins of sound change. In W. Labov (ed.), *Locating Language in Time and Space*, Academic Press, New York, pp. 251–65.

Labov, W. (1990) The intersection of sex and social class in the course of linguistic change. *Language Variation and Change* 2: 205–51.

Labov, W. (1994) *Principles of Linguistic Change. Vol.1: Internal Factors*, Blackwell, Oxford.

Lass, R. (1997) *Historical Linguistics and Language Change*, Cambridge University Press, Cambridge.

Lass, R. (1999) Phonology and morphology. In R. Lass (ed.), *The Cambridge History of the English Language, Volume III, 1476–1776*, Cambridge University Press, Cambridge, pp. 56–186.

Milroy, J. (1983) On the sociolinguistic history of /h/ dropping in English. In M. Davenport, E. Hansen, and H.F. Nielsen (eds.), *Current Topics in English Historical Linguistics*, University of Odense Press, Odense, pp. 37–53.

Milroy, J. (1992a) *Linguistic Variation and Change: On the Historical Sociolinguistics of English*, Blackwell, Oxford.

Milroy, J. (1992b) Middle English dialectology. In N. Blake (ed.), *The Cambridge History of the English Language, Volume II, 1066–1476*, Cambridge University Press, Cambridge, pp. 156–206.

Milroy, J. (2001) Language ideologies and the consequences of standardization. *Journal of Sociolinguistics* 5 (4): 530–55.

Milroy, J. (2002) The legitimate language: giving a history to English. In R. Watts and P. Trudgill (eds.), *Alternative Histories of English*, Routledge, London, pp. 7–25.

Milroy, J. (2005) Some effects of purist ideologies on historical descriptions of English. In N. Langer and W.V. Davies (eds.), *Linguistic Purism in the Germanic Languages*, Walter de Gruyter, Berlin, pp. 324–42.

Milroy, J. and Milroy, L. (1985) Linguistic change, social network and speaker innovation. *Journal of Linguistics* 21: 339–84.

Milroy, J. and Milroy, L. (1985/1999) *Authority in Language: Investigating Standard English* (3rd edn), Routledge, London.

Minkova, D. (2004) Philology, linguistics and the history of [hw]~[w]. In A. Curzan and K. Emmons (eds.), *Studies in the History of the English Language II*, Mouton de Gruyter, Berlin, pp. 7–46.

Mufwene, S. (2001) *The Ecology of Language Evolution*, Cambridge University Press, Cambridge.

Mühlhäusler, P. (1996) *Linguistic Ecology*, Blackwell, Oxford.

Potter, S. (1950) *Our Language*, Penguin, Harmondsworth.

Saussure, F. de (1916/1983) *A Course in General Linguistics* (trans. R. Harris), Duckworth, London.

Schieffelin, B.B., Woolard, K.A., and Kroskrity, P.V. (1998) *Language Ideologies: Practice and Theory*, Oxford University Press, Oxford.

Skeat, W.W. (1897) The proverbs of Alfred. *Transactions of the Philological Society*, 399–418.

Strang, B. (1970) *A History of English*, Methuen, London.

Sturtevant, E.H. (1917) *Linguistic Change*, University of Chicago Press, Chicago.

Thomason, S.G. and Kaufman, T. (1988) *Language Contact, Creolization and Genetic Linguistics*, University of California Press, Berkeley CA.

Weinreich, U. (1953) *Languages in Contact. Findings and Problems*, Mouton, The Hague.

Wyld, H.C. (1914/1927) *A Short History of English* (3rd edn), John Murray, London.

Wyld, H.C. (1920/1936) *A History of Modern Colloquial English* (3rd edn), Blackwell, Oxford.

32 Language Myths

RICHARD J. WATTS

1. Introduction: The 'Tunnel/Funnel View of the History of English'

In the introduction to Watts and Trudgill (2002a), we argued that the major reason for editing a collection of alternative histories of English was our concern that 'the' history of English, as it is presented in almost every introductory book on the subject, automatically leads novices in the field to the belief that a history of English is equivalent to a history of the standard language. We called this approach the 'tunnel view' of the history of English, a metaphor which projects from a source domain of the restriction, unidirectionality, and perhaps even darkness of passage through a tunnel onto the target domain of the abstract concept of language history. The 'traveler's' view is focused on the return of light at the end of the tunnel and the only possible enlightened goal of a language history is, according to this view, the standard language. In addition, the darkness of the tunnel can be interpreted as the lack of awareness of a world beyond the walls of the tunnel and a predefined narrow focus on emerging from the tunnel into the light. There is an implied teleology here that standard languages are the only valid objects of study for a language history, and that teleology depends on an ideological discourse driven by language myths.

But there is another way of conceptualizing the history of a language, viz. as a funnel rather than a tunnel. In the 'funnel view,' the wide top of the funnel represents a period in the past in which there was no standard and in which we can find a number of linguistic varieties that seem to be related enough to be grouped together as 'a language.' A funnel is used to direct liquid or a granular substance

The Handbook of Historical Sociolinguistics, First Edition. Edited by Juan Manuel Hernández-Campoy and Juan Camilo Conde-Silvestre.
© 2014 John Wiley & Sons, Ltd. Published 2014 by John Wiley & Sons, Ltd.

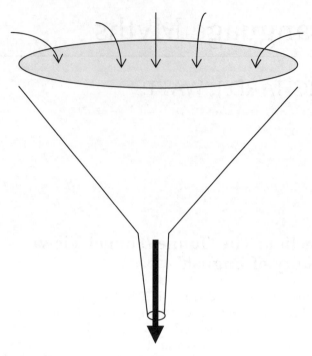

Figure 32.1.   The funnel view of the history of a language

into a single container, for example, for our purposes, a bottle. So, as we move through time, the wide top of the funnel narrows to a neck through which language varieties must pass. The bottle would then be the container for the standard, again giving a narrow focus and implying a predestined teleology. This view of language history also implies that the product collected in the bottle is composed of all the ingredients that were poured in at the top of the funnel and that tracing out the history of those ingredients is less important than the final product (see Figure 32.1):

In reality, however, the wide top of the funnel is riddled with holes through which other, non-standard varieties of the language drip out, although that, of course, is not part of the conceptualization of the history of the language.

Both metaphorical conceptualizations of language history exist, but they are presented as objective 'reality' rather than as metaphors. In the tunnel view, other varieties of the language are simply ignored, whereas in the funnel view, there is, at least, the recognition of a multidialectal input. The problem with the funnel view is that it displays a disregard for the historical trajectories of these varieties when a certain period of time is reached (in other words, when the narrow neck of the funnel is reached), and it is only marginally more realistic in terms of the discursive construction of the history of English than the tunnel view. Both views rely on a false teleology, that the goal of a history of English is to account for the emergence of the standard language. For this reason, throughout the remainder of this chapter, I refer to this conceptualization of the history of English as the 'tunnel/funnel view.' The tunnel/funnel view of the history of English goes back to the latter half of the nineteenth century and is determined by an ideological hegemonic discourse based on sets of myths about the nature of language, and it is those myths which lie at the heart of my argument (see also Chapter 31 in this *Handbook*).

2. The Discursive Construction of 'Knowledge'

The theoretical position I adopt is that every text, whether written, oral, or in some other semiotic medium, is an instantiation of a discourse, and through discourse sets of beliefs about various natural or social phenomena are constructed. Following Foucault (1969/1972), a discourse is

> . . . a body of statements (i.e. a subset of statements) belonging to a single system in the overall formation of statements, i.e. . . . it is a system of statements that is markedly distinct from other systems of statements. For Foucault statements are taken to be historically situated *events*. No human interaction can take place outside discursive formations, such that the individual comes to accept the statements, the events, as representing a 'true' state of affairs, 'true' not in the sense of logically true, i.e. true in a coherent logical system, but rather in the sense of a system of 'beliefs' shared (or believed to be shared) by others. (Watts 2011: 17)

A discourse always instantiates an ideology (a system of shared beliefs), perhaps a number of ideologies, and, again following Foucault (1969/1972), it is 'discontinuous,' that is, groups of statements might occur in any order, with any function, and they may be correlated in any way with other groups of statements. When a hegemonic discourse generates 'true' statements which constitute what Foucault calls "the law of what can be said, the system that governs the appearance of statements as unique events" (1969/1972: 129), it can be called a 'discourse archive.'

On the one hand, going against that law and challenging the archive is a risky business. On the other hand, if there are alternative beliefs that can be entertained to account for the phenomenon/phenomena concerned, the ideological beliefs constituting the discourse archive need to be unearthed (to use a similar metaphor to Foucault's notion of the 'archaeology of knowledge'). Beliefs about a phenomenon or a set of phenomena do not come from nowhere; they are socially constructed as frames, scripts, and schemata of knowledge in every individual's cognition through the discursive repetition of those beliefs in institutionalized settings of social interaction (or social practice) such as the family, the school, the media, friendship networks, the work-group, and other communities of practice (Wenger 1998; Eckert 2000; Eckert and McConnell-Ginet 2003). The basis of the constructions that we use to make sense of our worlds lies in narrative, in communal stories representing an accepted "'true' state of affairs," that is, in what I wish to call 'myths.' Since we are dealing, in the tunnel/funnel view of the history of English, with what can be considered to be a discourse archive – 'the law of what can be said' about the history of English – it becomes imperative to discover the language myths that drive the archive. It is also important to discover where the myths come from in the first place. My hypothesis is that the stories (the myths) are constructed from 'true' statements deriving from conceptual metaphors that we learn through socio-communicative verbal interaction in order to conceptualize, understand, and account for abstract notions such as LIFE, TIME, LOVE, ANGER, DEMOCRACY, and HONESTY. Unearthing the conceptual metaphors and the 'true' propositions derived from these metaphors, and understanding how the metaphors are used to construct the myths that drive the discourse, is essential to deconstructing the discourse archive. If the metaphors can be shown to offer insufficiently grounded projections from basic areas of human experience, the myths, the discourse, and the archives derived from them can be challenged.

A brief concrete example from the area of the Earth sciences might help the reader to conceptualize more easily what I mean. The canonical way of visualizing the Earth up to Wegener's work on continental drift (1912, 1915/1968), which sparked off the idea of tectonic plates, was based on the conceptual metaphor THE EARTH IS A SOLID BODY. It was possible to account for mountain ranges by accepting the theory of vertical crustal movement through a slight adjustment of the metaphor to THE EARTH'S CRUST IS A SOLID BODY, and volcanic activity appeared to support this theory. But the striking similarities between the outlines of different continents, which indicated that those continents must have been joined at some stage in the distant past, led to the notion of continental drift, which could only be explained by modifying the second metaphor. However, until Earth scientists knew a great deal more about the physical mechanisms governing the relationship between the liquid basalt magmas at the Earth's centre and what was still assumed to be the solid body of the Earth's crust, continental drift could not be explained. In 1956 the metaphor and the stories (myths) developed from it, which governed the dominant geological discourse of the time, were challenged by challenging the metaphor itself, and, on the basis of a large amount of solidly reliable data, the following new metaphor was constructed: THE EARTH'S CRUST IS A SET OF MOVABLE PLATES. The theory of tectonic plates, however, seemed so far from the original conceptualization of how the Earth was structured that the theory itself was treated like a myth. As we now know, that myth was closer to reality than the former myth, and it has driven the dominant geological discourse ever since.

In section 3 I define how I understand the term 'myth,' present a set of myths that occur in a Latin chronicle of the fourteenth century, all of which are still valid today, and hypothesize that there is an underlying 'master myth' driving beliefs about and attitudes towards language which I call the *myth of linguistic homogeneity*.[1] Section 4 shows how a selection of these myths became a discourse on language at the end of the sixteenth century immediately prior to the focus on the history of the standard language. The shift from a discourse to a dominant language ideology of the standard language and the creation of new myths from older ones is briefly presented in section 5, where I argue that the narrow end of the funnel or the tunnel was reached in the eighteenth century. Section 6 reviews the process from conceptual metaphor to discourse archive arguing that the tunnel/funnel view has become a discourse archive of the history of English. Finally, in section 7 I give concrete examples of some of the myths in the twentieth century and suggest ways in which alternative discourses may be set up to challenge the tunnel/funnel view.

3. Myths and Metaphors

The etymological origin of the term 'myth' lies in the Greek word μύθος ('story'), and the narrative aspect of the term has remained at the core of the nexus of meanings prompted by the lexeme ever since. In the modern world, however, to accuse someone of having articulated a myth can be interpreted as accusing her/ him of giving a false or untrue account, and 'myth' is often used as a term of abuse to discredit a statement or set of statements made by an interlocutor. But the nexus of meanings prompted by the lexeme 'myth' indicates that it is not by any means a personal story or an individual act of narration. Myths are not only transferred to individuals socially; they are also culturally constructed through a history of transference that has made them the 'cultural property' of a group. As we have seen, a myth provides a narrative cognitive embedding of a belief, or set of beliefs, about some aspect of a socio-cultural group and helps to set up a foundation for performing acts of identity in emergent social practice. Myths are not lies; they are not told to deceive us. On the contrary, they "fulfil a vital function in explaining, justifying and ratifying present behaviour by the narrated events of the past" (Watts 2000: 33).

Language myths are also communally shared stories, which, regardless of their factual status, are believed and propagated as the cultural property of a group. They form the basis of discursive ideologies, they are always present, and no amount of persuasion to the contrary will convince people to relinquish them. Examining language myths is unlikely to have much effect on how people, on an everyday basis, view language, but it is still important to locate and deconstruct instances in which myth has replaced historical fact in the presentation of the 'official' histories of a language. That is my purpose in this chapter.

A close look at statements that cluster together to form myths reveals that they are based on a restricted set of conceptual metaphors generating 'true' statements which form the narrative structure of the myths themselves. A conceptual metaphor should not be understood as an utterance, but as a cognitively stored projection from image schemata, stored frames of experience, or scripts of events onto mental spaces linked to abstract lexemes (for a more detailed explanation, see Watts 2011: Chapter 1).

3.1   Myths in the Polychronicon

The earliest text in which we find a concentration of statements specifically on language is Ranulph Higden's Latin chronicle the *Polychronicon*. The length of the extract is not much more than one page in length, but it is rich in its implications.

The *Polychronicon* was one of the last in a long line of Latin chronicles based on a plan taken from Scripture written before the age of printing, compiled by a Benedictine monk at the monastery of St. Werburg in Chester by the name of Ranulph Higden. Its full title is *Ranulphi Castrensis, cognomine Higdon, Polychronicon (sive Historia Polycratica) ab initio mundi usque ad mortem Edwardi III. in septem libros dispositum*, and it consists of seven books, the first presenting a geography of the known world, Books 2 to 4 a history of the world from the Creation to the time of the arrival of the Saxons in England, the fifth dealing with the invasion of the Danes, the sixth with the history of England until the time of the Norman Conquest and the final book completes the history as far as the time of Edward III, Higden's own time. There were at least three known translations of the work into English, the most famous of these being John de Trevisa's version, completed in 1387. The second was an anonymous translation copied out some time between 1432 and 1482, the year in which Caxton printed a reworking of Trevisa's translation. The fact that over 100 copies of the manuscript were made from the original attest to the enormous popularity of the *Polychronicon* in the fourteenth and fifteenth centuries, just before the advent of printing.

In Chapter LIX of Book 2, entitled "De incolarum linguis" ('Of the languages of the inhabitants'), Higden deals with the languages of Britain, and it is here that we find evidence of a complex of myths. I quote the passage in Latin with my own (somewhat free) translation into English:

Ranulphus. Ut patet ad sensum, quot in hac insula sunt gentes, tot gentium sunt linguæ; Scoti tamen et Wallani, uptote cum aliis nationibus impermixti, ad purum pæne pritinum retinent idioma: nisi forsan Scoti ex convictu Pictorum, cum quibus olim confœderati cohabitant, quippiam contraxerint in sermone.

Ranulphus. ① As is obvious to the understanding, there are as many races in this island as there are languages of the races. ② The Scots as well as the Welsh, even though they are intermixed with other nations, retain their languages almost in their former purity. ③ It might be the case that the Scots have taken on something in conversation from their intercourse with the Picts, with whom they lived together for some time.

Flandrenses vero, qui occidua
Walliæ incolunt, dimissa jam
barbariæ, Saxonice satis
proloquuntur. Angli quoque,
quamquam ab initio tripartitam
sortirentur linguam, austrinam
scilicet, mediterraneam, et
borealam, veluti ex tribus
Germaniæ populis procedentes,
ex commixtione tamen primo cum
Danis, deinde Normannis,
corrupta in multis patria lingua
peregrinos jam captant boatus et
garritus

Hæc quidem nativæ linguæ
corruptio provenit hodie multum
ex duobus; quod videlicet pueri
in scholis contra morem cæterum
nationum a primo Normannorum
adventu, derelicto proprio
vulgari, cosntruere Gallice
compelluntur; item quod filii
nobilium ab ipsis cunabulorum
crepundiis ad Gallicum idioma
informantur

Quibus profecto rurales homines
assimilari volentes, ut per hoc
spectabiliores videantur,
francigenare satagunt omni nisu.

Ubi nempe mirandum videtur,
quomodo nativa et propria
Anglorum lingua, in unica insula
coartata, pronunciatione ipsa sit
tam diversa; cum tamen
Normannica lingua, quæ
adventitia est, univocal maneat
penes cunctos.

De prædicta quoque lingua
Saxonica tripartita, quæ in paucis
adhuc agrestibus vix remansit,
orientales cum occiduis tanquam
sub eodem cœli climate lineati
plus consonant in sermone quam
boreales cum austrinis.

④ Indeed the Flemings who live in the
west of Wales, who set aside
barbarism long ago, speak Saxon well
enough. ⑤ The English, too, were
given three types of speech from the
beginning, i.e. southern, midland and
northern, as proceeding from three
peoples of Germany, but mainly from
a mixture with the Danes, and then
with the Normans, but their native
language has been corrupted in so
many ways that they now produce
foreign-sounding chattering and
bellowing. ⑥ Indeed this corruption of the native
tongue today is largely the result of
two factors; viz. contrary to the custom
of other nations, boys in schools, from
the first arrival of the Normans, leave
their own common tongue to one side
and are compelled to construe their
lessons in French. ⑦ On the other
hand, the sons of the nobles are taught
the language of the French from the
very rocking of their cradles.
⑧ Certainly, rural men who desire to
assimilate with these nobles and to be
seen as remarkable, labour with every
effort to speak French. ⑨ Of course, where something is seen as
being admirable, like the real native
language of the English enclosed
within one island, it is as diverse in its
pronunciation as the Norman
language – a language that is foreign
– remains "univocal" in the possession
of everyone. ⑩ In addition, with respect to the aforesaid
tripartite Saxon language, which still
lingers on with difficulty in a few wild
rustics, the speech of those in the east
sounds more like that of the men of the
west who live under the same climate
of the heavens than the men of the
north with those of the south.

Inde est quod Mercii sive
  Mediterranei Angli, tanquam
  participantes naturam
  extremorum, collaterales linguas
  arcticam melius intelligant quam
  adinvicem se intelligunt jam
  extremi.
Willelmus de Pontificibus, libro tertio.
  Tota lingua Northimbrorum,
  maxime inEboraco, ita stridet
  incondite, quod nos australes eam
  vix intelligere possumus; quod
  puto propter viciniam barbarorum
  contigisse, et etiam proper jugem
  remotionem regum Anglorum ab
  illis partibus, qui magis ad
  austrum diversati, si quando
  boreales partes adeunt, non nisi
  magno auxiliatorum manu
  pergunt.

⑪ The reason for this is that the
  Mercians or the Southern English,
  although they share nature at the
  extremities, understand languages
  close to them, northern and southern,
  better than those at the extremities
  understand one another.
Willelmus de Pontificibus, libro tertio.
  ⑫ The whole language of the
  Northumbrians, especially in York,
  hisses so confusedly that we of the
  south can scarcely understand it, so
  that I suppose it to have bordered on
  the vicinity of the barbarians, and
  even the perpetual removal of the
  kings of England from those parts,
  who have turned to the south,
  whenever they return to the northern
  parts they do not go there without a
  large group of auxiliary troops.

In sentence 1 Higden states that there are as many languages in Britain as there are 'peoples'/'races' (*gentes*), and he presents this as an indisputable fact (*ut patet ad sensum* 'as is clear to the understanding') rather than simply a belief. Every ethnic group is characterized by the fact that it possesses one distinct language, so that difference in language is a means of identifying one group from another. There is an underlying cognitive conceptualization from which this statement is drawn, but it is more in the nature of a metonymy than a metaphor:

- AN ETHNIC GROUP HAS A LANGUAGE

Sentences 2 and 3: Higden follows up on this 'fact' by strongly implying that the language of an ethnic group should be 'pure.' The ideal of 'purity' is almost reached in the Welsh and Scots, but possibly less so in the case of the Scots on account of language contact with the Picts. Statements such as these reveal a belief in the purity of language deriving from an underlying conceptual metaphor:

- A LANGUAGE IS A HUMAN BEING

It is not quite clear, however, whether the statement drawn from the metaphor – <a language is pure> – refers to a biological or a moral quality. At all events, Higden runs this part of the underlying metaphor to suggest that a language contact situation detracts from the ideal of purity. There is evidence here to suggest the existence of a *myth of language purity*, in which purity is compromised by language contact.

In sentence 4 Higden refers to a group of Flemings in West Wales (presumably Pembrokeshire) who speak Saxon "well enough," as they gave up barbarism long ago. The sentence displays a high degree of conceptual complexity. According to the conceptual metonymy AN ETHNIC GROUP HAS A LANGUAGE, they should speak Flemish. Instead they are said to speak Saxon (English, Anglo-Saxon?) "well enough," indicating that they do not speak "pure Saxon." On the other hand, the reason for them speaking Saxon at all is in some way connected to the fact that they gave up barbarism long ago. From this we can deduce the following:

> Although every ethnic group is characterized by its own language and although that language should be 'pure,' some ethnic groups are in a state of barbarism (presumably, they are heathens).

Hence, in Higden's own socio-cultural view of the world, there appears to be a hierarchy of ethnic groups: civilized groups at the top end and barbarous groups at the bottom. By the same token, the languages that they speak, whether or not they are pure, are ranged in the same positions on the hierarchy. Some languages are judged to be better than others by virtue of the fact that they are not barbarous. Saxon, in this case, is not barbarous. We have evidence here to support a further myth, the *myth of barbarians not speaking a proper language*. We have also drawn the inference from Higden's text that language contact leads to a decrease in purity, so what could be more natural than to assume that the greater the contact with a barbarous language, the greater the loss of purity?

Sentence 5: Higden finally turns to consider the state of English at the time of writing, in the middle of the fourteenth century. He uses Bede's description of the three ethnic groups who came to England in the fifth century, the Saxons, the Angles, and the Jutes, concluding that English is fragmented into three different dialect areas, and that it has become "corrupted" by contact with the Danes and the Normans. English is thus so very far from "purity" that its speakers produce "foreign-sounding chattering and bellowing," which comes close to denying the English and their language the status of being human. At this point, we need to ask what the difference is between Saxon and English for Higden. If Saxon is not barbarous, it must be Christian, and what Higden seems to refer to is an earlier, assumed state of purity in Anglo-Saxon, a purity which has been compromised through language contact, producing the hybrid, corrupt language, English. Up to this point in the text, I suggest that we have evidence of a complex of interwoven, closely related language myths: the *myth of the pure language*; the *myth of barbarians not speaking a proper language*; the *myth of language contact leading to corruption*.

Sentences 6, 7 and 8: Higden then turns his attention to two reasons for the current "corrupted" state of English. On the one hand, children can only be schooled in Anglo-Norman French, which automatically puts them at a disadvantage, and on the other, too many speakers of English, particularly in rural areas, are trying to learn French in order to assimilate to Anglo-Norman ways of life.

The assumption in this second suggestion is that the English are betraying their own language, since contact with Anglo-Norman French, in accordance with the **myth of language contact leading to corruption**, can only lead to the corruption and not to the purity of English.

Sentence 9: An interesting distinction is made here between English and Anglo-Norman French. English is said to be native to England and Anglo-Norman French to be foreign, even though it had been in use in England for almost 300 years at the time of writing. But whereas Anglo-Norman French is said not to vary in its phonology, English is "diverse in its very pronunciation."

Sentences 10 and 11: Higden's argumentation in these two sentences becomes somewhat unclear. In sentence 10, Saxon is said to linger on in the speech of "a few wild rustics" (*in paucis . . . agrestibus*). I need to digress just a little here. My translation is admittedly somewhat free, but the introduction of the adjective *wild* into the noun phrase indicates that the Latin *agrestis* ('a/the rustic') has a number of negative connotations in Latin, such as 'wild,' 'unmannered,' 'boorish,' 'untamed,' 'pertaining to the fields.' Higden may wish to imply at this point that Anglo-Saxon has been preserved not by those who cultivate the fields – by agriculturalists – but by those who drive sheep and/or cattle out into the fields – by pastoralists. Confirmation of this interpretation is given by Trevisa (in Babington 1865/1964: 126–28), who translates *in paucis . . . agrestibus* as "wiþ fewe vplondisshe men," in other words, men who live in the hills. But how are we to interpret this? Is the "pure" Saxon now only used by a few wild pastoralists while the hybrid English is used by agriculturalists? This would seem to contradict his statements about the group of Flemings in West Wales. I can only suggest that Higden is explicitly making a linguistic contrast between pastoralists and agriculturalists. However, he suggests later in the sentence that those in the South, West, and East live "under the same climate of the heavens," which implies that those living up in the hills, in the North, do not share the same climate. There is, in other words, slender – but only very slender – evidence to suggest another myth which does reappear, although not often, across the centuries: the **myth of a good climate providing fertile soil for a 'pure' language**. One of the conceptual metaphors for language in the nineteenth century is A LANGUAGE IS A PLANT, from which inferences similar to those made here by Higden might be drawn. If a language is a plant, it will need a good climate and fertile soil to allow it to develop.

Sentence 12 is adapted from William of Malmesbury's (c. 1095/96–c. 1143) *Gesta Pontificum Anglorum* ('Deeds of the English Bishops,' 1125/2007), and to some extent it supports my very tentative interpretation from sentence 10. William, or Higden through William, makes the comment that the language of the North "hisses so confusedly." This is a clear anthropomorphization of language, being derived from the conceptual metaphor A LANGUAGE IS A HUMAN BEING, and it is a negative evaluation of the forms of English beyond the Humber/Trent/Mersey divide. It is not made explicit whether the first person singular pronoun *I* refers to William or to Higden, but in either case the evaluator is from the South of the country. In addition, the speaker assumes that the reason for the incomprehensibility of the language of the North is that it has been in contact with a barbarous ethnic group (the Danes? the Scots?). This is the first realization in the literature of a very common and very English language myth, the *myth of the pure language of the South and the corrupted language of the North*. The myth is as alive today as it was in the time of William in the early twelfth century and it drives a language ideology whose aim is to discriminate against Northerners on the basis of their language. In addition, however, Trevisa's "vplondisshe men," Higden's *agrestes* and my "wild rustics" all tend to be situated, in the minds of Southerners, "in the North." I suggest that this is additional evidence to support the *myth of a good climate providing fertile soil for a 'pure' language*. If the wild rustics are pastoralists, their soil cannot be particularly fertile and the climate cannot encourage the growth of a 'pure' language. The additional taint from an assumed language contact with barbarians puts the seal on both myths, in particular making the *myth of the pure language of the South and the corrupted language of the North* one of the oldest and most robust myths of all.

In summary, the myths gleaned from this very brief extract from the *Polychronicon* are all interconnected, so much so that we can talk of a nexus of folk beliefs about English and other languages in the fourteenth century. Higden's general assessment of English is not particularly flattering. It is a hybrid language resulting from situations of language contact, it is structurally diverse, and it suffers from a chronic division between the North and the South. How, then, could this assessment have possibly given rise, through the myths that it generated, to the feeling that English was superior to other languages? It is clear that a bipartite division within English already exists in Higden's text (the North vs. the South), but we need to see how that split became first social, then political, and finally global.

3.2   *The underlying myth of linguistic homogeneity*

The key to this problem is to posit a basic language myth, probably one with universal validity, which channels the other myths in the direction of an ideal that can never be achieved. It rests on the assumption that a language can reach perfection and that it can be completely homogeneous. I shall call this underlying myth the *myth of linguistic homogeneity*. In Higden's text it reveals itself in the assumption that there can be such a thing as a 'pure' language. For Higden this would mean that it would have to be the language of a civilized ethnic group – in the case of Western Europe, a Christian ethnic group – rather than a barbaric ethnic group. It would have to avoid all contact with other languages, and it would have to have no dialect varieties and no variability. If such a language ever existed, it would not change from a state of perfect stasis, and each member of the ethnic group would be able to use it to the fullness of her/his ability. In addition, it would have to display total logical consistency and coherence in its constructions.

We are confronted at this point with the 'homogeneity/heterogeneity paradox.' 'A language' is not and can never be a totally homogeneous system (see Weinreich, Labov, and Herzog 1968). Those who are using it need flexibility at all times to adapt it to the purposes of ongoing social practice, and heterogeneity and variability would seem to be built into all human language. The totally homogeneous language does not and cannot ever exist, yet the *myth of linguistic homogeneity* drives dominant discourses which aim to produce it.

Many of the language myths constructed cognitively to explain, justify, and ratify the concept 'Language L' are based on notions of perfection, purity, and homogeneity. Now, it is quite obvious that in order to function as a 'ratified' member of a social group, each of us is constrained to acquire the linguistic constructions that others around us use for the simple reason that these are the only models available to us. So, in cognitive terms, it is logical that we project a metaphor in which these constructions are mapped onto a system independent of our own selves, the conceptual metaphor A LANGUAGE IS A HUMAN BEING. It is also only natural and logical that one of the 'true' statements emanating from this metaphor as well as from the conceptual metonymy AN ETHNIC GROUP HAS A LANGUAGE is <Language L is the property of group L>, as we saw in the brief interpretation of the extract from Higden's *Polychronicon*.

The construction of *a* language or *the* language is nothing more than the construction of a metaphorical blend that becomes embedded through repeated socialization in the minds of the members participating in the group's activities. It is also hardly surprising if the group or groups that perceive themselves to be using 'a language' construct communal stories (myths) to explain, justify, and ratify its existence. And again, at one and the same time, such 'myths' should have a historical underpinning and provide a means of distinguishing the group from other groups in present time. The paradox resides in the fact that the *myth of linguistic homogeneity* drives the construction of myths to achieve a goal which is not achievable. It is precisely this paradox between what the historical linguist and the sociolinguist have come to understand – that a language is a flexible, ever-changing, ever variable, heterogeneous system – and what the language community, the 'ethnic group' wishes to achieve – that 'their' language should strive to be a perfect, coherent, homogeneous system – which we need to understand when we examine the histories of English.

But how do we get to the tunnel/funnel view of the history of English from Higden? The first step is to identify other myths driven, from underneath, by the *myth of linguistic homogeneity*.

4. Puttenham, Carew, and Harrison

The *myth of the pure language* becomes properly active at the very beginning of the move towards the creation of a standard language, i.e. at the end of the sixteenth century and just before the narrow neck of the funnel is reached. At roughly the same time, two other closely related myths appear based on 'true' statements derived from the conceptual metaphor A LANGUAGE IS A HUMAN BEING:

1. <a noble language is a superior language>, <a noble language is a language with a heritage>, from which we can trace the *myth of the superiority of English*, and

2. <a morally pure language is a perfect language>, <a morally pure language has no blemish>, from which we can trace the *myth of the perfect language*.

The first explicit realization of the *myth of the pure language* is to be found in Book III, Chapter IV of George Puttenham's *The Arte of English Poesie* (1589) entitled "Of Language," although, as is usual in the late medieval and early modern periods, Puttenham might very well have taken over or 'translated' his ideas from previous texts. Puttenham describes the language to which budding poets should aspire as follows:

> . . . neither shall he follow the speech of a craftes man or carter, or other of the inferior sort, though he be inhabitant or bred in the best towne and Citie in this Realme, for such persons doe abuse good speaches by strange accents or ill shapen soundes, and false ortographie. But he shall follow generally the better brought vp sort, such as the Greeks call [*charientes*] men ciuill and graciously behauioured and bred. Our maker therfore at these dayes shall not follow *Piers Plowman* nor *Gower* nor *Lydgate* nor yet *Chaucer*, for their language is now out of vse with vs: neither shall he take the termes of Northern-men, such as they vse in dayly talke, whether they be noble men or gentlemen, or of their best clarkes all is a matter: nor in effect any speach vsed beyond the riuer of Trent, though no man can deny but that theirs is the purer English Saxon at this day, yet it is not so Courtly nor so currant as our Southerne English is, no more is the far Westerne mans speech: ye shall therfore take the vsuall speech of the Court, and that of London and the shires lying about London within lx. myles, and not much aboue. I say not this but that in euery shyre of England there be gentlemen and others that speake but specially write as good Southerne as we of Middlesex or Surrey do, but not the common people of euery shire, to whom the gentlemen, and also their learned clarkes do for the most part condescend, but herein we are already ruled by th'English Dictionaries and other bookes written by learned men, and therefore it needeth none other than direction in that behalfe. Albeit peraduenture some small admonition be not impertinent, for we finde in our English writers many wordes and speaches amendable, and ye shall see in some many inkhorne termes so ill affected brought in by men of learning as preachers and schoolemasters: and many straunge termes of other languages by Secretaries and Marchaunts and trauailors, and many dark wordes and not vsuall nor well sounding though they be dayly spoken in Court. (1589: 144–49)

When reading Puttenham's model for the language of would-be poets, one cannot help wondering whether he had read the *Polychronicon*, since most of the myths we discussed in the previous section are included here (shaded in gray). In addition, however, other criteria are listed as the best exemplars of English (shaded in black with white lettering). The pure language that Puttenham holds up as his model is socially and geographically restricted to "the vsuall speech of the Court, and that of London and the shires lying about London within lx. myles, and not much aboue." It is also the language of "men ciuill and graciously behauioured and bred." The same dichotomy that was in Higden between the North and the South is still there, but Puttenham adds a social dimension to it.

A new myth, implicit in Higden and briefly touched upon by Puttenham, is explicitly mentioned by Richard Carew in his 1586 essay "An Epistle concerning the Excellencies of the English Tongue" (in William Camden's 1605 *Remaines of a Greater Worke Concerning Britain*). We can call it the **myth of the superiority of English**, and it extols the superiority of English above all other languages. Superiority is generally located in a number of characteristics: greater beauty, greater logical powers of expression, greater nobility, greater simplicity of expression, and greater variety. One of the ways in which English is seen as being superior is precisely because of its dialectal variety, or what Carew calls "the Copiousness of English":

> Moreover the copiousness of our Language appeareth in the diversity of our Dialects, for we have Court and we have Countrey English, we have Northern and Southern English, gross and ordinary, which differ from each other, not only in the terminations, but also in many words, terms, and phrases, and express the same thing in divers sorts, yet all write English alike. (1605: ¶17)

Needless to say, Carew was copied almost verbatim in Guy Miège's *English Grammar* (1688/1969) at the end of the seventeenth century and again by Victor Peyton in his *Elements of the English Language* (1779/1971).

The **myth of the perfect language** finds its expression in William Harrison's essay "On the languages spoken in this land" in Holinshed's *Chronicles* (1577/1965):

> Afterward also, by diligent travel of Geffray Chaucer, and John Gower, in the time of Richard the second, and after then Iohn Scogan, and John Lydgate, monke of Berrie, our said toong was brought to an excellent passe, notwithstanding that it neuer came vnto perfection, vntill the time of Queen Elizabeth. (1577/1965: 25)

The narrow neck of the funnel is finally reached after 1688, when moral qualities of the underlying conceptual metaphor A LANGUAGE IS A HUMAN BEING are focused on in more detail, as we can see in the following section.

5. Entering the Tunnel or the Neck of the Funnel

The metaphorical tunnel, or, alternatively, the metaphorical neck of the funnel, in the canonical version of the history of English is reached just before the end of the seventeenth century. The unique focus on one variety, and later in the eighteenth century, one style, of English was motivated by the activation of 'true' statements generated by the positive moral qualities inherent in the conceptual metaphor A LANGUAGE IS A HUMAN BEING, above all statements like <A language is upright>, <A language is noble> and <A language is polished>. Prime movers in stressing these assumed qualities of a language were intellectual Whigs in the wake of the Glorious Revolution in 1688, such as John Locke, Daniel Defoe, William Congreve and, during the first decade of the eighteenth century, Joseph Addison, Richard Steele, and Anthony Ashley Cooper (the Third Earl of Shaftesbury), who were thoroughly dissatisfied with the intrigues of the Stuart Royal Court and sought to highlight the perceived values and lifestyles of the non-High Church country gentry as a model on which to construct a new approach towards language and society.

Just before the turn of the eighteenth century, in 1697, Defoe published his *Essay upon Projects*, and one of the projects he proposed was the establishment of a society to codify and 'police' the English language along the lines of the Académie Française in France. Members of the society should be selected from among the aristocracy and the gentry to the exclusion of scholars at the universities and members of the Royal Court, with a further set of members to be selected from among intellectuals who were not from the aristocracy or the gentry. The language that Defoe wished to promote was 'polite language,' which meant something rather different from the way we understand the term 'polite' at the beginning of the twenty-first century. For Defoe "polite language" was simply the language of the landed gentry and not of the universities or the Royal Court. It was 'polished' language, dignified language, the language of good breeding and decorum.

Defoe's ideas on 'polite language' were adopted by Anthony Ashley Cooper (Shaftesbury) and modeled into a full-scale philosophy of politeness in the first decade of the eighteenth century. They were also given expression by Joseph Addison and Richard Steele in the two periodicals *The Tatler* and *The Spectator*, in which the behavior (and of course the language) of the average gentleman was modeled on Shaftesbury's ideals. The insistence on polite English as the language appropriate to the upper echelons of British society – the gentry and the aristocracy – became the distinguishing feature of what was rapidly becoming 'Standard English.'

What had emerged in the years after 1688 was a new language myth, the ***myth of the polite language***, driven from below by the underlying ***myth of linguistic homogeneity***, and it was discursively transformed into the ideology of Standard English. The language of the polite circles of society was to provide what Shaftesbury required of polite society itself, viz. decorum and grace, beauty, symmetry, and order. The dominant discourse driven by this myth had become so influential by the middle of the eighteenth century that strenuous efforts were made to codify English through dictionaries, innumerable grammar books, pronouncing dictionaries, and books on elocution, etiquette, and 'good' style (see Fitzmaurice 1998; Watts 2003: Chapter 2; Watts 2011: Chapter 8; Tieken-Boon van Ostade 2008). The eighteenth-century emergence of the middle classes below the level of the gentry triggered a need, on their part, to acquire 'polite language' as a means of rising into the social class above them (Langford 1989). And as the social pressure on the gentry increased, so the definitions of 'polite language' became more stringent, more socially exclusive, and more dependent on the classical education received at the public and grammar schools. By the last two decades of the eighteenth century, British society had become excessively class-conscious (McIntosh 1998) and the style of English prose writing exaggeratedly 'classical.' The undeclared object of this discursive exercise, however, was to construct English as a classical language: to turn it into a 'truth' language[2] (or at the very least a *Kultursprache*),[3] and to exclude more than four fifths of the British population from participation in Standard English.

Since myths provide a narrative cognitive embedding of a belief, or set of beliefs, about some aspect of a socio-cultural group (Section 3), the slightest change in those beliefs may lead to an adaptation of the narrative cognitive embedding to account for that change and, as a consequence, the myth is subtly transformed. In the last two decades of the eighteenth century, the British political establishment was still recovering from the loss of the American colonies and struggling to keep ahead of the first stage of the Industrial Revolution, which it had set in motion by its own commercial activities. It was faced with the turmoil of the French Revolution and the fear of invasion during the first stages of the Napoleonic Wars. It was struggling to repress the upsurge of political Radicalism and a strong demand for human rights such as adequate wages and better working conditions, equality before the law, universal suffrage, and democratic participation in running the affairs of the country. The dominant language discourse became heavily politicized. Standard English was stylized into the 'refined' language, which was deliberately placed into opposition to the 'vulgar' language of the middle and lower classes of the population. Standard English, in its classical form, was considered to be the only form of language in which abstract notions such as 'government,' 'democracy,' and 'freedom' could possibly be expressed and was consciously used to exclude the middle and working classes from participation in education and the affairs of the state (see Smith 1984). The *myth of the polite language* had been subtly transformed into the *myth of the legitimate language*.

6. From Myths to Discourses and the Ideologies they Instantiate

Myths as communally shared stories have already begun to exert their influence on the structuring of a discourse as soon as they start circulating through a community. Once the statements come to be accepted as 'true' states of affairs within the discursive formation of a language, they need to be invested with an aura of authority, such as that which the dominant discourse of Standard English as the only 'legitimate' form of English in the nation-state began to acquire in the early eighteenth century and finally achieved in the middle of the nineteenth.[4]

But how does a language ideology that claims to constitute the 'only' legitimate way in which the history of English can be narrated arise? Put differently, how has it come to take on the status of a discourse archive, constituting what Foucault calls "the law of what can be said, the system that governs the appearance of statements as unique events" (1969/1972: 129)? Once the fictional aspect of the underlying myths has been obscured by their incorporation into a discourse that is increasingly accepted by members of the higher, more influential levels of social structure, the language ideology becomes factualized such that any alternative account is submitted to trivialization by the proponents of the 'official' account.

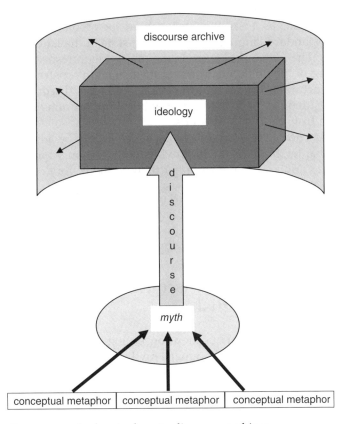

Figure 32.2. From conceptual metaphors to discourse archives

We can picture the process from myth to discourse archive in the above diagram (Figure 32.2):

In the first stage of the process, myths evolve out of the 'true' statements derived from the conceptual metaphors. We saw an example of this stage in the process in section 3. The frequent dissemination and circulation of myths through space and time allows them to be integrated into a discourse on language. The late sixteenth century provides examples of this in the work of Puttenham, Carew, and Harrison (section 4). The discourse becomes a dominant discourse and begins to instantiate an ideology, at which point the original myth fades from consciousness. The ideology of politeness, which drove the insistence on a 'polite' standard language and led to strenuous efforts at codification in the eighteenth century is an example of this stage in the process (see section 5). The more acceptable the ideology becomes, the more open it will be to developing into 'the law of what can be said' about language, thus to be transformed into a discourse archive. I have argued that is exactly what happened in the construction of the tunnel/funnel view of the history of English. The major thrust in this direction was the transformation of the *myth of the polite language* into the *myth of the legitimate language* and its use as a driving force behind the ideology of the 'legitimate,' homogeneous standard language of the nation-state in the latter half of the nineteenth century. The ideological stage in the process with respect to the history of English (the age of 'polite' English) was instrumental in constructing the dichotomous class structure in Britain, but the stage in which a discourse archive developed from the ideology had direct socio-political implications which only began to break down from the 1960s onwards.

In the final section I raise two questions which cannot be answered within the space of this chapter, but which will provide food for thought in later research on the histories of varieties of English rather than on the history of English:

1. Do we still find traces of the myths in contemporary instantiations of discourse, and if so, what do they tell us about lay conceptualizations of language?
2. Are there signs of a breakdown in the discourse archive of the tunnel/funnel view of the history of English, and why may this breakdown be taking place?

7. The Breakdown of a Discourse Archive on the History of English?

Let's begin by tackling the first question concerning traces of myths in contemporary instantiations of discourse. Language myths are not always easy to locate as concrete instantiations of social practice. But before we *can* locate them, we first need to be able to identify them historically and to trace their progress through time. Many of the myths that can be teased out of texts like Higden's *Polychronicon*, sometimes with the help of textual interpretation, have stood the test of time remarkably well, so much so that we would be foolish to assume that they were 'invented' by Higden himself. We know that versions of the language myths are likely to be verbalized in a variety of oral and written forms of socio-communicative interaction that takes place in a whole range of communities of practice in which we are ratified members. All we have to do is to go out, do empirical research, and find them.

An example from 1925 is given by James Milroy (2007: 137) in a school inspector's report:

> Come into a London elementary school and [...] [y]ou will notice that the boys and girls are almost inarticulate. They can make noises, but they cannot speak [...] listen to them as they 'play at schools'; you can barely recognise your native language.

The addressee of the school inspector's text is assumed to have a native language that is unrecognizable in the language produced by children at play in a London elementary school. There is very little difference between this school inspector's reaction and William of Malmesbury's reaction to the language of the inhabitants of York in the early twelfth century. William put it down to the influence of barbarians on the natives of York, directly verbalizing the *myth of barbarians not speaking a proper language*. The children observed by the school inspector, then, have been influenced by barbarians. Who are those barbarians? The only possible answer is their immediate family and friends. In this sense, both William of Malmesbury and the school inspector evoke the ***myth of language purity***, in that the addressee and the school inspector, but not the children, are assumed to speak a 'pure' English. There are also distinct shades in the quotation given above of the ***myth of language contact leading to corruption***, implying that the children have been corrupted through their social background and need to acquire Standard English at school in order to be 'saved,' or rather properly 'educated.' It was precisely the ideology that developed out of this complex of myths which led the Conservative Thatcher government in 1988 to attempt to return to the rote teaching of grammar in the National Curriculum for the teaching of English in schools (Cox 1991) in what I have called elsewhere the National Curriculum wars (Watts 2011: Chapter 10).

Lesley Milroy (1999: 176–77) gives an example from the British magazine *Bella*. An article entitled "Can your accent blight your life?" describes the experiences of Helen,

> a Manchester woman who moved to London in search of employment: ". . . in the arts where no-one has a regional accent . . . my CV was good enough to get me interviews, but . . . as soon as they heard me speak . . . I wasn't taken seriously". . . . and when Helen finally landed a job with a community theatre project in Islington, North London, she was told she'd only been selected because the area would benefit from a common touch. Helen encountered similar reactions in casual interpersonal encounters: "'People can't see further than my voice and assume I'm aggressive and common." (*Bella*, 24 January 1996).

This is an excellent example of the age-old ***myth of the pure language of the South and the corrupted language of the North***. It also has overtones of the ***myth of the legitimate language***, since we would expect Helen to encounter similar prejudices if she had had an East End of London pronunciation. Lesley Milroy's example is by no means an isolated occurrence. One story told in the corpus of conversations recorded from my own family concerns a man who was an inveterate user of the discourse marker *you know*, which began a lively impromptu discussion of discourse markers. The participants, my own family members, who were all from the South of England, expressed their distaste at the use of certain discourse markers which they perceived to be from the North. They did so quite openly and without realizing that they themselves occasionally used instantiations of those very same discourse markers during the ongoing conversation (Watts 1989). The story was just one more small instantiation of the ***myth of the pure language of the South and the corrupted language of the North***.

In our present-day world, compared with the data we have inherited from the past, we have the distinct advantage of being able to broadcast and record oral performances of discussions, arguments, casual conversations, school lessons and university lectures, parliamentary debates, and so on, in which rich evidence of the myths may be found. One small example must suffice. Cox (1991: 34) quotes

Conservative politician Norman Tebbitt openly stating in a program on Radio 4 in 1985 that "the decline in the teaching of grammar had led directly to the rise in football hooliganism." Tebbitt's statement instantiates a nexus of myths including the *myth of the legitimate language* and the *myth of barbarians not speaking a proper language*, in which the failure to learn Standard English had led to a moral decline involving hooliganism and violence.

Stories of this kind could be narrated almost endlessly. Given a large enough corpus of oral English, they are not hard to find if one is prepared to comb through the corpus by hand, rather than using a key word search. They offer the evidence that is required to substantiate the existence of the myths. The myths themselves cannot be said to represent objectively truthful accounts of the past, nor can we expect each telling of a myth to be the same. Many of them may contain grains of truth, and as such they are an eminently useful means of accounting historically for present attitudes towards language. For many, language myths may be represented as closer to truth than fiction, whereas for others, their fictional character may be much stronger. It should not be our goal to try and dissuade people from believing in language myths; this would be an utterly pointless undertaking. But the beliefs instantiated by myths still need to be taken seriously if hegemonic discourses on language are driven by those beliefs.

It has been my purpose in this chapter to highlight the significance of the term 'myth' in discussing the discursive construction of the history of English that I have called the tunnel/funnel view. I began by explaining what I understand by this term, but it was not my purpose to discuss all the myths that I have unearthed in my research. There are several more, and all of them are intertwined in one way or another. But to answer the second question above, the funnel/tunnel view of the history of English can only be challenged by providing solid evidence that it is ultimately based on a discourse driven by language myths. This is not to say that myths are untruths: far from it, but we are obliged to shift our attention to the histories of several other varieties of English than the standard language. This work has already begun, as is witnessed by Wales' book on Northern English (2006), Schreier's book on Tristan da Cunha (2003) and by the articles in Watts and Trudgill (2002b). We should never forget that many of the myths have a long history, and that, while it is not good policy to try to dissuade people outside the confines of academia from believing in them, it is certainly good policy to introduce the study of language myths into university-level courses on the history of English and to research further into the wide-ranging effects they can have on people's beliefs about and attitudes towards English.

NOTES

1   Myths will be presented throughout the paper in bold italic font.
2   The term 'truth' language was coined by Anderson (1983/2006) to refer to sacred languages such as Latin, Greek, and Arabic that were in the minds and mouths of those who had access

to the divine truth, such as clerics and priests, who were bilingual in the sacred language and their mother tongue and thus guardians of the 'truth' languages. The nation-state ideology of the past 200 years has focused on turning vernaculars like French, German, and English into "truth" languages by making them as 'classical' as the sacred languages, that is, by standardizing them through using myths such as the **myth of linguistic homogeneity**, the **myth of the pure language**, the **myth of the perfect language**, and the **myth of superiority** to construct dominant language ideologies.

3 The *Wildhagen-Heraucourt's German-English Dictionary* (Wildhagen and Heraucourt 1972) does not even give a translation for *Kultursprache*. The *online dictionary german-english* glosses the term into English as "language of a civilized people" (http://odge.de/index.php?ebene=Su che&kw=Kultursprache [accessed October 17, 2011]), which then forces us to define how we understand the term "civilized people." Vetter (2003: 282) uses the English expression "language of significant cultural heritage."

4 James and Lesley Milroy (1985/1999) call this dominant discourse "the ideology of the standard." Crowley (1989/2003) argues in a similar vein to the Milroys and myself, although he does not explicitly use the term "the ideology of the standard."

REFERENCES

Anderson, B. (1983/2006) *Imagined Communities: Reflections on the Origin and Spread of Nationalism* (2nd edn), Verso, London and New York.

Babington, C. (ed.) (1865/1964) *Polychronicon Ranulphi Higden Monachi Cestrensis, 7 Volumes: Together with the English translations of John Trevisa and of an unknown writer of the fifteenth century*, vol 2, Kraus Reprint, Wiesbaden.

Camden, W. (1605) *Remaines of a Greater Worke concerning Britain.* (ed. R.D. Dunn), University of Toronto Press, Toronto.

Carew, R. (1586) Epistle concerning the Excellencies of the English Tongue. London. In Camden, W. (ed. R.D. Dunn).

Cox, B. (1991) *Cox on Cox: An English Curriculum for the 1990s*, Hodder & Stoughton, London.

Crowley, T. (1989/2003) *Standard English and the Politics of Language* (2nd edn), Palgrave Macmillan, Basingstoke.

Defoe, D. (1697) *An Essay upon Projects.* Printed by R.R. for Tho. Cockerill, London.

Eckert, P. (2000) *Linguistic Variation as Social Practice*, Blackwell, Oxford.

Eckert, P. and McConnell-Ginet, S. (2003) *Language and Gender*, Cambridge University Press, New York.

Fitzmaurice, S. (1998) The commerce of language in the pursuit of politeness in eighteenth-century England. *English Studies* 79: 309–28.

Foucault, M. (1969/1972) *Archaeology of Knowledge* (2nd edn), Pantheon, New York.

Harrison, W. (1577) On the languages spoken in this land. In R. Holinshed (ed.). Higden, R. See under Babington, C.

Holinshed, R. (1577) *Chronicles of England, Scotland and Ireland* (ed. V.F. Snow, 1965), AMS, New York.

Langford, P. (1989) *A Polite and Commercial People: England 1727–1783*, Oxford University Press, Oxford.

McIntosh, C. (1998) *The Evolution of English Prose 1700–1800: Style, Politeness, and Print Culture*, Cambridge University Press, Cambridge.

Miège, G. (1688/1969) The English Grammar; or, the Grounds, and Genius of the English Tongue. In R.C. Alston Festeau, 1969 (ed.), *English Linguistics 1500–1800, a Collection of Facsimile Reprints*, Scholar Press, Menston.

Milroy, J. (2007) The ideology of the standard language. In C. Llamas, L. Mullany, and P. Stockwell (eds.), *The Routledge Companion to Sociolinguistics*, Routledge, London and New York, pp. 133–39.

Milroy, J. and Milroy, L. (1985/1999) *Authority in Language. Investigating Standard English*, Routledge, London.

Milroy, L. (1999) Standard English and language ideology in Britain and the United States. In T. Bex and R.J. Watts (eds.), *Standard English: The Widening Debate*, Routledge, London, pp. 173–206.

Peyton, V. (1779/1971) Elements of the English Language. London. In R.C. Alston Festeau, 1969 (ed.), *English Linguistics 1500–1800, a Collection of Facsimile Reprints*, Scholar Press, Menston.

Puttenham, G. (1589) *The Arte of English Poesie*. London (ed. G.D. Willcock and A. Walker, 1936), Cambridge University Press, Cambridge.

Schreier, D. (2003) *Isolation and Language Change. Contemporary and Sociohistorical Evidence From Tristan da Cunha English*, Palgrave Macmillan, London.

Smith, O. (1984) *The Politics of Language 1791–1819*, Oxford University Press, Oxford.

Tieken-Boon van Ostade, I. (ed.) (2008) *Grammars, Grammarians and Grammar-writing in Eighteenth-century England*, Mouton de Gruyter, Berlin.

Vetter, E. (2003) Hegemonic discourse in the Habsburg empire: The case of education. A critical discourse analysis of two mid 19th century government documents. In R. Rindler-Schjerve (ed.), *Diglossia and Power*, Mouton de Gruyter, Berlin, pp. 271–307.

Wales, K. (2006) *Northern English: A Social and Cultural History*, Cambridge University Press, Cambridge.

Watts, R.J. (1989) Taking the pitcher to the well: Native speakers' perceptions of their use of discourse markers in conversation. *Journal of Pragmatics* 13: 203–37.

Watts, R.J. (2000) Mythical strands in the ideology of prescriptivism. In L. Wright (ed.), *The Development of Standard English 1300–1800: Theories, Descriptions, Conflicts*, Cambridge University Press, Cambridge, pp. 29–48.

Watts, R.J. (2003) *Politeness*, Cambridge University Press, Cambridge.

Watts, R.J. (2011) *Language Myths and the History of English*, Oxford University Press, New York.

Watts, R.J. and Trudgill, P. (2002a) Introduction. In R.J. Watts and P. Trudgill (eds.), pp. 1–3.

Watts, R.J. and Trudgill, P. (eds.) (2002b) *Alternative Histories of English*, Routledge, London.

Wegener, A. (1912) Die Entstehung der Kontinente. *Geologische Rundschau* 3: 276–92.

Wegener, A. (1915/1968) *The Origin of Continents and Oceans*, Methuen, London.

Weinreich, U., Labov, W., and Herzog, M. (1968) Empirical foundations for a theory of language change. In W. Lehmann and Y. Malkiel (eds.), *Directions for Historical Linguistics*, University of Texas Press, Austin, TX, pp. 95–195.

Wenger, E. (1998) *Communities of Practice: Learning, Meaning and Identity*, Cambridge University Press, Cambridge.

Wildhagen, K. and Héraucourt, W. (compilers) (1972) *Wildhagen-Héraucourt's German–English, English–German Dictionary*, 2 volumes, Brandstetter, Wiesbaden.

William of Malmesbury (1125/2007) *Gesta pontificum Anglorum. Volume 1: Text and translation* (ed. and trans. M. Winterbottom), Oxford University Press, Oxford.

33 Linguistic Purism

NILS LANGER AND AGNETE NESSE

1. Introduction[1]

Linguistic Purism is one of the most noticeable areas of historical sociolinguistics since it very publicly deals with what speakers think of (particular) language use. It thus touches on the field of folk linguistics – as defined by Niedzielski and Preston (2000) – which places great importance on the *perception* of language varieties, rather than just the sociological significance of particular linguistic variables and variants. There is no agreement amongst academic linguists as to what counts as linguistic purism and what does not. The principal divisions lie, on the one hand, between those for whom an attempt to rid a language of *any* undesirable elements constitutes purism and those who define it more narrowly as an attempt to rid a language only of *foreign* elements, and on the other, between those who see linguistic purism as a completely unacceptable academic activity and those who feel that purism is sometimes a subject worthy of study for academic linguists, such as with regard to the protection of regional or minority languages, or the process of standardizing and codifying a language.

As it stands, the study of purism is connected to several important aspects of historical linguistics, including the process of standardizing languages, the use of language as a building block in the creation of nations, and the stigmatization of linguistic varieties or cultures as undesirable, or even a threat to one's identity. There are a number of publications on this subject, of which three in particular provide fairly recent and comprehensive overviews and case studies from different languages and historical periods: van der Sijs (1999), Brincat, Boeder, and Stolz (2003), and Langer and Davies (2005). In this chapter we will outline the key metalinguistic motivations, actors, and principal concerns in the area of linguistic purism.

The Handbook of Historical Sociolinguistics, First Edition. Edited by Juan Manuel Hernández-Campoy and Juan Camilo Conde-Silvestre.
© 2014 John Wiley & Sons, Ltd. Published 2014 by John Wiley & Sons, Ltd.

2. Current Definitions

The most fundamental presupposition for any puristic activity is that languages can be damaged, either by neglect on the part of a set of speakers or due to external influences, such as language contact. But languages are flexible systems of communication that will change over time depending on the – largely subconscious – changing communicative behaviors of those who use them. A language will always serve 'perfectly' those who communicate with it so there is no need to worry about change, in fact no point in worrying about it, resisting it, or making suggestions as to how to alter or improve a language.

As mentioned in the introduction, one of the most immediate disagreements between scholars on the subject of linguistic purism relates to whether it can be applied to foreign elements only, and we can see this contrast by comparing established definitions. Trask (1999) defines linguistic purism as:

> The belief that words (and other linguistic features) of foreign origin are a kind of contamination sullying the purity of a language. (Trask 1999: 254)

So for him, purism is a *belief*, not an activity, and is restricted to foreign influence on a language. Similarly, in his work on Scandinavian languages, Brunstad (2001) suggests that purism is only about foreign elements, which should be replaced by native (*heimlege*) forms.

By contrast, for Thomas (1991), purist activity is much more widely defined as:

> [A] desire on the part of the speech community [...] to preserve a language from, or rid it of, putative foreign elements, or other elements held to be undesirable (including those in dialects, sociolects, and styles of the same language). It may be directed at all foreign elements but primarily the lexicon. (Thomas 1991: 12)

For Thomas, purism extends to the removal of linguistic elements beyond those which are foreign to those which are 'undesirable' more generally, in other words, any deviation from a perceived norm.[2] This is echoed by van der Sijs (1999: 11) who defines purism as the conscious rejection of elements which are considered undesirable (*ongewenst*), rather than foreign. This usually but not exclusively applies to foreign elements.

3. Linguistic Purity

By its very name, the ultimate aim of puristic activity is to achieve purity. And like many other concepts used to describe states of a language (such as *language death, growth, decline,* or *development*) linguistic *purity* is analogous to descriptions in the natural sciences. In the natural sciences, purity might at least be achievable in theory since the object to be cleansed can be precisely defined: *water* is defined as H_2O, so any substance that contains elements other than hydrogen and oxygen cannot be 'pure' water (whether this is actually truly achievable is for a chemist to decide). However, when it comes to purifying languages, we would – by analogy to the water example – need to define *precisely* what a language is made of. If indeed there is such a thing as 'German,' what are its core or purest elements and which are the foreign elements of which we could, in principle, rid it?

One well-known and well-used way of defining the true essence of a particular language, particularly in lay discourse but also by educated journalists, for instance, is to equate it with its prestige standard variety, thus: German is standard written German. However, this is hardly satisfactory, since – accepting for the moment that we can actually speak of standard written German as a localizable variety – standard written German does, of course, contain numerous foreign influences: it is hardly 'pure' in a genealogical-historical sense. A second approach towards purity is to say that we define the pure state as that which has the grammatical and lexical properties of the oldest (surviving) texts, or as the oldest stage of the language as it was reconstructed during the era of historical comparative linguistics in the nineteenth century. However, which texts survived and which did not was largely accidental and thus hardly provides a good basis for a rigorously pure state. Furthermore, even the earliest texts of, for example, English or German, contain numerous identifiable lexical borrowings, such as in English *cheese*/German *Käse* (from the Latin *caseus*), English *church*/German *Kirche* (from the Greek *kyriakon*) and English *street*/German *Straße* (from the Latin *strata*), so these texts hardly represent pure Germanic language sources. One way to resolve this would be to trace all Greek and Latin influences (for example) and strip them out of these texts and present what is left as 'pure English' or 'pure German.' However, even then we would not arrive at a satisfactory result, principally for two reasons: firstly, we would not know which foreign elements we had failed to spot, such as borrowings from other, unattested, or unknown languages, or from minority languages that, having low prestige, were not searched as possible sources of loanwords into more prestigious languages. Secondly, words such as *church* and *cheese* are a fundamental part of several Germanic languages, even if, or maybe because, they are the result of language contact.

Language contact is one of the drivers of linguistic distinctiveness which ultimately contribute to the birth of new languages. Only because languages change because of cultural changes and because they come into contact with other languages, do particular languages become distinctive enough to warrant them being labeled a separate language[3] – thus without any change, there is no distinctiveness, and hence few needs to provide a separate name. A much cited example here could be the fact that the Norwegian spoken in Iceland in the Middle Ages changed less than the Norwegian in Norway, because Norwegian in Iceland was much less influenced by Low German than was Norwegian in Norway. Centuries later, the two varieties of Norwegian were identified as separate languages, and ironically, the variety closer to the older form (and thus the 'purer' form) was now no longer called Norwegian but Icelandic.

The crucial point for our discussion is that there is – strictly speaking – no such thing as linguistic purity: first because we can never determine the *Stunde Null*, the very beginning of a language – when, by definition, it was pure – and, secondly, because a new language is always the result of some degree of language contact; hence, even if we were able to pinpoint the actual birth of a language, it would contain some degree of influence from other languages.

This impossibility of conceiving linguistic purity as a real property of language is one of the crucial reasons why most academic linguists have traditionally ignored linguistic purism. However, as we will see below, this is not the case for all languages and for all periods. Grammarians working during the standardization-stage of a language often actively participate in the process of creating a linguistic norm (in the seventeenth century for German, or the nineteenth century for Norwegian). Creating a normative and prestige variety crucially involves two processes: saying not only what linguistic features are to be *in*cluded in, but also what features are to be *ex*cluded from, the new standard language. The process of excluding linguistic elements is *puristic* in the wider definition of purism suggested by Thomas (1991).

4. Puristic Discourses

A striking feature of the area of linguistic purism is the recurrence or at least overlap of particular lines of argument to justify the creation of a pure language, and the *ex*- or *in*clusion of particular linguistic features or varieties, in the puristic discourses of different languages or different historical periods. Thus we find the same, or at least very similar, objections to the use of English in modern Swedish expressed in eighteenth-century Germany with respect to French. Similarly, those who wanted Middle Low German elements removed from Norwegian used arguments about the dangers of linguistic infiltration similar to those heard in nineteenth-century Flanders. William J. Jones (1995, 1999) documents Germans' perception of foreign words from different sources since 1550, noting similarities and differences; and for Scandinavia, Helge Sandøy's project *Modern Loanwords in the Nordic Countries* has compared attitudes to the use of English in seven different speech communities, showing how puristic discourses are applied equally in different language settings and histories (Sandøy 2003, Kristiansen and Vikør 2006).

In his work on the history of lexical purism pertaining to German, Andreas Gardt (2001, see also Pfalzgraf 2009) identified four principal discourses that justify and carry puristic thought. These discourses concern linguistic structure (*sprachstruktureller Fremdwortdiskurs*), ideology (*sprachideologischer Fremdwortdiskurs*), pedagogy (*sprachpädagogisch-sprachsoziologischer Fremdwortdiskurs*), and metalinguistic considerations (*sprachkritischer Fremdwortdiskurs*), which can be found repeatedly at different historical stages in many languages and are not necessarily restricted to the lexical aspects of language. The *structural discourse* assumes that for each language there is a state of purity at which the linguistic system is perfectly balanced. The use of foreign words and constructions represents an interference that damages the system and can lead to a breakdown of the language; adherents of this view suggest replacing foreign with autochthonous elements, using archaic or dialectal forms or creating neologisms based on indigenous morphology. The *ideological discourse* emphasizes the superior quality of one's language based on its genealogical purity and great age, a belief in which forms a fundamental part of one's culture and history. Foreign elements in the language are thus seen as a corruption of cultural purity. The *pedagogical discourse* argues that the use of foreign words leads to social division within a society, since the less-educated and the elderly might not understand new borrowings introduced into specific domains such as youth language or technical registers[4]. Finally, the *metalinguistic discourse* more openly acknowledges that purism has to do with taste and aesthetics, rather than a general ability to communicate. The use of foreign words is scorned as chasing fashionable trends and giving the impression of being intellectual and modern, so is seen as superficial and pretentious behavior which should be rejected.

These four types of discourse typically overlap in practice, but distinguishing between them provides a useful way of understanding the different lines of argument suggested by purists. Ultimately, linguistic purism is not so much concerned with its ostensible aim, the purity of a given language, but is rather a social commentary on the (perceived) declining standards – linguistic, moral, and educational – of modern society.

5. Linguistic Purism and Standard Languages

Standard languages tend to have two principal purposes: firstly, they allow for smooth supraregional communication since most speakers in a larger community such as the UK, will at least have a good passive competence in the standard language, both written and spoken. The great functional advantage is undoubtedly that speakers from different regions can communicate with each other and that somebody in Bristol, for example, can effortlessly read a newspaper or listen to a radio program from Glasgow, even though the local dialects may be almost mutually incomprehensible. The second important function of standard languages is on the sociolinguistic level, rather than the purely functional, and that is their potential use as a community symbol; thus one of the main features which unites all Germans is the German language – this has been the case for many centuries and is quite independent of the existence of a standard language – and in order to maintain that this language is accepted as a prestigious aspect of German culture, a standard language used for higher-register discourse (*Distanzsprache*) was created some 400 years ago and has been cherished and codified ever since. A spin-off from the community-creating function of standard languages is obviously the power this function confers to exclude anyone from the community who does not have a command of the standard language; for instance, if speaking the standard language is a social requirement for participating in middle-class environments, then failure to speak the standard language will equate to a failure to be(come) middle class. The importance of speaking in the 'right' accent or variety becomes especially important at times when other factors that used to identify a person's class, such as clothes or education, lose their distinguishing power. We can see an example of this in the rapid rise in the publication of language manuals during the Age of Enlightenment, when speaking the 'correct' way became one of the prime identifiers of a person's class as other identifiers declined in importance. The destandardization-processes seen in many Northern European speech communities after 1968 can thus be seen as a means of weakening the importance of 'correct' speech for a person's potential to advance socially or at least of widening the range of linguistic variation still acceptable for a speaker to be judged to be speaking the standard or prestige language.

A standard language is thus not just a vehicle for supraregional communication but also a social norm, which allows a speaker to identify herself or himself as a member of an educated or non-low social class. According to van der Sijs (1999: 11), linguistic purism only occurs in standardized languages or in languages in the process of standardization. Thus purism and the existence of a standard language are inextricably linked: the removal of undesirable elements can only really be effective if it is clear what needs to be cleansed from the language, and this presupposes the existence of a norm, of the perception of one. Without a norm, speakers do not have a reference point as to what is incorrect or undesirable (but see Langer 2007 on the problems of locating linguistic norms). Linguistic standardization often coincides with – and may even be triggered by – changes in a community affecting its members' national or regional status. In particular, this takes place when a linguistic community suffers from an (at least perceived) communal insecurity arising from an external threat: for example, from a colonial language occupying particular high-status linguistic domains (French in nineteenth-century Flanders, Turkish in Bulgaria), from a cohabiting 'larger' language in the same area (Dutch in modern Western Frisia, French in medieval England), or from a hegemonizing world language, where language contact is largely restricted to 'fashion' or particular lexical fields (French in seventeenth-century Germany, English in most of the modern world).

Crucially, influences from non-threatening languages are not considered as a problem; for instance, in Wilhelmine Germany, objections were made to French and English words rather than to the much more prominent Latin and Greek influences in German, while in today's Europe, countless organizations and societies work towards the removal of English words from their national language, whilst there is little concern over the use of Italian words in banking and culinary areas. The case of the integration of foreign morphology in Norwegian demonstrates that foreign languages such as English and Italian are not being treated equally. There are two plural formations for the Norwegian word *konto*, borrowed from Italian *conto*, namely *konti* and *kontoer*, although the former is rarely used. However, though Italian suffixes are acceptable in Norwegian morphology, English suffixes are only rarely permitted; so, for example, *fotos* (< English *photos*) is not acceptable in educated discourse, although in actual speech it is much more likely to be encountered than *konti*. Thus there is a clear distinction between Italian and English borrowing for which the most likely explanation is that English is considered a threatening language, whilst Italian is not, thus mirroring the feelings found elsewhere in European languages.[5]

What is important for our purposes is that purism is often used as an important tool in the creation of standard languages and for strengthening their status in the community. Standardization tends to follow four generally recognized stages: selection, codification, implementation, and elaboration, as suggested by Haugen (1966/1997; for a recent application of his model to all Germanic languages, see Deumert and Vandenbussche 2003). Puristic efforts can affect all of these stages though they are most prominent in the process of codification, frequently by means of the process of exclusion, such as when foreign words are not included in modern dictionaries: the lexicographer Joachim Heinrich Campe (1746–1818) famously suggested thousands of loan-translations for foreign words in German – many of which are established words of modern German today: *Feingefühl* (Takt), *fortschrittlich* (progressiv), and *Hochschule* (Universität); moreover, one of the most striking oddities of the authoritative *Deutsches Wörterbuch* (1854–1960) by the Grimm brothers was their decision to exclude many foreign words, even those whose use was common and had been well-established for centuries. One result of their exclusion from such dictionaries is that they are denied their status as accepted words of the borrowing language; the crucial implication is that these dictionaries are not neutrally compiled lists of all existing words but, rather, subjective accounts of what ought to be part of a particular language. Incidentally, such practices of selectivity are by no means condemned even in modern times; the publication of a new edition of any important national dictionary is accompanied by a general outrage among the establishment, especially with regard to the inclusion of new words which come from nonstandard varieties or foreign languages.

It is a matter for debate to what extent any standardizing or normative process necessarily includes puristic tendencies, since standardization involves deciding not only what *is* standard but also what is *not* standard language. Thus codification cannot really take place without stigmatizing those words and constructions which are not to become part of the standard language. This would certainly be true for the broad interpretation of purism as the removal and exclusion of *anything* that is undesirable, rather than simply those elements that are foreign. As a consequence of this argument, the emergence of vernacular grammar-writing in post-Renaissance Europe would come to involve puristic efforts in the wider sense and therefore pave the way for a purism of the narrower definition[6].

The use of purism in standardizing efforts has a powerful effect on our perception of what constitutes a language proper: by elevating certain constructions as part of the standard language (e.g. in English: *you were*) and by excluding others (e.g. *you was*), the latter are rendered invisible even though they are still a part of the set of constructions used by native speakers of, in this case, English (Milroy 2005: 326).

6. Actors and Norms

Linguistic purism rests on an actual or idealized model of perfection. In seventeenth-century debates, this perfect linguistic variety was framed in a Biblical context: the perfect language was the language used in Paradise (either created or inspired by the Christian god) and what ought to be aimed for in contemporary puristic efforts was to either recreate the language of Paradise, or, failing that, to recreate the closest one could get to it, namely the principal languages or *Hauptsprachen* caused by the Confusion of the Languages after Babel (see Jones 1995, 1999, and also Eco 1994). By remodeling, for example, standard German by appealing to these ancient languages one would get as close as possible to the original, hence divinely perfect, language. However, linguistic models are also frequently based on more tangible though not necessarily very concrete forms: typically, the ideal language is that used by the reigning monarch[7], the language of the upper or middle classes in or near the capital city or royal court, the linguistic variety used in a particular region (see Mattheier 2003, 2005), the language used by an esteemed historical figure[8], or national institutions, such as linguistic academies like the *Academie Française*, or national media, such as the *Frankfurter Allgemeine Zeitung* or the *BBC*.[9] Academic linguists, too, often play a role, as discussed below.

An example of a very active role played by a national broadcasting company replacing certain elements of speech in a language can be seen in the attempts to change the way of counting in Norwegian. The traditional way of counting had been ones + tens, as in *enogtjue* 'one and twenty.' In 1950 the Norwegian parliament (*Storting*) decided that the post-war era characterized by modern technology and advanced communication required a new system of counting, and introduced a system with tens + ones, as in *tjueen* 'twenty one.' This recommendation was implemented by the *Norsk rikskringkasting* (NRK, Norwegian broadcasting association), which required all its correspondents to count in this way. It was also introduced in schools and as the written norm of the two standard languages, *bokmål* and *nynorsk*. After almost 60 years, most Norwegians count in both the old and the new ways, so it is clear that the introduction of the new counting system was only a partial success. A reason for this may have been that the old way of counting was (subconsciously) associated with dialect, and the new way with the standard language (Nesse 2008: 125). Therefore, as long as the spoken standard was used by all radio reporters and by others speaking in public domains, the new way of counting dominated the public domains. But the changed sociolinguistic climate in Norway from the mid-1960s, when it became more common and acceptable to use dialect in all domains, facilitated the use of the old way of counting in educated speech (see Table 33.1):

The introduction of the new way of counting (still referred to as such today) was supported by practical arguments and not founded on any ideological or cultural stereotype. For example, it was said that reading telephone numbers to be written down was easier in the new way, since in writing, the tens come first

Table 33.1. Counting in Norwegian radio, both reporters and interviewees. Based on a survey of 300 programs from 1936 to 1996 from the NRK local station in the county of Nordland (source: Nesse 2008: 125; reproduced by permission of Novus)

Period	New counting (tjueen)	Old counting (enogtjue)
1936–1950	0%	100%
1951–1960	75%	25%
1961–1970	50%	50%
1971–1980	47%	53%
1981–1987	40%	60%
1988–1996	48%	52%

and the units after. But this explanation may not be sufficient,[10] even though the initiative came from the national telephone company. It is at least possible that one of the key motivations for changing the way of counting was to create distance from German, since the old way of counting matched the German way (*einundzwanzig*), whilst the new way matched the English (*twenty one*). In the 1950s Norway – certainly as regards official circles – felt closely allied to the UK and the USA, whilst anything reminding people of Germany was seen in negative terms. This affinity towards the English-speaking world existed even before Word War II when the USA was seen as a progressive and liberal country and when many personal ties had been created by substantial migration from Norway to the USA. At the same time, the much older cultural ties with Germany were weakening. Changing the style of counting – with a top-down approach from the parliament to the speakers via the broadcasting association – is thus an intriguing purist method: removing elements that are indigenous to the language yet that become undesirable because they are similar or identical to an undesirable language. This process is by no means unique; for instance, one of the means of demonstrating the independence of Croatian from Serbian was to remove not just Serbian words, as would naturally be expected, but also words that were used in Serbian as well as Croatian: the highest degree of purity of 'Croatianness' was not simply that a word had always been part of Croatian but that it would *not* be found in Serbian (van der Sijs 1999: 21).

7. Linguistic Purism and Morale Decline

Having established that languages are flexible systems subject to continuous change according to the communicative behaviors of those who use them, it is somewhat surprising that linguistic purism continues not only to survive, but to thrive. There is no linguistic reason for this, as people in Germany or Norway, for example, are highly effective in communicating effortlessly with their peers even though German and Norwegian are full of relatively recent lexical, semantic, and even morphological borrowings. Concerns about linguistic purity are therefore separate from any real problems affecting communication: they are simply, as mentioned above, sociological concerns related to the perceived status of 'distinguished' languages, and in extreme cases, such as linguistic colonization, the very survival of endangered languages. It is important to stress that this has to do with perception: languages do not disappear as long as they are used, even though they may undergo massive linguistic changes: English is still considered a language despite having undergone massive changes since the time of its oldest surviving texts, because its speakers continued to speak it, write it, and call it English. Germans have thought of themselves as speaking German for many hundreds of years, even though the varieties they spoke in the Middle Ages would have been significantly different from each other and many mutually incomprehensible. Yet they would have claimed they all spoke German and this is part of the reason why in modern linguistic historiography we happily write histories of German beginning in the eighth, rather than the sixteenth or seventeenth century. *Perception* of unity plays a crucial part in the historiography – both academic and lay – of nations.

This brings us to the actors of linguistic purism. Traditionally, we identify members of the educated elites as the key players in puristic efforts, although in modern times these are only very rarely people with an academic training in linguistics (see, however, the next section), but in previous centuries, being a grammarian typically coincided with being a translator, a poet or writer, and a lexicographer. The emergence of linguistic purism in most European languages is causally linked to the desire to make one's vernacular language into a standard variety. In the seventeenth century several societies concerned with language emerged in many European countries, whose aim was to promote the use of vernacular languages. The foundation of such societies, whose members were typically drawn from the aristocracy and bourgeoisie, was prompted by an aversion to the use of foreign languages in educated discourse.[11]

Language societies in Germany stated quite explicitly in their constitutions that their task was to protect the German language and German virtues. With this aim in mind, these societies promoted the translation of classical texts into the vernacular to demonstrate that, for instance, German was a proper language capable of delivering fine literature and poetry. At a time when linguistic variation was seen to be a sign of chaotic weakness, in contrast to the much more uniform model languages of Latin and Greek, a further ambition was to provide a standardized language with a uniform grammar, an ideal pronunciation, and a pure lexicon. Language scholars, either as part of such societies or independently, pursued these aims by engaging in metalinguistic discussions and publications. Lexical purism was actively and openly pursued: in Germany, grammarians and lexicographers published lists of neologisms based on German(ic) roots to replace Latin- and Greek-based words (for example, *Verfasser* for *Autor* 'author,' *Anschrift* for *Adresse* 'address,' by Philipp von Zesen 1619–89) – a practice that has resurfaced from time to time and can be seen most vividly in the *Anglizismen-Index* issued by the private Society for the German Language (*Verein deutsche Sprache*, www.vds-ev.de). The principal flaw of any such list, of course, is the relative arbitrariness with which loanwords are identified as 'objectionable' vs. 'sufficiently well established to be acceptable.'[12] However, within the discourse of purism, such inconsistencies are not reflected upon since there tends to be a general consensus about which type of words pose a threat to one's language and which do not. One suggestion is that people object to those words which are borrowed after their own teenage years, that is, after their own 'golden age' (see Milroy 1998). Vikør (2007: 174) calls this "conservative purism:" an acceptance of the language the way it has become, combined with a reluctance to introduce new elements into the language. Opposed to this is what Vikør (2007:174) calls "regressive purism:" an attempt to rid the language of elements that have entered after the perceived 'golden age' of the nation (such as Norway in the thirteenth century). That different regimes have different goals, the example of Iran shows clearly: before 1979 there was an active, regressive purism, targeted at Arabic loan words, trying to replace them with Persian words. After the Islamic revolution in 1979, this process was reversed, and the Arabic words were taken back into the standard language (Vikør 2007:174).

It is striking that linguistic purists sometimes use scholarly arguments when it suits their endeavors, but more intuitive and emotional arguments when scholarship seems to go against them. The personification (hypostasis) of language is crucial for such arguments: by attributing organic and emotional values to a language, such as *health*, *disease*, *beauty*, or *warmth*, purists make a powerful case for defending something dear to one's heart from foreign and corrupting intrusions, without having to engage in complicated or objective arguments about the nature of language change (see also Chapters 31 and 32 in this *Handbook*).

8. Academic Linguists and Linguistic Purism

Milroy (2005) shows that apart from the more well-known type of 'sanitary purism' which largely corresponds to our discussion above, there is also 'genetic' or 'etymological' purism, aimed not so much at standardizing a language but at legitimizing it "by giving it a (preferably long and glorious) history and, in some cases, moving towards restoring the language to its ancient lawful state of purity" (Milroy 2005: 329; see also Chapter 31 in this *Handbook*). This kind of purism is evident in nineteenth-century efforts in English, but also, in our opinion, attempts to eliminate or downgrade foreign borrowings in Norwegian and Low German and to replace them with newly-created or previously extinct words with morphs drawn from the 'original source' language. The effect of this is to show linguistic continuity between the earliest stages of a language and its modern counterpart, an important demonstration if one is to justify the belief that one's language has a long history. This is particularly important for languages where the oldest attested stages bear little *linguistic* resemblance to the modern forms, such as English and High German. A famous example of practical steps towards linguistic purity is the creation of *Landsmål* (later renamed as *Nynorsk*), the written standard variety of Norwegian created by Ivar Aasen (1813–96) on the basis of Norwegian rural dialects, in order to oppose the existing Danish prestige language. Danish in Norway was later modified towards the spoken variety of the elite in the capital, and called *Riksmål* (later renamed as *Bokmål*). In his efforts at standardization, Aasen not only targeted Danish influence but also attempted to eradicate Low German influence, even though those elements had been part of Norwegian dialects since the Middle Ages. Intriguingly, however, he did not oppose the retention of morphemes and words from Latin and Greek, again, a position that is strikingly similar to puristic discourses found in many other European countries over the last 400 years or so, when only languages coming from cultural or political enemies (USA, France, Germany, or Serbia, for instance) were perceived as a danger to one's own language.

Aasen only argued for the removal of foreign words where they "were difficult for the people or disturbed the concept of the rules of the language" (Brunstad 2001: 317, our translation) but it is difficult to see how Latinate words such as *brev* ('letter' < Latin *breve scriptum*), *mil* ('mile' < Latin *milia passuum*) and *skriva* ('write' < Latin *scribere*) would be less semantically or morphologically obscure than the Middle Low German affixes *an-*, *be-*, *ge-* and *-heit*, especially since Norwegian words had been formed with these affixes for centuries. Aasen's model was an uncorrupted Old Norse which formed the basis for his standard language; for this reason, he focused on rather archaic, West Norwegian dialects, staying clear of both Southern Norwegian – with its dialectal similarities to Danish – and Northern Norwegian – which had enjoyed long-term and visible language contact with Sami and Finnish, a contact that, according to Aasen, had resulted in a morphology not suitable for the new language.

An area where Norwegian appears to be more liberal than other languages is spelling, in particular with regard to foreign words. Since the beginning of the twentieth century, Norway has had major spelling reforms roughly every twenty years, and in addition, the spelling of both Nynorsk and Bokmål has many optional variants, both for indigenous and foreign words, such as *service/sørvis*, *juice/jus* and *bag/bagg*. The combination of optional variants and frequent spelling reforms has meant that many Norwegians view correct spelling as a relative matter, which may play an important role in the implementation of the 'Norwegianization' of loan words.

This is in stark contrast to the situation in Denmark, where there is a more homogeneous, conservative written language, and where 'Danish' spelling of loan words is accepted to a much lesser degree. A striking example of this was the so called *majonæse-war* in the 1980s (Brunstad 2001: 155–59). The leader of the Danish language council suggested that words like *mayonnaise* and *creme* could have optional spellings: *majonæse* and *krem*. This was met by a massive protest from different layers of society, which in turn led to quiet opposition to the chair's proposal within the language council. Thus, an important difference between

Denmark and Norway with regard to the debates about the spelling of loan words in the 1990s lies in the approach of the members of the two language councils: careful, almost passive in Denmark, while active and (to many people) provocative in Norway.

A similarly charged discussion has arisen over the German spelling reform of 1998 and has led to greater uniformity in the spelling of some foreign elements, such as Greek <ph>, which can be spelled as <f> in many words. Both *Photo* and *Foto* had been possible even before the spelling reform, and by analogy, it is now also possible to spell dolphin as either *Delphin* or *Delfin*. However, the committee of regional education ministers vetoed the application of this rule to all instances of Greek <ph>, so some words considered to have a particularly high cultural value, such as philosophy, can *only* be spelled as *Philosophie*, not *Filosofie* (cf. Swedish, Danish, and Norwegian *filosofi*). This list of exceptions has led to great confusion amongst the populace, but, for our purposes, it shows how emotionally charged even the spelling of single words can be, regardless of their morphology.

How can these different approaches to the spelling of loan words be understood in the light of Thomas' theoretical framework (1991)? Are those in favor of spelling loan words in their original way purists because they try to avoid change? Or are those in favor of orthographical adjustment of loan words purists because they want to avoid foreignness in the spelling system? Or are neither 'language purists,' since neither is suggesting that borrowing should not take place? The spellings of *mayonnaise* and *service* are a defense for a spelling that has been used for decades, and the argument in favor of this traditional spelling is that any change (towards an orthographically adjusted spelling) would lead to decay in the language, and a general acceptance of 'mistakes.' These arguments are in line with the elitist purism "where prestige has to be defended against the democratising force" (Thomas 1991: 79). Change as such is considered to be 'bad,' so spelling should not be adapted even if the current spelling is difficult, foreign, or undemocratic. Others argue, however, that the appearance of language – including its spelling – ought to be uniform, so a modification of the spelling of loan words would make them easier to integrate into the borrowing language.

The well-known differences between the attitudes of Danes and Norwegians towards the spelling of loan words was one of the reasons behind the research project on *Modern Loanwords in the Nordic Countries* (Kristiansen and Sandøy 2010). This project investigates the *number* of loanwords in the individual Nordic languages, the frequency and usage of native *substitute forms*, the *adaptation* of loanwords to the domestic languages, the role of loan words in *official standardization*, and *attitudes* toward loanwords and substitute forms (Graedler 2004: 5–6), in order to determine whether differences in the attitudes of speakers and the policies of the different countries could be explained by differences in historical and present-day societal conditions. Attitudes were quite different in the two groups of countries, and not all these differences can be ascribed to their status as either former colonies (Finland, Norway, Iceland and the Faroe Islands) or former colonizers (Denmark and Sweden), although purism with regard to English appeared to be stronger in the former colonies. But where other factors were measured along with the attitudes towards English, different patterns emerged. In six of the seven speech communities, it was clear that liberal attitudes towards English were accompanied by liberal attitudes to the use of dialect in the public domains. Similarly, those who were purists with regard to English were also those who wanted to keep the standard languages pure from dialectal or sociolectal features. But in Norway the pattern was the opposite: informants in favor of dialect use in public domains were those most reluctant to the use of English (Kristiansen and Vikør 2006: 212–14).

9. Linguistic Historiography and Purism

Academic linguists provided – and still provide – accounts of the history of a language which show a wealth of linguistic variation until the period of standardization, focusing on the age and thus the venerability of the first surviving texts, in turn demonstrating the antiquity of the culture transmitted in these ancient texts. In the chapters covering the period of standardization and after, however, variation is ignored and the history of, for example, English, becomes the history of standard English. Sometimes regional varieties ('dialects') are given some consideration, in their role as modern relics of ancient times, but they are considered unimportant for the development of the language as a whole. Urban varieties are completely ignored and where mentioned, are seen as poisonous corruptions of the language proper. It really is quite striking that these – rather general – observations on the historiography of English (Milroy 2005; see also Chapters 31 and 32 in this *Handbook*) can be quite readily found in contemporary accounts of, for instance, German and presumably other languages with a similarly nationalist agenda (see Durrell 2009 and Leyhausen 2005 on the influence of German neogrammarians on our perception of language history and historiography). In fact, the mere observation that it is histories of 'German' or 'English' that are written suggests a rather monolithic perception of language history, given that both underwent intensive periods of lexical borrowing and both have changed beyond recognition – to a layperson – from the earliest surviving texts. Even though linguistics as an academic discipline has made great strides since the Romantic views of the Grimm brothers in the early nineteenth century, many of the principal divisions from those days are still part of accepted terminology; for instance, the name Old English (750–1050) suggests *linguistic* continuity with modern English despite the immense differences between the two historical varieties (see Milroy 2005: 336–39), and the term Old High German (750–1050) suggests a rather monolithic existence despite considerable regional variation at the time.

Such views have long persisted and we still speak today of different periods of the history of English as more or less heavily affected by lexical borrowings, rather than as phases of intense language contact – as in the case of English and French in Middle English – resulting in a completely new language[13]. The very name 'Middle English' for the linguistic period after Old English downgrades or even makes invisible the contribution of French or Norse. Milroy (2005) shows that such monolithic thinking is not restricted to historical accounts of language, and even reputable experts on language contact such as Einar Haugen or Uriel Weinreich spoke of linguistic 'abnormality,' 'suffering,' and 'violations' when two languages mix (Milroy 2005: 331). Few scholars have attempted to abandon the traditional classification of language according to the Indo-European model and actually write language history on the basis of what *is* rather than what fits the established model. Reichmann (2001, 2005) has shown that in lexical semantics, for example, a comparison of the semantic fields of even core words such as *house* results in a grouping of languages which does not correspond to the Indo-European model: the range of meanings of the German word *Haus* corresponds most closely with the Hungarian word *ház*, rather than, as we would expect, with its fellow West Germanic languages English or Dutch. He consequently pleads for a European, rather than a nation-based, language history. This ambition has been supported by a number of smaller studies which show how a pan-European look at language history can give deeper insights than a purely national approach: for instance, Johansson (1998) examines loss of grammatical case in different European languages, and comes to the conclusion that loss of case is more likely on the coast than inland, especially in areas where the largest cities are coastal.

10. Concluding Remarks: Linguistic Purism in Historical Sociolinguistics

A number of issues surface when we look at a range of examples and case studies of linguistic purism. First and foremost, purists are concerned about the state of their language – one never finds purists who are happy with the status quo – and feel that there is a need, sometimes urgent, to interfere, principally by removing corrupting and corrosive influences from their language. As discussed above, some believe that such influences are always foreign, while others define puristic activities as the objection to *any* kind of negative influence; crucially, the fact that it is fundamentally impossible to distinguish clearly between foreign and indigenous influences on language – because the complete set of 'indigenous' elements is not known for any language – does not prevent purists from focusing on foreign elements alone. Given, however, that the motivations for and discourses about attacking non-foreign elements, such as regionalisms and sociolectal elements, are strikingly similar to those that target foreign elements, it would seem useful for any academic linguist to follow the wider definition of purism, advocated, for example, by Thomas (1991).

   A second general observation is that for any particular example of puristic activity, only one set of corrupting influences is targeted; normally this means that only one foreign language (English for German and Norwegian, Low German for Nynorsk) or sociolect (youth language in many cases) is identified as a problem for the purity of one's language, even though there are other varieties with an equal or stronger degree of *actual* influence (Ancient Greek or Italian for German and Norwegian; old people's language for many examples). Thus linguistic purism is not about a general objection to language interference but only about

interference from undesirable languages and varieties (see van der Sijs's definition, discussed above).

Thirdly, linguistic purists want to protect a language that is worth protecting,
that is, a prestigious language. This does not mean that only standardized languages are subject to puristic activity, although this is the most common scenario.
However, there are a number of (romanticized) dialects and non-standardized
languages which also have protectors who are concerned, in particular, with the
corrupting influence of the modern(izing) world: for example, William Barnes
(1801–86) in nineteenth-century rural England, who wanted to give his Dorset
dialect the same status as that of standard English (Nevalainen and Tieken-Boon
van Ostade 2006: 273), or the current discussion about the High-Germanization
of Low German which, it is feared, could destroy its status as an independent
language.

Fourthly, linguistic purists justify the need to protect their language by attributing certain inherent values or properties to it, such as character or spirit (*Sprachgeist*,
Sprachgenius) which contains certain values (*manly, rational, warm*) and which are
likened to living organisms (*young, growing, blossoming, dying* languages). Such
metaphors are used to explain the perceived superiority of one's language: for
example, whilst eighteenth-century German was seen as manly and heroic, French
was seen as effeminate and weak by the same commentators (see Jones 1995 for
a long list of such statements). Similarly, French linguists argued for the superiority of their language because its syntax most closely matched the order of natural
logic (Lodge 1998). A common objection to English dialects is that they contain no
grammar – even though, of course, the morphology of English dialects is often
richer and more regular than that of standard English.

Finally, the identity of linguistic purists is hard to define. There are noticeable
tendencies that justify suggesting that linguistic purists are secure speakers
(Niedzielski 2005) who often have an above-average level of education and who
are in their tax-paying years; in other words, speakers who reminisce about the(ir)
golden age (Milroy 1998) when their own societal norms were formed and from
which any deviation is seen as a corruption. Such societal norms typically pertain
to social conduct, music, and fashion taste, and the level of linguistic impurity.
Broadly speaking, any foreign words which entered one's language during one's
golden age are accepted as part of the language, any words which enter *after* it
are seen as a corruption.

NOTES

1   Our gratitude goes to Debbie Pinfold (Bristol) for helping us resolve issues with our unor-
    thodox use of the English language.
2   The futility of any attempt to cleanse a language from foreign elements is, of course, clearly
    demonstrated by the practical and theoretical impossibility of identifying *all* native or
    foreign items in a language. It is only because we know about the Latin language and the

Roman Empire that we know such common and very native-sounding words like *Käse, kaas* (*'cheese'*) to be foreign borrowings; otherwise we would simply take them to be native German words.

3 Note that a language comes into existence because a particular linguistic variety is *called* a language, not because of any systemic changes (see Chambers and Trudgill 1980 for a discussion of the impossibility of radically distinguishing between language and dialects).

4 For German, it is striking that this line of argument is used to object to quite common and widespread anglicisms but rarely, if ever, to graecisms and Latinisms, which are generally much more obscure. This shows that the purpose of all these discourses is socio-political (based on the fear that Anglo-American culture will replace the German culture and language) rather than the provision of a sober argument about the communicative functions of language in society.

5 Note how the use of 'foreign' morphology is considered to be particularly sophisticated, provided that its origin is Greek or Latin: German *Kaktus*, pl. *Kakteen*, not *Kaktusse*, English *cactus*, pl. *cacti*, not *cactuses*. Note also that the German purists would object to *Atlasse* as the plural of *Atlas* (when it 'should' be *Atlanten*) whilst the English purist has no problem with *atlas*, pl. *atlases*. This demonstrates the apparent randomness of the selection of examples subjected to linguistic purification.

6 As testified by the many eighteenth-century dictionaries, grammars, and pamphlets which openly rejected foreign elements and produced elaborate, and often successful, replacements for these elements by indigenous – and mostly homemade – suggestions.

7 The Queen's English Society (QES) happily equates the best English with that used by the Queen but also expresses some caution over the suitability of Prince William's current use of English (www.queens-english-society.com).

8 For German, Martin Luther continues to be quoted as a language model even though as early as two generations after his death (1546), commentators stated that although Luther's German was still very good, some elements were a little dated.

9 On the difference between norm authorities and norm transmitters, see the discussions on the role of school teachers in the process of standardization offered by Wagner (2009) and Davies and Langer (2006).

10 Compare the use of the argument of 'communicative ease' in relation to capital letters in German, which are used for all nouns. This is often supported on the grounds of a better readability of texts, yet if this were really such an advantage, one wonders why German is the only language in the world which capitalizes all and only nouns.

11 The fashionable usage of French, the language of the most powerful nation in the eighteenth-century, was found particularly objectionable, as it was seen as a betrayal of one's own nation and language and a corruption of one's moral values.

12 For example, in German, few would object to the Latin borrowings *Käse, Mauer*, or *Ziegel*, yet they are just as much a product of language contact as *Handy, Email*, and *Post*.

13 This is not the place to discuss the academic merits of either view. The point here is the virtually complete absence of the latter view in any traditional textbook account of the history of English.

REFERENCES

Bauer, L. and Trudgill, P. (eds.) (1998) *Language Myths*, Penguin, London.

Brincat, J., Boeder, W., and Stolz, T. (2003) *Purism in Minor Languages, Endangered Languages, Regional Languages, Mixed Languages*, Brockmeyer, Bochum.

Brunstad, E. (2001) *Det reine språket. Om purisme i dansk, svensk, færøysk og norsk*, Ph.D. dissertation, Universitetet i Bergen.

Chambers, J.K. and Trudgill, P. (1980) *Dialectology*, Cambridge University Press, Cambridge.

Davies, W. and Langer, N. (2006) *The Making of Bad Language*, Peter Lang, Frankfurt.

Deumert, A. and Vandenbussche, W. (eds.) (2003) *Germanic Standardizations. Past to Present*, John Benjamins, Amsterdam.

Durrell, M. (2009) Deutsch: Teutons, Germans and Dutch? The Problems of Defining a Nation. In G. Horan, N. Langer, and S. Watts (eds.), pp. 169–88.

Eco, U. (1994) *The Search for the Perfect Language*, Blackwell, Oxford.

Gardt, A. (2001) Das Fremde und das Eigene. Versuch einer Systematik des Fremdwortbegriffs in der deutschen Sprachgeschichte. In G. Stickel (ed.), *Neues und Fremdes im deutschen Wortschatz. Aktueller lexikalischer Wandel*, Walter de Gruyter, Berlin, pp. 30–58.

Graedler, A.-L. (2004) Modern Loanwords in the Nordic Countries. Presentation of a project. *Nordic Journal of English Studies* 2: 5–22.

Haugen, E. (1966/1997) Language Standardisation. In N. Coupland and A. Jaworski (eds.), *Sociolinguistics: A Reader and a Coursebook*, Macmillan, London, pp. 341–52.

Horan, G., Langer, N., and Watts, S. (eds.) (2009) *Landmarks in the History of the German Language*, Peter Lang, Bern.

Johansson, C. (1998) Simulation som metod: vårt behov av syntes. In E.H. Jahr (ed.), *Språkkontakt i Norden i middelalderen, særlig i hansatida*, Norden, Copenhagen, pp. 101–18.

Jones, W.J. (1995) *Sprachhelden und Sprachverderber. Dokumente zur Erforschung des Fremdwortpurismus im Deutschen (1478–1750)*, Walter de Gruyter, Berlin.

Jones, W.J. (1999) *Images of Language. Six Essays on German Attitudes to European Languages*, John Benjamins, Amsterdam.

Kristiansen, T. and Sandøy, H. (eds.) (2010) *The Linguistic Consequences of Globalization: the Nordic Countries. International Journal of the Sociology of Language*. no. 204, de Gruyter, Berlin.

Kristiansen, T. and Vikør, L. (eds.) (2006) *Nordiske språkhaldingar. Ei meiningsmåling*, Novus, Oslo.

Langer, N. and Davies, W. (eds.) (2005) *Linguistic Purism in the Germanic Languages*, Walter de Gruyter, Berlin.

Langer, N. (2007) Finding Standard German – Thoughts on Linguistic Codification. In C. Fandrych and R. Salverda (eds.), *Standard, Variation und Sprachwandel in germanischen Sprachen*, Narr, Tübingen, pp. 217–41.

Leyhausen, K. (2005) 'Caution is not always the better part of valour' – Purism in the historiography of the German language. In N. Langer and W. Davies (eds.), pp. 302–23.

Lodge, A. (1998) French is a logical language. In L. Bauer and P. Trudgill (eds.), pp. 23–31.

Mattheier, K. (2003) German. In A. Deumert and W. Vandenbussche (eds.), pp. 211–44.

Mattheier, K. (2005) Dialect and written language: change in dialect norms in the history of the German language. In N. Langer and W. Davies (eds.), pp. 264–81.

Milroy, J. (1998) Children can't speak or write properly anymore. In L. Bauer and P. Trudgill (eds.), pp. 58–67.

Milroy, J. (2005) Some effects of purist ideologies on historical descriptions of English. In N. Langer and W. Davies (eds.), pp. 324–42.

Nesse, A. (2008) *Bydialekt, Riksmål og Identitet – Sett fra Bodø*, Novus, Oslo.

Nevalainen, T. and Tieken-Boon van Ostade, I. (2006) Standardisation. In R. Hogg and D. Denison (eds.), *A History of the English Language*, Cambridge University Press, Cambridge, pp. 271–311.

Niedzielski, N. (2005) Linguistic purism from several perspectives: views from the 'secure' and 'insecure.' In N. Langer and W. Davies (eds.), pp. 252–62.

Niedzielski, N. and Preston, D. (2000) *Folk Linguistics*, Mouton de Gruyter, Berlin.

Pfalzgraf, F. (2009) Linguistic purism in the history of German. In G. Horan, N. Langer, and S. Watts (eds.), pp. 137–68.

Reichmann, O. (2001) *Das nationale und das europäische Modell in der*

Sprachgeschichtsschreibung des Deutschen, Universitätsverlag, Fribourg.

Reichmann, O. (2005) Usefulness and uselessness of the term *Fremdwort*. In N. Langer and W. Davies (eds.), pp. 325–43.

Sandøy, H. (ed.) (2003) *Med "bil" i Norden i 100 år: ordlaging og tilpassing av utanlandske ord*, Novus, Oslo.

Thomas, G. (1991) *Linguistic Purism*, Longman London and New York.

Trask, R.L. (1999) *Key Concepts in Language and Linguistics*, Routledge, London.

van der Sijs, N. (1999) *Taaltrots*, Uitgeverij Contact, Amsterdam.

Vikør, L. (2007) *Språkplanlegging. Prinsipp og praksis*, Novus, Oslo.

Wagner, M. (2009) *Lay Linguistics and School Teaching*, Steiner, Stuttgart.

34 The Reconstruction of Prestige Patterns in Language History

ANNI SAIRIO AND MINNA PALANDER-COLLIN

1. Introduction

Prestige in language essentially refers to the social evaluations that speakers attach to a language rather than to the characteristics of the language system as such. The prestige of a language or a variety is closely connected to the prestige of its speakers, so a variety gains prestige if its speakers have prestige, while the variety of low-prestige people has low prestige. As quantifiable prestige (physical or material) is not easily achieved, it is "transferred to attributes of the prestigious persons," which are easier to imitate and acquire; such non-quantifiable attributes include language (Joseph 1987: 31). Prestige patterns relate to language variation and change, since in all societies there are different languages, regional dialects, and different ways of speaking (styles, registers, codes, or discourses), and speakers attribute different statuses to these different varieties in an ideological "hierarchy of languages" (Grillo 1989: 1–3) and select the linguistic forms they use accordingly. The reconstruction of prestige patterns in language history, therefore, deals with the reconstruction of attitudes of language users towards certain languages and varieties and the reconstruction of relationships between groups of people and the social dynamics of the community. It is also about exploring language in use and placing a language in its social, economic, and political contexts. To understand this type of "ecology of language," Haugen (1972: 336–37) suggests that the following questions have to be answered:

The Handbook of Historical Sociolinguistics, First Edition. Edited by Juan Manuel Hernández-Campoy and Juan Camilo Conde-Silvestre.
© 2014 John Wiley & Sons, Ltd. Published 2014 by John Wiley & Sons, Ltd.

(1) What is the classification of the language in relation to other languages?
(2) Who are the users?
(3) What are the domains of use?
(4) What concurrent languages are used?
(5) What internal varieties does the language show?
(6) What is the nature of written traditions?
(7) What kind of institutional support has the language won, e.g. in government, education, private organizations?
(8) What are the attitudes of the users towards the language?

As Haugen's list indicates, the reconstruction of prestige patterns is a multidisciplinary enterprise with links to many research fields, such as sociolinguistics, network studies, social history, and cultural evolution. In this chapter we examine the reconstruction of prestige patterns with respect to a range of interpretations of the concept. We focus first on prestige as a cultural and linguistic phenomenon and then consider the characteristics of prestigious individuals and their significance in language change (as per Henrich and Gil-White 2001; Milroy and Milroy 1985; Labov 1994, 2001; Rogers 1962/2003). Evidence that can be retrieved for people's attitudes to and awareness of language in the past (Burke 2004) will also be discussed, as will studies in historical sociolinguistics for the direct or indirect evidence of prestige which they provide, as prestige as such is not always the explicit focus of such studies. Finally, as prestige is not a stable attribute, and the loss of prestige by a high social group will lead to the loss of prestige of their language variant, the dynamics of this development are also addressed.

2. Prestige as a Cultural and Linguistic Phenomenon

Prestige is a significant factor in human societies affecting our everyday lives and the choices we make on many levels, not just that of language. Studies of cultural evolution suggest that prestige, as an evolutionary mechanism of cultural transmission, is essential for increasing the adaptive capacity of humans (see Henrich and Gil-White 2001). It is hypothesized that to improve the quality of information acquired through cultural transmission and the cost-effectiveness of this acquisition, people focus on prestigious rather than randomly-selected individuals as models. Henrich and Gil-White (2001: 175) further claim that humans are "default infocopiers," who first try to learn directly from others, thus easily adopting group values and norms and relying on prestigious individuals as models, only later seeking improvements through individual learning. Similarly, Rogers (1962/2003: 19) maintains that the diffusion of new ideas depends on the experience of near peers and is realized by way of modeling and imitating those who have already adopted an innovation.

According to Henrich and Gil-White's (2001: 171) interpretation, prestige is 'freely conferred deference' to an individual who excels in valued domains of activity (whatever they might be in a specific context), and is to be distinguished from dominance by force – although the same individual may have both prestige and dominance status. Prestige hierarchies can consequently be domain-specific, as valuable assets may vary depending on time and place (2001: 170). Along the same lines, communication accommodation theory (CAT) proposes that individuals' accommodation to each others' communicative behavior reflects their need to gain social approval or to identify with others. Moreover, the addressee's high social status influences the intensity of this need (Giles, Coupland, and Coupland 1991: 7, 18–19).

As we understand it today, linguistic prestige is often conferred on the standard variety, and standard languages tend to originate in a variety spoken by a prestige group with political or economic power and education. Moreover, the standard often has a literary history, having been the variety used by 'great' authors, and is spoken in a centrally located area (Stein 1994). However, the relationship of the standard to prestige is not a straightforward one, and may be even more complex when there is no codified standard on which people can model their language use. This was the case in the European context until the seventeenth and eighteenth centuries, when normative grammars, dictionaries, and regulating language academies started to emerge (Baggioni 1997; Burke 2004). However, social hierarchy and in-group motivations certainly also apply in these cases (Nevalainen and Raumolin-Brunberg 2003: 154). Echoing Henrich and Gil-White (2001), 'domain-specific prestige hierarchies' also seem to concern attitudes to language varieties. Milroy and Milroy (1985: 108–14) discuss this phenomenon in terms of a paradox: linguistic stratification is a reflection of social stratification with individuals who want to adopt the prestigious standard variety, but at the same time, socially disfavored varieties persist. This can be understood in terms of 'domain-specific' prestige in that the standard variety has *overt, status-oriented* prestige that is part of the process of social climbing up the status and/or power hierarchy. In seventeenth-century France, for example, the successful language varieties were said to be those of *la cour et la ville*, the court and the capital (Burke 2004: 99), and the importance of the court and London as models and gatekeepers of language change is also recognized in the history of English (Nevalainen and Raumolin-Brunberg 2003). In the term 'court,' Burke (2004: 99) includes the nobility as well as the clerks in the Chancery offices, whose language was "not infrequently taken as a model for writing by private individuals" particularly in the fifteenth and sixteenth centuries. In the seventeenth century, linguistic prestige came to be restricted to the upper end of French society (Burke 2004: 100). However, this type of status is not the valued asset in all contexts: non-standard varieties may have *covert, identity-oriented* prestige that is important in creating and maintaining group cohesion and in signaling an individual's belonging or aspiration to belong to a particular group (Milroy and Milroy 1985: 108–14). However, according to Labov (2001: 223), there is not much evidence of such conflicts involving overt and covert values, but "it may be that the further search for the social location of the leaders of linguistic change will throw light on this question." In the following section, we explore further the role of individuals and their networks in relation to linguistic prestige, and to language change in particular.

3. Prestigious Individuals and Language Change

Prestige has an important if not an uncontroversial role in language change, as it may contribute to the selection of a linguistic form. Prestigious individuals may be those whose language is imitated and have the power to propagate new linguistic forms in their community. Network studies in particular have addressed the role of individuals in change. In relation to the reconstruction of relationships between groups of people, prestige can be considered through Rogers's (1962/2003) framework of adopter categories in a social network, in which individuals are classified through their innovativeness in comparison with other members of the system.

'Opinion leaders' have an essential role in the spread and establishment of innovations, and they are the individuals who award prestige to linguistic forms. Rogers (1962/2003: 37–38) defines opinion leadership as "the degree to which an individual is able to influence informally other individuals' attitudes or overt behaviour in a desired way with relative frequency." 'Early adopters,' who are respected, successful, and well-integrated into their social network, have the greatest degree of opinion leadership, and they convey subjective evaluations to near-peers by means of interpersonal networks (Rogers 1962/2003: 27, 283). As a rule, prestigious individuals occupy an important position in the social system. They are found among the members of the French royal court, or the sixteenth-century clerks in the Chancery. If the upper levels of society had not adopted a new form in the period of early Modern English, it would not have been diffused (Nevalainen and Raumolin-Brunberg 2003: 150, 154). An eighteenth-century Spanish writer compares the legitimation of a new word with the legitimation of claims to status: if the word was "of known origin and expressive," two or three classic authors would be sufficient "testimonies to prove its nobility" (Burke 2004: 158). The legitimacy of a new word is thus directly linked to the value of its heritage, and the status of those who have been observed to use it.

Generally speaking, the innovators are neither prestigious nor overtly influential. They are relative outsiders in a local network, and thus freed from the constraints of that system, with wide-reaching interpersonal networks. Their judgment of new ideas is often distrusted and their influence is limited, but they are the gatekeepers who bring in new ideas from outside the system's boundaries (Rogers 1962/2003: 22, 281, 318). It is up to the opinion leaders to evaluate and potentially adopt these ideas. Opinion leaders react to change according to the norms of the society: they favor innovation when the system is so inclined, and are less innovative when the norms do not favor change (Rogers 1962/2003: 27, 318). Even if their criticism derives from personal prejudices, it is still often considered correct (Baugh and Cable 1951/2002: 259). In historical sociolinguistic research it is difficult to identify explicitly the source of an innovation or the innovators.

From the sociolinguistic point of view, Labov's (2001: 509) twentieth-century analysis of leaders of change emphasizes the role of upwardly-mobile women:

[I]n urban society [they] are able and energetic, non-conformist women who absorb and maintain lower class linguistic forms in their youth, and maintain them in their upwardly mobile trajectory in later years.

Overall, Labov's leaders and Rogers's early adopters have many similar qualities, such as their strong network ties and a respected position in their social system. Nevalainen and Raumolin-Brunberg (2003) suggest that, though there are no simple parallels between language change and its social embedding in the Early Modern English period, women were instrumental in language change, while the upper ranks were instrumental in generalizing and supralocalizing new forms (see also Chambers 1995), and that region (particularly the capital) and gender were the most influential external variables to correlate with ongoing change (Nevalainen and Raumolin-Brunberg 2003: 150, 200, 208).

How, then, do new forms spread and come to be established? A crucial point to consider is the phase of change. Milroy and Milroy (1985) argue that tight-knit networks do not promote change like loose-knit networks, which are formed of weak network ties, and that change is led by gatekeepers who have weak ties in the social system. Labov (2001), on the other hand, argues that the leaders of change are central and influential network members who have high-frequency contacts both within and outside their network. Raumolin-Brunberg (2006) considers the incipient leaders of the second person singular *you* and the first-wave leaders of the third person singular *-(e)s* in sixteenth and seventeenth century England, and her analysis seems to reconcile these approaches. The early leaders of change described in Raumolin-Brunberg (2006) were geographically mobile people with a number of weak links (as per Milroy and Milroy 1985), whereas the leaders of the new and vigorous stage of change can be compared with Labov's (2001: 130–31) central and influential network members. Raumolin-Brunberg (2006: 132) suggests that James and Lesley Milroy and William Labov focus on different phases of linguistic change: "[t]he Milroys seem to concentrate on the incipient phase, while Labov's arguments explicitly deal with new and vigorous changes." In other words, people with weak network ties lead the incipient stage of change, and when the innovation takes off, it is taken over by established network members or opinion leaders. A dense, multiplex network linked with strong network ties also functions as a norm enforcer, while loose-knit structures have been argued to promote linguistic variation (Milroy 1980/1987; see also Chapter 18 in this *Handbook*).

For social modeling to occur, individuals must be aware of the behavior of those in the network who have already adopted the innovation (Rogers 1962/2003: 359–60). Social prestige is the trigger for linguistic prestige, and when the origin of language change is considered in its social environment, we begin to perceive the elements which underlie it. Keller (1994: 88) argues that social success in its broad sense ("striving for everything concerning our social co-existence") is a driving force behind language change. Change from above is driven by high prestige groups, often takes place with full awareness, and occurs more frequently in formal styles. Change from below, on the other hand, begins in the vernacular, may be introduced by any social class (although Labov argues that the highest-status social groups have not been shown to act as innovators), and is barely noticed until it nears completion (Labov 1994: 78; Labov 2001: 274). Changes from above are often subject to hypercorrection, which is viewed as an aspect of social mobility rather than social insecurity (Labov 2001: 274, 277). For example, in sixteenth-century England, the intermediate ranks were generally more advanced in their use of innovative forms than the nobility or the lower ranks (Nevalainen 1996a).

Labov's Gender Paradox further proposes that women adopt prestige forms at a higher rate than men, whereas in change from below they act as the innovators: "[w]omen conform more closely than men to sociolinguistic norms that are overtly prescribed, but conform less than men when they are not" (Labov 2001: 293, 283). Nevertheless, Nevalainen and Raumolin-Brunberg (2003: 131) show that although Labov's "'long-standing cultural pattern' was already clearly in evidence" in Tudor and Stuart England, the Sex/Prestige pattern (see Hudson 1980/1996) is not a sociolinguistic universal; women of the early modern English period did not promote language change that emerged from the spheres of higher learning and professional use.

4. Historical Evidence of Linguistic Prestige

According to Burke (2004), language awareness increased in the early modern period, as shown in numerous treatises on language written in various parts of Europe at the time. These writings provide ample evidence of contemporary attitudes to language and testify to people's awareness of different aspects of language variation and their social evaluations of languages, sociolects, dialects, and accents (Burke 2004: 15–42). They also reveal that the complaint tradition and reactions against language change have a long history. In these writings different ways of speaking were generally identified as 'low' and 'high' varieties often corresponding to and reflecting social hierarchies, and Latin, for example, was criticized as the language of the ecclesiastical elite. In addition, other written sources such as dictionaries, travel descriptions, advertisements, and conduct and letter-writing manuals contain evaluations and attitudes by contemporaries (Burke 2004: 10–12). For instance, letter-writing manuals of the medieval and early modern periods clearly recognized social prestige patterns, and recommendations paid attention to the social standing of the recipient (see Palander-Collin 2010). One of the earliest English manuals, Angel Day's *The English Secretorie* (1586: 13), advised readers that the first thing to consider when writing a letter was "the estate and reputation of the partie, as whether hee be our better, our equal, or inferiour." Descriptions of runaway slaves and apprentices in advertisements sometimes contained notes of their speech habits ("plain," "slow," "broad Yorkshire," "speaks the Scotch tongue") (Burke 2004: 11–12). An Englishman traveling in France in the mid-seventeenth century noted that there was a "whining kind of querulous tone" in French peasants' speech, undoubtedly explained by "the pitiful subjection they are brought unto" (Burke 2004: 30). A glimpse of the contemporary perceptions of language and gender is seen in a sixteenth-century Englishman's assertion that "whereas commonly in all countries the women speak most neatly [...] [in Ireland they speak] so peevishly and faintly as though they were half sick and ready to call for a posset," a statement which might be one of the first formulations of female hypercorrectness (Burke 2004: 34). Seventeenth- and eighteenth-century satires (plays, poems, and even Samuel Johnson's *Dictionary*) that deal with the 'jargon' of learned women are characterized by Burke (2004: 35) as "the most sustained account of the sociolect of a group of women in the whole early modern period." In the seventeenth century, rural dialects were considered to be "corrupt and crude," "clownish language," and "rusticall speech." In advising his son on polite behavior, Lord Chesterfield (1787: 16) comments on several kinds of awkwardness, "such as, false English, bad pronunciation, old sayings, and common proverbs; which are so many proofs of having kept bad and low company." On the other hand, contemporary positive attitudes towards the vernacular languages can be detected, for instance, in the number of translations of literary texts into dialects (Burke 2004: 36–37).

Studies in historical sociolinguistics do not necessarily deal with prestige *per se*, but this aspect can be teased out when they are at least indirectly concerned with prestigious languages (such as in code-switching) or language variants (such as standard vs. stigmatized forms). In the following we look at case studies as evidence of contemporary evaluations of and reactions to prestige. Studies of code-switching in the history of English allow us to trace the recognition and standing of prestigious languages in actual usage. From the Old English to the Early Modern English period, Latin was the most frequently occurring foreign language in English texts (Pahta and Nurmi 2006: 205), which reflects its long-standing position as the international language of religion, administration, legislation, learning, and diplomacy. A notable exception is fifteenth- and sixteenth-century merchants' prominent use of French, which arose for practical reasons, mostly to do with foreign trade (Nurmi and Pahta 2004: 435). Nurmi and Pahta (2004) anticipated that fifteenth-century English letters might have contained remnants of the once prestigious Norman French, but this did not turn out to be the case. The material is "expressly selected as representative of English at the time," and might not reflect the overall language choices of the period (Nurmi and Pahta 2004: 447); however, according to Kahane and Kahane (1979: 186), the English nobility "switched allegiance to their English habitat" after the loss of Normandy in early thirteenth century, and considered itself totally English after 1250, so the results may reflect the disappearance of Norman French quite accurately. In eighteenth-century English correspondence, Latin switches still reflect the status of the language as the lingua franca of the educated, while the frequent switches to French and Italian can be viewed as an indication of the increasingly multiplex contacts of the upper classes to Europe (Pahta and Nurmi 2007). This is linked to the expansion of French in the seventeenth and eighteenth centuries to become the language of the European courts and eventually something of a lingua franca (Kahane and Kahane 1979; Burke 2004). However, the dominance of the French language also raised criticism. Samuel Johnson is told to have spoken Latin to his French visitors (Burke 2004: 87); Johnson also championed the "original Teutonick character" of English (Potkay 2000: 287); and rising nationalism and xenophobia eventually ended the considerable prestige of French in eighteenth-century Germany (Kahane and Kahane 1979: 189).

The next cases deal with social aspirations and language use. Labov maintains that the primary characteristic of twentieth-century leaders of linguistic change is their upward social mobility (2001: 509), and standardization and social ambition in present-day English speech communities are often observed to correlate positively with each other (Chambers 1995: 99). Social aspirers seem to be particularly aware of linguistic stigmas and accommodate their language use accordingly (Nevalainen and Raumolin-Brunberg 2003: 153). In what could be characterized as examples of change from above, successful sixteenth-century social climbers appear to have contributed the most to the disappearance of multiple negation in English (Nevalainen 1996b: 281; Nevalainen and Raumolin-Brunberg 2003: 150), and social aspirers of the period, aware of the then stigmatized status of the affirmative DO, used it significantly less than other groups (Nurmi 1999: 103, 105–6; see also Nevalainen and Raumolin-Brunberg 2003: 152–53; Raumolin-Brunberg 2009: 183). Aspirers were hesitant in their reaction to incoming forms in the sixteenth and seventeenth centuries, but quick to adopt when the stigma appears to have lifted (Nevalainen and Raumolin-Brunberg 2003: 152–53). Raumolin-Brunberg's (2009) study of lifespan changes in letters of three sixteenth and seventeenth century Englishmen shows grammatical changes to have taken place, probably linked to their social aspirations. The eighteenth-century bluestocking Elizabeth Montagu changed her language use significantly during the years of her transition towards literary and social recognition (Sairio 2009): among these changes are a significant increase of pied piping and a considerable decrease of the stigmatized preposition stranding, categorical avoidance of contracted verbs in letters to people of higher social status, and a temporary drop in contracted auxiliary verbs. They can be connected not only to the emerging normative tradition and changing printers' practices, but also to Montagu's increasingly influential social standing and her ventures into authorship, as well as her awareness of social hierarchy (Sairio 2009: 312–13).

Codification of a language does not, of course, make it inevitably the dominant dialect or sociolect (Burke 2004: 92), but standard variants are often associated with high prestige (Milroy 2001). In early modern England a codified standard did not yet exist, but the prestigious London/Court variety can be considered the incipient standard language of the period (Raumolin-Brunberg 2009: 172). The prestige of the emerging standard variants seems to have been particularly significant in eighteenth-century England, during which time both demands for the uniformity of spelling and criticism of variant forms increased (Haugland 1995; Baugh and Cable 1951/2002). Moreover, actual usage witnessed an increase in standard verb spellings and a decrease of contractions, which in certain cases began to be viewed as old-fashioned (Oldireva-Gustafsson 2002). Spelling had a social significance at the time (Tieken-Boon van Ostade 2006), and gender had a significant influence on eighteenth-century English letter-writers' choices between full and contracted verb spellings (Sairio 2009). Contractions occurred significantly more often in correspondence between female friends, in the most intimate and familiar kind of written communication (Sairio 2009), which suggests that they enjoyed covert, identity-oriented prestige. The overt, status-oriented prestige of standardized verb forms appears to have been less important in this context.

The suggestion that varieties used by high prestige speakers also come to enjoy prestige (Kahane 1986; Milroy 2001) is witnessed in eighteenth-century English grammarians' practice of presenting good usage through examples from individual authors. For example, George Campbell (1776) defines reputable use as "[w]hatever modes of speech are authorized as good by the writings of a good number, if not the majority of celebrated authors" (in Baugh and Cable 1951/2002: 284), and Finegan (1998: 551) notes that "[w]ith Lowth (1762: 52) grammarians were on safer ground citing as 'great authorities' Milton, Dryden, Addison, Prior, and Pope, whose written usage could be verified." Wright (1994) presents a list of the most frequently quoted sources in William Ward's *Essay on Grammar* (1765) and Fogg's *Principles of English Grammar* (1792–96). *The Spectator* and Joseph Addison are cited the most often, followed by Pope, Shakespeare, Dryden, Milton, and a number of early (but not later) eighteenth-century writers (Wright 1994: 244–45). In 1710 and 1711 Joseph Addison and Jonathan Swift criticized contractions in the *Tatler* and the *Spectator*; their comments were not immediately effective, but in the 1720s the grammarians also began to voice criticism, and the eventual influence of Swift and Addison can be detected in the numerous quotes of their arguments (Haugland 1995: 173–74). It should be noted that in the latter part of the century grammarians also began to scrutinize the best authors for instances of incorrect language and style (Fitzmaurice 1998).

5. Changes in Prestige Patterns

As prestige patterns emerge in varying social, economic, and political conditions, we can expect changes in the prestige and status of languages over time. For example, the status of English in 1596 was only marginal: an Italian treatise on diplomacy "declared that an ambassador should know seven languages – Latin, Greek, Italian, French, Spanish, German and Turkish – but not English. Until the eighteenth century, English had little prestige as far as continental Europeans were concerned" (Burke 2004: 115). Baggioni's (1997) three 'ecolinguistic' revolutions in European history around the years 1500, 1800 and 2000 map broad changes in the prestige of languages and link changes in the linguistic landscape with socio-political changes. The first ecolinguistic revolution is characterized by the demise of Latin as a prestigious language of formal usage and the increasing use of vernacular languages. The competition of the vernacular languages with Latin is linked to such societal trends as the development of nation states and the Reformation, which resulted in vernacular Bible translations and religious texts.

The printing press also gradually contributed to the spread of vernacular literature (Baggioni 1997: 112). The second revolution is characterized by the rise of the national consciousness and standard languages in different parts of Europe, particularly the elevation of vernaculars to the status of national languages and the consolidation of the ideology of 'one state, one nation, one language.' The most recent period is witnessing the spread of English as the language of international communication in the age of cheap travel, global business, and free movement of students and labor in the European Union.

Kahane (1986: 498), who discusses the major European prestige languages from antiquity through to modernity, including the Greek *koiné*, Latin, French, Old Provençal, and Italian, maintains that the rise of a prestige language is always followed by its decline. Kahane and Kahane (1979) establish a frequent pattern of sequences leading to the decline of a prestige language. The starting point is a diglossic system reflecting a class structure where a high-prestige variety coexists with a low-prestige variety. In the next stage, the low variety replaces the high variety, but the high variety does not disappear completely. It continues to be used, for example, in the lexicon of the new developing prestige variety that is the language of the educated middle strata, such as – in the medieval period – the clergy, administrators, and professionals. The low-prestige vernacular tends to supersede the high variety, as, for one thing, the prestige variety usually has to be learned separately in the educational system, which puts pressure on individual language acquisition. Moreover, education is not available to everyone. Other factors identified by Kahane and Kahane (1979) include sociological causes such as changes in class structure, religion, communications, and education as well as symbolic values attached to a language and language loyalty. According to Kahane (1986: 499), when the vernacular becomes the *koiné*, or "the linguistic medium of an ever-widening community," the prestige language is weakened. For example, the gradual decline of Latin and the subsequent loss of a lingua franca resulted in the increased importance of studying vernacular languages (Burke 2004: 113).

Dorian (1998) provides another perspective on the role of prestige in language maintenance and loss by looking at the prospects of small, indigenous languages vis-à-vis dominant prestige languages. In Dorian's words (1998: 17), "we understand the motivating factors in language shift [to the dominant language] far better than we understand the psychosocial underpinnings of long-sustained language maintenance." It is easy to understand that people whose language is associated with low prestige are willing to abandon their ancestral language in favor of the dominant language, particularly if dialects or ethnic minority languages are considered poor and crude, while the standard is seen as a rich and precise instrument of rational expression. But why should people in some cases retain the ancestral language? Dorian (1998: 5) describes tolerance towards cultural and linguistic diversity as a factor favoring the maintenance of small languages and suggests that in Western Europe the beginning of the industrial age and the rise of nationalism – Baggioni's (1997) second ecolinguistic revolution – coincide with less tolerant attitudes towards subordinate languages.

6. Conclusion

How does one proceed in the reconstruction of prestige patterns in language history? Historical research sheds light on the overtly prestigious high status groups in a given social system, and it is often possible to make hypotheses of prestige on the level of the individual. A wide range of contemporary texts provides evidence of people's attitudes to and awareness of languages and language varieties. But it is also necessary to determine what sort of prestige we are tracking. For example, do we consider prestige as a way of claiming higher status or group membership? Is the prestige variety on the ascent, which was the case with vernacular languages in the early modern period, or on the decline, like Latin at the same time? The standard language variety is often prestigious, but it does not necessarily entail covert, identity-oriented prestige. When carrying out, for example, micro-level research into a social network in which it may be difficult to predict the linguistic in-group signals, prestigious forms and prestigious network members may be identifiable from evidence of linguistic accommodation.

Prestige is related to language change, and studies on networks can shed more light on the role of individuals in the process. For instance, innovations do not have prestige until they are evaluated and potentially adopted by the individuals seen as opinion leaders (Rogers 1962/2003) or leaders of change (Labov 1994, 2001), a process which tends to take place in a tight-knit social network (Milroy 1980/1987; Rogers 1962/2003). Women pick up linguistic innovations (change from below) and adopt prestige forms (change from above) at a higher rate than men (Labov 1994, 2001), which links gender to the pursuit of status-oriented prestige, in particular, but also identity-oriented prestige, if we accept that non-standard vernacular varieties, which have an important role in the creation and maintaining of group cohesion and membership, reflect change from below.

Our final point in this chapter concerns the choice of academic research topics and shows that prestige plays a significant role. The historical linguist Henry Wyld (1934), when considering what kind of research into the English language would be relevant and valuable in the 1920s, argued for the superiority of the Received Standard (Milroy 2001). However, because of the contributions of rural dialects to the standard variety and the perception of their subsequent independent history (a very important point), rural dialects were awarded a degree of legitimacy (Milroy 2001). Burke (2004: 23, 169) points out that having little contact with foreign languages they were considered "free from contamination." Urban vernaculars, on the other hand, were seen as "illegitimate, not representative of 'language' at all and not part of the legitimate study of any particular language," as not having a history, and as a threat to the standard language. To study these variants for their own sake in the United Kingdom was not considered academically respectable, with the result that one of the earliest urban studies was carried out by a Norwegian scholar in 1960 (Milroy 2001: 547–48). Wyld and his ilk were prestigious enough to stigmatize the study of urban dialects for several decades of the twentieth century.

REFERENCES

Baggioni, D. (1997) *Langues et nations en Europe*, Payot, Paris.

Baugh, A.C. and Cable, T. (1951/2002) *A History of the English Language* (4th edn), Prentice Hall, Upper Saddle River, NJ.

Burke, P. (2004) *Languages and Communities in Early Modern Europe*, Cambridge University Press, Cambridge.

Campbell, G. (1776) *The Philosophy of Rhetoric*, W. Strahan and T. Cadell, London and W. Creech, Edinburgh.

Chambers, J.K. (1995) *Sociolinguistic Theory*, Blackwell, Oxford.

Chesterfield, P.D. Stanhope, Earl of (1787) *Lord Chesterfield's Advice to His Son, on Men and Manners. . . .* W. Gordon, Edinburgh. [*Eighteenth Century Collections Online*, Gale Cengage Learning, accessed on 25/11/2010.]

Day, A. (1586) *The English Secretorie. Wherein is contayned, A Perfect Method, for the inditing of all manner of Epistles and familiar Letters, . . .* R. Waldegrave, London [*Early English Books Online*, Chadwyck-Healey, accessed on 25/11/2010.]

Dorian, N.C. (1998) Western language ideologies and small-language prospects. In L.A. Grenoble and L.J. Whaley (eds.), *Endangered Languages: Language Loss and Community Response*, Cambridge University Press, Cambridge, pp. 3–21.

Finegan, E. (1998) English Grammar and Usage. In S. Romaine (ed.), *Cambridge History of the English Language, Vol. 4: 1776–1997*, Cambridge University Press, Cambridge, pp. 536–88.

Fitzmaurice, S. (1998) The commerce of language in the pursuit of politeness in eighteenth-century England. *English Studies* 4: 309–28.

Giles, H., Coupland, N., and Coupland, J. (1991) Accommodation theory: communication, context, and consequence. In H. Giles, J. Coupland, and N. Coupland (eds.), *Contexts of Accommodation: Developments in Applied Sociolinguistics*, Cambridge University Press, Cambridge, pp. 1–68.

Grillo, R. (1989) *Dominant Languages: Language and Hierarchy in Britain and France*, Cambridge University Press, Cambridge.

Haugen, E. (1972) *The Ecology of Language*, Stanford University Press, Stanford.

Haugland, K. (1995) "Is't allow'd or ain't it?" On contraction in early grammars and spelling books. *Studia Neophilologica* 67(2): 165–84.

Henrich, J. and J. Gil-White, F. (2001) The evolution of prestige: freely conferred deference as a mechanism for enhancing the benefits of cultural transmission. *Evolution and Human Behavior* 22: 165–96.

Hudson, R. (1980/1996) *Sociolinguistics* (2nd edn), Cambridge University Press, Cambridge.

Joseph, J.E. (1987) *Eloquence and Power: The Rise of Language Standards and Standard Languages*, Blackwell, Oxford.

Kahane, H. (1986) A typology of the prestige language. *Language* 62(3): 495–508.

Kahane, H. and Kahane, R. (1979) Decline and survival of Western prestige languages. *Language* 55(1): 183–98.

Keller, R. (1994) *On Language Change: The Invisible Hand in Language*, Routledge, London.

Labov, W. (1994) *Principles of Linguistic Change, Vol. 1: Internal Factors*, Blackwell, Oxford.

Labov, W. (2001) *Principles of Linguistic Change, Vol. 2: Social Factors*, Blackwell, Oxford.

Lowth, R. (1762) *A Short Introduction to English Grammar*, A. Millar, R. and J. Dodsley, London.

Milroy, J. (2001) Language ideologies and the consequences of standardization. *Journal of Sociolinguistics* 5(4): 530–55.

Milroy, J. and Milroy, L. (1985) *Authority in Language: Investigating Language Prescription and Standardization*, Routledge, London.

Milroy, L. (1980/1987) *Language and Social Networks* (2nd edn), Blackwell, Oxford.

Nevalainen, T. (1996a) Social Stratification. In T. Nevalainen and H. Raumolin-Brunberg (eds.), *Sociolinguistics and Language History: Studies Based on the Corpus of Early English Correspondence*, Rodopi, Amsterdam, pp. 57–76.

Nevalainen, T. (1996b) Social mobility and the decline of multiple negation in Early Modern English. In J. Fisiak and M. Krygier (eds.), *Advances in English Historical Linguistics*, Mouton de Gruyter, Berlin, pp. 263–91.

Nevalainen, T. and Raumolin-Brunberg, H. (2003) *Historical Sociolinguistics: Language Change in Tudor and Stuart England*, Longman Pearson Education, London.

Nurmi, A. (1999) *A Social History of Periphrastic* DO, Société Néophilologique, Helsinki.

Nurmi, A. and Pahta, P. (2004) Social stratification and patterns of code-switching in Early English letters. *Multilingua* 23: 417–56.

Oldireva-Gustafsson, L. (2002) *Preterite and Past Participle Forms in English 1680–1790: Standardisation Processes in Public and Private Writing*, Uppsala University, Uppsala.

Pahta, P. and Nurmi, A. (2006) Code-switching in the Helsinki Corpus: a thousand years of multilingual practices. In N. Ritt, H. Schendl, C. Dalton-Puffer, and D. Kastovsky (eds.), *Medieval English and its Heritage: Structure, Meaning and Mechanisms of Change*, Peter Lang, Frankfurt, pp. 203–20.

Pahta, P. and Nurmi, A. (2007) What we do *cón amore*: on structures of code-switching in eighteenth-century letters. In J. Pérez-Guerra, D. González-Álvarez, J.L. Bueno-Alonso, and E. Rama-Martínez (eds.), *'Of Varying Language and Opposing Creed': New Insights into Late Modern English*, Peter Lang, Bern, pp. 401–20.

Palander-Collin, M. (2010) Correspondence. In A.H. Jucker and I. Taavitsainen (eds.),

Handbook of Pragmatics: Historical Pragmatics, Mouton de Gruyter, Berlin, pp. 677–703.

Potkay, A. (2000) 'The structure of his sentences is French': Johnson and Hume in the history of English. *Language Sciences* 22: 285–93.

Raumolin-Brunberg, H. (2006) Leaders of linguistic change in Early Modern England. In R. Facchinetti, and M. Rissanen (eds.), *Corpus-based Studies of Diachronic English*, Peter Lang, Bern, pp. 115–34.

Raumolin-Brunberg, H. (2009) Lifespan changes in the language of three early modern gentlemen. In A. Nurmi, M. Nevala, and M. Palander-Collin (eds.), *The Language of Daily Life in England (1400–1800)*, John Benjamins, Amsterdam, pp. 165–96.

Rogers, E.M. (1962/2003) *Diffusion of Innovations* (5th edn), Free Press, New York.

Sairio, A. (2009) *Language and Letters of the Bluestocking Network: Sociolinguistic Issues in Eighteenth-Century Epistolary English*, Société Néophilologique, Helsinki.

Stein, D. (1994) Sorting out the variants: standardization and social factors in the English language 1600–1800. In D. Stein and I. Tieken-Boon van Ostade (eds.), pp. 1–17.

Stein, D. and Tieken-Boon van Ostade, I. (eds.) (1994) *Towards a Standard English 1600–1800*, Mouton de Gruyter, Berlin.

Tieken-Boon van Ostade, I. (2006) English at the onset of the normative tradition. In L. Mugglestone (ed.), *The Oxford History of English*, Oxford University Press, Oxford, pp. 240–73.

Wright, S. (1994) The critic and the grammarians: Joseph Addison and the prescriptivists. In D. Stein and I. Tieken-Boon van Ostade (eds.), pp. 243–84.

Wyld, H.C. (1934) The best English: a claim for the superiority of Received Standard English. *Society for Pure English* 4, Tract XXXIX, Clarendon Press, Oxford.

35 Written Vernaculars in Medieval and Renaissance Times

CATHARINA PEERSMAN

1. Introduction

In the first decade of the fourteenth century, Dante wrote his *De vulgari eloquentia*, a Latin treatise on eloquence in the vernacular. According to Boitani's literary history (2007), Dante, Boccaccio, and Petrarch connect the Middle Ages to modernity, with Italy becoming a cultural centre from which attitudes, ways of thinking, and writing were exported to the rest of the continent. Strikingly, Boitani defines two 'Middle Ages' before the cultural rise of Italy: the Latin and the French Middle Ages. Using a language to identify periods within the Middle Ages does not determine precisely when they occurred, but unlike a broad reference such as 'about 1500,' hints at sociolinguistic tendencies over a longer period of time. Fundamental to these tendencies is the rise of written vernaculars in Western Europe and growing literacy, which are considered to have unprecedented powers to engender historical change.

The topic of this chapter – written vernaculars in medieval and Renaissance times – is highly complex, covering not only a large period of time, but also a vast geographical area and diverse text genres. 'Medieval and Renaissance times' embraces more than a millennium during which social, political, religious, cultural, and economic (r)evolutions took place, not to mention the evolution of ideas and changes in mentality. Since it is impossible to address the inevitable nuances in such evolutions or the difficulties of chronological delimitation within the space of this chapter, we will address the topic of written vernaculars from a historical sociolinguistic point of view using a few key concepts. In doing so, we will be

The Handbook of Historical Sociolinguistics, First Edition. Edited by Juan Manuel Hernández-Campoy and Juan Camilo Conde-Silvestre.
© 2014 John Wiley & Sons, Ltd. Published 2014 by John Wiley & Sons, Ltd.

covering Western Europe during the Middle Ages, traditionally defined as beginning with the fall of the Western Roman Empire in 476 and ending during the eventful second half of the fifteenth century. This period includes a Carolingian renaissance in the eighth century and a twelfth-century renaissance, as well as the Italian quattrocento/cinquecento. Among the events traditionally considered to be crucial are the fall of Constantinople in 1453, the rapid spread of the printing press from 1454 onwards, and the discovery of the New World in 1492.[1] First, we will place the rise of the written vernaculars within the context of Latin literacy. This enables us to address the value of glosses, quotations, and macaronic texts. This brief description of the phenomenon on the textual level is followed by outlines of the diachronic and geographic spread of the written vernaculars. The last part of the chapter concentrates on the changes in mentality and language attitudes underlying the rise of the written vernaculars.

2. Latin Literacy

Throughout the Middle Ages, christianized Western Europe consisted of a variety of pre-nation states, a patchwork of socio-cultural and language communities. The only cohesive factor, apart from ecclesiastical influence, which was widespread, was the general use of Latin as a written language.[2] Literacy mostly meant literacy in Latin, generating a fundamental split between the spoken tongues, the vernaculars, of everyday oral use and the prestigious Latin used for writing. On the periphery of Latin culture stood England, with its Anglo-Saxon and Germanic civilization, at a meeting-point of languages and cultures.[3] As Clanchy (1979/1993: 16–21) rightly observes in his introduction to the revised edition of *From Memory to Written Record*, innovation can be easier on the fringes of a culture. Because of its position, therefore, England could assume a critical role not only in establishing the practice of writing in the vernacular, but also in the promotion of Latin literacy through the creation of a bureaucracy unprecedented since the fall of the Roman Empire. After all, the laws of Aethelbert of Kent had been written down in Old English, not Latin, as early as 597, and French first developed as a written language not in France, but in England in the century after the Norman Conquest.[4]

The shift from memory to written record, however, was not an exclusively English phenomenon: it was, at the least, western European. How and when the vernaculars came to be fully accepted as written languages is still an important question, both to linguists and historians, given that the evidence has still to be recorded and assessed across the region, the data so far available being insufficient for statistical analysis. During the nineteenth century, the main philological concern was the search for the oldest extant documents written in vernacular languages and the publication of text editions, tracing the outlines of the earliest appearances of the written vernaculars. During the last decades of the twentieth century, however, printed editions gave way to digitized text corpora, often initially based on printed text transcriptions or editions. Such corpora include the database of Middle Dutch texts *CD-rom Middelnederlands* (INL 1998), the digital

Middle High German Text Archive (Gärtner 2002) and *PhiloBiblon* (a database of Catalan, Galician, Portuguese, and Spanish manuscripts, coordinated by Charles Faulhaber, of the University of California, Berkeley). Today, the mass of unanalyzed medieval materials still hidden in private and official archives motivates researchers to present newly discovered texts immediately in digitized form. This applies, for example, to the French charter database *Chartae Galliae*, which contains digitized versions of existing printed editions as well as newly discovered charters in digitized form. These steadily growing databases allow research into the different types of medieval texts they present, steadily increasing the sources available for sociolinguistic in-depth enquiries.

2.1 Vernacular traces

Despite their different forms, most of the printed editions and databases of medieval texts that are available for sociolinguistic research share one important delimitation: they usually focus on one vernacular, one text genre, or one document collection. However, in order to describe and study the rise of the written vernaculars, we need to take into account all the available texts, across genres and languages, and the socio-historical parameters that allowed their redaction.[5] It is impossible to describe the rise of a vernacular language without assessing its relationship with Latin, which remained the most important written language throughout the Middle Ages. On a strictly textual level, Latin texts are the primary source of vernacular 'traces,' documenting the sketchy phase preceding the appearance of texts written entirely in the vernacular. The rise of the written vernaculars starts with different types of vernacular 'traces' discovered in Latin texts. The term 'traces' covers a variety of vernacular incursions considerably larger than the often barely Latinized names or toponyms and occasional loanwords: to illustrate the gradual evolution towards texts written wholly in the vernacular, we describe glosses, quotations, and macaronic texts.

2.1.1 Glosses Like names or loanwords, glosses can be classified mostly on the level of the individual word, offering interpretations or more current synonyms (*interpretamenta*) for Latin words that had become too rare or too learned to be understood immediately. The value of these sources for diachronic linguistics is obvious. For instance, the Reichenau glossary, dating from the end of the eighth century, consists of two lists of Latin words followed by proto-Romance *interpretamenta*, for example *arenam : sabulo* ('sand') and *semel : una vice* ('once') (Gullichsen 1999: 38, 43). Sometimes, however, a glossary offers much more than word-by-word equivalences. The early eighth-century Kassel glossary explains Latin, but more often Romance, terms in terms of their Old Bavarian synonyms, as in *manus: hant* ('hand') or *bouves : ohsun* ('oxen'). This more traditional part is followed by a small conversation manual in true Assimil-style: it translates practical phrases from Latin to Old Bavarian, such as "indica mihi quomodo nomen habet homo iste: sage mir uueo namun habet deser man" ('tell me the name of this man'). Not all items in the conversation manual are so neutral. The German scribe seized the opportunity to vent his animosity towards his French-speaking contemporaries by inserting a short sequence on the stupidity of the *romani* (those who speak Romance) as opposed to the wisdom of the Bavarians[6] (Gullichsen 1999: 44–46), providing us with an example of personal judgment and language attitude that is as amusing as it is rare. Glossatorial activity was a frequent and widespread practice throughout medieval Europe. As such, it was not necessarily restricted to the interaction of vernacular languages with Latin: it could also provide evidence for language contact between two vernaculars, as Porter (1999: 87, 88) points out for Old English and Old French. When it came to actual translations, the relationship between Latin and vernacular languages was not one-way, either.[7]

2.1.2   Quotations   Like glosses, quotations offer vernacular data inserted in a Latin text. During most of the Middle Ages, they are rather rare, because Latin served traditionally as the common medium of literacy in a multilingual and predominantly oral society. This means that, if a statement was recorded in a certain language (such as Latin), it had not necessarily originally been made in that language (Clanchy 1979/1993: 206). The length of quotations varies from a few words to several phrases. As an example of the latter, one of the earliest and best known on the European continent are the oaths of Strasbourg, recorded in Nithard's ninth[8]-century chronicles *De dissensionibus filiorum Ludovici Pii*. Marking an event of considerable political significance, the oaths were uttered in 842 by Charles the Bald and Louis the German, grandsons of Charlemagne, leaving us with early fragments of what is generally accepted to be proto-Romance on the one hand and Old High German on the other.

2.1.3   Macaronic texts   Although they provide us with valuable information on vernacular languages, glosses and quotations, despite existing within the Latin text, stand as clearly separate portions of that text. This is not the case with loanwords, whether introduced by a formula as *vulgariter dictu* or not. Loanwords are integrated into the Latin text, exerting a certain influence that is strictly limited to the lexical level. Macaronic phrases or entirely macaronic texts[9] attest to a more significant influence of the vernacular on the main Latin text, since grammatical systems are affected. The distinction between loanwords and macaronic texts, illustrating code-mixing and code-switching respectively (Fasold 1984: 180–82), provides a clear boundary between the common practice of loanwords and the type of vernacular incursions in what had been until then a strictly Latin environment.

Given the fact that code-switching marks a reassessment of the relation between two languages, the extant medieval macaronic texts mixing Latin with a vernacular seem to initiate the process of legitimizing the vernacular as an administrative and literary language (Kadens 2001: 115, 117). Moreover, macaronic texts have been preserved in different languages and very diverse text genres. Brunel (1922, 1926) made an extensive study of the rise of the *provençal* vernacular in South France charters, from *latin farci* charters[10] at the end of the tenth century to charters written in *provençal* in which only the salutation and the date formulas were still written in Latin at the end of the eleventh century. Code-switching is also quite frequent in Anglo-Saxon legal texts, influenced by various extra-linguistic variables, such as when the text was produced and the particular type of document, as well as the structural elements of the text (Schendl 2005; see also Chapter 28 in this *Handbook*). Nevertheless, legal texts are not the only text type to record code-switching in England or on the continent. Multilingual sermons and accounts, for instance, exist in several languages. Their literary counterparts seem to make a deliberate choice to demonstrate the capacity of multilingualism. For Old English, Schendl (2005) mentions the bilingual (Latin and Old-English) coda of the poem *Phoenix*. Very similar are the earliest forms of lyrical poetry in Ibero-Romance,[11] the *kharjas*, composed as a coda to an Arabic or Hebrew poem of the *muwashasha* type (Zwartjes 1997). The multilingual songs from the *Codex Buranus*, where Latin artfully intermingles with Middle High German or Old Provençal (Sayce 1992), are still performed today.[12]

Recent research establishes that mixing languages within and across sentences was established practice for business and legal writing and commonly used in composing sermons as well as medical and scientific texts (Davidson 2003: 473, 483). Since macaronic texts have been preserved in different languages and very diverse text genres, they might well have been a common feature of the switch from Latin to the vernacular in writing, a necessary stage preceding the writing of entire texts in the vernacular. However, code-switching in medieval texts was more than just that. On a purely textual level, from the perspective of the rise of the written vernacular, it constituted a necessary phase in the evolution of the vernacular towards an autonomous written medium. Secondly, as multilingual lyrical poetry suggests, code-switching could be used as a literary art form. Finally, like multilinguals today, late medieval speakers who possessed second-language ability could selectively mix languages as expressions of identity. Davidson (2003) analyzes convincingly how patterns of language-mixing as diverse as *The Chronicle of Pierre de Langtoft* (c. 1300), *The Canterbury Tales* (c. 1387–1400) and *Piers Plowman* (c. 1360–87) portray multilingual interactions in which speakers negotiate social positions through language choice. They selectively integrate Latin, French, and English in order to formulate expressions of linguistic membership. For instance, the allegorical Piers Plowman character Conscience linguistically affirms his belief that only bilingual clerks can correctly integrate Latin texts within English speech by using *intrasentential* switches as opposed to the simple *intersentential* quotation of his opponent, who is portrayed as a learned woman (Davidson 2003: 477). This conscious language mixing, serving to construct identity and authority, presupposes clearly defined positions of the languages involved with subsequent language attitudes, which is possible only in the late Middle Ages.

3. From the Page to the Map

Having considered the gradual growth of the vernacular languages on the textual level, we now trace the outlines of their geographic and diachronic evolution. The growing use of written vernaculars all over Latin Europe from the ninth century on implies a gradual diversification of text types. Given the scope of the phenomenon, the mass of unanalyzed materials and the fragmentary digitized corpora, a statistical study of the rise of written vernaculars on a European scale is not yet possible. This explains why a diachronic overview of the rise of the written vernacular across medieval Europe, taking into account different text genres, has not yet been attempted.[13] As a first attempt, the chronological Table 35.1 does not aim at exhaustiveness. It merely sketches the outlines of the rise of vernaculars in medieval Europe in terms of their first attested written appearances.[14] For that reason, the chronological framework ends in the middle of the thirteenth century. The texts mentioned by name (such as *Beowulf*, *Sente Servaes*, and *Ritmo Cassinense*) are usually literary texts.

Despite the necessarily incomplete nature of the table and the fact that dating medieval texts exactly is often impossible, this schematic structure allows us to point out some general tendencies in the rise of the written vernaculars. Geographically speaking, the use of the written vernacular spreads eastwards first, from England to the continent. On the continent, the movement towards the east continues, but at the same time the phenomenon spreads north- and southwards. This does not mean that the rise of the written vernacular was a homogeneous evolution: Kadens (2001: 119–22) observes two differences between the continental northern and southern regions. In the north, vernacular languages only become diplomatic languages in the wake of a literary tradition. For instance, charters written in German appear at the beginning of the thirteenth century, whereas German literary texts, such as the *Hildebrandslied*, are known to date back to the ninth century. Literary texts written down in the vernacular precede charters for Dutch and French (*langue d'oïl*), whereas Italian charters and literary texts appear around the same time.

The second difference between northern and southern Europe, as far as the rise of the written vernaculars is concerned, relates to the textual level; that is the macaronic phase in the evolution of the vernacular towards an autonomous written medium. From this perspective, documents issued in present-day French territory offer a particularly interesting case study. It appears that in the *langue d'oc* region (southern France), the transition phase took considerably longer than in the northern region of the *langue d'oïl*. The preserved macaronic fragments mixing Latin with southern French are numerous, whereas for the North of France, the evidence is extremely rare. A Latin rental from Cambrai (second half of the twelfth century) containing one French sentence and a list of payments due to the Saint-Vaast abbey in Arras (dating from about the same time) is already written entirely in French. Since no other preserved documents exist and a reliable dating of both texts is impossible, it is not possible to determine whether these texts are evidence of two different phases in the transition from Latin to written vernacular or whether both of them just appeared, illustrating two overlapping phases.

Table 35.1. The rise of written vernaculars in Western Europe

Chronology		Text and language
700	end 7th century	Anglo-Saxon writs and charters
800	8th century	*Beowulf* (Old English)
	early 9th century	*Hildebrandslied* (Old High German)
	+/− 830	*Heliand* (Old Low German)
	+/− 850	*Sermon sur Jonas* (Romance)
	880/881	*Séquence de Sainte-Eulalie* (Romance, proto-Picardian)
		Ludwigslied (Frankish)
900	960–963	proto-Italian oaths in Latin charters
	10th century	*Wachtendonckse Psalmen* (Old Dutch)
1000	early 11th century	*Glosas Emilianenses* (Ibero-Romance)
	11th century	macaronic charters in Latin-Provençal
	1060/1070	*Chanson de Sainte-Foy* (Old Ooccitan)
1100	+/− 1100	*Mittelfraenkische Reimbibel, Egmondse Williram* (Old Dutch)
	1136/8	*L'Estoire des Engleis* (Anglo-Norman)
	+/− 1170	*Sente Servaes* (Middle Dutch)
	1170–1200	Old French charters
	1175	*Noticia de Fiadores* (Galaïco-Portuguese)
	end 12th century	*Cantar de mio Cid* (Castillian)
1200	1170–1230	*Ritmo Cassinese, Ritmo su Sant'Alessio* (Italian)
	+/− 1200	Italian charters
		Old High German charters
		Old Norse charters
	early 13th century	nearly all official documents in Castillian
		Edda (Old Norse)
	1223	Galaïco-Portuguese troubadour poetry
	1225	Middle High German charters
	1249	Middle Dutch charters

This striking difference between northern and southern French can be explained in two ways. First, the presence of a macaronic phase could be due to the similarity between certain Romance dialects and written Latin, which we would expect to have facilitated the transfer from one to another. However, according to the hypothesis developed by Wright (1982, 1991/1996), the determining factor seems to have been the top-down influence of the Carolingian reforms. Wright argues that across the domain of the future Romance languages, written Latin was pronounced more or less the same as its evolved oral variety (the vernacular). In that way, Latin remained comprehensible even to illiterates if it was read aloud. The Carolingian reforms introduced a new pronunciation based on the Anglo-Saxon letter-by-letter model. The consequences were huge: where the reforms were successful, Latin was cut off from the influence of the spoken languages by an official barrier. In southern France, Spain, and Italy, where the reforms never took hold, Latin and its spoken derivative, the vernacular, continued to evolve on parallel tracks, with no official distinction between them. The gradual transition from Latin to the written vernacular was thus only possible in regions where the functional distance between Latin and the spoken language was not clearly delimited (Fishman 1972: 96, 102, 105). In other words, the diglossia institutionalized by the Carolingian reforms impeded alternation between the two languages, because they assumed different roles, different functions in society. If alongside the successful reforms there already existed a vernacular literature, the spoken and written language were separated. Macaronic fragments violate the official diglossia, a fact which is not self-evident. Since the reforms promoted the creation of vernacular literature for the regions subject to their impact, such as the *langue d'oïl* territory, the written vernacular becomes a diplomatic language only after it has already been a literary language.[15]

Further charting the rise of the written vernaculars in time and space, combined with an analysis of the socio-historical parameters that determined their existence, will help to define and explain the phenomenon. For now, the question remains as to whether this evolution was generated by a spontaneous generation of written vernaculars created by individual scribes or by a diffusion process, spreading out to many locations from a single starting-point. Both hypotheses have their supporting evidence (for instance, the preserved fragments revealing failed attempts for the first, the mobility of clerks and merchants for the latter), but the need for further research is indisputable, as has been pointed out by both historians and linguists.[16]

4. Language Attitudes

Whether glosses or macaronic texts, these vernacular intrusions into Latin 'territory' only illustrate how the switch from Latin to the written vernacular happened on a textual level. What caused the switch in mentality, however, is not revealed by the linguistic form of the preserved texts. The Middle Ages had formed a theory on what a text had to be. In an environment where the vernacular assumed more and more written functions, one or several innovators were capable of stretching the mental concept of written texts in such a way that it could cover documents written in a language different from Latin. In order to oppose the *auctoritas* and prestige of the Latin tradition, it is clear that a change in language attitudes was required both towards literacy[17] in general, as well as to the vernacular languages in particular.

An early indicator of change was the Roman church, the ultimate preserving institution for Latin, granting permission to use the written vernacular in certain circumstances. As early as 597, at the time of Augustine's mission, the practice of writing in some form of the English language (probably in runes), was sufficiently well established for the laws of Aethelbert of Kent to be written in Old English instead of Latin. This is an extraordinary instance of missionaries of the Roman church tolerating the writing of a barbarian language (Clanchy 1979/1993: 18), especially given the fact that official ecclesiastical authorization for the oral use of the vernacular in preaching came more than two centuries later, in 813.[18] At that time, Charlemagne's council of Tours stipulated in its seventeenth canon that sermons could be preached in the rustic Romance language or in German, in order to be understood more easily: "in rusticam Romanam linguam aut Theodiscam, quo facilius cuncti possint intellegere quae dicuntur."

The fundamental evolution of medieval society from memory to written record or from orality towards literacy[19] does not necessarily exclude the continuity of certain oral practices, such as the reading aloud of a Latin charter and its vernacular translation for the benefit of the witnesses. In a Latin charter given in 1244, for instance, the Flemish landlord Raas of Gavere authorizes his sergeant to perform a transaction in his name. The text of the authorization is quoted in Latin and then followed by the remark that, after these aforementioned letters had been read, they were translated to the vulgar language in the presence of the landlord's vassals and other men of quality: "sane lectis praedictis litteris et vulgariter in Teuthonica lingua expositis in praesentia hominum meorum feodatorum aliorum bonorum virorum."[20] Apparently, the oral translation of the Latin text was needed to guarantee that it would be understood by the landlord's vassals (Peersman 2008: 136–37). Similar side-references to the interaction between the oral and written mode can easily be found in medieval archives all over Europe. However, the overt debate about the appropriate role for Latin and the spoken tongues is also documented.

This debate arose early in the medieval history of Western Europe, reaching a peak during the twelfth and thirteenth centuries as literacy spread beyond the reach of a minute elite and vernacular literature came into its own (Haug 1997: 70–73, Lodge 2004, Lusignan 2005). Towards the end of the twelfth century, Walter Map is complaining about the unworthiness of any writing other than Latin, while his friend Gerald of Wales is expressing the hope that his *Expugnatio hibernica* will be translated into French. Meanwhile, on the continent, Chrétien de Troyes is proudly asserting that the Latin hegemony is a thing of the past. At this very moment no one, it seems, was paying much attention to the other great stride in the vernacularization of society: the change of the language of record. Unlike the creation of a vernacular literature, the diplomatic revolution that swept across Europe during the twelfth to fourteenth centuries incited little comment or criticism. Even in Flanders, where a century or two later the language of record would become – and remain – a point of bitter contention (Willemyns 1994, Vale 2005), the initial introduction of French and Dutch documents caused not a stir. This strange difference between literary and other texts, as described by Kadens (2001: 25–26), remains a mystery.

Since we have to wait for a explicit language policy until the late Middle Ages,[21] references and comments like those quoted in the preceding paragraphs are part of the data sociolinguists can work with, complementing research on the actual use of vernacular languages in different text genres. Case studies on individual vernacular languages and/or text genres have linked the socio-historical variables in the creation of a text to its linguistic form.

For different text genres, for instance, the 'patron' seems to have exercised decisive influence. It certainly comes as no surprise that support for the use of a certain vernacular on the part of powerful individuals, such as King Alfonso X el Sabio (1221–84) for Castillian, Duke William IX of Aquitaine (1086–1126) for Occitan, or Duke John I of Brabant (1252/3–94) for Middle Dutch, boosted the use of the vernacular concerned.[22] Although the examples all refer to men of the high nobility, patrons did not have to be male. Before the French *romancier* Chrétien de Troyes (c. 1135–c. 85) attached himself to Philip of Alsace, count of Flanders (1142–91), he acknowledged Countess Marie de Champagne (1174–1204) as his patroness. Eleanor of Aquitaine, grand-daughter of William IX and duchess of Aquitaine (1137–1204), is still considered the most fervent patroness of troubadour poetry. Through her successive marriages to the French and English kings (Louis VII and Henry II Plantagenet respectively), her influence was immense. Ladies belonging to the lower nobility could be significant as well: female patronage is known to have promoted the use of Anglo-Norman French in the Lincolnshire area (Short 1991: 243–44). The patron is obviously just one variable. Often, several socio-historic variables conspire to determine the use of the vernacular. As society changes, new institutions arise and the intended audience for texts changes, which implies a change in society's requirements for documentation. For instance, when in thirteenth-century Flanders communal benches of aldermen were created, most of them used the written vernacular straight away.

Generally speaking, the functions of literacy cross the boundaries of the clerical sphere as governmental institutions grow and the complexity of commercial and monetary transactions increases. At the same time, the need for persons educated in a very specific way becomes more and more pressing. This explains why urbanization and laicization are prominent among the causes suggested for the rise of the written vernaculars, alongside the birth status of the individual or his desire to express his identity.[23]

As the written vernaculars become more frequently used, their functions and text genres diversify. With the creation of language treatises, manuals, and grammars written in the vernacular, the vernaculars gradually but relentlessly move up the status scale, growing as they do so to carry the necessary weight and prestige. One of the earliest and most important works of instruction in a vernacular in Europe comes from England (again). Walter of Bibbesworth's *Tretiz de Langage*, also called *Femina*, is the first proper material for French instruction that is known for England.[24] Walter's vocabulary in verse form became *the* main material for teaching French in the thirteenth and fourteenth centuries and proved the most popular and widespread didactic French text of late medieval England in general (Kristol 1990: 294, 299–304).

Another huge step forward in the spread of the written vernaculars came when they were used for the writing of scholarly works, such as translations of and commentaries on Aristotle's *Problemata* (de Leemans and Goyens 2006), treatises on medicine (Taavitsainen and Pahta 2004), or manuals for confessional practice,[25] to name but three examples. The use of the spoken languages, however, did not necessarily imply the desire to make specific knowledge accessible to a less educated public (popularization). Texts on alchemy provide a particularly revealing case study, because of the tension between the requirements for secrecy that was a central tenet of alchemy and the potential expansion of readership that the use of the vernacular permitted.[26]

Alchemy was introduced into the Latin schools because of the wave of translations, mainly from Arabic into Latin (but also into and from Hebrew, sometimes with vernacular languages as intermediaries[27]) during the Renaissance of scientific thought in the twelfth century. This provided Latin culture with a hitherto unknown doctrine: the philosophical search for the agent of material perfection by means of the manipulation of base materials. Since alchemy as a doctrine was inseparable from laboratory practice, alchemical treatises can be considered examples of *Fachliteratur* as well as doctrinal writings, although they were never intended for university teaching. The alchemists were likely candidates for the use of the vernacular in writing, because their tradition implied linguistic transfers from the very start. Some of them had used the vernacular since the beginning of the fourteenth century. Vernacular languages were used in hundreds of alchemical recipes, which are to be found almost everywhere, on their own or within longer treatises. They demonstrate the generalized mixing of linguistic codes, especially the use of Latin formulas in vernacular recipes and vernacular names of substances in Latin recipes. Their presence should be viewed as a hint of the double regimen, oral and written, that characterized alchemy in its indissoluble mingling of practice and theory.

The evidence suggests that the use of vernacular languages in alchemy was neither limited to a single kind of alchemical text nor targeted at a single audience: both Latin and vernacular alchemical texts covered a similar range of uses. Except for the recipes, the existence of vernacular alchemical texts from the first half of the fourteenth century seems to have been fostered by the nonacademic status of sophisticated alchemists and by their experimental frame of mind. The first meant it was possible to use their native language instead of Latin even when writing, the second inspired them to do so. This, not any desire to popularize a subject for which secrecy was a central tenet, explains the early production of vernacular alchemical writings. Nevertheless, the very existence of these vernacular texts contributed to the diffusion of alchemy through ever larger sectors of society during the last two centuries of the Middle Ages.

Although it may not have been the intended effect of the use of vernacular languages – as we have observed for alchemical texts – knowledge was nevertheless popularized, in the sense that it spread beyond the audience originally intended for it. This diffusion of knowledge through the use of vernacular languages, and the explosion in the number of texts produced following the invention of the printing press, would bring Europe out of what the humanists claimed to be a millennium of medieval barbarism, into the classical light of knowledge and civilization.

5. Closing Remarks

During the Middle Ages, *the* model for literacy remained Latin, keeping the vernacular languages on the other side of the diglossic border. Dante, Boccaccio, Guillaume de Lorris, Jean de Meung, and Chaucer all bear ample testimony to this hierarchy in their apologies for writing in a different language: the vernacular. However, they not only acknowledge that difference, but also mark a historical shift in which the vernacular is no longer simply a spoken language, given the fact that each of them assumes for his own work the significance and authority traditionally associated only with the written form of Latin (Gellrich 1995: 14–15).

The shift from spoken to written vernaculars was a long and complex process, with respect to which the present chapter can only highlight a few aspects and problems. As an object of study, the evolution of written vernaculars still requires work in many fields: the composition and digitizing of corpora, statistical comparisons across western Europe, and in-depth analysis of specific text genres and of particular vernaculars. Above all, however, the complexity of the phenomenon needs to be viewed from an interdisciplinary angle and with the multivariable analytical model that historical sociolinguistics can provide.

NOTES

1   Given its huge impact on literacy, the printing press is by far the most important delimitation from a sociolinguistic point of view.
2   In medieval Latin, 'writing' (*scriptura*) and holy 'writ' (*scriptura*) became synonymous, as did office 'clerks' (*clerici*) and the church's 'clergy' (*clerici*) (Clanchy 1979/1993: 14).
3   Across the Channel to the south were the nations speaking Romance languages but writing in Latin. The seaways to the north were dominated by the Scandinavians writing in runes, and to the west lay the Celtic lands of Wales, Ireland, and the highlands and islands of Scotland, writing in ogams or Gaelic (Clanchy 1979/1993: 17).
4   More recent than Clanchy's work, but hugely indebted to it, is Machan (2003).
5   Among these variables are the spatio-temporal location of the text itself, and the social status and gender of the scribe (if he/she is known), the author (the person/institution on whose behalf the text is written) and the intended audience.

6 Latin: "stulti sunt romani – sapienti sunt paivari – modica est sapienti in romana – plus habent stultitia quam sapientia." Old Bavarian: "tole sint uualha – spahe sint peigera – luzic ist spahe in uualhum – mera habent tolaheiti denni spahi." ('The Romans (= French) are stupid, the Bavarians are intelligent, small is the wisdom of the French, they have more stupidity than wisdom').

7 A general introduction to the topic can be found in Mantello and Rigg (1996), especially the chapters on 'Latin and the vernacular languages' (122–128) and on 'Medieval translations: Latin and the vernacular languages' (728–733), where it is made very clear that the interaction between Latin and the vernaculars goes both ways.

8 The original text was ninth-century, but it is preserved in a single tenth- or eleventh-century manuscript.

9 'Macaronic' has been traditionally used to account for mixed-language medieval literature (Davidson 2003: 483, note 2).

10 Charters literally 'stuffed' with Latin.

11 A broad time basis for Ibero-Romance, as for Old English, is the period from the fifth to the twelfth century. Middle High German and Old Provençal, on the other hand, are located from the eleventh to the fourteenth and from the tenth to the fifteenth centuries respectively.

12 These examples only offer a very limited sample of the preserved multilingual materials. Thorough case-studies of multilingual manifestations and their cultural consequences can be found in the publications from the WUN-project *Multilingualism in the Middle Ages*; see Tyler (2011) and Kleinhenz and Busby (2010/11).

13 Throughout the twentieth century, partial overviews have been made of individual languages and/or specific text genres. Two of the most recent works are Brunner's (2009) overview of language use in charters from the eleventh to the fifteenth century, for almost all of present-day Europe, and Larsson (2009) on Swedish.

14 Kadens' (2001: 4) footnote on the rise of the written vernaculars inspired us to create this table. We completed the data using Frank, Hartmann, and Kürschner (1997), Ernst (2003), and Goyens and Verbeke (2003). We specifically consulted Brunel (1922, 1926) on *provençal*, Quak and Van Der Horst (2002) and van der Horst (2008) on medieval Germanic dialects, and Clanchy (1979/1993) and Schendl (2005) on Anglo-Saxon and Old English.

15 Conde-Silvestre's 2007 review of historical language contact from a sociolinguistic perspective makes use of the concept of diglossia. His account is illustrated with the case of Latin and the rise of romance vernaculars, as developed by Wright.

16 One of the possible research methods for the diffusion hypothesis is to look for language contact, for which evidence has been found in scriptologic studies (Brunner 2009: 71).

17 Clanchy (1979/1993) remains the reference work for this change in mentality, although his work is mainly a thorough case study of English documents. For a similar case study of Flemish documents, see Kadens (2001).

18 For England, macaronic sermons and hymns have been studied thoroughly (Jeffrey 1982; Wenzel 1994).

19 For further reading on the history of literacy in general and medieval literacy (500–1500 AD) in particular, see Ong (1982/2002), Enos (1991), and Clanchy (1979/1993: 335–345).

20 The charter concerned is one of the charters of the abbey of Ninove, number 197 of De Smet's (1841) edition.

21 Generally speaking, language policies began in the fifteenth century. We mention only two examples, concerning Dutch and French. The first language ordinance for Flanders was given in 1409 by Duke John the Fearless (Willemyns 1994). The first official measure setting a linguistic standard in France was the 1539 *Ordonnance de Villers-Cotterêts*, imposing French (the *Ile de France* dialect) as the official language in administration. Language policy and the resulting association between political power and language would ensure the transition

from the multilingual cultures of stratified society into separate, linguistically defined regional, and subsequently national, cultures, culminating in the nationalist tendencies of the nineteenth century.

22 Transposed to charters, the equivalent of the 'patron' is the issuer, the person(s) in whose name the charter is written and given. The influence the issuer could exercise on language use is similar to that of the patron.

23 On the medieval uses of language as a means of identification and the emergence of politicized linguistic consciousness, see Vale (2005).

24 The *Tretiz de langage* was written around 1235 at the request of Dionysia de Munchensi, a lady from the leading aristocratic circles. Until she asked for such help, only glosses, glossaries, and stray tables of French conjugations or declensions seem to have existed (Haas 2007: 141).

25 See Root (1997: 47–83) on vernacular confessional literature and the construction of the medieval subject.

26 In the following two paragraphs, we summarize Pereira's (1999) article on alchemy and the use of vernacular languages in the late Middle Ages.

27 Pereira (1999: 336, note 2) refers to the use of a vernacular language as an intermediary stage in the translations of a text into Latin, a process used by scholars all over medieval Europe.

REFERENCES

Boitani, P. (2007) *Letteratura europea e medioevo volgare*, Il Mulino, Bologna.

Brunel, C. (1922) Les premiers exemples de l'emploi du provençal dans les chartes. *Romania* 48: 335–64.

Brunel, C. (ed.) (1926) *Les plus anciennes chartes en langue provençale*, Picard, Paris.

Brunner, T.M. (2009) Le passage aux langues vernaculaires dans les actes de la pratique en Occident. *Le Moyen Age* 115 (1): 29–72.

Clanchy, M.T. (1979/1993) *From Memory to Written Record: England 1066–1307* (2nd edn), Blackwell, London.

Conde-Silvestre, J.C. (2007) *Sociolingüística histórica*, Gredos, Madrid.

Davidson, M.C. (2003) Code-switching and authority in late medieval England. *Neophilologus* 87: 473–86.

de Leemans, P. and Goyens, M. (eds.) (2006) *Aristotle's Problemata in Different Times and Tongues*, Leuven University Press, Leuven.

de Smet, J.J. (ed.) (1841) Codex diplomaticus abbatiae Ninoviensis. *Corpus Chronicorum Flandriae* II, Hayez, Bruxelles, pp. 751–893.

Enos, R.L. (ed.) (1991) *Oral and Written Communication. Historical Approaches*, Sage, London.

Ernst, G. (ed.) (2003) *Romanische Sprachgeschichte* II, X. Facteurs socioculturels dans l'histoire des langues romanes, Walter de Gruyter, Berlin.

Fasold, R. (1984) *The Sociolinguistics of Society*, Blackwell, Oxford.

Fishman, J. (1972) Societal bilingualism: stable and transitional. In A.S. Dil (ed.), *Language in Sociocultural Change. Essays by Joshua Fishman*, Stanford University Press, Stanford, pp. 135–52.

Frank, B, Hartmann, J., and Kürschner, H. (1997) *Inventaire systématique des premiers documents des langues romanes*, Narr, Tübingen.

Gärtner, K. (2002) Comprehensive digital text archives: a digital Middle High German text archive and its perspectives. *First EU/NSF Digital Libraries All Projects Meeting.* http://delos-noe.iei.pi.cnr.it/activities/internationalforum/All-Projects/RomeSlides/DTArchives.pdf

Gellrich, J.M. (1995) *Discourse and Dominion in the Fourteenth Century. Oral Contexts of Writing in Philosophy, Politics, and Poetry*, Princeton University, Press Princeton.

Goyens, M. and Verbeke, W. (eds.) (2003) *The Dawn of the Written Vernacular in Western Europe*, Leuven University Press, Leuven.

Gullichsen, H. (1999) Etude de deux glossaires anciens: les glossaires de Reichenau et de Kassel. *Romansk Forum 9* (1): 37–47.

Haas, R. (2007) Femina: female roots of 'foreign' language teaching and the rise of mother-tongue ideologies. *Exemplaria 19* (1): 139–62.

Haug, W. (1997) *Vernacular Literary Theory in the Middle Ages. The German Tradition, 800–1300, in its European Context* (trans. J.M. Catling), Cambridge University Press, Cambridge.

INL (Instituut voor Nederlandse Lexicologie) (1998) *CD-rom Middelnederlands*, Sdu Uitgevers – Standaard Uitgeverij, The Hague and Antwerp.

Jeffrey, D.L. (1982) Early English carols and the macaronic hymn. *Florilegium* 4: 210–22.

Kadens, E.E. (2001) *The Vernacular in a Latin World: Changing the Language of Record in Thirteenth-century Flanders*, Ph.D. thesis, Princeton University.

Kleinhenz, C. and Busby, K. (eds.) (2010/11) *Medieval Multilingualism. The Francophone World and its Neigbours*, Brepols, Turnhout.

Kristol, A.M. (1990) L'enseignement du français en Angleterre (XIIIe–XVe siècles): les sources manuscrites. *Romania* 111: 289–330.

Larsson, I. (2009) *Pragmatic Literacy and the Medieval Use of the Vernacular. The Swedish example*, Brepols, Turnhout.

Lodge, A. (2004) *A Sociolinguistic History of Parisian French*, Cambridge University Press, Cambridge.

Lusignan, S. (2005) *La résistible ascension du vulgaire. Le latin et le français dans les chancelleries de France et d'Angleterre à la fin du Moyen Âge*, L'Erma di Bretschneider, Rome.

Machan, T.W. (2003) *English in the Middle Ages*, Oxford University Press, Oxford.

Mantello, F.A.C. and Rigg, A.G. (eds.) (1996) *Medieval Latin: An Introduction and Bibliographical Guide*, The Catholic University of America Press, Washington, DC.

Ong, W. (1982/2002) *Orality and Literacy: The Technologizing of the word* (2nd edn), Routledge, New York.

Peersman, C. (2008) De opkomst van de volkstalen in de oorkonden van de abdij van Ninove. Casestudy van een bewogen eeuw (1250–1350). *Handelingen der Koninklijke Zuid-Nederlandse Maatschappij voor Taal- en Letterkunde en Geschiedenis* 61: 129–45.

Pereira, M. (1999) Alchemy and the use of vernacular languages in the late Middle Ages. *Speculum* 74 (2): 336–56.

Porter, D.W. (1999) The earliest texts with English and French. *Anglo-Saxon England* 28: 87–110.

Quak, A. and van der Horst, J. (2002) *Inleiding Oudnederlands*, Leuven University Press, Leuven.

Root, J. (1997) *Space to Speke: The Confessional Subject in Medieval Literature*, Peter Lang, New York.

Sayce, O. (1992) *Plurilingualism in the Carmina Burana: A Study of the Linguistic and Literary Influences on the Codex*, Kümmerle, Göppingen.

Schendl, H. (2005) 'Hec sunt prata to wassingwellan': aspects of code-switching in Old English charters. *Historical sociolinguistics and sociohistorical linguistics* 5 http://www.let.leidenuniv.nl/hsl_shl/index.html [accessed October 12, 2011].

Short, I. (1991) Patrons and polyglots: French literature in twelfth-century England. *Anglo-Norman Studies* 14: 229–50.

Taavitsainen, I. and Pahta, P. (eds.) (2004) *Medical and Scientific Writing in Late Medieval English*, Cambridge University Press, Cambridge.

Tyler, E.M. (ed.) (2011) *Conceptualizing Multilingualism in England, 800–1250*, Brepols, Turnhout.

Vale, M. (2005) Language, politics and society: the uses of the vernacular in the later Middle Ages. *English Historical Review* 120 (485): 15–34.

van der Horst, J. (2008) *Geschiedenis van de Nederlandse syntaxis*, Leuven University Press, Leuven.

Wenzel, S. (1994) *Macaronic Sermons: Bilingualism and Preaching in Late-medieval England*, University of Michigan Press, Ann Arbor.

Willemyns, R. (1994) Taalpolitiek in de Bourgondische tijd. *Verslagen en Mededelingen van de Koninklijke Academie voor Nederlandse Taal- en Letterkunde* 2–3: 162–77.

Wright, R. (1982) *Late Latin and Early Romance in Spain and Carolingian France*, Francis Cairns, Liverpool.

Wright, R. (1991/1996) The conceptual distinction between Latin and Romance: invention or Evolution. In R. Wright (ed.), *Latin and the Romance Languages in the Early Middle Ages* (2nd edn), University of Pennsylvania Press, Pennsylvania, pp. 103–13.

Zwartjes, O. (1997) *Love Songs from al-Andalus: History, Structure, and Meaning of Kharja*, Brill, New York and Leiden.

Index

Aarts, B. *et al.*, 399
Aasen, I., 618
Abad-Merino, M., 145–6
abbreviations in written
    text, 226–7
absolute standards, 48
Académie Française, 563
accents, attitudes towards,
    603; *see also* dialects
accommodation vs.
    dissociation, 388
Accountability Principle, 65
acculturation, 48, 55
actuation problem, 380,
    394–5
Adams, J., 557–8, 559–60
Adams, J. N., 523
adaptation vs. adoption,
    283
Addison, J., 200, 345–7, 634
Addison, J. and R. Steele,
    599
address terms, 296–7, 298
administrative texts,
    code-switching in,
    527–8
adoption vs. adaptation,
    283
adstratum languages, 559
advertisements in
    newspapers, 197–200,
    201–2
aesthetic variants in
    orthography, 218–19

aesthetics as force in lexical
    change, 281
Africa; *see also* South Africa
    colonialism in, 537–8
    as the cradle of language,
    354
Agard, F. B., 556
age
    as a factor in language
    change, 323–4
    as a factor in variants,
    265
    stereotypes, 317–18
age gradient in language
    shift, 53–4, 55–6
Ágel, V., 161
Ágel, V. and M. Hennig,
    160
Aitchison, J., 17, 376
Aitchison, J. and D. M.
    Lewis, 17–19
alchemy texts, vernaculars
    in, 649
Alford, H., 574
allophones, 237–8
Almqvist and Wiksell,
    430–31
Altenberg, B., 110–11
Al-Wer, E., 248–9
amanuenses *see* scribes
ambiguity, intentional, 17
American English
    the *Brown Corpus*, 105–6,
    110, 113–15

racial-color terminology,
    356–7
anachronisms, 82–4
anchor texts, 472
Ancient Greek (AGk) and
    lineal descent, 410–12
Andersen, H., 371, 373, 375,
    377, 392
Anderson, B., 604–5
Andrew, D. T., 198, 202
Anglo-Norman Delusion,
    134
Anglo-Romani, 56
Anglo-Saxon Gospels, 147
Anipa, K., 181, 186
Anson, C. M., 202
apparent-time model, 33–4,
    262–4, 429, 485–6
Appel, R. and P. Muysken,
    355
ARCHER (*A Representative
    Corpus of Historical
    English Registers*), 112,
    116, 194, 203
Archer, D. and J. Culpeper,
    101–2
Archer, D. *et al.*, 102
Aries, P., 83
Arnove, R. F. and H. J.
    Graff, 159
assigned gender, 348
*Atlas linguistique de la
    France (ALF)*, 481, 483,
    487

The Handbook of Historical Sociolinguistics, First Edition. Edited by Juan Manuel Hernández-Campoy
and Juan Camilo Conde-Silvestre.
© 2014 John Wiley & Sons, Ltd. Published 2014 by John Wiley & Sons, Ltd.

Index compiled by Kim Birchall